Encyclopedia
of Sociology

Second Edition

Editorial Board

Editor-in-Chief, Edgar F. Borgatta
Managing Editor, Rhonda J. V. Montgomery
Consulting Editor, Marie L. Borgatta

ADVISORY EDITORS

Duane Alwin
George W. Bohrnstedt
Karen S. Cook
Herbert L. Costner
Eileen Crimmons
William D'Antonio
Doris R. Entwistle
Amatai Etzioni
Archibald O. Haller
Maureen Hallinan
David Heise
Beth B. Hess
Charles Hirschman
Joan Huber
Yoshinori Kamo
David Knoke
Gladys E. Lang
Stanley Lieberson
Seymour Martin Lipset
J. Scott Long
Coral B. Marrett

David Mechanic
Margaret Mooney Marini
Peter V. Marsden
Douglas S. Massey
Jill Quadagno
Matilda White Riley
Pepper Schwartz
William H. Sewell
James F. Short, Jr.
Teresa A. Sullivan
James Teele
Marta Tienda
Nancy B. Tuma
Robin M. Williams, Jr.

INTERNATIONAL ADVISORY EDITORS

Vaneeta D'Andrea (Great Britain)
Mattei Dogan (France)
Alberto Gasperini (Italy)
Carl-Gunner Janson (Scandanavia)
Igor S. Kon (Soviet)
Judah Matra (Israel)
Georges Sabagh (Middle East)
Masamichi Sasaki (Japan)
Jacek Szmatka (Poland, Eastern Europe)
Vimal Shah (India)

Encyclopedia of Sociology

Second Edition

VOLUME 2

Edgar F. Borgatta
Editor-in-Chief
University of Washington, Seattle

Rhonda J. V. Montgomery
Managing Editor
University of Kansas, Lawrence

DOMINICAN UNIVERSITY LIBRARY
SAN RAFAEL, CALIFORNIA 94901

Macmillan Reference USA
an imprint of the Gale Group
New York • Detroit • San Francisco • London • Boston • Woodbridge, CT

Encyclopedia of Sociology
Second Edition

Copyright © 2000 by Edgar F. Borgatta and Rhonda J. V. Montgomery

All rights reserved. No part of this book may be reproduced or transmitted in any form or by any means, electronic or mechanical, including photocopying, recording, or by any information storage and retrieval system, without permission in writing from the Publisher.

Macmillan Reference USA
an imprint of The Gale Group
1633 Broadway
New York, NY 10019

Library of Congress Catalog in Publication Data
Encyclopedia of Sociology / Edgar F. Borgatta, editor-in-chief, Rhonda Montgomery,
    managing editor.—2nd ed.
        p. cm.
    Includes bibliographical references and index.
    ISBN 0-02-864853-6 (set: alk paper)—ISBN 0-02-864849-8 (v. 1: alk. paper)—
    0-02-864850-1 (v. 2)—0-02-864851-X (v. 3)—0-02-864852-8 (v. 4)—0-02-865581-8 (v. 5)
        1. Sociology—Encyclopedias. I. Borgatta, Edgar F., 1924- II. Montgomery,
    Rhonda J. V.

    HM425 .E5 2000
    301'.03—dc21   00-028402
                                                                         CIP

Printed in the United States of America by the Gale Group
Gale Group and Design is a trademark used herein under license.

Staff

Publisher
Elly Dickason

Project Editors
Timothy Prairie
Pamela Proffitt

Editorial Assistants
Shawn Beall
Wayne Yang

Assistant Manager, Composition
Evi Seoud

Buyer
Rhonda Williams

Senior Art Director
Michelle DiMercurio

E

ECOLOGY

See Demography; Environmental Equity; Environmental Sociology; Human Ecology and Environmental Analysis.

ECONOMIC DETERMINISM

NOTE: *Although the following article has not been revised for this edition of the Encyclopedia, the substantive coverage is currently appropriate. The editors have provided a list of recent works at the end of the article to facilitate research and exploration of the topic.*

Economic determinism refers to a kind of causality in which an economic variable x causes a condition of behavior y. This statement of direct causality contains very little actual economic determinism. But in stating that economic condition x is the most determining factor in causing behavior y, we have a model for economic determinism that is quite common in economics and sociology. This model appears in Weber's (1979) *Economy and Society*; in his discussion of domination he states:

> Nor does domination utilize in every case economic power for its foundation and maintenance. But in the vast majority of cases, and indeed in the most important ones, this is just what happens in one way or another and often to such an extent that the mode of applying economic means for the purpose of maintaining domination, in turn exercises a determining influence on the structure of domination. (p. 942)

The same model of economic determinism appears in Louis Althusser's (1970) *For Marx*, where the social formation has multiple determinants, but "the economy is determinant in the last instance" (p. 113). Neither model has the economic as a monocausal determinant of society, but economic categories, such as the economic market for Weber, clearly are part of a central structuring determination for society.

This model predates both Weber and Althusser and has its origins in eighteenth-century free market liberalism. In *The Federalist Papers*, James Madison assumes economic interests as the chief motivation of the people. In *The Wealth of Nations*, for Adam Smith it is "that in commercial society every man thus lives by exchanging, or becomes in some measure, a merchant" (1976, p. 26). For Smith people are buyers and sellers involved in production and consumption, and human behavior is an unending series of economic exchanges. Individuals pursue their own self-interest in rational ways, and their own self-interest consists of profit, which is regulated by competition in a predominantly self-regulating free market. In the pursuit of economic self-interest the individual promotes the social good, "led by an invisible hand to promote an end which was no part of his intention" (p. 477). In Smith's model an individual's pursuit of economic profit automatically structures the good for all of society.

Smith assumes an economic person who is always acting to optimize economic advantages. People here are determined by economic motives, that is, to increase profits and decrease losses.

Modern neoclassical economists, such as Milton Friedman and Gary Becker, have continued the tradition of Adam Smith. For them the only limitation on the free market model is the amount of information to which a rational actor has access. Since information is not perfect, mistakes can occur. But in the pursuit of profit a rational actor learns even from mistakes; mistakes therefore increase the amount of information that a rational actor acquires, thus increasing the chances of making correct choices in the future. Thus, the free market not only structures human behavior but determines the inevitability that these actors, in rationally pursuing profit, will acquire the information needed to produce profits continuously for themselves and to mold—even if unintentionally—the social good.

The model of economic determinism offers sociology an easily quantifiable object, a phenomenon that can be subjected to scientific procedures—observed, measured, tested, and verified. As a positivist social science, sociology requires a transhistorical and universal phenomenon such as the physical sciences have, and economic determinism provides it in economic concepts such as the market, money, the circulation of capital, and so forth. It allows sociologists to speak the language of science and to reduce all social phenomena to mathematical formulas.

All positivist social sciences use mathematical representations of social reality to understand society, and economic determinism is but one attempt at creating a scientific sociology. Still, the model has offered sociology a formula that possesses broad powers for explaining social factors and avoids problems of indeterminate multiple causes. This is what science traditionally means by lawfulness. These lawlike social categories are representations of social reality and provide a framework in which the aggregate behavior of individuals can be structured in terms of economic interests. This behavior is patterned and can be studied and subjected to scientific procedures. Thus, the model of economic determinism informs sociological analysis and research.

Exchange theory provides an example of a positivist methodology that is based on the model of economic determinism. In exchange theory, economic exchange is the determinant principle of behavior. George C. Homans, the originator of this form of analysis, combines this economic model with a behaviorist psychology, but the economic is the determining structure. In *Social Behavior: Its Elementary Forms*, Homans states, "Human behavior as a function of its payoff: in amount and kind it depends on the amount and kind of reward and punishment it fetches" (1961, p. 13). Human relations have been reduced to the exchange and circulation of commodities. Homans assumes that a social actor is an economic person existing in a free market where individuals make rational choices to maximize profits and reduce costs. This is stated partly in the language of behavioral psychology, but the conditions of economic exchange are dominant. Thus, Homans sounds more like Adam Smith than like B. F. Skinner when he writes "we define psychic profits as rewards less costs, and we argue that no exchange continues unless both parties are making a profit" (1961, p. 61).

This model allows Homans to analyze individuals who live in a group, make numerous rational choices, and yet live a stable, patterned life. Individuals calculating their possibilities and making rational choices are led by something like Smith's "invisible hand" to maintain group life in "practical equilibrium."

Homans believed that his analysis was a value-neutral attempt to expand the scope of a scientifically valid sociology of human behavior. But, while exchanges are an important aspect of human interaction, the reduction of all human behavior to elementary exchanges is problematic. Homans has universalized the relations of individuals in the capitalist marketplace, relations that are historically specific and not the basis of a universal psychology of human behavior. Homans's exchange theory is a conservative sociological theory in which pecuniary relations structure human behavior.

Another form of sociological analysis that uses the model of economic determinism is Marxist sociology. In Weber's *The Protestant Ethic and the Spirit of Capitalism*, Marx's analysis is called a "one-sided materialistic" interpretation (1958, p. 183). Marx provides evidence for Weber's contention when he argues that the economic base determines the ideological superstructure. In the preface to *A Contribution to the Critique of Political Economy*, Marx writes that "the totality of these relations of production constitutes the economic structure of society, the real foundation, on which arises a legal and political superstructure and to which correspond definite forms of social consciousness" (1970, p. 20). This famous passage, containing what is known as the base-superstructure model, became the hallmark statement for economic determinist Marxists from the Second International (Marxist Workers Congress) in 1889 to the present.

But Marx himself was not an economic determinist, even though many of his followers were. Marx theorized about a world in which human relations were subsumed under capitalist relations of production. His central concern was revolutionary change, which depended on the formation of a revolutionary class that could wage war against the dominant classes. But for Marx, class was determined not by economic conditions alone but by community and cultural conditions as well. Thus, he writes in *The Eighteenth Brumaire of Louis Bonaparte* on whether "small holding peasants" are or are not a class:

> *In so far as millions of families live under economic conditions of existence that separate their mode of life, their interests and their culture from those of other classes and put them in hostile opposition to the latter, they form a class. In so far as there is merely interconnection among these small holding peasants, and the identity of their interests begets no community, no national bond and no political organization among them, they do not form a class.* (Marx 1963, p. 124)

This is not "economics in the last instance" but a multivalent fitting together of a series of necessary conditions. Economic conditions are insufficient, and class formation and class struggle do not occur unless community occurs as well.

Later Marxists differ from Marx on a number of issues. First, many understand the base-superstructure model as a determinant condition of class. That is, class depends exclusively on the economic base for its formation. For Marx, however, it was an insufficient condition and a "moment" in his analysis of capitalism. Furthermore, economic determinist Marxists view class struggle as a secondary phenomenon, even though it is important. Finally, many Marxists have critiqued Marx's concept of class for its inability to predict revolutionary change with scientific accuracy. Erik

Olin Wright, for instance, calls Marx's concept of class "vague" and "random"; it is much too relativistic for use as a neat, lawlike scientific formula. In his important book *Classes*, Wright preserves the Marxian tradition of the Second International and attempts to erect a positivist Marxist sociology whose propositions can be empirically verified. It is upon the base-superstructure model that Wright builds this science. As in exchange theory, Wright's model suggests that in capitalism rational actors make rational choices in pursuing their economic advantages. But Wright also attempts to build a scientific base for an analysis of class struggle, and in *Classes* he provides the causal link between capitalist exploitation and the actions of individuals in society. He does this by demonstrating that class structure is determined by property relations, a central determinant in modern society:

> *Class structure is of pervasive importance in contemporary social life. The control over society's productive assets determines the fundamental material interests of actors and heavily shapes the capacities of both individuals and collectivities to pursue their interests. The fact that a substantial portion of the population may be relatively comfortable materially does not negate the fact that their capacities and interests remain bound up with property relations and the associated processes of exploitation.* (Wright 1985, pp. 285–286)

Economic factors are crucial for understanding the social world. But society is not reducible to economic determinants; it is too complex to be reduced to a set of economic propositions, or any single determinant set of propositions, that imply unilinear causality. Still, economic determinism is seductive because it offers a theory that has broad explanatory powers, is easily quantifiable, and can be reduced to simple mathematical formulas. Thus, it is not surprising to see it continue and expand, seemingly unaware of its limitations. For instance, George Gilder writes in *Wealth and Poverty*, "The man's earnings, unlike the woman's, will determine not only his standard of living but also his possibilities for marriage and children—whether he can be a sexual man" (1981, p. 109). The reduction of sex and marriage to economic determinants is highly problematic, both as science and as common sense. Yet generalizations about social life wholly based on economic causes persist, under the names of both science and myth. One can restate Max Weber's warning against monocausal theories in the social sciences:

But it is, of course, not my aim to substitute for a one-sided materialistic an equally one-sided spiritualistic causal interpretation of culture and of history. Each is equally possible, but each if it does not serve as the preparation, but as the conclusion of an investigation accomplishes equally little in the interest of historical truth. (1958, p. 183)

(SEE ALSO: *Capitalism; Economic Sociology; Marxist Sociology*)

REFERENCES

Albritton, Robert 1995 "Political Economy in the Making: A Response." *Rethinking Marxism* 8:125–129.

Aronowitz, Stanley 1988 *Science as Power: Discourse and Ideology in Modern Society*. Minneapolis: University of Minnesota Press.

Dahms, Harry F. 1997 "Theory in Weberian Marxism: Patterns of Critical Social Theory in Lukacs and Habermas." *Sociological Theory* 15:181–214.

Feenberg, Andrew 1992 "Subversive Rationalization: Technology, Power, and Democracy." *Inquiry* 35:3–4.

Gilder, George 1982 *Wealth and Poverty*. New York: Bantam.

Hodgson, Geoffrey M. 1995 "Varieties of Capitalism from the Perspectives of Veblen and Marx." *Journal of Economic Issues* 29:575–584.

Kennedy, Paul M., Andrew Levine, Elliott Sober, and Erik-Olin Wright 1987 *The Rise and Fall of the Great Powers: Economic Change and Military Conflict from 1500 to 2000*. New York: Random House.

Homans, George C. 1961 *Social Behavior: Its Elementary Forms*. New York: Harcourt, Brace, and World.

Marx, Karl (1859) 1970 *A Contribution to the Critique of Political Economy*.

—— (1852) 1963 *The Eighteenth Brumaire of Louis Bonaparte*. New York: International.

Rammert, Werner 1997 "New Rules of Sociological Method: Rethinking Technology Studies." *British Journal of Sociology* 48:171–191.

Resnick, Stephen A., and Richard D. Wolff 1987 *Knowledge and Class: A Marxian Critique of Political Economy*. Chicago: University of Chicago Press.

Sherman, Howard J. 1998. "Critique of the Critique: Analysis of Hodgson on Marx on Evolution." *Review of Social Economy* 56:47–58.

Smith, Adam 1976 *An Inquiry into the Nature and Causes of the Wealth of Nations*. Chicago: University of Chicago Press.

Weber, Max (1947) 1979 *Economy and Society: An Outline of Interpretive Sociology*. Guenther Roth and Claus Wittich, eds. and trans. Berkeley: University of California Press.

Wright Erik, O., Andrew Levine, and Elliott Sober 1992 *Reconstructing Marxism: Essays on Explanation and the Theory of History*. New York: Verso.

—— 1994 "Historical Materialism: Theory and Methodology." *Science and Society* 58:53–60.

—— (1904–1905) 1958 *The Protestant Ethic and the Spirit of Capitalism*. New York: Scribners.

Wright, Erik Olin 1985 *Classes*. London: Verso.

WILLIAM DiFAZIO

ECONOMIC DEVELOPMENT

See Industrialization in Less-Developed Countries, Modernization Theory; Rural Sociology .

ECONOMIC INSTITUTIONS

The analysis of economic institutions is central to the work of the classical figures of sociology-Marx, Weber, and Durkheim. These thinkers did not recognize a boundary line between sociological inquiry and economic inquiry; on the contrary, their efforts to make sense of the development of market capitalism led them to intensive analysis of market processes. Unfortunately, this thrust of sociological inquiry was largely abandoned by sociologists between World War I and the late 1960s. This was particularly true in the United States, where sociologists generally deferred to economists' claims of an exclusive mandate to study economic processes.

To be sure, there were a number of important intellectual figures during this period whose work integrated sociological and economic inquiry, but these individuals were rarely housed in sociology departments. Such economists as Thorstein Veblen, Joseph Schumpeter, and John Kenneth Galbraith have been retroactively recognized as sociologists. Similarly, the largely self-educated Hungarian scholar Karl Polanyi ([1944] 1957, 1971) is now acknowledged to have made seminal contributions to the sociological analysis of economic institutions. Yet scholars working in the sociological mainstream either ignored economic topics or tended to incorporate the perspectives of neoclassical economics.

Since the late 1960s, however, the lines of inquiry pioneered by the classical writers have been revitalized. Sociologists working in a number of different intellectual traditions and on diverse empirical topics have developed sophisticated analyses of economic processes (Swedberg 1987). No longer content to defer to the expertise of professional economists, many of these writers have developed powerful critiques of the work of neoclassical economists (Zukin and DiMaggio 1990).

Although this body of work explores a range of different economic institutions, much of it can be understood through its analysis of the way that markets work. (Analyses of other economic institutions, such as the division of labor, money, and corporate organizations, are presented elsewhere in this encyclopedia.) In particular, an emergent economic sociological conception of market processes can usefully be contrasted with the conception of the market that is implicit in most economic writings.

THE ORGANIZATION OF MARKETS

Neoclassical economists tend to assume an ideal market situation that allows changes in prices to equilibrate supply and demand. In this ideal market situation, there are multiple buyers and sellers whose transactions are fundamentally impersonal; information on the product and the price are the only relevant variables shaping the action of market participants. Contemporary economists recognize that this ideal market situation requires a basic symmetry in the information available to buyers and sellers. When there are significant differences in information, it is likely that the resulting price will diverge from the price that would effectively equilibrate supply and demand. Nevertheless, contemporary microeconomics rests on the assumption that most markets approximate the ideal situation, including information symmetry (Thurow 1983)

The sociological view of markets is fundamentally different. It stresses the embeddedness of behavior within markets, the central role of imitation in structuring markets, and the importance of blocked exchanges. The concept of embeddedness challenges the idea that impersonality is an important feature of actual market situations. While the individual actor in economic theory is a rational actor who is able to disregard his or her social ties in the market situation, the sociological actor is seen as embedded in a network of social relations at the time that he or she engages in market transactions. This embeddedness means that a wide range of social ties exert continuing influence over how the actor will both make and respond to price signals (Polanyi [1944] 1957; Granovetter 1985).

This view has two elements. First, the individual actor is decisively influenced by social ties. For example, a consumer might choose not to do business with retailers belonging to a stigmatized ethnic group, even when their prices are lower, because members of the consumer's ethnic group genuinely believe that the products of the other group will be inferior or that contact with the stigmatized group will jeopardize one's social position. The economists' argument that such an individual has a "taste for discrimination" does not adequately capture a reality in which discriminatory behavior often occurs with very little reflection because beliefs are deeply rooted. Second, the individual actor's dependence on social ties is necessary in order for him or her to accomplish a given economic goal. As Granovetter (1985) has pointed out, a purchasing officer at a corporation might well do business with a particular supplier regardless of price considerations because of longstanding ties to that individual. These ties provide assurance that the delivery will occur in a timely fashion and the merchandise will meet established quality standards. In other words, social bonds can provide protection against the uncertainties and risks that are always involved in transactions.

The standard economic view of markets tends to ignore these uncertainties; it is generally assumed that individuals will automatically obey the rules that make transactions possible. As Oliver Williamson (1975) has noted, this represents a profound inconsistency in economic analysis. While individuals are assumed to be self-interested, they are also expected to avoid guile and deception. In the real world, however, every transaction involves the risk that one party is deliberately cheating the other, and the more "impersonal" the transaction—that is, the less one party knows about the other—the greater the risk becomes.

This is one of the reasons that actual markets tend to develop structures and rules designed to constrain and to embed individual behavior. Although commodity markets and stock markets most closely resemble the pure markets of economic theory, in which rapid price changes serve to balance supply and demand, these markets tend to evolve complex social structures. At one level, such markets appear to be completely impersonal, in that there is no contact between buyers and sellers. On another level, however, the actual transactions are handled by a community of brokers who are well known to each other and who are expected to follow a particular etiquette for managing transactions. This structure has evolved to provide protection against unknown brokers who might prove unreliable and to assure that known brokers will be discouraged from cheating their colleagues and clients (Adler and Adler 1984; Baker 1984a; Burk 1988).

The central point, however, is that the particular ways in which market behaviors are embedded have real and significant consequences. On the one hand, embeddedness allows market processes to go forward by diminishing the opportunities for guile and deceit. On the other hand, embeddedness assures that factors besides price will influence the behavior of market participants, so it can no longer be assumed that price will automatically equilibrate supply and demand.

One of the main implications of the concept of embeddedness is that actual markets will be characterized by imitative behavior. Economists assume that each economic actor will calculate his or her preference schedule independently of all other actors. In the sociological view, however, actors are continually making their choices in reference to the behavior of others. In deciding the price to be asked for a particular commodity, a market participant will set it in comparison with the prices of competitors (White 1981). This is one of the key reasons that in actual markets there is often less price competition than would be suggested either by economic theory or by considerable differences across firms in the costs of production.

This role of imitation plays a particularly important role in financial panics and bubbles. Panics occur when many holders of a particular kind of asset rush to convert their holdings to cash, leading to precipitous price declines. Bubbles occur when enthusiasm for a particular asset drives prices far higher than can be justified by expected returns (Kindleberger 1978). Economists have trouble explaining the behavior of individuals in most panics or bubbles because rational actors with complete information would not engage in such irrational behavior; they would understand that the underlying value of an asset is not likely to change so dramatically in a short period of time. However, actual individuals have limited information, and they cope with uncertainty by observing the behavior of their friends and neighbors. Such observation makes them quite susceptible to the collective enthusiasms of panics and bubbles.

The threat of panics is another reason that financial markets develop institutional structures to embed individual behavior. The New York Stock Exchange, for example, has an elaborate system of specialist firms who have the responsibility to smooth out the market for particular stocks. Such firms are expected to be purchasers of last resort in situations where there are too many sellers of a stock (Baker 1984b). The idea is that such action should help to reduce the likelihood of panic. While such an institutional arrangement diverges from the economists' conception of a self-regulating market, it makes sense in the context of imitative behavior.

Furthermore, in their emphasis on the virtues of markets, neoclassical economists often suggest a vision of society as a giant bazaar in which everything is for sale. Sociologists, in contrast, are more likely to recognize that the viability of markets depends upon a wide variety of restrictions that block certain types of exchanges. Blocked exchanges are transactions that are in violation of the law or of widely shared ethical standards (Walzer 1983). Instances of blocked exchange include prohibitions on the resale of stolen merchandise, laws that prevent government officials from selling their services to the highest bidder, and the criminalization of prostitution and the purchase of certain drugs.

More subtle blocked exchanges play an important role in structuring the economy. Lawyers are not allowed to switch sides in the middle of a civil suit in response to an offer of a higher fee by the other side. Accountants are not supposed to produce a more favorable audit in response to a higher fee (Block 1990). Loan officers at a bank are prohibited from approving loans in exchange for side payments from the applicant. The members of a corporate board of directors are supposed to place their fiduciary responsibility to the shareholders ahead of their self-interest in contemplating offers to buy out the firm. In a word, there is a complicated and sometimes shifting boundary between legitimate and illegitimate transactions in contemporary economies.

The importance of blocked exchanges sheds further doubt on arguments that markets can regulate themselves without governmental interference (Polanyi [1944] 1957). The construction of any particular market involves rules as to what kinds of exchange are open and what kinds are blocked, but the incentives to violate these rules are often quite substantial. At the same time, the incentives for market participants to police each other are often lacking. Hence, there is often no alternative to a governmental role in policing the boundary between legitimate and illegitimate exchanges. Moreover, debates about social policy are often framed in a language of individual rights that is profoundly insensitive to the importance and pervasiveness of blocked exchanges. For example, when a woman serving as a surrogate mother in exchange for a fee decides she wants to keep the baby, the issue is often debated in terms of contract law. The more fundamental issue, however, is whether the society believes that the rental of wombs is a legitimate or illegitimate transaction (Rothman 1989).

VARIETIES OF MARKET SYSTEMS

A second important dimension of contemporary sociological work on economic institutions emphasizes the significant variations in the ways in which different market societies are institutionally organized. Against the common assumption that market societies will converge toward the same institutional arrangements, this work has used the comparative method to highlight significant and durable institutional differences. Out of this has come a rich body of literature on the wide variety of different "capitalisms" that can coexist at a particular moment in time. While there are a variety of typologies, this work has tended to identify an East Asian model, a Rhinish model that draws heavily on Germany and France, a social democratic model associated particularly with Sweden and Norway, and the Anglo-American model (Couch and Streeck 1997; Hollingsworth and Boyer 1997; Orru et al. 1997). While researchers have identified a wide variety of differences in economic institutions, much of this work has focused on examining differences in labor markets, capital markets, and in the markets for innovation.

The study of labor-market institutions encompasses variations in how the labor force acquires basic and advanced skills; variations in how social welfare provides citizens with income in the event of sickness, disability, unemployment, retirement, and other contingencies; variations in the rights and responsibilities that employees have in the workplace; and variations in the mechanisms for matching employees with job vacancies (Rogers and Streeck 1995; Wever and Turner 1995). The point is not simply that different countries are located on different points of a continuum in terms of variables such as union density or welfare generosity. It is rather that some of these variables tend to be grouped together, so that one can identify ideal typical complexes of institutions through which societies distribute some of the costs and benefits of economic growth. For example, studies by Dore (1997) and Streeck (1997) have sought to show how Japanese and German systems of industrial relations both differ dramatically from the Anglo-American model and work in tandem with other specific institutional features of those societies to create significant economic advantages for Japanese and German firms.

Comparative work on capital markets has generally contrasted the stock market-centered system in the United States and the United Kingdom with the bank-centered systems that have prevailed in Japan and in Continental Europe (Mizruchi and Stearns 1994; Zysman 1983). In the former firms rely primarily on stock and bond issues in impersonal markets to raise the funds required for expansion, while in the latter firms are more reliant on long-term loans from banks. This difference has important implications for corporate governance, for the size of the debt burden on corporations, for the time horizons of corporate executives, and for the openness of the economy to new entrepreneurial initiatives.

Finally, studies of the market for innovation have identified distinct varieties of what some analysts have called national innovation systems (Amable et al. 1997). This encompasses the research efforts of scientists and engineers, initiatives by government agencies to foster innovation, and the entrepreneurial activities of both public and private firms. The ways in which these elements are brought together vary significantly both in terms of the division of labor between the public sector and the private sector and the way that interactions between them are organized. Since innovation clearly weighs heavily in international economic success, some analysts have begun to examine the specific institutional features of nations that have been most effective in fostering successful innovation (Evans 1995).

This effort to identify different institutional types of capitalism has occurred during the same period in which the countries of Eastern Europe and the former Soviet Union have been making a transition from state socialism to capitalism. While some Western advisers acted as though the Anglo-American model was the only relevant model for former socialist countries to emulate, the process

of transition had the effect of deepening the awareness of the institutional variations among capitalist societies (Stark and Bruszt 1998). Hungary, for example, had to make a set of decision as to how much weight to give the stock market in corporate governance and in capital allocation. This, in turn, generated increasing interest in studies showing the important differences in the relative role of stock markets and banks in different market societies.

THE SCOPE OF MARKETS

A third important dimension of contemporary sociological work on economic institutions is a concern with the geographical scope of markets. Much of the sociological tradition has been oriented to the study of national societies or of subnational units. But an understanding of the scope of international markets calls that approach into question. Markets for raw materials, finished products, services, capital, and labor cross national boundaries and exert extraordinary influence over all aspects of social life (Swedberg 1987).

The most ambitious effort to date to chart the importance of these international markets has been the world-system theory of Immanuel Wallerstein (1974a, 1974b, 1980, 1989). Instead of using national societies as the basic unit of analysis, Wallerstein has sought to shift sociological analysis to the level of the capitalist world-system. For Wallerstein, this system is comprised of a world market and a competitive state system of divided sovereignties. Any analysis of patterns within a particular national society must begin by locating that society within the larger capitalist world-system. A nation's location at the core, the periphery, or the semiperiphery of the capitalist world-system can be expected to shape the nature of its economic and political institutions.

The existence of a single unified world market is central to Wallerstein's argument. Each nation that is part of the capitalist world-system must struggle for relative advantage in that market, and this has implications for both social relations within nations and for the political-military relations among nations. Moreover, it is a central part of

Wallerstein's project to detail the process by which various regions of the world have been incorporated into this unified world-system. The capitalist world-system began as a purely European phenomenon, but through colonization and the penetration of Western influence, this system became global. Regions that were once external to the system were progressively incorporated as peripheral areas that produced raw materials. Later-arriving nations such as the United States, Canada, and Japan moved to the semiperiphery and then to the core.

The contributions of Wallerstein and his followers have been extremely important in showing the systematic ways in which international markets shape developments within societies. The study of labor markets within the world-system, for example, has been particularly fruitful in making sense of international migrations-the massive movements of people across national boundaries-that loom so large in understanding both core and peripheral societies (Portes and Walton 1981).

Wallerstein's work, however, is vulnerable to criticism because it sometimes implies that there is a single unified world market for commodities, for labor, and for capital that operates quite similarly to the markets of economic theory. Critics have suggested that Wallerstein devotes too little attention to analyzing the specific institutional structures of global markets and that his work has not given sufficient weight to the institutional variations among capitalist societies. The response to the criticism is that the homogenizing logic of a global capitalist system will work itself out over time and will ultimately eliminate much of the variety in institutional forms.

Toward the end of the 1990s, debate over this precise issue has become increasingly important. The attention of a growing number of scholars is focused on the interactions between the varieties of market institutions at the national level and the dynamics of a global capitalist system. Particularly in discussions of "globalization" (see article in this encyclopedia), scholars ask whether there are-as Wallerstein suggests-powerful structural forces operating at the global level that are systematically forcing all market societies to adopt Anglo-American economic institutions. One British scholar posed the question polemically by asking if there were a new type of Gresham's Law in which "bad capitalisms were driving out good" (Gray 1999).

One set of events that intensified interest in this question were the deep problems of the Japanese economy during the 1990s and the Asian economic crisis that began in Thailand in July of 1997 and spread to Malaysia, Indonesia, South Korea, and ultimately to Russia and Brazil. Enthusiasm for an East Asian model of capitalism was considerably dampened by the severity of Japan's long-term problems, by South Korea's overnight transition from success story to severe financial crisis, and by doubts that the model could facilitate sustainable growth in poorer countries such as Thailand and Indonesia. At the same time, the crisis heightened awareness that the institutions of global capitalism, especially the International Monetary Fund, were exerting powerful pressures on East Asian countries to align themselves more fully with Anglo-American ways of organizing their economic institutions. Most specifically, in the aftermath of the crisis, there were pressures on nations to shift from bank-centered finance to stock market-centered finance (Wade and Veneroso 1998).

Finally, the Asian crisis also drew attention to the power of what one observer has labeled the "electronic herd" (Friedman 1999)-the global network of traders in markets for bonds, equities, foreign exchange, and more exotic financial instruments. When significant numbers of these traders decide that a particular economy on any continent is being poorly managed, they have the capacity to precipitate a major financial crisis just by taking positions in the market that assume a depreciation of the value of the country's financial assets and currency (Block 1996). To be sure, this power is not yet universal; China and Vietnam have been able to insulate themselves from these pressures by maintaining controls on capital movements, and Hong Kong and Malaysia were successful in foiling the speculative strategies of the traders. Nevertheless, the power wielded by these traders is further evidence that the global market might be able to force steadily greater homogenization in economic institutions and practices across nations.

These same concerns extend to the more developed economies of Western Europe. Scholars have argued that the rapid movement of capital across national boundaries has fundamentally weakened the social democratic model as an alternative way of organizing market societies (Scharpf 1991). And others have begun to wonder aloud as to how long the German model can resist the pressures to abandon its particular institutions for organizing labor markets and capital markets (Gray 1999; Streeck 1997). Developments such as the cross-border merger between Daimler-Benz and Chrysler might portend German accommodation to the Anglo-American model.

The question of whether the global economy will increasingly converge to a single type of capitalism based on the Anglo-American model or whether there will be continuing diversity of the institutional forms of market societies is far from being resolved. The outcome will depend on economic and political developments over the next few decades. However, if there is convergence, the results are likely to be highly unstable unless there is significant progress in increasing the regulatory capacities of global economic institutions. If one starts from neoclassical economic premises, one can imagine that a self-regulating global economy with relatively weak international institutions could be viable. However, a sociological view of markets evokes deep skepticism about the stability of such a system (Polanyi [1944] 1957). Just as sustained economic activity within nations requires both embeddedness of markets to minimize guile and deceit and enforcement of blocked exchanges, so an increasingly integrated global economy has similar needs. Moreover, since globalization tends to weaken regulatory mechanisms at the national level, the need for effective enforcement at the global level becomes more acute.

The Asian economic crisis of 1997 and 1998 revealed that the International Monetary Fund lacks the resources and the capacity to contain international financial panics. Moreover, since the global economy lacks an effective "lender of last resort," a financial panic could lead to a cascade of failures by large financial institutions on an enormous scale. But even when the need to expand global economic regulation is recognized, the political obstacles to the strengthening of international financial and regulatory institutions are enormous. Most national governments are extremely reluctant to cede sovereignty to international agencies. Since the same processes of globalization that increase the need for global regulation have already eroded the powers of national governments, political leaders are reluctant to limit their own authority even further. At the same time, while the United States has thrown its political and economic weight behind the forces of globalization, domestic political opposition in the United States to strengthened international agencies continues to be formidable. Hence, it appears unlikely that the globalized economy will soon have the regulatory institutions that it needs to function effectively.

(SEE ALSO: *Corporate Organizations; Division of Labor; Economic Sociology; Money; Transnational Corporations*)

REFERENCES

Adler, Patricia, and Peter Adler, eds. 1984 *The Social Dynamics of Financial Markets.* Greenwich, Conn.: JAI Press.

Amable, Bruno, Rémi Barré, and Robert Boyer 1997 "Diversity, Coherence, and Transformations of Innovation Systems." In Rémi Barré, Michael Gibbons, Sir John Maddox, Ben Martin, Pierre Papon et al., eds., *Science in Tomorrow's Europe.* Paris: Economica International.

Baker, Wayne 1984a "The Social Structure of a National Securities Market." *American Journal of Sociology* 89:775–811.

—— 1984b "Floor Trading and Crowd Dynamics." In Patricia Adler and Peter Adler, eds., *The Social Dynamics of Financial Markets.* Greenwich, Conn.: JAI Press.

Block, Fred 1990 *Postindustrial Possibilities: A Critique of Economic Discourse.* Berkeley: University of California Press.

—— 1996 "Controlling Global Finance." *World Policy Journal* (Fall): 24–34.

Burk, James 1988 *Values in the Marketplace: The American Stock Market Under Federal Securities Law.* New York: Walter de Gruyter.

Couch, Colin, and Wolfgang Streeck, eds. 1997 *Political Economy of Modern Capitalism: Mapping Convergence and Diversity.* Thousand Oaks, Calif.: Sage.

Dore, Ronald 1997 "The Distinctiveness of Japan" In Colin Crouch and Wolfgang Streeck, eds., *Political Economy of Modern Capitalism: Mapping Convergence and Diversity*. Thousand Oaks, Calif.: Sage.

Evans, Peter 1995 *Embedded Autonomy: States and Industrial Transformation*. Princeton, N.J.: Princeton University Press.

Friedman, Thomas 1999 *The Lexus and the Olive Tree* New York: Farrar, Straus & Giroux.

Granovetter, Mark 1985 "Economic Action and Social Structure: The Problem of Embeddedness." *American Journal of Sociology* 91:481–510.

Gray, John 1999 *False Dawn: The Delusions of Global Capitalism* New York: New Press.

Hollingsworth, J. Rogers, and Robert Boyer 1997 *Contemporary Capitalism: The Embeddedness of Institutions*. New York: Cambridge University Press.

Kindleberger, Charles P. 1978 *Manias, Panics, and Crashes*. New York: Basic Books.

Mizruchi, Mark S., and Linda Brewster Stearns 1994 "Money, Banking, and Financial Markets." In Neil J. Smelser and Richard Swedberg, eds., *The Handbook of Economic Sociology*. Princeton, N.J.: Princeton University Press.

Orru, Marco, Nicole Woolsey Biggart, and Gary G. Hamilton 1997 *The Economic Organization of East Asian Capitalism*. Thousand Oaks, Calif.: Sage.

Polanyi, Karl (1944) 1957 *The Great Transformation*. Boston: Beacon Press.

—— 1971 *Primitive, Archaic and Modern Economies*. Boston: Beacon Press.

Portes, Alejandro, and John Walton 1981 *Labor, Class, and the International System*. New York: Academic Press.

Rogers, Joel, and Wolfgang Streeck, eds. 1995 *Works Councils: Consultation, Representation and Cooperation in Industrial Relations*. Chicago: University of Chicago Press.

Rothman, Barbara Katz 1989 *Recreating Motherhood: Ideology and Technology in a Patriarchal Society*. New York: Norton.

Scharpf, Fritz 1991 *Crisis and Choice in European Social Democracy*, trans. Ruth Crowley and Fred Thompson. Ithaca, N.Y.: Cornell University Press.

Stark, Davis and Laszlo Bruszt 1998 *Postsocialist Pathways: Transforming Politics and Property in East Central Europe*. Cambridge, U.K.: Cambridge University Press.

Streeck, Wolfgang 1997 "German Capitalism: Does it Exist? Can it Survive?" In Colin Couch and Wolfgang Streeck, eds., *Political Economy of Modern Capitalism: Mapping Convergence and Diversity*. Thousand Oaks, Calif.: Sage.

Swedberg, Richard 1987 "Economic Sociology: Past and Present." *Current Sociology* 35:1–221.

Thurow, Lester 1983 *Dangerous Currents: The State of Economics*. New York: Random House.

Wade, Robert, and Frank Venoroso 1998 "The Asian Crisis: The High Debt Model Versus the Wall Street–Treasury–IMF Complex." *New Left Review* 228 (March–April): 3–25.

Wallerstein, Immanuel 1974a *The Modern World-System, I: Capitalist Agriculture and the Origins of the European World-Economy in the Sixteenth Century*. New York: Academic Press.

—— 1974b "The Rise and Future Demise of the Capitalist World-System: Concepts for Comparative Analysis." *Comparative Studies in Society and History* 16:387–415.

—— 1980 *The Modern World-System, II: Mercantilism and the Consolidation of the European World-Economy*. New York: Academic Press.

—— 1989 *The Modern World-System, III: The Second Era of Great Expansion of the Capitalist World-Economy, 1730–1840s*. New York: Academic Press.

Walzer, Michael 1983 *Spheres of Justice: A Defense of Pluralism and Equality*. New York: Basic Books.

Wever, Kirsen S., and Lowell Turner, eds. 1995 *The Comparative Political Economy of Industrial Relations*. Madison, Wis.: Industrial Relations Research Association.

White, Harrison 1981 "Where Do Markets Come from?" *American Journal of Sociology* 87:517–547.

Williamson, Oliver 1975 *Markets and Hierarchies: Analysis and Antitrust Implications*. New York: Free Press.

Zukin, Sharon, and Paul DiMaggio 1990 *Structures of Capital: The Social Organization of the Economy*. New York: Cambridge University Press.

Zysman, John 1983 *Governments, Markets, and Growth: Financial Systems and the Politics of Industrial Change*. Ithaca, N.Y.: Cornell University Press.

FRED BLOCK

ECONOMIC SOCIOLOGY

Economic sociology constitutes its own distinct subfield in sociology and can be briefly defined as *the sociological analysis of economic phenomena.* Economic sociology has a rich intellectual tradition and traces its roots to the founding fathers of sociology, especially to Max Weber and his *Economy and Society* (see Swedberg 1998). It should be noted that not only sociologists but also economists have made important contributions to economic sociology. This is particularly true for today's economic sociology, which is the result of works not only by sociologists (such as Mark Granovetter and Harrison White) but also by economists (such as Gary Becker and Oliver Williamson).

To define *economic sociology* as "the sociological analysis of economic phenomena" may seem bland and even tautological. It is therefore important to stress that it entails a definite conception of what topics may be studied by sociologists; that it implies a certain division of labor between economists and sociologists; and that it also has direct consequences for how the relationship between economic theory and sociology is conceived. That this is the case becomes very clear if we contrast this definition with two other ones that are commonly used: (1) that economic sociology primarily deals with a particular dimension of economic phenomena, namely their social dimension; and (2) that economic sociology is the study of social structures and organizations in the economy. That economic sociology deals with economic phenomena in general (our definition) means that it addresses issues not only at the periphery of the economy (such as, say, the influence of religious values on the economy or of ethnicity on entrepreneurship) but also at its core (such as the way markets operate or investment decisions are made). Sociological theory here emerges as either an alternative to economic theory or as a direct challenge to it. To look at the social dimension of economic phenomena (the first alternative definition) means, on the other hand, that sociologists only look at a limited number of economic issues, usually those that are left over once the economists have finished with their analyses. Economists may, for example, decide with the help of standard economic theory what salaries and prices are like in a certain industry, while sociologists, by looking at a factory or a work group as a social system, may

then add some additional information. Economic theory is not challenged by this type of economic sociology, since it only deals with those topics for which there is no economic theory. That economic sociology focuses on social structures or on organizations in the economy (the second alternative definition) means that a purely economic analysis may be regarded as economic sociology as long as it deals with certain topics. Why a firm rather than the market is used for a specific type of transaction may, for example, be explained by the fact that transaction costs are higher in this specific case in the market. This type of economic sociology is close to economic theory and basically dispenses with traditional sociology (although not necessarily with rational choice sociology; see, e.g., Coleman 1990).

These three ways of looking at economic sociology all have their followers. The one which emphasizes that the sociological perspective in principle can be applied to *all* types of economic phenomena is, however, the one that has been used most frequently throughout the history of economic sociology. That this is the case will become clear from the following brief overview of the field. That the two other definitions—economic sociology as the analysis of the social dimension of economic phenomena, and economic sociology as the study of social structures and organizations in the economy—also have their adherents will become obvious as well.

Since the mid-1980s economic sociology has been going through something of a renaissance in the sociological profession, not only in the United States but also in other countries. The advent of what is usually referred to as "new economic sociology" represents one of the most dynamic areas in contemporary sociology. Before the mid-1980s three separate attempts had been made to create a vigorous economic sociology, and something needs to be said about these. The first attempt was made in the early twentieth century by a group of German scholars of whom Max Weber is the most important. The second attempt was made during the same time period by Emile Durkheim and his followers in France. And the third attempt was made by some American sociologists, such as

Talcott Parsons and Neil Smelser, in the 1950s. A few words shall be said about each of these attempts before we discuss the contemporary situation.

HISTORICAL ATTEMPTS AT ECONOMIC SOCIOLOGY

The first significant attempt to create a solid economic sociology was made in Germany during the period 1890–1930 by a group of scholars who were all trained in economics. The three key figures were Max Weber, Werner Sombart, and Joseph Schumpeter. A major reason that economic sociology developed so forcefully in German-speaking academia was probably its strong tradition of historical economics. There was also the fact that toward the end of the nineteenth century Gustav von Schmoller, the leader of the historical school of economics, became embroiled in a bitter academic fight with Carl Menger, one of the founders of marginal utility analysis. By the time Weber and Sombart became active, German economics had been polarized into two camps through the so-called battle of the methods, or the *Methodenstreit*: one that was overly theoretical and one that was overly historical. The idea of "economic sociology" was conceived by both Sombart and Weber as an attempt to get out of this dead end and to function as a kind of bridge between economic history and economic theory. Economic sociology should be analytical in nature, but historically grounded. While Sombart, however, wanted economic sociology to totally replace economic theory, Weber thought differently. In his mind, a healthy science of economics (Weber used the term *Sozialoekonomie*, or "social economics") should be broad and simultaneously draw on economic theory, economic history, and economic sociology (Weber 1949). Schumpeter basically shared Weber's opinion, although economic theory would always rank higher in his mind than in Weber's. The idea of such a broad-based social economics, however, never caught on.

Weber, Sombart, and Schumpeter all made a series of first-rate contributions to economic sociology. For one thing, all of them produced major studies of capitalism: Weber ([1921-22] 1978) in *Economy and Society*; Sombart ([1902] 1987) in *Der moderne Kapitalismus*; and Schumpeter ([1942] 1976) in *Capitalism, Socialism and Democracy*. Weber emphasized that capitalism was becoming increasingly rationalized; Sombart was particularly interested in looking at the different historical stages of capitalism; and Schumpeter argued that modern capitalism was digging its own grave and was soon to be replaced by socialism. These visions of capitalism still dominate our thinking and are therefore of great interest. And so are many of the shorter studies by Weber, Sombart, and Schumpeter, such as Sombart's ([1906] 1976) study of why there is no socialism in the United States, Weber's ([1904–5] 1930) analysis of the relationship between Protestantism and the spirit of capitalism, and Schumpeter's ([1919] 1954, [1918] 1971) two superb articles on imperialism and the tax state.

A special mention must also be made of Georg Simmel's ([1907] 1990) *The Philosophy of Money*. This work contains an ingenious analysis of money that ranges from philosophy to sociology. No general theory of money is developed, but the author takes on a series of interesting topics, including credit, checks, and small change. Simmel should not only be credited with having made a serious attempt to develop a sociological approach of money; he was also the first sociologist to realize what an important role trust plays in economic life.

The only one to make a sustained effort to lay a theoretical foundation for economic sociology, however, was Max Weber. He did this in a chapter of *Economy and Society* (Weber [1921–22] 1978) entitled "Sociological Categories of Economic Action." When Weber lectured on this chapter to his students, they found his analysis abstract and dry. He therefore decided to give a lecture course in economic history to supplement his theoretical ideas. This course became what is today known as *General Economic History* (Weber [1923] 1981), and it should be read together with *Economy and Society*. In the latter work Weber carefully constructs the various analytical categories that are needed in economic sociology. He starts with "the concept of economic action" and ends with macroeconomic phenomena, such as "market economies and planned economies." He also defines and discusses such basic concepts as trade, money, and the market—all from a sociological perspective. At various points in his discussion Weber carefully underlines when economic theory and economic sociology differ. It is, for example, imperative for economic sociologists to use the concept of economic power in their analyses, while this plays no role in marginal utility theory. In economic theory it is assumed that consumers are price givers, but economic sociology assumes that they are price takers. In economic theory it is usually assumed that prices are simply the result of demand and supply, while in economic sociology it is necessary to look at the strength of the various social groups in order to understand the unfolding of the "price struggle." Finally, in economic sociology economic action must in principle be oriented to the behavior of others. Economists exclusively study rational economic action, Weber concludes, while sociologists have a much broader focus.

During about the same time that Weber, Sombart, and Schumpeter were active in Germany, a similar, though independent, effort to create an economic sociology was made in France. The key figures here are Emile Durkheim, Marcel Mauss, and François Simiand. All three felt that since economic theory is not a social theory (in the sense that it does not assign analytical priority to society as opposed to the individual), it should be replaced by a sociological approach to the economy or, more precisely, by economic sociology. In this they echoed Auguste Comte's critique in the early 1800s of economic theorists for ignoring the fact that the economy is part of society and that, as a consequence, there is no need for a separate economic theory (Swedberg 1987). The two most important studies in the French school of economic sociology are *The Division of Labor in Society* by Durkheim ([1893] 1964) and *The Gift* by Marcel Mauss ([1925] 1969) (see also Simiand 1932). The latter work not only covers gift-giving but also contains a series of brilliant remarks on credit, interest, and consumption. In *The Division of Labor in Society* Durkheim raises the question of how to bring about solidarity in industrial society. His answer, which is further elaborated in other works (see especially Durkheim [1928] 1962, [1950] 1983), is that no society in which the economic element

predominates can survive. Economic life has to be restrained by a moral element; without a common morality, all persons would be at war with one another.

Both German and French economic sociology petered out in the 1930s. At around this time European sociology was exhausting itself, while U.S. sociology was in ascendency. Among the multiple subfields that appeared at that time, several are of interest to economic sociology, such as industrial sociology, the sociology of professions, and stratification theory. None of these, however, dealt with core economic problems or with economic theory. Instead there was a firm division of labor in U.S. social science at this time between economists, who only studied economic topics, and sociologists, who only studied social topics. In the 1950s, however, some sociologists decided to challenge this division of labor, and their efforts have become known as the "economy and society approach," so called both because two works with this title now appeared (Moore 1955; Parsons and Smelser 1956) and because a conscious effort was made to bring closer together two bodies of thought in the social sciences—economics and sociology—that most social scientists felt should be kept separate (see also Polanyi et al. 1957). Talcott Parsons and Neil Smelser (1956) argued, for example, that the economy is part of society or, in their terminology, "the economic sub-system" is part of "the social system." In this sense they assigned a certain priority to society and implicitly to sociology. On the other hand, they also felt that economic theory was essentially correct—even if it needed to be complemented by a sociological approach. This dual position also informs the first textbook as well as the first reader in economic sociology—both produced by Smelser (1963, 1965).

NEW ECONOMIC SOCIOLOGY

During the late 1960s and the 1970s little of interest happened in economic sociology. Since the mid-1980s, however, there has been a sharp increase of interest in this topic, and a new type of economic sociology has come into being (see Friedland and Robertson 1990; Granovetter 1990;

Zukin and DiMaggio 1990). Not only sociologists but also economists have contributed to this development. Since the mid-1970s mainstream economists have become increasingly interested in the role of social structures and organizations in the economy. This has led to a movement usually referred to as "new institutional economics" (e.g., Eggertsson 1990). Sources of inspiration for this new institutionalism include transaction cost economics, agency–principal theory, and game theory. Gary Becker (1976), for example, has convinced many economists that social phenomena can be analyzed with the help of the economist's tools; Kenneth Arrow has written about the role of organizations in the economy; Thomas Schelling (1960) has used game theory to develop a science of "interdependent decision"; and Oliver Williamson (1975) has popularized the concept of transaction costs through his best-selling *Markets and Hierarchies* (see also Coase 1937; Swedberg 1990). Three Nobel Prizes have also been awarded to economists who in one way or another focus on the social aspects of the economy: R.H. Coase (1991), Gary Becker (1992), and Douglass North (1993). As a result of these and other events, mainstream economists today are interested not only in traditional issues relating to price formation but also in economic institutions and how these change. The last time this happened in the United States was in the early twentieth century, when American institutionalism was born (see, e.g., Commmons 1924; Gruchy 1947; Veblen [1899] 1973). There exists, however, an important difference between the old form of institutionalism and new institutional economics. While Thorstein Veblen and his contemporaries tried to analyze economic institutions with the help of an approach that was very close to that of sociology, Becker and other current theorists claim that the reason economic institutions work the way they do can be analyzed with the help of the economist's traditional tools (efficiency, rational choice, etc.). This approach has been severely criticized by some sociologists on the grounds that it simplifies and distorts the analysis (e.g., Etzioni 1988; Granovetter 1985).

Since the mid-1980s, as already mentioned, there has been a major revival of economic sociology, and what is usually referred to as "new economic sociology" has come into being. The date of birth of this movement is usually set to 1985, since that year a highly influential article, which was to create much interest in economic sociology, was published. This was Mark Granovetter's "Economic Action and Social Structure: The Problem of Embeddedness," published in *The American Journal of Sociology*. The very same year, it can be added, Granovetter introduced the notion of "new economic sociology" in a brief paper at the annual meeting of the American Sociological Association. In his 1985 article on embeddedness, Granovetter sharply attacked the attempts by economists to explain the functioning of social institutions and accused them of simplicity. Just as economists have a tendency to ignore social relations through an "undersocialized concept of man," Granovetter said, some sociologists view the individual as a reflex of the social structure, and they consequently have an "oversocialized concept of man." The proper way to proceed, Granovetter suggested, is to tread a middle way between these two opposites, and this can best be done by assuming that individual actions are always "embedded" in social networks.

Granovetter's article has been followed by a minor avalanche of writings in economic sociology, and there exist good reasons for arguing that new economic sociology today constitutes a minor school of its own. A large number of articles and quite a few monographs have been produced; a couple of introductory readers can be found on the market; and in the mid-1990s a huge *Handbook of Economic Sociology* was published (Smelser and Swedberg 1994). Other signs that a certain institutionalization of economic sociology has taken place is that a section in economic sociology has been organized at the American Sociological Association, which has also published a volume with course outlines and similar teaching materials (Green and Myhre 1996).

Before saying something about the concrete studies that have been produced since the mid-1980s, it should be pointed out that new economic sociology is primarily a creation of North American sociologists. In Europe and elsewhere in the world there also exists an interest in economic sociology, but it tends to manifest itself in a less cohesive form than in the United States, and it is not held together through recurring conferences and the like. This is especially true for Europe. Most of the major European sociologists have written on economic topics in some work or another, but this is rarely perceived as an interest in economic sociology (e.g., Boltanski 1987; Bourdieu 1986; Luhmann 1988). There also exist articles and monographs by European sociologists who identify themselves as economic sociologists—but, to repeat, these tend not to be much noticed, since they are not held together by a strong and self-conscious tradition (e.g., Beckert 1997; Dodd 1994; Gislain and Steiner 1995). Finally, quite a bit of economic sociology has also been produced under the auspices of the section on economy and society within the International Sociological Association (e.g., Martinelli and Smelser 1990).

New economic sociology has advanced the understanding of economic phenomena in a number of ways, and it has especially been successful in analyzing the following three topics: (1) the role that networks play in the economy, (2) the way that culture and values influence the economy, and (3) what causes firms to be organized the way they are. Something will be said about each of these topics, but before doing so it should be noted that some interesting advances have also been made in many other areas, such as consumption, finance, and the role of gender in the economy (e.g., Abolafia 1996; Biggart 1989; Warde 1997). Finally, social capital is a topic that has attracted attention from sociologists as well as from political scientists and economists (e.g., Bourdieu 1986a; Coleman 1988; for an overview, see Woolcock 1998).

Network Analyses. Network analyses are often empirical in nature and sophisticated in their methodology, and this is also true for network studies in economic sociology. This latter type of studies made its first appearance in the 1970s, something which Granovetter's well-known *Getting a Job* (1974) is a reminder of. The same is true for studies of interlocks, that is, studies of the kind of links that emerge when some individual is a member of more than one corporate board. Interlock studies became popular with Marxist sociologists, who felt that they had found a way to document how the ruling class controls corporations

(e.g., Mintz and Schwartz 1985). A more subtle version of this argument can be found in Michael Useem's *The Inner Circle* (1984), based on interviews with chief executive officers (CEOs), whose main point is that CEOs who are members of several boards have a better overview of the economy, something that enables them to better defend their interests.

The simplistic type of interlock studies have been severely critized, primarily on the grounds that it is unclear what the consequences are of the fact that two or more corporations are connected through interlocks. In one interesting study, it was also argued that if for some reason a link between two corporations was severed, it would have to be reconstituted relatively soon if this type of link indeed is as important as is often claimed. This study showed that only a minority of so-called broken ties were actually re-created (Palmer 1983; see also the discussion in Stearns and Mizruchi 1986). As of today, the opinion of many economic sociologists is that interlock studies can be quite valuable, but only on condition that they are complemented with other material, such as historical studies, interviews, and the like.

A few words must be said about Granovetter's *Getting a Job* (1974), since it represents a particularly fine example of what an empirically sophisticated and theoretically interesting study in economic sociology can look like. As Granovetter notes in the second edition of this work from 1995, his study has inspired quite a bit of research since its original publication in the 1970s. The main thrust of the study is to challenge the notion of mainstream economics that social relations can be abstracted from an analysis of how people get jobs. Through network data he had collected in a Boston suburb, Granovetter succeeded in showing that information about openings in the job market travels through social networks, and the more networks you belong to, the more likely you are to find this type of information. Having a few very close and helpful friends is not as effective in terms of getting information as being linked to many different networks ("the strength of weak ties"). A corollary of this thesis, Granovetter shows, is that people who have had several jobs are more likely to find a new position when they become unemployed than those who have had only one employer.

Since the mid-1980s network studies have become very popular in economic sociology, and a number of advances have been made (see the studies cited in Powell and Smith-Doerr 1994). Several new topics have also been added to the repertoire, including industrial regions and ethnic entrepreneurship. A special mention should be made of Ronald Burt's *Structural Holes* (1992), in which competition and entrepreneurship are analyzed from a network perspective. Burt's study is centered around the argument that when an actor is the one and only link between two networks, he or she is in a good position to exploit this situation (*tertius gaudens*, or "the third who benefits," in Simmel's terminology). Granovetter (1994) has also suggested that the network approach can be used to study so-called business groups, that is, the kind of social formations that are made up of corporations that are bound together in some formal or informal way and that display a certain amount of solidarity. The applicability of the notion of business groups to the Korean *chaebol* or to the Japanese *keiretsu* is obvious, but it also appears that business groups exist in most Western countries.

The Influence of Culture and Values. A few economic sociologists have approached the study of the economy from a different perspective and emphasize the way that culture and values influence economic phenomena. The two most prominent contributors to this type of economic sociology are Paul DiMaggio (1994) and Viviana Zelizer (1979, 1985, 1994); the studies they have produced are of two kinds—general theoretical statements and empirical studies of a historical and qualitative character. Zelizer (1988) has sharply critiqued what she sees as an attempt in much of current economic sociology to eliminate values and to reduce everything to networks. Economic sociology, she argues, needs to introduce culture and values into the analysis, while simultaneously paying attention to the social structure.

Zelizer has also produced three empirical studies in which she attempts to show the impact of culture and values on economic phenomena. In the first of these, Zelizer (1979) looks at the development of the life insurance industry in the United States, showing how difficult it was to get people to accept that an individual's life can be evaluated in purely monetary terms. In her second study, Zelizer (1985) looks at the same development but, so to speak, in reverse—namely, how something that had an economic value at one time in history can turn into something that has a sacred value at another. In the nineteenth century, as she shows, children were often seen as having an economic value, while today they have an exclusively emotional value. In her latest study, Zelizer (1994) looks at money, arguing that people usually distinguish between different types of money. Money—and this is the main point—is not some kind of homogeneous, asocial medium, as economists claim, but is social to its very core. Pin money, for example, differs from the kind of money that is set aside for ordinary expenses; and when money is given away as a gift, an effort is usually made to disguise its nature as money.

Organization Theory. For a number of reasons there exists a clear affinity between organization theory and economic sociology. One reason for this, no doubt, is that sociologists of organization often analyze economic organizations; another is that organization theory was to incorporate much of industrial sociology when this field disappeared in the 1970s. And, finally, roughly during the 1990s, business schools often hired sociologists to teach organization theory. Three schools or perspectives in organization theory have been of much importance to economic sociology: resource dependency, population ecology, and new institutionalism.

The basic idea of resource dependency is that an organization is dependent on resources in its environment to survive. This perspective, as especially Ronald Burt has shown, can be of some help in understanding how the economy works. At the center of Burt's work on resource dependency is his concept of structural autonomy, or the idea that a corporation has more room to maneuver the fewer competitors it has and the more suppliers and the more customers there are. That a corporation has more power if it is in a monopoly position is clear; from this it follows that suppliers as well as customers are less powerful the more competitors they have. If Corporation A, for example, has only one supplier and one customer, both of these can wield quite a bit of power over Corporation A. Using a huge input–output data set for U.S. industry, Burt has also shown that the idea of structural autonomy has some support in empirical reality; in brief, the more structurally autonomous a corporation is, the more likely it is that profits will increase (Burt 1983).

Population ecology, as opposed to resource dependency, uses as its unit of analysis not the single corporation but whole populations of organizations. That these populations go through fairly distinct phases of growth and decline has been shown through a number of empirical studies, many of which are highly relevant to economic sociology since the organizations being studied are often economic organizations. Population ecology also looks at competition between organizations and the processes through which new organizational forms become accepted. The fact that population ecology typically looks at large populations of organizations means that relatively high-powered statistical methods are used. There is, however, little theoretical renewal going on in population ecology, and unless this changes, this perspective risks being exhausted in a few years.

A considerably higher degree of flexibility and creativity characterizes new institutionalism, or the kind of organization theory that has emerged around the work of John Meyer (e.g., Meyer and Rowan 1977; cf. DiMaggio and Powell 1991). A fundamental thesis in this approach is that rationality is often only a thin veneer and that organizations usually look the way they do for other than rational reasons. There also exist more or less distinct models for what a certain type of organization should look like, and these models are typically diffused through imitation. Since new institutionalism has such a flexible core, it can be used to analyze a variety of topics, in contrast to population ecology, which is considerably more limited in scope.

Two studies that illustrate this flexibility are Neil Fligstein's *The Transformation of Corporate Control* (1990) and Frank Dobbin's *Forging Industrial Policy* (1994). The former is a study of the huge American corporation since the end of the nineteenth century that challenges several of Alfred Chandler's theses. According to Fligstein, U.S. corporations have created different concepts of control during different periods of time; by control, he means the general strategy that corporations follow for surviving and making money. While cartels, for example, represented a common strategy around the turn of the century in the United States, they were later replaced by vertical integration, the idea of conglomerates, and other concepts of control. Fligstein also shows not only that the famous multidivisional form was a response to the economic environment, as Chandler claimed, but also that it was diffused through imitation.

Fligstein, as opposed to Chandler, also points out that the state influences the way corporations operate and the way they decide on a certain concept of control. Dobbin makes a similar point in *Forging Industrial Policy* (1994), but the emphasis in this study is primarily on regulatory or industrial policy cultures. Drawing on empirical material of a historical character from France, England, and the United States in the nineteenth century, Dobbin shows how each of these countries developed different regulatory and industrial policy cultures, and in particular how they treated railroads in different ways. The state, for example, was actively involved in the railroad business in France but played a more passive role in England and the United States. Dobbin argues convincingly that there exists no single best way of doing things in the economy, as mainstream economists seem to think; what may seem natural and rational to do in one country does not seem so in another.

New economic sociology has also made some interesting progress in the analysis of the market. The reason this topic has attracted quite a bit of attention among sociologists is that the theory of the market constitutes the very heart of mainstream economics; and to challenge mainstream economics one first and foremost has to challenge its theory of the market. Of the empirical studies that sociologists have produced, the most innovative may well be Mitchell Abolafia's *Making Markets* (1996) (see also Uzzi 1996). Abolafia has investigated three important markets on Wall Street (bonds, stocks, and futures markets) through participant observation; in particular, he has looked at the way that these are regulated. His major conclusion is that markets are social constructions and that regulation is related to "cycles of opportunism." When the existing regulation of a market is mild, opportunistic actors will take advantage of this fact, which will lead to a tightening of the rules; when regulation has been strong and effective for some time, demands are likely to be raised that milder rules should be introduced.

While most empirical studies of the market have focused on some aspect of the market rather than on its core, there do exist a few theoretical attempts by sociologists to explain the very nature of the market. Two of these are particularly interesting, namely, the analyses of Harrison White (1981) and of Neil Fligstein (1996). White's argument, which takes its departure in the typical production market with only a handful of actors, can be summarized in the following way: When a few actors produce similar products at similar prices, they may, by watching one another, come to realize that they make up a market and also behave according to this perception. More precisely, it is by watching the terms-of-trade schedule that this process takes place; and as long as the producers feel that they fit into this schedule, the market will continue to exist. By modeling his argument about the terms-of-trade schedule, White is also able to show under which theoretical conditions a market can come into being and when it will unravel.

While only a few attempts have been made to work directly with White's so-called W(y)-model, its general impact has been large in new economic sociology, especially through White's argument that a market comes into being when actors orient their behavior to one another in a rolelike manner. The most suggestive of the studies that have been influenced in a general way by the W(y)-model is Fligstein's theory of markets. Like White, Fligstein uses the typical production market as his point of departure, but the emphasis in his theory is quite different. Market actors, according to Fligstein, fear competition, since this makes it hard to predict what will happen, and they therefore attempt to introduce stability into the market. This can be done in different ways, and for empirical illustration Fligstein draws on his study of the evolution of the huge American corporation (Fligstein 1990). In certain situations, competition can nonetheless be very strong, but this is usually accompanied by attempts to stabilize the market. As examples of this, Fligstein mentions the situation when a new market is coming into being, when a major innovation is introduced into an already existing market, and when some major social disturbance takes place.

POSSIBLE FUTURE DIRECTIONS

If one were to summarize the situation in economic sociology at the end of the twentieth century, it could be said that economic sociology, which played such an important role in the classic works of sociology, has once again come alive. New and provocative studies have been produced, and a steadily growing number of sociologists are becoming interested in economic sociology. If one adds to this that mainstream economists are increasingly realizing the importance of institutions in the economy, it may well be the case that economic sociology will become one of the most interesting fields in sociology during the twenty-first century.

REFERENCES

Abolafia, Mitchell 1996 *Making Markets: Opportunism and Restraint on Wall Street*. Cambridge, Mass.: Harvard University Press.

Arrow, Kenneth 1974 *The Limits of Organization*. New York: W.W. Norton.

Becker, Gary 1976 *The Economic Approach to Human Behavior*. Chicago: University of Chicago Press.

Beckert, Jens 1997 *Grenzen des Marktes*. Frankfurt: Campus Verlag.

Biggart, Nicole Woolsey 1989 *Charismatic Capitalism: Direct Selling Organizations in America*. Chicago: University of Chicago Press.

Boltanski, Luc 1987 *The Making of a Class: Cadres in French Society*. Cambridge, U.K.: Cambridge University Press.

——, and Laurent Thevenot 1987 *Les économies de la grandeur*. Paris: Presses Universitaires de France.

Bourdieu, Pierre 1986a "The Forms of Capital." In John G. Richardson, ed., *Handbook of Theory and Research for the Sociology of Education*. Westport, Conn.: Greenwood Press.

—— 1986b *The Distinction*. Cambridge, Mass.: Harvard University Press.

Burt, Ronald 1983 *Corporate Profits and Cooptation: Networks of Market Constraints and Directorate Ties in the American Economy*. New York: Academic Press.

—— 1992 *Structural Holes: The Social Structure of Competition*. Cambridge, Mass.: Harvard University Press.

Coase, Ronald H. 1937 "The Nature of the Firm." *Economica N.S.* 4:385–405.

Coleman, James 1988 "The Role of Social Capital in the Creation of Human Capital." *American Journal of Sociology* 94:S95–S120.

—— 1990 *Foundations of Social Theory*. Cambridge, Mass.: Harvard University Press.

Commons, John R. 1924 *The Legal Foundations of Capitalism*. New York: Macmillan.

DiMaggio, Paul 1994 "Culture and the Economy." In Neil Smelser and Richard Swedberg, eds., *Handbook of Economic Sociology*. Princeton, N.J., and New York: Princeton University Press and Russell Sage Foundation.

——, and Walter Powell, eds. 1991 *The New Institutionalism in Organizational Analysis*. Chicago: University of Chicago Press.

Dobbin, Frank 1994 *Forging Industrial Policy: The United States, Britain and France in the Railway Age*. Cambridge, U.K.: Cambridge University Press.

Dodd, Nigel 1994 *The Sociology of Money: Economics, Reason and Contemporary Society*. London: Polity Press.

Durkheim, Emile (1928) 1962 *Socialism*. New York: Collier Books.

—— (1893) 1964 *The Division of Labor in Society*. Glencoe, Ill.: Free Press.

—— (1950) 1983 *Professional Ethics and Civic Morals*. Westport, Conn.: Greenwood Press.

Eggertsson, Thráinn 1990 *Economic Behavior and Institutions*. Cambridge, U.K.: Cambridge University Press.

Etzioni, Amitai 1988 *The Moral Dimension: Towards a New Economics*. New York: Free Press.

Fligstein, Neil 1990 *The Transformation of Corporate Control*. Cambridge, Mass.: Harvard University Press.

—— 1996 "Markets as Politics: A Political-Cultural Approach to Market Institutions," *American Sociological Review* 61:656–673.

Friedland, Roger, and A. F. Robertson, eds. 1990 *Beyond the Marketplace: Rethinking Economy and Society*. New York: Aldine.

Gislain, Jean-Jacques, and Philippe Steiner 1995 *La sociologie économique 1890–1920*. Paris: Pressess Universitaires de France.

Granovetter, Mark (1974) 1995 *Getting a Job: A Study in Contacts and Careers*. Cambridge, Mass.: Harvard University Press.

—— 1985 "Economic Action and Social Structure: A Theory of Embeddedness." *American Journal of Sociology* 91:481–510.

—— 1990 "The Old and the New Economic Sociology: A History and an Agenda." In Roger Friedland and A. F. Robertson, eds., *Beyond the Marketplace*. New York: Aldine.

—— 1994 "Business Groups." In Neil Smelser and Richard Swedberg, eds., *Handbook of Economic Sociology*. Princeton, N.J. and New York: Princeton University Press and Russell Sage Foundation.

Green, Gary P., and David Myhre 1996 *Economic Sociology: Syllabi and Instructional Materials*. Washington, D.C.: American Sociological Association Teaching Resources.

Gruchy, Allan G. 1947 *Modern Economic Thought: The American Contribution*. New York: Prentice-Hall.

Luhmann, Niklas 1988 *Die Wirtschaft der Gesellschaft*. Frankfurt: Suhrkamp Verlag.

Martinelli, Alberto, and Neil Smelser, eds. 1990 *Economy and Society: Overviews in Economic Sociology*. London: Sage.

Mauss, Marcel (1925) 1969 *The Gift: Forms and Functions of Exchange in Archaic Societies*. London: Cohen & West.

Meyer, John, and Brian Rowan 1977 "Institutionalized Organizations: Formal Structure as Myth and Ceremony." *American Sociological Review* 83:340–363.

Mintz, Beth, and Michael Schwartz 1985 *The Power Structure of American Business*. Chicago: University of Chicago Press.

Moore, Wilbert E. 1955 *Economy and Society*. New York: Doubleday.

Palmer, Donald 1983 "Broken Ties: Interlocking Directorates, the Interorganizational Paradigm, and Intercorporate Coordination." *Administrative Science Quarterly* 28:40–55.

Parsons, Talcott, and Neil Smelser 1956 *Economy and Society: A Study in the Integration of Economic and Social Theory*. London: Routledge and Kegan Paul.

Polanyi, Karl, Conrad M. Arensberg, and Hartry W. Pearson, eds. 1957 *Trade and Market in the Early Empires*. Glencoe, Ill.: Free Press.

Powell, Walter, and Laurel Smith-Doerr 1994 "Networks and Economic Life." In Neil Smelser and Richard Swedberg, eds., *Handbook of Economic Sociology*. Princeton, N.J., and New York: Princeton University Press and Russell Sage Foundation.

Schelling, Thomas 1960 *The Strategy of Conflict*. Cambridge, Mass.: Harvard University Press.

Schumpeter, Joseph A. (1918) 1954 "The Crisis of the Tax State." *International Economic Papers* 4:5–23.

—— (1919) 1971 "The Sociology of Imperialisms." In *Imperialism and Social Classes*. New York: Meridian Books.

—— (1942) 1976 *Capitalism, Socialism and Democracy*. New York: Harper & Row.

Simiand, François 1932 *Le Salaire, l'Evolution Sociale et la Monnaie*. Paris: Alcan.

Simmel, Georg (1907) 1990 *The Philosophy of Money*, 2nd enlarged ed. London: Routledge.

Smelser, Neil 1963 *The Sociology of Economic Life*. Englewood Cliffs, N.J.: Prentice-Hall.

——, ed. 1965 *Readings on Economic Sociology*. Englewood Cliffs, N.J.: Prentice-Hall.

——, and Richard Swedberg, eds. 1994 *Handbook of Economic Sociology*. Princeton, N.J., and New York: Princeton University Press and Russell Sage Foundation.

Sombart, Werner (1906) 1976 *Why Is There No Socialism in the United States?* New York: Sharpe.

—— (1902) 1987 *Der moderne Kapitalismus*. Munich: Deutscher Taschenbuch Verlag.

Stearns, Linda Brewster, and Mark Mizruchi 1986 "Broken-Tie Reconstitution and the Function of Interorganizational Interlocks: A Reexamination." *Administrative Science Quarterly* 31:522–538.

Swedberg, Richard 1987 "Economic Sociology: Past and Present." *Current Sociology* 35(1):1–221.

—— 1990 *Economics and Sociology: On Redefining Their Boundaries. Conversations with Economists and Sociologists*. Princeton, N.J.: Princeton University Press.

—— 1998 *Max Weber and the Idea of Economic Sociology*. Princeton: Princeton University Press.

Useem, Michael 1984 *The Inner Circle: Large Corporations and the Rise of Business Political Activity in the U.S. and U.K.* New York: Oxford University Press.

Uzzi, Brian 1996 "The Sources and Consequences of Embeddedness for the Economic Performance of Organizations: The Network Effect." *American Sociological Review* 61:674–698.

Veblen, Thorstein (1899) 1973 *The Theory of the Leisure Class*. New York: Macmillan.

Warde, Alan 1997 *Consumption, Food and Taste*. London: Sage.

Weber, Max (1904–05) 1930 *The Protestant Ethic and the Spirit of Capitalism*. London: Allen & Unwin.

—— (1904) 1949 "'Objectivity' in Social Science and in Social Policy." In *The Methodology of the Social Sciences*. New York: Free Press.

—— (1921–22) 1978 *Economy and Society: An Outline of Interpretive Sociology*. Berkeley: University of California Press.

—— (1923) 1981 *General Economic History*. New Brunswick, N.J.: Transaction Books.

White, Harrison C. 1981 "Where Do Markets Come From?" *American Journal of Sociology* 87:514–547.

Williamson, Oliver 1975 *Markets and Hierarchies*. New York: Free Press.

Woolcock, Michael 1998 "Social Capital and Economic Development." *Theory and Society* 27:151–208.

Zelizer, Viviana 1979 *Morals and Markets: The Development of Life Insurance in the United States*. New York: Columbia University Press.

—— 1985 *Pricing the Priceless Child: The Changing Social Value of Children*. New York: Basic Books.

—— 1988 "Beyond the Polemics of the Market: Establishing a Theoretical and Empirical Agenda." *Sociological Forum* 3:614–634.

—— 1994 *The Social Meaning of Money*. New York: Basic Books.

Zukin, Sharon, and Paul DiMaggio, eds. 1990 *Structures of Capital: The Social Organization of the Economy*. Cambridge, U.K.: Cambridge University Press.

RICHARD SWEDBERG

EDUCATION AND DEVELOPMENT

It is safe to say that the current living standard is the highest since the beginning of human history.

We have achieved unprecedented levels of life expectancy, income per capita, and educational attainment over the past few decades. This unprecedented prosperity and achievement would probably not have been attained without the continuous technological progress of the peaceful era after World War II. Most people would acknowledge the role of education in the advancement of our socioeconomic development. The value of education is widely studied. For example, it has been found that better-educated farmers are more responsive to new technical possibilities and that better-educated women are more effective at allocating resources within the family, including those that enhance child survival (Cleland and Van Ginneken 1988; Lockheed et al. 1980; Mensch et al. 1985; Schultz 1979). This article examines the empirical relationship between education and development during recent decades. Included are a brief description of the history of world education and socioeconomic development since the early 1960s as well as discussions of theoretical background, data sources, research methodology, and findings.

EDUCATIONAL DEVELOPMENT IN RECENT DECADES

During the past few decades, a rapid expansion of educational provision at primary, secondary, and tertiary levels in much of the world has been documented (Shavit and Blossfeld 1993; World Bank 1998). Column 3 of Table 1 shows the primary school gross enrollment ratio from 1960 through 1990. The gross enrollment ratio is the ratio of total primary school enrollment, regardless of age, to the population of the age group that officially corresponds to the "usual" primary education years (World Bank 1998). The ratio for the world as a whole has increased from 86 per 100 population in primary school age group in 1960 to a virtually universal rate in 1990. Impressive gains have been observed for many areas of the world. In 1960, for example, the primary school enrollment ratio was only 39 per 100 for sub-Saharan Africa; by 1990, it had increased to 73 percent.

Similarly, the secondary school gross enrollment ratio for the world as a whole increased from 27 percent in 1960 to 54 percent in 1990. Progress was especially impressive in the Middle East and North Africa, where the enrollment ratio surged from 12 percent in 1960 to 57 percent in 1990. This gross enrollment ratio is lowest in sub-Saharan Africa, where only 4 percent and 22 percent of the population were enrolled in secondary school in 1960 and 1990, respectively.

One important reason for such educational expansion has been the adoption of a compulsory education policy by many countries. Egalitarian values regarding education have also emerged with increasing of modernization. According to Lenski (1966), the Western industrial nations began to subscribe to an egalitarian-democratic ideology, in which equality of educational opportunity is highly valued, after industrialization took place. Presumably this egalitarian-democratic ideology became part of the philosophy of the United Nations through the influence of Western countries. The United Nations General Assembly's Universal Declaration of Human Rights, Article 26, which proclaimed education as a basic right and demanded that elementary education should be compulsory and free resulted from post-World War II expansion of the conception of education as a fundamental human right. In addition, the demand for more skilled workers in today's economy has also played a role in the expansion of education.

SOCIOECONOMIC DEVELOPMENT IN RECENT DECADES

As discussed earlier, the overall progress in socioeconomic development during the past few decades has pushed our living standard to the highest level ever. The World Bank defines development as follows:

Development is about people and their well-being–about people developing their capabilities to provide for their families, to act as stewards of the environment, to form civil societies that are just and orderly. (World Bank 1998, p. 35)

At the national level, development is generally divided into two dimensions: social and economic. Indicators of social development include

World Education and Socioeconomic Development, 1960–1996

Region	Year	% Primary Enroll-ment	% Secondary Enroll-ment	Level of Indust-rialization	Level of Urban-ization	% with Radio	GNP per Capita (Constant 1987 US $)	Infant Mortality	Life Expec-tancy	Population Growth Rate	Total Fertility Rate
World											
	1960	86	27	39	33	.	.	.	.	.	.
	1970	83	31	45	37	9	$2,574	98	58.7	.	4.8
	1980	97	49	48	39	29	$3,037	80	62.7	1.7	3.7
	1990	103	54	51	43	36	$3,374	61	65.5	1.7	3.1
	1996	.	.	.	46	.	$3,502	54	66.7	1.4	2.8
Sub-Saharan Africa											
	1960	39	4	18	15	.	.	.	.	.	.
	1970	50	7	21	19	4	$508	137	44.2	2.7	6.6
	1980	78	14	28	23	9	$556	115	47.6	3.1	6.6
	1990	73	22	32	28	16	$488	100	50.7	2.9	6.0
	1996	.	.	.	32	.	$475	91	52.2	2.8	5.6
South Asia											
	1960	56	18	25	17	.	.	.	.	.	.
	1970	67	25	29	19	2	$233	139	48.8	2.4	6.0
	1980	76	27	31	22	4	$250	120	53.8	2.4	5.3
	1990	91	39	36	25	8	$348	89	59.2	2.2	4.0
	1996	.	.	.	27	.	$419	73	62.1	1.8	3.4
Middle East and North Africa											
	1960	54	12	41	33	.	.	.	.	.	.
	1970	68	24	50	41	11	.	134	52.8	2.7	6.8
	1980	87	42	53	48	17	$2,653	96	58.5	3.2	6.1
	1990	97	57	65	54	26	$2,016	61	64.5	2.8	4.9
	1996	.	.	.	57	.	.	50	67.0	1.9	4.0
East Asia and Pacific											
	1960	101	19	18	17	.	.	.	.	.	.
	1970	88	24	24	19	1	$147	79	59.2	2.7	5.8
	1980	111	43	28	21	7	$225	56	64.5	1.5	3.1
	1990	122	47	31	28	17	$391	42	67.3	1.6	2.4
	1996	.	69	.	32	.	$636	39	68.2	1.2	2.2
Latin America and Caribbean											
	1960	89	15	52	49	.	.	.	.	.	.
	1970	.	28	59	57	13	$1,386	84	60.6	2.6	5.2
	1980	106	42	66	65	26	$1,867	59	64.8	2.2	4.1
	1990	106	48	74	71	35	$1,675	42	68.1	1.9	3.2
	1996	.	.	.	74	.	$1,877	33	69.5	1.6	2.8
Europe and Central Asia											
	1960	.	.	54	45	.	.	.	.	.	.
	1970	.	.	67	52	.	.	.	.	.	2.6
	1980	97	84	73	58	.	$1,865	41	67.8	1.0	2.5
	1990	98	85	77	63	.	$2,154	27	69.3	0.7	2.3
	1996	.	.	.	66	.	$1,548	24	68.3	0.1	1.8
North America#											
	1960	113	66	90	69	.	.	27	.	.	3.7
	1970	101*	65*	94	75	.	$12,084	19	71.6	1.3	2.4
	1980	99	90	95	75	136	$15,079	12	74.2	1.1	1.8
	1990	103	97	97	76	155	$17,543	8	76.2	1.3	2.0
	1996	.	.	.	77	.	$18,265	7	77.9	1.0	1.9

Table 1

SOURCE: 1998 World Development Indicator, World Bank CD-ROM.

Table 1 - notes

NOTE: Primary enrollment ratio: The ratio of total primary school enrollment, regardless of age, to the population of the age group that officially corresponds to the "usual" primary education/years.

NOTE: Secondary enrollment ratio: The ratio of total secondary school enrollment, regardless of age, to the population of the age group that officially corresponds to the "usual" secondary education/years.

NOTE: Level of industrialization: The proportion of the total labor force recorded as not working in agriculture, hunting, forestry, or fishing.

NOTE: eization: The percentage of the total population living in urban areas.

NOTE: GNP per capita (constant 1987 US$): Gross national product divided by midyear population.

NOTE: *The average of U.S.A. and Canadian data.

NOTE: *Canadian data only.

life expectancy, infant mortality, and educational attainment. The most commonly used indicator for economic development is GNP per capita (the gross national product divided by midyear population).

Table 1 shows world education and socioeconomic development from 1960 through 1996. The selected indicators include level of industrialization, level of urbanization, percent of population with radio, GNP per capita, infant mortality, life expectancy, population growth rate, and total fertility rate. The results are summarized below.

Level of Industrialization. Level of industrialization is defined as the percent of the total labor force employed in areas other than agriculture, hunting, forestry, and fishing. In 1960, 39 percent of the world labor force was so employed; by 1990, this figure had risen to 51 percent. Similar gains were observed for all world regions. The Middle East and North Africa posted the largest change in the level of industrialization. For example, 41 percent of the labor force in the Middle East and North Africa was employed in areas other than agriculture, hunting, forestry, and fishing in 1960; by 1990, the figure had risen to 65 percent. On the other hand, the gain in North America was low: The level of industrialization increased from 90 percent to 97 percent during the same period. It should be noted that the level of industrialization in North America started at a very high level, This accounts for the low level of gains in North America.

Level of Urbanization. Urbanization is the process whereby the proportion of people in a population who live in urban places increases. As our world moves toward being a more industrial

one, more people migrate from rural to urban areas to pursue better economic opportunities. The push–pull theory of migration is often cited to account for rural-to-urban migration (Ravenstein 1898; Lee 1886). The push factors are the unfavorable internal and external conditions in the places of origin that push individuals to leave their jobs/residences. Unfavorable internal employment conditions include lack of economic opportunities, low pay, low prospect for upward mobility, poor interpersonal relations, lack of challenge in the job, poor working environments, and so forth. Individuals in such circumstances are more likely to be pushed out of their jobs. Adverse external conditions that push individuals away from their residences/jobs, include such unfavorable structural conditions as high crime rate, pollution, and traffic congestion.

On the other hand, pull factors are favorable conditions in the new place of employment that attract individuals to migrate there. Facing the pressures of population growth and deteriorating economic opportunities, rural residents are being pushed out of their villages and attracted to urban areas, where they find a variety of economic opportunities to raise their living standard. According to Table 1, only 33 percent of the world's population lived in urban areas in 1960; by 1996, this number had increased to 46 percent. All the world regions have experienced similar gains, with the Middle East/North Africa and Latin America/Caribbean countries posting the largest gain (about 25 percentage points). North America ranked first in level of urbanization in 1996, with 77 percent of the population living in urban areas.

Percent of Population with a Radio. Another indicator of development is the percent of population with a radio. This indicator is an indirect measure of exposure to modern values and ideas. In 1970, only 9 percent of the world's population had a radio; this figure had risen to 36 percent in 1990. South Asia has the lowest level of radio possession; in 1990, only 8 percent of the population in South Asia had a radio. North America has the highest level of radio possession; specifically, there were more than 1,500 radios per 1,000 population in 1990.

GNP Per Capita. GNP per capita is defined as the gross national product divided by midyear population. Based on Table 1, the GNP per capita (inconstant 1987 US$) increased for most world regions from 1970 through 1996. For example, the GNP per capita in the world increased from $2,574 in 1970 to $3,502 in 1996; in North America, it increased from $12,084 in 1970 to $18,265 in 1996; in South Asia, it increased from $233 in 1970 to $419 in 1996.

Life Expectancy. Life expectancy at birth is the number of years a newborn infant would live if prevailing patterns of mortality at the time of its birth were to stay the same throughout its life (World Bank 1998). According to Table 1, the life expectancy at birth for the world increased from 58.7 years in 1970 to 66.7 years in 1996. The gain is found for all world regions. The Middle East and North Africa posted the largest increase in life expectancy (from 52.8 in 1970 to 67 in 1996); the progress in South Asia has also been very impressive (from about 48.8 in 1970 to 62.1 in 1996). The observed increase in life expectancy from 1970 through 1996 is a strong indication of world socioeconomic development that enables newborns to live a longer life.

Infant Mortality Rate. Infant mortality rate (IMR) is defined as the number of deaths during the first year of life per 1,000 live births. The negative relationship between infant mortality and the level of economic development is often used as a barometer for economic development (United Nations 1982). Young (1993) found strong support for this relationship in developed countries. Krikshnan (1975) and Rodgers (1979) also reported a negative relationship between infant mortality and level of economic development for developing countries. Similarly, Berg (1973) and Gaise

(1979) also maintain that as a country's GNP increases, the standard of living improves, which leads to an improvement in nutrition and health services. Preston (1976), however, notes that one should not expect to find a direct relationship between mortality and per capita income, because per capita income is an average measure and does not take the distribution of income into account. The effects of income on mortality are likely to be greater at the lower end of the income distribution.

Table 1 shows that the world's IMR decreased from 98 in 1970 to 54 in 1996. All world regions experience a decreased IMR during the same period; for example, the IMR decreased from 137 to 91 for sub-Saharan Africa. The progress in reducing IMR was especially prominent in the Middle East and North Africa, where the IMR decreased from 134 in 1970 to 50 in 1996. North America had the lowest IMR—7—in 1996.

Total Fertility Rate. Total fertility rate is an estimate of the average number of children that would be born to a woman if the current age-specific birthrates remained constant. The reproductive revolution or the transition from high to low fertility is one of the dimensions of socioeconomic development. According to demographic transition theory, socioeconomic development facilitates fertility decline through the following mechanisms: 1) reducing infant/child mortality rate, 2) raising the status of women (including an increased level of education for women and an increased proportion of women employed in the nonagricultural sectors), 3) raising the marriage age and celibacy rate, 4) increasing the costs of raising children, and 5) reducing the economic value of children. Caldwell (1982) also argues that modernization creates reversed intergenerational wealth flows from parents to children. Such flow, unlike traditional wealth flow from children to parents, discourages couples to have high fertility. These changes coupled with accessible contraceptives, a higher value placed on smaller families, a latent demand for smaller families, and governmental family-planning policies are commonly cited factors that account for fertility decline. Moreover, diffusion/interaction theory (Bongaarts and Watkins 1886; Rosero-Boxby 1883; Casterline 1985) and ideational theory (Lesthaeghe 1883) also provide significant theoretical insights on fertility decline.

In 1970, the total fertility rate (TFR) for the world was 4.8 children per woman; it had dropped to 2.8 in 1996. Similar patterns of fertility decline are found for all world regions. The worldwide reduction in fertility is as predicted by the demographic transition theory. In most of the more developed countries and some East Asian countries (e.g., Taiwan, Singapore, South Korea, and Hongkong), the total fertility rate has reached the replacement level (when TFR=2.1) or even below replacement level. Hirschman and Young (1999) also found that the total fertility rate had dropped to below 2.0 for Thailand in 1990. (Impressively the reproductive revolution in Thailand occurred when its GNP per capita was only $1,470 in 1990 (World Bank 1994).)

In sum, the latest World Bank data show that we have made tremendous progresses in education and socioeconomic development over the past few decades. The central question, however, remains to be answered: What is the impact of education on socioeconomic development?

THEORETICAL BACKGROUND

The title "Education and Development" does not imply a straight, unidirectional causal effect of education on development. Actually, the relationship between education and development can well be covariational.

To identify the exact cause and effect between the two is a difficult task. For example, education can facilitate development by providing the better-educated human resources that are essential for socioeconomic development. Education also reduces the fertility rate and thus population growth rate. It also transforms the labor-force structure and promotes rural-to-urban migration. On the other hand, the level of socioeconomic development in a country is likely to influence the level of education for that country. As development progresses, countries would have more resources to invest in education (thus development affects education). According to the functionist theorists, the

rapidly changing technology of the twentieth century has generated a demand for a better-educated labor force. The expansion of schooling can be viewed as a direct response to these technological changes. Moreover, the need for a more skilled labor force would encourage government to invest more in education in order to keep the economy competitive in today's world economy.

Thus, the relationship between education and development can be best viewed as covariational. Here I assume that education and development are related to each other in the initial stage of development. My goal is to investigate the net impact of education in an early stage on later stages of socioeconomic development after controlling for early-stage development and other important intervening variables. There are three main theories (modernization, human capital, and world-system) that address the impact of education on development.

Modernization Theory. Modernization is a transformation of social and economic structures. The *International Encyclopedia of the Social Sciences* (1868) defines modernization as "the process of social change in which development is the economic component" (p. 387). From a comparative perspective, modernization can be viewed as the process of social change whereby less developed countries acquire characteristics common to more developed countries. Lasswell (1965) argued that modernization not only shapes economic factors but also reshapes all social values such as power, respect, rectitude, affection, well-being, skill, and enlightenment. Common characteristics of modernity include: (1) a degree of self-sustaining growth in the economy; (2) a measure of public participation in the polity; (3) a diffusion of secular-rational norms in the culture; (4) an increment of mobility in the society; and (5) a corresponding transformation in the modal personality that equips individuals to function effectively in a social order that operates according to the foregoing characteristics.

Proponents of modernization theory argue that the transformations of socioeconomic structures—such as the mechanization of agriculture, urbanization, a mass communication network, demographic transition, the expansion and integration of a national market, and an increase in political participation—are necessary preconditions for sustained economic growth (Apter 1965; Rostow 1960). Obviously, changes in these social forces create new opportunities, incentives, and normative influences that can affect (1) an individual's view on the world and (2) his or her behavior. Another thread of the modernization theory stresses that exposure to modern values leads to socioeconomic development. Inkeles and Smith (1975) maintain that modern people, as opposed to traditional people, are prepared to act on their world rather than fatalistically accept it; have a cosmopolitan rather than a local orientation; see the sense of deferring gratification; welcome rather than distrust change; are not constrained by irrational religious or cultural forms; and recognize the value of education. According to modernization theory, education plays a crucial role in making the route to modernization possible.

Macroeconomic studies have shown that education is positively correlated with overall economic growth, with one year of additional schooling of the labor force possibly leading to as much as a 9 percent increase in gross domestic product (GDP) for the first three years of schooling and a yearly 4 percent increase for the next three years (Summers 1994). Increased education has also been found to result in greater agricultural productivity, even in developing countries (Jamison and Lau 1982; Lockheed et al. 1980). The National Research Council (1986) also reported that "urbanization plays a beneficial role in the development process, providing an increasing share of population with access to relatively high-wage employment, education, health care, and other modern public services" (p. 76).

However, in a case study of Egypt, Faksh (1977) found that "educational expansion in modern Egypt thus far has not been conductive to development in the general configuration of the Egyptian polity" (p. 238).

Human Capital Theory. Human capital theory argues that education leads to development by increasing the efficiency and productivity of workers. Investment in human capital is a key element in achieving long-term sustainable economic growth. According to this perspective, "the main contribution of education to economic growth was to increase the level of cognitive skills possessed by the work force and consequently to improve their marginal productivity" (Benavot 1989, p. 15). According to the theory, the provision of education is not a form of consumption but a productive investment in society's "stock" of human capital. Investment in human capital is at least as profitable as investment in physical capital. At the national level, increasing the overall level of education will raise the stock of the human capital, which will have a positive impact on national productivity and economic growth. At the individual level, education level provides some indication of the ability of a person to perform certain duties and adapt to other work situations.

World-System/Dependency Theory. World-system and dependency theories suggest that the specialization of some countries in the export of raw materials and lightly processed goods is an important cause of their underdevelopment. Moreover, the world-system/dependency theories argue that the needs and interests of Western capitalism determine the pattern of education in developing countries. Education is seen as part of the process whereby peripheral countries are kept underdeveloped. The prevalence of foreign investment capital, the presence of multinational corporations, the concentration on exporting primary products, and the dependence on imported technologies and manufactured goods constrain long-term economic development (Bornschier and Chase-Dunn 1985; Delacroix and Ragin 1978). According to the theory, "education, far from a key component in development, modernization, self-sufficiency, and so on, is in fact yet another instrument of enslavement, a way of tightening, rather than loosening, the dependency bond." (Dale 1982, p. 412).

Each of the above theory examines the relationship between education and development from different angles. Each theory delineates part of the dynamics of the relationship. Due to the limitation

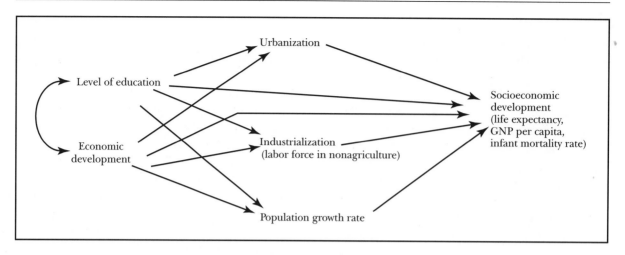

Figure 1. Analytical Model of Education and Development

of data, this article will examine only the validity of modernization theory.

DATA SOURCE, ANALYTICAL MODEL, MEASUREMENT, AND RESEARCH METHODS

Data Source. The World Bank compiles national data on education, demographics, and socioeconomic development from various years and sources. The data used for this research is from the World Bank's 1998 World Development Indicator CD-ROM.

Analytical Model. In this article, education and economic development are assumed to be related to each other in the initial stage of analysis (e.g., measures for both variables obtained in 1970). Both education and development are the independent variables. From there, I analyze how both 1970 factors affected the intervening variables (1980 level of industrialization, urbanization, and population growth rate). Finally, I estimate the net effect of 1970 education on 1990 development, after controlling for 1970 development and other 1980 intervening variables. The effect of education on development is also estimated for the 1980–1996 period. This model is shown in Figure 1.

Measurement. Education is defined as the formal schooling, although education can also be defined as an alternative to family education, an

instrument of state social policy, a site of civic reform, or a form of humanistic progress. Socioeconomic development is broadly defined as the progress in the areas of GNP per capita, infant mortality, and life expectancy.

There are three sets of variables—the independent, the intervening, and the dependent variables. The independent variables include the level of education and economic development observed at a earlier time period. The intervening variables, including urbanization, industrialization, and population growth rate, are controlled to mediate the effects of the independent variables on the dependent variable. Finally, the dependent variable is the level of socioeconomic development observed at a later period of time. Three indicators are used: GNP per capita, life expectancy, and infant mortality.

Level of education is defined as the secondary school gross enrollment ratio, defined in the previous section on "Educational Development in Recent Decades." I use this as the main independent variable rather than the primary school enrollment ratio because for many countries compulsory education is limited to the primary level. Lack of variation in primary school enrollment ratio could pose a threat to the validity of the study.

Socioeconomic development include three indicators: life expectancy, GNP per capita, and infant mortality rate. Lift expectancy at birth measures

Descriptive Statistics for All Variables in Panel Analyses

Variables	Mean	SD	Minimum	Maximum	N
1970–1990					
Independent variables					
Percent of secondary enrollment, 1970	31.6	26.4	1.0	102.0	128
Logged per capita GNP, 1970	7.2	1.5	4.5	11.0	119
Intervening variables					
Industrialization, 1980	57.1	28.0	5.6	98.7	173
Urbanization, 1980	45.9	24.1	3.9	100.0	195
Population growth rate, 1980	2.0	1.5	-2.4	9.7	194
Dependent variables					
Logged per capita GNP, 1990	7.4	1.4	4.7	10.3	159
Life expectancy, 1990	64.9	10.3	35.3	78.8	192
Infant mortality rate,1990	48.0	41.8	4.6	189.0	194
1980–1996					
Independent variables					
Education, 1980	49.37	31.56	3	114	147
Logged per capita GNP, 1980	7.42	1.47	4.8	10.72	136
Intervening variables					
Industrialization, 1990	62.36	28.28	5.88	99.63	173
Urbanization, 1990	50.41	23.73	5.2	100	194
Population growth rate, 1990	1.9	1.68	-4.87	14.12	199
Dependent variables					
Logged per capita GNP, 1996	7.23	1.44	4.55	10.32	138
Life expectancy, 1996	66.08	10.22	36.88	79.76	194
Infant mortality rate,1996	42.14	38.75	3.5	174.2	195

Table 2

the overall quality of life. It is defined as "the number of years a newborn infant would live if prevailing patterns of mortality at the time of its birth were to stay the same throught its life" (World Bank 1998: 19). The GNP per capita measures the economic aspect of progress. Infant death is the final biological expression of a process that is determined basically by the economic and social structure of a country of region. These conditions influence the occurrence and spread of disease as well as quality and availability of health care facilities, all of which are crucial to survival probabilities. The structural determinants are mediated at the family level, because the child's growth and development are heavily dependent on the living conditions of the family.

Intervening Variables. The intervening variables include urbanization of population in urban areas, industrialization of labor force in nonagricultural activities, and annual population growth rate. Time-lag path analysis is used to investigate

the direct and indirect effects of education at an earlier time (e.g., 1970) on socioeconomic development at the later time (e.g., 1990), after controlling for urbanization, population growth rate, and industrialization. Specifically, two models will be examined. The first model uses 1970 data for the independent variables, 1980 data for the intervening variables, and 1990 data for the dependent variables. The second model examines the periods between 1980 and 1996. That is, I use 1980 data for the independent variables, 1990 data for the intervening variables, and the 1996 data for the dependent variables. For both analyses, the unit of analysis is country.

Research Method. Path analysis will be used to study the proposed model. The path coefficient represents the standardized regression coefficient. The standardized regression coefficient (ß) represents the change in the standard deviation of the dependent variable associated with one standard deviation of change in the independent variable, when all other variables are controlled for.

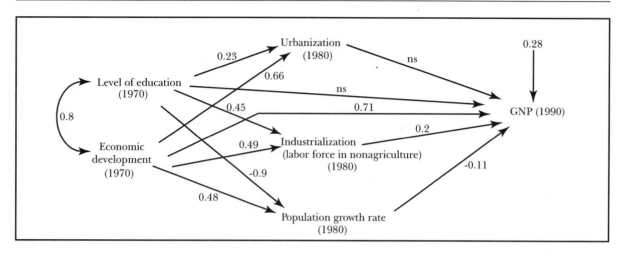

Figure 2. Education and Economic Development, 1970–1990.

The coefficient of alienation (defined as the square root of $1-R^2$) is also provided to show how well each development indicator is predicted by all the independent variables. A larger coefficient of alienation indicates that the development model has a smaller R^2 or coefficient of determination. On the other hand, if a development model has a smaller coefficient of alienation, then the independent variables in that model explain more variation in that development indicator.

FINDINGS AND DISCUSSION

Descriptive Statistics. Table 2 presents means, standard deviations, the minimum values, and the maximum values for all variables used in the analysis. The upper panel shows the data for 1970–1990 period and the lower panel for 1980–1996 period. There are two independent variables, percent of secondary school enrollment and logged GNP per capita. GNP per capita has an extremely skewed distribution. In regression analysis, normal distributions for all variables are expected. To correct this problem, I take the natural log of GNP per capita. The mean logged GNP per capita in 1970 was 7.2. The 1990 logged GNP per capita was 7.4.

The intervening variables include industrialization, urbanization, and population growth rate. Finally, the dependent variables include economic

Correlation Matrix of Variables Used in Panel Path Analyses

	(1)	(2)	(3)	(4)	(5)	(6)	(7)	(8)	(9)	(10)	(11)	(12)	(13)	(14)	(15)	(16)
1. Education, 1970	1.00															
2. GNP per capita, 1970	0.80	1.00														
3. Industrialization, 1980	0.81	0.84	1.00													
4. Urbanization, 1980	0.74	0.82	0.89	1.00												
5. Population growth rate, 1980	-0.52	-0.32	-0.36	-0.24	1.00											
6. GNP per capita, 1990	0.81	0.95	0.86	0.81	-0.32	1.00										
7. Life expectancy, 1990	0.79	0.73	0.88	0.73	-0.43	0.81	1.00									
8. Infant mortality rate,1990	-0.76	-0.70	-0.85	-0.69	0.43	-0.80	-0.96	1.00								
9. Education, 1980	0.92	0.78	0.81	0.72	-0.48	0.72	0.78	-0.77	1.00							
10. GNP per capita, 1980	0.76	0.98	0.87	0.83	-0.19	0.98	0.78	-0.75	0.78	1.00						
11. Industrialization, 1990	0.79	0.82	0.99	0.88	-0.35	0.88	0.88	-0.85	0.80	0.86	1.00					
12. Urbanization, 1990	0.70	0.80	0.87	0.98	-0.17	0.80	0.70	-0.66	0.68	0.82	0.87	1.00				
13. Population growth rate, 1990	-0.48	-0.17	-0.32	-0.16	0.75	-0.24	-0.37	0.38	-0.41	-0.12	-0.32	-0.13	1.00			
14. GNP per capita, 1996	0.84	0.94	0.81	0.78	-0.61	0.98	0.79	-0.77	0.69	0.97	0.80	0.76	-0.58	1.00		
15. Life expectancy, 1996	0.79	0.72	0.87	0.73	-0.41	0.80	0.99	-0.94	0.75	0.77	0.88	0.70	-0.35	0.79	1.00	
16. Infant mortality rate, 1996	-0.75	-0.68	-0.84	-0.68	0.41	-0.78	-0.96	0.99	-0.75	-0.73	-0.85	-0.66	0.36	-0.76	-0.95	1.00

Table 3

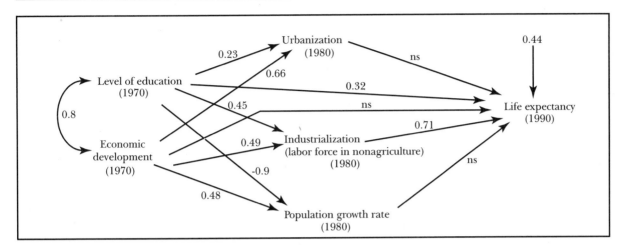

Figure 3. Education and Life Expectancy, 1970–1990

development (logged GNP per capita at a later year), life expectancy, and infant mortality.

Corelation Matrix. Table 3 shows the correlation matrix for all variables used in the two-panel analyses. All the correlation coefficients are significant at .01 level. Furthermore, the strengths of all correlations are substantially strong. Moreover, the direction of relationship is as expected by modernization theory. For example, there is a high correlation between 1970 education and 1990 socioeconomic development. Specifically, .81, .79, and −.76 are the correlations between 1970 education and 1990 logged GNP per capita, 1990 life expectancy, and 1990 infant mortality rate, respectively.

Similarly, there is also a high correlation between 1980 education and 1996 socioeconomic development. Specifically, the correlations between 1980 education and 1996 logged GNP per capita, 1996 life expectancy, and 1996 infant mortality rate are .69, .75, and −.75, respectively. Since the bivariate correlation between the independent variable and the dependent variables does not control for other causal mechanisms, I will be controlling for intervening variables in path analyses. The results of path analyses are reported below.

Path Models. Figure 2 shows the relationship between education and economic development during the 1970–1990 period. The path model shows that the level of education, as measured by secondary school enrollment rate in 1970, has no

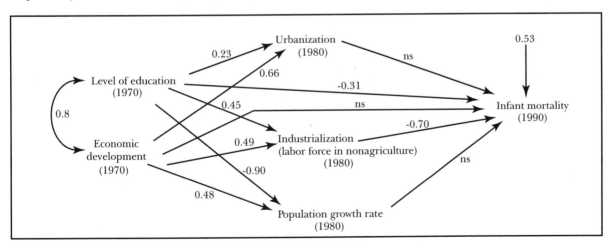

Figure 4. Education and Infant Mortality, 1970–1990

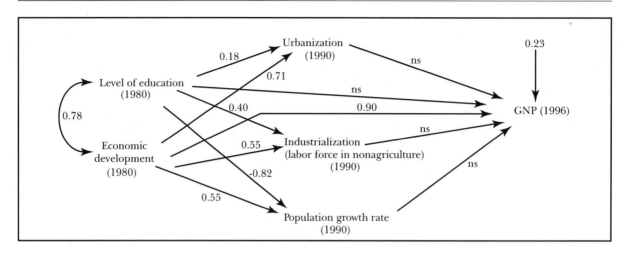

Figure 5. Education and Economic Development, 1980–1996

direct effect on economic development, as measured by GNP per capita in 1990, after the 1980 urbanization, 1980 industrialization, 1980 population growth rate, and 1970 economic development are held constant. Similarly, urbanization has no effect on economic development after other variables are controlled for, although cross-national studies suggest that urbanization is related to the level of economic development as measured by per capita income or GNP (Chenery and Syrquin 1975).

Nevertheless, education has indirect effects on economic development. The first indirect effect of .09 (.45×.02=.09) from education to economic development is through its effect on industrialization (the path coefficient is .45). High

enrollment rate in secondary school is found to have a moderate and positive effect on level of industrialization. Industrialization is found to have a positive direct effect on economic development (the path coefficient is .20). The second indirect path from education to economic development is through population growth rate. High secondary school enrollment rate lowers a country's population growth rate (path coefficient is −.90). A country's population growth rate is found to have a weak and negative effect on its economic development (the path coefficient is −.11). The second indirect effect of education on economic development is .10 (−.99×−.11=.10). The total indirect effect of education on economic development is .19 (.09+.10=.19).

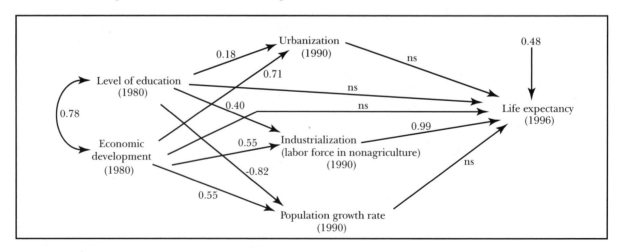

Figure 6. Education and Life Expectancy, 1980–1996

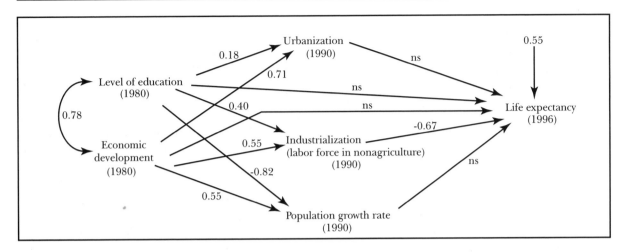

Figure 7. Education and Infant Mortality, 1980–1996

Figure 3 shows the relationship between education and life expectancy during the 1970–1990 period. The path model shows that the level of education in 1970, as measured by secondary school enrollment rate, has a positive and moderate direct effect on 1990 life expectancy (the path coefficient is .32), after 1980 urbanization, 1980 industrialization, 1980 population growth, and 1970 GNP per capita are controlled for. Countries that invest their resources in education can directly increase their population's life expectancy. Urbanization and population growth rate are found to have no effect on life expectancy. In addition to its direct effect on life expectancy, education also has an indirect effect on life expectancy. The indirect effect of .32 (.45×.71=.32) from education to life expectancy is through its effect on industrialization (the path coefficient is .45). High level of industrialization is found to have a very strong positive effect on life expectancy (path coefficient is .71). High proportion of population engaged in nonagricultural occupations increases a country's life expectancy. The total effect of education on life expectancy is .64 (the sum of direct effect, .32, + indirect effect, .32).

The last model for the relationship between education and development between 1970 and 1990, as measured by infant mortality, is shown in Figure 4. According to Figure 4, level of education in 1970 reduces the infant mortality rate in 1990. This finding is consistent with other studies based on individual-level analysis. Moreover, 1980 industrialization also has a direct and negative effect on

infant mortality. Countries with a low proportion of the labor force in nonagricultural activities are more likely to have higher infant mortality rate. The indirect effect of education on infant mortality through industrialization is −.32. (.45 × −.70 = −.32). The total effect on education on infant mortality is −.63 (−.32 + −.31 = −.63).

Figures 5, 6, and 7 examine the relationship between education and economic development, life expectancy, and infant mortality rate during 1980–1996. The intervening variables—urbanization, industrialization, and population growth rate—are based on 1990 data. Surprisingly, the results from Figure 5 shows that there was no direct or indirect effect of education on economic development during 1980–1996. Only 1980 GNP per capita had a direct impact on the 1996 GNP per capita.

Figure 6 shows that the level of education in 1980 had no direct effect on the 1996 life expectancy. However, it had an indirect effect on life expectancy through its effect on industrialization. The indirect effect of education on life expectancy is .31 (.40 − .77 = .31).

Similar to what was reported in Figure 6, Figure 7 shows that the level of education in 1980 had no direct effect on 1996 infant mortality. However, it had an indirect effect on infant mortality through its effect on industrialization. The 1980 industrialization has a substantially strong negative and direct effect on 1996 infant mortality rate (path coefficient= −.67). The indirect effect of education on infant mortality is −.27 (.40 × −.67 = −.27) for the 1980–1996 period. The level of economic development in 1960 is also found to have an indirect and negative impact on 1996 infant mortality rate. The indirect effect of economic development on infant mortality is −.37 (.55 × −.67 = −.37), which is stronger than the impact of education during this period.

There were some weaknesses in the study. The variables used in the study are period data. Period data are collected in a given year when their values are very much influenced by macro socioeconomic conditions. The time intervals between the independent and the dependent variables of 20 years (or 16 years for second model) may seem long. Finally, secondary school enrollment was used as the independent variable. Further studies may consider tertiary education as an indicator of education.

SUMMARY AND CONCLUSION

Modernization theory maintains that education promotes development. For many developing countries, education is a prominent means of attempting to narrow the knowledge gap between the highly industrialized countries and the developing countries.

This article reported the world's impressive education and socioeconomic developments over the past few decades. It also examined a diverse set of mechanisms through which education affects socioeconomic development for two periods: 1970–1990 and 1980–1996. The overall findings suggest that education has a positive effect on life expectancy for both time periods examined. Moreover, education was found to have had negative relationship to infant mortality for the 1970–1990 and 1980–1996 periods. However, the effect of education on economic development is more complicated. Education is found to have had a positive effect on economic development for only the 1970–1990 period, not for 1980–1996 period. Another interesting finding is that the effect of education on development was lower during 1980–1996 than the 1970–1990 period.

The study shows that education, industrialization, and development are inextricably interrelated. To achieve a higher level of socioeconomic development, policy makers would need to consider the complex relationship between education and development. Several countries have taken steps to improve their educational systems in order to bolster their economies and improve conditions in their nations. In recent history, for example, China and Taiwan have made attempts to modernize and strengthen their economies by encouraging people to further their education, especially in science and technology. It is clear from this study that to improve the welfare of the billions of people in the developing world, governments in developing countries need to continue and expand their investments in education for their population.

The sociology of education and the sociology of development have become very important areas in sociological research. As more advanced data become available, we will be able to do better research in this area by conducting more sophisticated and comprehensive studies. Examining modernization and other theories in the area of education and development will enable sociologists to provide solid knowledge about the mechanisms whereby education affects development, which can be important information for policy makers when they implement policies related to education and development.

REFERENCES

Apter, D. 1965 *The Politics of Modernization.* Chicago: University of Chicago Press.

Benavot, Aaron 1989 "Education, Gender, and Economic Development: A Cross-National Study." *Sociology of Education* 62(1):14–32.

Berg, B. 1973 "Nutrition and National Development." In Alan Berg, Neven S. Scrimshaw, and David L. Call, eds., *Nutrition, National Development and Planning.* Cambridge, Mass.: MIT Press.

Bornschier, Y., and C. Chase-Dunn 1985 *Transnational Corporations and Underdevelopment.* New York: Praeger Publishers.

Bongaarts, John, and Susan C. Watkins 1996 "Social Interactions and Contemporary Fertility Transitions." *Population and Development Review* 22:639–682.

Caldwell, John C. 1982 *Theory of Fertility Decline.* London: Academic Press.

Casterline, John B. ed. 1985 *The Collection and Analysis of Community Data.* Voorburg, Netherlands: International Statistical Institute.

Chenery, H., and M. Syrquin 1975 *Patterns of Development, 1950–1970*. New York: Oxford University Press.

Dale, Roger 1982 "Learning to Be . . .What? Shaping Education in Developing Societies." In Hamza Alavi and Teodor Shanin, eds., *Introduction to the Sociology of "Developing Societies."* New York: Monthly Review Press.

Delacroix, J., and C. Ragin 1978 "Modernizing Institutions, Mobilization, and Third World Development: A Cross-National Study." *American Journal of Sociology* 84:123–149.

Diebolt, Claude 1997 "Education and Economic Growth in Germany Before the Second World War." *Historical-Social-Research*.

Faksh, Mahmud A. 1977 "The Chimera of Education for Development in Egypt: The Socio-Economic Roles of Unversity Graduates." *Middle Eastern Studies* 13:229–240.

Gaise, S. K. 1979 "Some Aspects of Socioeconomic Determinants of Mortality in Tropical Africa" (WHO doc: DSI/SE WP/79:13).

Hirschman, Charles, and Yih-Jin Young 1999 "The Decline of Fertility in Thailand, Malaysia, Indonesia and the Philippines." In Ronald D. Lee and C. Y. Cyrus Chu, eds., *Economic Aspects of Demographic Transition in Asia-Pacific Countries. A supplement to Population and Development Review* (Forthcoming).

—— 1998 "Fertility Transition in Southeast Asia." Paper presented at the Conference on Economic Aspects of Demographic Transition: The Experience of Asian-Pacific Countries, Taipei, Taiwan, June 19–20, 1998.

Inkeles, Alex, and David Smith 1975 *Becoming Modern*. London: Heinemann.

Jamison, Dean, and Lawrence J. Lau 1982 *Farmer Education and Farm Efficiency*. Published for the World Bank. Baltimore: The Johns Hopkins University Press.

Lasswell, Harold D. 1965 "The Policy Sciences of Development." *World Politics* 17:286–309.

Lee, Everett 1966 "A Theory of Migration." *Demography* 3:47–57.

Lesthaeghe, Ron 1983 "A Century of Demographic and Cultural Change in Western Europe: An Exploration of Underlying Dimensions." *Population and Development Review* 9:411–435.

Lockheed, Marlaine E., Dean T. Jamison, and Lawrence Lau 1980 "Farmer Education and Farm Efficiency: A Survey." *Economic Development and Cultural Change* 29(1):37–76.

Mensch, B., H. Lentzner, and S. Preston 1985 *Child Mortality Differentials in Developing Countries*. New York: United Nations.

National Research Council 1986 *Population Growth and Economic Development: Policy Questions*. Washington, D.C.: National Academy Press.

Preston, Samuel H. 1976 *Mortality Patterns in National Populations: With Special Reference to Recorded Causes of Death*. New York: Academic Press.

Ravenstein, E. 1898 "The Laws of Migration." *The Journal of the Royal Statistical Society* 52:241–301.

Rodgers, G. B. 1979 "Income and Inequality as Determinants of Mortality: An International Cross-Section Analysis." *Population Studies* 33(2):343–351.

Rosero-Bixby, Luis, and John B. Casterline 1993 "Modelling Diffusion Effects in Fertility Transition." *Population Studies* 47:147–167.

Rostow, W. W. 1960 *The Stages of Economic Growth*. Cambridge, U.K.: Cambridge University Press.

Schultz, T. W. 1979 "Investment in Population Quality in Low Income Countries." In P. M. Haieser, ed., *World Population and Development: Challenges and Prospects*. Syracuse, N.Y.: Syracuse University Press.

Shavit, Yossi, and Hans-Peter Blossfeld, eds. 1993 *Persistent Inequality, Changing Educational Attainment in Thirteen Countries*. Boulder, Colo.: Westview Press.

Summers, Lawrence H. 1994 "Investing in All the People: Educating Women in Developing Countries" (EDI Seminar Paper No. 45), Washington, D.C.: Economic Development Institute of the World Bank.

United Nations 1982 "Levels and Trends of Mortality Since 1950: A Joint Study by the UN and WHO." New York: United Nations.

World Bank 1994 *World Tables 1994*. Baltimore: John Hopkins University Press.

—— 1998 *World Development Indicators 1998*. Washington, D.C.: The World Bank.

Young, Yih-Jin 1993 "A Macro-Comparative Analysis on Socioeconomic Development and Infant Mortality." Paper presented at the Canadian Association for the Study of International Development Ninth Annual Conference, Ottawa, Canada, June 1993.

YIH-JIN YOUNG

EDUCATION AND MOBILITY

One of the main reasons education is valued so highly in modern societies is the role it plays in relation to social mobility and reproduction. This role has long been debated between those who emphasize its contribution to social mobility and those who focus on its contribution to social reproduction. In order to understand this debate, it is useful to review the key concepts and theoretical perspectives before considering the empirical evidence and then offering a resolution.

Social stratification refers to institutionalized inequality, that is, to hierarchically structured social positions (strata) and to the inequality in social rewards received by people who belong to different strata. Social stratification is based mainly on class or status, although other forms of stratification exist (for elaboration, see Grusky and Takata 1992; Haller 1992). *Class* is the term preferred by theorists who view the social order as consisting of distinctive economic groupings struggling to maximize their interests vis-à-vis each other, while *status* is preferred by theorists who perceive a continuing distribution of socioeconomic variation without clear-cut divisions and conflict.

Social mobility is the movement from one class or status to another. The emphasis here, as with most studies of social mobility, is on *intergenerational mobility*, which refers to the change in class or status from parents to their adult children. An example of intergenerational mobility is when the daughter or the son of peasants becomes a doctor. In contrast, when the child of peasants ends up being a peasant, it is an example of *social reproduction.*

The class or status positions that individuals occupy in society are usually attributed to both *ascriptive* and *achievement* processes. These are generally viewed as opposite or contradictory processes involving either ascribed characteristics based on biological factors and family of origin or achieved characteristics based on individual traits and behaviors. Stratification systems that emphasize ascriptive characteristics for class or status placement are defined as "closed" and lead to status inheritance or class reproduction. Those stratification systems that emphasize achieved characteristics are defined as "open" and are expected to lead to social mobility.

The opposing positions are formalized in the functionalist and conflict theories of social stratification. With respect to the role of education in producing social mobility, functionalists argue that different social roles require different skills and abilities and that, if society is to function effectively, they must be filled by individuals possessing the appropriate skills and abilities (Davis and Moore

1945). The positions most valued by society are usually the most critical for societal functioning and the most demanding of individual skills and ability. In order to encourage individuals to invest the time and effort for training and to attract the best-qualified individuals, these positions have to be accompanied by higher social and economic rewards. Education is widely viewed as both developing and reflecting individual skills and abilities, and it is therefore used as a means of social selection. Thus, education enhances social mobility by providing for social selection based on achieved rather than ascribed characteristics of individuals.

Conflict theorists start with the premise that society consists of different groups with conflicting interest, and they argue that stratification exists because groups that acquired power, wealth, and prestige want to maintain and enhance their position at the expense of less privileged groups. In respect to education, most conflict theorists agree that schools help to reproduce and legitimize the stratification system by portraying attainment as an achieved individual characteristic, while in fact they select and process individuals on the basis of ascriptive characteristics (Bowles and Gintis 1976; Bourdieu 1977; Willis 1977).

Empirical research on the role of education in the process of social mobility or reproduction has produced conflicting evidence. The argument of mobility through education as suggested by functional theories depends on the validity of two general conditions: (1) Educational attainment must be used as a criterion of eventual class or status position, and (2) the level of educational attainment of individuals must not be influenced by the level of their family's class or status. Boudon (1976) calls these two conditions necessary for social mobility "meritocracy" and "equality of educational opportunity" respectively. It is important to note that social mobility exists only if both conditions are met and that each of them alone is a necessary but insufficient condition for social mobility.

These conditions necessitate a distinction, as far as the role of education is concerned, that is very rarely made between class and status. The role of education differs considerably in class and status mobility. Education plays a very weak role in class mobility or reproduction (Katsillis and Armer

1992). More specifically, the meritocracy condition is not satisfied, since education is almost never used as a criterion for class. Following Marx, most class theorists see two major classes, capitalists and workers, although the perception of the exact number of classes and their composition varies (see Poulantzas 1974; Wright 1978, 1985; for a discussion of the different views, see Grusky and Takata 1992). Education would play an important role in class reproduction only if it were a major criterion for becoming a capitalist or a worker and the vehicle through which the class of the parents is transferred to their children. But it is neither. In fact, if education were a principle determinant of class, one would expect most Ph.D.'s to be capitalists and a significant number of children from bourgeois families to become workers because of educational difficulties (Katsillis and Armer 1992).

A detailed discussion of the process through which class is reproduced is beyond the scope of this article. It suffices to say here that other institutions, such as the legal system and, more specifically, the inheritance and property transfer laws, are much more reliable and effective for the transfer of class from parents to their children. Whether these children have a high school or higher diploma may be important for other reasons, but it is clearly not essential for the reproduction of their class (Katsillis and Armer 1992).

In addition, educational attainment does not seem to be influenced by family class. Indeed, there is no reliable and consistent empirical evidence that supports such a relationship. When class is measured as determined by the relation of production and not as a status position, it has no effect on educational attainment, especially if the status position is held constant (see Katsillis and Armer 1992; Katsillis and Rubinson 1990; Katsillis and Spinthourakis 1997). At first glance, this would indicate that the equality of educational opportunity hypothesis is satisfied in relation to class. However, taking into account the absence of meritocracy in class determination, the lack of influence of class is more an indication of the weak role education plays in class reproduction or mobility than of its equalizing potential.

In contrast to class, education plays an important role in status allocation. Many studies have empirically tested the meritocracy hypothesis, and almost all have found a significant relationship between educational and later socioeconomic attainments (Blau and Duncan 1967; Duncan et al. 1972; Jencks et al. 1972; Sewell et al. 1969). Indeed, most studies in the United States have found educational attainment to be among the most important determinants of occupational and status attainment, although the findings regarding its relationship to income are not as conclusive (Jencks et al. 1972). In short, the meritocracy condition is well supported by empirical evidence.

However, other studies of social mobility have found that employing meritocracy in the allocation of occupational and social status does result in substantial increases in social mobility (Boudon 1974; Collins 1979). Boudon, using data from Western industrialized countries, and Collins, analyzing data from the United States, found that the tremendous expansion of education in the nineteenth and twentieth century left the opportunities for social mobility essentially unchanged. It did expand the educational attainment of many social groups, but, as the educational attainment of individuals from lower socioeconomic strata increased, individuals from higher strata acquired even more education, thus shifting the overall educational attainment of the population upward but keeping intact the stratification of educational attainment (Boudon 1974; Collins 1979). Given that meritocracy in the allocation of social positions exists, these findings suggest the lack of equality of educational opportunity.

In relation to the latter, the functionalist position is that schools do provide equality of opportunity. For empirical support, they point to the numerous empirical studies suggesting that the process of educational attainment is an achievement process. The best-known model of educational and status attainment in the United States, known as the Wisconsin model, describes the process as one whereby individual and background characteristics are translated into differential status attainment only after they have been transformed into individual performance and psychological variables (Sewell et al. 1969; 1970). Although this model has been criticized for excluding social constraints and related structural variables (see Kerckhoff 1976), its explanatory power remains strong, and it has withstood a number of replications (Alexander, Eckland, and Griffin 1978; Jencks et al. 1983). Indeed, most of the research on the social selection process that followed the Wisconsin model has shown that schools select, process, and reward students based on individual traits and achievements, such as aspirations and ability, and that educational attainment in turn is the major determinant of occupational status attainment.

Conflict theorists and researchers, by contrast, have not been very successful in describing and explaining a social selection process that leads to social reproduction. The explanations and the evidence as to why individuals from higher social strata acquire consistently better education have not been able to dispute or account for the fact that the educational selection process is ostensibly an "achievement" process. In general, the argument from a conflict perspective is that structural limitations imposed on the schooling of some groups restrict their educational success, thus helping to reproduce the educational and social hierarchies.

Some structural limitations on both the quality and quantity of educational opportunity of children from low socioeconomic strata do indeed exist. Differential quality and quantity of schooling may have been especially influential in the past, but it still exists today. Some of the best schools at all educational levels in the United States are private, with high tuition, and obviously not all social groups have equal access to or success in these institutions. Also, fewer institutions, especially at the postprimary levels, are available in rural or low-income areas. Nonetheless, the impact of variation in quality and quantity of schooling has been reduced over the years, and evidence does not indicate it as a major determinant of educational attainment. For example, the well-publicized report *Equality of Educational Opportunity* (Coleman et al. 1966) found that differences between public schools had no significant effect on student performance. In general, even though some relevant quality differences between schools may still exist today, this structural variable is a relatively weak factor in explaining differential educational attainment.

Other structural variables, such as curriculum tracking (Alexander, Cook, and McDill 1978) and differential treatment by teachers and counselors (Karabel 1972; Rist 1970), also have been found to exert significant influence on educational attainment. In addition, researchers have found that

cultural differences linked to differential social origin are also responsible for the unequal educational attainment of students from different social groups (Bourdieu 1977; Bourdieu and Passeron 1977; DiMaggio 1982). Overall, however, structural limitations and cultural deficiencies account for only a small amount of attainment differences as compared to the individual achievement variables.

Summarizing the findings on equality of educational opportunity and meritocracy presents a paradoxical picture of social stratification and leaves the issue of social mobility through education largely unresolved: Status attainment research has shown that educational and status attainment is a meritocratic process based on individual achievement variables, but it has not explained the relatively low social mobility rates. Critical research, on the other hand, has shown reproduction of social status, but it has not been able to unseat the equality of opportunity thesis resting on the association of individual achievement with educational status attainment.

This apparent paradox may be due in part to the fact that research on educational and social stratification in the last few decades has been dominated by the ascription–achievement controversy without necessarily examining the relationship between this controversy and the broader mobility–reproduction debate. The underlying assumption of this focus seems to have been that achievement leads to mobility and ascription leads to reproduction. But however important achievement and ascription may be, they do not address the same issues as mobility and reproduction. A way out of this impasse may be to challenge the assumed correspondence between what we traditionally consider individual achievements on the one hand and social mobility on the other. There is no reason to assume that an empirical finding of schooling as an achievement process is necessarily incompatible with a theoretical argument of schooling as a process of reproduction. As long as individual qualities and achievements are determined by the social origin of the student, educational systems can promote not only social reproduction and individual achievement but also social reproduction *through* achievement (Katsillis and Rubinson 1990).

One of the most consistent findings of the research on educational and status attainment is that the socioeconomic status of the family influences the whole educational process, including many, if not all, individual student achievements and abilities that lead to socioeconomic status attainment. Thus, once the assumption that achievement implies social status or class mobility is abandoned, there is no contradiction between the findings of status attainment research that indicate an achievement-oriented educational selection system and the findings of critical research that schools reproduce social status or class inequalities.

This, of course, poses some interesting questions, especially in relation to the meaning and the role of equality of educational opportunity as we understand it today: Does a process that transforms family status inequality into differential individual achievements or qualities and, subsequently, into unequal educational attainment constitute equality of educational opportunity? If it does not, what constitutes equality of educational opportunity, and how is it attained? We may have to rethink the whole process of equality of opportunity before we are able to provide satisfactory answers to the question of education and social mobility.

(SEE ALSO: *Equality of Opportunity*; *Social Mobility*; *Social Stratification*; *Sociology of Education*; *Status Attainment*)

REFERENCES

Alexander, K. L., M. A. Cook, and E. L. McDill 1978 "Curriculum Tracking and Educational Stratification: Some Further Evidence." *American Sociological Review* 43:47–66.

Alexander, K. L., B. K. Eckland, and L. J. Griffin 1978 "The Wisconsin Model of Socioeconomic Attainment: A Replication." *American Journal of Sociology* 81:324–342.

Blau, P. M., and O. D. Duncan 1967 *The American Occupational Structure*. New York: Wiley.

Boudon, R. 1974 *Education, Opportunity and Social Inequality*. New York: Wiley.

Bourdieu, P. 1977 "Cultural Reproduction and Social Reproduction." In J. Karabel and A. H. Halsey, eds., *Power and Ideology in Education*. New York: Oxford University Press.

——, and J. C. Passeron 1977 *Reproduction in Education, Society, and Culture*. Beverly Hills, Calif.: Sage Publications.

Bowles, S., and H. Gintis 1976 *Schooling in Capitalist America*. New York: Basic Books.

Coleman, J. S., E. Q. Campbell, C. J. Hobson, J. McPartland, A. M. Mood, F. D. Weinfall, and R. L. York 1966 *The Equality of Educational Opportunity*. Washington, D.C.: U.S. Department of Health, Education, and Welfare.

Davis, K., and W. Moore 1945 "Some Principles of Stratification. "*American Sociological Review* 10:242–249.

DiMaggio, P. 1982 "Cultural Capital and School Success: The Impact of Status Culture Participation on the Grades of U.S. High School Students." *American Sociological Review* 47:189–201.

Duncan, O. D., D. L. Featherman, and B. Duncan 1972 *Socioeconomic Background and Achievement*. New York: Seminar Press.

Grusky, D. B., and A. A. Takata 1992 "Social Stratification." In E. F. Borgatta and M. L. Borgatta, eds., *Encyclopedia of Sociology*. New York: Macmillan.

Jencks, C., J. Crouse, and P. Mueser 1983 "The Wisconsin Model of Status Attainment: A National Replication with Improved Measures of Ability and Aspirations." *Sociology of Education* 56:3–19.

Jencks, C., M. Smith, H. Acland, J. M. Bane, D. Cohen, H. Gintis, B. Heyns, and S. Michelson 1972 *Inequality: A Reassessment of Family and and Schooling in America*. New York: Basic Books.

Karabel, J. 1972 "Community Colleges and Social Stratification." *Harvard Educational Review* 42:521–562.

——, and A. H. Halsey, eds. 1977 *Power and Ideology in Education*. New York: Oxford University Press.

Katsillis, J., and J. M. Armer 1992 "Class Reproduction and Status Competition: Incompatible or Complementary Processes?" Paper presented at the annual meeting of the Southern Sociological Society, New Orleans, LA.

——and R. Rubinson 1990 "Cultural Capital, Student Achievement, and Educational Reproduction: The Case of Greece." *American Sociological Review* 55:270–279.

——and J. A. Spinthourakis 1997 "Social Determination of Language Learning in Greek High Schools." Paper presented at the Twelfth International Congress of the World Association for Educational Research (WAER), Rethymno, Crete.

Katsillis, J. M., C. Alexopoulos, P. Moustairas, and P. Skartsilas 1997 "Equality of Educational Opportunity and Social Equality: Concepts, Theory and Practice." In T. Moyne, ed. *Sociology of Greek Education: Review, New Research and Prospects*. Pp. 47–60, Patras, Greece: Achaikes Ekclosis. In Greek.

Kerckhoff, A. C. 1976 "The Status Attainment Process: Socialization or Allocation?" *Social Forces* 52:368–381.

Poulantzas, N. 1974 *Classes in Contemporary Capitalism.* London: Verso.

Rist, R. C. 1970 "Student Social Class and Teacher Expectations: The Self-Fulfilling Prophecy in Ghetto Education." *Harvard Educational Review* 40:411–451.

Sewell, W. H., A. O. Haller, and G. W. Ohlendorf 1970 "The Educational and Early Occupational Status Attainment Process: Replications and Revisions." *American Sociological Review* 34:1014–1027.

——, and A. Portes 1969 "The Educational and Early Occupational Status Attainment Process." *American Sociological Review* 34:82–92.

Willis, P. 1977 *Learning to Labor.* New York: Columbia University Press.

Wright., E. O. 1978 *Class Structure and Income Determination.* New York: Academic Press.

—— 1985 *Classes.* London: Verso.

JOHN KATSILLIS
J. MICHAEL ARMER

EDUCATIONAL ORGANIZATION

Education and schooling are not synonymous. Education is the more encompassing concept, referring to the general process by which a social group—whether an entire society, a family, or a corporation—transmits attitudes, beliefs, behaviors, and skills to its members. Within these broad boundaries, we can distinguish three general types of education—informal, nonformal, and formal—according to the location of instruction, the characteristics of the teachers, the methods of instruction, and what is learned.

Informal education takes place in the context of everyday life, and the educators include family members, peers, workmates, and the mass media. Formal education or schooling, meanwhile, takes place outside the family in institutions that specialize in education, is conducted by teachers who are not students' intimates and whose principal occupation is education, and stresses learning more through verbal and written description and guided inquiry than through observation and imitation. Finally, nonformal education—which takes such forms as on-the-job training, agricultural extension programs, and family-planning outreach programs—is more organized than informal education but has aims that are more specific and short term than those of formal education.

Virtually all societies utilize all three forms of education, but they differ in the relative predominance of these forms. In nonindustrialized societies, informal education dominates, with formal and nonformal education only marginally present. But in industrialized societies such as the United States, formal education rivals, if not exceeds, nonformal and informal education in importance and the use of society's resources. However, this is not to say that such agencies of informal education as the mass media do not have very profound effects. The ubiquity of the modern mass media and the fact that they are now held in relatively few hands allow them to widely and deeply shape many of our beliefs, attitudes, and behaviors (Bagdikian 1990; Herman and Chomsky 1988).

THE STRUCTURE OF NATIONAL SCHOOL SYSTEMS

School systems across the world are converging more and more in structure and content (Meyer, Kamens, and Benavot 1992; Meyer, Ramirez, and Soysal 1992). Yet school systems still differ considerably, even among countries comparable in economic development. One key axis of variation is relative size. Nations greatly differ in the proportion of their total population, especially the young, enrolled in school. For example, in 1994 the proportion of youth of secondary school age enrolled in school averaged 94 percent across twenty-one advanced industrial societies (sixteen European countries, the United States, Canada, Japan, Korea, and Australia). But the average percentage was 55 percent for eighteen less developed Asian countries (excluding Japan, Korea, Taiwan, Hong Kong, and Singapore) and 32 percent for fifteen African countries (U.S. National Center for Education Statistics 1997).

Clearly, differences in wealth and degree of industrialization explain a major part of this variation. But even when we control for these factors, we still find enormous differences among societies in the structure of their school systems.

Economically Advanced Countries. Even economically advanced societies differ greatly in how their school systems are governed and how their students' school careers are structured. Nations differ greatly in how much control the national government exercises over how schools are financed and operated. There are several countries that lodge governance primarily at the subnational or provincial level, such as the United States, Canada, and Germany. But most advanced societies vest control in a national central educational authority, usually a national Ministry of Education. For example, the Japanese Ministry of Education provides most of the funding for schooling, determines national curriculum requirements (the subjects to be taught and the depth in which they are to be covered), selects lists of acceptable textbooks, sets standards for teacher training and certification, and administers the 166 or so public universities. To be sure, local prefectural boards establish or close schools, hire and supervise teachers, and plan the curriculum. But they do all this within parameters set by the national ministry, which can veto their decisions (Kanaya 1994).

Nations with strongly centralized school governance leave much less room for local control and therefore for local variation in the content and structure of schooling. But the flip side of the coin is that such nations also suffer from much less inequality in school spending across localities and—because of class and racial segregation in housing—across social classes and races.

School systems in advanced industrial societies vary also in the structure of students' careers; that is, the timing of career selection and therefore curricular differentiation; the proportion of secondary students specializing in vocational studies; the strength of the tie between vocational training in secondary school and labor-market outcomes; the proportion of students entering and graduating from higher education; and the degree of differentiation within higher education, including whether there is an elite sector with privileged ties to elite public and private jobs (Brint 1998; Hopper 1977). The United States and Germany are nearly polar opposite on virtually all these dimensions.

The United States puts off occupational selection until very late. The main branching point comes after high school, when a student decides whether to go to college, which college to enter, and later what field to major in. As a result, U.S. high schools have a weak connection to the labor market. Because of this, many current educational reforms—such as school-to-work partnerships between schools and employers—are directed toward enhancing the connection between secondary school curricula and labor market opportunities.

Meanwhile, the proportion of students entering and graduating from higher education is huge. In 1996, 65 percent of high school graduates (or about 58 percent of all college-age youth, given a dropout rate of about 11 percent) entered higher education. According to the High School and Beyond Survey, about one-quarter of college entrants eventually receive a baccalaureate degree or higher and another one-fifth receive a one- or two-year certificate or degree. These figures for college entrance and graduation are about double those for Germany (Organization for Economic Cooperation and Development 1998; U.S. National Center for Education Statistics 1997). Because so many U.S. students go on to college and because student selection occurs to a great extent within college, U.S. higher education institutions are quite varied in curriculum, prestige, and student-body composition (see below).

Germany, meanwhile, has a very different school system. Student selection occurs at age ten, when students are divided between academic high school (Gymnasium) and two types of vocational secondary schooling (Realschule and Hauptschule). At age fifteen students graduate from the vocational high schools into either more advanced vocational schools or apprenticeship programs combining on-the-job and classroom training. Both are strongly connected to specific employment. Meanwhile, graduates of the Gymnasium go on to take the Abitur exam, which determines if they will be allowed into university. All told, only one-quarter of German students enter the university and only 15 percent get university degrees (Brint 1998; Organization for Economic Cooperation and Development 1998).

These differences in student careers fundamentally shape educational outcomes. A tightly coupled school career system, in which test results largely determine admission to the best schools and graduation from them in turn strongly shapes job placement, will tend to produce students who work hard at their schooling and their exam performance, as is the case in Japan (Brint 1998; Rohlen 1983). But the effects of school structure reach further. School systems that have small, highly selective higher educational sectors with little or no distinctions made among universities, as in the case of Germany, will tend to generate greater class consciousness and solidarity. In contrast, schools systems with large, internally heterogeneous higher education sectors, such as in the United States, foster weaker class consciousness (Brint 1998).

Economically Less Developed Countries. Economically less developed countries (LDCs) vary greatly as well in the size and structure of their school systems. For example, in Africa, the ratio of secondary school students to the secondary-age population ranges from 7 percent in Mozambique to 77 percent in Egypt (U.S. National Center for Education Statistics 1997). In addition, LDCs vary greatly in how socially exclusive their higher education systems are; for example, in 1985 the proportion of postsecondary students who are female ranged from 24 percent in sub-Saharan Africa to 52 percent in the Caribbean (Ramirez and Riddle 1991).

A major source of this diversity in size and structure is, of course, differences in degree and form of economic development even among less developed societies. But other factors also play an important role in causing this variation. Though most LDCs were at some point colonies or protectorates of one of the European powers or the United States, this colonial inheritance was not homogeneous. For example, the British and French colonial heritages were quite different, rooted in the different educational and political systems of those two countries. British colonies typically had higher rates of college attendance and lower rates of grade repetition than French colonies, echoing the differences between their colonial masters' own school systems (Brint 1998). Furthermore, the nature of the political elites—whether enthusiastic modernizers as in Turkey or Iraq or conservatives as in Saudi Arabia—has made a difference in how much emphasis they put on expanding the school system (Brint 1998).

Despite these variations, educational systems in economically less developed countries (LDCs) do exhibit considerable homogeneity in structure. A lack of resources has tended generally to force a lower level of educational provision (Brint 1998). In addition, many LDCs share a common colonial inheritance; for example, across the former British colonies in Africa and the Caribbean, secondary education remains dominated by the British "O-level" and "A-level" examinations (Brint 1998). Moreover, modernizing movements of quite various ideological stripes have seen education as a way of creating loyalty to and solidarity with their new ideas (Brint 1998; Meyer, et al. 1992). Finally, the World Bank has been playing a homogenizing role by strongly urging particular reforms (such as emphasizing primary over tertiary education and deemphasizing vocational education) on nations applying for loans (Brint 1998).

A CLOSER LOOK AT THE STRUCTURE OF THE U.S. SCHOOL SYSTEM

As noted above, the U.S. school system is quite unlike that of most other advanced industrial societies. The United States is virtually unique among advanced societies in that education is not mentioned in the national constitution and educational governance is not lodged with the national government (Ramirez and Boli-Bennett 1982). Instead, schooling in the United States is a state and local responsibility. Consequently, the United States has more than fifty separate sovereign educational authorities.

The United States has no national universities (except for the military academies and a few other specialized institutions). There is no required national exam for university entrance. While the Scholastic Assessment Test (SAT) and the American College Testing (ACT) exam are widely used, they are privately operated and individual colleges decide whether and how their results will be used.

The connection between educational credentials and workplace opportunities is comparatively weak in the United States (Collins 1979). Of course, for some occupations, the connection is quite strong, with a standardized curriculum preparing graduates for licensing examinations. But for most college graduates, the connection between their college major and their work careers is tenuous at best. Significant labor-market advantages go to those who attend and graduate from college, but the school system has relatively weak connections to most occupational sectors. Recent reforms, such as the 1994 federal School-to-Work Act, aim to tighten the links between secondary and postsecondary training and the labor market (Van Horn 1995). But it will take many years of such efforts before the United States even approximates Germany or Japan in the closeness of linkage between school and work.

These structural features have created an educational system in the United States that is wide open and characterized by very high enrollments and great student and institutional diversity. We make available a seat in some college somewhere for virtually everyone who wants to attend. Consequently, our secondary education system is less decisive than in most other countries, as "second-chance" opportunities abound. Secondary school students do not have to make hard decisions about their educational futures until quite late, often in college.

In order to better understand these unusual features of the American system, let us examine the structure of U.S. education in greater detail.

Elementary and Secondary Education. All elementary and secondary (K–12) school districts operate within the confines of the relevant state education law, which specifies requirements for graduation, certification of teachers, and so forth. State governments also provide on average about 47 percent of public school funding, with most of the rest coming from local taxes (U.S. National Center for Education Statistics 1997).

Private schools, too, must conform to state education law, but they are less restricted than are public schools. For example, in most states, the regulations governing teacher certification are less strict if one teaches in a private school than a public school. It is almost entirely up to the private school and its sponsors to generate financial support. No tax-derived funds may be used to support private K–12 schooling unless special conditions are met (for example, private schools may receive public aid if they enroll handicapped students). Interestingly, public aid flows much more easily to private colleges. They can receive student financial aid, grants to build academic facilities, and grants

and contracts to conduct research and run academic programs.

The operation of public education at the elementary and secondary levels largely rests with the local school district. In 1995–1996 there were about 16,000 separate school districts in the nation, each with its own school board, superintendent, and schools (U.S. National Center for Education Statistics 1997). Although smaller school districts have often been consolidated into larger ones, many states still have hundreds of separate districts. School district boundaries are usually coterminous with local political boundaries, but elected school boards are rarely identified with a political party. Localities provide about 46 percent of public school funding (U.S. National Center for Education Statistics 1997).

This reliance on local revenues derived from property taxes generates great disparities in per-pupil spending across property-rich and property-poor districts. Though states have increased their share of educational expenses, largely due to legal challenges to relying on local property taxes for funding, spending disparities have decreased only a little. The poorest districts do have more money to spend, but rich districts have increased their tax levels in order to maintain their spending lead (Ballantine 1997).

An important consequence of the U.S. pattern of considerable local control is that local concerns are more likely to be reflected in school policies and practices than is common in countries with more centralized educational systems. Citizens elect local school boards and frequently vote on budgets, property tax rates, and bond issues. Moreover, parents exercise considerable informal political power through parent–teacher associations, informal conferences with school teachers and administrators, and decisions about whether to send their children to a particular school or not. (See the section below on modes of influence over schools.)

Despite the absence of strong national control, U.S. elementary and secondary schools do share many similarities across the country. One reason is that the federal government does exercise a homogenizing influence through its policy recommendations and funding for particular programs. In addition, national professional associations of educators and regional nongovernmental accrediting agencies provide common definitions across states and localities of what constitutes good educational practice. Also, college admissions requirements, though they vary across colleges, are similar enough to influence the course offerings of secondary schools. Moreover, textbook writers and publishers, who provide instructional material for schools nationwide, influence what is taught and often how it is taught by marketing the same instructional materials nationwide (Apple 1986). Finally, the high geographic mobility of students and teachers has helped reduce the isolation and consequent diversity among schools.

Across the United States, formal public schooling generally begins at age six, but enrollment in preschool and kindergarten is widespread and growing. In 1995 about 61 percent of three- to five-year-olds were enrolled part time or full time in nursery schools or kindergartens (U.S. National Center for Educational Statistics 1997).

Elementary schools are smaller than secondary schools. They are also less differentiated internally, in that all students are exposed to essentially the same subject matter by their "home room" teacher. However, within the home room, teachers often do divide students into different groups that are supposed to learn the same material at different speeds. This within-class differentiation is often termed "ability grouping," but in actuality test scores are often only a weak predictor of group assignment. Nonetheless, this grouping by putative aptitude is an important source of later class and, less so, racial differences in achievement (Dougherty 1996).

While elementary schools are generally alike in organization and curriculum, they differ widely in student composition. Because they draw from neighborhoods differing in class and racial composition, they end up differing from each other in student composition.

Secondary schooling begins around age thirteen. For the most part, U.S. secondary schools are "comprehensive"; that is, intended as much for those who will not attend college as for those who will. The comprehensive high school provides college preparation, vocational education, and general secondary education under one roof (Clark 1985; Krug 1964, 1972).

The comprehensive nature of U.S. secondary schools is fairly atypical, for the usual pattern abroad is to have separate academic and vocational high schools. For example, in Germany, academic and vocational training is assigned to separate secondary schools, with nearly half of all students entering the latter (Brint 1998).

The United States is also atypical among industrialized societies in awarding secondary school diplomas qualifying their holders for college entrance solely on the basis of the number and kinds of courses taken. Most other countries require passage of a national exam to receive a degree that qualifies one for university entrance (Brint 1998). To be sure, seventeen U.S. states do use minimum-competency examinations for awarding high school degrees (Airasian 1987; U.S. National Center for Education Statistics 1997), but the country still does not have a European-style national examination that alone determines university entrance.

The exceptional devotion of the United States to comprehensive schooling is traceable to two factors. The strong local role in educational governance in the U.S. system makes it more likely that the demands of non-college-goers will be listened to. Moreover, the heterogeneity of the U.S. population has made social integration a more pressing concern than in most European societies. This is evident in the words of the highly influential 1918 report, *Cardinal Principles of Secondary Education*: "The comprehensive school is the prototype of a democracy in which various groups have a degree of self-consciousness as groups and yet are federated into a larger whole through the recognition of common interests and ideals. Life in such a school is a natural and valuable preparation for life in a democracy" (National Education Association 1918, p. 26).

While U.S. comprehensive schooling may have been successful in its aim of social integration, its diffuse character has also been widely criticized. As many recent critics have noted, the variety of curricular goals and educational and social purposes served by U.S. secondary schools blurs their academic mission. When large proportions of students are not particularly academically inclined, the rigor and sense of purpose necessary to motivate student effort are missing. Moreover, the huge size of many U.S. schools makes them impersonal and hard put to maintain the involvement and commitment of students (Cusick 1983; Goodlad 1984; Powell et al. 1985; Sizer 1985).

While the U.S. school system is much less differentiated than is typical abroad, U.S. secondary schooling is by no means entirely undifferentiated. To begin with, there is an extensive private sector. Ten percent of all U.S. K–12 students attend private schools. These schools vary enormously, from individual Montessori schools, Christian academies, and elite private schools to citywide systems of Catholic parochial schools. While small in numbers and enrollments, the elite private schools, which are variously termed "prep" or "boarding" or "country day" schools, carry great prestige and importance. Most areas of the United States have elite schools, but the most famous are the boarding schools of New England, such as Phillips Exeter, Choate/Rosemary Hall, Groton, Hotchkiss, and St. Paul's. These schools have enrolled such famous Americans as Franklin D. Roosevelt, John F. Kennedy, Adlai Stevenson, George Bush, and Nelson Rockefeller. The importance of these schools lies not only in the fact that they heavily enroll the sons and daughters of the upper and upper-middle classes, particularly those of long-established wealth and prominence, but also in the fact that they provide their students with privileged access to the top universities and, in turn, corporate and governmental leadership (Cookson and Persell 1985; Hammack and Cookson 1980).

But it is not just the public/private divide that provides differentiation within the U.S. system. Even the comprehensive public high schools provide alternatives within their walls in the form of different curricular groupings (college prep, vocational, and general) and courses at different levels of rigor. However, this phenomenon, typically termed "tracking," has been criticized as a significant source of class and racial inequality in educational attainment (Dougherty 1996). Consequently, a movement has developed to "detrack" schools by eliminating grouping and instead relying on "cooperative learning" within mixed-ability classrooms (Oakes and Lipton 1992; Wells and Oakes 1996).

In addition to different tracks, most U.S. urban school districts maintain specialized vocational and academic secondary schools. For example,

Boston, New York, Philadelphia, and San Francisco have maintained old and distinguished academic high schools such as Boston Latin.

Since about 1970, most urban school systems have introduced a wide variety of programs in order to meet demands for more choice, retain middle-class white students, and better motivate students (Dougherty and Sostre 1992). New York City provides a good example of how highly differentiated some urban school systems have become. The city does have a large number of general "academic/comprehensive neighborhood schools." However, within many of these schools, there are "academies" or other magnet programs, which are operationally independent and have some freedom to select their students from wider attendance areas. In fact, there are about fifty small alternative high schools that offer special curricular emphases and that are open to students citywide. New York City also has a variety of vocational schools. Special "educational opportunity" high schools are organized around vocational themes (such as health, business, or aviation) and have the right to select their students. On the other hand, there are also ordinary vocational schools that have no particular focus and have open admissions. Finally, the city boasts four very well-known college preparatory schools, such as the Bronx High School of Science, that grant entry solely on the basis of an examination or audition (Board of Education of the City of New York 1997).

In recent years, a new form of differentiation has arisen within the public schools: "charter schools." Since 1991, more than thirty-five states have passed legislation making these schools possible, and perhaps more than 1,000 of them are now operating. Once granted a "charter" by the state or other designated authority, these schools operate independently of many existing school regulations but are financed by funds that would otherwise go to the districts. Charter schools are accountable to the chartering authority, and the renewal of their charter depends on meeting the goals set forth in their mission statement. The idea behind these schools is to free public school parents, teachers, and administrators to create schools that "break the mold" of existing schools and, by competing with existing public schools for students, force them to improve their performance and attractiveness. Moreover, many charter advocates have seen charter schools as a way of meeting the growing parental demand for choice—among not only affluent white parents but also working-class minority parents—but keeping it from tipping into a demand for vouchers to allow student to attend private schools. Beyond these commonalities, charter schools are very diverse in size, mission, student composition, and sponsorship. And because of this variation and their youth, it is unclear what impact charter schools will ultimately have. The jury is still out on whether they will enroll more than a fraction of public school students, successfully "routinize the charisma" of their founders after those founders move on, significantly enhance the performance of their students, and effectively stimulate regular public schools to improve. Many fear that charter schools may simply cream off the most advantaged students and leave the regular public schools more segregated and academically impoverished than ever (Cobb and Glass 1999; Manno et al. 1998; Wells et al. 1999).

Higher Education. As with the K–12 system, the U.S. higher education system is also quite unusual. It is much larger than, and organized very differently from, most other nations' systems. As of 1995, the United States had 3,706 institutions of higher education enrolling 14.3 million students in credit-bearing courses, which corresponded to about 35 percent of the population age 18-21 (keeping in mind that many college students are older than twenty-one). In addition, there were some 6,300 noncollegiate postsecondary institutions enrolling 850,000 students (U.S. National Center for Education Statistics 1997). All these numbers are much larger than those for comparable advanced industrial societies.

Given their number, it is not surprising that American colleges are quite varied. This variation can be usefully categorized along three axes: control, degrees and programs offered, and student-body composition.

U.S. colleges are legally owned by a wide variety of bodies. Some 1,700 colleges are public, owned by local, state, and federal governmental bodies. They account for 45 percent of all colleges but 78 percent of all college enrollments. Meanwhile, about 2,000 colleges are private, owned either by religious groups, profit-making corporations, or nonsectarian, non-profit-making boards. The nonsectarian, nonprofit private institutions include both many of the most prestigious doctorate-granting universities in the world and many small, undistinguished liberal arts colleges (U.S. National Center for Education Statistics 1997).

The U.S. Department of Education distinguishes five kinds of colleges according to the degrees and programs that they offer. The first group is the 171 "doctoral" institutions that offer doctoral and professional programs and produce a large number of graduates with either Ph.D.'s or medical and dental degrees. "Comprehensive" institutions, numbering about 420, make up the second category. They offer graduate programs but graduate few people with doctoral or medical degrees. Rather, they specialize in undergraduate, master's, and law programs. Quite often these institutions are former teacher-training colleges that broadened into general liberal arts schools and added graduate programs. The nearly 700 "general baccalaureate" or "liberal arts" colleges emphasize undergraduate education and have very few, if any, graduate programs. "Specialized" colleges, which number about 600, emphasize one field, such as engineering or the arts, and offer either a baccalaureate or postbaccalaureate training. Finally, the nearly 1,500 "two-year colleges" specialize in two-year associate's degrees, one-year vocational certificates, and noncredit training, They enroll not only college-age students seeking academic or vocational training but also older adults seeking job retraining, skills upgrading, or avocational knowledge (Cohen and Brawer 1996; Dougherty 1994).

U.S. higher educational institutions also differ in their student-body composition. As one moves from universities to four-year colleges to two-year colleges, the proportion of students who are male, white, upper-class, or academically high-performing drops. In addition, some colleges serve distinct student populations; for example, nearly 200 colleges are single-sex and nearly 100 are all-black (U.S. National Center for Education Statistics 1997).

MODES OF INFLUENCE OVER SCHOOLS

The governance of education has been a repeated motif in our discussion above. We would now like to discuss it in greater detail. So far, in our discussion of control we have focused on political authority, whether exercised by national, state, or local governments or the citizens that elect them. But political authority is only one of several, often contradictory, mechanisms of influence over U.S. schooling. Also operative are market competition, bureaucratic power, professional authority, and ideological formation (Weiss 1990).

Political Authority. Political authority is vested in the various elected bodies of government and ultimately in the citizenry. State governors, legislatures, and boards of education control the schools through state funding (which amounts to nearly half of all public school revenues) and through laws specifying minimum curriculum and graduation requirements, the minimum length of the school day and year, required facilities, standards for teacher education and certification, standards for school plant, school district lines, and so forth (Campbell et al. 1990; Wirt and Kirst 1992).

However, state governments delegate political authority over the day-to-day operation of schools to local schools boards elected by local citizens. These local boards in turn have the power to hire and supervise district superintendents and school principals. The boards also vote on the school budget, the local tax rate (though usually subject to voter referendum), curriculum, teaching, facilities standards beyond state minimal, and the rules for hiring and supervising teachers (Campbell et al. 1990; Wirt and Kirst 1992).

The federal government, meanwhile, only contributes about 7 percent of K–12 public school revenues, mostly in the form of categorical aid (discussed below under "Market Competition"). However, through the federal courts, the federal government has had a profound effect on school policies involving the treatment of pupils, particularly women, racial and linguistic minorities, and the handicapped. Moreover, as will be discussed below, the federal government has also exercised great ideological power (Campbell et al. 1990; Wirt and Kirst 1992).

Citizens, finally, exert political authority. Very frequently they vote on who will represent them on a school board or in state office. They also exercise direct democratic control by voting on tax rates and bond issues through local and state referenda and initiative elections. And in states such as California and Washington, it has become commonplace for voters to vote on school policies such as affirmative action in student admissions and teacher hiring (Wirt and Kirst 1992).

However legitimate and powerful political authority is, it can also be ineffective, particularly in a highly decentralized political system such as that of the United States. When a host of different government bodies impose multiple, often conflicting, mandates on schools, the effectiveness and authority of any one given political body is undermined (Weiss 1990).

Market Competition. Market control is less coercive than political authority. Schools can refuse to act in the way a market actor wishes, but that actor achieves compliance by supplying or denying resources that the school values and that the school cannot easily acquire from alternative sources (Pfeffer and Salancik 1978). These resources include funds, students, teachers, and jobs. Market control is particularly obvious in the case of private schools, which usually do not have a guaranteed clientele or funds and must recruit new students every year. But public schools also face market competition. In fact, market control over public schooling is steadily rising with the current vogue for school choice, charter schools, performance-based funding, and other means of making public schools more "accountable."

Students and their parents exercise market control over schools through their decisions about which schools to attend (Spicer and Hill 1990; Weiss 1990). If many middle-class students desert a school district, it loses state funding, which is largely enrollment-driven. Moreover, local tax revenues may also decline. Real estate values are strongly affected by perceptions of the quality of local schools, and these perceptions are in turn shaped by how many middle-class and white students attend a school. But even if school revenues are not affected, the desertion of middle-class students can still affect schools by impinging on teachers' perceived quality of work. Teachers usually clamor for better-prepared students, and a loss of middle-class students can lead the better teachers to themselves desert a particular school.

In order to retain students, particularly middle-class white ones, school districts adopt a variety of expedients. They create "gifted" programs or "magnet" schools that attract such students not only by offering superior academic resources but also by largely segregating them from working-class and nonwhite students (Metz 1986; Wells 1993).

School competition for students has risen in the 1990s. It used to be that the main choices parents had available were between sending their children to public or private schools or between living in one school district versus another. But competition for students has increased with the advent of greater choice within the public schools in the form of magnet schools, charter schools, and interdistrict choice plans (Cookson 1994; Metz 1986; Wells 1993).

Students and their parents exert market power not only over schools overall but also over the classrooms within them. Student decisions about whether to take one or another course or whether or not to actively participate in class deeply shape the character of teaching and learning within classrooms. In order to attract students and then motivate them to work hard and actively participate, teachers often resort to such devices as giving students more choice over course selection or course content, making course content less abstruse and technical (more "relevant"), reducing academic demands, and grading less stringently (Powell et al. 1985; Weiss 1990).

But teachers themselves are also market actors. Teachers can choose whether to go to work for one or another district or, if they have enough seniority, work at one school versus another in the same district. Hence, school districts compete to hire and retain teachers, particularly if they are in fields such as math and science, where qualified teachers are scarce. Moreover, teachers have shaped the schools through their collective capacity to withhold their labor through unions. With the rapid growth of teacher unions since the early 1960s, teachers have been able to secure considerably higher salaries and greater voice in how schools run than they had before (Campbell et al. 1990; Kerchner et al. 1993).

Business also shapes schools through market control. For one thing, business controls jobs. Schools compete to place their students in good jobs because a good placement record can be used in turn to attract students. In order to get their students placed in good jobs, schools inculcate the kinds of skills, attitudes, and behaviors that business is looking for in new workers (Brint and Karabel 1989). In fact, business's influence based on its role as future employer of students has been institutionalized in the form of a myriad of business/school or school-to-work "compacts" or "partnerships" in which formal links are established and schools receive resources and job placements in return for greater responsiveness to business opinions about the desirable content of education (Gelberg 1997; Van Horn 1995).

In addition, business along with foundations and government influence schools through discretionary funding. Almost all business and foundation aid and most federal aid to schools takes the form of categorical grants. These funds will flow to a school only if it successfully competes with other schools to demonstrate that it is willing and able to engage in actions that the funder wishes to encourage. Moreover, this avenue of market control is increasing, as state governments establish not only more categorical grant programs but also performance funding, in which a certain portion of state formula aid is conditioned on meeting certain performance targets.

Market competition can be a very powerful control device, but it is also less effective than its evangelists believe. For example, greater student choice may not cause the deserted schools to change. The schools may not know why students are leaving, and the loss of funds, good students, and good teachers may impede its capacity to improve. Moreover, even if schools do react, they may get the wrong cues because students and their parents make bad choices due to lack of good information (Weiss 1990). Similarly, categorical aid often fails to accomplish its purpose. What schools do to secure the aid may bear little resemblance to how the aid is actually used. This has been a perennial problem with federal Title I funding for high-poverty schools. It often does not end up benefiting the students to which it is ostensibly targeted (Somini 1999).

Bureaucratic Power. Schools are bureaucratic organizations. They have explicit goals. Their work is done through a division of labor involving specialized jobs. There is a chain of command, with explicit differences in the authority of members according to their place in the organizational hierarchy. The members' actions are largely governed by formal rules and a norm of professionalism (impersonality). Organizational decisions are recorded through explicit and voluminous records. And personnel decisions are supposedly governed by merit (Bidwell 1965).

Within this bureaucratic structure, administrators—such as district superintendents or college presidents, school principals or deans—exercise great power. They create jobs and define their responsibilities, establish organizational rules, allocate scarce resources (money, space, staff, etc.), order specific actions, referee conflicts among subordinates, and hire and supervise subordinates (Campbell et al.; Weiss 1990).

Historically, teachers have been objects of administrative power. But increasingly, they themselves are participating in the exercise of administrative duties. The movement for school-based management has given teachers the potential to exercise greater power over how schools are run, though it is still not clear to what extent this has become a reality. In numerous communities, school councils have been set up that include teacher members. These councils have the authority to exercise considerable voice over such things as a school's budget, teacher hiring (what areas to hire in and whom to recommend to the district), and student discipline rules (Kerchner et al. 1993; Mohrman et al. 1994). However, this authority is often not exercised in practice. Between principal resistance to sharing authority and teacher reluctance to assume it, school councils often end up exerting much less authority than authorized.

Bureaucratic control had become perhaps the dominant form of school control by the end of the Progressive era. But despite its power, bureaucratic control does not handle localized, specific situations well. The general orientation of bureaucratic rulemaking is toward general prescriptions because the aim is to circumscribe the discretion of organizational staff (Weiss 1990). However, student-centered education—particularly in a highly diverse, politically decentralized society such as the United States—often does not fit easily within bureaucratic universalism.

Professional Authority. However bureaucratic schools are, they are also professional organizations because teachers make up such a large portion of the labor force and administrators are invariably former teachers. The main fount of professional authority lies in the fact that effective teaching requires the exercise of discretion—how teachers are to interact with students cannot be prescribed—and teachers largely monopolize the knowledge necessary to correctly exercise that discretion. Teachers use their professional authority to strongly shape curriculum, student evaluation, student discipline, proper classroom practices, and teacher training (Weiss 1990).

Nonetheless, teacher professional authority has always been uncertain and contested. This authority is at its apex in the classroom and fades as one goes up the bureaucratic hierarchy (Metz 1978; Weiss 1990). The weakness of teachers' claims for professional power and autonomy results from several factors. The majority of teachers are women, giving teaching less status than more male-dominated professions. Also, because of the unique complexity of the teacher–student relationship, teachers are less able to deliver consistent results than members of professions such as medicine and engineering. Finally, teachers must coexist with a powerful and numerous body of competitors for influence over students; namely, parents. (We discuss teacher–parent struggles for control below.) In the face of these limits to professional authority, teachers have increasingly resorted to market control, in the form of unionism, in order to bolster their influence over the schools.

Ideological Formation. Various actors can shape schools by the power of their ideas; that is, by their successful socialization of educational policy makers to certain values and beliefs (Weiss 1990). This ideological power has been strongly used by the federal government. Repeatedly, it has stimulated schools to take action by focusing attention on certain problems or offering exemplary solutions. One of the most notable examples has been the educational "excellence" movement of the 1980s and 1990s, which was strongly accelerated—though not really sparked—by the report of the National Commission on Excellence in Education, *A Nation at Risk* (1983). Within a year of its publication, many states and localities established commissions similar to the National Commission and passed laws implementing its recommendations. On a more global level, the power of ideological persuasion can be seen in the unusual homogeneity across the world in how nations have pursued the expansion and centralization of their educational systems. In large part this commonality of action is rooted in widespread support for a model of societal modernization that emphasizes national unification and development by means of the mass mobilization of citizens through a unified school system (Ramirez and Boli 1982).

Once established, ideological control can be extremely powerful and durable. Its main limitation is that it usually takes a long time to establish. And unlike the other forms of power, it is particularly dependent on the willing acquiescence of those who would be influenced (Weiss 1990).

Conflict Between Various Modes of Control. Many actors attempting to influence the schools utilize—wittingly or unwittingly—several of these modes of control. For example, state governments use political authority, market competition (through categorical aid), and ideological persuasion to get school personnel to act in certain ways. These different modes of influence can often yield great power if they are effectively meshed. But quite often they contradict each other.

Assertions of bureaucratic authority have been met by counterclaims by teachers in the name of professional authority or market control. Teachers have resisted state and local expansions of bureaucratic authority by mobilizing professional associations (for example, the National Council of Teachers of Mathematics) to shape the content of state curriculum standards (Massell 1994; Ravitch 1995). But because assertions of professional authority are often resisted, teachers have resorted as well to market control, in the form of teacher unionism.

But these assertions of power by teachers and by local and state school bureaucrats have in turn provoked democratic counterclaims by groups representing conservative parents concerned about parental prerogatives over education. These groups have strongly criticized teacher unionism and various curricular and pedagogical innovations advocated by teacher professional associations at the national, state, and local levels. These controversial innovations have included not only sex education and values clarification but also state content, performance, and evaluation standards. In California and Pennsylvania, parents associated with such New Right groups as Citizens for Excellence in Education, Focus on the Family, and Eagle Forum have vociferously attacked statewide goals and standards, performance-based assessment, whole-language instruction, and conceptually oriented math education. These groups reject such curricular and pedagogical reforms as ineffective and unwarranted educational experimentation on children that undermines parental prerogatives to determine the content of their children's education (Boyd et al. 1996; Kirst and Mazzeo 1995).

Interestingly, there has been little conflict between market control and democratic authority. For example, inadequate critical attention has been devoted to business/school partnerships and the question of how compatible are business desires and public interests in schooling. This absence of scrutiny may be due to the weakness of the socialist tradition in the United States. Because of this weakness, democracy and the market are seen in the popular mind as largely compatible. Both voting and buying tend to be seen similarly, as decisions by atomized actors operating on the basis of narrow self-interest. Public discussion and the public interest tend to be seen as no more relevant to voting than to buying. As a result, efforts to increase market competition within schooling through such devices as vouchers and charter schools are often portrayed in the U.S. as democratic innovations—because they "empower" individuals—whereas in Europe there is much more hesitation to equate consumer choice and citizen sovereignty (Whitty et al. 1998).

CONCLUSION

The sociology of U.S. schooling can benefit enormously from keeping in mind several features of that system. The educational system goes well beyond the schools to include such other institutions as families, the mass media, employers, and churches. Even when we focus on the schools, it is important to keep in mind that the U.S. school system is highly unusual compared to those in other advanced industrial societies. And when we turn to control of the U.S. system, we need to look beyond political authority to also consider other, often contradictory, mechanisms of influence over the schools: market competition, bureaucratic decision making, professional authority, and ideological formation.

REFERENCES

Airasian, Peter W. 1987 "State Mandated Testing and Educational Reform: Context and Consequences." *American Journal of Education* 95 (May):393–412.

Apple, Michael 1986 *Teachers and Texts*. New York: Routledge, Chapman and Hall.

Bagdikian, Ben 1990 *The Media Monopoly*, 3rd ed. Boston: Beacon Press.

Ballantine, Jeanne H. 1997 *The Sociology of Education: A Systematic Analysis*. Upper Saddle River, N.J.: Prenitce Hall.

Bidwell, Charles 1965 "The School as a Formal Organization." In James G. March, ed., *Handbook of Organizations*. Chicago: Rand McNally.

Board of Education of the City of New York 1997 *Directory of the Public High Schools, 1997–1998*. New York: Author.

Boyd, William Lowe, Catherine A. Lugg, and Gerald L. Zahorchak 1996 "Social Traditionalists, Religious Conservatives, and the Politics of Outcomes-Based Education." *Education and Urban Society* 28 (May):347–365.

Brint, Steven 1998 *Schools and Society*. Thousand Oaks, Calif.: Pine Forge Press.

Brint, Steven, and Jerome Karabel 1989 *The Diverted Dream*. New York: Oxford University Press.

Campbell, Roald F., Luvern L. Cunningham, Raphael O. Nystrand, and Michael D. Usdan 1990 *Organization and Control of American Schools*, 6th ed. Columbus, Ohio: Merrill.

Clark, Burton R. 1985 "The High School and the University: What Went Wrong in America" (2 parts). *Phi Delta Kappan* (February and March):391–397; 472–475.

Cobb, Casey D., and Gene V. Glass 1999 "Ethnic Segregation in Arizona Charter Schools." *Educational Policy Analysis Archives* 7 (January). http://epaa.asu.edu/epaa/v7n1z.

Cohen, Arthur M., and Florence Brawer 1996 *The American Community College*, 3rd ed. San Francisco: Jossey-Bass.

Collins, Randall 1979 *The Credential Society*. New York: Academic Press.

Cookson, Peter W., Jr. 1994 *School Choice: The Struggle for the Soul of American Education*. New Haven, Conn.: Yale University Press.

——, and Caroline Hodges Persell 1985 *Preparing for Power: America's Elite Boarding Schools*. New York: Basic Books.

Cusick, Philip 1983 *The Egalitarian Ideal and the American High School*. New York: Longman.

Dougherty, Kevin J. 1994 *The Contradictory College: The Conflicting Origins, Outcomes, and Futures of the Community College*. Albany: State University of New York Press.

—— 1996 "Opportunity to Learn Standards: A Sociological Critique." *Sociology of Education* 69(5):40–65.

——, and Lizabeth Sostre 1992 "Minerva and the Market: The Sources of the Movement for School Choice." *Educational Policy* 6 (June):160–179.

Gelberg, Denise 1997 *The "Business" of Reforming American Schools*. Albany: State University of New York Press.

Goodlad, John 1984 *A Place Called School: Prospects for the Future*. New York: McGraw-Hill.

Hammack, Floyd Morgan, and Peter W. Cookson, Jr. 1980 "Colleges Attended by Graduates of Elite Secondary Schools." *The Educational Forum* 44 (May):483–490.

Herman, Edward S., and Noam Chomsky 1988 *Manufacturing Consent*. New York: Pantheon.

Hopper, Earl 1977 "A Typology for the Classification of Educational Systems." In Jerome Karabel and A.H. Halsey, eds., *Power and Ideology in Education*. New York: Oxford University Press.

Kanaya, T. 1994 "Japan: System of Education." Pp. 3078-3086.In T. Husen and N. Postlethwaite, eds., *The International Encyclopedia of Education*. New York: Pergamon.

Kerchner, Charles Taylor, Julia Koppich, and William Ayers 1993 *A Union of Professionals: Labor Relations and Educational Reform*. New York: Teachers College Press.

Kirst, Michael, and Christopher Mazzeo 1995 "The Rise, Fall, and Rise of State Assessment in California." *Phi Delta Kappan* (December):319–325.

Krug, Edward 1964 *The Shaping of the American High School*, vol. 1. New York: Harper and Row.

—— 1972 *The Shaping of the American High School*, vol. 2. Madison, Wisc.: University of Wisconsin Press.

Manno, Bruce V., Chester E. Finn, Jr., Louann Bierlein, and Gregg Vanourek 1998 "Charter Schools: Accomplishments and Dilemmas." *Teachers College Record* 99 (Spring):537–558.

Massell, Diane 1994 "Setting Standards in Mathematics and Social Studies." *Education and Urban Society* 26 (February):118–140.

Metz, Mary Haywood 1978 *Classrooms and Corridors*. Berkeley: University of California Press.

—— 1986 *Different by Design: Politics, Purpose, and Practice in Three Magnet Schools*. Boston: Routledge and Chapman Hall.

Meyer, John W., David H. Kamens, and Aaron Benavot 1992 *School Knowledge for the Masses*. London: Falmer.

Meyer, John W., Francisco Ramirez, and Yasmin N. Soysal 1992 "World Expansion of Mass Education, 1870–1980." *Sociology of Education* 65:128–149.

Mohrman, Susan Albers, and Priscilla Wohlstetter 1994 *School Based Management.* San Francisco: Jossey-Bass.

National Commission on Excellence in Education 1983 *A Nation at Risk: The Imperative for Educational Reform.* Washington, D.C.: U.S. Government Printing Office.

National Educational Association 1918 *Cardinal Principles of Secondary Education.* Washington, D.C.: U.S. Department of the Interior, Bureau of Education.

Oakes, Jeannie, and Martin Lipton 1992 "Detracking Schools: Early Lessons from the Field." *Phi Delta Kappan* (February):448–454.

Organization for Economic Cooperation and Development 1998 *Education at a Glance.* Paris, France: Author.

Pfeffer, Jeffrey, and Gerald R. Salancik 1978 *The External Control of Organizations.* New York: Harper and Row.

Powell, Arthur, Eleanor Farrar, and David Cohen 1985 *The Shopping Mall High School: Winners and Losers in the Educational Marketplace.* Boston: Houghton Mifflin.

Ramirez, Francisco O., and John Boli-Bennett 1982 "Global Patterns of Educational Institutionalization." In Philip G. Altbach, Robert F. Arnove, and Gail P. Kelly, eds., *Comparative Education.* New York: Macmillan.

Ramirez, Francisco O., and Phyllis Riddle 1991 "The Expansion of Higher Education." In Philip G. Altbach, ed., *International Higher Education: An Encyclopedia,* vol. 1. New York: Garland.

Ravitch, Diane 1995 *National Standards in American Education.* Washington, D.C.: Brookings Institution.

Rohlen, Thomas P. 1983 *Japan's High Schools.* Berkeley: University of California Press.

Sizer, Theodore 1985 *Horace's Compromise: The Dilemma of the American High School,* Boston: Houghton Mifflin.

Somini, Sengupta 1999 "Integration Tool Bypasses Racially Isolated Schools in Queens." *New York Times* (February 23):B1, B5.

Spicer, Michael W., and Edward W. Hill 1990 "Evaluating Parental Choice in Public Education." *American Journal of Education* 98 (February):97–113.

U.S. National Center for Education Statistics 1997 *Digest of Education Statistics, 1997.* Washington, D.C.: U.S. Government Printing Office.

Van Horn, Carl E. 1995 *Enhancing the Connection Between Higher Education and the Workplace: A Survey of Employers.* Denver, Colo.: State Higher Education Executive Officers and Education Commission of the States.

Weiss, Janet A. 1990 "Control in School Organizations: Theoretical Perspectives." In William H. Clune and John F. Witte, eds., *Choice and Control in American Education,* vol. 1. Bristol, Pa.: Falmer.

Wells, Amy Stuart 1993 *Time to Choose.* New York: Hill and Wang.

——, and Jeannie Oakes 1996 "Potential Pitfalls of Systemic Reform: Early Lessons from Detracking Research." *Sociology of Education* 56(5):135–143.

——, Cynthia Grutzick, Sibyll Carnochan, Julie Slayton, and Ash Vasudeva 1999 "Underlying Policy Assumptions of Charter School Reform: The Multiple Meanings of a Movement." *Teachers College Record* 100:513–535.

Whitty, Geoff, Sally Power, and David Halpin 1998 *Devolution and Choice in Education: The School, the State, and the Market.* Bristol, Pa.: Open University Press.

Wirt, Frederick M., and Michael W. Kirst 1992 *Schools in Conflict.* San Francisco: McCutchan.

Kevin J. Dougherty
Floyd M. Hammack

ELITES

See Intellectuals; Social and Political Elites.

EMOTIONS

Emotions arise in individual experience, frequently with noticeable physiological signs, such as a racing heart, flushed or pallid face, tense gut, cold hands, and so forth, and thus may seem an unsuitable topic for sociological examination. This attitude, however, reckons without the incontrovertible facts that *most human emotions result from real, imagined, recollected, or anticipated outcomes of social interaction* and that interaction is the fundamental stuff of sociological analysis. Thus emotions are empirically linked to the social by virtue of their being a consequence of involvement in interaction. But emotions are also precursors of the social, by virtue of their mobilizing energy and motivation for the accomplishment of major social tasks, not the least of which is social solidarity itself.

Although emotions are thus important features of social life, they have had a varying place in the history of sociology. Early recognized as important by the great founders of the field—Marx, Durkheim, Weber, and Simmel—emotions declined in importance after the 1920s, as behavioral and cognitive approaches came to the fore in the social sciences. (Although these two approaches are thoroughly antagonistic to each other, they have agreed that emotions are irrelevant or unamenable to sociological analysis.) Resurrected after a long hiatus, emotions have once again come into their own and are now recognized both as exerting causal effects as well as serving as important results of social endeavors.

This article covers both early and present-day approaches to what has come to be known as the sociology of emotions and examines the role of emotions as both independent and dependent variable.

THE PLACE OF EMOTIONS IN NINETEENTH-CENTURY SOCIOLOGY

In the great effort to topple the entrenched structures of monarchy and clergy in eighteenth-century Europe, a signal weapon was *reason*. By virtue of the application of reason to traditional modes of thought and conduct, philosophers and political theorists concluded that the domininion of kings and priests was falsely premised and that all men were created equal. That reason alone could lead to such a startling conclusion for that day was the result of the conquest by reason in another domain, namely natural science. In astronomy, physics, chemistry and biology, the work of reason had accomplished transformations of thought and understanding of a revolutionary nature. The success of reason here gave social thinkers confidence that reason applied to social life would produce results equally significant. And, indeed, it did in form of the upheavals that culminated in the American and French Revolutions.

What had been only thought was put into practice and the tradition of a thousand years swept away. In the ensuing years, reason was enshrined, a new god replacing the old ones that had been discarded. But as this occurred, a counterrevolutionary ideological process was getting under way. In England, Thomas Burke, at first partial to the aims of the French Revolution, recoiled in horror at its excesses—reason had run amok, with a degree of passion and emotion that was terrifying. Burke argued that society was not amenable to quick constructions or reconstructions. Rather, a slow accretion of time-tested ways that ultimately refined the social rules and customs was the only reliable method for attaining a safe, stable, and satisfactory social order. Opposing the worship of reason, Burke posed rather the validity of an emotional basis for social solidarity. Longstanding mores garnered emotional support and, by virtue of this, violent social change, with its attendant upheaval, was averted.

Burke's conservative message, which rejected the application of reason to social forms, was to lie fallow for a century, until it was resurrected in a more systematic sociological way by Émile Durkheim. In the interim, Karl Marx, also an exponent of reason in the reorganization of society, had propounded his comprehensive historical theory of the growth and decay of societal organization. Yet in developing his understanding of how society, particularly capitalist society, works, Marx ([1842–1844] 1971, [1867] 1967; Engels [1846] 1947) also produced a paradigm for how to examine emotions sociologically. His approach remains important today, even if the specific political and ideological interests of Marxism are no longer attached to it.

Marx propounded the view that forms of social organization—feudalism, capitalism, socialism—were products of such factors as technology and the division of labor, which he termed the *mode of production*, and certain forms of authority and property rights, which he termed the *relations of production*. A given historical mode of production gave rise, for Marx, to a necessary set of relations of production. In feudal times, the relatively primitive technology required a great deal of hand labor, as exemplified in craft production, where producers owned their tools, their raw materials, and the products of their labor. Property rights and social relations were in line with the division of labor made possible by the technology of the time.

After the Industrial Revolution, with its relatively advanced technology, a new form of division of labor and property rights emerged. The factory system entailed labor sold by its owners, the workers, as if it were any other commodity. Factory workers owned neither the tools, the raw materials, nor the products of their labor. Thus a new set of property and authority relations came into existence because of the more advanced technology and the division of labor this enabled.

Here Marx looked closely at the horrible conditions of early entrepreneurial capitalism. The principal, although not the only, defect of capitalism was that workers were reduced to a state of what Marx called "immiseration," a condition fostered by subsistence wages. Poor housing, poor food, poor health, and impoverishment of spirit were the common lot of factory workers. Beyond this was the state of "alienation," a concept Marx adopted from the work of philosopher Georg Frederick Hegel. Hegel had reflected on the sad fate that befell human effort, which, once crystallized in material objects, exists separately and apart from the individual who exerted it and, in this sense, was alienated from its producer. Marx used this concept to forge a theory of emotional consequences for workers under capitalism.

The primary form of workers' alienation was the fundamental experience of chagrin, bitterness, and resentment because of the loss, or alienation, of the product of their labor to the capitalist, who did not labor or produce anything. According to Marx, this was the main emotional result of a system in which those who produced things were not the same ones who owned them.

A second form of alienation resulted from the boring and mentally numbing tasks of factory-based production. Instead of the inherent satisfactions of earlier craft forms of work, workers in modern industry, with its extensive division of labor, obtained little pleasure from their largely repetitive tasks.

A third form of alienation was the emotional isolation and competitive envy of others: both owners and fellow workers. This led to the breakdown of solidarity and community, the comfortable sense of belonging to a group in which one was an accepted member. Melvin Seeman (1959) translated Marx's forms of alienation into five elements: (1) powerlessness, or a feeling that one had no control over one's fate; (2) meaninglessness,

or a sense of confusion about the value and significance of one's efforts; (3) self-estrangement, or a feeling of distance between what one felt oneself to be and what one was required to do at work; (4) isolation, or the longing for a sense of connection with others; and (5) normlessness, or the feeling that one's efforts lacked aim or goal.

Even if Marx's critique of capitalism is ignored, it is important to recognize his innovation in sociological analysis, what today we would call social psychology; that is, how social organization affects individual variables. In Marx's case view, how the social patterns by which labor is organized and its benefits distributed affects emotions. This mode of analysis, designated by the term *social structure*, is one of the two main types of approach to the analysis of emotions in current sociology. The other, designated as *culture*, was fostered by the work of Max Weber.

Although he recognized the power and utility of Marx's social structural analysis of capitalism and its emotions, Weber cast a different light on the process and examined different emotions. In his most famous work, *The Protestant Éthic and the Spirit of Capitalism*, Weber ([1904–1905] 1958) engaged Marx in an intellectual battle over who better understood the historical processes that led to capitalism. According to Marx, the economic infrastructure of society—the mode and relations of production—gave rise to the superstructures of society; namely, the way in which other institutions, such as the family, religion, politics, art, and so on, were organized. Further, Marx contended that the infrastructure even determined ideas. And here Weber demurred. Instead, Weber sought to show that capitalism was the product of a distinct set of religious ideas, along with the emotions that those ideas fostered.

For Weber, the crucial ideational matrix for capitalism was the Calvinist doctrine of predestination. This is the view that salvation in the religious sense is determined for everyone prior to birth. Some, the elect, are destined to be saved and the remainder, doomed to eternal damnation. According to this doctrine, there is nothing one can do to change one's fate—no action, no amount of devotion can change one's predestined fate. For many today, this seems like an odd doctrine, and many wonder how it could have held sway. But in

Geneva and other places where Calvinism reigned for a while, the belief was of the utmost importance, since it spelled out the possible eternal fate of one's soul.

Weber conjectured that such a doctrine must have been accompanied by some powerful emotions, mainly a terrible anxiety. At this point, Weber argues, a reaction formation of necessary optimism intervened to forestall despair. Calvinists came to believe that somehow, contrary to doctrine, they might change a dire fate by the most faithful and dedicated service to God's commandments. One of the most important ways in which to do this was in one's God-given *Beruf*, or vocation; that is, one's life's work, whether it be as a farmer, artisan, merchant, and so forth. Pursuing one's daily work in so dedicated a fashion would perhaps avert the severity of a predestined fate.

But such religiously and emotionally driven attention to one's occupation brought an unsought consequence: It led to worldly success. This in itself, despite doctrinal objections, seemed like a divine signal. Those who succeeded in worldly pursuits began to see this as a hopeful sign that they were among the elect. And, if this were so, then even greater worldly success would ensure that prognosis. Given that Calvinism also inveighed against material display, it led the successful to plow their profits back into their work. In other words, said Weber, it led to the routine practice of the capitalist method of doing business, thus giving rise to that historic form of entrepreneurship. In Weber's view, anxiety and a form of coping with it were central to the emergence of capitalism.

In the terms of the present-day sociology of emotions, Marx originated an approach based on *social structure*, while Weber fostered an approach based on *culture*. The effects of this distinction will be elaborated below.

Émile Durkheim also entered the debate against Marx, but on a different front from Weber. Marx had viewed religion as an opiate, offering hope to and dulling the pain felt by workers who suffered from the extremes of dislocation and poverty, especially during the early stages of capitalism. Marx supposed that when socialism conquered, it would obviate the need for religious belief and practice. Durkheim ([1915] 1965) viewed this as a form of ultrarationalism and sought to uncover the universal wellsprings of religion, which, he believed, would flourish regardless of what form society took. In order to investigate religious phenomena at their simplest—and hence most likely to prove universal—Durkheim examined the religion of Australian Aborigines, a group that appeared to be about as primitive as one could find according to nineteenth-century understanding.

First Durkheim proposed a distinction between religious behavior and everyday behavior, the sacred and the profane. He saw the two as segregated by time and place as well as by behavior. Among the Aborigines, the sacred emerged during clan gatherings, with the worship of totems—animals that stood for the clan and with whom clan members identified. Worship was a matter of ritual practice involving highly emotional activities—rhythmic chanting, frenetic dancing, sexual intercourse—with individuals giving over emotional control to the impulses of the moment. Durkheim reasoned that in these moments of heightened emotional arousal, individuals felt themselves to be in the grip of forces greater than themselves, providing a sense of the presence of something greater than any single individual—a spirit, a god. But Durkheim argued that the only supraindividual entity present was the group itself; that is, the co-presence of the members of the group, giving themselves over to strong emotions, provided the sense of a superior force. In worshiping that force, group members were, unwittingly, worshiping the group itself.

Durkheim generalized this point, arguing that ritual conduct, with its element of emotional arousal, leads to a sense of solidarity among those who engage in the ritual. Thus, religious ritual, far from representing the dead hand of the past, as Marx would have it, enabled group members to cleave to each other and make group continuity possible. This is true, said Durkheim, even when the shared emotion is sadness. Indeed, in examining funerary rites, he showed that coming together on the death of a group member stirred up emotions that transcended the sadness itself. Remarkably, a feeling of strength and renewed vitality emerged from the co-presence of other mourners. Emotions, thus, are not merely individual phenomena; they are crucial to the existence of human groups.

Society itself is possible only because its members periodically share emotions, whether elation over great victory or sadness over great loss.

EMOTIONS IN MODERN PERSPECTIVE

Although present-day sociologists of emotions treat them differently in many ways than did the founders of the field, they nonetheless hue close to the main insight of the founders; namely, that emotions are socially constituted. This means several things.

First, emotions emerge from episodes of interaction in which valued outcomes are at stake. Second, emotions have a socially normative component. Thus, when one's emotions deviate from the normative emotional prescription, there is some constraint to adjust one's emotions to what is normatively specified. Third, over time, as social conditions change, emotional requirements change as well. New conditions mean a somewhat new recipe for emotional life.

In the present-day sociology of emotions, two major sociological traditions converge on the social constitution of emotions, but they do so in different ways. The *social structural* approach examines emotions as direct products of social interaction and its outcomes. For example, insult leads to anger; deflated ego leads to shame; threat leads to fear; and so on. In each case, the end result of the social interaction is experienced as an emotion.

By contrast, the *cultural* approach looks mainly at the regulation of emotional expression by social rules. For example, we are enjoined to be happy at weddings, sad at funerals, angry at injustice, and so on. In each case, the individual who is emotionally out of line with what is expected in the situation confronts the possibility of emotional deviance.

The social structural and the cultural approaches form the main body of work in the modern sociology of emotions, and we discuss each in turn.

Social Structural Approaches. The earliest modern sociologist of emotion was Erving Goffman (1959, 1967, 1981), a transitional figure between the works of the founders, especially Durkheim, and later approaches. He focused powerfully on ordinary conversation as one of the main settings of social interaction. In the social interaction we call conversation, he found high emotional drama. Although conversation most often proceeds without conscious reflection about it by the participants, a conversation has only to break down to receive considerable and sometimes perplexed attention. Goffman saw that conversation actually comprises a miniritual, much in the manner Durkheim described, and that a successful conversation is like a successful ritual: Everyone plays a necessary prescribed role, even if the exact content of the role is not prescripted. In a successful conversation, participants experience a degree of self-realization that produces the kind of satisfaction that ensues from a whole-hearted and authentic participation in a religious ritual. Indeed, there is a similar sacred aspect to conversation, with the most important sacred object on display being the participant's self. In conversation, that self is accorded a due reverence by other participants or is demeaned by them.

Goffman proposed that in a conversation every actor offers a "line" about him- or herself, one which the other participants are expected to take at face value. For example, one has just been promoted to a higher position, or one has sacrificed dearly for a loved one, or one has learned how to play a Bach partita, and so on. If one carries off the line in the conversation such that others confirm one's projected persona, one feels confident and self-assured. But if one stumbles conversationally and the projected self becomes noncredible, then embarrassment ensues. Unless the actor has what Goffman calls "poise," which is the ability to mask one's embarrassment, the conversation falters.

Since conversation by its nature is interactional, other participants must cooperate in sustaining the viability of the conversational interaction. Except in unusual circumstances, Goffman saw in ordinary talk a precarious social order that is supported by the emotions of the participants, requiring their cooperation and emotional sensibility to succeed. The social order of ordinary talk is an instance of social order in general. Although Goffman did not pursue the larger questions of social order in society, his point about the emotional underpinnings of the micro order was extended to the social macro order, especially in the formal precedence orders of social power and status. Randall Collins and Arlie Russell Hochschild examined this question in the domain of stratification.

Stratification is the division of the social order into a hierarchy of power, status, and benefits. Some individuals have more and some have less of these desirable attributes and commodities. Since so many life chances are tied up in the stratification order, it is understandable that emotions are focal here, too.

According to Collins (1975, 1981, 1990), social systems, whether large or small, are arenas of conflict in which power, status, and benefits are sought by the participants. In modern societies, the main field of conflict is in organizations devoted to work. Here there are order-givers and order-takers, whose daily interactions are fraught with emotional consequences. Relative to order-takers, order-givers are secure, confident, and charged with emotional energy. This is because they are at the head of organizational units that support their initiatives and legitimate their orders. Order-takers, on the other hand, are relatively resentful, indifferent, and alienated. They are under constraint from the organizational coalitions headed by the order-givers; they will be punished if they do not obey.

Following Durkheim's model, Collins views the daily interactions of order-givers and order-takers as a ritual in which the former display their social value by providing information, evaluating the performances of others, and mobilizing the morale and energies of group members. The order-takers are the objects of the ritual, which is intended to arouse them to the same pitch of organizational commitment experienced by the order-givers. But since the order-givers, as the main beneficiaries of the system of organizational stratification, are most aroused in the ritual, they are most likely to cleave loyally to the symbols of the organizations they represent. As beneficiaries of far less, order-takers are also aroused—but with different emotions that are less conducive to good feelings, high energy, and loyal commitment.

Hochschild (1979, 1983) examined some of the emotional accompaniments of labor in service organizations. In an exemplary study of airline flight attendants, she found these workers to be often conflicted in their emotions. Although they were trained specifically to do what Hochschild called emotional labor—namely, to cater to passengers' expectations in situations of high time and space constraints, as well as passengers' sometimes impolite or obstreperous behavior—flight attendants' own emotions had to be suppressed. Insulted by a passenger, they were required to suppress anger; disgusted by a passenger's conduct, they were required to overlook their own emotion; and so on—all in the service of not alienating customers. According to Hochschild, this left many of the flight attendants emotionally numb from the overpractice of emotion suppression. Hochschild generalized these findings to the service economy at large, where most of the occupations that require emotional labor are staffed disproportionately by women.

Taking a broader perspective on social structure, Theodore Kemper (1978, 1987, 1989, 1990) proposed that most emotions could be examined as resultants of interaction outcomes in two dimensions; namely, power and status. Power is a relationship in which one actor compels another actor to do something the latter does not want to do. This entails the employment or threat of employment of a variety of noxious stimuli—from physical and verbal violence, through withholding of deserved rewards, to subtle manipulations such as lying and deception. Power is exercised pandemically, whether in informal social interactions or in organizations that carry out the broad work of society.

Status (or status-accord), on the other hand, is a social relationship in which actors voluntarily provide rewards and gratification to other actors. Coercion plays no part here. Status-giving is the basis of true social solidarity, and individuals who voluntarily share membership with each other in a social group are normally motivated to provide each other with the benefits of status, the ultimate degree of which is love.

Kemper proposed that outcomes of interaction in power and status terms give rise directly to emotions. For a sense of how this works, it is important to see that a relatively simple model of social relational outcomes suffices for the analysis. Every relational exchange takes place along the dimensions of power and status. For each actor, the outcomes can be: an increase in power and/or status, a decline, or no change. This produces 12 possible outcomes (2 actors × 2 dimensions × 3 results), but only 4 of these will actually occur, namely a power and status outcome for each actor A. Emotions will flow from these.

In the power dimension, the available evidence suggests that actor A loses power or actor B gains it, the emotional outcome for actor A is some degree of fear or anxiety. If actor A gains power and/or actor B loses it, the emotional outcome for actor is likely to be a sense of security. In the status domain, the outcomes are a bit more complex. If actor A gains status, he is likely to feel contented, satisfied, and happy. If actor A loses status, the emotional outcome depends on the felt sense of agency: Who was ultimately responsible for the status loss? If actor B is held culpable, the emotional result is anger. If the self is held culpable, the emotional result is shame or, more seriously, depression, if actor A feels that the situation is irremediable.

When the situation is one in which actor A gives status to actor B, we may expect satisfaction and contentment on the part of actor A. When actor A withholds or withdraws status from actor B, several emotional outcomes are possible. If actor B is deemed responsible ("deserving" this treatment), the result is likely to be satisfaction of a self-righteous kind on the part of actor A. If actor B was not responsible (not "deserving" the treatment), then two emotions are possible, either singly or jointly. If actor A deems that he or she did not live up to his or her character standing—that is, the amount of status with which he or she is generally credited by others as deserving—he or she will feel shame. On the other hand, if actor A concentrates on the harm or hurt he or she did to actor B, guilt is likely to ensue. In the instance of shame, actor A recognizes that he or she has acted in such a way as not to deserve the status he or she has been accorded. In the case of guilt, actor A recognizes that he or she has used an excess of power against actor B.

Some aspects of emotion also follow from anticipations that are either confirmed or disconfirmed by subsequent interaction. Thus, the actor who anticipated losing power but did not should feel especially secure. The actor who did not anticipate receiving status but received it is likely to feel especially pleased. In general, disconfirmations of expectations tend to exert a multiplier effect on the emotions that would ordinarily be felt from the power–status outcome in the situation.

Kemper's approach to emotions through power and status analysis also allows a social relational perspective on love and on its frequently confused near-relation, liking. Kemper defines a love relationship as one in which at least one actor gives or is prepared to give extreme amounts of status (for terminological purposes, status is equated with affection) to another actor. The definition includes nothing about power, but since power is a feature of all relationships, including it allows for seven different ideal-typical love relationships: (1) *Adulation*, in which one actor gives or is prepared to give extreme affection to another who may not even know of the other's existence. Neither actor has or uses power. (2) *Ideal love*, in which each actor gives or is prepared to give extreme amounts of affection to the other. Neither actor has or uses power. (3) *Transference* or *mentor love*, in which each actor gives or is prepared to give extreme amounts of affection to the other, but one of the actors also has a great deal of power over the other. This pattern is prevalent in ideal teacher–student, therapist–client, or mentor–mentee relationships, in which the former in each case is the one with power over the latter. (4) *Romantic love*, in which each actor gives or is prepared to give extreme amounts of love to the other, but each actor also has a great deal of power over the other. This is the kind of relationship in which each can suffer intensely from the real or imagined withdrawal of affection by the other. (5) *Unfaithful love*, in which only one actor gives or is prepared to give extreme amounts of affection to the other, but both actors have a great amount of power. Infidelity is a case of this kind of relationship; the betrayer has withdrawn affection from the betrayed, although the betrayed still has a great deal of power, which is why most infidelities are kept secret. (6) *Infatuation* or *unrequited love*, in which one actor gives or is prepared to give extreme amounts of affection to the other but has no power, while the other actor gives no affection but has a great deal of power. (7) *Parent–Infant Love*, in which the parent gives extreme amounts of affection to the infant and the

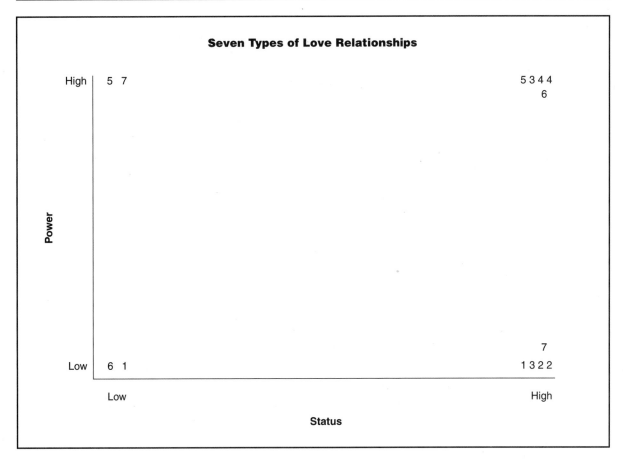

Figure 1

NOTE: 1-1 Adulation
NOTE: 2-2 Ideal Love
NOTE: 3-3 Transference or Mentor Love
NOTE: 4-4 Romantic Love
NOTE: 5-5 Unfaithful Love
NOTE: 6-6 Inatuation or Unrequited Love
NOTE: 7-7 Parent-Infant Love

infant gives nothing in return, while the parent has a great deal of power and the infant has none. These seven relationships can also be represented visually in a two-dimensional space according to their power and status (affection) locations (See figure 1).

Kemper (1989; and Reid 1997) distinguishes love from liking as follows: one feels love for another when the other's qualities match one's standards to an extremely high degree. It does not matter what the standards are; they may be trivial (e.g., he dresses well; she dances well) or they may be profound (e.g., he is a noble man who would

risk his life to preserve others; she is compassionate woman whose concern is with the well-being of others). In either case, if one has standards that are met by these qualities in the other, then it is likely that feelings of love will be induced. Ordinarily, more than one standard must be met by the qualities of the other in order for love to bloom. No small standard in Western culture is appearance, which often dominates all others, at least among the young. Love thus has to do with the qualities of the other and how they match our standards.

Liking, on the other hand, according to Kemper, is the pleasant feeling that arises when the other gives us status or affection. Liking requires that the other act well toward us; love has no such requirement, as shown by such types (above) as adulation, unfaithful love, infatuation or unrequited love, and parent–child love. In each of these, one party loves another who gives no affection in return. In love this is possible; in liking, it is not.

Kemper's use of power and status is matched by Heise (1979) and his colleagues (Smith-Lovin and Heise 1988; MacKinnon 1994) in another structural approach to emotions known as affect control theory (ACT). Heise's model of interaction and emotions stems from a linguistic paradigm, most notably the semantic differential (SD), which purports to get at fundamental categories of meaning in the use of language. Supported by many cross-cultural studies, the proponents of the SD have found three fundamental dimensions: potency (power), evaluation (status), and activity. Kemper does not include activity in his approach to emotions, although it has a place in a more general social organizational framework as standing for technical activity in the division of labor.

Working with the potency, evaluation, and activity dimensions, Heise and his colleagues have developed a mathematically sophisticated set of formulas to predict a variety of outcomes, including emotions. First, common language terms—nouns, verbs, adjectives—are rated by samples of respondents for their potency, evaluation, and activity standing. For example, the term *father* may stand relatively high on each of these; on the other hand, the term *criminal* may stand high on potency and activity but low on evaluation. Heise has compiled a large dictionary of such terms whose potency, evaluation, and activity values can be entered into complex regression equations to predict emotions.

The basic notion in ACT is that individuals behave so as to maintain their fundamental identity. If something has occurred—whether action by oneself or another—that questions the validity of that identity, an emotion results. For example, a parent may usually be loving to his or her child, but if the parent acts out of character by behaving cruelly or indifferently to the child, there is a felt need to reequilibrate the relationship and reclaim the identity of loving parent. The emotion, whether it is shame or guilt, provides some of the

motivational energy to repair the relationship and maintain the fundamental identity.

In some examples of how this works, Heise and his colleagues found that when a father serves a son, the father's emotions were predicted to be pleased, contented, and relieved, while the son's emotions (the emotions of the recipient of interaction can also be predicted) were predicted to be amused, light-hearted, and euphoric. If a judge sentences a gangster, the judge's emotions were predicted to be contented, relieved, and proud, while the gangster's emotions were predicted to be uneasy and awestruck. Several emotions are usually generated by the ACT equations because they have approximately equal value in potency, evaluation, and activity terms for the given situation.

Heise has examined complex instances in which an individual is observed to perform an act and reveal a number of emotions. How others will judge the actor is predicted to be based on the emotions the focal actor reveals. For example, when a man kisses a woman, if he is cheerful, he is identified as a gentleman, pal, or mate, identities that gain significantly in evaluation, with some loss in the potency dimension. On the other hand, if he kisses a woman and manifests disgust, he is identitified at a much lower evaluation level, but with his potency remaining unchanged. If he displays nervousness, he is identified as having lower standing in both evaluation and potency.

Heise's method also allows for a distinction between emotions and moods. For example, if a father ignores a son, the father is predicted to feel unhappy. ACT now predicts that the father will act to reinstate his identity as a father who does not ignore his son. In contrast to the father who became unhappy over his act, there is the unhappy father, a fundamental identity combining a social position with an emotion. Heise identifies this as a mood. According to ACT, moods give rise to consistent behavior; for example, the unhappy father might neglect or attack the son.

In all, the structural theorists of emotion are concerned with predicting emotions from the social locations and relationships of actor. This assumes that there is a natural (or pancultural) universal reaction to certain kinds of social relational outcomes. For example, insult evokes anger. One of the most important differences between the social structural and cultural approaches (to be discussed next) hinges on whether this assumption is correct.

Cultural Approaches to Emotions. In contrast with the social structural view of emotions as direct results of social relations between actors, the cultural approach inserts an intervening stage; namely, the normative definition of situations and the specification of what emotions are appropriate in them. Hochschild proposes that these "feeling rules" define and regulate the expression of emotion. Examining emotions from this perspective leads to a strong emphasis on the study of how emotions are managed so that they conform with the normative requirements of given situations. Culturally oriented sociologists of emotion are also concerned with how emotions contribute to social order. Guilt and shame are significant emotions for this purpose.

The cultural approach to emotions is partial to cognitive and idealist models, since these concern themselves with mental processes that come to determine emotions. The fundamental source of the cultural approach is *symbolic interactionism*. In this school, whose prime practitioner and exemplar was George Herbert Mead (1934), the fundamental notion is that virtually nothing, not even mind or self, precedes social interaction. Thus social interaction actually constitutes or constructs these fundamental categories.

Mead proposed that after some cooperative interactions with another person, we have the capacity to call up in ourself the probable reaction of the other to any proactive behavior of our own. This is based on the recollection of the pattern of interactions with the other when one or another behavior on our part elicited one or another response on the part of the other. The ability to recapitulate all this in our head prior to any actual behavior is what Mead termed *mind* and the process, *thinking*.

Having derived mind from prior social interaction, Mead went further and located the origin of the self in the same kinds of interactive encounters with others. In Mead's terms, we become capable of putting ourself in the place of the other and looking at ourself as if we were an object. This

mental operation provides us with a sense of self–our identity–as derived from the perspective of another. The actual self of the individual is some composite of the many selves that are available when one takes the perspective of the many others with whom one interacts.

The most widely known approach to emotions from the symbolic interactionist perspective is offered by Hochschild (1979, 1983). She posits that emotions arise in a somewhat natural way in situations or frames. But the emotion is then subjected to examination as more or less appropriate from the perspective of the normative borders of the situation. Expressed as "feeling rules," the norms specify the required emotions in given frames: happy at birthday parties, sad at funerals, and so on. Because most people react emotionally to situations in more or less the ways that the rules require, they are rarely conscious of the rules. But should there be a discrepancy between the emotion and the rule, there is a sense of discomfort and a felt pressure to adapt. Hochschild offers a number of likely strategies that are used to manage one's emotions in such emotionally deviant situations. Principally, one may engage in either surface or deep acting. In the former, one puts on the manifest signs of the emotion even if one does not authentically feel it; for example, smiling at the host of a party, despite the fact that one despises him. In deep acting, the individual actually tries to evoke the prescribed emotion.

For Hochschild, emotion essentially results from a discrepancy between what we perceive and what we expected. The inchoate feeling is labeled by cultural fiat as anger, fear, shame, and so on, and this provides a reservoir of cultural associations with the significance, meaning, implications, and so on of having such an emotion. These may ramify into modifying or seeking to change the emotion. Thus culture, the aggregate of normative understandings derived from others, intervenes early in the emotion process, leading to the judgment that emotion is a social construction. For example, shame is constructed from five perceptions: motive (I want to do right); possession (I have done wrong); value (I disapprove); agency (I am the cause of the event); and self–agent relations (the audience for my act is better than I am).

Hochschild's (1983) widely cited study of emotion management among airline flight attendants has led to a significant body of research that has focused on the *emotional* effects of managing emotions. These studies are reviewed by Morris and Feldman (1996) and Gibson (1997).

Peggy Thoits (1990) has taken Hochschild's ideas on emotion management to another level. In her view, emotions are comprised of four elements: situational cues, physiological changes, expressive gestures, and an emotion label. These are so connected in memory and behavior pattern that the elicitation of one evokes the others. Thoits proposes that when emotions and feeling rules are discrepant, the actor can manage this through either cognitive or behavioral manipulation of the four elements of emotion. For example, one can withdraw when a deviant emotion is felt (behavior-situational), or one can exercise or take drugs to change the physiological base of the emotion (behavior-physiological), or one can redefine the situation so that its implication for emotion changes (cognitive-situational), and so on.

Thoits also expands Hochschild's notion of emotional deviance through proposing four situations that might dispose toward it: multiple role occupancy, subcultural marginality, role transition, and rigid rules governing ongoing roles or ceremonial occasions. Thoits also proposes that a deviant emotion not only violates the feeling rules but also includes emotions that are too prolonged, too intense, or directed at the wrong target. Yet even deviant emotions may become legitimate if they are widely shared, thus leading to a change in social norms. An example is the change in national sentiment brought about by the protests of the antiwar movement during the Vietnam period.

In another fundamentally symbolic interactionist approach to emotions, Clark (1997) examines sympathy, an emotion treated importantly by Adam Smith ([1759] 1853) in his *Theory of Moral Sentiments*. Clark sees sympathy as a pervasive emotion, making society possible, for without it there would be no "social glue." Indeed, since sympathy is so important, "sympathy entrepreneurs," emerge to facilitate the evocation and display of this emotion. These are voluntary organizations designed to mobilize sympathy for specific victims (for example, Mothers Against Drunk Driving [MADD]) or commercial organizations, such as greeting card companies, that facilitate expressions of sympathy by large publics. Clark also sees what she refers to as "sympathy margins" as regular features of social relationships. These are earned credits, so to speak, that enable individuals to call on the understanding, sympathy, and forgiveness of others when they are caught out, or caught short, or have otherwise become hapless victims.

Steven Gordon (1981) is another exponent of the social constructionist view of emotions. Although he acknowledges that emotions per se are elemental and biological, he contends that shortly after childhood they are culturally transformed into what he calls "sentiments." For example, the elemental emotion of anger is converted into such sentiments as resentment, righteous indignation, moral outrage, and so on. This is presumed to be the fate of all emotions. Since sentiments are socially formed, they can be invented or even abandoned.

Gordon stands within the tradition of Norbert Elias (1978a, 1978b), who offered an insightful historical perspective on the emergence of the emotion of shame as an important feature of social relations between different social classes. Elias examined especially the relations between the rising bourgeousie of the fifteenth and sixteenth centuries and the aristocrats who disdained them. In many instances the nobility, seeking to insulate itself from the incursions of lower-status merchants and traders, refined their practices in the execution of common daily chores involving dining, self-cleansing, toilet functions, and so on. Those who could not match the newly defined limits of gentility were exposed to ridicule and shaming. For a long historical period, the aristocracy were the arbiters of manners, that is, what passed for acceptable social conduct. Those who were ill trained in the ultrarefinements thus properly felt shame.

Although symbolic interactionism has been used to refute the idea of fixity in the domain of emotions, Susan Shott (1979) and Thomas Scheff (1979, 1988, 1994, 1997) have also employed it to show how emotions underlie social order and stability. The fact that pattern and predictability exist in much of social life, rather than chaos and randomness, poses one of the longstanding problems in sociological analysis. It is generally acknowledged that the reverse side of social order is social control, indicating that society manages somehow to instill in individuals a propensity to comply with required social forms and that deviance from these forms, though greater in some periods than in others, is actually quite limited. How is this accomplished?

There are two main answers to the question, and both of them turn on emotion. First, social order may be imposed by dominant and powerful groups. Their tactic is to evoke fear for nonconforming behavior. Although it has been argued by some, such as Talcott Parsons, that such regimes cannot be stable in the long run, in the short run they can have remarkable sticking power. Decades or even centuries may elapse before a feared government is overthrown.

The second ground for social order entails acceptance of the existing pattern of things. And here sociologists have split on what is accepted. On the one hand, social order can flow from belief in the validity of the social norms. One pays one's taxes, serves in the armed forces, does not steal even when there is an opportunity to do so undetected, and so on because the rules are deemed valid and it feels morally right to abide by them. A second view, which has come to prominence, is that underlying social order is an emotional order. Without an emotional basis, social order would not be possible.

Attacking the question from a symbolic interactionist perspective, Shott proposes a set of "role-taking emotions" that are central to social control: guilt, shame, embarrassment, pride, and vanity. Each of these involves the central symbolic interactionist mechanism of putting oneself in the place, or taking the role, of the other person and thereby evoking his or her perspective. The result of such role-taking can be an emotion directed toward the self, because it evokes in the self the judgment that others are making about the self. Guilt involves the self- and (presumed) other-judgment of "moral inadequacy." Shame entails the self- and (presumed) other-rejection of an "idealized self-image." Embarrassment arises from the realization that others view one's self-presentation as "inept." Pride comes from placing oneself in the position of others and regarding oneself with approbation; vanity is a reduced form of this, in that one is not sure of other's approval.

These emotions (with perhaps the exception of vanity) operate homeostatically. Individuals are moved to reduce the incidence of such unpleasant emotions as guilt, shame, and embarrassment and

increase the incidence of pleasant emotions such as pride. How is this done? Obviously, one avoids the unpleasant emotions by avoiding conduct that would earn the disapprobation of others. One gains pleasant emotions by engaging in conduct of which others approve. In general, the emotions fit one into the moral requirements of others, who are themselves governed by the same set of pre- and proscriptions for social conduct.

Shott suggests that the role-taking emotions are an inexpensive way for society to obtain social order, since they make each person his or her own guardian in ensuring that the emotional tone of one's life remains, on balance, more pleasant than painful. Where such self-control fails, the prospects of social order are not entirely dim, for the emotions that ensue—guilt, shame, or embarrassment—motivate reparative action to reequilibrate the social order as well as others—therefore, one's own—opinion of oneself. Thus, guilt and shame have been shown to increase compensatory altruism toward others, and embarrassment has been shown to evoke compensatory supererogation or attainment as a way of reequilibrating the judgments of others about the self to return to a positive balance.

Finally, Shott proposes a role-taking emotion that is not reflexive, in that it does not pertain to a judgment of the self. This is empathy, which allows one to feel what the other person in the situation is feeling, or what one would likely feel if one were in the place of the other person. Empathy makes any emotion vicariously accessible. Where the emotion reveals the other to be in a socially vulnerable place, one has the embodied sense of the need that other has for social rescue, and the likelihood of engaging in that rescue is enhanced. Thus empathy allows for the evocation of solidarity with others and the preservation of social order through protective behaviors that take up the slack when others are unable to act suitably in their own behalf.

Scheff is also concerned with social order, but he focuses on shame and pride as the ne plus ultra emotions in this regard. He takes a cue from Charles Horton Cooley's ([1902] 1922) famous looking-glass metaphor: "Each to each a looking glass, reflects the other that doth pass" (p. 184). Cooley asserted that pride and shame were the emotional engines for getting individuals to conform to the requirements of their fellow members in society. Scheff proposes that individuals are continuously in a state of either pride or shame. But then the question arises as to why, if these emotions are so important, there is so little evidence of them.

Scheff proposes that shame is a recursive emotion. That is, once present it has a tendency to evoke more shame, or even anger, over the fact that one is ashamed. This can lead to a spiral of emotion about emotion about emotion . . . that leads to both an inability to escape the emotion and a tendency to hide it from others—a frequent response when coping with shame. This hiddenness, proposed as a defining feature of shame, ties in with the work of Helen Block Lewis (1971), whose intensive analysis of psychotherapy protocols revealed two types of "unacknowledged" shame: *overt, undifferentiated shame* and *bypassed shame*. The former is manifested by painful feelings and self-derogation ("I am stupid, foolish, feckless, incompetent," and the like). Often this is accompanied by stammering, unnecessary word repetition, averted gaze, and declining audibility of speech. Both the verbal, paralinguistic and proxemic forms are means of hiding the self from the evaluating gaze of others.

Bypassed shame, on the other hand, leads to covert such symptoms as obsessive focusing on the episode that evoked the inadequate response, as if the replay could retrieve the lost status. Thought and speech are hyperactive, actually preventing one from participating with others in the natural rhythm of conversational flow. Both types of shame share the common characteristic of low visibility, thus demonstrating the power of shame as the emotional foundation of social control. Only those with sufficient self-esteem can acknowledge their shame and thus discharge it. But self-esteem itself, as proposed by Mead, derives from the good opinion of others, which itself arises when one conforms to their normative requirements; that is, when there has been social control.

This formulation, implying catharsis in the discharge of shame, ties into Scheff's work on the problem of undischarged emotions. Scheff proposes that catharsis of these residual emotions can only occur in properly "distanced" settings. Here Scheff adopts the concept of "aesthetic distance," employed by Bullough in his analysis of drama. According to Bullough (1912), an audience can experience a dramatic presentation in various ways according to its emotional distance from what appears on stage. Too little distance involves the audience so deeply that it forgets it is merely watching a play and wants to mount the stage in defense of the hero. Too much distance leaves the audience uninvolved, indifferent to whatever murder or mayhem may be happening on stage. Optimum, or aesthetic, distance, like the last of Goldilocks's porridge bowls and beds, is "just right," providing a comfortable level of emotional arousal that leads to the "purgation of pity and terror," which according to Aristotle was the aim of drama.

In a similar vein, Scheff proposes that troublesome residual emotions may also be purged in social settings where there is optimum distance. To do so, he suggests, requires that the expressive emotional content be retrieved (for example, crying, trembling, sweating), but in a context in which the individual can be both participant and observer of his or her own emotional display. When these conditions for emotional aesthetic distance are met, catharsis occurs. This is signaled by an anomalous emotional outcome: even though the residual emotion may be unpleasant, discharging it is not unpleasant, and there is a succeeding state of clarity of thought, relaxation, renewed energy or exhilaration. Although the catharsis paradigm is somewhat different from the social control paradigm, the two are joined in that unacknowledged shame, which is not discharged, often leads to spirals of emotion (e.g., anger over shame over fear) that incapacitate individuals in their social interactions, leading sometimes to violent outbursts that break though all the bonds of social control.

Robert Thamm (1992) builds a theory of emotions on the foundations of Talcott Parsons's and Edward Shils's scheme for a general theory of action. In their formulatiion, social actors are linked in reciprocal forms of action and response through expectations and sanctions. In social settings, individuals have expectations of each other, and in light of those expectations they reward or fail to reward each other's behavior. From each actor's perspective, according to Thamm, this leads to four questions: (1) Is the self meeting expectations? (2) Is the self receiving rewards? (3) Is the other meeting expectations? (4) Is the other receiving rewards? These constitute a social matrix for the production of emotions. As the answers to these questions vary from yes (+) to no (−) to don't know (0), different emotions result. A given state of the system of self and other's expectations and sanctions can be coded by a pertinent series of pluses, minuses, and zeros. For example, if the answer to all four questions is yes, the coding is [++++]; if the answer to all four is no, the coding is [−−−−]; if the answer to the first two is yes and the last two is no, the coding is [++−−].

Based on the permutations of the many possible states of the expectations–sanctions system, Thamm hypothesizes a variety of emotional resultants. For example, when the self meets expectations [+000], the self feels pleased with itself. When the self does not meet expectation [−000], the self feels disappointed with itself. When the other does not meet expectations [00−0], the self feels disappointed in the other. When the self meets expectations but is not rewarded [+−00], the self feels powerless. When the other does not meet expections, so that the self is not rewarded [0−−0], the self feels anger at the other. Many additional hypotheses follow from the variations along the spectrum of expectations–sanctions possibilities.

The reliance of the cultural approach to emotions on mental structions susceptible to socialization and variable according to historical conditions of change, directly conflicts with at least some elements of the social structural position. The latter places more emphasis on universal situational determinants of emotion and on some biological mechanisms that articulate with the situation–emotion nexus. Kemper (1987) has attempted to reconcile some of the opposing views through a syncretic analysis, focusing on the issue of primary and secondary emotions.

Kemper proposes that a large body of cross-cultural, phylogenetic, autonomic, social relational, and classificatory evidence leads to a model of four primary emotions: fear, anger, sadness, and joy (or nominal variants of these). Since there are additional emotions, the question is: What is their source? Kemper proposes that emotions beyond the primary ones may arise from a specific pattern of socialization in which a social definition and label are applied to a situation in which one of the primary emotions is being felt. For example, pride may be derived from socialization to the idea of self-regard for accomplishment in a context of joy.

Shame may result from socialization to the idea of self-rejection in a context of anger. And guilt may derive from socialization to the idea of self-rejection for what is defined as a morally wrong action in the context of fear. The primary emotion contexts are important because they provide the autonomic, therefore specifically emotional, underpinnings of the secondary emotions. The cultural components, such as situational definitions and emotional labels, are important because they help the person differentiate and ascribe the feeling to particular social and behavior contexts.

Gibson (1997) offers a different approach to the reconciliation of the structural and cultural approaches to emotions by incorporating aspects of both in his model for feeling and expression of emotions in organizations. Both structural conditions and display rules operate to instigate and control emotions in organizational contexts.

REASON AND EMOTION

One of the longest-standing problems in the study of emotions is the relationship between emotions and reason. This question has engaged two millennia of philosophers and psychologists, including Aristotle, Aquinas, Spinoza, Hume, and Freud. Sociologists are latecomers here, but have substantially and persuasively claimed that reason is not an isolated domain of human action, but is imbued with emotion (Kemper 1993), a point that a sociological approach makes particularly clear.

Max Weber ([1922] 1947) set the stage by distinguishing between *Zweckrational*, or expedient action, and at least two types of emotional action: *Affectuel*, or impulsive action, and *Wertrational*, or value-oriented action. But he did little to develop the relationship between the two emotional types and the strictly expedient type. The latter is the prototypical action of economic theory, where means are examined and selected to attain the best possible outcome. In the economic version, money is the usual yardstick for the efficacy of the decision based on expediency. Other considerations are treated more or less as "noise," disturbing the adequacy of the model. The sociological version of this economic approach is rational choice theory.

In a radical confrontation with rational choice theory, Collins (1993) throws down the gauntlet to economically based theories. He argues that the main preference order is based on emotional currency, namely emotional energy (EE) which is acquired in successful interactions with others (see earlier description of Collins' work). The good feelings—confidence and enthusiasm—that individuals derive from participation in interaction are the *summum bonum*, and this is what individuals are attempting to maximize in their so-called rational choices, regardless of what the currency may appear to be—money, status, practical or aesthetic enjoyment of material goods, and so on.

Lawler and Thye (1999) approach the rational choice issue through the window of social exchange theory, in which self-interested actors are trying to obtain something of value from other self-interested actors. They examine the *context* of exchange, which ordinarily will have a certain emotional tone and emotional requirements, the *processes* of exchange, which may make actors feel satisfied, excited, or otherwise emotionally aroused, and the *outcome* of exchange at which point actors may feel gratified or angry, prideful or crestfallen. In a useful schematic formulation, Lawler and Thye organize the context, process, and outcome features of exchange according to six different mainly sociological approaches to the study of emotions. For context, the *cultural-normative* approach (Hochschild 1979) and the *structural-relation* approach (Collins 1975, Kemper 1978); for processes, a psychologically oriented *social-cognitive* approach (Bower 1991) and a *sensory-informational* approach (Heise 1979); and for outcomes, a *social attribution* approach (Weiner 1986) and a *social formations* approach (Collins 1981 and Lawler and Yoon 1998). This schematic formulation enables analysts to move easily into the examination of motions in social exchange situations.

EMOTIONS AND MACROPROCESSES

Most sociological examinations of emotion are social-psychological; that is, social structures, processes, or outcomes of these are seen to produce emotions in the individuals involved, with emotions differing according to where in the structure, process, or outcome the individual stands. Jack Barbalet (1998) provides an important exception to this social-psychological approach, conceiving of emotion as integral to social relations and social processes themselves. Emotion is felt by individuals—this cannot be escaped—but as an aspect of societal patterns of social organization in terms of class, gender, race, and the like. This leads to another perspectival difference: Most sociological approaches to emotion examine social processes and social relations as the independent variables—they cause or produce emotions. Barbalet reverses this and examines how emotions cause or produce social processes and social relations. Furthermore, this is conceived at the macro level, engaging societal, as opposed to interpersonal, processes.

For example, working-class individuals might be expected to harbor social resentment against those who are better off, but such resentment is scant in the United States and has led to no effective political movements. Following Bensman and Vidich (1962), Barbalet tries to explain this in part by locating different sectors of the working class in different places in normal trade cycles in capitalist societies. A dynamic economy contains both expanding (e.g., computers) and contracting (e.g., textiles) industries, and workers in the different industries cannot be expected to experience the same emotions, thus vitiating any theory or program that views workers in a monolithic way.

In another venture into the macrosociology of emotions, Barbalet examines the emotion, mood, or feeling of confidence as an important feature of social process. Particularly in the business community, confidence is a necessary condition of investment. Indeed, in Barbalet's view, confidence dominates even rational calculation. This is because rational business planning is limited by the fact that it is future-oriented and the information that rational assessment requires is unavailable—it can only unfold in the future. Therefore, to undertake action under conditions of limited rationality, the business community must rely on its intuition that investment will be profitable. Put otherwise, it must have confidence. Government is an important constituent of the situation, sometimes enhancing and sometimes depressing business confidence. Barbalet proposes that what differentiates these effects of government policy is whether they reflect "acceptance and recognition" of the business community. For example, government spending on infrastructure or the bailout of the savings and loan industry reflect such appreciation. On the other hand, business interests feel slighted when the government proposes strict policies to reduce global warming, and business confidence falls accordingly. In both examples—those of the working class and business—the emotions are aggregated products of many individuals that then act as a discrete force in society.

In an unusually strong entry of a macrosociological approach into the domain of emotions, Jasper (1998) and Goodwin and Jasper (1999) have argued for the overlooked importance of emotions in the understanding of large scale social movements. Social movements, they argue, are awash in emotions. Anger, fear, envy, guilt, pity, shame, awe, passion and other feelings play a part either in the formation of social movements, in their relations with their targets who are either antagonists or possible collaborators, and in the lives of potential recruits and members. Without the emotions engaged in movement environments, dynamics, and structure it would be hard to explain how social movements arise, amass critical levels of support, maintain such support in long enduring campaigns in the face of often intense opposition, and provide means for recruiting and sustaining supporters, both as active members and as favorably disposed publics and bystanders. Understanding the dynamics of emotions thus clarifies social movement dynamics.

CONCLUSION

The sociology of emotions has a long history but only a short recent life. It is a diverse speciality, reflecting many of the axial divisions that currently rend the field, but one that lends itself to the illumination of a large number of problem areas from the micro to the macro level. The main requirement for the present-day sociology of emotions is, as Peggy Thoits (1989) has argued, to pursue empirical support for its many theories. Only in this way will it become clear in which direction theory can most fruitfully go.

(SEE ALSO: *Affect Control Theory and Impression Formation; Rational Choice ; Social Exchange Theory*)

REFERENCES

Barbalet, Jack 1998 *Emotion, Social Theory and Social Structure: A Macrosociological Analysis*. Cambridge, U.K.: Cambridge University Press.

Bensman, Joseph, and Arthur Vidich 1962 "Business Cycles, Class and Personality." *Psychoanalysis and the Psychoanalytic Review* 49:30–52.

Bower, G. H. 1991 "Mood Congruity of Social Judgments." In J. Forgas, ed., *Emotion and Social Judgments*. Oxford: Pergamon.

Bullough, Edward 1912 "Psychic Distance as a Factor in Art and as an Aesthetic Principle." *British Journal of Psychology* 5: 669–679.

Clark, Candace 1997 *Misery and Company: Sympathy in Everyday Life*. Chicago: University of Chicago Press.

Collins, Randall 1975 *Conflict Sociology*. New York: Academic Press.

——1981 "On the Microfoundations of Macrosociology." *American Journal of Sociology* 86: 984–1014.

——1990 "Stratification, Emotional Energy, and the Transient Emotions." In T. D. Kemper, ed., *Research Agendas in the Sociology of Emotions*. Albany: State University of New York Press.

——1993 "Emotional Energy as the Common Denominator or Rational Action." *Rationality and Society* 5: 203–230.

Cooley, Charles H. (1902) 1922 *Human Nature and the Social Order*, Rev. ed. New York: Scribner's.

Durkheim, Émile (1915) 1965 *The Elementary Forms of the Religious Life*, trans. J. W. Swain. New York: Free Press.

Elias, Norbert 1978a *The Civilizing Process*. New York: Urizen Books.

——1978b *The History of Manners*. New York: Urizen Books.

Gibson, Donald E. 1997 "The Struggle for Reason: The Sociology of Emotions in Organizations." In R. J. Erickson and B. Cuthbertson-Johnson, eds., *Social Perspectives on Emotion*, Vol. 4. Greenwich, Conn.: JAI Press.

Goffman, Erving 1959 *The Presentation of Self in Everyday Life*. Garden City, N.Y.: Doubleday.

——1967 *Interaction Ritual*. Garden City, N.Y.: Doubleday.

——1981 *Forms of Talk*. Philadelphia, Pa.: University of Pennsylvania Press.

Goodwin, Jeff, and James M. Jasper 1999 "Caught in a Winding, Snarling Vine: The Structural Bias of Political Process Theory." *Sociological Forum* 14: 27–54.

Gordon, Steven L. 1981 "The Sociology of Sentiments and Emotions." In M. Rosenberg and R. S. Turner, eds., *Social Psychology: Sociological Perspectives*. New York: Basic Books.

Heise, David R. 1979 *Understanding Events: Affect and the Construction of Social Action*. New York: Cambridge University Press.

Hochschild, Arlie Russell 1979 "Emotion Work, Feeling Rules, and Social Structure." *American Journal of Sociology* 85:551–575.

—— 1983 *The Managed Heart: Commercialization of Human Feelings*. Berkeley: University of California Press.

Jasper, James M. 1998 "The Emotions of Protest: Affective and Reactive Emotions in and Around Social Movement." *Sociological Forum* 13: 397–424.

Kemper, Theodore D. 1978 *A Social Interactional Theory of Emotions*. New York: Wiley.

—— 1987 "How Many Emotions Are There? Wedding the Social and the Autonomic Components." *American Journal of Sociology* 93:263–289.

—— 1989 "Love and Like and Love and *Love*." In D. D. Franks and E. D. McCarthy, eds., *The Sociology of Emotions: Original Essays and Research Papers*. Greenwich, Conn.: JAI Press.

—— 1990 "Social Relations and Emotions: A Structural Approach." In T. D. Kemper, ed., *Research Agendas in the Sociology of Emotions*. Albany: State University of New York Press.

—— 1993 "Reason in Emotions or Emotions in Reason." *Rationality and Society* 5: 275–282.

—— and Muriel T. Reid 1997 "Love and Liking in the Attraction and Maintenance Phases of Long-Term Relationships." In R. Erickson and B. Cuthbertson-Johnson, eds., *Social Perspectives on Emotion*, Vol. 4. Greenwich, Conn.: JAI Press.

Lawler, Edward J., and Jeongkoo Yoon 1998 "Network Structure and Emotion in Exchange Relations. "*American Sociological Review* 63: 871–894.

—— and Shane R. Thye 1999 "Bringing Emotions into Social Exchange Theory." In K. Cook and J. Hagan, eds., *Annual Review of Sociology*, Vol. 25. Palo Alto, Calif.: Annual Reviews.

Lewis, Helen B. 1971 *Shame and Guilt in Neurosis*. New York: Wiley.

MacKinnon, Neil J. 1994 *Symbolic Interaction as Affect Control*. Albany: State University of New York Press.

Marx, Karl (1842–1844) 1971 *The Early Texts*, Ed. D. McLellan, Oxford: Blackwell.

—— (1867) 1967 *Capital: A Critique of Political Economy*. New York: International Publishers.

—— and Friedrich Engels (1846) 1947 *The German Ideology*. New York: International Publishers.

Mead, George H. 1934 *Mind, Self, and Society*. Chicago: University of Chicago Press.

Morris, J. Andrew, and Daniel C. Feldman 1996 "The Dimensions, Antecedents, and Consequences of Emotional Labor." *Academy of Management Review* 21: 986–1010.

—— 1979 *Catharsis in Healing, Ritual, and Drama*. Berkeley: University of California Press.

—— 1988 "Shame and Conformity: The Deference-Emotion System." *American Sociological Review* 53:395–406.

Scheff, Thomas J. 1994 *Bloody Revenge: Emotions, Nationalism, and War*. Boulder, Colo.: Westview Press.

—— 1997 *Emotions, the Social Bond, and Human Reality: Part/Whole Analysis*. New York: Cambridge University Press.

Seeman, Melvin 1959 "On the Meaning of Alienation." *American Sociological Review* 24: 783–791

Shott, Susan 1979 "Emotion and Social Life: A Symbolic Interactionist Analysis." *American Journal of Sociology* 84:1317–1334.

Smith, Adam (1759) 1853 *The Theory of Moral Sentiments*. Rev. ed. London: G. Bell and Sons.

Smith-Lovin, Lynn, and David R. Heise 1988 *Analyzing Social Interaction: Advances in Affect Control Theory*. New York: Gordon and Breach.

Thamm, Robert 1992 "Social Structure and Emotion." *Sociological Perspectives* 35:649–671.

Thoits, Peggy 1989 "The Sociology of Emotions." *Annual Review of Sociology* 15:317–342,

—— 1990 "Emotional Deviance: Research Agendas." In T. D. Kemper, ed., *Research Agendas in the Sociology of Emotions*. Albany: State University of New York Press.

Weber, Max (1904–1905) 1958 *The Protestant Ethic and the Spirit of Capitalism*, trans. T. Parsons. New York: Scribner's.

Weiner, Bernard 1986 *An Attributional Theory of Motivation and Emotion*. New York: Springer-Verlag.

THEODORE D. KEMPER

ENVIRONMENTAL EQUITY

The scientific study of the social distribution of environmental impacts has quickly become an important area of inquiry within environmental sociology. Scholarly interest in this topic—which has been referred to as environmental justice, environmental equity, or environmental racism—does not derive from formal theories of differential environmental impacts, but rather has been inspired by the rapidly evolving environmental justice movement. Sociologists have studied both the social movement itself and the claims of environmental inequity made by the movement's proponents. The study of environmental justice has important implications for other areas of sociology, including stratification, race relations, sociology of health, and the study of social movements.

THE ENVIRONMENTAL JUSTICE MOVEMENT

Origins of the Movement. In the summer of 1978, the state of New York finally acknowledged what the residents of Love Canal had suspected for some time—that some of the 21,000 tons of chemical waste that had been dumped into an abandoned canal between 1942 and 1952 were now leaking into the basements of nearby homes and percolating into the playgrounds of the elementary school that had been built directly above the filled canal (Levine 1982). The situation presented "great and imminent peril to the health of the general public residing at or near the site," according to the New York state commissioner of health (as quoted in Levine 1982, p. 7). This announcement galvanized the concerns and suspicions of many residents of this working-class community, who for years had endured bad smells, mysterious sinkholes, skin irritations, respiratory problems, spontaneous abortions, and birth defects. Soon after this announcement, the private concerns of individual people began to develop into an organized social protest that pressured the state and federal governments to take action to protect the health, safety, and property of the citizens.

The events at Love Canal continued to make national headlines for the next two years. In 1979, before the media or the public could forget about environmental health risks, an accident occurred at the Three Mile Island nuclear power plant near Harrisburg, Pennsylvania (Walsh 1981). Large quantities of radioactive gas and water were released, and over 100,000 residents within a 15-mile radius of the plant were evacuated. Overnight, public support rallied behind local anti-nuclear groups that had previously been viewed as radical.

Soon after, grassroots anti-toxics movements began to proliferate in the United States. In addition to the media attention given to Love Canal and Three Mile Island, a number of other factors set the stage for the emergence of these movements. The growing popularity of the mainstream environmental movement and books such as Rachel Carson's *Silent Spring* (1962) had made much of the public aware that there were health hazards surrounding man-made chemicals, that citizens could be exposed to them unknowingly, and that technical and political solutions to such problems were not readily available (Cable and Shriver 1995; Freudenberg and Steinsapir 1992; Szasz 1994). In addition, problems associated with the unsafe disposal practices used during the post-World War II industrial boom began to surface at this time, causing increasing discovery of new toxic contamination problems.

Racial issues quickly became central to the environmental justice movement. The first environmental justice protest organized by African Americans took place in 1982 in Warren County, North Carolina, where the state proposed to build a landfill for the disposal of hazardous polychlorinated biphenyls (PCBs) that had been illegally dumped in 14 different North Carolina counties (Bullard 1994). This was a poor, mostly black, rural community. Why had this community been chosen to receive the landfill? Local residents believed that race was a deciding factor. They called upon black civil rights leaders for support, and a protest was organized. Although the landfill was eventually constructed, the Warren County protest was a landmark in the history of the environmental justice movement. Since then numerous other communities of color, primarily African American, Hispanic, and Native American, have become active in the environmental justice movement (for examples, see Bullard 1993 or Hofrichter 1993).

The formation of local-level anti-toxics movements has tended to follow a general pattern (Cable and Benson 1993; Cable and Shriver 1995). The first stage is the recognition that there is a local toxics hazard. Often, this recognition is a result of health problems among members of the community. Thus it is frequently women, particularly housewives, who are the first to become involved with toxics issues, since they are most likely to take responsibility for the health of the family (Krauss 1993; Brown and Masterson-Allen

1994). Once a toxics problem is perceived by community members, they typically turn to official administrative and regulatory bodies for correction of the problem. The results are usually disappointing, and residents often come to believe that these institutions actually serve the interests of polluters more than the interests of residents (Bullard 1994; Cable and Benson 1993; Krauss 1989; Levine 1982; Molotch 1970). A sense of injustice, and often a deep sense of betrayal, develops among local activists, and they begin to pursue alternative means of social control through social movement organizations.

Most anti-toxics movements emerge in poor, working class, or minority communities (Brown and Masterson-Allen 1994; Freudenberg and Steinsapir 1992). Many activists and analysts alike argue that this is due to the disproportionate share of toxic pollution borne by these communities (Austin and Schill 1991; Bullard 1994). More affluent communities have more resources to draw on—including adequate funding, an educated membership, access to professional advice, and social networks that overlap with local power structures—and thus they are better able to control pollution problems through the political and regulatory processes (Hurley 1995; Molotch 1970).

The notion that less powerful communities have been targeted for polluting facilities was further reinforced by the widespread circulation among the grassroots community of a report written by the consulting firm Cerrell Associates, Inc. for the California waste industry. The report recommended that waste incinerators would most easily be sited in communities least likely to generate political resistance (i.e., communities that have populations that are older, more conservative, less educated, and have lower average incomes) (Cerrell Associates, Inc. 1984; Cable and Shriver 1995).

Relationship to Mainstream Environmental Groups. The environmental justice movement differs significantly from the "mainstream" environmental movement in terms of its membership, values, and tactics. The mainstream environmental movement has focused primarily on issues of conservation of natural resources and preservation of natural beauty. Membership in mainstream environmental organizations grew rapidly in the United States from 1960 to 1990, with three groups—the Sierra Club, the National Wildlife Federation, and the National Audubon Society— each claiming more than 500,000 members (Mitchell et al. 1991). Mainstream environmental groups have professional staffs, generate funds through large foundation grants and membership dues, and work primarily within the system by using lobbying and litigation to influence government action.

Mainstream environmentalism has often been characterized as an elite movement. Early studies supported this general view when they found the greatest support for environmental causes among people who are young, white, well-off, urban, well-educated, and politically liberal (Buttel 1979; Buttel and Flinn 1974; Kreger 1973; Morrison et al. 1972). Some more research has confirmed these findings (Jones and Dunlap, 1992). However, one longitudinal study suggests the well-educated and well-off were simply the first to embrace environmentalism (Kanagy et al. 1994).

There has been some debate about the role of race in mainstream environmentalism. It has been common for social scientists to assume that African Americans will be less supportive of environmentalism than whites, but most evidence suggests that when it comes to environmental concern, there is no significant difference between blacks and whites (Jones and Carter 1994). Blacks *are* less likely, however, to be involved in mainstream environmental action (Taylor 1989; Mohai 1990). One explanation for this lag in environmental action is that blacks are more likely to experience a variety of stressors which detract from their ability to act upon environmental concerns. As Robert Bullard put it: "Decent and affordable housing, for example, is a top environmental problem for inner-city blacks" (1994, pp. 10–11).

In contrast to mainstream environmentalism, environmental justice movements tend to develop in poor, working class, or minority communities (Brown and Masterson-Allen 1994; Freudenberg and Steinsapir 1992). The two movements also have different goals —concerns about local health threats are central to the environmental justice movement. Protests often focus on pollution-generating facilities, such as factories, landfills, toxic waste dumps, incinerators, or nuclear power plants. Participants in these movements are generally people who believe they are personally at risk from the facility. Thus, at least initially, these protests are generally grassroots-generated, and locally focused.

This focus on local issues has prompted some members of the mainstream environmental movement to charge that environmental justice activists are mere "NIMBY" (Not In My BackYard) protesters (Freudenberg and Steinsapir 1992). They accuse environmental justice activists of lacking concern for the environment in general and of acting out of pure self-interest. In turn, environmental justice activists have accused the mainstream environmental movement of representing elite interests and being content to let disadvantaged groups bear the toxic burden of modern affluence. As relative newcomers to environmental activism, members of the environmental justice movement have generally been disappointed with the lack of assistance given their cause from the larger, more established environmental groups (Bullard and Wright 1992; Taylor 1992).

Grassroots environmental protests have tended to use different tactics than the mainstream environmental groups. They typically lack the funds or the political clout to lobby and negotiate with elites. Thus they are more likely to use disruptive and attention-getting tactics, such as public protests, sit-ins, letter writing campaigns, and attendance at public hearings (Bullard 1994). In one extreme example, a group of residents in Love Canal took an EPA official hostage for several hours in an effort to generate media attention (Levine 1982). Environmental justice groups have also made use of the courts, primarily through tort actions that seek reparations for damage to health and property.

These differences between the two movements have had conflicting implications for social movement theory. The elite membership of mainstream environmental groups has often been viewed as support for *resource mobilization theory*. This theory proposes that the emergence of social movements has little to do with the existence or extent of grievances experienced by movement participants. Grievances are a given, everyone has them, and the development of active social movements depends upon the availability of resources available to particular groups of people to advance their causes (McCarthy and Zald 1977). In contrast, the environmental justice movement is based on grievances and is comprised of members with relatively little resources. Current social movement theory appears inadequate to explain the environmental justice movement (Brown and Masterson-Allen 1994; Masterson-Allen and Brown 1990; Walsh 1981; Walsh et al. 1993).

Expansion of the Environmental Justice Movement. The environmental justice movement has evolved beyond its origin in the late 1970s as a collection of isolated local protests. Regional coalitions, such as the Southern Organizing Committee and the Southwest Network for Environmental and Economic Justice, have formed to facilitate the sharing of ideas, resources, and networks among geographically dispersed groups. A number of national support organizations have also been formed, most notably the Citizen's Clearing House for Hazardous Waste (led by Lois Gibbs of Love Canal) and the National Toxics Campaign Environmental Justice Project (Moore and Head 1993). These organizations provide resources and information to smaller groups, and have conducted their own organizing and lobbying campaigns at the national level. Activists have also connected with the academic community, and a number of research and support centers for environmental justice have been established. These include the Environmental Justice Resource Center at Clark Atlanta University in Atlanta and the Deep South Center for Environmental Justice at Xavier University in New Orleans, among others (Wright 1995). Members of the environmental justice movement have increasingly sponsored meetings and panels that bring together activists, scholars, and the media.

Institutional responses to the environmental justice movement have also increased at the national level. In 1992 the Environmental Protection Agency established an Office of Environmental Equity (Cutter 1995). In 1994, President Clinton signed Executive Order 12898, which requires every federal agency to adhere to principles of environmental justice in its operations (Clinton 1994). The issue of racial disparity has allowed activists to file administrative complaints under Title VI of the 1964 Federal Civil Rights Act.

A New Worldview—Ecological Democracy. Many scholars have noted the profound change in worldview that often results from individual participation in the environmental justice movement. As noted earlier, environmental justice activists often become disillusioned with the ability of the government to protect them from toxic contamination. This change is often conceived as a reframing of the toxics problem: what was initially perceived as an isolated technical or regulatory problem is now seen as a larger social issue involving the relative power of corporations and citizens, the role of the state, and conceptions of social justice (Capek 1993; Brown and Masterson-Allen 1994; Cable and Shriver 1995). Capek (1993) argues that, especially for black communities, the civil rights movement provided a "master frame" which legitimated the quest for environmental equality and permitted critical analysis of the social structure that created the inequity.

This new, broader perspective now dominates discourse on the causes of environmental inequity. As Heiman (1990) puts it, the Not In My BackYard perspective has become the Not In Anybody's BackYard critique. When challenged as to where hazardous facilities should be located, rather than try to locate them in someone else's backyard, environmental justice activists have responded by questioning the assumption that such facilities are a public good that must be sited somewhere. "The not-in-anybody's-backyard stand forces the debate away from the suitability of specific waste treatment facilities of locations, and toward a more fundamental reassessment of the propriety of a production system under private control where, in the quest for profit, the public is exposed to known risks" (Heiman 1990, p. 361).

This new perspective was expressed in the *Principles of Environmental Justice*, a document created in 1991 by a group of activists at the People of Color Environmental Leadership Summit. Among the 17 principles adopted are these:

1. Environmental Justice affirms the sacredness of Mother Earth, ecological unity and the interdependence of all species, and the right to be free from ecological destruction. 3. Environmental justice mandates the right to ethical, balanced and responsible uses of land and renewable resources in the interest of a sustainable planet for humans and other living things. 5. Environmental justice affirms the fundamental right to political, economic, cultural and environmental self-determination of all peoples. 6. Environmental justice demands the cessation of the production of all toxins,

hazardous wastes, and radioactive materials, and that all past and current producers be held strictly accountable to the people for detoxification and the containment at the point of production. 7. Environmental justice demands the right to participate as equal partners at every level of decision-making including needs assessment, planning, implementation, enforcement and evaluation. (Reprinted in Hofrichter, 1993, pp.237–239)

In searching for the causes of environmental inequity, many analysts—academics and activists alike—have come to see issues of environmental justice as a result of an inherent contradiction within the liberal democratic capitalist state (Cable and Benson 1993; Hamilton 1993; Heiman 1990; Krauss 1989; see also O'Connor 1973). The essence of this argument is that the state is charged with two conflicting goals: to further the accumulation of capital and profits for private industry; and to protect the interests of individual citizens and communities. Particularly in terms of environmental regulation, these two goals are at odds because environmental regulations protect citizens from industrial externalities at the expense of profits.

This line of reasoning is compatible with that of social ecologists and eco-Marxists. For example, Faber (1998) states:

The roots of America's ecological problems and injustices are grounded in the expansionary dynamics of the global capitalists system . . . . To sustain the process of capital accumulation and higher profits in the new global economy, American capital is increasingly relying on ecologically and socially unsustainable forms of production. . . . In so doing, America's corporate ruling class, the 1 percent of the population that owns 60 percent of all corporate stock and business assets, is serving its own narrow material interests at the expense of the environment, communities, and the health of working people. The reason is that corporate expenses related to human health and environmental quality do not typically increase labor productivity (hence potential profits) sufficiently to outweigh such expenditures. . . . It costs capital and the state much less to displace environmental health problems onto people who lack health care insurance, possess lower incomes and property values, and as unskilled or semiskilled laborers are more easily replaced if they become sick or die. In this sense, environmental inequalities in all forms, whether they be class, race, gender, or geographically based, are socially constructed features grounded in the systemic logic of capitalist accumulation. (pp. 2–5)

The emergence of this theoretical model of environmental justice has inspired some writers to call for a restructuring of society and a return to basic principles of democracy. They reject the false contradiction between individuals rights and social goods. In particular, they are challenging corporate power and control over production decisions (Pullido 1994; O'Connor 1993; Hamilton 1993). They favor a new social contract with the state to create an economic democracy in which decision making is decentralized. For example, O'Connor (1993) states:

For the people to regain their sovereignty and restore their environment, fundamental changes in the structure of government are required that permit effective discussion, debate, and decision making. Every citizen, regardless of wealth, should be given an equal opportunity to bring ideas to stop environmental decline directly to the American people. In addition, each citizen will need new rights, in relation to polluting or poisonous industries, in order to allow citizens an opportunity to protect themselves and their communities from the everyday abuses of economic power, against which no level of regulation or conventional governance can fully protect them. (p. 52)

Global Issues in Environmental Justice. The global dimensions of environmental justice issues have been receiving increased attention. Third World environmental problems, particularly natural resource depletion, have generally been viewed by established international authorities (particularly the United Nations) as the result of insufficient development and a lack of advanced technology (World Commission on Environment and Development, 1987). Alternatively, however, critical scholars see Third World environmental problems as the legacy of colonialism and continuing exploitation of the periphery by core nations (Esteva 1992; Harvey 1997; Redclift 1987; Sachs 1997; Weissman 1993). Plans to promote development

in the Third World often involve large-scale construction projects (often funded by the World Bank) that cause large-scale destruction of natural resources such as forests, rivers, farmlands, or native species. Agyeman and Evans (1996) explain the situation this way:

The well-entrenched belief endemic to Northern societies is that the extant economic and social conditions of many Southern societies legitimately permit commercial behaviour that would not be accepted in the North, often justified in terms of bringing employment to areas of no work. However, the implicit, unstated position is fundamentally racist, in that such commercial behaviour is deemed as appropriate for black people whereas it is inappropriate for white people. It is far away from the economic power centres of the North, and any local representations concerning pollution or environmental degradation are likely to be muted for fear of unemployment. (pp. 74–75)

A case in point is the Union Carbide pesticide factory near Bhopal, India that released a cloud of poisonous gasses in 1984, killing an estimated 6,600 people and injuring as many as 600,000. Such a massive facility probably could never have been sited in a Northern country, and it would have required much more expensive safety measures.

The involvement of U.S. environmental groups in Third World environmental issues has been strongest in the protection of forests and natural habitat, and has generally involved mainstream environmental groups and other organizations dedicated to global justice and equity (Keifer and Benjamin, 1993). One popular intervention is the debt-for-nature swap, in which a Northern environmental group pays a portion of a Third World country's debt on the condition that the recipient nation will establish a nature preserve or other conservation program. These types of programs are increasingly resented by the nations of the South, who view them as paternalistic extensions of the North's colonial control that interfere with local self-determination. One alternative that has been developed is the debt-for-Indian-stewardship swap, in which indigenous people gain control over parcels of land in exchange for debt relief (Alston and Brown 1993).

The export of toxic waste to Third World nations has also become a major political issue. As the cost of disposal rises, facilities in the United States and Western Europe are increasingly looking for new locations to dispose of their wastes. For example, a ton of waste that costs $200 to store in the United States will cost $40 to dispose in Benin (Mpanya 1992). About half of all African nations have been approached by Western interests to serve as dump sites. At least 25 African nations have agreed, motivated by payments of $10 to $25 million that can be used to make payments on international debt. There have also been several rather widely publicized cases (and probably many undiscovered cases) where toxic waste has been imported into Third World counties under false pretenses, often labeled as fertilizer or construction material. For example, 4,000 tons of toxic incinerator ash from Philadelphia were unloaded on a beach in Haiti, falsely labeled as fertilizer. The attempt to repatriate the toxic ash has dragged on for years (Bruno, 1998).

The economic logic of these practices was revealed in a leaked internal World Bank memo, written in 1991 by then chief economist Lawrence Summers, which was subsequently published in *The Economist* (September 8, 1992). It reads in part:

Just between you and me, shouldn't the World Bank be encouraging more migration of the dirty industries to the LDC's (Lesser-Developed-Countries)? I can think of three reasons: 1) The measurement of the costs of health-impairing pollution depends on the foregone earnings from increased morbidity and mortality. From this point of view a given amount of health-impairing pollution should be done in the country with the lowest cost, which will be the country with the lowest wages. I think the economic logic behind dumping a load of toxic waste in the lowest-wage country is impeccable and we should face up to that. 2) The costs of pollution are likely to be non-linear as the initial increments of pollution probably have very low cost. I've always thought that under-populated countries in Africa are vastly under-polluted; their (air pollution) is probably vastly inefficiently low compared to Los Angeles or Mexico City. Only the lamentable facts that so much pollution is generated by non-tradable industries (transport, electric generation) and that the unit transportation costs

of solid waste are so high prevent world welfare-enhancing trade in air pollution and waste. 3) The demand for a clean environment for aesthetic and health reasons is likely to have very high income elasticity. The concern over an agent that causes a one in a million change in the odds of prostate cancer is obviously going to be much higher in a country where people survive to get prostate cancer than in a country where under-5 mortality is 200 per thousand. Also, much of the concern over industrial atmosphere discharge is about visibility of particulates. These discharges may have little direct health impact. Clearly trade in goods that embody aesthetic pollution concerns could be welfare enhancing.

In an attempt to address the problem of increasing toxic exports, the United Nations organized a convention held in Basel, Switzerland regarding the international movement of toxic waste. In 1989, 118 nations signed the Basel Convention on the Control of Transboundary Movements of Hazardous Waste and their Disposal. The Basel Convention prohibits the transfer of toxic wastes from member nations of the Organization for Economic Cooperation Development (OECD—an organization comprising the most industrialized and developed nations in the world) to non-OECD countries. However, many nations, including the United States, have yet to ratify the treaty and make it the law of the land. Furthermore, other international agreements, particularly international trade agreements such as the North American Free Trade Agreement (NAFTA) and the General Agreement on Tariffs and Trade (GATT) actually make it more difficult for individual nations to restrict the flow of toxic substances across their borders, since such restrictions can present impediments to free trade.

EMPIRICAL RESEARCH ON ENVIRONMENTAL EQUITY

Research Findings. For many environmental justice activists, the existence of inequitable environmental impacts along race and class lines is a reality. For sociologists and other scholars, however, the nature and extent of these inequities needs to be established through systematic and objective research. The protest against the Warren County landfill (described above) launched the current interest in empirical investigation into claims of disproportionate siting of environmentally hazardous facilities in disadvantaged communities. One of the activists involved in the Warren County protest was Congressman Walter E. Fauntroy, who initiated a study by the General Accounting Office (GAO) of hazardous landfill siting in the South (GAO 1983). The GAO study, though limited in scope and analysis, found a relationship between the siting of landfills and the racial and economic characteristics of residents in surrounding communities. A more comprehensive study, also in response to the Warren County protest, was conducted by the Commission for Racial Justice of the United Church of Christ (United Church of Christ 1987). This study analyzed the presence of hazardous waste treatment, storage, and disposal facilities (TSDFs) in all zip codes in the United States, and concluded that racial composition was the strongest predictor of the presence of a TDSF. This study was circulated widely within the civil rights community and is considered to be the seminal investigation into racial bias in environmental risk. Interestingly, as Szasz and Mueser (1997) point out, the United Church of Christ analysis was not the first study of environmental justice. A number of investigations conducted in the 1970s, which focused more on social class than on race, had already found disparities in exposures to environmental risks, but these studies were largely ignored by the social science community. It took the politicizing force of the charge of racism to get scholars to take up serious investigation of the distribution of environmental hazards.

Since the United Church of Christ report, research on this topic has grown rapidly. Most studies, with some significant exceptions, have reported some type of social disparity in the distribution of environmental hazards. (See Szasz and Meuser 1997 for a comprehensive review of environmental justice research.) Higher levels of environmental hazards in places with lower socioeconomic status have been found by the United Church of Christ (1987), Burke (1993), Pollack and Vittas (1995), Been (1997), Boer et al. (1997), Brooks and Sethi (1997), Ringquist (1997), Kreig (1998), and Daniels and Friedman (1999). Similar findings for minority communities have been reported by the United Church of Christ (1987), Burke (1993), Zimmerman (1993), Perlin et al. (1995), Pollack

and Vittas (1995), Been (1997), Boer et al. (1997), Brooks and Sethi (1997), Ringquist (1997), Kreig (1998), Stretesky and Hogan (1998), and Daniels and Friedman (1999). Research by Anderton et al. (1994; 1997), Bowen et al. (1995), and Cutter et al. (1996), however, found no significant evidence of race or class disparity in the distribution of environmental hazards.

Methodological Issues. It is important to note that the studies mentioned above have used a variety of different research designs, and thus are not entirely comparable. For example, researchers have studied a wide range of geographic locations, ranging in size from the entire United States to a single metropolitan area, and results from one location may have little bearing on the situation in others. Furthermore, some of these differences in design point to important methodological issues that need to be considered in evaluating environmental equity.

One of the most important methodological issues involves the conceptualization and measurement of pollution. What constitutes a hazard? A wide variety of environmental risks have been discussed in the literature, including lead poisoning, pesticide exposure, toxic fish consumption, occupational hazards, nuclear facilities, municipal landfills, hazardous waste sites, and industrial emissions. Empirical research to date has most often used data on three types of hazards: hazardous waste treatment storage and disposal facilities (TSDFs) (United Church of Christ 1987; Anderton et al. 1994; Cutter et al. 1996; Been 1997; Boer et al. 1997); Superfund sites or other sites known to be contaminated with hazardous wastes (Anderton et al. 1997; Cutter et al. 1996; Kreig 1998; Stretesky and Hogan 1998; Zimmerman 1993); and data on industrial toxic releases from the EPA's Toxics Release Inventory (TRI) (Burke 1993; Bowen et al. 1995; Brooks and Sethi 1997; Daniels and Friedman 1999; Perlin et al. 1995; Pollack and Vittas 1995; Ringquist 1997). The focus on these particular environmental hazards stems partially from the seriousness of their potential impacts on human health, but it is also due to the simple fact that there are publicly available data for these hazards.

The extent of the risk posed by these forms of pollution is an important variable that sociologists have yet to fully address. Some researchers have tried to take this issue into account by measuring the distance of resident populations from the hazard (Pollack and Vittas 1995), and others have included data on the toxicity of released chemicals in their analyses (Bowen et al. 1995). However, we still have relatively little information about exposure pathways and the risks to health that result from the environmental hazards under study. Epidemiologists, statisticians, and others have reported associations between the proximity of various environmental hazards and heightened morbidity and mortality (e.g., Geschwind et al. 1992; Kelsall 1997), but there are currently many more questions than answers about the mechanisms by which pollutants cause disease, the dose-response relationships involved, and potential synergistic effects (National Research Council 1991). These issues, although outside the domain of sociological inquiry, are highly relevant to the study of environmental equity, since adverse health outcomes lie at the core of citizen concerns about environmental contamination.

Another methodological issue involves a controversy in the literature concerning the appropriate geographic unit for the study of environmental equity. Some analysts have declared that, due to their smaller size, census tracts or block groups are more appropriate than zip codes, counties, or regions (Anderton et al. 1994; Bowen et al. 1995; Cutter et al. 1996). They suggest that findings of racial inequity such as that found in the United Church of Christ study are the result of an ecological fallacy resulting from the use of too large a geographic unit. Large units can mask significant heterogeneity in the distribution of residents, hazards, or both. Whether the ecological fallacy has played a role in findings of environmental inequity is still unresolved, as attempts to address the issue have been inconclusive. Bowen et al. (1995) claimed to compare two geographic levels in their study of environmental equity in Ohio, however, they analyzed first all counties in Ohio and then census tracts only in Cuyahoga County. Thus it is impossible to know if differences between the two levels were due to the unit of analysis or the area of study. Cutter et al. (1996) studied environmental justice in South Carolina at the county, tract, and block group levels. While they did observe that bivariate relationships changed significantly across geographic units, they found little evidence of

environmental inequity in South Carolina at any level, and thus no evidence of the ecological fallacy.

Future Directions. Evidence is mounting that disparities do exist in the distribution of environmental hazards according to race and class. But there is still much to know with regard to which groups of people are exposed to which hazards. As noted above, there are many types of environmental hazards and they may have very different distributions and impacts.

Perhaps the most significant question raised by this line of research is the question of process. How have disadvantaged communities come to be associated with greater environmental risks? Which came first—are hazardous facilities sited in already disadvantaged communities, or do poor and minority residents tend to settle near already existing facilities? This question is particularly significant because the answers may have important implications for policies intended to remedy inequities. Szasz and Meuser (1997) suggest six possible scenarios, ranging from overt discrimination in the siting process to market rationality. Most of the empirical research has been cross-sectional in design, and thus cannot address this important issue. One major barrier has been the lack of good historical data on environmental hazards. A few longitudinal studies have been conducted, but the results have been inconclusive (Been 1994; Been 1997; Oakes et al. 1996). Evidence about process from case studies of polluted communities, while perhaps not generalizable, suggests the operation of complex reciprocal processes (Hersch 1995; Hurley 1995). Traditional heavy industry in Pittsburgh, Pennsylvania and Gary, Indiana, for example, appears to have been located in places near raw materials and transportation. Initially, the lack of transportation meant that more-affluent white workers lived closer to the factories. Over time, a number of processes brought African Americans and poor whites into closer proximity to pollution. Improved transportation and affluence, combined with housing segregation, allowed middle-class whites to move away from the factories into new housing on the suburban fringe, while blacks moved into downtown locations. As the cities grew and environmental regulation increased, it became necessary to locate sites for the disposal of wastes. Affluent communities with more political clout were able to keep such facilities outside their borders. Less advantaged communities were more vulnerable to the siting of waste facilities due to a lack of effective zoning regulations, a reluctance to protest anything that might bring jobs, and a lack of information about the types of facilities that were being proposed for construction.

This question of process points to the need to establish links between existing sociological theories and the issues raised by the environmental justice movement regarding the distribution of environmental impacts. What larger social forces have had a role in producing these outcomes? As noted above, some scholars have begun to link environmental inequities to general theories of capitalist production. In order to demonstrate the relevance of these ideas (or other theories, for that matter) to environmental justice, more specific mechanisms of inequity must be identified. Several factors have been suggested, including housing discrimination, the market dynamics of land values, occupational segregation, and procedural inequities in environmental regulation. Hopefully, future research will begin to address these challenging issues.

REFERENCES

Agyeman, Julian, and Bob Evans 1996 "Black on Green: Race, Ethnicity and the Environment." In Susan Buckingham-Hatfield and Bob Evans, eds., *Environmental Planning and Sustainability*. New York: John Wiley and Sons.

Alston, Dana, and Nicole Brown 1993 "Global Threats to People of Color." In Robert D. Bullard, ed., *Confronting Environmental Racism: Voices from the Grassroots*. Boston: South End Press.

Anderton, Douglas L., Andy B. Anderson, John Michael Oakes, and Michael R. Fraser 1994 "Environmental Equity: The Demographics of Dumping." *Demography* 31:2 (May) 229–248.

——, John Michael Oakes, and Karla L. Egan 1997 "Demographics of the Discovery and Prioritization of Abandoned Toxic Sites." *Evaluation Review* 21(1):3–26.

Austin, Regina, and Michael Schill 1991 "Black, Brown, Poor, and Poisoned: Minority Grassroots Environmentalism and the Quest for Eco-Justice." *The Kansas Journal of Law & Public Policy* 1(1):69–82.

Been, Vicki 1997 "Coming to the Nuisance or Going to the Barrios? A Longitudinal Analysis of Environmental Justice Claims." *Ecology Law Quarterly* 24(1):1–56.

—— 1994 "Locally Undesirable Land Uses in Minority Neighborhoods: Disproportionate Siting or Market Dynamics?" *The Yale Law Journal* 103:6 (April):1383–1422.

Boer, J. Tom, Manuel Pastor, Jr., James L. Sadd, and Lori D. Snyder 1997 "Is There Environmental Racism? The Demographics of Hazardous Waste in Los Angeles County." *Social Science Quarterly* 78(4):793–810.

Bowen, William M., Mark J. Salling, Kingsley Haynes, and Ellen J. Cyran 1995 "Toward Environmental Justice: Spatial Equity in Ohio and Cleveland." *Annals of the Association of American Geographers* 85(4):641–663.

Brooks, Nancy, and Rajiv Sethi 1997 "The Distribution of Pollution: Community Characteristics and Exposure to Air Toxics." *Journal of Environmental Economics and Management* 32:233–250.

Brown, Phil, and Susan Masterson-Allen 1994 "The Toxic Waste Movement: A New Type of Activism." *Society and Natural Resources* 7:269–287.

Bruno, Kenny 1998 "Philly Waste Go Home." *Multinational Monitor* (February).

Bullard, Robert D., ed. 1993 *Confronting Environmental Racism: Voices from the Grassroots*. Boston: South End Press.

—— 1994 *Dumping in Dixie: Race, Class, and Environmental Quality*, 2nd ed. San Francisco: Westview Press.

——, and Beverly H. Wright 1992 "The Quest for Environmental Equity: Mobilizing the African-American Community for Social Change." In Riley E. Dunlap and Angela G. Mertig, eds., *American Environmentalism: The U.S. Environmental Movement*. New York: Taylor and Francis.

Burke, Lauretta M. 1993 "Race and Environmental Equity: A Geographic Analysis in Los Angeles." *Geo Info Systems* (October):44–50.

Buttel, Frederick H. 1979 "Age and Environmental Concern: A Multivariate Analysis." *Youth and Society* 10(3):237–256.

Buttel, F. H., and W. L. Flinn 1974 "The Structure of Support for the Environmental Movement, 1968–1970." *Rural Sociology* 39:56–69.

Cable, Sherry, and Michael Benson 1993 "Acting Locally: Environmental Injustice and the Emergence of Grass-roots Environmental Organizations." *Social Problems* 40(4):464–477.

——, and Thomas Shriver 1995 "Production and Extrapolation of Meaning in the Environmental Justice Movement." *Sociological Spectrum* 15(4):419–442.

Capek, Stella M. 1993 "The 'Environmental Justice' Frame: A Conceptual Discussion and an Application." *Social Problems* 40(1):5–24.

Carson, Rachel 1962 *Silent Spring*. New York: Fawcett.

Cerrell Associates, Inc. 1984 *Political Difficulties Facing Waste-to-Energy Conversion Plant Siting*. Los Angeles: Cerrell Associates.

Clinton, William J. 1994 "Executive Order 12898 of February 11, 1994: Federal Actions to Address Environmental Justice in Minority Populations and Low-Income Populations." *The Federal Register* 59:32 (February 16):7629–7633.

Cutter, Susan L. 1995 "Race, Class and Environmental Justice." *Progress in Human Geography* 19(1):111–122.

———, Danika Holm, and Lloyd Clark 1996 "The Role of Geographic Scale in Monitoring Environmental Justice." *Risk Analysis* 16(4):517–526.

Daniels, Glynis, and Samantha R. Friedman 1999 "Spatial Inequality and the Distribution of Industrial Toxic Releases: Evidence from the 1990 TRI." *Social Science Quarterly* 80(2):244–262.

Esteva, Gustavo 1992 "Development." In Wolfgang Sachs, ed., *The Development Dictionary: A Guide to Knowledge as Power*. London: Zed Books.

Faber, Daniel 1998 "The Struggle for Ecological Democracy and Environmental Justice." In Daniel Faber, ed., *The Struggle for Ecological Democracy: Environmental Justice Movements in the United States*. New York: Guildford Press.

Freudenberg, Nicholas, and Carol Steinsapir 1992 "Not in Our Backyards: The Grassroots Environmental Movement." In Riley E. Dunlap and Angela G. Mertig, eds., *American Environmentalism*. New York: Taylor and Francis.

General Accounting Office 1983 *Siting of Hazardous Waste Landfills and Their Correlation with Racial and Economic Status of Surrounding Communities*. (June 1) Washington, D.C.: U.S. General Accounting Office.

Geschwind, Sandra A., Jan A. J. Stolwijk, Michael Bracken, Edward Fitzgerald, Alice Stark, Carolyn Olsen, and James Melius 1992 "Risk of Congenital Malformations Associated with Proximity to Hazardous Waste Sites." *American Journal of Epidemiology* 135(11):1197–1207.

Hamilton, Cynthia 1993 "Environmental Consequences of Urban Growth and Blight." In Richard Hofrichter, ed., *Toxic Struggles: The Theory and Practice of Environmental Justice*. Philadelphia: New Society Publishers.

Harvey, David 1997 "The Environment of Justice." In Andy Merrifield and Erik Swyngedouw, eds., *The Urbanization of Injustice*. New York: New York University Press.

Heiman, Michael 1990 "From 'Not in My Backyard!' to 'Not in Anybody's Backyard!' Grassroots Challenge to Hazardous Waste Facility Siting." *Journal of the American Planning Association* 56:359–362.

Hersch, Robert 1995 "Race and Industrial Hazards: An Historical Geography of the Pittsburgh Region, 1900–1990." Discussion Paper 95–18. Washington, D.C.: Resources for the Future.

Hofrichter, Richard, ed. 1993 *Toxic Struggles: The Theory and Practice of Environmental Justice*. Philadelphia: New Society Publishers.

Hurley, Andrew 1995 *Environmental Inequalities: Class, Race, and Industrial Pollution in Gary, Indiana, 1945–1980*. Chapel Hill, N.C.: University of North Carolina Press.

Jones, Robert Emmet, and Riley E. Dunlap 1992 "The Social Bases of Environmental Concern: Have They Changed Over Time?" *Rural Sociology* 57(1):28–47.

Kanagy, Conrad L., Craig R. Humphrey, and Glenn Firebaugh 1994 "Surging Environmentalism: Changing Public Opinion or Changing Publics?" *Social Science Quarterly* 75(4):804–819.

Kelsall, J. E., J. M. Samet, S. L. Zeger, and J. Xu 1998 "Air Pollution and Mortality in Philadelphia, 1974–1988." *American Journal of Epidemiology* 146(9):750–762.

Kiefer, Chris, and Medea Benjamin 1993 "Solidarity with the Third World: Building an International Environmental-Justice Movement." In Richard Hofrichter, ed., *Toxic Struggles: The Theory and Practice of Environmental Justice*. Philadelphia: New Society Publishers.

Krauss, Celene 1993 "Blue Collar Women and Toxic Waste Protests." In Richard Hofrichter, ed., *Toxic Struggles: The Theory and Practice of Environmental Justice*. Philadelphia: New Society Publishers.

——— 1989 "Community Struggles and the Shaping of Democratic Consciousness." *Sociological Forum* 4(2):227–239.

Kreger, Janet 1973 "Ecology and Black Student Opinion." *Journal of Environmental Education*. 4(3):30–34.

Kreig, Eric J. 1998 "The Two Faces of Toxic Waste: Trends in the Spread of Environmental Hazards." *Sociological Forum* 13(1):3–23.

Levine, Adeline Gordon 1982 *Love Canal: Science, Politics, and People*. Lexington, Mass.: Lexington Books.

Masterson-Allen, Susan, and Phil Brown 1990 "Public Reaction to Toxic Waste Contamination: Analysis of a Social Movement." *International Journal of Health Services* 20(3):485–500.

McCarthy, John D., and Mayer N. Zald 1977. "Resource Mobilization and Social Movements: A Partial Theory." *American Journal of Sociology* 82:1212–1241.

Mitchell, Robert Cameron, Angela G. Mertig, and Riley E. Dunlap 1991 "Twenty Years of Environmental Mobilization: Trends Among National Environmental Organizations." *Society and Natural Resources* 4(3):219–234.

Mohai, Paul 1990 "Black Environmentalism." *Social Science Quarterly* 71:745–765.

Molotch, Harvey 1970 "Oil in Santa Barbara and Power in America." *Sociological Inquiry* 40 (Winter):131–144.

Moore, Richard, and Louis Head 1993 "Acknowledging the Past, Confronting the Present: Environemtnal Justice in the 1990s." In Richard Hofrichter, ed., *Toxic Struggles: The Theory and Practice of Environmental Justice*. Philadelphia: New Society Publishers.

Morrison, D. E., K. E. Hornback, and W. K. Warner 1972 "The Environmental Movement: Some Preliminary Observations and Predictions." In W. R. Burch, Jr., N. H. Cheek Jr., and L. Taylor, eds., *Social Behavior, Natural Resources, and the Environment*. New York: Harper and Row.

Mpanya, Mutombo 1992 "The Dumping of Toxic Waste in African Countries: A Case of Poverty and Racism." In Bunyan Bryant and Paul Mohai, eds., *Race and the Incidence of Environmental Hazards: A Time for Discourse*. San Francisco: Westview Press.

National Research Council 1991 *Environmental Epidemiology: Public Health and Hazardous Wastes*. Washington, D.C.: National Academy Press.

Oakes, John Michael, Douglas L. Anderton, and Andy B. Anderson 1996 "A Longitudinal Analysis of Environmental Equity in Communities with Hazardous Waste Facilities." *Social Science Research* 25:125–148.

O'Connor, James R. 1973 *The Fiscal Crisis of the State*. New York: St. Martin's Press.

O'Connor, John 1993 "The Promise of Environmental Democracy." In Richard Hofrichter, ed., *Toxic Struggles: The Theory and Practice of Environmental Justice*. Philadelphia: New Society Publishers.

Perlin, Susan A., R. Woodrow Setzer, John Creason, and Ken Sexton 1995 "Distribution of Industrial Air Emissions by Income and Race in the United States: An Approach Using the Toxic Release Inventory." *Environmental Science & Technology* 29(1):69–80.

Pollock, Phillip H., III, and M. Elliot Vittas 1995 "Who Bears the Burdens of Environmental Pollution? Race, Ethnicity, and Environmental Equity in Florida." *Social Science Quarterly* 76(2):294–310.

Pullido, Laura 1994 "Restructuring and the Contraction and Expansion of Environmental Rights in the United States." *Environment and Planning A* 26:915–936.

Redclift, Michael 1987 *Sustainable Development: Exploring the Contradictions*. New York: Routledge.

Ringquist, Evan J. 1997 "Equity and the Distribution of Environmental Risk: The Case of TRI Facilities." *Social Science Quarterly* 78(4):811–829.

Sachs, Wolfgang 1997 "Sustainable Development." In Michael Redclift and Graham Woodgate, eds., *The International Handbook of Environmental Sociology*. Northhampton, Mass.: Edward Elgar Publishing, Inc.

Stretesky, Paul, and Michael J. Hogan 1998 "Environmental Justice: An Analysis of Superfund Sites in Florida." *Social Problems* 45(2):268–287.

Szasz, Andrew 1994 *Ecopopulism: Toxic Waste and the Movement for Environmental Justice*. Minneapolis: University of Minnesota Press.

———, and Michael Meuser 1997 "Environmental Inequalities: Literature Review and Proposals for New Directions in Research and Theory." *Current Sociology* 45(3):99–120.

Taylor, Dorceta 1992 "Can the Environmental Movement Attract and Maintain the Support of Minorities?" In Bunyan Bryant and Paul Mohai, eds., *Race and the Incidence of Environmental Hazards: A Time for Discourse*. San Francisco: Westview Press.

Taylor, Dorceta E. 1989 "Blacks and the Environment: Toward an Explanation of the Concern and Action Gap Between Blacks and Whites." *Environment and Behavior* 21:175–205.

United Church of Christ (Commission for Racial Justice) 1987 *Toxic Wastes and Race in the United States: A National Report on the Racial and Socioeconomic Characteristics of Communities with Hazardous Waste Sites*. New York: United Church of Christ.

Walsh, Edward J. 1981 "Resource Mobilization and Citizen Protest in Communities Around Three Mile Island." *Social Problems* 29(1):1–21.

———, Rex Warland, and D. Clayton Smith 1993 "Backyards, NIMBYs, and Incinerator Sitings: Implications for Social Movement Theory." *Social Problems* 40(1):25–38.

Weissman, Robert 1993 "Corporate Plundering of Third World Resources." In Richard Hofrichter, ed., *Toxic Struggles: The Theory and Practice of Environmental Justice*. Philadelphia: New Society Publishers.

World Commission on Environment and Development 1987 *Our Common Future*. Oxford: Oxford University Press.

Wright, Beverly 1995 "Environmental Equity Justice Centers: A Response to Inequity." In Bunyan Bryant, ed., *Environmental Justice: Issues, Policies, and Solutions*. Washington, D.C.: Island Press.

Zimmerman, Rae 1993 "Social Equity and Environmental Risk." *Risk Analysis* 13(6):649–666.

GLYNIS DANIELS

ENVIRONMENTAL SOCIOLOGY

Environmental sociology is a relatively new area of inquiry that emerged largely in response to increased societal recognition of the seriousness of environmental problems. Many areas of sociology have similarly arisen as a result of societal attention to problematic conditions, including poverty and inequality, racial and gender discrimination, and crime and delinquency. Environmental sociology is unique, however, in that sociological attention to environmental problems had to overcome strong disciplinary traditions that discouraged giving attention to nonsocial conditions such as environmental quality. Consequently, the growth of sociological work on environmental issues has been accompanied by a critique and reassessment of core sociological assumptions and practices, with the result that environmental sociology has a somewhat ambivalent stance toward its parent discipline.

We begin with a brief examination of the nature and evolution of environmental problems, in order to clarify the kinds of issues that are of concern to environmental sociologists. Then we describe the emergence of societal attention to environmental problems, highlighting sociological work on environmental activism and related topics. Next we describe sociology's response to the increased salience of environmental problems, including the development of environmental sociology as an area of inquiry as well as its critique of mainstream sociology's neglect of environmental issues. Then we review some important emphases of the field, including analyses of the causes of environmental problems, examinations of the social impacts of these problems, and analyses of solutions to such problems. We end with a brief overview of recent trends and debates in the field.

SOCIETAL–ENVIRONMENTAL INTERACTIONS AND THE EVOLUTION OF ENVIRONMENTAL PROBLEMS

Environmental sociology is typically defined as the study of relations between human societies and their physical environments or, more simply, "societal–environmental interactions" (Dunlap and Catton 1979). Such interactions include the ways in which humans influence the environment as well as the ways in which environmental conditions (often modified by human action) influence human affairs, plus the manner in which such interactions are socially construed and acted upon. The relevance of these interactions to sociology stems from the fact that human populations depend upon the biophysical environment for survival, and this in turn necessitates a closer look at the functions that the environment serves for human beings.

Three Functions of the Environment. The biophysical environment serves many essential functions for human populations, as it does for all other species (Daily 1997), but three basic types can be singled out. First, the environment provides us with the resources that are necessary for life, ranging from air and water to food to materials needed for shelter, transportation, and the vast range of economic goods we produce. Human ecologists thus view the environment as providing the "sustenance base" for human societies, and we can also think of it as a "supply depot." Some resources, such as forests, are potentially renewable while others, like fossil fuels, are nonrenewable or finite. When we use resources faster than the environment can supply them, even if they are potentially renewable (such as clean water), we create resource shortages or scarcities (Catton 1980).

Second, in the process of consuming resources humans, like all species, produce "waste" products; indeed, humans produce a far greater quantity and variety of waste products than do other species. The environment must serve as a "sink" or "waste repository" for these wastes, either absorbing or recycling them into useful or at least harmless substances (as when trees absorb carbon dioxide and return oxygen to the air). When land was sparsely populated and utilization of resources was minimal, this was seldom a problem. Modern and/or densely populated societies generate more waste than the environment can process, however, and the result is the various forms of "pollution" that are so prevalent worldwide.

Humans, like other species, must also have a place to exist, and the environment provides our home—where we live, work, play, travel, and spend our lives. In the most general case, the planet Earth provides the home for our species. Thus, the third function of the environment is to provide a "living space" or habitat for human populations. When too many people try to live in a given space, the result is overcrowding, a common occurrence in many urban areas (especially in poorer nations). Some analysts suggest that the entire planet is now overpopulated by human beings, although efforts to determine the number of people the Earth can support has proven to be difficult and contentious (Cohen 1995).

When humans overuse an environment's ability to fulfill these three functions, "environmental problems" in the form of pollution, resource scarcities, and overcrowding and/or overpopulation are the result. However, not only must the environment serve all three functions for humans, but when a given environment is used for one function its ability to fulfill the other two is often impaired. Such conditions of functional competition often yield newer, more complex environmental problems.

Competition among environmental functions is especially obvious in conflicts between the living-space and waste-repository functions, as using an area for a waste site typically makes it unsuitable for living space. When an area is used as a garbage landfill or hazardous waste site, for example, people don't even want to live near it, much less on it (Freudenburg 1997). Likewise, if hazardous materials escape from a waste repository and contaminate the soil, water, or air, the area can no longer serve as a supply depot for drinking water or for growing agricultural products. Finally, converting farmland or forests into housing subdivisions creates more living space for people, but it means that the land can no longer function as a supply depot for food or timber (or as habitat for wildlife).

The Evolution of Environmental Problems.
Understanding these three functions played by the environment provides insight into the evolution of

environmental problems, or the problematic conditions created by human overuse of the environment. In the 1960s and early 1970s when awareness of environmental problems was growing rapidly in the United States, primary attention was given to air and water pollution and to litter—problems stemming from the environment's inability to absorb human waste products—as well as to the importance of protecting areas of natural beauty. The "energy crisis" of 1973 highlighted the dependence of modern industrialized nations on fossil fuels and raised the specter of resource scarcity in general. The living-space function came to the forefront in the late 1970s when it was discovered that a neighborhood in Niagara Falls, New York, was built on an abandoned chemical waste site that had begun to leak toxic materials. Love Canal came to symbolize the growing problems of using an area as both waste repository and living space.

New environmental problems continually emerge, the result of humans trying to make incompatible uses of given environments. Global warming is an excellent example. It is primarily a consequence of a rapid increase in carbon dioxide in the Earth's atmosphere produced by a wide range of human activities—especially burning fossil fuels (coal, gas, and oil), wood, and forest lands. This buildup of carbon dioxide (CO_2) traps more of the Sun's heat, thus raising the temperature of the Earth's atmosphere. While global warming results from overuse of the Earth's atmosphere as a waste site, the resulting warming may in turn produce changes that make our planet less suitable as a living space (not only for humans, but especially for other forms of life). A warmer climate may also affect the Earth's ability to continue producing natural resources, especially food supplies (Stern et al. 1992).

These examples of how human activities are harming the ability of the environment to serve as our supply depot, living space, and waste repository involve focusing on specific aspects of particular environments (e.g., a given river's ability to absorb wastes without becoming polluted). However, it is increasingly recognized that the health of entire ecosystems is being jeopardized as a result of growing human demands being placed on them. An *ecosystem* is an interacting set of living organisms (animals and plants) and their nonliving environment (air, land, water) that are bound together by a flow of energy and nutrients (e.g., food chains); it can range in size from a small pond, to a large region such the Brazilian rainforest, to the entire biosphere—the Earth's global ecosystem (Freese 1997). Technically, it is not "the environment" but "ecosystems" that serve the three functions for humans—and for all other living species.

Exceeding the capacity of a given ecosystem to fulfill one of the three functions may disrupt not only its ability to fulfill the other two but its ability to continue to function at all. As a recent U.S. Environmental Protection Agency (EPA) report notes, "Ecological systems like the atmosphere, oceans, and wetlands have a limited capacity for absorbing the environmental degradation caused by human activities. After that capacity is exceeded, it is only a matter of time before those ecosystems begin to deteriorate and human health and welfare begin to suffer" (EPA Science Advisory Board 1990, p. 17). Human overuse of ecosystems thus creates "ecological disruptions" that become "ecological problems" for humans. As more and more people require places to live, use resources, and produce wastes, it is likely that ecological problems will worsen and that new ones will continue to emerge.

The notion that human societies face "limits to growth" was originally based on the assumption that we would run out of natural resources such as oil, but nowadays it is recognized that the ability of ecosystems to fulfill any of the three necessary functions can be exceeded. Ozone depletion, for example, stems from exceeding the atmosphere's limited ability to absorb chlorofluorocarbons (CFCs) and other pollutants. Thus, it is not the supply of natural resources per se, but the finite ability of the global ecosystem to provide us with resources, absorb our wastes, and still offer suitable living space (all of which, as we have seen, are interrelated) that constrains human societies. The emergence of problems such as ozone depletion, climate change, species extinction, and rainforest destruction are indications that modern societies may be taxing the limits of the global ecosystem (see, e.g., Daily 1997).

This brief sketch of the nature and evolution of environmental problems reveals the rich subject matter studied by environmental sociologists. While broadly construed as the study of relations between human societies and their physical environments, the field focuses primary attention on the ways in which modern societies are altering their environments and the ways in which such alterations eventually create problematic conditions for our societies—as well as the ambiguities and controversies involved in assessing and responding to these alterations and impacts (Hannigan 1995). Despite improvements in specific environmental problems, such as urban air quality and the quality of many streams and lakes, in the last quarter of the twentieth century, newer and often more serious environmental problems—often affecting wider geographic areas—have continued to emerge as greater effort is made to monitor the quality of the environment. Consequently, it seems safe to assume that environmental sociology will have no shortage of subject matter in the foreseeable future.

SOCIETAL RESPONSE TO ENVIRONMENTAL PROBLEMS

Environmental concerns first attained considerable prominence in the United States with the rise of the progressive conservation movement in the late 1800s and early 1900s in response to reckless exploitation of the nation's resources. This movement included both "utilitarians" like Gifford Pinchot, who sought to manage natural resources such as forests wisely to ensure their continued availability, and "preservationists" like John Muir, who sought to preserve areas of natural beauty for their own sake. Although these two factions eventually came into conflict, their joint efforts led to legislation establishing national parks and agencies such as the U.S. Forest Service while also spawning organizations such as the Sierra Club and National Audubon Society.

These "conservation" organizations and agencies continued to exist and grow periodically throughout the first half of the twentieth century, but they did not become highly visible until the 1950s and 1960s, when preservationist organizations such as the Sierra Club achieved renewed visibility by fighting for the protection of areas of natural beauty such as the Grand Canyon (which had been threatened by damming). The older preservationist concern with natural areas gradually coalesced with concerns about issues such as pesticide contamination—publicized by Rachel Carson's *Silent Spring*—and air and water pollution and other urban-based problems (Taylor 1997). These newer "environmental" problems tended to be more complex in origin (often stemming from new technologies), and had delayed, complex, and difficult-to-detect effects that were consequential for human (as well as nonhuman) health and welfare. Encompassing pollution and loss of recreational and aesthetic resources, and ultimately the consequences of overusing all three functions of the environment, such problems were increasingly viewed as threats not only to "environmental quality" but to our "quality of life" (Dunlap and Mertig 1992).

By the late 1960s the older conservation movement had evolved into a modern "environmental movement," as traditional conservation organizations joined with newer, multi-issue organizations, such as the Natural Resources Defense Council and Environmental Defense Fund, to pursue a wide range of environmental goals. The transformation from conservationism to environmentalism—symbolized by celebration of the first "Earth Day" in 1970—is reflected by the growth of an "environmental" discourse that largely supplanted the older conservation/preservation discourses (Brulle 1996) as well as by the explosive growth of both local and national environmental organizations concerned with a wide range of issues in the 1970s (McLaughlin and Khawaja 1999). With a reported 20 million participants, "E-Day" not only launched the contemporary environmental movement but mobilized a far greater base of support for environmentalism than had ever been achieved by the earlier conservation movement (Dunlap and Mertig 1992).

Environmental sociologists quickly tried to explain the emergence of the modern environmental movement. Besides highlighting the crucial roles played by older conservation organizations (such as the Sierra Club) in mobilizing public support, they pointed to the following factors: growth of scientific knowledge about problems such as pesticides and smog; intense media coverage devoted to incidents such as the 1969 Santa Barbara oil spill; rapid increase in outdoor recreation that brought more and more people into direct contact with threatened environments; widespread post–World War II affluence that stimulated increasing concern with quality of life over

more materialistic pursuits; and, finally, the general climate of social activism that grew out of the civil rights, anti–Vietnam War and student-power movements (see, e.g., Morrison et al. 1972). More recent analyses have emphasized the decline of class politics and materialist concerns and the subsequent emergence of new social movements devoted to quality-of-life goals as the broad socio-cultural context in which environmentalism developed (e.g., Buttel 1992).

The last three decades of the twentieth century have seen enormous changes in the nature of environmentalism, often chronicled by sociologists. The large national organizations, like the Sierra Club, constituting the core of the "environmental lobby" have remained strong, but their limited ability to produce effective results and the continual emergence of new issues that escape their purview have resulted in the emergence of numerous alternative strands of environmental activism. The result is that environmentalism is far more diverse than in the older days of the utilitarian–preservationist bifurcation (Dunlap and Mertig 1992). A major divide is that between the national organizations and the burgeoning number of local, grassroots groups that are typically concerned with hazardous conditions in their communities. A particularly potent form of grassroots activism has arisen in response to evidence of environmental racism, or the disproportionate location of hazardous facilities in minority communities, and the "environmental justice" movement spearheaded by people of color is the result (Taylor 1997). A variety of other splinter groups, including radical environmentalism (exemplified by the direct-action tactics pursued by Earth First!), deep ecology (a biocentric philosophy urging the equality of all forms of life), and ecofeminism (which links environmental degradation to the exploitation of women), along with the increasing internationalization of environmental organizations, make the contemporary environmental movement a highly complex entity (Brulle 1996).

Regardless of its historical causes, the establishment and continued existence of a viable environmental movement has ensured that environmental issues remain on the nation's policy agenda. Several pieces of landmark legislation aimed at protecting and improving environmental quality were passed in the late 1960s and early 1970s, including the National Environmental Policy Act requiring environmental impact assessments and establishment of the Environmental Protection Agency. Despite some ups and downs, environmental quality has remained a major national goal for the last three decades of the twentieth century, with new concerns continually emerging—often in response to specific "crises" such as the *Exxon Valdez* oil spill in Alaska.

The environmental movement has been widely criticized for failing to halt environmental degradation in our nation (and the world). Nonetheless, compared to other social movements, environmentalism has clearly been one of the most influential movements of the last half of the twentieth century, ranking with the women's movement, civil rights movement, and peace/antiwar movements as having changed the contours of contemporary life. Environmental concerns are now institutionalized throughout our society, not only in government laws and agencies, but in the form of environmental education (K–12) and college-level environmental studies, environmental reporters and news beats among major media, environmental affairs offices within major corporations, the growing involvement of mainstream religions with environmental problems, and a reasonably well funded and institutionalized discipline of environmental science. To these institutional indicators one can add cultural changes such as the emergence of an environmental discourse throughout society, including advertising; the ubiquity (if not effectiveness) of recycling and the gradual growth of green consumer behaviors; and the normative disapproval of outright assaults on environmental quality whether by governments or industry. Despite the intermittent emergence of open opposition to environmentalism—as represented by the current "wise-use" movement that seeks to lift governmental restrictions on use of natural resources (Switzer 1997)—the overall trends toward "environmentalization" validate claims that we are witnessing a "greening" of society at both the institutional and cultural levels (Buttel 1992).

DISCIPLINARY RESPONSE: THE BIRTH OF ENVIRONMENTAL SOCIOLOGY

Although there was scattered sociological attention to natural resource issues prior to the 1970s, environmental sociology developed in that decade as sociology's own response to the emergence of environmental problems. At first sociologists tended to pay more attention to societal response to environmental problems than to the problems themselves. As noted earlier, analyses of the environmental movement were popular, as were studies of public attitudes toward environmental issues. Prime topics included identifying the social sectors from which environmental activists were drawn and the social bases of pro-environmental attitudes among the general public (Dunlap and Catton 1979). Broader analyses of the ways in which "environment" was being constructed as a social problem, and the vital roles played by both activists and the media in this process, also received attention (Albrecht 1975). In addition, rural sociologists conducted a growing number of studies of natural resource agencies, while other sociologists examined environmental politics and policy making. In general, sociological work on environmental issues typically employed perspectives from the larger discipline to shed light on societal awareness of and response to environmental problems. In today's parlance, these initial efforts largely involved analyses of aspects of the "social construction of environmental problems" and represented what was termed a "sociology of environmental issues" (Dunlap and Catton 1979).

As sociologists paid more attention to environmental issues, a few began to look beyond societal attention to environmental problems to the underlying relationships between modern, industrialized societies and the physical environments they inhabit. Concern with the causes of environmental pollution was supplemented by a focus on the social impacts of pollution and resource constraints. In some cases there was explicit attention to the reciprocal relationships between societies and their environments, or to the "ecosystem-dependence" of modern societies (Dunlap and Catton 1994). These concerns were bolstered by the 1973–1974 "energy crisis," as the interrupted flow of oil from Arab nations generated dramatic and widespread impacts and vividly demonstrated the vulnerability of modern industrial societies to an interruption of their fossil fuel supplies and—by extension—to natural resources in general (Rosa et al. 1988). Sociologists were quick to respond with numerous studies of the impacts, particularly the inequitable distribution of negative ones, of energy shortages (Schnaiberg 1975).

Sociological interest in the impacts of energy and other resource scarcities accelerated the emergence of environmental sociology as a distinct area of inquiry by heightening awareness that "environment" was more than just another social problem, and that environmental conditions could indeed have societal consequences. Studies of the societal impacts of energy shortages thus facilitated a transition from the early "sociology of environmental issues" to a self-conscious "environmental sociology" focused explicitly on societal–environmental relations. In retrospect, it is apparent that this concern also contributed to a rather one-sided view of such interactions, however, as the effects of resource constraints on society received far more emphasis than did the impacts of society on the environment (something that has been rectified in more recent research on the causes of environmental degradation).

The nascent environmental sociology of the 1970s was quickly institutionalized via formation of interest groups within the national sociological associations. These groups provided an organizational base for the emergence of environmental sociology as a thriving area of specialization and attracted scholars interested in all aspects of the physical environment—from environmental activism to energy and other natural resources, natural hazards and disasters, social impact assessment, and housing and the built environment (Dunlap and Catton 1983). The late 1970s was a vibrant era of growth for American environmental sociology, but momentum proved difficult to sustain during the 1980s, as the Reagan era was a troublesome period for the field and social science more generally. Ironically, however, sociological interest in environmental issues was beginning to spread internationally, and by the late 1980s and the 1990s environmental sociology was not only reinvigorated in the United States but was being institutionalized in countries around the world and within the International Sociological Association (Dunlap and Catton 1994).

The resurgence of environmental sociology in the United States and its emergence internationally benefited from key societal events. Publicity surrounding Love Canal and other local environmental hazards stimulated interest in the impacts of such hazards on local communities, while major accidents at Three Mile Island, Bophal (India), and

Chernobyl dramatized the importance of technological hazards and helped generate sociological interest in the environmental and technological risks facing modern societies (Short 1984). More recently, growing awareness of global environmental problems such as ozone depletion, global climate change, and tropical deforestation have served to enhance sociological interest in environmental problems—particularly at the global level (Dunlap and Catton 1994).

ENVIRONMENTAL SOCIOLOGY AND THE LARGER DISCIPLINE

As previously noted, early sociological work on environmental issues typically involved application of standard sociological perspectives drawn from social movements, social psychology, social problems, and so forth to empirical work focusing on societal response to environmental issues. Efforts to theorize about environmental matters were rare, and they tended to involve demonstrations of the utility of established theoretical perspectives, such as Parsonian theory, for viewing environmental issues rather than asking whether such perspectives were adequate for understanding the relations between modern societies and their biophysical environments (Klausner 1971). Since sociologists interested in theorizing about the relations between modern societies and their environments found little guidance from the larger discipline, they drew heavily upon other disciplines, such as general ecology (Catton 1976), or combined ecological and sociological insights in order to develop new theoretical perspectives (Schnaiberg 1975).

Unlike the larger society, in the 1970s mainstream sociology was remarkably oblivious to the relevance of environmental matters. This disciplinary blindness stemmed from a long period of neglect of such matters stimulated by both societal developments and disciplinary traditions. The Durkheimian emphasis on explaining social phenomena only in terms of other "social facts," plus an aversion to earlier excesses of biological and geological "determinisms," had led sociologists to ignore the physical world. These disciplinary traditions were further strengthened by sociology's emergence during an era of unprecedented growth and prosperity, when limits to resource abundance and technological progress were unimaginable, and increased urbanization, which reduced direct contact with the natural environment. With modern, industrialized societies appearing to be increasingly independent of the biophysical world, sociology came to assume that the exceptional features of *Homo sapiens*—language, technology, science, and culture more generally—made these societies "exempt" from the constraints of nature. Thus, the core task of sociology was to examine the uniquely social determinants of contemporary human life (Dunlap and Catton 1979, 1983). In short, mainstream sociology offered infertile ground for planting sustained interest in the relations between societies and their biophysical environments.

It is not surprising, therefore, that efforts to establish environmental sociology as a legitimate and important area of inquiry included criticism of the larger discipline's blindness to environmental matters. Indeed, efforts to define and codify the field of environmental sociology were accompanied by explication and critique of the "human exemptionalism paradigm" (HEP) on which contemporary sociology was premised. While not denying that human beings are obviously an exceptional species, environmental sociologists argued that our special skills and capabilities nonetheless failed to exempt us from the constraints of the natural environment. Consequently, it was argued that the HEP needed to be replaced by a more ecologically sound perspective, a new ecological paradigm (NEP), that acknowledges the ecosystem-dependence of human societies (Catton and Dunlap 1978, 1980). It was further argued that much of environmental sociology, particularly examinations of the relations between social and environmental factors (as opposed to analyses of the social construction of environmental issues), entailed at least implicit rejection of the HEP with its assumed irrelevance of nonsocial phenomena to modern societies (Dunlap and Catton 1979, 1983).

The call for revision of mainstream sociology's dominant paradigm, and particularly the urging of adoption of an ecological perspective, has been a controversial feature of environmental sociology. While regarded as a core element of the field's commitment to ensuring that the material bases of modern societies are no longer neglected by sociology, the argument has been criticized for deflecting efforts to utilize classical and mainstream theoretical perspectives in environmental sociology (Buttel 1996, 1997). Fortunately, debate about the need for an ecological perspective versus the relevance of mainstream sociological theories has taken a new turn in recent years, as several environmental sociologists have independently begun to develop ecologically informed versions of classical theoretical perspectives. Efforts to develop "green" versions of Durkheimian, Weberian, and especially Marxian macro-sociologies as well as micro-level perspectives, such as symbolic interactionism, bear the fruit of integrating an ecological paradigm with classical theoretical traditions (see Foster 1999 and references in Dunlap 1997).

Increasing awareness of the societal significance of ecological conditions has not only stimulated efforts to develop greener sociological theories but also opened the floodgates of empirical research on societal–environmental relations. Studies such as those conducted by Freudenburg and Gramling (1994) on oil development in coastal waters, which convincingly show how development depends on *both* environmental conditions and social forces, and by Couch and Kroll-Smith (1985) on community hazards, which demonstrates the differing impacts of natural versus human-made disasters, clearly violate the disciplinary tradition of ignoring all but the social causes of social facts (as do many of the studies to be reviewed later).

While the empirical thrust of environmental sociology thus represents at least implicit rejection of mainstream sociology's "exemptionalist" orientation by continually demonstrating the relevance of environmental factors in modern, industrialized societies, the situation regarding adoption of an ecological paradigm or perspective is less clear. Some environmental sociologists follow Catton's (1980) lead in applying ecological theory and concepts to human societies (e.g., Fischer-Kowalski 1997), and others employ an ecological perspective as an "orienting strategy" that encourages them to raise questions about issues such as the long-term sustainability of current consumption patterns in the wealthy nations (Redclift 1996). However, some environmental sociologists express caution regarding the utility of ecological *theory* as a guiding framework for environmental sociology (Buttel 1997) or disavow its utility altogether (Macnaghten and Urry 1998). These differing orientations stem from the inherent ambiguities involved in applying concepts and findings from general ecology to human societies (Freese 1997) as well as differences of opinion about the roles of paradigms versus theories in empirical inquiry.

SOME CURRENT RESEARCH EMPHASES

Over the last three decades of the twentieth century, sociological research on environmental issues has focused on a wide range of topics, and we cannot begin to do justice to the full body of work by environmental sociologists. Fortunately, several existing reviews and compilations provide fairly comprehensive overviews of this research, covering the 1970s (Dunlap and Catton 1979), 1980s (Buttel 1987; Rosa et al. 1988), and 1990s (Buttel 1996; Dunlap and Catton 1994; Redclift and Woodgate 1997). Consequently, we limit our attention to sociological work on three particularly important theoretical and policy-relevant topics: the causes of environmental problems, the impacts of such problems, and the solutions to these problems.

Causes of Environmental Problems. Given that environmental sociology arose largely in response to increased recognition of environmental problems, it is not surprising that a good deal of work in the area has been devoted to trying to explain the origins of environmental degradation. Much of the early work, however, was devoted more to analyses and critiques of the rather simplistic views of the causes of environmental degradation that predominated in the literature rather than original studies. The need for such analyses stemmed from the fact that the predominant conceptions of the origins of environmental problems tended to emphasize the importance of single factors such as population growth (emphasized by Paul Ehrlich) or technological development (stressed by Barry Commoner), rather than recognizing the multiplicity of factors involved, and also ignored or simplified the distinctively social causes of environmental degradation. In this context, environmental sociologists tended to explicate the competing range of explanations (Dunlap and Catton 1983) and to criticize the most widely accepted ones for their shortcomings (Schnaiberg 1980).

The most powerful sociological critique of common conceptions of the origins of environmental problems in general, and those by biologists such as Ehrlich and Commoner in particular, was provided by Schnaiberg (1980). Schnaiberg criticized Ehrlich's view by noting the enormous variation in environmental impact between populations of rich and poor nations as well as between the wealthy and poor sectors within individual nations, emphasized that population growth is interrelated with factors such as poverty—which induces poor people to have more children for work-force and security reasons. Similary, Commoner's perspective was criticized for viewing technology as an autonomous force, ignoring the degree to which technological developments are driven by political and especially economic forces—particularly the need for profit and capital accumulation.

Besides demonstrating the oversimplification involved in attributing environmental degradation to either population or technology, Schnaiberg also critiqued a third factor widely mentioned as a cause—the wasteful lifestyles of consumers. In particular, Schnaiberg distinguished between the production and consumption spheres of society, arguing that the former is the more crucial contributor to environmental degradation. Attributing environmental degradation to the affluence of consumers ignores the fact that decisions made in the production realm (e.g., as to what types of transportation will be available to consumers) are far more significant than are the purchasing behaviors of individual consumers. Consequently, Schnaiberg emphasized the "treadmill of production," or the inherent need of market-based economic systems to grow and the powerful coalition of capital, state, and labor supporting such growth, as the most fundamental contributor to environmental degradation.

While Schnaiberg's analysis, which he has continued to update and refine (see, e.g., Schnaiberg and Gould 1994), has become highly influential within environmental sociology (Buttel 1987, 1997), it has proven difficult to translate into concrete empirical research beyond local case studies of organized opposition to treadmill processes (Gould et al. 1996). Consequently, a new generation of sociological analysts, while cognizant of Schnaiberg's insights, have adopted a broader framework for investigating the causes of crucial environmental problems, particularly pressing global problems.

Ironically, one line of this new work has involved revisiting the Ehrlich–Commoner debate over the relative importance of population and technological factors in generating environmental degradation. As their debate progressed, both sides realized that they could not totally ignore the other's preferred cause, or more distinctively social factors, and the debate became encapsulated in differing interpretations of a simple formulation known as the "IPAT" equation. Both Ehrlich and Commoner came to agree that environmental impact = population × affluence × technology, although debate continued over which factor on the right side of the equation had the most impact on environmental degradation (for more on this debate, see Dietz and Rosa 1994; Dunlap et al. 1994).

In recent years environmental sociologists have begun to reassess the IPAT model's utility, particularly as a means of examining the crucial causal forces generating global-level environmental problems such as tropical deforestation and global climate change. Taking into account earlier critiques of the IPAT model, Dietz and Rosa (1994; see also Rosa and Dietz 1998) have proposed a major revision that they label "STIRPAT," for "stochastic impacts by regression on population, affluence and technology." Whereas IPAT is an accounting equation that assumes direct proportionality between impact and each of the other three factors, such that a 10-percent increase in population (or technology or affluence) is assumed to produce a 10-percent increase in impact, STIRPAT treats such linkages as hypotheses to be tested. In addition, it allows both for decomposition of the individual factors (e.g., population size versus growth rate) in the model and the consideration of cultural, institutional, and political factors as additional sources of environmental impact.

While the STIRPAT model can be applied to any environmental impact, the initial application has been to global climate change, where the basic model was used to estimate CO_2 emissions (Dietz and Rosa 1997). Two interesting results emerged: First, diseconomies of scale apparently exist at the largest population sizes, as countries with the largest populations (e.g., China and India) have a disproportionate impact on CO_2 loads. Second, the results also replicated recurrent findings by economists that suggest the existence of an environmental Kuznets curve. Economists argue in these studies that as affluence increases, environmental impact per unit of affluence decreases, producing an inverted U curve, or a Kuznets curve, named as the relationship between development and inequality posited by Simon Kuznets (see Dietz and Rosa 1997 for citations).

A related sociological study, involving a longitudinal analysis of national CO_2 emissions, challenges the economists' faith that economic development will lessen environmental impacts because of the Kuznets curve. Roberts and Grimes (1997) conclude that since the energy crisis of the 1970s, affluent nations have become more carbon-efficient, producing more gross national product per unit of CO_2 emissions, but that the carbon efficiency of middle-income nations has gone down slightly and that of the poor nations has dropped substantially. Consequently, the poorest nations are locked into a pattern of high and even increasing environmental impact per unit of affluence, while wealthy nations may indeed follow the patterns proposed by development theorists. If true, this challenge to development theory suggests that the continued development of poor but populous nations like China and India will lead to increasing levels of CO_2 and other pollutants rather than the pattern observed in wealthy nations.

Tropical deforestation is another global-level problem that has attracted increasing attention by environmental sociologists seeking to understand its causes. A series of studies by Rudel and colleagues (see Rudel and Roper 1997) employ a variety of theoretical models encompassing population, technology, and affluence (the components of the IPAT and STIRPAT models) as well as a wide range of both national and international social-structural variables such as level of inequality, urbanization, and international debt. These studies typically find a significant impact of population growth in general, and patterns of rural versus urban growth in particular, on deforestation rates, but these effects are moderated by a wide range of environmental conditions and social-structural factors. Importantly, but not surprisingly, Rudel finds that deforestation is partly a function of the size of nations' forests and the topography of forest land as well as political and economic decisions to invest capital in forestry, levels of economic development, and international indebtedness.

Sociological studies of global-level problems such as deforestation and emissions of greenhouse gases, both of which directly contribute to global climate change, are yielding important findings as well as conceptual and methodological strategies for developing a better understanding of the driving forces producing global environmental change and other environmental problems (Rosa and Dietz 1998). As such, they represent an important supplement to natural-science research programs on these topics.

Impacts of Environmental Problems. As noted earlier, environmental sociology was just emerging at the time of the 1973–1974 energy crisis, and it is not surprising that a good deal of effort was made to identify real as well as potential social impacts of energy and other natural resources in this early period of the field. While diverse impacts, from regional migration to consumer lifestyles, were investigated, heavy emphasis was placed on investigating the "equity" impacts of both energy shortages and the policies designed to ameliorate them (Rosa et al. 1988). A general finding was that both the problems and policies often had regressive impacts, with the lower socioeconomic strata bearing a disproportionate cost due, for example, to rising energy costs (Schnaiberg 1975).

Equity has been a persistent concern in environmental sociology, and researchers gradually shifted their attention to the distribution of exposure to environmental hazards (ranging from air and water pollution to hazardous wastes). Again, a persistent finding has been that exposure to environmental hazards is generally negatively correlated with socioeconomic status. A growing number of studies have also found that minority populations are disproportionately exposed to environmental hazards, in part because of their lower-than-average socioeconomic levels but perhaps also because of conscious decisions to locate hazardous sites in minority communities. Such findings, which a few recent studies have challenged, have led to charges of "environmental racism" and efforts to achieve "environmental justice." At a broader level, international equity is attracting the attention of environmental sociologists, who are investigating the export of polluting industries from wealthy to poor nations, the disproportionate contribution of wealthy nations to many global-level problems, and the consequent hurdles these phenomena pose for international cooperation to solve environmental problems (Redclift and Sage 1998).

Sociologists have not limited themselves to investigating the equity impacts of environmental problems, and studies of communities exposed to technological or human-made hazards (such as Love Canal) offer particularly rich portrayals of the diverse impacts caused by discovery of community hazards. Whereas natural hazards—such as floods, hurricanes, and earthquakes—have been found to result in a therapeutic response in which communities unite in efforts to help victims, repair damage, and reestablish life as it was before the disaster struck, technological disasters have been found to have very different impacts (Freudenburg 1997). Although a putative hazard often appears obvious to those who feel affected by it, the ambiguities involved in detecting and assessing such hazards often generate a pattern of intense community conflict. Unlike those affected by natural hazards, the "victims" often find themselves at odds not only with public officials but also with other residents who fail to acknowledge the seriousness of the hazard (for fear of economic loss in terms of property values, jobs, etc.). In many cases, such conflicts have resulted in a long-term erosion of community life as well as exacerbation of the victims' personal traumas stemming from their exposure to the hazards (Couch and Kroll-Smith 1985).

Solutions to Environmental Problems. As was true for the causes of environmental problems, early work by environmental sociologists interested in solutions to these problems often involved explications and critiques of predominant approaches. Early on Heberlein (1974) noted the predilection of the United States for solving environmental problems via a "technological fix," or developing and applying new technologies to solve problems such as air and water pollution. Understandably popular in a nation with a history of technological progress, such a solution is appealing because it avoids mandating behavioral and institutional change. Unfortunately, solving problems with new technologies sometimes creates even more problems, as illustrated by attempts to solve energy shortages with nuclear power. Consequently, as the seriousness and pervasiveness of environmental problems became more obvious, attention was given to a variety of "social fixes," or efforts to change individual and institutional behaviors.

Expanding on Heberlein's analysis, other sociologists (e.g, Dunlap et al. 1994) have identified three broad types of social fixes, or implicit policy types: (1) the cognitive (or knowledge) fix, which assumes that information and persuasion will suffice to produce the necessary changes in behavior, illustrated by campaigns encouraging energy conservation and recycling; (2) the structural fix, which relies on laws and regulations that mandate behavioral change, reflected in highway speed limits or enforced water conservation; and (3) the intermediary behavioral fix, which employs incentives and disincentives to encourage changes in behavior, as illustrated by pollution taxes (penalties) and tax credits (rewards) for installing pollution-abatement technology (see Gardner and Stern 1996 for a more refined typology of policy approaches and detailed examples of each).

Environmental sociologists, in conjunction with other behavioral scientists, have conducted a range of studies that bear on the efficacy of these differing strategies for solving environmental problems, ranging from field experiments to test the effectiveness of information campaigns in inducing energy and water conservation to evaluations of alternative strategies for generating participation in recycling programs (see Gardner and Stern 1996 for a good summary). A noteworthy sociological study was Derksen and Gartrell's (1993) investigation of recycling in Edmonton, Alberta, which found that individuals' level of environmental concern (and, by implication, knowledge about the importance of recycling) was not as important in predicting recycling behavior as was ready access to a curbside recycling program. While sociologists have conducted numerous field experiments and evaluations of community environmental programs, typically investigating the efficacy of one or more of the above-noted "fixes," they have generally left examinations of national and international environmental policy making to political scientists and economists. However, sociologists have begun to pay attention to efforts to negotiate international agreements to achieve reduction of greenhouse gases (Redclift and Sage, 1998), and we expect more sociological work along these lines.

CURRENT TRENDS AND DEBATES

As the foregoing illustrates, environmental sociology not only emerged in response to societal attention to environmental problems but has focused much of its energy on understanding these problems, especially their causes, impacts, and solutions. The field has proved to be more than a passing fad, becoming well institutionalized and also increasingly internationalized. But in the process, fundamental assumptions that once served to unify the field—agreement over the reality of environmental degradation; diagnoses of such degradation as inherent to modern, industrialized societies; and the sense that mainstream sociology was largely blind to the significance of environmental matters—have become matters of debate (Buttel 1996, 1997).

The emergence of environmental problems provided the raison d' etre for environmental sociology, and the seriousness of such problems was seldom challenged. While environmental sociologists from the outset paid attention to ways in which claims about environmental conditions are socially constructed and become the subject of societal conflict (e.g., Albrecht 1975), such efforts seldom questioned the objective existence of environmental problems. In recent years, however, environmental sociology has felt the effects of the larger discipline's turn toward more cultural and interpretative orientations. A growing number of scholars, particularly in Europe, have not only highlighted the contested nature of claims about environmental problems but—in the postmodern tradition—concluded that there is no reason for privileging the claims of any parties to these debates, including those of environmental scientists as well as activists (Macnaghten and Urry 1998).

Such work has led to the emergence of a strong constructivist/interpretative orientation in environmental sociology that challenges the objectivist/realist perspective that has traditionally been dominant. Whereas the realist orientation assumes that the environment is a biophysical entity existing independent of humans, thereby providing the setting for study of human–environment interactions as the core of environmental sociology, the constructivist orientation leads its adherents to adopt an agnostic view of such interactions, preferring instead to examine knowledge claims—and the social forces they reflect—about these interactions (Macnaghten and Urry 1998). These competing perspectives can be readily seen in sociological work on global environmental change (GEC), where those in the realist camp have sought to complement natural-science research by examining, for example, societal processes leading to tropical deforestation and greenhouse gas emissions (noted previously), while constructivists have highlighted the uncertainties in scientific evidence for GEC and the social, political, and historical forces that have made GEC a central topic of scientific and policy-making interest (see Rosa and Dietz 1998). These differing orientations have led to debate among environmental sociologists, with realists pointing to shortcomings of the constructivist approach (Dickens 1996; Murphy 1997) and constructivists demonstrating the utility of their perspective (Hannigan 1995). Fortunately promising syntheses of constructivist and realist perspectives are beginning to emerge (Rosa 1998).

Another source of debate is the inevitability of continued environmental degradation, particularly on the part of advanced, industrialized nations. Whereas environmental sociologists have traditionally seen the drive toward capital accumulation inherent in such societies as making environmental degradation inevitable (as epitomized by Schnaiberg's "treadmill of production" argument), European scholars have increasingly suggested that this may not be the case. Obvious successes in environmental amelioration within advanced European nations have led them to build upon economic models of "industrial ecology," which suggest that modernization of industrial processes can permit production with ever-decreasing levels of material input and pollution output, heralding a new era of "ecological modernization" (Spaargaren and Mol 1992).

This perspective not only adopts a more sanguine image of the future of industrialized societies but, as Buttel (1996, 1997) notes, involves a shift in focus for environmental sociology: from a preoccupation with the origins of environmental degradation to efforts to explain the institutionalization of environmental amelioration (via technological innovation, policy incentives, pressures from citizens' groups, etc.). While representing an important complement to traditional perspectives in the field and building on larger sociological debates about the future of "modernity," ecological modernization is vulnerable to criticism. First, its development in northern Europe leads to concerns that ecological modernization is not applicable to less wealthy and technologically disadvantaged nations. Second, although nations such as the Netherlands have made considerable advances

in protecting their own environments, their import of natural resources and export of pollution creates a large "ecological footprint" well beyond their borders (Wackernagel and Rees 1996). Finally, even if continual progress is made in creating cleaner, more efficient production processes, these gains may be offset by continued economic growth and consumption and consequent increased demand for materials and energy (Bunker 1996).

The trends toward adoption of more constructivist/interpretative frameworks and models of ecological modernization are related to a third trend in environmental sociology—the ongoing reassessment of its relationship to the larger discipline. As noted earlier, the emergence of environmental sociology was marked by criticism of mainstream sociology's neglect of the ecosystem-dependence of modern, industrialized societies and consequent inattention to the challenge posed by environmental problems. This critical orientation led many environmental sociologists to look to other disciplines (such as ecology and environmental science) for guidance and probably contributed to a somewhat insular perspective vis-à-vis mainstream sociology.

But in the 1990s environmental problems, particularly global-level threats like climate change, have caught the attention of growing numbers of eminent sociologists, such as Giddens (1990), who have recognized that such problems cannot be ignored in analyses of the future course of industrial societies. Greater interaction between environmental and mainstream sociology has resulted, and the penetration of currently fashionable perspectives, such as cultural/interpretative frameworks and theories of the nature of late modernity into environmental sociology has followed—as exemplified by the popularity of the constructivist and ecological modernization perspectives. This is resulting in considerable debate and self-reflection among environmental sociologists, something that a maturing field can afford. Hopefully, environmental sociology will emerge with renewed relevance to the larger discipline of sociology as well as continued relevance to societal efforts to ensure an ecologically sustainable future for humankind.

(SEE ALSO: *Environmental Equity*)

REFERENCES

Albrecht, Stan L. 1975 "The Environment as a Social Problem." In A. L. Mauss, ed., *Social Problems as Social Movements.* Philadelphia: J. P. Lippincott.

Brulle, Robert J. 1996 "Environmental Discourse and Social Movement Organizations." *Sociological Inquiry* 66:58–83.

Bunker, Stephen G. 1996 "Raw Material and the Global Economy: Oversights and Distortions in Industrial Ecology." *Society and Natural Resources* 9:419–430.

Buttel, Frederick H. 1987 "New Directions in Environmental Sociology." *Annual Review of Sociology* 13:465–488.

—— 1992 "Environmentalization: Origins, Processes, and Implications for Rural Social Change." *Rural Sociology* 57:1–27.

—— 1996 "Environmental and Resource Sociology: Theoretical Issues and Opportunities for Synthesis." *Rural Sociology* 61:56–76.

—— 1997 "Social Institutions and Environmental Change." In M. Redclift and G. Woodgate, eds., *The International Handbook of Environmental Sociology.* Cheltenham, U.K.: Edward Elgar.

Catton, William R., Jr. 1976 "Why the Future Isn't What It Used to Be." *Social Science Quarterly* 57:276–291.

—— 1980 *Overshoot: The Ecological Basis of Revolutionary Change.* Urbana: University of Illinois Press.

—— and Riley E. Dunlap 1978 "Environmental Sociology: A New Paradigm." *The American Sociologist* 13:41–49.

——, and Riley E. Dunlap 1980 "A New Ecological Paradigm for Post-Exuberant Sociology." *American Behavioral Scientist* 24:15–47.

Cohen, Joel E. 1995 *How Many People Can the Earth Support?* New York: Norton.

Couch, Stephen R., and J. Stephen Kroll-Smith 1985 "The Chronic Technical Disaster: Toward a Social Scientific Perspective." *Social Science Quarterly* 66:564–575.

Daily, Gretchen C., ed. 1997. *Nature's Services: Social Dependence on Natural Ecosystems.* Washington, D.C.: Island Press.

Derksen, Linda, and John Gartrell 1993 "The Social Context of Recycling." *American Sociological Review* 58:434–442.

Dickens, Peter 1996 *Reconstructing Nature: Alienation, Emancipation and the Division of Labour.* London: Routledge.

Dietz, Thomas, and Eugene A. Rosa 1994 "Rethinking the Environmental Impacts of Population, Affluence and Technology." *Human Ecology Review* 1:277–300.

—— 1997. "Effects of Population and Affluence on CO_2 Emissions." *Proceedings of the National Academy of Sciences* 94:175–179.

Dunlap, Riley E. 1997 "The Evolution of Environmental Sociology." In M. Redclift and G. Woodgate, eds., *The International Handbook of Environmental Sociology.* Chelterham, U.K.: Edward Elgar.

——, and William R. Catton, Jr. 1979 "Environmental Sociology." *Annual Review of Sociology* 5:243–273.

——, and William R. Catton, Jr. 1983 "What Environmental Sociologists Have in Common (Whether Concerned with 'Built' or 'Natural' Environments)." *Sociological Inquiry* 53:113–135.

——, and William R. Catton, Jr. 1994. "Struggling with Human Exemptionalism: The Rise, Decline and Revitalization of Environmental Sociology." *The American Sociologist* 25:5–30.

——, and Angela G. Mertig, eds. 1992 *American Environmentalism: The U.S. Environmental Movement: 1970–1990.* Bristol, Pa.: Taylor and Francis.

——, Loren A. Lutzenhiser, and Eugene A. Rosa 1994 "Understanding Environmental Problems: A Sociological Perspective." In B. Burgenmeier, ed., *Economy, Environment, and Technology.* Armonk, N.Y.: M.E. Sharpe.

EPA Science Advisory Board 1990 *Reducing Risk: Setting Priorities and Strategies for Environmental Protection.* Washington, D.C.: U.S. Environmental Protection Agency.

Fischer-Kowalski, Marina 1997 "Society's Metabolism." In M. Redclift and G. Woodgate, eds., *The International Handbook of Environmental Sociology.* Cheltenham, U.K.: Edward Elgar.

Foster, John Bellamy 1999 "Marx's Theory of Social-Ecological Metabolism and the Critique of Capitalist Society: Classical Foundations for Environmental Sociology." *American Journal of Sociology:* 105:366–405.

Freese, Lee 1997 *Environmental Connections.* Supplement 1 (Part B) to *Advances in Human Ecology.* Greenwich, Conn.: JAI Press.

Freudenburg, William R. 1997 "Contamination, Corrosion and the Social Order: An Overview." *Current Sociology* 45:41–57.

——, and Robert Gramling 1994 *Oil in Troubled Waters: Perceptions, Politics, and the Battle over Offshore Drilling.* Albany: State University of New York Press.

Gardner, Gerald T., and Paul C. Stern 1996 *Environmental Problems and Human Behavior.* Boston: Allyn and Bacon.

Giddens, Anthony 1990 *The Consequences of Modernity.* Stanford, Calif. Stanford University Press.

Gould, Kenneth A., Allan Schnaiberg, and Adam S. Weinberg 1996 *Local Environmental Struggles: Citizen Activism in the Treadmill of Production*. New York: Cambridge University Press.

Hannigan, John A. 1995 *Environmental Sociology: A Social Constructionist Perspective*. London: Routledge.

Heberlein, Thomas 1974 "The Three Fixes: Technological, Cognitive and Structural." In D. R. Field, J. C. Barron, and B. F. Long, eds., *Water and Community Development: Social and Economic Perspectives*. Ann Arbor, Mich.: Ann Arbor Science.

Klausner, Samuel A. 1971 *On Man in His Environment*. San Francisco, Jossey-Bass.

Macnaghten, Phil, and John Urry 1998 *Contested Natures*. London: Sage Publications.

McLaughlin, and Marwan Khawaja 1999 "The Organizational Dynamics of the U.S. Environmental Movement." *Rural Sociology*: In press.

Morrison, Denton E., Kenneth E. Hornback, and W. Keith Warner 1972 "The Environmental Movement: Some Preliminary Observations and Predictions." In W. R. Burch, Jr., N. H. Cheek, Jr., and L. Taylor, eds., *Social Behavior, Natural Resources, and the Environment*. New York: Harper and Row.

Murphy, Raymond 1997 *Sociology and Nature: Social Action in Context*. Boulder, Colo.: Westview Press.

Redclift, Michael 1996 *Wasted: Counting the Costs of Global Consumption*. London: Earthscan.

——, and Colin Sage 1998 "Global Environmental Change and Global Inequality: North/South Perspectives." *International Sociology* 13: 499–516.

——, and Graham Woodgate, eds. 1997 *The International Handbook of Environmental Sociology*. Cheltenham, U.K.: Edward Elgar.

Roberts, J. Timmons, and Peter E. Grimes 1997 "Carbon Intensity and Economic Development 1962–1991: A Brief Exploration of the Environmental Kuznets Curve." *World Development* 25:191–198.

Rosa, Eugene A. 1998 "Metatheoretial Foundations for Post-Normal Risk." *Risk Analysis* 1:15–44.

——, and Thomas Dietz 1998 "Climate Change and Society: Speculation, Construction, and Scientific Investigation." *International Sociology* 13:421–455.

——, Gary E. Machlis, and Kenneth M. Keating 1988 "Energy and Society." *Annual Review of Sociology* 14:149–172.

Rudel, Thomas K., and Jill Roper 1997 "The Paths to Rain Forest Destruction: Crossnational Patterns of Tropical Deforestation, 1975–90" *World Development* 25:53–65.

Schnaiberg, Allan 1975 "Social Syntheses of the Societal–Environmental Dialectic: The Role of Distributional Impacts." *Social Science Quarterly* 56:5–20.

—— 1980 *The Environment: From Surplus to Scarcity*. New York: Oxford University Press.

——, and Kenneth Alan Gould 1994 *Environment and Society: The Enduring Conflict*. New York: St. Martin's Press.

Short, James F., Jr. 1984 "The Social Fabric at Risk: Toward the Social Transformation of Risk Analysis." *American Sociological Review* 49:711–725.

Spaargaren, Gert, and Arthur P.J. Mol 1992 "Sociology, Environment, and Modernity: Ecological Modernization as a Theory of Social Change." *Society and Natural Resources* 5:323–344.

Stern, Paul C., Oran R. Young, and Daniel Druckman, eds. 1992 *Global Environmental Change: Understanding the Human Dimensions*. Washington, D.C.: National Academy Press.

Switzer, Jacqueline Vaughn 1997 *Green Backlash*. Boulder, Colo.: Lynne Rienner.

Taylor, Dorceta E. 1997 "American Environmentalism: The Role of Race, Class and Gender in Shaping Activism, 1820–1995." *Race, Gender and Class* 5:16–62.

Wackernagel, Mathis, and William Rees 1996 *Our Ecological Footprint: Reducing Human Impact on the Earth*. Philadelphia: New Society Publishers.

RILEY E. DUNLAP
EUGENE A. ROSA

EPIDEMIOLOGY

Epidemiology is the study of the distribution of disease and its determinants in human populations. Epidemiology usually takes place in an applied public health context. It focuses on the occurrence of disease by time, place, and person and seeks to identify and control outbreaks of disease through identification of etiological factors. Its approach is to identify associated risk factors and then work back to causes.

Historically, the focus of epidemiology was on large outbreaks, usually of infectious disease. The substance and methods of epidemiology have been applied to most forms of acute and chronic disease and many other physical and mental health conditions. Along with the broadening of the subject matter of epidemiology has come more focus on its methods. Along with the specialization of epidemiological methods has come the professional identification of persons as epidemiologists. In this entry, we address the origins, methodology, current topics, and professional issues related to epidemiology.

PROFESSIONAL ROLE

Epidemiology is the professional identification of an increasing number of persons who have received specialized training in departments of epidemiology in schools of public health. Many complete approved courses of study at the master's or doctoral level leading to an M.P.H., Dr. P.H., or Ph.D. with epidemiology as an area of concentration. Some schools offer the M.P.H. to physicians after an abbreviated course of study. Like most other developing professions, graduate epidemiologists are protective of their professional identification and would seek to differentiate their professional credentials from those who have found their ways to epidemiological roles from other educational backgrounds. The problem in this developing professionalism is how to define a unique intellectual content or theory of epidemiology, when the applied nature of the discipline demands that the latest theories and methods of investigating disease be incorporated into any ongoing investigation.

ORIGINS

Langmuir (Roeché 1967, p. xiii) traces the origins of epidemiology as far back as Hypocrites' report of an outbreak of mumps among Greek athletes, but the written history of mankind is full of major outbreaks of disease, which the practitioners of the time attempted to control with methods ranging from folk remedies and the available medicine, to religion and witchcraft, and even to civil and sanitary engineering. It was the careful and scientific observation of these outbreaks that led to the development of modern epidemiology.

Perhaps the most famous early epidemiological inquiry was John Snow's careful observation of the house-by-house locations of incident cases of cholera during epidemics in London in the 1840s and 1850s. Snow's correlation of new cases with some water supply systems, but not others, changed the conventional medical wisdom about how cholera was spread and did so before the microbial nature of the disease was discovered. Roeché's *Annals of Epidemiology* provides a number of examples of the application of epidemiological methods in relation to local outbreaks in the earlier part of the twentieth century. More recent well-known investigations have included those relating to Legionnaires' disease and AIDS.

Epidemiology as a discipline has grown along with the many associated disciplines of public health and medicine. Microbiology has identified the organisms and modes of transmission for many infectious diseases. Biochemistry, physiology, virology, and related basic medical sciences have provided the scientific background to support the development of the epidemiology of infectious disease. Other sciences ranging from genetics to sociology have contributed to the various specializations within epidemiology, which are broadly classified as infectious disease, chronic disease, cancer, cardiovascular disease, genetic, perinatal, reproductive, oral, occupational, environmental, air pollution, respiratory, nutritional, injury, substance abuse, psychiatric, social, and health care epidemiology as well as pharmaco-epidemiology.

A CONCEPTUAL PARADIGM

A typical paradigm in epidemiology focuses on the interaction of: host, agent, and environment. The host is typically a person but is sometimes another species or organism which provides a reservoir of infection that is subsequently transmitted to humans. In the presence of an epidemic, one tries to understand the characteristics of the host that provide susceptibility to the epidemic condition. Characteristics that are frequently considered are: (1) genetic characteristics; (2) biological characteristics, such as immunology, physiology, and anatomy; (3) demographic characteristics, such as age, sex, race, ethnicity, place of birth, and place of residence; (4) social and economic factors, such as socioeconomic status, education, and occupation; and (5) personal behaviors, such as diet, exercise, substance use, and use of health services.

The agents in this paradigm have classically been rats, lice, and insects. They may be biological, such as viruses or bacteria, as is the case in most infectious disease epidemiology. Typhus, cholera, smallpox, the Ebola virus, Legionnaires' disease, and AIDS follow this model. Chemical agents have also contributed to significant epidemics. Some have been physiological poisons such as the mercury once used in hatmaking, lead in old paint, water pipes, or moonshine liquor; others have been carcinogens such as tobacco or PCBs found as a contaminant in oil spread on roads. Recent focus has been on alcohol and other drugs of abuse. Other physical agents have included asbestos, coal dust, and radioactive fallout. Guns, automobiles, and industrial equipment are also agents of injury and mortality. Sometimes the "agent" has been a nutritive excess or deficiency, demonstrated in Goldberger's 1915 discovery that a deficiency of niacin, part of the vitamin B complex, causes pellagra. Similarly, stress and other elements of lifestyle have been investigated as contributors to cardiovascular disease. An element in the consideration of agents is the degree of exposure and whether the agent alone is a necessary or sufficient cause of the disorder.

The third element of this paradigm is the environment, which may promote the presence of an agent or increase host susceptibility to the agent. Many elements of the environment may be relevant to the disease process, including (1) the physical environment, such as climate, housing, and degree of crowding; (2) the biological environment, including plant and animal populations, especially humans; and (3) the demographic and socioeconomic environments of the host.

At the core of this simple paradigm is the potential for multiple paths of causation for an epidemic. Rarely is a single cause sufficient to ensure the onset of a disease or condition. Thus the approach considers alternative modes of transmission, such as the influence of a common agent versus transmission from host to host. For many agents there is an incubation period, with delayed onset after "infection" or contact with the agent. Further, exposure may lead to a spectrum of disease with variation in the type and severity of the response to the agent. An important element to observe in any outbreak is *who* is not affected and whether that is due to immunity or some other protective factor.

METHODOLOGY

Field Methods. The historical method of epidemiology began with the observation that an epidemic was present, with the initial response beginning with "shoe leather" investigation of who was affected and how. The initial approach focused on identified cases and their distribution over time and place, leading to a methodology that was often able to discern the risk factors for a disease even before a particular pathogen could be identified. The description of cases in terms of geography and environment as well as various demographic characteristics and exposures remains at the core of epidemiology.

Essential complements to epidemiologic field methods are careful clinical observation, measurement, and classification of the disorder, as well as laboratory identification of any pathogens and identification of potential risk factors for the observed disorder. This methodology is drawn from the methods of associated fields such as pathology, bacteriology, virology, immunology, and molecular genetics. Efforts at classification of pathogens have been augmented by the collection of libraries of reference specimens from past outbreaks.

A problem with the investigation of known outbreaks is that many types of epidemic may develop unobserved until a significant proportion of the population is affected. This has led to the development of surveillance strategies. Among these have been the reporting of multiple causes on death certificates and the mandatory reporting to the health department of many communicable diseases, such as tuberculosis and sexually transmitted diseases. The early detection and reporting of outbreaks make various public health interventions possible. Statistical analysis of mortality and morbidity has become a major component of the public health systems of most countries.

Case Registers. An extension to this approach involves case registers, in which identified mortality or morbidity is investigated and compiled in a statistical database, with subsequent investigation of the detailed context for each case. Case registers for particular types of diseases typically identify a case and then collect additional information through review of medical charts and direct field investigations and interviews. Although not as detailed as most case registers, large databases of treated disorders are gathered by various funders or providers of health services. These include the Health Care Finance Administration (Medicare and Medicaid) and various private insurance companies.

The systematic analysis of large databases, whether case registers or those of administrative agencies, makes it possible to monitor the prevalence of various conditions and to detect increases in prevalence or outbreaks long before they would be detected by individual clinicians. Analyses of mortality and morbidity are presented by most public health agencies. Typical methods include the presentation of rates of disorder, such as the number of cases per 100,000 population for geographic and demographic subpopulations. Analyses might ask whether rates are higher in one place compared to another, for a particular birth cohort, or for persons of a particular socioeconomic status. Such comparisons may be crude or adjusted for factors such as age and sex, which may bias such comparisons. Sometimes the analyses provide detailed age- and sex-specific comparisons or breakouts by other risk factors. Yet this approach is dependent on people with diseases being identified through the health system.

Prevalence Surveys. In order to discover the true prevalence of various conditions and risk factors, it is possible to conduct sample surveys of the population of a country or other geographic unit. This approach avoids potential reporting bias from the health care system and can identify conditions that might not otherwise be recognized or reported. Typically a representative sample of persons would be interviewed about their health, and sometimes various examinations or tests would be administered. Large comprehensive surveys of health and nutrition are conducted regularly by the National Center for Health Statistics. More specialized surveys of particular conditions such as blood pressure, substance use, and mental health have been conducted by federal, state, and private agencies. Because participation in most such surveys is voluntary, investigative procedures are usually limited to interviews and test procedures with little discomfort or risk. The limitation of prevalence surveys is that they are expensive and may have respondent selection biases. On the other hand, they have great potential for collecting detailed information about disorders and potential risk factors.

Case-Control Studies. The case-control method is used extensively in epidemiology. This approach typically starts with a sample of cases of a particular disorder and identifies one or more samples of persons who appear similar but who do not have the disorder. Careful comparison of the groups has potential for identifying risk factors associated with having the disorder or, alternatively, factors that are protective. The most important issue in designing case-control studies is the designation of an appropriate control group in such a way that the process selecting controls neither hides the real risk factors nor pinpoints apparent but false ones. Control groups are frequently designated by geographic or ecological variables and are often matched on individual characteristics such as age and sex. These methods are somewhat similar to those used in natural experiments, in which two groups differ on one or more risk factors and the rates of disorder are compared, but the case-control method starts with identified cases.

Cohort Studies. Unlike the prevalence survey and most case-control studies, which are cross-sectional or retrospective in nature, a cohort study endeavors to identify groups of persons who do not have the disorder or disorders in question and then follows them prospectively through the occurrence of the disease, with ascertainment of factors likely to contribute to the etiology of the disease. Such studies may start with a general sample of the population or may select groups based on the presence or absence of hypothesized risk factors prior to onset of the disorder. They then follow the samples for incident disorder. Unlike cross-sectional studies, cohort studies provide the possibility of determining causal order for risk factors and thus avoid the possibility that apparent risk factors are simply consequences of the disease. The main problem with true cohort studies is that they must last as long as it takes for the disease to develop, which may even take longer than the working life of the investigator. Sometimes, however, cohorts can be found that have been identified and assessed historically and thus can be compared in the present. Examples may be insurance groups, occupational groups, or even residents of certain areas. Then the task is to gather the information on exposure and relate it to health outcomes.

Experimental and Quasi-Experimental Methods. A true experiment is dependent on random assignment of persons or groups to conditions, but one would hardly assign a person to a condition known to produce a serious disease. Nonetheless, there are research designs that approximate true experiments. The most direct is an intervention study in which an intervention that cannot be provided to everyone is provided to one group but not another—or provided to the alternative group at a later time. A quasi-experimental design would identify a group that has been exposed to a risk factor and compare it to another that has not. If the factors that govern the initial exposure appear to be truly accidental, then the quasi-experiment may be nearly as random as a true experiment. In such circumstances or in true randomization, one can determine the effect of the risk factor on outcomes with little risk of the outcome determining the status of the risk factor.

Alternative Methods. There are a number of research designs found in epidemiology. Those presented above are typical but certainly not exhaustive of the alternatives. At the core of nearly all of these methods, however, is the identification of factors associated with the incidence or prevalence of particular types of disorder.

CURRENT ISSUES

In recent epidemiological literature there has been some concern about the future development of epidemiology. A part of this discussion focuses on the basic paradigm being used and whether it has shifted from an ecological approach consistent with the spread of infectious disease and related pathogens to individual risk factors that are more closely related to the current emphasis on chronic diseases. The growing influence of molecular and genetic methods increases this tendency. It has been suggested that this focus on individual and proximate causes blames the individual rather than fixing the prior cause. Some authors have suggested that epidemiology should regain its public health orientation by focusing more on ecological issues affecting the risk status of groups rather than on individual-level factors, and one suggested that the primary focus should be on fighting poverty. A more integrative approach has been suggested by Susser and Susser (1996a, 1996b), who criticize the field for continuing to rely on a multiple risk factor "black box" approach, which is of declining utility, in favor of an approach that encompasses multiple levels of organization and causes from the molecular to the societal.

A second area of concern, identified by Bracken (1998), is the relationship of epidemiology to corporate litigation when various rare disorders are related to sources of risk such as cellular telephones, breast implants, and the like. The issue is the extent to which epidemiologists can provide risk information to journalists and the public without undue burden from unbridled discovery and from the inconsistencies of findings of rare exposures related to rare diseases.

A third issue appears to be the search for professional identity in a discipline that has applicability across the full range of health professions, human and otherwise. The professional positions identified in a 1999 Internet search indicated that there is a continuing market for persons with epidemiological training but that these positions are distributed widely in departments supporting specific disciplines or located in various public health settings. Thus the job titles are often designated in a hyphenated form, such as psychiatric-epidemiologist, cancer-epidemiologist, and genetic-epidemiologist. For a more complete introduction to the principles and methods of epidemiology see Kleinbaum, Kupper, and Morgenstern (1982), Littlefeld and Stolley (1994), or MacMahon and Trichopolous (1996).

REFERENCES

Ahlbom, Anders, and Staffan Norell 1990 *Introduction to Modern Epidemiology.* Newton Lower Falls, Mass.: Epidemiology Resources, Inc.

Bracken, M. B. 1998 "Alarums False, Alarums Real: Challenges and Threats to the Future of Epidemiology." *Annals of Epidemiology* 8(2):79–82.

Friedman, Gary D. 1980 *Primer of Epidemiology,* 2nd ed. New York: McGraw-Hill.

Lilienfeld, David E., and Paul D. Stolley 1994 *Foundations of Epidemiology.* New York: Oxford University Press.

MacMahon, Brian, and Dimitrios Trichopoulos *Epidemiology: Principles and Methods 2nd ed.* Boston: Little, Brown.

Roueché, Berton 1967 *Annals of Epidemiology.* Boston: Little, Brown.

Susser M., and E. Susser 1996a "Choosing a Future for Epidemiology: I. Eras and Paradigms." *American Journal of Public Health* 86(5):630–632.

—— 1996b "Choosing a Future for Epidemiology: II. From Black Box to Chinese Boxes and Eco-Epidemiology." *American Journal of Public Health* 86(5):674–677.

CHARLES E. HOLZER, III

EPISTEMOLOGY

The term *epistemology* is used with two separate meanings according to different cultural traditions. In English-speaking countries, epistemology denotes the philosphical theory of knowledge in general: in this sense, it includes themes and problems such as the question of the possibility of valid knowledge, the analysis of the nature of such validity, the foundation of knowledge on reason or on experience and the senses, the analysis of different types of knowledge, and the limits of knowledge. In continental Europe, the above issues are considered part of the field of the more general discipline of *gnoseology* (*gnoséologie* in French, *gnoseologia* in Italian and Spanish) or *theory of knowledge* (*Erkenntnistheorie* in German), whereas the aim of epistemological inquiry is restricted to scientific knowledge.

In this second sense, with particular respect to social sciences (and sociology, in particular) the fundamental epistemological question becomes: "Is it possible to acquire any valid knowledge of human social reality? And, if so, by what means?" As these questions show, epistemological issues are inescapably interconnected with methodological problems; however, they cannot be reduced to simple technical procedures and their validity, as a long empiricist tradition among sociologists has tried to do. A full epistemological awareness, from a sociological point of view, should cope with at least four main issues:

1. Is the nature of the object of social sciences (i.e., social reality) fundamentally different from that of the object of natural sciences (i.e., natural reality)?

2. Consequently, what is the most appropriate gnoseological procedure with which to study and understand social reality?

3. Are we sure that the particular knowledge we get by studying a particular social reality can be generalized?

4. What kind of causality can we postulate between social events, if any?

Historically, the various sociological traditions or schools have answered these four questions differently. We shall trace them by following the three main epistemological debates that took place between three pairs of opposing schools of sociological and epistemological thinking: positivism versus historicism, logical empiricism versus dialectical theory, and realism versus constructivism.

POSITIVISM VERSUS HISTORICISM

At the beginning of the nineteenth century, the discipline of sociology originated as the positivistic science of human society and aligned itself against metaphysical and philosophical speculation about social life. This, according to Auguste Comte, the founder of sociology, implied the straight application of the scientific method used in physics and the other natural sciences to the analysis of human society. His *social physics* (Comte 1830–42) is the expression of the new culture of the Industrial Revolution and of its practical ambition of a totally planned social life. Comte's positivistic doctrine is organic and progressive and holds a naive faith in the possibility of automatically translating scientific knowledge of the laws of society into a new harmonious social order.

The uncritical assumptions of Comte as to the reliability and universal applicability of scientific method were at least partially tempered by John Stuart Mill, who considered illiberal and doctrinaire Comte's idea that, once sociological laws are established by the same scientific method of natural science, they can no longer be questioned. Mill objected that scientific knowledge never provides absolute certainties, and he organically settled the British empiricist tradition in his *A System of Logic, Ratiocinative and Inductive* (1834). Starting from the epistemological positions of David Hume, Mill considered knowledge as fundamentally grounded on human experience, and the induction as its proper method. The possibility of inductive generalization is based on the idea of regularity and uniformity of human nature, ordinated by laws; and even social events are correlated in the form of empirical laws, which we can understand using the scientific method, considered as a formal logical structure independent from human subjectivity.

The individualistic and liberal features (based on utilitarian ethics) of British positivism were particularly evident in Herbert Spencer, who opposed to Comte's organicistic view of society the greater importance of the particular with respect to the organic whole. His central focus on the concept of evolution supplied him with a synthetic perspective with which to study reality as a whole, using the analogy of biological and inorganic evolution to consider social evolution (1876–1896). However, the most complete development of a positivistic epistemology in sociological thought is certainly contained in Emile Durkheim's work *Les régles de la méthode sociologique* (1895). What he terms *faits sociaux* (social facts) can be characterized according to four criteria: two of the criteria are related to the subjects observed, whereas the other two are concerned with the sociologist observing them.

The first criterion considers the social facts as a reality external to the individual conscience: social institutions have their own life independent from individual life. The second criterion is that this external, objective nature of social facts consequently confers upon them a normative, coercive power over the individual: these social facts impose themselves on him, even without his will. Morals, public opinion, law, customs are all examples of this. These two features of social facts require, on the part of the social scientist observing them, the observance of two further qualifying criteria. Firstly, they should be considered as "things," that is, they should be studied as an external, objective reality, separate from the individual consciousness. Secondly, consistent with their nature, social facts can be explained only by other social facts: the nature of social causality is specific, and can be reduced neither to psychological causes of individual behavior, nor to biological causality, as Spencer's evolutionism suggested. The emerging nature of social phenomena from the level of psychological and biological phenomena grounds their autonomous, distinct reality: this, in turn, constitutes the specific field of sociology and of the other social sciences. To explain social phenomena, sociology should adopt a unilinear concept of causation: the same effect always corresponds to the same cause. Any plurality of causes, according to Durkheim, involves the impossibility of sorting a scientific principle of causality.

In sum, we can say that the classic positivistic paradigm of sociology is characterized by the recognition of the specific nature of social facts as emerging from the other spheres of reality. However, this implies an idea of sociology as a naturalistic science of society, using the same methods already applied with success in natural sciences (*methodological monism*), and grounded on experience as perceived by the senses and generalized on the basis of universal human nature (*induction*). Finally, a proper explanation of social facts should take into account only one cause for each effect (*mono-causal determinism*).

A serious challenge to this epistemological view of sociology came from the German Historical School: the debate about the method (*methodenstreit*) which took place in Germany during the last decades of the nineteenth century is the first example of epistemological debate in sociological history. It started with Wilhelm Dilthey, the major representative of German historicism, who argued against Comte and Mill's proposal of introducing the methods of physics into the "moral sciences." What he termed "spiritual sciences" (*Geisteswissenschaften*) were of a radically different type from the natural sciences and therefore they could not share the same method (Dilthey 1833). In fact, their objects were states of mind, spiritual experiences that could be apprehended only by means of an "empathic understanding" (*Verstehen*): "we explain nature, we understand psychic life" (ibid.). In the first phase of Dilthey's thought, this understanding, on which the sociohistorical nature of the spiritual sciences is grounded, was not considered to be mediated by sense perception, but rather as producing a direct and immediate intuitive knowledge-by-acquaintance. In the second phase of his thought (1905), however, he believed that psychic life was not immediately understandable, but would require the hermeneutic interpretation of its objective displays in cultural life. In any case, his distinction between the aim of natural sciences (to explain *erklären* data by means of external senses) and the scope of human sciences (to understand *verstehen* through an intrapsychic experience) was posited as a long-lasting distinction in the social sciences.

Wizhelm Windelband and Heinrich Rickert, two other adherents of German historicism, criticized Dilthey's distinction between nature and spirit and the related sciences, since they considered human knowledge as always a spiritual activity, without regard to its *object*. In its place, they proposed a distinction based on the *form* and on the different type of *methods* used: whereas the *idiographic* method is a description of singular events, the *nomothetic* method is concerned with the inquiry of regularities and general laws (Windelband 1894). The first type of procedure is typical of—though not exclusive to—the *sciences of the particular*, the sciences of culture that, being historical, had to interpret and understand the individual character of the historical event; the second type of method is more typical of the *sciences of the general*, natural sciences that are aimed at establishing general laws. Knowledge is always a simplification of reality, which is a heterogeneous continuum (*eterogenes Kontinuum*); knowledge can either proceed by making a homogeneous *Kontinuum*, as the natural sciences do, or by sectionalizing a portion of heterogeneous *Diskretum*, such as the sciences of culture do. Rickert (1896) further developed the necessity of referring to values as a foundation for sociohistorical knowledge: the sciences of culture (*Kulturwissenschaft*) are not idiographic disciplines only, they should also refer to *value relevences* (*Wertbeziehung*) if they want to understand the actual meaning of sociohistorical events.

The most significant attempt to reconcile the two antitheses (understanding/explanation and idiographic/nomothetic) has been carried out by Max Weber, the founder of German sociology, who was profoundly influenced by German historicism, although critical of its idealistic orientation. In his methodological essays (1904–17) and in subsequent works, Weber undertakes an inquiry into the nature and validity of methods used in the social sciences and presents a general epistemological framework for his *interpretive sociology* (*Verstehende Soziologie*). He argued in particular for the necessity of when investigating social actions, 1) resorting to an *interpretive understanding*, which is not separated by *causal explanation*, 2) while avoiding *value judgements*, establishing *value relevances* (*Wertbeziehungen*) of the subject matter as criteria for its cultural importance and scientific pertinence, and 3) preserving the social and cultural uniqueness of the historical event, using the *ideal-type* methodology. These three points constitute

Weber's main elaboration of the epistemological tenets of German historicism.

With regard to the first point, Weber criticized Wilhelm Wundt and George Simmel (who were influenced by Dilthey), who reduced socio-historical knowledge to psychological understanding, since this position cannot support an objective knowledge: to properly understand a socio-historical event requires establishing some relations of cause and effect in order to test our interpretive comprehension. Therefore, Weber conceived an idea of sociology as both a generalizing, nomothetic and interpretive, idiographic science, arguing for the complementarity of interpretive understanding and causal explanation: that is, a researchers personal understanding should be balanced by empirical and statistically established regularities of scientific explanation (1913).

Secondly, Weber distinguishes *value judgements*, based on personal faith and belief, and *fact judgements*, based on science. Scientific knowledge cannot be neutral, in the sense that the values of the researcher inevitably influence his choices of relevance—the specific selection of problems and focus. However, it can be *nonevaluative* and *objective* in the sense that, once its priorities have been selected according to the researcher's personal values, the researcher should proceed by testing empirical evidence supporting his hypotheses, thus expressing fact judgements only.

Finally, the ideal-type concept was employed by Weber to explain certain unique historical events using a model of *plural causality*: a singular event is always the effect of a multiplicity of historical connections. The problem becomes, in the infinite flow of events, to sort out the proper model of factors that under certain conditions and at a certain time can *probably* explain that effect. This also implies a *probabilistic* idea of causation, which gets beyond the deterministic approach typical of positivistic unilinear causation by a model of plural probabilistic-causal connections.

LOGICAL EMPIRICISM VERSUS DIALECTICAL THEORY

The epistemological legacy of German historicism—with its *dualistic* approach to the relationship between social and natural sciences, its preferential bias for a gnoseological model based on *interpretive understanding*, and its *probabilistic* model of *multiple causality*—has undoubtedly influenced a significant part of contemporary twentieth century sociology, such as the School of Chicago (Park's contacts with Windelband and Simmel are well known) and, more strongly, the later interpretive sociology (through Weber and Simmel) and the phenomenological tradition in sociology (through Schutz). Its impact is manifest even in the antipositivistic methodological choices of many sociologists as different as Pitrim Aliksandrovič Sorokin (1959) and Charles Wright Mills (1959). Altogether, these different currents answer negatively the epistemological question about the possibility of acquiring knowledge of human social reality by means of empirical data alone. They reject the methodological unity of the natural and social sciences and do not accept the straight application of the scientific method to sociological analysis. When researchers undertake empirical research, they resort to methodological perspectives that result from the researcher's epistemological choices: they tend to reject technical terminologies and statistical quantification, to privilege common-sense conceptualization and language, and to take the point of view of the social actor instead of that of the researcher and of the scientific community. Qualitative methodologies of this kind are also favored by those microsociologies—such as symbolic interactionism, ethnomethodology, and sociologies of daily life of different varieties—that have not been directly influenced by the idealistic and antipositivistic tenets of the German historicism. Although seldom explicitly stated, their epistemological foundations, which tacitly direct their choice of methods and tools of social research, are mostly consonant with those of interpretive and phenomenological sociologies.

The large majority of sociologists, however, followed an empirical-quantitative approach and accepted the scientific method borrowed from natural sciences as the appropriate and valid method of social sciences. The positivistic epistemological foundations of this *mainstream* sociology are quite evident in its most significant representatives Lazarsfeld and Lundberg, and in their utilization of the *social survey* as the main research tool of sociological inquiry. Lazarsfeld, in particular, although reluctant during his work at Columbia University to directly tackle epistemological issues

while preferring practical empirical research, was well known for his neo-positivistic convictions (Gallino 1973:27), which were rooted in his mathematical and psychological background within the Vienna philosophical movements of the post-World War I period.

In fact, during the twenties and thirties of the twentieth century, a new group of positivists, the so-called "Vienna Circle," arose in the Austrian capital, profoundly influenced by the work of the physicist Ernst Mach, the pioneers of mathematical logic Gottlob Frege, Bertrand Russell, Alfred North Whitehead, and Ludwig Wittgenstein, and by the French *conventionalism* of Pierre Duhem and Jules-Henri Poincaré. Mach considered science not a fact-finding but a fact-related activity: it cannot claim to discover the absolute truth about reality, since its laws are not absolute but, at best, "limitations of possibilities." Russell, among the pioneers of mathematical logic, attempted a logical foundation of mathematics that considers the element of necessity present in both disciplines. This can be considered as the basis of the logical structure of thinking. Finally, Duhem and Poincaré suggested an idea of scientific theories as being purely hypothetical and conventional constructions of the human mind.

On these premises, the main representatives of the "Vienna Circle"—Moritz Schlick, Rudolf Carnap, and Otto Neurath—preferred the label of *logical empiricism* or *neopositivism* to distinguish themselves from classical positivism, since they discarded its sensist view—the idea that knowledge originates from experience ganied only through the senses, and from the observation and verification of that experience. They rejected direct observation of experience as the only means of hypothesis testing, and they considered verification as "testability in principle." In this way, they accepted theoretical constructs without direct empirical referents as meaningful. They renewed empiricism on the new basis of the logical analysis of language: in fact, they argued that linguistic statements can be shown to be true or false by appeal to both logic and experience, and that both means, being factual, can be considered meaningful.

Logical empiricism still mantained some fundamental epistemological tenets of classical positivism, however, such as the idea that only empirically verifiable knowledge was meaningful, that science was a cumulative process based on induction, that the method of physics was the method of all sciences including social sciences (*methodological monism*), and that the discovery of natural and general laws was the fundamental aim of any science. The criticism of Karl Popper was aimed at most of these foundations and reversed them in a sort of *negativism* (Cipolla 1990). Since his first major publication (Popper 1934), the Austrian philosopher formulated his tenets in opposition to the main assumptions of the neopositivist: first and foremost, the *induction* as an appropriate method to infer general laws from the observation of a singular case. He argued that one case is enough to demonstrate the falsity of induction and that verification always depends on observational theories that are often derived from substantially the same theory from which hypotheses under test have been deducted, making their test logically inconclusive. Popper dropped the notion of *verification* itself in favor of that of *falsification*, and proposed a *hypothetic–deductive* method, based on the assumption that a hypothesis can be definitely considered false if it fails an adequate test, while if it is congruent with data this does not necessary mean it is true. In any case, Popper argued that a theory is maintained as true only provisionally, and it always remains a conjectural hypothesis that can be confuted in the future. In this way, scientific knowledge is never a closed, completed system, but always remains open to new possibilities. And even though Popper believed in the *methodological monism*— the unified theory of method—this is not absolute but conjectural, critical, and subject to falsification (1963).

A substantial refusal of *methodological monism* is represented by the Frankfurt School with its "critical theory of society" that advocates the necessity of the dialectical method in sociology. Its epistemological tenets are derived partly from Weber's thought on Western reason and rationalization and partly from the young Hegel-influenced Marx of the *Philosophical-Economical Manuscripts* of 1844. It was also strongly influenced by the two critical Marxists Lukacs and Korsch and by the psychoanalysis of Freud. Dialectical epistemology implies:

1. The *holistic* approach, that is, the necessity of considering the totality in order to understand the parts, which are mediated by totality.

2. The denial of the separation of history and sociological theory in order to grasp the dialectical process of change.

3. A demystifying attitude in undertaking critical analysis of society and of the irrationality of Enlightenment reason once it has become purely instrumental and separated from its goals, that is, when it's become a pure means of domination over men and society.

In 1961 the second most significant debate in the history of sociological epistemology took place at Tübingen between Theodor Adorno and Jurgen Habermas (two of the most prominent representatives of the Frankfurt School) on one side and Karl Popper and Hans Albert on the other (Adorno et al. 1969). The neopositivistic epistemology of the latter two was strongly questioned by the former two, who criticized its dialectic nature and who considered it a sort of logical formalism without any connection with its contents and that was incapable of understanding the social reality. The aim of sociology is to go beyond apparent phenomena, to grasp social contradictions and conflicts by interpreting society as a totality. This implies a refusal of the individualistic approach of positivism, of its *monism* with regard to the scientific method, of its measurement and *quantification* of social reality. Beyond Popper and Albert, the actual target of the Frankfurt scholars was the American school of sociology, whose positivistic analytical framework (theoretical categories and their translation into research tools) was considered an ideological reflection of the domination structures in the late capitalistic society.

REALISM VERSUS CONSTRUCTIVISM

Since the 1960s, logical empiricism, under criticism from many sources, has dissolved in a plurality of *postpositivistic* approaches, whose common denominator is a reformulation of positivistic tradition. This allows them to be grouped under the label of *scientific realism*, which asserts the absolute or relative independence of the reality under scientific scrutiny from the human researcher studying it. This, in turn, is based on the fundamental distinction between the objectivity of the reality observed and the subjectivity of the scientific observer studying it. The common tenet of realisms of all types is that the observer does not belong to the reality he observes; by means of his techniques of scientific inquiry, he should avoid any involvement and influence on reality, maintaining a neutral position. In this way, the subjectivity of the observer is limited to his "discovery" of the objective reality.

One of the first attacks on the neopositivistic legacy was by Willard Van Ormand Quine (1952), who proposed a holistic view of knowledge, considered as a field of forces whose limiting conditions are constituted by experience. In turn, Mary Hesse (1974) considered scientific language as a dynamic system whose continuing growth is due to metaphorical extension of the natural language. Thomas Kuhn (1962) greatly contributed to the growing consciousness of the reality of scientific change by analyzing its actual historical development, challenging the common-sense concept of science as a purely rational enterprise. Taking scientific practice into account, he showed how it is usually ruled by a *paradigm*, a world view, legitimized by the scientific community, that remains dominant until a new paradigm replaces it.

Paul K. Feyerabend, with his "methodological anarchism" (1975), proposed a paradoxical and extreme view of science. In Feyerabend's view, the scientific method remains the only rational procedure for deciding and agreeing upon which theory is more adequate to describe and explain a state of affairs in the natural as well as in the social worlds. Of course, rationality depends on common premises and procedures: the advantage of accepting them is great because it is through them that intersubjectivity is achieved. Scientific objectivity resides neither in the object of knowledge, as classical positivism maintained, nor in the subject, as idealists tend to believe, but rather in the intersubjectivity that results when researchers adopt the same procedures and accept the premises on which those procedures are based. It is the reproducibility of the methods, techniques, and tools of scientific research that secures the replicability of results. And their reproducibility is due largely to their being public procedures, easily scrutinized and reapplied. The results of the research in the natural sciences may be more objective than those in the social sciences, but this is due to the standardization and publicity of procedures in the natural sciences. There is no ground for supposing that

natural sciences possess a special objective attitude, while social scientists possess a value-oriented attitude. The problem is that many research procedures in the social sciences are not reproducible, because they often reflect a private state of mind communicated through linguistic expression full of connotative meanings, often not shared by all in the research community.

The *critical realism* of Roy Bashkar (1975) proposes an ontology based on the distinction of three spheres: the *real*, the *actual*, and the *empiric*, arguing in favor of the existence of structures or hidden mechanisms that can work independently from our knowledge, but whose power can be empirically investigated both in closed and open systems. This realistic view of science is supported also by Rom Harré (1986), who stresses the role of models in the development of theory. The new realists also suggest a *relational paradigm* for sociology in order to overcome the traditional antinomy between structure and action by a theory of *structuralization* (Giddens 1984) and by a *transformative model of social activity* (Bhaskar 1989). According to this new paradigm, the social structure should be considered as both the omnipresent condition and the continuously reproduced outcome of the intentional human action. This view is shared by the *applied rationalism* of Pierre Bourdieu, who systematically applies relational concepts and methodically compares his theoretical models with the empirical material that is the result of different research methodologies (Bourdieu et al. 1973). The critical view of science taken by the new realists, joined with their transformative conception of social reality, has produced a *critical naturalism* that considers both the positivist and the historicist traditions as dependent on the same positivistic conception of the natural sciences. This critical naturalism holds that, in actuality, both the human social life and the natural life are liable to scientific explanation, although of a different kind (Bhaskar 1989).

This realistic view has been seriously challenged in the 1980s and 1990s by the *constructivistic movement*, giving rise to the third, and still ongoing, epistemological debate in the history of sociology. Constructivism proposes the unification of the objective reality observed with the subjective reality of the observer. The rationale is that the reality investigated and the science used to investigate it have an equally subjective origin, which implies that the reality observed "depends" on the observer. This does not mean that constructivism denies the actual existence of an autonomous reality from the observer, but rather that an "objective" representation of this external reality by scientific knowledge is not possible. All that can be said about reality is inevitably a "construction" of the observer (von Foerster 1984), who, in turn, being part of this reality, is a "black box" whose internal components are unobservable. Therefore, even for the constructivists, reality is an elusive objectivity, with its autonomous existence which cannot be reduced to a simple subjective and arbitrary experience. What is "constructed" is the knowledge and not the reality (Von Glasersfeld 1987).

There are different types of constructivism. The most radical (Von Glasersfeld 1995) maintains that nothing can be said even by the observer, apart from the trivial verification that he observes. An unknowable observer faces an unknowable reality. A more moderated type of constructivism considers still possible a theory of the observer, even though it denies the same possibility for the reality observed (Maturana 1988). And finally, there is a constructivism which accepts both a theory of the observer and of the observed, considering them as mental systems (Luhmann 1990).

TOWARDS AN INTEGRATED AND PLURALISTIC PARADIGM

As the current debate between realism and constructivism shows, the positions only appear distant. Especially when they move from the more abstract theory to the empirical research, the respective positions become more ambiguous, vague, and overlapping. Moreover, there are clear indications that the old cleavages between positivistic and interpretive sociologies may slowly fade away. Even though quantitative research techniques appear more precise and rigorous—with their standardization and reproducibility features—than qualitative methods, it is difficult to justify using quantification for all types of sociological data. Many sociologists believe that not all aspects of social phenomena could be subject to the rules of quantification. And most of them start out thinking that quantitative and qualitative methods and techniques are complementary. Yet, such an integrated and pluralistic methodology needs to be justified by an explicit epistemology. Therefore,

the times seem ripe for a new epistemological foundation of an emerging integrated and pluralistic methodology, even though a few attempts have been made towards this goal.

The first attempt was the *ecological paradigm* of Gregory Bateson (1972). Strongly influenced by his participation in the 1940s in the interdisciplinary research group on cybernetics composed of Von Neumann, Shannon, Von Foerster, and Wiener, among others, he then organized all his subsequent work in different fields around a few central cybernetics concepts, including schismogenesis, circular communication, and feedback. On the ground of this new theoretical perspective, he built up an epistemology aimed at getting beyond the boundaries between the internal and the external components of the observer, the "mind," conceived as a network of founding relationships. In this process, the identity of the observing subject is dissolved into its ecological environment, in the relationship between subjective meanings, action, and action objective. Even though Bateson's epistemology precedes the debate between realism and constructivism, it has clearly inspired most of the constructivistic approach.

A second attempt, historically, can be traced in Edgar Morin's attempt to set up a new general method (Morin 1977, 1980, 1986), which can be applied in every field of knowledge according to a methodological *plurivers*. In this way, he tries to overcome the shortcomings of the traditional scientific paradigm, which he considers *disjointed*, *reductive*, and *simplified*, since it does not take into account the complexity of reality. The *multidimensional* character of reality is precisely the starting point of his very comprehensive attempt to found a new epistemology based on the *auto-eco-organizing* principle. An attempt, however, which for the most part is affected by a biologistic bias, seems quite inappropriate for the social sciences.

Finally, Costantino Cipolla has proposed a new *correlational* paradigm based on an *epistemology of tolerance* (Cipolla 1997) which prefers an "inter-" and "co-" perspective linking together and integrating the traditionally opposite epistemological poles in an attempt to reassemble them into a new pluralistic approach. Closer to the sociological tradition of the first two attempts, this new correlational paradigm takes into account the reasons of both the realists and the constructivists and focuses its attention on the connection, the relation, and the link between the objective reality and the subjective observer in order to avoid any absolutism of either of the poles. It is starting from this bivalent conception of reality—which considers reality as both autonomous in itself and "constructed" by the subject, who is in turn the outcome of the real social forces, so that each pole is considered only partially autonomous and strictly interconnected with the other—that it should be possible to re-found the sociological epistemology on the ground of the methodological research questions of the discipline, in recognition of the fundamental ambivalence of reality and of the need of an *adductive* procedure as a "double movement" between induction and deduction, particular and general, theoretical hypotheses and social reality beyond any self-contained reductivistic monism.

REFERENCES

Adorno, T. W. et al. 1969 *Der Positivismusstreit in der deutschen Soziologie*. Berlin: Luchterhand.

Bateson, G. 1972 *Steps to an Ecology of Mind*. San Francisco: Chandler.

Bhaskar, R. (1975) 1978 *A Realist Theory of Science*. Hemel Hempstead: Harvester Wheatsheaf.

—— 1989 *The Possibility of Naturalism*. Hemel Hempstead: Harvester Wheatsheaf.

Bourdieu, P. et al. (1973) 1991 *The Craft of Sociology: Epistemological Preliminaries*. Berlin and New York: De Gruyter.

Cipolla, C. 1990 *Dopo Popper*. Roma: Borla.

—— 1997 *Epistemologia della tolleranza*. vol. 5 Milano: Angeli.

Comte, A. 1830–42 *Cours de philosophie positive*. Paris: Bachelier.

Dilthey, W. (1883) 1966 *Einleitung in die Geisteswissenschaften*. Vol 1 of *Gesammelte Schriften*. Stuttgart: Teubner.

—— 1905 *Kritik der historischen Vernunft*. Stuttgart: Taubner.

Durkheim, E. 1895 *Les régles de la méthode sociologique*. Paris: Alcan.

Feyerabend, P. K. 1975 *Against Method: Outline of an Anarchist Theory of Knowledge*. London: NBL.

Gallino, L. 1973 "Metodologia neopositivistica e teoria sociologica." In *Quaderni di Sociologia*. XXII, 1.

Giddens, A. 1984 *The Constitution of Society*. Cambridge: Polity Press.

Harré, R. 1986 *Varieties of Realism*. Oxford: Blackwell.

Hesse, M. 1974 *The Structure of Scientific Inference*. London: Macmillan.

Kuhn, T. S. 1962 *The Structure of Scientific Revolutions*. Chicago: University of Chicago Press.

Luhmann, N. 1990 *Die Wissenschaft der Gesellschaft*. Frankfurt am Mein: Suhrkamp.

Maturana, H. 1988 "Reality: the Search for Objectivity and the Quest for a Compelling Argument." *The Irish Journal of Psychology*, Special Issue, 9,1.

Morin, E. 1977 *La methode 1. La nature de la nature*. Paris: Seuil.

—— 1980 *La methode 2. La vie de la vie*. Paris: Seuil.

—— 1986 *La methode 3. La conaissance de la conaissance*. Paris: Seuil.

Mill, J. Stuart (1834) 1947 *A System of Logic, Ratiocinative and Inductive*. New York: Longman.

Mills, C. Wright 1959 *The Sociological Imagination*. New York: Oxford University Press.

Popper, K. 1939 *Logik der Forschung*. Wien: Springer.

—— 1963 *Conjectures and Refutations*. London: Routledge and Kegan Paul.

Quine, W. V. O. (1952) 1963 *From a Logical Point of View*. New York: Harper and Row.

Rickert, H. (1896) 1913 *Die Grenzen der naturwissenschaftlichen Begriffsbildung*. Tübingen: Mohr.

Sorokin, P. A. 1959 *Fads and Foibles in Modern Sociology and Related Sciences*. New York: Henry Regnery.

Spencer, H. 1876–96 *The Principles of Sociology*. London: Williams and Norgate.

Von Foerster, H. 1984 "Erkenntnistheorien und Selbstorganisation." *Delphin* 4:6–19.

Von Glasersfeld, E. 1987 *The Construction of Knowledge*. Seaside, Calif.: Intersystems Publishers.

—— 1995 *Radical Constructivism. A Way of Knowing and Learning*. London: Falmer Press.

Weber, M. (1904–17) 1949 *The Methodology of the Social Sciences*. New York: Free Press.

—— (1913) 1968 "Über einige Kategorien der verstehenden Soziologie." In *Gesammelte Aufsätze zur Wissenschaftslehre*. Tübingen: Mohr.

Windleband, W. (1894) 1914 "Geschichte und Naturwissenschaft." In W. Wildeband, ed., *Präludien*. Tübingen: Mohr.

CostantinO Cipolla
Guido Giarelli

EQUALITY OF OPPORTUNITY

Equality of opportunity refers to the fairness of processes through which individuals with different backgrounds or from different social groups reach particular outcomes, such as educational or occupational goals. Sociologists have developed several alternative approaches to defining and assessing equality of opportunity in each outcome domain, including trends in demographic gaps, residual differences after relevant qualifications are taken into account, process differences in the variables linking individual attributes to outcomes, and structural differences in the barriers encountered in preparing for, learning about, or obtaining particular educational or occupational achievements. Each approach has advantages and disadvantages for particular scientific, policy, and practical purposes.

TRENDS IN DEMOGRAPHIC GAPS

Equality of opportunity is usually judged with reference to major demographic groupings, such as race, sex, or socioeconomic status. When there are significant changes over an extended period of time in educational or occupational outcome gaps for major subgroups, inferences may be made that changes in opportunity structures underlie the trends. This argument is best made when confidence is high on the accuracy of the outcome trend data, the timing of changes in outcomes and specific opportunity processes can be matched, and other subgroup differential changes in personal resources can be discounted as nonexistent or following a different time sequence.

In education, changes in racial/ethnic gaps in achievement scores and college attendance rates have been subjected to trend analyses to pinpoint opportunity processes. The test score gap showing higher average achievement in basic skills by white students compared to African-American students has shown a significant narrowing since the 1970s, although the covergence may have stalled or begun to reverse on some tests by the end of the century (Jencks and Phillips 1998). Since the largest gains during this period occurred for African-American students who entered school between the late 1960s and late 1970s, particularly in the South, some have credited the antipoverty legislation and school desegregation enforcements of the time aimed at increasing educational opportunities for minorities. Trends in college entry among gender and racial/ethnic groups show interesting patterns in recent decades that invite explanations of changing opportunities for selected groups. After a long-term upward trend from the 1940s to the mid 1970s, when college entry increased more for African Americans than whites to narrow the gap in educational attainments, college entry actually declined among African-American high school graduates from the mid 1970s to the mid 1980s, with some signs of recovery in black initial college enrollments in the 1990s that still did not match the progress of whites during the same period. Careful analyses to match various contemporaneous changes to the college entry trends through the 1980s ruled out most changes in personal resources, such as family income and academic achievement, although modifications in college financial aid policies from grants to loans in the face of rapidly rising college costs may account for minority college entry declines (Hauser 1993).

Racial/ethnic gaps in college degree attainments, after gradually closing for successive decades, still remain very large and recently also have begun to grow even larger. The number of African-American recipients of either bachelor or advanced degrees has actually declined since the beginning of the 1980s, which can be tied to numerous inequalities of access and support in the American education system across the grades and the court-inspired decline of racial considerations in the admissions policies of some colleges (Miller 1995; Orfield and Miller 1998).

Economic changes over recent decades in the distribution of income have also been subjected to trend analyses. Income inequality as measured by the gaps in the percentage of annual income held by different social groups, such as the top fifth versus bottom fifth of the population, showed moderate improvements, with only small periods of slight reversals over the years following World War II through the end of the 1970s. But the period since 1980 has been one in which income inequality increased sharply, sometimes called the shrinking middle class, as the rich got richer, acquiring a higher percent of total income, while productivity growth eliminated jobs or decreased earnings for many less educated workers (Levy,

1995). Numerous factors have been associated with recent trends, including reduced access to employment opportunities due to the movement of jobs from many urban locations where poor minority workers live (Wilson 1996).

RESIDUAL DIFFERENCES IN EQUALITY OF OPPORTUNITY

Even when major outcome gaps are observed, the issue remains whether individuals from major population subgroups have had the same chances to achieve educational or occupational success, assuming that they possess the same distributions of personal attributes to qualify for success. Because any initial average outcome gaps between subgroups can be due to unequal possession of relevant qualifications, as well as to unfair access to the opportunities that link qualifications to achievements, it is necessary to take into account differences in personal qualifications before deciding that unequal opportunities exist.

Researchers have frequently tested for inequalities of opportunity by estimating the residual gap between the educational or occupational success of selected race, sex, or social-class groups after individual differences in relevant credentials or competencies and educational or labor market locations have been statistically controlled for. The usual methodology is to estimate a prediction equation or to use other methods of standardization for selected individual resource variables that permit a researcher to compare the actual group difference in an educational or occupational outcome with the residual gap that would be expected if one group's productivity resources were replaced by the average resources of the other group (Farley and Allen 1987, Chap. 11). For example, the actual average difference in annual earnings of African-American and white workers in the North would be compared against the residual earnings gap when one assumes that African-American workers' resources (such as education and labor-market experience) deliver the same rate of return in earnings as that experienced by white workers. Some problems are inherent in this approach, including the risk of overestimating the residual gap if some important qualification variables are omitted or poorly measured and the chance of underestimating the residual gap when some groups

are deprived of relevant qualifications due to earlier unequal opportunities not reflected in the estimation methodology. Nevertheless, several important residual race, sex, or social-class gaps have been identified for various important educational and occupational outcomes. However, these gaps are often associated with some subgroups but not others, and some gaps have been changing more rapidly than others in recent years.

Numerous national and regional studies have been conducted since the 1960s to estimate the inequality of job opportunities, including research that examines residual subgroup differences in unemployment rates, occupational distributions, and dollar returns from holding a job. Studies of race, sex, and social-class residual gaps in earnings and income of employed workers have been particularly noteworthy, with more than twenty-five major national studies having been published since 1965 (Farley and Allen 1987).

The research on earnings gaps that estimates the "cost of being black" due to inequality of job opportunities has contrasted the experiences of male and female workers and reported the continuing but declining significance of race. After taking into account differences in educational attainment, age or years of potential labor-market experience, hours of work, and regional location, large residual gaps in earnings are found between male African-American and white workers, with African Americans earning 10 to 20 percent less than comparable whites in various regions and at various educational levels. Women continue to earn much less than men of the same race with similar educational credentials, but the residual race gap for women is no longer the same as reported for men. In 1960, African-American women earned less than white women at all educational levels except college graduate, but this gap had been eliminated or reversed by 1980, when college-educated African-American women actually reported greater earnings, largely because of greater hours of employment. The residual race gap in earnings for employed workers also appeared to grow somewhat smaller, for men between 1960 and the 1990s, but it still remains between 10 and 15 percent at all educational levels.

At the same time, evidence is mounting that racial gaps in rates of unemployment are significant and have been growing worse since the 1960s for African-American men in most age and education categories; they are especially severe for unmarried young African-American men in the North who have limited educational attainments (Farley and Allen 1987, chaps. 8–11; Jaynes and Williams 1989, Chap. 6). While the economic boom period in the 1990s benefited the average employment prospects and median incomes of all race/ethnic and gender groups, the lower levels of the income distribution and the poorly educated did not keep pace and actually fell behind in some of these years.

Race inequalities of accumulated wealth have also been investigated after statistically taking into account factors that affect how individuals encounter financial opportunity structures. Measured by either the net worth of a household total assets less any debts or as net financial assets that exclude equity accrued in a home or vehicle that is more difficult to convert into other resources, very large racial differences are found in wealth that have grown even larger in recent years. The average black family held $3,779 in mean net worth in 1967, which rose to $19,736 in 1984 and $23,818 in 1988, in comparison to the average white family's mean net worth, which stood at $20,153, $76,267, and $95,667 for the same time periods, for a race gap that widened by $40,000 during these years and reached $71,849 by 1988. After controlling for differences in age, annual household income, household composition, and professional and self-employed status, nearly three-quarters of the racial gap is left unexplained. Institutional and policy factors that may account for the residual race differentials in wealth include mortgage loan and interest rate practices, evaluation of different neighborhoods, and various inheritance mechanisms whereby status and resources can be transmitted across generations (Oliver and Shapiro 1995).

Inequalities of educational opportunity have been examined by estimating residual race, sex, or social-class gaps in outcomes net of initial resources, especially for college enrollment and completion rates. Among the earliest evidence of a social-class gap in college attendance net of academic ability is data from the 1960s showing that even after controlling on standardized test performance, students from lower categories of socioeconomic status are much less likely to enter college

within five years of high school graduation. The talent loss due to unequal social-class background was estimated to be 50 percent of top-ability students who do not enter college from the lowest socioeconomic quartile, compared with a loss of only 5 percent of high-ability students from the highest socioeconomic quartile (U.S. Department of Health, Education and Welfare 1969). The importance of social-class factors for educational equity was reinforced by extensive research on Wisconsin high school students that included measures of race as well as student achievement on standardized tests. Social-class disparities in educational attainment net of academic ability were again in evidence, as it was reported that top-ability students were only half as likely to attend college or to graduate from college if they came from the lowest quarter, rather than the highest quarter, in socioeconomic status (Sewell and Hauser 1980). These studies also estimated that observed African-American–white differences in years of educational attainment can largely be accounted for by social-class differences between the racial groups.

However, race differences in students' achievement test performance are not so well explained by socioeconomic status alone. A study of seven national probability samples of adolescents from 1965 to 1996 described trends in black–white test score gaps after adjustments had been made for social class, family structure, and community variables. About a third of the test score gap is accounted for by racial differences in social class, so a major race gap remains in adjusted test scores; this gap has narrowed somewhat since 1965, although the rate of closure seems to have decreased or reversed since 1972. Group differences at the extremes of the distribution reveal contrasting gaps and the importance of social-class factors. Social-class–adjusted differences at the bottom of the distribution are closing more rapidly, especially in reading, but differences at the top of the achievement distribution are large and they are neither improving over time nor due to relative changes in social class (Hedges and Nowell 1999). This supports that argument that gaps in test scores are due to factors other than social class and family structure, such as discrimination, residential segregation, and the quality of schooling available to African Americans (Jaynes and Williams 1989).

PROCESS DIFFERENCES IN OPPORTUNITIES

Another approach to assessing equality of opportunity is to compare the attainment processes that link personal resources or investments to educational or occupational achievements for different social groups. Opportunities can be defined as unequal when the major avenues to advancement used by one group are not as effective for another. Researchers have frequently reported attainment process differences in the degree to which various population subgroups have been able to capitalize on advantages of family background or have experienced a high rate of return on investments in building relevant competencies or credentials. Some of this work has been criticized for possible shortcomings of methodology and interpretation.

Studies of social-group differences in an attainment process are important because they help to estimate the long-run prospects for closing existing achievement gaps (Featherman and Hauser 1978, Chap. 6). The prospects are positive if each subgroup has access to an attainment process that will translate improvements of personal and family resources into achievement outcomes, especially when programs and policies are available for investments in upgrading resources of groups that at present are weak. But if some groups are lagging in relevant skills and credentials, and are exposed only to attainment processes that provide poor returns in comparison with other groups, then the prospects are dim for closing existing gaps.

Studies of general social mobility processes have identified the special problems of African American males in translating any advantages from the family of origin into attainments in their own adult lives. For the white male population in this country, clear intergenerational processes have been evidenced in which sons can build upon a middle- or upper-class family background, as shown by the strong relationship between father's and son's occupational status for whites over many recent decades. In contrast, through the 1960s, African-American males have not been as able to capitalize on any family advantages in building their occupational careers, as shown by the weak relationship for intergenerational mobility and the frequency with which substantial proportions of African-American males from nonmanual or white-collar households are downwardly mobile

and unable to benefit from their family advantages. There is some indication that since the 1970s race differences for males in the opportunities to benefit from any inheritance of family social-class advantages have closed (Farley and Allen 1987; Featherman and Hauser 1978.)

Race differences in the processes of school effects on achievement have been reported in two national studies by the sociologist James S. Coleman and his research coworkers. In a 1966 national study of public schools, differences in school resources and learning environments were found to have larger average effects on African-American students' achievement than on white students' achievement (Coleman et al. 1966). The result was interpreted as a differential sensitivity of disadvantaged students to school improvements, because these students from poor families relied more on good schools for their development of academic skills. A similar race difference in educational processes was found in the 1980s with national data from public and private high schools (Coleman and Hoffer 1987). African Americans, Latinos, and students from low socioeconomic backgrounds were found to do better in Catholic schools than in public high schools, in terms of both higher test scores and lower dropout rates. It was argued that these students especially benefited from the greater academic demands that can be enforced by the sense of community established by Catholic schools, which compensates for family disadvantages of many of these students. Again, minority and disadvantaged students were found to be more responsive to changes in school environments that have effects on high school students' achievement and completion rates. Other researchers have questioned the recent results on the grounds that key student/family self-selection variables were not controlled in the analyses of public–Catholic school differences and that the sizes of the race interaction effects were not impressive by conventional statistical standards (Alexander and Pallas 1985; McPartland and McDill 1982).

Research has indicated that race inequalities are currently much less evident in educational attainment processes than in occupational attainment processes. Analyses using appropriate statistical tests of the processes that yield important educational achievements—such as additional years of schooling and scholastic outcomes, including grades and test scores—have found great similarities between African Americans and whites (Gottfredson 1981; Wolfle 1985). Thus, not only have African-American–white differences in the frequency of high school graduation and college education been diminishing, the processes that link social background and school input variations to educational achievements have become very similar for African Americans and whites. At the same time, race gaps in school test scores have been closing more slowly, and serious disparities persist in the level of financing and concentration of single-race and disadvantaged student bodies in schools attended by racial minorities, even though education attainment processes would translate improvements of such inputs into attainments for African Americans (Jaynes and Williams 1989).

However, major race and sex differences continue in the occupational domain regarding both the processes of attainment and the gaps in achievement. Labor-market disparities by race and sex are much more apparent than differences in educational opportunities, but the disparities are exhibited in complex patterns or processes according to individuals' social-class position, labor-market location, career stage, and other factors (Farley and Allen 1987; Featherman and Hauser 1978; Jaynes and Williams 1989; Wilson 1987). The chances are equally good for African Americans and whites of each sex who are highly educated to gain entry to good jobs, but advancement opportunities to higher positions at later career stages are more likely to be missed by African Americans. At the same time, African-American male workers with less advanced credentials are much more likely to have periods of unemployment or reduced hours, and to be paid less when employed, than white males with equivalent years of schooling. The greatest race discrepancies are observed for poorly educated young African-American males, who are much more likely than comparable whites to be unemployed, to have dropped out of the labor force, or to report no annual earnings. William J. Wilson (1980) has developed a theory of the "declining significance of race" that considers the growing social-class gaps within the African-American population in occupational success, as well as the special difficulties faced by poorly educated African-American males in urban racial ghettos, whom he views as "the truly disadvantaged" (Wilson 1987).

STRUCTURAL BARRIERS TO EDUCATIONAL OPPORTUNITIES

While careful studies of residual differences and attainment process differences can document the existence of unequal opportunities, other research is required on specific interactions and practices in schools or labor markets to understand the actual barriers that unfairly inhibit individuals because of their sex, race, or social-class position. For education, research on differential access to specific components of schooling, studies of tracking and grouping policies in elementary and secondary schools, and examinations of financial aid practices in higher education have identified some specific structural barriers in educational opportunities.

A landmark study was conducted in response to a congressional request under the 1964 Civil Rights Act and published in 1966 with the title *Equality of Educational Opportunity*. Also known as the "Coleman Report," after the sociologist James S. Coleman who directed the research, it was both influential and controversial for the way it examined educational opportunities and for its major findings (Coleman et al. 1966). Based on a large national survey of students and schools at both elementary and secondary levels, the Coleman Report collected the most comprehensive data available at that time on equity issues in education. It was not satisfied to compare only the average school input resources experienced by different race and ethnic groups—such as textbooks, libraries and laboratories, per pupil expenditures, teacher qualifications, or class size. The Coleman Report also considered race and ethnic differences on student outcomes as measured by standardized tests in major subjects, and asked how different school components contributed to student learning, in order to weigh inequalities of school inputs by their importance for student outcomes. The simultaneous examination of school inputs, student outcomes, and their relationships to one another had not been attempted before in assessing equity issues, and the published results have been a continuing source of reanalysis and reinterpretation.

The Coleman Report did find large differences in test scores between white and most racial and ethnic minority groups that existed from the time students began school and were not reduced, on the average, as students moved from grade 1 to grade 12. These differences in student outcomes could not be explained by variations in the school input factors measured by the Coleman Report surveys, because within each region no great disparities of school inputs appeared for different racial and ethnic groups, and these factors did not relate strongly to student outcomes in any case after family background and social-class factors were statistically controlled. In fact, when school factors were combined into three clusters for analysis—(1) instructional materials and resources, (2) teacher and staff characteristics, and (3) student body composition—the most important component in accounting for variations in student test scores net of family background was the attributes of fellow students. Thus, the large observed group differences in student outcomes were not found to be accounted for by existing variations in conventional school and teacher components, although attending a school with fellow students who were college-bound did seem to make a positive contribution to the learning environment.

Subsequent investigations have shown that improvements in school factors, such as smaller class size, better-qualified teachers, and well-directed extra resources, can actually make a significant difference for student learning (Burtless 1996; Jencks and Phillips 1998). But the general picture drawn by the Coleman Report has been confirmed of an educational system that does little to reduce the large racial and ethnic differences in academic test scores with which students begin elementary grades (Jencks et al. 1972; Puma et al. 1997).

The Coleman Report data did not measure within-school differences in educational resources and learning environments, and consequently was unable to analyze major barriers to equal opportunities from specific internal school practices, such as tracking and ability grouping. Other research has shown that when students are tracked into separate programs or separate courses according to their earlier test scores or grades, those in the lower-level groups are likely to encounter serious barriers to their educational growth and progress. Lower tracks and lower-level courses have been shown to offer weaker educational resources, such as fewer expert teachers and poorer educational climates with lower academic expectations, that can lead to lower average student achievement test scores and decreased probabilities of completing

high school and continuing education in college (Gamoran 1986; Hallinan 1988; Oakes 1985). Tracking is now seen as a major barrier to equal educational opportunities because tracking and ability grouping are very common practices in American schools, and minorities and socioeconomically disadvantaged students are much more likely to be assigned to the lower-level programs and courses within their schools (Oakes 1985).

Moreover, the educational resources available at the school level are thought to be more unequal for minorities and disadvantaged students at the present time than they were found to be in the 1966 Coleman Report assessments (Smith and O'Day 1991). Since the 1960s, demographic trends have created greater concentrations of poverty in large urban schools, and changes in funding support for public education in central city districts have reduced those districts' relative ability to purchase adequate classroom supplies and materials, and to recruit and retain highly qualified teachers. In addition, trends in school desegregation, which produced increasing numbers of racially mixed schools with improved learning environments for minorities because of court decisions from 1954 through the 1970s, were reversed in the late 1980s and early 1990s, when school segregation grew in most regions and in the nation as a whole (Orfield and Eaton, 1996). Consequently, school-level barriers to equal educational opportunities have worsened since the 1960s, because the changing urban demographics and negative fiscal trends have dramatically altered the student body composition and the quality of the teaching staff that the Coleman Report found to be the most important factors of a good school.

Barriers have been identified in college educational opportunities, which also may have gotten worse, especially for African-American males, in recent years. Minorities have long been underrepresented as students at four-year colleges, in scientific major fields, and in obtaining advanced degrees (Trent and Braddock 1987). Some of these gaps had been closing through the 1970s, but since that time, uniform progress is no longer evident and some actual downturns in minority enrollments and attainments have been recorded (Jaynes and Williams 1989; Miller 1995; Wirt et al. 1998)African-American and Latino students often encounter special problems in pursuing college programs because of insufficient social and academic support on campus or inadequate prior educational experiences (Green 1989). Recent reversals in minority enrollments have been explained by increasing tensions related to race and ethnicity on some college campuses and to changes from grants to loans in many financial assistance programs which poor students are less likely to receive or use (Blackwell 1990).

STRUCTURAL BARRIERS TO OCCUPATIONAL OPPORTUNITIES

To help account for residual sex or race gaps in job success and in the career attainment process, research has identified specific structural barriers to sex equality and to racial equality in occupational opportunities.

Studies of the large average earnings differences between men and women workers show that very large gaps remain after statistically controlling on individual differences in input variables such as education and experience, but these gaps are substantially reduced by adding measures of each person's occupation or occupational group. This result indicates that sex gaps in earnings have much of their source in the extreme job segregation by sex in the American labor market—many occupations are primarily filled by women or primarily filled by men—and the wage levels are much lower for "female" occupations (Treiman and Hartmann 1981). Since fully two-thirds of men and women would have to change jobs to achieve similar representation of each sex across occupations, full enforcement of antidiscrimination laws against unequal pay for men and women in the same occupation can achieve only modest improvements in wage differentials by sex. Other suggested approaches to reducing sex segregation of jobs and associated wage gaps—such as enriching the socialization experiences toward a wider range of career exposures for children and youth of both sexes, or incorporating policies of "comparable worth" that establish wage rates by job features, irrespective of sex or race of incumbents (Hartmann 1985; Marini 1989)—have not yet made large inroads.

To specify how occupational opportunities continue to be unequal for racial or ethnic minorities, research has identified structural barriers at each stage of the occupational career process.

Barriers can appear at the job candidate stage, when employers are recruiting the pool of candidates for job openings; at the job entry stage, when an individual is actually selected to fill a vacancy; and at the job promotion stage, when transfers are made within a firm to fill spots at higher levels (Braddock and McPartland 1987; Feagin and Feagin 1978; Marini 1989).

At the job candidate stage, qualified minorities of either sex may fail to learn about many desirable job openings because they are excluded from useful social networks that provide others with information about and contacts for particular employment opportunities. Employers find job candidates more frequently from walk-ins and friends of current employees (the result of informal social networks) than any other recruitment means for lower- and middle-level jobs. The social contacts used by many minorities are racially segregated networks that on the average are not as well tied to good job information as the social networks available to whites. This barrier to equal opportunities at the job candidate stage is partially kept in place by the continued racial segregation of the schools and neighborhoods that create many social networks and by the underrepresentation of minorities in the upper levels of firms, where informal information for friends and relatives about job openings is often best acquired (Crain 1970; Rossi et al. 1974).

At the job entry stage, otherwise qualified minorities are often not selected because of barriers of statistical discrimination and information bias. Employers who do not wish to invest much to obtain extensive information about job applicants will often use a group identifier, such as sex or race, in hiring decisions when they believe that traits on which subgroups may differ statistically predict job performance. For example, such "statistical discrimination" can occur when an employer selects a white over a minority applicant for a job requiring good academic skills, based on a belief in average racial group differences on academic test scores rather than on actual individual candidates' differences in academic skills shown on tests administered or obtained by the employer during the screening process (Bielby and Baron 1986; Braddock et al. 1986; Thurow 1975).

Even when qualification data from individuals are relied upon in hiring decisions, other barriers to equal opportunities occur due to "information bias" of data on minority candidates. References and recommendations from school or employment officials for African-American applicants may be viewed as less credible by white employers who are less familiar with an African-American school, a member of the African-American clergy, or an African-American firm, or who may be more wary of information provided by minority sponsors due to stigmas or stereotypes attached to these sources. Similarly, minority job applicants who grow up in communities that have high youth unemployment rates will be less able to satisfy prospective employers' interests in previous employment experiences and references (Braddock and McPartland 1987).

At the job promotion stage, minorities may face unfair barriers due to internal recruitment methods or because they are poorly positioned within internal labor markets. However, findings from a national study indicate the potential benefits to minorities of seeking internal promotions: The average pay differential between African-American and white workers is less for jobs filled from inside a firm than for jobs filled from outside for individuals of the same sex and education level, suggesting that unfair selection is reduced when employers process information on applicants' actual job performance within their firm. On the other hand, the same study showed that unless an internal vacancy is widely advertised within a firm, whites are more likely to be sought out for available promotions (Braddock and McPartland 1987). Moreover, research has shown that minorities are less likely to have entered a firm on a career ladder that ordinarily leads to promotion opportunities, so they may never be eligible to compete for advancement through an internal labor market (Rosenfield 1980).

POLICIES AND PRACTICES

Governments and courts have established policies and practices in recent decades that are intended to eliminate race and sex discrimination and to ensure equality of opportunity. These range from the 1954 Supreme Court decision against segregated schools to the civil rights legislation of the 1960s and the executive orders to establish affirmative action guidelines in employment (Burstein 1985; Jaynes and Williams 1989). However, in the final decades of the twentieth century, major court decisions have stepped back from considerations of race in school attendance patterns, college admissions policies, and employment selection practices (Orfield and Eaton 1996; Orfield and Miller 1998). At the same time, the expectation of high performance in elementary and secondary schools by students regardless of race or ethnicity has become widespread national and state policy, as a common-core academic curriculum is being mandated for all learners. It has yet to be determined how testing of students will combine with higher standards to influence access to educational opportunities and the gaps in dropout rates and achievement scores.

Although it is difficult to distinguish the effects of one governmental action from those of another in improving the life chances of women and minorities, clear advances have been made that can be attributed to the combined impacts of various public policies for equal rights. For example, from 1970 to 1990 the race gaps in academic test scores of schoolchildren decreased between 25 and 50 percent for different age groups (Smith and O'Day 1991). Reductions in the race gaps in terms of years of school completed have been dramatic, especially among female students. Greater equity is also evident in some labor-market behaviors, including the distribution of occupations by race within sex groups. On the other hand, inequalities in the distribution of income have grown in recent years, with a much higher share going to the top earners; average racial improvements are not evident in employment rates and income levels of adult males; some stagnation or reversals have occurred in upward trends of minority test scores and college attainment rates; and extensive racial segregation of housing and schooling remains a dominant feature of American life. The increasing diversity of minority groups in this country will amplify issues of equality of opportunity that concern language and cultural background differences in the population (Harrison and Bennett 1995).

Controversy continues to accompany further efforts to sustain current policies and to institute new practices for equal opportunities. The differences are most evident on whether outcome-based policies are required to overcome systemic barriers—for instance, affirmative action programs that use guidelines and timetables—or whether efforts should concentrate only on intentional discrimination or on specific aspects of the processes that inhibit equal rights (Levinger 1987).

(SEE ALSO: *Affirmative Action; Discrimination; Education and Mobility; Ethnicity; Equity Theory; Social Mobility; Race*)

REFERENCES

Alexander, Karl A., and Aaron M. Pallas 1985 "School Sector and Cognitive Performance." *Sociology of Education* 58:115–127.

Bielby, William T., and James N. Baron 1986 "Men and Women at Work: Sex Segregation and Statistical Discrimination." *American Journal of Sociology* 91:759–799.

Blackwell, James E. 1990 "Current Issues Affecting Blacks and Hispanics in the Educational Pipeline." In Gail E. Thomas, ed., *U.S. Race Relations in the 1980s and 1990s*. New York: Hemisphere.

Braddock, Jomills H., II, and James M. McPartland 1987 "How Minorities Continue to Be Excluded from Equal Employment Opportunities: Research on Labor Market and Institutional Barriers." *Journal of Social Issues* 43(1):5–39.

——, et al. 1986 "Applicant Race and Job Placement Decisions: A National Survey Experiment." *International Journal of Sociology and Social Policy* 6:3–24.

Burstein, Paul 1985 *Discrimination, Jobs and Politics: The Struggle for Equal Employment Opportunity in the United States Since the New Deal*. Chicago: University of Chicago Press.

Burtless, Gary, ed. 1996 *Does Money Matter? The Effect of School Resources on Student Achievement and Adult Success*. Washington, D.C.: Brookings Institution Press.

——, and Thomas Hoffer 1987 *Public and Private High Schools*. New York: Basic Books.

—— et al. 1966 *Equality of Educational Opportunity*. Washington, D.C.: U.S. Government Printing Office.

Crain, Robert L. 1970 "School Integration and Occupational Achievement of Negroes." *American Journal of Sociology* 75:593–606.

Farley, Reynolds, and Walter R. Allen 1987 *The Color Line and the Quality of Life in America*. New York: Russell Sage Foundation.

Feagin, J. R., and C. B. Feagin 1978 *Discrimination American Style: Institutional Racism and Sexism*. Englewood Cliffs, N.J.: Prentice-Hall.

Featherman, David L., and Robert M. Hauser 1978 *Opportunity and Change*. New York: Academic Press.

Gamoran, Adam 1986 "Instructional and Institutional Effects of Ability Grouping." *Sociology of Education* 59:185–198.

Gottfredson, Denise C. 1981 "Black–White Differences in the Educational Attainment Process: What Have We Learned?" *American Sociological Review* 46:542–557.

Granovetter, Mark S. 1974 *Getting a Job: A Study of Contacts and Careers*. Cambridge, Mass.: Harvard University Press.

Green, Madeleine F. 1989 *Minorities on Campus: A Handbook for Enhancing Diversity*. Washington, D.C.: American Council on Education.

Hallinan, Maureen T. 1988 "Equality of Educational Opportunity." *Annual Review of Sociology* 14:249–268.

Harrison, Roderick J., and Claudette E. Bennett 1995 "Race and Ethnic Diversity." In Reynolds Farley, ed., *State of the Union: America in the 1990s: vol. 2. Social Trends*. New York: Russell Sage Foundation.

Hartmann, Heidi I., ed. 1985 *Comparable Worth: New Directions for Research*. Washington, D.C.: National Academy Press.

Hauser, Robert M. 1993 "The Decline in College Entry Among African Americans: Findings in Search of Explanations." In Paul M. Snideman, Philip E. Tetlock, and Edward G. Carmines, eds., *Prejudice, Politics, and the American Dilemma*. Stanford, Calif.: Stanford University Press.

Hedges, Larry V., and Amy Nowell 1999 "Changes in the Black–White Gap in Achievement Test Scores." *Sociology of Education* 72:111–135.

Jaynes, Gerald David, and Robin M. Williams, Jr., eds. 1989 *A Common Destiny: Blacks and American Society*. Washington, D.C.: National Academy Press.

Jencks, Christopher, and Meredith Phillips, eds. 1998 *The Black–White Test Score Gap*. Washington, D.C.: Brookings Institution Press.

Jencks, Christopher, et al. 1972 *Inequality: A Reassessment of the Effect of Family and Schooling in America*. New York: Basic Books.

Levinger, George (ed.) 1987 "Black Employment Opportunities: Macro and Micro Perspectives." *Journal of Social Issues* 43:1–156.

Levy, Frank 1995 "Incomes and Income Inequality." In Reynolds Farley, ed., *State of the Union: America in the 1990s: vol. 1. Economic Trends*. New York: Russell Sage Foundation.

Marini, Margaret Mooney 1989 "Sex Differences in Earnings in the United States." *Annual Review of Sociology* 15:343–380.

McPartland, James M., and Edward L. McDill 1982 "Control and Differentiation in the Structure of American Education." *Sociology of Education* 55:65–76.

Miller, L. Scott 1995 *An American Imperative: Accelerating Minority Educational Advancement*. New Haven, Conn.: Yale University Press.

Oakes, Jeannie 1985 *Keeping Track*. New Haven, Conn.: Yale University Press.

Oliver, Melvin L., and Thomas M. Shapiro 1995 *Black Wealth/White Wealth: A New Perspective on Racial Inequality*. New York: Routledge.

Orfield, Gary, and Susan E. Eaton 1996 *Dismantling Desegregation*. New York: New Press.

Orfield, Gary, and Edward Miller, eds. 1998 *Chilling Admissions: The Affirmative Action Crisis and the Search for Alternatives*. Cambridge, Mass.: Harvard Education Publishing Group.

Puma, M.J., N. Karweit, Price C., Ricciuti, A., Thompson, W., and Vaden-Kiernan, M. 1997. *Prospects: Final report on student outcomes*. Bethesda, MD: Abt Associates, Inc.

Rosenfield, Rachel A. 1980 "Race and Sex Differences in Career Dynamics." *American Sociological Review* 45:583–609.

Rossi, Peter H., Richard A. Berk, and Betty K. Eidson 1974 *The Roots of Urban Discontent: Public Policy, Municipal Institutions and the Ghetto*. New York: Wiley.

Sewell, William H., and Robert M. Hauser 1980 "The Wisconsin Longitudinal Study of Social and Psychological Factors in Aspirations and Achievements." In Alan C. Kerckhoff, ed., *Research in Sociology of Education and Socialization*, vol. I. Greenwich, Conn.: JAI Press.

Smith, Marshall S., and Jennifer O'Day 1991 "Educational Equality: 1966 and Now." In Deborah Verstegen, ed., *Spheres of Justice in American Schools*. New York: Harper Business.

Thurow, Lester 1975 *Generating Inequality*. New York: Basic Books.

Treiman, Donald J., and Heidi I. Hartmann, eds. 1981 *Women, Work and Wages: Equal Pay for Jobs of Equal Value*. Washington, D.C.: National Academy Press.

Trent, William T., and Jomills Henry Braddock II 1987 "Trends in Black Enrollment and Degree Attainment." In John B. Williams, ed., *Title VI Regulation of Higher Education: Problems and Progress*. New York: Teachers College Press.

U.S. Department of Health, Education and Welfare 1969 *Toward a Social Report*. Washington, D.C.: U.S. Government Printing Office.

Wilson, William Julius 1980 *The Declining Significance of Race: Blacks and Changing American Institutions*, 2nd ed. Chicago: University of Chicago Press.

—— 1987 *The Truly Disadvantaged: The Inner City, the Underclass and Public Policy*. Chicago: University of Chicago Press.

—— 1996 *When Work Disappears: The World of the New Urban Poor*. New York: Knopf.

Wirt, John, Tom Snyder, Jennifer Sable, Susan P. Choy, Yupin Baes, Janis Stennett, Allison Gruner, and Marianne Perie 1998. *The Condition of Education 1998* Washington, D.C.: U.S. Department of Education, National Center for Education Statistics.

Wolfle, Lee M. 1985 "Postsecondary Educational Attainment Among Whites and Blacks." *American Educational Research Journal* 22:501–525.

JOMILLS HENRY BRADDOCK II
JAMES M. MCPARTLAND

EQUILIBRIUM THEORY

See Cognitive Consistency Theories; Social Dynamics.

EQUITY THEORY

See Social Justice.

ETHICS IN SOCIAL RESEARCH

The immediacy of subject matter in social science underscores the importance of ethical issues in research by social scientists. This is particularly true in sociology. A rather small percentage of sociologists use historical documents or cultural products as data. The majority rely upon interviews with actively cooperating subjects, records relating to persons still living or recently alive, unobtrusive observation of live actors, or participant studies within interacting groups. Sociological research typically focuses on relatively large study populations and poses questions relevant to many dimensions of individual and social life. Both the process and application of sociological inquiry may conceivably affect large numbers of subjects in an adverse manner. Thus, the question of "right" and "wrong" in research has been a continual (though not always powerful or explicit) concern within the profession.

Ethics may be conceptualized as a special case of norms governing individual or social action. In any individual act or interpersonal exchange, ethics connotes principles of obligation to serve values over and above benefits to the people who are directly involved. Examination of ethical standards in any collectivity provides insights into its fundamental values; identification of ethical issue provides clues to its basic conflicts. This is as true of sociology as a profession as it is of other social systems.

The most abstract and general statements about ethics in sociological literature reflect broad agreement about the values that social inquiry should serve. Bellah (1983) writes that ethics constitutes an important, though typically implicit, topic in the thinking of sociology's founders (such as Durkheim and Weber) and leading modern practitioners (such as Shils and Janowitz). Even while consciously striving to distinguish their emerging discipline as a science free of values and moralizing, the early sociologists appeared to have a distinct ethical focus. The discipline's founders implied and sometimes stated that sociology necessarily involved ethical ends, such as identification of emerging social consensus or the development of guidelines for assessing social good. Modern sociologists have emphasized improvement of society's understanding of itself as the discipline's principal ethical end, as opposed to determining a specific direction or developing technology for social change. In the broadest sense, contemporary sociologists seem to consider the raising of consciousness as quintessentially ethical activity and social engineering by private or parochial interests as ethically most objectionable. In the phraseology of Edward Shils, this means contributing to "the self-understanding of society rather than its manipulated improvement" (Shils 1980, p. 76).

Dedication to advancement of society's understanding of itself through diverse scientific approaches may comprise the fundamental ethic of sociology. A Code of Ethics published by the American Sociological Association (ASA) in 1989 (American Sociological Association 1989) gave concrete expression to this ethic. Concentrating primarily on research, the Code of Ethics emphasized three specific areas of concern: (1) full disclosure of motivations for and background of research; (2) avoidance of material harm to research subjects, with special emphasis on issues of confidentiality;

and (3) qualifications to the technical expertise of sociology.

The first area appeared concerned primarily with a fear among sociologists that agencies of social control (such as military or criminal justice units) may seek intelligence under the guise of social research. Thus, the code advised sociologists not to "misuse their positions as professional social scientists for fraudulent purposes or as a pretext for gathering intelligence for any organization or government." The mandate for disclosure has implications involving relations among professionals, between professionals and research subjects, and between professionals and the public. Another provision of the code read, "Sociologists must report fully all sources of financial support in their publications and must note any special relation to any sponsor." (p. 1)

The second area of concern in the code placed special emphasis on assurance of confidentiality to research subjects. It stressed the need for extraordinary caution in making and adhering to commitments. As if to recognize the absence of legal protection for confidentiality in the research relationship and to mandate its protection nevertheless, the code stated: "Sociologists should not make any guarantees to respondents, individuals, groups, or organizations—unless there is full intention and ability to honor such commitments. All such guarantees, once made, must be honored" (p. 2).

As a subject of professional ethics, the third area is extraordinary. Provisions mandating disclosure of purpose and assurance of confidentiality might appear in the code of ethics of any profession dealing regularly with human clients or subjects. But it is surprising to find, as a provision in the 1989 ASA Code of Ethics, the mandate that sociologists explicitly state the shortcomings of methodologies and the openness of findings to varying interpretation. The following quote illustrates provisions of this nature:

Since individual sociologists vary in their research modes, skills, and experience, sociologists should always set forth ex ante the limits of their knowledge and the disciplinary and personal limitations that condition the validity of findings. To the best of their ability, sociologists should . . . disclose details of their theories, methods and research designs that might bear upon interpretation of research findings. Sociologists should take particular care to state all significant qualifications on the findings and interpretations of their research. (p. 2)

Themes in the 1989 *Code of Ethics* dealing with disclosure and confidentiality reflect widely shared values and beliefs in the profession. Historically, sociology has stood out among the learned professions as critical of the authority of established institutions such as governments and large business firms. But propositions about the limitations of theories and methodologies and the openness of findings to varying interpretation suggest conflict. In the late twentieth century, sociological methodologies encompassed both highly sophisticated mathematical modeling of quantitative data and observation and theory building based entirely on qualitative techniques. Acknowledgment of the legitimacy of these differences in an *ethical* principle reflects a strenuous attempt by sociology as a social system to accommodate subgroups whose basic approaches to the discipline are inconsistent with each other in important respects.

A more recent formulation of the ASA *Code of Ethics*, published in 1997 (American Sociological Association 1997), restates the basic principals of serving the public good through scientific inquiry and avoiding harm to individuals or groups studied. But a shift in emphasis appears to have occurred. The 1989 *Code* explicitly cited the danger of governmental or corporate exploitation of the sociologist's expertise. The 1997 *Code*, though, stresses ethical challenges originating primarily from the researcher's personal objectives and decisions.

The 1997 *Code of Ethics*, for example, contains a major section on conflict of interest. According to this section, "conflicts of interest arise when sociologists' *personal or financial* interests prevent them from performing their professional work in an unbiased manner" (p. 6; emphasis added). A brief item on "disclosure" asserts an obligation by sociologists to make known "relevant sources of financial support and relevant personal or professional relationships" that may result in conflicts of interest vis-a-vis to employers, clients, and the public (p. 7).

The two most extensive sections in the 1997 *Code* are those on confidentiality and informed cnsent. The directives addressing confidentiality place extraordinary responsibility on the individual sociologist. Pertinent language states that "confidential information provided by research participants, students, employees, clients, or others is treated as such by sociologists *even if there is no legal protection or privilege to do so*" (emphasis added). The *Code* further instructs sociologists to "inform themselves fully about all laws and rules which may limit or alter guarantees of confidentiality" and to discuss "relevant limitations on confidentiality" and "foreseeable uses of the information generated" with research subjects (p. 9). It is recommended that information of this kind be provided at the "outset of the relationship." Sociologists are neither absolutely enjoined from disclosing information obtained under assurances of confidentiality nor given clear guidance about resolving pertinent conflicts. The *Code of Ethics* states:

Sociologists may confront unanticipated circumstances where they become aware of information that is clearly health- or life-threatening to research participants, students, employees, clients, or others. In these cases, sociologists balance the importance of guarantees of confidentiality with other priorities in [the] Code of Ethics, standards of conduct, and applicable law. (p. 9)

The section on informed consent, the most extensive in the 1997 *Code of Ethics*, reflects a frequent dilemma among sociologists. The basic tenets of informed consent as stated here approximate those in all fields of science. Obtaining true consent requires eliminating any element of undue pressure (as might occur in the use of students as research subjects) or deception regarding the nature of the research or risks and benefits associated with participation. In social research, however, statement of the objectives of an investigation may affect attitudes and behavior among research subjects in a manner that undermines the validity of the research design. Recognizing this possibility, the *Code* acknowledges instances when deceptive techniques may be acceptable. These include cases where the use of deception "will not be harmful to research participants," is "justified by the study's prospective scientific, educational, or applied value," and cannot be substituted for by alternative procedures (p. 12).

A review of historical developments, events, and controversies of special importance to sociologists in the decades preceding the 1989 and 1997 *Codes of Ethics* promotes a further appreciation of the concerns they embody. Perhaps the most far-reaching development in this era was the introduction of government funding into new areas of the sociological enterprise. In sociology, as in many areas of science, government funding provided opportunities to expand the scope and sophistication of research, but it created new ethical dilemmas and accentuated old ones.

Increased government funding created interrelated problems of independence for the sociological researcher and anonymity for the research subject. A report by Trend (1980) on work done under contract with the U.S. Department of Housing and Urban Development (HUD) illustrates one aspect of this problem. Possessing a legal right to audit HUD's operations, the General Accounting Office (GAO) could have examined raw data complete with individual identifiers despite written assurances of confidentiality to the subjects by the research team. Sensitivity on the part of the GAO and creativity by the sociologists averted an involuntary though real ethical transgression in this instance. But the case illustrates both the importance of honoring commitments to subjects and the possibility that ethical responsibilities may clash with legal obligations.

Legal provisions designed explicitly to protect human subjects emerged in the 1970s. Regulations developed by the U.S. Department of Health and Human Services (DHHS) require that universities, laboratories, and other organizations requesting funds establish institutional review boards (IRBs) for protection of human subjects. The 1997 ASA *Code of Ethics* makes frequent reference to these boards as a resource for resolution of ethical dilemmas.

Sociologists, however, have not always expressed confidence in the contributions of IRBs. One commentary (Hessler and Freerks 1995) argues that IRBs are subject to great variability in protecting the rights of research subjects at the local level. Others contend that deliberations of these boards take place in the absence of appropriate standards or methods of analysis. The expertise and concerns of IRBs may not apply well to actual risks posed by sociological research methods. Biomedical research, the primary business of most IRBs, potentially poses risks of physical injury or death to the research subject. Except in extraordinary circumstances, sociological techniques expose subjects at worst to risks of embarrassment or transient emotional disturbance. IRB requirements often seem inappropriate or irrelevant to sociology. In the words of one commentator, the requirement by IRBs that researchers predict adverse consequences of proposed studies encourages sociologists to engage in exercises of "futility, creativity, or mendacity" (Wax and Cassell 1981, p. 226).

Several instances of highly controversial research have helped frame discussion of ethics among sociologists. Perhaps most famous is the work of Stanley Milgram (1963), who led subjects to believe (erroneously) that they were inflicting severe pain on others in a laboratory situation. This experiment, which revealed much about the individual's susceptibility to direction by authority figures, was said by some to present risk of emotional trauma to subjects. Milgram's procedure itself seemed to duplicate the manipulative techniques of authoritarian dictators. Distaste among sociologists for Milgrom's procedure helped crystallize sentiment in favor of public and professional scrutiny of research ethics.

The Vietnam era saw increasing suspicion among sociologists that government might use its expertise to manipulate populations both at home and abroad. A seminal event during this period was the controversy over a U.S. Army–funded research effort known as Project Camelot. According to one commentator, Project Camelot aimed at ascertaining "the conditions that might lead to armed insurrections in . . . developing countries so as to enable United States authorities to help friendly governments eliminate the causes of such insurrections or to deal with them should they occur" (Davison 1967, p. 397). Critical scrutiny by scholars, diplomats, and congressional committees led to cancellation of the project. But provisions in the1989 *Code of Ethics* on disclosure and possible impacts of research clearly reflect its influence.

The end of the Cold War and increasing litigiousness among Americans may help explain the shift in emphasis between the 1989 and 1997

ASA *Codes of Ethics.* As noted above, the later *Code* appears to emphasize ethical issues facing sociologists as individuals rather than as potential tools of government and big business. Many sociologists have stories to tell about actual or potential encounters with the legal system over the confidentiality of data obtained from research subjects. The visibility and frequency of such encounters may have helped shape the 1997 *Code*'s section on confidentiality.

The most celebrated confrontation of a sociologist with the law involved Rik Scarce, who was incarcerated for 159 days for refusing to testify before a grand jury investigating his research subjects. Scarce's case is described by Erikson (1995):

> *Scarce found himself in an awful predicament. He was engaged in research that rested on interviews with environmental activists, among them members of the Animal Liberation Front. One of his research subjects came under investigation in connection with a raid on a local campus, and Scarce was ordered to appear before a grand jury investigation. He refused to answer questions put to him, was found to be in contempt, and was jailed for more than five months.*

Some evidence suggests that the institutional structure surrounding social research has proven an uncertain asset in personal resolution of ethical issues such as Scarce's. The 1997 ASA *Code of Ethics* advises sociologists confronting dilemmas regarding informed consent to seek advice and approval from institutional review boards or other "authoritative [bodies] with expertise in the ethics of research." But IRBs typically serve as reviewers of research plans rather than consultative bodies regarding issues encountered in execution of research; the phrase "authoritative [bodies] with expertise in the ethics of research" has a vague ring. Lee Clark's (1995) description of his search for guidance in responding to a law firm's request for his research notes illustrates the limitations of IRBs and related individuals and agencies:

> *. . . I talked with first amendment attorneys, who said academic researchers don't enjoy journalists' protections. . . . I was told that if I destroyed the documents, when there was reason to expect a subpoena, then I would be held in contempt of court. I talked with ASA officials and the chair of ASA's Ethics Committee, all*

> *sympathetic but unable to promise money for an attorney. They were equally certain of my obligations according to the Ethics Code. . . . I talked with lawyers from Stony Brook [where Clark had performed his research], who told me that the institution would not help. Lawyers for Rutgers, where I was . . . employed, said they wouldn't help either.*

In all human activity, individuals ultimately face ethical issues capable of resolution only through personal choice among alternatives. But increasingly, sociologists seem to face these choices unaided by distinct guidelines from their profession. This default to personal responsibility derives in part from the ambiguity in two philosophical principles widely encountered in sociological discourse, utilitarianism and moral relativism.

As an ethical principle, utilitarianism seems to provide a convenient rule ofr making decisions. The prevailing morality among modern cosmopolitans, utilitarianism applies the principle of the greatest net gain to society in deciding questions of research ethics. This perspective places emphasis on degrees of risk or magnitude of harm that might result from a given research effort. Under this perspective, Project Camelot (cited above) may have deserved a more favorable reception. Davison (1967) suggests that completion of the project would probably not have caused appreciable harm. He comments:

> *If past experience is any guide, it would have contributed to our knowledge about developing societies, it would have enriched the literature, but its effects on this country's international relations would probably have been tangential and indirect.* (p. 399)

Several well-known and ethically controversial studies may be justified on utilitarian grounds. Among the best known is Laud Humphreys's study of impersonal sex in public places (1975). Humphreys gained access to the secret world of male homosexuals seeking contacts in public restrooms by volunteering his services as a lookout. Despite its obvious deception, Humphreys's work received the support of several homophile organizations (Warwick 1973, p. 57), in part because it illustrated the prevalence of sexual preferences widely considered abnormal. In his study of mental institutions, Rosenhan (1973) placed normal (i.e., nonpsychotic) observers in psychiatric wards without the knowledge or consent of most staff. His study generated highly useful information on the imperfections of care in these institutions, but the deception and manipulation of his subjects (hospital staff) are undeniable.

As a rule for making decisions, though, utilitarianism presents both practical and conceptual problems. Bok (1978) points out the difficulty in estimating risks of harm (as well as benefits) from any research activity. The subtle and uncertain impacts of sociological research techniques (as well as associated findings) make prospective assessment of utilitarian trade-offs extremely problematical. Many traditional ethical constructs, moreover, contradict utilitarianism, implying that acts must be assessed on the basis of accountability to abstract principles and values (e.g., religious ones) rather than the practical consequences of the acts themselves.

Moral relativism provides some direction to the uncertainty implicit in utilitarianism. This principle assumes that "there are no hard and fast rules about what is right and what is wrong in all settings and situations" (Leo 1995). Under this principle, ethical judgment applies to ends as well as means. Moral relativism might provide ethical justification for a sociologist who, believing that the public requires greater knowledge of clandestine police practices, misrepresents his personal beliefs or interests in order to observe these practices. The very relativism of this principal, however, invites controversy.

The 1997 ASA *Code of Ethics* restates the profession's fundamental ethic as striving to "contribute to the public good" and to "respect the rights, dignity, and worth of all people" (p. 4). Regarding research activity, the *Code* places primary emphasis on informed consent, protection of subjects from harm, confidentiality, and disclosure of conflicts of interests. But the *Code*, the institutional milieu of sociology, and the practical conditions under which sociological research takes place preclude strong direction for individuals in the ethical dilemmas they encounter.

REFERENCES

American Sociological Association 1989 *Code of Ethics*. Washington, D.C.: Author.

—— 1997 *Code of Ethics*. Washington, D.C.: Author.

Bellah, R. N. 1983 "The Ethical Aims of Sociological Inquiry." In N. Haan, R. N. Bellah, P. Rabinow, and E. M. Sullivan, eds., *Social Science as Moral Inquiry*. New York: Columbia University Press.

Bok, S. 1978 "Freedom and Risk." *Daedalus* 107 (Spring):115–127.

Clark. L. 1995 "An Unethical Ethics Code?" *The American Sociologist* 26(2):12–21.

Davison, W. P. 1967 "Foreign Policy." In P. F. Lazarsfeld, W. H. Sewell, and H. L. Wilensky, eds., *The Uses of Sociology*. New York: Basic Books.

Erikson, K. 1995 "Commentary." *The American Sociologist* 26(2):4–11.

Hessler, R. M., and K. Freerks 1995 "Privacy Ethics in the Age of Disclosure: Sweden and America Compared." *The American Sociologist* 26(2):35–53.

Humphreys, L. 1975 *Tearoom Trade: Impersonal Sex in Public Places*. Chicago: Aldine.

Leo, R. A. 1995 "The Ethics of Deceptive Research Roles Reconsidered: A Response to Kai Erikson." *The American Sociologist* 27(1):122–128.

Milgram, S. 1963 "Behavioral Study of Obedience." *Journal of Abnormal and Social Psychology* 67:371–378.

Rosenham, D. L. 1973 "On Being Sane in Insane Places." *Science* 179 (January 1973):250–258.

Shils, E. 1980 *The Calling of Sociology: Essays on the Pursuit of Learning*. Chicago: University of Chicago Press.

Trend, M. G. 1980 "Applied Social Research and the Government: Notes on the Limits of Confidentiality." *Social Problems* 27:343–349.

Warwick, D. P. 1973 "*Tearoom Trade*: Ends and Means in Social Research." *The Hastings Center Studies* 1:27–38.

Wax, M. L., and J. Casell 1981 "From Regulation to Reflection: Ethics in Social Research." *The American Sociologist* 16:224–229.

HOWARD P. GREENWALD

ETHNIC CLEANSING

See Genocide.

ETHNICITY

Ethnicity is a salient feature of numerous societies throughout the world. Few societies are ethnically homogeneous, even when they proclaim themselves to be. Consequently, ethnicity has been a preoccupation of sociologists since the early days of the discipline (although more so in the United States than elsewhere).

Yet there is not complete agreement on how the subject should be defined. In the past, it was common to highlight cultural difference as an essential feature of ethnic distinctiveness (see, e.g., van den Berghe 1967). Recently, this has lost favor on the grounds that cultural differences may vary from one setting to another and from one historical period to another. Following an approach attributed to Frederik Barth (1969), recent definitions have therefore focused on the existence of a recognized social boundary. But still among the most useful definitions is the classic one of Max Weber ([1922] 1968): An ethnic group is one whose members "entertain a subjective belief in their common descent because of similarities of physical type or of customs or both, or because of memories of colonization and migration" Weber adds insightfully, "It does not matter whether or not an objective blood relationship exists" (p. 389).

Despite definitional disagreements, there is general recognition that a number of characteristics appear as hallmarks of ethnicity; not all of them will be present in every case, but many will be. They include features shared by group members, such as the same or similar geographic origin, language, religion, foods, traditions, folklore, music, and residential patterns. Also typical are special political concerns, particularly with regard to a homeland; institutions (e.g., social clubs) to serve the group; and a consciousness of kind, or sense of distinctiveness from others (for the full listing, see Thernstrom et al. 1980, p. vi).

There is controversy over whether race should be viewed as a form of ethnicity. In this context, "race" should not be understood as a bundle of genetically determined traits that of themselves generate social differences—a view that has been repudiated by the vast majority of social scientists—but as a kind of social classification used by members of a society. Many scholars distinguish between ethnicity and race. For example, Pierre van den Berghe (1967) defines race as a social classification based on putative physical traits and ethnicity as a classification based on cultural ones

(see also Omi and Winant 1994). The contrast between the two can also be formulated in terms of volition vs. external constraint, with racial categories seen as more imposed by outsiders and ethnic ones as more claimed by the group members themselves (see, e.g., Waters 1990). But equally commonly, race is seen as a variant of ethnicity: A racial group is, then, an ethnic group whose members are believed, by others if not also by themselves, to be physiologically distinctive. This is the approach adopted in this article for several reasons. Not only do racial groups typically have the characteristics of ethnic groups (e.g., cultural distinctiveness), but many seemingly nonracial ethnic groups may also be believed to possess some distinctive physical features (e.g., the olive skin tone of Italians). The distinction between the two types of groups is therefore not hard and fast, a conclusion that is underscored by the historical transmutation of some racial groups into nonracial ones, for example, the Irish (Ignatiev 1995; Roediger 1991).

Sociologists recognize that the imprint of history on the contemporary ethnic relations of any society is deep, and this gives rise to another distinction that is potentially central to any discussion of ethnicity. It pertains to the mode of entry of a group into a society, and it has been formulated by Stanley Lieberson (1961; see also Blauner 1972) in terms of the situation that obtains just after contact between an indigenous group and one migrating into an area. One possibility is that the migrant group dominates, typically through conquest (often aided by the introduction of new diseases)—this is exemplified in the contacts between indigenes and European settlers in Australia and the United States. The other is that the indigenous group dominates, as occurred during the century of mass immigration (1830–1930) to the United States. The crux of the matter here is whether a group is incorporated into a society through force or through more or less voluntary migration. Lieberson argues that a group's mode of entry is fateful for its trajectory of development in a society, and this is amply borne out in the literature on ethnicity.

Stated in very broad terms, three approaches have dominated the sociological study of ethnicity; a fourth and much newer one appears to hold the promise of eventual parity with them. Of the older approaches, one, the *assimilation* perspective, focuses on social processes and outcomes that tend to dissolve ethnic distinctions, leading to the assimilation of one ethnic group by another or by the larger society. The second approach could be labeled as *stratification*. As the name implies, it addresses the origins and consequences of inequalities of various kinds among ethnic groups. The third approach focuses on *ethnic-group resources*, and encompasses processes, such as mobilization and solidarity, by which the members of ethnic groups attempt to use their ethnicity to compete successfully with others. The newest approach is a *social constructionist* one. It stems from the recognition that ethnic boundaries are malleable and is concerned with the ways by which such boundaries are created, maintained, and transformed.

No one of these approaches could be described as preeminent; each is a major presence in contemporary research on ethnicity and has shown that it has something to contribute. Other approaches are possible but are not as theoretically and empirically developed as these four. One other approach seeks a basis for ethnicity in sociobiology, viewing it as a form of genetic nepotism, a generalization of the universal tendency among animals to favor kin. van den Berghe (1981) has been an exponent of such an approach, but as yet no body of evidence has been developed to distinguish it from more sociological approaches; other sociologists have not followed his lead. Ethnicity has also been viewed as "primordial," deriving from deeply seated human impulses and needs that are not eradicated by modernization (Isaacs 1975). But this viewpoint has not led to sociologically interesting research, and it has lacked exponents in recent decades. Another attempt, stemming from "rational choice theory" (Banton 1983; Hechter 1987), seeks to explain ethnic phenomena in terms of the efforts of individuals to maximize their advantages (or, in technical language, utilities). Research using rational choice theory is still too immature to draw up a meaningful balance sheet on it.

The assimilation approach has deep roots in classical social theory as well as in American sociology, where it is often traced to Robert E. Park's 1926 formulation of a race relations cycle of "contacts, competition, accommodation, and eventual assimilation" (quoted from Park 1950, p. 150; cf. Lal 1990). The canonical statement of the assimilation approach is by Milton Gordon (1964; for an

updated revision, see Alba and Nee 1997). Although Gordon was addressing the role of ethnicity in the United States, his formulation is so general that it can be readily applied to other societies. At the heart of his contribution is the recognition that assimilation is a multidimensional concept. He distinguished, in fact, among seven types of assimilation, but the critical distinction lies between two of them: acculturation and structural (or social) assimilation. *Acculturation* means the adaptation by an ethnic group of the cultural patterns of the dominant, or majority, group. Such acculturation encompasses not only external cultural traits, such as dress and language, but also internal ones, such as beliefs and values. Gordon (1964) theorized that acculturation is typically the first of the types of assimilation to occur and that the stage of "'acculturation only' may continue indefinitely" (p. 77)—hence the importance of the second assimilation type, structural assimilation. *Structural assimilation* is defined by Gordon to mean the entry of an ethnic group's members into close, or primary, relationships with members of the dominant group (or, at least, with ethnic outsiders). The cardinal hypothesis in Gordon's (1964) scheme is that structural assimilation is the key that unlocks all other types: "Once structural assimilation has occurred . . . all of the other types of assimilation will naturally follow" (Gordon 1964, p. 81). Once structural assimilation occurs, the way is open to widespread intermarriage, an abating of prejudice and discrimination, and the full participation of ethnic-group members in the life of a society.

Gordon discussed certain models, or theories, of the assimilation process (they might also be described as ideologies because of their value-laden character). Although these were, again, developed for the U.S. context, Gordon's discussion is so lucid that the models have passed into more general application. One is labeled as "Anglo-conformity" by Gordon, and it describes an assimilation that is limited to acculturation to the behavior and values of the core ethnic group, taken to be Protestants with ancestry from the British Isles in the American context. A second model is that of the "melting pot." It envisions an assimilation process that operates on cultural and structural planes. One outcome is a culture that contains contributions from numerous ethnic groups and is adopted by their members. A parallel outcome on a structural plane is a pattern of widespread marriage across ethnic lines, in which the members of all ethnic groups participate and which leads ultimately to population made up of individuals of quite intermixed ancestry. The melting-pot idea corresponds with some popular notions about U.S. society, but so does the last model explicated by Gordon—namely, "cultural pluralism." Cultural pluralism corresponds with a situation in which ethnic groups remain socially differentiated, often with their own institutions and high rates of in-group marriage, and retain some culturally distinctive features. It is, in fact, an apt description of many societies throughout the world.

Urban ecology, dating back to the origins of the Chicago School of American sociology, is quite compatible with the assimilation approach. A core tenet of this tradition is that the spatial separation of one group from another mirrors the social distance between them and changes as this does. This ultimately implies a model of *spatial assimilation* (Massey 1985), according to which residential mobility follows from the acculturation and socioeconomic mobility of ethnic-group members and is often an intermediate step on the way to more complete—that is, structural—assimilation. The model envisions an early stage of residential segregation, as the members of ethnic groups—typically, immigrants and their children—are concentrated in urban enclaves, which frequently results in the displacement of other groups. But as the members of an ethnic group acculturate and establish themselves in the labor markets of the host society, they attempt to leave behind less successful co-ethnics and to convert socioeconomic and assimilation progress into residential gain by "purchasing" residence in places with greater advantages and amenities. This process implies, on the one hand, a tendency toward dispersion of an ethnic group, opening the way for increased contact with members of the ethnic majority, and, on the other hand, greater resemblance in terms of residential characteristics between successful ethnic-group members and their peers from the majority group.

The assimilation perspective has been successfully applied to American ethnic groups derived from European immigration. In a review of the evidence, Charles Hirschman (1983) documents the abating of ethnic differences in the white population in terms of socioeconomic achievement, residential location, and intermarriage. To cite some representative research findings, Stanley Lieberson and Mary Waters (1988), comparing the occupations of men of European ancestry in 1900 and 1980, find a marked decline in occupational concentrations, although these still show traces of the patterns of the past. These authors and Richard Alba (1990) also demonstrate the great extent to which interethnic marriage now takes place within the white population: Three of every four marriages in this group involve some degree of ethnic boundary crossing. The assimilation perspective as applied to European Americans has not been without its critics; Andrew Greeley (1971) has done the most to assemble evidence of persisting ethnic differences.

There can be no doubt that African Americans do not exemplify the patterns expected under the assimilation perspective (e.g., Massey and Denton 1993). A question that now motivates much debate and research is the degree to which the assimilation patterns will be found among contemporary immigrants and their descendants (see Alba and Nee 1997; Portes and Rumbaut 1996). It is too early to answer the question, but reflecting on the potential differences between past and contemporary immigrations, Portes and Zhou (1993) have added a new concept to the ethnicity arsenal—namely, *segmented assimilation*, which acknowledges that the strata of American society into which individuals assimilate may vary considerably. In their view, the children of dark-skinned, working-class immigrants who grow up in the inner city are at great risk of assimilating into the indigenous lower class and thus experiencing assimilation with little or no upward mobility.

Much of the evidence on assimilation and ethnic change is derived from cross-sectional studies rather than those done over time; the latter are difficult to conduct because of the limited availability of comparable data from different time points. Cross-sectional analyses involve some dissection of an ethnic group into parts expected to display a trajectory of change. One basis for such a dissection is generational groups. *Generation* here refers to distance in descent from the point of entry into a society. (By convention, generations are numbered with immigrants as the "first," so that their children are the "second," their grandchildren are the "third," etc.) Generally speaking, later generations are expected to be more assimilated than earlier ones. Another basis for dissection is *birth cohorts*, defined as groups born during the same period. Cohort differences can provide insight into historical changes in a group's position. Both kinds of differences have been used to study ethnic changes in the United States (for an application of the generational method, see Neidert and Farley 1985; for the cohort method, see Alba 1988).

The second major approach to the study of ethnicity and race, labeled above as "stratification," is considerably less unified than the assimilation approach, encompassing quite diverse theoretical underpinnings and research findings. Yet there are some common threads throughout. One is an assumption that ethnic groups generally are hierarchically ordered: There is typically a dominant, or *superordinate*, group, which is often described as the *majority* group (even though in some societies, such as South Africa, it may be a numerical minority of the population). There are also *subordinate* groups, often called *minorities* (although they may be numerical majorities). Second, these groups are assumed to be in conflict over scarce resources, which may relate to power, favorable occupational position, educational opportunity, and so forth. In this conflict, the dominant group employs a variety of strategies to defend or enhance its position, while minority groups seek to challenge it. Often, the focus of the stratification approach is on the mechanisms that help preserve ethnic inequalities, although there has also been some attention to the means that enable minorities successfully to challenge entrenched inequality.

One tradition in ethnic stratification research has looked to mechanisms of inequality that are rooted in ideologies and outlooks that are then manifested in the behavior of individuals. This is, in fact, a common meaning for the word *racism*. A longstanding research concern has been with *prejudice*, which is generally defined as a fixed set of opinions, attitudes, and feelings, usually unfavorable, about the members of a group (Allport 1954). Prejudice is frequently an outgrowth of *ethnocentrism*, the tendency to value positively one's own group and denigrate others. It can lead to *discrimination*, which is a behavior: the denial of equal treatment to a group's members, exemplified by the refusal to sell homes in certain neighborhoods to minority-group members. The investigation of

prejudice was one of the early testing grounds for survey research. In the United States, this research uncovered a dimension of *social distance*, expressing the specific gradations of social intimacy the majority is willing to tolerate with the members of various ethnic groups (Bogardus 1928). Recent research has revealed a paradoxical set of changes: on the one hand, a secular decline in traditional prejudice, most notably the prejudiced attitudes and beliefs held by whites about blacks; on the other, little increase in support for government policies that implement principles of racial equality (Schuman et al. 1998). This divergence has led many scholars to theorize about the emergence of modern forms of prejudice, exemplified by the concept of *symbolic racism* (Kinder and Sears 1981).

However persuasive as explanatory factors prejudice and discrimination may appear to the layperson, sociologists have in recent decades more and more neglected them in favor of *institutional*, or *structural*, mechanisms of inequality (see, e.g., Bonilla-Silva 1997). One reason for this shift has been skepticism that prejudice and individual-level discrimination by themselves are adequate to account for the depth and durability of racial and ethnic cleavages in industrial societies, especially since these purported explanatory factors have seemed to decline in tandem with rising educational levels. (However, the emphasis on structural mechanisms can itself be faulted for neglecting the ideological component in racism.)

One expression of the focus on structural factors has been the notion of *institutional racism* (Blauner 1972). According to it, inequality among racial and ethnic groups depends not so much on individual acts of discrimination as it does on the workings of such institutions as the schools and the police, which process and sort individuals according to their racial and ethnic origins and ultimately impose very different outcomes on them. An assumption of this approach is that this sort of discrimination can occur on a wide scale without equally widespread prejudice. Indeed, it may even be possible without any discriminatory intent on the part of individuals in authority; an example would be educational tracking systems, which sort students according to racial background based on culturally and socially biased cues that are presumed by teachers and administrators to be related to intellectual ability. Studies deriving from the notion of institutional racism have in fact provided some compelling analyses of the perpetuation of inequalities (on education, see Persell 1977), although they also can easily descend into controversy, as when any unequal outcome is declared to indicate the operation of racism.

A crucial arena in which both institutional and individual forms of racism operate to produce inequality is that of residence. Residential segregation is probably the most prominent indicator of the persisting importance of race in the United States; and it is critical to many other inequalities because life chances, especially for children, vary sharply across neighborhoods, which differ in many ways, from the qualities of the housing and schools they contain to the risks that their residents will be victims of crime. Decades of research with highly refined data and measures, such as the well-known Index of Dissimilarity, have shown that levels of neighborhood segregation by race are quite high and, at best, moderating very slowly (Farley and Frey 1994; Massey and Denton 1993). The pattern in many American cities can be described as one of *hypersegregation*, in the sense that the overwhelming majority of African Americans reside in large, consolidated ghettos containing virtually no whites and few members of other groups (Massey and Denton 1993). Residential segregation is not much explained by the economic inequalities between whites and blacks. So-called audit studies, involving matched pairs of white and black housing applicants, reveal considerable outright discrimination in the housing market. While whites are now more willing than in the past to accept blacks as neighbors, it appears that their tolerance is usually limited to small numbers. Contemporary segregation is also the consequence of government policies, past and present. The policies of the Federal Housing Administration, which effectively led in the 1930s to the modern mortgage instrument but were biased against mortgage lending in areas with many black residents, have had an enduring impact of American residential patterns, reflected in the division between largely white suburbs and largely nonwhite cities. (For a thorough discussion of the mechanisms behind segregation, see Massey and Denton 1993.)

A major theme in the stratification approach is the often complicated relationship, or interaction, between ethnicity and social class. One viewpoint is that ethnicity is, to some degree at least, a manifestation of deeply rooted class dynamics. This has led to analyses that emphasize the economic and material foundations of what appear superficially to be cultural and ethnic distinctions. Analyses of this type have sometimes been inspired by Marxism, but they are hardly limited to Marxists. For example, Herbert Gans ([1962] 1982), in an influential analysis of second-generation Italians in a Boston neighborhood, argued that many of their distinctive traits could be understood as a function of their working-class position, which was not greatly changed from the situation of their southern Italian ancestors. In a related vein, Stephen Steinberg (1989) argues that cultural explanations of ethnic inequalities, which impute "undesirable" characteristics to some groups and "desirable" ones to others, are often rationalizations of economic privilege.

It is sometimes argued that inequalities that once rested on an ethnic basis now rest primarily on one of class. An important, if controversial, instance is William J. Wilson's (1978, 1987) claim of a "declining significance of race" for American blacks. One part of Wilson's argument focuses on an increasing socioeconomic division within the black population. This is held to result from the increasing opportunities available to young, well-educated African Americans since the 1960s. However, while improvements have been registered for a minority of the group, the lot of the black poor has not improved—it has even worsened. Wilson describes their situation as one of an *underclass*, which he defines in terms of isolation from the mainstream economy and society. His explanations for the emergence of the underclass are structural, not individualistic, and include the spatial concentration of the black poor in run-down urban neighborhoods, which have been stripped of their institutional fabric and middle-class residents, and the exodus of suitable job opportunities from central cities to suburbs and Sunbelt areas. In opposition to Wilson, others have argued that the emergence of underclass ghettos is better understood as a consequence of racism, as exemplified in residential segregation (e.g., Massey and Denton 1993).

An economic approach has also been used to explain ethnic conflict, which is seen as an outgrowth of the conflicting material interests of different ethnic groups. An exempler is provided by the theory of the ethnically *split labor market* (Bonacich 1972). Such a labor market develops when two ethnically different groups of workers compete (or could compete) for the same jobs at *different costs to employers*. It is typical in such situations for the higher-priced group of workers to have the same ethnic origins as employers, and therefore for the lower-priced group to be ethnically different from both. Nevertheless, it is in the interest of employers to substitute lower-priced workers for higher-priced ones wherever possible, despite the ethnic ties they share with the latter. Intense ethnic conflict can therefore develop between the two groups of workers, as the higher-priced group seeks to eliminate the threat to its interests. Two strategies may be employed: exclusion of the lower-priced group (for example, through legal restrictions on the immigration of its members) or creation of a caste system, that is, the limitation of the lower-priced group to a separate sphere of undesirable jobs. Split-labor-market theory has been applied to black–white relations in South Africa and the United States.

Yet, even in terms of a strictly economic approach, the precise genesis of the conflict between different ethnic groups of workers is open to question, and the theory of *segmented labor markets* draws another picture (Piore 1979). This theory divides the economies and labor markets of advanced capitalist societies into a primary sector, which contains relatively secure, well-paid jobs with decent working conditions and the opportunity for advancement, and a secondary sector, made up of insecure, dead-end jobs at low wages. Regardless of their class position, workers from the dominant group prefer to avoid jobs in the secondary sector, and usually they can manage to do so. Even unemployment may not be sufficient to force them into the secondary sector, since the benefits and resources available to most members of the dominant group, such as relatively generous unemployment compensation and seniority rights, enable them to wait out periodic unemployment. Hence, there is a need for another supply of workers, typically drawn from minorities and immigrants, who have no alternative but to accept employment in the secondary sector. Immigrants, in fact, are often willing to take these jobs because, as sojourners, they find the social stigma attached to the work to be less meaningful than do the native-born. In contrast to the theory of the split labor market, which takes the existence of an ethnic difference among workers as a given, segmented-labor-market theory can explain why ethnic differences, especially between natives and immigrants, are so prevalent and persistent in the industrial societies of the West.

An economic explanation of ethnic differences is sometimes placed in a context of worldwide colonialism and capitalist exploitation (Rex 1981). Indeed, ethnic inequalities within a society are sometimes seen as the consequence of international relations between colonizers and the colonized. The notion that subordinate groups form economically exploited *internal colonies* in Western societies is an expression of this view (Blauner 1972). This notion is compatible with a hypothesis of a *cultural division of labor,* according to which positions in the socioeconomic order are assigned on the basis of cultural markers and hence ethnic origin (Hechter 1975).

The stratification approach need not focus exclusively on socioeconomic differences. Some scholars, in fact, prefer to see inequalities of power as more fundamental (Horowitz 1985; Stone 1985). This is a very general perspective on ethnic stratification, which is quite compatible with such fundamental notions as dominant and subordinate groups. According to it, social-class relations are but one instance, no matter how important, of the institutionalized inequalities between ethnic groups. Equally important, ethnic dominance cannot be reduced to, or explained solely in terms of, social-class mechanisms. (An implication is that class analysis of ethnic relations can be reductionist, an attempt to explain away ethnicity's causal independence.) Thus, the antagonism and sectarian violence between Catholics and Protestants in Northern Ireland is not comprehensible solely in terms of a social-class analysis, even though aggregate class differences between the groups exist as a result of centuries-long Protestant domination. This domination, the legacy of the colonial treatment of Ireland by the British, is manifest in a number of areas—in separate residential neighborhoods and schools, in social relations between members of the two groups, and in the political system. In short, domination encompasses much more than social-class privilege and gives even working-class members of the Protestant group a sense of status and superiority.

Distinguishing empirically between ethnic stratification based on power and that rooted in economic structure has proven difficult. In one attempt, Hubert Blalock (1967) formulated a *power threat hypothesis*, to be contrasted with one derived from economic competition between groups. These two hypotheses can be tested in the relationship between discrimination and the size of a minority group. In particular, threats to the power of the dominant group are expected to result in discrimination that rises sharply with increases in the size of a minority; the same is not true for economic competition. So far, this test has been applied mainly to the American South (Tolnay and Beck 1995).

Theories concerning power differentials among ethnic groups border on the third major approach to the study of ethnicity, with its focus on ethnic-group resources. This approach, like the preceding one, takes its point of departure from the inequalities among groups. However, its vision is less one of the domination of some groups over others than it is of a more balanced competition that is affected by characteristics of the groups, such as their numbers, their solidarity, and their ability to form separate ethnic subeconomies. Such characteristics can give the group and its members relative advantages, or disadvantages, in this competition. Insofar as advantages are conferred, there may incentives for individuals to maintain their attachments to a group rather than assimilate. In a sense, theories of ethnic-group resources can be seen as counterarguments to assimilation theories.

This is certainly clear in Nathan Glazer and Daniel Patrick Moynihan's ([1963] 1970) politically based explanation for the continuing importance of ethnicity in the United States. These authors acknowledge that immigrant cultures fade quickly under the impact of the assimilation process; assimilation is accomplished to this degree. However, ethnicity comes to coincide with differences in American circumstances, such as residential and occupational concentrations, which are similarly affected by government policies and actions. Hence, ethnicity takes on importance in the political sphere: Ethnic groups become "interest groups," reflecting the interests of many similarly situated individuals. This role breathes new life into what might otherwise languish as an Old World social form. Glazer and Moynihan give many examples of the working of such interest groups in New York City.

Others have argued that ethnicity has become "politicized" in many contemporary societies, including many industrialized ones, and this leads to an unanticipated ethnic "resurgence." Daniel Bell (1975) states one basis for this point of view, claiming that politics is increasingly replacing the market as the chief instrument of distribution and that politics recognizes only group claims, thus enhancing ethnicity's political import. (The direction of change seems to have shifted since then, however.) In a more general fashion, Francois Nielsen (1985) contends that ethnicity offers a wider basis for political recruitment than the chief alternative, social class, and therefore ethnic-based movements have a greater chance for success. Addressing the situation in Third World societies, Donald Horowitz (1985) sees the ethnic political conflict that troubles many of them as originating in part in colonial policies and then being intensified by the anxieties of groups over their status in the postcolonial order.

Students of ethnic politicization have focused especially on the phenomenon of ethnic mobilization, which is epitomized in separatist movements in modern states, as in the Congo, Quebec, and Tibet (Olzak 1983). Mobilization can be regarded as one manifestation of the state of ethnic solidarity, a core concept in the literature on ethnicity. Ethnic groups marked by *solidarity* can be defined as self-conscious communities whose members interact with each other to achieve common purposes, and *mobilization* occurs when members take some collective action to advance these purposes. Recent research on ethnic movements appears to demonstrate that they are not generally interpretable in modern polities as the vestiges of traditional loyalties that have yet to be submerged by the modernization processes attendant upon development; rather, such movements can be outcomes of these processes and thus increase as economic development proceeds. The specific causes of this linkage are disputed, however (Olzak 1983).

Culture is another domain in which the search for group resources has been carried out. The group-resources approach is compatible with the cultural-pluralist description of society, described earlier. More commonly in the past than today, the relative success of ethnic groups has been explained in terms of cultural traits. Quite often, the advantages these give have been analyzed in social-psychological terms. A well-known attempt along these lines was that of Bernard Rosen (1959), who matched American ethnic groups against the profile of the "achievement syndrome," a configuration of values that was presumed to predispose individuals to success. Included was an orientation to the future rather than the past and a downplaying of fatalism. In Rosen's analysis, the presence or absence of these traits in the culture of a group was explained according to the group's history and experience, and frequently in terms of the culture of the society from which it came. This sort of analysis, presuming stable cultural traits and rooting socioeconomic success in social-psychological prerequisites, has fallen into disfavor of late. In fact, it is often seen more as popular myth than as social science (Steinberg 1989). Cultural explanations, however, are not limited to the social-psychological realm. As one example, Ivan Light (1972) has devised an intriguing partial explanation for the entrepreneurial proclivities of different groups—in terms of the extent to which their cultures sponsor mechanisms that generate capital for the start-up of small businesses. Light argues that the business success of some Asian groups can be understood in part as an outcome of the rotating-credit association, a traditional social form imported from their home societies. Nevertheless, sociologists recently have stressed the malleability of culture and have tended to view it more as an adaptation to, and hence outcome of, socioeconomic position than as a cause of it. Consequently, cultural interpretations currently play only a minor role in the study of ethnicity. This may be a neglect engendered by cyclical intellectual fashion—in the future, they may loom larger, especially in the analysis of the immigrant groups proliferating in many societies (see, e.g., Zhou and Bankston 1998).

A focus of intense interest in recent years has been on the economic resources some groups are able to attain and thus on the advantages and opportunities adhering to ethnicity for their members. This interest is expressed in somewhat divergent research streams, running along distinctive conceptual channels. One has been carved out around the linkage that appears in many societies between minority-group status and entrepreneurial activity. This linkage makes sense in terms of the disadvantages borne by many minority groups in mainstream economies, where they may suffer from various forms of discrimination and be channeled into low-status positions. Entrepreneurial activity, then, represents an attempt to evade these economic disadvantages. But, as many observers have pointed out, this hypothesis alone cannot account for the wide variation in entrepreneurial levels and forms among groups (Light 1984). An early attempt at a general theory is that of middle-man minorities, which begins from the observation that a few groups, such as the Chinese and Jews, have occupied entrepreneurial niches in numerous societies (Bonacich 1973). The theory views entrepreurialism, especially in commercial forms, as consistent with the sojourner status and interstititial position of these groups, between elites and masses. Yet this theory is too specific to account for contemporary immigrant entrepreneurialism, which frequently, for instance, involves nonsojourner groups. Therefore, Ivan Light (1984) has turned toward broader conceptual accounting schemes, seeing a range of ethnic and class resources as behind entrepreneurialism. Very intriguing here is the notion of ethnic resources, which include the established ethnic networks that train newly arrived immigrants and set them up in business. This notion helps to account for the clustering that is so obvious in ethnic small business, such as the concentration of New York's Koreans in greengroceries and dry cleaning.

A second stream of research builds partly on the immigrant proclivity toward entrepreneurialism. The theory of the ethnic enclave, developed by Alejandro Portes and various collaborators, holds that some groups are able to form ethnic subeconomies, which shelter not only entrepreneurs but also workers from the disadvantages they would face in the secondary sectors of the mainstream economy (Portes and Bach 1985). Enclave theory is particularly interesting because it provides a material motive for resisting assimilation. As exemplified in the case of the Cubans of Miami, enclave-forming groups typically contain a high-status stratum composed of individuals with professional occupations, capital, or both, along with lower-status strata of workers seeking employment. A key to a full-fledged enclave is the establishment of networks of firms in interrelated economic sectors. The success of these firms is predicated on ethnic loyalties to an important degree. Workers and bosses may find mutual advantage where they share the same ethnicity. Workers may be willing to work longer hours or for lower wages, thus enhancing the profitability of a business, because they are able to work in a culturally familiar environment (usually speaking their mother tongue, for example). Workers may also have the opportunity to learn about running a business, and some eventually graduate to become entrepreneurs themselves. Enclave economies may be sustained in part by servicing the needs of their own ethnic communities, but if they are to be truly robust, they must also plug into the mainstream economy. This is the case, for instance, with the many ethnic firms in the American garment industry.

Despite its attractiveness on theoretical grounds, the implications of the enclave economy are disputed. One criticism is that such an economy offers few benefits for workers; the economic gains accrue to ethnic entrepreneurs (Sanders and Nee 1987). In addition, there is growing recognition that fully formed enclave economies are uncommon (Logan et al. 1994). These problems have led investigators to reinvigorate a broader notion, that of the *ethnic niche*, which refers to any economic position where a group is sufficiently concentrated to draw advantage from it, typically by being able to steer its own members into openings (Model 1997; Waldinger 1996). Thus, one can speak of an entrepreneurial niche, such as the Koreans have established in various lines of small business, or of an occupational niche, exemplified by the former dominance of the Irish in municipal employment in numerous cities. The ethnic-niche idea implicates other notions, such as the operation of ethnic networks that assist group members in finding positions in a niche. The niche idea is also frequently linked to that of an ethnic queue, an hierarchical ordering among minority groups, and to demographic and socioeconomic shifts. The latter open up niches, as exemplified by the withdrawal of white ethnics from some lines of small business in American cities, and the former determine which other groups are best positioned to take advantage of the openings (Waldinger 1996).

Oddly, a relatively neglected dimension of the ethnic-resources perspective concerns ethnic communities themselves, despite an almost universal recognition among scholars that some ethnics prefer to live in communities where their fellow ethnics are a numerous, if not the predominant, element of the population. Ethnic neighborhoods continue to be a salient aspect of metropolitan life in the United States and connected to inequalities that affect the well-being and life chances of their residents; and now they are emerging on a substantial scale in suburban settings (Horton 1995). A longstanding idea is that the residents of "institutionally complete" communities are less likely to assimilate (Breton 1964). Given the burgeoning of immigrant communities in the United States and elsewhere, it seems certain that this scholarly neglect will soon be repaired.

The final orientation, the social constructionist one, is so new that it cannot yet be said to have accumulated a substantial corpus of findings (for general reviews, see Nagel 1994; Omi and Winant 1996). This is not to deny its roots in the classical conception of ethnicity, as exemplified by the Weberian definition cited earlier, with its emphasis on the subjective view and, implicitly, on the relation of ethnic boundaries to social closure. As its name implies, this perspective stresses that ethnic boundaries and meanings are not preordained but malleable and thus that an understanding of ethnic distinctions must generally be sought in contemporary, rather than historical, circumstances. This perspective is especially attuned to the possible emergence of new forms of ethnicity, as some see, for instance, in the cultural hybridity associated with the rising frequency of mixed racial ancestry in the United States. There is also an emphasis on heightened ethnic fluidity, even the potential for revolutionary shifts, in the present because of the rise of the global economy and associated phenomena, such as large-scale migrations across borders, cultural diffusions, and transnational networks (Sassen 1988).

The most striking findings to emerge from this perspective concern historical shifts in racial boundaries, confounding the lay view that racial distinctions are determined by impossible-to-overlook physical differences among humans. Yet, historically, such boundaries have shifted in the United States within relatively brief intervals. During their immigrations, Irish Catholics, Italians, and

Eastern European Jews were all perceived as racially different from native-born whites, as nineteenth-century cartoon depictions of the Irish demonstrate. Today, the racial element in the perception of ethnic differences among whites has disappeared. The limited historical studies have not yet fully explicated the decades-long process by which this happened but make clear that it was not benign, as immigrants used violence and stereotyping, among other means, to create social distance between themselves and African Americans and thereby make plausible their candidacy for "whiteness" (see Ignatiev 1995; Roediger 1991). Then, their acceptability to other white Americans grew as they climbed the social ladder and mixed occupationally and residentially with other whites.

In conclusion, one must acknowledge that the literature on ethnicity remains unsettled in its theoretical core. The persistence—perhaps even the resurgence—of ethnic difference and conflict in societies throughout the world has attracted much attention from sociologists and other social scientists. But the paradoxes associated with ethnicity, evidenced in the United States by the assimilation of some groups and the continued separateness and even subordination of others, have yet to be resolved. They remain fruitful for sociology, nevertheless: The study of ethnicity has produced some of the discipline's most striking findings and, no doubt, will continue to do so.

REFERENCES

Alba, Richard 1988 "Cohorts and the Dynamics of Ethnic Change." In Matilda White Riley, Bettina J. Huber, and Beth B. Hess, eds., *Social Structures and Human Lives*. Newbury Park, Calif.: Sage.

—— 1990 *Ethnic Identity: The Transformation of White America*. New Haven, Conn.: Yale University Press.

——, and Victor Nee 1997 "Rethinking Assimilation for a New Era of Immigration." *International Migration Review* 31:826–874.

Allport, Gordon 1954 *The Nature of Prejudice*. New York: Addison-Wesley.

Banton, Michael 1983 *Racial and Ethnic Competition*. Cambridge, U.K.: Cambridge University Press.

Barth, Frederik 1969 "Introduction." In Frederik Barth, ed., *Ethnic Groups and Boundaries*. Boston, Mass.: Little, Brown.

Bell, Daniel 1975 "Ethnicity and Social Change." In Nathan Glazer and Daniel Patrick Moynihan, eds., *Ethnicity: Theory and Experience*. Cambridge, Mass.: Harvard University Press.

Blalock, Hubert 1967 *Toward a Theory of Minority-Group Relations*. New York: Capricorn.

Blauner, Robert 1972 *Racial Oppression in America*. New York: Harper and Row.

Bogardus, Emory 1928 *Immigration and Race Attitudes*. Boston: D.C. Heath.

Bonacich, Edna 1972 "A Theory of Ethnic Antagonism: The Split Labor Market." *American Sociological Review* 37:547–559.

—— 1973 "A Theory of Middleman Minorities." *American Sociological Review* 38:583–594.

Bonilla-Silva, Eduardo 1997 "Rethinking Racism: Toward a Structural Interpretation." *American Sociological Review* 62:465–480.

Breton, Raymond 1964 "Institutional Completeness of Ethnic Communities and the Personal Relations of Immigrants." *American Journal of Sociology* 70:193–205.

Farley, Reynolds, and William Frey 1994 "Changes in the Segregation of Whites from Blacks During the 1980s: Small Steps Towards a More Integrated Society." *American Sociological Review* 59:23–45.

Gans, Herbert (1962) 1982 *The Urban Villagers: Group and Class in the Life of Italian Americans*. New York: Free Press.

Glazer, Nathan, and Daniel Patrick Moynihan (1963) 1970 *Beyond the Melting Pot: The Negroes, Puerto Ricans, Jews, Italians, and Irish of New York City*. Cambridge, Mass.: MIT Press.

Gordon, Milton 1964 *Assimilation in American Life*. New York: Oxford University Press.

Greeley, Andrew 1971 *Why Can't They Be Like Us?* New York: Dutton.

Hechter, Michael 1975 *Internal Colonialism: The Celtic Fringe and British National Development*. Berkeley: University of California Press.

—— 1987 *Principles of Group Solidarity*. Berkeley: University of California Press.

Hirschman, Charles 1983 "America's Melting Pot Reconsidered." *Annual Review of Sociology* 9:397–423.

Horowitz, Donald 1985 *Ethnic Groups in Conflict*. Berkeley: University of California Press.

Horton, John 1995 *The Politics of Diversity: Immigration, Resistance, and Change in Monterey Park, California*. Philadelphia: Temple University Press.

Ignatiev, Noel 1995 *How the Irish Became White*. New York: Routledge.

Isaacs, Harold 1975 "Basic Group Identity: The Idols of the Tribe." In Nathan Glazer and Daniel Patrick Moynihan, eds., *Ethnicity: Theory and Experience.* Cambridge, Mass.: Harvard University Press.

Kinder, Donald, and David Sears 1981 "Prejudice and Politics: Symbolic Racism Versus Threats to the Good Life." *Journal of Personality and Social Psychology* 40:414–431.

Lal, Barbara Ballis 1990 *The Romance of Culture in an Urban Civilization: Robert E. Park on Race and Ethnic Relations in Cities.* London: Routledge.

Lieberson, Stanley 1961 "A Societal Theory of Race and Ethnic Relations." *American Sociological Review* 26:902–910.

——, and Mary Waters 1988 *From Many Strands: Ethnic and Racial Groups in Contemporary America.* New York: Russell Sage Foundation.

Light, Ivan 1972 *Ethnic Enterprise in America: Business and Welfare Among Chinese, Japanese, and Blacks.* Berkeley: University of California Press.

—— 1984 "Immigrant and Ethnic Enterprise in North America." *Ethnic and Racial Studies* 7:195–216.

Logan, John, Richard Alba, and Thomas McNulty 1994 "Ethnic Economies in Metropolitan Regions: Miami and Beyond." *Social Forces* 72:691–724.

Massey, Douglas 1985 "Ethnic Residential Segregation: A Theoretical Synthesis and Empirical Review." *Sociology and Social Research* 69:315–350.

——, and Nancy Denton 1993 *American Apartheid: Segregation and the Making of the Underclass.* Cambridge, Mass.: Harvard University Press.

Model, Suzanne 1997 "Ethnic Economy and Industry in Mid-Twentieth Century Gotham." *Social Problems* 44:445–463.

Nagel, Joane 1994 "Constructing Ethnicity: Creating and Recreating Ethnic Identity and Culture." *Social Problems* 41:152–176.

Neidert, Lisa, and Reynolds Farley 1985 "Assimilation in the United States: An Analysis of Ethnic and Generation Differences in Status and Achievement." *American Sociological Review* 50:840–850.

Nielsen, Francois 1985 "Toward a Theory of Ethnic Solidarity in Modern Societies." *American Sociological Review* 50:133–149.

Olzak, Susan 1983 "Contemporary Ethnic Mobilization." *Annual Review of Sociology* 9:355–374.

Omi, Michael, and Howard Winant 1994 *Racial Formation in the United States: From the 1960s to the 1990s,* 2nd ed. New York: Routledge and Kegan Paul.

Park, Robert 1950 *Race and Culture.* New York: Free Press.

Persell, Caroline 1977 *Education and Inequality: The Roots of Stratification in America's Schools.* New York: Free Press.

Piore, Michael 1979 *Birds of Passage: Migrant Labor and Industrial Societies.* Cambridge, U.K.: Cambridge University Press.

Portes, Alejandro, and Robert Bach 1985 *Latin Journey: Cuban and Mexican Immigrants in the United States.* Berkeley: University of California Press.

Portes, Alejandro, and Ruben Rumbaut 1996 *Immigrant America: A Portrait,* 2nd ed. Berkeley: University of California Press.

Portes, Alejandro, and Min Zhou 1993 "The New Second Generation: Segmented Assimilation and Its Variants." *The Annals* 530:74–96.

Rex, John 1981 "A Working Paradigm for Race Relations Research." *Ethnic and Racial Studies* 4:1–25.

Roediger, David 1991 *The Wages of Whiteness: Race and the Making of the American Working Class.* New York: Verso.

Rosen, Bernard 1959 "Race, Ethnicity, and the Achievement Syndrome." *American Sociological Review* 24:47–60.

Sanders, Jimy, and Victor Nee 1987 "Limits of Ethnic Solidarity in the Ethnic Enclave." *American Sociological Review* 52:745–767.

Sassen, Saskia 1988 *The Mobility of Capital and Labor.* Cambridge, U.K.: Cambridge University Press.

Schuman, Howard, Charlotte Steeh, Lawrence Bobo, and Maria Krysan 1998 *Racial Attitudes in America: Trends and Interpretations,* rev. ed. Cambridge, Mass.: Harvard University Press.

Steinberg, Stephen 1989 *The Ethnic Myth: Race, Ethnicity, and Class in America.* Boston: Beacon.

Stone, John 1985 *Racial Conflict in Contemporary Society.* London: Fontana Press/Collins.

Thernstrom, Stephan, Ann Orlov, and Oscar Handlin 1980 *Harvard Encyclopedia of American Ethnic Groups.* Cambridge, Mass.: Harvard University Press.

Tolnay, Stewart, and E. M. Beck 1995 *A Festival of Violence: An Analysis of Southern Lynchings, 1882–1930.* Urbana: University of Illinois Press.

van den Berghe, Pierre 1967 *Race and Racism: A Comparative Perspective.* New York: Wiley.

—— 1981 *The Ethnic Phenomenon.* New York: Elsevier.

Waldinger, Roger 1996 *Still the Promised City? African-Americans and New Immigrants in Postindustrial New York.* Cambridge, Mass.: Harvard University Press.

Waters, Mary 1990 *Ethnic Options: Choosing Identities in America.* Berkeley: University of California Press.

Weber, Max (1922) 1968 *Economy and Society*. New York: Bedminster Press.

Wilson, William J. 1978 *The Declining Significance of Race: Blacks and Changing American Institutions*. Chicago: University of Chicago Press.

—— 1987 *The Truly Disadvantaged: The Inner City, the Underclass, and Public Policy*. Chicago: University of Chicago Press.

Zhou, Min, and Carl Bankston 1998 *Growing Up American: How Vietnamese Children Adapt to Life in the United States*. New York: Russell Sage Foundation.

RICHARD D. ALBA

ETHNOCENTRISM

See Ethnicity; Nationalism.

ETHNOGRAPHY

Ethnographic research (also referred to as *field research* or *participant observation*) is a qualitative social science method that involves the observation of the interactions of everyday life, whether in public parks, business organizations, or mental health clinics. It is social constructionist, exploring intersubjective cultural meanings rather than positivist "social facts," or laws. The theoretical intent of ethnography is inductive, generating concepts and theories from the data. However, in sociology, ethnography is also associated with micro-level theories such as symbolic interactionism, ethnomethodology, labeling theory, and dramaturgy. In particular, the theories of everyday life developed by Georg Simmel (1950) and Erving Goffman (1959) form part of the disciplinary repertoire from which workers in the field draw their concepts. Some field researchers also link their ethnography to critical, macro-theoretical frameworks emphasizing power relations within hierarchies of gender, class, race, age, nationality, or sexual orientation (Diamond, 1993).

The goal of field research is on the development of analytic descriptions or grounded theories (Glaser and Strauss, 1967) of the social world, usually written but sometimes audio- or videotaped. As Clifford Geertz (1988) notes, "thick description" is the foundation of ethnography.

But equally important is analysis: the generation of concepts, patterns, or typologies from thick description, and their linkage to concepts, theories, and literatures already established in the discipline. Although some academic fieldworkers may have other goals (such as helping the people in the setting), most seek to publish their ethnographic work as books or articles. There are also some field researchers who have turned to alternative forms of inscription, such as poems or plays, to try to bring to life the social worlds they study or (as in autoethnography) inhabit.

HISTORIES OF ETHNOGRAPHY

The contemporary origins of sociological ethnography are traced to the "Chicago School" of 1915–1940 (Bulmer 1984), and to nineteenth century sociological theory, reformist endeavors, and anthropological exploration. "Origin myths" seek the roots of ethnography in the writings of ancient and medieval travelers who sought first-hand knowledge of other cultures. Herodotus, for example, has been called the father of both history and sociology. In the fifth century B.C.E., Herodotus traveled to distant lands and recorded comments about the peoples and customs he found there; throughout the centuries into modern times, European, Persian, and Chinese explorers, traders, and missionaries followed suit. But it was in the nineteenth century, with the development of sociology as a discipline, that first-hand observation became part of the modern methodological repertoire.

Although the canonical work of the nineteenth century European theorists such as Karl Marx, Max Weber, and Émile Durkheim was macro-level and comparative-historical, the works are read for their ethnographic warrant. In particular, Weber's concept of *verstehen*, read as an interpretive immersion into the subjective worlds of respondents, is cited as an epistemological foundation of contemporary ethnography. Feminist ethnographers of the late twentieth century have added the names of prominent nineteenth and early twentieth century women to the histories of field research, citing Harriett Martineau's interest in the everyday lives of women and children, and Charlotte Perkins Gilman's "autoethnographic" account of her moral treatment for neurasthenia (Bailey 1996).

Anglo-American reform movements also played a part in the development of nineteenth and early twentieth century observational methods. With an Enlightenment focus on reason and the scientific method, reform efforts came to be accompanied by observational studies of the problems seen as needing remediation, from conditions in mental hospitals to poverty in the streets of London or New York. The work of reformist scholars such as Beatrice Webb and Charles Booth in Victorian London among the poor involved the use of survey and field research methods. During the same era, Beatrix Potter took a position in a London sweatshop in order to document working conditions and attempt to change them (Bailey 1996).

British and American anthropology, following Bronislaw Malinowski's lead, instituted several of the key elements of field research: the time commitment, immersion in the geographical space of the respondents, the use of cultural insiders as key informants, and the inscription of observations and thoughts. Other aspects of ethnographic research are traced to the Chicago School, with its eclectic mix of pragmatist philosophy, symbolic interaction, journalistic interests, and reformist tendencies (Bulmer 1984; Becker 1999). Robert Park's injunction to his Chicago students has been taught to subsequent generations of ethnographers:

> go and sit in the lounges of the luxury hotels and on the doorsteps of the flophouses; sit on the Gold Coast settees and on the slum shakedowns; sit in the Orchestra Hall and in the Star and Garter Burlesk. In short, gentlemen, go get the seat of your pants dirty in real research (Bulmer 1984; 97).

The Chicago School sociologists pioneered the case study method, which included oral histories, documents, statistical surveys, and some fieldwork. And it was from Chicago that the themes of 1950s to 1970s fieldwork emerged: the focus on studies of everyday life exemplified by the work of Goffman (1959), and on labeling and deviance by Howard Becker (1963) and others. The methods learned by contemporary sociological ethnographers are grounded in the Chicago, neo-Chicago (Fine 1995) and "California" schools (Adler and Adler 1987), while there has also been convergence with other disciplines practicing ethnography, such as anthropology, education, and business.

DOING ETHNOGRAPHIC RESEARCH

Introductory texts on ethnographic research (for example, Bailey 1996; Lofland and Lofland 1995) emphasize the nonlinear aspect of the method: the reflexive interplay of data collection, writing, and analysis. However, two distinct sets of activities are involved in doing ethnography: interacting within the "field" and inscription. Inscription occurs in the form of field notes (and perhaps diaries, memos, analytic notes, and other writings) and drafts of the ethnographic paper or monograph. Interaction within the field poses the usual everyday life issues of roles and relationships, together with more particular concerns such as human subjects regulations, research ethics, and entrée. Thus, the methodology of field research poses intertwined issues of representation and interaction.

Before initiating research in the field, the ethnographer selects a setting, and makes her preparations for attempting entrée. These preparations may be as simple as walking across the road to the local park, or as complex as negotiating with the governments of Cuba and the United States for permission to travel and stay in Havana. For many studies, especially funded team ethnography, it is necessary for the ethnographer to obtain permission to do the study from Institutional Review Boards (IRBs) at her University, and perhaps at the organization she wishes to study, for example, a prison or mental hospital. These Institutional Review Boards ensure that the fieldworker's plans are in compliance with the basic tenets of human subjects protections: informed consent (which is often not possible in non-interview based field research) and protection of confidentiality (in practice, not naming respondents, nor providing identifying details in published work).

All fieldwork in public places, and some fieldwork in other places, is exempt from IRB scrutiny, but no fieldwork is exempt from ethical considerations. Ethical issues that have preoccupied ethnographers for several decades are those associated with the deception of respondents. In covert fieldwork, where the ethnographer pretends to be a member of the setting (for example, Alcoholics Anonymous), the respondents are deceived about the researcher's identity and purposes. This level of deception is probably less common than it was up until the early 1980s. More common, however, is fieldwork in settings where the researcher is already a member or participant, such as a bar where he is employed, or a bisexual or gay organization of which he is a member. In this type of "nonstranger" research, the fieldworker's identity is known, but she may or may not share her new research purposes with the other members.

Entrée and Incorporation. In a setting where she is initially a stranger, the ethnographer must negotiate entrée into the setting. If this is a public park, she simply goes and sits on a park bench. If this is an organization, she will have already negotiated initial entrée with an administrative "gatekeeper," and now must thread her way through the geographical and relational space of the setting, from the first to the last time she does fieldwork there. It is a truism of field research that entrée is not a one-time event: both physical and relational entrée must continually be negotiated and renegotiated throughout the field study. Initial setting gatekeepers may be followed by new gatekeepers of other parts of the setting, while "freeze outs" bar the door to some occasions or locales.

Once in the door, hoping to be allowed to stay and move about (and perhaps conduct formal or informal interviews), the researcher is incorporated into the setting: assigned a physical and conceptual space within the field by each individual respondent, and by groups of people within the setting. The language of incorporation, as against that of role playing, highlights the reciprocal nature of the interaction between the respondents and the ethnographer, in which the researcher cannot just "decide" what kind of role to play, but, rather, is assigned a place by the people in the setting. The ethnographer's personal and status characteristics—gender, age, nationality, appearance—are an important aspect of incorporation, and determine the place that will be afforded him within the setting. These characteristics may, indeed, preclude or smooth access to particular persons, events, or parts of the field. Much has been written about gender and ethnography (Warren and Hackney 2000, since gender and sexuality are focal elements of hierarchy, interactions, and relationships within many settings.

Incorporation is a powerful emotional force field for many ethnographers, drawing them into the web of relationships in the field. Old hands at fieldwork warn of the necessity—if an analytic description is to be written—of balancing immersion with distance, touching cognitive and emotional base with both disciplinary concepts and out-of-setting roles in order to avoid engulfment in the field (Pollner and Emerson 1988). Researchers who begin as members of the setting they are studying sometimes report the opposite, becoming more detached as they move from immersed membership to analytic observer: the field, once warmly familiar, can become a place of distance and even alienation.

In the classic language of the "research bargain," ethnographers may find that they are approached and sometimes used as economic, medical, status, labor, or even sexual resources in the organizations or communities where they conduct their fieldwork. Fieldwork "warnings and advice," although they avoid the positivist language of bias, note that such research bargains may take a toll on researchers in the form of time, emotions or funds. And at times, the incorporation of the ethnographer into the setting makes leaving the field emotionally difficult, although practically necessary. Some ethnographers, anthropologists in particular, revisit "their" fields at intervals of years or months in order to document change over time. But, once out of the field, the researcher is faced with the disciplinary requisite of starting or finishing the ethnographic writing of the inscription already begun in the field.

Ethnographic Representation. The endpoint of fieldwork is ethnographic representation: an article or book about the field, published in a scholarly journal, or as a monograph or trade book. Two major publication outlets for sociological ethnographies are the *Journal of Contemporary Ethnography* and *Qualitative Sociology*; fieldworkers may also publish in general, specialty (for example, gerontology or education), or anthropology journals. Many published ethnographies are "realist tales" (Van Maanen 1988), written in the traditional style of the analytic description: "I am here and this is what is going on here." Some are "confessional tales" which focus on the writer rather than on the respondents, while others experiment with alternative representational forms such as poetry or plays. There is also a well-established tradition of visual sociology which includes photography, film, video, and the internet together with more contemporary genres such as performance ethnography.

Written ethnographic representations begin with fieldnotes: the inscription of the field (Emerson et al. 1995). Fieldworkers are taught and exhorted to write down everything they can, including verbatim conversations, in the service of thick description. This exhortation approaches feasibility in bounded settings such as a self-help group meeting that occurs once a week for fifty minutes. It becomes more problematic when the ethnographer is faced with an entire village, or even perhaps a large urban area. In practice, fieldworkers often take note of, and inscribe, aspects of events and persons to which they habitually attend; for example, one person studying a restaurant takes note of spatial patterns, while another inscribes social types by appearance and clothing, and still another notes the interaction between servers and cooks.

The inscription of fieldnotes is vital to the traditional ethnographic enterprise, since the identification of analytic patterns is difficult without an adequate amount of field notes (what is "adequate" varying with the size and complexity of the field). Alongside fieldnotes (separated by parentheses, or on separate pieces of paper), fieldworkers write memos, diaries, and analytic notes which record their own feelings and thoughts, analytic ideas and possibilities, and sometimes events which they do not want recorded in their formal fieldnotes. Although most fieldnotes have no audience but the self, fieldnotes written for graduate seminars or funded team research may be read by instructors, supervisors, or co-workers. In inscribing the Other, fieldnotes also inscribe the self (Warren 2000).

POSTMODERN ETHNOGRAPHY AND BEYOND

Ethnography, like most corners of the social sciences, has been affected by postmodernism. As representations, both fieldnotes and published ethnographies are open to the postmodern critiques of social scientific representation, critiques which began in sociology with the work of Joseph Gusfield (1976) on the literary rhetoric of sociological writing. One result of this postmodern critique is the deconstruction of realist or traditional ethnography, which, in turn, has resulted in a withdrawal from the field (the Other) into the text or the self. This movement away from traditional fieldwork has given rise to an ironic reversal of earlier exhortations to "get out of the armchairs and into the streets." There is a joke in ethnographic circles today that goes something like this: Respondent to Ethnographer: "Well, enough about you. Why don't we talk a bit about me?"

While the postmodern ethnography of the 1990s sometimes takes place in the armchair and away from the streets, dwelling upon the self rather than upon the Other, it is likely that the new century and millenium will see a renewed concern with the activities, as well as the representations, of ethnography. Those sociologists concerned with relations of power and hierarchy—of gender, race, class, and nation—are particularly concerned that a focus on textual discourse and polyvocality (attending equally to the voices of the ethnographer and those of all the respondents) does not erase the critical function of ethnographic research. Jaber Gubrium and James Holstein (1997) suggest that contemporary ethnographers attend to both the "what" (the field), and the "how" (the representations of fieldwork), becoming "self-consciously attentive to both the world researched and the researcher" (1997: 212). This is the reflexivity toward which our ethnographic practice strives at the beginning of the twenty-first century.

REFERENCES

Adler, Patricia A., and Peter Adler 1987 *Membership Roles in Field Research.* Newbury Park: Sage.

Bailey, Carol A. 1996 *A Guide to Field Research.* Thousand Oaks, Calif.: Pine Forge Press.

Becker, Howard S. 1999 "The Chicago School, So-Called." *Qualitative Sociology* 22 (Spring): 3–12.

Becker, Howard S. 1963 *Outsiders: Studies in the Sociology of Deviance.* New York: Free Press.

Bulmer, Martin 1984 *The Chicago School of Sociology.* Chicago: University of Chicago Press.

Diamond, Tim 1993 *Making Grey Gold: Narratives of Nursing Home Care.* Chicago: University of Chicago Press.

Emerson, Robert M., Rachel I. Fretz, and Linda L. Shaw 1995 *Writing Ethnographic Fieldnotes.* Chicago: University of Chicago Press.

Fine, Gary Alan, ed. 1995 *A Second Chicago School?* Chicago: University of Chicago Press.

Geertz, Clifford 1988 "Toward an Interpretive Theory of Culture." In Robert M. Emerson, ed., *Contemporary Field Research.* Prospect Heights, Ill.: Waveland Press.

Glaser, Barney and Anselm L. Straus 1967 *The Discovery of Grounded Theory*. Chicago: Aldine.

Goffman, Erving 1959 *The Presentation of Self in Everyday Life*. Garden City, NY: Anchor Books.

Gubrium, Jaber F. and James A. Holstein 1997 *The New Language of Qualitative Research*. New York: Oxford University Press.

Gusfield, Joseph 1976 "The Literary Rhetoric of Science: Comedy and Pathos in Drinking Driver Research." *American Sociological Review* 41 (February): 16–34.

Lofland, John and Lyn H. Lofland 1995 *Analyzing Social Settings*. third; ed. Belmont: Wadsworth.

Pollner, Melvin and Robert M. Emerson 1988 "The Dynamics of Inclusion and Distance in Field Research." In Robert M. Emerson, ed., *Contemporary Field Research*. Prospect Heights, Ill.: Waveland Press.

Simmel, Georg 1950 *The Sociology of Georg Simmel*, trans./ed. Kurt H. Wolff. New York: Free Press.

Van Maanen, John 1988 *Tales of the Field: on Writing Ethnography*. Chicago: University of Chicago Press.

Warren, Carol A.B. 2000 "Writing the Other, Inscribing the Self." *Qualitative Sociology*. Forthcoming.

——, and Jennifer K. Hackney 2000 *Gender Issues in Ethnography*. 2nd ed. Thousand Oaks, Calif.: Sage.

Wolff, Kurt H., ed. 1950 *The Sociology of Georg Simmel*. New York: Free Press.

CAROL A.B. WARREN

ETHNOMETHODOLOGY

Ethnomethodology is a field of sociology that studies the commonsense resources, procedures, and practices through which the members of a culture produce and recognize mutually intelligible objects, events, and courses of action. The field emerged in the late 1960s in reaction to a range of sociological perspectives, most prominently structural functionalism, which treated conduct as causally determined by social structural factors. In contrast, ethnomethodology stressed that social actions and social organization are produced by knowledgeable agents who guide their actions by the use of situated commonsense reasoning. Rather than treating the achievement of social organization as a given from which the analysis of social structure could proceed, ethnomethodological research was directed at the hidden social processes underlying that achievement. The resulting research focus on the properties of commonsense knowledge and reasoning represents one strand of what has been termed the "cognitive revolution" in the social sciences. As a sociological perspective however, ethnomethodology deals with the socially shared and publicly accountable nature of commonsense reasoning rather than with psychological aspects of cognitive processes. Its primary research stance has been descriptive and naturalistic rather than explanatory or experimental.

BACKGROUND AND DEVELOPMENT

The basic outlook of ethnomethodology was developed by Harold Garfinkel (1967a) during a twenty-year period spanning graduate research at Harvard under the supervision of Talcott Parsons through an extensive number of empirical investigations at UCLA. Garfinkel's starting point was the vestigial treatment in the sociological analyses of the 1950s of how actors employ knowledge to understand and act in ordinary social contexts (Heritage 1984). With respect to the prevailing treatment of internalized norms as motivational "drivers" of behavior, Garfinkel noted that the achievement of goals requires actions based on knowledge of real circumstances and that where coordinated action is necessary, that knowledge must be socially shared. What is the character of this knowledge? How is it implemented and updated? By what means are shared and dynamically changing knowledge and understanding concerning actions and events sustained? Merely to raise these questions was to point to fundamental deficiences in the theory of action.

In developing answers to these questions, Garfinkel drew on the theoretical writings of the phenomenological sociologist Alfred Schutz (Schutz 1962–1966). Schutz observed that each actor approaches the social world with a "stock of knowledge at hand" made up of commonsense constructs and categories that are primarily social in origin. The actor's grasp of the real world is achieved through the use of these constructs, which, Schutz stressed, are employed presuppositionally, dynamically, and in a taken-for-granted fashion. Schutz also observed that these constructs are held in typified form, that they are approximate and revisable, that actions are guided by a patchwork of "recipe knowledge," and that intersubjective understanding between actors who employ these constructs is a constructive achievement that is sustained on a moment-to-moment basis. Ethnomethodology took shape from Garfinkel's efforts to develop these theoretical observations into a program of empirical research.

A major component of these efforts took the form of the famous "breaching experiments," which were inspired by the earlier "incongruity experiments" pioneered by Solomon Asch and Jerome Bruner. The breaching experiments employed a variety of techniques to engineer drastic departures from ordinary expectations and understandings about social behavior. By "making trouble" in ordinary social situations, Garfinkel was able to demonstrate the centrality of taken-for-granted background understandings and contextual knowledge in persons' shared recognition of social events and in their management of coordinated social action. He concluded that understanding actions and events involves a circular process of reasoning in which part and whole, foreground and background, are dynamically adjusted to one another. Following Karl Mannheim, he termed this process "the documentary method of interpretation." In this process, basic presuppositions and inferential procedures are employed to assemble linkages between an action or an event and aspects of its real worldly and normative context. The character of the action is thus grasped as a "gestalt contexture" (Gurwitsch 1966) that is inferentially and procedurally created through the interlacing of action and context. Here temporal aspects of actions and events assume a central significance (Garfinkel 1967a), not least because background and context have to be construed as dynamic in character. Within this analysis, presuppositions, tacit background knowledge, and contextual detail are the inescapable resources through which a grasp of events is achieved.

Garfinkel (1967a) also showed that the recognition, description, or coding of actions and events is an inherently approximate affair. The particulars of objects and events do not have a "one-to-one" fit with their less specific representations in descriptions or codings. The fitting process thus inevitably involves a range of approximating activities that Garfinkel terms "*ad hoc* practices" (Garfinkel 1967a). This finding is, of course, the inverse of his well-known observation that descriptions, actions, and so forth have *indexical* properties: Their sense is elaborated and particularized by their contextual location. An important consequence of these observations is that shared understandings cannot be engendered by a "common culture" through a simple matching of shared words or concepts but rather can only be achieved constructively in a dynamic social process (Garfinkel 1967a). Similar conclusions apply to the social functioning of rules and norms.

In summary: Garfinkel's researches indicate that every aspect of shared understandings of the social world depends on a multiplicity of tacit *methods of reasoning*. These methods are procedural in character, they are socially shared, and they are ceaselessly used during every waking moment to recognize ordinary social objects and events. A shared social world, with its immense variegation of social objects and events, is jointly constructed and recognized through, and thus ultimately rests on, a shared base of procedures of practical reasoning that operationalize and particularize a body of inexact knowledge.

In addition to functioning as a base for understanding actions, these procedures also function as a resource for the production of actions. Actors tacitly draw on them so as to produce actions that will be *accountable*—that is, recognizable and describable—in context. Thus, shared methods of reasoning are publicly available on the surface of social life because the results of their application are inscribed in social action and interaction. As Garfinkel (1967a) put it: "The activities whereby members produce and magage the settings of organized everyday affairs are identical with members' procedures for making these settings account-able" (p. 1).

While the results of Garfinkel's experiments showed that the application of joint methods of reasoning is central to the production and understanding of social action, they also showed that the application of these methods is strongly "trusted" (Garfinkel 1963, 1967a). This "trust" has a normative background and is insisted upon through a powerful moral rhetoric. Those whose actions could not be interpreted by means of this reasoning were met with anger and demands that they explain themselves. Garfinkel's experiments thus showed the underlying *morality* of practical reasoning and that the procedural basis of action and understanding is a part—perhaps the deepest part—of the moral order. Such a finding is consistent with the view that this procedural base is foundational to organized social life and that departures from it represent a primordial threat to the possibility of sociality itself.

CONTEMPORARY RESEARCH INITIATIVES

Garfinkel's writings have stimulated a wide range of commentary, theoretical reaction, and empirical initiatives. In what follows, only the latter will be described. Empirical research in ethnomethodology will be discussed under three headings: (1) social structures as normal environments, (2) the creation and maintenance of social worlds, and (3) studies of work. A fourth, and possibly the most conspicuous, initiative—conversation analysis —is discussed elsewhere in this Encyclopedia.

Social Structures as Normal Environments. In his theoretical writings, Schutz (1962) argued that human consciousness is inherently typifying and that language is the central medium for the transmission of socially standarized typifications. In a number of his empirical studies, Garfinkel developed this idea in relation to social process, noting the ways in which commonsense reasoning is used—often within a moral idiom—to typify and normalize persons and events. A number of influential ethnomethodological studies have taken up this theme and focused on the ways in which particpants may be actively or tacitly engaged in creating or reproducing a texture of normality in their everyday affairs.

Much of this work was focused in the fields of deviance and bureaucratic record keeping. This focus was far from accidental. In both fields, the participants are concerned with the administration of socially consequential categories and in both—with their indigenous preoccupation with classification and definition—normalizing processes were close to the surface of organizational life and were somewhat easier to track. Pioneering studies in this area included Sudnow's (1965) analysis of "normal crimes," in which he showed that California lawyers employed models of "typical" offenders and offences in plea-bargaining procedures that departed substantially from the provisions of the California criminal code. Zimmerman's (1969) work on record keeping in a public welfare agency showed that bureaucratic records employed typifications of clients that could only be interpreted by reference to detailed background knowledge of the organization's procedures (see also Garfinkel 1967a, pp. 186–207). Wieder's (1974) work on a halfway house for paroled narcotics offenders showed that a "convict code" profoundly shaped how staff and inmates perceived events inside the institution—with disastrous consequences for its success.

Related works on deviance—by Cicourel (1968) on the policing of juveniles and by Atkinson (1978) on suicide—crystallized points of friction between ethnomethodology and more traditional approaches to the study of deviant behavior. Both studies examined the social processes underlying the classification of deviants. Each of them detailed a complex of commonsense considerations that enter into the determination of the nature of a deviant act and (in the case of juvenile offenders) the treatment of its perpetrator.

Cicourel's study showed that police treatment of juveniles was informed by a lay theory that posited a connection between juvenile offenses and the home background of the offender. Offenses by juveniles from "broken homes" were treated more seriously than offenses by those from other social backgrounds. In consequence, offenses by juveniles from broken homes were more likely to be officially reported, were more commonly the object of court proceedings, and had a greater tendency to result in custodial sentences. Police records, Cicourel showed, embodied a related process of idealization and typification in which case records, as they were developed through the system, became increasingly concise, selective, and consistent with the assumptions, objectives, and dispositions of the legal agencies. At the core of Cicourel's argument was the claim that the processing of juvenile offenders exhibits a circular process. Basic assumptions about the causal factors associated with juvenile crime were being used to normalize offenders and were built into the differential treatment of juveniles. From this point, these assumptions became built into police records and statistics and, finally, into social scientific treatments of the statistics that "recovered" the initial assumptions as valid explanations of juvenile crime.

Similar conclusions were reached by Atkinson (1978) in relation to the treatment of suicide.

Drawing on the work of Garfinkel (1967G) and Douglas (1967), Atkinson argued that police conceptions of "typical suicides" profoundly influenced how particular cases of sudden death were investigated and treated. These conceptions not only influenced individual verdicts but, through the accumulation of verdicts, the official statistics on suicide. Atkinson concluded that sociological studies of suicide based on official statistics are unavoidably engaged in decoding the commonsense typifications of suicide that were constitutive in the recognition of, and verdicts on, individual cases and that accumulate in the statistical record.

In sum, ethnomethodological studies of typification in relation to deviance and organizational records have had both "constructive" and "deconstructive" moments. New and important social processes that inform the categorial activities of public agencies of various kinds have been uncovered. At the same time, these discoveries have challenged traditional sociological treatments of official statistics. The "deconstructive" conclusion that official statistics of social phenomena may be largely artifactual and, in many cases, can tell us only about the kinds of assumptions and practices that animate the relevant officials has provoked debates in the discipline that are unresolved to the present date.

The Creation and Maintenance of Social Institutions and Social Worlds. An important aspect of ethnomethodological theorizing is the notion that social institutions are sustained as real entities through vocabularies of accounts (or accounting frameworks) through which the events of the social world are recognized and acted upon. Although this idea can be traced back to C. Wright Mills (1940), it found vivid expression in Garfinkel's (1967a) analysis of a transsexual individual, which he used as an occasion to investigate the nature of gender as (1) the achievement of a particular individual that (2) was made possible by the person's grasp of, and subscription to, appropriately "gendered" practices and accounting frameworks that are generally hidden or taken for granted by normally sexed persons.

A number of subsequent studies have developed this preoccupation with the role of accounting frameworks that are employed in the taken-for-granted production and reproduction of social institutions and social realities. An early and influential work was Wieder's (1974) study of the role of the "convict code" in a halfway house for paroled narcotics offenders. Wieder showed the ways in which the code—which prescribed a range of activities hostile to staff members—functioned both as a fundamental way of seeing "what was going on" in the halfway house and as a resource that could be invoked in accounting for noncompliant conduct in interaction with staff members. Of particular interest is Weider's finding that the "code" functioned in these ways among both offenders and staff despite their distinctive and conflicting perspectives on the activities of the halfway house. In transcending the formal power structure of the institution, the code was the predominant medium through which events were defined and acted upon by all participants and, for this reason, served as a source of power and control for the offenders.

At a still more general level, Pollner (1974; 1987) has explored the ways in which a version of reality is socially sustained within a collectivity. Our sense of reality, he argues, is a social institution that is sustained by particular socially organized practices, which he labels "mundane reason." Within this framework of practices, we start from the presumption that real-world objects and events are intersubjectively available as determinate, definite, noncontradictory, and self-identical. That this presumption is actively sustained, he shows, emerges in environments—ranging from everyday events to more specialized contexts such as the law courts, mental hospitals, and research science—where witnesses disagree in their depiction of objects and events. In such contexts, Pollner observes, a range of procedures are invoked that discount one version of events and privilege the other. The invocation of such procedures sustains (by restoring or repairing) persons' belief in a single noncontradictory reality. "Explaining away" a witness's testimony—by, for example, arguing that he couldn't have seen what he saw, was not competent to do so, or was lying or even insane—functions in the way described by Evans-Pritchard (1937) as the "secondary elaboration of belief." Such secondary elaborations, Pollner observes, are inevitably used in defense of the factual status of all versions of the world. They are the universal repair kit of the real. Pollner's work has stimulated a range of empirical studies in a variety of settings, ranging from mental hospitals (Coulter, 1975) to a research community of biochemists (Gilbert and Mulkay 1984), and has strongly influenced the recent "discourse analysis" movement in social psychology.

Workplace Studies. In recent years, ethnomethodological research has been most prominently visible in social studies of science (Lynch 1995) and in studies of knowledge and action in the workplace (Button 1993). These studies are continuous with earlier investigations in that they examine the practical context and practical achievement of scientific and workplace activities. However they also radicalize earlier studies in their demonstrations of the practical contingencies that underly the production and use of "hard" scientific and technological findings just as much as they do more ephemeral cultural objects such as sketch maps (Garfinkel 1996, in press).

The workplace studies began with a focus on embodied courses of practical reasoning and action that are involved in the technically competent performance of work tasks that range from playing jazz (Sudnow 1978) to proving a mathematical theorem (Livingston 1986), laboratory work in brain science (Lynch 1985), or astronomical discovery (Lynch et al. 1983). Work in these fields was studied for the detailed texture of the shop-talk and workbench practices that comprise the recognizably competent performance of work tasks. A further focus on workplace studies has emerged from Lucy Suchman's (1987) pioneering study of human–machine communication. A very large body of ethnomethodological work has focused on a variety of aspects of machine-mediated observation and communication (for representative studies from a large corpus, see Button 1993, Luff et al. in press), as well as fundamental aspects of the relationship among computers, human action, and communication (Agre 1997; Button et al. 1995). Another set of studies addresses disciplinarily specific processes of representation in science (Lynch and Woolgar 1990), police work in courtroom testimony (Goodwin 1994), and historical events in the political context of congressional hearings (Lynch and Bogen 1996). Finally, a new body of work by Lynch and his collaborators (see Jordan and Lynch 1998) examines the nature and application of scientific techniques concerned with DNA sequencing in a variety of contexts, ranging from research and industrial to forensic contexts. This research explores the contigencies that support the stability and objectivity of these techniques in some contexts, while subverting them in others.

CONCLUSION

Since its emergence in the 1960s, ethnomethodology has developed as a complex set of research initiatives that have raised topic areas, problems, and issues for analysis where none were previously seen to exist or perceived to be relevant. A number of these initiatives have had a pronounced "deconstructive" dimension that has sometimes appeared iconoclastic or even nihilistic (Pollner 1991). Yet in its oscillation between constructive and deconstructive tendencies, ethnomethodology has been a significant site of theoretical and empirical innovation within sociology. It is exerting a continuing impact on the sensibility of the discipline. Finally, it has also had a wide ranging influence on a range of adjacent disciplines that are concerned with knowledge systems, communication, action, and practical reasoning

(SEE ALSO: *Conversation Analysis*)

REFERENCES

Agre, P. 1997. *Computation and Human Experience*. Cambridge, U.K.: Cambridge University Press.

Atkinson, J.M. 1978 *Discovering Suicide: Studies in the Social Organization of Sudden Death*. London: Macmillan.

Button, G., ed. 1993 *Technology in Working Order: Studies of Work, Interaction and Technology*. London: Routledge.

——, Jeff Coulter, John Lee, and Wesley Sharrock 1995 *Computers, Minds and Conduct*. Oxford: Blackwell.

Cicourel, A.V. 1968 *The Social Organization of Juvenile Justice*. New York: Wiley.

Coulter, J. 1975 "Perceptual Accounts and Interpretive Asymmetries." *Sociology* 9:385–396.

Douglas, J. 1967 *The Social Meanings of Suicide*. Princeton, N.J.: Princeton University Press.

Evans-Pritchard, E. E. 1937 *Witchcraft, Oracles and Magic Among the Azande*. Oxford: Oxford University Press.

Garfinkel, H. 1963 "A Conception of, and Experiments with, 'Trust' as a Condition of Stable Concerted Actions." In O. J. Harvey, ed., *Motivation and Social Interaction*. New York: Ronald Press.

—— 1967a *Studies in Ethnomethodology*. Englewood Cliffs, N.J.: Prentice Hall.

—— 1967b "Practical Sociological Reasoning: Some Features of the Work of the Los Angeles Suicide Prevention Center." In E. S. Schneidman, ed., *Essays in Self-Destruction*. New York: International Science Press.

—— 1996. "Ethnomethodology's Program." *Social Psychology Quarterly* 59(1):5–21.

—— in press. *A Catalogue of Ethnomethodological Investigations*, ed. Anne Warfield Rawls. Boston: Basil Blackwell.

——, M. Lynch, and E. Livingston 1981 "The Work of a Discovering Science Construed with Materials from the Optically Discovered Pulsar." *Philosophy of the Social Sciences* 11:131–158.

Gilbert, G. N., and M. Mulkay, 1984 *Opening Pandora's Box: A Sociological Analysis of Scientists' Discourse*. Cambridge, U.K.: Cambridge University Press.

Goodwin, C. 1994 "Professional Vision." *American Anthropologist* 96(3):606–633.

Gurwitsch, A. 1966 *Studies in Phenomenology and Psychology*. Evanston, IL: Northwestern University Press.

Heritage, J. 1984 *Garfinkel and Ethnomethodology*. Cambridge, Mass.: Polity Press.

Jordan, K. and M. Lynch 1998 "The Dissemination, Standardization and Routinization of a Molecular Biological Technique." *Social Studies of Science*, 28:773–800.

Livingston, E. 1986 *Ethnomethodological Foundations of Mathematics*. London: Routledge.

Luff, P., J. Hindmarsh, and C. Heath, eds., in press. *Workplace Studies: Recovering Work Practice and Informing System Design*. Cambridge, U.K.: Cambridge University Press.

Lynch, M. 1985 *Art and Artifact in Laboratory Science*. London: Routledge.

—— 1995 *Scientific Practice and Ordinary Action: Ethnomethodology and Social Studies of Science*. Cambridge, U.K.: Cambridge University Press.

——, and D. Bogen 1996 *The Spectacle of History: Speech, Text and Memory at the Iran–Contra Hearings*. Durham, N.C.: Duke University Press.

——, E. Livingston, and H. Garfinkel 1983 "Temporal Order in Laboratory Work." In K. Knorr-Cetina and M. Mulkay, eds., *Science Observed*. London: Sage.

——, and S. Woolgar, eds. 1990 *Representation in Scientific Practice*. Cambridge, Mass.: MIT Press.

Mills, C. W. 1940 "Situated Actions and Vocabularies of Motive." *American Sociological Review* 5:904–913.

Pollner, M. 1974 "Mundane Reasoning." *Philosophy of the Social Sciences* 4:35–54.

—— 1987 *Mundane Reason: Reality in Everyday and Sociological Discourse*. Cambridge, U.K.: Cambridge University Press.

—— 1991 "Left of Ethnomethodology," *American Sociological Review* 56:370–380.

Schutz, A. 1962 "Commonsense and Scientific Interpretation of Human Action." In A. Schutz, *Collected Papers: Vol. 1. The Problem of Social Reality*, ed. by M. Natanson. The Hague: Martinus Nijhoff.

——1962–1966 *Collected Papers*, 3 vol. The Hague: Matinus Nijhoff.

Suchman, L. 1987 *Plans and Situated Action*. Cambridge, U.K.: Cambridge University Press.

Sudnow, D. 1965 "Normal Crimes." *Social Problems* 12:255–276.

—— 1978 *Ways of the Hand*. Cambridge, Mass.: Harvard University Press.

Wieder, D. L. 1974 *Language and Social Reality*. The Hague: Mouton.

Zimmerman, D. 1969 "Record Keeping and the Intake Process in a Public Welfare Agency." In S. Wheeler, ed., *On Record: Files and Dossiers in American Life*. Beverly Hills, Calif.: Sage.

JOHN HERITAGE

EUTHANASIA

See Death and Dying.

EVALUATION RESEARCH

BRIEF HISTORY

There is no uniformly accepted definition of what constitutes evaluation research. At perhaps its narrowest point, the field of *evaluation research* can be defined as "the use of scientific methods to measure the implementation and outcomes of programs for decision-making purposes" (Rutman 1984, p. 10). A broader, and more widely accepted, definition is "the systematic application of social research procedures for assessing the conceptualization, design, implementation, and utility of social intervention programs" (Rossi and Freeman 1993, p. 5). A much broader definition is offered by Scriven (1991), who suggests that evaluation is "the process of determining the merit, worth and value of things" (p. 1). In the latter definition, the notion of what can be evaluated is not limited to a social program or specific type of intervention but encompasses, quite literally, everything.

Any description of the history of evaluation research depends on how the term is defined. Certainly, individuals have been making pronouncements about the relative worth of things since time immemorial. In the case of social programs, proficiency requirements to guide the selection of public officials using formal tests were recorded as early as 2200 B.C. in China (Guba and Lincoln 1981). Most observers, however, date the rise of evaluation research to the twentieth century. For example, programs in the 1930s established by the New Deal were viewed as great opportunities to implement social science methods to aid social planning by providing an accounting of program effects (Stephan, 1935). Modern evaluation research, however, underwent explosive growth in the 1960s as a result of several factors (Shadish et al. 1991). First, the total amount of social programming increased tremendously under the administrations of Presidents Kennedy, Johnson, and Nixon. New programs were directed toward social issues such as education, housing, health, crime, and income maintenance. Second, along with these huge financial investments came the concern by Congress about whether these programs were achieving their intended effect. As a result, Congress began mandating evaluations. Third, program managers were concerned whether programs were being implemented in the manner intended, and consequently data were required to monitor program operations. In addition, there were intellectual issues about how best to implement programs and the relative effectiveness of various approaches to offsetting various social ills. Outcome data were needed to compare competing approaches. The result was a burgeoning demand for trained evaluators; and the large number of scientists involved in the common enterprise of evaluation became sufficient to support the development of evaluation research as a scientific specialty area.

The field of evaluation research is no longer expanding at the rate it was in the 1960s and 1970s (Freeman 1992). By the 1980s, there was a substantial decline in the funding for evaluation activities that was motivated, in part, by the budget cuts of the Reagan administration. By then, however, the field of evaluation research had been established.

It continues to thrive for several reasons (Desautels 1997). First, difficult decisions are always required by public administrators and, in the face of continuing budget constraints, these decisions are often based on accountability for results. Second, an increasingly important aspect of service provision by both public and provide program managers is service quality. Monitoring quality requires information about program practices and outcomes. Third, there is growing public demand for accountability in government, a view increasingly echoed by government representatives. Meeting these demands requires measurement of results and a management system that uses evaluation for strategic planning and tactical decision making.

Early in its history, evaluation was seen primarily as a tool of the political left (Freeman 1992). Clearly, that is no longer the case. Evaluation activities have demonstrated their utility to both conservatives and liberals. Although the programs of today may be different from those launched in the 1960s, evaluation studies are more pervasive than ever. As long as difficult decisions need to be made by administrators serving a public that is demanding ever-increasing levels of quality and accountability, there will be a growing market for evaluation research.

PURPOSES OF EVALUATION RESEARCH

A wide variety of activities are subsumed under the broad rubric of "evaluation research." This diversity proceeds from the multiplicity of purposes underlying evaluation activities. Chelimsky (1997) identifies three different purposes of evaluation: evaluation for accountability, evaluation for development, and evaluation for knowledge.

Accountability. From the perspective of auditors and funding agencies, evaluations are necessary to establish accountability. Evaluations of this type frequently attempt to answer the question of whether the program or policy "worked" or whether anything changed as a result. The conceptual distinction between program and policy evaluations is a subtle but important one (Sonnad and Borgatta 1992). Programs are usually characterized by specific descriptions of what is to be done, how it is to be done, and what is to be accomplished. Policies are broader statements of objectives than programs, with greater latitude in how they are implemented and with potentially more diverse outcomes. Questions addressed by either program or policy evaluations from an accountability standpoint are usually cause-and-effect questions requiring research methodology appropriate to such questions (e.g., experiments or quasi-experiments). Studies of this type are often referred to as summative evaluations (Scriven 1991) or impact assessments (Rossi and Freeman 1993). Although the term "outcome" evaluation is frequently used when the focus of the evaluation is on accountability, this term is less precise, since all evaluations, whether conducted for reasons of accountability, development, or knowledge, yield outcomes of some kind (Scriven 1991).

Development. Evaluation for development is usually conducted to improve institutional performance. Developmental evaluations received heightened importance as a result of public pressure during the 1980s and early 1990s for public management reforms based on notions such as "total quality management" and "reinventing government" (e.g., see Gore 1993). Developmental evaluations often address questions such as: How can management performance or organizational performance be improved? What data systems are necessary to monitor program accomplishment? What are appropriate indicators of program success and what are appropriate organizational goals? Studies designed primarily to improve programs or the delivery of a product or service are sometimes referred to as formative or process evaluations (Scriven 1991). In such studies, the focus is on the treatment rather than its outcomes. Depending on the specific question being addressed, methodology may include experiments, quasi-experiments, or case studies. Data may be quantitative or qualitative. Formative or process evaluations may be sufficient by themselves if a strong relationship is known to exist between the treatment and its outcomes. In other cases, they may be accompanied by summative evaluations as well.

Knowledge. In evaluation for knowledge, the focus of the research is on improving our understanding of the etiology of social problems and on detailing the logic of how specific programs or policies can ameliorate them. Just as evaluation for accountability is of greatest interest to funding or oversight agencies, and evaluation for performance is most useful to program administrators, evaluation for knowledge is frequently of greatest interest to researchers, program designers, and evaluators themselves. Questions might include such things as the causes of crime, homelessness, or voter apathy. Since these are largely cause-and-effect questions, rigorous research designs appropriate to such questions are generally required.

CONTEMPORARY ISSUES IN EVALUATION

Utilization of Findings. Implicit in the enterprise of evaluation research is the belief that the findings from evaluation studies will be utilized by policy makers to shape their decisions. Indeed, such a view was espoused explicitly by Campbell (1969), who argued that social reforms should be regarded as social experiments and that the findings concerning program effectiveness should determine which programs to retain and which to discard. This process of rational decision making, however, has not been consistently embraced by policy makers and has been a source of concern and disillusionment for many evaluators. Rossi (1994) sums up the situation by noting:

> Although some of us may have entertained hopes that in the "experimenting society" the experimenter was going to be king, that delusion, however grand, did not last for long. It often seemed that programs had robust lives of their own, appearing, continuing, and disappearing following some unknown processes that did not appear responsive to evaluations and their outcomes. (p. 26)

One source of the utilization problem, as Weiss (1975, 1987) has noted, is the fact that evaluations take place in a political context. Although accomplishing its stated objectives is important to program success, it may not be the only—or even the most important—measure of program success. From this perspective, it is not that administrators and policy makers are irrational—they simply use a different model of rationality than do evaluators. Indeed, the view of policy makers and program administrators may be more "rational" than that of evaluators because it has been shown repeatedly that programs can and do survive negative evaluations. Programs are less likely, however, to survive a hostile congressional committee, negative press, or lack of public support. There are generally multiple stakeholders, often with competing interests, associated with any large program. Negative findings are of very little use to individuals whose reputations and jobs are dependent on program success. Thus, rather than bemoaning a lack of utilization of findings, evaluators need to recognize that evaluation findings represent only one piece of a complex political process.

Evaluators concerned with utilization frequently make a distinction between the immediate or instrumental use of findings to make direct policy decisions versus the conceptual use of findings, which serves primarily to enlighten decision makers and perhaps influence later decision making (Leviton and Hughes 1981). In a related vein, Scriven (1993) makes an important distinction between "lack of implementation" and "lack of utilization." Lack of implementation merely refers to a failure to implement recommendations. In contrast, utilization is more ambiguous. It is often not clear what outcomes or actions actually constitute a utilization of findings. Evaluation findings can have great utility but may not necessarily lead to a particular behavior. For example, a consumer can read an evaluation of a product in a publication such as *Consumer Reports* and then decide not to buy the product. Although the evaluation did not lead to a particular behavior (i.e., purchasing the product), it was nonetheless extremely useful to the consumer, and the information can be said to have been utilized. Some observers have noted that the concern about underutilization of evaluation findings belies what is actually happening in the field of evaluation research. Chelimsky and Shadish (1997) provide numerous examples of how evaluation findings have had substantial impacts on policy and decision making, not only in government but also in the private sector, and not only in the United States but internationally as well.

Quantitative Versus Qualitative Research. The rise of evaluation research in the 1960s began with a decidedly quantitative stance. In an early, influential book, Suchman (1967) unambiguously defined *evaluation research* as "the utilization of scientific research methods and techniques" (p. 7) and cited a recent book by Campbell and Stanley (1963) on experimental and quasi-experimental designs as providing instruction on the appropriate methodology. It was not long, however, before the dominance of quantitative methods in evaluation research came under attack. Cook (1997) identifies two reasons. First, there has been a longstanding debate, especially in sociology, over the merits of qualitative research and the limits of quantitative methods. Sociologists brought the debate with

them when they entered the field of evaluation. Second, evaluation researchers, even those trained primarily in quantitative methods, began to recognize the epistemological limitations of the quantitative approach (e.g., Guba and Lincoln 1981). There were also practical reasons to turn toward qualitative methods. For example, Weiss (1987) noted that quantitative outcome measures are frequently too insensitive to detect program effects. Also, the expected time lag between treatment implementation and any observed outcomes is frequently unknown, with program effects often taking years to emerge. Moreover, due to limited budgets, time constraints, program attrition, multiple outcomes, multiple program sites, and other difficulties associated with applied research, quantitative field studies rarely achieved the potential they exuded on the drawing board. As a result, Weiss recommended supplementing quantitative with qualitative methods.

Focus on the quantitative–qualitative debate in evaluation research was sharpened when successive presidents of the American Evaluation Association expressed differing views on the matter. On the qualitative side, it was suggested that the focus on rigor associated with quantitative evaluations may have blinded evaluators to "artistic aspects" of the evaluation process that have traditionally been unrecognized or simply ignored. The time had come "to move beyond cost benefit analyses and objective achievement measures to interpretive realms" in the conduct of evaluation studies (Lincoln 1991, p. 6). From the quantitative perspective, it was acknowledged that while it is true that evaluations have frequently failed to produce strong empirical support for many attractive programs, to blame that failure on quantitative evaluations is akin to shooting the messenger. Moreover, at a time when research and statistical methods (e.g., regression discontinuity designs, structural equations with latent variables, etc.) were finally catching up to the complexities of contemporary research questions, it would be a shame to abandon the quantitative approach (Sechrest 1992). The ensuing controversy only served to polarize the two camps further.

The debate over which approach is best, quantitative or qualitative, is presently unresolved and, most likely, will remain so. Each paradigm has different strengths and weaknesses. As Cook (1997) points out, quantitative methods are good for generalizing and describing causal relationships. In contrast, qualitative methods are well suited for exploring program processes. Ironically, it is the very differences between the two approaches that may ultimately resolve the issue because, to the extent that their limitations differ, the two methods used jointly will generally be better than either used singly (Reichardt and Rallis 1994).

Research Synthesis. Evaluation research, as it was practiced in the 1960s and 1970s, drew heavily on the experimental model. The work of Donald Campbell was very influential in this regard. Although he is very well known for his explication of quasi-experimental research designs (Campbell and Stanley 1963; Cook and Campbell 1979), much of his work actually de-emphasized quasi-experimentation in favor of experiments (Shadish et al. 1991). Campbell pointed out that quasi-experiments frequently lead to ambiguous causal inferences, sometimes with dire consequences (Campbell and Erlebacher 1970). In addition, he noted that experiments have wide applicability, even in applied settings where random assignment may not initially seem feasible (Campbell and Boruch 1975). Campbell also advocated implementing such rigorous methods in the evaluation of social programs (Campbell 1969). As a result, Campbell is frequently credited with proposing a rational model of social reform in which a program is first evaluated using rigorous social science methods, such as experiments, when possible, and then a report is issued to a decision maker who acts on the findings.

Whatever its source, it was not long before the rational model was criticized as being too narrow to serve as a template for evaluation research. In particular, Cronbach and colleagues (Cronbach et al. 1980) argued that evaluation is as much a political process as a scientific one, that decisions are rarely made but more likely emerge, that there is rarely a single decision maker, and that programs are often amorphous undertakings with no single outcome. From Cronbach's perspective, the notion that the outcome of a single study could influence the existence of a program is inconsistent with the political realities of most programs.

Understanding the ensuing controversy requires an understanding of the notion of validity. Campbell distinguished between two types of validity: internal and external (Campbell 1957; Campbell and Stanley 1963). Internal validity refers to whether the innovation or treatment has an effect. In contrast, external validity addresses the issue of generalizability of effects; specifically, "To what populations, settings, treatment variables, and measurement variables can this effect be generalized" (Campbell and Stanley 1963, p. 5). Campbell clearly assigned greater importance to internal validity than to external validity. Of what use is it, he asked, to generalize experimental outcomes to some population if one has doubts about the very existence of the relationship that one seeks to generalize (Shadish et al. 1991)? Campbell's emphasis on internal validity was clearly consistent with his focus on experiments, since the latter are particularly useful in examining causal relationships.

In contrast, Cronbach (1982) opposed the emphasis on internal validity that had so profoundly shaped the approach to evaluation research throughout the 1960s and 1970s. Although experiments have high internal validity, they tend to be weak in external validity; and, according to Cronbach, it is external validity that is of greatest utility in evaluation studies. That is, decision makers are rarely interested in the impact of a particular treatment on a unique set of subjects in a highly specific experimental setting. Instead, they want to know whether a program or treatment, which may not always be administered in exactly the same way from agency to agency, will have an effect if it is administered on other individuals, and in other settings, from those studied in the experimental situation. From Cronbach's perspective, the rational model of evaluation research based on rigorous social research procedures is a flawed model because there are no reliable methods for generalizing beyond the factors that have been studied in the first place and it is the generalized rather than the specific findings in which evaluators are interested. As a result, Cronbach viewed evaluation as more of an art than a scientific enterprise.

The debate over which has priority in evaluation research, internal or external validity, seems to have been resolved in the increasing popularity of research syntheses. Evaluation syntheses represent a meta-analytic technique in which research results from numerous independent evaluation studies are first converted to a common metric and then aggregated using a variety of statistical techniques. The product is a meaningful summary of the collective results of many individual studies. Research synthesis based on meta-analysis has helped to resolve the debate over the priority of internal versus external validity in that, if studies with rigorous designs are used, results will be internally valid. Moreover, by drawing on findings from many different samples, in many different settings, using many different outcome measures, the robustness of findings and generalizability can be evaluated as well.

Although meta-analysis has many strengths, including increased power relative to individual studies to detect treatment effects, the results are obviously limited by the quality of the original studies. The major drawback to meta-analysis, then, deals with repeating or failing to compensate for the limitations inherent in the original research on which the syntheses are based (Figueredo 1993). Since many evaluations use nonexperimental designs, these methodological limitations can be considerable, although they potentially exist in experiments as well (e.g., a large proportion of experiments suffer from low external validity).

An emerging theory underlying research syntheses of experimental and nonexperimental studies, referred to as critical multiplism (Shadish 1993) and based on Campbell and Fiske's (1959) notion of multiple operationalism, addresses these issues directly. "Multiplism" refers to the fact that there are multiple ways of proceeding in any research endeavor, with no single way being uniformly superior to all others. That is, every study will involve specific operationalizations of causes and effects that necessarily underrepresent the potential range of relevant components in the presumed causal process while introducing irrelevancies unique to the particular study (Cook 1993). For example, a persuasive communication may be intended to change attitudes about an issue. In a study to evaluate this resumed cause-and-effect relationship, the communication may be presented via television and attitudes may be assessed using paper-and-pencil inventory. Clearly, the medium used underrepresents the range of potential persuasive techniques (e.g., radio or newspapers might have been used) and the paper-and-pencil task introduces irrelevancies that, from a measurement perspective, constitute sources of error. The term "critical" refers to the attempt to identify biases in the research approach chosen. The logic, then, of critical multiplism is to synthesize the results of studies that are heterogeneous with

respect to sources of bias and to avoid any constant biases. In this manner, meta-analytic techniques can be used to implement critical multiplist ideas, thereby increasing our confidence in the generalizability of evaluation findings.

The increasing use of research syntheses represents one of the most important changes in the field of evaluation during the past twenty-five years (Cook 1997). Research synthesis functions in the service of increasing both internal and external validity. Although it may seem that the use of research syntheses is a far cry from Campbell's notion of an experimenting society, in reality Campbell never really suggested that a single study might resolve an important social issue. In "Reforms as Experiments" (1969) Campbell states:

> Too many social scientists expect single experiments to settle issues once and for all. . . . Because we social scientists have less ability to achieve "experimental isolation," because we have good reason to expect our treatment effects to interact significantly with a wide variety of social factors many of which we have not yet mapped, we have much greater needs for replication experiments than do the physical sciences. (pp. 427–428)

Ironically, perhaps, the increasing use of research syntheses in evaluation research is perfectly consistent with Campbell's original vision of an experimenting society.

DIRECTIONS FOR THE FUTURE

The field of evaluation research has undergone a professionalization since the early 1970s. Today, the field of evaluation research is characterized by its own national organization (the American Evaluation Association), journals, and professional standards. The field continues to evolve as practitioners continue the debate over exactly what constitutes evaluation research, how it should be conducted, and who should do it. In this regard, Shadish and colleagues (1991) make a compelling argument that the integration of the field will ultimately depend on the continued development of comprehensive theories that are capable of integrating the diverse activities and procedures traditionally subsumed under the broad rubric of evaluation research. In particular, they identify a number of basic issues that any theory of evaluation must address in order to integrate the practice of evaluation research. These remaining issues include knowledge construction, the nature of social programming and knowledge use, the role of values, and the practice of evaluation.

Knowledge Construction. A persisting issue in the field of evaluation concerns the nature of the knowledge that should emerge as a product from program evaluations. Issues of epistemology and research methods are particularly germane in this regard. For example, the controversy over whether quantitative approaches to the generation of knowledge are superior to qualitative methods, or whether any method can be consistently superior to another regardless of the purpose of the evaluation, is really an issue of knowledge construction. Other examples include whether knowledge about program outcomes is more important than knowledge concerning program processes, or whether knowledge about how programs effects occur is more important than describing and documenting those effects. Future theories of evaluation must address questions such as which types of knowledge have priority in evaluation research, under what conditions various knowledge-generation strategies (e.g., experiments, quasi-experiments, case studies, or participatory evaluation) might be used, and who should decide (e.g., evaluators or stakeholders). By so doing, the field will become more unified, characterized by common purpose rather than by competing methodologies and philosophies.

Social Programming and Knowledge Use. The ostensible purpose of evaluation lies in the belief that problems can be ameliorated by improving the programs or strategies designed to address those problems. Thus, a social problem might be remediated by improving an existing program or by getting rid of an ineffective program and replacing it with a different one. The history of evaluation research, however, has demonstrated repeatedly how difficult it is to impact social programming. Early evaluators from academia were, perhaps, naive in this regard. Social programs are highly resist to change processes because there are generally multiple stakeholders, each with a vested interest in the program and with their own constituencies to support. Complicating the matter is the fact that knowledge is used in different ways in different circumstances. Several important distinctions concerning knowledge use

can be made: (1) use in the short term versus use in the long term, (2) information for instrumental use in making direct decisions versus information intended for enlightenment or persuasion, and (3) lack of implementation of findings versus lack of utilization of findings. These different types of use progress at different rates and in different ways. Consequently, any resulting program changes are likely to appear slow and sporadic. But the extent to which such change processes should represent a source of disappointment and frustration for evaluators requires further clarification. Specifically, theories of evaluation are needed that take into account the complexities of social programming in modern societies, that delineate appropriate strategies for change in differing contexts, and that elucidate the relevance of evaluation findings for decision makers and change agents.

Values. Some evaluators, especially in the early history of the field, believed that evaluation should be conducted as a value-free process. The value-free doctrine was imported from the social sciences by early evaluators who brought it along as a by-product of their methodological training. This view proved to be problematic because evaluation is an intrinsically value-laden process in which the ultimate goal is to make a pronouncement about the value of something. As Scriven (1993) has cogently argued, the values-free model of evaluation is also wrong. As proof, he notes that statements such as "evaluative conclusions cannot be established by any legitimate scientific process" are clearly self-refuting because they are themselves evaluative statements. If evaluators cling to a values-free philosophy, then the inevitable and necessary application of values in evaluation research can only be done indirectly, by incorporating the values of other persons who might be connected with the programs, such as program administrators, program users, or other stakeholders (Scriven 1991). Obviously, evaluators will do a better job if they are able to consider explicitly values-laden questions such as: On what social values is this intervention based? What values does it foster? What values does it harm? How should merit be judged? Who decides? As Shadish and colleagues (1991) point out, evaluations are often controversial and explosive enterprises in the first place and debates about values only make them more so. Perhaps that is why values theory has gotten short shrift in the past. Clearly, however, future theory needs to address the issue of values, acknowledging and clarifying their central role in evaluation research.

The Practice of Evaluation. Evaluation research is an extremely applied activity. In the end, evaluation theory has relevance only to the extent that it influences the actual practice of evaluation research. Any theory of evaluation practice must necessarily draw on all the aforementioned issues (i.e., knowledge construction, social programming and information use, and values), since they all have direct implications for practice. In addition, there are pragmatic issues that directly affect the conduct of evaluation research. One important contemporary issue examines the relationship between the evaluator and individuals associated with the program. For example, participatory evaluation is a controversial approach to evaluation research that favors collaboration between evaluation researchers and individuals who have some stake in the program under evaluation. The core assumption of participatory evaluation is that, by involving stakeholders, ownership of the evaluation will be shared, the findings will be more relevant to interested parties, and the outcomes are then more likely to be utilized (Cousins and Whitmore 1998). From an opposing perspective, participatory evaluation is inconsistent with the notion that the investigator should remain detached from the object of investigation in order to remain objective and impartial. Not surprisingly, the appropriateness of participatory evaluation is still being debated.

Other aspects of practice are equally controversial and require clarification as well. For example: Who is qualified to conduct an evaluation? How should professional evaluators be trained and by whom? Should evaluators be licensed? Without doubt, the field of evaluation research has reached a level of maturity where such questions warrant serious consideration and their answers will ultimately determine the future course of the field.

REFERENCES

Campbell, Donald 1957 "Factors Relevant to the Validity of Experiments in Social Settings." *Psychological Bulletin* 54: 297–312.

—— 1969 "Reforms as Experiments." *American Psychologist* 24:409–429.

——, and Robert Boruch 1975 "Making the Case for Randomized Assignment to Treatments by Considering the Alternatives: Six Ways in Which Quasi-Experimental Evaluations in Compensatory Education Tend to Underestimate Effects." In C. Bennett and A. Lumsdaine, eds., *Evaluation and Experiments: Some Critical Issues in Assessing Social Programs*. New York: Academic Press.

——, and Albert Erlebacher 1970 "How Regression Artifacts Can Mistakenly Make Compensatory Education Programs Look Harmful." In J. Hellmuth, ed., *The Disadvantaged Child: vol. 3. Compensatory Education: A National Debate*. New York: Brunner/Mazel.

——, and Donald Fiske 1959 "Convergent and Discriminant Validity by the Multitrait–Multimethod Matrix." *Psychological Bulletin* 56:81–105.

——, and Julian Stanley 1963 *Experimental and Quasi-Experimental Designs for Research*. Chicago: Rand McNally.

Chelimsky, Eleanor 1997 "The Coming Transformations in Evaluation." In E. Chelimsky and W. Shadish, eds., *Evaluation for the Twenty-first Century*. Thousand Oaks, Calif.: Sage.

——, and William Shadish 1997 *Evaluation for the Twenty-first Century*. Thousand Oaks, Calif.: Sage.

Cook, Thomas 1993 "A Quasi-Sampling Theory of the Generalization of Causal Relationships." In L. Sechrest and A. Scott, eds., *Understanding Causes and Generalizing About Them* (New Directions for Program Evaluation, No. 57). San Francisco: Jossey-Bass.

—— 1997 "Lessons Learned in Evaluation over the Past 25 Years. "In Eleanor Chelimsky and William Shadish, eds., *Evaluation for the Twenty-first Century*. Thousand Oaks, Calif.: Sage.

——, and Donald Campbell 1979 *Quasi-Experimentation: Design and Analysis Issues for Field Settings*. Chicago: Rand McNally.

Cousins, J. Bradley, and Elizabeth Whitmore 1998 "Framing Participatory Evaluation." In Elizabeth Whitmore, ed., *Understanding and Practicing Participatory Evaluation* (New Directions for Evaluation, No. 80). San Francisco: Jossey-Bass.

Cronbach, Lee 1982 *Designing Evaluations of Educational and Social Programs*. San Francisco: Jossey-Bass.

——, Sueann Ambron, Sanford Dornbusch, Robert Hess, Robert Hornik, D. C. Phillips, Decker Walker, and Stephen Weiner 1980 *Toward Reform of Program Evaluation*. San Francisco: Jossey-Bass.

Desautels, L. Denis 1997 "Evaluation as an Essential Component of 'Value-for-Money.'" In Eleanor

Clemimsky and William R. Shadish, eds., *Evaluation for the Twenty-first Century*. Thousand Oaks, Calif.: Sage.

Figueredo, Aurelio 1993 "Critical Multiplism, Meta-Analysis, and Generalization: An Integrative Commentary. "In L. Sechrest, ed., *Program Evaluation: A Pluralistic Enterprise* (New Directions for Program Evaluation, No. 60). San Francisco: Jossey-Bass.

Freeman, Howard 1992 "Evaluation Research." In E. Borgatta and M. Borgatta, eds., *Encyclopedia of Sociology*. New York: Macmillan.

Gore, Albert 1993 *From Red Tape to Results: Creating a Government That Works Better and Costs Less*. New York: Plume/Penguin.

Guba, Egon, and Yvonna Lincoln 1981 *Effective Evaluation*. San Francisco: Jossey-Bass.

Leviton, Laura, and Edward Hughes 1981 "Research on the Utilization of Evaluations: A Review and Synthesis." *Evaluation Review* 5:525–548.

Lincoln, Yvonna 1991 "The Arts and Sciences of Program Evaluation." *Evaluation Practice* 12:1–7.

Reichardt, Charles, and Sharon Rallis 1994 "The Relationship Between the Qualitative and Quantitative Research Traditions." In Charles Reichardt and Sharon Rallis, eds., (New Directions for Program Evaluation, No. 61). San Francisco: Jossey-Bass.

Rossi, Peter 1994 The War Between the Quals and the Quants. Is a Lasting Peace Possible? In Charles Reichardt and Sharon Rallis, eds., *The Qualitative–Quantitative Debate: New Perspectives* (New Directions for Program Evaluation, No. 61). San Francisco: Jossey-Bass.

——, and Howard E. Freeman 1993 *Evaluation*, fifth ed. Newbury Park, Calif.: Sage.

Rutman, Leonard 1984 *Evaluation Research Methods*. Newbury Park, Calif.: Sage.

Scriven, Michael 1991 *Evaluation Thesaurus*, fourth ed. Newbury Park, Calif.: Sage.

—— 1993 *Hard-Won Lessons in Program Evaluation* (New Directions for Program Evaluation, No. 58). San Francisco: Jossey-Bass.

Sechrest, Lee 1992 "Roots: Back to Our First Generations." *Evaluation Practice* 13:1–7.

Shadish, William 1993 "Critical Multiplism: A Research Strategy and Its Attendant Tactics." In L. Sechrest, ed., *Program Evaluation: A Pluralistic Enterprise* (New Directions for Program Evaluation, No. 60). San Francisco: Jossey-Bass.

——, Thomas Cook, and Laura Leviton 1991 *Foundations of Program Evaluation: Theories of Practice*. Newbury Park, Calif.: Sage.

Sonnad, Subhash, and Edgar Borgatta 1992 "Evaluation Research and Social Gerontology." *Research on Aging* 14:267–280.

Stephan, A. Stephen 1935 "Prospects and Possibilities: The New Deal and the New Social Research." *Social Forces* 13:515–521.

Suchman, Edward 1967 *Evaluative Research: Principles and Practice in Public Service and Social Action Programs*. New York: Russell Sage Foundation.

Weiss, Carol 1975 "Evaluation Research in the Political Context." In Marcia Guttentag and Elmer Struenning, eds., *Handbook of Evaluation Research*, vol. 1. Beverly Hills, Calif.: Sage.

—— 1987 "Evaluating Social Programs: What Have We Learned?" *Society* 25:40–45.

KARL KOSLOSKI

EVENT HISTORY ANALYSIS

Event history analysis is a collection of statistical methods for the analysis of longitudinal data on the occurrence and timing of events. As used in sociology, event history analysis is very similar to linear or logistic regression analysis, except that the dependent variable is a measure of the likelihood or speed of event occurrence. As with other regression methods, event history analysis is often used to develop causal or predictive models for the occurrence of events. Event history analysis has become quite popular in sociology since the mid 1980s, with applications to such diverse events as divorces (Bennett et al. 1988), births (Kallan and Udry 1986), deaths (Moore and Hayward 1990), job changes (Carroll and Mayer 1986), organizational foundings (Halliday et al. 1987), migrations (Baydar et al. 1990), and friendship choices (Hallinan and Williams 1987).

Although event history methods have been developed and utilized by statistical practitioners in a variety of disciplines, the term *event history analysis* is primarily used in sociology and closely allied disciplines. Elsewhere the methodology is known as survival analysis (biology and medicine), failure-time analysis (engineering), or duration analysis (economics). Introductory treatments for social scientists can be found in Teachman (1983), Allison (1984, 1995), Tuma and Hannan (1984), Kiefer (1988), and Blossfeld and Rohwer (1995).

For a biostatistical point of view, see Collett (1994), Kleinbaum (1996), or Klein and Moeschberger (1997).

EVENT HISTORY DATA

The first requirement for an event history analysis is event history data. An event history is simply a longitudinal record of when events occurred for an individual or a sample of individuals. For example, an event history might be constructed by asking a sample of people to report the dates of any past changes in marital status. If the goal is a causal analysis, the event history should also include information on explanatory variables. Some of these, such as race and gender, will be constant over time while others, such as income, will vary. If the timing of each event is known with considerable precision (as with exact dates of marriages), the data are called continuous-time data. Frequently, however, events are only known to have occurred within some relatively large interval of time, for example, the year of a marriage. Such data are referred to as discrete-time data or grouped data.

Event history data are often contrasted with panel data, in which the individual's status is known only at a set of regular, fixed points in time. For example, employment status and other variables may be measured in annual interviews. Panel data collected at frequent intervals can often be treated as discrete-time event history data. But if the intervals between data collections are long, one of the major attractions of event history analysis can be lost—the ability to disentangle causal ordering. While this capability is by no means unequivocal, the combination of event history data and event history analysis is perhaps the best available nonexperimental methodology for studying causal relationships.

PROBLEMS WITH CONVENTIONAL METHODS

Despite the attractiveness of event history data, they typically possess two characteristics that make conventional statistical methods highly unsuitable. Censoring is the most common problem. Suppose, for example, that the aim is to study the causes of divorce. The sample might consist of a number of couples who married in 1990 and who are followed for the next five years. For the couples who get divorced, the length of the marriage is the principal variable of interest. But a large fraction of the couples will not divorce during the five-year interval. Marriages that are still in progress when the study ends are said to be *censored*. The problem is to combine the data on timing with the data on occurrence in a statistically consistent fashion. Ad hoc methods, such as excluding the censored cases or assigning the maximum length of time observed, can lead to substantial biases or loss of precision.

The second problem is time-varying explanatory variables (also known as time-dependent covariates). Suppose, in our divorce example, that the researcher wants to include number of children as a predictor of divorce. But number of children may change over the marriage, and it is not obvious how such a variable should be included in a regression model. If there were no censored cases, one might be tempted to regress the length of the marriage on the number of children at the end of the marriage. But longer marriages are likely to have produced more children simply because more time is available to have them. This would produce a spurious positive relationship between number of children and the length of the marriage.

One method for dealing with the censoring problem has been around since the seventeenth century and is still widely used—the *life table*. The life table is one example of a variety of methods that are primarily concerned with estimating the *distribution* of event times without regard for the effects of explanatory variables. For a comprehensive survey of such methods, see Elandt-Johnson and Johnson (1980). The remainder of this article focuses on regression methods that estimate the effects of explanatory variables on the occurrence and timing of events.

ACCELERATED FAILURE-TIME MODELS

Suppose the goal is to estimate a model predicting the timing of first marriages, and the sample consists of women who are interviewed at age twenty-five. For each woman ($i=1,\ldots,n$), we learn her age in days at the time of the marriage, denoted by T_i.

For women who still were not married at age twenty-five (the censored cases), T_i^* is their age in days at the time of the interview. We also have data on a set of explanatory variables $x_{i1}, \ldots, x_{i1}$. For the moment, let us suppose that these are variables that do not change over time, such as race, parents' education, and eighth-grade test scores.

One class of models that is appropriate for data such as these is the accelerated failure-time (AFT) model. The general formulation is

$$\log T_i = \beta_0 + \beta_1 x_{i1} + \ldots + \beta_2 x_{i2} + \varepsilon_i \qquad (1)$$

By taking the logarithm on the left-hand side, we ensure that T_i is always greater than 0, regardless of the values of the x variables. Specific cases of this general model are obtained by choosing particular distributions for the random disturbance ε_i. The most common distributions are normal, extreme-value, logistic, and log-gamma. These imply that T_i has distributions that are, respectively, lognormal, Weibull, log-logistic, and gamma, which are the names usually given to these models. The disturbance term ε_i is assumed to be independent of the x's and to have constant variance.

If there are no censored data, these models can be easily estimated by ordinary least-squares regression of log T on the x's. The resulting coefficients are best linear unbiased estimators. But the presence of censored data requires a different method. The standard approach is maximum likelihood, which combines the censored and uncensored data in an optimal fashion. Maximum likelihood estimation for these models is now widely available in several statistical packages (e.g., BMDP, LIMDEP, SAS, SYSTAT, Stata).

Here's an example from criminology. In the early 1970s, 432 inmates from Maryland state prisons were followed for one year after their release (Rossi et al. 1980). The event of interest is the first arrest that occurred to each person during the one-year observation period. Only 26 percent of the released inmates were arrested. We'll use the following variables:

ARREST   1 if arrested, otherwise 0

WEEK   Week of first arrest for those who were arrested (ranges 1 to 52); for those not arrested, week 52

FIN   1 if they received financial aid after release, otherwise 0

AGE   Age in years at the time of release

RACE   1 if black, otherwise 0

MAR   1 if married at the time of release, otherwise 0

PRIO   Number of prior convictions

Using these data, I estimated a Weibull version of the accelerated failure time model by maximum likelihood with the SAS® statistical package. Results are shown in Table 1. Looking first at the p-values, we see that race and marital status do not have a significant impact on the timing of arrests. On the other hand, we see highly significant effects of age and number of prior convictions, and a just barely significant effect of financial aid.

The negative coefficient for PRIO tells us that having more prior convictions is associated with *shorter* times to arrest. The positive coefficient for AGE tells us that inmates who were older when they released have *longer* times to arrest. Similarly, those who got financial aid have longer times to arrest. We can interpret the magnitudes of the coefficients by applying the transformation $100[\exp(\beta)-1]$, which gives the percentage change in time to event for a 1-unit increase in a particular independent variable. For PRIO we get $100[\exp(-.071)-1]=-6.8$, which tells us that each additional conviction lowers the time to arrest by 6.8 percent, controlling for other variables in the model. For FIN we get $100[\exp(.268)-1]=31$. Those who got financial aid have times to arrest that are 31 percent longer than those who did not get financial aid.

In addition to the Weibull model, I also estimated gamma, lognormal, and log-logistic models. Results were very similar across the different models.

PROPORTIONAL HAZARDS MODELS

A second class of regression models for continuous-time data is the proportional hazards model. To explain this model, it is first necessary to define the hazard function, denoted by $h(t)$, which is the fundamental dependent variable. Let $P(t+\Delta t)$ be the conditional probability that an event occurs in the time interval $(t+\Delta t)$, given that it has not already

Results from Weibull Regression Model Predicting the Time of First Arrest

Variable	Coefficient	Standard Error	Chi-Square	*p*-value
FIN	.268	.137	3.79	.05
AGE	.043	.015	8.00	.004
RACE	-.226	.220	1.06	.30
MAR	.353	.269	1.73	.19
PRIO	-.071	.020	12.85	.0003
Intercept	4.037	.402		

Table 1

occurred prior to t. To get the hazard function, we divide this probability by the length of the interval Δt, and take the limit as Δt goes to 0:

$$h(t) = \lim_{\Delta t \to 0} \frac{P(t, t + \Delta t)}{\Delta t} \qquad (2)$$

Other common symbols for the hazard function are $r(t)$ and $\lambda(t)$. The hazard may be regarded as the instantaneous likelihood that an event will occur at exactly time t. It is not a probability, however, since it may be greater than 1.0 (although never less than 0).

If $h(t)$ has a constant value c, it can be interpreted as the expected number of events in a 1-unit interval of time. Alternatively, $1/c$ is the expected length of time until the next event. Suppose, for example, that the events are residence changes, time is measured in years, and the estimated hazard of a residence change is .20. That would imply that, for a given individual, the expected number of changes in a year is .20 and the expected length of time between changes is $1/.20$ = 5 years.

Like a probability (from which it is derived), the hazard is never directly observed. Nevertheless, it governs both the occurrence and timing of events, and models formulated in terms of the hazard may be estimated from observed data.

The general proportional hazards (PH) model is given by

$$\log h_i(t) = \alpha(t) + \beta_1 x_{i1} + \ldots + \beta_k x_{ik} \qquad (3)$$

where $\alpha(t)$ may be any function of time. It is called the proportional hazards model because the ratio of the hazards for any two individuals is a constant over time. Notice that, unlike the AFT model,

there is no disturbance term in this equation. That does not mean that the model is deterministic, however, because there is random variation in the relationship between $h(t)$ and the observed occurrence and timing of events.

Different versions of the PH model are obtained by choosing specific forms for $\alpha(t)$. For example, the Gompertz model sets $\alpha(t) = \alpha_i + \alpha_2 t$, which says that the hazard is an increasing (or decreasing) function of time. Similarly, the Weibull model has $\alpha(t) = \alpha_i + \alpha_2 \log t$. (The Weibull model is the only model that is a member of both the AFT class and the PH class.) The exponential model—a special case of both the Weibull and the Gompertz models—sets $\alpha(t) = \alpha$, a constant over time. For any specific member of the PH class, maximum likelihood is the standard approach to estimation.

In a path-breaking paper, the British statistician David Cox (1972) showed how the PH model could be estimated without choosing a specific functional form for $\alpha(t)$, using a method called partial likelihood. This method is very much like maximum likelihood, except that only a part of the likelihood function is maximized. Specifically, partial likelihood takes account only of the ordering of events, not their exact timing. The combination of partial likelihood and the proportional hazards model has come to be known as Cox regression. The method has become extremely popular because, although some precision is sacrificed, the resulting estimates are much more robust. Computer programs that implement this method are now available in most full-featured statistical packages (SPSS, SAS, LIMDEP, BMDP, S-Plus, Stata, SYSTAT).

As an example, we'll estimate a proportional hazards model for the recidivism data discussed

Results from Cox Regression Model Predicting the Hazard of First Arrest

Variable	Coefficient	Standard Error	Chi-Square	*p*-value
FIN	-.373	.191	3.82	.05
AGE	-.061	.021	8.47	.004
RACE	.317	.308	1.06	.30
MAR	-.493	.375	1.73	.19
PRIO	.099	.027	13.39	.0003
Intercept	4.037	.402		

Table 2

earlier. The chi-squares and *p*-values shown in Table 2 for the five variables are remarkably similar to those in Table 1 that were obtained with maximum likelihood estimation of a Weibull model. On the other hand, the coefficients are noticeably different in magnitude and even have signs that are reversed from those in Table 1. The sign reversal is a quite general phenomenon that stems from the fact that the dependent variable is the time of the event in the AFT model and the hazard of the event in the PH model. People with high hazards are very likely to have events at any point in time, so their times to events tend to be short. By contrast, people with low hazards tend to have long times until event occurrence.

To interpret the magnitudes of the coefficients, we can use the same transformation used for the AFT models. Specifically, $100[\exp(\beta)-1]$ gives the percentage change in the hazard of an event for a 1-unit increase in a particular independent variable. Thus, for FIN we have $100[\exp(-.373)-1] = -31$, which says that those who got financial aid have hazards of arrest that are 31 percent lower than those who did not get aid. For AGE we have $100[\exp(-.061)-1] = -6$. Each additional year of age at release yields a 6 percent reduction in the hazard of arrest. Finally, each additional conviction is associated with $100[\exp(.099)-1] = 10.4$ percent increase in the hazard of an arrest.

The partial likelihood method also allows one to easily introduce time-varying explanatory variables. For example, suppose that the hazard for arrest is thought to depend on both financial aid (x_1) and employment status (x_2, coded 1 for employed, 0 for unemployed). A suitable PH model might be

$$\log h(t) = \alpha(t) + \beta_1 x_1 + \beta_2 x_2(t) \qquad (4)$$

which says that the hazard at time t depends on financial aid, on employment status at time t, and on time itself. If longitudinal data on income are available, models such as this can be estimated in a straightforward fashion with the partial likelihood method. How to do this is shown in Chapter 5 of Allison (1995).

MULTIPLE KINDS OF EVENTS

To this point, it has been assumed that all events can be treated alike. In many applications, however, there is a compelling need to distinguish among two or more types of events. For example, if the events of interest are job terminations, one might expect that explanatory variables would have vastly different effects on voluntary and involuntary terminations. For recidivism studies, it might be desirable to distinguish arrests for crimes against persons and crimes against property. The statistical analysis should take these distinctions into account.

All of the methods already discussed can be easily applied to multiple kinds of events. In essence, a separate model is estimated for each kind of event. In doing an analysis for one kind of event, one simply treats other kinds of events as though the individual were censored at the time when the event occurred, a method known as "competing risks." Thus, no new methodology is required to handle this situation.

An alternative approach is to estimate a single event history model for the timing of events, without distinguishing different event types. Then, after eliminating all the individuals who did not have events (the censored cases), one estimates a logistic regression model for the determinants of the type of event. This method of analysis is most appropriate when the different kinds of events are functionally alternative ways of achieving a single objective. For example, the event might be purchase of a computer and the two different types might be a Windows-based computer versus a Macintosh computer.

REPEATED EVENTS

The discussion so far has presumed that each individual experiences no more than one event. Obviously, however, such events as childbirths, job changes, arrests, and car purchases can occur many times over the life of an individual. The methods already described have been routinely applied to cases of repeated events, taking one of two alternative approaches. One approach is to do a separate analysis for each successive event. For example, one event history model is estimated for the birth of the first child, a second model is estimated for the birth of the second child, and so on. The alternative approach is to break each individual's event history into a set of intervals between events, treat each of these intervals as a distinct observation, and then pool all the intervals into a single analysis.

Neither of these alternatives is entirely satisfactory. The sequential analysis is rather tedious, wastes information if the process is invariant across the sequence, and is prone to selection biases for later events in the sequence. The pooled analysis, on the other hand, makes the rather questionable assumption that the multiple intervals for a single individual are independent. This can lead to standard errors that are biased downward and test statistics that are biased upward.

Several methods are available for dealing with the lack of independence. One is to estimate standard errors and test statistics using the robust method developed by White (1982). These robust standard errors have been incorporated into some Cox regression programs (e.g., Stata, S-Plus). Another is to do a "fixed-effects" Cox regression that stratifies on the individual (Allison 1996; Yamaguchi 1986). These models can be estimated with most Cox regression software, and they have the advantage of automatically controlling for all stable

characteristics of the individual. On the other hand, fixed-effects models cannot produce coefficient estimates for stable characteristics such as sex or race. Finally, there are "random-effects" or "frailty" models that explicitly build the dependence into the model as an additional random disturbance. Unfortunately, there is little commercial software available to estimate random-effects event history models.

DISCRETE-TIME METHODS

When event times are measured coarsely, the continuous-time methods already discussed may yield somewhat biased estimates. In such cases, methods specifically designed for discrete-time data are more appropriate (Allison 1982). Moreover, such methods are easily employed and are particularly attractive for handling large numbers of time-varying explanatory variables.

Suppose that the time scale is divided into a set of equal intervals, indexed by $t = 1, 2, 3, \ldots$ The discrete-time analog of the hazard function, denoted by P_t, is the conditional probability that an event occurs in interval t, given that it has not occurred prior to t. A popular model for expressing the dependence of P_t on explanatory variables is the logit model

$$\log\left(\frac{P_{it}}{1-P_{it}}\right) = \alpha_t + \beta_1 x_{i1} + \ldots + \beta_2 x_{i2} \qquad (5)$$

where the subscript on α_t indicates that the intercept may differ for each interval of time. Similarly the explanatory variables may take on different values at each interval of time. This model can be estimated by the method of maximum likelihood, using the following computational strategy:

1. Break each individual's event history into a set of discrete time units, for example, person-years.

2. Create a dependent variable that has a value of 1 for time units in which events occurred; otherwise use 0. Explanatory variables are assigned whatever values they had at the beginning of the time unit.

3. Pool all these time units, and estimate a logistic regression model using a standard maximum likelihood logit program.

Other models and computational methods are also available for the discrete-time case. These methods can be easily extended to allow for multiple kinds of events and repeated events.

REFERENCES

Allison, Paul D. 1982 "Discrete Time Methods for the Analysis of Event Histories." In Samuel Leinhardt, ed., *Sociological Methodology 1982*. San Francisco: Jossey-Bass.

—— 1984 *Event History Analysis*. Beverly Hills, Calif.: Sage.

—— 1995 *Survival Analysis Using the SAS® System: A Practical Guide*. Cary, N.C.: SAS Institute.

—— 1996 "Fixed Effects Partial Likelihood for Repeated Events." *Sociological Methods and Research* 25:207–222.

Baydar, Nazli, Michael J. White, Charles Simkins, and Ozer Babakol 1990 "Effects of Agricultural Development Policies on Migration in Peninsular Malaysia." *Demography* 27:97–110.

Bennett, Neil G., Ann Klimas Blanc, and David E. Bloom 1988 "Commitment and the Modern Union: Assessing the Link Between Premarital Cohabitation and Subsequent Marital Stability." *American Sociological Review* 53:127–138.

Blossfeld, Hans-Peter, and Götz Rohwer 1995 *Techniques of Event History Modeling: New Approaches to Causal Modeling*. Mahwah, N.J.: Lawrence Earlbaum.

Carroll, Glenn R., and Karl Ulrich Mayer 1986 "Job-Shift Patterns in the Federal Republic of Germany: The Effects of Social Class, Industrial Sector, and Organizational Size." *American Sociological Review* 51:323–341.

Collett, D. 1994 *Modelling Survival Data in Medical Research*. London: Chapman and Hill.

Cox, David R. 1972 "Regression Models and Life Tables." *Journal of the Royal Statistical Society*, Series B, 34:187–202.

Elandt-Johnson, R. C., and N. L. Johnson 1980 *Survival Models and Data Analysis*. New York: Wiley.

Halliday, Terence C., Michael J. Powell, and Mark W. Granfors 1987 "Minimalist Organizations: Vital Events in State Bar Associations, 1870–1930." *American Sociological Review* 52:456–471.

Hallinan, Maureen, and Richard A. Williams 1987 "The Stability of Students' Interracial Friendships." *American Sociological Review* 52:653–664.

Kallan, Jeffrey, and J. R. Udry 1986 "The Determinants of Effective Fecundability Based on the First Birth Interval." *Demography* 23:53–66.

Kiefer, Nicholas M. 1988 "Economic Duration Data and Hazard Functions." *Journal of Economic Literature* 26:646–679.

Klein, John P., and Melvin Moeschberger 1997 *Survival Analysis: Techniques for Censored and Truncated Data*. New York: Springer-Verlag.

Kleinbaum, David G. 1996 *Survival Analysis: A Self-Learning Text*. New York: Springer-Verlag.

Moore, David E., and Mark D. Hayward 1990 "Occupational Careers and Mortality of Elderly Men." *Demography* 27:31–53.

Rossi, P. H., R. A. Berk, and K. J. Lenihan 1980 *Money, Work and Crime*. New York: Academic Press.

Teachman, Jay D. 1983 "Analyzing Social Processes: Life Tables and Proportional Hazards Models." *Social Science Research* 12:263–301.

Tuma, Nancy Brandon, and Michael T. Hannan 1984 *Social Dynamics: Models and Methods*. Orlando, Fla.: Academic Press.

White, Halbert 1982 "Maximum Likelihood Estimation of Misspecified Models." *Econometrica* 50:1–25.

Yamaguchi, Kazuo 1986 "Alternative Approaches to Unobserved Heterogeneity in the Analysis of Repeated Events." In Nancy Brandon Tuma, ed., *Sociological Methodology 1986*. Washington, D.C.: American Sociological Association.

PAUL D. ALLISON

EVOLUTION: BIOLOGICAL, SOCIAL, CULTURAL

The diverse forms of life on earth have emerged probably from a common source, through a process of evolution that has the following characteristics:

1. The course of evolution does not always proceed along a straight path (for example, from simple to complex forms). Instead, it can meander like a stream, directed largely by environmental circumstances, although also affected by limitations on the capacities of organisms to respond to environmental challenges, and by unpredictable "chance" factors. Occasionally it reverses direction in certain respects, as when our own distant monkey-like ancestors became adapted to life in

the trees, and our more recent ancestors readapted to living on the ground. When the course of evolution does reverse direction, it generally does so with respect to comparatively few features only, not all features. Thus, we humans retain various characteristics evolved earlier in connection with life in the trees: stereoscopic vision, visual acuity, reduced sense of smell, and hands adapted for grasping.

2. Different groups of organisms sometimes evolve in similar directions in certain respects when exposed to similar environmental conditions. Thus whales—descendants of mammals that lived on land—acquired fishlike shapes when they adapted to life in the water. However, parallelism in evolutionary development generally remains limited: different evolutionary lines do not come close to "merging." Whales, even though living in the ocean and acquiring fishlike shapes, retain basic anatomical and physiological features of mammals, quite different from those of fish.

The life cycle of a human being involves fixed stages (infancy, childhood, adolescence, adulthood, old age) that represent an unfolding of innate potentialities and that culminate in inevitable death. The evolution of a new biological species, by contrast, is a unique historical development involving movement in directions shaped primarily by environmental pressures, without any inevitable "death" or other pre-determined end state.

A "Lamarckian" evolutionary process (named after Jean Baptiste Lamarck, 1744–1829), would involve inheritance of acquired characteristics. Thus, if evolution followed the Lamarckian pattern, giraffes might have acquired their long necks because in each generation necks were stretched (perhaps to obtain food high up in trees, or to detect approaching enemies), and because the effect of each generation's stretching tended to be inherited by the generation that followed. However, Lamarckian ideas were found to be invalid long ago.

A different approach developed by Charles Darwin (1859) and others does not assume that

acquired characteristics (such as effects of neck-stretching) are inherited. Rather, it assumes (1) random or randomlike variation among the offspring in each generation (with some giraffes happening by chance to have longer necks than others); (2) natural selection, involving tendencies for certain variants (longer-necked giraffes) to survive and reproduce more than others; and (3) preservation through inheritance of the effects of natural selection (longer-necked giraffes tending to have similarly long-necked offspring, although—as suggested above—there would still be some random variation among these offspring with respect to neck length).

Darwinian ideas challenged traditional Christian religious beliefs by suggesting (1) that we are descended from ape-like creatures and, ultimately, from elementary life forms; (2) that our evolution was basically an unplanned outcome of diverse environmental pressures rather than something planned in advance; and (3) that the earth is old enough for evolutionary processes to have had time to produce the variety and complexity of life forms that we actually find. Although today still resisted by many on religious grounds, Darwinian theory ultimately came to be generally accepted by biologists, with important modifications and certain disagreements about details, and in combination with new knowledge in other areas of biology and other scientific disciplines that was not available to Darwin (see Gould 1982; Stebbins and Ayala 1985; Mayr and Provine 1998).

An inherited trait that has evolved over a long period of time (like the giraffe's long neck) has very likely evolved because it makes some contribution to the survival and reproduction of the organisms possessing it, and because it has consequently emerged and persisted through the Darwinian mechanisms outlined above. However, some traits may appear and persist that are neutral in their implications for survival and reproduction, and even traits that have negative implications may appear and persist if they happen to be linked with traits whose implications are positive.

Bioevolutionary explanations of human social phenomena, sometimes under the label of "sociobiology" (see Wilson 1975), pose a challenge to sociology, as the following example suggests. Stepparents tend to abuse their stepchildren more than biological parents tend to abuse their own children. Sociologists would ordinarily seek to explain this in a way that utilizes sociological and social-psychological concepts only, avoiding assumptions about inherited and biologically evolved traits. A sociobiologist, by contrast, would be more likely to view it as a human manifestation or extension of a biologically evolved tendency prevailing widely among nonhuman mammals: a tendency for individual mammals in stepparent-like positions to kill their "stepchildren," thus increasing their own prospects for producing survivable offspring and perpetuating their own genes (see Beckstrom 1993, pp. 23–29).

An evolutionary explanation of an aspect of human life or society may present that aspect as having emerged (1) as a part of, or a continuation of, biological evolution (as illustrated in the discussion of stepparental child abuse above), or (2) through a process analogous to biological evolution but nevertheless distinct from it, that is, a process of social or cultural evolution. Concepts analogous to those of biological evolution are especially applicable to aspects of culture such as science (Hull 1988) and technology (Basalla 1988) in which the cumulative character of culture is most strongly manifested. Competing scientific hypotheses are the "randomlike variations" in science as an evolutionary process. Research results that evaluate such hypotheses select some of them for survival and others for extinction, and the knowledge that constitutes the outcome of this process in any given generation of scientists is "inherited" by subsequent generations through textbooks, teaching, and research publications. In technological evolution, positive selection (i.e., acceptance) of variations (innovations) depends not only on research results (i.e., on how well they "work") but also on costs, competitive pressures, compatibility with prevailing culture, and other factors.

The evolutionary model is not appropriately applied to social or cultural changes that are cyclical, easily reversed, primarily planned, or repetitive. It may be usefully applied when a complex social or cultural transformation that would be hard to repeat or to reverse occurs gradually without being planned, through environmentally determined selections from among divergent alternative directions of change, and with enough

stability to preserve the results of past environmental influence (see Campbell 1965; Richter 1982, pp. 19-34).

Not every process that is called "evolutionary" seems to deserve that label. Some theories pertaining to major transformations of society illustrate this point.

The idea that human society evolves from simple beginnings through comparatively fixed stages came to be commonly accepted in the nineteenth century, although different theorists had different conceptions of what these stages were. Thus we find analyses of transitions from theological to metaphysical to "positivistic" thought-styles (Comte 1875); from savagery to barbarism to civilization (Morgan 1877); from tribalism to slavery, feudalism, capitalism, and then communism (Marx and Engels [1846] 1947); and from simple to compounded, doubly compounded and then triply compounded societies (Spencer [1885–1886] 1967).

When societies, cultures, or civilizations are said to pass from childhood to adulthood, and then to old age, or are said to grow and then decline, we have an analogy not with the evolution of a species but rather with the human life cycle, as illustrated in the works of Oswald Spengler and Arnold J. Toynbee. Nineteenth century "social-evolutionary" theories departed from the life-cycle model in that they did not involve the idea of decline or old age followed by death as the end point of a cycle. Quite the opposite: the trends they described tended to culminate in triumphant achievements—"positivism" (Comte), "civilization" (Morgan), "communism" (Marx and Engels), and societies "compounded" many times (Spencer). In this one respect, but only in this respect, these theories resembled the bioevolutionary model: biological species do not have to become extinct—even though many of them actually do—in the same sense that individuals have to die. However, these theories nevertheless reflect a life-cycle model, insofar as they involve one society after another following essentially the same pattern of development, just as one infant after another follows the same general route to adulthood. And they do not appear to involve, in any major way, the evolutionary mechanisms of random variation and selection. In fact, they are primarily theories of progress, not of evolution in any sense that biologists would recognize, regardless of the "evolutionary" label commonly attached to them (Nisbet 1969).

The social-evolutionary idea fell into disfavor among sociologists around the turn of the twentieth century, but was revived several decades later with, for example, Talcott Parsons' analysis of primitive, intermediate, and modern societies (1977), and Lenski and Lenski's (1982) analysis of transitions from hunting-and-gathering to horticultural, agrarian, and industrial societies. Although based on more accurate and more extensive facts than were available in the nineteenth century, these newer schemes pertaining to the evolution of whole societies are nevertheless basically similar to their nineteenth century predecessors in that they present various societies as passing through specific stages in a predominantly unidirectional pattern, which, as noted above, represents a divergence from the bioevolutionary model. This is not necessarily a defect: the development of societies of new types may simply not be a process to which concepts of a bioevolutionary sort are fully applicable.

Evolutionary concepts have been used not only in attempts to understand some social and cultural phenomena, as discussed above, but also in attempts to formulate and justify certain social policies. In the late nineteenth and early twentieth centuries, evolutionary concepts and associated slogans such as "survival of the fittest" appeared to provide rationales for what have been labelled "Social Darwinist" policies. Focusing on the selective (rather than on the random-variation) phase of the evolutionary process, various business, political, ideological, and military leaders in several countries, along with some scholars in several disciplines (including the sociologists Herbert Spencer and William Graham Sumner), emphasized the importance of the struggle for survival in maintaining a hardy population and a vigorous society, and opposed social welfare measures that they thought would mitigate that struggle. Supporters of this approach differed in several ways: some emphasized individual struggle, others, group (e.g., racial or national) struggle; some emphasized nonviolent means (e.g., economic competition), and others, armed conflict (see Hofstadter 1955).

A statement by Darwin himself illustrates the basic idea underlying "Social Darwinism." Although Darwin did not oppose smallpox vaccination, he worried about its effects: "There is reason to believe that vaccination has preserved thousands, who from a weak constitution would formerly have succumbed to smallpox. Thus the weak members of civilized societies propagate their kind. No one who has attended to the breeding of domestic animals will doubt that this must be highly injurious to the race of man" (Darwin [1871] 1897, p. 134).

Darwin did not believe that war led to the selective survival of the fittest people, as he thought smallpox tended to do. Quite the opposite: he saw war as destroying "the finest" young men while those with "poor constitutions" would avoid fighting and thus survive and reproduce.

But evolutionary concepts can be applied at diverse levels. Nineteenth-century war might have led to the selective survival of societies or governments that were "fittest" in some sense, even if not to the survival of the "fittest" young men within particular societies. Some Social Darwinists adopted that perspective. Thus: "Storm purifies the air and destroys the frail trees, leaving the sturdy oaks standing. War is the test of a nation's political, physical and intellectual worth. The State in which there is much that is rotten may vegetate for a while in peace, but in war its weakness is revealed. . . . It is better to spend money on armaments and battleships than luxury, motormania and other sensual living" (Baron Karl von Stengel, cited by Angell 1911, p. 168).

There is a problem here: what an exceedingly powerful storm is most likely to leave standing are not sturdy oaks but blades of grass. And this leads to a question: what does "survival of the fittest" actually mean? Defining the fittest as "those who survive" would make the phrase tautological, but any other definition would very likely make it untrue except under a limited range of conditions. In any case, "fitness" is not necessarily equivalent to "desirability" as we might define that, or to what the people of a society actually desire.

The problem of defining "fitness" may be illustrated by examining what Darwin said about smallpox. Suppose people who would have succumbed to smallpox if not vaccinated, but who were actually saved by vaccination, have descendants who inherit their potential vulnerability to that disease. In this respect, such descendants might be considered relatively "unfit." But if these descendants are all protected from smallpox by vaccination, or if smallpox itself is permanently eliminated, then "potential vulnerability to smallpox" might have no practical implications and might not entail "unfitness" in any practically relevant sense.

If the term "Social Darwinism" is to be applied to attempts to improve society through competition and struggle that eliminate some variants while perpetuating others, then attempts to improve society by improving people within society (through education, health care, and so on) might reasonably be labelled "Social Lamarckism." The fact that Lamarckian ideas have been empirically disconfirmed and rejected in explanations of biological evolution has no bearing on the question of the reasonableness of analogous ideas in the sociocultural realm. And, in both biological and sociocultural contexts, Lamarckian and Darwinian ideas can logically coexist and have done so. Darwin himself accepted the validity of Lamarckian ideas in explaining biological evolution, even while he was developing different ideas of his own; the decisive rejection of Lamarckism by evolutionary biologists came after Darwin had died. And Herbert Spencer, who coined the Darwinian phrase "survival of the fittest" and has traditionally been considered a major Social Darwinist, has also been called a Social Lamarckist (Bowler 1995, p. 113) on the ground that he was more committed to struggle as a (Lamarckian) means for invigorating and improving the individuals who participate in it, than to struggle as a (Darwinian) means for eliminating the "unfit."

Partial artificial control over reproduction and hence over the evolutionary process is illustrated by methods used to develop new variants of farm animals, work animals, laboratory animals, and pets. Improvements in these methods have ultimately led to "cloning," which involves total and exact replication of individuals' inherited characteristics without mating. Control over human reproduction was sought on a limited basis by a "eugenics" movement that emerged in the late nineteenth century, founded by Darwin's cousin Francis Galton. This movement achieved some successes, including arrangements for sterilization of some criminals and mentally ill people in various jurisdictions. However, it also faced problems, including: lack of consensus about the traits to be targeted; complexities in the process of hereditary transmission (for example, the fact that parents may transmit to their offspring a defect that they do not manifest themselves); political and legal obstacles to compulsory eugenic measures in societies with well-established traditions of democracy and personal freedom; and, the difficulty of distinguishing between traits transmitted through heredity and traits transmitted through socialization. Supporters of eugenics did not always care about this last point: they sometimes assumed that preventing people with undesirable traits from having children would reduce the prevalence of people bearing these traits regardless of how the traits themselves were transmitted from one generation to the next.

The eugenics movement developed in a tragically racist direction. Some major leaders of the movement in the United States thought that white people of northern European ancestry constituted a superior race and regarded as genetically inferior the southern and eastern Europeans who were immigrating to the country in large numbers. The movement came to be discredited after its ideas came to be used in Hitler's Germany to support genocidal killings of Jews and members of various other groups.

REFERENCES

Angell, Norman 1911 *The Great Illusion*. New York: Putnam.

Basalla, George 1988 *The Evolution of Technology*. New York: Cambridge University Press.

Beckstrom, John H. 1993 *Darwinism Applied: Evolutionary Paths to Social Goals*. Westport, Conn.: Praeger.

Bowler, Peter J. 1995 "Social Metaphors in Evolutionary Biology, 1870–1930." In Sabine Maasen, Everett Mendelsohn, and Peter Weingart, eds., *Biology as Society, Society as Biology: Metaphors*. Dordrecht: Kluwer Academic Publishers.

Campbell, Donald T. 1965 "Variation and Selective Retention in Socio-Cultural Evolution." In Herbert R. Barringer, George I. Blanksten, and Raymond W. Mack, eds., *Social Change in Developing Areas*. Cambridge, Mass.: Schenkman.

Comte, Auguste 1875 *The Positive Philosophy*, 2nd ed. Harriet Martineau, trans. and cond. London: Trubner.

Darwin, Charles 1859 *On the Origin of Species*. London: Murray.

Darwin, Charles 1897 *The Descent of Man*. New York: D. Appleton.

Gould, Stephen Jay 1982 "Darwinism and the Expansion of Evolutionary Theory." *Science* 216:380–387.

Hofstadter, Richard 1955 *Social Darwinism in American Thought*. Boston: Beacon Press.

Hull, David L. 1988 *Science As a Process*. Chicago: University of Chicago Press.

Lenski, Gerhard, and Jean Lenski 1982 *Human Societies: An Introduction to Macrosociology*. New York: McGraw-Hill.

Marx, Karl, and Friedrich Engels 1947 *The German Ideology*. New York: International Publishers.

Mayr, Ernst, and William B. Provine, eds., 1998 *The Evolutionary Synthesis*. Cambridge, Mass.: Harvard University Press.

Morgan, Lewis H. 1877 *Ancient Society*. Chicago: Charles H. Kerr and Co.

Nisbet, Robert A. 1969 *Social Change and History*. London: Oxford University Press.

Parsons, Talcott 1977 *The Evolution of Societies*. Jackson Toby, ed. Englewood Cliffs, N.J.: Prentice-Hall.

Richter, Maurice N., Jr. 1982 *Technology and Social Complexity*. Albany, N.Y.: State University of New York Press.

Spencer, Herbert 1967 *The Evolution of Society*. Robert L. Carneiro, ed. Chicago: University of Chicago Press. Excerpted from *Principles of Sociology*, vols. 1 and 2, rev. ed. London: Williams and Margate, 1885–1886.

Stebbins, G. Ledyard, and Francisco J. Ayala 1985 "The Evolution of Darwinism." *Scientific American* 253:72–82.

Wilson, Edward O. 1975 *Sociobiology: The New Synthesis*. Cambridge, Mass.: The Belknap Press of Harvard University Press.

MAURICE N. RICHTER, JR.

EXCHANGE THEORY

See Social Exchange Theory.

EXPECTATION STATES THEORY

Expectation states theory is a well-established, ongoing research program investigating various aspects of group interaction. The focus is on small, task-oriented groups; the central interest is in both the processes through which group members assign levels of task competence to each other and the consequences this assignment has for their interaction. Originating as a single theory developed by Joseph Berger (1958), expectation states theory has grown to include various branches sharing a core of basic concepts, definitions, and propositions about group interaction processes, as well as methodological and metatheoretical assumptions. Thus, the program in fact contains not just one theory but several. (Unless otherwise specified, the expression "expectation states theory" refers here to the entire program rather than to any particular theory within it.) Expectation states theory has received strong support from extensive empirical research.

Two key concepts in the program are "status characteristics" and "performance expectations." A status characteristic is any valued attribute implying task competence. Such characteristics are viewed as having at least two levels (e.g., being either high or low in mechanical ability, being either male or female), one carrying a more positive evaluation than the other. They are also defined as varying from specific to diffuse, depending on the range of their perceived applicability. For instance, mechanical ability is usually considered to be relatively specific, or associated with well-defined performance expectations. Gender, on the other hand, is frequently treated as diffuse, or carrying both limited and general performance expectations. The "diffuseness" refers to the fact that since there is no explicitly set limit to the expectations, the characteristic is viewed as relevant to a large, indeterminate number of different tasks. Other attributes commonly treated as diffuse status characteristics are ethnicity, skin color, socio-economic class, level of education, organizational rank, age, and physical attractiveness.

Performance expectations link status characteristics to observable behavior. Thus, levels of these characteristics are associated with levels of competence and corresponding expectations that, in turn, determine what is known as "the power and prestige order of the group." This concept refers to a set of interrelated behaviors, namely, the unequal distribution in the offer and acceptance of opportunities to perform, the type of evaluations received for each unit of performance, and the rates of influence exerted among group members. Note, then, that performance expectations are distinguished from evaluations of units of performance: while the latter are evaluations of a single act, the former refer to the level of competence that a person is predicted to exhibit over a number of such performances. Once formed, expectations tend to be stable, since the behaviors that make up the power and prestige order of a group operate in a way that reinforces the status quo.

Research in expectation states theory follows a situational approach. Propositions are formulated from the point of view of an individual (also referred to as "self" or "focal actor") who performs a given task with a partner ("other"). Performance expectations are therefore relative to a specific pair of actors, and an individual is not seen as holding high (or low, or medium) expectations for self but, rather, an "expectation state" that is defined in terms of self *and* other. In other words, the focal actor is said to hold expectations for self that are either higher than, lower than, or equal to, the expectations he or she holds for the partner. Such expectations are also conceptualized as relative to a particular situation. Thus, for example, with a different partner or in the context of a different task, a person's expectation state could vary. It should also be noted that an expectation state is a theoretical construct, not an observable phenomenon. In particular, although expectations are seen as reflecting a person's beliefs about the distribution of task competence in the group, they are *not* assumed to be self's conscious calculations of advantage (or disadvantage, or equality) in this respect. Rather, what is proposed are models to be used to predict the focal actor's behavior, and this person is to be seen only *as if* he or she performed the operations specified in the models.

Propositions in expectation states theory also have been formulated within well defined scope conditions, or clauses specifying the limits within which the propositions apply. Since scope conditions are part of the theory, they are expressed in abstract terms (as are the key concepts of "status characteristic," "performance expectations," and "power and prestige order"). Three important scope conditions are that the focal actor is assumed to: (1) value the task in question (he or she views it as having two or more possible outcomes, none due exclusively to chance, and considers one of these to be success and the other failure); (2) be task-oriented (motivated to do the task well); and (3) be collectively oriented (prepared to accept the partner's ideas if they are thought to contribute to the task solution). In other words, the third scope condition specifies that solving the task must be

more important to the focal actor than any other considerations (such as having his or her individual contributions accepted, or being liked by the partner).

The situational approach and the use of scope conditions are part of an overall theory-construction strategy whereby the initial focus is on the simplest contexts, which are studied with the aid of minimum assumptions. Complexities are then added gradually as knowledge accumulates. More recent expectation states research has, for example, extended the investigation from dyads to larger groups. Similarly, the scope condition of collective orientation has been relaxed in some of these studies, with results showing that status still affects expectations under such circumstances.

The core of the theory investigates the performance expectations an individual forms about self and other in settings where the two are engaged in the joint solution of a task. As indicated previously, the focal actor is assumed to value the task and to be both task-oriented and collectively oriented. A valued task implies that competence at the task is more desirable than incompetence, and therefore that levels of task ability constitute a status characteristic for that actor. Basically, the assignment of levels of this characteristic and corresponding performance expectations may occur in one of two ways: directly, from actual evaluations of task performance, or indirectly, on the basis of other status characteristics of the performers that self perceives to be relevant to the task. For simplicity, I first consider situations where expectations are formed exclusively in one fashion or the other. These two ways comprise the major branches of expectation states theory, the former focusing on the effects of performance evaluations and the latter on the effects of other status information. These branches and their development are described below. (Because of space limitations, the emphasis in this article is on the basic ideas, and specific references can only be given for a sample of the theoretical and empirical work done in the program. This sample consists of key earlier pieces and a selection of the more recent research. It should be noted, however, that expectation states theory has been a collaborative effort from its beginnings and that a considerable number of researchers have worked in it. For references to their individual contributions at the various stages of the program, see the reviews and edited collections, as well as the examples of research, mentioned at the end of this article.)

Initial work in the first branch of the theory investigated the formation of performance expectations in situations where two persons begin their interaction as status equals (i.e., they have no information from either inside or outside the group that would enable them to assign different levels of task competence to each other). In this case, the assignment of levels of competence that eventually occurs is the result of a generalization from evaluations of units of performance. These evaluations may be made by the performers themselves as they resolve disagreements between them regarding the correct solution to the task (Berger and Conner 1969; Berger and Snell 1961) or by a "source" or third party with the right to evaluate the performers (Crundall and Foddy 1981; Webster 1969; Webster and Sobieszek 1974). Moreover, the evaluations may or may not be made through the use of objective criteria. Various other topics were later investigated within this branch. These include the effects on expectations of the type of evaluations received (e.g., either positive or negative; either highly or moderately positive), the consistency of these evaluations (e.g., across performances or across sources), and the types of attributes that confer evaluative competence on a source (such as level of task competence or vicarious exposure to the task). Other recent work has dealt with the effects of applying either strict or lenient standards for competence (as well as for lack of competence) to the processing of evaluations. The study of second-order expectations (those based on self's perceptions of the expectations held by the partner) also has received attention in this program, and is of direct relevance to this branch.

The second branch of the theory is primarily concerned with situations where the actors differ in status. It is in this branch, which has come to be known as "status characteristics theory," that a large proportion of expectation states research has been conducted. This work started with the investigation of situations in which two persons are differentiated with respect to a single diffuse status characteristic (Berger et al. [1966] 1972; Moore 1968). Furthermore, this difference constitutes the only information that the focal actor has about self and other, and he or she treats the attribute as a diffuse status characteristic (i.e., attaches different evaluations to its various levels

and holds different performance expectations, specific as well as general, for each level).

The basic proposition in this branch states that unless the focal actor believes the characteristic to be irrelevant to the task at hand, he or she will use the status difference between self and other to organize their interaction. In other words, performance expectations for the task will be the result of importing status information from outside the group. This process is known as "status generalization." Let us consider gender as an example (with "man" carrying a more positive valuation than "woman") and assume that the focal actor is a man and that his partner is a woman. The theory predicts different expectations, depending on what the individual believes the sex linkage of the task to be. If the task is perceived as masculine (one at which, in general, men do better than women), self will use this information to infer that he is the better of the two. If he has no information about its sex linkage (perceives the task as neither associated with nor dissociated from sex differences), the "burden-of-proof principle" will apply: those of lower status will be considered to have inferior task competence, unless they demonstrate the opposite. Accordingly, also in this situation, the man will expect to be more competent at the task than his female partner. On the other hand, the theory predicts that he will *not* form expectations of his own superiority if the task has been explicitly dissociated from gender. Finally, if the valued task is perceived to be one at which women generally excel, the prediction is that the male actor will consider himself inferior to his female partner.

It is important to emphasize that the above predictions assume that gender is a diffuse status characteristic for the focal actor (and that, in this example, "man" carries a higher value than "woman"). If gender is not such a characteristic, the propositions do not apply. Because of the inclusion of this scope condition, the theory is able to incorporate cultural, historical, and individual differences. Thus, through this condition, it incorporates the fact that although gender is a diffuse status characteristic in most societies, it is more so in some than in others. The extent to which this is the case also may vary within a given society and from one historical period to another. Furthermore, the theory reflects the fact that even in strongly sexist societies there are likely to be individuals who are less sexist than the majority, and perhaps some who are not sexist at all. (This may be due, for example, to variations in socialization practices within a given culture, and/or to the different degrees of success of these practices). Note that the theory assumes that women, *as well as* men, may treat gender as a diffuse status characteristic and devalue women's performances. (For a theoretical account of the social construction of status beliefs, see Ridgeway 1991).

Let us then reanalyze the earlier example from the point of view of the female actor, and assume that she considers gender to be a diffuse status characteristic to the same degree as her male partner does. The theory predicts that she will then form expectations that are exactly complementary to those of her partner. Thus, if she either views the task as masculine or relates it to sex differences through a burden-of-proof process, she will consider herself the less competent of the two performers. (She will not form such expectations if she sees the task as dissociated from gender, and will believe herself to be the better performer if she views the task as feminine.) However, as with most status systems, those persons who benefit from the existing order can be expected to be more supportive of it than those who do not, socialization practices notwithstanding. Thus it could be that men tend to meet this scope condition more than women do. This is not an issue about the theory itself but an empirical matter regarding the particular instances to which it applies. Note, also, that while the preceding discussion has been limited to gender for the sake of providing an example, the comments are meant to apply to any diffuse status characteristic. In general, the strength of the link between status and expectations is a function of the extent to which the attribute is a status characteristic for the focal actor.

Performance expectations formed through status generalization may, of course, be affected by other factors. Accordingly, the basic ideas of the initial formulation of status characteristics theory have been expanded and elaborated in several directions. In particular, these include the study of situations where actors possess more than one status characteristic. These may be either specific or diffuse, or either consistent or inconsistent with each other in terms of the levels of competence

they imply. Furthermore, as a set, they may either equate or differentiate the performers to various degrees (Berger et al. 1977). This extended formulation specifies the conditions under which the available status items will become salient (or "activated"), as well as the rules by which they will be processed. It is proposed that all (and only) activated items will be used and that they will be combined according to the following principles: inconsistent information will have more impact than consistent information, and each additional item of consistent information will have less weight than it would by itself. Furthermore, this version includes referent actors (nonparticipating actors who serve as objects of comparison for the performers) and their role in the formation of expectations.

The two main branches of the program have not developed independently of each other. In fact, the branches touch and intertwine at various points, as expectations are formed on the basis of *both* performance evaluation and status information. For example, the extent to which the focal actor accepts the evaluations from a source is often affected by the diffuse status characteristics (and their levels) of everyone involved in the situation. Of particular interest is the resilience of status-based expectations when these are contradicted by actual performance evaluations. This resistance shows itself in, for example, the higher level of performance that lower-status actors have to achieve in order to escape the effects of status generalization. The inconsistency between performance evaluation and status information is of course a special case of the extension of status characteristics theory to more than one attribute. A recent theoretical proposal in this area links the resilience to the use of double (or even multiple) standards for both competence and incompetence that protect higher-status actors and penalize lower-status ones.

Other expectation states research, also of relevance to both branches, has included a rich variety of topics. For example, theoretical and empirical work has investigated the relationship between performance expectations and reward expectations, the status-value view of distributive justice, the transfer of expectations across actors and situations, and the legitimation of status positions. The latter work examines how and why individuals come to view the status hierarchies in which they are involved as right and proper. Also of special interest is the analysis of the way in which task settings generate emotional reactions and how these, in turn, affect performance expectations. Other important areas have been: The extension of status characteristics theory to include self-fulfilling effects of status on performance; the study of the role that status cues (such as accent, dress, demeanor) have in the assignment of task competence; and the work on how the attribution of personality characteristics (such as friendly, rigid, outgoing) and moral characteristics (such as honest, fair, selfish) affects this assignment and is, in turn, affected by it.

No review of expectation states theory would be complete without a discussion of three features that, together with those mentioned earlier, serve to characterize this program. *First*, a sizable portion of the research has used a standardized experimental situation involving two subjects (Webster and Sobieszek 1974, Appendices 1 and 2). The utilization of an experimental approach clearly is well suited to the program's analytical strategy of investigating the effects of a few variables at a time, and the standardized setting has contributed to cumulativeness in the research findings by allowing comparability across studies. In this setting, the task consists of a series of trials, each involving a binary choice regarding visual stimuli, with subjects allowed to interact only indirectly (as opposed to face-to-face) with each other. The situation consists of two phases. In the first phase, performance expectations are formed on the basis of information controlled by the experimenter. This may include evaluations of each person's task performance, cues regarding the participants' other status characteristics, or a combination of the two. In the second phase, each trial consists of an individual initial choice, the experimentally controlled communication of the partner's choice, and a final individual choice. In most trials, the communication indicates that the partner disagrees with the subject. The dependent variable of central interest is the amount of influence (one of the components of the power and prestige order of the group) that a partner exerts on the subject in the resolution of those disagreements. Several versions of this setting, including computerized ones, have now been developed. (Additional bases of empirical support for the theory include direct evidence from research conducted in discussion groups, classrooms, and various other settings—such as those mentioned below—as well as indirect evidence from work originating in several other theoretical traditions. These studies corroborate and extend the knowledge gained through the use of the standardized setting. For a review of the different types of support for the theory, see Berger et al. 1989).

Second, the program has been characterized by a strategy of stating propositions as part of deductive systems. These systems have been formalized to various extents, and different techniques (such as stochastic models, a Bayesian approach, graph theory, fuzzy set theory) have been used. The most comprehensive of these formulations is the graph theoretic model of the extended version of status characteristic theory (Berger, Fisek, Norman, and Zelditch 1977). This model has also been used to formalize other areas of the program, such as the formation of expectations in groups where members initially are status equals, and the legitimation and delegitimation of status hierarchies.

Third, from its beginnings, researchers in the program have shown a definite interest in applications and interventions designed to understand and alleviate specific social problems. A large portion of this work has included the development of techniques to reduce the effects of status generalization, particularly those based on skin color and ethnic background, in classroom settings (Cohen 1972, 1982; Cohen and Lotan 1997; Entwisle and Webster 1972). It is important to note that this research has progressed in close association with theoretical work; thus applications and interventions have both stimulated and benefited from the development of abstract formulations.

Expectation states theory continues to generate strong interest among researchers in group processes and related areas, and to develop in several directions. For example, the refinement, expansion, and integration of various aspects of the program are currently under way. There are also some exciting new areas of research, such as the study of the relationship between status and various other factors in the assignment of task competence, namely affect (emotions and sentiments), formal authority, power, dominance, and social identity. Furthermore, the notion of an "expectation state" has been generalized from its original reference to status-based processes, to incorporate those concerning affect and control. Finally, the research methodology has been extended to comprise a wide range of settings and tasks, including face-to-face contexts, larger groups, interactions where selected aspects of formal organizations have been re-created, vignette studies, computerized tasks, and settings where actors are not required to be collectively oriented.

For reviews and assessments of the expectation states program at various stages, see Berger (1988); Berger, Rosenholtz, and Zelditch (1980); Berger, Wagner, and Zelditch (1985, 1989); Meeker (1981); Ridgeway and Walker (1995); Wagner and Berger (1993); Webster and Foschi (1988a). For edited collections of work on various topics, see Berger, Conner, and Fisek (1974); Berger and Zelditch (1985; 1998b); Szmatka, Skvoretz, and Berger (1997); Webster and Foschi (1988b). For examples of the more recent research, see Balkwell, Berger, Webster, Nelson-Kilger, and Cashen (1992); Cohen and Zhou (1991); Foschi (1996); Foschi, Lai, and Sigerson (1994); Gerber (1996); Lovaglia and Houser (1996); Lovaglia, Lucas, Houser, Thye, and Markovsky (1998); Riches and Foddy (1989); Ridgeway (1989); Ridgeway, Boyle, Kuipers, and Robinson (1998); Ridgeway and Johnson (1990); Shelly and Webster (1997) Stewart and Moore (1992); Troyer and Younts (1997); Wagner, Ford, and Ford (1986); Webster and Whitmeyer (1999). For discussions of the program's methodological and metatheoretical assumptions, see Berger and Zelditch (1998a); Berger, Zelditch, and Anderson (1972); Cohen (1989, esp. chap. 6); Zelditch (1969).

REFERENCES

Balkwell, James W., Joseph Berger, Murray Webster, Jr., Max Nelson-Kilger, and Jacqueline Cashen 1992 "Processing Status Information." *Advances in Group Processes* 9:1–20.

Berger, Joseph 1958 "Relations Between Performance, Rewards, and Action-Opportunities in Small Groups." Ph.D. diss., Harvard University.

——1988 "Directions in Expectation States Research." In Murray Webster, Jr., and Martha Foschi, eds., *Status Generalization: New Theory and Research*. Stanford, Calif.: Stanford University Press.

——, Bernard P. Cohen, and Morris Zelditch, Jr. 1966 "Status Characteristics and Expectation States." In Joseph Berger, Morris Zelditch, Jr., and Bo Anderson, eds., *Sociological Theories in Progress*, vol. 1. Boston: Houghton Mifflin.

——, Bernard P. Cohen, and Morris Zelditch, Jr. 1972 "Status Characteristics and Social Interaction." *American Sociological Review* 37:241–255.

——, and Thomas L. Conner 1969 "Performance Expectations and Behavior in Small Groups." *Acta Sociologica* 12:186–198.

——, Thomas L. Conner, and M. Hamit Fisek, eds., 1974 *Expectation States Theory: A Theoretical Research Program*. Cambridge, Mass.: Winthrop.

——, M. Hamit Fisek, Robert Z. Norman, and Morris Zelditch, Jr. 1977 *Status Characteristics and Social Interaction: An Expectation-States Approach*. New York: Elsevier.

——, Susan J. Rosenholtz, and Morris Zelditch, Jr. 1980 "Status Organizing Processes." In Alex Inkeles, Neil J. Smelser, and Ralph H. Turner, eds., *Annual Review of Sociology*, vol. 6. Palo Alto, Calif.: Annual Reviews.

——, and J. Laurie Snell 1961 "A Stochastic Theory for Self-Other Expectations." Technical Report no. 1. Stanford, Calif.: Laboratory for Social Research, Stanford University.

——, David G. Wagner, and Morris Zelditch, Jr. 1985 "Expectation States Theory: Review and Assessment." In Joseph Berger and Morris Zelditch, Jr., eds., *Status, Rewards and Influence: How Expectations Organize Behavior*. San Francisco: Jossey-Bass.

——, David G. Wagner, and Morris Zelditch, Jr. 1989 "Theory Growth, Social Processes, and Metatheory." In Jonathan H. Turner, ed., *Theory Building in Sociology: Assessing Theoretical Cumulation*. Newbury Park, Calif.: Sage.

——, and Morris Zelditch, Jr., eds., 1985 *Status, Rewards, and Influence: How Expectations Organize Behavior*. San Francisco: Jossey-Bass.

——, and Morris Zelditch, Jr. 1998a "Strategies of Theory Construction." In Joseph Berger and Morris Zelditch, eds., *Status, Power and Legitimacy: Strategies and Theories*. New Brunswick, N.J.: Transaction.

——, and Morris Zelditch, Jr., eds., 1998b *Status, Power and Legitimacy: Strategies and Theories*. New Brunswick, N.J.: Transaction.

——, Morris Zelditch, Jr., and Bo Anderson 1972 "Introduction." In Joseph Berger, Morris Zelditch, Jr., and Bo Anderson, eds., *Sociological Theories in Progress*, vol. 2. Boston: Houghton Mifflin.

Cohen, Bernard P. 1989 *Developing Sociological Knowledge: Theory and Method*, 2nd ed. Chicago: Nelson-Hall.

——, and Xueguang Zhou 1991 "Status Processes in Enduring Work Groups." *American Sociological Review* 56:179–188.

Cohen, Elizabeth G. 1972 "Interracial Interaction Disability." *Human Relations* 37:648–655.

——1982 "Expectation States and Interracial Interaction in School Settings." In Ralph H. Turner and James F. Short, Jr., *Annual Review of Sociology*, vol. 8. Palo Alto, Calif.: Annual Reviews.

——, and Rachel A. Lotan, eds., 1997 *Working for Equity in Heterogeneous Classrooms: Sociological Theory in Practice*. New York: Teachers College Press.

Crundall, Ian, and Margaret Foddy 1981 "Vicarious Exposure to a Task as a Basis of Evaluative Competence." *Social Psychology Quarterly* 44:331–338.

Entwisle, Doris R., and M. Webster, Jr. 1972 "Raising Children's Performance Expectations: A Classroom Demonstration." *Social Science Research* 1:147–158.

Foschi, Martha 1996 "Double Standards in the Evaluation of Men and Women." *Social Psychology Quarterly* 59:237–254.

——, Larissa Lai, and Kirsten Sigerson 1994 "Gender and Double Standards in the Assessment of Job Applicants." *Social Psychology Quarterly* 57:326–339.

Gerber, Gwendolyn L. 1996 "Status in Same-Gender and Mixed-Gender Police Dyads: Effects on Personality Attributions." *Social Psychology Quarterly* 59:350–363.

Lovaglia, Michael J., and Jeffrey A. Houser 1996 "Emotional Reactions and Status in Groups." *American Sociological Review* 61:867–883.

——, Jeffrey W. Lucas, Jeffrey A. Houser, Shane R. Thye, and Barry Markovsky 1998 "Status Processes and Mental Ability Test Scores." *American Journal of Sociology* 104:195–228.

Meeker, Barbara F. 1981 "Expectation States and Interpersonal Behavior." In Morris Rosenberg and Ralph H. Turner, eds., *Social Psychology: Sociological Perspectives*. New York: Basic Books.

Moore, James C., Jr. 1968 "Status and Influence in Small Group Interactions." *Sociometry* 31:47–63.

Riches, Phoebe, and Margaret Foddy 1989 "Ethic Accent as a Status Cue." *Social Psychology Quarterly* 52:197–206.

Ridgeway, Cecilia L. 1989 "Understanding Legitimation in Informal Status Orders." In Joseph Berger, Morris Zelditch, Jr., and Bo Anderson, eds., *Sociological Theories in Progress: New Formulations*. Newbury Park, Calif.: Sage.

——1991 "The Social Construction of Status Value: Gender and Other Nominal Characteristics." *Social Forces* 70:367–386.

——, and Cathryn Johnson 1990 "What Is the Relationship Between Socioemotional Behavior and Status in Task Groups?" *American Journal of Sociology* 95:1189–1212.

——, Elizabeth H. Boyle, Kathy J. Kuipers, and Dawn T. Robinson 1998 "How Do Status Beliefs Develop? The Role of Resources and Interactional Experience." *American Sociological Review* 63:331–350.

——, and Henry A. Walker 1995 "Status Structures." In Karen S. Cook, Gary A. Fine, and James S. House, eds., *Sociological Perspectives on Social Psychology*. Boston: Allyn and Bacon.

Shelly, Robert K., and Murray Webster, Jr. 1997 "How Formal Status, Liking, and Ability Status Structure Interaction: Three Theoretical Principles and a Test." *Sociological Perspectives* 40:81–107.

Stewart, Penni A., and James C. Moore, Jr. 1992 "Wage Disparities and Performance Expectations." *Social Psychology Quarterly* 55:78–85.

Szmatka, Jacek, John Skvoretz, and Joseph Berger, eds., 1997 *Status, Network, and Structure: Theory Development in Group Processes*. Stanford, Calif.: Stanford University Press.

Troyer, Lisa, and C. Wesley Younts 1997 "Whose Expectations Matter? The Relative Power of First- and Second-Order Expectations in Determining Social Influence." *American Journal of Sociology* 103:692–732.

Wagner, David G., and J. Berger 1993 "Status Characteristics Theory: The Growth of a Program." In Joseph Berger and Morris Zelditch, Jr., eds., *Theoretical Research Programs: Studies in the Growth of Theory*. Stanford, Calif.: Stanford University Press.

——, Rebecca S. Ford, and Thomas W. Ford 1986 "Can Gender Inequalities Be Reduced?" *American Sociological Review* 51:47–61.

Webster, Murray, Jr. 1969 "Source of Evaluations and Expectations for Performance." *Sociometry* 32:243–258.

——, and Martha Foschi 1988a "Overview of Status Generalization." In Murray Webster, Jr. and Martha Foschi, eds., *Status Generalization: New Theory and Research*. Stanford, Calif.: Stanford University Press.

——, and Martha Foschi, eds., 1988b *Status Generalization: New Theory and Research*. Stanford, Calif.: Stanford University Press.

——, and Barbara Sobieszek 1974 *Sources of Self-Evaluation: A Formal Theory of Significant Others and Social Influence*. New York: Wiley.

——, and Joseph M. Whitmeyer 1999 "A Theory of Second-Order Expectations and Behavior." *Social Psychology Quarterly* 62:17–31.

Zelditch, Morris, Jr. 1969 "Can You Really Study an Army in the Laboratory?" In Amitai Etzioni, ed., *A Sociological Reader on Complex Organizations*, 2nd ed. New York: Holt, Rinehart and Winston.

MARTHA FOSCHI

EXPERIMENTS

Sociologists usually reserve the term *experiment* for studies in which the researcher manipulates one or more key independent variables; that is, for studies in which the experimenter controls the decision as to which subjects are exposed to what level of the independent variable. Although experiments comprise a minority of sociological research studies, they are still quite common. Laboratory versions are traditional in much of sociological social psychology (examples are Bonacich 1990; Molm 1990). Field experiments are prominent in program evaluations, particularly in applied areas such as education (e.g., Slavin and Karweit, 1985), criminal justice (e.g. Rossi et al. 1980; see also Zeisel, 1982), and even large-scale social policy efforts such as studies of a proposed guaranteed minimum income (Hannon et al. 1977). Questionnaire experiments (such as Schuman and Presser 1981) test various methodological questions, while "vignette" experiments (such as Rossi and Nock 1982) have become popular approaches to the study of attitudes.

The primary attraction of the experimental method is undoubtedly that it is more persuasive than other methods in its fit with causal arguments (Kish 1987). Campbell and Stanley, whose 1963 book is the most influential discussion of experiments for contemporary sociologists, call this "internal validity" (for other historically important discussions of experiments, see especially Cochran and Cox 1957; Fisher 1935). To them, "true" experiments are studies in which subjects are randomly allocated into "experimental" and "control" groups. The former receive a "treatment," such as an educational program, while the latter do not. Randomization allows the researcher to assume the similarity of groups at the beginning of the treatment, with known statistical chances of error, and to avoid a variety of "threats" to the validity of the conclusion that the treatment "caused" any found differences between the groups in post-treatment behavior or other outcome. In contrast, "quasi-experiments" (most other forms of research), which do not use randomization, require a variety of additional, often heroic, assumptions in order to make causal inferences (see Lieberson 1985 for an argument that these assumptions may be generally unacceptable).

A MODEL

Consider an experiment to test the proposition that increasing the sensitivity to Hispanic cultures of non-Hispanic second-grade teachers will improve the performance of Hispanic children in their classes, particularly students with poor English-language skills. Teachers are randomly assigned to attend one of three seminars on Hispanic cultures that vary in intensity (experimental treatments) or a seminar on Asian culture (control). Following the approach of Alwin and Tessler (1974), Figure 1 presents a model of this experiment. Our proposition is tested by estimating the relationship between two "unobservable" variables—student performance in second grade (Y) and the sensitivity of their teachers (X). The variables are "unobservable" in the sense that we cannot unambiguously and directly measure the rather complex concepts we have. For example, true "student performance" probably includes facility with mathematics, language aquisition, and many other components, each of which we can measure only imperfectly. The model also contains two other variables that may be unobservable—the "Hispanic intensity" of the course (T), and the English-language skill of the student (L)—and might include a fifth unobservable variable (as indicated by the broken line), which is the student's performance in first grade (P). Including P would allow us to test for the effect of taking the seminar on *change* in student performance.

As is conventional in such models, each unobservable variable is measured by indicators (x_1, x_2, t_1, etc.) and is affected by a stochastic term (e_X, e_T, etc.) representing our inability to measure the concept perfectly with our indicators as well. It is obvious that student performance (Y and P) would be best measured by a series of indicators such as teacher's ratings, grades in various topics, and performances on standardized tests. Since similar or identical measures of Y and P might be used, errors could be correlated, as shown by the curved line between e_{y2} and e_{p2}, thereby biasing

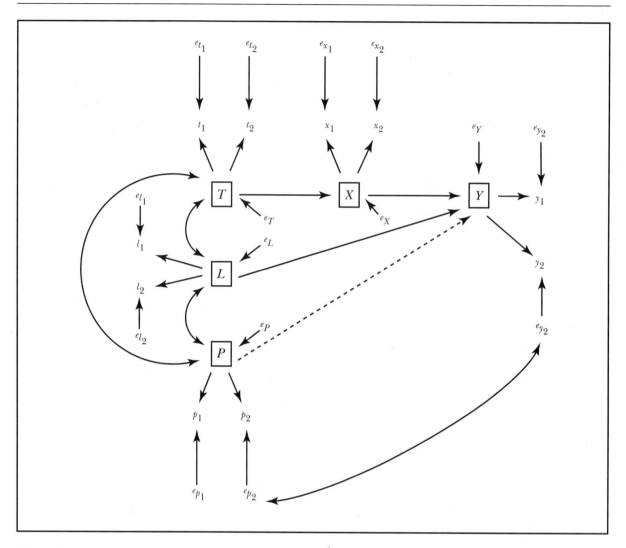

Figure 1

NOTE: Model based on Alwin and Tessler

results. This is why Campbell and Stanley (1963) argue in favor of generally using "post-test only" designs.

Alwin and Tessler call x_1 and x_2 "manipulation checks." Hispanic culture seminars (T) may or may not change a given teacher's sensitivity toward Hispanic students (X). It is even possible that Asian culture seminars make teachers more sensitive to all minorities, including Hispanics. Heckman and Smith (1995) also point out that subjects who do not get the "treatment" in field experiments can sometimes find "substitutes." For example, the teachers assigned to Asian culture seminars might feel they also need sensitivity to Hispanic

culture and take courses in the subject voluntarily. All these possibilities point out that if we simply assume that T successfully manipulated X, we might be making a grave error. There may actually be little difference in Hispanic sensitivity (X) between experimentals and controls. We will have to check, which means that we will have to measure X.

VARIATIONS IN TREATMENT

Experimenters rarely realize that they often need to measure T as well as Y, even if T is "under their control." If the treatment is complicated, assigning a subject to be treated does not guarantee that he or she receives the treatment that is intended. The instructor in one of the culture seminars might do a poor job of presenting the materials. A teacher might be ill and miss one of the sessions. Most experimenters assume that the relationship between T and X is 1.0, but that is frequently, perhaps mostly, not the case. To estimate the actual effect of T on X, various "treatment checks" (t_1, t_2) would be required.

Note that a sophisticated experimental design may often require many levels of the "treatment" and even of the "control." Or there may be no "control" at all, just comparison among different treatments. If X is conceptualized as a continuous variable, such as the intensity of the seminar (where T may be number of sessions), there is no reason to have only three levels of T. Instead, we might randomly assign each member of the treatment group to a different number of sessions from one to a whole semester (if the seminar was being offered at the university anyway). This is particularly important in something like a guaranteed income experiment, where a wide range of levels of guaranteed income are possible. We might even wish to have every family receive a different level of income support, so as to well represent the possible range and thus help us choose the best level of support for an actual program.

Furthermore, note that in our example the control group is not comprised of teachers who get no seminars at all. This is to avoid what has been commonly termed the "Hawthorne effect," in which experimental subjects respond to the attention they get by being sent to a seminar rather than to the content (Hispanic culture) of the seminar itself. Designs that do not attend to the effects of just being treated are always subject to errors of interpretation. Of course, an even more sophisticated design might include a second control group of teachers who were not even informed that others were attending seminars (and perhaps other control groups at various levels of "intensity" of the Asian culture seminar, as well). The "no seminar" group would provide data that allow us to estimate the size of the difference in class performance between students whose teachers had attended sensitivity seminars and students in a school system with no sensitivity program at all.

The Hawthorne effect is actually only one example of a general class of problems that might arise in interpreting found relationships (or nonrelationships) between T and Y. Smith (1990) argues that even if T does manipulate X as designed, it might also affect some additional unmeasured and perhaps untheorized variable (A) that in turn has an important effect on Y. This is particularly a problem for "real-world" experiments. For example, teachers who take the Hispanic culture seminars might be treated with more respect by their Hispanic principal, who feels closer to them. These teachers may have no greater sensitivity, but may work harder and teach better in response to the principal's behavior. If A is not in the causal model, the effects of A on Y will be misattributed to X. Thus, some of the difficulties with nonexperimental research designs can affect complex experimental research as well.

BLOCKING

In most studies, a number of variables other than X may seem to the researcher to be probable causes of Y. Unlike A, above, these variables are both theorized and measurable. However, these variables cannot be manipulated, either because such manipulation is impossible or because it is otherwise undesirable. For example, English-language facility (L) would probably affect the performance of most second-grade students in the United States. The experimenter cannot manipulate this characteristic of the subjects. Because of randomization we expect T, and hence X, to be uncorrelated with L (see Figure 1) and with all other variables. However, sampling variation means that we might be unlucky, so that T and L are empirically correlated among the students we are actually studying. Under these conditions our estimate of the relationship between X and Y may be unbiased, but it is also less efficient than when L is controlled, because we add sampling error to other sources of error.

We can increase the efficiency of the estimate by using L as a "blocking variable," perhaps by using their ranks on L to create matched pairs of students. We then randomly assign one of the two highest-rated students to the experimental group and the other to the controls, one of the two second-highest-rated students to the experimental group and the other to the controls, and so forth, until the lowest L pair is assigned. We thus guarantee a correlation of 0 between T and L. In our analysis, we can statistically estimate the effects of blocked variables, such as L on Y, and reduce the variance that we attribute to "error."

COST

Efficiency is particularly important because experiments are often very expensive. When "real life" manipulates the independent variables—for example making one person male and the other female, one born to rich parents another to poor—the researcher does not have to pay for the "treatment." But experiments usually require the researcher to get the subject to do something, which can often be done only through pay, and then to do something to the subject, which also usually costs money. In our example, the teachers will have to be paid for their time spent going to the seminars, and so will the instructors of those seminars. These costs generally mean that experimenters very much need to keep the number of subjects they study small, which threatens the internal (and external, see below) validity of the research.

GENERALIZATION

The most frequent criticism of experiments is that their results are often difficult to generalize, a problem Campbell and Stanley (1963) call "external invalidity." Because treatments tend to require special arrangements, the sample studied is usually restricted to some relatively "special" group, which is therefore unrepresentative (Kish 1987) of the population to whom we might like the results to apply. For example, getting students from more than one or two school systems to participate in our study is hard to imagine. Certainly a random sample from all the Hispanic students in the whole country is impossible. Yet the school system to which we have access, and within which we do the study, might be very atypical. For example, it may be a suburb whose Hispanic community is comparatively well-off. A strong relationship between X and Y might exist in a poorer community, but our study might estimate the relationship as 0. It *is* possible to do representative samples in experiments (see Marwell and Ames 1979), particularly those involving such things as question wording (e.g., Schuman and Presser 1981). However, such opportunities are rare.

Experiments also usually prescribe strong "control" over various extraneous conditions. To assure that they all get the identical treatment, the teachers might be brought to a tightly run seminar at the university. However, if the program were actually implemented as a regular policy by a number of school systems, many of the seminars would be taught at the schools, at various times, by various leaders, and so forth. Can one generalize from the experiment to everyday practice? As Kish (1987) points out, experiments are often necessarily weak on the *reality* of the conditions they impose on subjects.

Campbell and Stanley spend much of their time discussing the possibility that the very process of measuring the variables of interest may make the experiment unrepresentative of other situations. For example, if we measure performance in both the second (Y) and first (P) grades with the same standardized test, some students might have had their learning during the second grade affected by taking the test in the first grade. They might have become sensitized to the material asked in the early test and "learned" it more than would students in the "real world" who had not been tested. Again, the issue is whether what appear to be the effects of X on Y might not be the effects of some interaction between X and P—and therefore not be generalizable to the usual situation in the school. This is one reason Campbell and Stanley recommend using "post-test only" designs (i.e., without P) where feasible, relying on randomization to make groups equivalent.

In fact, interactions with nonmanipulated independent variables are a particular problem for experiments. For example, the sensitivity program may work only with Hispanic students who are at least second-generation Americans. First-generation Hispanics have such language problems that "sensitivity" matters much less than other skills. If our community contains only first-generation students, we may falsely assume that sensitivity training was generally worthless (Smith 1990).

CONCLUSIONS

Although recognizing the advantages of experimental studies for making causal inferences, sociologists have tended to associate experiments with laboratory-based studies and to denigrate the possibility of generalizing from their results. A broader view of experiments sees them as serving a variety of purposes in a variety of settings, while retaining the association with causal models that makes them attractive.

One of the less recognized of these advantages is that experiments tend to force the researcher to clarify the causal model underlying his or her argument, since such theoretical clarity is necessary for the development of an effective design.

The future of experiments in sociology seems particularly uncertain at this time. On the one hand, the growth of observational and historical studies, along with the continuing influence of econometric methods and large data sets, all appear to be reserving for experiments a smaller and smaller part of the research agenda. The study of group structure and group behavior, perhaps the sociological area most suffused with experimental research, appears to be shifting out of sociological centers and journals and into business schools and publications. Technically skilled economists and sociologists such as Heckman and Smith have been rethinking the problems of experiments and have been making clearer their shortcomings, even for causal assertions.

On the other hand, work on sociological topics done in business schools, sometimes by trained sociologists, need not be interpreted as a decline in interest or activity by the field. Within sociology there has been a growth of attention to social networks, and some of the work in this area has used experiments to good effect.

The reconsideration of experiments by economists has followed a surge of interest in experimental methods by a growing number of economists, with the institutionalization of a journal called *Experimental Economics*, a book with same title (Davis and Holt 1993), and even a *Handbook of Experimental Economics* (Kagel and Roth 1991). The growth of interest by economists is largely (although not entirely) driven by the increasing willingness of government and other large funders to undertake experimental evaluations of social programs in areas such as welfare reform, education, and criminal justice. Sociologists have played a continuing and central role in these efforts, and the end of such investments does not seem in sight.

REFERENCES

Alwin, Duane F., and Richard C. Tessler 1974 "Causal Models, Unobservable Variables, and Experimental Data." *American Journal of Sociology* 80:58–86.

Bonacich, Philip 1990 "Communication Dilemmas in Social Networks: An Experimental Study." *American Sociological Review* 55:427–447.

Campbell, Donald T., and Julian C. Stanley 1963 *Experimental and Quasi-Experimental Designs for Research*. Chicago: Rand McNalley.

Cochran, W. G., and G. Cox 1957 *Experimental Designs*. New York: John Wiley.

Davis, Douglas D., and Charles A. Holt 1993 *Experimental Economics*. Princeton, N.J.: Princeton University Press.

Fisher, R. A. 1935 *The Design of Experiments*. London: Oliver and Boyd.

Hannan, Michael, Nancy Brandon Tuma, and Lyle Groenveld 1977 "Income and Marital Events." *American Journal of Sociology* 82:1186–1211.

Heckman, James J., and Jeffrey A. Smith 1995 "Assessing the Case for Social Experiments." *Journal of Economic Perspectives* 9:85–110.

Kagel, J., and A. Roth, eds. 1991 *Handbook of Experimental Economics*. Princeton, N.J.: Princeton University Press.

Kish, Leslie 1987 *Statistical Design for Research*. New York: John Wiley.

Lieberson, Stanley 1985 *Making It Count: The Improvement of Social Research and Theory*. Berkeley: University of California Press.

Marwell, Gerald, and Ruth Ames 1979 "Experiments on the Provision of Public Goods, I: Resources, Interest, Group Size and the Free Rider Problem." *American Journal of Sociology* 84:1335–1360.

Molm, Linda 1990 "Structure, Action and Outcomes: The Dynamics of Power in Social Exchange." *American Sociological Review* 55:427–447.

Rossi, Peter H., Richard A. Berk, and Kenneth J. Lenihan 1980 *Money, Work, and Crime: Experimental Evidence*. New York: Academic Press.

Rossi, Peter H., and Steven L. Nock 1982 *Measuring Social Judgments: The Factorial Survey Approach*. Beverly Hills, Calif.: Sage.

Schuman, Howard, and Stanley Presser 1981 *Questions and Answers in Attitude Surveys: Experiments on Question Form, Wording, and Context*. Orlando, Fla.: Academic Press.

Slavin, Robert E., and Nancy C. Karweit 1985 "Effects of Whole Class, Ability Grouped and Individual Instruction on Mathematics Achievement." *American Educational Review Journal* 22:351–367.

Smith, Herbert L. 1990 "Specification Problems in Experimental and Nonexperimental Social Research." *Sociological Methodology* 20:59–92.

Zeisel, Hans 1982 "Disagreement over the Evaluation of a Controlled Experiment." *American Journal of Sociology* 88:378–389.

GERALD MARWELL

EXTREME INFLUENCE – THOUGHT REFORM, HIGH CONTROL GROUPS, INTERROGATION AND RECOVERED MEMORY PSYCHOTHERAPY

That social influence is ever present and pervasive is one of the most fundamental observations that may be made about social life. While we are both guided and constrained by the influence factors present at every moment in our lives, we typically fail to fully appreciate how much of an effect cultural, community, and interpersonal influences have on our values, beliefs, and choices. This is in part due to the fact that we rarely find ourselves in situations in which essentially all of the influence forces to which we are exposed are strongly organized and directed in support of a particular ideology, perception, and/or set of actions—rather we usually find ourselves in social situations in which the factors pressuring us to act in one way are offset somewhat by opposing pressures directing us toward different value positions, understandings of the world, and/or different actions. The variability and diversity of the influences to which we are exposed allow us to maintain a sense that we are the source of our choices and actions and contribute to our sense of personal autonomy, freedom of choice, and individuality.

The substantial power of community and interpersonal influence to shape perceptions and actions can most clearly be appreciated through the study of social environments in which influence factors are hyper-organized rather than relatively loosely knit together. It is through the study of influence environments that have been consciously designed to elicit conformity, promote radical change in a person's values and beliefs, and influence an individual's choices that it is possible to gauge the extent to which our sense of personal autonomy and individuality is rooted in social organization. Four examples of environments constructed for the purpose of inducing radical and dramatic shifts in major components of persons' values or perceptions, or both, or environments designed to induce a shift on a single, but nevertheless important decision will be briefly reviewed herein—programs of thought reform or coercive persuasion (such as programs of political reeducation attempted in China under Mao); programs of indoctrination carried out by ideologically focused high control groups (groups labeled as cults and organizations that market experiences that are alleged to psychologically transform an individual); modern police interrogation tactics that, through psychological means, elicit false confessions from innocent suspects; and quack psychotherapy treatments in which patients are led to mislabel hypnotic fantasies, dreams, and hunches as "recovered memories" of lengthy histories of sexual abuse that were entirely unknown to them prior to entering treatment.

REEDUCATION PROGRAMS

Coercive persuasion and *thought reform* are alternate names for programs of social influence capable of producing substantial behavior and attitude change through the use of coercive tactics, persuasion, and/or interpersonal and group-based influence manipulations (Schein 1961; Lifton 1961). Such programs have also been labeled "brainwashing" (Hunter 1951), a term more often used in the media than in scientific literature. However identified, these programs are distinguishable from other elaborate attempts to influence behavior and attitudes, to socialize, and to accomplish social control. Their distinguishing features are their totalistic qualities (Lifton 1961), the types of influence procedures they employ, and the organization of these procedures into three distinctive subphases of the overall process (Schein 1961; Ofshe and Singer 1986). The key factors that distinguish coercive persuasion from other training and socialization schemes are (1) the reliance on intense interpersonal and psychological attack to destabilize an individual's sense of self to promote compliance, (2) the use of an organized peer group, (3) applying interpersonal pressure to promote conformity, and (4) the manipulation of the totality of the person's social environment to stabilize behavior once modified.

Thought-reform programs can vary considerably in their construction. The first systems studied ranged from those in which confinement and physical assault were employed (Schein 1956; Lifton 1954; Lifton 1961, pp. 19–85) to applications that were carried out under nonconfined conditions, in which nonphysical coercion substituted for assault (Lifton 1961, pp. 242–273; Schein 1961, pp. 290–298). The individuals to whom these influence programs were applied were in some cases unwilling subjects (prisoner populations) and in other cases volunteers who sought to participate in what they believed might be a career-beneficial, educational experience (Lifton 1961, p. 248).

Significant differences existed between the social environments and the control mechanisms employed in the two types of programs initially studied. Their similarities, however, are of more importance in understanding their ability to influence behavior and beliefs than are their differences. They shared the utilization of coercive persuasion's key effective-influence mechanisms: a focused attack on the stability of a person's sense of self; reliance on peer group interaction; the development of interpersonal bonds between targets and their controllers and peers; and an ability to control communication among participants. Edgar Schein captured the essential similarity between the types of programs in his definition of the coercive-persuasion phenomenon. Schein noted that even for prisoners, what happened was a subjection to "unusually intense and prolonged persuasion" that they could not avoid; thus, "they were coerced into allowing themselves to be persuaded" (Schein 1961, p. 18).

Programs of both types (confined/assaultive and nonconfined/nonassaultive) cause a range of cognitive and behavioral responses. The reported cognitive responses vary from apparently rare instances, classifiable as internalized belief change (enduring change), to a frequently observed transient alteration in beliefs that appears to be *situationally adaptive* and, finally, to reactions of nothing less than firm intellectual resistance and hostility (Lifton 1961, pp. 117–151, 399–415; Schein 1961, pp. 157–166).

The phrase *situationally adaptive belief change* refers to attitude change that is *not* stable and *is environment dependent*. This type of response to the influence pressures of coercive-persuasion programs is perhaps the most surprising of the responses that have been observed. The combination of psychological assault on the self, interpersonal pressure, and the social organization of the environment creates a situation that can only be coped with by adapting and acting so as to present oneself to others in terms of the ideology supported in the environment (see below for discussion). Eliciting the desired verbal and interactive behavior sets up conditions likely to stimulate the development of attitudes consistent with and that function to rationalize new behavior in which the individual is engaging. Models of attitude change, such as the theory of Cognitive Dissonance (Festinger 1957) or Self-Perception Theory (Bem 1972), explain the tendency for consistent attitudes to develop as a consequence of behavior.

The surprising aspect of the situationally adaptive response is that the attitudes that develop are unstable. They tend to change dramatically once the person is removed from an environment that has totalistic properties and is organized to support the adaptive attitudes. Once removed from such an environment, the person is able to interact with others who permit and encourage the expression of criticisms and doubts, which were previously stifled because of the normative rules of the reform environment (Schein 1961, p. 163; Lifton 1961, pp. 87–116, 399–415; Ofshe and Singer 1986). This pattern of change, first in one direction and then the other, dramatically highlights the profound importance of social support in the explanation of attitude change and stability. This relationship has for decades been one of the principal interests in the field of social psychology.

Statements supportive of the proffered ideology that indicate adaptive attitude change during the period of the target's involvement in the reform environment and immediately following separation should not be taken as mere playacting in reaction to necessity. Targets tend to become genuinely involved in the interaction. The reform experience focuses on genuine vulnerabilities as the method for undermining self-concept: manipulating genuine feelings of guilt about past conduct; inducing the target to make public denunciations of his or her prior life as being unworthy; and carrying this forward through interaction with peers for whom the target develops strong bonds. Involvement developed in these ways prevents the target from maintaining both psychological distance or emotional independence from the experience.

The reaction pattern of persons who display adaptive attitude-change responses is not one of an immediate and easy rejection of the proffered ideology. This response would be expected if they had been faking their reactions as a conscious strategy to defend against the pressures to which they were exposed. Rather, they appear to be conflicted about the sentiments they developed and their reevaluation of these sentiments. This response has been observed in persons reformed under both confined/assaultive and nonconfined/nonassaultive conditions (Schein 1962, pp. 163–165; Lifton 1961, pp. 86–116, 400–401).

Self-concept and belief-related attitude change in response to closely controlled social environments have been observed in other organizational settings that, like reform programs, can be classified as total institutions (Goffman 1957). Thought-reform reactions also appear to be related to, but are far more extreme than, responses to the typically less-identity-assaultive and less-totalistic socialization programs carried out by organizations with central commitments to specifiable ideologies, and which undertake the training of social roles (e.g., in military academies and religious-indoctrination settings (Dornbush 1955; Hulme 1956).

The relatively rare instances in which belief changes are internalized and endure have been analyzed as attributable to the degree to which the acquired belief system and imposed peer relations function to fully resolve the identity crisis that is routinely precipitated during the first phase of the reform process (Schein 1961, p. 164; Lifton 1961, pp. 131–132, 400). Whatever the explanation for why some persons internalize the proffered ideology in response to the reform procedures, this extreme reaction should be recognized as both atypical and probably attributable to an interaction between long-standing personality traits and the mechanisms of influence utilized during the reform process.

Much of the attention to reform programs was stimulated because it was suspected that a predictable and highly effective method for profoundly changing beliefs had been designed, implemented, and was in operation. These suspicions are not supported by fact. Programs identified as thought reforming are not very effective at actually changing people's beliefs in any fashion that endures apart from an elaborate supporting social context. Evaluated only on the criterion of their ability to genuinely change beliefs, the programs have to be judged abject failures and massive wastes of effort.

The programs are, however, impressive in their ability to prepare targets for integration into and long-term participation in the organizations that operate them. Rather than assuming that individual belief change is the major goal of these programs, it is perhaps more productive to view the programs as elaborate role-training regimes. That is, as resocialization programs in which targets are being prepared to conduct themselves in a fashion appropriate for the social roles they are expected to occupy following conclusion of the training process.

If identified as training programs, it is clear that the goals of such programs are to reshape behavior and that they are organized around issues of social control important to the organizations that operate the programs. Their objectives then appear to be behavioral training of the target, which result in an ability to present self, values, aspirations, and past history in a style appropriate to the ideology of the controlling organization; to train an ability to reason in terms of the ideology; and to train a willingness to accept direction from those in authority with minimum apparent resistance. Belief changes that follow from successfully coercing or inducing the person to behave in the prescribed manner can be thought of as by-products of the training experience. As attitude-change models would predict, they arise "naturally" as a result of efforts to reshape behavior (Festinger 1957; Bem 1972).

The tactical dimension most clearly distinguishing reform processes from other sorts of training programs is the reliance on psychological coercion: procedures that generate pressure to comply as a means of escaping a punishing experience (e.g., public humiliation, sleep deprivation, guilt manipulation, etc.). Coercion differs from other influencing factors also present in thought reform, such as content-based persuasive attempts (e.g., presentation of new information, reference to authorities, etc.) or reliance on influence variables operative in all interaction (status relations, demeanor, normal assertiveness differentials, etc.). Coercion is principally utilized to gain behavioral compliance at key points and to ensure participation in activities likely to have influencing effects; that is, to engage the person in the role-training activities and in procedures likely to lead to strong emotional responses, to cognitive confusion, or to attributions to self as the source of beliefs promoted during the process.

Robert Lifton labeled the extraordinarily high degree of social control characteristic of organizations that operate reform programs as their totalistic quality (Lifton 1961). This concept refers to the mobilization of the entirety of the person's social, and often physical, environment in support of the manipulative effort. Lifton identified eight themes or properties of reform environments that contribute to their totalistic quality: (1) control of communication, (2) emotional and behavioral manipulation, (3) demands for absolute conformity to behavior prescriptions derived from the ideology, (4) obsessive demands for confession, (5) agreement that the ideology is faultless, (6) manipulation of language in which clichés substitute for analytic thought, (7) reinterpretation of human experience and emotion in terms of doctrine, and (8) classification of those not sharing the ideology as inferior and not worthy of respect (Lifton 1961, pp. 419–437, 1987).

Schein's analysis of the behavioral sequence underlying coercive persuasion separated the process into three subphases: *unfreezing, change,* and *refreezing* (Schein 1961, pp. 111–139). Phases differ in their principal goals and their admixtures of persuasive, influencing, and coercive tactics. Although others have described the process differently, their analyses are not inconsistent with Schein's three-phase breakdown (Lifton 1961; Farber, Harlow, and West 1956; Meerloo 1956; Sargent 1957; Ofshe and Singer 1986). Although Schein's terminology is adopted here, the descriptions of phase activities have been broadened to reflect later research.

Unfreezing is the first step in eliciting behavior and developing a belief system that facilitates the long-term management of a person. It consists of attempting to undercut a person's psychological basis for resisting demands for behavioral compliance to the routines and rituals of the reform program. The goals of unfreezing are to destabilize a person's sense of identity (i.e., to precipitate an identity crisis), to diminish confidence in prior social judgments, and to foster a sense of powerlessness, if not hopelessness. Successful destabilization induces a negative shift in global self-evaluations and increases uncertainty about one's values and position in society. It thereby reduces resistance to the new demands for compliance while increasing suggestibility.

Destabilization of identity is accomplished by bringing into play varying sets of manipulative techniques. The first programs to be studied utilized techniques such as repeatedly demonstrating the person's inability to control his or her own fate, the use of degradation ceremonies, attempts to induce reevaluation of the adequacy and/or propriety of prior conduct, and techniques designed to encourage the reemergence of latent feelings of guilt and emotional turmoil (Hinkle and Wolfe 1956; Lifton 1954, 1961; Schein 1956, 1961; Schein, Cooley, and Singer 1960). Contemporary programs have been observed to utilize far more psychologically sophisticated procedures to accomplish destabilization. These techniques are often adapted from the traditions of psychiatry, psychotherapy, hypnotherapy, and the human-potential movement, as well as from religious practice (Ofshe and Singer 1986; Lifton 1987; Singer and Lalich 1995).

The *change* phase allows the individual an opportunity to escape punishing destabilization procedures by demonstrating that he or she has learned the proffered ideology, can demonstrate an ability to interpret reality in its terms, and is willing to participate in competition with peers to demonstrate zeal through displays of commitment. In addition to study and/or formal instruction, the techniques used to facilitate learning and the skill basis that can lead to opinion change include scheduling events that have predictable influencing consequences, rewarding certain conduct, and manipulating emotions to create punishing experiences. Some of the practices designed to promote influence might include requiring the target to assume responsibility for the progress of less-advanced "students," to become the responsibility of those further along in the program, to assume the role of a teacher of the ideology, or to develop ever more refined and detailed confession statements that recast the person's former life in terms of the required ideological position. Group structure is often manipulated by making rewards or punishments for an entire peer group contingent on the performance of the weakest person, requiring the group to utilize a vocabulary appropriate to the ideology, making status and privilege changes commensurate with behavioral compliance, subjecting the target to strong criticism and humiliation from peers for lack of progress, and peer monitoring for expressions of reservations or dissent. If progress is unsatisfactory, the individual can again be subjected to the punishing destabilization procedures used during unfreezing to undermine identity, to humiliate, and to provoke feelings of shame and guilt.

Refreezing denotes an attempt to promote and reinforce behavior acceptable to the controlling organization. Satisfactory performance is rewarded with social approval, status gains, and small privileges. Part of the social structure of the environment is the norm of interpreting the target's display of the desired conduct as demonstrating the person's progress in understanding the errors of his or her former life. The combination of reinforcing approved behavior and interpreting its symbolic meaning as demonstrating the emergence of a new individual fosters the development of an environment-specific, supposedly reborn social identity. The person is encouraged to claim this identity and is rewarded for doing so.

Lengthy participation in an appropriately constructed and managed environment fosters peer relations, an interaction history, and other behavior consistent with a public identity that incorporates approved values and opinions. Promoting the development of an interaction history in which persons engage in cooperative activity with peers that is not blatantly coerced and in which they are encouraged but not forced to make verbal claims to "truly understanding the ideology and having been transformed," will tend to lead them to conclude that they hold beliefs consistent with their actions (i.e., to make attributions to self as the source of their behaviors). These reinforcement procedures can result in a significant degree of cognitive confusion and an alteration in what the person takes to be his or her beliefs and attitudes while involved in the controlled environment (Bem 1972; Ofshe et al. 1974).

Continuous use of *refreezing* procedures can sustain the expression of what appears to be significant attitude change for long periods of time. Maintaining compliance with a requirement that the person display behavior signifying unreserved acceptance of an imposed ideology and gaining other forms of long-term behavioral control requires continuous effort. The person must be carefully managed, monitored, and manipulated through peer pressure, the threat or use of punishment (material, social, and emotional) and through the normative rules of the community (e.g., expectations prohibiting careers independent of the organization, prohibiting formation of independent nuclear families, prohibiting accumulation of significant personal economic resources, etc.) (Whyte 1976; Ofshe 1980; Ofshe and Singer 1986).

The rate at which a once-attained level of attitude change deteriorates depends on the type of social support the person receives over time (Schein 1961 pp. 158–166; Lifton pp. 399–415). In keeping with the *refreezing* metaphor, even when the reform process is to some degree successful at shaping behavior and attitudes, the new shape tends to be maintained only as long as temperature is appropriately controlled.

One of the essential components of the reform process in general and of long-term *refreezing* in particular is monitoring and controlling the contents of communication among persons in the managed group (Lifton 1961; Schein 1960; Ofshe et al. 1974). If successfully accomplished, communication control eliminates a person's ability to safely express criticisms or to share private doubts and reservations. The result is to confer on the community the quality of being a spy system of the whole, upon the whole.

The typically observed complex of communication-controlling rules requires people to self-report critical thoughts to authorities or to make doubts known only in approved and readily managed settings (e.g., small groups or private counseling sessions). Admitting "negativity" leads to punishment or reindoctrination through procedures sometimes euphemistically termed "education" or "therapy." Individual social isolation is furthered by rules requiring peers to "help" colleagues to progress, by reporting their expressions of doubt. If it is discovered, failure to make a report is punishable, because it reflects on the low level of commitment of the person who did not "help" a colleague to make progress.

Controlling communication effectively blocks individuals from testing the appropriateness of privately held critical perceptions against the views of even their families and most-valued associates. Community norms encourage doubters to interpret lingering reservations as signs of a personal failure to comprehend the truth of the ideology; if involved with religious organizations, to interpret doubt as evidence of sinfulness or the result of demonic influences; if involved with an organization delivering a supposed psychological or medical therapy, as evidence of continuing illness and/or failure to progress in treatment.

The significance of communication control is illustrated by the collapse of a large psychotherapy organization in immediate reaction to the leadership's loss of effective control over interpersonal communication. At a meeting of several hundred of the members of this "therapeutic community" clients were allowed to openly voice privately held reservations about their treatment and exploitation. They had been subjected to abusive practices which included assault, sexual and economic exploitation, extremes of public humiliation, and others. When members discovered the extent to which their sentiments about these practices were shared by their peers they rebelled (Ayalla 1998).

Two widespread myths have developed from misreading the early studies of thought-reforming influence systems (Zablocki 1991). These studies dealt in part with their use to elicit false confessions in the Soviet Union after the 1917 revolution; from American and United Nations forces held as POWs during the Korean War; and from their application to Western missionaries held in China following Mao's revolution.

The first myth concerns the necessity and effectiveness of physical abuse in the reform process. The myth is that physical abuse is not only necessary but is the prime cause of apparent belief change. Reports about the treatment of POWs and foreign prisoners in China documented that physical abuse was present. Studies of the role of assault in the promotion of attitude change and in eliciting false confessions even from U.S. servicemen revealed, however, that it was ineffective. Belief change and compliance was more likely when physical abuse was minimal or absent (Biderman 1960). Both Schein (1961) and Lifton (1961) reported that physical abuse was a minor element in the understanding of even prison reform programs in China.

In the main, efforts at resocializing China's nationals were conducted under nonconfined/nonassaultive conditions. Millions of China's citizens underwent reform in schools, special-training centers, factories, and neighborhood groups in which physical assault was not used as a coercive technique. One such setting for which many participants actively sought admission, the "Revolutionary University," was classified by Lifton as the "hard core of the entire Chinese thought reform movement" (Lifton 1961, p. 248).

Attribution theories would predict that if there were differences between the power of reform programs to promote belief change in settings that were relatively more or less blatantly coercive and physically threatening, the effect would be greatest in less-coercive programs. Consistent with this expectation, Lifton concluded that reform efforts directed against Chinese citizens were "much more successful" than efforts directed against Westerners (Lifton 1961, p. 400).

A second myth concerns the purported effects of brainwashing. Media reports about thought reform's effects far exceed the findings of scientific studies—which show coercive persuasion's upper limit of impact to be that of inducing personal confusion and significant, but typically transitory, attitude change. Brainwashing was promoted as capable of stripping victims of their *capacity* to assert their wills, thereby rendering them unable to resist the orders of their controllers. People subjected to "brainwashing" were not merely influenced to adopt new attitudes but, according to the myth, suffered essentially an alteration in their psychiatric status from *normal* to *pathological*, while losing their capacity to decide to comply with or resist orders.

This lurid promotion of the power of thought-reforming influence techniques to change a person's capacity to resist direction is entirely without basis in fact: No evidence, scientific or otherwise, supports this proposition. No known mental disorder produces the loss of will that is alleged to be the result of brainwashing. Whatever behavior and attitude changes result from exposure to the process, they are most reasonably classified as the responses of normal individuals to a complex program of influence.

The U.S. Central Intelligence Agency seems to have taken seriously the myth about brainwashing's power to destroy the will. Due, perhaps, to concern that an enemy had perfected a method for dependably overcoming will—or perhaps in hope of being the first to develop such a method—the Agency embarked on a research program, code-named MKULTRA. It was a pathetic and tragic failure. On the one hand, it funded some innocuous and uncontroversial research projects; on the other, it funded or supervised the execution of several far-fetched, unethical, and dangerous experiments that failed completely (Marks 1979; Thomas 1989).

Although no evidence suggests that thought reform is a process capable of stripping a person of their will to resist, a relationship does exist between thought reform and changes in psychiatric status. The stress and pressure of the reform process cause some percentage of *psychological casualties*. To reduce resistance and to motivate behavior change, thought-reform procedures rely on psychological stressors, induction of high degrees of emotional distress, and on other intrinsically dangerous influence techniques (Heide and Borkovec 1983). The process has a potential to cause psychiatric injury, which is sometimes realized. The major early studies (Hinkle and Wolfe 1961; Lifton 1961; Schein 1961) reported that during the *unfreezing* phase individuals were intentionally stressed to a point at which some persons displayed symptoms of being on the brink of psychosis. Managers attempted to reduce psychological pressure when this happened, to avoid serious psychological injury to those obviously near the breaking point.

Contemporary programs speed up the reform process through the use of more psychologically sophisticated and dangerous procedures to accomplish destabilization. In contemporary programs the process is sometimes carried forward on a large group basis, which reduces the ability of managers to detect symptoms of impending psychiatric emergencies. In addition, in some of the "therapeutic" ideologies espoused by thought-reforming organizations, extreme emotional distress is valued positively, as a sign of progress. Studies of contemporary programs have reported on a variety of psychological injuries related to the reform process. Injuries include psychosis, major depressions, manic episodes, and debilitating anxiety (Glass, Kirsch, and Parris 1977, Haaken and Adams 1983, Heide and Borkovec 1983; Higget and Murray 1983; Kirsch and Glass 1977; Yalom and Lieberman 1971; Lieberman 1987; Singer and Ofshe 1990; Singer and Lalich 1995, 1996).

HIGH CONTROL GROUPS AND LARGE GROUP AWARENESS TRAINING

Political reeducation in China was backed by the power of the state to request, if not to compel participation. Contemporary examples of the use of extreme influence that rise to the level of attempting to induce a major shift in belief typically lack the power to coerce someone into remaining involved long enough for the persuasive procedures of the program to unfreeze, change, and refreeze a person's values, perceptions, and preferences. Rather, participants must be attracted to the group and participate long enough for the tactics utilized during the unfreezing phase to destabilize the person's sense of identity so that he or she will be motivated to adopt the new world view or the new perceptions promoted by the program's managers, will desire to maintain association with committed believers in the new perspective, and will thereby obtain the long-term social support necessary to restabilize his or her identity.

Contemporary thought-reform programs are generally far more sophisticated in their selection of both destabilization and influence techniques than were the programs studied during the 1950s (Ofshe and Singer 1986; Singer and Lalich 1995, 1996). For example, hypnosis was entirely absent from the first programs studied but is often observed in modern programs. In most modern examples in which hypnosis is present, it functions as a remarkably powerful technique for manipulating subjective experience and for intensifying emotional response. It provides a method for influencing people to imagine impossible events such as those that supposedly occurred in their "past lives," the future, or during visits to other planets. If persons so manipulated misidentify the hypnotically induced fantasies, and classify them as previously unavailable memories, their confidence in the content of a particular ideology can be increased (Bainbridge and Stark 1980).

Hypnosis can also be used to lead people to allow themselves to relive actual traumatic life events (e.g., rape, childhood sexual abuse, near-death experiences, etc.) or to fantasize the existence of such events and, thereby, stimulate the experience of extreme emotional distress. When imbedded in a reform program, repeatedly leading the person to experience such events can function simply as punishment, useful for coercing compliance.

Accounts of contemporary programs also describe the use of sophisticated techniques intended to strip away psychological defenses, to induce regression to primitive levels of coping, and to flood targets with powerful emotion (Ayalla 1998; Haaken and Adams 1983; Hockman 1984; Temerlin and Temerlin 1982; Singer and Lalich 1996). In some instances stress and fatigue have been used to promote hallucinatory experiences that are defined as therapeutic (Gerstel 1982). Drugs have been used to facilitate disinhibition and heightened suggestibility (Watkins 1980). Thought-reform subjects have been punished for disobedience by being ordered to self-inflict severe pain, justified by the claim that the result will be therapeutic (Bellack et al. *v.* Murietta Foundation et al.).

Programs attempting thought reform appear in various forms in contemporary society. They depend on the voluntary initial participation of targets. This is usually accomplished because the target assumes that there is a common goal that unites him or her with the organization or that involvement will confer some benefit (e.g., relief of symptoms, personal growth, spiritual development, etc.). Apparently some programs were developed based on the assumption that they could be used to facilitate desirable changes (e.g., certain rehabilitation or psychotherapy programs). Some religious organizations and social movements utilize them for recruitment purposes. Some commercial organizations utilize them as methods for promoting sales. In some instances, reform programs appear to have been operated for the sole purpose of gaining a high degree of control over individuals to facilitate their exploitation (Ofshe 1986; McGuire and Norton 1988; Watkins 1980).

Virtually any acknowledged expertise or authority can serve as a power base to develop the social structure necessary to carry out thought reform. In the course of developing a new form of rehabilitation, psychotherapy, religious organization, utopian community, school, or sales organization, it is not difficult to justify the introduction of thought-reform procedures.

Perhaps the most famous example of a thought-reforming program developed for the ostensible purpose of rehabilitation was Synanon, a drug-treatment program (Sarbin and Adler 1970, Yablonsky 1965; Ofshe et al. 1974). The Synanon environment possessed all of Lifton's eight themes. It used as its principle coercive procedure a highly aggressive encounter/therapy group interaction. In form it resembled "struggle groups" observed in China (Whyte 1976), but it differed in content. Individuals were vilified and humiliated not for past political behavior but for current conduct as well as far more psychologically intimate subjects, such as early childhood experiences, sexual experiences, degrading experiences as adults, etc. The coercive power of the group experience to affect behavior was substantial as was its ability to induce psychological injury (Lieberman, Yalom, and Miles 1973; Ofshe et al. 1974).

Allegedly started as a drug-rehabilitation program, Synanon failed to accomplish significant long-term rehabilitation. Eventually, Synanon's leader, Charles Diederich, promoted the idea that any degree of drug abuse was incurable and that persons so afflicted needed to spend their lives in the Synanon community. Synanon's influence program was successful in convincing many that this was so. Under Diederich's direction, Synanon evolved from an organization that espoused nonviolence into one that was violent. Its soldiers were dispatched to assault and attempt to murder persons identified by Diederich as Synanon's enemies (Mitchell, Mitchell, and Ofshe 1981).

The manipulative techniques of self-styled messiahs, such as People's Temple leader Jim Jones (Reiterman 1982), and influence programs operated by religious organizations, such as the Unification Church (Taylor 1978) and Scientology (Wallis 1977; Bainbridge and Stark 1980), can be analyzed as thought-reform programs. The most controversial recruitment system operated by a religious organization in recent American history was that of the Northern California branch of the Unification Church (Reverend Moon's organization). The influence program was built directly from procedures of psychological manipulation that were commonplace in the human-potential movement (Bromley and Shupe 1981). The procedures involved various group-based exercises as well as events designed to elicit from participants information about their emotional needs and vulnerabilities. Blended into this program was content intended to slowly introduce the newcomer to the group's ideology. Typically, the program's connection with the Unification Church or any religious mission was denied during the early stages of the reform process. The target was monitored around the clock and prevented from communicating with peers who might reinforce doubt and support a desire to leave. The physical setting was an isolated rural facility far from public transportation.

Initial focus on personal failures, guilt-laden memories, and unfulfilled aspirations shifted to the opportunity to realize infantile desires and idealistic goals, by affiliating with the group and its mission to save the world. The person was encouraged to develop strong affective bonds with current members. They showed unfailing interest, affection, and concern, sometimes to the point of spoon-feeding the person's meals and accompanying the individual everywhere, including to the toilet. If the *unfreezing* and *change* phases of the program succeeded, the individual was told of the group's affiliation with the Unification Church and assigned to another unit of the organization within which *refreezing* procedures could be carried forward.

POLICE INTERROGATION AND FALSE CONFESSIONS

Police interrogation in America was transformed in the twentieth century from a method of gaining compliance relying largely on physical coercion into one that relies almost exclusively on psychological means (Leo 1992). Psychological methods of interrogation were developed to influence persons who know they are guilty of a crime to change their decision to deny guilt, to admit responsibility for the crime, and to confess fully to their role in the crime (see Hilgendorf and Irving 1981; Ofshe and Leo 1997a,b). Compared to the other extreme influence environments described in this entry, a police interrogation is of relatively short duration and is entirely focused on the single issue of eliciting a confession. It is nevertheless an environment in which a person can be influenced to make a dramatic shift in position—from denial of guilt to confession.

The techniques and tactics that lead a guilty suspect to admit guilt constitute an impressive display of the power of influence to change a person's decision even when the consequence of the shift is obviously disadvantageous. If the procedures of interrogation are misused, modern interrogation methods can have an even more impressive result. If the influence procedures and techniques of modern interrogation methods are directed at innocent persons, some false confessions will result (Bedau and Radelet 1987; Leo and Ofshe 1998). In most instances when an innocent person is led to give a false confession the cause is coercion—the use of a threat of severe punishment if the person maintains that he is innocent and an offer of leniency if he complies with the interrogator's demand to confess. Most persons who decide to comply and offer a false confession in response to coercion remain certain of their innocence and know that they are falsely confessing in order to avoid the most severe possible punishment.

Under some circumstances, however, interrogation tactics can cause an innocent person to give what is called a persuaded false confession—a false confession that is believed to be true when it is given. Influence procedures now commonly used during modern police interrogation can sometimes inadvertently manipulate innocent persons' beliefs about their own innocence and, thereby, cause them to falsely confess. Confessions resulting from accomplishing the *unfreezing* and *change* phases of thought reform are classified as persuaded false confessions (Kassin and Wrightsman 1985;

Gudjonsson and MacKeith 1988; Ofshe and Leo 1997a). Although they rarely come together simultaneously, the ingredients necessary to elicit a temporarily believed false confession are: erroneous police suspicion, the use of *certain* commonly employed interrogation procedures, and some degree of psychological vulnerability in the suspect. Philip Zimbardo (1971) has reviewed the coercive factors generally present in modern interrogation settings. Richard Ofshe and Richard Leo (1989, 1997a) have identified those influence procedures that if present in a suspect's interrogation contribute to causing *unfreezing* and *change*.

Techniques that contribute to *unfreezing* include falsely telling a suspect that the police have evidence proving the person's guilt (e.g., fingerprints, eyewitness testimony, etc.). Suspects may be given a polygraph examination and then falsely told (due either to error or design) that they failed and the test reveals their unconscious knowledge of guilt. Suspects may be told that their lack of memory of the crime was caused by an alcohol- or drug-induced blackout, was repressed, or is explained because the individual is a multiple personality.

The techniques listed above regularly appear in modern American police interrogations. They are used to lead persons who know that they have committed the crime at issue to decide that the police have sufficient evidence to convict them or to counter typical objections to admitting guilt (e.g., "I can't remember having done that."). In conjunction with the other disorienting and distressing elements of a modern accusatory interrogation, these tactics can sometimes lead innocent suspects to doubt themselves and question their lack of knowledge of the crime. If innocent persons subjected to these sorts of influence techniques do not reject the false evidence and realize that the interrogators are lying to them, they have no choice but to doubt their memories. If the interrogator supplies an explanation for why the suspect's memory is untrustworthy, the person may reason that "I must have committed this crime."

Tactics used to *change* the suspect's position and elicit a confession include maneuvers designed to intensify feelings of guilt and emotional distress following from the suspect's assumption of guilt.

Suspects may be offered an escape from the emotional distress through confession. It may also be suggested that confession will provide evidence of remorse that will benefit the suspect in court.

RECOVERED MEMORY PSYCHOTHERAPY

The shifts in belief and conduct promoted during political reeducation concern an intellectual analysis of society and one's role it; in the context of high control groups the beliefs are about theology and one's role in a community; and in police interrogation the newly created beliefs concern a crime the suspect has no knowledge of having committed. The progression in these illustrations is from influence efforts directed at an intellectual or philosophical assumption to that of an influence effort directed at changing beliefs about a single fact—Did the suspect commit a crime and not know of it due to a memory defect? The final example of extreme influence and belief change is arguably the most dramatic example of the power of interpersonal influence and particular influence techniques to change a person's beliefs about the historical truth relating to a major dimension of his or her life history, such as whether or not he or she had been viciously raped and horribly brutalized by a parent (or parents, or siblings, or teachers, or neighbors, etc.) for periods of as long as two decades.

Psychotherapy directed at causing a patient to retrieve allegedly repressed and therefore supposedly unavailable memories (e.g., of sexual abuse, and/or having spent one's life suffering from an unrecognized multiple personality disorder, and/or having spent one's childhood and teenage years as a member of a murderous satanic cult) is one of the most stunning examples of psychological/psychiatric quackery of the twentieth century. It is also perhaps the most potent example of the power of social influence to predictably create beliefs (in this case beliefs that are utterly false) and thereby alter a person's choices and conduct (Loftus 1994; Perdergrast 1995; Ofshe and Watters 1994; Spanos 1996).

The elements of a thought-reforming process are visible in the steps through which a patient undergoing recovered memory therapy is manipulated. The patient's identity is destabilized by the therapist's insistence that the reason for the patient's distress or mental illness is that she or he suffered a series of sexual traumas in childhood that he or she don't know about because he or she has *repressed* them. Recovered memory therapists organize their treatment programs on the presumption that repression exists despite the fact that the notion of repression was never more than a fanciful, unsubstantiated speculation that was long ago rejected as useless by the scientific community that studies human memory (Loftus 1994; Crews 1998; Watters and Ofshe 1999). Recovered memory therapists rely on assertions of authority, claims of expertise, and outright trickery (e.g., inducing the patient to experience hypnotic fantasies of sexual abuse that they lead patients to misclassify as memories and interpreting the patient's dreams as proof that they suffer from repressed memories) to convince the patient of the existence of repression. Recovered memory therapists rely on the alleged "repression mechanism" to undermine patients' confidence in their normal memories of their lives. If patients can be successfully convinced that repression exists and that the hypnotic fantasies that the therapist suggests to them are memories of events that happened during their lives, they can no longer trust that they know even the broad outlines of their life histories.

Once the patient's identity has been destabilized, the therapist guides the patients to build a new identity centered on his or her status as victim of sexual abuse. This victim role may include requiring the patient to learn to act as if she or he suffers from multiple personality disorder, or suggesting that the patient publicly denounce, sue, or file criminal charges against the persons who supposedly abused them.

CONCLUSION

Extreme influence environments are not easy to study. The history of research on extreme influence has been one in which most of the basic descriptive work has been conducted through posthoc interviewing of persons exposed to the influence procedures. The second-most frequently employed method has been that of participant observation. In connection with work being done on police interrogation methods, it has been possible to analyze contemporaneous recordings of interrogation sessions in which targets' beliefs are actually made to undergo radical change. All this work

has contributed to the development of an understanding in several ways.

Studying these environments demonstrates that the extremes of influence are no more or less difficult to understand than any other complex social event. The characteristics that distinguish extreme influence environments from other examples of social settings are influence in the order in which the influence procedures are assembled and the degree to which the target's environment is manipulated in the service of social control. These are at most unusual arrangements of commonplace bits and pieces.

As it is with all complex, real-world social phenomena that cannot be studied experimentally, understanding information about the thought-reform process proceeds through the application of theories that have been independently developed. Explaining data that describe the type and organization of the influence procedures that constitute an extreme influence environment depends on applying established social-psychological theories about the manipulation of behavior and attitude change. Assessing reports about the impact of the experiences on the persons subjected to intense influence procedures depends on the application of current theories of personality formation and change. Understanding instances in which the thought-reform experience appears related to psychiatric injury requires proceeding as one would ordinarily in evaluating any case history of a stress-related or other type of psychological injury.

(SEE ALSO: *Attitudes; Persuasion; Social Control*)

REFERENCES

Ayalla, Marybeth 1998 *Insane Therapy*. Philadelphia: Temple University Press.

Bainbridge, William S., and Rodney Stark 1980 "Scientology, to Be Perfectly Clear." *Sociological Analysis* 41:128–136.

Bedau, Hugo, and Michael Radelet 1987 "Miscarriages of Justice in Potentially Capital Cases." *Stanford University Law Review* 40:21–197.

Bellack, Catherine et al. *v.* Murietta Foundation et al. United States District Court, Central District of California. Civil No. 87–08597.

Bem, Darryl 1972 "Self-Perception Theory." In Leonard Berkowitz, ed., *Advances in Experimental Social Psychology*, vol 6. New York: Academic.

Biderman, Albert D. 1960 "Social-Psychological Needs and Involuntary Behavior as Illustrated by Compliance in Interrogation." *Sociometry* 23:120–147.

Bromley, David G., and Anson D. Shupe, Jr. 1981 *Strange Gods*. Boston: Beacon Press.

Dornbush, Sanford M. 1955 "The Military Academy as an Assimilating Institution. *Social Forces* 33:316–321.

Farber, I. E., Harry F. Harlow, and Louis J. West 1956 "Brainwashing, Conditioning and DDD: Debility, Dependency and Dread." *Sociometry* 20:271–285.

Festinger, Leon 1957 *A Theory of Cognitive Dissonance*. Evanston, Ill.: Row Peterson.

Gerstel, David 1982 *Paradise Incorporated: Synanon*. Novato, Calif.: Presidio.

Glass, Leonard L., Michael A. Kirsch, and Frederick A. Parris 1977 "Psychiatric Disturbances Associated with Erhard Seminars Training: I. A Report of Cases." *American Journal of Psychiatry* 134:245–247.

Goffman, Erving 1957 "On the Characteristics of Total Institutions." Proceedings of the Symposium on Preventive and Social Psychiatry. Washington, D.C.: Walter Reed Army Institute of Research.

Gudjonsson, Gisli, and Bent Lebegue 1989 "Psychological and Psychiatric Aspects of a Coerced-Internalized False Confession." *Journal of Forensic Science* 29:261–269.

Gudjonsson, Gisli H., and James A. MacKeith 1988 "Retracted Confessions: Legal, Psychological and Psychiatric Aspects." *Medical Science and Law* 28: 187–194.

Haaken, Janice, and Richard Adams 1983 "Pathology as 'Personal Growth': A Participant Observation Study of Lifespring Training." *Psychiatry* 46:270–280.

Heide, F. J., and T. D. Borkovec 1984 "Relaxation Induced Anxiety: Mechanism and Theoretical Implications." *Behavior Research and Therapy* 22:1–12.

Higget, Anna C., and Robin M. Murray 1983 "A Psychotic Episode Following Erhard Seminars Training." *Acta Psychiatria Scandinavia* 67:436–439.

Hilgendorf, Edward, and Barrie Irving 1981 "A Decision-Making Model of Confession." In S.M.A. Loyd-Bostock, ed., *Psychology in Legal Contexts*. London: Macmillan.

Hinkle, L. E., and Harold G. Wolfe 1956 "Communist Interrogation and Indoctrination of Enemies of the State." *Archives of Neurology and Psychiatry* 20:271–285.

Hochman, John A. 1984 "Iatrogenic Symptoms Associated with a Therapy Cult: Examination of an Extinct 'New Therapy' with Respect to Psychiatric Deterioration and 'Brainwashing'." *Psychiatry* 47:366–377.

Hulme, Kathryn 1956 *The Nun's Story*. Boston: Little, Brown.

Hunter, Edward 1951 *Brain-washing in China*. New York: Vanguard.

Kassin, Saul, and Lawrence Wrightsman 1985 "Confession Evidence." In Samuel Kassin and Lawrence Wrightsman, eds., *The Psychology of Evidence and Trial Procedure*. London: Sage.

Kirsch, Michael A., and Leonard L. Glass 1977 "Psychiatric Disturbances Associated with Erhard Seminars Training: II. Additional Cases and Theoretical Considerations." *American Journal of Psychiatry* 134: 1254–1258.

Leo, Richard 1992 "From Coercion to Deception: The Changing Nature of Police Interrogation in America." *Journal of Criminal Law and Social Change* 88, 27–52.

—— and Richard Ofshe 1998 "The Consequences of False Confessions. *Journal of Criminal Law and Criminology* 88, 2:429–496.

Lieberman, Morton A. 1987 "Effect of Large Group Awareness Training on Participants' Psychiatric Status." *American Journal of Psychiatry*, 144:460–464.

——, Irvin D. Yalom, and M. B. Miles 1973 *Encounter Groups: First Facts*. New York: Basic Books.

Lifton, Robert J. 1954 "Home by Ship: Reaction Patterns of American Prisoners of War Repatriated from North Korea." *American Journal of Psychiatry* 110:732–739.

—— 1961 *Thought Reform and the Psychology of Totalism*. New York: Norton.

—— 1986 *The Nazi Doctors*. New York: Basic Books.

—— 1987 "Cults: Totalism and Civil Liberties." In Robert J. Lifton, ed., *The Future of Immortality and Other Essays for a Nuclear Age*. New York: Basic Books.

Loftus, Elizabeth, and Katherine Ketcham 1994 *The Myth of Repressed Memory*. New York; St. Martins.

Marks, John 1979 *The Search for the Manchurian Candidate*. New York: Dell.

McGuire, Christine, and Carla Norton 1988 *Perfect Victim*. New York: Arbor House.

Meerloo, Jorst A. 1956 *The Rape of the Mind: The Psychology of Thought Control, Menticide and Brainwashing*. Cleveland, Ohio: World Publishing.

Mitchell, David V., Catherine Mitchell, and Richard J. Ofshe 1981 *The Light on Synanon*. New York: Seaview.

Ofshe, Richard J. 1980 "The Social Development of the Synanon Cult: The Managerial Strategy of Organizational Transformation." *Sociological Analysis* 41: 109–127.

—— 1986 "The Rabbi and the Sex Cult." *Cultic Studies Journal* 3:173–189.

—— 1989 "Coerced Confessions: The Logic of Seemingly Irrational Action." *Cultic Studies Journal* 6:1–15.

—— 1992 "Inadvertent Hypnosis During Interrogation: False Confession Due to Dissociative State; Mis-Identified Multiple Personality and the Satanic Cult Hypothesis." *International Journal of Clinical and Experimental Hypnosis* 40, (3):125–156.

——, and Richard Leo 1997a "The Social Psychology of Police Interrogation: The Theory and Classification of True and False Confessions." *Studies in Law, Politics and Society* 16: 190–251.

——, 1997b "The Decision to Confess Falsely: Rational Choice and Irrational Action." *Denver University Law Review* 74, 4:979–1122.

Ofshe, Richard and Margaret T. Singer 1986 "Attacks on Peripheral Versus Central Elements of Self and the Impact of Thought Reforming Techniques." *Cultic Studies Journal* 3:3–24.

——, Nancy Eisenberg, Richard Coughlin, and Gregory Dolinajec 1974 "Social Structure and Social Control in Synanon." *Voluntary Action Research* 3:67–76.

Ofshe, Richard, and Ethan Watters 1994 *Making Monsters*. New York: Scribners.

Perdergrast, Mark 1995 *Victims of Memory*. Hinesberg, Vt.: Upper Access.

Reiterman, Timothy, and Dan Jacobs 1982 *The Raven*. New York: Dutton.

Sarbin, Theodore R., and Nathan Adler 1970 "Self-Reconstitution Processes: A Preliminary Report." *Psychoanalytic Review* 4:599–616.

Sargent, William 1957 *Battle for the Mind: How Evangelists, Psychiatrists, and Medicine Men Can Change Your Beliefs and Behavior*. Garden City, N.Y.: Doubleday.

Schein, Edgar W. 1961 *Coercive Persuasion*. New York: Norton.

——, W. E. Cooley, and Margaret T. Singer 1960 *A Psychological Follow-up of Former Prisoners of the Chinese Communists*, Part I, *Results of Interview Study*. Cambridge: MIT.

Shurmann, Franz 1968 *Ideology and Organization in Communist China*. Berkeley: University of California Press.

Singer, Margaret, and Janja Lalich 1995 *Cults in Our Midst*. San Francisco: Jossey-Bass.

—— 1996 *Crazy Therapies*. San Francisco: Jossey-Bass.

Singer, Margaret T., and Richard J. Ofshe 1990 "Thought Reform Programs and the Production of Psychiatric Casualties." *Psychiatric Annals* 20:188–193.

Taylor, David 1978 "Social Organization and Recruitment in the Unification Church." Master's diss., University of Montana.

Temerlin, Maurice K., and Jane W. Temerlin 1982 "Psychotherapy Cults: An Iatrogenic Phenomenon." *Psychotherapy Theory, Research Practice* 19:131–41.

Thomas, Gordon 1989 *Journey Into Madness*. New York: Bantam.

Wallis, Roy 1977 *The Road to Total Freedom*. New York: Columbia University Press.

Watkins, Paul 1980 *My Life With Charles Manson*. New York: Bantam.

Whyte, Martin K. 1976 *Small Groups and Political Behavior in China*. Berkeley: University of California Press.

Wright, Stewart 1987 *Leaving Cults: The Dynamics of Defection*. Society of the Scientific Study of Religion, Monograph no. 7, Washington, D.C.

Yablonski, Louis 1965 *The Tunnel Back: Synanon*. New York: Macmillan.

Yalom, Irvin D., and Morton Lieberman 1971 "A Study of Encounter Group Casualties." *Archives of General Psychiatry* 25:16–30.

Zablocki, Benjamin 1991 *The Scientific Investigation of the Brainwashing Conjecture*. Washington D.C.: American Association for the Advancement of Science.

Zimbardo, Philip G. 1971 "Coercion and Compliance." In Charles Perruci and Mark Pilisuk, eds., *The Triple Revolution*. Boston: Little, Brown.

RICHARD J. OFSHE

F

FACTOR ANALYSIS

Factor analysis is a mathematical and statistical technique for analyzing differences among units of analysis and the structure of relationships among variables assessing those units. The units of analysis may be persons, groups, organizations, ecological units, or any other justifiable basis of aggregation although persons are most often the focus of analysis. The chief purpose of the method is the attainment of scientific parsimony, which is achieved by positing a set of latent common factors that underlie the data. The factor model was developed by Charles Spearman (1904a, 1927) to be used to describe economically the correlations among mental test scores observed for persons. Spearman's famous bi-factor model of intelligence held that measures of mental abilities had two major sources: a factor common to all measures of ability, which he called the g-factor (factor of general ability), and a specific component of variation (an s-factor) unique to the test. For example, a test of numerical ability may be affected in part by a general factor of intelligence as well as a factor specific to numerical aptitude. This model, although never the predominant psychological theory of mental tests, has persisted in the culture in the sense that people often believe there is a general factor of intelligence underlying performance across different domains (see Gould 1981 for a critique of this view).

Although Spearman's work did not go very far beyond such a simple model, his approach to model construction and theory testing using tetrad differences has provided the basis for much further work (see, e.g., Glymour et al. 1987). Many contemporaries of Spearman—Cyril Burt, Karl Pearson, Godfrey Thomson, J. C. Maxwell Garnett, and others—working in the fields of human abilities and statistics also contributed to the development of factor analysis. Several worked to modify Spearman's bi-factor model to include multiple factors of intelligence. But the most radical departure from the g-factor view of human intelligence came with Thurstone's (1938) publication of *Primary Mental Abilities*, in which he demonstrated empirically through the application of *multiple factor analysis* that several common factors were necessary to explain correlations among measures of human abilities. While Thurstone (1947) is usually credited with the popularization of this more general technique, the concept of multiple factor analysis first arose in the work of Garnett (1919–1920; see Harmon 1976).

Multiple factor analysis proved to be a major advance over the Spearman model, which was later to be seen as a special case (the one-factor case). Multiple factor analysis permitted a general solution to the possibility of positing multiple factors (k) in a set of variables (p). Within this framework, two competing research strategies emerged, each resting on distinct principles. One was based on Pearson's principle of *principal axes*, which was later developed by Hotelling (1933) as the method of *principal components*. This approach emphasized the objective of "extracting" a maximum of variance from the set of p variables so that the k factors explained as much of the variance in the variables as they could. This tradition still exists in approaches to factor analysis that rely on principal components analysis, and, although many researchers use the technique, they are likely to be unaware of the objectives underlying the approach (see Harman 1976).

In contrast to the strategy of maximizing the variance explained in the variables, the other basic strategy—more squarely in the tradition of Spearman—emphasized the objective of reproducing the observed correlations among the variables. These two objectives—one emphasizing the extraction of maximum variance in the variables and the other emphasizing the fit to the correlations among the variables—eventually became the object of serious debate. However, with time there has emerged a consensus that the "debate" between these approaches rested on a misconception. The method of principal axes, which is the basis of principal components analysis—involving the analysis of a correlation matrix with unities in the diagonal—is now better understood as a computational method and not a model, as the factor analysis approach is now considered (see Maxwell 1977).

The early developments in the field of factor analysis and related techniques were carried out primarily by psychometricians. These early developments were followed by many important contributions to estimation, computation, and model construction during the post–World War II period. Some of the most important contributions to the method during the 1950s were made by a sociologist, Louis Guttman. Guttman made important contributions to the resolution of the issue of deciding upon the best number of latent factors (Guttman 1954), the problem of "factor indeterminacy" (Guttman 1955), and the problem of estimating communalities (Guttman 1956), among many others. Guttman (1960) also invented yet a third model, called *image analysis*, which has a certain elegance but is rarely used (see Harris 1964; Kaiser 1963).

Research workers in many fields made contributions to the problem of deciding how best to represent a particular factor model in a theoretical/geometrical space, via the transformation or rotation of factors. Methods of rotation included the quartimax (Neuhaus and Wrigley 1954), varimax (Kaiser 1958), and oblimax (Harman 1976), among

others. Several contributions were made during the early development of factor analysis with respect to the most useful strategies for estimating factor scores (see reviews by Harris 1967 and McDonald and Burr 1967) and for dealing with the problem of assessing factorial invariance (e.g., Meredith 1964a, 1964b; Mulaik 1972). Beginning in the mid-1960s the advances in the field of factor analysis have focused on the development of maximum-likelihood estimation techniques (Lawley and Maxwell 1971; Jöreskog 1967; Jöreskog and Lawley 1968); alternative distribution-free techniques (Bentler 1983, 1989; Bentler and Weeks 1980; Browne 1974, 1984; Browne and Shapiro 1988); the development of confirmatory factor analysis, which permits the setting of specific model constraints on the data to be analyzed (Bentler 1989; Jöreskog 1966, 1967, 1970, 1971a, 1973; Jöreskog and Sörbom 1986); and the development of factor analysis strategies for categoric variables (Christofferson 1975; Jöreskog and Sörbom 1988; Muthén 1983, 1988).

Factor analysis is used extensively by sociologists as a research tool. It is used in at least four related ways. *First*, it is frequently used as a data reduction or item analysis technique in index construction. *Second*, it is used as an exploratory device for examining the dimensional structure of content within a well-specified domain. *Third*, it is used as a confirmatory, hypothesis-testing tool aimed at testing prior hypotheses about the dimensional structure of a set of variables. And *fourth*, it is used to conceptualize the relationships of multiple indicators of latent variables in a causal modeling framework in which a factor model is assumed for the relationships between latent variables and their indicators. After a brief introduction to each of these four ways in which factor analytic tools are used in sociological research, this discussion covers the basic factor model and issues that arise in its application, either in the *exploratory* or *confirmatory* frameworks of analysis.

DATA REDUCTION APPROACHES

When a researcher wishes to build a composite score from a set of empirical variables, factor analysis and related techniques are often useful. Indeed, it is perhaps in this area of "index construction" that factor analysis is most often used by sociologists. There are various related data reduction approaches that fall under the heading of "dimensional analysis" or "cluster analysis," but the basic goal of all these techniques is to perform some decomposition of the data into sets of variables, each of which is relatively independent and homogeneous in content. When factor analysis is used in this way the researcher is essentially interested in determining the sets of linear dependence among a set of variables that are intended to measure the same general domain of content. The factor analysis of such variables may proceed in a number of different ways, but the basic goal is to determine the number of clusters of homogeneous content and the extent of relationship among various clusters or factors. Relationships among factors may be conceptualized either in terms of uncorrelated (or orthogonal) sets of factors or in terms of correlated (or oblique) factors. Such analyses are often supplemented with information on how to build "factor scores," with item-analysis information, such as item-to-total score correlations, and with information estimating the "internal consistency" or "reliability" of such composite scores (see Greene and Carmines 1979; Maxwell 1971).

When using factor analysis and related techniques as a basis for index construction, one of two situations is typically the case. Either the investigator has some a priori basis for expecting that items in a set have a common factor (or common factors) underlying them, and therefore the investigator has certain well-founded expectations that the items can be combined into a scale, *or* the investigator has no a priori set of hypotheses for what clusters will be found and is willing to let the inherent properties of the data themselves determine the set of clusters. In the first case confirmatory factor models are appropriate, whereas in the second case exploratory methods are mandated. In either case the use of factor analysis as a data reduction tool is aimed at the development and construction of a set of "scores," based on factor analysis, that can then be introduced as variables in research.

Exploratory Factor Analysis. As noted above, in situations where the researcher has no a priori expectations of the number of factors or the nature of the pattern of loadings of variables on factors, we normally refer to applications of factor analysis as exploratory. In the case of exploratory factor analysis the goal is to find a set of k latent dimensions that will best reproduce the correlations among the set of p observed variables. It is usually desirable that k be considerably less than p and as small as possible. In exploratory factor analysis one typically does not have a clear idea of the number of factors but instead begins with uncertainty about what the data will reveal. The most common practice is to find k orthogonal (uncorrelated) dimensions that will best reproduce the correlations among the variables, but there is nothing intrinsic to the factor analytic model that restricts the conceptual domain to several orthogonal dimensions.

Confirmatory Factor Analysis. Confirmatory factor analysis, in contrast, refers to situations in which the investigator wishes to test some hypotheses regarding the structure of relationships in the presence of a strong set of assumptions about the number of factors, the values of the factor pattern coefficients, the presence or absence of correlations of factors, or other aspects of the model. In confirmatory factor analysis it is essential that one begin with a theory that contains enough detailed specification regarding constraints that should be imposed on the data in order to provide such a test, whereas in exploratory factor analysis there is no requirement that one specify the number of factors and expected relationships to be predicted in the data. Confirmatory approaches are thus more theory-driven, whereas exploratory approaches are more data-driven (see Alwin 1990). However, much of the so-called confirmatory factor analysis that is carried out in modern social and behavioral science is in fact exploratory, and much current research would be more realistically appraised if such confusion did not exist. Often, there is considerable tinkering with "confirmatory" models in order to improve their fit to the data, either by removing variables or by loosening up (or "freeing") certain parameters. It is also often the case that the "confirmatory" factor analyses are actually preceded by an exploratory analysis, and then a confirmatory model based on these results is fit to the same data. Although very common, this approach "capitalizes" on chance and gives an illusory sense that one has confirmed (or verified) a particular model. Placed in the proper perspective, there is nothing in principal wrong with the approach, as long as the "test" of the model is cross-validated in other data.

FACTOR ANALYSIS AND MULTIPLE INDICATOR CAUSAL MODELS

In the 1960s and 1970s, with the introduction of causal modeling strategies in social science (see Blalock 1964; Duncan 1966, 1975; Heise 1968), a fundamental shift occurred in the nature and uses of the common factor models by sociologists. Methods and the logic of causal modeling with nonexperimental statistical designs had been around for a long time. Due largely to the influence of Lazarsfeld (1968), causal inference strategies had been prevalent especially among analysts of sample survey data since the 1940s, but the research strategies were based on tabular presentation of data and the calculation of percentage differences. In the early 1960s there was a general infusion of techniques of causal modeling in sociology and other social science disciplines. Path analysis, principal of these newly adopted techniques, of course, was invented before 1920 by the great geneticist Sewall Wright, but his contributions were not appreciated by social and behavioral scientists, including the psychometricians responsible for the development of factor analysis. Wright (1921) developed path models as *deductive* systems for deriving correlations of genetic traits among relatives of stated degree. He also used the method inductively to model complex economic and social processes using correlational data (Wright 1925).

Psychometricians, like Spearman, had been dealing with models that could be thought of as "causal models," which could be understood in Wright's path analysis framework—common factors were viewed as the causes underlying the observed variables—but Spearman and others who developed common factor models were unfamiliar with Wright's work. None of the early psychometricians apparently recognized the possibility of causal relationships among the latent variables of their models, or for that matter among their indicators. However, with the publication of work by Jöreskog (1970) and others working in the "new" field of *structural equation models* (see Goldberger 1971, 1972; Goldberger and Duncan 1973; Hauser and Goldberger 1971); the convergence and integration of linear models in the path analysis tradition and those in the factor analysis tradition provided a basic "breakthrough" in one of the major analytic paradigms most prevalent in social science. These developments were assisted by the interest in conceptualizing measurement errors within a causal analysis framework. A number of researchers began to incorporate conceptions of measurement error into their causal analyses (Alwin 1973a, 1974; Blalock 1965, 1969, 1970; Costner 1969; Duncan 1972; Heise 1969; Siegel and Hodge 1968), ushering in a new approach that essentially combined factor models and path models.

At about this same time, Karl Jöreskog and his colleagues were developing efficient procedures for estimating the parameters of such models—called LISREL models, named after Jöreskog and his colleagues' computer program, LISREL—and this provided a major impetus for the widespread use of confirmatory approaches to the estimation of structural equation models. Jöreskog's (1967) early contributions to maximum-likelihood factor analysis became readily applied by even the most novice of analysts. Unfortunately, the widespread availability of these techniques to researchers who do not understand them has led to serious risks of abuse. This can be true of any technique, including the techniques of exploratory factor analysis. In any event, the proper use and interpretation of the results of LISREL-type model estimation is a significant challenge to the present generation of data analysts.

THE COMMON FACTOR MODEL

The formal mathematical properties of the common factor model are well known and can be found in many of the accompanying references. It is useful for purposes of exposition briefly to review its salient features. Although the model can be most compactly represented using vector and matrix notation, it is normally best to begin with a scalar representation for the data, such as in equation 1.

$$
\begin{aligned}
z_1 &= a_{11}f_1 + a_{12}f_2 + \dots + a_{1k}f_k + u_1 \\
z_2 &= a_{21}f_1 + a_{22}f_2 + \dots + a_{2k}f_k + u_2 \\
&\dots \\
z_p &= a_{p1}f_1 + a_{p2}f_2 + \dots + a_{pk}f_k + u_p
\end{aligned}
\tag{1}
$$

Here the z variables are empirical quantities observed in a sample of units of observation (e.g., persons, groups, ecological units), and for present purposes the variables are standardized to have a mean of zero and standard deviation of unity. This scaling is not a requirement of the model. In fact, in confirmatory factor models, it is often desirable to leave the variables in their original metric, especially when comparing the properties of these models across populations or subpopulations (see Alwin 1988b).

According to the common factor model, each observed z variable is, then, a linear function of a set of k latent or unobserved variables and a residual variable, ui, (also unobserved), which contains variation specific to that particular variable and random measurement error. The a coefficients in equation 1 are "factor loadings." They reflect the linkage between the "observed" variables and the "unobserved" factors. In the case of uncorrelated factor these loadings equal the correlations of the variables with the factors. The loadings thus provide a basis for interpreting the factors in the model; factors obtain their meaning from the variables to which they are linked and vice versa. Thus, in many investigations the primary objective is to estimate the magnitudes of these factor loadings in order to obtain a meaningful understanding of the nature of the data.

The k latent variables are called *common* factors because they represent common sources of variation in the observed variables. As such, these common factors are thought to be responsible for covariation among the variables. The unique parts of the variables, by contrast, contribute to lack of covariation among the variables. Covariation among the variables is greater when they measure the same factors, whereas covariation is less when the unique parts of the variables dominate. Indeed, this is the essence of the model—variables correlate because they measure the same things. This was the basis of Spearman's original reasoning about the correlations among tests of mental ability. Those tests correlated *because* they measured the same general factor. In the general case those variables that correlate do so because of their multiple sources of common variation.

Common variation in the aggregate is referred to as *communality*. More precisely, a variable's communality is the proportion of its total variation that is due to its common sources of variation. The communality of variable i is denoted h^2_i. A variable's *uniqueness*, denoted u^2_i, is the complement of the communality; that is, $u^2_i = 1.0 - h^2_i$. The

uniqueness is thought of as being composed of two independent parts, one representing *specific* variation and one representing *random measurement error* variation; that is, $u^2_i = s^2_i + e^2_i$. (This notation follows traditional psychometric factor analysis notation. Each of these quantities is a variance, and, thus, in the covariance modeling or structural equation modeling tradition these quantities would be represented as variances, such that $\sigma^2_{ui} = \sigma^2_{1i} + \sigma^2_{ei}$ [see below].) Specific variance is *reliable* variance, and thus the reliability of variable i can be expressed as $r^2_i = h^2_i + s^2_i$. Unfortunately, because of the presence of specific variance in most variables, it is virtually impossible to use the traditional form of the common factor model as a basis for reliability estimation (see Alwin 1989; Alwin and Jackson 1979). The problem is that the common factor model typically does not permit the partitioning of u^2_i into its components, s^2_i and e^2_i. In the absence of specific variance, classical reliability models may be viewed as a special case of the common factor model, but in general it is risky to assume that $e^2_i = u^2_i$. Alwin and Jackson (1979) discuss this issue in detail. Some attempts have been made to augment the traditional latent "trait" model inherent in the common factor model by adding "method" factors based on the *multitrait–multimethod* design of measurement within the framework of confirmatory factor models (see Alwin 1974; Alwin and Jackson 1979; Werts and Linn 1970). This provides a partitioning of the specific variance due to method, but it does not provide a general solution to the problem of handling specific variance.

Returning to the above example (in equation 1), in Spearman's case (the one-factor case) each variable contains a common factor and a specific factor, as shown in equation 2.

$$
\begin{aligned}
z_1 &= a_{11}f_1 + s_1 \\
z_2 &= a_{21}f_2 \text{ n } s_2 \\
&\cdots \\
z_p &= a_{p1}f_1 + s_p
\end{aligned}
\tag{2}
$$

In this case $h^2_i = a^2_i$ and $u^2_i = s^2_i$. Spearman's (1927) theory in essence assumes perfect measurement, not unlike most common factor models. However, unlike researchers of today, Spearman was very concerned about measurement errors, and he went to great lengths to correct his observed correlations for imperfections due to random errors of measurement (Spearman 1904b). Thus, when applied to such corrected correlational data, these assumptions may be appropriate.

As can be seen from the equations for Spearman's model (equation 2), the correlations among variables z_i, and z_j $r_y = E[z_i z_j]$ (the expected value of the cross-products of the z scores for the two variables) may be written as $r_y = a_i a_j$. For example, if $p = 3$, the correlations among the variables can be written as $r_{12} = a_i a_2$, $r_{13} = a_i a_3$, and $r_{23} = a_2 a_3$. In vector notation (introduced in greater detail below), the common parts of the correlations among the variables of the model are composed of the matrix product AA'. In the case where $p = 3$, the matrix A is written as in equation 3,

$$\begin{bmatrix} a_1 \\ a_2 \\ a_3 \end{bmatrix} \quad (3)$$

and the product AA' is written as in equation 4.

$$\begin{bmatrix} a_1 a_1 & a_1 a_2 & a_1 a_3 \\ a_2 a_1 & a_2 a_2 & a_2 a_3 \\ a_3 a_1 & a_3 a_2 & a_3 a_3 \end{bmatrix} \quad (4)$$

The variances of the variables are also affected by the common factors, but, as indicated in the foregoing, there is a residual portion of variance containing specific and unreliable variance. In Spearman's model the variance of variables i is as shown in equation 5.

$$\sigma_{z_i}^2 = 1.0 = a_i^2 + \sigma_{u_i}^2$$
$$= a_i^2 + \sigma_{s_i}^2 + \sigma_{e_i}^2 \quad (5)$$

Then it can be seen that the correlation matrix is equal to $R = AA' + U^2$, where the matrix U^2 for the $p = 3$ case is written in matrix form as in equation 6.

$$\begin{bmatrix} \sigma_{u_i}^2 & 0 & 0 \\ 0 & \sigma_{u_2}^2 & 0 \\ 0 & 0 & \sigma_{u_3}^2 \end{bmatrix} \quad (6)$$

These results have general applicability, as will be seen below.

ESTIMATION AND TESTING OF THE FACTOR MODEL

Before proceeding to the more general uses of the model, it is important to review the logic behind Spearman's approach. In the general Spearman case, the correlation of two variables is equal to the product of their loadings on the general factor; that is, $r_{ij} = a_i a_j$. Recall that under this model the a coefficients represent the correlations of the variables with the factor. Spearman reasoned therefore that if the model were true (that is, if a single unobserved common factor could account for the correlations among the observed variables), then certain things had to hold in the empirical data.

Spearman reasoned that, if the single factor model holds, the partial correlation between any two variables, holding constant the underlying common factor, r_{ijf} should be zero. This stems from the fact that the numerator of this partial correlation, $r_{ij} - r_{if} r_{jf}$, is zero, because *under the model* $r_{ij} - a_i a_j = a_i a_j - a_i a_j = 0$. Of course, it is not possible to calculate such a partial correlation from the data because the factor score, f, does not exist except in the theory. Spearman, however, recognized a specific pattern to the components of the correlations *under the model*. He noted that, if the single factor model held for $p = 4$, the intercorrelations of the variables had to satisfy two independent conditions, referred to by Spearman (1927) as *vanishing tetrads*, shown in equation 7.

$$r_{12}\, r_{34} - r_{14}\, r_{23} = 0$$
$$r_{13}\, r_{24} - r_{14}\, r_{23} = 0 \quad (7)$$

Note that the case of $p = 3$ is a trivial case, since a one-factor model can always be used to describe the intercorrelations among three variables. For $p = 5$ there are $[p(p - 1)\,(p - 2)\,(p - 3)]/8$ different tetrads (see Harman 1976), which equals fifteen. Not all of the possible tetrad differences formed from these fifteen are independent, and for one factor to explain the correlations, there are $p\,(p - 3)/2$ independent tetrad differences. Thus, in the case of five variables there are five tetrad differences that must vanish, and for six there are nine, and so forth.

Although in recent years there has been a revival of interest in Spearman's vanishing tetrads for sets of four variables (Glymour et al. 1987), at the time he developed this logic there was little that could be done computationally with very large problems. Thurstone (1947) developed the *centroid* method as an approximation to the principal axes approach involved in Spearman's early work, which was in common use during the 1940s and 1950s, but with the development of the high-speed computer, principal axes methods became (and remain) quite common in many applications of the model.

In exploratory factor analysis, where the number of factors of the model is not known beforehand, estimation is carried out by way of an eigenvalue/eigen-vector decomposition of some matrix, either R or some estimate of $R - U^2$. There is a wide variety of types of factor analyses that can be done—principal component factor analysis (which analyzes the p first nonzero components of R), communality-based factor analysis (which analyzes R with a communality estimate in the diagonal), alpha factor analysis, canonical factor analysis, or image analysis (see Harris 1963, 1964). Few developments have been made in these approaches since the 1960s, although there continues to be considerable debate about the desireable properties of these various approaches (e.g., see Widaman 1991).

Perhaps the most important development affecting exploratory factor analysis since the 1960s has been the development of maximum-likelihood factor analysis. Maximum-likelihood estimation, however, requires the prior estimate of the number of factors. These methods are most often discussed in connection with confirmatory factor analysis, although the approach to exploratory factor analysis discussed by Lawley and Maxwell (1971) illustrates how a form of traditional exploratory factor analysis can be done by setting minimal constraints on the model and testing successive hypotheses about the number of factors. A discussion of these models occurs in a subsequent section on confirmatory factor analysis. Before this, a more formal presentation of the factor model in matrix form is given, along with a discussion of several of the longstanding problems that dominate the literature on factor analysis, specifically the problem of estimating communality, the problem of estimating factor scores, and the problem of determining factorial invariance.

THE FACTOR MODEL IN MATRIX NOTATION

We can generalize the model given above for the case of multiple factors, k, in matrix notation. And again, the factor model can be easily represented in terms of the data matrix at hand. (The model can also be written compactly in vector notation for populations of interest. This is the approach taken in the subsequent discussion of confirmatory factor analysis.) The data matrix in this case can be represented as a p by n array of variable scores. Let Z' symbolize this p by n data matrix. Using this notation, write the common factor model for a set of p variables as $Z' = AF' + UW'$ where Z' is as defined above, A is a p by k *factor pattern matrix* (in the case of uncorrelated factors A is called the *factor structure matrix*), F' is a k by n matrix of hypothetical factor scores, U is a p by p diagonal matrix of unique-score standard deviations (defined such that the element u_i is the square root of the unique variances, $\sigma^2 u_i$), and W' is a p by n matrix of hypothetical unique scores. Note that the factors (both common and unique) are never observed—they exist purely at the hypothetical level. Note also that because we have standardized the variables (the z's) to be centered about the mean and to have standard deviations of unity, the factor scores in this model are theoretically standardized in the same fashion. In other words, $E(F'F) = I_k$, and the variances of the unique scores are equal to $E(W'W) = U^2$, assumed to be a diagonal matrix.

Traditionally, the factor model assumed that the factors of this model were uncorrelated, that the unique parts of the data (the W) are uncorrelated with the common parts (the F), and that the unique variation in variable i is uncorrelated with the unique variation in variable j, for all i and j. In matrix notation, the factor model assumes that $E(F'F) = I_k$, $E(W'W) = U^2$, and $E(F'W) = E(W'F) = 0$. In other words, the factors of the model are uncorrelated with one another and have variances of unity. Also, the common factors and unique factors are uncorrelated, and the unique factors are uncorrelated among themselves.

This type of notation helps clarify the fact that factor analysis is in effect interested in the "reduced" data matrix, $Z' - UW'$, rather than Z'. Consequently, the factor model is concerned with the decomposition of the matrix $R - U^2$ (the correlation matrix with communalities in the diagonal) rather than R (the correlation matrix with unities in the diagonal), since in equation 8 we demonstrate the following:

$$R = E(Z'Z) = E(AF' + UW')(AF' + UW')'$$

$$= AA' + U^2 \qquad (8)$$

and $R - U^2 = AA'$.

This demonstrates an often misunderstood fact —namely, that factor analysis focuses on the reduced-correlation matrix, $R - U^2$, rather than on the correlation matrix (with 1s in the diagonal). As will be clarified below, this is the fact that differentiates factor analysis from principal components analysis—the latter operates on the correlation matrix. In factor analysis, then, one must begin with some estimate of $I - U^2$ or H^2, the matrix of communalities, and then work on the decomposition of $R - U^2$. This poses a dilemma, since neither the common nor unique factors are observed, and it is therefore not possible to know U^2 and H^2 beforehand. The objective is to come up with an estimate of H^2 that retains a positive semidefinite property to $R - U^2$. At the same time, H^2 is one aspect of what one wants to discover from the analysis, and yet in order to estimate the model one must know this matrix beforehand. The solution to this problem is to begin with an "estimate" of the communalities of the variables, and then through an iterative procedure new estimates are obtained and the solution is reached through convergence to some criterion of fit.

COMMUNALITY ESTIMATION AND THE NUMBER OF FACTORS

Determining the number of factors in exploratory factor analysis is one of the fundamental problems involved in arriving at a solution to the parameters of the factor model. The problem essentially involves determining the rank, k, of the matrix $R - U^2$, where these matrices are as defined above. Technically, we want to find a matrix U^2 that will retain the property of positive semidefiniteness in $R - U^2$ with the smallest possible rank (Guttman 1954). The rank of this matrix in this case is the minimum number of factors necessary to reproduce the off-diagonal elements of R. Thus, the problem of determining k is closely related to the communality estimation problem, that is, determining an estimate for the diagonal of $R - U^2$, that is, H^2.

Guttman (1954) outlined the problem of deciding on the number of factors and compared three principles for estimating k via solutions to the communality estimation problem. He described a "weak lower bound" on the number of factors, k_1, as the nonnegative roots (eigen values) of the matrix $R - I$. This is equivalent to the number of roots of R greater or equal to unity, since R and $R - I$ differ only by I, and their roots differ therefore only by unity. Guttman shows that k_1 is a lower bound to k, that is, $k \geq k_1$. A second principle, one that also implies another approach to estimating communality, is based on the matrix $R - D$, where D is a diagonal matrix whose elements, $1 - r_j^2 (j = 1, p)$, are the result of unity minus the square of the largest correlation of variable j with any of the $p - 1$ other variables. Guttman shows that k_2 is also a lower bound to k, such that $k \geq k_2$. A third and perhaps the most common approach to estimating communalities is based on the idea that the squared multiple correlation for each variable predicted on the basis of all the other variables in the model is the upper limit on what the factors of the model might reasonably explain. If we define the matrix $R - C^2$, where C^2 is a diagonal matrix whose elements $C_j^2 (1, p)$ are equal to $1 - r_j^2$, where r_j^2 is the squared multiple correlation of variable j with the remaining $p - 1$ variables. Guttman shows that k_3 is also a lower bound to k. This third lower bound is often referred to as Guttman's *strong* lower bound since he showed the following relationships among the lower bounds: $k \geq k_3 \geq k_2 \geq k_1$. In practice, k_1 may be adequate but it could be wrong, and, if wrong, it is likely to be too small. The use of k_1 is probably questionable in the general case. The use of k_2 is obsolete and not practicable. It estimates communality in the way of the Thurstone centroid method, which is only a rough approximation to a least-squares approach. Perhaps the best solution is the choice of k_3. It is less likely to overlook common factors, as k_1 might, since $1 - s_j^2$ is a lower bound to h_j^2. It should be pointed out that the lower bounds k_1 and k_3 are what distinguish the two main approaches to factor analysis, namely an incomplete principal components decomposition (referred to as principal components factor analysis) and the principal factor method of analysis.

FACTOR ANALYSIS VERSUS PRINCIPAL COMPONENTS ANALYSIS

It was mentioned above that it is not understood well enough that factor analysis is concerned mainly with the matrix $R - U^2$ rather than with R. This is in fact one of the things that distinguishes factor analysis from principal components analysis. However, the differences between the two are more fundamental. Factor analysis is based on a *model*, a particular theoretical view (hypothesis, if you like) about the covariance (or correlational) structure of the variables. This model states (as given above) that the correlation matrix for a set of variables can be partitioned into two parts—one representing the common parts of the data and one representing uniqueness—that is, $R = A'A + U^2$. The factor model states, first, that the off-diagonal elements of $A'A$ equal the off-diagonal elements of R and, second, that the elements of U^2 (a diagonal matrix) when added to the diagonal elements of $A'A$ give the diagonal elements of R. Thus, the factor model posits a set of k hypothetical variables ($k << p$) that can account for the interrelationships (or correlations) of the variables but not for their total variances.

In contrast to this, principal components is not a model in the same sense—it is best viewed as a method. It is one method for obtaining an initial approximation to the common factor model (see Guttman's weak lower bound, discussed above), but it is extremely important to distinguish such an "incomplete" principal components solution (one associated with the roots of R that are equal to or greater than unity) from the full-rank principal components decomposition of R (see Maxwell 1977).

Any square symmetric nonsingular matrix, for example, $R = R'$, can be written in the form $R = QD^2Q'$, where D^2 is a diagonal matrix of order p containing eigen values ordered according to decreasing magnitude, and Q is a matrix of unit-length eigen vectors (as columns) associated with the eigen values. Q is an orthonormal matrix, $Q'Q = I = QQ'$. This model is referred to as the principal components decomposition of R. Typically, one either analyzes a correlation matrix with 1s in the diagonal, or a covariance matrix with variances in the diagonal, in the application of this decomposition. In this model the correlation matrix, R, is formed by a centered or deviation-score data matrix scaled so that the variables have variances of unity. Let Z' be the $p \times n$ data matrix, as above. Note that the expected value of $Z'Z = QD^2Q'$, since $Z' = QDY'$.

If the correlation matrix is of full rank, then there will be p columns in Q. This means that in this case the principal components model involves a transformation of p variables into a set of p orthogonal components. When the correlation matrix is singular, meaning that the rank of the matrix is less than p, the principal components decomposition is said to be incomplete, but from the point of view of factor analysis this is often irrelevant since it is the matrix $R - U^2$ that is of interest to the factor analyst.

If P is an $r \times p$ components matrix ($P = QD$), and $r = p$, then it is well known that $Y' = (P'P)^{-1}P'Z' = P^{-1}Z'$, where Y' is a set of r component scores, P is as defined above, and Z' is a $p \times n$ data matrix involving p variables and n units of observation (e.g., persons, cities, social organizations). In other words, component scores (in contrast to factor scores) are directly calculable.

THE ROTATION PROBLEM–CORRELATED VERSUS UNCORRELATED FACTORS

Principal components are by definition *uncorrelated* with one another. The basic objective of the method is to obtain a set of p orthogonal (uncorrelated) new variables via a linear transformation of the p original variables. Factors are different. Factors may be uncorrelated, and in classical exploratory factor analysis one always begins with a set of uncorrelated factors, but in general this is not a requirement. Indeed, in exploratory factor analysis the factors one obtains are uncorrelated because of the nature of the methods used, but normally one performs a transformation or rotation of these factors to achieve a more pleasing representation for interpretation purposes.

Two types of rotations are available—those that preserve the uncorrelated nature of the factors, such as the varimax and quartimax rotations (see Kaiser 1958; Neuhaus and Wrigley 1954), and those that allow the factors to be correlated. The latter are called "oblique" rotations because they move the factors out of the orthogonal reference into a vector space that reduces the geometric angles between them. Using either of these approaches, the basic goal of rotation is to achieve what Thurstone called *simple structure*, the principle that variables should simultaneously load highly on one factor and low on all other factors. These rotational approaches are relatively straightforward and discussed in all of the textbook descriptions of factor analysis.

FACTORIAL INVARIANCE

Following Thurstone's (1938, 1947) discussions of factor analysis, students of the method have frequently been concerned with the problem of the correspondence between factors identified in separate studies or in subgroups of the same study. Using Thurstone's terminology, a concern with the correspondence of factors refers to the *invariance* of factors. The concern with factorial invariance has generated an array of methods for comparing factors (see Mulaik 1972). The most common approach to the problem involves the computation of an index of *factor similarity* for corresponding factors given estimates of a factor model using the same variables in two or more samples. The details of various strategies for estimating factor similarity will not be covered here, as descriptions can be found in a variety of factor analysis textbooks.

These approaches were developed primarily for results obtained from exploratory factor analysis, and it can be argued that the issues of factorial invariance can be more fruitfully addressed using the methods of confirmatory factor analysis (see Jöreskog 1971b; Lawley and Maxwell 1971). The technical aspects of these methods will not be reviewed here, as they have been exposited elsewhere (see Alwin and Jackson 1979, 1981). Suffice it to say that issues of factorial invariance can be phrased, not only with respect to the correspondence of the factor pattern coefficients (the A matrix) across populations, but also with respect to other parameters of the model as well, particularly the matrix of factor interrelationships (correlations and covariances) and the matrix of disturbance covariances.

It is perhaps useful in this context to raise a more general question regarding the nature of factorial invariance that is sought in the analysis of the factorial content of measures. In general there

is no consensus regarding whether stronger or weaker forms of invariance are necessary for comparisons across populations or subpopulations. Horn and associates (1983), for example, suggest that rather than the "equivalence" of factor structures across populations, weaker "configurational" forms of invariance are "more interesting" and "more accurate representations of the true complexity of nature." By contrast, Schaie and Hertzog (1985, pp. 83–85) argue that the condition of factorial invariance, that is, "the equivalence of unstandardized factor loadings across multiple groups," is critical to the analysis of differences among groups and developmental changes within groups.

Clearly, these represent extremes along a continuum of what is meant by the question of factorial invariance. On the one hand, for strict comparison of content across groups, it is necessary to have the same units of measurement, that is, invariance of metric. This requires the same variables measured across populations, and some would also argue that such invariance of metric requires that the relationships of the variables and the factors be equivalent across populations (see Jöreskog 1971a). On the other hand, if the same pattern of loadings seems to exist, it may be an example of misplaced precision to require equivalence in the strictest sense. Of course, the resolution of these issues has implications for other uses to which factor analysis is typically put, especially the construction of factor scores and the use of causal modeling strategies to compare substantive processes across groups.

THE PROBLEM OF FACTOR SCORE ESTIMATION

Researchers using the common factor model as a data reduction tool typically engage in the estimation of such models in order to obtain scores based on the factors of the model, which can then be used to represent those factors in further research. As will be shown here, *factor scores* can never be computed directly (as in the case of *component scores*). Factor scores are always estimated, and, due to the nature of the factor model, "estimated factor scores" never correlate perfectly with the underlying factors of the model. An important alternative to factor scores is what have come to be called "factor-based" scores, which are scores derived from the results of the factor analysis, using unit versus zero weightings for the variables instead of the factor score weights derived from one or another method of estimating factor scores. Factor-based scores, which are frequently more easy to justify and much more practical, typically correlate so highly with factor score estimates as to make one skeptical of the need for factor score estimates at all (see, e.g., Alwin 1973b).

However, it is important that factor analysts understand the nature of the factor score estimation problem, regardless of whether factor score estimates become any more appealing than the simpler and more stable factor-based scores. The factor score estimation problem can best be seen in terms of an interest in solving for the matrix F' in the above matrix representation of the common factor model, $Z' = AF' + UW'$. This can be done analytically, but, as will be seen, it is not possible to do so empirically because of the nature of the model. To solve for F' in this model we arrive at the following representation (without going through all of the necessary steps): $F' = (A'A)^{-1} A' [Z' - UW']$. The calculations implied by this expression cannot actually be carried out because one never knows W'. This is known as the "factor measurement problem," which results in the fact that factor scores cannot be computed directly and must therefore be estimated.

The question, then, becomes whether it is possible to estimate factor scores in a manner that is useful, given what is known–Z, A, and U^2. Several approaches have been set forth for estimating the factors, all of which involve some transformation of the data matrix Z' into a set of k scores that vary in their properties (see Harris 1967; McDonald and Burr 1967). Most of these methods bear some resemblance to the analytic solution for F' above, but there are some technical differences. One of the most commonly misunderstood facts involved in the estimation of factor scores is that the factor pattern coefficient matrix, A, *cannot* be applied directly to the estimation of factors; that is, F' cannot be estimated by $A'Z'$. This, of course, should be clear from the above representation, but it is often used, probably due to ignorance of the more "correct" factor score estimation strategies.

There are four recognized strategies for estimating scores representing the common factors of the model, given Z, A, and U^2 (Alwin 1973b). All of these approaches are typically discussed for a model such as that discussed above, namely a set of uncorrelated factors scaled to have 0 means and standard deviations of 1. It is not the purpose of the present discussion to evaluate the properties of these various approaches to factor score estimation, but a brief summary can perhaps provide a guide to the technical literature on this topic. It is important to emphasize that *none* of these approaches produces factor score "estimates" that are perfectly correlated with the underlying factors of the model. Some of these approaches produce *univocal* score estimates, meaning that each factor score correlates *only* with the factors they are intended to measure and not with factors they are not intended to measure. Only one of the approaches produces a set of factor score estimates that reflect the property of uncorrelated factors with unit standard deviations. But it is difficult in practice to evaluate the desirability of any of the properties of factor score estimates.

METHODS OF CONFIRMATORY FACTOR ANALYSIS

Confirmatory factor analysis, unlike the methods of exploratory factor analysis, begins with prior knowledge regarding the number of factors and something about the nature of their relationships to the observed variables. In the absence of such knowledge, confirmatory factor analysis is not appropriate. In the typical situation of confirmatory factor analysis, then, the investigator begins with some specific theoretical hypotheses involving a model that can be tested against the data. Naturally, there is an extremely large number of such possible models, so it should be obvious that the techniques cannot easily be used to "search" for the best possible set of restrictions involving k factors (but see Glymour et al. 1987).

The bulk of this review has been devoted to the use of exploratory techniques of factor analysis. This imbalance is perhaps justified, given what is known within sociology about the common factors in our data. Exploratory factor analysis techniques are likely to be much more useful, especially at a stage where less knowledge has been developed. And within a field like sociology, where there is a broad variety of competing concepts and paradigms, exploration of data may often be the most salutary strategy. There are, however, clear-cut instances where the use of confirmatory factor analysis techniques is in order, and the remainder of this discussion focuses on these situations.

Consider the following model for a set of p variables: $y = v + \lambda \eta + \varepsilon$, where v is a vector of location parameters or constants representing the origins of measurement of the p observed variables, η is a vector of k latent variables or factors, and ε is a vector of random disturbances for the p observed variables. The covariance properties associated with η and ε are basically the same as those discussed in the section on exploratory factor analysis for F and W, except that in general these are not required to be uncorrelated within the common factor set. And, of course, there is no restriction on the metric of the variables; that is, the p variables and k factors are not necessarily standardized to have 0 means and standard deviations of unity. The coefficient matrix, λ, is a matrix of regression coefficients relating the p observed variables to the k latent factors. In the case of a single population, one can easily consider the p variables centered (which would remove the vector of location constants) and scaled to have unit variance, but in the situation where one wants to compare populations neither of these constraints is probably desirable.

The use of these models requires the distinction between constrained and unconstrained parameters. Typically, one refers to parameters of the model as *fixed* if they are constrained to have a particular value, such as a factor loading of 0 or, in the case of the variance of a latent factor, a variance of unity. By contrast, the unknown parameters of the model, for example the λs, are referred to as *free* parameters, which means that they are estimated in the model under the constraints specified for *fixed* parameters. Thus, one speaks of fixed or constrained parameters on the one hand and free or estimable parameters on the other. The major breakthrough in the use of this type of model was the development of computer programs that allow one to fix certain parameters of the model to known quantities while estimating the free parameters under these constraints. The general approach also allows one to specify causal connections among the latent factors of the model, and it allows one to specify correlations among the errors in the variables and the errors in the equations connecting the latent factors.

Consider the factor model for the situation where there are $p = 4$ variables and $k = 2$ factors, with the pattern of factor pattern coefficients shown in equation 9, where the first two variables are believed to measure η_1 and the third and fourth variables are said to measure η_2. This is the kind of situation described by Costner (1969), who developed an approach to confirmatory factor analysis using Spearman's tetrad differences. Of course, there are more efficient estimation strategies than those proposed by Costner. In any event, the point of this example is that the investigator begins not only with a specific number of factors in mind but also with a specific set of assumptions about the pattern of loadings.

$$\Lambda = \begin{bmatrix} \lambda_{11} & 0.0 \\ \lambda_{21} & 0.0 \\ 0.0 & \lambda_{32} \\ 0.0 & \lambda_{42} \end{bmatrix} \quad (9)$$

In the general case the covariances and correlations of the common factors of the model, $E(\eta'\eta)$, can be symbolized by ψ (sometimes this matrix is denoted as Φ, but there are many ways in which to symbolize these quantities), and the covariances of the disturbances (or errors) on the variables can be symbolized by θ_e. Neither of these two matrices, ψ and θ_e, is required by the model to be diagonal, although in the simplest form of the confirmatory model, θ_e is often assumed to represent a set of uncorrelated disturbances. In more complicated forms of the model, within constraints placed by the identification problem, both of these matrices can be nondiagonal. In either case, the model here is written with the assumption that the investigator has prior theoretical knowledge regarding the number of sources of common variation and that the η vector exhausts those sources.

Any application of this model requires that it be *identified*, which essentially means that there must be enough independent information within the covariance and correlation structure being analyzed sufficient to solve for the unknown parameters of the model. In general, there need to be k^2 constraints on a particular common factor model, that is, in the parameters in λ and ψ. Other constraints, of course, are possible. Space does not permit the discussion of these matters, but a detailed treatment of these issues can be found elsewhere (see Alwin 1988a; Alwin and Jackson 1979).

The True-Score Models. It can be shown that a well-known class of measurement models that form the basis for *classical test theory* (Lord and Novick 1968) can be specified as a special case of confirmatory factor analysis (see Alwin and Jackson 1979; Jöreskog 1971a). In brief, by placing particular constraints on the λ and θ, matrices of the model, one can estimate the parameters of models that assume the measures are *parallel, tau-equivalent,* or *congeneric.* Of course, as indicated earlier, in order to use the common factor model in such a fashion, one must be reasonably sure that there is little or no specific variance in the measures. Otherwise, one runs the risk of confusing reliable specific variance with measurement error variance.

Multitrait–Multimethod Models. In addition to the application of confirmatory factor analysis to the estimation of classical true-score models, several attempts have been made to augment the traditional latent "trait" model, inherent in the classical model, by the addition of "method" factors based on the *multitrait–multimethod* design of measurement within the framework of confirmatory factor models (see Alwin 1974; Alwin and Jackson 1979; Werts and Linn 1970). This provides a partitioning of the specific variance due to method, but it does not provide a general solution to the problem of handling specific variance. While these models can be very useful for partitioning item-level variance into components due to trait, method, and error, they place relatively high demands on the measurement design. And while the required designs are relatively rare in practice, these models help sensitize the researcher to problems of correlated method error (see e.g., Costner 1969). Recent work in this area has shown that the multitrait-multimethod model can be fruitfully applied to questions of survey measurement quality, assessing the extent to which correlated measurement errors account for covariation among survey measures (see Alwin, 1997; Scherpenzeel, 1995).

Multiple-Indicator, Multiple-Cause Models. One of the simplest forms of causal models involving latent common factor models is one in which a single latent endogenous variable having several indicators is determined by several perfectly having measured exogenous variables. Jöreskog (1974) and Jöreskog and Goldberger (1975) refer to this as a *multiple-indicator, multiple-cause* (MIMC) model. This kind of model has certain similarities to the canonical correlation problem (see Hauser and Goldberger 1971).

Analysis of Change—Simplex Models. One type of model that can be viewed as a confirmatory factor model, and is useful in analyzing change with respect to the latent common factors over time, falls under the rubric of *simplex* models (Jöreskog 1974). Such models are characterized by a series of measures of the same variables separated in time, positing a Markovian (lag-1) process to describe change and stability in the underlying latent variable. This model can be used in situations where there is a single variable measured over time (see Heise 1969) or in situations where there are multiple measures of the latent variable at each time (see Wheaton et al. 1977).

These models have proven to be valuable in the study of human development and change, especially applied to panel studies of individual lives over time (Alwin 1994, 1995a; Alwin and Krosnick 1991; Alwin et al. 1991; Asendorf 1992.); A related set of models in this area are latent growth curves, in which levels and trajectories of the growth in latent factors can be conceptualized and estimated (e.g., Karney and Bradbury 1995; McArdle 1991; McArdle and Anderson 1990; Willett and Sayer 1994). In such applications the focus is on the nature of growth processes and the correlates/predictors of individual change in latent factors over time. This is a natural extension of traditional methods of confirmatory factor analysis and causal modeling strategies within the context of longitudinal data.

Causal Modeling of Factors. If one obtains multiple measures of factors, for which common factor models are believed to hold, and the factors can be specified to be causally related, then it is possible to use confirmatory techniques to estimate the causal influences of factors on one another. Of course, one must be able to justify these models strongly in terms of theoretical considerations, and there must be considerable prior knowledge (as in the use of confirmatory factor analysis) that justifies the specification of such measurement models. The logic involved in dealing with the linkage between observed and unobserved variables is essentially that involved in confirmatory factor analysis, while the logic applied in dealing with the causal linkages among factors is that involved in path analysis and structural equation modeling. The main point is that the parameters of models that essentially contain two parts—a measurement part specifying a model linking observed and latent variables and a structural model linking the latent variables—can be estimated within the framework of LISREL-type models. The measurement part can typically be viewed within the framework of confirmatory factor analysis, although in some cases an "induced variable" model is more appropriate (Alwin, 1988b).

CONCLUSION

This review is designed to provide an overview of the major issues involved in the use of factor analysis as a research tool, including both exploratory and confirmatory techniques. There are several useful textbook discussions of factor analysis that will aid those who desire further study. Among these, the texts by Gorsuch (1984), Harman (1976), Mulaik (1972), McDonald (1985), and Lawley and Maxwell (1971) are some of the best sources on exploratory factor analysis. There are some recent texts offering instruction on the conceptual understanding and practical guidance in the use of these confirmatory factor analysis and causal modeling strategies (e.g., Bollen 1989; Loehlin 1992). The newest developments in the area involve advances in the analysis of categorical and ordinal data, statistical estimation in the presence of incomplete data, the provision of graphic interfaces for ease of specification of causal models. There are now several major competitors in the area of software packages that can be used to estimate many of the confirmatory factor models discussed here. Although these several packages offer largely comparable material, each offers a somewhat special approach. The LISREL approach to the analysis of covariance structures was first made available in the early 1970s. It is now in its

eighth version and offers many improvements to its use (Jöreskog and Sörbom 1996a). The LISREL8 program is now supplemented by PRELIS (Jöreskog and Sörbom 1996b), which provides data transformaton capabilities, and by SIMPLIS (Jöreskog and Sörbom 1993), which provides a simple command language for formulating LISREL-type models. There are several alternatives to the LISREL approach, including EQS (Bentler 1992), AMOS (Arbuckle 1997), and Mplus (Muthén and Muthén 1998), among others, which provide many attractive features (see West, 1997).

(SEE ALSO: *Causal Inference Models; Measurement; Multiple Indicator Models; Validity*).

REFERENCES

Alwin, D. F. 1973a "Making Inferences from Attitude–Behavior Correlations." *Sociometry* 36:253–278.

——1973b "The Use of Factor Analysis in the Construction of Linear Composites in Social Research." *Sociological Methods and Research* 2:191–214.

——1974 "Approaches to the Interpretation of Relationships in the Multitrait-Multimethod Matrix." In H. L. Costner, ed., *Sociological Methodology* 1973–74. San Francisco: Jossey-Bass.

——1988a "Structural Equation Models in Research on Human Development and Aging." In K. Warner Schaie, Richard T. Campbell, William Meredith, and Samuel C. Rawlings, eds., *Methodological Issues in Aging Research*. New York: Springer.

——1988b "Measurement and the Interpretation of Coefficients in Structural Equation Models." In J. S. Long. ed., *Common Problems/Proper Solutions: Avoiding Error in Quantitative Research*. Beverly Hills, Calif.: Sage.

——1989 "Problems in the Estimation and Interpretation of the Reliability of Survey Data." *Quality and Quantity* 23:277–331.

——1990 "From Causal Theory to Causal Modeling: Conceptualization and Measurement in Social Science." In J. J. Hox and J. De-Jong. Gierveld, eds., *Operationalization and Research Stategy*. Amsterdam: Swets and Zeitlinger.

——1994 "Aging, Personality and Social Change." In D. L. Featherman, R. M. Lerner, and M. Perlmutter, eds., *Life-Span Development and Behavior*, vol. 12. Hillsdale, N.J.: Lawrence Erlbaum.

——1995a "Taking Time Seriously: Social Change, Social Character Structure, and Human Lives." In P.

Moen, G. H. Elder, Jr., and K. Lüscher, eds., *Examining Lives in Context: Perspectives on the Ecology of Human Development*. Washington, D.C.: American Psychological Association.

——1995b "Quantitative Methods in Social Psychology." In K. Cook, G. Fine, and J. House, eds., *Sociological Perspectives on Social Psychology*. New York: Allyn and Bacon.

——1997 "Feeling Thermometers Versus 7-Point Scales—Which Are Better?" *Sociological Methods and Research* 25:318–340.

——, R.L. Cohen, and T.M. Newcomb 1991 *Political Attitudes Over the Life-Span: The Bennington Women After 50 Years*. Madison: University of Wisconsin Press.

——, and D. J. Jackson 1979 "Measurement Models for Response Errors in Surveys: Issues and Applications." In K. F. Schuessler, ed., *Sociological Methodology 1980*. San Francisco: Jossey-Bass.

——, 1981 "Applications of Simultaneous Factor Analysis to Issues of Factorial Invariance." In D. J. Jackson and E. F. Borgatta, eds., *Factor Analysis and Measurement in Sociological Research*. Beverly Hills, Calif.: Sage.

——, and D. J. Jackson 1982 "Adult Values for Children: An Application of Factor Analysis to Ranked Preference Data." In R. M. Hauser et al. eds., *Social Structure and Behavior*. New York: Academic Press.

——, and J. A. Krosnick. 1991 "Aging, Cohorts and the Stability of Socio-Political Orientations Over the Life-Span. *American Journal of Sociology* 97:169–195.

——, and R. C. Tessler. 1974 "Causal Models, Unobserved Variables, and Experimental Data." *American Journal of Sociology* 80:58–86.

Arbuckle, J. L. 1997 *Amos Users' Guide*. Version 3.6. Chicago: SmallWaters Corporation.

Asendorpf J. B. 1992 "Continuity and Stability of Personality Traits and Personality Patterns." In J. B. Asendorpf and J. Valsiner, eds., *Stability and Change in Development*. Newbury Park, Calif.: Sage.

Bentler, P. M. 1983 "Some Contributions to Efficient Statistics for Structural Models: Specification and Estimation of Moment Structures." *Psychometrika* 48:493–517.

——1989 *EQS Structural Equations Program Manual, Version 3.0*. Los Angeles: BMDP Statistical Software.

——, and D. G. Weeks 1980 "Linear Structural Equations with Latent Variables." *Psychometrika* 45:289–308.

Blalock, H. M., Jr. 1964 *Causal Inferences in Nonexperimental Research*. Chapel Hill: University of North Carolina Press.

——1965 "Some Implications of Random Measurement Error for Causal Inferences." *American Journal of Sociology* 71:37–47.

——1969 "Multiple Indicators and the Causal Approach to Measurement Error." *American Journal of Sociology* 75:264–272.

——1970 "Estimating Measurement Error Using Multiple Indicators and Several Points in Time." *American Sociological Review* 35:101–111.

Bollen, K. A. 1989 *Structural Equations with Latent Variables*. New York: John Wiley and Sons.

Browne, M. W. 1974 "Generalized Least Squares Estimators in the Analysis of Covariance Structure." *South African Statistical Journal* 8:1–24.

——1984 "Asymptotically Distribution-Free Methods for the Analysis of Covariance Structures." *British Journal of Mathematical and Statistical Psychology* 37:62–83.

——, and A. Shapiro 1988 "Robustness of Normal Theory Methods in the Analysis of Linear Latent Variate Models." *British Journal of Mathematical and Statistical Psychology* 41:193–208.

Christofferson, A. 1975 "Factor Analysis of Dichotomized Variables." *Psychometrika* 40:5–32.

Costner, H. L. 1969 "Theory, Deduction, and Rules of Correspondence." *American Journal of Sociology* 75:245–263.

Duncan, O. D. 1966 "Path Analysis: Sociological Examples." *American Journal of Sociology* 72: 1–16.

——1972 "Unmeasured Variables in Linear Models for Panel Analysis." In H. L. Costner, ed., *Sociological Methodology 1972*. San Francisco: Jossey-Bass.

——1975 *Introduction to Structural Equation Models*. New York: Academic Press.

Garnett, J. C. M. 1919–20 "On Certain Independent Factors in Mental Measurement." *Proceedings of the Royal Society of London* A. 96:91–111.

Glymour, C., R. Scheines, P. Spines, and K. Kelly 1987 *Discovering Causal Structure: Artificial Intelligence, Philosophy of Science, and Statistical Modeling*. New York: Academic Press.

Goldberger, A. S. 1971 "Economics and Psychometrics: A Survey of Communalities." *Psychometrika* 36:83–107.

——1972 "Structural Equation Models in the Social Sciences." *Econometrika* 40:979–999.

——, and O. D. Duncan 1973 *Structural Equation Models in the Social Sciences*. New York: Seminar Press.

Gorsuch, R. L. 1984 *Factor Analysis*, 2d ed. Hillsdale, N.J.: Lawrence Erlbaum.

Gould, S. J. 1981 *The Mismeasure of Man*. New York: Norton.

Greene, V. L., and E. G. Carmines 1979 "Assessing the Reliability of Linear Composites." In K. F. Schuessler, ed., *Sociological Methodology 1980*. San Francisco: Jossey-Bass.

Guttman, L. 1954 "Some Necessary Conditions for Common Factor Analysis." *Psychometrika* 19:149–161.

——1955 "The Determinacy of Factor Score Matrices with Implications for Five Other Basic Problems of Common-Factor Theory." *British Journal of Statistical Psychology* 8:65–81.

——1956 "'Best Possible' Systematic Estimates of Communalities." *Psychometrika* 21:273–285.

——1960 "The Matrices of Linear Least-Squares Image Analysis." *British Journal of Statistical Psychology* 13:109–118.

Harman, H. H. 1976 *Modern Factor Analysis*. Chicago: University of Chicago Press.

Harris, C. W. 1963 "Canonical Factor Models for the Description of Change." in C. W. Harris, ed., *Problems in Measuring Change*. Madison: University of Wisconsin Press.

——1964 "Some Recent Developments in Factor Analysis." *Educational and Psychological Measurement* 24:193–206.

——1967 "On Factors and Factor Scores. *Psychometrika* 32:193–379.

Hauser, R. M. 1972 "Disaggregating a Social Psychological Model of Educational Attainment." *Social Science Research* 1:159–188.

——, and A. S. Goldberger 1971 "The Treatment of Unobservable Variables in Path Analysis." In H. L. Costner, ed., *Sociological Methodology 1971*. San Francisco: Jossey-Bass.

Heise, D. R. 1968 "Problems in Path Analysis and Causal Inference." In E. F. Borgatta, ed., *Sociological Methodology 1969*. San Francisco: Jossey-Bass.

——1969 "Separating, Reliability and Stability in Test–Retest Correlation." *American Sociological Review* 34:93–101.

——1972 "Employing Nominal Variables, Induced Variables, and Block Variables in Path Analysis." *Sociological Methods and Research* 1:147–174.

——, and G. W. Bohrnstedt 1970 "The Validity, Invalidity, and Reliability of a Composite Score. In E. F. Borgatta and G. W. Bohrnstedt, eds., *Sociological Methodology 1970*. San Francisco: Jossey-Bass.

Horn, J. L., J. J. McArdle, and R. Mason 1983 "When Is Invariance Not Invariant?: A Practical Scientist's Look at the Ethereal Concept of Factor Invariance." *The Southern Pschologist* 1:179–188.

Hotelling. H. 1933 "Analysis of a Complex of Statistical Variables into Principal Components." *Journal of Educational Psychology* 24:417–441, 498–520.

Jöreskog. K. G. 1966 "Testing a Simple Structure Hypothesis in Factor Analysis." *Psychometrika* 31: 165–178.

——1967 "Some Contributions to Maximum-Likelihood Factor Analysis." *Psychometrika* 32:443–482.

——1970 "A General Method for Analysis of Covariance Structures." *Biometrika* 56:239–251.

——1971a "Simultaneous Factor Analysis in Several Populations." *Psychometrika* 36:409–426.

——1971b "Statistical Analysis of Sets of Congeneric Tests." *Psychometrika* 36:109–133.

——1973 "A General Method for Estimating a Linear Structural Equation System." In A. S. Goldberger and O. D. Duncan, eds., *Structural Equation Models in the Social Sciences*. New York: Seminar Press.

——1974 "Analyzing Psychological Data by Structural Analysis of Covariance Matrices." In D. H. Kranz, et al., eds., *Measurement, Psychophysics, and Neural Information Processing*. San Francisco: Freeman.

——, and A. S. Goldberger 1975 "Estimation of a Model with Multiple Indicators and Multiple Causes of a Single Latent Variable." *Journal of the American Statistical Association* 70:631–639.

——, and D. N. Lawley 1968 New Methods in Maximum-Likelihood Factor Analysis." *British Journal of Mathematical and Statistical Psychology* 21:85–96.

——, and D. Sörbom 1986 *LISREL: Analysis of Linear Structural Relationships by the Method of Maximum-Likelihood*. User's Guide. Version 6. Chicago: Scientific Software.

——, and D. Sörbom 1988 *PRELIS: A Program for Multivariate Data Screening and Data Summarization (A Preprocessor for LISREL)*. Version 1.8, 2d ed. Chicago: Scientific Software.

——, and D. Sörbom 1996a *LISREL8: User's Reference Guide*. Chicago: Scientific Software International.

——, and D. Sörbom 1996b *PRELIS2: User's Reference Guide*. Chicago: Scientific Software International, Inc. 7383 N. Lincoln Avenue. Chicago IL 60646-1704.

——, and D. Sörbom 1993. *LISREL8: Structural Equation Modeling with the SIMPLIS Command Language*. Chicago: Scientific Software International.

Kaiser, H. F. 1958 "The Varimax Criterion for Analytic Rotation in Factor Analysis." *Psychometrika* 23:187–200.

——1963 "Image Analysis." In C. W. Harris, ed., *Problems in Measuring Change*. Madison: University of Wisconsin Press.

Karney, B. R., and T. N. Bradbury 1995 "Assessing Longitudinal Change in Marriage: An Introduction to the Analysis of Growth Curves." *Journal of Marriage and the Family* 57:1091–1108.

Lawley, D. N., and A. E. Maxwell 1971 *Factor Analysis as a Statistical Method*. London: Butterworths.

Lazarsfeld, P. F. 1968 "The Analysis of Attribute Data." In D. L. Sills, ed., *International Encyclopedia of the Social Science*, vol. 15. New York: Macmillan and Free Press.

Loehlin, J. C. 1992 *Latent Variable Models: An Introduction to Factor, Path, and Structural Analysis*. Hillsdale, N.J.: Lawrence Erlbaum.

Lord, F. M., and M. L. Novick 1968 *Statistical Theories of Mental Test Scores*. Reading. Mass.: Addison-Wesley.

Maxwell, A. E. 1971 "Estimating True Scores and Their Reliabilities in the Case of Composite Psychological Tests." *British Journal of Mathematical and Statistical Psychology* 24:195–204.

——1977 *Multivariate Analysis in Behavioral Research*. London: Chapman and Hall.

McArdle, J.J. 1991 "Structural Models of Developmental Theory in Psychology." *Annals of Theoretical Psychology* 7:139–160.

McArdle, J.J., and E. Anderson. 1990 "Latent Variable Growth Models for Research on Aging." In J.E. Birren and K.W. Schaie, eds., *Handbook of the Psychology of Aging*, 3rd ed. New York: Academic Press.

Meredith, W. 1964a "Notes on Factorial Invariance." *Psychometrika* 29:177–185.

——1964b "Rotation to Achieve Factorial Invariance." *Psychometrika* 29:187–206.

Mulaik, S. A. 1972 *The Foundations of Factor Analysis*. New York: McGraw-Hill.

——1975 "Confirmatory Factor Analysis." In D. J. Amick and H. J. Walberg, eds., *Introductory Multivariate Analysis for Educational, Psychological, and Social Research*. Berkeley: McCutchan Publishing Corp.

Muthén, B. 1978 "Contributions to Factor Analysis of Dichotomous Variables." *Psychometrika* 43:551–560.

——1983 "Latent Variable Structural Equation Modeling with Categorical Data." *Journal of Econometrics* 22:43–65.

——1988 *LISCOMP–Analysis of Linear Structural Equations with a Comprehensive Measurement Model: A Program for Advanced Research*. Version 1.1. Chicago: Scientific Software.

——, and B.O. Muthén 1998 *Mplus–The Comprehensive Modeling Program for Applied Researchers*. User's Guide Version 1.0. Los Angeles: Muthen and Muthen.

Neuhaus, J. O., and C. Wrigley 1954 "The Quartimax Method: An Analytical Approach to Orthogonal Simple Structure." *British Journal of Statistical Psychology* 7:81–91.

Schaie, K. W., and C. Hertzog 1985 "Measurement in the Psychology of Adulthood and Aging." In J. E. Birren and K. W. Schaie, eds., *Handbook of the Psychology of Aging*. New York: Van Nostrand.

Scherpenzeel, A. 1995 "A Question of Quality: Evaluating Survey Questions By Multitrait–Multimethod Studies." Unpublished doctoral dissertation, University of Amsterdam, The Netherlands.

Siegel, P. M., and R. W. Hodge 1968 "A Causal Approach to Measurement Error." In H. M. Blalock, Jr. and A. B. Blalock. eds., *Methodology in Social Research*. New York: McGraw-Hill.

Spearman, C. 1904a "'General Intelligence,' Objectively Determined and Measured." *American Journal of Psychology* 15:201–293.

——1904b "The Proof and Measurement of Association between Two Things." *American Journal of Psychology* 15:88–103.

——1927 *The Abilities of Man*. New York: Macmillan. Thurstone, L. L. 1931 "Multiple Factor Analysis." *Psychological Review* 38:406–427.

——1938 *Primary Mental Abilities*. Psychometric Monographs, no. 1. Chicago: University of Chicago Press.

——1947 *Multiple Factor Analysis*. Chicago: University of Chicago Press.

Werts, C. E., and R. L. Linn 1970 "Path Analysis: Psychological Examples." *Psychological Bulletin* 74:194–212.

Wheaton, B., et al. 1977 "Assessing Reliability and Stability in Panel Models." In D. R. Heise, ed., *Sociological Methodology 1977*. San Francisco: Jossey-Bass.

West, Joel 1997 "Structural Equation Software." http://www.gsm.uci.edu/~joelwest/SEM/Software.htm.

Widaman, K. 1991 "Common Factor Analysis vs. Component Analysis: Differential Bias in Representing Model Parameters." Department of Psychology, University of California, Riverside. Typescript.

Wiley, D. E., and J. A. Wiley 1970 "The Estimation of Measurement Error in Panel Data." *American Sociological Review* 35:112–117.

Willett, J. B., and A. G. Sayer 1994 "Using Covariance Structure Analysis to Detect Correlates and Predictors of Individual Change Over Time." *Psychological Bulletin* 116:363–381.

West, Joel 1997 "Structural Equation Software." http:// www.gsm.uci.edu/~joelwest/SEM/Software.htm.

Wright, S. 1921 "Systems of Mating." *Genetics* 6:111–178.

——1925 *Corn and Hog Correlations*. U.S. Dept. of Agriculture, Bulletin no. 1300L1-60. Washington, D.C.: U.S. Government Printing Office.

DUANE F. ALWIN

FAMILISM

See Filial Responsibility; Family and Household Structure; Intergenerational Relations; Intergenerational Resource Transfers.

FAMILY AND HOUSEHOLD STRUCTURE

The family system of the United States is often characterized as consisting of nuclear-family households—that is, households consisting of no more than the parent(s) and dependent children, if any (Lee 1999). This is certainly true of the great majority of family households. In fact, there has never been a point in American history in which extended-family households predominated statistically (Ruggles 1994a; Seward 1978). In 1997 only about 4.1 percent of all families in the United States were "related subfamilies"—a married couple or single parent with children living with a related householder (U.S. Bureau of the Census 1998, Table 69). However, an analysis of census data from 1970 through 1990 by Glick and colleagues (1997) showed that the percentage of all households containing nonnuclear kin increased from 9.9 percent in 1980 to 12.2 percent in 1990, reversing a nearly century-long pattern of decline. In 1910 about 20 percent of the households of white families and 24 percent of those of black families contained nonnuclear kin (Ruggles 1994b). Apparently we have seen a long-term decline in the prevalence of extended-family households, very slightly counterbalanced by an increase in the 1980s; what happened in the 1990s is not yet known.

Not all of the of the households that do not contain extended families consist of the stereotypical nuclear family of two parents and their dependent children, however. There is great diversity among American families and households, and this diversity is increasing. Table 1 presents data on the composition of American households and families from 1960 to 1998. Even over this relatively brief period, substantial changes are apparent. The average size of both households and families decreased dramatically from 1960 to 1990, although they have both been stable in the 1990s. Many fewer households contain families and married couples in the late 1990s than in 1960, while the proportion of nonfamily households has more than doubled and the proportion of single-person households has nearly doubled. Female householders have increased substantially as a proportion of both all households and all families.

There are many factors responsible for these changes. To understand them, changes in marriage rates and age at marriage, divorce and remarriage rates, rates of nonmarital cohabitation, the departure of children from their parents' homes, and the predilection of unmarried persons to live alone will be briefly examined. Each of these factors has affected family and household structure.

Marriage rates have declined considerably since 1960 (see Table 2). This is not readily apparent from the "crude" marriage rate (the number of marriages per 1,000 population) because this rate does not take the marital status or age distributions of the population into account. The crude marriage rate was artificially low in 1960 because, as a result of the postwar baby boom, a large proportion of the population consisted of children too young to marry. The rates per 1,000 unmarried women (for both ages 15 and over and ages 15 to 44) show the frequency of occurrence of marriage for persons exposed to the risk of marriage, and here there is clear evidence of decline. Some of this, however, is attributable to increases in the median age at first marriage, which declined throughout the twentieth century until about 1960, but has been increasing rapidly since 1970. As age at marriage increases, more and more people temporarily remain unmarried each year, thus driving the marriage rate down. The best evidence (Oppenheimer et al. 1997) indicates that a major cause of delayed marriage is the deteriorating economic circumstances of young men since the

Changes in U.S. Households and Families Since 1960

	1960	1970	1980	1990	1998
Number of households (in 1,000s)	52,799	63,401	80,776	93,347	102,528
Average size	3.35	3.14	2.76	2.63	2.62
Family households (%)	85.04	81.15	73.72	70.80	69.13
Married-couple households (%)	74.34	70.54	60.79	56.04	52.97
Female householder (%)	8.38	8.67	10.77	11.66	12.34
Nonfamily households (%)	14.95	18.84	26.27	29.19	30.86
Single-person households (%)	13.10	17.11	22.65	24.63	25.67
Number of families (in 1,000s)	45,111	51,586	59,550	66,090	70,880
Average size of families	3.67	3.58	3.29	3.17	3.18
Married-couple families (%)	87.18	86.75	82.47	79.16	76.63
Female householder (%)	9.99	10.83	14.61	16.47	17.81

Table 1

SOURCE: U.S. Bureau of the Census (1998; Table 69), and Current Population Reports, P20-509 and earlier reports.

1970s. Perhaps the improving economy of the later 1990s will eventually produce some change in this trend.

The rising divorce rate has also contributed greatly to the declining proportion of married-couple households and the increases in female householders and single-person households. The crude divorce rate rose from 2.2 per 1,000 in 1960 to 5.2 in 1980 (reaching peaks of 5.3 in both 1979 and 1981) but has declined modestly since then to 4.3 in 1996. The rate of divorce per 1,000 married women 15 and older followed a similar pattern, reaching a high of 22.6 in 1980 and declining to 19.5 in 1996. Some of this decline is illusory, because the large baby boom cohorts are aging out of the most divorce-prone years (Martin and Bumpass 1989). However, although the divorce rate remains high, it has not been increasing since 1980.

Sweeney (1997) notes that, for recent cohorts, about half of all marriages have involved at least one previously married partner. However, rates of remarriage after divorce have been declining steadily. Annual remarriage rates were 204.5 per 1,000 divorced men and 123.3 per 1,000 divorced women in 1970; by 1990 they had decreased to 105.9 for men and 76.2 for women (U.S. Bureau of the Census 1998).

Decreasing marriage and remarriage rates and increasing divorce rates have combined to produce increases in single-person and single-parent households. This trend is mitigated, however, by the increasing prevalence of nonmarital heterosexual cohabitation. Most such unions (those without children) appear as nonfamily households in Table 1. Evidence from the National Survey of Families and Households (Bumpass 1994; Waite 1995) shows that, in the early 1990s, nearly one-quarter of all unmarried adults aged 25 to 29 were cohabiting. This percentage declines with age, but still exceeded 20 percent for those in their late thirties. The National Survey of Family Growth found that, in 1995, more than 41 percent of all women aged 15 to 44 had cohabited or were currently cohabiting (National Center for Health Statistics 1997). Of course many of the women who had not cohabited at the time of the survey will do so in the future. The best estimates suggest that more than half of all couples who marry now cohabit prior to marriage; further, about 60 percent of all cohabiting unions eventuate in marriage (Bumpass 1994; Bumpass et al. 1991).

To a considerable extent the increase in cohabitation has offset the decline in marriage. This is particularly the case among blacks, for whom the decrease in marriage rates over the past several decades has been much more precipitous than it has been for whites (Raley 1996; Waite 1995). Although cohabiting unions are less stable than marriages, ignoring cohabitation results in substantial underestimates of the prevalence of heterosexual unions in the United States.

In spite of the increase in cohabitation, changes in marriage and divorce behavior have had substantial effects on household and family structure

Changes in U.S. Marriage and Divorce Since 1960

	1960	1970	1980	1990	1996
Number of marriages (in 1,000s)[1]	1,523	2,159	2,390	2,443	2,344
Rate per 1,000 population	8.5	10.6	10.6	9.8	8.8
Rate per 1,000 unmarried women, age 15+	73.5	76.5	61.4	54.5	49.7
Rate per 1,000 unmarried women, age 15–44	148.0	140.2	102.6	91.3	81.5
Median age at first marrage[2]					
Males	22.8	23.2	24.7	26.1	27.1
Females	20.3	20.8	22.0	23.9	24.8
Divorce and annulments (in 1,000s)[3]	393	708	1,189	1,182	1,150
Rate per 1,000 population	2.2	3.5	5.2	4.7	4.3
Rate per 1,000 married women 15+	9.2	14.9	22.6	20.9	19.5

Table 2

NOTE: 1. Monthly Vital Statistics Report, Vol. 43, No. 12 (S), July 14, 1995 for 1960–90; and U.S. Bureau of the Census (1988): Table 156 for 1996.

2. U.S. Bureau of the Census, Current Population Reports, P20–514 (March 1998) and earlier reports for 1960–90; and U.S. Bureau of the Census web site for 1996.

3. Monthly Vital Statistics Report, Vol. 43, No. 9 (S), March 22, 1995 for 1960–90; and U.S. Bureau of the Census (1998): Table 156 for 1996.

in the United States over the past four decades. Fewer people are marrying, those who marry are doing so at later ages, more married people are divorcing, and fewer divorced people are remarrying. This means that Americans are living in smaller households than they did in 1960, but there are more of them. The rate of growth in the number of households has substantially exceeded the rate of growth in the number of families. Referring back to Table 1, from 1960 to 1998 the number of households increased by more than 94 percent, while the increase in the number of families was only about 57 percent. Over the same time period, the total population of the United States increased by just under 50 percent (U.S. Bureau of the Census 1998, Table 2). Our population, therefore, is distributed in a larger number of smaller households than was the case in 1960.

One cause of the decline in household size shown in Table 1 is decreased fertility. The fertility rate (number of births per 1,000 women aged 15 to 44) was 118.0 in 1960; by 1997 it had decreased to 65.0, although most of the decrease occurred prior to 1980 (National Center for Health Statistics 1999). The trend toward smaller households and families is reflective to some extent of decreases in the number of children per family.

A larger cause of the decrease in household size, however, is the proliferation of single-person households, as shown in Table 1. Single-person households consist of three types of persons: the never-married, who are primarily young adults; the divorced and separated without coresident children, who are primarily young and middle-aged; and the widowed who live alone, who are primarily elderly. Each of these types has increased, but for somewhat different reasons. Each must therefore be examined separately.

As shown in Table 2, average ages at marriage have risen markedly since 1960, and the percentage of young adults who have never married has increased proportionately (Waite 1995). This has been accompanied by a long-term decline (since prior to World War II) in the average age of leaving the parental home (Goldscheider 1997). Prior to 1970 most of this decline was driven by decreasing ages at marriage, but since then it has reflected an increasing gap between leaving the family of orientation and beginning the family of procreation. More young adults are living independently of both parents and spouses. Some of them are cohabiting, of course, but increasing numbers are residing in either single-person or other nonfamily households (Goldscheider 1997; White 1994).

Since about 1970 there has been some increase in the proportion of young adults who live with their parents. This marks the reversal of a long-term decline in age at leaving home (White 1994). This is, in part, a by-product of increasing age at marriage. However, decreases in exits from parental homes to marriage have been largely offset by increases in exits to independent living, so this recent increase in young adults living with parents is actually very small (Goldscheider 1997). On the other hand, there is increasing evidence that the process of launching children has become much more complex than in previous years. Goldscheider (1997) also shows that the proportion of young adults who return to their parents' homes after an initial exit has more than doubled from the 1930s to the 1990s; increases have been particularly striking since the early 1960s. This is a response, in part, to the rising divorce rate, but also an indication that it has gotten increasingly difficult for young adults, particularly young men, to make a living (Oppenheimer et al. 1997). Nonetheless, the proportion of young adults living independently of both parents and spouses continues to increase, contributing to the prevalence of nonfamily households.

The increase in divorce and decrease in remarriage have contributed to the rise in single-person households, as formerly married persons establish their own residences and, increasingly, maintain them for longer periods of time. They have also contributed to the rise in family households that do not contain married couples. As shown in Table 1, families headed by females (without husband present) increased from 10 percent of all families in 1960 to nearly 18 percent in 1998. Families headed by males (without wife present) also increased, from 2.8 percent of all families in 1960 to 5.5 percent in 1998. Among families with children under 18 in 1998, 20 percent were headed by women without spouses and 5 percent by men without spouses (U.S. Bureau of the Census 1998, Table 70).

As a consequence of these changes plus the rise in nonmarital childbearing, the proportion of children under 18 living with both parents decreased from 88 percent in 1960 to 68 percent in 1997 (U.S. Bureau of the Census 1998, Table 84). In addition, there is a large race difference in the living arrangements of children. Only 35 percent of black children lived with both parents in 1997, compared to 75 percent of white children. More than half (52 percent) of all black children lived

with their mothers only, as did 18 percent of white children. Further, 8 percent of black children and 3 percent of white children lived with neither parent. Some of these children are living with, and being cared for by, their grandparents (Pebley and Rudkin 1999). This raises the issue of the living arrangements of older persons.

A somewhat longer perspective is necessary to observe changes in the living arrangements of older persons. Ruggles (1994a) has shown that, in 1880, nearly 65 percent of all elderly whites and more than 57 percent of all elderly nonwhites lived with a child. Since about 18 percent of all older persons had no living children, Ruggles estimates that about 78 percent of whites and 70 percent of nonwhites who had children lived with a child. By 1980 the percentages living with children had decreased to 16 for whites and 29 for nonwhites. There is little evidence of major changes in the proportion living with children since 1980. Further, Ruggles (1996) found that only 6 percent of all elderly women and 3 percent of elderly men lived alone in 1880. By 1997 the percentages living alone had increased to 41 for women and 17 for men (U.S. Bureau of the Census 1998, Table 50). The growth of single-person households among older people has been particularly rapid since about 1940.

Two sets of factors appear to be primarily responsible for the "migration" of older people from typically sharing households with their children in the late nineteenth century to living alone (or with their spouses only) in the late twentieth century. First, the family life cycle was quite different in 1900 than today. People married a bit later (and markedly later than in the 1960s and early 1970s), had more children, and had children later in life. Consequently, a significant proportion of people in their sixties had unmarried children who simply had not yet left the parental home. Ruggles (1994a) shows that, in 1880, about 32 percent of all unmarried elders and 57 percent of the married resided with a never-married child. Of course many of these children may have remained home precisely in order to care for their aging parents. Unmarried elders were more likely to live with married children.

Second, economic factors played a major role. Social Security did not exist until 1940. In 1900, 85 percent of all men between the ages of 65 and 69 were in the labor force, as were 49 percent of all men 85 and over (Smith 1979). However, this option was much less available to women; the comparable proportions in the labor force were 12 and 6 percent. Many older persons, particularly women, had no means of support other than their children. Rates of coresidence of aging parents with their adult children have decreased as the prosperity of the elderly has increased; more can now afford to live independently.

However, Ruggles (1994a) found that wealthier older people were more likely to share a household with children than were poorer elders in the nineteenth century, and the majority of multigenerational families lived in households headed by the elderly parent(s). These facts suggest that adult children benefited economically from coresidence and that the possibility of inheriting a farm or business from aging parents may have motivated many adults to coreside with parents. Today coresidence is more common among poorer than wealthier people (Ruggles 1994a, 1996).

As of March 1998, 41 percent of all women aged 65 and older lived alone, as did 17 percent of all older men. These percentages increase to 53 percent and 22 percent for women and men, respectively, for those age 75 and over (U.S. Bureau of the Census Web site). The reason for this large gender difference, of course, is the difference in marital status between men and women. Among men 75 and over, nearly two-thirds are married and less than one-quarter are widowed; among women these figures are almost exactly reversed. According to 1980 census data, the proportion of all elderly persons living alone increases from 22 percent among those 65 to 69 to more than 41 percent in the 85–89 age category, then drops to 33 percent for those 90 and over (Coward et al. 1989), after which the modal category becomes living with children. Older persons who have lost their spouses through death are clearly exhibiting a tendency to live alone as long as possible, which for many of them extends into the latest years of life.

Older persons now constitute nearly 13 percent of the total population of the United States, compared to about 4 percent in 1900. With so many of them maintaining their own residences,

either with their spouses or alone following widowhood, their contribution to the proliferation of small and single-person households is substantial.

If so many older persons lived with their children in the late nineteenth century, why were there so few extended-family households? Ruggles (1994a) shows that just under 20 percent of the households of whites contained extended families in both 1880 and 1900; this compares to less than 7 percent in 1980, but it was still very much a minority statistical pattern. There were three primary reasons. First, because of more limited life expectancies and relatively high fertility rates, there were proportionally few older people in the population, so where they lived made less difference to the nation's household structure. Second, as noted above, many older persons lived with an unmarried child; unless other relatives are present, this arrangement constitutes a nuclear-family household regardless of the age of the parent. Third, while these cohorts of older persons typically had many children (an average of 5.4 per woman in 1880), these children did not live together as adults, so older persons could live with only one; their remaining children lived in nuclear families. Ruggles (1994a) estimates that more than 70 percent of all elders who could have lived with a child actually did so in 1880; the comparable percentage in 1980 was 16. In comparison to the last century, older persons today are much less likely to live with children and much more likely to live alone, contributing to the proliferation of small and single-person households.

To this point, factors that have contributed to long-term decreases in household and family size, and consequent increases in the numbers of households and families, have been elucidated. There is evidence of changes in these directions in all age segments of the population. These trends do not mean, however, that more complex family households are not part of the contemporary American experience.

As noted at the beginning of this entry, the United States has never been characterized by a statistical predominance of extended-family households, although it appears that the preference was for intergenerational coresidence in the form of stem families (families containing an older parent or parents and one of their married children) until the early years of the twentieth century. But extended family households do occur today. At any single point in time, they constitute less than 10 percent of all households (Glick et al. 1997; Ruggles 1994a). However, a dynamic perspective presents a somewhat different picture.

Beck and Beck (1989) analyzed the household compositions of a large sample of middle-aged women who were followed from 1969 to 1984. The presence of nonnuclear kin in their households was noted for specific years and was also calculated for the entire fifteen-year period. In 1984, when these women were between the ages of 47 and 61, only 8 percent of white married women and 20 percent of white unmarried women lived in households containing their parents, grandchildren, or other nonnuclear kin. The proportions were higher for comparable black women: 27 percent of the married and 34 percent of the unmarried. However, over the fifteen years covered by the survey, about one-third of all white women and fully two-thirds of the black women lived in a household containing extended kin at some point.

These and other data (Ruggles 1994a, 1994b) show that today blacks are more likely than whites to live in extended-family households. This was not the case until about 1940. What has happened is that the decrease in intergenerational coresidence since the late nineteenth century has been much steeper for whites than for blacks. This is probably connected to much lower rates of marriage among blacks; living in multigenerational households is much more common for unmarried than for married persons. It may also reflect the shift in the distribution of extended families from the wealthier to the poorer segments of the economic structure. Rather than serving as a means of ensuring inheritance and keeping wealth in the family, extended family living today is more likely to be motivated by a need to share and conserve resources.

The family and household structure of the United States has changed dramatically over the past century, in spite of the fact that our family system has remained nuclear in at least the statistical sense. More and more Americans are living in single-person households before, between, and after marriages. More are living in single-parent households. Collectively Americans are spending smaller proportions of their lives in families of any description than they did in the past (Watkins et al.

1987). However, they are more likely than ever before to live in nonmarital heterosexual unions, and many of them live in households that contain nonnuclear kin at some point in their lives. In fact, there is evidence (Glick et al. 1997) that the proportion of extended-family households increased between 1980 and 1990.

The growth of small and single-person households is in many ways indicative of the fact that more Americans can now afford to remain unmarried, leave unhappy marriages, and maintain their own residences in later life. The proliferation of households represents the proliferation of choices. The consequences of these choices remain to be seen.

REFERENCES

Beck, Rubye W., and Scott H. Beck 1989 "The Incidence of Extended Households Among Middle-Aged Black and White Women: Estimates from a 15-Year Panel Study." *Journal of Family Issues* 10:147–168.

Bumpass, Larry L. 1994. "The Declining Significance of Marriage: Changing Family Life in the United States." Paper presented at the Potsdam International Conference, "Changing Families and Childhood."

——, James A. Sweet, and Andrew J. Cherlin 1991 "The Role of Cohabitation in Declining Rates of Marriage." *Journal of Marriage and the Family* 53:913–927.

Coward, Raymond T., Stephen Cutler, and Frederick Schmidt 1989 "Differences in the Household Composition of Elders by Age, Gender, and Area of Residence." *The Gerontologist* 29:814–821.

Glick, Jennifer E., Frank D. Bean, and Jennifer V. W. Van Hook 1997 "Immigration and Changing Patterns of Extended Family Household Structure in the United States: 1970–1990." *Journal of Marriage and the Family* 59:177–191.

Goldscheider, Frances 1997 "Recent Changes in U.S. Young Adult Living Arrangements in Comparative Perspective." *Journal of Family Issues* 18:708–724.

Lee, Gary R. 1999 "Comparative Perspectives." In Marvin B. Sussman, Suzanne K. Steinmetz, and Gary W. Peterson, eds., *Handbook of Marriage and the Family*, 2nd ed. New York: Plenum.

Martin, Teresa Castro, and Larry L. Bumpass 1989 "Recent Trends in Marital Disruption." *Demography* 26:37–51.

National Center for Health Statistics 1997 "Fertility, Family Planning, and Women's Health: New Data from the 1995 National Survey of Family Growth."

Vital and Health Statistics, Series 23, No. 19. Hyattsville, Md.: Public Health Service.

—— 1999 "Births: Final Data for 1997." *National Vital Statistics Reports*, series 47, no. 18. Hyattsville, Md.: National Center for Health Statistics.

Oppenheimer, Valerie K., Matthijs Kalmijn, and Nelson Lim 1997 "Men's Career Development and Marriage Timing During a Period of Rising Inequality." *Demography* 34:311–330.

Pebley, Anne R., and Laura L. Rudkin 1999 "Grandparents Caring for Grandchildren: What Do We Know?" *Journal of Family Issues* 20:218–242.

Raley, R. Kelly 1996 "A Shortage of Marriageable Men? A Note on the Role of Cohabitation in Black–White Differences in Marriage Rates." *American Sociological Review* 61:973–983.

Ruggles, Steven 1994a "The Transformation of American Family Structure." *American Historical Review* 99:103–128.

—— 1994b "The Origins of African American Family Structure." *American Sociological Review* 59:136–151.

—— 1996 "Living Arrangements of the Elderly in the United States." In Tamara K. Hareven, ed., *Aging and Intergenerational Relations: Historical and Cross-Cultural Perspectives*. Berlin, Germany: de Gruyter.

Seward, Rudy R. 1978 *The American Family: A Demographic History*. Thousand Oaks, Calif.: Sage.

Smith, Daniel Scott 1979 "Life Course, Norms, and the Family System of Older Americans in 1900." *Journal of Family History* 4:285–298.

Sweeney, Megan M. 1997 "Remarriage of Women and Men After Divorce." *Journal of Family Issues* 18:479–502.

U.S. Bureau of the Census 1998 *Statistical Abstract of the United States*, 118th ed. Washington, D.C.: U.S. Government Printing Office.

—— 1998 "Marital Status and Living Arrangements: March 1998." http://www.gov/population/www/socdemo/ms-la.html.

Waite, Linda J. 1995 "Does Marriage Matter?" *Demography* 32:483–507.

Watkins, Susan Cotts, Jane A. Menken, and Jon Bongaarts 1987 "Demographic Foundations of Family Change." *American Sociological Review* 52:346–358.

White, Lynn 1994 "Coresidence and Leaving Home: Young Adults and Their Parents." *Annual Review of Sociology* 20:81–102.

GARY R. LEE
PADMA SRINIVASAN

FAMILY AND POPULATION POLICY IN LESS DEVELOPED COUNTRIES

In 1798, Thomas Malthus penned his famous dictum that agricultural productivity increases arithmetically while populations increase geometrically. Ever since that time, scholars have concerned themselves with the relationship between population dynamics and economic development. With the rise of the modern nation-state, interest grew in how governmental family and population policies might affect the health of national economies. At the turn of twenty-first century comes, accelerating economic globalization, the decline of communism, and the growing influence of the United Nations and other international organizations provide an increasingly complex context within which to understand family and population policy in less developed countries.

The designation of countries as "less developed" or "more developed" (or "developing" versus "developed", "newly industrializing" versus "industrialized") relies on a multidimensional construct of development, ranging from the conditions of education and health to agricultural surplus generation, industrialization, and capital accumulation (Staudt 1997). Perhaps the best single measure of development is a country's real gross domestic product (GDP) per capita (Crenshaw et al. 1997). However, while meager per capita productivity is characteristic of less developed countries, these nations fall along a productivity continuum of considerable range. Less developed countries also vary greatly in size, geographic location, and quality of natural resources. A study of population dynamics in seventy-five developing nations included countries as diverse as Mexico, Brazil, Sierra Leone, Rwanda, Egypt, Pakistan, Malaysia, and the Philippines (Crenshaw et al. 1997).

Like more developed nations, some of these countries have highly centralized governments; others are weak states with little coordination of productive or distributive activities. All, however, are perceived as promoting some form of family policy. In many of these countries, policies that attempt to regulate the family per se as a social institution are not explicitly articulated. Rather, policies regarding the family often operate indirectly through measures directed toward population control (e.g., family-planning programs and restrictions on internal migration) or economic development (e.g., agrarian reform and import-substitution policies). In some parts of the developing world (e.g., China, India, the Islamic states), extensive legal and political measures attempt to govern the formation, functioning, and dissolution of families more directly through, for example, laws on inheritance, dowry, divorce, and filiation. These more explicit family policies often bear the traces of traditional religious interests, but they may also reflect attempts to "modernize" countries by weakening traditional patriarchal control over the disposition of property and the labor of family members. Thus, family policy in less developed countries, whether indirect or explicit, is inextricably bound to questions of economic development, including those concerning the relationship between population and resources.

As a result, few social scientists today treat comparative family policy as an arena of inquiry separate or distinct from comparative studies of population or economic development policy. In fact, attempts to define "family policy" as a distinct object of study have been conspicuously absent from the scholarly literature since the late 1970s (for an example of one such attempt, see Kamerman and Kahn 1978). In part, waning efforts to define and examine family policy per se reflect heated debates about whether a uniform definition of the "family" is useful or appropriate. Feminist critiques in particular have challenged uniform definitions of the family as overly monolithic, static, and undifferentiated, claiming that these definitions ignore the diversity of family patterns not only in less developed nations but also in "modern" countries such as the United States (Beneria and Roldan 1987; Collins 1991; Baca Zinn 1990).

These definitional disputes have given rise to different concepts of what the family is. For example, some scholars argue that variations in household and kinship relations exist worldwide; they tend to prefer the term "household" to "family," defining the former as a residential unit wherein people live in close proximity and organize activities to meet daily needs (Chow and Berheide 1994). Others, however, argue that adopting the household as the unit of analysis, with an attendant focus on how households respond "strategically" to the external economic and political environment, obscures conflicts of interest that arise within households (Bourque and Warren 1987; Wolf

1992). These critics tend to conceptualize the family or household not as a unit or entity but as a site that offers a cultural and moral context for the interaction of personalities, for the production and consumption of goods, and for the reproduction of populations (Acker 1988). This view of the family tends to emphasize how different interests within families are shaped by gender and age—interests that are themselves related to competition and conflict between larger systems of authority and of control over labor (e.g., capitalism, socialism, patriarchy) within national settings.

Athough the study of family policy in less developed nations has largely been overtaken by more fundamental debates about the "proper" unit of analysis, some of these arguments provoke new ways of thinking about *why* developing nations have an interest in the regulation of families. The question of what constitutes a "family" for the purposes of analyzing policy might be found in answers to the question: What is it that families do, in addition to their contributions to population dynamics and economic development, that captures the interest of governments? That is, why do states have a "compelling interest" in families?

Part of an answer may be found in Cherlin's (1999) definition of the "public family," a definition that attempts to locate the contribution of families to the public welfare in their caring for dependent members of the population, such as children, the sick, and the elderly. Adapting Cherlin's definition to a global context, public families may be defined as one adult, or two or more adults who are related by marriage, kin ties, shared parenthood, or coresidence, who is/are taking care of dependents and the dependents themselves. In nearly every society, most caretaking of dependents is performed within a small web of relations like those defined above. Although this work is largely unpaid, it is of great social value, being necessary for the reproduction of a society from one generation to the next. Hence the state's interest in how well families manage the care of dependents. But government interest extends beyond merely ensuring the replenishment of a population. As Folbre (1994) argues, the caretaking that goes on within families can result in the production of valuable public goods—most notably through the rearing of children who will grow up to be productive adult members of a society. Thus, governments have an interest in promoting caretaking within families that gives rise to positive collective benefits (productive members of the next generation, including those who will continue to provide caretaking within families).

Policies that provide explicit incentives for family caretaking in the form of tax breaks or government subsidies for day care, parental leave, or child allowances tend to emerge in countries with a highly developed welfare-state appartus, which presumes the existence of large, stable (if not expanding) public revenues. That is, these policies tend to presume an already-high level of economic development that ensures stable public revenues. The European social democracies—in particular, Sweden—are examples in this regard (Acker 1994). However, some developing countries, such as China, have instituted policies that support caretaking in the form of parenting education programs, child allowances, maternity leave, and planning for social security for the aged (Chow and Chen 1994). The difference in the Chinese case, as in that of other less developed nations, is that these policies are tethered to population policies and goals. The Chinese government, for example, makes eligibility for forms of caretaking support contingent on compliance with its one-child policy, levying penalties in the form of fines, wage deductions, possible job demotion, and forfeiture of other social benefits on parents who have a second child (Chow and Chen 1994). Thus, caretaking policies in the developing world are often put into place as a mechanism for achieving family planning or development goals that aim, over the long term, to ensure national prosperity; they less often derive from such prosperity to begin with, as in the West. The extent to which developing countries manage to implement such "conditional" caretaking policies depends on the strength of the state—in particular, on whether this strength relies on autocratic forms of rule (e.g., China). In developing countries with weaker governments or less autocratic systems of power, support for caretaking more often arises from the adoption of programs or initiatives that are funded by international organizations committed to population control and/or globally organized economic growth. These programs often take the form of children's health initiatives, such as immunization and nutritional-support projects sponsored by the World Health Organization and the World Bank.

A second aspect of governmental interest in the family among less developed countries concerns the role of family and kin networks as the matrix for traditional authority relations. In many emerging nation-states, political power remains locally controlled by clans or confederations of kin that resist attempts by central governments to consolidate power. Loyalties to religious or ethnically based claims to authority also tend to be coupled closely with loyalties to family and larger kin groups. Thus, the emergence of explicit family policies in less developed countries may reflect attempts on the part of central governments to wrest political control from clans or lineages (such as in sub-Saharan Africa; see Migdal 1988). In some parts of the developing world, changes in family law and policy are a function of competition between bureaucratic state interests and traditional religious claims to authority. For example, in the mid-1950s the government of Tunisia outlawed "repudiation," or the husband's Quranic, unilateral prerogative to terminate a marriage at will without judicial involvement. Prior to this time, family matters had been regulated by traditional Islamic doctrine, with allegiance to Islamic law being regionally based and deeply rooted in kin loyalties (Charrad 1994). Changes in the Tunisian civil code to abolish repudiation and make judicial intervention mandatory for divorce had the effect of unifying and strengthening the judicial system by creating a national network of courts. In terms of actual implementation of the new code, judges found themselves shifting between the values of traditional Islamic doctrine and the principles of reform. Nonetheless, the new policy has had a transformative effect on the structure of Tunisian rule, strenthening and consolidating the power of civil law. The case of the Philippines offers another example of how government policy toward families reflects competition between religious and more secular authority claims; the 1986 Philippine constitutional statement about the family reflects an uneasy compromise between Roman Catholic groups and more liberal elements of Filipino society ("Proceedings of the Constitutional Commission" 1986).

In short, despite widespread disagreement in the literature over definitions of "family" and the scope of "family policy," government policies in less developed nations reveal interests in the caretaking of dependents and in the consolidation and centralization of authority that might be usefully thought of as targeting "the family." In contrast to the field of family policy, the terrain of population policy is much more clearly defined, though no less marked by controversy. Population policies differ from family policies because the former are designed to meet specific demographic goals. The most common population policies found in less developed countries are those that attempt to ameliorate population growth by reducing birthrates, for example, through programs in family-planning education and in the distribution of contraceptives (International Institute for Sustainable Development 1994). Other population policies attempt to control migration flows from, for example, rural to urban economic sectors in an attempt to control the mobility of labor and patterns of economic development. These migration policies are especially prevalent in sub-Saharan African countries, where increasing urbanization and the influx of wartime refugees from neighboring areas have placed severe pressures on cities and depleted the supply of labor for rural agriculture. For example, in the 1980s Zambia took steps to curb rural-to-urban migration and promote the resettlement of rural areas through such measures as removing subsidies for commodities in urban areas, a "back to the land" policy, and youth training programs in agriculture and farm management, carpentry, and other rural community-building skills (Mijere and Chilivumbo 1994).

Several demographic problems are a source of shared concern among less developed nations. Concern over rapid population growth has motivated a variety of family-oriented laws and programs, including raising the minimum legal age for marriage in order to shorten the reproductive span during which women are exposed to regular sexual activity (Piepmeier and Hellyer 1977), providing free family-planning services, and, as in China, offering incentives and disincentives for childbearing that involve the provision or withholding of housing, paid maternity leave, and medical or educational services (Greenhalgh 1990; Quah 1990).

Another demographic problem faced by many less developed countries is the lengthening of childhood dependency through adolescence and the concomitant rise of an independent youth culture brought about by the earlier onset of puberty and rising ages at marriage (United Nations 1989). A number of governments in Asia have established sex education or "family life education" policies and programs that target burgeoning adolescent populations, partly as a way of maintaining government family-planning programs in the face of declining levels of marital fertility (Xenos 1990). Other governments have increasingly differentiated youth from adults in their constitutions (Boli-Bennett and Meyer 1978), and programs that explicitly target adolescents and youth are an increasingly important element of social policy in less developed nations (see Central Committee on Youth 1988; Paxman 1984).

Another emerging demographic problem affecting many less developed countries is the growth of the aged population, a situation that typically arises whenever birthrates fall. While less developed nations may have a clear and compelling interest in the production of children as "public goods," the question of how to care for a growing population of the aged amid declining birthrates and the emergence of smaller families raises thorny issues. In some countries, policies are being considered to keep this burden within families rather than making it a government responsibility, reflecting the state's reluctance to absorb the costs of dependency among those who are no longer members of the productive work force.

All three of the above concerns—about rapid population growth, an expanding youth culture, and care for the aged—mark the recent history of policy in China. The Chinese one-child policy was adopted in 1979 to ameliorate population pressure on China's food supply and to reduce state expenditures. Later, it developed into a policy promoting modernization and economic development, with the Chinese government offering several rationales for planned fertility: It would foster better health care for children and mothers, establish better social conditions for the rearing of future generations, increase work efficiency and political awareness, and promote equality of the sexes (Huang 1982). The government created a number of assistance programs, such as fertility education, free birth control and abortion, and planning for social security for the aged; it also offered numerous economic incentives for compliance, such as extra maternity leave, housing or farmland, free doctor visits, day care, and wage bonuses.

Overall, these provisions appear to have relieved China's population crisis: As of 1994, population growth rates were the lowest since 1949, and the percentages of women marrying at an early age and bearing more than one child have declined (Beijing Review 1995). But because enforcement of the one-child policy is left to local jurisdictions, implementation and outcomes vary by location. The policy appears to have gained greater acceptance in the wealthier, more urban provinces, where the incentives are more abundant. Even in these areas, however, the policy has had an important, unanticipated consequence: The preciousness of the single child has led parents, especially mothers, to spend more time on child care and housework than parents in multiple-child households. Instead of promoting women's greater participation in employment, the policy has led to a reassertion of women's traditional roles as homemakers and nurturers. The policy's weakening of the traditional Chinese system of old-age dependence on adult children (primarily sons) was more readily anticipated, but an alternative system of old-age support has yet to emerge.

As the aims (though not the consequences) of the Chinese policy illustrate, another area of concern involves global social movements, including those supporting equal rights for women and other oppressed groups (Bandarage 1997; Chow and Berheide 1994; Staudt 1997). A second global trend is that of environmentalism (McMichael 1996). A variety of "green" movements have emerged that question the assumptions behind unrestricted economic growth and have redefined the debate about development in Third World countries, focusing on the need for agricultural sustainability, the protection of ecologically vulnerable habitats (particularly in the tropical zones), and the maintenance of biodiversity. Concerns about the environmental degradation sometimes wrought by development projects are often coupled with concerns about the rights and well-being of oppressed groups—particularly in Africa, where mining and rural development policies have differentially affected female-headed households

and, as in the case of South Africa, magnified racial inequalities (Schonfield 1994).

Emerging global viewpoints and the sanction given to them by international organizations represent another trend that is likely to influence future policy concerning families in developing countries. In the 1990s alone, various arms of the United Nations offered explicit recommendations on a range of policies, including those on education, family health, women's labor-force participation, and the family (International Institute for Sustainable Development 1994, 1995). Often these recommendations arose from the participation of nongovernmental organizations (NGOs) in planning and development activities. Such recommendations have been closely tied to the system of international aid that includes donors such as the World Bank and the U.S. Agency for International Development. However, the growing visibility of NGOs at U.N. conferences such as the 1994 Cairo Conference on Population and Development and the 1995 Beijing Conference on Women in part reflects the NGOs' lack of efficacy at the national level: These conferences provide forums for NGOs that have encountered resistance from national governments or have failed to mobilize support from the local populace (Baden and Goetz 1997).

Local and national resistance to NGO or multilateral initiatives regarding families sometimes stems from the belief that these initiatives have been "co-opted" by large international aid agencies that neglect the needs of local populations and their families (Mukherjee 1993). For example, donor-influences policies in Malawi have disadvantaged female-headed households, favoring households headed by men, even though the traditional culture recognizes the mother–child pair as the most important family unit (Rodgers 1980; Spring 1986). Donor-influenced structural adjustment policies (SAPs) have become another source of conflict about policy. In response to recent economic stagnation and the Third World debt crisis, these adjustments have involved reducing levels of government employment, "floating" national currencies, and cutting tariffs and subsidies, while encouraging export-driven economic growth through labor-intensive manufacturing. In many countries, women have responded by increasing their participation in home-based industries, often to provide themselves with security should a spouse lose a formal-sector or government job as a result of structural adjustment (Osirim 1994).

The case of Zimbabwe provides an example of how these SAPs can come into conflict with the aims of government policies concerning families. In the early 1980s, Zimbabwe passed laws that ensured women's claims to property in the event of divorce and allowed married women to obtain loans and property in their own names to establish businesses. These laws, supplemented by government loan and training programs to assist women entrepreneurs, were designed to encourage the greater participation of women in national development and to advance their civil rights. However, the advent of Zimbabwe's SAP in 1990 signaled a shift in priorities toward "shrinking the state." The resulting increases in transportation, wholesale, and licensing costs for businesses were particularly hard on women entrepreneurs, some of whom had become the sole wage earners of their families after their husbands had lost a government job (Osirim 1994).

The increasing involvement of transnational social movements, international donor agencies, and nongovernmental organizations in policy development raises an important issue: the strain in many less developed countries between a Western vision of the family that may be supported by the government, NGOs, or international aid agencies, and the traditional family forms supported at the local, grassroots level. In many less developed countries, the government vision of the family may result from the colonial experience, the exposure of elites to Western society, or the perception that a more Westernized family system fits better with other governmental goals, such as economic development or undermining the traditional authority of kin, religious, or ethnic groups. Wherever political struggle focuses on family and population policies, however, the underlying issue often at stake—to which debates in the literature attest—is competition between alternative definitions of the family.

REFERENCES

Acker, Joan 1998 "Class, Gender, and the Relations of Distribution." *Signs* 13:473–497.

—— 1994 "Women, Families, and Public Policy in Sweden." In Esther Ngan-Ling Chow and Catherine White Berheide, eds., *Women, The Family, and Policy* Albany, N.Y.: State University of New York Press.

Baca Zirr, Maxine 1990 "Family, Feminism, and Race in America." *Gender and Society* 4:68–82.

Baden, Sally, and Anne Marie Goetz 1997 "Who Needs [Sex] When You Can Have [Gender]: Conflicting Discourses on Gender at Beijing." In Kathleen Staudt, ed., *Women, International Development, and Politics: The Bureaucratic Mire*. Philadelphia: Temple University Press.

Bandarage, Asoka 1997 *Women, Population, and Global Crisis: A Political-Economic Analysis*. London: Zed Books.

Beijing Review 1995. *State Statistics Bureau 38:26*. Beijing: Beijing Review.

Beneria, Lourdes, and Martha Roldan 1987 *The Crossroads of Class and Gender*. Chicago: University of Chicago Press.

Boli-Bennett, John, and John W. Meyer 1978 "The Ideology of Childhood and the State: Rules Distinguishing Children in National Constitutions, 1870–1970." *American Sociological Review* 43:797–812.

Bourque, Susan, and Kay Warren 1987 "Technology, Gender, and Development." *Daedalus* 116:173–197.

Central Committee on Youth 1988 *Report on Youth Policy*. Hong Kong: Author.

Charrad, Mounira 1994 "Repudiation versus Divorce: Responses to State Policy in Tunisia." In Esther Ngan-ling Chow and Catherine White Berheide, eds., *Women, The Family, and Policy*. Albany, N.Y.: State University of New York Press.

Cherlin, Andrew 1999 *Public and Private Families: An Introduction*. Boston: McGraw-Hill.

Chow, Esther Ngan-ling, and Catherine White Berheide 1994 "Studying Women, Families, and Policies Globally." In Esther Ngan-ling Chow and Catherine White Berheide, eds., *Women, The Familym and Policy*. Albany, N.Y.: State University of New York Press.

——, and Kevin Chen 1994 "The Impact of One-Child Policy on Women and the Patriarchal Family in the People's Republic of China." In Esther Ngan-ling Chow and Catherine White Berheide, eds., *Women, The Family, and Policy*. Albany, N.Y.: State University of New York Press.

Collins, Patricia Hill 1991 *Black Feminist Thought: Knowledge, Consciousness, and The Politics of Empowerment.* New York: Routledge.

Crenshaw, Edward M., Ansari Z. Ameen, and Matthew Christenson 1997 "Population Dynamics and Economic Development: Age-Specific Population Growth Rates and Economic Growth in Developing Countries, 1965 to 1990." *American Sociological Review* 62:974–984.

Folbre, Nancy 1994 "Children as Public Goods." *American Economic Review* 84:86–90.

Greenhalgh, Susan 1990 *State–Society Links: Political Dimensions of Population Policies and Programs, with Special Reference to China.* (Research Division Working Papers No. 18). New York: Population Council.

Huang, Lucy Jen 1982 "Planned Fertility of One-Couple/One-Child Policy and Gender Equality in the People's Republic of China." *Journal of Marriage and the Family* 44:775–784.

International Institute for Sustainable Development 1994 "International Conference on Population and Development." *Earth Negotiations Bulletin* 6 (40). Author.

—— 1995 "Summary of the Fourth World Conference on Women." *Earth Negotiations Bulletin* 14 (21). New York Author.

Kamerman, Sheila B., and Alfred J. Kahn, eds. 1978 *Family Policy: Government and Families in Fourteen Countries.* New York: Columbia University Press.

McMichael, Philip 1996 *Development and Social Change: A Global Perspective.* Thousand Oaks, Calif.: Pine Forge Press.

Migdal, Joel S. 1988 *Strong Societies and Weak States: State–Society Relations and State Capabilities in the Third World.* Princeton, N.J.: Princeton University Press.

Mijere, Nsolo, and Alifeyo Chilivumbo 1994 "Rural-Urban Migration and Urbanization in Zambia during the Colonial and Postcolonial Periods." In Ezekiel Kalipeni, ed., *Population, Growth and Environmental Degradation in Southern Africa.* Boulder, Colo.: Lynne Rienner Publishers.

Mukherjee, Vanita Nayak 1993 *Shaping a Better Future: Women's Perspectives on Alternative Economic Framework and Population and Reproductive Rights.* Kuala Lumpur, Malaysia: Asian and Pacific Development Centre.

Osirim, Mary 1994 "Women, Work, and Public Policy: Structural Adjustment and the Informal Sector in Zimbabwe." In Ezekiel Kalipeni, ed., *Population Growth and Environmental Degradation in Southern Africa.* Boulder, Colo.: Lynne Rienner.

Paxman, John M. 1984 *Law, Policy, and Adolescent Fertility: An International Overview.* London: International Planned Parenthood Federation.

Piepmeire, Katherine B., and Elizabeth Hellyer 1977 "Minimum Age at Marriage: 20 Years of Legal Reform." *People* 4 (3):

"Proceedings of the Constitutional Commission on the Family, 1986 (Part 1)" *1986 Philippine Population Journal* 2(1–4):135–156.

Quah, Stella R. 1990 "The Social Significance of Marriage and Parenthood in Singapore: Policy and Trends." In S. R. Quah, ed., *The Family as an Asset: An International Perspective on Marriage, Parenthood, and Social Policy.* Singapore: Times Academic Press.

Rodgers, Barbara 1980 *The Domestication of Women: Discrimination in Developing Societies.* New York: St. Martin's Press.

Schonfield, Anne 1994 "Securing the Future: Environmental Issues as a Priority in South Africa." In Ezekiel Kalipeni, ed., *Population Growth and Environmental Degradation in Southern Africa.* Boulder, Colo.: Lynne Rienner Publishers.

Spring, Anita 1986 "Men and Women Smallholder Participants in a Stall-Feeder Livestock Program in Malawi." *Human Organization* 45(2):154–161.

Staudt, Kathleen 1997 "Gender Politics in Bureaucracy: Theoretical Issues in Comparative Perspective." In Kathleen Staudt, ed., *Women, International Development, and Politics.* Philadephia: Temple University Press.

United Nations 1989 *Adolescent Reproductive Behaviour: Evidence from Developing Countries*, vol. 2. New York: Author.

Wolf, Diane 1992 *Factory Daughters.* Berkeley: University of California Press.

Xenos, Peter 1990 "Youth, Sexuality and Public Policy in Asia: A Research Perspective." In S. R. Quah, ed., *The Family as Asset: An International Perspective on Marriage, Parenthood, and Social Policy.* Singapore: Times Academic Press.

JULIE BRINES

FAMILY AND RELIGION

Social scientific notions of the disappearance or vestigialization of religion and family are deeply rooted in our theoretical conceptions of the social processes that created the modern world and that now are transforming that modernity into postindustrial, postmodern society. Theories of modernization envision social change as entailing the rationalization of all spheres of existence. In a statement characterizing the classic modernization approach, Moore (1963, p. 79) says, "A major feature of the modern world . . . is that the rational orientation is pervasive and a major basis for deliberate change in virtually every aspect of man's concerns." There is little room for the seemingly irrational and unscientific impulses of religion, primary emotions, and familial concerns.

With this approach, the secularization of religion is a given. Moore (1963, p. 80) states, "Even with regard to the role of religion in human affairs, the 'rational spirit' takes the form of *secularization*, the substitution of nonreligious beliefs and practices for religious ones." Though religion survives, it addresses "personal misfortune and bereavement" above all else in modern society (Moore 1963, p. 104).

Furthermore, "economic modernization" tends to have "negative consequences for extended kinship systems" and leads to "extensive 'family disorganization'" accompanying the "breakdown of traditional patterns and the incomplete establishment of new institutions" (Moore 1963, p. 102). For modernization theorists, although families remain significant as consumption units, the "decline" of the family (Popenoe 1988) is, at minimum, a metaphor for its consignment to a peripheral societal role. The analogue of the notion of linear secularization of religion is the idea of the loss of family functions (Vago 1989, pp. 150–157). Shaped in the eighteenth and nineteenth centuries, modernization views have continued to dominate public opinion and much of social scientific discourse. In general, according to modernization theories, both family and religion are relegated to the "private" sphere, set apart from the broader social processes and, thus, less significant than those broader processes.

Despite this widespread orientation, a revolution in the social sciences has been gaining momentum over the last twenty years or so. The message of this revolution is that the modernization perspective is no longer an adequate vision for understanding the dynamics of modernity or the potentials of postmodernity for religion and family. In the sociology of religion, the paradigm shift moves social science away from a focus on religion as a disconnected phenomenon to a much more complex view of the nature of religious inter-institutional relations. Reflecting this shift, numerous scholars have begun to examine religion as an influence on and as an effect of varied social, political, and economic variables (e.g., Carter 1996; Cousineau 1998; Hammond 1985; Misztal and Shupe 1992; Roberts 1995; Rubenstein 1987; Shupe and Misztal 1998; Swatos 1992; Witte 1993). A market model of religion, based in rational choice propositions, has become the most strongly debated version of the new way of looking at the religious institution (Hadden 1995; Warner 1993; Young 1997).

Similarly for the family, there are many who now argue that, in spite of its changing forms and functions, the family as an institution remains crucially central to social processes and to the patterns of change determining the future of human societies (cf. Cherlin 1996). If not taken into consideration, family processes themselves are liable to torpedo efforts at planned social change and to deflect the vectors of unplanned change in unexpected directions (Settles 1996).

Attuned to the inter-institutional perspective, this article examines the linkage between family and religion. Then, after discussing social change processes, we make the point that the religion and family linkage today is important not only in the burgeoning private sphere but in the public realm as well. In spite of its importance, sociologists have given relatively little attention to family and religion together (Thomas and Cornwall 1990). A few journal articles and four collected volumes have addressed this institutional linkage. D'Antonio and Aldous (1983) and Thomas (1988) edited general volumes, and a collection by Ammerman and Roof (1995) focused on family and religion in relation to work. As of 1999, only one book (Houseknecht and Pankhurst 2000) had taken an international comparative approach to the topic. (An expanded discussion of some of the themes presented here can be found in the introduction of the latter volume.)

THE RELIGION AND FAMILY LINKAGE

In order to understand the significance of religion and family for both the private and public spheres, we must see clearly their unique characteristics and how they interrelate. The inter-institutional relations between family and religion are strong and qualitatively different from other institutional relationships. Berger (1967) noted that in premodern societies kinship was permeated with religious meaning, and in modern societies religion remains closely connected to the family. Hargrove (1979), in her systematization of the sociology of religion, argued that religion and family have had a close relationship throughout history in both Western and non-Western societies. D'Antonio and colleagues (1982) also stressed the significance of the connections between these two institutions.

Both the familial and religious institutions are characterized by what MacIver (1970, p. 45) called cultural rather than secondary interests. In other words, associations within the religious and familial spheres pursue interests for their own sake, because they bring direct satisfaction, not because they are means to other interests, as in the case of economy and polity. Both family and religion are devoted to organizing primary group relations. They stand out as the only two institutions that deal with the person as a whole rather than just segmented aspects of individual lives. These various similarities that religion and family share serve to strengthen the inter-institutional ties between them.

The interrelations between the institutions of religion and family are reciprocal (Thomas and Henry 1985; Thornton 1985). Religion provides the symbolic legitimation for family patterns (cf. Berger 1969), and the family is a requisite for a vigorous religious system because it produces members and instills them with religious values. In fact, numerous familial events are marked in religious contexts (e.g., weddings and funerals), and many religious observances take place within the familial setting (e.g., prayers at meals and bedtime).

The special affinity of religion and family as institutions takes varied forms. Almost everywhere, religion provides ritual support for family and kinship structures. This is the case even in a highly secularized society such as Sweden (Trost and Palm 2000). In some societies, this ritual support may be seen in ancestor rites or memorialization, for example, in Cameroonian Kedjom rites (Diduk and Maynard 2000), Japan's core religion (Smith 2000), Taiwan's folk religion (Yang et al. 2000), and French Mormonism (Jarvis 2000). Such practices support family life and, at the same time, fulfill a central function for religion itself (cf. Berger 1969, p. 62). In fact, Jarvis argues that the familism of Mormonism, expressed both ritually and in church values, is its greatest asset in the eroding environment for traditional families in France. Moreover, utopian experiments and new religious movements often take the family as their essential focus. According to Christiano (2000), in the Unification Church ("Moonies"), the family serves as more than the organizing metaphor for the group: It provides a basic model for the church's self-conception.

FAMILY, RELIGION, AND SOCIAL CHANGE

The institutions of family and religion, in their interactions with each other and with the rest of society, can be considered in terms of two broad social change patterns—institutional differentiation and institutional dominance. Secularization can be seen as a special instance of institutional differentiation, and we discuss the concept and its use below, indicating the value of religious economy models over the conventional secularization approach.

Institutional Differentiation. Underlying all the dimensions of social change is the notion of institutional differentiation. This phenomenon implies greater specialization. Although the paths and extent of institutional differentiation vary across societies, when differentiation does proceed, we see fundamental changes in inter-institutional relations (cf. Alexander and Colomy 1990; Beckford 1989). Institutional differentiation affects all institutions, and we argue more broadly that one cannot assume inter-institutional isolation of religion and family in the private sphere, even in highly differentiated societies. The effects of these institutions are always felt across inter-institutional divisions in some measure. In this section, we examine the issue of differentiation of religion and family conceptually.

Our previous description of the religion and family linkage as involving special affinity and reciprocity was not to say that religion and family always and everywhere are, or must be, equally intimately entangled. We can see a continuum in the level of differentiation of these institutions. On the one end of the continuum, Islam in Egypt (Houseknecht 2000) displays a lack of differentiation, an elaborate interweaving of the two institutions that makes each strongly dependent on the other. And research on the Cameroonian Kedjom funerary rites (Diduk and Maynard 2000) provides an example of religious practices that are hardly differentiated from the kinship context; they are precisely an affirmation of the kinship patterns of Kedjom society.

On the opposite end of the spectrum, Sweden, a country in which the Lutheran Church is officially established and a large majority of the population are nominal members, is highly secular. Developments in the family there have widely diverged from the traditional model that Protestant Christianity had advocated. In Sweden, the two institutions are intertwined only in limited ways (Trost and Palm 2000). It is primarily in regard to life-cycle rites that the two intersect. The individualized faith of many Americans also accompanies a highly differentiated system of institutional relationships (Christiano 2000).

Secularization Theories. Secularization is a special process of differentiation in which that which was previously under the "sacred canopy" (Berger 1969) of religion is removed from that realm and placed in a nonreligious institutional context. Allegedly, education, the acceptance of science, urbanization, industrialized work-life, and the like take away the mystery of religion and strip it of its "plausibility" in many areas of concern. Thus, cure of disease, protection from misfortune, explanation of the universe, and so forth are made

rational and thus not subject to religious intervention. In this approach, religion remains relevant only for very personal spiritual quests and solace in the private sphere, and most of its social institutional ramifications become, first, empty shells, and eventually vanish.

The notion of a unilinear process of secularization has long troubled many sociologists (cf. Hadden and Shupe 1986; Hadden 1987; Hammond 1985). Some have developed variants that see secularization as a cyclical process with long historical waves. Nisbet (1970), for example, reminds us of the rationality of the eras of classical Greece and of the Renaissance and Age of Reason, with the period from first century Rome to the Renaissance having Christianity "virtually eliminating secular rationalism from the European continent for more than a thousand years" (p. 391). Though we are now in a rationalizing or secularizing age, "To argue permanence for this age would be, on the testimony of history, absurd" (p. 391). Recently, as we shall see, sociologists of religion have focused upon shorter waves of secularization and have viewed the process as self-limiting. The most prominent versions of this approach apply economic models to religious markets, putting aside the notion that religion must be irrational or otherwise antimodern. Some of these postsecularization theorists argue for a rational choice approach to religion (Young 1997), an approach that is largely alien to the mode of thought underlying secularization theory.

In the long debate about the validity of notions of secularization within the sociology of religion, it has become clear that secularization cannot be understood in a simplistic way, if one wants to keep the concept at all. While certain evidence of secularization seems apparent, there are counter-movements suggesting that religion is truly vital in the modern world (cf. Marty and Appleby 1995). The spread of Liberation Theology throughout Latin America in the 1970s and 1980s (Berryman 1987; Smith 1991), followed by the more recent explosion of evangelical, fundamentalist, and pentecostal Protestantism in the same world region (Martin 1990), suggest the power of the human concern regarding spiritual or nonempirical matters. Similarly, the tenacious attachment of Americans to belief in God (Greeley 1989, 1992; cf. Wald

1986), their high levels of religious activity, and the numerical growth and public voice of evangelical Protestantism indicate that religious sentiment of some sort is compatible even with a society that is highly developed socioeconomically. Going beyond the simple Marxist assertion that religion is illusion, even if religious claims are often masks for the interests of power or wealth, religion must be understood as a very real and consequential part of sociocultural life.

Casanova (1994) carried out one of the most extensive recent cross-cultural analyses of religion, a close examination of the conditions of evangelical Protestantism and Catholicism in the United States and of Catholicism in Brazil, Spain, and Poland. He argued that the social scientific literature depicts secularization as having three correlated dimensions, but his research challenges this idea by convincingly showing that the three dimensions are not always present together. First, Casanova accepts the validity of claims that secularization entails a structural differentiation of the religious institution from other institutions as societal modernization takes place. This differentiation means, in particular, the "emancipation of the secular spheres from religious institutions and norms" (Casanova 1994, p. 6). However, the second dynamic often subsumed under secularization—the decline in religious beliefs and practices—cannot be taken for granted, and it does not necessarily follow from the first. The third dynamic, which is the core of the privatization thesis, is that religion will sequester itself in the private sphere under modernity, and, according to some analysts, will be marginalized there. However, this process, too, cannot be assumed to be associated with secularizing institutional differentiation. The second and third dynamics are unwarranted correlates of the first. While Casanova would have us accept the first as the true essence of secularization, he argues that the second and third are not supported by empirical evidence and should not be seen as part of the secularization process.

While there is no question that institutional differentiation is a sort of master process of the modern era, we cannot assume that it has progressed equally far everywhere. As already noted, cases like modern Egypt and Cameroon, though both experiencing significant pressures toward greater differentiation, evidence far less differentiation between family and religion, and between these two and other institutions, than does, for example, the United States or Sweden. Furthermore, even if there is great differentiation, one cannot presume that the influences of the religious and familial institutions end. As the debates on abortion policy illustrate, even in a highly differentiated society like the United States, there is plenty of room for religious assertions beyond the alleged parameters of secularized religion and into political life. This circumstance indicates that we cannot take for granted notions of the irrelevance of religion for social policy, as secularist analysts are prone to do.

In addition, it also is possible for there to be de-differentiation in a highly differentiated society. Some of this has happened in Belarus during the post-Soviet period (Vardomatskii and Pankhurst 2000). Better known to the U.S. public is the recent passage of laws in Russia favoring the Russian Orthodox Church (Pankhurst 1998) after many decades of antireligious, extremely secularist communist control under the Soviets and after a brief period of strict legal disestablishment of all religions between 1991 and 1997. Here are instances of seeming de-differentiation, where the gap between politics and religion is narrowed. Similarly, the debate in Indonesia over divorce law indicates efforts to reassert religious authority over a legal arena that had been under state control for several decades (Cammack et al. 2000).

Religious and Familial Markets. The notion of unilinear secularization seems untenable, but there are certainly processes of decline and growth in religious phenomena that must be explained. The general inter-institutional perspective focuses attention on relationships that are important for these variations in the strength and character of religion. In addition, sociologists of religion have found market model approaches useful, within the general inter-institutional perspective, for generating testable hypotheses about several aspects of religion and family in various societies.

Social differentiation approaches, including secularization theories, start from observations of society from the top down. An alternative approach is to look from the bottom up, moving from the level of individual social action toward the institutional structures that the aggregation of such action creates. Such an approach is found in rational choice theories, which begin by analyzing patterns of individual behavior according to the economic logic of consumer choice. In rational choice approaches to religion, churches and other religious organizations are seen as firms offering a variety of goods and services to consumer-believers and consumer-parishioners. When patterns of individual consumer choice are aggregated, market structures become apparent. Such markets provide the context within which patterns of supply and demand are worked out. They distribute goods and services to consumers, as well as "market share" to religious firms. Seen from the market model viewpoint, the issue of the strength of religion boils down to the likelihood on the part of potential consumer-believers to buy into a given religious belief or practice, or to affiliate with a given religious firm such as a temple or a missionary organization. Just as the level of economic purchases rises and falls over time, so does the level of various religious "products," like church membership or belief in God, rise and fall. What governs variation in purchases or adoptions (or church membership or belief in God) is the logic of rational choice among the options in the marketplace that are available to the consumer-believers or the consumer-members. Religious organizational leaders, like business executives, proffer a variety of products to the consuming public and vary the price of such products in order to attract consumer-believers. The leaders seek market share in the religious market.

This emerging "new paradigm" for understanding religious change relies upon economic models of the religious market to understand differing levels of religious group affiliation and participation (Hadden 1995; Warner 1993; Young 1997). Stark and Bainbridge (1987) provide an elaborate deductive theory of religion based upon rational choice principles, and this theory provides the backdrop for a series of more recent studies by these authors and collaborators (Hadden 1996). Perhaps most prominent among the studies developed in connection with this theoretical approach is Finke and Stark's (1992) analysis of American religion, which shows that, over the last three centuries, it has grown, rather than declined, in number of participants and proportion of the U.S. population, contrary to what secularization theory would predict. The authors argue that the growth is the result of competition in a pluralistic market. The economist Laurence Iannaccone (1995, 1997, and works cited in these sources) has elaborated several propositions in line with the theory and expanded the application of economic modeling.

The approach seems to hold greater promise for explaining and predicting the dynamism of religious phenomena than do other approaches that are primarily based in traditional functionalist secularization theorizing. For present purposes, its primary wisdom is that secularization processes are self-limiting. That is, when "the processes that erode commitments to a particular set of supernatural assumptions" (Stark and Bainbridge 1987, p. 311) advance far enough, the religious market will be open to new options. These options, according to Stark and Bainbridge (1987), take the form of either schisms from established groups, sects, or cults.

One of the great assets of the cultural market approach is that it is inter-institutional while at the same time giving individuals agency. That is, market-based institutions are structured by the individual patterns of choice that are aggregated in any society. Simultaneously, institution building is regulated by relationships with other institutions in an interactive process. Clearly, there are many avenues for development of other theoretical approaches to these issues. In particular, conflict theory, social movement theory, and Weberian theory have valuable traditions of analysis that apply to family and religion. Theoretically and conceptually, there are similarities between the market approach and these other approaches. But the market approach, which has assimilated numerous insights from other approaches, establishes a greater balance between micro and macro elements.

The economic model in which the market approach is rooted certainly has its own limitations. Perhaps its biggest problem for many readers is the use of a language that has its own implications that do not and should not apply to religious and familial processes. From a strict theoretical perspective, perhaps the most daunting criticism of the theory argues that religious choice by its nature cannot be strictly rational (cf., Chaves 1995; Demerath 1995; Neitz and Mueser 1997). It is this point of view that has discredited the theory most strongly in the religious studies field, where its advocates are relatively few. In his review of Finke and Stark's (1992) revisionist study of American religious history, Martin Marty (1993, p. 88) writes that their "world contains no God or religion or spirituality, no issue of truth or beauty or goodness, no faith or hope or love, no justice or mercy; only winning and losing in the churching game matters." The work, Marty says, is reductionistic, oversimplifying complex issues. Further, James Spickard (1998, p. 110), though expressing considerable sympathy for the rational choice model, has argued that "a rational-choice [sic] model can duplicate the overall structure of a religious marketplace, but it cannot demonstrate that individual people think in market terms."

Some sociologists (Ammerman 1997; Ellison 1995; Sherkat 1997) have contended that the notion of rational choice does not adequately take into account the structuring of individual preferences by a host of contextual, cultural, or environmental variables. Several have argued that the value of the approach in analyzing the open, pluralistic market of the United States may not extend to other societies (cf. Warner 1997). The approach also has been charged with being androcentric (Carroll 1996) and with ignoring gender as a variable (Neitz and Mueser 1997). These criticisms are important, but they do not, in our eyes, undermine the approach so much as indicate an agenda for research and further conceptual development.

At this juncture, it should be noted that much of the logic that has just been applied in the discussion of religion could presumably be extended to families. Among many social scientists, there is an overgeneralization from patterns of differentiation related to families that is similar to that which Casanova identified in secularization thinking about religion (cf. Hargrove 1985). There is a widespread notion that changing patterns in the family (related to institutional differentiation) mean that the family is not centrally important in the modern age. From this premise, we are led to focus on the "private" family to the neglect of the "public" functions that the family retains (Cherlin 1996). It is as if the many "problems" of families remove the family from useful consideration. While scholars often take families for granted, there is clearly no more powerful socializer of the young and no other viable means for the reproduction of society through the birthing of new members than the family, whatever form it takes. If we assume the phenomenon can be identified by its function, that is, by what it does, rather than by its form, then we cannot imagine a society without families and without the effects that families by definition have.

Family sociologists and economists have long examined the economic side of families in its own right, looking at the effects on families of work, the household division of labor, the patterns of money and time budgets, and the like. There also have been significant studies using the market analogy to understand strictly familial phenomena. The economist Gary Becker (1973, 1974, 1976, 1981; Becker et al. 1977) has been the most deliberate in applying analytical tools from economics to family matters. (His impact on the religious economy approach is acknowledged by Iannaccone, 1997.) Others using economic analytical tools in studies of aspects of families that are not formally economic include Grossbard (1978), Huber and Spitze (1980), and Johnson (1980).

In an open "family market"—a notion that deserves much more elaboration and evaluation than we can give it here—the adoption of one family form over another (say, single parenting over dual parenting, isolated nuclear households over interconnected extended kin networks, or formal marriage over nonmarital cohabitation) would relate to the evaluation by participants of the costs and rewards associated with the adoption of the given form. Costs and rewards would be assessed by the individual taking into account the surrounding culture and relevant subcultures, which would presumably restrict options for "choice" in numerous ways. Trost and Palm (2000) have outlined the conditions for a fairly open familial market system in Sweden.

As some work in the economic approaches to religion shows, one can include consideration of contextual variables in developing criteria of "choice" in such matters (see, for example, Ellison 1995; Iannaccone 1997; Sherkat 1997). Among significant influences on choice would be individual religious beliefs or the values of the religious affiliation a person may have, both of which are the product, to some degree, of the family socialization and community experience of the person. We can extend this line of thought by including a range of cultural variables that allow the research to be fully comparative, potentially applicable to any society or subsocietal unit. In short, conceptually exploiting the analogy with economic markets has potential for the analysis not only of religion but of family matters as well. In the end, such an approach would identify the conditions under which particular choices in the realm of families can be seen as signs of the strength of adaptive families rather than compromises of weak and ineffectual families.

Finally, it is interesting and important to note that the economic approach to religion relies on an understanding of religious choices as based in the household as much as in the individual. Religious "goods" are "household commodities" that the household invests other goods, labor, and skills in producing, according to Iannaccone (1997). In this imagery of the *household* producing religion, then, we again emphasize the intimate connection between religion and family. From this point, we need to establish its place in the larger sociocultural context.

Institutional Dominance in Modern Societies. Modern structures of institutional dominance—a concept first articulated by Williams in ([1955] 1970)—do not negate the importance of the religious and familial institutions. In many societies today, family and religion do not rank high in the relative dominance of major societal

institutions. On the contrary, there usually is some other institution that dominates the entire social system, most often the economy (as in Sweden and the United States, for example). Although this means that the economy is much more likely to be the instigator of social change in the less powerful institutions than vice versa, it does not follow that family and religion cannot initiate change as well. They can and they do, although such occurrences are much less frequent than in the case of the dominant institution(s).

Sometimes the question is asked, Do family and religion facilitate or hinder social change? But this question is an inappropriate one to ask. It is one that never is asked about the economy or the polity. Perhaps it is raised in the case of religion and family because these two institutions are viewed as conservative—as part of the past that is slowing down forward motion. This view, however, is untenable. All societal institutions—including family, religion, polity, economy, education, health care, welfare, and so forth—both facilitate and hinder social change. The direction of their effects depends on what best meshes with their interests at a particular point in time. Research on Brazil and Mexico illustrate facilitating effects of religion for change in gender roles. In fact, according to Rosado Nunes (2000), Catholicism in Brazil did more than facilitate—it orchestrated dramatic changes in women's roles, restricting women to a very limited range of options within the household by the nineteenth century. Fortuny Loret de Mola (2000) showed how the mobilization of Protestantism in Mexico has provided for certain aspects of authority and legitimacy for women that the dominant Catholic culture did not support, that is, religion has fostered change in gender roles in a direction opposite to that of Brazilian Catholicism. While these examples evidence the change-oriented qualities of religion and family, work on Egypt (Houseknecht 2000) provides a good contrasting example in that it describes the hindering influences that religion and family can have with regard to social change in other institutions. Finally, in Godsell's (2000) study of South Africa, we see examples of both facilitation and hindrance of social change by the religious and familial institutions. While the East Asian Hindu and Muslim networks promote entrepreneurship, the black African Christian ones tend to inhibit the development of entrepreneurial activities.

In the modern world, the intersection of institutions is largely in the realm of economic issues—because of the dominance of the economic institution. This is true even in the interactions of noneconomic institutions, since the values and norms of the dominant institution "permeate a great many areas of life and enter into the operation of other institutions" (Gouldner and Gouldner 1963, p. 496).

RELIGION AND FAMILY IN THE PRIVATE AND PUBLIC SPHERES

Although analysts have tended to see family and religion as institutions of the private sphere, there is no question but that they are both found in the public sphere as well. In the following sections, we elaborate on the dynamics that are found within and between these spheres.

The Private Sphere. Some theorists have argued that "privatization" (Luckmann 1967; Berger 1967) characterizes religion in modern societies and that the private sphere is shared by the family (Berger 1969). With modernization, these two institutions tend to become more specialized and to take on new forms as they structure and give substance to the private sphere. A high degree of differentiation, though, does not put an end to the family and religion connection, even though it weakens the relationships that they have with each other and with other societal institutions. The private sphere may seem to be, in a macro sense, peripheral in the modern world, but it nevertheless is where we find a bedrock of mutually reinforcing relations between family and religion. As noted earlier, both of these institutions focus on primary relations, and, in the past, primary relations were much more encompassing of all interinstitutional relations. This meant that the points of intersection that these two institutions had with each other and with other societal institutions were many. In modernized societies, though, the relevance of primary relations has come to be

limited more to the private sphere than in the past. And it is in the private sphere where we see what is really unique about the family and religion linkage. It is here that the connection is cut to the bare bones, and it is here that we see the affinity (although reduced) that persists despite differentiation.

With modernization and postmodernity, the private sphere has emerged as a unique social phenomenon. Although family and religion come to be dominated by other societal institutions in the modern setting, the private sphere that they constitute is of growing importance. It is a buffer zone in which individuals receive support that helps them absorb the stresses and strains brought on by their public activities in other institutional spheres. Because the public and private domains become less and less well integrated, the need for retreat to privacy grows. Not only is the private sphere an essential retreat, but it is also a place where people can devote more and more of the bounty of economic development—increased leisure time, less constant concern with mere survival, and greater financial and other material assets. In short, the private sphere is expanding in the modern world both because of the social psychological need for it and because of the availability of greater resources that can be devoted to it.

The growth of the private sphere signifies one way that the importance of family and religion is growing. Roof (1993) and Wuthnow (1994a) have argued that a primary form of contemporary American religion is found in the self-help or support group (which is frequently located within the context of the church, though it need not be). Aimed at solving problems of individual adaptation, interpersonal relationships, and local community issues, such groups would seem to represent a therapy technique for private troubles. As the private sphere grows, this function grows to match. However, both Roof and Wuthnow also claim that these groups are, in fact, linking mechanisms which bring the private sphere and the public sphere into connection. They are means of overcoming one-dimensional individualism and of connecting the individual with the broader community.

The Public Sphere. The recognition that the private functions of religion and family are vital and even expanding in modern societies is not inconsistent with the fact that the public side of these two institutions retains significance (cf. Beyer 1994). Both family and religion provide important public functions that, in the end, demand our attention. They are public functions that are in crisis in many ways in modern and globalizing societies, and understanding them clearly should aid those who seek to overcome the crises. Following the work of Cherlin (1996) on families and of Casanova (1994), Cochran (1990), and Wuthnow (1994b) on religion, we note that both these institutions provide a range of significant public goods. Such goods are general benefits for the society; they cannot be denied to those who did not participate in producing them, and they often are in short supply due to the tendency for nonproducers to "free-ride" on the efforts of those voluntary actors who take part in the production.

Families provide the public good of children—they give birth to them and raise them to be contributing members of society. These children, then, by being productive, paying taxes, and paying into Social Security and other pension systems, help support all persons in the society, but particularly persons who have aged past the productive years. In addition to reproduction, Cherlin (1996) asserts that, in bearing the burden of dependence created mostly by care for children and care for the frail elderly, families are providing public goods. These public functions are fewer than the public functions of families in the past (Demos 1970), but they are nevertheless extremely important in the modern world.

In a similar vein, religion provides important public goods as well. The first of these is moral values. In modern societies, many citizens do not nurture moral values through church participation and support, and yet the Ten Commandments are nearly universally honored as moral values. Although derived from religious sources and cultivated and rehearsed in religious settings on a regular basis, they are not perceived as sectarian or limited in applicability. They are the concrete form of broad societal values that are not, for the most part, in dispute. Still, it is only the religious groups—aided and abetted by families, of course—who spend the time reminding us of the importance of these fundamentals. Even atheists profit from the order and social stability that such an emphasis nurtures (cf. Cochran 1990). While Durkheim (1973) thought that adequate progress would lead to the usurpation of this moral production role of religion by education, with schools sustaining the essential values for the modern society, this situation has not yet arrived. The difficulty in designing a moral program that can be taught in the schools seems only more and more dependent upon the interpretation of relevant faith traditions. The schools, rather than displacing religious groups in this task, seem to be calling upon them for clarification and support (cf. Wuthnow 1994b).

Cochran (1990) stresses that religion is also important as a forum for public participation, that is, a place where people come together and discuss, evaluate, lobby, and generally keep informed about public issues and problems. In fact, while the private side of religion focuses upon individual salvation, there is also the supremely public side of "prophetic" religion, to use Weber's ([1922] 1963) term for the kind of religion that challenges and calls for reform in society. As a forum for participation, the church, synagogue, mosque, or temple provides a venue in which individuals and families work out their positions vis-à-vis the politics and economics of their communities.

Casanova (1994) argues that religions today are more and more asserting their influence and enunciating their interest in secular affairs, mostly rising against the presumptions of the state and the market to prevent their incursion into religious matters. There is a new era, he asserts, of "public religion." The core of Casanova's argument is that, instead of a retreat by religion into a segregated and marginalized private sphere, there is today a "deprivatization" of religion in the world as one after another faith reasserts its claims to an active role in the broader society, especially in politics and economics. The mobilization of religious groups around the abortion debate in the United States is one such example, with the well-known engagement of American Catholic and conservative Protestant groups in unexpected political contestation with the government (cf. Pankhurst and Houseknecht 1983). Another form of this deprivatization is the demand that the church not ally itself with the political and economic elites when the latter create and enforce policies or patterns of control that disenfranchise segments of the population, such as the poor or minorities. From within the faith, there has arisen the counterdemand that the poor be given a chance to improve and to escape the bonds of poverty. We can see these counterdemands dramatically stated in the Liberation Theology of the 1980s in Latin America. They also are advocated by a variety of Christian groups in the United States (Hart [1992] 1996).

In the end, such processes indicate the reinvigoration of public religion around the world. For Casanova (1994), even Islamic movements can be seen in this light and should not be consigned to a peripheralized "fundamentalist reaction" to modernization. Whether progressive or conservative, public religions' calls for a new vision of politics and economic life are an essential characteristic of the present era. We cannot, then, think of religion as circumscribed by the private sphere, Casanova argues, and must not neglect the public roles that religions play if we are to perceive the modern world clearly.

In sum, religion and family, both public and private, are essential components of modern life. If anything, their future roles seem to be growing rather than shrinking. Biomedical advances promise to play out most dramatically the questions of life and death, spirit and body in the public church and the public family, which will have to adapt to longer life and, perhaps, longer periods of dependency for the elderly. The need to prepare children for appropriate careers in the new fields being created by technological advances will have to be addressed in the personal councils around the kitchen table that always so strongly influence the occupational choices that young people make. Those occupational choices will rely, in some indirect but profound ways, on the economic ethic that is espoused in the religious community that the family adheres to. In the Third World, development hinges, to some degree, on the fertility decisions made in the family under the influence of the faith that defines appropriate sexual and reproductive behavior. In the process of economic and political change that so many societies experience as disruption and disorganization, family and religion provide important sources of stability and order, even as they adapt to the changing circumstances they find themselves in. It is there that one should go to find the processes working out the morality for the new age and the lifestyles for the new era.

REFERENCES

Alexander, Jeffrey C., and Paul Colomy, eds. 1990 *Differentiation Theory and Social Change: Comparative and Historical Perspectives*. New York: Columbia University Press.

Ammerman, Nancy Tatom 1997 "Religious Choice and Religious Vitality: The Market and Beyond." In Lawrence A. Young, ed., *Rational Choice Theory and Religion: Summary and Assessment*. New York: Routledge.

Ammerman, Nancy Tatom, and Wade Clark Roof, eds. 1995 *Work, Family, and Religion in Contemporary Society*. New York: Routledge.

Becker, Gary S. 1973 "A Theory of Marriage: Part I." *Journal of Political Economy* 81(4):413–446.

—— 1974 "A Theory of Marriage: Part II." *Journal of Political Economy* 82(2):511–526.

—— 1976 *The Economic Approach to Human Behavior*. Chicago: University of Chicago Press.

—— 1981 *A Treatise on the Family*. Cambridge, Mass.: Harvard University Press.

Becker, Gary S., Elisabeth M. Landes, and Robert T. Michael 1977 "An Economic Analysis of Marital Instability." *Journal of Political Economy* 85(6):1141–1187.

Beckford, James A. 1989 *Religion and Advanced Industrial Society*. London: Unwin Hyman.

Berger, Peter L. 1967 "Religious Institutions." In Neil J. Smelser, ed., *Sociology: An Introduction*. New York: John Wiley and Sons.

—— 1969 *The Sacred Canopy: Elements of a Sociological Theory of Religion*. Garden City, N.Y.: Doubleday Anchor Books.

Berryman, Phillip 1987 *Liberation Theology: The Essential Facts About the Revolutionary Movement in Latin America*. New York: Pantheon Books.

Beyer, Peter 1994 *Religion and Globalization*. London: Sage.

Cammack, Mark, Lawrence A. Young, and Tim B. Heaton 2000 "The State, Religion, and the Family in Indonesia: The Case of Divorce Reform." In Sharon K. Houseknecht and Jerry G. Pankhurst, eds., *Family, Religion and Social Change in Diverse Societies*. New York: Oxford University Press.

Carroll, Michael P. 1996 "Stark Realities and Androcentric/Eurocentric Bias in the the Sociology of Religion." *Sociology of Religion* 57(3):225–239.

Carter, Lewis F., ed. 1996 *The Issue of Authenticity in the Study of Religions* (Religion and the Social Order Series, Volume 6). Greenwich, Conn.: JAI Press.

Casanova, Josè 1994 *Public Religions in the Modern World*. Chicago: University of Chicago Press.

Chaves, Mark 1995 "On the Rational Choice Approach to Religion." *Journal for the Scientific Study of Religion* 34(1):98–104.

Cherlin, Andrew 1996 *Public and Private Families: An Introduction*. New York: McGraw-Hill.

Christiano, Kevin J. 2000 "Religion and Family in Modern American Culture." In Sharon K. Houseknecht and Jerry G. Pankhurst, eds., *Family, Religion and Social Change in Diverse Societies*. New York: Oxford University Press.

Cochran, Clarke E. 1990 *Religion in Public and Private Life*. New York: Routledge.

Cousineau, Madeleine, ed. 1998 *Religion in a Changing World: Comparative Studies in Sociology*. Westport, Conn.: Praeger.

D'Antonio, William V., and Joan Aldous, eds. 1983 *Families and Religions: Conflict and Change in Modern Society*. Beverly Hills, Calif.: Sage.

D'Antonio, William V., William A. Newman, and Stuart A. Wright 1982 "Religion and Family Life: How Social Scientists View the Relationship." *Journal for the Scientific Study of Religion* 21(3):218–225.

Demerath, N. J., III 1995 "Rational Paradigms, A-Rational Religion, and the Debate over Secularization." *Journal for the Scientific Study of Religion* 34(1):105–112.

Demos, John 1970 *A Little Commonwealth: Family Life in Plymouth Colony*. Oxford: Oxford University Press.

Diduk, Susan E., and Kent Maynard 2000 "A Woman's Pillow and the Political Economy of Kedjom Family Life in Cameroon." In Sharon K. Houseknecht and Jerry G. Pankhurst, eds., *Family, Religion and Social Change in Diverse Societies*. New York: Oxford University Press.

Durkheim, Emile 1973 *Emile Durkheim: On Morality and Society; Selected Writings* Chicago: University of Chicago Press.

Ellison, Christopher G. 1995 "Rational Choice Explanations of Individual Religious Behavior: Notes on the Problem of Social Embeddedness." *Journal for the Scientific Study of Religion* 34(1):89–97.

Finke, Roger, and Rodney Stark 1992 *The Churching of America, 1776–1990: Winners and Losers in Our Religious Economy*. New Brunswick, N.J.: Rutgers University Press.

Fortuny Loret de Mola, Patricia 2000 "Converted Women Redefining Their Family Roles In Mexico." In Sharon K. Houseknecht and Jerry G. Pankhurst, eds., *Family, Religion and Social Change in Diverse Societies*. New York: Oxford University Press.

Godsell, Gillian 1999 "Religious and Familial Networks as Entrepreneurial Resources in South Africa." In Sharon K. Houseknecht and Jerry G. Pankhurst, eds., *Family, Religion and Social Change in Diverse Societies*. New York: Oxford University Press.

Gouldner, Alvin W., and Helen P. Gouldner 1963 *Modern Sociology: An Introduction to the Study of Human Interaction*. New York: Harcourt, Brace and World.

Greeley, Andrew M. 1989 *Religious Change in America*. Cambridge, Mass.: Harvard University Press.

—— 1992 "Religion in Britain, Ireland and the USA." In R. Jowell, L. Brook, G. Prior, and B. Taylor, eds., *British Social Attitudes: The 9th Report*. Social and Community Planning Research. Brookfield, Vt.: Dartmouth Publishing.

Grossbard, Amyra 1978 "Towards a Marriage Between Economics and Anthropology and a General Theory of Marriage." *American Economic Review* 68(2):33–37.

Hadden, Jeffrey K. 1987 "Toward Desacralizing Secularization Theory." *Social Forces* 65:587–611.

—— 1995 "Religion and the Quest for Meaning and Order: Old Paradigms, New Realities." *Sociological Focus* 28:83–100.

—— 1996 "Foreword" to the paperback edition. In Rodney Stark and William Sims Bainbridge *A Theory of Religion*. New Brunswick, N.J.: Rutgers University Press.

Hadden, Jeffrey K., and Anson Shupe 1986 "Introduction." In Jeffrey K. Hadden and Anson Shupe, eds., *Prophetic Religions and Politics: Religion and the Political Order*, vol. 1. New York: Paragon House.

Hammond, Phillip E. 1985 *The Sacred in a Secular Age: Toward Revision in the Scientific Study of Religion*. Berkeley: University of California Press.

Hargrove, Barbara 1979 *The Sociology of Religion: Classical and Contemporary Approaches*. Arlington Heights, Ill.: AHM Publishing.

—— 1985 "Gender, the Family, and the Sacred." In Phillip E. Hammond, ed., *The Sacred in a Secular Age: Toward Revision in the Scientific Study of Religion*.Berkeley: University of California Press.

Hart, Stephen (1992) 1996 *What Does the Lord Require: How American Christians Think about Economic Justice*. New Brunswick, N.J.: Rutgers University Press.

Houseknecht, Sharon K. 2000 "Social Change in Egypt: The Roles of Religion and Family." In Sharon K. Houseknecht and Jerry G. Pankhurst, eds., *Family, Religion and Social Change in Diverse Societies*. New York: Oxford University Press.

Houseknecht, Sharon K., and Jerry G. Pankhurst, eds. 2000 *Family, Religion, and Social Change in Diverse Societies*. New York: Oxford University Press.

Huber, Joan, and Glenna Spitze 1980 "Considering Divorce: An Expansion of Becker's Theory of Marital Instability." *American Journal of Sociology* 86:75–89.

Iannaccone, Laurence R. 1995 "Voodoo Economics? Reviewing the Rational Choice Approach to Religion." *Journal for the Scientific Study of Religion* 34(1):76–89.

—— 1997 "Rational Choice: Framework for the Scientific Study of Religion." In Lawrence A. Young, ed., *Rational Choice Theory and Religion: Summary and Assessment*. New York: Routledge.

Jarvis, John 2000 "Mormonism in France: The Family as a Universal Value in Globalizing Religion." In Sharon K. Houseknecht and Jerry G. Pankhurst, eds., *Family, Religion and Social Change in Diverse Societies*. New York: Oxford University Press.

Johnson, Robert Alan 1980 *Religious Assortative Marriage in the United States*. New York: Academic Press.

Luckmann, Thomas 1967 *The Invisible Religion*. New York: Macmillan.

MacIver, Robert M. 1970 *On Community, Society and Power*. Chicago: University of Chicago Press.

Martin, David 1990 *Tongues of Fire: The Explosion of Protestantism in Latin America*. Oxford: Basil Blackwell.

Marty, Martin 1993 Review of *The Churching of America, 1776–1990: Winners and Losers in Our Religious Economy* (Rutgers University Press, 1992). *Christian Century*, January 27, p. 88.

Marty, Martin E., and R. Scott Appleby 1995 *The Fundamentalism Project*. Chicago: University of Chicago Press.

Misztal, Bronislaw, and Anson Shupe, eds. 1992 *Religion and Politics in Comparative Perspective: Revival of Religious Fundamentalism in East and West*. Westport, Conn.: Praeger.

Moore, Wilbert E. 1963 *Social Change*. Englewood Cliffs, N.J.: Prentice-Hall.

Neitz, Mary Jo, and Peter R. Mueser 1997 "Economic Man and the Sociology of Religion: A Critique of the Rational Choice Approach." In Lawrence A. Young, ed., *Rational Choice Theory and Religion: Summary and Assessment*. New York: Routledge.

Nisbet, Robert A. 1970 *The Social Bond: An Introduction to the Study of Society*. New York: Alfred A. Knopf.

Pankhurst, Jerry G. 1998 "Russia's Religious Market: Struggling with the Heritage of Russian Orthodox Monopoly." In Madeleine Cousineau, ed., *Religion in a Changing World: Comparative Studies in Sociology*. Westport, Conn.: Praeger.

Pankhurst, Jerry G., and Sharon K. Houseknecht 1983 "The Family, Politics and Religion in the 1980s: In Feat of the New Individualism." *Journal of Family Issues* 4:5–34.

Popenoe, David 1988 *Disturbing the Nest: Family Change and Decline in Modern Societies*. New York: Aldine de Gruyter.

Roberts, Richard H., ed. 1995 *Religion and the Transformations of Capitalism: Comparative Approaches*. London: Routledge.

Roof, Wade Clark 1993 *A Generation of Seekers: The Spiritual Journey of the Baby Boom Generation*. New York: HarperCollins.

Rosado Nunes, Maria Jose Fontelas 2000 "Women, Family and Catholicism in Brazil: The Issue of Power." In Sharon K. Houseknecht and Jerry G. Pankhurst, eds., *Family, Religion and Social Change in Diverse Societies*. New York: Oxford University Press.

Rubenstein, Richard L., ed. 1987 *Spirit Matters: The Worldwide Impact of Religion on Contemporary Politics*. New York: Paragon House.

Settles, Barbara H. 1996 "The International Study of Families and Rapid Social Change: Issues for Family Sociologists and their Professional Organizations." Paper presented at the annual meeting of the American Sociological Association, August 16–20, New York.

Sherkat, Darren E. 1997 "Embedding Religious Choices: Integrating Preferences and Social Constraints into

Rational Choice Theories of Religious Behavior." In Lawrence A. Young, ed., *Rational Choice Theory and Religion: Summary and Assessment*. New York: Routledge.

Shupe, Anson, and Bronislaw Misztal, eds. 1998 *Religion, Mobilization, and Social Action*. Westport, Conn.: Praeger.

Smith, Christian 1991 *The Emergence of Liberation Theology: Radical Religion and Social Movement Theory*. Chicago: University of Chicago Press.

Smith, Stephen R. 2000 "Land of the Rising Son? Domestic Organization, Ancestor Worship, and Economic Change in Japan." In Sharon K. Houseknecht and Jerry G. Pankhurst, eds., *Family, Religion and Social Change in Diverse Societies*. New York: Oxford University Press.

Spickard, James V. 1998 "Rethinking Religious Social Action: What is 'Rational' About Rational Choice Theory?" *Sociology of Religion* 59(2):99–115.

Stark, Rodney, and William Sims Bainbridge 1987 *A Theory of Religion*. New York: Peter Lang.

Swatos, William H., ed. 1992 *Twentieth-Century World Religious Movements in Neo-Weberian Perspective*. Lewiston, N.Y.: Edwin Mellen Press.

Thomas, Darwin L., ed. 1988 *The Religion and Family Connection: Social Science Perspectives*. Provo, Utah: Religious Studies Center, Brigham Young University.

Thomas, Darwin L., and Marie Cornwall 1990 "Religion and Family in the 1980s: Discovery and Development." *Journal of Marriage and the Family* 52:983–992.

Thomas, Darwin L., and Gwendolyn C. Henry 1985 "The Religion and Family Connection: Increasing Dialogue in the Social Sciences." *Journal of Marriage and the Family* 47(2):369–379.

Thornton, Arland 1985 "Reciprocal Influences of Family and Religion in a Changing World." *Journal of Marriage and the Family* 47(2):381–394.

Trost, Jan, and Irving Palm 2000 "Family and Religion in Sweden." In Sharon K. Houseknecht and Jerry G. Pankhurst, eds., *Family, Religion and Social Change in Diverse Societies*. New York: Oxford University Press.

Vago, Steven 1989 *Social Change*, 2nd ed. Englewood Cliffs, N.J.: Prentice-Hall.

Vardomatskii, Andrei, and Jerry G. Pankhurst 2000 "Belarus on the Cusp of Change: The Relationship Between Religion and Family in a Newly Open Religious Market." In Sharon K. Houseknecht and Jerry G. Pankhurst, eds., *Family, Religion and Social Change in Diverse Societies*. New York: Oxford University Press.

Wald, Kenneth 1986 *Religion and Politics in the United States*. New York: St. Martin's Press.

Warner, Stephen R. 1993 "Work in Progress Toward a New Paradigm for the Sociological Study of Religion in the United States." *American Journal of Sociology* 98(5):1044–1093.

—— 1997 "Convergence Toward the New Paradigm: A Case of Induction." In Lawrence A. Young, ed., *Rational Choice Theory and Religion: Summary and Assessment*. New York: Routledge.

Weber, Max (1922) 1963 *The Sociology of Religion*. Boston: Beacon Press.

Williams, Robin M., Jr. (1955) 1970 *American Society: A Sociological Interpretation*, 3rd ed. New York: Alfred A. Knopf.

Witte, John, Jr., ed. 1993 *Christianity and Democracy in Global Context*. Boulder, Colo.: Westview Press.

Wuthnow, Robert 1994a *Sharing the Journey: Support Groups and America's New Quest for Community*. New York: Free Press.

—— 1994b *Producing the Sacred: An Essay on Public Religion*. Urbana: University of Illinois Press.

Yang, Li-shou, Arland Thornton, and Thomas Fricke 2000 "Religion and Family Formation in Taiwan: The Decline of Ancestral Authority." In Sharon K. Houseknecht and Jerry G. Pankhurst, eds., *Family, Religion and Social Change in Diverse Societies*. New York: Oxford University Press.

Young, Lawrence A., ed. 1997 *Rational Choice Theory and Religion: Summary and Assessment*. New York: Routledge.

JERRY G. PANKHURST
SHARON K. HOUSEKNECHT

FAMILY LAW

Family law is that body of law having to do with creating, ordering, and dissolving marital and family groups. Although the exact scope of family law is given differently by different authors, at its core family law is concerned with such issues and events as marriage, separation, divorce, alimony, custody, child support, and adoption, as well as the more arcane topics of annulment, paternity, legitimacy, artificial insemination, and surrogate parenting.

This entry on family law in the United States should be read with two important caveats in mind. First, it is somewhat misleading to write of "United States" family law. Because the power to regulate domestic life is not one of the powers delegated to the federal government by the Constitution, in the United States most family law has been "a virtually exclusive province of the states" (*Sosna v. Iowa*, 419 U.S. 393 [1975]). Despite considerable variation in state law, however, certain general trends can be identified. Moreover, researchers have identified similar trends in a number of European countries (Glendon 1989).

Second, many kinds of law that affect the family cannot be discussed here. These include laws that are not ordinarily listed under the rubric of "family law" but that have significant effects on family life in this country. These range from the laws of inheritance to zoning regulations and regulations about social welfare programs. While the impact on the family of a diversity of laws seems to become increasingly significant, this is not a uniquely modern phenomenon. For example, 200 years ago poor laws affected family life in ways that anticipated the impact of modern welfare laws (tenBroek 1964).

As was typical of much of early law in this country, most American family law was received from English law; but family law was atypical in that much of it was not derived from secular or "temporal" English law. In England, from the late twelfth century (Pollock and Maitland 1898, Vol. 2, p. 367) until the passage of the Matrimonial Causes Act of 1857, issues pertaining to marriage and divorce were governed by canon law, and most family matters were thus subject to the jurisdiction of ecclesiastical courts. While the American colonies had no ecclesiastical courts, English canonical rules concerning family relations were incorporated—either by statute or by common law tradition—into the laws of the colonies and, later, the states (Clark 1980).

Notwithstanding its religious heritage, family law in this country was completely secular. Although marriages were frequently performed by members of the clergy, the authority to solemnize marriages was vested in them by the state, not the church. In legal theory, at the basis of the family was a marriage that was a civil contract and not a religious sacrament.

This contractual view of marriage had some interesting consequences. For example, it led to official recognition of informal as well as formal marriage. This informal union, the so-called common law marriage, was effected by the simple express agreement of a man and a woman to be married, followed by their cohabitation. (Contrary to popular myth, common law marriages did not require a specific number of years to go into effect.) While today they are recognized only in fourteen states, until the twentieth century common law marriages were as valid as formal marriages in nearly every state (Wardle et al. 1988, § 3:17). Recognition of common law marriage meant that settlers on the geographic fringes of society, without access to officials, could enjoy the same protection of their property rights and their children's legitimacy as was afforded in formal marriages. In 1833, Chief Justice Gibson of Pennsylvania ruled that rigid marriage laws were "ill adapted to the habits and customs of society as it now exists." Not recognizing common law marriage, or so Gibson suggested, would "bastardize the vast majority of children which have been born within the state for half a century" (*Rodenbaugh v. Sanks*, 2 Watts 9).

After the Civil War, there was a movement to strengthen state regulation of marriage. Most states already required marriage licenses, but in antebellum America, courts had treated these licenses as a means "to register, not to restrict marriage" (Grossberg 1985, p. 78). By the end of the nineteenth century, however, marriage licenses had clearly become a means of social control. Because the process of acquiring a marriage license brought the couple under scrutiny of some official, licensing requirements helped states prevent marriages of people who were too young or too closely related, either by blood (consanguinity) or marriage (affinity). Official scrutiny of those seeking to wed also helped to enforce laws against bigamy and polygamy.

But legislators, encouraged by eugenicists who believed that crime, mental illness, and other social ills could be traced to hereditary biological factors, also enacted laws enumerating other kinds of forbidden marriages. For example, marriage was prohibited to those not mentally capable of contracting owing to conditions variously labeled as insanity, lunacy, idiocy, feeblemindedness, imbecility, or unsound mind (Clark 1968, pp. 95–96). Marriage was also prohibited to those physically incapable of performing the "marriage essentials." Generally, this latter criterion involved only the capacity to have "normal" or "successful" sexual intercourse, not necessarily the ability to procreate. As one author explained it, "Copula, not fruitfulness, is the test" (Tiffany 1921, p. 29).

Eugenics also justified, scientifically, laws that prohibited people with certain diseases (e.g., epilepsy, tuberculosis, and venereal disease) and statuses (e.g., habitual criminal, rapist) from marrying. In most cases, such obstacles could be overcome only if the person consented to sterilization. Many believed such statutes were necessary to "prevent the demise of civilized-society" (Linn and Bowers 1978, p. 629). Even some of the most respected legal thinkers joined the eugenicists. Justice Oliver Wendell Holmes of the United States Supreme Court, for example, wrote that it would be "better for all the world, if instead of waiting to execute degenerate offspring for crimes, or to let them starve for their imbecility, society can prevent those who are manifestly unfit from continuing their kind" (*Buck v. Bell*, 274 U.S. 200 [1927]).

The most notorious marriage impediment was race. By 1930, thirty states had enacted statutes prohibiting interracial marriages (Clark 1968, p. 91). For the most part, these antimiscegenation laws forbade marriages between whites and blacks, but in several cases the prohibition was extended to, for example, white and Malays, whites and Mongolians, whites and Native Americans, and blacks and Native Americans (Kennedy 1959, pp. 59–69).

Divorce was even more strictly regulated than marriage. However, the absence of ecclesiastical restrictions made divorces much easier to obtain in the United States than in England. This was especially true in the northern states. A few states even allowed divorce simply where the cause seemed "just and reasonable." Connecticut, for example, permitted divorce for conduct that "permanently destroys the happiness of the petitioner and defeats the purpose of the marriage relation" (Clark 1968, p. 283). During the latter part of the nineteenth century such generous statutes were repealed, and divorce was allowed only in response to specific types of fault—usually adultery, desertion, cruelty, or long-term imprisonment.

Despite stringent regulation of entrance to and exit from marriage, husbands and wives in intact marriages were generally protected from legal scrutiny. Indeed, traditionally, the principle of nonintervention was so strong that neither husbands nor wives could invoke the law to resolve marital disputes even when they wished to. In one case, for example, the wife of a well-to-do but stingy husband asked the Nebraska courts to require him to pay for indoor plumbing and to provide a reasonable allowance to her. The court agreed that, given his "wealth and circumstances," the husband's attitude "leaves little to be said in his behalf." But, said the court, "the living standards of a family are a matter of concern to the household and not for the courts to determine" (*McGuire v. McGuire*, 157 Neb. 226, 59 N.W.2d 336 [1953]). Similarly, the courts preferred a hands-off approach to parent–child relationships. As the United States Supreme Court ruled in 1944, "the custody, care, and nurture of the child reside first in the parents, whose primary function and freedom include preparation for obligations the state can neither supply nor hinder. . . . It is in recognition of this that [earlier] decisions have respected the private realm of family life which the state cannot enter" (*Prince v. Massachusetts*, 321 U.S. 158 [1944]).

The extent of the courts' reluctance to intervene in family matters or, as it was sometimes put, to "disrupt family harmony," was shown in the rule that spouses could not sue one another for personal torts or injuries. If, for example, a husband assaulted or battered his wife, she was enjoined from taking legal action against him in civil court (Keeton et al. 1984, pp. 901–902). In theory, the husband could be prosecuted in criminal court, but police and criminal courts too were reluctant to interfere in domestic matters (Pleck 1987, p. 187).

The practice of nonintervention was carried a step further at the turn of the century when the courts invented the doctrine of "parental immunity." Owing to reasons of "sound public policy, designed to subserve the repose of families and the best interests of society" (*Hewellette v. George*, 68 Miss. 703, 9 So. 885 [1891]), an unemancipated minor was barred from suing his or her parents for negligent or intentional wrongdoing.

Owing to the state's reluctance to intervene, the family has had a great deal of autonomy in this country, even to the extent that some have referred to the family as a "minisovereignty" (O'Donnell and Jones 1982, p. 7). In recent times, this autonomy has been justified on the basis of privacy rights. Speaking of the married couple's right to make decisions about the use of contraception, the United States Supreme Court said in 1965, for example, "we deal with a right of privacy older than the Bill of Rights" (*Griswold v. Connecticut*, 381 U.S. 479 [1965]).

But things began to change in the late twentieth century. First, beginning in the 1960s, strict regulation of entrance to and exit from marriage began to unravel. In the 1967 case of *Loving v. Virginia*, the United States Supreme Court ruled unconstitutional all antimiscegenation laws, saying that the states had no right to "prevent marriages between persons solely on the basis of racial classification." "Marriage," said the Court, "is one of the 'basic civil rights of man,' fundamental to our very existence and survival" (388 U.S. 1; quoting *Skinner v. Oklahoma*, 316 U.S. 535 [1942]). Since *Loving*, many other marriage restrictions have been repealed or eased. Age requirements in many states have been lowered; the mental ability needed to contract marriage has been ruled to be less than that required for other sorts of contracts; and the necessary mental competency is presumed to be present unless there is "clear and definite" proof to the contrary. Moreover, "there is a trend in modern times to abolish affinity restrictions" (Wardle et al. 1988, § 2:09); only one state (Missouri) still prohibits epileptics to marry (Wardle et al. 1988, § 2:47), and in many states, even prison inmates are deemed to have a right to marry (*In re Carrafa*, 77 Cal. App.3d 788 [1978]).

These changes reflect the courts' willingness to protect the rights of individuals to make their own choices about marriage and related matters. The decision to marry, according to the Supreme Court, is among "the personal decisions protected by the right to privacy" (*Zablocki v. Redhail*, 434 U.S. 374 [1978]).

Presumably, much the same can be said about the decision to divorce; recent changes in divorce laws have, if anything, been even more dramatic than changes in marriage laws. Implicitly accepting the principle that there is a right to divorce, the Supreme Court ruled in 1971 that welfare recipients could not be denied access to divorce courts because they could not afford to pay court costs and fees (*Boddie v. Connecticut*, 101 U.S. 371 [1971]). By the mid-1980s, every state had either replaced fault-based divorce laws with no-fault laws or added no-fault grounds to existing laws (Freed and Walker 1986, p. 444). No longer, then, must there be a "guilty" and an "innocent" party in a divorce. Instead, one spouse simply needs to assert that the couple is no longer getting along or has been living apart for a certain amount of time.

While regulations governing entrance to and exit from marriage and family life have decreased, there has been a corresponding increase in regulations affecting relations in ongoing families. Spousal immunity has been abolished in most states. Moreover, in many states the law recognizes the crime of "marital rape." Similarly, children now have more rights that can be asserted against their parents. For example, minors have the right to obtain information about and to use birth control without a parent's consent (*Carey v. Population Services International*, 431 U.S. 678 [1977]); to receive psychiatric care (*In re Alyne E.*, 113 Misc. 2d 307, 448 N.Y.S.2d 984 [1982]); and perhaps even to separate from their parents should the parents and children prove "incompatible" (*In re Snyder*, 85 Wash. 2d 182. 532 P.2d 278 [1975]). At base, says the Supreme Court, children "are 'persons' under the Constitution" and have rights that should be protected by the state (*Tinker v. Des Moines Independent School District*, 393 U.S. 503 [1969]).

Both the easing of marriage and divorce restrictions and the loss of family autonomy can be traced to the growth of individual rights that began in the 1960s. The idea of family autonomy and privacy and, hence, the policy of nonintervention were traditionally based on "paternal" authority; the authority of the family patriarch. This pattern can be traced back to the Roman idea of *patria potestas*–or the right of the father to exert absolute control over his family, including the power of life or death.

Family autonomy and privacy that is based on paternal power is viable only when other members of the family are unable to invoke the power of the state against the father. It was for this reason, then, that traditionally the woman's power to invoke the law was suspended from the moment of her marriage (Blackstone [1769] 1979, Vol. 1, p. 430). Children, likewise, had no legal standing until they reached the age of majority.

Things are much different today: While children still have many "legal disabilities," they can no longer be regarded as chattel. Women have achieved at least technical legal equality (though whether this has served to their advantage in divorce law is still subject to debate–compare Weitzman 1985 and Jacob 1988). Although the courts still speak of "family privacy," it is becoming clear that such privacy is based on family members' individual rights and exists only as long as family members are not in serious conflict about how they wish to assert those rights.

Some mourn the loss of near total family autonomy; the family, they say, has lost its integrity (Peirce 1988). There is no doubt that the notion of family autonomy or privacy served an important value: It has been "a convenient way for dealing with a problem . . . [that is] especially acute in the United States–that of devising family law that is suited to the needs and desires of persons with different ethnic and religious backgrounds, different social status, and different standards of living" (Glendon 1989, p. 95). In many instances, however, nonintervention created private Hobbesian jungles in which the strong ruled and the weak could not call upon the law for help.

As we move into the twenty-first century, families will continue to play an important role in society, and there can be little doubt that family relations will continue to be regarded as legally different from other relations and worthy of special legal protection. The question is, To whom is the law's protection to be extended in domestic matters as the United States embarks upon the twenty-first century? Traditionally, lawmakers have extended this protection to a limited variety of relations–the father–mother–children household. If present trends continue, however, the traditional ideal-typical nuclear family will be something that is achieved (and perhaps aspired to) by only a small fraction of Americans (Difonzo 1997; Estlund and Nussbaum 1998; McIntyre and Sussman 1995; Reagin 1999).

As we move through the first decades of this new century, new and more complex family legal issues will emerge as people construct new communal arrangements, call them family, and seek the protections accorded by the law to more traditional arrangements (Dolgin 1999; Edwards 1999; Minow 1993). The most pressing question facing lawmakers is this: Will the law continue to afford its protections only to those domestic arrangements that mirror traditional family *forms*, or will it embrace and protect domestic arrangements insofar as they fulfill traditional family *functions*?

(SEE ALSO: *Family and Household Structure*)

REFERENCES

Blackstone, William (1769) 1979 *Commentaries on the Laws of England*, 4 vols. Chicago: University of Chicago Press.

Clark, Homer H., Jr. 1968 *Law of Domestic Relations*. St. Paul, Minn.: West.

——1980 *Cases and Problems on Domestic Relations*. 3rd ed. St. Paul, Minn.: West.

Difonzo, J. Herbie 1997 *Beneath the Fault Line: The Popular and Legal Culture of Divorce in the Twentieth Century*. Charlottesville: University Press of Virginia.

Dolgin, Janet L. 1999 *Defining the Family: Law, Technology and Reproduction in an Uneasy Age*. New York: New York University Press.

Edwards, Jeanette 1999 *Technologies of Procreation: Kinship in the Age of Assisted Conception*. New York: Routledge.

Estlund, David M. and Martha C. Nussbaum 1998 *Sex, Preference, and Family: Essays on Law and Nature*. New York: Oxford University Press.

Freed, Doris J., and Timothy B. Walker 1986 "Family Law in the Fifty States: An Overview." *Family Law Quarterly* 20:439–587.

Glendon, Mary A. 1989 *The Transformation of Family Law, State, Law, and Family in the United States and Western Europe*. Chicago: University of Chicago Press.

Grossberg, Michael 1985 *Governing the Hearth: Law and Family in Nineteenth-Century America*. Chapel Hill: University of North Carolina Press.

Jacob, Herbert 1988 *Silent Revolution*. Chicago: University of Chicago Press.

Keeton, W. Page, Dan B. Dobbs, Robert E. Keeton, and David G. Owen 1984 *Prosser and Keeton on the Law of Torts*, 5th ed. St. Paul, Minn.: West.

Kennedy, Stetson 1959 *The Jim Crow Guide to the USA*. London: Lawrence and Wishart.

Linn, Brian J., and Lesly A. Bowers 1978. "The Historical Fallacies Behind Legal Prohibitions of Marriages Involving Mentally Retarded Persons: The Eternal Child Grows Up." *Gonzaga Law Review* 13:625–690.

Long, Joseph R. 1905 *A Treatise on the Law of Domestic Relations*. St. Paul, Minn.: Keefe-Davidson.

McIntyre, Lisa J. and Marvin Sussman 1995 *Families and Law*. New York: Haworth Press.

Minow, Martha 1993 *Family Matters: Readings on Family Lives and the Law*. New York: New Press.

O'Donnell, William J., and David A. Jones 1982 *The Law of Marriage and Marital Alternatives*. Lexington, Mass.: D. C. Heath.

Peirce, Dorothy S. 1988 "*BRI v. Leonard*: The Role of the Courts in Preserving Family Integrity." *New England Law Review* 23:185–219.

Pleck, Elizabeth 1987 *Domestic Violence: The Making of American Social Policy Against Family Violence from Colonial Times to the Present*. New York: Oxford University Press.

Pollock, Frederick, and Frederic W. Maitland 1898 *The History of English Law Before the Time of Edward I*, 2 vols. Cambridge: Cambridge University Press.

Reagin, Milton C. *Alone Together: Law and the Meanings of Marriage*. New York: Oxford University Press.

tenBroek, Jacobus 1964 *Family Law and the Poor*. Westport, Conn.: Greenwood.

Tiffany, Walter C. 1921 *Handbook on the Law of Personal and Domestic Relations*. 3rd ed. St. Paul, Minn.: West.

Wardle, Lynn D., Christopher L. Blakesley, and Jacqueline Y. Parker 1988 *Contemporary Family Law: Principles, Policy, and Practice*, 4 vols. Deerfield, Ill.: Callaghan.

Weitzman, Lenore 1985 *The Divorce Revolution*. New York: Free Press.

LISA J. MCINTYRE

FAMILY PLANNING

The ability of couples to plan the size of their family and the timing of births has important sociological implications for both individual families and society as a whole. Women's roles and labor-force participation, the socialization of children, social and economic development, and ultimately the ability of the earth to sustain human life are all affected in one way or another by the ability of couples to practice family planning and the success with which they do so. In the United States, women expect to complete their childbearing with an average of 2.2 children per woman (Abma et al. 1997), and, on average, women have 2.0 births over their lifetime (Ventura et al.). Throughout the world, the average number of children desired varies from about two in most industrialized nations to between six and eight in some African nations (Alan Guttmacher Institute 1995). In order to limit lifetime births to the number desired, couples must abstain from intercourse, have high levels of contraceptive use, or resort to abortion. Indeed, sexually active women would average eighteen births over their lifetime if they used no contraception and no induced abortion (Harlap et al. 1991). This article summarizes information regarding sexual activity; the risk and occurrence of unplanned pregnancy; contraceptive use and failure; and the provision of family planning–related information, education, and services in the United States. For comparison, worldwide variation in the planning status of pregnancies and births and the use and availability of contraception are also presented.

EXPOSURE TO THE RISK OF PREGNANCY

Most Americans begin to have intercourse during their late adolescence and continue to be sexually active throughout their reproductive lives. In 1995, 55 percent of all men aged 15–19 in the United States had had intercourse (Sonenstein et al. 1998). Similarly, about half of all women aged 15–19 report ever having had sex (Table 1). These data, collected in 1995, indicate a leveling off in the trend toward earlier ages of sexual initiation. Whereas the percentage of adolescents who reported being sexually experienced rose steadily throughout most of the 1980s, the percentage of adolescent females who had ever had sex did not change significantly between 1988 and 1995 and the percentage of adolescent males who were sexually experienced actually fell during that period (Singh and Darroch 1999).

Once sexually active, most women become at risk for an unintended pregnancy. Table 1 shows information on the percentage of all U.S. women aged 15–44 who are at risk for becoming pregnant by age and union-status groups (currently married, cohabiting, formerly married or never married). The proportion who are not at risk of an unintended pregnancy because they have never had intercourse decreases quickly from 50 percent of teenagers 15–19 to only 1 percent of all women aged 35–44. Five to seven percent of women in all age groups have had intercourse but are not currently in a sexual relationship (i.e., they have not had sex within the last three months). Some 5 percent of women are infertile, or noncontraceptively sterile, because of illness, surgery (that was not for contraceptive purposes), menopause, or some other reason. The proportion that is infertile increases steadily with age, from 1 to 2 percent of women under 30 to about 13 percent of those aged 40–44. Some women, especially those in their twenties and early thirties, are not at risk of an *unintended pregnancy* because they are already pregnant, postpartum, or seeking pregnancy. Eleven to fifteen percent of women aged 20–34 are in this category.

Women who are at risk for an unintended pregnancy account for more than two-thirds of all women ages 15–44 at any point in time. Women at risk are those who are currently in a sexual relationship, are fertile, and wish to avoid becoming pregnant. The proportion of women at risk of

unintended pregnancy increases from less than 40 percent of teenagers to about three-quarters of all women ages 25–44. Women who are currently married or cohabiting are most likely to be at risk for unintended pregnancy—81 to 83 percent of them are at risk, compared with 72 percent of formerly married women and 49 percent of never-married women. The most common reason some married or cohabiting women are not at risk of unintended pregnancy is that they are pregnant, postpartum, or trying to become pregnant. Among women who have never been married, never having had intercourse or no recent intercourse are the most common reasons.

OCCURRENCE OF UNINTENDED PREGNANCY

Nearly one-half of all pregnancies (49 percent) in the United States are unintended (Henshaw 1998), that is, they occur to women who want to have a baby later but not now (generally called "mistimed") or to women who did not want to have any (more) children at all (called "unwanted") (Table 2). The proportion of pregnancies that are unintended is highest among adolescents—78 percent—and varies considerably by age. The percentage of pregnancies that are unintended is lowest among women aged 30–34 (33 percent) and rises again among older women to 51 percent among women aged 40 and older. Unintended pregnancies are also relatively more likely to occur among never-married women (78 percent), black women (72 percent), and low-income women (61 percent for women under 100 percent of the federal poverty level).

The percentage of pregnancies that are unintended has declined in recent years—from 57 percent in 1987 to 49 percent in 1994 (see Table 2). These declines have occurred across all age categories but have been more significant among older women. These declines have also been more significant among low-income women. In 1987, 75 percent of all pregnancies to women with family incomes under 100 percent of the poverty level were unintended. This dropped to 61 percent in 1994. In comparison, the percentage of unintended pregnancies to women with incomes 200 percent or more of the federal poverty level fell from 45 percent in 1987 to 41 percent in 1994.

Percentage Distribution of Women Aged 15–44 According to Exposure to the Risk of Unintended Pregnancy, by Age and Union Status, National Survey of Family Growth, 1995

| | Total | AGE | | | | | | UNION STATUS | | | |
		15–19	20–24	25–29	30–34	35–39	40–44	Currently Married	Cohabiting	Formerly Married	Never Married
Total	100	100	100	100	100	100	100	100	100	100	100
At risk of unintended pregnancy	**69**	**37**	**70**	**74**	**77**	**77**	**77**	**81**	**83**	**72**	**49**
Using contraception	64	30	64	69	73	73	71	76	78	67	43
Not using contraception	5	7	6	5	4	4	5	4	5	6	7
Not at risk	**31**	**63**	**31**	**26**	**23**	**23**	**24**	**19**	**18**	**28**	**51**
Infertile	5	1	1	2	4	9	13	6	5	8	2
Pregnant/postpartum seeking pregnancy	9	5	11	15	12	7	3	13	12	4	3
No recent intercourse*	6	7	7	6	5	6	7	1	1	16	13
Never had intercourse	11	50	12	4	3	1	1	0	0	0	33

Table 1

SOURCE: Alan Guttmacher Institute tabulations of the 1995 National Survey of Family Growth (Cycle V).

NOTE: *Have not had intercourse in the past three months.

Among all unintended pregnancies, more than half (54 percent) end in an abortion while 46 percent result in an unintended birth. This relationship differs for adolescents, who, in recent years, have been more likely to resolve unintended pregnancies with a birth. More than one-half of all unintended pregnancies to adolescents result in an unintended birth (55 percent), while 45 percent are resolved with an abortion. These percentages represent a significant change in the resolution of unintended pregnancies among adolescents. Throughout the 1980s, adolescents who were pregnant unintentionally were more likely to obtain an abortion (55–53 percent) than to carry the pregnancy to term.

Nearly half (48 percent) of all women aged 15–44 have had at least one unintended pregnancy at some time in their lives; 28 percent have had one or more unplanned births, 30 percent have had one or more abortions, and 11 percent have had both. Given current rates of pregnancy and abortion, by the time they are 45 years old, the typical woman in the United States will have experienced 1.42 unintended pregnancies and 43 percent will have had an abortion.

Women who are using no contraceptive method account for about 8 percent of all women at risk of unintended pregnancy, but, because they are more likely to become pregnant than are those using a method, they account for nearly one-half of all unplanned pregnancies, an estimated 47 percent. Significant reductions in unintended pregnancy and abortion could occur with increased contraceptive use, with more effective use of existing methods, and with the development and marketing of additional methods.

CONTRACEPTIVE USE

Women and men in the United States rely on a variety of contraceptive methods to plan the timing and number of children they bear and to avoid unintended pregnancies. Surgical contraceptive sterilization is available to both men and women. Oral contraceptives, Depo Provera injectibles, Norplant implants, the IUD, and female barrier methods such as the diaphragm and the cervical cap are available from physicians and clinic providers. Other methods—condoms and spermicidal foam, cream, jelly, and film—can be purchased over the counter in pharmacies or other stores. Instruction in periodic abstinence is available from physicians and other family planning providers as well as through classes where only that method is taught.

More than nine in ten women aged 15–44 in 1995 who were at risk of unintended pregnancy

Percentage of All Pregnancies (Excluding Miscarriages) That are Unintended by Women's Age, Marital Status, Race, Ethnicity and Poverty Status, 1987 and 1995

WOMEN'S CHARACTERISTICS	% OF ALL PREGNANCIES THAT ARE UNINTENDED	
	1987*	1994**
All women	**57.3%**	**49.2%**
Age		
15–19	81.7%	78.0%
20–24	60.6%	58.5%
25–29	45.2%	39.7%
30–34	42.1%	33.1%
35–39	55.9%	40.8%
40–44	76.9%	50.7%
Marital status		
Currently married	40.1%	30.7%
Formerly married	68.5%	62.5%
Never married	88.2%	77.7%
Race		
White	NA	42.9%
Black	NA	72.3%
Other	NA	50.0%
Ethnicity		
Hispanic	NA	48.6%
Non-Hispanic	NA	49.3%
Poverty status		
<100% poverty	75.4%	61.4%
100–199% poverty	64.0%	53.2%
200+% poverty	45.0%	41.2%

Table 2

SOURCE: *Forrest (1994); **Henshaw (1998).

NOTE: na=not available.

were using a contraceptive method, as shown in Table 3. Thirty-six percent relied on contraceptive sterilization of themselves or their partner, 52 percent used reversible medical methods, 5 percent used nonmedical methods such as withdrawal and periodic abstinence, and 7.5 percent were currently using no contraceptive, even though they were at risk of unintended pregnancy.

Patterns of contraceptive use differ by age. Younger women at risk of unintended pregnancy are more likely than older women to use no method of contraception. Nearly one in five teenage women at risk use no method, compared to 6 to 7 percent of women at risk aged 25 and older. The proportion using reversible medical methods declines steeply with age—from more than four out of five women aged 20–24 to less than one-quarter

of those ages 40–44. Oral contraceptives are the most commonly used method among women under 30, used by 35 to 48 percent of these women. Condoms are second in popularity among this age group, used by 23 to 30 percent of women. Although fewer than 3 percent of women at risk use Depo Provera injectible contraceptives, this method has grown in popularity since its introduction into the United States, particularly among young women. Eight percent of teenagers at risk used this method. As women become older and complete their families, male and female contraceptive sterilization become increasingly common, rising steeply from 5 percent of women at risk aged 20–24 to one in five women in their late twenties and to two out of three women aged 40–44. Among women in their twenties, female sterilization is about four times more common than vasectomy. The margin narrows among older women to between two and two and a half times more common.

The proportion of women at risk of unintended pregnancy who use no contraceptive method is highest among never-married women, 14 percent as compared to 5 percent of those who are currently married or cohabiting and 8 percent of formerly married women. Sterilization is the most frequently used method among women who are currently married (46 percent) as well as formerly married women (50 percent). The pill is the most commonly used method among never-married women (38 percent) and cohabiting women (34 percent). Condoms are most likely to be used by never-married women (28 percent).

Although poor women and minority women at risk of unintended pregnancy have, in the past, been more likely than higher-income and non-Hispanic white women to be using no contraceptive method, these differences have lessened. Compared to the 1980s, in 1995 there were no significant race/ethnicity or poverty differences in the percentages of women at risk of unintended pregnancy who used no method of contraception. However, there is some variation in the types of methods used among these subgroups. Low-income women are less likely to rely on reversible methods and more likely to rely on sterilization than higher income women. Forty percent of women at risk of unintended pregnancy who are under

Percentage Distribution of Women at Risk of Unintended Pregnancy by Contraceptive Method Use and Age, Union Status, Race/Ethnicity and Poverty, National Survey of Family Growth, 1995

Contraceptive Method Used	Total at Risk of Unintended Pregnancy	AGE						UNION STATUS				RACE/ETHNICITY				POVERTY STATUS		
		15–19	20–24	25–29	30–34	35–39	40–44	Currently Married	Cohabiting	Formerly Married	Never Married	NonHispanic White	Black	Other	Hispanic	0–149%	150–299%	300%+
Total	100	100	100	100	100	100	100	100	100	100	100	100	100	100	100	100	100	100
Sterilization	36	0	5	20	38	56	66	46	27	50	8	36	38	29	37	40	37	32
Female	26	0	4	16	28	39	47	30	23	47	8	23	36	21	34	37	27	19
Male	10	0	1	4	10	18	19	16	4	3	0	13	2	8	4	3	10	14
Reversible medical methods	52	76	83	68	51	33	23	43	63	39	74	52	49	57	49	48	50	55
Oral contraceptives	25	35	48	37	27	11	6	19	34	19	38	27	21	18	21	22	25	26
Male condom	19	30	24	23	17	16	12	17	18	14	28	18	18	34	19	16	18	21
Depo Provera injectible	3	8	6	4	2	1	0	2	4	2	5	2	5	2	4	5	3	2
Barrier methods*	2	0	1	1	3	3	3	3	2	1	1	2	1	1	1	1	2	3
Norplant (implant)	1	2	3	2	1	0	0	1	2	1	2	1	2	2	2	3	1	1
Spermicides	1	1	1	1	1	1	1	1	2	1	1	1	1	1	1	1	1	1
IUD	1	0	0	1	1	1	1	1	1	1	0	1	1	1	1	1	1	1
Nonmedical methods	5	5	4	5	6	6	5	6	5	4	4	5	3	9	5	4	5	6
Withdrawal	3	3	3	4	3	3	2	3	3	3	3	3	1	4	3	3	3	3
Periodic abstinence	2	1	1	1	3	3	2	3	2	1	1	2	1	5	2	1	2	3
No method	8	19	9	6	6	6	7	5	5	8	14	7	10	5	9	8	8	7

Table 3

SOURCE: Alan Guttmacher Institute tabulations of the 1995 National Survey of Family Growth (Cycle V).

NOTE: *Female barrier methods include the diaphragm, cervical cap, sponge, and female condom.

150 percent of the poverty level use sterilization compared to 32 percent of women at 300 percent of the poverty level and above. Poor women relying on sterilization are much more likely than higher-income women to have been sterilized themselves rather than have a partner who has had a vasectomy. Female sterilization accounts for 92 percent of all contraceptive sterilization among poor women, compared with 58 percent among those with higher incomes.

CONTRACEPTIVE EFFECTIVENESS

Pregnancies occur to couples using contraceptive methods for two reasons—because of the inadequacy of the method itself or because it was not used correctly or consistently. Estimates have been made (either theoretically or empirically during clinical trials) regarding the efficacy of each contraceptive method given perfect use (Trussell 1998). In addition, estimates are made that measure the typical use effectiveness of each method, which relates to the experience of an actual group of users. The most recent estimates of typical use contraceptive effectiveness by method have been made using the 1995 National Survey of Family Growth, corrected for abortion underreporting and standardized for variation in the proportions of women from different subgroups using certain methods (Fu et al. 1999). Failure rates differ by method, with some methods consistently showing higher effectiveness than other methods. Rates also differ by sociodemographic subgroup within study populations.

Table 4 provides estimates of method-specific failure rates given both perfect use and typical use for the most commonly used reversible contraceptive methods. For each contraceptive method, the typical failure rates observed among women are substantially higher than the estimated rates given perfect use, and the rates differ widely among marital status, age, and poverty of women subgroups. The lowest failure rates are achieved with long-acting hormonal contraceptives that require little user compliance. Among methods that women must use daily or per coital episode, oral contraceptives are most effective, while spermicides, withdrawal, and periodic abstinence have the highest failure rates. In general, women who are young,

Estimated Percentage of Women Who Would Experience a Contraceptive Failure During the First Twelve Months of Perfect Method Use* and the Corrected Use-failure Rates Given Typical Method Use** for all Users and for Age, Poverty, and Marital Status Subgroups of Women Experiencing the Lowest or Highest Use-failure Rates

METHOD	Perfect Use*	Typical Use**
Total		13.1
Norplant implants	0.05	2.0
Depo Provera injectible	0.3	3.5
Oral contraceptives	.1 to .5	8.5
Diaphragm/cervical cap	6/9 to 26	13.2
Male condom	3	14.9
Spermicides	6	28.2
Withdrawal	4	26.0
Periodic abstinence	1 to 9	21.8

Table 4

SOURCES: *Trussell (1998), Table 31–1, p. 800. The ranges presented correspond to different formulations of the method, except for the cervical cap, where the range is due to woman's parity status. **Fu et al., (1999), (From corrected Table 1, available on http://www.agi-usa.org/pubs/journals/3105699.html).

unmarried or cohabiting, and poor have higher failure rates. The differences in failure rates between methods and between subgroups of women are much greater than what any difference in method effectiveness or in the biology of women would cause and are assumed primarily to reflect differences in the correctness and consistency of method use (although reporting errors may also play a role).

FAMILY PLANNING INFORMATION AND EDUCATION

Rising public concern over the occurrence of unintended pregnancy and, particularly, of unintended, nonmarital adolescent pregnancy and childbearing in the United States has drawn attention to the manner in which young people are educated about sexuality, contraception, and how to avoid pregnancy and other negative consequences of sexual activity. Parents and other adults have long played a key role in controlling the sexual behavior of adolescents and in providing basic information about sex and pregnancy avoidance. During the past twenty-five years, there has been a proliferation of organized efforts to augment the information, education, and support traditionally provided by families. Beginning with programs and services for young pregnant women, these efforts have expanded to include legislative mandates regarding the teaching of sexuality or family life education in schools, development and distribution of a variety of sexuality-education curricula, as well as integrated community interventions and media involvement. Organized efforts to implement sexuality education and related activities have also been influenced by growing public concern and awareness of HIV/AIDs and the need to provide young people with the information and means to avoid infection.

Increasingly, policies and programs to encourage abstinence among unmarried teenagers have become popular. Some of these programs attempt to accomplish this objective by giving young people encouragement, offering moral support and teaching interpersonal skills to resist pressures to become sexually active. Others, which seek to convince teenagers that sex before marriage is immoral, emphasize the negative consequences of sexual intercourse, occasionally withhold or distort information about the availability and effectiveness of contraception (Alan Guttmacher Institute 1994a). In fact, although most public schools provide some sort of sexuality education to middle or junior and senior high school students, the education provided is often too little, too late.

On a broader scale, community and service organizations have implemented interventions aimed at increasing the life options of disadvantaged young people through, for example, role models and mentoring, community service projects, job training, and activities aimed at reducing risky behaviors. Such interventions are expected indirectly to reduce levels of unintended teenage pregnancy, childbearing, and sexually transmitted infections, based on the belief that teenagers who are more positive about their futures are less likely to participate in risk-taking behaviors, including risky sexual practices.

Other policies or programs implemented with the hope of reducing unprotected teenage sexual behavior include (1) comprehensive school-based sexuality-education curricula that include discussion of abstinence but also include information about contraceptive methods and services; (2) programs that address the social pressures faced by teenagers to have sex and that provide modeling and practice of communication, negotiation, and refusal skills; (3) condom availability programs in schools; and (4) multicomponent programs that include communitywide activities—such as media involvement, social marketing, and links between school-based activities and contraceptive service providers (Alan Guttmacher Institute 1994a).

Evaluations of a variety of programs and approaches aimed at affecting teenage sexual and reproductive behavior, although still somewhat inconclusive, have shown that some programs have had a positive effect on the behavior of youth. In addition, results of multiple studies indicate that the provision of contraceptive information and access does not encourage young people to become sexually active at younger ages. Reviews of the evaluation research point to the need for integrated approaches that both address the antecedents of sexual risk taking (e.g., poverty, violence, social disorganization) and provide young people (who will soon become adults) with the information, skills, and resources to make responsible decisions about sexual behavior and the avoidance of unintended outcomes (e.g., Kirby 1997).

CONTRACEPTIVE SERVICE PROVISION

In the United States, women can receive contraceptive services from private practice general and family practitioners and obstetrician-gynecologists, as well as from publicly supported clinics run by hospitals, health departments, community health centers, and Planned Parenthood affiliates or independent clinic providers. In addition, some teenage and young adult women receive contraceptive services from school-based clinics and college or university health centers.

Private practice physicians are the most numerous providers in the United States that are available to women seeking contraceptive information and services. More than 40,000 family practice doctors and nearly 30,000 obstetrician-gynecologists provide office-based outpatient services (Alan Guttmacher Institute 1997). About seven in ten women seeking family planning services report going to a private practitioner or health maintenance organization (HMO) for their care (Aloma et al. 1997).

Annually, some 6.5 million U.S. women receive contraceptive services, supplies, and information from more than 7,000 publicly supported family planning clinics, located in 85 percent of all U.S. counties (Frost 1996). Family planning clinics, using a combination of federal, state, and local funds, provide care to those who cannot afford services from private physicians or who cannot use private physicians for other reasons. In most clinics, fees are based on the client's ability to pay, confidential services to teenagers are assured, and a full range of contraceptive methods are offered. As a result, family planning clinic clients are primarily low-income (57 percent are below 100 percent of the federal poverty level, and 33 percent are between 100 percent and 249 percent of the federal poverty level) and young (20 percent are under age 20; 50 percent are aged 20–29). Although a majority of clinic clients are non-Hispanic whites, nearly 40 percent are minority women (19 percent are black, 14 percent are Hispanic, and 7 percent are Asian or other races) (Frost and Bolzan). Lower-income women go to clinics primarily because they cannot afford physicians' fees, because the clinic is more conveniently located, or because the clinic will accept Medicaid payment. Adolescents often go to clinics because of the free or low-cost services and because they are afraid a private physician will tell their parents about their contraceptive use. In addition, some women, especially teenagers who have never been to a physician on their own, go to clinics because they do not know a physician who would serve them. Clinic clients usually shift to private physicians when their incomes rise and as they become older.

Sixty percent of all publicly supported clinics receive federal Title X support and must therefore follow federal standard of care guidelines. These guidelines provide medical protocols as well as mandates regarding confidentiality and key areas of outreach that clinics should seek to address. As a result, many publicly supported clinics provide outreach and information or education in local schools or in other community locations. These clinics often seek to reach out to women (and men) in need of contraceptive care who have special needs or risk factors for unintended pregnancy (e.g., because of homelessness, drug or alcohol abuse, domestic violence, or other reasons).

The provision of contraceptive services, like all areas of health care, has been affected by changes in the structure of health care financing and the rise of managed care. In the past, most privately insured women had employer-based indemnity health insurance plans that rarely covered either routine gynecological checkups or reversible contraceptive services and supplies. However, such plans often covered sterilization services. Today, most privately insured women are enrolled in managed care plans. These plans are more likely to cover preventative care, including routine gynecological checkups and some reversible contraceptive services and supplies. However, not all managed care plans cover all or even most methods, and often the process of obtaining contraceptive services within managed care plans places additional burdens on women seeking contraceptive care. These burdens include prior authorization requirements that may cause some women to delay care or forgo sensitive care that a woman may not want to disclose to her primary care physician (Alan Guttmacher Institute 1994b, 1996).

INTERNATIONAL COMPARISONS

Women in the United States have both similarities and differences with women throughout the world in their efforts to plan the number and timing of children. In adolescence, American women are somewhat less successful in their attempts to prevent unplanned pregnancies than are young women in most other industrialized countries. Table 5 presents recent birthrates among women aged 15–19 for selected European and North American countries. Although there is no evidence that young women in the United States are more (or less) sexually active than young women in many other industrialized countries, the United States has adolescent birthrates that are nine to ten times higher than the rates for the Netherlands and Sweden and more than twice as high as the rates for Canada, England, and Wales. The factors responsible for these differences are not entirely clear; however, it is likely that they are due in part to differences in the levels of disadvantage among countries, to variation in the family planning education and services provided to youth and to greater or lesser openness regarding sexuality among countries.

In developing countries, young women marry earlier and have children at younger ages than in the United States. More than half of the young women in sub-Saharan Africa bear a child during the teenage years and about one-third of the young women in Asia, North Africa, the Middle East, and Latin America bear children as teens, compared to just one-fifth of teenage women in the United States. Although the situation is improving and the proportion of adolescents using contraception is increasing in many developing countries, few married adolescents use contraceptive methods and high percentages of sexually active unmarried adolescents rely on traditional nonmedical methods, such as withdrawal and periodic abstinence. Greater use of reliable contraceptive methods by adolescents worldwide is often hampered by inadequate or inaccurate information, poor access to services, and community expectations that value early childbearing within marriage and punish sexual activity outside of marriage. As a result, a substantial proportion of births to adolescents are unplanned—40 to 60 percent in several Latin American and sub-Saharan African countries, and 20 percent or more even in countries where almost all births are to married adolescents. By comparison, 66 percent of adolescent births in the United States are unplanned (Alan Guttmacher Institute 1998).

The patterns of pregnancy, childbearing, and contraceptive use among women of all ages vary from region to region throughout the world. Table 6 presents information on pregnancy rates

Adolesecent Birthrates for Selected European and North American Countries, Mid-1990s

COUNTRY	BIRTHS PER 1,000 WOMEN AGED 15–19
Switzerland	5.7
Netherlands	5.8
Italy	6.9
Sweden	7.7
Spain	7.8
Denmark	8.3
Belgium	9.1
Slovenia	9.3
Finland	9.8
France	10.0
Greece	13.0
Germany	13.2
Norway	13.5
Austria	15.6
Czech Republic	20.1
Portugal	20.9
Poland	21.1
Iceland	22.1
Canada	24.2
England and Wales	28.4
Hungary	29.5
Slovak Republic	32.3
Estonia	33.4
Belarus	39.0
Bulgaria	49.6
Russian Federation	45.6
United States	54.4

Table 5

SOURCE: Singh et al. (2000).

(per 1,000 women aged 15–44), planning status of pregnancy, abortion, and contraceptive use for women in different regions of the world. Women in Africa experience the highest rates of pregnancy, the lowest percentage of pregnancies aborted, and the highest percentage of married women using no contraceptive method. Although women in the United States have somewhat higher pregnancy rates than women in most of Europe and other North American countries, they have significantly lower pregnancy rates than most of the women in the rest of the world. The percentage of pregnancies that are planned varies considerably among the different regions of the world, from only 25 percent of pregnancies in eastern Europe being planned to 54 percent of African pregnancies being planned. Similarly, there is variation in the percentage of pregnancies that are aborted and in the patterns of contraceptive use. Compared to other regions of the world, the percentage of U.S. pregnancies that are aborted is similar to that in most of Europe and Latin America but less than half the percentage in eastern Europe. In terms of contraceptive use, married women in the United States are more likely than women in most other regions of the world (except for East Asia) to choose sterilization as their method of contraception. Married women in Africa and in Europe (both eastern and western Europe) rarely choose sterilization, and high percentages of Europeans rely on nonmedical methods, such as withdrawal.

Worldwide, only 47 percent of all pregnancies (including miscarriages) are planned and, at the same time, 42 percent of married women are using no method of contraception. In most regions of the world, one-third or more of married women use no method. Ensuring greater information, education, and access to family planning services worldwide has the potential to greatly reduce the level of unplanned pregnancy and abortion.

(SEE ALSO: *Birth and Death Rates; Family Size; Fertility Determinants; Pregnancy and Pregnancy Termination*)

REFERENCES

Abma, J. C., et al. 1997 "Fertility, Family Planning, and Women's Health: New Data from the 1995 Survey of Family Growth." *Vital and Health Statistics*, Series 23, No. 19, Table 1.

Alan Guttmacher Institute 1994 *Sex and America's Teenagers.* New York: Alan Guttmacher Institute.

—— 1994b *Uneven and Unequal: Insurance Coverage and Reproductive Health Services.* New York: Alan Guttmacher Institute.

Total Number of Pregnancies per 1,000 Women Aged 15–44, Percentage of Pregnancies Planned and Aborted, and Contraceptive Use Among Married Women, Major Regions of the World, 1990s

	TOTAL PREGNANCY RATE*	% OF PREG-NANCIES PLANNED**	% OF PREG-NANCIES ABORTED**	Contraceptive Use by Married Women Aged 15–49				
				Sterili-zation	Reversible Methods	Nonmedical Methods	No Method	Total
World	160	47%	22%	23	27	8	42	100
Africa	262	54%	12%	2	14	4	80	100
East Asia	123	47%	30%	44	38	1	17	100
Rest of Asia	182	51%	17%	17	17	8	58	100
Latin America	159	33%	23%	30	28	8	34	100
Eastern Europe	157	25%	57%	2	29	38	31	100
Rest of Europe	81	52%	21%	8	48	18	26	100
North America	100	41%	23%	27	34	6	33	100
United States	107	43%	23%	37	35	5	24	100

Table 6

SOURCES: columns z–4: Alan Guttmacher Institute (1999); columns 5–9: United Nations (1999).

NOTE: *Per 1,000 women aged 15–44.

NOTE: **Pregnancies include miscarriages in this table.

——— 1995 *Hopes and Realities: Closing the Gap Between Women's Aspirations and Their Reproductive Experiences.* New York: Alan Guttmacher Institute.

——— 1996 *Improving the Fit: Reproductive Health Services in Managed Care Settings.* New York: Alan Guttmacher Institute.

——— 1997 *Contraceptive Needs and Services.* New York: Alan Guttmacher Institute.

——— 1998 *Into a New World: Young Women's Sexual and Reproductive Lives.* New York: Alan Guttmacher Institute.

——— 1999 *Sharing Responsibility: Women, Society and Abortion Worldwide.* New York: Alan Guttmacher Institute.

Forrest, J. D. "Epidemiology of Unintended Pregnancy and Contraceptive Use." *American Journal of Obstetrics and Gynecology* 170(5):1485–1489.

Frost, J. 1996 "Family Planning Clinic Services in the United States, 1994." *Family Planning Perspectives* 28(3)92–100.

———, and M. Bolzan 1997 "The Provision of Public Sector Services by Family Planning Agencies in 1995." *Family Planning Perspectives* 29(1)6–14.

Fu, H., J. E. Darroch, T. Haas, and N. Ranjit 1999 "Contraceptive Failure Rates: New Estimates from the 1995 National Survey of Family Growth." *Family Planning Perspectives* 13(2):56–63.

Harlap, S., K. Kost, and J. D. Forrest 1991 *Preventing Pregnancy, Protecting Health: A New Look at Birth Control Choices in the United States.* New York: Alan Guttmacher Institute.

Henshaw, S. K. 1998 "Unintended Pregnancy in the United States." *Family Planning Perspectives* 30(1)24–29, 46.

Kirby, D. 1997 "No Easy Answers: Research Findings on Programs to Reduce Teen Pregnancy." (Research review commissioned by The National Campaign to Prevent Teen Pregnancy Task Force on Effective Programs and Research, Washington, D.C.)

Singh, S., and J. E. Darroch 1999 "Trends in Sexual Activity Among Adolescent American Women: 1982–1995." *Family Planning Perspectives* 31(5):212–219.

———, and J. E. Darroch, Forthcoming "Adolescent Pregnancy and Childbearing: Levels of Trends in Developed Countries." *Family Planning Perspectives.*

Sonenstein, F. L., et al. 1998 "Changes in Sexual Behavior and Condom Use Among Teenaged Men: 1988 to 1995." *American Journal of Public Health* 88(6):956–959.

Trussell, J. 1998 "Contraceptive Efficacy." In R. A. Hatcher et al., eds., *Contraceptive Technology*, 17th rev. ed. New York: Ardent Media.

United Nations 1999 *Levels and Trends of Contraceptive Use as Assessed in 1998*. New York: United Nations.

Ventura, S. J., et al. 1998 "Births and Deaths: Preliminary Data for 1997." *National Vital Statistics Reports* 47(4):4.

JENNIFER J. FROST
JACQUELINE E. DARROCH

FAMILY POLICY IN WESTERN SOCIETIES

The dramatic growth in the industrial capacities and economic power of the United States and the countries of Western Europe since World War II has demonstrably improved the per capita income and quality of life of the average citizen in these countries. Based on such indicators as available health services, declining death rates, unemployment protection, and retirement benefits, it is reasonable to infer that, more than at any other time in human history, the majority of the people in these countries are assured that they can obtain the basic elements necessary for their survival and the survival of their families. Moreover, their quality of life, as measured by education, availability and quality of housing, ownership of automobiles and other durable goods, and available leisure time, suggests a lifestyle heretofore reserved only for the rich.

It is ironic that this unparalleled affluence has been accompanied by fundamental changes in family structure and family relationships—changes that challenge our basic conceptions of how families are organized and function. Marital stability and the size of the birthrate are common indicators of family health (Kittrie 1997). Over the early 1970s, virtually all the highly industrialized countries have experienced accelerating increases in divorce, decreased family size, increases in pregnancies among unmarried women, and an increase in childless marriages. Unlike many Third World countries, where population is growing at a rapid rate, birthrates in Western countries are below the level of population replacement (see Van de Kaa 1987 for Western Europe; Sweet and Bumpass 1987 for the United States). According to Census Bureau data, the American family reached its smallest size in 1990.

There is general agreement among family scholars that these changes are due, at least in part, to the expanding number of married women in the labor force. In 1920, about 9 percent of the families in the United States included wives who were employed outside the home (Hayghe 1990, p. 14). By 1987 the number of dual-earner families outnumbered families in which the husband was the only breadwinner by two to one (Lerner 1994). This situation does not change appreciably when children enter the family. Labor-force participation for married women with children under the age of six increased from 18.6 percent of all married women in 1960 to 63.6 percent in 1997. For married women with children between the ages of six and thirteen, the rate peaked in 1997 at 76.5 percent. Similar data exist for countries in Western Europe. Haavio-Mannila and Kauppinen (1990) note that full-time homemaking has almost disappeared in the Nordic countries. These changes have had a direct impact on the division of labor in the family and an indirect effect on marital-role relationships. Closely linked to women's growing labor-market activity is the fact that they are making better use of the educational opportunities available to them. There is evidence that educational achievement is converging for males and females in most of the Western world (Haavio-Mannila 1988).

As both educational and occupational career opportunities increase for women, there is a tendency to delay marriage. In the United States, the median age for first marriage peaked in 1996 for men (27.1 years) and in 1997 for women (25.0 years). Moreover, with growing educational equality and an increased ability to compete effectively for jobs in markets that value the skills obtained through education, the time such women spend raising children becomes more costly, both economically and psychologically (Sweet and Bumpass 1987). The result is fewer children per family and less time spent in parent–child interaction in those families with offspring (Lerner 1994).

These changes have altered marital and parental roles in families. Sweet and Bumpass (1987), describing the situation for U.S. families, claim that although husbands have made only a modest contribution to sharing household duties, they can no longer claim the role of "breadwinner." The conception of the prototypical family as consisting of a legally married husband and wife living together for a lifetime, raising children in a household managed by the wife and mother and financially supported by the husband and father, is anachronistic. Indeed, such family structures constitute less than 7 percent of families in the United States (Lerner 1994).

Many scholars regard this decline in traditional family structures with considerable alarm. The decline is associated with values that emphasize individualistic and self-oriented goals over family well-being and, by extension, concern for others in the community. It is argued that these values lead to social isolation, growing levels of interpersonal distrust, and the the involvement by individuals in an endless and empty search for gratification (Elshtain 1997).

Other scholars, though not sanguine about the human problems created by these changes, tend to consider them as inevitable consequences of increased individual opportunity and freedom. Such freedom can only occur when developed societies establish equality between the sexes and underwrite the financial and social risks of illness, job loss, and aging. To the extent that greater individual autonomy and freedom of opportunity are gained at the cost of stable family relations, that cost should be borne (Myrdal 1967). Most important, those who look positively upon these changes point with approval to the changing role of women. The increased participation of women in the labor force in all industrialized countries has increased women's freedom to choose their own lifestyles, both in the world of work and in the family (Lerner 1994). If changes in family structure contribute to greater equality and greater opportunities for women to achieve their full potential, then, it is argued, society as a whole benefits (Lanca 1997).

Interestingly, people on both sides of the debate tend to define themselves as pro-family. Virtually everyone seems to acknowledge the social importance of the family in caring for and socializing children. There is also a perception of the family as a sanctuary that provides its members with protection, affection, and succor in what is often a hostile and, generally, impersonal environment. For the most part, advocates of both perspectives accept as problematic the fact that, increasingly, families fail to carry out these functions.

The high divorce rate, single-parent households, teenage pregnancy, and domestic violence are disturbing components in modern family life, and there is general agreement that something should be done about these problems. There is a consensus in all the advanced industrialized countries that the family is a proper concern of public policy. There are, however, fundamental differences in the conceptions of what that policy should be, what institutions or groups should be responsible for implementing policy, and what types of families or individuals should be the targets of such policy.

A conservative movement seeks to reverse the trends discussed above by shoring up the traditional family. They advocate reinforcing the importance of legal marriages, making divorce more difficult, emphasizing parental responsibility for the care and protection of children, and, more generally, strengthening the family by protecting it from government intrusions. Governments, from this perspective, should be restrained from taking over responsibilities that "rightfully" belong to the family. In this view, only limited indirect support in the form of tax relief or tax credits to help families care for their dependent members and to make homeownership easier are considered appropriate forms of government involvement (Carlson 1988). Advocates of restricting government involvement maintain that families, if left alone, would function quite well. Some critics of government involvement in family life argue for the privatization of most social services geared toward helping families. The essential claim is that privately organized and funded services to families would be more efficient and would protect the right of the family to make choices for itself (Brodkin and Young 1989).

Related to this position is the argument that a weakening of the family can be attributed to constitutional neglect—a failure to define and protect the status of the family as a publicly recognized institution (Kittrie 1997). Additionally, it is argued that contemporary social policy emphasizes individualistic interests rather than family concerns, thus reducing the family to a contractual arrangement rather than a socially recognized institution.

At the other extreme there are those who believe that the appropriate role of government is to assist the family in maximizing individual potential for each family member. They maintain that, in democratic societies, government should mediate among various interest groups, each seeking its own advantages. Only the government, responsible to the electorate, is in a position to protect the public interest. Far from weakening the family, the government, it is argued, is the only institution in a position to use its resources to support and strengthen families and their members. This is especially true for families with children living under current conditions of rapid social change. Thus, it is argued that "social and demographic changes have combined to diminish the likelihood that families can assure their children's healthy growth and development without help from outside the family" (Schorr et al. 1986).

Some have maintained that the question of government intervention is a moot point, since governments (as political entities) serve the purposes of their most influential constituencies. For example, they point to government tax incentives to assist businesses, the building of highways in the 1950s to benefit the automobile industry, and the government's readiness to come to the aid of large corporations, banks, and savings and loan associations during times of crisis. In brief, for many observers, the notion of "minimalist government"—the ideal advocated in the rhetoric of the Reagan administration in the 1980s—is not a reality in any modern country (Kahn and Kamerman 1975). The real question is not whether government should come to the aid of its citizens, but which citizens will be the beneficiaries of such aid.

William J. Wilson's (1987) answer to the question is that government services should be as universal as possible. Rather than limiting services to crisis intervention and emergencies or providing aid just to the disadvantaged, public services should be expanded to cover all citizens. Wilson maintains that only when public programs serve all segments of a society will it be possible to prevent system breakdowns and integrate all elements as productive members of the society.

The disagreements about what is appropriate family policy are so basic that it is hard to identify "objective" investigations or investigators. Policy implies advocacy, and advocacy implies bias. As a consequence, debates circle around such fundamentals as what is meant by the phrase *family policy*; indeed, there is disagreement on what is meant by *family*. Consider the following three

definitions: (1) "The family is a society limited in members but nonetheless a true society, anterior to every state or nation, with rights and duties of its own, wholly independent of the commonwealth" (Pope Leo XIII, quoted in Strong and DeVault 1989, p. 6). (2) "The family consists of two or more persons living together and related by blood, marriage or adoption" (U.S. Bureau of the Census 1990). (3) "One or more adults related by blood, marriage, or affiliation who cooperate economically, share a common dwelling place, and may rear children" (Strong and DeVault 1996, p. 15). Note that definition (1) places the family as independent and free from the state. By implication, what goes on in the family is none of the government's business. Definition (2) restricts the family to shared residence and formal kin ties determined by blood or legal marriage, whereas definition (3), by introducing the vague term *affiliation*, is intended to include under the family label such "family" forms as cohabiting families and gay and lesbian families.

Still other definitions point to the fact that families need not always reside in the same household to maintain familial bonds and obligations, suggesting that emotional ties may be more salient than biological ties when defining family. A recent public opinion poll found that only 22 percent of respondents defined the American family in terms of blood, marriage, or adoption (Footlick 1990).

Those who define the family as the Census Bureau does are more likely to advocate policies that support only households whose members are linked through legally defined ties of kinship. Those who adhere to definition (3), on the other hand, are more likely to advocate government recognition of and assistance to different kinds of heterosexual and same-sex unions formed only by the consent of the participants without any state recognition or sanction. Adherents of definitions (1) or (2) are more likely to maintain that governmental aid to some of the groups that fit definition (3) is not aid to families but a major contribution toward the declining significance of the family in modern life (Kittrie 1997).

Despite disagreements concerning an adequate definition, some shared understanding of what is meant by "family" is necessary to provide a referent for the discussion that follows. The working definition provided below is designed to incorporate essential elements that make up most definitions. It is, however, not likely to satisfy staunch advocates of any particular policy orientation. The family is defined here as *any group of individuals who are bound together by publicly acknowledged and socially sanctioned kinship ties.* The key to this definition is in the concept of *kinship.* Kinship is a special type of social relationship determined by ancestry, marriage, and adoption. In every society certain kin have designated duties toward and responsibilities for other members of the kin group. These responsibilities are obligatory; the only way an individual can free him- or herself from such obligations is by ceasing to be kin, a difficult, if not impossible, task. These obligations tend to be lifelong. For key kin the obligations can pertain to virtually all physical and emotional needs of family members. For example, in modern industrial societies parents are expected not only to care for their children's physical needs but to provide them with love and affection and to prepare them to function effectively in the real world. Failure to do so can result in severe sanctions against the parent. Thus all Western industrialized countries have laws designed to require that parents provide financial support and care for their children, even if the husband and wife are separated. Each country also has laws designed to sanction parents for physically abusing or neglecting their minor children. Similar obligations accrue as a consequence of marriage. Formal marriages are legal entities sanctioned by the state (and often the church), and violations of the marital agreement are monitored and adjudicated by reference to secular laws, sacred laws, or both.

Whereas the care, nurturance, and socialization of children continue to be the responsibility of parents, the care of aging parents by adult children is becoming less common. Social Security and retirement pensions, national health programs, and public support for housing for the elderly have been introduced in all highly industrialized countries. As these programs increase, family obligations tend to decline.

The tendency toward declining family responsibility for its members extends beyond care for the elderly. Over the years, as modes of production have changed, the family has gradually relinquished responsibility for providing either employment or occupational training for its members.

The family is no longer directly responsible for formal and religious education, and, more recently, responsibility for child care has tended to be relegated to nonfamily institutions. As the family gives up these functions to the workplace, schools, and churches, its relative power and influence on the economic and political life of the society diminishes. The issue thus becomes whether public policy, established and administered by agents of the governmental or economic segments of society, should be used to assist this weakened institution. More specifically, the question arises whether public services in the form of health care, housing, unemployment insurance, support for education, maternity benefits, support for child care, and so forth help to strengthen the family in its remaining responsibility for the care, nurturance, and socialization of its members or further weaken it by making family members dependent on nonfamily sources for benefits and social support. This is the key question surrounding the debate over what is a proper family policy in the Western world.

The term *policy*, like *family*, is burdened with multiple meanings and definitions. It has been variously described as the means for focusing on fundamental problems of individuals in relation to societies (Lasswell 1968), a set of decisions designed to support an agreed-upon course of action (Zimmerman 1988), or as governmental goals (Dumon and Aldous 1979). Thus the different definitions have covered the gamut, from means to process to goals. Kahn's (1969) conception of policy incorporates these elements within a context that gives it specific meaning. He refers to policy as "the general guide to action, the cluster of overall decisions relevant to the achievement of the goal, the guiding principles, the standing plan" (p. 131). Thus, a definition that seems to have some consensual meaning would hold that policy is a commitment to action that utilizes a consciously designated strategy designed to attain specified goals.

Although some writers insist that the term *policy* is applicable only to governmental action, the more general view is that any actor, whether an individual or a large collectivity, can make and implement policy (Zimmerman 1988). What is important, and the source of considerable debate, is the fit between the policy goals and the actor's ability to implement those goals. For example, individual families of moderate means are not likely, by themselves, to be able to implement a policy for attaining high-standard, low-cost day care for their children; conversely, neither national governments nor national corporations are likely to be able effectively to develop policies for resolving neighborhood conflicts between ethnic groups. The difficulty is not only in matching appropriate levels of scale (e.g., community problems are best solved by community organizations); it also lies in the actor's ability to bring the right resources to bear on a given problem. This requires access to relevant information, the ability to recruit appropriate personnel, and control over the appropriate resources. The debate about family policy generally focuses on three primary issues: goals, the strategies designed to attain those goals, and the appropriate agencies for implementing these strategies. The sharpest differences concerning these issues are apparent at the national level.

The differences among policy goals, strategies, and designated agents are most evident when we compare the approach to family policy in the United States with the industrialized nations of Western Europe. As noted earlier, the United States shares many of the same family problems with these countries. The solutions offered in the form of public policy, however, differ considerably. The United States, often referred to as the "reluctant welfare state," has tended to be less forthcoming than the European countries in providing funds or services for its families or individuals. Moreover, there has been a strong inclination to have agencies other than government administer and implement social programs. America's revolutionary history has left its citizens with a pervasive distrust of government; rather than viewing government as a source of aid and assistance to its people, they often consider it a threat capable of usurping individual freedom and autonomy (Schorr 1979). Where the family is considered, this fear of government is enhanced by the tradition in Anglo-Saxon jurisprudence of noninterference in family life (Glendon 1989).

Differences in approach to family policy in the United States and Western Europe are also affected by the different cultural, racial, and ethnic compositions of the various countries. For example, despite the recent immigration of foreign workers to European countries such as West Germany, Switzerland, and Sweden, no European country approximates the United States in its ethnic and racial heterogeneity. Whereas minorities make up between 6 and 7 percent of the population of countries like West Germany and Sweden, the nonwhite and Hispanic minorities in the United States represent 20 percent of the population (*Statistical Abstract of Sweden 1990; Statistisches Jahrbuch fur die Bundesrepublik Deutschland* 1989; U.S. Bureau of the Census 1990).

Also important are the differences between the countries in the extent to which governments are centralized and can make policy at the national level. With the exception of Switzerland, the Western European countries tend to be more centralized. This makes it possible to have a meaningful national debate about the pros and cons of a national family policy. Such a debate in the United States is less conclusive, principally because decision-making power on such an issue is distributed among federal, state, and local governments (Dumon and Aldous 1979).

These factors tend to contribute to one incontrovertible fact: The United States has less legislation directly concerned with assisting families and provides less financial support designated to aid families than any other advanced Western industrial society (Kahn and Kamerman 1983; Kittrie 1997).

Americans have been more reluctant than Europeans to pass legislation that might be interpreted as violating the sanctity and the privacy of the family. Legislators in most European countries seem willing to write laws designed to protect the child's safety, health, and psychological well-being without great concern that such legislation might interfere with family prerogatives (Glendon 1989). Although the reluctance of the U.S. courts to venture into the family domain is gradually changing, especially in the areas of child-support enforcement and prevention of domestic violence, they have moved much more slowly and reluctantly in this area than their counterparts in the Scandinavian countries, France, the Netherlands, and West Germany. It would be unheard of, for example, for courts or legislatures in the United States to follow the Swedish example and forbid parents to spank their children (Davis 1997).

Although divorce is a common condition in all the Western developed countries, the United States and England have been hesitant to interfere in the financial arrangements resulting from divorce on behalf of the children involved. This is not the case in the Nordic countries or in continental Europe, where, according to Glendon (1989), there is "genuine judicial supervision of the spouses' financial arrangements for children: mechanisms to ensure that child support is fixed at realistic and fair levels; highly efficient collection systems; 'maintenance advance systems' in which the state not only collects unpaid child support, but partially absorbs the risk of non-payment of advancing support up to a fixed amount in cases of default" (pp. 236–237).

The available data indicate that, with the possible exception of Social Security benefits for the elderly, the United States is not as generous as most of the European countries with regard to funding programs designed to assist families (Kahn and Kamerman 1983). This is most apparent when we consider families with children. The United States has tended to limit its assistance to such programs as Aid to Families with Dependent Children, which was geared toward providing financial aid to single-parent families living below the poverty line. Some additional assistance is provided to poor families through food stamps (unique to the United States) and, in the short run, unemployment insurance. Financial assistance to all families with children generally takes the form of a standard income tax deduction of $2,700 for each dependent child. For families whose income is below $10,000 an earned income credit is provided.

Most of the countries of Western Europe, on the other hand, provide direct cash payments to families for each child. These payments are tax-free and serve as family income supplements. The per-child payments tend to increase with increased family size. Funds are also provided to assist families during the childbearing phase in the form of direct grants to cover income loss and pre- and postnatal medical care (Kamerman and Kahn 1981).

The Nordic states and Western continental Europe also provide direct housing assistance for both rental and homeownership payments. Housing allowances generally decrease as income rises, thus providing an income leveling mechanism in these countries (Herrstrom 1986). Unlike the U.S. policy of tax deductions for interest paid on mortgages, which benefit better-off families, the European housing allowances tend to favor lower-income families (Kahn and Kamerman 1983; Herrstrom 1986).

In addition to these direct income-transfer programs, many of the countries in Western Europe provide a variety of benefits designed to assist families with the child-rearing challenges associated with both parents' working outside the home. Sweden, for example, provides a guaranteed pregnancy leave as well as a nine-month parental leave at 90 percent of salary and an additional three months at a flat rate (Lerner 1994). Austria, Germany, Norway, and the Netherlands have policies of at least three months of paid leave at 100 percent salary. Denmark and France have policies of at least sixteen weeks at 90 percent of salary, and Finland has a policy of eleven months at 80 percent of salary (Lerner 1994). Efforts are underway in Finland to extend this type of parental leave to three years. In the Nordic countries parents during the first three years of a child's life can choose to obtain state support for one parent to remain home with the child or to use the funds for day-care services. By comparison, the Family Support Act, passed in 1988 in the United States, renewed the requirement that a proportion of mothers receiving public assistance find employment (Michel 1998). At the same time, efforts to pass universal child-care legislation failed. Until January 1993, the United States was the only industrialized nation without a national parental leave policy (Lerner 1994).

Regardless of the merits of the American and European approaches to family policy, one significant current fact differentiates family conditions in the United States from those in the developed countries of continental Europe: In 1993, 40.1 percent of children under age six living in the United States were poor (U.S. Bureau of the Census 1994). This high level of poverty in the midst of affluence has produced a growing sense of despair and hopelessness concerning the life chances of these children. Miller (1990) summarizes the available data as follows: "Many studies have documented the much poorer health status of poor and minority children, the greater rates of child abuse, the higher incidence of injuries and death attributable to violence and crime, high rates of illiteracy, teenage pregnancy, educational failure and school dropouts." He goes on to note that the communities in which these children live are more dangerous, the schools are less adequate, and the rates of drug abuse are higher than in the general population. A sizable proportion of these children, but by no means all, are African American Hispanic, or Native American. The majority live in female-headed, single-parent families, a phenomenon increasingly referred to as the "feminization of poverty" in the United States.

Thus, the essential issue concerning family policy for Americans is inextricably linked with the questions of poverty and what to do about it. The fact that this situation does not exist in the advanced countries of Europe (with the possible exception of the United Kingdom) raises the inevitable question whether the family policies of these "welfare states" have anything to offer Americans in their search for solutions to the problem of family poverty.

It will come as no surprise that expert opinion on this issue is greatly divided. Differences exist even among those who usually share the same ideological perspective. Some who are concerned with providing greater equality in our society advocate programs such as those in Western Europe. Wilson (1987, p. 149) refers to such programs as "universal programs of reform," that is, programs that provide services for all citizens rather than earmarking aid for just minorities or the poor. The advantages of such programs are that since all citizens benefit, there is no stigma attached to being a recipient and no resentment among nonrecipients that taxes are being spent to benefit others.

This position is not universally shared even among those committed to egalitarian solutions. Some feel strongly that massive resources must be put into play to assist only those families at the greatest risk of being trapped in an abyss of poverty and hopelessness (Schorr 1988).

Predictably, those more concerned with issues of freedom than equality have argued that the problem of poverty in the United States is not the result of inadequate public services but rather is a consequence of such services. According to Carlson (1988), the "matriarchal welfare state has produced family disruptive results" and the "poverty crisis, the ageism crisis, the teen pregnancy crisis, the overpopulation crisis, the juvenile delinquency crisis, the eugenics crisis, the child abuse crisis, the youth suicide crisis" have all contributed to expanding the power of the state at the expense of the family (p. 273). Charles Murray (1984) compiled an impressive amount of data that purports to illustrate that public services designed to reduce poverty in the United States were ineffectual. Murray's data have been challenged by a number of investigators, and the ensuing debate reaffirms the difficulty in interpreting data relevant to this issue in ways that are free of bias. The difficulty is that socioeconomic conditions change so rapidly that it is not likely that any single factor can or should be justified as constituting the cause for poverty.

Whatever the causes, poverty is a reality in the United States, and, increasingly, the discrepancies in the distribution of wealth in this country demand the attention of policy makers (Phillips 1990). It also seems apparent that, given the ubiquity of the family in social life, any policy regarding poverty must also be a policy pertaining to families. Whether that policy will be concerned with all families or just the poor remains to be seen; whether it will be a national policy or policies instigated and implemented at the state levels, and whether its funding will be in the form of direct grants or tax benefits and incentives, is also hard to predict. It is likely, however, given American traditions and the deep differences that exist within the country about family policy, that the eventual solutions and compromises reached will be different from those that have evolved in Europe. Nevertheless, in this world of instant communication and visibility, the state of the family in Europe and the resources available to European families must have an impact on the policy decisions made in the United States.

(SEE ALSO: *Alternative Life styles; American Families; Family Law; Family Planning; Family Size; Fertility Determinants; Marriage and Divorce Rates*)

REFERENCES

Brodkin, Evelyn Z., and Dennis Young 1989 "Making Sense of Privatization: What Can We Learn from Economic and Political Analysis?" In Sheila B. Kamerman and Alfred J. Kahn, eds., *Privatization and the Welfare State*. Princeton, N.J.: Princeton University Press.

Carlson, Allan C. 1988 *Family Questions: Reflections on the American Social Crisis*. New Brunswick, N.J.: Transaction Books.

Davis, Phillip W. 1997 "The Changing Meanings of Spanking." In Arlene S. Skolnick and Jerome S. Skolnick, eds., *Family in Transition*, 9th ed. New York: Longman.

Dumon, Wilfried, and Joan Aldous 1979 "European and United States Political Contexts for Family Policy Research." In Gerald W. McDonald and F. Ivan Nye, eds., *Family Policy*. Minneapolis: National Council on Family Relations.

Elshtain, Jean Bethke 1997. "Reflections on the Family at Century's End." In Gordon L. Anderson, ed., *The Family in Global Transition*. St. Paul, Minn. PWPA/ Paragon House.

Footlick, Jerold 1990 "What Happened to the American Family?" *Newsweek* (December 1990): 18.

Glendon, Mary Ann 1989 *The Transformation of Family Law: State, Law, and Family in the United States and Western Europe*. Chicago: University of Chicago Press.

Haavio-Mannila, Elina 1988 "Converging Tendencies in Gender Roles." Paper presented at symposium, Can America Continue to Learn from Sweden and Finland?, University of Delaware, Newark, Del. October.

——Kaisa Kauppinen 1990 "Women's Lives and Women's Work in the Nordic Countries." In Hilda Kehore and Janet Giele, eds., *Women's Lives and Women's Work in Modernizing and Industrial Countries*. Boulder, Colo.: Westview Press.

Hayghe, Howard V. 1990 "Family Members in the Work Force." *Monthly Labor Review* 113(3):14–19.

Herrstrom, Staffan 1986 "Swedish Family Policy. "*Current Sweden* 348 (September).

Kahn, Alfred J. 1969 *Theory and Practice in Social Planning*. New York: Russell Sage Foundation.

——, and Sheila B. Kammerman 1983 *Income Transfers for Families with Children*. Philadelphia: Temple University Press.

—— 1981 *Child Care, Family Benefits, and Working Parents: A Comparative Study*. New York: Columbia University Press.

Kittrie, Nicholas N. 1997 "Policy, Law and Family Stability: From Antiquity to the Dawn of the Third Millennium." In Gordon L. Anderson, ed., *The Family in Global Transition*. St. Paul, Minn.: Paragon House.

Lanca, Patricia 1997 "Feminism and the Family." In Gordon L. Anderson, ed., *The Family in Global Transition*. St. Paul, Minn.: Paragon House.

Laswell, Harold 1968 "The Policy Orientation." In Daniel Lerner and Harold Lasswell, eds., *Policy Sciences*. Stanford, Calif.: Stanford University Press.

Michel, Sonya 1998 "The Politics of Child Care in America's Public/Private Welfare State." In Karen V. Hansen and Anita Ilta Garey, eds., *Families in the U.S.: Kinship and Domestic Politics*. Philadelphia: Temple University Press.

Miller, Gary J. 1990 "A Contextual Approach to Child Development" (Working Paper No. 9) Minneapolis: The City Inc.

Myrdal, Alva 1967 "Forward." In Edmund Dahlstrom, ed., *The Changing Roles of Men and Women*. London: Gerald Duckworth.

Murray, Charles 1984 *Losing Ground: American Social Policy, 1950–1980*. New York: Basic Books.

Myrdal, Alva 1967 "Forward." In Edmund Dahlstrom, ed., *The Changing Roles of Men and Women*. London: Gerald Duckworth.

Phillips, Kevin 1990 *The Politics of Rich and Poor: Wealth and the American Electorate in the Reagan Aftermath*. New York: Random House.

Schorr, Alvin L. 1979 "Views of Family Policy." In Gerald McDonald and F. Ivan Nye, eds., *Family Policy*. Minneapolis: National Council on Family Relations.

Schorr, Lisbeth B. 1988 *Within Our Reach*. New York: Anchor Books.

——, C. Arden Miller, and Amy Fine 1986 "The Social Policy Context for Families Today." In Michael W. Yogman and T. Berry Brazeiton, eds., *In Support of Families*. Cambridge, Mass.: Harvard University Press.

Statistical Abstract of Sweden 1990 Stockholm: Statis-tiska Centralbyran.

Statistisches Jahrbuch fur die Bundesrepublik Deutschland 1989 Bonn: W. Kohlhammer.

Sweet, James A., and L. L. Bumpass 1987 *American Families and Households*. New York: Russell Sage Foundation.

U.S. Bureau of the Census 1990 *Statistical Abstract of the United States*. Washington, D.C.: U.S. Government Printing Office.

Van de Kaa, Kirk J. 1987 "Europe's Second Demographic Transition." *Population Bulletin* 42:1–57.

Wilson, William Julius 1987 *The Truly Disadvantaged: The Inner City, the Underclass, and Public Policy*. Chicago: University of Chicago Press.

—— 1988 *Understanding Family Policy*. Newbury Park, Calif.: Sage Publications.

Irving Tallman
Ginna M. Babcock

FAMILY ROLES

See Alternative Life Styles; American Families; Parental Roles.

FAMILY SIZE

Family size may be considered from two perspectives. At the individual (micro) level, it defines one aspect of an individual's family background or environment. As such, it represents a potential influence on the development and accomplishments of family members. At the societal (macro) level, family size is an indicator of societal structure that may vary over time, with concomitant implications for individual development and social relations in different cohorts. In this essay, consideration is given to both aspects of family size, as it is reflected in sociological theory and research.

While the term *family size* is sometimes used to represent the total number of individuals comprising a family unit, Treas (1981) argues convincingly for decomposing the concept into two components: numbers of children and numbers of adults in the household. This distinction is important, as observed patterns of change in overall family size may be attributable to one component or the other, as may effects of overall family size. In the present discussion, family size is defined in terms of the number of children in the household.

A further distinction is made between family size in the parental and filial households, sometimes referred to as the family of origin (or orientation) and the family of procreation. Some use the term *sibship size* to refer to the number of children in an individual's parental family (Blake 1989; Ryder 1986). However, the two are not directly comparable: Mean family size takes into account those families which have no children, while mean sibship size is necessarily restricted to families with children.

Family size can also be differentiated from fertility, which reflects the aggregate numbers of births relative to the numbers of women in the population, without regard for the distribution of those births across family units. Fertility and family size are both important characteristics of cohorts; however, for assessing relationships at the individual level, family size or sibship size is the more meaningful construct (Ryder 1986).

The subsequent sections address the following aspects of family size: demographic trends in family size, antecedents and correlates of family size, and implications of sibship size and family size for child and adult members of the family.

DEMOGRAPHIC TRENDS

The twentieth century has witnessed substantial change in both fertility and family size (as indicated by the number of children in the household), with the overall trend being toward smaller families. Such trends can be examined through comparisons of fertility rates and mean family size, and also through investigation of parity distributions—that is, the numbers of families with zero, one, two (and so on) children.

Drawing on fertility tables compiled by the National Center for Health Statistics, Ryder (1986) presents time-series data for successive cohorts of women in the United States born between 1867 and 1955 (and who would thus be bearing children between approximately 1885 and 1975) that show the following general trends in fertility and family size:

1. Total fertility declined by 52 percent in the period being considered, from 4.00 for women born in 1867–1870 to 1.92 for women born in 1951–1955. A similar rate of decline occurred in marital fertility.

2. This decline was punctuated by a temporary upsurge in fertility for women born in 1916–1940, who were bearing children during the two decades following World War II (the "baby boom" years).

3. Variation in fertility rates increased for cohorts through 1910 and since then has consistently decreased, suggesting that in recent years there have been fewer women bearing no children or large numbers of children and an increasing concentration of families of moderate size.

4. Family size (the mean number of children in the family) decreased by 61 percent from a high of 7.3 for women born in 1867–1870 to 2.8 for women born in 1951–1955.

It thus appears that during the period under consideration, mean family size decreased at an even faster rate than fertility. Further, the increased fertility during the baby boom years appears to have been offset by reduced variation in fertility for those cohorts of women, with the result that mean family size held relatively constant during that period, then continued its pattern of decline.

Treas (1981) examined changes in family size between 1955 and 1978 for whites and for nonwhites, using data from the March Current Population Surveys. Throughout the period, nonwhites consistently had larger families than did whites: In 1955 the mean number of children was 1.26 in white families and 1.80 in nonwhite families; in 1978 the corresponding figures were 1.04 and 1.56. During this period Treas found similar patterns of increases in family size through the 1960s, followed by decreasing family size in the 1970s, for both groups. However, the shifts were considerably more pronounced among nonwhite families.

Data obtained from the U.S. Census on the distribution of family sizes (parity distributions) provide further insight on the trend toward smaller families. During the years between 1970 and 1988 the proportion of families with no children under eighteen increased substantially, from 44 percent to 51 percent, while the proportion of families with one child or two children increased only slightly (from 18 percent to 21 percent and from 17 percent to 18 percent, respectively). However, the proportion of families with three or more children decreased markedly, from 20 percent to 10 percent during this period. Among black and Hispanic families, the increase in families with no children was not as pronounced as among white families, but the increases in families with one or two children were greater, as were the decreases in families with three or more children (U.S. Bureau of the Census 1990, p. 51).

Further insight into the decline in family size is provided by investigations of parity progression, or the probability of having (or intending to have) an additional child at each parity level. Decomposing his time-series data into parity progressions, Ryder (1986) reports that the baby boom was the result of an increase in progression from parities one and two, but that progression from parities three and higher have shown consistent declines. Similarly, data on intended parities show that the proportions intending progression from parity one have increased over time, while the intended progression ratios for parity three and higher have declined.

Other data on ideal, or normative, family sizes support this pattern of increasing concentration of smaller families. West and Morgan (1987) cite historical data showing that fertility norms have fluctuated in parallel with fertility rates and family sizes: During the 1930s and early 1940s two- and three-child families were preferred. During the post–World War II era three- and four-child families became the ideal, but in the late 1960s preferences reverted to the two- or three-child family. They further report that, among a sample of contemporary adults, a significant majority (64.8 percent) view the two-child family as ideal; that belief was surprisingly consistent across various subgroups defined by current family size, marital status, race, and religion.

At the same time that families have tended to become smaller on average, there has been increased variability in the timing of childbearing. One trend that has been widely noted has been the increase in childbearing among teenagers, particularly among those who are of lower socioeconomic statues (SES), nonwhite, and less academically able youth (Card and Wise 1978). At the same time, there has been an increase in the proportion of women who delay childbearing until their early and mid-thirties or who remain childless (Bloom and Trussell 1984). As will be discussed below, the timing of the first birth has implications for the eventual family size and thus for the development and accomplishment of family members.

In sum, in the United States there appears to have been a strong shift toward smaller families, with the ideal being a two- or three-child family. A similar trend toward smaller families is found in other developed countries, while in developing countries families are more likely to be larger (Lopreato and Yu 1988). One exception to this generalization concerns countries, such as the People's Republic of China, that are trying to implement a policy of restricting families to one child. However, while the policy appears to have led to lower mean family sizes, numerous families have continued to have two or more children, and a preferred family size of two continues to be the mode (Whyte and Gu 1987).

ANTECEDENTS AND CORRELATES OF FAMILY SIZE

Determinants of family size have been investigated at both the societal and the individual level. At the societal level, researchers have sought to account for differences in fertility and family size over time or between societies. Easterlin (1980) advanced the theory that changes in fertility and family size over time are a function of individuals' economic resources and aspirations. He attributes the baby boom surge in fertility and family size to the generation of young men following World War II who experienced high wages, as a result of the expanding economy, and had relatively low material aspirations, as a result of being raised during the Depression. Conversely, the baby boom generation confronted increased competition for jobs, which, combined with higher aspirations, led to the "baby bust" of the 1970s and 1980s. One implication of Easterlin's theory is that smaller birth cohorts are likely to experience more favorable labor markets, resulting in higher fertility.

A variation of this theory is espoused by Devaney (1983), who argues that the decline in fertility observed during the 1960s and 1970s can be attributed to increases in female wages and female employment, which in turn served to depress fertility, rather than to conscious decisions to limit fertility in the face of disadvantageous economic conditions. Her analyses, based on national fertility data and data on female labor-force participation rates and male and female earnings, suggest (1) that female labor-force participation and fertility are highly and negatively correlated and (2) that female wage rates are the dominant factor in explaining recent variations in fertility and female employment. While this model differs from Easterlin's in terms of the process by which economic factors are thought to influence fertility, they are similar in viewing fertility as a response to economic market conditions.

Studies of developing countries have focused on several sociocultural as well as socioeconomic factors associated with fertility and family size:

modernization (Levy 1985); contraceptive use and family-planning programs (Koenig et al. 1987); and cultural attitudes and values, such as the perceived old-age security value of children (Rani 1986) or the view of children as risk insurance (Robinson 1986).

At the individual level, researchers have examined the extent to which fertility and family size may vary depending on individuals' family backgrounds, social and psychological characteristics, or economic status. Inverse relationships between social class and family size have been documented in a number of data sets: Individuals from larger families tend to have less-well-educated fathers who have lower-status occupations. Also, farm background is associated with larger family sizes (Blake 1989).

Parents' sibship size (the number of siblings that each parent had) is a second major determinant of family size: Women and men from larger families are more likely to have larger families (Ben-Porath 1975; Thornton 1980). This gives rise to an apparent paradox: While there is an overall trend toward small families, a high proportion of children come from larger families (Blake 1989). This paradox arises from the distinction noted above between cohort fertility rates, which are based on all women or all families, and children's sibship sizes, which are necessarily limited to women or families who have had children.

Retherford and Sewell (1988) investigated the relationship between intelligence and family size in their analysis of data from the Wisconsin Longitudinal Study of the High School Class of 1957, finding that the overall relationship between IQ and family size was negative for both sexes. However, the relationship proved to be much stronger for females, who showed consistent declines in family size as IQ increased. Among men the relationship was less consistent. Retherford and Sewell also reviewed the results of other, earlier studies, noting that the negative relationship between IQ and family size appears to have become more pronounced in the post–baby boom cohorts.

Additional factors associated with family size pertain primarily to family and achievement-related characteristics of the mother: More education, later age at marriage, longer interval between marriage and the birth of the first child, and employment status are all associated with smaller families—that is, fewer children (Wagner et al. 1985). Family configuration has also been found to be associated with increased family size, with the probability of having an additional child being higher in families with all children of the same sex (Gualtieri and Hicks 1986). Also, only children are disproportionately likely to come from broken families (Blake 1989).

The interaction between wives' employment and childbearing has been a topic of much study, as women have increasingly entered or remained in the work force, but the results obtained are inconsistent. Waite and Stolzenberg (1976) found a significant negative relationship between wife's work and family size. However, based on analyses of longitudinal data that allowed for the study of recursive processes as well as inclusion of several additional measures, Bagozzi and Van Loo (1988) found no causal relationships between wife's employment and family size; they suggested that both labor-force participation and family size are codetermined by the wife's achievement motivation, sex-role norms, and perceived value of children.

Oropesa (1985) used data from the National Opinion Research Center (NORC) General Social Surveys to test the hypotheses represented in Easterlin's model at the micro level, using relative affluence as the predictor and expected family size as the outcome of interest. He found that relative affluence is more likely to be associated with expected births for women than for men, and that the effects are stronger with regard to expected births in the short term than with total expected family size.

The research cited above focuses on static determinants of childbearing and family size. However, some investigators have examined fertility and childbearing decisions as a dynamic process, influenced by life situation and life events, that may change over time, as well as by relatively fixed individual characteristics. One line of investigation has focused on timing of first birth as a determinant of eventual family size. Card and Wise (1978) and Hofferth and Moore (1979) demonstrated that early first births are associated with larger families; Bloom and Trussell (1984) similarly demonstrated that delayed childbearing is associated with smaller average family sizes, as well as with childlessness.

A second line of research has investigated the relationships between parity level and fertility decisions. Udry (1983) examined the relative influence of initial fertility plans and intervening life events (such as births during the interval, change in household income, change in education, female work status, change in marital satisfaction) on couple's fertility decisions at different parity levels. He found that including intervening events in the analyses improved the prediction of both fertility plans and, especially, actual fertility behavior, providing support for a sequential model of fertility decision making. White and Kim (1987) investigated whether the determinants of fertility choices vary by parity; they found a nonlinear relationship between fertility determinants and childbearing, especially with regard to factors related to women's roles. Both sex-role traditionalism and achievement in nonfamily roles were associated with a higher probability of having a child at parity zero or one, but a lower probability of having a child among women at higher parities. These findings are somewhat contrary to those based on cross-sectional analyses of family size, suggesting the importance of taking parity level into account in such investigations.

IMPLICATIONS OF SIBSHIP AND FAMILY SIZE

The effects of sibship/family size and family composition on children and on adults has long been a topic of popular interest and in recent years has become the focus of a considerable body of sociological and psychological inquiry. In particular, attention has been directed to effects of sibship size on children's cognitive development, physical and social-psychological development, educational attainment, and socioeconomic attainment and mobility. Consideration is also given to effects of family size on parents and on family well-being.

Cognitive Development. Interest in the relationship between sibship size and intelligence dates back to Anne Anastasi's (1956) review, which found an inverse relationship between the two. Subsequent empirical studies, in the United States as well as in Europe, using various measures of ability and controlling for family background characteristics, have confirmed this finding (Belmont and Marolla 1973; Breland 1974; Claudy et al. 1974). Blake (1989) provides a comprehensive review of this literature, including a discussion of limitations and weaknesses in the prior studies.

Only children present a special case. Numerous studies have reported that only children do not perform as well on intelligence measures as do children from two-child families. Indeed, in the Belmont and Marolla study (1973), only children were found to be lower in intelligence than first-borns in families up to size four, and lower than second-borns in families up to size three. Claudy and associates (1974) obtained similar results after controlling for differences in SES. However, when differences in family composition were taken into account by restricting the sample to only children in two-parent families, the differences between only children and first-born children in larger families became nonsignificant (Claudy et al. 1979).

In an effort to account for the observed relationships between sibship size and intellectual ability, Zajonc (1976) introduced the "confluence model," which postulates that the intellectual environment in the home, defined by the combined intellectual levels of the parents and children, accounts for the observed relationships. According to his theory, the intellectual level is at its peak in families with two adults and no children; as the number of children in the home increases, the intellectual environment afforded to any individual child is effectively diluted. There are two implications of the "confluence model": Children from smaller families should show higher intelligence, and children born earlier in families should show higher intelligence. While the former hypothesis has been supported by a number of empirical studies, the latter did not account for the findings pertaining to only children. In response, Zajonc expanded the confluence model, postulating that younger siblings provide an opportunity for teaching, thus enriching the intellectual experience of older children; the lower intellectual performance of only children is attributed to the fact that they cannot avail themselves of this opportunity. While the confluence model has generated considerable discussion and debate, particularly regarding possible interactions between family size and birth order, and with family SES (for example, see Steelman 1985; Zajonc 1986), a systematic test of the model remains to be conducted.

Blake (1989) identifies two limitations in the previous work: lack of differentiation of various kinds of intellectual ability (such as verbal and nonverbal) and potential interactions with SES. She finds that the inverse relationship between sibship size and intelligence holds for measures of verbal skill, but not for measures of nonverbal ability, and that the verbal ability deficits observed among children in large families are not limited to those from more disadvantaged backgrounds.

Physical and Social-Psychological Development. Compared with other outcome measures, relatively little attention has been given to the study of sibship-size effects on children's physical and social-psychological development. Mednick and associates (1985) and Wagner and associates (1985) provide brief reviews of this literature. Family size has been found to be inversely related to children's height and weight; it is also positively correlated with morbidity and mortality. With regard to social-psychological development, children from larger families have been found to have poorer self-concepts, to value conformity and self-control rather than independence and self-expression, and to show a greater tendency toward antisocial behavior. They are also less likely to be interested in white-collar occupations.

Blake (1989) investigated the relationship between sibship size and educational expectations, using data from three different cohorts of youth, and found that young people from smaller families, as well as from higher-status families, tend to have higher educational goals. These effects, however, are mediated through ability and grades as well as through parents' expectations.

Educational Attainment. Blake's (1989) book *Family Size and Achievement* provides the most comprehensive assessment to date of this area. Two sets of questions are addressed: First, does sibship size affect educational expectations and attainment, and if so, where in the educational process? Second, what is the relative importance of sibship size, relative to other measures of family background?

With regard to the first question, sibship size does appear to have a substantial effect on educational attainment. Individuals from small families had approximately two additional years of schooling, relative to their peers from larger families—net of differences attributable to parental characteristics. The greatest impact on education occurred at the high school level, with individuals from larger families more likely to drop out of high school.

With regard to the second question, relative to other background variables in the analysis, sibship size was consistently second in importance for years of schooling, behind father's education. However, the negative effects of large families were somewhat mitigated by high parental SES and by membership in certain religious or ethnic groups. Similarly, the effects of parental SES were somewhat mitigated for youth in small families.

Some have argued that sibship size is simply a proxy for otherwise unmeasured characteristics of parents' family background and does not exert any independent effect on education in its own right. To address this concern, Blake (1989) examined the extent to which children from different-sized families have different home environments that might, in turn, influence educational attainment. In particular, attention was given to characteristics of the home setting (such as time spent reading newspapers, reading books, watching television) and to parental behaviors directed toward the child (such as encouragement, correction, goal setting). Children from smaller families were more likely to spend time in intellectual and cultural pursuits, to spend time playing alone, to have been read to as children, and to have had music or dance lessons. However, no significant differences were found in parental values for their children or in parenting style after parents' education and SES were taken into account. Thus, while there appear to be differences in the home environments afforded to children in smaller versus larger families, these differences do not appear to be attributable to differences in parental values or parenting style.

Socioeconomic Attainment and Mobility. A long tradition of research has addressed the question of how family background conditions or constrains individuals' socioeconomic attainment and social mobility. While primary consideration has been given to the impact of family social resources (father's education and occupation) on children's attainment, sibship size also was found to be related to occupational attainment (Blau and Duncan 1967). Among both women and men, those from larger families were more likely to have lower-status jobs and lower earnings, even after adjusting for differences in fathers' SES and educational attainment, both of which are correlated

with family size. Among women, the effect of sibship size on earnings was stronger than the effect of father's occupation (Featherman and Hauser 1976). Using path analysis to model both indirect and direct relationships, however, Duncan and associates (1972) found that the negative effect of sibship size on men's occupational status could be accounted for primarily by the effect of sibship size on educational attainment. This finding lends some support to arguments that larger families result in a dilution of family economic resources, thus constraining the opportunities available to children.

Parents' Economic Well-Being. Duncan and associates (1972) examined the impact of family size (as contrasted with sibship size) as a contingency in men's socioeconomic attainment, finding a slight and negative effect on occupational status but a positive effect on earnings, net of other background variables. Studies that included women found evidence of reciprocal relationships between family size and labor-force participation, which in turn affected women's career attainment (Waite and Stolzenberg 1976). However, as noted previously, Bagozzi and Van Loo (1988) suggested that women's work and family size are not causally related but are mutually dependent on other, achievement-related characteristics of the wife.

Relationships have been reported between the timing of childbearing and subsequent economic well-being. Card and Wise (1978) found that teenage parents of both sexes tended to have less education, lower job prestige, and lower earnings, relative to later childbearers, net of differences in background characteristics. Investigating this relationship in greater depth, Hofferth and Moore (1979) found that the effects of early childbearing on women's subsequent earnings were primarily attributable to the larger family sizes of these women and to the consequent implications for (less) work experience. However, they also found that early childbearing was less of a handicap for black women, due to weaker relationships between early childbearing and subsequent education and employment. Hofferth (1984) found that among women aged 60 or over, the number of children per se was not related to measures of economic well-being, but that the timing of childbearing was: Those who delayed the first birth until after age thirty had higher family incomes and higher standards of living than did women

975

whose first child was born before age thirty. This relationship was most pronounced among delayed childbearers who had small families, suggesting an interaction between timing of childbearing and family size.

Massagli (1987) has argued for a life-cycle model of the process of stratification that incorporates information on family size in both the parental and the filial generations. He hypothesizes that sibship size does not affect socioeconomic attainment directly but, rather, is related to the timing of early life-cycle transitions and to marital fertility; the observed negative effects of sibship size on attainment are attributed to the product of the relationship with life-cycle transitions and marital fertility and the negative effect of marital fertility on attainment.

Parental Attitudes and Well-Being. Wagner and associates (1985) review a number of studies of effects of family size on parental attitudes and parental health. They find that parental attitudes and treatment of children vary with family size: Larger families are more family centered, with a greater role played by fathers; at the same time, parents in larger families tend to be more authoritarian and more inclined to treat all children alike. Parents in larger families have also been found to have poorer marital relations. Finally, men and women who have many children are at greater risk of hypertension and other physical ailments.

In sum, sibship size and family size both appear to exert significant influence on the children and on the parents. Sibship size is closely related to family socioeconomic background, however, which is also a major influence on children's development and attainment. As a result, care must be taken to differentiate between effects of sibship size per se and effects of socioeconomic background. Similarly, family size among adults (the number of children they have) is highly correlated with socioeconomic status, intelligence, and other characteristics; again, it is important to consider the effects of family size net of these other factors. In many instances, the effects of sibship size and family size appear to be indirect. For example, sibship size is highly correlated with educational attainment and thus with subsequent occupational attainment. Similarly, among adults, family size is correlated with employment and thus with socioeconomic attainment. Finally, family size is often closely related to other characteristics of the family: Among children, it may be related to birth order, and among parents, it may be related to the timing of childbearing. Understanding these indirect as well as direct relationships yields a better understanding of the ways in which, and the extent to which, sibship size and family size may affect the lives of children and adults.

AT THE TURN OF THE CENTURY

The United States—as well as other developed and developing countries—has witnessed significant changes in fertility patterns and in family structure, which together combine to impact family size. This closing section reviews the more salient of these developments and examines how they have been reflected in recent sociological and demographic research.

Family Size and Fertility. Because family size is inextricably linked to fertility, it has been impacted by the fertility transition (i.e., the change from higher to lower rates of fertility) that has been well documented in the United States and is now being seen in both developed and developing societies elsewhere in the world. In the United States fertility has remained relatively constant since the early 1980s, ranging from 1.7 to 1.9 births per woman. However, this apparent stability masks a dramatic shift toward having children at later ages, especially among white women (Chen and Morgan 1991) and more highly educated women (Rindfuss et al. 1996).

The stability seen in the United States is in sharp contrast to Europe, where most countries have experienced significant declines in fertility during this period, and to many developing countries, which are also now evidencing fertility declines (Rutenberg and Diamond 1993; Thomas and Muvandi 1994). Global fertility projections for the twenty-first century (released by the United Nations in 1992) range from 1.7 to 2.5 births per woman (Cohen 1996). These declines have been linked to three factors:

1. Widespread changes in the *social and economic roles and opportunities* available to women, including the increased availability of child care (Hirschman and Guest 1990; Mason and Kuhlthau 1992; Rindfuss et al. 1996)

2. Increased availability of *contraception and family-planning services*, as well as in some developing countries policies supporting fertility limitation in some developing countries (Axinn 1992; DeGraff 1991; Lavely and Freedman 1990; Njogu 1991)

3. Changes in the *social norms governing childbearing and child rearing*, including the emerging concept of "numeracy" about children—that is, the idea of having a particular family size as a goal—in developing countries (van de Walle 1992)

Corresponding decreases in actual and expected family size are also seen for this period. The average family size in 1993 was 3.16, down from 3.29 in 1980; similarly, the proportion of family households with three or more children had fallen by half since 1970 (Dortch 1993). On the 1994 General Social Survey 55 percent of Americans reported that they preferred two-child families—up from 41 percent in 1972—while the percentage of preferring substantially larger families declined commensurately. By 1988, the proportion of women expecting to remain childless had increased to 9 percent (National Center for Health Statistics 1996).

Family Size and Family Structure. Family size is also closely linked to family structure and to changes in patterns of family formation. Two somewhat related changes in particular have significantly impacted the size of family units: increased rates of marital dissolution and increased rates of out-of-wedlock births, both of which have contributed to a dramatic increase in single-parent family units.

Rates of *marital dissolution* have increased dramatically, both in the United States and elsewhere. In the United States more than half of all marriages are now expected to end in divorce; in less developed countries, approximately 25 percent of first marriages, on average, have dissolved as a result of death, divorce, or separation (Bruce et al. 1995). Not only does marital dissolution contribute directly to smaller family size (Lillard and Waite 1993); it also has an indirect effect—maternal divorce not followed by remarriage substantially reduces children's preferred family size (Axinn and Thornton 1996).

Beginning in the 1980s, women were increasingly likely to have *children out of wedlock*, signaling a significant change in the norms governing childbearing. By the early 1990s, 2 out of 3 black children and nearly 1 of 4 white children were born to unmarried mothers (Smith et al. 1996). One-fourth of these out-of-wedlock births were to cohabiting couples (Bumpass 1990). Thus, while fewer women were marrying and staying married, alternative family structures involving children were emerging.

The number of *single-parent families* in the United States grew dramatically from 1960 (10.5 percent) to 1990 (23.3 percent) (Garasky and Meyer, 1996). As a result, it is estimated that half of today's young children will spend some time in single-parent family (Bumpass 1990). While the majority of single-parent family units are headed by the mother, the number of father-only families has grown at nearly twice the rate as the number of mother-only families. Nor is this phenomenon limited to the United States: In the former Soviet Union, the proportion of households headed by a single parent doubled in the fifteen-year period from 1980 to 1995 to 20 percent; in developing countries, the incidence of female-headed households as of 1995 ranged from 11 percent in the Philippines, to 13 percent in Mexico, to 19 percent in Cameroon, to more than 25 percent in Hong Kong (Bruce et al. 1995).

Implications for the Study of Family Size. Returning to the framework initially presented in this essay, what are the implications of these trends and developments for the conceptualization of the "family" and "family size," and for research on the correlates and implications of family size?

Conceptualization of the "family" and "family size." The decreasing variance in family size is being offset by increasing complexity in family structure. In addition to the growing interest in single-parent families—and within that category, differentiation of mother-only and father-only families—researchers also identify nonmarital cohabitation (Bumpass 1990), parent-stepparent and blended families (Astone and McLanahan 1991; Dortch 1993; Wojtkiewicz 1993), and intergenerational households (Macunovich and Easterlin 1990). This evolving conceptualization of the family and—in particular—family structure is of interest not only in its own right but also for its implications for models of intergenerational transmission of status, resources, and values (Smith et al. 1996).

Correlates of changes in family size and structure. Increasingly research is directed toward linking social change at a macro level to individual-level fertility behavior. Structural factors, including increased labor-force participation of women (Rindfuss et al 1996), availability of contraceptive technology (Lavely and Freedman 1990), and availability of child care (Mason and Kuhlthau 1992; Rindfuss et al. 1996), continue to be a subject of study in both developed and developing countries. Of equal interest is the social context surrounding childbearing decisions, including the husband's and wife's own values regarding desired family size (Thomson 1997; Thomson et al. 1990), their parents' preferences and behavior (Axinn et al. 1994; Axinn and Thornton 1996), and societal norms (van de Walle 1992). As increasing attention is given to fertility transitions occurring in other countries, attention is also being given to identifying cultural factors that can potentially bias data and findings, such as nonresponse or qualitative responses to questions about expected or desired family size (Hermalin and Liu 1990; Riley et al. 1993).

Implications of changes in family size and structure. Considerable attention continues to be devoted to studying the impact of family size and structure on children's achievement. The inverse relationship between family size and children's attainment that has been widely documented in the United States is also observed in a number of developing countries, including Thailand (Knodel and Wonsith 1991), Vietnam (Anh et al. 1998), Ghana (Lloyd and Gage-Brandon 1995), and Israel (Shavit and Pierce 1991). Research is increasingly focusing on delineating the processes underlying these relationships, including the greater availability of parental economic and interpersonal resources in smaller families (Downey 1995; Macunovich and Easterlin 1990; Powell and Steelman 1993). Similarly, studies of the negative impact of marital disruption on children's achievement also explore how social factors such as reductions in parental expectations and involvement mediate this relationship (Astone and McLanahan 1991; Wojtkiewicz 1993).

These changes in family size and structure have significant implications for policy as well as for research. Domestically, Dortch (1993) raises the question of how the trend toward smaller families will impact caring and support relationships for older family members, especially as the number of older American increases over the next few decades. In developing countries, where many governments are proactively working to foster economic development and social well-being, policies supporting lower fertility and smaller families may have both direct and indirect benefits: As the number of children coming from smaller families increases, so too should their prospects for educational and economic attainment (Knodel and Wonsith 1991).

(SEE ALSO: *Family Planning; Family Policy in Western Societies; Fertility Determinants*)

REFERENCES

Anastasi, A. 1956 "Intelligence and Family Size." *Psychological Bulletin* 53:187–209.

Anh, Truong Si, John Knodel, David Lam, and Jed Friedman 1998 "Family Size and Children's Education in Vietnam." *Demography* 35(1):57–70.

Astone, Nan M., and Sara S. McLanahan 1991 "Family Structure, Parental Practices, and High School Completion." *American Sociological Review*, 56 (June):309–320.

Axinn, William G. 1992 "Family Organization and Fertility Limitation in Nepal." *Demography* 27(4):503–521.

——, Marin E. Clarkberg, and Arland Thornton 1994 "Family Influences on Family Size Preferences." *Demography* 31(1):65–79.

——, and Arland Thornton 1996 "The Influence of Parents' Marital Dissolutions on Children's Attitudes Toward Family Formation." *Demography* 33(1):66–81.

Bagozzi, Richard P., and M. Frances Van Loo 1988 "An Investigation of the Relationship Between Work and Family Size Decisions over Time." *Multivariate Behavioral Research* 23:3–34.

Belmont, L., and F. A. Marolla 1973 "Birth Order, Family Size, and Intelligence." *Science* 182:1096–1101.

Ben-Porath, Y. 1975 "First-Generation Effects on Second-Generation Fertility." *Demography* 12:397–405.

Blake, Judith 1986 "Number of Siblings, Family Background, and the Process of Educational Attainment." *Social Biology* 33:5–21.

——1989 *Family Size and Achievement.* Berkeley: University of California Press.

Blau, Peter M., and Otis D. Duncan 1967 *The American Occupational Structure.* New York: Free Press.

Bloom, David E., and James Trussell 1984 "What Are the Determinants of Delayed Childbearing and Permanent Childlessness in the United States?" *Demography* 21:591–611.

Breland, H. M. 1974 "Birth Order, Family Configuration, and Verbal Achievement." *Child Development* 45:1011–1019.

Bruce, Judith, Cynthia B. Lloyd, and Ann Leonard 1995 *Families in Focus: New Perspectives on Mothers, Fathers, and Children.* New York: Population Council.

Bumpass, Larry L. 1990 "What's Happening to the Family? Interactions Between Demographic and Institutional Change." *Demography* 27(4):483–498.

Card, Josefina J., and Lauress L. Wise 1978 "Teenage Mothers and Teenage Fathers: The Impact of Early Childbearing on the Parents' Personal and Professional Lives." *Family Planning Perspectives* 10:199–205.

Chen, Renbao, and S. Philip Morgan 1991 "Recent Trends in the Timing of First Births in the United States." *Demography* 28(4):513–533.

Claudy, John G., William S. Farrell, Jr., and Charles W. Dayton 1979 "The Consequences of Being an Only Child: An Analysis of Project TALENT Data." Final report. Palo Alto, Calif.: American Institutes for Research.

Claudy, John G., David E. Gross, and Rebecca D. Strause 1974 "Two Population Studies: I. Family Size, Birth Order, and Characteristics of Young Adults, and II. A Study of Married Couples in Knox County, Tennessee." Final report. Palo Alto, Calif.: American Institutes for Research.

Cohen, Joel E. 1996 "How Many Can the Earth Support?" *American Demographics.*

DeGraff, Deborah S. 1991 "Increasing Contraceptive Use in Bangladesh: The Role of Demand and Supply Factors." *Demography* 28(1):65–81.

Devaney, Barbara 1983 "An Analysis of Variations in U.S. Fertility and Female Labor Force Participation Trends." *Demography* 20:147–161.

Dortch, Shannon 1993 "The Future of Kinship." *American Demographics.*

Downey, Douglas B. 1995 "When Bigger Is Not Better: Family Size, Parental Resources, and Children's Educational Performance." *American Sociological Review* 60 (October):746–761.

Duncan, Otis D., David L. Featherman, and Beverly Duncan 1972 *Socioeconomic Background and Achievement.* New York: Seminar Press.

Easterlin, Richard A. 1980 *Birth and Fortune.* New York: Basic Books.

Featherman, David L., and Robert M. Hauser 1976 "Sexual Inequalities and Socioeconomic Achievement." *American Sociological Review* 41:462–483.

Garasky, Steven, and Daniel R. Meyer 1996 "Reconsidering the Increase in Father-Only Families." *Demography* 33(3):385–393.

Gualtieri, C. Thomas, and Robert E. Hicks 1986 "Family Configuration and Family Size." *Social Biology* 33:146–147.

Hermalin, Albert I., and Xian Liu 1990 "Gauging the Validity of Responses to Questions on Family Size Preferences in China." *Population and Development Review* 16(2):337–354.

Hirschman, Charles, and Philip Guest 1990 "Multilevel Models of Fertility Determination in Four Southeast Asian Countries: 1970 and 1980." *Demography* 27(3):369–396.

Hofferth, Sandra L. 1984 "Long-Term Economic Consequences for Women of Delayed Childbearing and Reduced Family Size." *Demography* 21:141–155.

——, and Kristin A. Moore 1979 "Early Childbearing and Later Economic Well Being." *American Sociological Review* 44:784–815.

Knodel, John, and Malinee Wonsith 1991 "Family Size and Children's Education in Thailand: Evidence from a National Sample." *Demography* 28(1):119–131.

Koenig, Michael A., James F. Phillips, Ruth S. Simmons, and Mehrab A. Khan 1987 "Trends in Family Size Preferences and Contraceptive Use in Matlab, Bangladesh." *Studies in Family Planning* 18:117–127.

Lavely, William, and Ronald Freedman 1990 "The Origins of the Chinese Fertility Decline." *Demography* 27(3):357–367.

Levy, Victor 1985 "Cropping Pattern, Mechanization, Child Labor, and Fertility Behavior in a Farming Economy: Rural Egypt." *Economic Development and Cultural Change* 33:777–791.

Lillard, Lee A., and Linda J. Waite 1993 "A Joint Model of Marital Childbearing and Marital Disruption." *Demography* 30(4):653–681.

Lloyd, Cynthia B., and Anastasia J. Gage-Brandon. 1995 *Does Sibsize Matter? The Implications of Family Size for Children's Education in Ghana* (Working Paper no. 45). New York: Population Council.

Lopreato, Joseph, and Mai-yu Yu 1988 "Human Fertility and Fitness Optimization." *Ethology and Sociobiology* 9:269–289.

Macunovich, Diane J., and Richard A. Easterlin 1990 "Life Cycle Demographic Decisions and the Economic Status of Young Children." *Population and Development Review* 16(2):301–325.

Mason, Karen O., and Karen Kuhlthau 1992 "The Perceived Impact of Child Care Costs on Women's Labor Supply and Fertility." *Demography* 29(4): 523–543.

Massagli, Michael P. 1987 "Effects of Family Size on the Process of Stratification: A Structural Equation Model for White Couples in the U.S. in 1962 and 1973." In Robert V. Robinson, ed. *Research in Social Stratification and Mobility*, vol. 6. Greenwich, Conn.: JAI Press.

Mednick, Birgitte R., Robert L. Baker, and Dennis Hocevar 1985 "Family Size and Birth Order Correlates of Intellectual, Psychosocial, and Physical Growth." *Merrill-Palmer Quarterly* 31:67–84.

National Center for Health Statistics 1996 "Birth Expectations of Women in the United States, 1973–88."

Njogu, Wamucii 1991 "Contraceptive Use in Kenya: Trends and Determinants." *Demography* 28(1): 83–99.

Oropesa, R. S. 1985 "Subject Relative Affluence and Expected Family Size." *Sociology and Social Research* 69:501–515.

Powell, Brian, and Lala Carr Steelman 1993 "The Educational Benefits of Being Spaced Out: Sibship Density and Educational Progress." *American Sociological Review* 58 (June):367–381.

Rani, Usha D. 1986 "Old Age Security Value of Children and Fertility in Relation to Social Policy." Paper presented at the annual meeting of the International Sociological Association.

Retherford, Robert D., and William H. Sewell 1988 "Intelligence and Family Size Reconsidered." *Social Biology* 35:1–40.

Riley, Ann P., Albert I. Hermalin, and Luis Rosero-Bixby 1993 "A New Look at the Determinants of Non-Numeric Response to Desired Family Size: The Case of Costa Rica." *Demography* 30(2):159–174.

Rindfuss, Ronald R., S. Philip Morgan, and Kate Offutt 1996 "Education and the Changing Age Pattern of American Fertility: 1963–1989." *Demography* 33(3):277–290.

Robinson, W. C. 1986 "High Fertility as Risk-Insurance." *Population Studies* 40:289–298.

Rutenberg, Naomi, and Ian Diamond 1993 "Fertility in Botswana: The Recent Decline and Future Prospects." *Demography* 30(2):143–157.

Ryder, Norman B. 1986 "Observations on the History of Cohort Fertility in the United States." *Population and Development Review* 12:617–643.

Shavit, Yossi, and Jennifer L. Pierce 1991 "Sibship Size and Educational Attainment in Nuclear and Extended Families: Arabs and Jews in Israel." *American Sociological Review* 56 (June):321–330.

Smith, Herbert L., S. Philip Morgan, and Tanya Koropeckyj-Cox 1996 "A Decomposition of Trends in the Nonmarital Fertility Ratios of Blacks and Whites in the United States, 1960–1992." *Demography* 33(2):141–151.

Steelman, Lala C. 1985 "A Tale of Two Variables: A Review of the Intellectual Consequences of Sibship Size and Birth Order." *Review of Educational Research* 55:353–386.

Thomas, Duncan, and Ityai Muvandi 1994 "The Demographic Transition in Southern Africa: Another Look at the Evidence from Botswana and Zimbabwe." *Demography* 31 (2):185–207.

Thomson, Elizabeth 1997 "Couple Childbearing Desires, Intentions, and Births." *Demography* 34(3):343–354.

——, Elaine McDonald, and Larry L. Bumpass 1990 "Fertility Desires and Fertility: Hers, His, and Theirs." *Demography* 27(4):579–600.

Thornton, A. 1980 "The Influence of First Generation Fertility and Economic Status on Second Generation Fertility." *Population and Environment* 3:51–72.

Treas, Judith 1981 "Postwar Trends in Family Size." *Demography* 18:321–334.

Udry, J. Richard 1983 "Do Couples Make Fertility Plans One Birth at a Time?" *Demography* 20:117–128.

U.S. Bureau of the Census 1990 *Statistical Abstract of the United States: 1990*. Washington, D.C.: U.S. Government Printing Office.

van de Walle, Etienne 1992 "Fertility Transition, Conscious Choice, and Numeracy." *Demography* 29(4):487–502.

Wagner, Mazie E., Herman J. P. Schubert, and Daniel S. P. Schubert 1985 "Family Size Effects: A Review." *Journal of Genetic Psychology* 146:65–78.

Waite, Linda J., and Ross M. Stolzenberg 1976 "Intended Childbearing and Labor Force Participation of Young Women: Insights from Nonrecursive Models." *American Sociological Review* 41:235–252.

West, Kirsten K., and Leslie A. Morgan 1987 "Public Perceptions of the Ideal Number of Children for Contemporary Families." *Population and Environment* 9:160–171.

White, Lynn K., and Hyunju Kim 1987 "The Family-Building Process: Childbearing Choices by Parity." *Journal of Marriage and the Family* 49:271–279.

Whyte, Martin K., and S. Z. Gu 1987 "Popular Response to China's Fertility Transition." *Population and Development Review* 13:471–494.

Wojtkiewicz, Roger A. 1993 "Simplicity and Complexity in the Effects of Parental Structure on High School Graduation." *Demography* 30(4):701–717.

Zajonc, Robert B. 1976 "Family Configuration and Intelligence." *Science* 192:227–236.

——1986 "Family Factors and Intellectual Test Performance: A Reply to Steelman." *Review of Educational Research* 56:365–371.

LAURI STEEL

FAMILY VIOLENCE

Physical violence of all types, from slaps to murder, probably occurs more frequently in the family than in any other setting or group except the armed services or police in time of war or riot. This article summarizes the prevalence rates and examines reasons for the high rates, with emphasis on the characteristics of the family as a social institution and on social inequality.

Physical violence is defined as an act carried out with the intention or perceived intention of causing physical pain or injury to another person (Gelles and Straus 1979). For certain purposes, the term "assault" is preferable because much intrafamily violence is a statutory crime. However, not all violence is criminal. Hitting a misbehaving child is legal and expected in all but a few countries. Corporal punishment of an "errant wife" was legal under common law in the United States until the 1870s (Calvert 1974).

Child abuse was not regarded as a widespread social problem by sociologists, family therapists, or the public until the 1960s (Nelson 1984; Pfohl 1977), and wife beating not until the women's movement made it a national issue in the mid-1970s. The subsequent emergence of public concern about and research on these and other aspects of family violence reflects major social changes, including the following:

1. The social activism of the 1960s, which sought to aid oppressed groups of all types, was extended to this aspect of the oppression of children and women.

2. The rising homicide and assault rates, violent political and social protest and assassinations, terrorist activity, and the Vietnam War sensitized people to violence.

3. Disenchantment with the family in the 1960s and early 1970s facilitated the perception of negative features of family life, including violence.

4. The growth of paid employment by married women provided the economic means for them no longer to tolerate the abuse that had long been the lot of women.

5. The reemerged women's movement made battering a central issue in the mid-1970s and gave it wide publicity.

6. The creation by the women's movement of a new social institution—shelters for battered women—did more than provide material assistance. Shelters were ideologically important because they concretized and publicized a phenomenon that had previously been ignored.

7. Changes in theoretical perspectives in sociology put the consensus model of society under attack by conflict theory. The inevitability of conflict in all human groups, including the family, was recognized, along with the possibility of violent conflict.

PREVALENCE OF FAMILY VIOLENCE

Homicide. In the United States, about one-quarter of all murders involve family members (Straus 1986). In other industrialized countries the percentage is much higher, for example, 40 percent in Canada and 67 percent in Denmark (Straus 1987). These high percentages occur because Canada has a low homicide rate and Denmark an even lower one: The few family homicides that occur are a large proportion of the low overall rate. This suggests that when homicide has been almost eliminated in a society, such as in Denmark, the family is the setting in which it is most likely to persist. Homicides of domestic partners have been decreasing in the United States since the mid 1970s (Greenfeld et al. 1998) and in Canada (Fedorowycz 1999).

OFFICIAL STATISTICS ON CHILD ABUSE AND SPOUSE ABUSE

National statistics on child abuse in the United States have been published since 1976. These statistics vastly underestimate the actual extent of child abuse. Many times more children are severely beaten each year but do not come to public attention. Officially reported cases grew from about 600,000 in 1976 to about 3 million annually in the mid-1990s. However, rather than being a 400 percent increase, the growth in cases reported to child protective services reflects social changes such as mandatory child abuse reporting laws, hot lines, child abuse education campaigns, an increasingly educated population, and a growth in professionals concerned with aiding and protecting children. These changes led the public and professionals to report cases that previously would have been ignored. This is consistent with historical and survey evidence suggesting that the true incidence of physical child abuse has been slowly decreasing since the late seventeenth century (Radbill 1987; Straus and Gelles 1986).

There are no official statistics for the United States on violence between spouses because the Uniform Crime Reporting System used by almost all police departments does not record the relationship between victim and offender. A new "incident-based reporting system" includes that information and is now being used in twelve states. However, because only about 7 percent of domestic assaults come to the attention of the police (Kaufman Kantor and Straus 1990), the new system will uncover only a small fraction of the cases. A similar problem makes the U.S. National Crime Survey (Gaquin 1977–1978; U.S. Department of Justice 1980) vastly underestimate the incidence of wife beating (Straus 1999). The public tends to consider assault by a spouse as a "family problem" rather than a "crime" and rarely informs the survey interviewer of such events.

The National Family Violence Surveys. National surveys of U.S. families were conducted in 1975 (Straus et al. 1980) and 1985 (Gelles and Straus 1988), and national surveys focused on specific aspects of family violence were conducted in 1992 (Kaufman Kantor et al. 1994) and 1995 (Straus et al. 1998). These studies provide a better estimate of the prevalence of family violence than is possible from police statistics or crime studies. They were made possible by the development of the "Conflict Tactics Scales" to measure family violence (Straus 1990; Straus et al. 1996). The resulting rates, which are based on the 6,002 households surveyed in 1985, are many times greater

than rates based on cases known to child welfare professionals, the police, shelters, or the National Crime Survey, but they are still believed to be lower-bound estimates.

Sixteen percent of the couples surveyed reported one or more incidents involving physical violence during the previous twelve months. Attacks by husbands on wives that were serious enough to warrant the term "wife beating" (because they involved punching, biting, kicking, choking, etc.) were reported for 3.2 percent of wives, resulting in a lower-bound estimate of 1.7 million beaten women. The National Family Violence Surveys, and all other studies of marital violence that do not use samples selected from the clientele of shelters and similar agencies, find that women assault their husbands at about the same rate as men assault their wives (Straus 1999); however, women are injured at seven times the rate of injury to men (Stets and Straus 1990; Straus 1990).

The most violent role within the family is that of parent, because almost all parents use corporal punishment (Straus and Stewart 1999). More than a third of the parents of infants in the 1995 survey reported hitting their child that year. Ninety-four percent of parents of three- to five-year-old children used corporal punishment. The percentage decreased steadily from age five on, but one-third of parents of children in their early teens reported hitting the child that year.

Child abuse is more difficult to operationalize than *corporal punishment* because the line differentiating *abuse* from *physical punishment* is to a considerable extent a matter of social norms. If one includes hitting a child with an object such a belt, paddle, or hairbrush, the 1995 national survey data found a rate of 4.9 percent (Straus et al. 1998), which is twelve times higher than the rate of cases reported to protective service agencies in 1995.

Intrafamily relationships between children are also extremely violent. But, like the violence of parents, it is not perceived as such because there is an implicit normative tolerance. Almost all young children hit a sibling, and more than a third hit a parent. Even in their late teens (age fifteen to seventeen), the rate of violence between siblings is enormous: More than two-thirds of that age group hit a sibling during the year of the survey.

EXPLANATIONS OF FAMILY VIOLENCE

Numerous family characteristics affect the level of family violence, several of which are discussed below.

High Level of Family Conflict. One characteristic of the family that helps account for the high rate of violence is its inherently high level of conflict. One reason for high conflict is that, as in other primary groups, family members are concerned with "the whole person." Consequently, there are more issues over which conflict can occur than in nonprimary relationships. Moreover, when conflict does occur, the deep commitment makes arguments emotionally charged. A disagreement about music with colleagues at work is unlikely to have the same emotional intensity as when children favor rock and parents favor Bach. The likelihood of conflicts is further multiplied because families usually consist of both males and females and parents and children, thus juxtaposing differences in the orientations and interests of different genders and generations. The family is the prime locus of the "battle of the sexes" and the "generation gap."

Norms Tolerating or Requiring Violence. Although conflict is endemic in families, it is not the only group or institution with a high level of conflict. Conflict is also high in academic departments and congressional committees, yet physical violence is practically nonexistent in those groups. Additional factors are needed to explain why violence is so much more frequent in the family than in other groups. One of these is the existence of cultural norms that tolerate or require violence. The clearest example is the right of parents to use corporal punishment to correct and control a child. At least two-thirds of Americans believe that "it is sometimes necessary to discipline a child with a good hard spanking" (Straus and Mathur 1996). These norms contrast with those prevailing within other institutions. Even prison authorities are no longer permitted to use corporal punishment.

Similar norms apply to husband–wife relations. However, they are implicit and taken for granted, and therefore largely unrecognized. Just as parenthood gives the right to hit, so the marriage license is also an implicit hitting license (Gelles and Straus 1988; Greenblat 1983). As with other licenses, rules limit its use. Slapping a spouse, for example, is tolerable if the spouse is perceived to be persisting in a serious wrong and "won't listen to reason." Many of the men and women interviewed by Gelles (1974) expressed this normative principle with such phrases as "I asked for it" or "She needed to be brought to her senses" (p. 58).

The common law right of a husband to use corporal punishment on an "errant wife" was recognized by U.S. courts until the late nineteenth century (Calvert 1974). Informally, it lived on in the behavior of the public, the police, and the courts, and it continues to do so. Under pressure from the women's movement, this is changing, but slowly. There have been major reforms of police and legal procedures, but the general public and many police officers continue to believe that "it's their own business" if spouses are violent to each other, provided the blow is not severe enough to cause an injury that requires medical treatment, whereas they would not tolerate a similar pattern of assault in an office, factory, or church. Only a very small percent of men believe that a legal sanction would be likely if they assaulted their wife (Carmody and Williams 1987). In one study, of the more than 600 women who were assaulted by their husbands, the police were involved in only 6.7 percent of the incidents and an arrest was made in only five cases (Kaufman Kantor and Straus 1990). The probability of legal sanction for assaulting a wife is even less than the .008 indicated by those five cases, because two-thirds of the 600 women were assaulted more than once during the year of the survey.

Family Socialization in Violence. In a certain sense it begs the question to attribute the high rate of family violence to norms that tolerate, permit, or require violence because it does not explain why the norms for families are different from those for other social groups or institutions. There are a number of reasons, but one of the most fundamental is that the family is the setting in which physical violence is first experienced and in which the normative legitimacy of violence is learned. As noted above, corporal punishment is experienced by at least 94 percent of American children (Straus and Stewart 1999). Corporal punishment is used to teach that certain types of behavior are not condoned, but simultaneously, social learning processes teach the legitimacy of and behavioral script for violence.

The example of corporal punishment also links love with violence. Since corporal punishment begins in infancy, parents are the first, and usually the only, ones to hit an infant. From the earliest level of psychosocial development, children learn that those to whom they are most closely bonded are also those who hit. Second, since corporal punishment is used to train the child in morally correct behavior or to teach about danger to be avoided, it establishes the normative legitimacy of hitting other family members. Third, corporal punishment teaches the cultural script for use of violence. For example, parents often refrain from hitting until their anger or frustration reaches a certain point. The child therefore learns that anger and frustration justify the use of physical force.

As a result of these social learning processes, use of violence becomes internalized and generalized to other social relationships, especially such intimate relationships as husband and wife and parent and child. The National Family Violence Surveys found that the more corporal punishment experienced as a child, the higher the probability of hitting a spouse (Straus et al. 1980; Straus and Yodanis 1996). Many children do not even need to extrapolate from corporal punishment of children to other relationships because they directly observe role models of physical violence between their parents.

Gender Inequality. Despite egalitarian rhetoric and the trend toward a more egalitarian family structure, male dominance in the family and in other spheres remains an important cause of family violence (Straus 1976). Most Americans continue to think of the husband as the "head of the family," and many believe that status gives him the right to have the final say. This sets the stage for violence, because force is ultimately necessary to back up the right to have the final say (Goode 1974).

Numerous structural patterns sustain the system of male dominance: The income of women employed full time is about a third lower than the income of men, and money is a source of power. Men tend to marry women who are younger, shorter, and less well educated; and age, physical size, and education form a basis for exercising power. Thus, the typical marriage begins with an advantage to the man. If the initial advantage changes or is challenged, many men feel morally justified in using their greater size and strength to maintain the right to have the final say, which they perceive to have been agreed on at the time of the marriage (LaRossa 1980). As a result, male-dominant marriages have been found to have the highest rate of wife beating (Coleman and Straus 1986; Straus et al. 1980), and societies in which male-dominant marriages prevail have higher rates of marital violence than more egalitarian societies (Levinson 1989; Straus 1994).

The privileged economic position of men also helps to explain why beaten wives so often stay with an assaulting husband (Kalmuss and Straus 1983). Women with full-time jobs earn only about 65 percent of what men earn (U.S. Bureau of the Census 1992). When marriages end, children stay with the mother in about 90 percent of the cases. Child support payments are typically inadequate and often defaulted on after a year or two. No-fault divorce has worked to the economic disadvantage of women (Weitzmen 1986). Consequently, many women stay in violent marriages because the alternative is bringing up their children in poverty.

Other Factors. Many other factors contribute to the high rate of intrafamily violence in the United States, even though they do not explain why the family is, on the average, more violent than other groups. Space permits only some of these to be identified briefly.

The empirical evidence shows that the greater the number of stressful events experienced by a family, the higher the rate of marital violence and child abuse (Makepeace 1983; Straus 1980; Straus and Kaufman Kantor 1987). In addition to specific stressful events that impinge on families, chronic stresses, such as marital conflict and poverty, are also strongly associated with child abuse and spouse abuse.

Almost all studies find a strong association between drinking and family violence (Coleman and Straus 1983; Kaufman Kantor and Straus 1987). However, even though heavy drinkers have two to three times the violence rate of abstainers, most heavy drinkers do *not* engage in spouse abuse or child abuse (Kaufman Kantor and Straus 1987).

The higher the level of nonfamily violence in a society, the higher the rate of child abuse and spouse abuse (Levinson 1989; Straus 1977). The nonfamily violence can be in the form of violent crime or socially legitimate violence such as warfare. The carryover of violent behavior from one sphere of life to another may be strongest when the societal violence is "legitimate violence" rather than "criminal violence," because most individual acts of violence are carried out to correct some perceived wrong. Archer and Gartner (1984) and Huggins and Straus (1980) (1980) found that war is associated with an increase in interpersonal violence. Straus constructed an index to measure differences between the states of the United States in the extent to which violence was used or supported for socially legitimate purposes, such as corporal punishment in the schools or expenditure per capita on the National Guard (Baron and Straus 1989). The higher the score of a state on this Legitimate Violence Index, the higher the rate of *criminal* violence such as homicide (Baron and Straus 1988) and rape (Baron and Straus 1989).

Family violence occurs at all social levels, but it is more prevalent at the lowest socioeconomic level and among disadvantaged minorities. Socioeconomic group differences in corporal punishment of children or slapping of spouses are relatively small, but the more severe the violence, the greater the socioeconomic difference. Thus, punching, biting, choking, attacking with weapons, and killing of family members occur much more often among the most disadvantaged sectors of society (Linsky et al. 1995; Straus et al. 1980).

The Overall Pattern. No single factor, such as male dominance or growing up in a violent family, has been shown to account for more than a small percentage of the incidence of child abuse or spouse abuse. However, a study of the potential effect of twenty-five such "risk factors" found that in families where only one or two of the factors existed, there were no incidents of wife beating during the year studied. On the other hand, wife beating occurred in 70 percent of the families with twelve or more of the twenty-five factors (Straus et al. 1980). Similar results were found for child abuse. Thus, the key to unraveling the paradox of family violence appears to lie in understanding the interplay of numerous causal factors.

THE FUTURE

During the period 1965 to 1985, the age-old phenomena of child abuse and wife beating underwent an evolution from "private trouble" to "social problem" and, in the case of wife beating, to a statutory crime. Every state in the United States now employs large numbers of "child protective service" workers, and there are national and local voluntary groups devoted to prevention and treatment of child abuse. There are more than 1,000 shelters for battered women, whereas none existed in 1973. There are growing numbers of treatment programs for batterers and of family dispute mediation programs. Criminal prosecution of violent husbands, although still the exception, has become frequent, often with mandated participation in a treatment program as an alternative to fines or incarceration (Sherman et al. 1992). After lagging behind the states for more than a decade, in 1994 Congress passed the Violence Against Women act, which provides funds for services, education, and research. In the 1990s there was also an exponential growth of family therapy by psychologists and social workers, and psychology replaced sociology as the discipline most active in research on family violence.

Comparison of the 1975, 1985, and 1992 National Family Violence Surveys found a substantial reduction in the rates of child abuse and wife beating (Straus 1995; Straus and Gelles 1986; Straus et al. 1997). However, domestic assaults *by* women remained about the same, perhaps because there has been no national effort to confront this aspect of family violence and perhaps because it is a perverse aspect of the movement toward gender equality. These decreases in family violence are an acceleration of a centuries-long trend. The acceleration probably results from a combination of the educational programs, services, and legal changes discussed in this article; as well as from changes in characteristics of the family and the society that lie at the root of family violence. These include increases in the educational level of the population, later marriages, and fewer children, all of which reduce family stress; parent education programs and media, which help parents manage children without corporal punishment or more severe violence; greater equality between men and women, which reduces some of the power struggles that lead to violence; and wives in paid jobs and a greater acceptability of divorce, which (along with shelters for battered women) enables more women to escape from violent marriages. Although child abuse and spouse abuse rates have declined, they are still extremely high. American society still has a long way to go before a typical citizen is as safe in his or her own home as on the streets or in the workplace.

REFERENCES

Archer, D., and R. Gartner 1984 *Violence and Crime in Cross-National Perspective.* New Haven, Conn.: Yale University Press.

Baron, L., and M. A. Straus 1988 "Cultural and Economic Sources of Homicide in the United States." *The Sociological Quarterly* 29(3):371–190.

—— 1989 *Four Theories of Rape in American Society: A State-Level Analysis.* New Haven, Conn.: Yale University Press.

Calvert, R. 1974 "Criminal and Civil Liability in Husband–Wife Assaults." In S. K. Steinmetz and M. A. Straus, eds., *Violence in the Family.* New York: Harper and Row.

Carmody, D. C., and K. R. Williams 1987 "Wife Assault and Perceptions of Sanctions." *Violence and Victims* 2(1):25–38.

Coleman, D. H., and M. A. Straus 1983 "Alcohol Abuse and Family Violence." In E. Gottheil, K. A. Druley, T. E. Skolada, and H. M. Waxman, eds., *Alcohol, Drug Abuse and Aggression.* Springfield, Ill.: Thomas.

—— 1986 "Marital Power, Conflict, and Violence in a Nationally Representative Sample of American Couples." *Violence and Victims* 1(2):141–157.

Fedorowycz, O. 1999 "Homicide in Canada–1998." *Juristat: Canadian Centre for Justice Statistics,* 19(10).

Gaquin, D. A. 1977–1978 "Spouse Abuse: Data from the National Crime Survey." *Victimology* 2:632–643.

Gelles, R. J. 1974 *The Violent Home: A Study of Physical Aggression Between Husbands and Wives.* Beverly Hills, Calif.: Sage.

——, M. A. Straus 1979 "Determinants of Violence in the Family: Toward a Theoretical Integration." In W. R. Burr, F. Rueben Hill, I. Nye, and I. L. Reiss, eds., *Contemporary Theories About the Family.* New York: Free Press.

——, and M. A. Straus 1988 *Intimate Violence.* New York: Simon and Schuster.

Goode, W. J. 1974 "Force and Violence in the Family." In S. K. Steinmetz and M. A. Straus, eds., *Violence in the Family.* New York: Harper and Row.

Greenblat, C. S. 1983 "A Hit Is a Hit Is a Hit . . . Or Is It? Approval and Tolerance of the Use of Physical Force by Spouses." In D. Finkelhor, R. J. Gelles, G. T. Hotaling, and M. A. Straus, eds., *The Dark Side of Families.* Beverly Hills, Calif.: Sage.

Greenfeld, L. A., M. R. Rand, P. Craven, P. A. Klaus, C. A. Perkins, C. Ringel, G. Warchol, C. Maston, and J. A. Fox 1998 *Violence by Intimates: Analysis of Data on Crimes by Current or Former Spouses, Boyfriends, and Girlfriends* (Bureau of Justice Statistics Factbook: No. NCJ-167237). Washington, D.C.: U.S. Department of Justice.

Huggins, M. D., and M. A. Straus 1980 "Violence and the Social Structure as Reflected in Children's Books from 1850 to 1970." In M. A. Straus and G. T. Hotaling, eds., *The Social Causes of Husband-Wife Violence.* Minneapolis: University of Minnesota Press.

Kalmuss, D. S., and M. A. Straus 1983 "Feminist, Political, and Economic Determinants of Wife Abuse Services in American States." In D. Finkelhor, R. J. Gelles, G. T. Hotaling, and M. A. Straus, eds., *The Dark Side of Families: Current Family Violence Research.* Newbury Park, Calif.: Sage.

Kaufman Kantor, G., J. L. Jasinski, and E. Aldarondo 1994 "Sociocultural Status and Incidence of Marital Violence in Hispanic Families." *Violence and Victims* 9:207–222.

Kaufman Kantor, G., and M. A. Straus 1987 "The 'Drunken Bum' Theory of Wife Beating." *Social Problems* 34(3):213–230.

—— 1990 "Response of Victims and the Police to Assaults on Wives." In M. A. Straus and R. J. Gelles, eds., *Physical Violence in American Families: Risk Factors and Adaptations to Violence in 8,145 Families.* New Brunswick, N.J.: Transaction Publishers.

Larossa, R. 1980 "And We Haven't Had Any Problems Since: Conjugal Violence and the Politics of Marriage." In M. A. Straus and G. T. Hotaling, eds., *The Social Causes of Husband-Wife Violence.* Minneapolis: University of Minnesota Press.

Levinson, D. 1989 *Family Violence in Cross-Cultural Perspective,* vol. 1. Newbury Park, Calif.: Sage.

Linsky, A. S., R. Bachman, and M. A. Straus 1995 *Stress Culture and Aggression.* New Haven, Conn.: Yale University Press.

Makepeace, J. M. 1983 "Life Events Stress and Courtship Violence." *Family Relations* 32(January):101–109.

Nelson, B. J. 1984 *Making an Issue of Child Abuse: Political Agenda Setting for Social Problems.* Chicago: University of Chicago Press.

Pfohl, S. J. 1977 "The Discovery of Child Abuse." *Social Problems* 24(February):310–323.

Radbill, S. X. 1987 "Children in a World of Violence: A History of Child Abuse and Infanticide." In R. E. Helfer and C. H. Kempe, eds., *The Battered Child*, 4th ed. Chicago: University of Chicago Press.

Sherman, L. W., D. A. Smith, J. D. Schmidt, and D. P. Rogan 1992 "Crime, Punishment, and Stake in Conformity: Legal and Informal Control of Domestic Violence." *American Sociological Review* 57:680–690.

Stets, J. E., and M. A. Straus 1990 "Gender Differences in Reporting of Marital Violence and its Medical and Psychological Consequences." In M. A. Straus and R. J. Gelles, eds., *Physical Violence in American Families: Risk Factors and Adaptations to Violence in 8,145 Families*. New Brunswick, N.J.: Transaction Publishers.

Straus, M. A. 1976 "Sexual Inequality, Cultural Norms, and Wife-Beating." In E. C. Viano, ed., *Victims and Society*. Washington, D.C.: Visage Press.

—— 1977 "Societal Morphogenesis and Intrafamily Violence in Cross-Cultural Perspective." *Annals of the New York Academy of Sciences* 285:718–730.

—— 1980 "Social Stress and Marital Violence in a National Sample of American Families." *Annals of the New York Academy of Sciences* 347:229–250.

—— 1986 "Domestic Violence and Homicide Antecedents." *Bulletin of the New York Academy of Medicine* 62:446–465.

—— 1987 "Primary Group Characteristics and Intra-Family Homicide." Paper Presented At the Third National Conference For Family Violence Researchers, Family Research Laboratory, Durham, NH.

—— 1990 "The Conflict Tactics Scales and its Critics: An Evaluation and New Data on Validity and Reliability." In M. A. Straus and R. J. Gelles, eds., *Physical Violence in American Families: Risk Factors and Adaptations to Violence in 8,145 Families*. New Brunswick, N.J.: Transaction Publishers.

—— 1994 "State-to-State Differences in Social Inequality and Social Bonds in Relation to Assaults on Wives in the United States." *Journal of Comparative Family Studies* 25(1):7–24.

—— 1995 "Trends in Cultural Norms and Rates of Partner Violence: An Update to 1992." In S. Stith and M. A. Straus, eds., *Understanding Partner Violence: Prevalence, Causes, Consequences, and Solutions*. Minneapolis, Minn.: National Council on Family Relations.

—— 1999 "The Controversy over Domestic Violence by Women: A Methodological, Theoretical, and Sociology of Science Analysis." In X. Arriaga and S. Oskamp, eds., *Violence in Intimate Relationships*. Thousand Oaks, Calif.: Sage.

——, and R. J. Gelles 1986 "Societal Change and Change in Family Violence from 1975 to 1985 as Revealed by Two National Surveys." *Journal of Marriage and the Family* 48:465–479.

——, R. J. Gelles, and S. K. Steinmetz 1980b *Behind Closed Doors: Violence in the American Family*. New York: Doubleday/Anchor.

——, S. L. Hamby, S. Boney-Mccoy, and D. B. Sugarman 1996 "The Revised Conflict Tactics Scales (CTS2): Development and Preliminary Psychometric Data." *Journal of Family Issues* 17(3):283–316.

——, S. L. Hamby, D. Finkelhor, D. W. Moore, and D. Runyan 1998 "Identification of Child Maltreatment with the Parent-Child Conflict Tactics Scales: Development and Psychometric Data for a National Sample of American Parents." *Child Abuse and Neglect* 22:249–270.

——, and G. Kaufman Kantor 1987 "Stress and Child Abuse." In R. E. Helfer and R. S. Kempe, eds., *The Battered Child*, 4th ed. Chicago: University of Chicago Press.

——, G. Kaufman Kantor, and D. W. Moore 1997 "Change in Cultural Norms Approving Marital Violence: From 1968 to 1994." In G. Kaufman Kantor and J. L. Jasinski, eds., *Out of the Darkness: Contemporary Perspectives on Family Violence*. Thousand Oaks, Calif.: Sage.

——, and A. K. Mathur 1996 "Social Change and Change in Approval of Corporal Punishment by Parents from 1968 to 1994." In D. Frehsee, W. Horn, and K.-D. Bussmann, eds., *Family Violence Against Children: A Challenge for Society*. New York: Walter deGruyter.

——, and J. H. Stewart 1999 "Corporal Punishment by American Parents: National Data on Prevalence, Chronicity, Severity, and Duration, in Relation to Child and Family Characteristics." *Clinical Child and Family Psychology Review* 2(2):55–70.

——, and C. L. Yodanis 1996 "Corporal Punishment in Adolescence and Physical Assaults on Spouses Later in Life: What Accounts for the Link?" *Journal of Marriage and the Family* 58(4):825–841.

U.S. Bureau of the Census 1992 *Statistical Abstract of the United States*. Washington, D.C.: Author.

U.S. Department of Justice 1980 *Intimate Victims: A Study of Violence Among Friends and Relatives* (A National Crime Survey Report). Washington, D.C.: Bureau of Justice Statistics.

Weitzmen, L. J. 1986 *The Divorce Revolution*. New York: Free Press.

Murray A. Straus

FEMINIST THEORY

The term *feminist theory* is an invention of the academic branch of the mid- and late twentieth-century feminist movement. It refers to generating systematic ideas that define women's place in society and culture, including the depiction of women—large questions, indeed. The task of feminist theorists is necessarily monumental. It requires the wisdom, courage, and perseverance that Penelope displayed as she wove and unwove her tapestry to trick the suitors who sought to appropriate her kingdom and so steal her child's birthright.

For many reasons the task of feminist theorists is difficult. First, it is interdisciplinary. Literary critics, art historians, musicologists, historians, and philosophers—to name some specialists associated with the humanities—have all offered powerful and sometimes conflicting ideas about women in society and culture. So have sociologists, anthropologists, economists, psychologists, and psychoanalysts. Although the biological and physical sciences do not usually make fruitful contributions to contemporary debates about social and cultural issues, feminist scientists have posed questions that challenge the presuppositions of their own fields. They, too, have augmented the scope of feminist theory. Indeed, specialists in so many disciplines have offered apt ideas that no one essay or writer can even pretend to outline the scope of contemporary feminist theory. This presentation will concentrate on ideas developed in the social sciences.

Second, because feminist theory has its basis in the current women's movement, it is necessarily infused with the political concerns of the contemporary era. (Any system of arranging facts, including the writing of history, is necessarily influenced by the dominant concerns and ideologies of its times.) The most important of these is the relationship among race (ethnicity), gender, and class, both cross-culturally and historically. For even as Americans and Europeans have sought to confront institutionalized racism and sexism, as well as the unequal distribution of income and wealth in their own nations, women in developing nations have posed issues regarding the application of generalizations based on those experiences to their own situations. So, too, historical research has raised the challenge of process—namely, the problem that any particular historical outcome is not predetermined, so that the development of relationships among gender, class, and race (or ethnicity) may vary greatly. Such variations make the act of generalizing hazardous, if not foolhardy.

Third, feminist theory has not merely existed in a sociopolitical context but has been informed by it. This means that many theorists realize that their ideas have been influenced by their own material conditions and cultures. Thus, they have had to confront epistemological issues, including the meaning of objectivity and the way male dominance has shaped notions important to all branches of human inquiry. Put somewhat differently, theorists have broached two issues: (1) the inextricable association between ideas and methods of inquiry, and (2) how both dominant ideas and methods have been influenced by the male hegemony over academic and scientific discourse. As is true in most contemporary fields of study, each of these issues is controversial.

Given these challenges, one might well wonder why anyone would try to generate feminist theory. But feminist academics felt that they could make a significant contribution by using their training first to document and later to analyze women's place in society. When the feminists of academe began to debate their understandings of women's place in society and culture, no sure path seemed available. With the exception of Simone de Beauvoir's *The Second Sex* (1952), men had penned the two canonized (nineteenth-century) texts most familiar to these academics, namely John Stuart Mill's *The Subjection of Women* and Frederick Engels's *The Origins of Private Property, the Family, and the State*. Although Western women had debated their own situation since at least 1400, when, as Joan Kelly (1982) notes, Christine de Pisan "sparked . . . the four-century-long debate . . . known as the *querelle des femmes*," twentieth-century academics were largely ignorant of that polemical tradition. Instead, they had been schooled in the thought of great men—whose writings were included in the first anthologies of feminist thought, such as Miriam Schneir's *Feminism: The Essential Historical Writings* (1972) and Alice Rossi's *The Feminist Papers* (1973). Such anthologies also introduced American academics to great women outside their own fields.

Nonhistorians learned of the generative ideas of participants in the Seneca Falls convention of 1848, as well as about Susan B. Anthony, Emma Goldman, and the British activist Emily Pankhurst; noneconomists met Charlotte Perkins Gilman; nonliterary critics met Virginia Woolf. Although feminist intellectuals might find strength in the knowledge that other women had provided trail markers to guide their way, antifeminists were not convinced that gender inequality still existed.

Thus, the first task confronting feminist theory was to document both past and present inequalities. Many of the early writings addressing this project discussed women as either "other" or "victim." These characterizations ran through writings that might be classed as either liberal (the belief that women have the same capabilities as men and should receive equal treatment); socialist Marxist (variations of the notion that capitalism created or augmented gender inequality); or radical feminist (versions of the idea that women are inextricably different from men and at least equal, and possibly superior, to them).

WOMAN AS OTHER AND AS VICTIM

To some extent the notions of "other" and "victim" are implicit in any mid-twentieth-century demonstration of inequality. Those who are maltreated for unacceptable reasons appear to be victims, as implicit in the late 1960s' and early 1970s' political slogan "Don't blame the victim." They seem to be "others" because of the historical and cross-cultural tendency of dominant groups to justify discriminatory actions by arguing that members of subdominant groups are "alien," not fully human, or simply "not like us." (In the American case, blacks were deemed "not fully human" when procedures for counting the male population were defined in the early years of the Republic.) This dichotomy between "subject" and "object," "self" and "other," has also been crucial to modern European thought, including the philosophic basis for de Beauvoir's *The Second Sex*, which was Jean-Paul Sartre's concept of existentialism. Such notions seemed to provide a conceptual framework with which to document *sexism*, a term introduced by those members of the American women's movement who had participated in the civil rights movement and who wished for a term that

reverberated with connotations of despicable conduct implicit in the more familiar term *racism*. That is, academic feminists could view themselves as demonstrating how specific practices or institutions viewed women as "others," maltreated them, and so transformed them into "victims" not responsible for their "despised" status. Once those processes were identified, feminist activists could seek to reform or to revolutionize the relevant institutions.

Social scientists provided confirmation of victimization by gathering data comparing women and men. Men were more likely to dominate professions (even such "female work" as grade school teaching and librarianship, in which men were likely to be principals and department heads), earn more money, receive higher education, be awarded scholarships and fellowships, earn advanced degrees, hold positions of political leadership, be granted credit cards, be treated as legally responsible for their actions, and be permitted to make decisions about their own bodies. (Both theorists and activists hotly discussed the "body issues" such as abortion, incest, rape, and sexual harassment and wife battering.) Psychologists and psychiatrists pointed out that their colleagues had equated mental health with supposedly male characteristics. Humanists demonstrated that in art, music, and literature, men had inscribed themselves in the "cultural canon." Not only did the canon identify men's accomplishments as the "most important" Western works, but the so-called Western cultural tradition also represented history, literature, art, and philosophy from a male point of view. Sometimes these great works dwelled on the dichotomy between the concepts of madonna and whore; sometimes on the secular objectification of women's sexuality (as seen in renditions of the female nude). Whether religious or secular, both the cultural canon and academic knowledge were discovered to ignore or belittle women in various ways, as well as to devalue their contributions to civic and cultural life throughout the centuries.

Feminists confronted the dilemma of what to do about this devaluation. Liberal feminists seemed to echo one theme implicit in de Beauvoir's *The Second Sex* and Mill's *The Subjection of Women*: Become more like men—that is, remove the barriers preventing women from having the same opportunities as men, and, in the future, women will accomplish as much as men. Because, as some psychologists argued, there is no innate difference between women and men, equal treatment and equal opportunity will result in equal accomplishment.

The solution offered by Marxist and socialist feminists was not all that different from the ideas of liberals. They, too, believed that the eradication of obstacles would liberate women. But Marxist and socialist feminists were haunted by the "problem of the hyphen." That is, for them, the barriers confronting women were not simply posed by what all feminists termed "patriarchy" (shorthand for "male dominance"). Rather, as they saw it, patriarchy was itself inextricably related to capitalism. So, disentangling that relationship was a complex task. If capitalism had been a primary cause of women's inferior position, then women should have found greater equality in noncapitalist nations. In actuality, women had *not* prospered under the brands of communism found in the Soviet Union, Eastern Europe, or China. In those nations, too, women were clustered in jobs that paid less than those filled by men of equivalent education.

As feminists learned, communist lands had treated women favorably while still in their revolutionary stages. For example, in the Soviet Union of the 1920s, "changes in property relationships and inheritance laws weakened the family as an economic unit and reduced the dominance of the male household head, while new family codes undermined the legal and religious basis of marriage and removed restriction on divorce" (Lapidus 1978, p. 60). By undercutting the power of both the church and the traditional family, these measures strengthened the state. Once the Communist party had institutionalized its power and declining birthrates challenged economic growth, however, it redefined the family as "the bulwark of the social system, a microcosm of the new socialist society . . . [supposed] to serve above all as a model of social order" (Lapidus 1978, p. 112). Divorce became difficult; motherhood was defined as a contradiction, simultaneously a joy and the "supreme obligation of Soviet women." As in capitalist countries, the Soviet Union then began to glorify women's role in the family (what feminist theory identified as the private sphere).

The discrepancy that arose between communist practice and socialist theory created a theoretical dilemma. One might insist that the so-called communist countries had radically departed from the theoretical ideal, and so the impact of socialism on women's lives had yet to receive a valid test. One might point to the relatively enlightened laws of the Scandinavian societies, where social policies assisted women who tried to combine work and family life. But even in these nations, women assumed more of the responsibility for children than did men. Although Scandinavian laws enabled father or mother to take parental leave after the birth or adoption of a child, few men exercised that legal right. Thus, another option seemed necessary: One might seek to reconceptualize the link between private property and patriarchy.

Anthropologists and historians were among the first feminists to attempt that (re)vision. Three of their solutions were particularly influential. First, drawing on de Beauvoir, some anthropologists (and at least one sociologist) returned to the idea of woman as other (see Rosaldo and Lamphere 1974). They suggested that extant societies embodied an analogy: Woman is to nature as man is to culture. That is, traditional and industrialized societies assumed that woman is closer to nature than man is. Men had supposedly thrust themselves upon nature and transformed it.

Second, some theorists incorporated Marxist notions by pointing out that men had defined women as private property. Rubin (1975) offered the most influential argument about what she termed "the sex/gender system." Assuming that women and men are more like than unlike one another, she asked how societies create "difference" or transform sex into gender. Answering her question, she retained her anthropologist's conviction that kinship relations are at the basis of society while she drew on her own "freely interpretive" readings of Claude Levi-Strauss and Sigmund Freud. In essence, Rubin argued, men exchange women to create and to cement their own social relationships. This exchange "does imply a distinction between gift and giver. If women are the gifts, then men are the exchange partners. And it is the partners, not the presents, upon whom reciprocal exchange confers its quasi-mystical powers of social linkage. The relations of such a system are such that women are in no position to realize the benefits of their own circulation. As long as the relations specify that men exchange women, it is the men who are the beneficiaries of the product of such exchanges—social organization" (Rubin 1975, p. 174).

Prohibitions on incest keep this exchange system going because they intend to ensure the availability of women to be exchanged. Yet the women must be willing to be "gifts"; that is, they must have internalized the appropriate societal norms. Supposedly, what Freud describes as the Oedipal complex provides that internalization. According to Rubin, the Oedipal complex is a record of "how [contemporary] phallic culture domesticates women" (1975, p. 198). Furthermore, psychoanalytic findings about women's inferiority to men is a palimpsest "of the effects in women of their domestication" (p. 198). Thus, any society based on the exchange of women has molded the inequalities of the sex/gender system into its very essence. According to Rubin, this generalization is as applicable to today's industrialized societies as to nonindustrial societies. What feminists term *patriarchy* is actually the operation of the sex/gender system. By implication, to achieve equality, feminists had to challenge the sex/gender system.

Third, some historians and anthropologists responded to the conflation of capitalism and patriarchy by seeking nonindustrial models where women held power. Mainly they sought examples of women as a force in the public sphere. Eleanor Leacock wrote about one classic case, the Iroquois. In the Iroquois Confederation, women elected the (male) chiefs and were also empowered to remove them from office. In medieval society, Joan Kelly maintained, (aristocratic) women had power over the education of their daughters. During the Renaissance, men absconded with that power, devalued the knowledge women had shared, deprived women of the right to educate one another, and also denied women equal access to the then newly discovered "classics." Kelly concluded her article by suggesting that the Renaissance had a different meaning for women and men; and so, by challenging historians' periodization, another conclusion was also possible. One might infer that during the Renaissance, men transformed women into victims.

By viewing women as either other or victim, all these theorists were implicitly accepting the male assumption that the public sphere is more important than the private. Even the search for examples of women who had once collectively held significant political power can be viewed as an affirmation of the dominant (male) view that the public sphere is more important than the private (home).

However, the third approach—the search for examples of institutionalized female power—also foreshadowed a new phase of feminist theory: "the (re)vision of public and private spheres." As introduced by the poet Adrienne Rich, the term *(re)vision* is a deliberate pun referring to both a reconsideration of past ideas and a new vision of women's role in society.

THE (RE)VISION OF PUBLIC AND PRIVATE SPHERES

In the late 1970s, the feminist movement was maturing; many middle- and upper-class women (including nonfeminists) began to flock to the male-dominated professional schools from which they had once been excluded. Feminists in several fields began to reassess the value of activity in the private sphere—the world of the home in which most women were ensconced. Could the private sphere serve as a launchpad for social change? Had it ever done so? Are these spheres indeed separate, or does the persistence of this dichotomy conflate the errors of nineteenth-century thought? (A reconsideration of the relationship between the public and private spheres is implicit in the titles of such books as *Beyond Separate Spheres* and *Private Woman, Public Stage*. In sociology, Marxist and sociolist feminists use different language to discuss women's and men's spheres.)

Nineteenth-century social theories had implied that the private sphere was of equal importance to the public world of work. Although the early nineteenth-century "cult of domesticity" banished women to the home, where they were to serve as models of religiosity and virtue, they were also enshrined as "mothers of civilization"—a role that might imply power. But from the vantage of the late twentieth century, the role of "mother of civilization" did not seem so vital. If the private sphere was so important, why was the role of "parent of civilization" not available to men, who historically seemed almost to have monopolized positions of power? If the roles of women and men (wives and husbands) were of equal importance, as Talcott Parsons had implied, why were American women more likely than men to complain of the sorts of physical and mental ailments associated with an inferior social position?

Yet, in the late 1970s, historians, anthropologists, and some sociologists began to find positive aspects of women's role in the private sphere. According to historians, women had used their roles to initiate social reforms. They had been especially active in trying to ameliorate some of the social problems resulting from the transformation of an agricultural society into an industrial one. For example, through voluntary associations, middle- and upper-class women in New York tried to decrease the destructive impact of poverty on the poor, especially on poor women. In Oneida County, they sought to reform the behaviors of the many single men who had moved to the city from the farms, lived in boarding houses, and sometimes disrupted the civil order. That the activities of the volunteers resulted in the enshrinement of women in the home once their activities had been successful is a historical irony (Ryan 1981). But that outcome is irrelevant to the main theoretical point offered by feminist theorists: Activity that nineteenth-century women had viewed as an extension of their roles in the private sphere had indeed influenced the public sphere. Put somewhat differently, the domestic and public spheres are not necessarily dichotomous.

Yet problems remain. First, variations suggest that generalization is premature. Second, rejection of the dichotomy between domestic and public spheres challenges the residues of nineteenth-century thought remaining in twentieth-century theories but does not necessarily lead to new theoretical formulation. Indeed, neither historical nor anthropological discoveries of variations on the common pattern—male dominance—*necessarily* facilitate theorizing. Rather, they might and did lead some feminists to search for the origins of male dominance (as in the article by Gayle Rubin) and to champion causal explanations.

Yet the (re)vision of public and private spheres did enable some feminist theorists to ask new questions. The anthropologist M. Z. Rosaldo (1980) explains:

Sexual asymmetry can be discovered in all human social groups, just as can kinship systems, marriages, and mothers. But asking "Why?" or "How did it begin?" appears inevitably to turn our thoughts from an account of the significance of gender for the organization of all human institutional forms (and reciprocally, of the significance of all social facts to gender) toward dichotomous

assumptions that link the roles of men and women to the different things that they, as individuals, are apt to do.

Rosaldo (1980) continues:

What traditional social scientists have failed to grasp is not that sexual asymmetries exist but that they are as fully social as the hunter's or the capitalist's role, and that they figure in the very facts, like racism or social class, that social science claims to understand. A crucial task for feminist scholars emerges, then, not as the relatively limited one of documenting pervasive sexism as a social fact–or showing how we can now hope to change or have in the past been able to survive it. Instead, it seems that we are challenged to provide new ways of linking the particulars of women's lives, activities, and goals to inequalities wherever they exist.

To advance beyond naivete, feminist theories must grasp *how* meanings of gender are constructed, not why they exist.

Sociologist Nancy Chodorow provided one such demonstration in her now-classic but still controversial *The Reproduction of Mothering.* Using psychoanalytic object-relations theory and some elements of Marxist thought, she argued that in contemporary capitalist societies the roles of women and men within the family (re)produce the roles women and men are expected to fill in Western societies. Because women are responsible for the care of small children, young girls and boys initially identify with their mothers. Girls are encouraged to continue this relational identification with their mothers; boys are not. For girls, the omnipresence of women in early childhood leads to a problem of boundaries—of knowing where their mothers end and they begin. As adults, this lack of boundaries may be advantageous: Out of their ability to see the world as others do, they may have a richer emotional life than men and also be more emphatic than they are. For boys, the omnipresence of women means that men learn the meaning of masculinity through the eventual demand that they separate from their mothers and identify with a role (male gender). Theirs is a positional identification. Ultimately, Chodorow argues, these scenarios play themselves out so that women and men try to reproduce the sorts of

992

modern families in which they were reared. Additionally, Chodorow (1978) claims,

> An increasingly father-absent, mother-involved family produces in men a personality that both corresponds to masculinity and male dominance as these are currently constituted in the sex-gender system, and fits appropriately with participation in capitalist relations of production. Men continue to enforce the sexual division of spheres as a defense against powerlessness in the [capitalist] labor market. Male denial of dependence and of attachment to women helps to guarantee both masculinity and performance in the world of work.

She continues,

> The relative unavailability of the father and the overavailability of the mother create negative definitions of masculinity and men's fear and resentment of women, as well as the lack of inner autonomy in men that enables, depending on the particular family constellation and class origin, either rule-following or the easy internalization of the values of the organization.

Chodorow's theory is controversial. Some liberals object to the inference that women are more empathetic than men. They claim that psychological studies show that women and men have the same innate emotional capabilities. Nevertheless, radical feminists—people who believe that male dominance is the primary cause of women's subjugation—sometimes celebrate women's alleged superiority to men.

Others challenge Chodorow's theory by questioning whether any theory about the modern American family can possibly be applied to other historical epochs or cultures. Yet this objection misses the point in two ways. First, Chodorow discusses a specific time and place—contemporary America. Her contrast between how women and men learn their (relational or positional) roles should be even more important today than it was in 1978 when *The Reproduction of Mothering* was first published. Since 1978 the percentage of female-headed households has increased. Concomitantly, more young boys have even less contact with men; they must form the positional identifications that, Chodorow claims, prepare them to uphold the orientations to work and

family required to maintain postindustrial capitalism. Second, Chodorow anticipated Rosaldo's call to understand how gender is socially constructed to articulate with other roles. She did not ask the origin of all sex/gender systems.

Chodorow's argument is important in a third way: She transforms "normal" understandings of men's and women's roles. She turns one current interpretation of Freud's thought, object-relations theory, on its head. Woman-centered (written from the perspective of a feminist) yet comparative (examining both women and men), Chodorow's book anticipated the challenge that feminist scholarship currently offers other theoretical projects.

CHALLENGING CONVENTIONAL INTERPRETATIONS

The theme of difference is key to Carol Gilligan's *In a Different Voice* (1981). Extending and (re)vising Lawrence Kohlberg's work on the development of moral judgments among men, Gilligan argues that Kohlberg's scale of moral maturity slights women. Kohlberg argues that the highest stages of maturity involve the application of "rules to universal principles of justice" (Gilligan 1981, p. 18). In Kohlberg's model, women seem stuck at an intermediate stage because of their lack of opportunity to enter the public sphere and so to master and to apply those universal principles. Gilligan contends that Kohlberg has erred in his assessment of women (and other subordinated groups). In the case of women, he has not understood how their concepts of morality are based on their socialization. On the basis of her empirical studies and Chodorow's argument, Gilligan concludes that women do not make inferior moral judgments but different ones. They employ a relational ethic that stresses interpersonal caring, including a responsibility for self and others.

Gilligan's theory is as controversial as Chodorow's—perhaps even more so. Radical feminists cite this theory to argue again that women are morally superior to men. Some liberal feminists, who are interested in pushing for women's entry to upper levels of corporate management, use Gilligan's theory to claim that women are better equipped than men to develop innovative management styles that bind teams to the corporation. Other liberals (e.g., Epstein 1989) insist that there are no *innate* psychological distinctions between women and men.

However, both Chodorow and Gilligan raise an additional issue, potentially more controversial than the debates about "innate" gender differences. They try at one and the same time to follow the practices of their respective disciplines and to view social life from a woman's perspective. Since science, social science, and the literary canon are based on male perspectives (as is true of Kohlberg's studies), how are we to forge an epistemology (and hence a methodology) that can simultaneously claim veracity and be true to women's experience of the social world? Can any theory that is either androcentric (man-centered) or gynocentric (woman-centered) be valid?

FEMINIST THEORY AND THE PROBLEM OF KNOWLEDGE

Some scientists or social scientists might believe that the question of validity applies only to explicitly interpretive work. After all, many decades have passed since Heisenberg enunciated his famous principle that the technologies (and by extension the theories and methods) used to view a phenomenon necessarily influence what is viewed. Supposedly, scientists and social scientists have been taking this principle into account as they explain how their generalizations apply "all other things being equal." But feminist theorists, like postmodern theorists, have challenged the very basis of the deductive methods at the heart of contemporary science and social science. They "question the very foundation of post-Enlightenment science and social science: the 'objectivist illusion' (Keller 1982) that observation can be separated from explanation, the knower from the known, theory from practice, the public from the private, culture from nature, and other dualisms that undergird systems of social stratification" (Hess 1990, p. 77). The feminist challenge differs from other deliberations about epistemology because, as Hess observes, it is "more political."

The work of scientist Evelyn Fox Keller is exemplary of this controversy. Keller has written rather abstract philosophic essays on such issues as Plato's epistemology and Bacon's notions of mastery and obedience to argue that modern science is infused with "male" notions. Rather than attempt to present these complex arguments briefly, let us concentrate on a more concrete work, Keller's biography of biologist Barbara McClintock, *A Feeling for the Organism* (1982).

In this biography, Keller claims that McClintock accomplished her Nobel Prize–winning research on the transposition of genes in part because McClintock's research style radically departed from the dominant male model, molecular genetics. According to Keller, the dominant model presumed a hierarchical structure of genetic organization that resembles organizational charts of corporate structure and assumes a unidirectional flow of information. That assumption permitted the quick payoffs in research on the structure of specific bacteria that facilitates significant scientific findings (and so careers). The hierarchical model, though, is also supposedly a "male" model.

McClintock, however, believed in a more complex and less hierarchical "old-fashioned" model: "To McClintock, as to many other biologists, mechanism and structure have never been adequate answers to the question 'How do genes work?' To her an adequate understanding would, by definition, have to include an account about how they function in relation to the rest of the cell, and, of course, to the organism as a whole" (Keller 1985, p. 168). In this view, even a genome is an organism, and it, too, must be considered in relation to its environment.

Keller does not claim that McClintock's model was female: McClintock was trained by men. Keller does argue that many biologists have missed the essence of McClintock's vision. Keller includes among them biologists who are trying to incorporate McClintock's work on transposition into the hierarchical model. And, Keller believes,

The matter of gender never does drop away. . . . The radical core of McClintock's stance can be located right here. Because she is not a man, in a world of men, her commitment to a gender-free science has been binding; because concepts of gender have deeply influenced the basic categories of science, that commitment has been transformative. In short, the relevance of McClintock's gender in this story is to be found not in its role in her personal socialization but precisely in the role of gender in the construction of science. (Keller 1982, p. 174)

For, Keller explains, contemporary science names the object of its inquiry (nature) "as female and the parallel naming of subject (mind) as male" (1982 pp. 174). Thus, women scientists are faced with a necessary contradiction between their roles in the world and their role as scientist. Even as the social structure of science tends to place women on the periphery of the invisible colleges that constitute the scientific world, that contradiction may limit the creative scientific imagination of both women and men.

However, as Keller readily admits, not all men believe in the hierarchical model. Nor, to paraphrase Keller, have they all "embraced" the notion of science as a female to be put on the rack and tortured to reveal her secrets. But, Keller insists, both the naming of subject and object and the hierarchical model are androcentric and limit the possibilities of scientific inquiry.

Keller's work has been challenged on a number of grounds. Stephen Jay Gould has launched the most telling attack. His field, paleontology, is also dominated by men but rejects the hierarchical "male" model. Unlike nineteenth-century evolutionary thought, contemporary theories do not view human beings as the proud culmination of the past. Other lifeforms have been more successful. Furthermore, to reconstruct the past, paleontologists must grasp "wholes." Cynthia Fuchs Epstein adds that one cannot even argue that, as social scientists, women have been more empathic or observant than men. Epstein's counterexample is Erving Goffman, whose ability to "see" is almost legendary among sociologists.

For the purposes of this article, it is irrelevant whether Keller, Gould, or Epstein is correct. What matters is that developments in feminist theory have led feminists to participate in the postmodern debate about the nature of knowledge. During the late 1980s, this debate was at the center of controversies in the social sciences and the humanities. It will probably remain important for some years to come. The debate infuses interpretations of literary works, reconstructions of the past, and understandings of social scientific models. It seems to transcend schools of thought. Marxists are divided about postmodernism, as are liberals and, within the feminist community, radicals. Feminist theory has followed the course of all contemporary theories because feminists, too, are members of the societies about which they write and which they are trying to change.

Throughout this essay, terms such as *liberal*, *Marxist* or *socialist*, and *radical* feminists have been intended to distinguish different political orientations and experiences that shaped each group of feminists, as so well documented in histories and sociologies of the mid-twentieth-century feminist movement. By 1990, these very different groups of feminists had become self-consciously aware; that is, many understood that even as feminism had sought social change, it, too, had shaped and been shaped by its environment. For instance, Stacey (1990) argued that in the late 1960s and early 1970s, as feminism stressed female participation in the public sphere and denigrated motherhood, it contributed to rising divorce rates and the devaluation of feminine tasks.

In the 1990s, feminist theory has maintained its own questions and has continued to be divided into camps that emphasize either the similarities between women and men or the differences between them. However, as is axiomatic, all enterprises are embedded in and shaped by their structural contexts. Feminist theory has not been an exception to this well-known rule.

In the 1990s, feminist theories have been influenced by general tendencies in other academic specialties. Although it is still rare (and perhaps because it is still rare) for someone to receive a Ph. D. from an academic department called "women's studies," "gender studies," or "feminism," feminist theory has become increasingly influenced by movements toward specialization within the social sciences. These movements have included the ever more narrow delineation of topics of inquiry, such that a business school course on women in nonprofit organizations may share few if any readings with a sociology course on women and the professions and a course on men and masculinity taught in a school of family studies may not overlap an anthropology course on cross-cultural notions of masculinity. Additionally, within the social sciences, academic disciplines are so beset by specialized theories that researchers may encourage a thousand flowers to bloom by ignoring one another's ideas rather than by addressing the basic and competing philosophic premises on which their theoretical systems are built. Within sociology, for instance, the articles of feminist theorists who pledge allegiance to rational choice theory rarely cite the works of feminist theorists who use key ideas of the symbolic interactionists—and vice versa. Indeed, they may not even agree to call themselves feminist theorists, but rather speak of themselves as rational choice theorists interested in the problems of gender or as symbolic interactionists exploring theories about how women experience their bodies under the parameters set by a national medical system.

Nonetheless, there have been some general ideas about which feminist theorists have come to agree. Perhaps the most important of these is a problem central to all social science: to wit, the theoretical tension between approaches that emphasize individuals as the agents of social stability and social change and approaches that stress how either macro- or microstructures influence and shape both individuals and their decisions. Indeed, as more social scientists have come to agree that nature and nurture interact, the theoretical problems posed by agency and structure have become more salient.

One basic way that feminist theorists have dealt with these problems is to redefine gender itself. In the past, gender has been thought of as a cultural phenomenon—either normative patterns of behaviors, roles, or scripts. Today gender itself is being viewed as a structural phenomenon. This means that many feminist theorists now define gender as an institution, as basic to social structure as the economy, religion, education, and the state—and perhaps more basic than the family (Connell 1995; Lorber 1994). Such theorists emphasize that in some societies there are more than two (dichotomous) genders and that socially and historically embedded notions of gender influence the operation of all institutions, even as they are influenced by other sociohistoric institutions. Further, these theorists continue, identification of gender as an institution enables one to recognize that gender is stratified and that it is also processual (part of unfolding social processes). Thus, this redefinition of gender enables theorists to link structure and agency by discussing how individuals' gendered behavior (re)produces gendered social structures, much as Giddens's (1984) structuration theory seeks to marry structural and agentic approaches. Furthermore, the recognition of gender as an institution entails such a broad paradigmatic shift that, at one and the same time, it refocuses

how theorists view gender and facilitates work within different theoretical traditions. Adherents of symbolic interactionism, neofunctionalism, or rational choice theory could all absorb this notion into their work and test its implications with their method of choice (Ferree et al. 1999).

(SEE ALSO: *Comparable Worth; Gender; Social Movements*)

REFERENCES

Chodorow, Nancy 1978 *The Reproduction of Mothering*. Berkeley: University of California Press.

Connell, R. W. 1995 *Masculinities*. Berkeley: University of California Press.

de Beauvoir, Simone 1952 *The Second Sex*. New York: Alfred A. Knopf.

Ferree, Myra Marx, Judith Lorber, and Beth Hess, eds. 1999 *Revisioning Gender*. Thousand Oaks, Calif.: Sage.

Giddens, Anthony 1984 *The Constitution of Society*. Berkeley: University of California Press.

Gilligan, Carol 1981 *In a Different Voice*. Cambridge, Mass.: Harvard University Press.

Hess, Beth 1990 "Beyond Dichotomies: Drawing Distinctions and Embracing Differences." *Sociological Forum* 5:75–94.

Keller, Evelyn Fox 1982 *A Feeling for the Organism*. New York: W. H. Freeman.

——1985 *Reflections on Gender and Science*. New Haven, Conn.: Yale University Press.

Kelly, Joan 1982 "Early Feminist Theory and the *Querelle des femmes*, 1400–1789." *Signs* 8:4–28.

Lapidus, Gail 1978 *Women in Soviet Society*. Berkeley: University of California Press.

Lorber, Judith 1994 *Paradoxes of Gender*. New Haven, Conn: Yale University Press.

Rosaldo, M. Z. 1980 "The Uses and Abuses of Anthropology." *Signs* 5:389–417.

——and Louise Lamphere, (eds.) 1974 *Women, Culture, and Society*. Stanford, Calif.: Stanford University Press.

Rossi, Alice S., ed. 1973 *The Feminist Papers*. New York: Columbia University Press.

Rubin, Gayle 1975 "The Traffic in Women: Notes on the Political Economy of Sex." In Rayna Rapp Reiter, ed., *Toward an Anthropology of Women*. New York: Monthly Review Press.

Ryan, Mary P. 1981 *Cradle of the Middle Class*. New York: Cambridge University Press.

Schneir, Miriam, ed. 1972 *Feminism: The Essential Historical Writings*. New York: Random House.

Stacey, Judith 1990 *Brave New Families*. Berkeley: University of California Press.

GAYE TUCHMAN

FEMININITY/MASCULINITY

Femininity and masculinity, or one's *gender identity* (Burke et al. 1988; Spence 1985), refer to the degree to which persons see themselves as masculine or feminine given what it means to be a man or woman in society. Femininity and masculinity are rooted in the social (one's gender) rather than the biological (one's sex). Societal members decide what being male or female means (e.g., dominant or passive, brave or emotional), and males will generally respond by defining themselves as masculine while females will generally define themselves as feminine. Because these are social definitions, however, it is possible for a person to be female and see herself as masculine or male and see himself as feminine.

It is important to distinguish *gender identity*, as presented above, from other gender-related concepts such as *gender roles*, which are shared expectations of behavior given one's gender. For example, gender roles might include women investing in the domestic role and men investing in the worker role (Eagly 1987). The concept of gender identity is also different from *gender stereotypes*, which are shared views of personality traits often tied to one's gender, such as instrumentality in men and expressiveness in women (Spence and Helmreich 1978). And gender identity is different from *gender attitudes*, which are the views of others or situations commonly associated with one's gender, such as men thinking in terms of justice and women thinking in terms of care (Gilligan 1982). Although gender roles, gender stereotypes, and gender attitudes influence one's gender identity, they are not the same as gender identity (Katz 1986; Spence and Sawin 1985).

From a sociological perspective, gender identity involves all the meanings that are applied to oneself on the basis of one's gender identification. In turn, these self-meanings are a source of motivation for gender-related behavior (Burke 1980). A person with a more masculine identity should act more masculine, that is, engage in behaviors whose meanings are more masculine such as behaving in a more dominant, competitive, and autonomous manner (Ashmore et al. 1986). It is not the behaviors themselves that are important, but the meanings implied by those behaviors.

Beginning at birth, self-meanings regarding one's gender are formed in social situations, stemming from ongoing interaction with significant others such as parents, peers, and educators (Katz 1986). Although individuals draw upon the shared cultural conceptions of what it means to be male or female that are transmitted through institutions such as religion or the educational system, they may come to see themselves as departing from the masculine or feminine cultural model. A person may label herself female, but instead of seeing herself in a stereotypical female manner, such as being expressive, warm, and submissive (Ashmore et al. 1986), she may view herself in a somewhat stereotypically masculine manner, such as being somewhat instrumental, rational, and dominant. The point is that people view themselves along a feminine–masculine continuum, some seeing themselves more feminine, some as more masculine, and some as a mixture of the two. It is this self-perception along the feminine–masculine continuum that is their gender identity, and it is this that guides their behavior.

THE ROOTS OF FEMININITY/ MASCULINITY

In Western culture, men are stereotypically seen as being aggressive, competitive, and instrumentally oriented while women are seen as being passive, cooperative, and expressive. Early thinking often assumed that this division was based on underlying innate differences in traits, characteristics, and temperaments of males and females. In this older context, measures of femininity/masculinity were often used to diagnose what were understood as problems of basic gender identification, for example, feminine males or masculine females (cf. Terman and Miles 1936).

We now understand that femininity and masculinity are not innate but are based upon social and cultural conditions. Anthropologist Margaret Mead addressed the issue of differences in temperament of males and females in *Sex and Temperament in Three Primitive Societies* (1935). This early study concluded that there are no necessary differences in traits or temperaments between the sexes. Observed differences in temperament between men and women are not a function of their biological differences. Rather, they result from differences in socialization and the cultural expectations held for each sex.

Mead came to this conclusion because the three societies showed patterns of temperament that varied greatly with our own. Among the Arapesh, both males and females displayed what we would consider a "feminine" temperament (passive, cooperative, and expressive). Among the Mundugamor, both males and females displayed what we would consider a "masculine" temperament (active, competitive, and instrumental). Finally, among the Tchambuli, men and women displayed temperaments that were different from each other, but opposite to our own pattern. In that society, men were emotional and expressive while women were active and instrumental.

Mead's study caused people to rethink the nature of femininity/masculinity. Different gender-related traits, temperaments, roles, and identities could no longer be inextricably tied to biological sex. Since Mead's study, the nature–nurture issue has been examined extensively, and with much controversy, but no firm conclusions are yet clear (Maccoby and Jacklin 1974). While there may be small sex differences in temperament at birth (and the evidence on this is not consistent), there is far more variability within each sex group (Spence and Helmreich 1978). Further, the pressures of socialization and learning far outweigh the impact of possible innate sex differences in temperament. We examine this next.

THE DEVELOPMENT OF FEMININITY AND MASCULINITY

There are at least three major theories that explain the development of femininity and masculinity: psychoanalytic theory (Freud 1927), cognitive-developmental theory (Kohlberg 1966), and learning theories that emphasize direct reinforcement (Weitzman 1979) and modeling (Mischel 1966). In all of these theories, a two-part process is involved. In the first part, the child comes to know that she or he is female or male. In the second part, the child comes to know what being female or male means in terms of femininity or masculinity.

According to psychoanalytic theory, one's gender identity develops through identification with the same-sex parent. This identification emerges out of the conflict inherent in the oedipal stage of psychosexual development. By about age 3, a child develops a strong sexual attachment to the opposite-sex parent. Simultaneously, negative feelings emerge for the same-sex parent that are rooted in resentment and jealousy. By age 6, the child resolves the psychic conflict by relinquishing desires for the opposite-sex parent and identifying with the same-sex parent. Thus, boys come to learn masculinity from their fathers and girls to learn femininity from their mothers.

A later formulation of psychoanalytic theory suggests that mothers play an important role in gender-identity development. According to Chodorow (1978), mothers are more likely to relate to their sons as different and separate because they are not of the same sex. At the same time, they experience a sense of oneness and continuity with their daughters because they are of the same sex. As a consequence, mothers will bond with their daughters, thereby fostering femininity in girls. Simultaneously, mothers distance themselves from their sons, who respond by shifting their attention away from their mother and toward their father. Through identification with their father, boys learn masculinity.

Cognitive-developmental theory is another psychological theory of gender-identity development (Kohlberg 1966). Like psychoanalytic theory, it suggests that certain critical events have a lasting effect on gender-identity development, but these events are seen as cognitive rather than psychosexual in origin. Unlike psychoanalytic theory and learning theory (which is discussed next), cognitive-development theory sees the development of a gender identity as preceding rather than following from identification with the same-sex parent. Once a child's gender identity becomes established, the self is then motivated to display gender-congruent attitudes and behaviors, well before same-sex modeling takes hold. Same-sex modeling simply moves the process along.

Kohlberg identifies two crucial stages of gender identity development: (1) acquiring a fixed gender identity and (2) establishing gender-identity constancy. The first stage begins with the child's identification as male or female when hearing the labels "boy" or "girl" applied to the self. By about age 3, the child can apply the appropriate gender label to the self. This is when gender identity becomes fixed. By about age 4, these gender labels are appropriately applied to others. Within another year or two, the child reaches the second critical phase, that of gender constancy. This is the child's recognition that his or her gender will not change despite changes in age or outward appearance.

The most social of the theories of gender-identity development are the learning theories. In these theories, it is the social environment of the child, such as parents and teachers, that shapes the child's gender identity. Here, parents and teachers instruct the child on femininity and masculinity, either directly through rewards and punishments or indirectly through acting as models to be imitated. Direct rewards or punishments are often given for outward appearance, such as what to wear (girls in dresses and boys in pants); object choice, such as toy preferences (dolls for girl and trucks for boys); and behavior (passivity and dependence in girls and aggressiveness and independence in boys). Through rewards and punishments, children learn appropriate appearance and behavior. Indirect learning of one's gender identity emerges from modeling same-sex parents, teachers, peers, or models in the media. Children imitate rewarded models' thoughts, feelings, or behavior because they anticipate that they will receive the same rewards that the models received.

MEASURING MASCULINITY AND FEMININITY: A PSYCHOLOGICAL VIEW

Conceptualizing masculinity and femininity and measuring these orientations in men and women originated in the work of Lewis Terman and Catherine Cox Miles (1936), who created a 455-item test to detect masculinity and femininity. They called it the Attitude Interest Analysis Test (AIAT) to conceal its purpose from subjects. The test included such things as word associations, inkblot associations, interest items, and introversion–extroversion items. For example, on the interest items, persons got femininity points for liking (and masculinity points for disliking) "nursing," "babies," and "charades." Individuals received masculinity points for liking (and femininity points for disliking) "people with loud voices" and "hunting." On the introversion–extroversion items, persons got

femininity points for agreeing (and masculinity points for disagreeing) that they "always prefer someone else to take the lead" and that they are "often afraid of the dark." And they got masculinity points for agreeing (and femininity points for denying) that "as children [they were] extremely disobedient" and that they can "stand as much pain as others." The responses did discriminate between the sexes, with men displaying higher masculinity and women displaying higher femininity.

Terman and Miles's masculinity–femininity (M–F) scale became a model for M–F scales for more than three decades (see Morawski 1985 for a review). The M–F scales that followed shared four assumptions with the scale created by Terman and Miles. These included the assumptions that masculinity and femininity were: (1) deep-seated, enduring characteristics of people, (2) not readily apparent in overt behavior, (3) linked to mental health (an incongruence in sex and masculinity and femininity signaled problems in psychological adjustment), and (4) opposite ends of a continuum (Morawski 1987).

By the 1970s, researchers had become disenchanted with M–F scales, a timing that coincided with the reemergence of the women's movement. Three criticisms had developed: (1) The early M–F scales fostered research that exaggerated the differences between men and women, (2) the feminine characteristics in M–F scales often carried negative connotations, and (3) the bipolar conception of masculinity–femininity was seen as problematic, that is, one could be masculine or feminine but not both (Morawski 1987). From the third criticism arose the concept of *androgyny* and scales to assess it (see Morawski 1987 for a review of the problems surrounding the concept of androgyny).

Androgyny is a combination or balance of masculinity and femininity, allowing for the possibility that individuals can express both. Instead of conceptualizing masculinity and femininity as opposite ends of a continuum, where masculinity on one end precludes one from being feminine on the other end, in androgyny, masculinity and femininity are separate dimensions that can be combined. People can be masculine, feminine, or both (androgynous). Two of the more famous inventories that emerged from the impetus to measure masculinity and femininity on separate, independent dimensions were in psychology: the Bem Sex

Role Inventory (BSRI) (Bem 1974) and the Personal Attributes Questionnaire (PAQ) (Spence and Helmreich 1978).

Both the BSRI and PAQ listed attributes that are positively valued for both sexes but are more normative for either males or females to endorse. These are known as the masculine scale and feminine scale, respectively. In the BSRI, respondents indicate the degree to which a series of descriptions are true about them. Examples of descriptions for the masculine scale include "acts as a leader," "makes decisions easily," and "willing to take risks." Examples of descriptions for the feminine scale include being "affectionate," "gentle," and "sensitive to the needs of others."

In the PAQ, respondents rate themselves on a series of bipolar items. For the masculine scale, the items range from masculine to not masculine, while the items for the feminine scale range from feminine to not feminine. Examples of items from the masculine scale include "very independent" (vs. "not at all independent") and "can make decisions easily" (vs. "has difficulty making decisions"). The feminine scale includes bipolar items such as "very emotional" (vs. "not at all emotional") and "very helpful to others" (vs. "not at all helpful to others"). In addition to the masculinity and femininity scales, the PAQ has a third scale, labeled masculinity–femininity, that is in keeping with the bipolar M–F measurement tradition. The bipolar items for this scale are culturally appropriate for males on one end, and culturally appropriate for females on the other. Typical items include "very dominant" (vs. "very submissive") and "feelings not easily hurt" (vs. "feelings easily hurt").

With separate measures of masculinity and femininity, it is possible to ask about the relationship between the measure of masculinity and the measure of femininity. When this relationship was examined, it was found that the two scales were not strongly negatively related, as would be expected if masculinity were the opposite of femininity. Instead, using either the BSRI or the PAQ, the two ratings were relatively unrelated; a person's score on one scale did not predict that person's score on the other scale (Bem 1974; Spence and Helmreich 1978). People had all combinations of scores. Initially, people who combined high scores on masculinity with high scores on femininity were labeled

as androgynous (Bem 1977; Spence and Helmreich 1978). Later, androgyny was indicated by a small difference between masculinity and femininity scores, representing balanced levels of these two characteristics. The other classifications were masculine (high M and low F scores), feminine (high F and low M scores), and undifferentiated (low F and low M scores).

The BSRI and the PAQ are embedded in very different theories about how gender-related characteristics are organized. For Bem (1981, 1993), scores on the BSRI measure not only the different dimensions of masculinity and femininity; more importantly, the scores measure an underlying unidimensional construct known as *gender schematization*. Gender schematization is an internalized tendency to see the world in gendered terms. One who is gender-schematic classifies stimuli as male or female rather than other according to other dimensions that could equally be used. Those who score high on masculinity or high on femininity are gender-schematic because they tend to organize information along gender lines. Androgynous people are gender-aschematic.

Spence (1984, 1993), on the other hand, suggests that gender phenomena are multifactorial. In this view, there are numerous attributes, attitudes, and behaviors that culturally distinguish between men and women, but these are not bound together as a single underlying property such as gender schematization. For Spence (1985; Spence and Sawin 1985) the important underlying construct is *gender identity*, or one's sense of being masculine or feminine. Culturally defined personality traits, physical attributes, abilities, and occupational preferences, among other things, all contribute to one's gender identity in unique and individualized combinations. Individuals draw upon these gender characteristics and choose those qualities that are compatible for them as they define themselves as masculine or feminine and ignore other gender qualities. Thus, while societal members may agree on the representation of masculinity and femininity, one's own masculinity and femininity tends to be more variable and idiosyncratic in nature.

Rather than conceptualizing the items on the PAQ and the BSRI as referring to the broad categories of masculinity and femininity, Spence maintains that these items tap into socially desirable instrumental and expressive traits in men and women, respectively (Spence and Helmreich 1978, 1980). While these traits are related to masculinity and femininity, they do not define one's overall gender identity. They are simply one of the set of contributors to one's gender-based self-image. This is supported by the fact that scores on the PAQ and BSRI are not strongly relate to scores on other measures of gender attitudes, attributes, and behaviors (Spence 1993; Spence and Sawin 1985).

MEASURING MASCULINITY AND FEMININITY: A SOCIOLOGICAL VIEW

In sociology, the symbolic interactionist view of masculinity–femininity (Burke 1989; Burke et al. 1988; Burke and Tully 1977) shares much in common with the view held by the psychologist Spence and her colleagues. For symbolic interactionists, gender identity is understood in the context of a body of research known as identity theory (Stryker 1980). According to identity theory, the self is an organized collection of hierarchically arranged identities (self-meanings) that serve as a source of motivation for our behavior (Burke 1980). Identities are organized as control systems that act to maintain congruency between the internalized self-meanings (one's identity standard) and perceptions of the meaning of the self in ongoing social situations (Burke 1991). The key in this is one's self-meanings (Osgood et al. 1957).

Individuals' gender identity as masculine or feminine is based on the meanings they have internalized from their association with the role of male or female, respectively, in society. Since these are self-meanings, they cannot be directly observed; they must be inferred from behaviors and expressions in which people engage. Gender identity is one of many role identities people hold. In sociology, we assume that roles do not stand in isolation but presuppose and are related to counterroles (Lindesmith and Strauss 1956). For example, the role of teacher takes on meaning in connection with the role of student, the role of mother takes on meaning in relation to the role of child, and so on. The same is true of identities.

Just as the meaning of student (the student identity) is understood in relation to that of teacher (the teacher identity), so too is the meaning of

male (masculinity) relative to that of female (femininity). The meanings of masculine and feminine are necessarily contrastive. To be male (masculine) is to be not female (feminine) and vice versa (Storms 1979). Gender meanings thus relate to one another as opposite ends of a single continuum, returning to the bipolar conceptualization of masculinity and femininity. Indeed, masculinity and femininity are negatively related when individuals are asked to judged themselves based on the self-descriptors "masculine" and "feminine" (Spence 1993). Interestingly, young children initially do not see masculine and feminine characteristics as opposites, but as they get older, their views of the genders become increasingly bipolar (Biernat 1991). This contrasting of masculinity and femininity in self-meanings does not necessarily hold for behaviors, since one can engage in both masculine and feminine behaviors.

The procedure that symbolic interactionists use to measure gender identity is based on the method devised by Burke and Tully to measure self-meanings (1977). In an analysis of middle school children's gender identities, Burke and Tully first collected sets of adjectives from children that the children themselves used to describe the images of boys and girls. These adjectives, together with their opposites, were used as adjective pairs to form a semantic differential scale to measure the meanings of the male and female roles (Osgood et al. 1957). The stem for the semantic differential was "Usually [boys, girls] are . . . "Then, through a statistical procedure known as discriminant function analysis, the researchers selected those items that best discriminated between the meanings of boys and girls. Examples of items that best distinguished "girl" meanings from "boy" meanings for these children included "soft" (vs. "hard"), "weak" (vs. "strong"), and "emotional" (vs. "not emotional"). After selecting the most discriminating items, children's self-descriptions ("As a [boy, girl] I usually am . . .") were then summed to form a scale of gender identity.

A gender identity scale constructed along the lines described above has certain properties. First, the scale evolves out of the meanings of maleness in relation to femaleness that actually are held in the population from which the sample is drawn. This procedure contrasts with much research that uses attributes that are assumed to carry meanings of masculinity and femininity with no attempt to check whether they have these meanings for respondents. Second, the measure outlined above incorporates the assumption that meaning is contrastive. The meaning of female is in contrast to the meaning of male and vice versa. Third, by focusing upon self-meanings, we separate issues of who one is (gender identity) from what one does (gender roles) or what one believes (gender attitudes and stereotypes). From this perspective, androgyny may be thought of not as combining masculine and feminine meanings, but as being flexible in the kinds of behaviors in which one engages (sometimes more masculine in meaning, sometimes more feminine in meaning). We now review some of the important research on gender identity that has emerged out of the Burke–Tully method, for which the symbolic interactionist perspective has served as the backdrop.

RESEARCH ON FEMININITY AND MASCULINITY

The symbolic interactionist perspective suggests that the self is defined through interactions with others. Burke and Tully's (1977) work found that children with cross-sex identities (boys who thought of themselves in ways similar to the way most girls thought of themselves and vice versa) were more likely than children with gender-appropriate identities: (1) to have engaged in gender-inappropriate behavior, (2) to have been warned about engaging in gender-inappropriate behavior, and (3) to have been called names like "tomboy," "sissy," or "homo." Not surprisingly, boys and girls with cross-sex gender identities were more likely to have low self-esteem.

Another symbolic interactionist tenet is that people will choose behaviors that are similar in meaning to the meanings of their identities (Burke and Reitzes 1981). Burke (1989) found that among middle school children, boys and girls with a more feminine gender identity earned higher grades than those with a more masculine gender identity. This was true independent of the child's sex, race, or grade, the subject area, or the sex of the teacher. Since the early years of schooling are more likely to be "feminized" because there are more female

than male teachers (Lipman-Blumen 1984), children with a more feminine identity will likely perform better in a "feminine" institution. Among college students, research has shown that males and females with a more feminine gender identity are more likely to inflict and sustain both physical and sexual abuse in dating relationships (Burke et al. 1988). People with more feminine gender identities are likely to be more emotionally expressive and relationship-oriented. Aggression may be used as a last resort to attain a closer relationship.

Within the symbolic interactionist tradition, research demonstrates that the meanings that people attribute to themselves as masculine or feminine (their gender identity) are sometimes more important in predicting how they will behave than is their gender (male or female). For example, early research on conversational behavior reported that males were more likely than females to use more dominant and assertive speech patterns in interaction, such as interrupting (West and Zimmerman 1983) and talking more (Aries 1976). However, a later review of the many empirical studies on interruptions and time spent talking showed that gender had inconsistent effects (James and Clarke 1993; James and Drakich 1993). This inconsistency might be explained through an analysis of gender identity rather than gender. For example, research shows that persons with a more masculine gender identity, irrespective of their gender as male or female, are more likely to use overlaps, interruptions, and challenging statements in a conversation (Drass 1986; Spencer and Drass 1989).

While gender identity may sometimes be more important than gender in determining outcomes, it is also possible for one's gender (male or female) and one's gender identity (masculine or feminine) to each result in different displays of behavior. For example, in an analysis of problem-solving discussions between newly married spouses, females and those with a more masculine gender identity were more likely to express negative, oppositional, and dominating behavior, such as complaining, criticizing, or putting down their spouse (Stets and Burke 1996). While masculinity more than femininity should increase dominating behavior (as discussed above), it was surprising that females engaged in more dominating behavior than males.

It was discovered that this dominating behavior emerged especially from females who were viewed by their spouses as being in a weak, subordinate position in our society. These women were apparently using coercive communication to counteract the (subordinate) view of them and gain some control. The problem is that in compensating for their weaker status by behaving in a dominant fashion, women may unwittingly be reminding men of their weak position.

While one's gender identity is generally stable over time, it sometimes changes in response to different experiences. To examine stability and change in gender identity, Burke and Cast (1997) examined the gender identities of newly married couples over the first three years of marriage, finding that the year-to-year stability in gender identity was moderately high. This means that while the gender identities of the respondents did change over this period of time, they did not change markedly. Looking from month to month or week to week, there was almost no observable change.

Identity theory suggests that identities are most likely to change in the face of persistent changes in the environment. The birth of a first child represents a dramatic and persistent change in the environment that confers femininity on women and masculinity on men. Burke and Cast showed that when a couple had their first child, women's gender identities became more feminine and men's gender identities become more masculine. Social psychological processes may also modify one's gender identity. Burke and Cast also found that the more a spouse took the perspective of the other in the marriage, the more the spouse shifted his or her gender identity in the direction of the other's gender identity. The other's gender identity was thus verified and supported by the spouse, which may act to minimize marital conflict.

THE FUTURE

We mention below several avenues of possible future work in femininity/masculinity. Many more avenues could be identified, for this is an area rich for continuing investigation, but our space is limited. First, we are only beginning to understand issues of stability and change in one's gender identity. How might gender identities be modified through participation in societal institutions such as the economy, religion, and politics? For example, to what extent and in what ways might employers socialize employees into particular views of being masculine or feminine in order to maintain a smooth flow of work and profit? Are some people more resistant to this socialization than others? Is this issue tied to how relevant gender identity is to individuals?

Related to the above is a second avenue of research, that is, the salience of gender identity across individuals, groups, even cultures. Salience refers to the probability that a particular identity will be invoked in a situation (Stryker 1980). This will vary by situation, but it also varies across individuals. For some, gender is not very relevant, and for others gender is almost always relevant. This returns us to Bem's notion of gender schematization, or the tendency to see the world in gendered terms. What makes gender identity more or less salient for people, and what are the consequences of that?

Third, we know very little about subcultural, cultural, and cross-cultural differences in the meanings that are attached to femininity and masculinity. Most of what we know concerns Western cultures, yet as Margaret Mead discovered long ago, these patterns are not universal. We need to investigate the variation in the meanings of being masculine and feminine. Such studies may help us understand a society's division of labor, its differential power and status structure, and how its privileges and responsibilities are allocated. To modify the social system may mean first modifying individual beliefs about masculinity and femininity.

REFERENCES

Aries, Elizabeth 1976 "Interaction Patterns and Themes of Male, Female, and Mixed Groups." *Small Group Behavior.* 7:7–18.

Ashmore, Richard D., Frances K. Del Boca, and Arthur J. Wohlers 1986 "Gender Stereotypes." In Richard D. Ashmore and Frances K. Del Boca, eds., *The Social Psychology of Female-Male Relations: A Critical Analysis of Central Concepts.* New York: Academic Press.

Bem, Sandra, L. 1974 "The Measurement of Psychological Androgyny." *Journal of Consulting and Clinical Psychology* 42:155–162.

—— 1977 "On the Utility of Alternative Procedures for Assessing Psychological Androgyny." *Journal of Consulting and Clinical Psychology* 45:196–205.

—— 1981 "Gender Schema Theory: A Cognitive Account of Sex Typing." *Psychological Review* 88:354–364.

—— 1993 *The Lenses of Gender: Transforming the Debate on Sexual Inequality*. New Haven, Conn.: Yale University Press.

Biernat, Monica 1991 "Gender Stereotypes and the Relationship Between Masculinity and Femininity: A Developmental Analysis." *Journal of Personality and Social Psychology* 61:351–365.

Burke, Peter J. 1980 "The Self: Measurement Implications from a Symbolic Interactionist Perspective." *Social Psychology Quarterly* 43:18–29.

—— 1989 "Gender Identity, Sex, and School Performance." *Social Psychology Quarterly* 52:159–169.

—— 1991 "Identity Processes and Social Stress." *American Sociological Review* 56:836–849.

——, and Alicia D. Cast 1997 "Stability and Change in the Gender Identities of Newly Married Couples." *Social Psychology Quarterly* 60:277–290.

——, and Donald C. Reitzes 1981 "The Link Between Identity and Role Performance." *Social Psychology Quarterly* 44:83–92.

——, Jan E. Stets, and Maureen A. Pirog-Good 1988 "Gender Identity, Self-Esteem, and Physical and Sexual Abuse in Dating Relationships." *Social Psychology Quarterly* 51:272–285.

——, and Judy Tully 1977 "The Measurement of Role/Identity." *Social Forces* 55:880–897.

Chodorow, Nancy 1978 *The Reproduction of Mothering: Psychoanalysis and the Sociology of Gender*. Berkeley: University of California Press.

Drass, Kriss A. 1986 "The Effect of Gender Identity on Conversation." *Social Psychology Quarterly* 49:294–301.

Eagly, Alice H. 1987 *Sex Differences in Social Behavior: A Social-Role Interpretation*. Hillsdale, N.J.: Lawrence Erlbaum.

Freud, Sigmund 1927 "Some Psychological Consequences of the Anatomical Distinction Between the Sexes." *International Journal of Psychoanalysis* 8:133–142.

Gilligan, Carol 1982 *In a Different Voice: Psychological Theory and Women's Development*. Cambridge, Mass.: Harvard University Press.

James, Deborah, and Sandra Clarke 1993 "Women, Men and Interruptions: A Critical Review." In Deborah Tannen, ed., *Gender and Conversational Interaction*. New York: Oxford University Press.

——, and Janice Drakich 1993 "Understanding Gender Differences in Amount of Talk: A Critical Review of Research." In Deborah Tannen, ed., *Gender and Conversational Interaction*. New York: Oxford University Press.

Katz, Phyllis A. 1986 "Gender Identity: Development and Consequences." In Richard D. Ashmore and Frances K. Del Boca, eds., *The Social Psychology of Female-Male Relations: A Critical Analysis of Central Concepts*. New York: Academic Press.

Kohlberg, Lawrence 1966 "A Cognitive-Developmental Analysis of Children's Sex-Role Concepts and Attitudes." In Eleanor E. Maccoby, ed., *The Development of Sex Differences*. Stanford, Calif.: Stanford University Press.

Lindesmith, Alfred R., and Anselm L. Strauss 1956 *Social Psychology*. New York: Holt, Rinehart and Winston.

Lipman-Blumen, Jean 1984 *Gender Roles and Power*. Englewood Cliffs, N.J.: Prentice-Hall.

Maccoby, Eleanor E., and Carol N. Jacklin 1974 *The Psychology of Sex Differences*. Stanford, Calif.: Stanford University Press.

Mead, Margaret 1935 *Sex and Temperament in Three Primitive Societies*. New York: Dell.

Mischel, Walter 1966 "A Social-Learning View of Sex Differences in Behavior." In Eleanor E. Maccoby, ed., *The Development of Sex Differences*. Stanford, Calif.: Stanford University Press.

Morawski, J. G. 1985 "The Measurement of Masculinity and Femininity: Engendering Categorical Realities." In Abigail J. Stewart and M. Brinton Lykes, eds., *Gender and Personality: Current Perspectives on Theory and Research*. Durham, N.C.: Duke University Press.

Morawski, J. G. 1987 "The Troubled Quest for Masculinity, Femininity, and Androgyny." In Phillip Shaver and Clyde Hendrick, eds., *Sex and Gender*. Newbury Park, Calif.: Sage.

Osgood, Charles E., George J. Succi, and Percy H. Tannenbaum 1957 *The Measurement of Meaning*. Urbana: University of Illinois Press.

Spence, Janet T. 1984 "Masculinity, Femininity, and Gender-Related Traits: A Conceptual Analysis and Critique of Current Research." In B. A. Maher and W. Maher, eds., *Progress in Experimental Research*. San Diego: Academic Press.

—— 1985 "Gender Identity and Implications for Concepts of Masculinity and Femininity." In T. B.

Sonderegger, ed., *Nebraska Symposium on Motivation: Psychology and Gender*. Lincoln: University of Nebraska Press.

—— 1993 "Gender-Related Traits and Gender Ideology: Evidence for a Multifactorial Theory." *Journal of Personality and Social Psychology* 64:624–635.

——, and Robert L. Helmreich 1978 *Masculinity and Femininity: Their Psychological Dimensions, Correlates, and Antecedents*. Austin: University of Texas Press.

——, and Robert L. Helmreich 1980 "Masculine Instrumentality and Feminine Expressiveness: Their Relationships with Sex Role Attitudes and Behaviors." *Psychology of Women Quarterly* 5:147–163.

——, and Linda L. Sawin 1985 "Images of Masculinity and Femininity: A Reconceptualization." In Virginia E. O'Leary, Rhoda Kesler Unger, and Barbara Strudler Wallston, eds., *Women, Gender, and Social Psychology*. Hillsdale, N.J.: Lawrence Erlbaum.

Spencer, J. William, and Kriss A. Drass 1989 "The Transformation of Gender into Conversational Advantage: A Symbolic Interactionist Approach." *The Sociological Quarterly* 30:363–383.

Stets, Jan E., and Peter J. Burke 1996 "Gender, Control, and Interaction." *Social Psychology Quarterly* 59:193–220.

Storms, Michael D. 1979 "Sex Role Identity and its Relationships to Sex Role Attitudes and Sex Role Stereotypes." *Journal of Personality and Social Psychology* 37:1779–1789.

Stryker, Sheldon 1980 *Symbolic Interactionism*. Menlo Park, Calif.: Benjamin/Cummings.

Terman, Lewis M., and Catherine C. Miles 1936 *Sex and Personality*. New York: McGraw-Hill.

Weitzman, Lenore J. 1979 *Sex Role Socialization*. Palo Alto, Calif.: Mayfield.

West, Candace, and Don H. Zimmerman 1983 "Small Insults: A Study of Interruptions in Cross-Sex Conversations Between Unacquainted Persons." In Barrie Thorn, Chris Kramarae, and Nancy Heuley, eds., *Language, Gender, and Society*. Rowley, Mass.: Newbury House.

JAN E. STETS
PETER J. BURKE

FERTILITY DETERMINANTS

There have been two periods of intense interest in the determinants of fertility by demographers.

The first period, which encompasses the late nineteenth and early twentieth centuries, was dominated by a concern about differential fertility within Western countries; in this period, leaders of the eugenics movement enlisted the services of demographers to learn how these differentials could be reduced, either by increasing the fertility of some groups or lowering the fertility of others. The second period, encompassing the 1940s to the late 1980s, was dominated by concern about differences in fertility (and thus in population growth rates) between Western countries and those countries known variously as, "less developed," "developing," "Third World," and, most recently, "Southern." In this period, there was little effort to raise fertility in low-fertility societies but a great deal of effort by an international population movement composed of neo-Malthusians and family planners to lower fertility in high-fertility societies by promoting the use of modern contraception. Again, policy makers turned to demographers to learn about the determinants of fertility. At the end of the twentieth century, fertility appears to have a lower place on the agenda of demographers. In some Western countries where national population growth rates are below replacement, there is increasing concern about fertility that is considered to be too low; groups that have fertility considered to be too high are largely adolescents and, in some countries, immigrants. Many Southern countries and some Western policy makers, however, remain concerned about levels of fertility, particularly in poor countries where fertility declines are just beginning. I begin by describing fertility determinants in pretransition societies (those characterized by an absence of deliberate attempts to limit family size) and then describe fertility transitions in Europe and the Third World.

DEFINITIONS

Fertility refers to the actual childbearing performance of individuals, couples, groups, or populations. Fertility transitions are best defined not in terms of a change in level (from high to low) but rather in terms of reproductive practices. Pretransition societies are those in which *married* couples do not effectively stop childbearing once they reach the number of children they desire; correspondingly, the onset of a fertility transition is marked by the adoption of practices to stop childbearing before the woman's physiological capacity to reproduce is exhausted. More precisely, in pretransition societies behavior is not parity-specific; that is, it does not depend on the number of children the couple has already borne (Henry 1961). At some point in time, presumably all societies were pretransition; currently, there are few societies where fertility remains high (most are in sub-Saharan Africa) and even fewer where there are no signs that a fertility transition may have begun (Bongaarts and Watkins 1996).

FERTILITY DETERMINANTS IN PRETRANSITION SOCIETIES

Despite the absence of parity-specific control in pretransition societies, fertility varies across individuals, couples, and groups: Observed total fertility rates for a population are as high as twelve (married Hutterites in the 1920s) and as low as four to five (the Kung hunters and gatherers in the 1970s and rural Chinese farmers around 1930). Important advances in understanding the sources of this variation followed a distinction between the "proximate" determinants of fertility and the "true" determinants of fertility, a distinction that owed much to an earlier systematic classification of influences on fertility made by Kingsley Davis and Judith Blake (1956). The proximate determinants are *direct* determinants of fertility, the combination of biological and behavioral channels through which the "true" determinants—the social, economic, psychological, and environmental factors—affect fertility (Bongaarts 1978).

In pretransition societies, the two most important of the proximate determinants of the overall level of fertility are marriage patterns and breast-feeding patterns. The other proximate determinants—fecundability (the monthly probability of conceiving among women who menstruate regularly but do not practice contraception), the use of contraception, the risk of spontaneous intrauterine mortality, and induced abortion—play a lesser role in accounting for variations in fertility (Bongaarts

and Menken 1983). Marriage patterns are important, since in most societies childbearing occurs within marriage. Thus, the proportion of women who are currently married at the ages at which reproduction is physiologically possible has a major influence on fertility. There is a striking difference between the marriage patterns of Western Europe and countries of European settlement, such as the United States, Australia, and New Zealand, and societies in other parts of the world, particularly Asia and Africa. In the former, marriage has been relatively late at least since the fourteenth century, and substantial proportions of women remain lifelong spinsters. In Africa and Asia, the typical pattern has been that marriage for women is early (usually as soon as a woman is able to bear a child she marries), and virtually all women marry. Obviously, the reproductive span in Western countries has been on average shorter than that in Asian and African societies. The peculiar Western European marriage pattern is associated with a nuclear family household ideal. In Western countries, couples typically set up their own households after marriage; in Asia and Africa, in contrast, the ideal has usually been that sons bring wives into their parents' household, while daughters go to live in the parental households of their husbands (Laslett 1972). Since the ability to support one's own household is associated with age, it is not surprising that the age of marriage has been later in Western countries than elsewhere.

Within marriage, the major determinants of variations in fertility across groups in populations in which little or no contraception is practiced is breast-feeding, since nursing inhibits the return of ovulation. In addition, in some societies a period of abstinence from sexual intercourse is prescribed by local custom, often because it is believed that intercourse during this period will harm the mother or the child. Post-partum abstinence taboos have been found to vary from a few weeks to as much as a year; if these are followed, they can account for substantial variations in marital fertility. Little research has been done on the determinants of post-partum abstinence. They are clearly cultural, in the sense that they characterize societies of interacting individuals, but they may also be linked to other factors.

Although differences in marriage patterns and breast-feeding patterns account for much of the observed differences in fertility across groups in pretransition societies, it is unlikely that their variation reflects variation in desired family size, for either the individual or the couple. Whether marriage was early or late, or whether breast-feeding was short or long, seems largely the outcome of other social concerns (Kreager 1982). It is probable that these patterns were determined by community norms or social structures, rather than individual preferences: Communities seem to have differed more in these respects than did individuals within these communities (Watkins 1991).

FERTILITY TRANSITIONS

It is conventional to distinguish between fertility transitions in Western societies and those in other parts of the world. There are evident differences not only in geography but also in timing, with Western fertility transitions occurring earlier. In addition, fertility transitions in non-Western countries were promoted by an international population movement that played a major role in making modern contraception accessible in the Third World, whereas fertility declines in the West occurred without such efforts by governments or social movements. There have recently been a number of reviews of the determinants of fertility change; taken together, they show little consensus on similarities or differences in other determinants of fertility change (Hirschman 1994; Kirk 1996; Mason 1997), although most include mortality decline, the perception that large numbers of children are increasingly unaffordable, the attitudes and moralities concerning family life, and the costs of birth control (Casterline in press).

The earliest sustained fertility transitions at the national level occurred in France, where fertility decline began around the time of the French Revolution, and in the United States, where fertility control was evident in a number of New England communities by the end of the first quarter of the nineteenth century and widespread among women who married on the eve of the Civil War (David and Sanderson 1987). Other fertility transitions spread throughout Europe between 1870

and 1930 (Coale and Watkins 1986), with similar timing in Australia. These changes began in the core countries of northwest Europe and occurred later in the periphery of Central Europe and the Mediterranean countries. In contrast, most analysts agree that there was little evidence of efforts to deliberately stop childbearing or a decline in marital fertility anywhere in the developing world before 1960, except for Argentina, Uruguay, and Chile (largely populated by settlers from Western Europe).

The observation was nearly universal that industrialization was causing this decline, with those who were in more industrial settings (i.e., cities) having lower fertility than rural populations. Industrialization was thought to produce a rising standard of living, an increasingly complex division of labor, an open class system, a competitive social milieu, and individualism. These changes, most thought, induced a desire for smaller families (Hodgson and Watkins 1997). What most concerned observers of fertility changes was the differential fertility by class and ethnicity; the latter was particularly important in late nineteenth- and early twentieth-century America, a period of massive immigration from Eastern, Central, and Southern Europe (Watkins 1994). Although some early observers saw the declining fertility of the wealthy and the urban as fostering prosperity, by the last quarter of the nineteenth century most emphasized the consequences of differential fertility for the composition of the population. For example, U.S. President Theodore Roosevelt decried the "race suicide" of upper-class women who were avoiding marriage or having small families: "The greatest problem of civilization is to be found in the fact that the well-to-do families tend to die out; there results, in consequence, a tendency to the elimination instead of the survival of the fittest" (1907, p. 550). At the time, eugenicists worried that the "prudent and thoughtful" would be the ones to practice birth control, while knowledge of birth control was unlikely to affect the fertility of the "reckless" lower classes (Hodgson and Watkins 1997, pp. 473–474). Women, according to most commentators, were the instigators of fertility decline, and many linked their turn to abortion and contraception to their reassessment of the value of motherhood. The problem was seen to be particularly acute among elite women. When initial attempts to persuade elite women to bear more children failed, attention was turned to persuading others to have fewer, and access to contraception was gradually liberalized. In Western countries the concerns of demographers and policy makers with domestic population composition faded with the widespread low fertility of the 1930s, and the eugenics movement was dealt a serious blow by its association with Nazi Germany in the 1930s and 1940s.

In the 1950s, Western attention turned to population growth rates in developing countries, many of which had until recently been colonies of Western countries. Mortality was declining, but until the 1960s, fertility in most developing countries was relatively high and apparently stable, aside from brief fluctuations associated with wars, famines, and other upheavals. This stimulated the formation of an international population movement, an alliance of neo-Malthusians, who emphasized the problems consequent on rapid population growth, and birth-controllers, who emphasized the importance of providing women with the means to control their reproduction. Subsequently, the previous pattern of stable reproduction came to an abrupt halt with the onset of rapid fertility transitions in a majority of countries. Between the early 1960s (1960–1965) and the late 1980s (1985–1990), the total fertility rate of the developing world as a whole declined by an estimated 36 percent—from 6.0 to 3.8 births per woman (United Nations 1995). Declines have been most rapid in Asia and Latin America (−42 and −43 percent respectively), less rapid but still substantial in the Middle East and North Africa (−25 percent), and almost nonexistent in sub-Saharan Africa. These averages conceal wide variations among countries in the timing of the onset of transitions and their subsequent pace. At one end of the spectrum of experience are a few countries (e.g., Hong Kong and Singapore) where a fertility transition started around 1960, followed by swift further reductions to the replacement level. At the other extreme are other countries, mostly in sub-Saharan Africa, that have not yet entered the transition.

These remarkable trends in reproductive behavior have been extensively documented in censuses and surveys, and the empirical record is not in dispute (Bongaarts and Watkins 1996). The causes of these trends, however, are the subject of often-contentious debate. Conventional theories of fertility decline, from the modernization versions dominant in the 1950s and 1960s to neoclassical economic and rational actor versions of recent decades, assume the fundamental importance of socioeconomic change, much as did nineteenth-century theories about industrialization and fertility decline. Socioeconomic development results in shifts in the costs and benefits of children and hence in the demand for them. As desired family size declines, fertility reduction soon follows with the widespread adoption of birth control, especially when governments make contraceptive services available through family-planning programs. While this broad explanation is widely accepted, analysts vigorously debate the precise variables and processes involved in this chain of causation. These disagreements have been stimulating and fruitful, producing a wide variety of increasingly refined and detailed views that have guided empirical investigations.

Although rises in female marriage age have contributed to the decline in fertility, this decline is largely due to the adoption of new behavior in marriage: More precisely, it is due to the adoption of parity-specific control using modern contraceptives. In Europe, fertility declines were accomplished initially by the use of abortion, withdrawal, and/or abstinence by married couples to stop childbearing, and only later by the use of modern contraceptives to space children as well as to limit their number. In the Third World, fertility decline was closely associated with the use of modern contraceptives.

Why did fertility decline? Why did couples start to deliberately limit the number of children they bore? What are the "true" determinants of fertility? While a comprehensive theory of fertility would account for both the shift from high to low fertility and variations in fertility at each stage of the fertility transition, most of the attempts to understand the social, economic, and cultural influences on fertility have focused on attempts to understand the onset of the fertility transition. Almost anything that distinguishes traditional from modern societies has been considered relevant to the explanation of the fertility decline (Cleland 1985; see also reviews of fertility determinants by Hirschman 1994; Kirk 1996; Mason 1997).

The most influential theories that have guided demographic research into the determinants of fertility over the last four decades have been those that assume the fundamental importance of economic factor. Predominant in the 1960s and 1970s was the theory of the demographic transition (classic statements are Davis 1963; Freedman 1961–1962; Notestein 1953; Thompson 1929). Demographic transition theory is based on the assumption that the means of fertility control used in the early stages of the Western fertility transition were always known. Hence, fertility declines can be attributed to changes in the motivations of individuals or couples, changes thought to be related to "modernization," especially increasing literacy, urbanization, the shift to paid, nonagricultural labor, and declines in infant and child mortality. Neoclassical economic theory, and in particular the New Home Economics associated with Gary Becker (1991), provides a translation from macro-level structural changes to the micro-level calculus of parents (for a more thorough review, see Pollak and Watkins 1993).

Empirical examinations driven by these theories gave them some support. It is now generally acknowledged that economic factors—often described in terms of the "costs" and "benefits" of children—are important determinants of fertility decline. It is, however, also acknowledged that economic factors do not provide a complete explanation. Currently, interesting research focuses on several additions to classical demographic transition theory and to neoclassical economic approaches.

Much attention has been devoted to evaluating the role of family-planning programs in the fertility decline in the Third World, where it seems that the methods used initially in the West were either not known or considered too costly in personal terms (Knodel et al. 1984). In the 1950s, it became evident that population growth rates in Third World countries were high because of declining mortality but stable fertility. This was believed to have substantial consequences, ranging from changes in the composition of the world's population (an increasing proportion of which was projected to come from Third World countries) to effects on Third World countries themselves, including famine, political instability, and the constraints that population growth was expected to place on the ability of these countries to develop economically and to modernize more generally. This led to concerted efforts by international agencies, Western governments, and Third World countries themselves to reduce fertility by making modern contraception desirable and accessible in the Third World (Hodgson and Watkins 1997). There has been considerable debate about the effectiveness of these efforts, with some according them little importance (e.g., Pritchett 1994) and others giving them more weight (e.g., Bongaarts 1997). There was a significant impact on fertility levels in the late 1980s, but whether this program effect operates primarily by affecting the timing of the onset of the transition or by the pace of fertility decline cannot be determined with available data (Bongaarts and Watkins 1996).

There has also been considerable interest in institutional determinants of fertility change. These are typically social institutions (e.g., systems of landholding) but occasionally are emergent properties of the collective behavior of individuals (Smith 1989). Therefore, in understanding the frequent association between education and fertility decline, for example, it may be more relevant to ask what proportion of the community has attended school than to ask whether a particular individual has. Similarly, both class relations and gender relations are aspects of the community rather than the individual, and both are likely to be associated with fertility change.

Another perspective emphasizes ideational change. Ideational changes are sometimes broadly, sometimes more narrowly, defined. Among the former is a shift in ideational systems toward individualism, which offered justification for challenging traditional authorities and practices, including those that concerned reproduction

(Lesthaeghe 1983). In a similar vein, John Caldwell argues that much of the fertility decline in developing countries can be explained in terms of the introduction of images of the egalitarian Western family into the more patriarchal family systems of the developing world. It was not so much that the relative balance of costs and benefits of children changed, but that the moral economy shifted: It came to be seen as inappropriate to derive economic benefit from one's children (Caldwell 1982). Among the narrower ideational changes are reevaluations of the acceptability of controlling births within marriage (Watkins in press) and changes in the acceptability of modern family planning (Cleland and Wilson 1987). Explanations for fertility declines in terms of ideational change are often linked to a focus on diffusion as an important mechanism of change, where diffusion can be postulated as stemming from a central source such as the media (e.g., Westoff and Rodríguez 1995) and/or from person to person in global, national, and/or local networks of social interaction (Bongaarts and Watkins 1996). It is likely that personal networks influence fertility through social learning and the exercise of social influence (Montgomery and Casterline 1996). Intensive efforts to examine local networks of social interaction and their relation to fertility are currently underway in several countries (Agyeman et al 1995; Behrman et al. 1999; Entwistle et al. 1997).

What will happen to fertility in the future? In Western countries, fertility is close to replacement level, although in some (e.g., Italy, Spain) it is well below. There is less variation in fertility than there was either in pretransition societies or during the transition (Watkins 1991). Most couples desire only a few children (rarely more than two), and most use effective means to achieve their desires. Accordingly, analysts have concentrated on the determinants of fertility in specific subgroups of the population, such as teenagers or ethnic or racial minorities. In doing so, they have drawn on much the same combination of socioeconomic characteristics, institutional factors, and ideational change. For example, the higher fertility of teenagers is usually explained in terms both of their differing socioeconomic characteristics and of their lesser access to effective contraception, as well as to an unwillingness to use it.

Few expect fertility to rise, and there seems to be a consensus that fertility will either remain around replacement level or decline further (see, e.g., Lesthaeghe and Willems 1999). The predictions of even lower fertility in the West are based on a combination of proximate and true determinants. Since the 1960s, marriage age has risen sharply in most developed countries, as have divorce rates; if these trends continue—and as long as most children continue to be born within marriage—lower fertility will follow. There has also been some increase in the proportion who are unable to bear children, in part because some couples postpone marriage and childbearing so long that they are unable to have the children they want, and in part because it is likely that involuntary sterility associated with sexually transmitted diseases may have increased at least slightly (Menken 1985). But the major predictions of lower fertility in the future emphasize the characteristics of modern societies that make childbearing less rewarding compared to the other opportunities available to women and the continued inroads into the family that individualism is making (Keyfitz 1986; Preston 1986; Schoen et al. 1997).

Similarly, fertility is likely to begin to decline in Third World countries that have not yet begun a fertility transition and to continue to decline in those where this process has begun. The course of fertility decline in countries where fertility is now low suggests that once the process of the fertility transition has started, fertility levels decline monotonically until very low levels are reached. Moreover, there is no turning back: The new reproductive behavior is not abandoned. Thus, it is likely that past differences in fertility both within and across countries will diminish.

(SEE ALSO: *Demographic Transition*; *Family and Population Policy in Less Developed Nations*; *Family Planning*; *Family Policy in Western Societies*; *Family Size*)

REFERENCES

Agyeman, D., P. Aglobitse, C. Fayorse, J. Casterline, and M. Montgomery 1995 "Social Networks and Fertility

Control in Ghana." Paper presented at the annual meeting of the Population Association of America, San Francisco, April 6–8.

Becker, Gary S. 1991 *Treatise on the Family*. Cambridge, Mass.: Harvard University Press.

Behrman, Jere R., Peter Kohler, and Susan C. Watkins 1999 "Family Planning Programs and Social Interaction: Exploration of Two Dimensions of Specification." Manuscript Submitted for Publication.

Bongaarts, John 1978 "A Framework for Analyzing the Proximate Determinants of Fertility." *Population and Development Review* 4(1):105–132.

——— 1997 "The Role of Family Planning Programmes in Contemporary Fertility Transitions." In G. W. Jones, R. M. Douglas, J. C. Caldwell, and R. M. D'Souza, eds., *The Continuing Demographic Transition* Oxford: Clarendon Press.

———, and Jane Menken 1983 "The Supply of Children: A Critical Essay." In R. Bulatao and R. Lee, eds., *Determinants of Fertility in Developing Countries*, vol. 1. New York: Academic Press.

———, and Susan C. Watkins 1996 "Social Interactions and Contemporary Fertility Transitions." *Population and Development Review* 22(4):639–682.

Caldwell, John C. 1982 *Theory of Fertility Decline*. New York: Academic Press.

Casterline, John B. in press "The Onset and Pace of Fertility Transition." *Population and Development Review*.

Cleland, John 1985 "Marital Fertility Decline in Developing Countries: Theories and the Evidence." In J. Cleland and J. Hobcraft, eds., *Reproductive Change in Developing Countries: Insights from the World Fertility Survey*. London: Oxford University Press.

———, and Chris Wilson 1987 "Demand Theories of the Fertility Decline: An Iconoclastic View." *Population Studies* 41:5–30.

Coale, Ansley J., and Susan C. Watkins, eds. 1986 *The Decline of Fertility in Europe*. Princeton, N.J.: Princeton University Press.

David, Paul A., and Warren C. Sanderson 1987 "The Emergence of a Two-Child Norm Among American Birth-Controllers." *Population and Development Review* 13(1):1–41.

Davis, Kingsley 1963 "The Theory of Change and Response in Modern Demographic History." *Population Index* 29(4):345–366.

———, and Judith Blake 1956 "Social Structure and Fertility: An Analytic Framework." *Economic Development and Cultural Change* 4(3):211–235.

Entwisle, Barbara, Ronald R. Rindfuss, Stephen J. Walsh, Tom P. Evans, and Sara R. Curran 1997 "Geographic Information Systems, Spatial Network Analysis, and Contraceptive Choice." *Demography* 34(2):171–187.

Freedman, Ronald 1961–1962 "The Sociology of Human Fertility." *Current Sociology* 10/11(2):35–119.

Henry, Louis 1961 "Some Data on Natural Fertility." *Eugenics Quarterly* 8(2):81–91.

Hirschman, Charles 1994 "Why Fertility Changes." *Annual Review of Sociology* 20:203–233.

Hodgson, Dennis, and Susan Cotts Watkins 1997 "Feminists and Neo-Malthusians: Past and Present Alliances." *Population and Development Review* 23(3):469–523.

Keyfitz, Nathan 1986 "The Family That Does Not Reproduce Itself." *Population and Development Review* 12(suppl.):139–154.

Kirk, Dudley 1996 "Demographic Transition Theory." *Population Studies* 50(3):361–387.

Knodel, John, Havanon Napaporn, and Anthony Pramualratana 1984 "Fertility Transition in Thailand: A Qualitative Analysis." *Population and Development Review* 10(2):297–328.

Kreager, Philip 1982 "Demography in Situ." *Population and Development Review* 8(2):237–266.

Laslett, Peter 1972 "Introduction: The History of the Family." In P. Laslett and R. Wall, eds., *Household and Family in Past Time*. Cambridge, U.K.: Cambridge University Press.

Lesthaeghe, Ron 1983 "A Century of Demographic and Cultural Change in Western Europe." *Population and Development Review* 9(3):411–435.

———, and Paul Willems 1999 "Is Low Fertility a Temporary Phenomenon in the European Union?" *Population and Development Review* 25(2):211–228.

Mason, Karen O. 1997 "Explaining Fertility Transitions." *Demography* 34:443–454.

Menken, Jane A. 1985 "Age and Fertility: How Late Can You Wait?" *Demography* 22(4):469–483.

Montgomery, Mark R., and John B. Casterline 1996 "Social Learning, Social Influence and New Models of Fertility." *Population and Development Review* 22(suppl.):151–175.

Notestein, Frank 1953 "Economic Problems of Population Change." In *Proceedings of the Eighth International*

Conference of Agricultural Economists. London: Oxford University Press.

Pollak, Robert A., and Susan C. Watkins 1993 "Cultural and Economic Approaches to Fertility: A Proper Marriage or a Mésalliance?" *Population and Development Review* 19(3):467–496.

Preston, Samuel H. 1986 "Changing Values and Falling Birth Rates." *Population and Development Review* 12(suppl.):176–195.

Pritchett, Lant H. 1994 "Desired Fertility and the Impact of Population Policies." *Population and Development Review* 20(1):1–56.

Roosevelt, Theodore 1907 "A letter from President Roosevelt on race suicide." *American Monthly Review of Reviews* 35(5):550–551.

Schoen, Robert, Young J. Kim, Constance A. Nathanson, Jason Fields, and Nan M. Astone 1997 "Why Do Americans Want Children?" *Population and Development Review* 23(2):333–358.

Smith, Herbert L. 1989 "Integrating Theory and Research on the Determinants of Fertility." *Demography* 26(2):171–184.

Thompson, Warren S. 1929 "Population." *American Journal of Sociology* 34:959–975.

United Nations 1995 *World Population Prospects: The 1994 Revision*. New York: United Nations.

Watkins, Susan C. 1991 *From Provinces into Nations: Demographic Integration in Western Europe, 1870–1960*. Princeton, N.J.: Princeton University Press.

—— 1994 *After Ellis Island: Newcomers and Natives in the 1910 Census*. New York: Russell Sage Foundation.

—— in press "Local and Foreign Models of Reproduction in Nyanza Province, Kenya." *Population and Development Review*.

Westoff, Charles F., and Germán Rodríguez 1995 "The Mass Media and Family Planning in Kenya." *International Family Planning Perspectives* 21(1):26–31, 36.

SUSAN COTTS WATKINS

FIELD RESEARCH METHODS

See Case Studies; Ethnography; Ethnomethodology; Sociocultural Anthropology; Qualitative Methods.

FIELD THEORY

It was perhaps only the youthful optimism of a new science that allowed Kurt Lewin and his colleagues to believe that they had within their grasp the key elements of a "field theory of the social sciences." Social psychology made great strides in 1930s and 1940s. Lewin and Lippitt (1938) seemed to have demonstrated in the laboratory the inherent superiority of democracy over autocracy. Lewin (1948) provided a theoretical framework for resolving social conflicts, and after his death his colleagues quickly shaped his legacy into a social scientific theory (Lewin, 1951). How could they resist? The physicists had just announced developments that shook the foundations of Newtonian physics. It was expected that Einstein, safely ensconced in the Institute for Advanced Studies, would any day announce the "unified field theory" that would once again make the physical world an orderly place. Could they ask less of the social sciences?

By 1968 one of Lewin's former students, Morton Deutsch, would declare field theory—and all other grand theories of social psychology—moribund. A few years later, Nicholas Mullins (1973) would eulogize the entire field of small group research as "the light that failed," a victim of the untimely death of its only real intellectual leader, Kurt Lewin. Mullins's borrowing of the Kipling title is compelling not only because it suggests that small group research promised much and failed to deliver but also because it suggests that field theory extended its reach beyond its grasp. In recent years there has been a revival of interest in field theory, though, for better or worse, much of the youthful optimism has faded.

LEWIN AND THE ORIGINS OF FIELD THEORY

Lewin's (1935) *A Dynamic Theory of Personality* called for a shift in psychology from the Aristotelian to the Galilean mode of thought. Epitomized by the now-classic formulation "behavior is a function of personality and environment," or $B=f(PE)$, the new perspective placed social psychology squarely at the intersection of psychology and sociology.

It required abandoning the hope that social behavior could be explained by reference to personality variables and seeking explanations in the dynamic relationships among actors and situations. In this book, Lewin defined the building blocks of the field theory that was to come: force (a vector directed at a point of application), valence (the push or pull of the force), and conflict (the opposition of roughly equivalent forces). At this point, he clearly had in mind a metric space of social life, the concepts of vector and direction having limited meaning in topological (or nonmetric) space.

The young field of topological mathematics soon freed Lewin from the necessity of defining a metric space of social life. In *Principles of Topological Psychology*, he defined the new nonmetric space: "By this term is meant that we are dealing with mathematical relationships which can be characterized without measurement. No distances are defined in topological space" (Lewin 1936, p. 53). The concept was a failure; his presentation to the mathematicians at MIT made it clear that he had overreached. He had ventured into the murky realm of topology when, in fact, he always intended to return to metric space. Two additional difficulties also appear in this volume. First, Lewin insisted that the new topological psychology deal with the entire life-space of the individual. Much as Simmel (1917) conceived of the individual as lying at the intersection of various "social circles," Lewin saw the individual life-space as made up of the totality of available social rations. For practical purposes, this made the specification of a single life-space almost impossibly complex. If one then tried to understand even a small group of actors by merging life-spaces, the problem became overwhelming. Second, Lewin often seemed to think of life-space in terms of physical space. Thus, locomotion almost literally meant moving from one physical location to another. This confusion of metaphor with reality prevented Lewin from proposing a consistent conceptual space of the sort suggested by Borgatta (1963), Bales (1985), and others.

A collection of Lewin's (1948) more applied American papers, *Resolving Social Conflicts*, appeared the year he died. Lewin translated concrete conflicts into abstract life-space "capsules." They were designed to illustrate the concept of "range of free movement" as "a topological region encircled by other regions that are inaccessible" (Lewin 1948, p. 5). The researchers who followed him have since used his graphic depiction of life-space as capsules only rarely. In the same volume, Lewin defined two useful characteristics of the boundaries between sectors of the life-space: sharpness (the clarity of boundaries) and rigidity (the ease with which boundaries may shift). *Field Theory in the Social Sciences*, a collection of Lewin's more theoretical writings, appeared in 1951. In these papers, Lewin introduced the most crucial concepts. Conflict is defined as "the overlapping of two force fields," force as "the tendency toward locomotion," and position as "a spatial relation of regions" (1951, pp. 39–40). The example of a conflict between husband and wife illustrates Lewin's concept of "subjective" and "objective" social fields. The subjectively defined life-spaces of two people differ, and so a single interpersonal act may have very different meanings for the two actors. Repeated reality testing is necessary to bring the individuals to a consensually defined "objective" social life-space.

Lewin never really succeeded in developing a predictive theory of group dynamics: "The clarification of the problems of past and future has been much delayed by the fact that the psychological field which exists at a given time contains the views of that individual about his future and past" (Lewin 1951, p. 53). The field is still struggling with this problem, lacking an adequate theory of even state-to-state transition.

In the years following Lewin's death, the focus shifted from the theoretical to the applied. Much of the work done at the University of Michigan's Research Center for Group Dynamics and at the National Training Laboratory's facilities in Bethel, Maine, was been only very loosely tied to the concepts of field theory. While Lewin is often credited with founding the field of organizational development (Weisbord 1987), his careful work on the nature of the social field is often ignored in favor of deceptively simple quotes such as "There's nothing so practical as a good theory." While Lewin believed that he could not be sure that he had fully understood a social situation unless he could change it, he never assumed that the ability to bring about change implied understanding. Only in the past several years has attention returned to the difficult legacy of an incomplete field theory.

THE CURRENT STATE OF FIELD THEORY

The Society for the Advancement of Field Theory was founded at a Temple University conference in 1984. Stivers and Wheelan (1986) have since published the proceedings of the conference as *The Lewin Legacy*. Later, papers from the two subsequent biennial conferences have been published as *Advances in Field Theory* (Wheelan et al. 1990).

The Lewin Legacy includes historical essays and applications of field theory to therapy, education, organizational development, and community psychology. A brief set of papers at the end calls for a revitalization of Lewinian thought, particularly within the tradition of action research. It is clear, however, that the authors are responding more to Lewin's research philosophy than to the theoretical constructs of his field theory.

Advances in Field Theory continues to focus on application, but with more explicit reference to theory. Gold's (1990) paper titled "Two Field Theories" addresses the issue of whether field theory is a "real theory" or simply an "approach." It distinguishes between the theory as described above and the approach—or "metatheory"—that has served as the guide for the generations of scholars that followed Lewin. Pointing out that much of social psychology has drifted away from the consideration of social life-space toward the understanding of internal cognitive processes, the author calls for a revitalization of the Galilean mode of thought. The remainder of the volume is once again directed toward the solution of practical problems. The authors deal with families, psychiatry, human development, education, conflict, organizations, and cross-cultural concerns. Virtually all of this work seems to draw on Lewin's "approach," or "metatheory," rather than his "specific field theory."

All of this is not to deny the tremendous impact that Lewin and his students have had on both academia and the resolution of social problems. What impressed his students most was Lewin's commitment to democracy and fairness. This commitment started in the research community, where he unselfishly gave of his time and intellect to help his students and colleagues expand their understanding of society. It extended to society at large. He and his students worked on behalf of the war effort during World War II and actively combated prejudice at home. As Weisbord (1987) has pointed out, the field of organizational development (OD) probably owes its existence and current shape to Lewin and his students. Organizational development is as much an ideology as a theory of change; its democratic value orientation owes much to the ideas of Kurt Lewin. Citing Marrow's (1969) excellent biography of Lewin, Weisbord draws parallels between the lives of Frederick Taylor and Kurt Lewin. Lewin's "humanization of the Taylor system" can be thought of as a blueprint for achieving the central goal of organizational development: increasing organizational effectiveness through the application of social science knowledge. In the seminal work in the field, *The Human Side of Enterprise*, Douglas McGregor (1960) blends the social science of Kurt Lewin with the humanistic psychology of Abraham Maslow (1954). The origins of participatory management, teambuilding, feedback, process consultation, and third-party intervention lie in both the theoretical and empirical work of Lewin and his colleagues: Ronald and Gordon Lippett, Ralph White, Kurt Back, Kenneth Beene, Dorwin Carwright, Alvin Zander, and others.

REKINDLING THE LIGHT: ATTEMPTS AT SYNTHESIS

The group process school, with its origins in Parsonian functionalism, has recently moved toward integration with the group dynamics school. Bales (1985), tracing the origins of field theory to Dewey's (1896) "reflex arc," suggested that his three-dimensional conceptual space of social interaction made possible a new field theory. He argued for the universality of the dimensions but stopped short of offering the integration: "The new field theory of social psychology is the needed framework, I believe, for the long-desired integration of social psychology. But to explore that thesis is a major undertaking, and here we must be content with a tentative case for the major dimensions of the framework" (Bales 1985, p. 17). Bales's colleagues (Hare et al. 1996) have since announced the existence of this "new field theory," but it has yet to be published in full and the academic community seems not to be eager to accept it as a major theoretical advance. Whether or not opinion changes as a result of the forthcoming publication of Bales's *Social Interaction Systems: Theory and Measurement* (1999) remains to be seen, but Bales's past efforts have been seen as much stronger in measurement than in theory. To the extent that Bales's new field theory has succeeded, it has been an operationalization of Lewin's concept of subjective life-space. His current theories of polarization are organized around positive and negative images in the minds of individual participants, not around consensual social reality.

Polley (1989) validated an updated set of dimensions and offered a series of explicit operational definitions for the basic concepts of Lewinian field theory. Figure 1 presents a "field diagram" that illustrates some of the basic principles. Two dimensions of interpersonal behavior (friendly–unfriendly and conventional–unconventional) define the plane of the diagram, and the third (dominant–submissive) is represented by circle size. Larger circles represent more dominant members, while smaller circles represent less dominant members. Members close together in the plane of the field diagram are drawn closer by vectors of positive valence, while distinct subgroups repel one another by vectors of negative valence. Members positioned at right angles to the central conflict between two subgroups tend to serve as mediators if they lie toward the "friendly" side of the space and as scapegoats if they lie toward the "unfriendly" side of the space. Both have the potential to draw opposing subgroups together, reducing the severity of the conflict. These analyses are based on "group average" perceptions and so are an attempt to operationalize Lewin's "objective" or consensual life-space. In 1994, Polley and Eid attempted an integration of the three major fields of

small group theory: Lewin's group dynamics, Bales's group process, and Moreno's sociometry. But again, while the methodology and theory are in use at a number of research centers, there has been no consensus among the academic community that either the synthesis or the operationalization of field theory have succeeded.

Two additional lines of research have drawn heavily on field theory concepts. Both developed observation systems based for the measurement of temporal patterns in groups. McGrath's (1991) research group developed a theory known as time, interaction, and performance (TIP) and an observation system known as TEMPO. Wheelan's (1999) research group is seeking to develop a model of group development based on a synthesis of Lewinian group dynamics and Bion's psychodynamic theory of groups. (For more information on these two lines of research, see Observation Systems.)

THE FUTURE OF FIELD THEORY

It now appears that Deutsch's announcement of the death of field theory was essentially correct, though there are a few signs of life, as indicated above. However, neither *Psychological Abstracts* nor *Sociological Abstracts* have listed "field theory" as a research topic in recent years. A search of the years 1985–1999 using *PsyINFO* revealed 177 books and articles under the key phrase "field theory." Of those, 65 dealt not with social field theory but with unrelated concepts that simply happened to share the same name. Of the remaining 112 citations, 31 were historical in nature and 63 used field theory as what Gold (1990) refers to as a "general approach" rather than as a specific theory capable of generating testable hypotheses. The remaining 18 articles use field theory as a specific theory. The applications of specific field theory are varied; the articles summarized below are not inclusive but should serve to give the flavor of the impact of Lewinian field theory.

Houston and associates (1988) and Dube and associates (1991) have applied field theoretic concepts to the study of customer evaluation of quality of service. Their model integrates concepts from marketing with those from Lewinian field theory

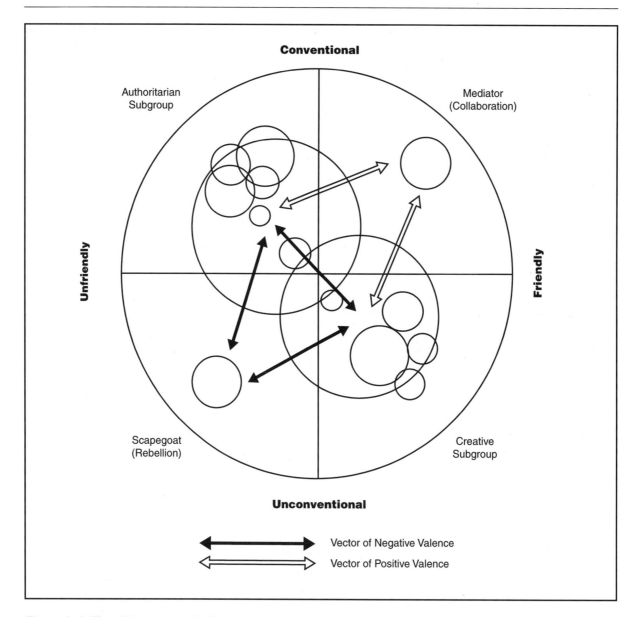

Figure 1. A Three-Dimensional Field Diagram, Showing Two Subgroups, a Mediator, and a Scapegoat.

to develop a deeper understanding of customer satisfaction. Granberg and Holberg (1986) compared behavioristic theory with field theory in attempting to explain voting behavior in Sweden and the United States. They conclude that field theory provides greater explanatory power than behavioristic psychology. In a related series of studies, Dillbeck (1990) and Assimakis and Dillbeck (1995) have employed field theory concepts to explain the effect of a Transcendental Meditation program on social change and perceptions of quality of life. Viser (1994) pitted field theory against Lazarsfeld's sociological model of voting behavior and contends that field theory provides a better explanation of voter choice. Greenberg (1988) employed field theory concepts of competing force fields to develop a model of employee theft behavior. Diederich (1997) used field theory as the basis for her multiattribute dynamic decision model (MADD), which she uses to predict decision making under time constraints. In the field of communications, Hample (1997) and

Greene (1997) have based theories of "message production" on the Lewinian concepts of life-space and planes of reality and unreality. In the realm of therapy, Barber (1996) has employed field theory to the understanding of the educational community as an agent of change. Dube and Schmitt (1996) tested field theory–based predictions of perceived time judgments. They demonstrated that "unfilled intervals" were perceived to be longer if they occurred during a social process rather than before or after the process. Smith and Smith (1996) identified the concept of the social field as necessary and sufficient for the explanation of social behavior. Finally, Diamond (1992) contrasted field theory and rational choice as explanations for social policy choices and concluded that field theory explains many effects that are dismissed as "irrational" by the rational choice model. This brief tour of empirical research is not intended as comprehensive, but it does suggest that field theory as a specific theory continues to be taken seriously in a variety of disciplines.

There may never be a widely accepted "grand theory" of social psychology. Certainly, the attempts that we have seen so far have not received widespread support from sociologists and psychologists. Still, Kurt Lewin's legacy is alive and well—as a philosophical orientation in a number of applied fields, such as organizational development, social work, conflict management, and therapy; as a general orientation for researchers in sociology and psychology; and even as a specific theory that continues to generate testable hypotheses. His all-too-brief career has served, and will likely continue to serve, as a guiding light to generations of researchers, practitioners, and social activists.

REFERENCES

Assimakis, Panayotis D., and Michael Dillbeck 1995 "Time Series Analysis of Improved Quality of Life in Canada: Social Change, Collective Consciousness, and the TM-Sidhi Program." *Psychological Reports* 76:1171–1193.

Bales, Robert F. 1985 "The New Field Theory in Social Psychology." *International Journal of Small Group Research* 1:1–18.

—— 1999 *Social Interaction Systems: Theory and Measurement*. Somerset, N.J.: Transaction Publishers.

Barber, Paul 1996 "The Therapeutic 'Educational' Community as an Agent of Change: Towards a Lewinian Model of Peer Learning." *Therapeutic Communities: The International Journal for Therapeutic & Supportive Organizations* 12:241–252.

Borgatta, Edgar 1963 "A New Systematic Interaction Observation System." *Journal of Psychological Studies* 14:24–44.

Deutsch, Morton 1968 "Field Theory in Social Psychology." In G. Lindsey and E. Aronson, eds., *The Handbook of Social Psychology*. Reading, Mass.: Addison-Wesley.

Dewey, John 1896 "The Reflex Arc Concept in Social Psychology." *Psychological Review* 3:357–370.

Diamond, Gregory A. 1992 "Field Theory and Rational Choice: A Lewinian Approach to Modeling Motivation." *Journal of Social Issues* 48:79–94.

Diederich, Adele 1997 "Dynamic Stochastic Models for Decision Making Under Time Constraints." *Journal of Mathematical Psychology* 41:260–274.

Dillbeck, Michael 1990 "Test of a Field Theory of Consciousness and Social Change." *Social Indicators Research* 22:399–418.

Dube, Laurette, and Bernd H. Schmitt 1996 "The Temporal Dimension of Social Episodes: Position Effect in Time Judgments of Unfilled Intervals." *Journal of Applied Social Psychology* 26:1816–1826.

Dube, Laurette, Bernd H. Schmitt, and France Leclerc 1991 "Consumers' Affective Response to Delays at Different Phases of a Service Delivery." *Journal of Applied Social Psychology* 21:810–820.

Gold, Martin 1990 "Two Field Theories." In S. Wheelan, E. A. Pepitone, and V. Apt, eds., *Advances in Field Theory*. Newbury Park, Calif.: Sage Publications.

Granberg, Donald, and Soeren Holberg 1986 "Prior Behavior, Recalled Behavior, and the Prediction of Subsequent Voting Behavior in Sweden and the U.S." *Human Relations* 39:135–148.

Greenberg, Jerald 1998 "The Cognitive Geometry of Employee Theft: Negotiating 'The Line' Between Taking and Stealing." In Ricky Griffing and Anne O'Leary-Kelly, eds., *Dysfunctional Behavior in Organizations*, vol. 23. Stamford, Conn.: JAI Press.

Greene, John O., ed. 1997 *Message Production: Advances in Communication Theory*. Mahwah, N.J.: Lawrence Erlbaum.

Hample, Dale 1997 "Framing Message Production Research with Field Theory." In John O. Greene, ed., *Message Production: Advances in Communication Theory*. Mahwah, N.J.: Lawrence Erlbaum.

Hare, A. Paul, Sharon E. Hare, and Robert J. Koenigs 1996 "Implicit Personality Theory, Social Desirability, and Reflected Appraisal of Self in the Context of the New Field Theory (SYMLOG)." *Small Group Research* 27:504–531.

Houston, Mark B. Lance A. Bettencourt, and Sutha Wenger 1998 "The Relationship Between Waiting in a Service Queue and Evaluations of Service Quality: A Field Theory Perspective." *Psychology and Marketing* 15:735–753.

Lewin, Kurt 1935 *A Dynamic Theory of Personality*. New York: McGraw-Hill.

—— 1936 *Principles of Topological Psychology*. New York: McGraw-Hill.

—— 1948 *Resolving Social Conflicts*. New York: Harper.

—— 1951 *Field Theory in the Social Sciences*. New York: Harper.

——, and Ronald Lippitt 1938 "An Experimental Approach to the Study of Autocracy and Democracy: A Preliminary Note." *Sociometry* 1:292–300.

Marrow, Alfred 1969 *The Practical Theorist*. New York: Basic Books.

Maslow, Abraham 1954 *Motivation and Personality*. New York: Harper and Row.

McGrath, Joseph E. 1991 "Time, Interaction, and Performance (TIP): A Theory of Groups." *Small Group Research* 22:147–174.

McGregor, Douglas 1960 *The Human Side of Enterprise*. New York: McGraw-Hill.

Mullins, Nicholas C. 1973 *Theories and Theory Groups in Contemporary American Sociology*. New York: Harper and Row.

Polley, Richard B. 1989. "Operationalizing Lewinian Field Theory." In E. J. Lawler and B. Markovsky, eds., *Advances in Group Processes: Theory and Method*. Greenwich, Conn.: JAI Press.

——, and J. Eid 1994 "First Among Equals: Leaders, Peers, and Choice." *Journal of Group Psychotherapy, Psychodrama and Sociometry* 47:59–76.

Simmel, Georg 1955 *Conflict and the Web of Group Affiliation* (K. H. Wolf and R. Bendix, trans.). New York: Free Press.

Smith, Noel W., and Lance L. Smith 1996 "Field Theory in Science: Its Role as a Necessary and Sufficient Condition in Psychology." *Psychological Record* 46:3–19.

Stivers, Eugene, and Susan Wheelan 1986 *The Lewin Legacy*. New York: Springer-Verlag.

Viser, Max 1994 "The Psychology of Voting Action." *Journal of the History of the Behavioral Sciences* 30:43–52.

Weisbord, Marvin R. 1987 *Productive Workplaces*. San Fransisco: Jossey-Bass.

Wheelan, Susan A., ed. 1999 "Group Development." *Small Group Research* (special issue) 30:3–129.

——, Emmy A. Pepitone, and Vicki Apt, eds. 1990 *Advances in Field Theory*. Newbury Park, Calif.: Sage Publications.

RICHARD B. KETTNER-POLLEY

FILIAL RESPONSIBILITY

The term *filial responsibility* denotes the "responsibility for parents exercised by children. The term emphasizes duty rather than satisfaction and is usually connected with protection, care, or financial support" (Schorr, 1980, p. 1). Although it is popularly believed that the obligation of children to care for their parents has ancient origins based on widely held moral beliefs, both historical and sociological evidence suggests that neither element of this belief is true (Finch 1989; Schorr 1980).

LEGAL MANDATES FOR FINANCIAL SUPPORT

One source of the persistent belief in both the historical existence of filial responsibility and its moral derivation stems from an equally persistent belief that there was a time in the past when "the family" had a stronger sense of responsibility for looking after its aging members (Finch 1989). However, a literature on the history of families and demographic trends has emerged that consistently refutes this belief (Laslett 1972). Central to this literature is an understanding of the effects of the demographic transitions, medical advancements, and changes in social and health practices that have resulted in a significant increase in the numbers of persons living into old age. Together these factors have resulted in dramatic changes in the population structure of modern societies wherein the aging segments account for a significantly higher proportion of the population than ever before (Himes 1994). Put simply, until recently only an extremely small segment of the population survived into an extended and dependent old age (Anderson 1980).

Furthermore, due to the nature of the preindustrial economy, those persons who did survive into old age were not dependent upon the goodwill of or a sense of obligation on the part of their children to assure their financial support. In preindustrial economies both land and businesses, which served as the family's source of sustenance, were owned by the oldest generation and passed down to the younger generation only at death. Hence, it was not the oldest generation that was dependent upon the younger generation, but rather the younger generation that was dependent on the older generation for housing and income. What care may have been provided to parents was, therefore, not necessarily based on a sense of moral obligation but instead stemmed from economic necessity (Haber and Gratton 1994; Schorr 1980).

As long as this economic basis for support existed, there was no need for filial responsibility laws (Schorr 1980). Only with the introduction of an industrial economy that provided a means for children to leave the parental home and obtain an income was there a need for the community to regulate filial responsibility. As Finch (1989, p. 84) notes:

> Much of the historical evidence. . . suggests that under the harsh conditions of poverty which prevailed for most people in the early industrial period, family relationships necessarily were highly instrumental, with support being offered only if there was. . . hope of mutual benefit precisely because anything else would have been an unaffordable luxury (p. 84).

The shift to an industrial economy changed the financial base of the family and introduced the possibility of independent access to financial resources by children. This shift effectively emphasized the possibility of elders becoming destitute (Bulcroft et al. 1989).

LEGAL MANDATES FOR FINANCIAL SUPPORT

From their first inception in Roman and English codes, filial responsibility laws were enacted as a means to protect the public purse (and minimize the financial responsibility of the wealthy class) (Jacobson 1995). The aim of such laws was to enable public authorities to recover the costs of maintaining paupers by making claims on those relatives assumed to be naturally bound by normal obligations of kinship to offer support. The poor laws established for the first time in history that the community would help an indigent parent only after the means of his child had been exhausted (Schorr 1980). These laws were not simply about poverty; they were laws intended to govern the lower class in order to keep down public expenditure. This motivation continues to underlie current laws and practices concerning the care of the elderly in both England and the United States. Despite the moral rhetoric in which filial responsibility laws are often couched, these laws emerged not as a result of moral values but in response to the threat of the growing financial burden that dependent elders posed to an industrial society (Jacobson 1995; Montgomery 1999).

Perhaps this absence of a moral basis for filial responsibility laws accounts for the inconsistency among states in the statement of filial responsibility. Filial responsibility laws, which in 1999 existed in some form in twenty-two states, are variously located in domestic statutes, poor laws, penal codes, and human resource laws. The nature of the fiscal responsibility incorporated into these statutes varies widely and tends to be quite vague. There are variations in the specificity as to which members of the family are responsible and the conditions under which they are responsible. Moreover, these laws are inconsistently enforced (Narayanan 1996), and many questions have been raised about their constitutionality and practicality (Jacobson 1995). For the most part, filial responsibility as incorporated in laws is limited to financial support; and these laws have generally gone unenforced. In fact, several court challenges to Medicaid laws have affirmed the illegality of states' requiring adult children to pay for care provided under Medicaid regulations (Jacobson 1995; Kline 1992).

ATTITUDES TOWARD FILIAL RESPONSIBILITY

Just as the discrepancy between the existence of filial responsibility laws and the lack of enforcement suggests an equivocal attitude toward children's responsibilities, results of attitude surveys about filial responsibility have been inconsistent.

While there is evidence that both parents and children acknowledge the existence of filial responsibility as a social expectation, individuals' reports of filial responsibility have been found to differ as a function of the type of support (Ganong et al. 1998), geographic distance from parents (Finley et al. 1988), income (Lee, Netzer and Coward 1994), and ethnicity (Lee et al. 1998; Stein et al. 1998). Findings regarding gender differences in attitudes toward responsibility have been mixed (Ganong et al. 1998).

Surveys generally yield respectable percentages of responses favoring filial responsibility as long as the question is limited to ethical and general terms (Schorr 1980). However, a majority of aged persons oppose filial responsibility when the question is reframed to introduce an individual's personal responsibility or to force a choice between the child and governmental/ community sources as the primary source of support (Schorr 1980). Recent studies have revealed a general trend in both Western and Asian cultures toward acceptance of the government or insurance programs as the source most appropriately responsible for financial support of the elderly (Sung 1990). The introduction of Social Security and Supplemental Security Income (SSI) in the United States and the introduction of national health care programs for the elderly in most other developed countries exemplify this trend. In a similar trend, adult children and their parents express a preference for independent living arrangements for the two generations even in Asian countries, where filial piety has long been a central value (Bleiszner and Hamon 1992).

Current practices of filial responsibility in the form of financial support correspond to these expressed preferences. For most families, the flow of financial support between generations is primarily from the oldest generation to the younger generation; and in most developed countries the two generations most commonly reside in separate housing units (Goldscheider and Lawton 1998). When parents and adult children do live together, it is usually due to the needs of the younger generation or the mutual benefits for both generations. The situation of a parent moving into the home of an adult child is relatively rare and is usually associated with a need for personal care rather than a need for housing.

FILIAL RESPONSIBILITY AS DIRECT PARENT CARE

The assumption by large numbers of adult children of responsibilities for the welfare and direct care of their parents has been the most significant change in family roles and filial responsibility practices in recent history. Although the motives that prompt adult children to care for their frail parents are not well understood, the predominance of adult children among informal caregivers is undisputed when all types and levels of assistance are considered. The prevalence of children as sources of emotional support, assistance with transportation and banking matters, and help with household chores and activities of daily living has been widely documented over the past two decades (e.g., Brody 1985; Merrill 1997).

Gender Differences. There is, however, a significant difference between sons and daughters in their caregiving activities and experience. Almost uniformly, studies have shown that greater numbers of daughters than sons assist their parents with a wider range of tasks. Daughters' predominance is especially strong with respect to direct personal assistance to their impaired parents (Merrill 1997). As a rule, daughters are more likely than sons to help elders with household chores, especially food preparation and laundry chores, as well as with personal care tasks that require hands-on care and daily assistance (Montgomery 1992). In contrast, sons tend to concentrate their efforts on tasks that are more circumscribed and sporadic, such as occasional shopping trips and annual yard and house maintenance activities.

The difference in the types of tasks that sons and daughters assume is related to the types of caregiving roles that the each group tends to assume. Daughters are not only more likely to engage in caregiving tasks; they are also more likely to assume the role of primary caregiver (Merrill 1997). As such, they are more likely to provide "routine" care over longer periods of time (Matthews and Rosner 1988; Stoller 1990). Sons, in contrast, assume supportive roles that require commitments over shorter periods of time; they tend to be peripheral helpers within a caregiving network rather than the central actors (Matthews 1995).

There is evidence that gender differences in patterns of care persist across cultures and classes. However, these patterns are mediated by the level of dependency of the elder and the size and gender composition of the family network (Coward and Dwyer 1990; Matthews 1995). Fewer gender differences are observed in patterns of care for parents with low levels of disability. Also, sons from family networks that do not include daughters tend to provide care in a style that is more similar to that of daughters.

Numerous explanations have been advanced to account for the observed divergence of caregiving behaviors between sons and daughters. Most of these explanations center on differences between male and female *roles* and gender differences in power within the family and within society in general (see Finley 1989). However, there is little evidence to support any of the hypothesized explanations, and none of them account for the persistence of divergent parent care activities.

Class Variations. Patterns of parent care have also been found to differ within the United States by class and income. Lower-class and working-class caregivers are more likely to live with the elder and to provide direct care. In contrast, higher economic status has been found to be associated with larger financial gifts and help with procuring services (Merrill 1997). This tendency for wealthy families to purchase care for the elderly has also been noted in a wide range of countries at different stages of development throughout the world (Kosberg 1992).

Cultural Variations. Cultural differences in informal care have been the focus of a number of studies. However, evidence of cultural differences in parent care within the United States remains equivocal. Greater levels of kin support among African Americans and Hispanics than among whites have been documented in a few studies (Lee et al. 1998; Tennstedt and Chang 1998); but other researchers have reported no differences in informal support (Belgrave and Bradsher 1994) or have documented greater use of informal supports by whites (Silverstein and Waite 1993). These inconsistencies in findings are likely due to differences in sampling designs and the confounding of ethnicity with socioeconomic status.

AFFECTION AND OBLIGATION

The persistence of parent care activities, despite the absence of legal or economic imperatives,

has often led researchers and policy makers to focus on affection as the primary motivation for these filial responsibility practices (Jarrett 1985). Numerous studies have noted the relationship between affection and the felt obligation to provide for parent care (Blieszner and Hamon 1992) as well as the importance of attitudes of obligation as correlates of contact with and assistance to parents (Walker et al. 1990). However, there is a growing literature that questions the importance of "affection" as the primary force underlying filial responsibility and/or the performance of caregiving tasks. Repeatedly, it has been shown that there can be emotional closeness between parent and child without contact or aid being given (Walker et al. 1989). At the same time, it has been shown that children who do not feel a great amount of affection for their parents are still able and willing to provide needed assistance (Lee and Sung 1997; Walker et al. 1990). Furthermore, there is growing evidence that caregiving is governed by a cluster of motives that encompass both affection and obligation (Belgrave and Bradsher 1994). For many children, affection may influence the way in which responsibilities are experienced, but these children frequently provide care simply because parents need care (Litwin 1994) or because they perceive few alternatives (Guberman et al. 1992).

PARENT CARE AS A CONSEQUENCE
SOCIAL POLICY

It has been suggested that the lack of alternatives for parent care is due to existing social policy, which incorporates assumptions about filial responsibility although it does not necessarily explicitly legislate this responsibility (Finch 1989; Montgomery 1999). Specifically, as implemented and practiced, policies and programs concerned with services for the elderly in both developed and developing countries reflect the belief that there is a latent willingness, presumably based upon a residual sense of responsibility that can be activated. The decline in economic liability of children for their parents, which has resulted from the introduction of old-age pensions and health care programs for the elderly, has not been accompanied by a decline in expectations that children will care for and support their parents. In fact, the general trend in long-term care policy, which has emphasized the benefits of community-based care, has been accompanied by a greater expectation of family care (Finch 1989; Hendricks and Hatch 1993). This expectation for relatives to provide direct care, however, remains more implicit in current long term-care policies than the fiscal liability of relatives, which was explicitly written into the original English poor laws and later adopted by many states (Doty 1995; Kapp 1995). For example, changes in Medicare coverage that are related to the prospective payment system have resulted in shorter hospital stays for elders, who are now being discharged with greater needs for assistance (Estes et al. 1993). The assumption appears to be that family members are, or should be, available to provide such care. Another example of the way in which current policy delegates the direct care responsibilities to family members is found in eligibility guidelines for (SSI), which reduce benefits for beneficiaries who live with other persons or who receive in-kind contributions from them (Hendricks and Hatch 1993). Built into this provision is the expectation that family members will provide the beneficiary with needed care at no cost. Although these regulations assure minimal financial commitment for states that otherwise would be responsible for nursing home care, they differ from fiscal responsibility laws in that the assignment of such responsibility is more diffuse (Doty 1995).

Most often, the delegation of responsibility for direct care to family is implicit rather than explicit. Expectations for direct care are often conveyed directly and indirectly to adult children by case-workers and physicians who serve as gatekeepers for community services (Doty 1995). Even when elders are eligible for assistance through formal providers, there is often pressure placed on family members to perform care (Guberman et al. 1992). When resources are scarce and must be rationed, the living arrangement of the elder as well as the gender and location of relatives become criteria for the distribution of services. The effect of these family characteristics on distribution of home- and community-based services is contingent upon the elder's level of functioning. For elders with low- to mid-level disability, priority for in home care services is given to those who live alone, with the expectation that family members will provide the necessary care for elders who live with them (Greene and Coleman 1995). In contrast, elders with high levels of disability who live with family members are more likely to receive home care services than those who live alone because discharge planners and case managers view such supports as supplemental but not sufficient for an elder living alone to remain in the community (Doty 1995).

Regardless of the elder's level of functioning, when practitioners convey expectations for care to family members, they are often influenced by cultural and gender norms regarding the division of labor within households (Walker 1983). Cumulative results overwhelmingly show that long-term care, like housework and child care, has been institutionalized as women's work (Keith 1995). Practitioners, who serve as gatekeepers for community resources, tend to offer greater supports to male caregivers and convey lower expectations for sons to provide direct care services (Doty 1995). The impact of these practices has been observed by researchers, who report care-sharing patterns that are associated with gender and note that sons tend to receive more assistance from formal service providers than do daughters (Merrill 1997).

The clear line between long-term care policies and family care patterns provides evidence that care patterns are not simply a result of choices made by family members to adhere to some "inherent" moral order. Rather, these patterns of care emerge as a consequence of laws and practices that limit the alternatives available to family members (Neysmith 1993). Taken together, the evidence regarding filial responsibility suggests trends in laws and practice that reflect a decline in expectations for financial support of the elderly but a simultaneous growth in expectations for children, especially daughters, to support parents in more direct ways. There is also an indication that filial responsibility, as practiced in terms of both financial and direct care, stems largely from necessity and is created by social policies and practices that tend to invoke a questionable or mythical moral basis for such responsibility.

REFERENCES

Anderson, M. 1980 *Approaches to the History of the Western Family 1500–1914*. London, U.K.: Macmillan.

Belgrave, Linda, and Julia Bradsher 1994 "Health as a Factor in Institutionalization: Disparities between African Americans and Whites." *Research on Aging* 16:115–141.

Blieszner, R., and R. R. Hamon 1992 "Filial Responsibility: Attitudes, Motivators and Behaviors." In J. W. Dwyer and R. T. Coward, eds., *Gender, Families and Elder Care*. Newbury Park, Calif.: Sage.

Brody, E. M. 1985 "Parent Care as a Normative Family Stress." *The Gerontologist* 25:19–29.

Bulcroft, K., J. Van Leynseele, and E.F. Borgatta 1989 "Filial Responsibility Laws: Issues and State Statutes." *Research on Aging* 11:374–393.

Coward, R. T., and J. W. Dwyer 1990 "The Association of Gender, Sibling Network Composition, and Patterns of Parent Care by Adult Children." *Research on Aging* 12:158–181.

Doty, P. 1995 "Family Caregiving and Access to Publicly Funded Home Care." In R. A. Kane and J. D. Penrod, eds., *Family Caregiving in an Aging Society*. Thousand Oaks, Calif.: Sage Publications.

Estes, C. L., J. H Swan, J. H and Associates 1993 *The Long Term Care Crisis*. Newbury Park, Calif.: Sage Publications.

Finch, J. 1989 *Family Obligations and Social Change*. Cambridge, U.K.: Polity Press and Basil Blackwell.

Finley, N. J. 1989 "Theories of Family Labor as Applied to Gender Differences in Caregiving for Elderly Parents." *Journal of Marriage and the Family* 51:79–86.

Finley, N. J., M. D. Roberts, and B. F. Banahan, III 1988 "Motivators and Inhibitors of Attitudes of Filial Obligation Toward Aging Parents." *The Gerontologist* 28:73–78.

Ganong, L., M. Coleman, K. McDaniel, and T. Killian 1998 "Attitudes Regarding Obligations to Assist an Older Parent or Stepparent Following Later-Life Remarriage." *Journal of Marriage and the Family* 60:595–610.

Goldscheider, F. K., and L. Lawton 1998 "Family Experiences and the Erosion of Support for Intergenerational Coresidence." *Journal of Marriage and the Family* 60:623–632.

Greene, V., and P. D. Coleman 1995 "Direct Services for Family Caregivers." In R. A. Kane and J. D. Penrod, eds., *Family Caregiving in an Aging Society: Policy Perspectives*. Thousand Oaks, Calif.: Sage Publications.

Guberman, N., P. Maheu, and C. Maille 1992 "Women as Family Caregivers: Why Do They Care? *The Gerontologist* 32:607–617.

Haber, C., and B. Gratton 1994 *Old Age and the Search for Security*. Bloomington: Indiana University Press.

Hendricks, J., and L. R. Hatch 1993 "Federal Policy and Family Life of Older Americans." In J. Hendricks and C. J. Rosenthal, eds., *The Remainder of Their Days: Domestic Policy and Older Families in the United States and Canada*. New York: Garland Publishers.

Himes, Christine 1994 "Parental Caregiving by Adult Women: A Demographic Perspective." *Research on Aging* 16:191–211.

Jacobson, R. 1995 "Americana Healthcare Center v. Randall: The Renaissance of Filial Responsibility." *South Dakota Law Review* 40:518–545.

Kapp, M. B. 1995 "Legal and Ethical Issues in Family Caregiving and the Role of Public Policy." In R. A. Kane and J. D. Penrod, eds., *Family Caregiving in an Aging Society*. Thousand Oaks, Calif.: Sage Publications.

Kline, T. 1992 "The Rational Role for Filial Responsibility Laws in Modern Society." *Family Law Quarterly* 26(3):193–210.

Keith, C. 1995 "Family Caregivng Systems: Models, Resources and Values." *Journal of Marriage and the Family* 57:179–189.

Kosberg, Jordan 1992 *Family Care of the Elderly: Social and Cultural Changes*. Thousand Oaks, Calif.: Sage Publications.

Laslett, P. 1972 "Introduction: The History of Family." In P. Laslett and R. Wall, eds., *Household and Family in the Past Time*. Cambridge, U.K.: Cambridge University Press.

Lee, Gary R., J. K Netzer, and Raymond T. Coward 1994 "Filial Responsibility Expectations and Patterns of Intergenerational Assistance." *Journal of Marriage and the Family* 56:559–565.

Lee, Gary R, Chuck Peek, and Raymond T. Coward 1998 "Race Differences in Filial Responsibility Expectations Among Older Parents." *Journal of Marriage and the Family* 60:404–412.

Lee, Yoon-Ro, and Kyu-Taik Sung 1997 "Cultural Differences in Caregiving Motivations for Demented Parents: Korean Caregivers Versus American Caregivers." *International Journal of Aging and Human Development* 44:115–117.

Litwin, Howard 1994 "Filial Responsibility and Informal Support Among Family Caregivers of the Elderly in Jerusalem: A Path Analysis." *International Journal of Aging and Human Development* 38:137–151.

Matthews, S. 1995 "Gender and the Division of Filial Responsibility Between Lone Sisters and Their Brothers." *Journals of Gerontology: Social and Behavioral Sciences* 50B:S312–S320.

—— and T. T. Rosner 1988 "Shared Filial Responsibility: The Family as the Primary Caregiver." *Journal of Marriage and the Family* 50:185–195.

Merrill, D. M. 1997 *Caring for Elderly Parents*. Westport, Conn.: Auburn House.

Montgomery, R. J. V. 1992 "Gender Difference in Patterns of Child-Parent Caregiving Relationships." In J. Dwyer and R. Coward, eds., *Gender, Families, and Elder Care*. Newbury Park, Calif.: Sage.

—— 1999 "The Family Role in the Context of Long-Term Care." *Journal of Aging and Health* 11(3):401–434.

Narayanan, U. 1996 "The Government's Role in Fostering the Relationship Between Adult Children and Their Elder Parents: From Filial Responsibility Laws to. . . What?, A Cross-Cultural Perspective." *The Elder Law Journal* 4(2):369–406.

Neysmith, S. M. 1993 "Developing a Home Care System to Meet the Needs of Aging Canadians and Their Families." In J. Hendricks and C. J. Rosenthal, eds., *The Remainder of Their Days: Domestic Policy and Older Families in the United States and Canada*. New York: Garland Publishers.

Schorr, Alvin L. 1980 *Thy Father and Thy Mother. . . A Second Look at Filial Responsibility and Family Policy*. Washington D.C.: Government Printing Office.

Silverstein, M., and L. J. Waite 1993 "Are Blacks More Likely Than Whites to Receive and Provide Social Support in Middle and Old Age? Yes, No, and Maybe So." *Journals of Gerontology: Social Sciences* 48:S212–S222.

Stein, Catherine, Virginia A. Wemmerus, Marcia Ward, Michelle E. Gaines, Andrew L. Freeberg, and C. Jewell Thomas 1998 "Because They're My Parents: An Intergenerational Study of Felt Obligation and Parental Caregiving." *Journal of Marriage and the Family* 60:611–622.

Stoller, E. P. 1990 "Males as Helpers: The Role of Sons, Relatives, and Friends." *The Gerontologist* 30:228–235.

Sung, K. 1990 "A New Look at Filial Piety: Ideals and Practices of Family-Centered Parent Care in Korea." *The Gerontologist* 30:610–617.

Tennstedt, S., and B. Chang 1998 "The Relative Contribution of Ethnicity Versus Socioeconomic Status in Explaining Differences in Disability and Receipt of Informal Care." *Journals of Gerontology: Social Sciences* 53B(2):S61–S70.

Walker, A. 1983 "Care for Elderly People: A Conflict Between Women and the State." In J. Finch and D. Groves, eds., *A Labour of Love: Women, Work and Caring*. Boston: Routledge and Kegan Paul.

—— C. C. Pratt, H.-Y. Shin, and L. L. Jones 1990 "Motives for Parental Caregiving and Relationship Quality." *Family Relations* 39:51–56.

RHONDA J. V. MONTGOMERGY

THE FRENCH SCHOOL OF SOCIOLOGY

The French School of Sociology was formed during the last decade of the nineteenth century and the first quarter of the twentieth century. The nucleus of the school was created by Emile Durkheim (1858–1917), to whose work was joined the crystalizing efforts in the new science that were performed by the team of *L'Année sociologique*, which was founded in 1898. In recent times, scholars have undertaken the examination of the effects of this major contribution to the field by studying the vicissitudes of Durkheim's legacy from the period between the two world wars and onward. We have also concentrated on clarifying the methods that permitted the exploitation and application of this legacy. In this regard, from 1979 to 1982, P. Besnard has fully informed us on the establishment and functioning of assistance strategies in the university and publishing fields. As important as the stakes of power may be, they are much less so than the thematic orientations that Durkheim and his disciples assigned to the science that, in 1838, Comte publicly baptized "sociology." Thus, in this entry, we will first apply ourselves to the task of recalling the path that was forged by the French School of Sociology; we will then examine schematically how it was charted and, finally, discuss the new directions in which sociological research is currently headed.

PRINCIPAL BRANCHES OF THE FRENCH SCHOOL OF SOCIOLOGY

Problems of periodization are particularly acute in the field of the history of ideas. They are associated with problems related to affiliations, to influences, to rupture and continuity in thought, and to collaboration. Of what, precisely, does "a group," "a school," or "a generation" in a given discipline consists? In his amply documented and unjustly maligned *Manuel de sociologie* (first published in 1950), A. Cuvillier resolved the question a priori: In the history of sociology there exists a "before" and "after" Comte, a series of national schools as well as an ensemble of disciplinary cross-currents. Today, one would more likely delineate a "before" and "after" Durkheim and to regard differently those who are situated upstream of him. At present, it is more precisely posited that "sociological tradition," formed in the nineteenth century, begins to have meaning with and after the appearance of four Durkheim masterpieces—*De la division du travail social* (1993), *Les règles de la méthode sociologique* (1995), *Le Suicide* (1997), *Les Formes élémentaires de la vie religieuse* (1912)—and that this tradition finds its origins in the works of Montesquieu and Rousseau, who are considered to be "the precursors of sociology." As a rule, innovators tend to undervalue the works of those who preceded them. As the founder of scientific sociology, Durkheim does not escape this rule. He is even considered an obstacle according to a whole current of opinion, the perpetual ignorance of which has even given rise to the belief in a "blank" between Comte and Durkheim in the development of the discipline (cf. Yamashita 1995).

The concept of a scientifically based sociology was thus imposed. This concept affirms the specificity of social context; it pays close attention to the morphological substratum. While accenting collective tendencies, "forces which are just as real as cosmic forces," it shows that "social life is essentially made up of representations." From the introduction of the concept of anomie in the dissertation of 1893 to the analysis of the sacred and of beliefs that was developed in the 1912 work, the principal themes of a general sociology and those of specialized sociologies are freed from prejudices and preconceptions by a rigorously codified approach. Almost entirely, the domains in which they were implemented were "covered" with Durkheimians: judicial sociology by, notably, H. Lévy-Bruhl, economic sociology by F. Simiand (1873–1935), moral and political sociology by P. Fauçonnet and especially C. Bouglé (1870–1940), and religious sociology being particularly well by H. Hubert and M. Mauss (1872–1950). Again, the latter does not limit himself to this one sector, any more than M. Halbwachs (1877–1945) does to social morphology, or L. Lévy-Bruhl (1857–1939) to the writing of a masterpiece, *La morale et la science des moeurs*, published in 1903. Many other specialists—G. Bourgin, L. Gernet, M. Granet, C. Lalo, and so forth— produced works that, combined with those of their master, had a profound influence abroad. It was thus understood that every new development in the discipline had to rest upon the base that Durkeimism had furnished.

The fact that this vigorously formulated concept of sociology provoked the marginalization of other trends is not at all surprising. Such was the case with the School of Social Reform, founded by F. Le Play (1806–1888), with the dissident school of E. Emolins, and with all the more or less obedient followers of Le Play whose allegiance inspired the family of monographs gathered together in *Les Ouvriers européens* (1855–1879) and *Les Ouvriers des deux mondes* (1857–1885): P. Bureau, E. Cheysson, P. Descamps, P. du Maroussem, P. de Rousiers, and the abbot of Tourville, all of whom were forgotten innovators, but all of whom were recently discovered by Kalaora and Savoya (1989). One will simply note that the collections of *La Réforme sociale* (from 1881 onward), those of *La Science sociale*, directed by Demolins after 1886, and those of *Le Musée social* (which became *Cahiers du Musée social* after 1945) comprise a documentary corpus parallel to that of *L'Année sociologique*. The same may be said for the *Revue internationale de sociologie*, published from 1893 onward by René Worms (1867–1926), who was the director of the International Sociological Library from 1896, the author of an important work, *Philosophie des sciences sociales* (3 vol., 1903–1907), and, most notably, the founder in 1894 of the International Institute of Sociology and in 1895 of the Society of Sociology of Paris.

One may, however, extend to sociology the relation that R. Aron extended for the field of history expanded into historiography: Every society produces the social science that it needs. Durkheim's brand of sociology, strongly tinged with morality, was necessary to the Third Republic, which had been badly shaken by successive crises (Panama, boulangisme, the Dreyfus affair). Scholars have often stressed the concerns that are raised in Durkheim's work about political thought, which is itself centered on social integration and cohesion; these concerns are evidenced by the course he taught in 1902–1903 entitled *L'Education Morale*. With regard to these concerns, what could be worth provoking objections raised in the name of old-fashioned individualism, and what interest could this "intermental" psychology present—that is, a collective conceptualized by G. Tarde (1843–1904), author of *Lois de l'imitation* (1890) and of *Logique sociale* (1894)—against which Durkheim polemicizes so effectively and so unjustly? A number of ruptures were deliberately intentional on Durkheim's part; it was against psychology that he intended to build sociology, while refusing moreover to consider history to be a science and simultaneously reducing economics to nothing more than an incarnation of metaphysics. He was so effective that, whereas in Germany sociology could be developed at the crossroads of history, economics, and psychology, in France all the conditions were right for it to be defined in opposition to these disciplines.

Perhaps this sociological tradition was ordered at a later date. One has only to refer to the *Eléments de sociologie* by C. Bougle and J. Raffault (first edition, 1926; second edition, 1930) to measure the reshaping that occurred between the two world wars. The range of this anthology is wide open, from Bonald to Jaurès, and passing by way of Constant, Tocqueville, and Guizot. Texts by Le Play and Tarde figure alongside those of Durkheim and some of the Durkheimians who, of course, carve out the lion's share. Spencer, Frazer, Jhering, and Mommsen are among the others who are cited, while excerpts of *Principes historiques du droit* by the Russian, P. Vinogradoff, are presented. Yet, more than because of the authors they assemble, these selected pieces interest us because of whom they exclude: Tönnies, Weber, Simmel, Michels, Mosca, Pareto, and Comte, who is only cited a single time! Shortly thereafter, Aron introduced *Sociologie allemande contemporaine* (1935) to French researchers, but for a long while he remained closed to the sociology of Pareto. Other perspectives finally emerged on the eve of World War II: a major contribution to this process was made by Stoetzel, who was the founder of the IFOP in 1938 and of the review *Sondages* in 1939 upon his return from the United States, where he became acquainted with Gallup's works; he would later devote his doctoral thesis to a *Esquisse d'une théorie des opinions* (1943). With Stoetzel was born in France an electoral psychosociology during the electoral ecology inaugurated in 1913 by A. Siegfried's *Tableau politique de la France de l'Quest*. Other important contributors to the broadening of perspectives were G. Bataille, R. Caillois, and M. Leiris, who were reunited within the College of Sociology between 1938 and 1939; as brief as the existence of this institution was, it was the framework for interdisciplinary contributions on myth, the sacred, the imaginary, and the problems of the age (democracy and totalitarianism) that are still striking today for their modernity.

FRENCH SOCIOLOGIES OF TODAY

Rupture or continuity? For M. Verret, co-author with H. Mendras of a collection of studies entitled *Les Champs de la sociologie française* Mendras and Verret (1988), there is no doubt about the answer: "French contemporary sociology cannot be understood without taking into consideration the great rupture between the two world wars; 1940 was a terrible critical test for French society.... There is nothing surprising about the fact that during this disaster, French sociology was also on the rocks. This includes not only Durkheimian sociology which constituted the latest face of it, but all the tradition from which it proceeded." The rereading of the fundamental chapters of *Traité de sociologie générale* (2 vols., 1958–1960), begun by G. Gurvitch (1897–1965) a dozen years after the end of World War II, leads one to nuance this assessment, which links devastation and reconstruction. A number of their authors began their careers before the rupture of 1940: This is the case of the taskmaster himself, whose *L'Idée de droit social* was published in 1932; of G. Friedman, who, beginning in 1936, inaugurated in France research in industrial sociology; and of J. Stoetzel. Others began during the Occupation: for example, A. Girard, working within the framework of the Alexis Carrel Foundation, which was tranformed upon the Liberation into the National Institute of Demographic Studies. The documentation upon which they rely owes a great deal to Durkheim and his disciples.

May one say that these authors, senior and junior—F. Bourricaud, J. Cazeneuve, H. Mendras, and others—approach the study of social phenomena in a radically new spirit by breaking the connections established in the twentieth century between knowledge and power over society, by abandoning the research of the great consonance targeted by Durkheimism, and by stripping the discipline of its conquering aspects? It would seem not. A degree of optimism characterized the works of sociologists during the two and a half decades that followed the end of World War II. This is indicated by a flourishing of publications, all marked by a certain voluntarism, like the essays gathered together through the initiative of the French Society of Sociology under the title *Tendances et volontés de la société française* (1966). In a number of areas, people trusted this young science: One expected from its application a decisive improvement in the government of mankind and in the management of things: various adjustments in the highly industrialized societies and in the developing countries such that they might contribute to the realization of the chosen model of growth.

However, many changes took place behind this permanence that had found its incarnation in a Durkheimian orthodoxy. G. Davy (1883–1973), whose *Eléments de sociologie* (1932) was republished in 1950, beginning in 1931, gathered together "sociologists of yesterday and sociologists of today" who were in the pursuit of the same goals. Those which are easiest to identify are of an institutional nature: the creation, under the auspices of the National Center of Scientific Research, of the Center for Sociological Studies, organizer of important "sociological weeks" that treated various issues such as *Industrialisme et technocratie* (1948), *Villes et campagnes* (1951), and *La Famille contemporaine* (1954); the constitution of numerous research groups (such as the Social Ethnology group run by P.-H. Chombart de Lauwe) and of associations like the one for the Development of the Sociology of Work; and the launching of new reviews, for example, the *Cahiers Internationaux de Sociologie*, founded in 1946 by G. Gurvitch, then, ten years later, the *Archives de Sociologie des Religions*, an organ of the sociology of religions group over which G. Le Bras presided, and two more in 1960. *La Revue Française de Sociologie* by J. Stoetzel, and *Sociologie du travail* by G. Friedman. On the academic front, sociology integrated with the study of philosophy became an entirely separate discipline with the creation of a B.A. in Sociology in 1958; this was the beginning of full academic recognition, which would lead to the institution of an *aggrégation* in Social Science in 1976.

To these organizational transformations are added conflicts of paradigms. They are linked to the affirmation of, to use the expression of D. Lerner (1959), the "American concept," that is, to the diffusion of a concept and a practice of sociology that had come from the far side of the Atlantic. Without oversimplifying, one can, in fact, say that during the period under consideration, the study of social facts was pursued on the one hand within the framework of functionalism, and on the other, on the bases of historical and dialectical materialism. It occurred on a basis of debate, called upon in the 1960s to take a polemical and ideological turn, when one wrongly and sterilely opposed the descriptive and the explicative, the qualitative and the quantitative, empirical research and theoretical speculation, the exploitation of investigation and of social criticism.

Against the sociological scientism with which one assimilated the new American referent (whether it concern the sociometry of J.-L Moreno or the functionalism of T. Parsons, the works of R. K. Merton or those of P. Lazarsfeld), the tenets of the dialectic hark back to C. W. Mills, who denounced the invasion of bureaucratic techniques into the social sciences (in *The Sociological Imagination*, 1957), and to P. Sorokin, vigorous critic of the compulsion to enumerate which then reigned, notably in electoral sociology. Imported into France, the German quarrel in the social sciences which, in the beginning of the 1960s, pitted T. Adorno, one of the principal representatives of the Frankfurt School, against K. Popper, the great epistemologist of Vienna, underlined the rift between the protagonists of both camps. Caught up in the turbulence of the late 1960s, sociology then entered a period of crisis (cf. R. Boudon 1971). The gulf widened between the functionalist sociologists, who adhered to systemic analysis, which could be denounced (and not without reason) for its schematism, its optimism, and its conservatism, and their adversaries who countered with a critical rhetoric that often sounded hollow, unsubstantiated as it was by precise data concerning controversial problems such as social change.

The major event of this period would remain, for French sociology, the coming of structuralism, with, in the background, the antagonistic conceptual orientations of G. Gurvitch, who was a proponent of the study of global societies, and of R. Aron, who shared the open perspective of Tocqueville. With the replacement of the Marxist explicative schema by the theorized structural analysis of C. Lévi-Strauss, a mutation of knowledge occurred: A paradigm centered on the idea of conflict was replaced by another that was formed of the stable elements of structure; new modes of conceptualization appeared and with them, new intellectual modes. The history of ideas shows how, in the succession of such modes, a model that has been dominant is shaken, and how it loses or even exhausts the merit that has been attributed to it. The reemergence of structuralism, which one must take care not to confuse with structural analysis, and whose range and limits have been stressed, permitted the subsistence of four theoretical orientations that P. Ansart (1990) has clearly identified. These have certain affinities with the four schools distinguished by A. Touraine (1988): genetic structuralism, dynamic sociology, the functionalist and strategic approach, and, finally, methodological individualism.

These theoretical models reflect different visions of the world. Thus, P. Bourdieu's analyses lead to a highlighting of the division of society into classes; studies of the frequenting of museums or of the *grandes écoles* reveal practices that differ widely according to origin and to class. Associated with the study of determining structures, which is the goal of genetic structuralism, are the analyses of the author of *La Distinction* (1979) and those of the research team he conducts, who publish their works in *Actes de la recherche en sciences sociales*. The epistemology they display can be qualified as "poststructuralist" because of the introduction of the concept of *habitus* and because of the importance of the developments that support this conceptual proposition. Associated with the study of social dynamism are the names G. Balandier and A. Touraine. The former, beginning with African societies, conceptualized economic and social change; the latter, working from a base of the sociology of work, theorized collective action and social movement. Individual behavior and the problems posed by their aggregation occupies a central place in the work of R. Boudon, notably in *Effets pervers et ordre social* (1977), in *La Logique du social* (1979), and in *La Place du désordre* (1984).

One will note the cleavage that separates the latter two theoretical constructions (M. Crozier, R. Boudon) from the preceding ones. These latter constructions reveal the same structural social model of social determinations: The former prioritize the strategy of the participant and value the individual; nevertheless, their openness to social psychology remains distinct. Thus, M. Crozier reproaches several interactionist models for treating interaction as a generalizable element, as though interaction revealed the totality of the regulations of a system of action. One is aware, on the other hand, of the close relationship between individualism and social interactionism.

It is not only the radical position that exists between the principles applied by genetic structuralism and those which prevail in methodological individualism that must here be noted, the "epistemological distance" being perfectly measured by the debate on the inequality of chance. A nodal point of divergence appears, constituted by the conception of this *subject*. What is, in fact, the subject in generic structuralism and in a strategic conception of individual actions? Whether it be a question of the analysis of conflicts and of the representation of social relationships that it implies, a question of symbolic systems which contemporary sociologists are working to rethink, or finally a question of the place, the role and the function of the sociologist in the city, it clearly appears, as P. Ansart (1990) notes, that "the works of R. Boudin mark a critical position with regard to other sociological paradigms . . . , and, like every explicitly critical position, this position clearly marks the divergences, the points of disagreement which can be taken to be, on the epistemological level, insurmountable" (p. 285).

To conclude, these four theoretical orientations prolong and renew tendencies that were charted in the nineteenth century. In a certain manner, P. Bourdieu carries on the ambition of the first sociologists of the nineteenth century, which was picked up by Durkheim: that of constituting a science of social phenomena, with the certitude that social reality is indeed a reality and that it is ponderable by means of strictly codified rules. One can also say that dynamic sociology retains a vision of the world that has its origins in the works of Saint-Simon, Comte, Marx, and Spencer, insofar as these thinkers posed the problem of social change and proposed explicative models for it. One also recognizes without difficulty that in the background of methodological individualism may be distinguished the influence of Tocqueville, Weber, the Austrian marginalist school, and the debates of the Vienna Circle. As for the functionalist and strategic approach, one may consider it to be the inheritor of an administrative science that, with M. Vivien and M. Block, was put into place in the second half of the nineteenth century.

CONCLUSION

What, all in all, is sociology in France at the end of the twentieth century? The statement made at the beginning of the 1990s by J.-M. Berthelot in *La*

Construction de la sociologie (1991) is still valid. The programmatical crossovers that have been identified and the new uncertainties that have been discerned have been both confirmed and emphasized. To these, one adds a transformation of the very objective of sociology by reason of a notable subjectivization of social material. Often denounced as a fetishistic idea, society tends to be thought of as an ensemble of forms and networks of *sociability*, in the same way that *individual*, a simple statistical element passively submitted to diverse sorting operations, tends to be substituted by a complex *individuality*, more or less free of contradictions, the subject of a statement that claims to be "personal" and, in all cases rebellious to classification, recalcitrant toward enumeration and cut off from the "masses". To weigh the new relationships maintained by the individual and society, one has recourse to sociologies that, unlike those of Durkheim and his followers, remained engaged in the psychological givens: Such is indeed the direction of interest aroused by the recent translations of G. Simmel's works, in which, in the analysis of phenomena under study, the content is less important than the form and the part more significant than the whole.

One sees to what degree, in this perspective, the rereading of "sociological tradition" is imposed, as well as the reintegration into the discipline's history of contributions that had more or less been excluded from it, and of reflections on the epistemology of the social sciences. Concurrently being pursued is a *conceptual clarification*, including the admirable *Dictionnaire critique de la sociologie*, continually reedited since its appearance in 1982 by R. Boudon and F. Bourricaud, which is its point of departure and canonical example. At the same time, also being pursued is the analysis of *social problems* related to the evolution of mores (the family, the young, the relations between generations, etc.) and to economic transformations (unemployment, exclusion, social justice, etc.). Finally, parallel to these pursuits is the research being conducted on the improvement of descriptive and explicative models of the changes that society is witnessing today. One points out in this regard the exemplary character of the investigation being conducted by Louis Dirn (anagram for *lundi soir*), that is, the group of sociologists who meet at the beginning of each week in the company of H. Mendras and M. Forsé. Thus, for the most part freed from past dogmatisms, French sociology today asserts its vitality by better adjusting its procedures for examining social objects and phenomena to which it is working to give a sense.

Bibliography

Ansart, P. 1990 *Les Sociologies contemporaines*. Paris: Seuil.

Berthelot, J.-M. 1991 *La Construction de la sociologie*. Paris: P.U.F.

Besnard, P. dir. 1979 "The Durkheimians", *Revue française de sociologie*, January–March, XX-1.

—— 1981 "Sociologies françaises au tournant du siècle." *Revue française de sociologie*, July–September, 1981, XXII-3.

—— 1985 "La Sociologie française dans l'entre-deux-guerres." *Revue française de sociologie*, April–June, 1985, XXVI-2.

Boudon, R. 1971 *La Crise de sociologie*. Geneva: Droz.

Hollier, D. 1979 *Le Collège de sociologie*. Paris: Gallimard.

Kalaora, B., and Savoye. A. 1989 *Les Inventeurs oubliés: Le Play et ses continuateurs*. Paris: Champ Vallon.

Lerner, D. 1959 "De la tradition européene au concept américan. Esprit (January): pp. 3–17.

Mendras, H. and Verret, M. 1988 *Les Champs de la sociologie française*. Paris: A. Colin.

Touraine, A. 1988 "Sociologies et sociologues." In *L'état des sciences sociales*. Paris: La Découverte.

Valade, B. 1989 "La Sociologie depuis la Seconde Guerre mondiale." In the *Encyclopédie philosophique universelle*, vol. 1. Paris: P. U. F.

—— with R. Fellieule 1996 *Introduction aux sciences sociales*. Paris: P.U.F.

Yamashita, M. 1995 La Sociologie française entre Auguste Comte et Emile Durkheim." in *L'Année sociologique*, vol. 45, 1995, I.

BERNARD VALADE

FUNCTIONALISM AND STRUCTURALISM

Sociology's first theoretical orientation was functionalism. In trying to legitimate the new discipline of sociology, Auguste Comte (1830–1842,

1851–1854) revived analogies made by the Greeks and, closer to his time, by Hobbes and Rousseau that society is a kind of organism. In so doing, Comte effectively linked sociology with the prestige of biological science. For functional theory, then, society is like a biological organism that grows, and as a consequence, its parts can be examined with respect to how they operate (or function) to maintain the viability of the body social as it grows and develops. As Comte emphasized (1851–1854, p. 239), there is a "true correspondence between Statical Analysis of the Social Organism in Sociology, and that of the Individual Organism in Biology" (1851–1854, p. 239). Moreover, Comte went so far as to "decompose structure anatomically into *elements, tissues,* and *organs*" (1851–1854, p. 240) and to "treat the Social Organism as definitely composed of the Families which are the true elements or cells, next the Classes or Castes which are its proper tissues, and lastly, of the cities and Communes which are its real organs" (pp. 211–212). Yet, since these analogies were not systematically pursued by Comte, his main contribution was to give sociology its name and to reintroduce organismic reasoning into the new science of society.

It was Herbert Spencer who used the organismic analogy to create an explicit form of functional analysis. Drawing upon materials from his monumental *The Principles of Biology* (1864–1867), Spencer's *The Principles of Sociology* (1874–1896) is filled with analogies between organisms and society as well as between ecological processes (variation, competition, and selection) and societal evolution (which he saw as driven by war). Spencer did not see society as an actual organism; rather, he conceptualized "superorganic systems" (organization of organisms) as revealing certain similarities in their "principles of arrangement" to biological organisms (1874–1896, part 2, pp. 451–462). In so doing, he introduced the notion of "functional requisites" or "needs," thereby creating functionalism. For Spencer, there were three basic requisites of superorganic systems: (1) the need to secure and circulate resources, (2) the need to produce usable substances, and (3) the need to regulate, control, and administer system activities (1874–1896, part 2, p. 477). Thus, any pattern of social organization reveals these three classes of functional requisites, and the goal of sociological analysis is to see how these needs are met in empirical social systems.

Later functionalists produced somewhat different lists of requisites. Émile Durkheim argued that sociological explanations "must seek separately the efficient cause [of a phenomenon]—and the function it fulfills" (1895, p. 96), but, in contrast to Spencer, he posited only one functional requisite: the need for social integration. For Durkheim, then, sociological analysis would involve assessment of the causes of phenomena and their consequences or functions for meeting the needs of social structures for integration.

Were it not for the activities of theoretically oriented anthropologists, functionalism probably would have died with Durkheim, especially since Spencer's star had faded by World War I (Turner and Turner 1990). As the traditional societies studied by early anthropologists were generally without a written history, anthropologists were confronted with the problem of explaining the existence of activities and structures in these societies. The explanatory problem became particularly acute in the post–World War I period with the demise of evolutionism and diffusionism as deciphering tools (Turner and Maryanski 1979). Functional analysis provided a novel alternative: Analyze structures such as kinship or activities such as rituals in terms of their functions for maintaining the society. It was A. R. Radcliffe-Brown ([1914] 1922, 1924, 1935, 1952) who sustained the Durkheimian tradition by emphasizing the importance of integrative needs and then analyzing how structures—most notably kinship systems—operate to meet such integrative requisites. In contrast, Bronislaw Malinowski (1913, 1944) extended functional analysis in a more Spencerian direction, emphasizing that there are distinct system levels (biological, social, and cultural), each of which reveals its own distinctive requisites. Extending Spencer and anticipating Talcott Parsons, Malinowski (1944) posited four basic requisites at the social system level: (1) production and distribution, (2) social control and regulation, (3) education and socialization, and (4) organization and integration.

Thus functionalism was carried to the midpoint of the twentieth century by anthropological work. Then during the 1930s, a group of Harvard sociologists—led by a graduate student, Robert Merton (1949)—began thinking about functional analysis, especially as it had been carried forth by

Radcliffe-Brown and Malinowski (Turner and Maryanski 1979). As a result, many of Merton's fellow students became the leading figures in the revival of functionalism in sociology. This revival began with Kingsley Davis and Wilbert Moore's classic article on "Some Principles of Stratification" (1945), followed by Davis's basic text, *Human Societies* (1948), and a variety of articles and books by others listing the "functional requisites" of societies (e.g., Levy 1952). But it was Talcott Parsons, a young Harvard instructor during Merton's tenure as a graduate student, who was to become the archfunctionalist of modern times (Parsons 1951; Parsons et al. 1953). For Parsons, the social universe was conceptualized in terms of four distinct types and levels of "action systems" (culture, social, personality, and organismic/behavioral), with each system having to meet the same four functional needs: (1) adaptation (securing and distributing environmental resources), (2) goal attainment (mobilizing resources to goals or ends), (3) integration (coordinating system parts), and (4) latency (managing tensions within parts and generating new parts). The operation and interchanges of structures and processes within and between system levels were then analyzed with respect to these basic requisites.

As functional theorizing became dominant in American theory in the 1950s and 1960s, criticism escalated. Opposition came from several different quarters and took a number of distinctive lines of attack. From interactionist theorizing came criticism about functionalism's failure to conceptualize adequately the nature of actors and the process of interaction (Blumer 1969); from Marxist-inspired theory, which was just emerging from the academic closets in the post-McCarthy era, came attacks on the conservative and static nature of analysis that emphasized the functions of phenomena for maintaining the status quo (e.g., Coser 1956; Dahrendorf 1958; Mills 1959); from theory construction advocates came questions about the utility of excessively classificatory or typological theories that pigeonholed phenomena in terms of their functions (e.g., Merton 1957, pp. 44–61); and from philosophers and logicians came questions about tautology and illegitimate teleology in explanations that saw phenomena as meeting needs and needs as generating phenomena (e.g., Dore 1961). The result was the decline of functional theorizing in the early 1970s.

Functionalism has never fully recovered from these criticisms, although there persist vibrant modes of functional analysis in many disciplines, both within and outside of the social sciences. Within sociology, functionalism adapted to a hostile intellectual environment in several ways. One was to downplay functional requisites in a "neofunctionalism" (Alexander 1985; Alexander and Colomy 1985) and, instead, emphasize the dynamics that had always been at the center of functional analysis: differentiation and social change. As with Parsons, neofunctionalism maintains the analytical distinctions among culture, social system, and personality; and as with Durkheim and Radcliffe-Browne, integration among (1) cultural symbols, (2) differentiating social systems, and (3) persons is given emphasis without, however, the baggage of functional requisites. Another strategy was to maintain Parsons's functional requisites, expanding and elaborating his scheme, but at the same time generating testable propositions (Münch, 1982). In this way, the criticism that Parsons's theory was, in reality, a category system could be mitigated because a system of categories could be used to generate propositions and hypotheses. Still another approach was to downplay the notion of functional requisites, as was done by neofunctionalists, and analyze specific institutional systems in terms of their consequences for overcoming the problem of system complexity generated by differentiation (Luhmann 1982). Yet another effort emphasized cultural processes and the functions of rituals, ideology, and values for integrating social structures (Wuthnow 1987). A final strategy has been to translate the notion of functional requisites into a more ecological perspective, with the notion of requisites being translated into selection pressures in a way that corresponds to the notion of functions in the biological sciences (Turner 1995). That is, function becomes a shorthand way to summarize selection processes as they operated in the past to create a new structure. When this logic is applied to sociocultural processes, function is simply a name given to selection forces; and the analysis shifts from listing requisites to assessing how selection pressures increases or deceases for certain types of sociocultural formations.

Aside from changing under the impact of critiques leveled against it, functionalism has also spawned a number of other theoretical traditions. The most obvious is structuralism, which will be examined in more detail shortly, but there is another that is equally important in sociology, namely, human ecology. Human ecology is a perspective that comes from Spencer's and Durkheim's sociology. Both Spencer and Durkheim recognized that any social structure or system of symbols exists in a resource environment and that there is often competition for resources among alternative structures and symbols when social density increases. Thus, religious or political ideologies must compete for adherents, or businesses or governmental agencies must compete in their respective resource niche. Ecological reasoning came initially via the Chicago School's interest in how areas of cities were utilized, and like Durkheim and Spencer before them, members of the Chicago School visualized the competition for space created by dynamic real estate markets in Darwinian terms (e.g., Park 1936; Park et al. 1925; Hoyt 1939). Later others (Hannan and Freeman 1977) applied the idea of niche, niche density, competition, and selection to populations of organizations to examine their rates of success and failure. Thus, one of the more visible theoretical perspectives in sociology comes from early functionalists, who not only borrowed an image of society as being like an organism but also developed ideas that paralleled those of Darwin in examining the mechanisms behind sociocultural differentiation (or "social speciation"). For them, differentiation is both the context of niche specialization and the result of previous competitions, as sociocultural forms compete with each other, with those unable to compete in one niche dying, moving to a new niche, or creating a new niche (and, thereby, increasing the level of differentiation).

The other major offspring of functionalism were various lines of structuralism that were inspired primarily by Durkheim's and various collaborators' work. Durkheim (1893, 1895) implicitly borrowed Comte's distinction between statics and dynamics, although Durkheim conceptualized social statics in Montesquieu's terms as social "morphology." Static or morphological analysis was seen to involve an assessment of the "nature," "number," "interrelations," and "arrangement" of parts in a systemic whole (Durkheim 1895, p. 85). For Durkheim, sociological explanation still sought to discover "cause" and "function," but the basic structural units of sociological analysis—that is, the "things" that are caused and functioning—are to be classified by "the nature and number of the component elements and their mode of combination" (Durkheim 1895, p. 81).

FRENCH STRUCTURALISM

French structuralism stood Durkheim on his head through Claude Lévi-Strauss's (1945a, [1949] 1969, 1963) adoption of ideas in less sociologically prominent works by Durkheim and his nephew, Marcel Mauss. In Durkheim's "Incest: The Nature and Origin of the Taboo" (1898) as well as his and Mauss's *Primitive Classification* ([1903] 1963), emphasis shifts to the origins and functions of rules of exogamy and to human classification systems and modes of symbolic thought. For Durkheim and Mauss, the way that humans cognitively perceive and classify the world reflects the morphological or material structure of society (nature, number, arrangement, and combination of parts). In developing this argument, which Durkheim repeats in less extreme form in *Elementary Forms of the Religious Life* (1912), Durkheim and Mauss posit all the basic elements of Lévi-Strauss's (1963) structuralism. First, although societies differ in their evolutionary development, they are all fundamentally similar because they are based upon the same "underlying principles" (Durkheim and Mauss [1903] 1963, p. 74), and these principles provide individuals with a basis for classifying and constructing their universe. Second, "mythology" is a universal method of classification. Third, such classification systems represent "relations of things" to each other and "are thus intended, above all, to connect ideas, to unify knowledge" (p. 81). Fourth, classification systems are, in essence, created by oppositions in the material social world—sacred–profane, pure–impure, friends–enemies, favorable–unfavorable.

This last idea, which Lévi-Strauss was to conceptualize as "binary oppositions," is carried further by Mauss (in collaboration with Henri Beuchat) in *Seasonal Variations of the Eskimo: A Study in Social Morphology* ([1904–05] 1979), where the sharp dualisms of Eskimo life are outlined as they are created by the seasonal nature of Eskimo activities. Later, in *The Gift* ([1925] 1941), Mauss reasserts Durkheim's earlier conclusion that activity, such as the famous Kwakiutl potlatch, is a surface exchange reflecting a "deeper" and "more complex" underlying structure in which gifts symbolize and assure the continuation of social relations among diverse groups.

Lévi-Strauss regarded *The Gift* as the inauguration of a new era in the social sciences and saw Mauss as a new Moses "conducting his people all the way to a promised land whose splendour he would never behold" (Lévi-Strauss [1950] 1987, pp. 41–45). Following directly in Mauss's footsteps, Lévi-Strauss ennobled the concept of exchange as a "total social phenomena" by arguing in his first major work, *The Elementary Structures of Kinship*, that a "principle of reciprocity" is the most general and universal property of society, with the exchange of women as the most fundamental expression of this principle (Lévi Strauss [1949] 1969, pp. 60–62).

Yet it is doubtful that these ideas alone would have produced structuralism. Two other scholars are critical to Lévi-Strauss's transmutation of Durkheim and Mauss. One is Robert Hertz, a young member of Durkheim's "Année School." Before his death in World War I, Hertz produced a number of essays, the two best-known ones being published in *Death and the Right Hand* ([1909] 1960). In this work, Hertz continues the Durkheim–Mauss theme of the duality in the structure of society and documents how this is reflected in ideas about society (myths, classifications, and other "representations"), but the imagery is much more like modern structuralism in that the goal of inquiry is (1) to show the meaning of observed facts in their interrelations and (2) to uncover the underlying structural principles beneath the surface of such observed phenomena.

The final and perhaps most critical influence on Lévi-Strauss's reversal of Durkheim is the Swiss linguist Ferdinand de Saussure ([1915] 1966), whose lectures, posthumously published under the title *Course in General Linguistics*, serve as the pioneering and authoritative work for modern-day structural linguistics. Saussure appears to have influenced Lévi-Strauss indirectly through Nikolai Trubetzkoi ([1949] 1964, 1968) and Roman Jakobson (1962, 1971), but they simply extend Saussure's key insight that language is a system whose units—whether sounds or morphemes—are only points in an overall structure. Moreover, while speech

(*parole*) can be directly observed, it reflects an underlying system or language structure (*langue*), and, thus, it is critical to use *parole* to discover the *langue*.

In Lévi-Strauss's hands, this combined legacy was to produce French structuralism. At times, Lévi-Strauss is critical of Durkheim, but he concludes in the end that Durkheim's work "is an inspiration" (Lévi-Strauss 1945b, p. 522) and that "the entire purpose of the French school lies in an attempt to break up the categories of the layman, and to group the data into a deeper, sounder classification" (Lévi-Strauss 1945b, pp. 524–525). In early work such as *The Elementary Structures of Kinship* (Lévi-Strauss [1949] 1969), there is a clear debt to Durkheim and Mauss as Lévi-Strauss seeks to uncover the underlying principles (such as "reciprocity") of bridal exchanges, but he soon turns to the methods of structural linguistics and sees surface social structures (Durkheim's "morphology") as reflecting a more fundamental reality, lodged in the human unconscious and the biochemistry of the human brain and involving "rules and principles" to organize "binary oppositions" that are used to create empirically observable patterns of social reality (Lévi-Strauss 1953). But these empirical patterns (e.g., myths, beliefs, kinship structures) are not the "really real" structure; they are like *parole* is to *langue*, a reflection of a deeper structural reality of which existing phenomena are only the surface realizations.

Thus, by the middle of the twentieth century, Lévi-Strauss (1953) had created a structuralism concerned with understanding cultural and social patterns as reflections of universal mental processes rooted in the biochemistry of the human brain. His basic argument can be summarized as follows: (1) The empirically observable must be viewed as a system of relations, whether these be a kinship system, elements of myth or folk tales, or any sociocultural pattern. (2) Statistical models of these observable systems need to be developed in order to summarize the empirically observable relations among components. (3) These models are, however, only surface manifestations of more fundamental reality and must, therefore, be used to construct mechanical models in which the organization of binary oppositions is organized by basic rules lodged presumably in the human brain. (4) These mechanical models are the more "real" since they get at the underlying processes by which sociocultural systems are generated by the biology and neurology of the brain.

Marshall Sahlins (1966) once sarcastically remarked of Lévi-Strauss's scheme that "what is apparent is false and what is hidden from perception and contradicts it is true." But Levi-Strauss was not alone in this kind of neurological reasoning. Within linguistics, Noam Chomsky (1980) was making a similar argument, asserting that the brain is wired to produce generative grammars that are less the result of the sociocultural environment of humans than of the structure of their brains. We might term these kinds of structuralisms "biostructuralism" because they all argue that the social world as it is perceived and structured is being systematically generated by rules of organization that are part of the neurobiology of the human brain.

Not all structuralists went this far. Most were content to argue that symbol systems and social structures are organized by rules that need to be discovered. Since the rules are not obvious when examining symbols and text, the task of structural analysis is to uncover the underlying rules, programs, principles, and other generative forces that have produced a particular system of symbols or social structure. The presumption that these rules are built into the neurology of the brain was rarely invoked in most structuralist analysis, whether in the social sciences or the humanities.

Within sociology proper, structuralism exerted a rather vague influence. For a time in the 1970s and 1980s, it was quite faddish to search for the underlying structure of texts, social structures, cultural systems, and virtually any phenomena studied by sociologists. Jargon from structuralism appeared in the works of prominent theorists, such as Anthony Giddens's (1984) use of the notion of "structural principles" as part of the explanation for how the "rules and resources" are implicated in "structuration." Others such as Richard Harvey Brown (1987) proclaimed that we should conceptualize "society as text" in which methods of structural linguistics can get at the underlying forms that organize societies. A variety of texts and edited books on structuralism began to appear (e.g., Rossi 1982), but in the end this kind of analysis did not take a firm hold in American

sociology. It had a much greater influence in continental Europe, but here, too, structuralist sociology did not last very long (Giddens 1987).

But arising out of structuralism came "poststructuralism," which was even more vague than structuralism. Still, poststructuralism did take hold and evolved into or merged with what is now called "postmodernism." Ironically, postmodernism is generally anti-science and highly relativistic, emphasizing that there are no grand narratives. All is text, and none should enjoy a privileged voice. By the time poststructuralism had become part of a broad postmodern movement, then, it bore little resemblance to the scientific stance of structuralists, who were not only decidedly pro-science but also were committed to discovering the universal principles by which texts and all other human systems are generated, giving such a discovery a highly privileged voice.

Despite its origins in structural linguistics, French structuralism became ever more vague. In contrast, structuralism took a very different turn in England and the United States, evolving into one of the most precise ways of conceptualizing structures. While French-inspired structuralism got much of the press, British and American versions of network analysis have endured. These approaches also come out of Durkheim, particularly the British line but also the American line, although today the two approaches are the same.

BRITISH STRUCTURALISM

Radcliffe-Brown's early works were decidedly functional in the Durkheimian tradition of analyzing sociocultural patterns in terms of their functions for the larger social whole. Radcliffe-Brown also began to develop a conception of structure that was very close to Durkheim's emphasis on the number, nature, and relations among parts. And increasingly, Radcliffe-Brown emphasized structural analysis over functional analysis, stressing the importance of examining relations among entities. Radcliffe-Brown's disagreement with Lévi-Strauss is clear in a letter: "I use the term 'social structure' in a sense so different from yours as to make discussion so different as to be unlikely to be profitable. While for you, social structure has nothing to do with reality but with models that are built up, I regard social structure as a reality" (quoted in Murdock 1953). A key British figure in the transition from Durkheim's emphasis on relations among entities was S. F. Nadel (1957), a social anthropologist who separated structural from functional analysis and emphasized that structural analysis must concentrate on the properties of relations that are invariant and always occur rather than the nature of the actors in these relations. For Nadel, structure is to be viewed as clusters of networks of relations among positions or actors. This point of view was developed into network analysis by J. Clyde Mitchell (1974) and John A. Barnes (1972), who took Nadel's imagery and converted it into a more pure form of network analysis.

AMERICAN STRUCTURALISM

At the same time that French-inspired structuralism was making inroads into American intellectual life, social psychologists in the United States were developing an alternative way to examine structure. Jacob Moreno (1953) was critical here, as he developed the methodology of sociograms in which a matrix of relations among a set of actors was plotted and then converted into a line drawing of relations. Studies by Alex Bavelas (1948) and Harold Leavitt (1951) on communication in groups were the first to assess how the network structure of groups influenced patterns of communication. At about the same time, gestalt and balance theory approaches by Fritz Heider (1946), Theodore Newcomb (1953), and Dorwin Cartwright and Frank Harray (1956) used network graphs to examine patterns of balance in groups. Concurrently within mathematics, a more formal system of notation for networks was being developed (Luce and Perry, 1949), and it is from this system that modern-day network analysis emerged.

THE MERGER OF BRITISH AND AMERICAN STRUCTURALISM INTO NETWORK ANALYSIS.

The British and American lines of what became network analysis are now merged in a view of structure that emphasizes (1) nodes or positions in a system, (2) mapping the relations among these nodes, and (3) examining generic patterns and forms of ties along such dimensions as the nature,

number, direction, reciprocity, transitivity, centrality, equivalence, density, and strength of ties. A fairly standard vocabulary and set of analytic techniques have emerged from network analysis, and the approach is now used in many other areas of sociological analysis. Thus, Durkheim's original vision of structure has been more fully realized in contemporary network analysis.

FUNCTIONALISM AND STRUCTURALISM TODAY

Functionalism and structuralism share common roots, especially the works of Durkheim and Mauss, and hence it should not be surprising that these two theoretical traditions reveal certain affinities. First, both emphasize that the subject matter of sociology is to be relations among parts. Second, both stress part–whole analysis—the functions of parts for sustaining the whole in functionalism, and the view that parts are understood only as elements of a more inclusive whole, revealing underlying properties, in structuralism. Beyond these affinities, however, functionalism and structuralism diverge. French structuralism moves toward a highly vague view of underlying structures below visible phenomena whose generative processes constitute reality, whereas the merger of British and American network approaches moves toward analysis of the form of relations among interrelated units. In contrast, functionalism sustains an emphasis on how units meet the needs of larger social wholes, or it moves toward models of system differentiation during historical change and, alternatively, toward ecological models of population differentiation. It is safe to say that, today, all forms of functionalism and structuralism, even the network branch of structuralism, have little in common besides part–whole analysis. But even here, this kind of part–whole approach is conducted in very different ways by functionalists and structuralists.

Moreover, neither functionalism nor structuralism represented coherent approaches as we enter the twenty-first century. Functionalism was plagued by its emphasis on functional requisites, whereas French structuralism was always handicapped by a vagueness about what structure is. And so, few sociologists today would proclaim themselves to be either functionalists or structuralists;

these labels have negative connotations, and most seek to avoid such stigmatizing labels. If they perform elements of functional or structuralist analysis, they do so by another name.

REFERENCES

Alexander, Jeffrey C., ed. 1985 *Neofunctionalism*. Beverly Hills, Calif.: Sage.

——, and Paul Colomy 1985 "Toward Neofunctionalism." *Sociological Theory* 3:11–32.

Barnes, John A. 1972 "Social Networks." Menlo Park, Calif.: Addison-Wesley Module No. 26.

Bavelas, Alex 1948 "A Mathematical Model for Group Structures." *Applied Anthropology* 7:16–30.

Blumer, Herbert 1969 *Symbolic Interaction: Perspective and Method*. Englewood Cliffs, N.J.: Prentice-Hall.

Brown, Richard Harvey 1987 *Society as Text: Essays on Rhetoric, Reason, and Reality*. Chicago: University of Chicago Press.

Cartwright, Dorin, and Frank Harary 1956 "Structural Balance: A Generalization of Heider's Theory." *Psychological Review* 63:277–293.

Chomsky, Noam 1980 *Rules and Representations*. New York: Columbia University Press.

Comte, Auguste 1830–1842 *Cours de Philosophie Positive*, 5 vols., Paris: Bachelier.

—— 1851–1854 *Système de Politique: ou, Traité de Sociologie, Instituant la Religion de L'Humanité*. Paris: L. Mathias.

Coser, Lewis A. 1956 *The Functions of Social Conflict*. London: Free Press.

Dahrendorf, Ralf 1958 "Out of Utopia: Toward a Reorientation of Sociological Analysis." *American Journal of Sociology* 74:115–127.

Davis, Kingsley 1948 *Human Societies*. New York: Macmillan.

——, and Wilbert Moore 1945 "Some Principles of Stratification." *American Sociological Review* 4:431–442.

Dore, Phillip Ronald 1961 "Function and Cause." *American Sociological Review*. 26:843–853.

Durkheim, Émile 1893 *The Division of Labor in Society*. New York: Free Press.

—— 1895 *The Rules of the Sociological Method*. New York: Free Press.

—— 1898 "Incest: The Nature and Origin of the Taboo." *Année Sociologique* 1:1–70.

—— 1912 *Elementary Forms of the Religious Life*. New York: Macmillan.

——, and Marcell Mauss (1903) 1963 *Primitive Classification*. London: Cohen and West.

Giddens, Anthony 1984 *The Constitution of Society: Outline of the Theory of Structuration*. Berkeley: University of California Press.

—— 1987 "Structuralism, Post-structuralism and the Production of Culture." In A. Giddens and J. Turner, eds., *Social Theory Today*. Cambridge, U.K.: Polity Press.

Hannan, Michael, and John Freeman 1977 "The Population Ecology of Organizations." *American Journal of Sociology* 82:929–964.

Heider, Fritz 1946 "Attitudes and Cognitive Orientation." *Journal of Psychology* 2:107–112.

Hertz, Robert (1909) 1960 *Death and the Right Hand*. London: Cohen and West.

Hoyt, Homer 1939 *The Structure and Growth of Residential Neighborhoods in American Cities*. Washington, D.C.: Federal Housing Authority.

Jakobson, Roman 1962 *Selected Writings I: Phonological Studies*. The Hague: Mouton.

—— 1971 *Selected Writings II: Word and Language*. The Hague: Mouton.

Leavitt, Harold J. 1951 "Some Effects of Certain Communication Patterns on Group Performance." *Journal of Abnormal and Social Psychology* 36:38–50.

Lévi-Strauss, Claude 1945a "The Analysis of Structure in Linguistics and in Anthropology." *Word* 1:1–21.

—— 1945b "French Sociology." In Georges Gurvitch and Wilbert E. Moore, eds., *Twentieth Century Sociology*. New York: Philosophical Library.

—— (1949) 1969 *The Elementary Structures of Kinship*. Boston: Beacon Press.

—— (1950) 1987 *Introduction to the Work of Marcel Mauss*. London: Routledge and Kegan Paul.

—— 1953 "Social Structure." In A. Kroeber, ed., *Anthropology Today*. Chicago: University of Chicago Press.

—— 1963 *Structural Anthropology*. New York: Basic Books.

Levy, Marion J. 1952 *The Structure of Society*. New Haven, Conn.: Yale University Press.

Luce, R. Duncan, and A. D. Perry 1949 "A Method of Matrix Analysis of Group Structure." *Psychometrika* 14:94–116.

Luhmann, Niklas 1982 *The Differentiation of Society*. New York: Columbia University Press.

Malinowski, Bronislaw 1913 *The Family Among the Australian Aborigines*. New York: Schocken.

—— 1944 *A Scientific Theory of Culture.* Chapel Hill: University of North Carolina Press.

Mauss, Marcel, with Henry Beuchat (1904–1905) 1979 *Seasonal Variations of the Eskimo: A Study in Social Morphology.* London: Routledge and Kegan Paul.

—— (1925) 1941 *The Gift, Forms and Functions of Exchange in Archaic Societies.* New York: Free Press.

Merton, Robert K. 1949 "Manifest and Latent Functions." In *Social Theory and Social Structure.* New York: Free Press.

—— 1957 *Social Theory and Social Structure,* rev. ed. New York: Free Press.

Mills, C. Wright 1959 *The Sociological Imagination.* New York: Oxford University Press.

Mitchell, J. Clyde 1974 "Social Networks." *Annual Review of Anthropology* 3:279–299.

Moreno, Jacob 1953 *Who Shall Survive?,* rev. ed. New York: Beacon House.

Münch, Richard 1982 *Theory of Action: Reconstructing the Contribution of Talcott Parsons, Emile Durkheim and Max Weber,* 2 vols. Frankfurt: Suhrkamp.

Murdock, George P. 1953 "Social Structure." In Sol Tax, Loren Eiseley, Irving Rouse, and Carl Voegelin, eds., *An Appraisal of Anthropology Today.* Chicago: University of Chicago Press.

Nadel, S. F. 1957 *The Theory of Social Structure.* New York: Free Press.

Newcomb, Theodore M. 1953 "An Approach to the Study of Communicative Acts." *Psychological Review* 60:393–409.

Park, Robert 1936 "Human Ecology." *American Journal of Sociology* 42:1–15.

——, Ernest Burgess, and Roderick D. McKenzie 1925 *The City.* Chicago: University of Chicago Press.

Parsons, Talcott 1951 *The Social System.* New York: Free Press.

——, Robert F. Bales, and Edward Shils 1953 *Working Papers in the Theory of Action.* New York: Free Press.

Radcliffe-Brown, A. R. (1914) 1922 *The Andaman Islanders.* Cambridge, U.K.: Cambridge University Press.

—— 1924 "The Mother's Brother in South Africa." *South African Journal of Science* 21:42–63.

—— 1935 "On the Concept of Function in Social Science" (reply to Lesser 1935). *American Anthropologist* 37:394–402.

—— 1952 *Structure and Function in Primitive Society.* London: Cohen and West.

Rossi, Ino, ed. 1982 *Structural Sociology.* New York: Columbia University Press.

Sahlins, Marshall D. 1966 "On the Delphic Writings of Claude Lévi-Strauss." *Scientific American* 214:134.

Saussure, Ferdinand de (1915) 1966 *Course in General Linguistics.* New York: McGraw-Hill.

Spencer, Herbert 1864–1867. *The Principles of Biology,* 3 vols. New York: D. Appleton.

—— 1874–1896 *The Principles of Sociology,* 3 vols. New York: D. Appleton.

Trubetzkoi, Nikolai (1949) 1964 *Principes de Phonologie.* Paris: Klincksieck.

—— 1968 *Introduction to the Principles of Phonological Description.* The Hague: Martinus Nijhoff.

Turner, Jonathan H. 1995 *Macrodynamics: Toward a General Theory on the Organization of Human Populations.* New Brunswick, N.J.: Rutgers University Press.

——, and Alexandra Maryanski 1979 *Functionalism.* Menlo Park, Calif: Benjamin Cummings.

Turner, Stephan Park, and Jonathan H. Turner 1990 *The Impossible Science: An Institutional Analysis of Sociology.* Newbury Park, Calif: Sage.

Wuthnow, Robert 1987 *Meaning and Moral Order: Explorations in Cultural Analysis.* Berkeley: University of California Press.

ALEXANDRA MARYANSKI
JONATHAN H. TURNER

FUTURES STUDIES AS HUMAN AND SOCIAL ACTIVITY

Future thinking has always been part of human history, for humans become human when they think about the future, as John McHale (1969) wrote. Some form of future thinking exists in almost all known societies; it is a universal phenomenon, as Wendell Bell (1997) writes, that ranges from divination, which involves the unveiling of the unknown, to the recent development of futures studies. Divination may be related to decisions taken by whole tribes and nations, just as the aim of scientifically rigorous futures studies is to support decision making.

In this particular context, it is important to trace the development of future thinking and the formalization of futures studies after World War II.

TERMINOLOGY

As in most disciplines, issues of terminology in futures studies are related as much to the word itself as to the underlying concept expressed by it.

From the 1940s to the 1970s, *forecasting* was the most important concept of futures studies. In 1967, Eric Jantsch defined *forecasting* "as a probabilistic statement, on a relatively high level of confidence about the future" (p. 15). In this rigorous definition, the use of the adverb "relatively" indicates the element of uncertainty that is always present in futures studies in general.

In France and in Spanish-speaking countries, however, they tend to prefer the term *prospective*. The term and the concept were actually born in France in the 1950s when Gaston Berger (1958) described *prospective* as "a way of focusing and concentrating on the future by imagining it full-blown rather than by drawing deductions from the present" (p. 3). In *prospective*, the main element is a project for the future. The idea is that by understanding the past (which cannot be changed but only interpreted), one can, in the present, choose from among the many possible and probable futures the one that is more desirable. According to Bertrand de Jouvenel (1967), the present cannot be changed either, as it is but a fleeting moment. Hence, the future is the only space we have to influence. Clearly, the prospective approach is completely different from the forecasting approach, as Michel Godet (1979) has correctly underlined.

The term *prevision*, as indicated by Barbieri Masini (1993) is not used in English or in French. In English it is thought to have the specific meaning of *pre*-vision, or seeing ahead (something not possible, as the future does not exist); in French it is not used because of its theological associations. In Italian the term *previsione* is used because a term equivalent to prospective does not exist. *Prospettiva* has a different meaning and projection is closer to forecast, which, as already mentioned here and discussed by Godet (1979), does not have the implications of prospective. Consequently when the term *previsione* is used in Italian it is necessary to qualify it. For example, *previsione umana* and *previsione sociale*, which has in itself the capacity to build a set of futures that are different from the past and the present (as with prospective) but with the addition of some other qualifications, as indicated by Barbieri Masini and Medina (1993). In this meaning, to build the future is seen simultaneously as a need, a choice, and a way of life that are related to the human being and to a given society. The need is due in part to the rapidity of change in modern times but also to an ethical requirement to create a future that is humane, as Josef Fuchs (1977) says, and at the same time social, as related to social choices. According to Barbieri Masini (1993), embedded in *previsione umana e sociale* is the need to build the future, but with a choice in terms of deciding to propose one or many alternative futures. It is a way of life, as it goes beyond a discipline and becomes a distinguishing feature of a group of people. Hence, *previsione umana e sociale* has the following basic functions: It is geared to a project of the future; it clarifies the goals of a given person or social group; and it is educational, in terms of helping to create responsibility for the future.

Prognosis is a term that is very much used in German-speaking countries and in Central and Eastern Europe. It is very close to forecast and forecasting.

Among the many other terms, it is important to mention *futuribles*, which was used by Bertrand de Jouvenel (1967) to indicate the many possible, probable and desirable futures that exist. In the debate about futuribles, Jouvenel's thinking is reminiscent of the thinking of many in the Middle Ages, especially the emphasis put on freedom by the Jesuit Molina (in 1588), whose writings were published in 1876 in France. Jouvenel, in the conceptual discussion of terms, especially "futuribles," refers to the discussion of the symmetry between the past and the future that took place in the eighteenth century and goes back to 1588 to the Jesuit Molina who had favored the position of human freedom of choice in relation to the interpretation of the past and the choice of the future.

An interesting more recent term is *foresight*. Actually it was first used by D.H. Wells in 1932 in a speech for the BBC advocating the need for experts in foresight. As described by Irvin and Martin (1984), nowadays the term is mostly used in the sense of outlook, meaning a cluster of systematic attempts to look ahead and to choose more effectively. Foresight takes into account the fact that there is not one future but many—only one of which, however, will occur. Foresight is also used at the national level as a support for national planning, to identify the possible technological futures and their environmental and social impact.

As regards the actual discipline, in addition to *futures studies*—a very broad term that contains all the different ways of looking at the future, from projection to utopia—there is the term *futurology*, which was defined by Ossip Flechtheim (1966) as the search for the logic of the future in parallel to the search for the logic of the past in history. Unfortunately, this concept has lost its correct meaning and is now used casually to refer to any fantasy about the future.

Futuristics is another term that is often used, especially in North America. Its meaning is similar to that of futures studies.

A BRIEF HISTORY OF FUTURES STUDIES

It is hard to establish a definite date for the beginning of futures studies. Many indicate the period immediately after World War II with the development in the United States of what was called *technological forecasting* at RAND (Research and Development) Corporation. According to Wendell Bell (1997), this can be linked to the *operational research* conducted in the United Kingdom to predict and project the moves of the German bombers.

More or less in the same period, the Europeans also contributed to what may be considered the "beginnings" of futures studies—in France, Bertrand de Jouvenel with futuribles and Gaston Berger with prospective, followed by Pierre Massé and many others; Pater in the Netherlands, Fred Polak with his important books *The Image of the Future* and *Prognosis: A Science in the Making*.

The three major organizations dealing with futures studies were established at the end of the 1960s: the World Futures Studies Federation, which started in embryo in Oslo in 1967 and was formally founded in Paris at UNESCO in 1973; the World Future Society, essentially a North American organization founded by Edward Cornish in 1967; and the Club of Rome, founded in Rome by Aurelio Peccei and Alexander King in 1968. The latter in particular had a major impact on decision making with the project "The Limits to Growth," which is still relevant both in relation to the limits

of the earth and of the need to look at the future in the long term, and in relation to a cluster of human and social issues (the global problematic).

The 1970s posed a serious challenge to futures studies. The severe economic crisis of that period showed that in looking at the future it is necessary to address many aspects and paces of change, given that economic and technological changes are much more rapid than social and cultural changes, for example. The 1970s also challenged the concept of the future as being linear development of the present and the past. There was a reappraisal of futures studies in the 1980s, especially in Europe. In countries such as the Netherlands, Sweden, and Finland, futures studies acquired political importance. In the 1990s developing countries also started to make use of futures studies; with the exception of India, China, and certain Latin American countries, most developing countries had had little interest in futures studies up until then. In the same period, futures studies reemerged very strongly in the United States with the launching of such major projects as the Millennium Project, supported by the United Nations University and the Smithsonian Institute. The Millenium Project, directed by Jerome C. Glenn and Theodore J. Gordon, studies the major threats and challenges of the future and produces the "state of the future" report. The debate on methodologies was also revived, sparking the publication of many basic texts that became prominent in the world debate. Schools of futures studies emerged in Finland and Hungary, and there was increased interest in Australia.

Numerous sociologists have made important contributions to futures studies: William F. Ogburn was appointed by President Herbert Hoover to chair the Research Committee on Social Trends as early as 1929. Harold Lasswell, who laid the foundations for the science of political choices also wrote many less well-known articles on futures perspectives. Daniel Bell wrote the famous report of the Commission Toward the Year 2000 for the American Academy of Arts and Sciences in 1967. John McHale wrote many books and contributed to the founding of the World Futures Studies Federation in the 1960s and 1970s. Elise Boulding greatly contributed with her work on peace in the future and the role of women in the future. One could mention many more names. The main point to stress is that futures studies and sociology have not always been considered two separate and distinct disciplines.

CHARACTERISTICS OF FUTURES STUDIES

Many characteristics of futures studies relate to the linking of present action with future results. Barbieri Masini (1993) identifies seven characteristics in particular:

1. *Transdisciplinary.* Futures studies go beyond the interdisciplinary nature of social science. Futures studies needs the parallel approaches of different disciplines as well as the combined effort of many approaches in addressing the complexity of present problems in a rapidly changing society. It needs disciplinary approaches that identify common assumptions and use common methodologies. In terms of methodologies, examples of such approaches are the Delphi and the scenario-building methods, which function with the support of mathematics, statistics, economics, sociology, history, and psychology. To quote Fred Polak: "all kinds of separate, fragmented portions of the jigsaw puzzle are of little avail, unless they are fitted together in the best possible way, to form an image of the future depicting a number of main areas of development" (1971, p. 261).

2. *Complex.* This represents the other side of the transdisciplinary nature of futures studies. As a concept, complexity was much debated in futures studies, even before it became a clear issue in social sciences, because it is related to uncertainty: The greater the complexity of a given situation, the greater the level of uncertainty; the greater the number of variables needed to describe a social situation, the greater the uncertainty. Because the future is so uncertain, futures studies has to devise methods for lowering the level of uncertainty: One such method is alternative scenario building.

3. *Global.* Its global nature is probably the best-known characteristic of futures studies. It is now generally accepted that the future is determined by a continuous interplay between local issues and global issues. Some issues emerge as local and then become global, such as an economic crisis in a given country or part of the world. Some issues are born global and subsequently affect the local level such as the greenhouse effect.

4. Normative. The impact of the normative is much greater in futures studies than is usually the case in social sciences. Frameworks of values and systems of values can never be completely eliminated in futures studies. Many methods try to lower the level of impact of the normative, but it is always present: Thinking about the future, making decisions about the future, is always related to some hope or fear.

5. Scientific. This is the most debated characteristic of futures studies, precisely because the normative is always present. Great effort has been made to invent devices and methods for increasing the scientific level of futures studies. If it is not possible to define futures studies as scientific, then it must be absolutely rigorous in terms of application and methods. It must be used according to strict scientific rules. Yehezkel Dror (1974) stresses the importance of combining a clinical and a human approach.

6. Dynamic. Futures studies is very dynamic: It is constantly in search of stronger foundations, of better approaches, and of more effective methods for facing the rapidity of change.

7. Participatory. There is less consensus on this characteristic of futures studies than on the previous ones. It is obvious that futures studies methods should be developed with the participation of those who are responsible for choosing the future, that is, decision makers at every level. This may not be possible at every step in the application of methods, but it is certainly something to strive for. Participation is definitely an essential characteristic of scenario-building and Delphi applications.

LIMITS OF FUTURES STUDIES

Like all disciplines futures studies has limits. Barbieri Masini (1993) has singled out six such limits.

1. *Self-altering.* The moment a forecast, or the result of a futures study, becomes public, it produces consequences that alter the reality in which it operates. In other words, a self-realizing or a self-defeating effect may invalidate the value of the forecast. This danger was underlined long ago by Robert Merton ([1938] 1973) and is still valid today.

2. *Psychological aspects.* These are crucial in futures studies, as inevitably in looking ahead one is influenced by hopes and fears. Fear of the unknown is ever present and can have a negative impact on the need to think in alternative terms as the future requires. It is also easy to underestimate the changes that will occur in the future.

3. *Irrational aspects.* In future processes and events there is always an irrational element that cannot be quantified or evaluated; for example, the whims of a given head of state or the religious reaction of a given population.

4. *Implicit hypotheses.* These are present in any futures exercise. This aspect is of course related to the normative characteristic mentioned earlier, however, in using futures studies, it is essential to detect the implicit hypotheses.

5. *A posteriori verification.* A definite limit of futures studies is that it is only possible to verify the validity of a given study after the events forecast have occurred. This is often done and is an extremely useful way of learning more about the application of methods.

6. *Availability of reliable data.* This clearly is a crucial aspect: Any future-oriented study must be able to rely on good quantitative and qualitative data. There may, for example, be a lack of historical data on which to base a forecast or a lack of relevant ad hoc surveys. This is one of the most important limits of futures studies, for if forecasts are to be reliable, data must be rigorously evaluated.

METHODS

Before entering the debate on methods, it is important to underline the accepted typology of futures studies methods. Futures studies can be *extrapolative* (opportunity-oriented) or *normative* (mission-oriented). The definitions in parenthesis are those of Eric Jantsch (1967). In other words, to extrapolate from the past to the present and into the future constitutes one group of methods, of which projections are one. Another is to start from what is needed in the future—an image, a goal, an objective—and work backward, searching in the present for possible and probable ways of realizing it. Nowadays futures studies are never wholly

extrapolative or normative; they usually emphasize one or the other aspect, given the normative characteristic of futures studies.

SCENARIOS

The term and method were introduced by Herman Kahn during the 1960s. Nowadays *scenario* is a general term that is used to refer to different approaches: those of the Stanford Research Institute (SRI), of the Battelle Institute, of the studies by Michel Godet and others. A scenario can be defined as an ensemble created to describe a future situation and the sequence of events leading from the present situation to a future one.

Theoretically speaking, scenarios are a synthesis of several different hypothetical routes (events, actors, strategies) that lead to different possible futures. Practically speaking, scenarios often describe specific sets of events and variables that have been put together with the aim of focusing on causal processes and related decision-making. According to Herman Kahn (1967), scenarios answer the following basic questions: How does a situation evolve step by step from the present to the future? What are the possible alternatives that different actors in the different moments of decision making can use in order to anticipate, change, or facilitate the process?

From an epistemological point of view, scenarios are analytical and empirical constructions. They are hypotheses that do not "predict" the future but rather indicate a series of options and probable situations. No scenario will ever precisely anticipate the occurrence of a given event; rather it will suggest alternatives with the aim of sensitizing decision makers to what might happen. Hypotheses are never invented but are founded on a rational, consistent diagnosis of the forces that may model events. According to Michel Godet (1995), the scenario hypothesis should respond to the following five conditions. They must be: pertinent, coherent, realistic, important, and transparent.

Scenarios are instruments for better decision making. Their aim is to lower the level of uncertainty and increase the level of understanding of the consequences of actions in the present.

In looking at scenarios, one presumes an awareness on the part of the author of the rapidity and interrelatedness of change, which will affect both decisions and the understanding of consequences, which can change a preexistent situation, either completely or in part. Scenarios are both synoptic and simultaneous: They can be used to analyze many variables at once and identify the respective turning points in terms of decision-making in steps of five, ten, or twenty years. Timing depends on the area of interest. For example, in the economic area the time span considered will be much shorter than in the educational area.

In recent years, use of the scenario technique has increased greatly, as have its applications. The scenario method seems to be particularly useful in the following situations: (1) to detect long-term trends that can help to formulate alternative within a given context; (2) to identify potential discontinuities and situations and alert organizations, countries, or regions to foresee them and thus prepare contingency plans; (3) to alert organizations, regions, or countries of possible interrelated changes as a reference for planning; (4) to provide a basis for analyzing risks as interactions between socioeconomic areas that may lead to risks and are not understandable if seen only in a specific and isolated area; (5) to evaluate the results of different strategies in different areas that may not have been developed in the awareness of interrelations.

In the public sector the best-known applications include the following. In the 1960s, Herman Kahn used scenarios connected to military and strategic studies that were developed at the RAND corporation. In the 1960s and 1970s, territorial planning by DATAR was used in France. Scenarios derived from systems analysis and global models, such as *The Limits to Growth* by Meadows and Meadows (1972), analyzed the global consequences of the interrelated growth of population, agricultural production, industrial development, environmental pollution, and use of natural resources. Finally, Jacques Lesourne directed an important exercise of Interfutures for the Organization for Economic Cooperation and development (OECD), which identified the alternatives of the relationships between the North and the South regions of the world.

In scenario building the private sector intervened, perhaps late, but in a sophisticated manner. Shell International Petroleum Company (Royal Dutch/Shell Group) used scenarios before the energy crises of 1973 and before the debacle of the Soviet Union, its major competitor in the petroleum area. Other large oil companies followed Shell's example and made extensive use of scenarios—ARGO in the late 1970s and, more recently, Pacific Gas and Electric.

In the private sector scenarios are used by enterprises in many sectors. Financial services have used scenarios to understand competitors and regulate uncertainty. Insurance companies, such as the Allied Irish Bank, have used scenarios to support strategic planning within a constantly changing context.

REFERENCES

Barbieri Masini, Eleonora 1993 *Why Futures Studies?* London: Grey Seal.

——, and Javier Medina Vasquez 2000 "Scenarios as Seen From a Human and Social Perspective." In *Technological Forecasting and Social Change.* Amsterdam: Elsevier.

Bell, Wendell 1997 *Foundations of Futures Studies* 2 vols. News Brunswick, N.J.: Transaction Publishers.

Berger, Gaston 1958 *L'Attitude.* Paris: Presses Universitaires de France.

Dror, Yehezkel 1974 "Futures Studies—Quo Vadis?" In *Human Futures, Needs–Societies–Technologies.* London: IPC Science and Technology Press.

Flechteim, Ossip 1966 *History and Futurology* Verlag Anton Main Meisenheim, Arn Glam.

Fuchs, Josef 1977 "Morale come progettazione del futuro del'uomo" [Ethics as Building the Human Future]. In P. C. Beltrao, ed., *Pensare il futuro (Thinking the Future).* Rome: Edizioni Paoline.

Glenn, Jerome C., Gordon Theodore, Jr. 1999 *State of the Future, Challenges We Face at the Millenium.* American Council of United Nations Universes.

Godet, Michel 1995 "From Anticipation to Action." *A Book of Strategic Prospectice, Future Oriented Studies.* Paris: UNESCO Publishing.

—— 1995 "Global Scenarios: Morphological and Probability Analysis." In *Scenario Building, Convergence, and Differences* Profutures Workshop, Institute for Prospective Technological Studies (IPTS). European Commission Joint Research Council, 17–30.

—— 1995 "From Anticipation to Action: A Book of Strategic Prospective." Paris: UNESCO Publishing.

—— 1979 *The Crisis in Forecasting and the Emergence of the Prospective Approach, UNITAR.* New York: Pergamon.

Hatem, Fabrice 1993 "Introduction à la prospective." Paris: *Gestion-Economica*. 86–89.

—— 1996 "La prospective. Pratiques et méthodes." *Gestion-Economica*. 222–232.

Irvin, J., and B. Martin, B. 1984 *Foresight in Science, Picking the Winners*. London: Pinter Publishers.

Jantsch, Eric 1967 *Technological Forecasting in Perspective*. Paris: Ocse.

Jouvenel, Bertrand de 1967 *The Art of Conjecture*. New York: Basic Books.

Kahn, Herman, and Anthony Wiener 1967 *The Year 2000–A Framework for Speculation in the Next 33 Years*. London: Macmillan.

Malaska, Pentti 1995 "Survey of the Use of the Multiple Scenario Approach in Big European Companies Since 1973." In *Scenario Building, Convergence, and Differences*. Profutures Workshop, Institute for Prospective Technological Studies (IPTS), European Commission Joint Research Council, 42–46.

McHale, John 1969 *The Future of the Future*. New York: George Braziller.

Merton, Robert K. (1938) 1973 *The Sociology of Science*. Chicago: University of Chicago Press.

Norse, David 1979 "Scenario Analysis in Interfutures." *Futures*. (October):412–428.

Ozbekahn, Hasan 1970 "Verso una teoria generale della pianificazione." (Towards a General Theory of Planning). *Futuribili* (October):25–128.

Polak, Fred 1971 *Prognosis: A Science in the Making*. Amsterdam: Elsevier.

—— 1973 *The Image of the Future*. (ed. and abridged by Elise Boulding). New York: Elsevier.

Schwartz, Peter 1996 "The Art of the Long View." *Planning for the Future in an Uncertain World*. New York: Doubleday.

——, and Kees Van der Heijden 1996 "Culture d'entreprise et planification par scénarios: une relation de coévolution." In Jacques Lesourne and Christian Stoffaes, eds., *La prospective stratégique d'entreprise*. Paris: Intereditions.

Wack, Peter 1985 "Scenarios: Shooting the Rapids." *Harvard Business Review* (November/December):139–150.

—— 1985 "Scenarios: Uncharted Waters Ahead." *Harvard Business Review* (September/October):73–89.

Wilson, Ian 1995 "Linking Intuition and Structure: an Integrated Approach to Scenario Development." In *Scenario Building, Convergence, and Differences*, Profutures Workshop, Institute for Prosepctive Technological Studies (IPTS), European Commission, Joint Research Council, 31–41.

—— 1978 "Scenarios." In Jib Fowles, ed., *Handbook of Futures Research*. Westport, Conn.: Greenwood Press.

ELEONORA BARBIERI MASINI

G

GAME THEORY AND STRATEGIC INTERACTION

A *game* is a situation that involves two or more decision makers (called *players*), where (1) each player faces a choice between at least two behavioral options, (2) each player strives to maximize utility (i.e., to achieve the greatest payoff possible), and (3) the payoff obtained by a given player depends not only on the option that he or she chooses but also on the option(s) chosen by the other player(s). In virtually all games, some or all of the players have fully or partially opposing interests; this causes the behavior of players to be proactive and strategic.

The *theory of games* is a branch of applied mathematics that rigorously treats the topic of optimal behavior in two-person and *n*-person games. Its origins go back at least to 1710, when the German mathematician-philosopher Leibniz foresaw the need for a theory of games of strategy. Soon afterward, James Waldegrave (in Montmort 1713; 1980) formulated the concept of maximin, a decision criterion important to game theory. In his book *Mathematical Psychics*, Edgeworth (1881; 1995) made explicit the similarity between economic processes and games of strategy. Later, theorists such as Zermelo (1913) stated specialized propositions for certain games (e.g., chess). Not until the work of Borel ([1921–1927] 1953) and von Neumann (1928), however, did the foundations of a true theory of games appear. A landmark of the modern era, von Neumann and Morgenstern's *Theory of Games and Economic Behavior* (1944), extended game theory to problems involving more than two players. Luce and Raiffa (1957) published the first widely used textbook in game theory. For more details regarding the early history of game theory, see Dimand and Dimand (1996) and Weintraub (1992).

Game theory has continued to develop substantially in recent years. Many introductory presentations of the modern mathematical theory are available. Among these are Friedman (1990), Jones (1980), Myerson (1991), Owen (1982), Romp (1997), and Szep and Forgo (1985).

Beyond its status as a branch of applied mathematics, game theory serves social scientists as a tool for studying situations and institutions with multiple decision makers. Some of these investigations are empirical, while others are primarily analytic in character. The dependent variables of central concern in games include allocation of payoffs (i.e., who receives what rewards or bears what costs) and formation of coalitions (i.e., which of various possible alliances among players occur in a game.) Other concerns include whether outcomes of a game are stable or not, whether outcomes are collectively efficient or not, and whether outcomes are fair or not in some specific sense.

GAME-THEORETIC CONCEPTS

Mathematical game theory provides three main tools that assist in the analysis of multiperson decision problems. These include a descriptive framework, a typology of games, and a variety of solution concepts.

Descriptive Framework. At base, a description of any game requires a list of all players, the strategies available to each player, the logically possible outcomes in the game, and the payoff of each outcome to each player. In some instances, a game's description also includes a specification of the dynamic sequence of play and of the (possibly limited or incomplete) information sets available to players. Payoffs in a game are expressed in terms of *utility*; this provides a standard means of comparing otherwise diverse outcomes.

An analyst can model or represent a game in various forms. *Extensive form* depicts all possible strategies of players in a tree format. It is especially useful for modeling games in which play occurs in stages or over time. *Strategic form* (also called normal form or a "payoff matrix") shows payoffs to players as a function of all strategy combinations. *Characteristic function form* lists the minimum payoffs assured for each of the coalitions in a game. Whereas extensive and normal forms pertain to virtually all types of games, characteristic function form pertains only to cooperative games (i.e., games that permit coalitions).

Typology of Games. The second tool from game theory is a general typology of games. This provides a means of codifying or classifying games vis-à-vis one another. At base, there are four major types of games. Games can be either *static* (i.e., single time period) or *dynamic* (multiple time periods), and they can involve either *complete information* (all relevant information is shared and held in common) or *incomplete information* (some information is private and held only by some players). Much of classic game theory was formulated with reference to static games involving complete information; more recent developments have extended the theory to dynamic games and also to games involving incomplete information.

Games can be *two-person* or *n-person* (more than two players), and they can be further classified as *cooperative* or *noncooperative*. Cooperative games permit players to communicate before reaching decisions and include some mechanism that enables players to make binding agreements regarding coordination of strategies. Noncooperative games do not permit players to communicate or to form binding agreements prior to play. In other words, cooperative games enable players to form coalitions whereas noncooperative games do not.

Among cooperative games, some are *sidepayment games* while others are *nonsidepayment games*. Sidepayment games permit players to transfer payoffs (utility) within coalitions; nonsidepayment games do not. A further distinction applicable to cooperative sidepayment games is that between *simple games* and *nonsimple games*. Simple games are those in which the characteristic function assumes only two values, whereas nonsimple games are those in which the characteristic function has more than two values. Analysts use simple games primarily to model social processes with binary outcomes (e.g., win–lose, succeed–fail, etc.)

Solution Concepts. The third set of tools provided by game theory is a variety of solution concepts. A *solution concept* is theory of equilibrium that predicts (behaviorally) or prescribes (normatively) the allocation of payoffs to players in games. In other words, a solution concept specifies how a game will turn out when played. For this reason, solution concepts are among the most important contributions of game theory.

Game theorists have developed numerous solution concepts. These differ not only in the underlying assumptions but also in the predictions they make. For static noncooperative games, the most prominent solution is the Nash equilibrium (Nash 1951); there are many extensions of this concept (summarized in van Damme 1987). Other approaches to the solution of noncooperative games are those of Harsanyi and Selten (1988) and Fraser and Hipel (1984).

For static cooperative games, there are several classes of solution concepts. One prominent class consists of solutions that predict outcomes which are collectively rational (i.e., imputations). Included in this class are the core (Aumann 1961; Gillies 1959), the Shapley value (Shapley 1953), and the nucleolus (Schmeidler 1969). Other solutions in this class are the disruption nucleolus (Gately 1974; Littlechild and Vaidya 1976), the disruption value (Charnes et al. 1978), the p-center solution (Spinetto 1974), and the aspiration solution (Bennett 1983). Another class of solutions for cooperative games includes concepts that make payoff predictions contingent upon the coalition structures that form during play; these payoff allocations are usually coalitionally rational. Included are the $M_1(i)$ bargaining set (Aumann and Dreze 1974; Aumann and Maschler 1964), the competitive bargaining set (Horowitz 1973), the kernel (Davis and Maschler 1965), the Myerson–Shapley solution (Aumann and Myerson 1988; Myerson 1977), the equal division kernel (Crott and Albers 1981), and the alpha-power solution (Rapoport and Kahan 1982). Recently, a third class of solutions has emerged for cooperative games. Solutions in this class attempt not only to determine endogenously which coalition structure(s) will emerge but also to specify the associated payoffs to players. One solution in this class is the central-union theory (Michener and Au 1994; Michener and Myers 1998), which predicts coalition formation probabilistically. Another solution in this class is the viable proposals theory (Sengupta and Sengupta 1994).

EXPERIMENTAL STUDIES OF GAMES

Laboratory experimentation on two-person and n-person games commenced in the early 1950s (e.g., Flood 1952) and it continues to the present. Some gaming studies are primarily descriptive in nature, whereas others investigate the predictive accuracy of various solution concepts.

Experiments of Two-Person Games. Investigators have conducted literally thousands of experiments on two-person games. Most of these treat noncooperative games, although some do treat cooperative games in various forms. Some studies investigate constant-sum games, whereas others treat non-constant-sum games (primarily such archetypal games as the prisoner's dilemma, chicken, battle of the sexes, etc.).

The major dependent variables in the two-person studies are the strategies used by players (particularly the frequency of cooperative choices) and the payoffs received by players. Independent variables include the type of game, strategy of the confederate, information set, interpersonal attitudes of players, sex of players, motivational orientation of players, and magnitude and form of payoffs.

Some of this research seeks to understand how differences in game matrices affect play (Harris 1972; Rapoport et al. 1976). Another portion describes how players' strategies vary as a function of the confederate's strategy (i.e., partner's history of play over time); this is reviewed in Oskamp (1971). Another portion of this work investigates

the extent to which predictions from the minimax theorem approximate observed payoffs in constant-sum games; Colman (1982, ch. 5) reviewed these findings. Still other work covers cooperative bargaining models; Roth (1995) reviewed research on bargaining experiments. Some experimentation on two-person games has addressed the impact of players' value orientation on cooperation (McClintock and Liebrand 1988; Van Lange and Liebrand 1991). General reviews of experimental research on two-person games appear in Colman (1982), Komorita and Parks (1995), and Pruitt and Kimmel (1977).

Experiments of n-Person Noncooperative Games. There are several lines of experimentation on n-person noncooperative games. One line investigates multiperson compound games derived from 2×2 matrices (e.g., n-person chicken, n-person battle of the sexes, etc.). Important among these is the n-person dilemma (NPD) game, wherein individually rational strategies produce outcomes that are not collectively rational. The NPD serves as an abstract model of many phenomena, including conservation of scarce natural resources, voluntary wage restraint, and situations involving the tragedy of the commons (Hardin 1968; Hartwick and Yeung 1997; Moulin and Watts 1997). The literature contains many experimental studies of the NPD and other social dilemmas (e.g., Liebrand et al. 1992; Rapoport 1988). In addition to varying the payoff matrix itself, studies of this type investigate the effects of such factors as group identity, self-efficacy, perceptions of other players, value orientation, uncertainty, and players' expectations of cooperation. Reviews of research on NPDs and similar games appear in Dawes (1980), Kollock (1998), Komorita and Parks (1999), Liebrand and colleagues (1992), Liebrand and Messick (1996), and Messick and Brewer (1983).

A related line of research is that by experimental economists on markets and auctions (Smith 1982). This work investigates market structures (such as competitive exchange, oligopoly, and auction bidding) in laboratory settings (Friedman and Hoggatt 1980; Plott and Sunder 1982). Many of these structures can be viewed as noncooperative games. Plott (1982) provides a review of studies investigating equilibrium solutions of markets—the competitive equilibrium, the Cournot model, and the monopoly (joint maximization) model.

There is an increasingly large experimental literature on auctions, some of which is game-theoretic in character. Since auctions usually entail incomplete information (buyers have private information about their willingness to pay and ability to pay), these studies investigate the effects on bidding behavior of such variables as differential information, asymmetric beliefs, and risk aversion. They also investigate different institutional forms, such as English auctions, Dutch auctions, double auctions, and sealed bid–offer auctions (e.g., Cox et al. 1984; Smith et al. 1982). Reviews of the theoretical literature on auctions appear in Engelbrecht-Wiggans (1980), Laffont (1997), and McAfee and McMillan (1987). Kagel (1995) provides a survey of experimental research on auctions.

Experiments of *n*-Person Weighted Majority Games. Weighted majority games are an important subclass of cooperative, sidepayment, simple games. They serve as models of legislative or voting systems. Theorists have developed many special solution concepts for these games. Early theories applicable to weighted majority games are the minimum power theory and minimum resource theory (Gamson 1961). Riker's size principle predicts the formation of minimal winning coalitions in these games. Other theories for weighted majority games include the bargaining theory (Komorita and Chertkoff 1973; Kravitz 1986) and the equal excess model (Komorita 1979). The bargaining theory posits that players in a coalition will divide payoffs in a manner midway between equality and proportionality to resources (votes) contributed. The equal excess model is similar but uses the equal excess norm instead of proportionality.

Numerous experiments on coalition bargaining in weighted majority games have tested these and related theories (e.g., Cole et al. 1995; Komorita et al. 1989; Miller and Komorita 1986). Results of these studies generally support the bargaining theory and the equal excess model over the others, although all have deficiencies. Reviews of some experiments in this line appear in Komorita (1984) and Komorita and Kravitz (1983).

Experiments of Other *n*-Person Cooperative Games. Beyond NPD and weighted majority games, investigators have studied a wide variety of *n*-person cooperative games in other forms. The primary objective of the work is to discover which game-theoretic solution concepts predict most accurately the outcomes of these games.

Numerous studies have investigated cooperative sidepayment games in characteristic function form (e.g., Michener et al. 1986; Murnighan and Roth 1980; Rappaport 1990). Other studies have investigated similar games in strategic form. This work shows that in games with empty core, solution concepts such as the nucleolus and the kernel predict fairly well; in games with a nonempty core, however, the Shapley value is often more accurate. Reviews of parts of this research appear in Kahan and Rapoport (1984), Michener and Potter (1981), and Murnighan (1978).

Other studies have investigated cooperative nonsidepayment games. Some of this research pertains to bargaining models in sequential games of status (Friend et al. 1977). Other research tests various solution concepts (such as the core and the lambda transfer value) in nonsidepayment games in strategic form (McKelvey and Ordeshook 1982; Michener et al. 1985; Michener and Salzer 1989).

Another line of experimentation on cooperative nonsidepayment games is that conducted by political scientists interested in committee games or spatial voting games. These are *n*-person voting games in which policies are represented as positions in multidimensional space. For the most part, this research attempts to test predictions from alternative solution concepts (Ferejohn et al. 1980; Ordeshook and Winer 1980). Some of this work has led to new theories, such as the competitive solution (McKelvey and Ordeshook 1983; McKelvey et al. 1978), and to further developments regarding established ones, such as methods for computing the Copeland winner (Grofman et al. 1987). Experimental research on spatial games is reviewed in McKelvey and Ordeshook (1990).

DYNAMIC GAMES

Although early developments in game theory centered primarily on static games (i.e., games in which interaction among players is single-period or single-play in nature), many subsequent developments have addressed *dynamic games* occurring over time. In a dynamic game, time (or stage) is an important consideration in strategy, and the choices and actions of players at any stage are conditional on the history of prior choices in the game. There is a growing theoretical literature on various classes of dynamic games, including repeated games, differential games, and evolutionary games. Introductions to the topic of dynamic games appear in Friedman (1990), Fudenberg and Tirole (1991), Owen (1982), and Thomas (1984). The empirical literature on dynamic games is still small relative to that on static games, although experimental studies of repeated games appear increasingly often.

The term *supergame* refers to a sequence of (ordinary) games played by a fixed set of players. One important type of supergame is the *repeated game*, wherein the same constituent game is played at each stage in the sequence. For instance, if some players play a prisoner's dilemma game again and again, they are engaging in a repeated game. At this point in historical time, the dominant paradigm for the study of dynamic strategic behavior is that of repeated games. Certain repeated games are of interest because they allow collectively rational outcomes to result from noncooperative equilibrium strategies. Axelrod (1984) has analyzed the development of cooperation in repeated games. Selten and Stoecker (1983) have used a learning theory approach to model end-game behavior of players in repeated prisoner's dilemma games. Aumann and Maschler (1995) have studied repeated games with incomplete information. A survey of literature on repeated games appears in Mertens and colleagues (1994a,b,c).

Theorists have developed various solution concepts applicable to repeated games and multistage games. Among these are the backward induction process, the subgame perfect equilibrium (Selten 1975), and the Pareto perfect equilibrium (Bernheim et al. 1987). Cronshaw (1997) describes computational techniques for finding all equilibria in infinitely repeated games with discounting and perfect monitoring.

Another class of dynamic games is the *differential game*, played in continuous time. Much of the literature on differential games focuses on the two-person zero-sum case. Some applications of differential games are military, such as pursuit games, where the goal of, say, a pursing aircraft is to minimize time or distance required to catch an evading aircraft (Hajek 1975). The classic works on differential games include Friedman (1971) and Isaacs (1965). Models of differential games with more than two players are discussed in Leitman

(1974). Other useful works on differential games include Basar and Bernard (1989) and Lewin (1994). The vector-valued maximin for these games is discussed in Zhukovskiy and Salukvadze (1994).

Biologists and economists have used game theoretic concepts to study *evolutionary games*, which are dynamic models of social evolution that explain why certain inherited traits (i.e., behavioral patterns) arise in a human or animal population and remain stable over time. In some evolutionary games (especially those with animal populations), the individuals are modeled as having neither rationality, nor conscience, nor expectations, so strategy selection and equilibrium derive from behavioral phenotypes rather than from rational thought processes. Models of this type often incorporate such phenomena as mutation, acquisition (learning), and the consequences of random perturbations. Theorists have advanced various concepts of evolutionary stability and evolutionarily stable strategies (Amir and Berninghaus 1998; Bomze and Potscher 1989; Gardner et al. 1987; Maynard Smith 1982). Summaries and extensions of work on evolutionary games appear in Bomze (1996), Friedman (1991, 1998), Samuelson (1997), and Weibull (1995).

INSTITUTIONAL ANALYSIS VIA GAME THEORY

Economists and political scientists have long used game theory in the analysis of social institutions. In work of this type, an analyst specifies an institution (such as a Cournot oligopoly or an approval voting system) in hypothetical or ideal-typical terms and then applies game-theoretic solution concepts to see which payoff allocation(s) may result at equilibrium. Through this approach, an analyst can compare the outcomes of alternative institutional forms with respect to stability, efficiency, and fairness. Broad discussions and reviews of this literature appear in Schotter (1981, 1994), Schotter and Schwodiauer (1980), and Shubik (1982, 1984).

Economic Institutions. Von Neumann and Morgenstern (1944) were among the first to explore the role of *n*-person game theory in economic analysis. Since that time, economists have analyzed a variety of institutions in game-theoretic terms, including *oligopoly and other imperfect markets*. Markets in which there are only a few sellers (oligopoly), two sellers (duopoly, a type of oligopoly), one buyer and one seller (bilateral monopoly), and so on, lend themselves to game-theoretic analysis because the payoffs to each player depend on the strategies of the other players.

Economists have modeled oligopolies both as noncooperative games and as cooperative games. Several analyses of oligopolies as noncooperative games show that the standard Chamberlin price-setting strategy is equivalent to a Nash equilibrium in pure strategies (Telser 1972). Beyond that, various analyses have treated oligopoly as a noncooperative multistage game. These analyses have produced generalizations concerning the effects of adjustment speed, demand and cost functions, and incomplete information regarding demand on the dynamic stability of the traditional Cournot solution and other equilibria (Friedman 1977; Radner 1980).

Analyses of collusion among oligopolists usually view this as a cooperative game. These treatments analyze outcomes via such solution concepts as the core or the bargaining set (Kaneko 1978). Reviews and discussions of game-theoretic models of oligopoly appear in deFraja and Delbono (1990), Friedman (1983), Kurz (1985), and Shubik (1984). Game theoretic literature on collusive equilibria is surveyed in Rees (1993).

A second topic of interest to game-theoretic economists is general equilibrium in a *multilateral exchange economy*. An early paper (Arrow and Debreu 1954) modeled a general competitive exchange economy (involving production, exchange, and consumption) as a noncooperative game, and then showed that a generalized Nash equilibrium existed for the model. Other theorists have modeled a multilateral exchange economy as a cooperative *n*-person game. Shubik (1959) showed that the core of such a game is identical to Edgeworth's traditional contract curve. More generally, Debreu and Scarf (1963) showed that the core converges to the Walrasian competitive equilibrium. Telser (1996) discussed the core as a tool for finding market-clearing prices in economies with many inputs and outputs. Roth and Sotomayor (1990) discussed the matching problem in labor and marriage markets.

By representing an economy as an *n*-person cooperative game, analysts can investigate general equilibrium even in markets that do not fulfill the neoclassical regularity assumptions (e.g., convexity of preferences, divisibility of commodities, absence of externalities) (Rosenthal 1971; Telser 1972). Beyond that, some economists model general equilibrium in game-theoretic terms because they can introduce and analyze a variety of alternative institutional arrangements. This includes, for instance, models with or without trade, with or without production, with various types of money (commodity money, fiat money, bank money, accounting money), and with various types of financial institutions (shares, central banks, bankruptcy rules, and the like) (Dagan et al. 1997; Dubey and Shubik 1977; Karatzas et al. 1997). Depending on the models used, such cooperative solutions as the core, Shapley value, and nucleolus play an important role in these analyses, as does the Nash noncooperative solution.

A third concern of game-theoretically oriented economists is the analysis of *public goods and services* (e.g., bridges, roads, dams, harbors, libraries, police services, public health services, and the like). Of special relevance is the pricing and cross-subsidization of public utilities; a central issue is how different classes of customers should divide the costs of providing public utilities.

Theorists can model such problems by letting the cost function of a public utility determine the characteristic function of a (cooperative) cost-sharing game. Games of this type are amenable to analysis via such solution concepts as the Shapley value (Loehman and Whinston 1974), the nucleolus (Littlechild and Vaidya 1976; Nakayama and Suzuki 1977), and the core (Littlechild and Thompson 1977), each of which represents alternative cost-sharing criteria. Moulin (1996) compared alternative cost-sharing mechanisms under increasing returns. Other work has used game-theoretic concepts to model negotiation with respect to provision of public goods (Dearden 1998; Schofield 1984a). A survey of experimental research on public goods appears in Ledyard (1995).

Political Institutions. Like economists, political scientists have analyzed a variety of institutions in game-theoretic terms. One broad line of work—termed the study of *social choice*—investigates various methods for aggregating individual preferences into collective decisions (Moulin 1994). Of special concern is the stability of outcomes produced by alternative *voting systems* (Hinich and Munger

1997; Nurmi 1987; Ordeshook 1986). Analysts have studied many different voting systems (e.g., majority voting, plurality voting, weighted voting, approval voting, and so on.) Strikingly, this work has demonstrated that in majority voting systems where voters choose among more than two alternatives, the conditions for equilibria (i.e., the conditions that assure a decisive winner) are so restrictive as to render equilibria virtually nonexistent (Fishburn 1973; Riker 1982).

Topics in voting include the detailed analysis of cyclic majority phenomena (generalized Condorcet paradox situations), the analysis of equilibria in novel voting systems such as weighted voting (Banzhaf 1965) and approval voting (i.e., a method of voting wherein voters may endorse as many candidates as they like in multicandidate elections) (Brams and Fishburn 1983), and the development of predictive solution concepts for voting systems that possess no stable equilibrium (Ferejohn and Grether 1982).

A second line of work by game theorists concerns the strategic manipulation of political institutions to gain favorable outcomes. One topic here is the consequences of manipulative *agenda control* in committees (Banks 1990; Plott and Levine 1978). Another topic is the effects of *strategic voting*—that is, voting in which players strive to manipulate the decision by voting for candidates or motions other than their real preferences (Cox and Shugart 1996; Feddersen and Pesendorfer 1998; Niemi and Frank 1982). Analyses by Gibbard (1973) and Satterthwaite (1975) showed that no voting procedure can be completely strategy-proof (in the sense of offering voters no incentive to vote strategically) without violating some more fundamental condition of democratic acceptability. In particular, any voting mechanism that is strategy-proof is also necessarily dictatorial. An important issue here is how to design voting systems with at least some desirable properties that encourage sincere revelation of preferences.

A third broad line of work concerns the *indexing of players' power* in political systems (Owen 1982, ch. 10). Frequently this entails assessing differences in a priori voting strength of members of committees or legislatures. For example, a classic study applied the Shapley–Shubik index of power to the U.S. legislative system and assessed the relative power of the president, senators, and representatives (Shapley and Shubik 1954). Other measures of power include the Banzhaf–Coleman index (Banzhaf 1965; Dubey and Shapley 1979) and Straffin's probabilistic indices (Straffin 1978).

A fourth game-theoretic topic is *cabinet coalition formation*, especially in the context of European governments. This topic is of interest because political fragmentation can produce instability of cabinet coalitions, which in turn can lead to collapse of entire governments. Work on this problem ties in with that on spatial voting games and weighted majority games, discussed above. Some cabinet coalition models stress policy (or ideological) alignment among members, while other models stress the transfer of value (payoffs) among members. Important theoretical models include DeSwaan (1973), Grofman (1982), Laver and Shepsle (1996), and Schofield (1984b).

REFERENCES

Amir, M., and S. Berninghaus 1998 "Scale Functions in Equilibrium Selection Games." *Journal of Evolutionary Economics* 8(1):1–13.

Arrow, K. J., and G. Debreu 1954 "Existence of an Equilibrium for a Competitive Economy." *Econometrica* 22:265–290.

Aumann, R. J. 1961 "The Core of a Cooperative Game Without Sidepayments." *Transactions of the American Mathematical Society* 98:539–552.

——, and J. H. Dreze 1974 "Cooperative Games with Coalition Structures." *International Journal of Game Theory* 3:217–237.

——, and M. Maschler 1964 "The Bargaining Set for Cooperative Games." In M. Dresher, L. S. Shapley, and A. W. Tucker, eds., *Advances in Game Theory* (Annals of Mathematics Studies, No. 52), Princeton, N.J.: Princeton University Press.

——, and M. B. Maschler, with R. E. Stearns 1995 *Repeated Games with Incomplete Information.* Cambridge, Mass.: MIT Press.

——, and R. B. Myerson 1988 "Endogenous Formation of Links Between Players and of Coalitions: An Application of the Shapley Value." In A. E. Roth, ed., *The Shapley Value: Essays in Honor of Lloyd S. Shapley.* New York: Cambridge University Press.

Axelrod, R. 1984 *The Evolution of Cooperation.* New York: Basic Books.

Banks, J. S. 1990 "Monopoly Agenda Control and Asymmetric Information." *Quarterly Journal of Economics* 105(2):445–464.

Banzhaf, J. F., III 1965 "Weighted Voting Doesn't Work: A Mathematical Analysis." *Rutgers Law Review* 19:317–343.

Basar, T. S., and P. Bernard, (eds.) 1989 *Differential Games and Applications*. New York: Springer-Verlag.

Bennett, E. 1983 "The Aspiration Approach to Predicting Coalition Formation and Payoff Distribution in Sidepayment Games." *International Journal of Game Theory* 12:1–28.

Bernheim, B. D., B. Peleg, and M. Whinston 1987 "Coalition-Proof Nash Equilibria. I: Concepts." *Journal of Economic Theory* 42:1–12.

Bomze, I. M. 1996 "Evolutionary Stability Is Not a Foolish Game." *Central European Journal for Operations Research and Economics* 4(1):25–56.

——, and B. M. Potscher 1989 *Game Theoretic Foundations of Evolutionary Stability*. Berlin: Springer-Verlag.

Borel, E. (1921–1927) 1953 "'The Theory of Play and Integral Equations with Skew Symmetric Kernels,' 'On Games That Involve Chance and the Skill of the Players,' and 'On Systems of Linear Forms of Skew Symmetric Determinant and the General Theory of Play,'" trans. L. J. Savage. *Econometrica* 21:97–117.

Brams, S. J., and P. C. Fishburn 1983 *Approval Voting*. Cambridge, Mass.: Birkhauser.

Charnes, A., J. Rousseau, and L. Seiford 1978 "Complements, Mollifiers, and the Propensity to Disrupt." *International Journal of Game Theory* 7:37–50.

Cole, S. G., P. R. Nail, and M. Pugh 1995 "Coalition Preference as a Function of Expected Values in a Tetradic Weighted-Majority Game." *Basic and Applied Social Psychology* 16:109–120.

Colman, A. M. 1982 *Game Theory and Experimental Games*. Oxford: Pergamon Press.

Cox, J. C., V. L. Smith, and J. M. Walker 1984 "Theory and Behavior of Multiple Unit Discriminative Auctions." *Journal of Finance* 39:983–1010.

Cox, G. W., and M. S. Shugart 1996 "Strategic Voting under Proportional Representation." *Journal of Law, Economics, and Organization* 12(2):299–324.

Cronshaw, M. B. 1997 "Algorithms for Finding Repeated Game Equilibria." *Computational Economics* 10(2):139–168.

Crott, H. W., and W. Albers 1981 "The Equal Division Kernel: An Equity Approach to Coalition Formation and Payoff Distribution in *n*-Person Games." *European Journal of Social Psychology* 11(3):285–305.

Dagan, N., R. Serrano, and O. Volij 1997 "A Noncooperative View of Consistent Bankruptcy Rules." *Games and Economic Behavior* 18(1):55–72.

Davis, M., and M. Maschler 1965 "The Kernel of a Cooperative Game." *Naval Research Logistics Quarterly* 12:223–259.

Dawes, R. M. 1980 "Social Dilemmas." *Annual Review of Psychology* 31:169–193.

Dearden, J. A. 1998 "Serial Cost Sharing of Excludable Public Goods: General Cost Functions." *Economic Theory* 12(1):189–198.

Debreu, G., and H. E. Scarf 1963 "A Limit Theorem on the Core of an Economy." *International Economic Review* 4:235–246.

deFraja, G., and F. Delbono 1990 "Game Theoretic Models of Mixed Oligopoly." *Journal of Economic Surveys* 4(1):1–17.

DeSwaan, A. 1973 *Coalition Theories and Cabinet Formation*. San Francisco: Jossey-Bass.

Dimand, M. A., and R. W. Dimand 1996 *A History of Game Theory*. New York: Routledge.

Dubey, P., and L. S. Shapley 1979 "Mathematical Properties of the Banzhaf Power Index." *Mathematics of Operations Research* 4:99–130.

Dubey, P., and M. Shubik 1977 "Trade and Prices in a Closed Economy with Exogenous Uncertainty, Different Levels of Information, Money and Compound Future Markets." *Econometrica* 45:1657–1680.

Edgeworth, F. Y. 1881 *Mathematical Psychics*. London: Kegan Paul.

—— 1995 *Foundations of Mathematical Economics Series*, vol. 3. San Diego, Calif.: James and Gordon.

Engelbrecht-Wiggans, R. 1980 "Auctions and Bidding Models: A Survey." *Management Science* 26:119–142.

Feddersen, T., and W. Pesendorfer 1998 "Convicting the Innocent: The Inferiority of Unanimous Jury Verdicts Under Strategic Voting." *American Political Science Review* 92(1):23–35.

Ferejohn, J. A., M. P. Fiorina, and E. W. Packel 1980 "Nonequilibrium Solutions for Legislative Systems." *Behavioral Science* 25:140–148.

Ferejohn, J. A., and D. M. Grether 1982 "On the Properties of Stable Decision Procedures." In P. C. Ordeshook and K. A. Shepsle, eds., *Political Equilibrium*. Boston: Kluwer-Nijhoff Publishing.

Fishburn, P. C. 1973 *The Theory of Social Choice*. Princeton, N.J.: Princeton University Press.

Flood, M. M. 1952 "Some Experimental Games." Research Memorandum RM-789. Santa Monica, Calif.: The Rand Corporation.

Fraser, N. M., and K. W. Hipel 1984 *Conflict Analysis: Models and Resolutions*. New York: Elsevier Science.

Friedman, A. 1971 *Differential Games*. New York: John Wiley.

Friedman, D. 1991 "Evolutionary Games in Economics." *Econometrica* 59(3):637–666.

—— 1998 "On Economic Applications of Evolutionary Game Theory." *Journal of Evolutionary Economics* 8(1):15–43.

Friedman, J. W. 1977 *Oligopoly and the Theory of Games.* Amsterdam: North-Holland.

—— 1983 *Oligopoly Theory.* New York: Cambridge University Press.

—— 1990 *Game Theory with Applications to Economics,* 2nd ed. New York: Oxford University Press.

——, and A. C. Hoggatt 1980 "An Experiment in Noncooperative Oligopoly." *Research in Experimental Economics,* vol. 1, supplement 1. Greenwich: Conn.: JAI Press.

Friend, K. E., J. D. Laing, and R. J. Morrison 1977 "Game-Theoretic Analyses of Coalition Behavior." *Theory and Decision* 8:127–157.

Fudenberg, D., and J. Tirole 1991 *Game Theory.* Cambridge, Mass.: MIT Press.

Gamson, W. A. 1961 "A Theory of Coalition Formation." *American Sociological Review* 26:373–382.

Gardner, R., M. R. Morris, and C. E. Nelson 1987 "Conditional Evolutionarily Stable Strategies." *Animal Behaviour* 35(2):507–517.

Gately, D. 1974 "Sharing the Gains From Regional Cooperation: A Game Theoretic Application to Planning Investment in Electric Power." *International Economic Review* 15:195–208.

Gibbard, A. 1973 "Manipulation of Voting Schemes: A General Result." *Econometrica* 41:587–601.

Gillies, D. B. 1959 "Solutions to General Non-Zero-Sum Games." *Annals of Mathematics Studies* 40:47–85.

Grofman, B. 1982 "A Dynamic Model of Protocoalition Formation in Ideological *N*-Space." *Behavioral Science* 27:77–90.

——, G. Owen, N. Noviello, and A. Glazer 1987 "Stability and Centrality in Legislative Choice in the Spatial Context." *American Political Science Review* 81:539–552.

Hajek, O. 1975 *Pursuit Games.* New York: Academic Press.

Hardin, G. 1968 "The Tragedy of the Commons." *Science* 162:1243–1248.

Harris, R. J. 1972 "An Interval-Scale Classification System for All 2 × 2 Games." *Behavioral Science* 17:371–383.

Harsanyi, J. C., and R. Selten 1988 *A General Theory of Equilibrium Selection in Games.* Cambridge, Mass.: MIT Press.

Hartwick, J. M., and D. W. K. Yeung 1997 "The Tragedy of the Commons Revisited." *Pacific Economic Review* 2(1):45–62.

Hinich, M. J., and M. C. Munger 1997 *Analytical Politics.* New York: Cambridge University Press.

Horowitz, A. D. 1973 "The Competitive Bargaining Set for Cooperative *n*-Person Games." *Journal of Mathematical Psychology* 10:265–289. (Erratum: 1974, 11:161).

Isaacs, R. 1965 *Differential Games.* New York: John Wiley.

Jones, A. J. 1980 *Game Theory: Mathematical Models of Conflict.* Chichester, U.K.: Ellis Horwood.

Kagel, J. H. 1995 "Auctions: A Survey of Experimental Research." In J. H. Kagel and A. E. Roth, eds., *Handbook of Experimental Economics.* Princeton, N.J.: Princeton University Press.

Kahan, J. P., and Am. Rapoport 1984 *Theories of Coalition Formation.* Hillsdale, N.J.: Lawrence Erlbaum.

Kaneko, M. 1978 "Price Oligopoly as a Cooperative Game." *International Journal of Game Theory* 7:137–150.

Karatzas, J., M. Shubik, and W. D. Sudderth 1997 "A Strategic Market Game with Secured Lending." *Journal of Mathematical Economics* 28(2):207–247.

Kollock, P. 1998 "Social Dilemmas: The Anatomy of Cooperation." *Annual Review of Sociology* 24:183–214.

Komorita, S. S. 1979 "An Equal Excess Model of Coalition Formation." *Behavioral Science* 24:369–381.

—— 1984 "Coalition Bargaining." In L. Berkowitz, ed., *Advances in Experimental Social Psychology,* vol. 18. New York: Academic Press.

——, K. F. Aquino, and A. L. Ellis 1989 "Coalition Bargaining: A Comparison of Theories Based on Allocation Norms and Theories Based on Bargaining Strength." *Social Psychology Quarterly* 52(3):183–196.

——, and J. M. Chertkoff 1973 "A Bargaining Theory of Coalition Formation." *Psychological Review* 80:149–162.

——, and D. A. Kravitz 1983 "Coalition Formation: A Social Psychological Approach." In P. B. Paulus, ed., *Basic Group Processes.* New York: Springer-Verlag.

——, and C. D. Parks 1995 "Interpersonal Relations: Mixed-Motive Interaction." *Annual Review of Psychology* 46:183–207.

——, and C. D. Parks 1999 "Reciprocity and Cooperation in Social Dilemmas: Review and Future Directions." In D. V. Budescu, I. Erev, and R. Zwick, eds., *Games and Human Behavior: Essays in Honor of Amnon Rapoport.* Mahwah, N.J.: Lawrence Erlbaum.

Kravitz, D. A. 1986 "Extensions of Komorita and Chertkoff's (1973) Bargaining Theory to Simple

Weighted Majority Games in Which Players Lack Alternative Minimal Winning Coalitions." In R. W. Scholz, ed., *Current Issues in West German Decision Research: Vol. 4, Psychology of Decisions and Conflict*. Frankfurt, Federal Republic of Germany: Peter Lang Publishing.

Kurz, M. 1985 "Cooperative Oligopoly Equilibrium." *European Economic Review* 27(1):3–24.

Laffont, J. J. 1997 "Game Theory and Empirical Economics: The Case of Auction Data." *European Economic Review*, 41(1):1–35.

Laver, M., and K. A. Shepsle 1996 *Making and Breaking Governments: Cabinets and Legislatures in Parliamentary Democracies*. New York: Cambridge University Press.

Ledyard, J. O. 1995 "Public Goods: A Survey of Experimental Research." In J. H. Kagel and A. E. Roth, eds., *Handbook of Experimental Economics*. Princeton, N.J.: Princeton University Press.

Leitmann, G. 1974 *Cooperative and Non-Cooperative Many Player Differential Games*. New York: Springer-Verlag.

Lewin, J. 1994 *Differential Games: Theory and Methods for Solving Game Problems with Singular Surfaces*. New York: Springer-Verlag.

Liebrand, W. B. G., and D. M. Messick, (eds.) 1996 *Frontiers in Social Dilemmas Research*. New York: Springer.

——, and H. A. M. Wilke, (eds.) 1992 *Social Dilemmas: Theoretical Issues and Research Findings*. Oxford: Pergamon Press.

Littlechild, S. C., and G. E. Thompson 1977 "Aircraft Landing Fees: A Game Theory Approach." *Bell Journal of Economics* 8:186–207.

Littlechild, S. C., and K. G. Vaidya 1976 "The Propensity to Disrupt and the Disruption Nucleolus of a Characteristic Function Game." *International Journal of Game Theory* 5:151–161.

Loehman, E., and A. Whinston 1974 "An Axiomatic Approach to Cost Allocations for Public Investments." *Public Finance Quarterly* 2:236–251.

Luce, R. D., and H. Raiffa 1957 *Games and Decisions: Introduction and Critical Survey*. New York: John Wiley.

Maynard Smith, J. 1982 *Evolution and the Theory of Games*. Cambridge, U.K.: Cambridge University Press.

McAfee, R. P., and J. McMillan 1987. "Auctions and Bidding." *Journal of Economic Literature* 25:699–738.

McClintock, C.G., and W. B. G. Liebrand 1988. "Role of Interdependence Structure, Individual Value Orientation, and Another's Strategy in Decision Making: A Transformational Analysis." *Journal of Personality and Social Psychology* 55:396–409.

McKelvey, R. D., and P. C. Ordeshook 1982 "An Experimental Test of Solution Theories for Cooperative Games in Normal Form." In P. C. Ordeshook and K. A. Shepsle, eds., *Political Equilibrium*. Boston: Kluwer-Nijhoff Publishing.

—— 1983 "Some Experimental Results That Fail to Support the Competitive Solution." *Public Choice* 40(3):281–291.

—— 1990 "A Decade of Experimental Research on Spatial Models of Elections and Committees." In J. M. Enelow and M. J. Hinich, eds., *Advances in the Spatial Theory of Voting*. New York: Cambridge University Press.

——, and M. D. Winer 1978 "The Competitive Solution for n-Person Games without Transferable Utility, with an Application to Committee Games." *American Political Science Review* 72:599–615.

Mertens, J.-F., S. Sorin, and S. Zamir 1994a "Repeated Games Part A: Background Material" (CORE Discussion Paper No. 9420). Universite Catholique de Louvain.

—— 1994b "Repeated Games Part B: The Central Results" (CORE Discussion Paper No. 9421). Universite Catholique de Louvain.

—— 1994c "Repeated Games Part C: Further Development" (CORE Discussion Paper No. 9423). Universite Catholique de Louvain.

Messick, D. M., and M. D. Brewer 1983 "Solving Social Dilemmas: A Review." In L. Wheeler and P. Shaver, eds., *Review of Personality and Social Psychology*, vol. 4. Beverly Hills, Calif.: Sage.

Michener, H. A., and W. T. Au. 1994 "A Probabilistic Theory of Coalition Formation in n-Person Sidepayment Games." *Journal of Mathematical Sociology* 19:165–188.

Michener, H. A., D. C. Dettman, J. M. Ekman, and Y. C. Choi 1985 "A Comparison of the Alpha- and Beta-Characteristic Functions in Cooperative Non-Sidepayment n-Person Games." *Journal of Mathematical Sociology* 11:307–330.

Michener, H. A, G. B. Macheel, C. G. Depies, and C. A. Bowen 1986 "Mollifier Representation in Non-Constant-Sum Games: An Experimental Test." *Journal of Conflict Resolution* 30:361–382.

Michener, H. A., and D. J. Myers 1998 "Probabilistic Coalition Structure Theories: An Empirical Comparison in Four-Person Superadditive Sidepayment Games." *Journal of Conflict Resolution* 42(6):853–883.

Michener, H. A., and K. Potter 1981 "Generalizability of Tests in n-Person Sidepayment Games." *Journal of Conflict Resolution* 25:733–749.

Michener, H. A., and M. S. Salzer 1989 "Comparative Accuracy of Value Solutions in Non-Sidepayment Games with Empty Core." *Theory and Decision* 26:205–233.

Miller, C. E., and S. S. Komorita 1986 "Changes in Outcomes in Coalition Bargaining." *Journal of Personality and Social Psychology* 51(4):721–729.

Montmort, P. R. de 1713 *Essay d'Analyse sur les Jeux de Hazard*, 2nd ed. Paris: Quillau.

Moulin, H. 1994 "Social Choice." In R. J. Aumann and S. Hart, eds., *Handbook of Game Theory with Economic Applications*, vol. 2. New York: Elsevier, North-Holland.

—— 1996 "Cost Sharing under Increasing Returns: A Comparison of Simple Mechanisms." *Games and Economic Behavior* 13(2):225–251.

——, and A. Watts 1997 "Two Versions of the Tragedy of the Commons." *Economic Design* 2(4):399–421.

Murnighan, J. K. 1978 "Models of Coalition Behavior: Game Theoretic, Social Psychological, and Political Perspectives." *Psychological Bulletin* 85:1130–1153.

——, and A. E. Roth 1980 "Effects of Group Size and Communication Availability on Coalition Bargaining in a Veto Game." *Journal of Personality and Social Psychology* 39:92–103.

Myerson, R. B. 1977 "Graphs and Cooperation in Games." *Mathematics of Operations Research* 2:225–229.

—— 1991 *Game Theory: Analysis of Conflict*. Cambridge, Mass.: Harvard University Press.

Nakayama, M., and M. Suzuki 1977 "The Cost Assignment of Cooperative Water Resource Development: A Game Theoretical Approach." In R. Henn and O. Moeschlin, eds., *Mathematical Economics and Game Theory*. Berlin: Springer-Verlag.

Nash, J. F., Jr. 1951 "Non-Cooperative Games." *Annals of Mathematics* 54:286–295.

Niemi, R. G., and A. Q. Frank 1982 "Sophisticated Voting Under the Plurality Procedure." In P. C. Ordeshook and K. A. Shepsle, eds., *Political Equilibrium*. Boston: Kluwer-Nijhoff Publishing.

Nurmi, H. 1987 *Comparing Voting Systems*. Dordrecht: D. Reidel.

Ordeshook, P. C. 1986 *Game Theory and Political Theory*. New York: Cambridge University Press.

——, and M. Winer 1980 "Coalitions and Spatial Policy Outcomes in Parliamentary Systems: Some Experimental Results." *American Journal of Political Science* 24:730–752.

Oskamp, S. 1971 "Effects of Programmed Strategies on Cooperation in the Prisoner's Dilemma and Other Mixed Motive Games." *Journal of Conflict Resolution* 15:225–259.

Owen, G. 1982 *Game Theory*, 2nd ed. New York: Academic Press.

Plott, C. R. 1982 "Industrial Organization Theory and Experimental Economics." *Journal of Economic Literature* 20:1485–1527.

——, and M. E. Levine 1978 "A Model of Agenda Influence on Committee Decisions." *American Economic Review* 68:146–160.

——, and S. Sunder 1982 "Efficiency of Experimental Securities Markets with Insider Information." *Journal of Political Economy* 90:663–698.

Pruitt, D. G., and M. J. Kimmel 1977 "Twenty Years of Experimental Gaming: Critique, Synthesis, and Suggestions for the Future." *Annual Review of Psychology* 28:363–392.

Radner, R. 1980 "Collusive Behavior in Noncooperative Epsilon-Equilibria of Oligopolies with Long but Finite Lives." *Journal of Economic Theory* 22:136–154.

Rapoport, Amnon 1988 "Experiments with *N*-Person Social Traps II: Tragedy of the Commons." *Journal of Conflict Resolution* 32(3):473–488.

—— 1990 *Experimental Studies of Interactive Decisions*. Dordrecht, Netherlands: Kluwer Academic Publishers.

——, and J. P. Kahan 1982 "The Power of a Coalition and Payoff Disbursement in Three-Person Negotiable Conflicts." *Journal of Mathematical Sociology* 8:193–224.

——, M. Guyer, and D. G. Gordon 1976 *The 2 × 2 Game*. Ann Arbor: University of Michigan Press.

Rees, R. 1993 "Tacit Collusion." *Oxford Review of Economic Policy* 9(2):27–40.

Riker, W. 1982 "Implication from the Disequilibrium of Majority Rule for the Study of Institutions." In P. C. Ordeshook and K. A. Shepsle, eds., *Political Equilibrium*. Boston: Kluwer-Nijhoff Publishing.

Romp, G. 1997 *Game Theory: Introduction and Applications*. New York: Oxford University Press.

Rosenthal, R. W. 1971 "External Economies and Cores." *Journal of Economic Theory* 3:182–188.

Roth, A. E. 1995 "Bargaining Experiments." In J. H. Kagel and A. E. Roth, eds., *Handbook of Experimental Economics*. Princeton, N.J.: Princeton University Press.

——, and M. A. O. Sotomayor 1990 *Two-Sided Matching*. New York: Cambridge University Press.

Samuelson, L. 1997 *Evolutionary Games and Equilibrium Selection*. Cambridge, Mass.: MIT Press.

Satterthwaite, M. A. 1975 "Strategy-Proofness and Arrow's Conditions: Existence and Correspondence Theorems for Voting Procedures and Social Welfare Functions." *Journal of Economic Theory* 10:187–217.

Schmeidler, D. 1969 "The Nucleolus of a Characteristic Function Game." *SIAM Journal of Applied Mathematics* 17:1163–1170.

Schofield, N. 1984a "Bargaining over Public Goods." In M. J. Holler, ed., *Coalitions and Collective Action*. Wurzburg, Germany: Physica-Verlag.

—— 1984b "Political Fragmentation and the Stability of Coalition Governments in Western Europe." In M. J. Holler, ed., *Coalitions and Collective Action*. Wurzburg, Germany: Physica-Verlag.

Schotter, A. 1981 *The Economic Theory of Social Institutions*. New York: Cambridge University Press.

—— 1994 *Microeconomics: A Modern Approach*. New York: HarperCollins.

——, and G. Schwodiauer 1980 "Economics and the Theory of Games: A Survey." *Journal of Economic Literature* 18:479–527.

Selten, R. 1975 "Reexamination of the Perfectness Concept for Equilibrium Points in Extensive Games." *International Journal of Game Theory* 4:25–55.

——, and R. Stoecker 1983 *End Behavior In Sequences of Finite Prisoner's Dilemma Supergames: A Learning Theory Approach*. Bielefeld, Germany: Institut fur Mathematische Wirtschaftsforschung an der Universitat Bielefeld.

Sengupta, A., and K. Sengupta 1994 "Viable Proposals." *International Economic Review* 35(2):347–359.

Shapley, L. S. 1953 "A Value for *n*-Person Games." In H. W. Kuhn and A. W. Tucker, eds., *Contributions to the Theory of Games, II* (Annals of Mathematics Studies, No. 28). Princeton, N.J.: Princeton University Press.

——, and M. Shubik 1954 "A Method of Evaluating the Distribution of Power in a Committee System." *American Political Science Review* 48:787–792.

Shubik, M. 1959 "Edgeworth Market Games." In A. W. Tucker and R. D. Luce, eds., *Contributions to the Theory of Games*, vol. 4 (Annals of Mathematics Studies, No. 40). Princeton, N.J.: Princeton University Press.

—— 1982 *Game Theory in the Social Sciences*. Cambridge, Mass.: MIT Press.

—— 1984 *A Game-Theoretic Approach to Political Economy*. Cambridge, Mass.: MIT Press.

Smith, V. L. 1982 "Microeconomic Systems as an Experimental Science." *American Economic Review* 72:923–955.

——, A. W. Williams, W. K. Bratton, and M. G. Vannoni 1982 "Competitive Market Institutions: Double Auctions vs. Sealed Bid–Offer Auctions." *American Economic Review* 72:58–77.

Spinetto, R. 1974 "The Geometry of Solution Concepts for *n*-Person Cooperative Games." *Management Science* 20:1292–1299.

Straffin, P. D., Jr. 1978 "Probability Models for Power Indices." In P. C. Ordeshook, ed., *Game Theory and Political Science*. New York: New York University Press.

Szep, J., and F. Forgo 1985 *Introduction to the Theory of Games*. Dordrecht, Holland: D. Reidel.

Telser, L. 1972 *Competition, Collusion, and Game Theory*. Chicago: Aldine-Atherton.

—— 1996 "Competition and the Core." *Journal of Political Economy* 104(1):85–107.

Thomas, L. C. 1984 *Games, Theory and Applications*. Chichester, U.K.: Halsted Press.

van Damme, E. 1987 *Stability and Perfection of Nash Equilibria*. Berlin: Springer-Verlag.

Van Lange, P. A., and W. B. Liebrand 1991 "The Influence of Other's Morality and Own Social Value Orientation on Cooperation in the Netherlands and the U.S.A. *International Journal of Psychology* 26(4):429–499.

von Neumann, J. 1928 "Zur Theorie der Gesellschaftsspiele." *Mathematische Annalen* 100:295–320.

——, and O. Morgenstern 1944 *Theory of Games and Economic Behavior*. Princeton, N.J.: Princeton University Press.

Weibull, J. W. 1995 *Evolutionary Game Theory*. Cambridge, Mass.: MIT Press.

Weintraub, E. R., (ed.) 1992 *Toward a History of Game Theory*. Durham, N.C.: Duke University Press.

Zermelo, E. 1913 "Uber eine Anwendung der Mengenlehre auf die Theorie des Schachspiels." In E. W. Hobson and A. E. H. Love, eds., *Proceedings of the Fifth International Congress of Mathematicians*, vol. 2. Cambridge, U.K.: Cambridge University Press.

Zhukovskiy, V. I., and M. E. Salukvadze 1994 *The Vector-Valued Maximin*. Boston: Academic Press.

H. ANDREW MICHENER

GANGS

See Criminal and Delinquent Subcultures; Juvenile Delinquency.

GENDER

Gender, race, ethnicity, and social class are the most commonly used categories in sociology. They represent the major social statuses that determine the life chances of individuals in heterogeneous societies, and together they form a hierarchy of access to property, power, and prestige.

Gender is the division of people into two categories, "men" and "women." Through interaction with caretakers, socialization in childhood, peer pressure in adolescence, and gendered work and family roles, women and men are socially constructed to be different in behavior, attitudes, and emotions. The gendered social order is based on and maintains these differences.

In sociology, the main ordering principles of social life are called *institutions*. Gender is a social institution as encompassing as the four main institutions of traditional sociology—family, economy, religion, and symbolic language. Like these institutions, gender structures social life, patterns social roles, and provides individuals with identities and values. And just as the institutions of family, economy, religion, and language are intertwined and affect each other reciprocally, as a social institution, gender pervades kinship and family life, work roles and organizations, the rules of most religions, and the symbolism and meanings of language and other cultural representations of human life. The outcome is a gendered social order.

The source of gendered social orders lies in the evolution of human societies and their diversity in history. The gendered division of work has shifted with changing means of producing food and other goods, which in turn modifies patterns of child care and family structures. Gendered power imbalances, which are usually based on the ability to amass and distribute material resources, change with rules about property ownership and inheritance. Men's domination of women has not been the same throughout time and place; rather, it varies with political, economic, and family structures, and is differently justified by religions and laws. As an underlying principle of how people are categorized and valued, gender is differently constructed throughout the world and has been throughout history. In societies with other major social divisions, such as race, ethnicity, religion, and social class, gender is intricately intertwined with these other statuses.

As pervasive as gender is, it is important to remember that it is constructed and maintained through daily interaction and therefore can be resisted, reformed, and even rebelled against. The social construction perspective argues that people create their social realities and identities, including their gender, through their actions with others—their families, friends, colleagues. It also argues that their actions are hemmed in by the general rules of social life, by their culture's expectations, their workplace's and occupation's norms, and their government's laws. These social restraints are amenable to change—but not easily.

Gender is deeply rooted in every aspect of social life and social organization in Western-influenced societies. The Western world is a very gendered world, consisting of only two legal categories—"men" and "women." Despite the variety of playful and serious attempts at blurring gender boundaries with androgynous dress and desegregating gender-typed jobs, third genders and gender neutrality are rare in Western societies. Those who cross gender boundaries by passing as a member of the opposite gender, or by sex-change surgery, want to be taken as a "normal" man or woman.

Although it is almost impossible to be anything but a "woman" or a "man," a "girl" or a "boy" in Western societies, this does not mean that one cannot have three, four, five, or more socially recognized genders—there are societies that have at least three. Not all societies base gender categories on male and female bodies—Native Americans, for example, have biological males whose gender status is that of women. Some African societies have females with the gender status of sons or husbands. Others use age categories as organizing principles, not gender statuses. Even in Western societies, where there are only two genders, we can think about restructuring families and workplaces so they are not as rigidly gendered as they are today.

WHY GENDER AND NOT SEX

Gender was first conceptualized as distinct from sex in order to highlight the social and cultural processes that constructed different social roles for females and males and that prescribed sex-appropriate behavior, demeanor, personality characteristics, and dress. However, *sex* and *gender* were often conflated and interchanged, to the extent that this early usage was called "sex roles" theory. More recently, gender has been conceptually separated from sex and also from sexuality.

Understanding gender practices and structures is easier if what is usually conflated as sex/gender or sex/sexuality/gender is split into three conceptually distinct categories—sex (or biology, physiology), sexuality (desire, sexual preference, sexual orientation, sexual behavior), and gender (social status, position in the social order, personal identity). Each is socially constructed but in different ways. Gender is an overarching category—a major social status that organizes almost all areas of social life. Therefore bodies and sexuality are gendered—biology and sexuality, in contrast, do not add up to gender.

Conceptually separating sex and gender makes it easier to explain how female and male bodies are socially constructed to be feminine and masculine through sports and in popular culture. In medicine, separating sex from gender helps to pinpoint how much of the differences in longevity and propensity to different illnesses is due to biology and how much to socially induced behavior, such as alcohol and drug abuse, which is higher among men than women. The outcome is a greater number of recorded illnesses but longer life expectancy for women of all races, ethnicities, and social classes when compared to men with the same social characteristics. This phenomenon is known in social epidemiology as "women get sicker, but men die quicker."

SOCIAL CONSTRUCTION OF GENDER

As with any other aspect of social life, gender is shaped by an individual's genetic heritage, physical body, and physiological development. Socially, however, gendering begins as soon as the sex of the fetus is identified. At birth, infants are placed in one of two sex categories, based on the appearance of the genitalia. In cases of ambiguity, since Western societies do not have a third gender for hermaphrodites as some cultures do, the genitalia are now "clarified" surgically, so that the child can be categorized as a boy or a girl. Gendering then takes place through interaction with parents and other family members, teachers, and peers ("significant others"). Through socialization and gendered personality development, the child develops a gendered identity that, in most cases, reproduces the values, attitudes, and behavior that the child's social milieu deems appropriate for a girl or a boy.

Borrowing from Freudian psychoanalytic theory, Nancy Chodorow developed an influential argument for the gendering of personalities in the two-parent, heterogendered nuclear family. Because women are the primary parents, infants bond with them. Boys have to separate from their mothers and identify with their fathers in order to establish their masculinity. They thus develop strong ego boundaries and a capacity for the independent action, objectivity, and rational thinking so valued in Western culture. Women are a threat to their independence and masculine sexuality because they remind men of their dependence on their mothers. However, men need women for the emotional sustenance and intimacy they rarely give each other. Their ambivalence toward women comes out in heterosexual love–hate relationships and in misogynistic depictions of women in popular culture and in novels, plays, and operas.

Girls continue to identify with their mothers, and so they grow up with fluid ego boundaries that make them sensitive, empathic, and emotional. It is these qualities that make them potentially good mothers and keep them open to men's emotional needs. But because the men in their lives have developed personalities that make them emotionally guarded, women want to have children to bond with. Thus, psychological gendering of children is continually reproduced.

To develop nurturing capabilities in men and to break the cycle of the reproduction of gendered personality structures would, according to this theory, take fully shared parenting. There is little data on whether the same psychic processes produce similarly gendered personalities in single-parent families, in households where both parents are the same gender, or in differently structured families in non-Western cultures.

Children are also gendered at school, in the classroom, where boys and girls are often treated differently by teachers. Boys are encouraged to develop their math abilities and science interests; girls are steered toward the humanities and social sciences. The result is that women students in the United States outnumber men students in college, but only in the liberal arts; in science programs, men still outnumber women. Men also predominate in enrollment in the elite colleges, which prepare for high-level careers in finance, the professions, and government.

This data on gender imbalance, however, when broken down by race, ethnicity, and social class, is more complex. In the United States, upper- and middle-class boys are pushed ahead of girls in school and do better on standardized tests, although girls of all social statuses get better grades than boys. African-American, Hispanic, and white working-class and poor boys do particularly badly, partly because of a peer culture that denigrates "book learning" and rewards defiance and risk taking. In the context of an unresponsive educational structure, discouraged teachers, and crowded, poorly maintained school buildings, the pedagogical needs of marginal students do not get enough attention; they are also much more likely to be treated as discipline problems.

Children's peer culture is another site of gender construction. On playgrounds, girls and boys divide up into separate groups whose borders are defended against opposite-gender intruders. Within the group, girls tend to be more cooperative and play people-based games. Boys tend to play rule-based games that are competitive. These tendencies have been observed in Western societies; anthropological data about children's socialization shows different patterns of gendering. Everywhere, children's gender socialization is closely attuned to expected adult behavior.

GENDER AND WORK

Whether they have fully internalized Western society's gender binarism and social construction of gender differences or rebelled against gender typing, adults encounter a gendered work world. The workplaces in industrialized societies are either gender-segregated or composed of all one gender. During the 1970s and 1980s, decades in which women were thought to have made inroads into many occupations previously dominated by men in the United States, about 6 percent of occupations saw an increase of women workers that was significantly greater than the increase of women

overall in the paid labor force during that period. Rather than desegregating occupations, most of the new women workers went into occupations where most of the employees were women, and those who went into occupations where the employees were predominantly men soon found that their coworkers became predominantly women. Some U.S. occupations that went from having a predominance of workers who were men to mostly women workers were personnel, training, and labor relations specialists; computer operators; and insurance adjusters, examiners, and investigators. These occupations had *resegregated*. When women and men work in nontraditional occupations, gender typing is often maintained symbolically, as when policewomen view their work as social work and men nurses emphasize the technical and physical strength aspects of what they do.

The processes that sort women and men of different racial and ethnic groups into different types of work include a matching of ranked workers and jobs, or *queues* of workers and jobs. Workers are ranked by employers from their first picks to their last. Jobs are ranked by workers similarly. Lower-ranked workers get the chance to move into better jobs than they have held in the past when these jobs are abandoned by favored workers or there are too few of these workers to go around, such as in wartime. The process works the other way, too; when there are too few of the best jobs for the preferred workers, as in a recession, only the best qualified or experienced among them will be hired; those with fewer credentials and less seniority move down the queue, bumping out lower-ranked workers. When workers are moving up, the most preferred on the basis of race, ethnicity, and gender usually get the better jobs. If gender segregation is so rigid that men will not apply or be hired for "women's work," when manufacturing jobs decline or are taken elsewhere, women in service, sales, and clerical work may continue to work as men's unemployment rates rise.

Workers rank jobs on the basis of payoff for education and experience in salaries and also in fringe benefits, prestige, autonomy, security, and chances of promotion. For some workers, having any job may be an improvement over economic dependency. Employers' preferences for workers, however, are not so uniform. Some will rank gender and race above qualifications; others will choose the most highly qualified of the preferred race and gender and then go down the line, looking for the most qualified each time. Another variable employers factor in is the going pay scale for the workers they want; they may have to settle for less preferred workers to see more of a profit or sacrifice some profits to avoid protests from highly paid entrenched workers.

Although worker demographics, industry growth, and employer preferences produce changes in occupational gender composition, the main factor that redistributes workers of different races and genders is change in the structure of the work process and in the quality of particular jobs within occupations, which can be manipulated by employers. That is, jobs can be automated and deskilled or made part time or home based to justify reducing labor costs, with a few better-paid workers retained in supervisory positions.

During shifts of labor queues up and down the job ladder, the potential for conflict between women and men as well as between members of dominant and subordinated racial and ethnic groups is high. Dominant men want to perpetuate the work conditions that justify their high pay; employers who want to reduce their labor costs degrade the work process so they can hire cheaper labor, and then these new workers are accused of depressing the job's qualifications and skills. Gender segregation of jobs is historically the way employers have kept their men workers satisfied, while expanding the number of cheaper women workers. Such job divisions undercut unions that want to organize women and demand the same pay for them as similarly situated men workers. In a growing or stable job market, dominant men are much less resistant to incoming new types of workers, since they do not see them as competition. In those cases, the job may come closer to being integrated along lines of gender and race.

Occupational gender segregation does not result in separate but equal jobs. Rather, women's work tends to be lower in pay, prestige, and fringe benefits, such as health insurance. Workers themselves rate jobs where most of the employees are women as inferior to jobs where most of the employees are men. The criteria are number and flexibility of hours, earnings, educational requirements, on-the-job training, having a union contract, extent of supervision and place in the hierarchy, repetitiveness, risk of job loss, and being a

government employee. Workers rate women's jobs as better in vacation days and not getting dirty at work, even though changing bedpans is as "dirty" as changing oil pans. If wages were used to compensate for unattractive nonmonetary job characteristics, women's jobs would have to pay four times as much as men's jobs for workers to rate them equally. Nor is there a trade-off of pay for compatibility with child care—most full-time jobs held by mothers are incompatible with parenting demands; flexibility of schedules and control and timing of work-related tasks are the prerogatives of men managers, not their women secretaries.

The best-paid jobs are shaped on an ideal, dominant man's career—long-term, continuous work in the same occupation, with steady pay raises and a pension at retirement. Men's gender status is an advantage to them as workers; they are expected to earn more money when they marry and when they have children, so employers tend to view them as better workers than women. Women workers are felt to be entitled only to supplementary wages, whether they are married or single, because they are not considered legitimate workers but primarily wives and mothers. In actuality, research has shown that married women with children work harder and are more productive than married men with children.

The structured patterns of opportunities and access far override most individual employers' tastes or individual workers' motivations, ambitions, personal desires, and material needs. By the 1970s in the United States, adolescent girls were considerably less likely than in previous years to plan on entering an occupation in which most of the workers were women, especially if they lived in a woman-headed household. But they continued to value working with people, helping others, using their abilities, and being creative; boys wanted jobs with status, high earnings, freedom from supervision, and leadership potential. The jobs women are likely to end up in are more gender typed and less fulfilling than their occupational aspirations, but ambitious and hard-working men can often reach their early goals.

Women of all educational levels and men disadvantaged because of race, immigrant status, lack of education, or outmoded job skills are profitable workers because they tend to receive low wages; they also get promoted less frequently and therefore receive fewer raises. Many work part time and get no benefits. They can be paid little because the pool of such workers is larger that of privileged men workers. The size and social characteristics of the pool of low-waged workers are affected by state policies encouraging or discouraging the employment of women, the influx of immigrants, and the flight of capital from one area of a country to another or offshore.

Other processes that segregate and stratify occupations are *segmentation* and *ghettoization*. Segmented occupations are horizontally or vertically divided into sectors with different educational or credential requirements for hiring, different promotion ladders, different work assignments, and different pay scales. Typically, these segments are gendered and frequently also exhibit racial and ethnic clustering. However, occupations in which almost all the workers are of one gender can also be segmented. For instance, in the United States, doctors and nurses are gender-segregated segments in hospitals. Physicians are segmented between those in primary care and those who are hospital-based specialists, who have more prestige and power and higher incomes. Women physicians are often found in primary care. Nursing is also segmented into registered nurses, licensed practical nurses, nurses' aides, and home health workers. Nurses are virtually all women, but the segments are racially differentiated: The majority of registered nurses tend to be white or Asian-American; most of the lower-paid health workers tend to be black or Hispanic. Men who go into nursing tend to specialize in the more lucrative specializations and become administrators.

Segmentation is legitimized by bureaucratic rules or legal requirements for qualifying credentials, but ghettoization separates the lower-paid "women's" jobs from the better-paid "men's" jobs within an occupation through informal gender typing. What is dubbed "women's work" or "men's work" has a sense of normality and naturalness, an almost moral quality, even though the justification for such typing is usually an after-the-fact rationalization. The assumption is that the skills, competence, strength, and other qualities needed to do a job are tied up with masculinity and femininity, but gendered identities as workers are constructed in the gendered organization of the workplace and reinforced in training and organizational sociability, such as company golf games and sports teams.

Within gender-typed occupations, jobs or specialties may be gender typed in the opposite direction. For example, the majority of physicians are men in the United States and women in Russia, but the same specialties are seen as appropriate for one gender—pediatrics for women and neurosurgery for men. In both countries, neurosurgery pays better and has more prestige than pediatrics.

Both structural segmentation and gender typing that puts some jobs into a low-wage ghetto have the same results. They limit the extent of competition for the better positions, make it easier for privileged workers to justify their advantageous salary scales, and create a group of workers whose lack of credentials or requisite skills legitimate their lower pay. Credentials and skills, however, as well as experience, are manipulated or circumvented to favor workers with certain social characteristics, as when men with less lower-rank experience in women's jobs are hired as supervisors. In addition, femaleness and maleness are stereotypically linked to certain capabilities, such as finger dexterity and physical strength; gender then becomes the discriminant criterion for hiring, not what potential employees can actually do with their hands, backs, and heads.

Promotion ladders are also gender segregated. Women and men who are not of the dominant racial or ethnic group tend not to rise to the top in their work organization, unless practically all the workers are women or men of the same racial or ethnic group. White men tend to dominate positions of authority whether or not they are numerically predominant. This pattern is known as the *glass ceiling*—the lid on women's rise to the top of their work organizations. In occupations where the majority of the workers are women, positions of authority tend to be held by men—elementary school teachers are predominantly women in the United States, but principals and superintendents are predominantly men. That is, token men in a woman's occupation tend to be promoted faster than the women workers. This parallel phenomenon has been dubbed the *glass escalator*.

These pervasive patterns of occupational segregation and stratification are the result of deliberate actions and also inaction on the part of governments, owners and managers, and organized groups of workers—and change has to come from the same sources. Since gender segregation involves occupations and professions, job titles, and specific work sites, integration has to involve more than simply increasing the numbers of women. True occupational gender equality would mean that women and men would have the same opportunities to obtain professional credentials and occupational training, and would be distributed in the same proportions as they are in the paid work force across workplaces, job titles, occupations, and hierarchical positions. Instead, in most industrialized countries, women are overrepresented in clerical and service jobs, low-prestige professional and technical work, and sales. In developing countries, and in areas of industrialized countries where there are concentrations of poor people and recent immigrants, women tend to be concentrated in labor-intensive factory work, agriculture, and the informal (off-the-books) economy.

This gendered organization of paid labor dovetails with the gendered organization of domestic labor. Low pay, uninteresting jobs, and the glass ceiling encourage single women to marry and married women to devote energy and attention to child rearing and domestic work. The job market encourages women to be a reserve army of labor—available for full-time work in times of scarce labor, but fired or put on part-time schedules when there is less work. Better job opportunities are offered to men of the dominant racial and ethnic groups to encourage them to give their all to the job. Employers (mostly men) benefit from women's cheap labor and men's need to earn more to support a family; men who live with women benefit from women's unpaid labor at home. Highly educated and professional women are caught in the structural conflicts of these two forms of labor; in order to compete with the men of their status, they have to hire "wives"—other women to do their domestic work. This pool of paid domestic labor historically is made up of the least advantaged women—native poor and recent immigrants of a variety of racial and ethnic groups.

GENDER INEQUALITY

Gender inequality takes many different forms, depending on the economic structure and social organization of a particular society and on the culture of any particular group within that society. Although we speak of *gender* inequality, it is usually women who are disadvantaged when compared to similarly situated men. In the job market, women often receive lower pay for the same or comparable work and are frequently blocked in their chances for advancement, especially to top positions. There is usually an imbalance in the amount of housework and child care a wife does compared to her husband, even when both spend the same amount of time in waged work outside the home. When women professionals are matched with men of comparable productiveness, men get greater recognition for their work and move up career ladders faster. On an overall basis, work most often done by women, such as teaching small children and nursing, is paid less than work most often done by men, such as computer programming and engineering. Gender inequality also takes the form of girls getting less education than boys of the same social class. It often means an unequal distribution of health care services between women and men, and research priorities that focus on diseases men are more likely to get than women.

Gender inequality takes even more oppressive and exploitative forms. Throughout the world, women are vulnerable to beatings, rape, and murder—often by their husbands or boyfriends, and especially when they try to leave an abusive relationship. The bodies of girls and women are used in sex work—pornography and prostitution. They undergo cosmetic surgery and are on display in movies, television, and advertising in Western cultures. In other cultures, their genitals are mutilated and their bodies are covered from head to toe in the name of chastity. They may be forced to bear children they do not want or have abortions or be sterilized against their will. In countries with overpopulation, infant girls are much more often abandoned in orphanages than infant boys. In cultural groups that value boys over girls, if the sex of the fetus can be determined, it is girls who are aborted.

Gender inequality can also disadvantage men. In many countries, only men serve in the armed forces, and in most countries, only men are sent into direct combat. It is mostly men who do the more dangerous work, such as firefighting and policing. Although women have fought in wars and are entering police forces and fire departments, the gender arrangements of most societies assume that women will do the work of bearing and caring for children, while men do the work of protecting them and supporting them economically.

Most women in industrial and postindustrial societies do not spend their lives having and caring for babies, and most women throughout the world do paid and unpaid work to supply their families with food, clothing, and shelter, even while they are taking care of children. The modern forms of gender inequality are not a complementary exchange of responsibilities, but a social system within which women are exploitable. In a succinct summary of gender inequality, it was estimated by a United Nations report in 1980 that women do two-thirds of the world's work, receive 10 percent of the world's income, and own 1 percent of the world's property.

The major social and cultural institutions support this system of gender inequality. Religions legitimate the social arrangements that produce it, justifying them as right and proper. Laws support the status quo and also often make it impossible to redress the outcomes—to prosecute husbands for beating their wives, or boyfriends for raping their girlfriends. In the arts, women's productions are so often ignored that they are virtually invisible, which led Virginia Woolf to conclude that Anonymous must have been a woman. Much scientific research assumes that differences between women and men are genetic or hormonal and looks for data to support these beliefs, ignoring findings that show gender overlaps or input from the social environment. In the social sciences, gender is entered into research designs only as a binary, erasing the effects of racial, social class, and ethnic variations.

Except for the Scandinavian countries, which have the greatest participation of women in government and the most gender-equal laws and state policies, most governments are run by socially dominant men, and their policies reflect their interests. In every period of change, including those of revolutionary upheaval, men's interests, not women's, have prevailed, and many men, but few women, have benefited from progressive social policies. Equality and justice for all usually means for men only. Women have never had their revolution because the structure of gender as a social institution has never been seriously challenged. Therefore, all men benefit from the "patriarchal dividend"—women's unpaid work maintaining homes and bringing up children; women's low-paid work servicing hospitals, schools, and myriad other workplaces.

Gender inequality is deeply ingrained in the structure of Western, industrialized societies. It is built into the organization of marriage and families, work and the economy, politics, religion, sports, the arts and other cultural productions, and the very language we speak. Making women and men equal, therefore, necessitates social, not individual, solutions.

CHANGING GENDER

Changing a gendered society entails structural and institutional change. Attitudes and values must change, too, but these are often altered when social policies and practices shift. Which changes have occurred since the beginning of the feminist movement of the early 1970s and which have not? What kind of programs target institutions and social structures? What is still needed for gender equality?

Affirmative action and comparable worth pay scales were two efforts to effect structural change—one to desegregate occupations and the other to distribute economic rewards for work on a gender-neutral basis. Affirmative action (hiring women in occupations dominated by men and men for work usually done by women) was widely implemented in the United States and did desegregate some occupations, but without continuous effort, gender segregation reestablishes itself as jobs and work organizations change. Another effort to establish gender-neutral work policies was comparable worth pay scales—assessing the characteristics of the job and paying on the basis of type of work done, not on who does the work. These programs were not widely implemented; women's work continues to be paid less than men's even when a man does the work. Women have entered the professions, especially medicine and the law, in large numbers and have moved up career ladders, but in most large-scale corporations and professional organizations, the top positions of authority are still held by men.

Sexual harassment guidelines have been another effective effort at changing thinking about acceptable behavior, and again, while the results are imperfect (and the guidelines are being used in ways that do not empower women), thinking about what was "normal" behavior in the workplace did change drastically.

In Europe, but not in the United States, subsidized parental leave for either parent and child care for every mother has changed mothering from a full-time occupation to something that can be combined with paid work out of the home without a constant struggle. The Scandinavian countries provide "daddy days"—leave time in the first year of a newborn's life that the father must take or it is forfeited.

A radical effort at restructuring government has taken place in France—a proposed program for mandating equal numbers of women and men representatives at the national level of government. Parity is not likely to become a widespread policy, but even redressing gender imbalance would give women and men a more equal opportunity to make laws and influence social policy. Gender differences in voting patterns in the United States indicate that women do have a different perspective on many issues. For women to be elected in greater numbers, powerful men now in politics would have to encourage young women to consider a career in politics, foster their advancement through mentoring, nominate them for national offices, and campaign with them and raise money for them when they run for office. Paradoxically, it has seemed easier for women to become heads of state than for these same states to vote in an equal number of women and men in their governing bodies. It has also been easier for women to become heads of parliamentary governments, where a party chooses the prime minister. The appointment of women to high positions, such as Madeleine Albright as U.S. Secretary of State, has also been welcomed. Yet when it comes to directly putting women into leadership positions of great authority, whether in government or in major corporations, there is still a public reluctance to grant women as much power as men.

On a more personal level, some people have structured their families to be gender-equal on every level—domestic work, child care, and financial contribution to the household economy. However, as long as work is structured for a married-man-with-wife career pattern, and men's work is paid better than women's work, gender-equal families will be very hard to attain by the majority of people. Other heterosexual couples have reversed roles—the woman is the breadwinner and the man cares for the children and keeps house. Here, the problem is that the domestic world is so gendered that male househusbands suffer from ostracism and isolation, as well as from a suspicion of homosexuality. Oddly, lesbian and gay couples who have reared children in a variety of family arrangements have blended more easily into hetero-coupled social worlds, at least in some communities. Corporate and government policies that offer health insurance and other benefits to any couple in a long-term household arrangement have also helped to restructure family life in ways that do not assume heterosexuality and marriage. Note, however, that communal domestic households have waned in popularity in Western countries, although they are the norm in polygamous cultures.

Least amenable to change have been the gendered divisions of work in the global economy. Financed by capital from developed countries, work organizations around the world exploit the labor of young, unmarried women under sweatshop-like conditions, while reserving better-paid jobs and support for entrepreneurship to men. The policies of the International Monetary Fund and other financial restructuring agencies do not include among their goals gender desegregation or encouraging women's education and access to health resources. In many developing countries, violence and sexual exploitation, as well as the heterosexual spread of AIDS, seriously undermine efforts to upgrade the lives of women and girls.

In sum, to change gendered social orders to be more equal (or, alternatively, less gendered) will take individual effort and modification of gender-stereotyped attitudes and values, but most of all, a restructuring of work and family through the policies and practices of large-scale corporations and the governments of dominant nations.

REFERENCES

Acker, J. 1989 *Doing Comparable Worth: Gender, Class, and Pay Equity*. Philadelphia: Temple University Press.

Barrett, M. 1988 *Women's Oppression Today*, rev. ed. London: Verso.

Bart, P. B., and E. G. Moran (eds.) 1993 *Violence Against Women*. Thousand Oaks, Calif.: Sage.

Berk, S. F. 1985 *The Gender Factory: The Apportionment of Work in American Households*. New York: Plenum.

Boserup, E. 1987 *Women's Role in Economic Development*, 2nd ed. New York: St. Martin's Press.

Butler, J. 1990 *Gender Trouble*. New York and London: Routledge.

Chafetz, J. S. 1990 *Gender Equity*. Thousand Oaks, Calif.: Sage.

Chodorow, N. 1978 *The Reproduction of Mothering*. Berkeley: University of California Press.

—— 1994 *Femininities, Masculinities, Sexualities*. Lexington: University Press of Kentucky.

Collins, P. H. 1990 *Black Feminist Thought*. Boston: Unwin Hyman.

Connell, R. W. 1987 *Gender and Power*. Stanford, Calif.: Stanford University Press.

—— 1995 *Masculinities*. Berkeley: University of California Press.

Coontz, S., and P. Henderson 1986 *Women's Work, Men's Property: The Origins of Gender and Class*. London: Verso.

Epstein, C. F. 1988 *Deceptive Distinctions: Sex, Gender and the Social Order*. New Haven, Conn.: Yale University Press.

Ferree, M. M., J. Lorber, and B. B. Hess, (eds.) 1998 *Revisioning Gender*. Thousand Oaks, Calif.: Sage.

Herdt, G., (ed.) 1994 *Third Sex Third Gender: Beyond Sexual Dimorphism in Culture and History*. New York: Zone Books.

Hochschild, A. 1989 *The Second Shift*. New York: Viking.

hooks, b. (1984) 1990 *Yearning: Race, Gender, and Cultural Politics*. Boston, Mass.: South End Press.

Kanter, R. M. 1977 *Men and Women of the Corporation*. New York: Basic Books.

Keller, E. F. 1985 *Reflections on Gender and Science*. New Haven, Conn.: Yale University Press.

Kessler, S. J. 1998 *Lessons from the Intersexed*. New Brunswick, N.J.: Rutgers University Press.

Kessler, S. J., and W. McKenna 1978 *Gender: An Ethnomethodological Approach*. Chicago: University of Chicago Press.

Laqueur, T. 1990 *Making Sex: Body and Gender from the Greeks to Freud*. Cambridge, Mass.: Harvard University Press.

Laslett, B., S. G. Kohlstedt, H. Longino, and E. Hammonds, (eds.) 1996 *Gender and Scientific Authority*. Chicago: University of Chicago Press.

Lorber, J. 1994 *Paradoxes of Gender*. New Haven, Conn.: Yale University Press.

—— 1998 *Gender Inequality: Feminist Theories and Politics*. Los Angeles: Roxbury.

MacKinnon, C. A. 1989 *Toward a Feminist Theory of the State*. Cambridge, Mass.: Harvard University Press.

Melhuus, M., and K. A. Stolen, (eds.) 1997 *Machos, Mistresses, Madonnas: Contesting the Power of Latin American Gender Imagery*. New York and London: Verso.

Messner, M. A., and D. F. Sabo, (eds.) 1990 *Sport, Men, and the Gender Order*. Champaigne, Ill.: Human Kinetics.

Oyewúmí, O. 1997 *The Invention of Women: Making an African Sense of Western Gender Discourses*. Minneapolis: University of Minnesota Press.

Peterson, V. S., (ed.) 1992 *Gendered States: Feminist (Re)visions of International Relations Theory*. Boulder, Colo.: Lynne Rienner.

Potuchek, J. L. 1997 *Who Supports the Family? Gender and Breadwinning in Dual-Earner Marriages*. Stanford, Calif.: Stanford University Press.

Redclift, N., and M. T. Stewart, (eds.) 1991 *Working Women: International Perspectives on Women and Gender Ideology*. New York and London: Routledge.

Reskin, B. F., (ed.) 1984 *Sex Segregation in the Workplace: Trends, Explanations, Remedies*. Washington, D.C.: National Academy Press.

Reskin, B. F., and P. A. Roos 1990 *Job Queues, Gender Queues*. Philadelphia: Temple University Press.

Risman, B. 1997 *Gender Vertigo: Toward a Post-Gender Family*. New Haven, Conn.: Yale University Press.

Rothman, B. K. 1989 *Recreating Motherhood*. New York: Norton.

Sainsbury, D., (ed.) 1994 *Gendering Welfare States*. Thousand Oaks, Calif.: Sage.

Segal, M. T., and V. Demos, (eds.) 1996–98 *Advances in Gender Research*, vols. 1–3. Greenwich, Conn.: JAI.

Smith, D. E. 1987 *The Everyday World as Problematic*. Toronto: University of Toronto Press.

—— 1990 *The Conceptual Practices of Power*. Toronto: University of Toronto Press.

—— 1990 *Texts, Facts, and Femininity*. New York and London: Routledge.

Staples, R. 1982 *Black Masculinity*. San Francisco: Black Scholar Press.

Thorne, B. 1993 *Gender Play: Girls and Boys at School*. New Brunswick, N.J.: Rutgers University Press.

Tilley, L. A., and P. Gurin, (eds.) 1990 *Women, Politics, and Change*. New York: Russell Sage.

Van den Wijngaard, M. 1997 *Reinventing the Sexes: The Biomedical Construction of Femininity and Masculinity*. Bloomington: Indiana University Press.

Walby, S. 1997 *Gender Transformations*. New York and London: Routledge.

West, C., and D. Zimmerman 1987 "Doing Gender." *Gender and Society* 1:125–151.

Williams, C. L. 1995 *Still a Man's World: Men Who Do Women's Work*. Berkeley: University of California Press.

JUDITH LORBER

GENERAL LINEAR MODEL

See Analysis of Variance and Covariance; Causal and Inference Models; Correlation and Regression Analysis.

GENOCIDE

When, in 1881, the German anti-Semite Dühring urged a "final settling of accounts" with the Jews, he spoke, rather obliquely, of the need for a "Carthaginian" solution (p. 113f.). This was not merely a euphemism, however, as it might now seem. On the contrary, it was well known that Rome had utterly destroyed Carthage in the last Punic War. Hence Dühring's meaning was clear. But his phrasing remained cryptic because the vocabulary of mass death had not yet attained technical precision. Not until World War II, in fact, were the terms "genocide" and "crimes against humanity" introduced. Thus, in December 1948, when the United Nations declared the willful destruction of an entire people to be a breach of international law—a principle enshrined in the U.N. Convention for the Prevention and Punishment of the Crime of Genocide—the very word for mass murder was still novel.

CONCEPTUAL ROOTS

The word "genocide" was coined by the jurist Raphaël Lemkin in his book *Axis Rule in Occupied Europe*. "New conceptions require new terms," Lemkin wrote. "By 'genocide,' we mean the destruction of a nation or... ethnic group"—that is, "murder, though on a vastly greater scale" (1944, pp. 79, 91).

Mass murder, of course, is hardly new. But only since the French Revolution has there been widespread concern with what the philosopher Hegel called "the fanaticism of destruction," which aims, Hegel said, to eliminate all enemies, real or imagined ([1821] 1991, p. 38). An early expression of this concern came from Gracchus Babeuf, the leading socialist in the French Revolution, who decried the "exterminating wheel" of Robespierre's Terror. Robespierre's "general system of government," Babeuf contended, is also a "general system of extermination" ([1794] 1987, pp. 96–98). In a similar spirit, the liberal poet August von Platen deplored the Russian repression of the Polish revolution of 1831 as an instance of *"Volksmurder"* (Jonassohn 1998, p. 140). Others later made similar charges. But it was not until the Nazi Holocaust that the international community felt the need to adopt a special term for the attempted murder of a people.

In 1945, soon after Lemkin's book appeared, the defeated Nazi rulers were charged with "deliberate and systematic genocide." A year later the United Nations ratified a working definition of genocide as the "denial of the right of existence of entire human groups" (Kuper 1981, pp. 22–23). Lemkin's new coinage had won swift acceptance. Since then, it has become universally popular—and equally controversial.

GLOBAL VIOLENCE

The popularity of the idea of genocide reflects its continuing relevance in today's world. Globally, there were at least forty-four state-organized mass slaughters in the period from 1945 to 1989, many of which were quasi-genocidal by almost any definition. These massacres resulted in an average of 1.6 million to 3.9 million deaths per annum—significantly more, that is, than the total number of fatalities caused by all wars and natural disasters in this period. And in every decade since 1945 another 1.85 million people have died in wars and civil wars (Gurr and Harff 1989). Nor has the picture improved since 1989. In 1993, for example, there were twenty-three wars, 25 million refugees, and a record number of armed U.N. interventions in conflicts around the world (Gurr and Harff 1994). In 1994, a genocidal massacre in Rwanda caused roughly 850,000 deaths (Smith 1998). Elsewhere—in Burundi, east Timor, and myriad other places—similar if smaller tragedies have unfolded.

Many groups, in other words, have been victims of systematic violence in the recent past, and allegations of genocide abound. Yet the concept itself remains elusive—partly, indeed, thanks to its own success. So many people now equate genocide with evil that nearly every conflict is marked by charges and countercharges of genocide. Abortion, birth control, forced sterilization, intermarriage, and desegregation are just a few of the countless practices that have been labeled genocidal. Almost anything controversial, it seems, can be called genocide.

For social scientists, plainly, the matter is more complex. This was clear from the outset in Lemkin's work, which remains paradigmatic in many ways.

TOTAL WAR

Sociologically, Lemkin believed that the Holocaust was not a contingent feature of German Nazism but rather an expression of intrinsic Nazi tendencies. As an absolutist form of nationalism, Nazism claimed absolute sovereignty over non-Germans on the ground of purported German racial-national superiority. This, in turn, led to a Nazi conception of war as Total War—the conviction, that is, that wars are not merely struggles between states but rather inevitable racial contests between peoples, with total victory or defeat as the ultimate outcomes. And the Nazi repudiation of universalist ethics inspired the belief that, in Total War, enemy peoples may be totally destroyed without ethical qualms.

Genocide was not, however, the entire Nazi agenda. On the contrary, in Lemkin's view, genocide was a single part of a many-sided strategy. The ultimate Nazi goal was to build a German empire, and in pursuing this goal only certain types of enemies were slated for annihilation: Jews, who were seen as the poisonous racial antithesis of everything German; so-called Gypsies, who were regarded as racially inferior pests; and a variety of others (including democratic intellectuals, Marxists, and resistance fighters) whom the Nazis saw as irreconcilable political foes. Enemies of other kinds, however, were to be ruled rather than massacred. Some, indeed, were to be incorporated into the Nazi empire as lesser "Germanic" peoples (including the Dutch, Flemings, and Scandinavians). Others, including Russians, Serbs, and Poles, were to be enslaved and reduced in numbers (by limits on birthrates, food rationing, etc.) but were not to be liquidated per se.

AN AGE OF ABSOLUTES

For Lemkin, that is, genocide was a strand in the fabric of Nazi war aims. And though the genocidal aspect of Nazi policy had historical precedents, it was also uniquely modern in many ways. Neither of the two pillars of the Holocaust ("master-race mythology and aggressive technology") could be grasped apart from specifically modern forces, including science and industry, nationalism, racism, and statism. Nor could modern German militarism be equated with the warrior ethics of times past. Other peoples had periodically committed mass murder, but German militarism had risen to new heights of virulence, driven, Lemkin concluded, by an acute "national and racial emotionalism" that was given a uniquely destructive force by modern technology (1944, p. xiv).

The consequence, as the sociologist Jessie Bernard noted shortly after the war ended (1949, p. 652), is that "ethnic conflict in our day has taken an unexpectedly brutal turn," even reaching the level of "exterminating whole peoples—genocide." Previous conflicts, however brutal, now seemed relatively small and unsystematic by comparison.

VARIETIES OF GENOCIDE

This is not to say, however, that genocide is entirely unique to modernity. In recent decades, sociologists have tended to agree that the willful destruction of entire peoples is, in fact, an ancient practice, common to many cultures. But it is also widely accepted that mass murder has assumed new forms in the twentieth century (as Lemkin said). This change is not merely quantitative but qualitative, and it is often framed in terms of a contrast between two ideal-types: (1) *instrumental genocide*, or mass murder to achieve pragmatic goals; and (2) *ideological genocide*, or mass murder as an end in itself.

Save for a relatively small proportion of cases that prefigure contemporary trends (e.g., wars of religion like the Crusades), most premodern genocides were essentially instrumental in nature. Modern genocides, in contrast, are often said to be largely if not primarily ideological—though instrumental motives remain powerful as well.

THE ORIGIN OF MASS MURDER

Many scholars, like Kurt Jonassohn, believe that genocides have occurred "throughout history in all parts of the world" (Jonassohn 1988, in Chalk and Jonassohn 1990, p. 415). Leo Kuper, in a classic study, called genocide "an odious scourge which has inflicted great losses on humanity in all periods of history" (1981, p. 11). Sociobiologists, meanwhile, have been even bolder, claiming that genocide is not only universal for humanity but for our closest evolutionary relatives as well (including chimpanzees and our evolutionary ancestors; cf. Diamond 1991, p. 264). E. O. Wilson, the founder of sociobiology, has speculated that genocide may be a "primitive cultural capacity," rooted in "the possession of certain genes," that confers a selective advantage on predatory groups that wish to spread their genes at the expense of their neighbors (1980, p. 298).

In reality, however, there is very little evidence of anything like genocidal violence in the evolutionary or historical record until comparatively recently. Sociobiologists who defend the idea that people and chimps share "a continuous, 5-million-year habit of lethal aggression" have offered, as their best evidence, the testimony of witnesses who report that, in more than 100 years of observation at four sites, seven chimps were assaulted by groups from neighboring chimp communities; and though none of the victims were killed on the spot, several later died or disappeared (Wrangham and Peterson 1996, pp. 16–21, 63).

This, it seems plain, is slight evidence for the large claim that people and their relatives and ancestors are genocidal by nature. Little else in the ethological or evolutionary record seems to lend credibility to this claim. Nor does history before the discovery of agriculture show significant evidence of mass murder.

To date, the earliest known evidence of collective violence is a gravesite in the Nile Valley containing fifty-nine men, women, and children, most of whom were killed by weapons with projectile points. This massacre, dating back 12,000–14,000 years, was "almost certainly" a consequence of disruptions produced by a crisis in the proto-agricultural system that was evolving in the region (Reader 1998, p. 146). The only other authenticated evidence of mass violence in remote antiquity is a similar but smaller burial ground in Bavaria dating back 7,700 years (Frayer 1997).

PLOUGHSHARES INTO SWORDS

In general, archaeological evidence makes it clear that wars, massacres, and even murders were comparatively rare in pre-agricultural days (Ferguson 1997). And the ethnographic evidence shows that, while hunter-gatherers are seldom entirely non-violent, they have significantly fewer wars, internal conflicts, and interpersonal violence than agrarian peoples (Ember and Ember 1997; Ross 1993). Even the famously "fierce" Yamomami of northern Brazil and Venezuela seem to have been driven to violence as much by the influence of outside forces as by internal pressures (Ferguson 1992). "It seems unlikely," as the genocide scholars Chalk and Jonassohn conclude, "that early man engaged in genocide during the hunting and gathering stage" (1990, p. 32).

For some peoples, this stage lasted until the recent past. For humanity as a whole, hunting and foraging remained universal until roughly 11,000 years ago. Shortly afterwards, agriculture arose in the Middle East; and then, in succession, in China 11,000 years ago in Papua, Mexico, and the Andes 10,000 years ago in West Africa 6,000 years ago and elsewhere.

Once agriculture had appeared, mass violence assumed new dimensions.

EMPIRE AND TERROR

The first weapons of war, and the earliest signs of mass warfare, appeared at the dawn of the agrarian era. In the ensuing millenia the first true wars were fought (Ferrill 1997, pp. 18–19). The intent of these wars was usually instrumental—to win land and labor, to keep enemies at bay, to build states and empires. This was the context in which mass violence became familiar. Genocide in particular was almost always linked to empire building in this period.

Historically, empire builders generally seek tribute or servile labor from the peoples they conquer, which leads them to spare the lives of noncombatants, especially peasants. This was the spirit in which Sumerian, Hittite, and Babylonian epics of remote antiquity warned of the folly of genocide (Cohn 1996). But as fortified cities emerged as obstacles in the path of empire, conquest sometimes took more brutal forms. And peasant resistance often provoked vengeful repression. Hence, by the third millenium B.C.E., genocidal conquests had become comparatively common in the early Egyptian empire (Jonassohn 1998). Elsewhere, genocidal massacres seem to have become common by the first millenium B.C.E.

The Assyrians in particular became legendary for their merciless assaults on fortified cities, including Babylon, which Sennacherib decimated in 689 B.C.E. The goal of such assaults was usually to destroy an imperial or commercial rival. The preferred method was to lay siege to a city and starve its citizens into submission by burning crops and destroying livestock. Once a campaign of this kind triumphed, the conquerors would often raze the defeated city, salt the earth, and slaughter the citizens. The legalistic Romans dubbed this practice "devastation."

Early "devastations" included the destruction of Melos by Athens in 416 B.C.E. (for refusing to take sides in the Peloponnesian Wars); the destruction of two Sicilian cities by Carthage in 409 B.C.E.; and the annihilation of Carthage by Rome in 146 B.C.E. In the latter case, as many as 150,000 people are said to have died.

THE CONTINUATION OF WAR BY OTHER MEANS

Sociologists have identified a range of motives for instrumental genocide. Chalk and Jonassohn, for example, say that most genocides of this type (which they call "utilitarian") have been prompted by the wish to acquire wealth, to terrorize real or potential enemies, or to avert threats (1990, pp. 34–36). Until comparatively recently, motives of this kind have been the main effective spurs to genocide both in the circum-Mediterranean world and elsewhere. In brief, it seems that whenever empires fight, great opportunities and equally great dangers are at stake. In such cases, genocidal massacres can become the extraordinary means of attaining goals that, in other contexts, would be pursued by ordinary statecraft.

Examples abound. Canton was gutted in 879 C.E. and its population was decimated. In the twelfth century C.E., Afghan conquerors from Ghur destroyed the city of Ghazni and all its men. In the next century the Mongols laid waste to Transoxania and Khurasan, evidently killing hundreds of thousands of people. Not long afterwards, all 12,000 of the Meos people (south of Delhi) were killed in the wake of a failed uprising. Many events in the sixteenth-century Spanish conquest of the Americas were plainly genocidal. And many other examples of this kind can be cited as well (Chalk and Jonassohn 1990; Jonassohn, 1998).

A related form of genocide accompanied the rise of modern colonialism. In the Americas, for example, the English Puritans liquidated the Pequot in 1637, the French destroyed the Natchez in 1731, and Argentine settlers virtually eliminated the Araucanians in 1878–1885. In Africa, many peoples have been devastated by colonial conquests; some (including the Herero of Namibia and the Matumbi of Tanzania) have suffered mass destruction. Many indigenous peoples in Australia have been destroyed, and in Tasmania the entire aboriginal population was extinguished by 1876.

These are just a few of the many cases in which genocide has accompanied instrumental conquest.

IDEOLOGICAL GENOCIDE

In some cases, however, genocide is not an instrumental means to an end, but rather an end in itself. Genocides of this type, in which the destruction of entire peoples is sought for intrinsic reasons, are generally classified as "ideological" (Fein 1993; Smith 1987). These massacres, which are typically fueled by religious or ethnoracial fanaticism, are often among the deadliest of genocides, since they seek to destroy targeted peoples for reasons of "principle," not simply expediency. And they are often instrumentally irrational in an almost chemically pure sense. In 1994, for example, the rulers of Rwanda were so preoccupied by the wish to annihilate an unarmed ethnic minority that they left themselves virtually defenseless against an army of invading rebels from Uganda (Des Forges 1999). Between 1975 and 1979, the Pol Pot regime wrought havoc across the length and breadth of Cambodia in a vain effort to purge Cambodia of every trace of foreign, urban, and intellectual influence (Kiernan

1996). In the Nazi Holocaust, the German leaders diverted vital resources from the Russian front to fuel the militarily useless operations of the death camps (Postone 1980). Earlier, during World War I, Turkey failed to finish the strategically crucial Berlin–Bagdad railway largely because the Turkish rulers were so intent on destroying the Armenians that they liquidated large numbers of Armenian construction workers (Jonassohn 1998).

Genocides of this type are thus doubly destructive—first, because they are prosecuted with systematic ruthlessness; and second, because they often hurt the perpetrators as well as the victims.

BEFORE IDEOLOGY?

Only a few instances of premodern mass violence are clearly ideological in inspiration—including, for example, the Crusades and the persecution of Cathar heretics in thirteenth-century Languedoc. But many other early cases also reveal a noninstrumental side.

Beginning in 1634, for example, the Iroquois fought a series of "mourning wars" against the Hurons, which resulted in large-scale massacres of Huron men and women. The main object, in this case, was to "requicken," in the bodies of Huron children, the spirits of Iroquois who had died in epidemics. This was perhaps not an "ideological" motive in the modern sense, but it was clearly inspired by religious belief (Richter 1992). Similarly, the genocidal massacres that accompanied the Mongol conquests were fueled, in part, by apocalyptic faith in Mongol destiny (Jagchid and Hyer 1979). And several Indian cases recorded by Jonassohn (1998) were largely religious in character—for example, the massacre of Jains by the Hindu king of Pandya in the eleventh century C.E., the destruction of the Buddhist majority of Bihar by Muslim conquerors in the twelfth century C.E., and the persistent efforts of Bahmani sultans to exterminate or convert Hindus in the Deccan region in the period 1347–1482 C.E.

Broadly defined, in other words, ideological genocide may have been more common in the past than scholars have tended to say. But it is nonetheless plain that the twentieth century marked a new departure. Only in this century did mass murder routinely followed paths defined by doctrine.

A NEW SELF-CONSCIOUSNESS

Raphaël Lemkin had been well aware that genocidal practices predated the twentieth century (Fein 1993). But he believed that the absolutist racism and nationalism of the modern era gave contemporary mass murder decisive new features. Above all, genocide was now pursued with heightened self-consciousness. In the characteristic genocides of the twentieth century—most notably the liquidation of Armenians by Turkey in World War I, the Nazi Holocaust during World War II, and the postwar massacres of minority groups by governments in Indonesia, Pakistan, Cambodia, Burundi, and Rwanda—the intent was genocidal from the start. Entire groups were sentenced to death for ideological as well as geopolitical reasons. And these sentences were pronounced with full awareness of their antihumanistic implications, since they defied the humanitarian trend, rooted in Puritanism and bourgeois constitutionalism (Tergel 1998; Troeltsch [1912] 1958), which had swept the Euro-Atlantic world in the nineteenth century.

What explains this genocidal intent? What gives "ideological" genocide its compelling force? For Lemkin the answer lies, in part, in social psychology. He sees evidence, in particular, of such psychological tendencies as cynicism, denial, "contempt for the victim," and "exaggerated pride," among others (1992, pp. 189–235). This line of reasoning is richly developed in the research literature on the personality traits most relevant to genocide: aggressiveness, submissiveness, and punitiveness. It was first shown, in a flawed but classic study (Adorno et al. 1950), that these three traits systematically covary in structured and intelligible ways. Later research has significantly refined this original discovery.

It is now well understood that certain kinds of harsh personal experience tend to make people (1) *submissive* to leaders and (2) *aggressive* toward—outsiders. And people imbued with this dually obedient and violent tendency are often exceptionally willing to persecute or fight those who are authoritatively defined as their "enemies" (Altemeyer 1996; Hopf 1993; Lederer and Schmidt 1995). The significance of this fact for the study of genocide was revealed by Ross, who showed that conflict intensity is strongly related to personality variables of just this type. While objective social divisions tend to determine *who fights whom*—class versus class, nation versus nation, and so forth—personality-forming experiences play an exceptionally large role in determining the destructiveness of any given conflict. Ross found, after systematically studying the interplay of forty-one variables in ninety nonindustrial societies, that "the more affectionate and warm and the less harsh the socialization in a society, the lower the level of political conflict and violence" (1993, p. 99); and indeed, no other single factor has a greater impact.

DIVIDED SOCIETIES

Patterns of socialization are thus highly relevant to the study of genocide. No less relevant are structural determinants—few of which, however, have yet received systematic attention. This is largely due to the fact that the sociology of genocide is still just a few decades old. While studies of anti-Semitism, ethnocentrism, and the Holocaust have been common throughout the postwar era, the study of genocide as a phenomenon *sui generis* was first pursued in the 1970s by a small cohort of sociologists—Dadrian, Kuper, Fein—who have remained central to the enterprise ever since.

Leo Kuper, the "doyen of genocide scholars" (Charny 1994, p. 64), set the stage for much of the research that was to follow. Focusing entirely on the twentieth century, Kuper noted that genocide in this century has been distinctive in several ways. In addition to the rising influence of ideological motives, Kuper observed that contemporary genocides are also exceptionally likely to occur within divided societies, as autocratic states seek to defend their monopoly of power against the challenges of domestic rivals. Genocidal massacres are still common in the conflicts between societies as well—especially, Kuper says, when imperialist motives are at work—but internal conflicts are now especially acute. This is particularly true in postcolonial societies, many of which were profoundly destabilized by the experience of colonial rule. Such societies are often pure artifacts of the colonial imagination, rigidly stratified and ethnically divided in new and untenable ways. When dissent arises in these "new nations," the rulers—*sans* consent—resort to coercion, often on a grand scale. Hence the state-sponsored massacres in such postcolonial realms as Indonesia, the former "East Pakistan" (now Bangladesh), Rwanda, and Burundi. And communal divisions in these nations run so deep that genocidal massacres often unfold entirely within civil society, unbidden by the state (Kuper 1981).

Many of Kuper's themes were adapted from classical texts by Sartre (1968) and Cohn (1967), and many later scholars have pursued variations on these themes (see Andreopolous 1994; Totten et al. 1995). Except for Jonassohn, who delves into remoter history, most social scientists continue to focus mainly on twentieth-century cases (Dadrian 1995; Mazian 1990; Melson 1992; Wallimann and Dobkowski 1987). Much has been learned about these cases. Yet in many ways genocide remains as elusive as ever. Part of the problem is definitional.

DUELLING DEFINITIONS

As the study of genocide proves, definitions are deeply political. This was apparent from the beginning of the United Nations debate over genocide in 1948. For the Russian delegates, "genocide" was a logical effect and extension of fascist doctrine, revolving around the victimization of racial and ethnic groups. Others argued that social classes and political groups can also be the victims of genocide. When the final vote was taken, religious as well as national and ethnic groups were identified as possible targets of genocide, but political groups were excluded. And the United Nations further limited the applicability of its definition by specifying that genocide entails an "intent to destroy" some group, "in whole or in part." Since proving intent is notoriously difficult, some delegates questioned whether the Genocide Convention, so restricted, could ever be enforced. Similar doubts were voiced about the idea of "destroying" a group. Lemkin, in his original formulation, had said that genocide can take cultural as well as physical forms. But does this mean that efforts to sabotage the culture, language, or religion of a group are just as much "acts of genocide" as attempts to physically destroy the group?

Questions of this kind quickly proved to have direct political relevance. In 1951, W. E. B. Du Bois, Paul Robeson, and others addressed a book-length petition to the United Nations accusing the U.S. government of systematically genocidal actions against African Americans (Patterson et al. 1951). Reluctance to entertain charges of this kind led many U. S. senators to oppose the Genocide Convention; and, indeed, the United States did not endorse the Convention until 1986 (LeBlanc 1991). Nor did the United Nations prove eager to enforce the Convention. Not until the Rwandan massacres of 1994, in fact, did the United Nations classify a postwar event as "genocide"—and even this came after the fact. It has remained extremely difficult, in short, for policy makers to operationally define or apply the notion of genocide.

Scholars, meanwhile, have spent considerable time on definitional issues. Kuper offered an influential distinction between genocide and "genocidal massacre" as a means of distinguishing the attempted murder of entire peoples from large-scale massacres that are not prompted by the wish to destroy groups *in toto*. He did not, however, establish clear criteria for this distinction, which limits its utility. Nor has any other approach won consensus. Thus, debate rages over the classification of many events: "the rape of Nanking," Stalin's purges, the nuclear bombing of Hiroshima, the carpet bombing of Vietnam, "human-made" famine in Mao's China, and similar events. Other debates pivot on questions of principle. Are there unintended genocides? Is genocide distinct from the destruction of a culture? Does genocide belong on a continuum with other forms of destructiveness, or is it qualitatively unique?

THE LIMITS OF CLASSIFICATION

Many answers have been given to these questions, but it remains far from clear that "genocide" is, indeed, a unitary phenomenon or amenable to general explanation. Most scholars have tended to focus on relatively clear cases of mass murder inspired by modern racial-national ideologies, but even these vary in significant respects. Another approach, proposed by the psychologist Charny (1994), is to subsume the full range of mass-destructive practices into a wider matrix; but it seems unlikely that the criterion of mass destructiveness alone is sufficient to justify treating ecological catastrophe, ethnic slaughter, and cultural repression as elements in a unified field of events.

For fuller, more nuanced understanding, comparative research is needed on a widening scale. Whether the general notion of "genocide" will continue to prove compelling remains to be seen.

REFERENCES

Adorno, Theodor W. Else Frenkel-Brunswik, Daniel Levinson, and R. Nevitt Sanford 1950 *The Authoritarian Personality*. New York: Harper and Bros.

Altemeyer, Bob 1996 *The Authoritarian Specter*. Cambridge, Mass.: Harvard University Press.

Andreopoulos, George J., (ed.) 1994 *Genocide: Conceptual and Historical Dimensions*. Philadelphia: University of Pennsylvania Press.

Babeuf, Gracchus (1794) 1987 *La guerre de la Vendée et le système de dépopulation*. Paris: Tallandier.

Bernard, Jessie 1949 *American Community Behavior*. New York: Dryden.

Chalk, Frank, and Kurt Jonassohn 1990 *The History and Sociology of Genocide*. New Haven, Conn.: Yale University Press.

Charny, Israel W. 1994 "Toward a Generic Definition of Genocide." In George J. Andreopoulos ed., *Genocide*. Philadelphia: University of Pennsylvania Press.

Cohn, Norman 1967 *Warrant for Genocide*. New York: Harper and Row.

—— 1996 *Noah's Flood*. New Haven, Conn.: Yale University Press.

Dadrian, Vahakn N. 1995 *The History of the Armenian Genocide*. Providence, R.I.: Bergahn.

Des Forges, Alison 1999 *Leave None to Tell the Story: Genocide in Rwanda*. New York: Human Rights Watch.

Diamond, Jared 1991 *The Rise and Fall of the Third Chimpanzee*. London: Radius.

Dühring, Eugen 1881 *Die Judenfrage als Racen-, Sitten- und Culturfrage*, 2nd ed. Leipzig and Karlsruhe: H. Reuther.

Ember, Carol R., and Melvin Ember 1997 "Violence in the Ethnographic Record." In Debra L. Martin and David W. Frayer, eds. *Troubled Times*. Amsterdam: Gordon and Breach.

Fein, Helen 1993 *Genocide: A Sociological Perspective*. Newbury Park, Calif.: Sage.

Ferguson, R. Brian 1992 "A Savage Encounter." In R. Brian Ferguson and Neil L. Whitehead, eds. *War in the Tribal Zone*. Santa Fe, N. Mex.: School of American Research Press.

—— 1997 "Violence and War in Prehistory." In Debra L. Martin and David W. Frayer, eds. *Troubled Times*. Amsterdam: Gordon and Breach.

Ferrill, Arther 1997 *The Origins of War*. Boulder, Colo.: Westview.

Frayer, David W. 1997 "Ofnet." In Debra L. Martin and David W. Frayer, eds. *Troubled Times*. Amsterdam: Gordon and Breach.

Gurr, Ted Robert, and Barbara Harff 1994 *Ethnic Conflict in World Politics*. Boulder, Colo.: Westview.

—— 1989 "Victims of the State." *International Review of Victimology* 1(1):23–41.

Hegel, G. W. F. (1821) 1991 *Elements of the Philosophy of Right*. New York: Cambridge University Press.

Hopf, Christel 1993 "Authoritarians and Their Families." In William F. Stone, Gerda Lederer, and Richard Christie, eds., *Strength and Weakness: The Authoritarian Personality Today*. New York: Springer-Verlag.

Jagchid, Sechin, and Paul Hyer 1979 *Mongolia's Culture and Society*. Boulder, Colo.: Westview.

Jonassohn, Kurt with Karin Solveig Björnson 1998 *Genocide and Gross Human Rights Violations in Comparative Perspective*. New Brunswick, N.J.: Transaction.

Kiernan, Ben 1996 *The Pol Pot Regime: Race, Power, and Genocide in Cambodia Under the Khmer Rouge, 1975–79*. New Haven, Conn.: Yale University Press.

Kuper, Leo 1981 *Genocide: Its Political Use in the Twentieth Century*. New Haven, Conn.: Yale University Press.

LeBlanc, Lawrence J. 1991 *The United States and the Genocide Convention*. Durham, N.C.: Duke University Press.

Lederer, Gerda, and Peter Schmidt, (eds.) 1995 *Autoritarismus und Gesellschaft*. Opladen, Germany: Leske + Budrich.

Lemkin, Raphaël 1944 *Axis Rule in Occupied Europe*. Washington D.C.: Carnegie Endowment for International Peace.

—— 1992 *Not Guilty? Raphael Lemkin's Thoughts on Nazi Genocide*. In Steven L. Jacobs, ed. Lewiston, U.K.: Edwin Mellen.

Mazian, Florence 1990 *Why Genocide? The Armenian and Jewish Experiences in Perspective*. Ames: Iowa State University Press.

Melson, Robert 1992 *Revolution and Genocide*. Chicago: University of Chicago Press.

Patterson, William, W. E. B. Du Bois, et al. 1951 *We Charge Genocide: The Historic Petition to the United Nations for Relief from a Crime of the United States Government Against the Negro People*. New York: Civil Rights Congress.

Postone, Moishe 1980 "Anti-Semitism and National Socialism." *New German Critique* 19:97–116.

Reader, John 1998 *Africa*. New York: Knopf.

Richter, Daniel K. 1992 *The Ordeal of the Long House*. Chapel Hill: University of North Carolina Press.

Ross, Marc Howard 1993 *The Culture of Conflict*. New Haven, Conn.: Yale University Press.

Sartre, Jean-Paul 1968 *On Genocide*. Boston: Beacon Press.

Smith, David Norman 1998 "The Psychocultural Roots of Genocide: Legitimacy and Crisis in Rwanda." *The American Psychologist* 53(7): 743–753.

Smith, Roger W. 1987 "Human Destructiveness and Politics." In Isidor Wallimann and Michael N. Dobkowski, eds., *Genocide and the Modern Age*. New York: Greenwood.

Tergel, Alf 1998 *Human Rights in Cultural and Religious Traditions*. Uppsala: Acta Universitatis Upsaliensis.

Totten, Samuel, William S. Parsons, and Israel W. Charny, (eds.) 1995 *Genocide in the Twentieth Century: Critical Essays and Eyewitness Accounts*. New York: Garland.

Troeltsch, Ernst (1912) 1958 *Protestantism and Progress*. Boston: Beacon Press.

Wallimann, Isidor, and Michael N. Dobkowski, (eds.) 1987 *Genocide and the Modern Age*. New York: Greenwood.

Wilson, E. O. 1980 *Sociobiology*, 2nd ed. Cambridge, Mass.: Harvard University Press.

Wrangham, Richard, and Dale Peterson 1996 *Demonic Males: Apes and the Origins of Human Violence*. Boston: Houghton Mifflin.

DAVID NORMAN SMITH

GERONTOLOGY

See Aging and the Life Course; Cohort Perspectives; Filial Responsibility; Intergenerational Relations; Intergenerational Resource Transfer, Long Term Care, Long Term Care Facilities; Retirement; Widowhood.

GERMAN SOCIOLOGY

NOTE: *Although the following article has not been revised for this edition of the Encyclopedia, the substantive coverage is currently appropriate. The editors have provided a list of recent works at the end of the article to facilitate research and exploration of the topic.*

"German Sociology" has two specific traits: It is part of the general humanities tradition of German culture—that is, it has a philosophical orientation—and it emphasizes epistemological reflection, favoring the understanding of human action through *verstehen* (intuitive oneness with the explanandum). This is the way in which Raymond Aron (1935) characterized sociology in Germany, studying it at the time of the Nazi regime, when it was mainly a memory and not a living field of knowledge or profession.

Since then a large number of books and essays in the United States have treated sociology as practiced in Germany, at least some of which broaden the image (Nisbet 1966; Fletcher 1971; Oberschall 1965, 1972; Schad 1972; Freund 1978). The dominant meaning of the intellectual commodity called German sociology—as continued in the works of Salomon (1945), Barnes (1938), Coser (1977), Zeitlin (1981), and especially Meja, Misgeld, and Stehr (1987)—is that of grand theory with a teleological meaning. This "German Sociology" is only a small part of sociology in Germany, but it is the aspect to which the intellectual community at large reacts; and it is reinforced by selectivity in translation and citation. For the social sciences in the United States, those parts of sociology in other countries which are least like American sociology are searched out as welcome completions.

THE CLASSICAL PERIOD

By the turn of the twentieth century, sociology had become an exciting intellectual concern in the United States, France, England, and Germany. Since an educated person at that time was expected to know English, German, and French, there was intensive direct interaction. Of special importance were the exchanges among Albert Schäffle (1884), Ferdinand Tönnies (1887), Emile Durkheim (e.g., 1887), and Georg Simmel (1890). Durkheim first made a name for himself in France by reviewing German social science literature by authors such as Wilhelm Wundt and, especially, Ferdinand Tönnies, and was therefore attacked as a Germanophile. Tönnies's distinction *Gemeinschaft* (community) and *Gesellschaft* (society) influenced Durkheim's dichotomy mechanical and organic solidarity, and Tönnies in turn commented on Durkheim's notion of the division of labor as the central element in social evolution (Gephardt 1982). Initially the builders of large "systems," such as Ludwig Gumplowitz (1883), Gustav Ratzenhofer (1893), and Theodore Abel (1929), dominated German sociological literature.

In a review of the period up to 1914, Leopold von Wiese (1959) lists Ferdinand Tönnies, Max Weber, and Werner Sombart as the most important sociologists; the list should also include Alfred Vierkandt, Franz Oppenheimer, Alfred Weber, Roberto Michels, and Hermann Kantorowicz (Käsler 1984). This inner circle of sociologists of the "classical period" is still influential today.

In the closing days of the German empire, sociology was established in an elitist academy with Tönnies as president, Sombart as vice president, and von Wiese as the eminence gris. Simmel and Weber were considered to be the leading scholars within this academy, even though both had become merely observers. In 1912, after numerous editions, Tönnies's *Gemeinschaft und Gesellschaft*, first published in 1887, at last achieved wide recognition among the educated public, paralleling the impact of Edward A. Ross's *Social Control* in the United States.

THE WEIMAR PERIOD

Upon the reestablishment of sociology in 1919, von Wiese was able to retain bureaucratic control over the policy of the academy and largely over its conventions. Not until the end of the 1920s was the first chair of sociology instituted in Frankfurt. However, during the fourteen years of the Weimar Republic, forty professorships were created that combined sociology with another discipline, such as economics, philosophy, or law. Eight periodicals had *Sociology* in their titles, and another eight regularly published sociological contributions. Von Wiese was instrumental in founding the first permanent research institute at the University of Cologne, Forschungsinstitut für Sozial- und Verwaltungswissenschaften, in 1919 (Alemann 1978), followed in 1923 by the Institut für Sozialforschung in Frankfurt (Jay 1973). In the early 1930s nearly all universities in Germany regularly offered courses in sociology, and by the mid-1920s the Deutsche Gesellschaft für Soziologie had begun to question the wisdom of opposing a degree curriculum in the universities.

The 1920s were a time of abrasive partisanship in German intellectual life. René König groups the various positions along a dividing line between left and right Hegelians, the Kantian tradition having paled in the humanities (König 1987). Left Hegelian translates into Marxism, but that itself was very heterogeneous. When Eisenstadt and Curelaru (1976, p. 122) and Zeitlin (1981, p. v) maintain that "a critical reexamination of Marxism" is a main focus of German sociology, this is an error; Marxists and non-Marxists mostly tended to ignore each other, although not in the 1920s.

"In the 1920s there was no dominant figure in sociology, which evolved in a number of milieus with little common direction. Even within its local centers in the Weimar Republic there was practically no paradigmatic unity" (Lepsius 1987, p. 40). These local centers were Frankfurt, Cologne, Berlin, and (later) Leipzig. In this characterization of the Weimar turmoil, there are two omissions: Max Weber's influence is not mentioned, and the Frankfurt School is bypassed. In both cases it is done for the same reason: at that time they were not very important for sociology. Shortly after accepting a professorship in Munich, Weber died in 1920. Some of his most important works on religion had appeared during the war, and his magnum opus, *Wirtschaft und Gesellschaft* (Economy and Society) was published posthumously by his wife Marianne Weber. Other works by Weber were not readily available until after about 1925.

The Institut für Sozialforschung in Frankfurt did not see itself as an institute for sociologists. Felix J. Weill, who obtained the funds for the institute from his grain merchant father, would have preferred to call it Institute for Marxism, but it was then judged prudent to choose the neutral title Social Research. All of the members shared an aesthetic disgust with bourgeois society, though they themselves were from well-off-to-very-rich families, and they wanted to convert fellow intellectuals to this view. The most important effect of the institute until the 1940s, however, was to give younger social scientists a chance to develop their talents: Max Horkheimer, Karl August Wittfogel, Franz Borkenau, Leo Löwenthal, Herbert Marcuse, and Theodor Adorno. "Although without much impact in Weimar, and with even less during the period of exile that followed, the Frankfurt School was to become a major force in the revitalization of Western European Marxism in the postwar years" (Jay 1973, p. 4).

AN END TO SOCIOLOGY

It is easier to name sociologists who did not emigrate as the Nazi regime came to power than to list the émigrés. Of all the sociologists with a reputation, only the social philosopher Hans Freyer welcomed the new regime. Werner Sombart, who during his lifetime took just about every political stance available, was in an anticapitalist anti-Semitic phase around 1933. It must have protected him when, in 1938, he ridiculed racism and the glorification of the people. Franz Oppenheimer and Eric Vögelin were eventually forced to emigrate, even though they tried to remain. Othmar Spann lost his professorship in 1938 and was imprisoned. Ferdinand Tönnies, whose show of opposition bordered on the suicidal, was ostracized. Alfred Weber was dismissed. Alfred Vierkandt had to cease lecturing. Alfred von Martin resigned. The Deutsche Gesellschaft für Soziologie was suspended in 1934 by von Wiese in order to avoid a takeover. Von Wiese stopped publishing the *Kölner Zeitschrift* in the same year, and from then on, lectured only on the history of economic thought. René König, a young candidate for a professorial career who had to emigrate in 1935, attributes to the Nazis a complete stoppage of sociology worthy of its name (König 1978, p. 14).

A SECOND BEGINNING

Sociology after 1945 could not have been a continuation of a tradition; and even if it had been possible, it would not have been a discipline in which basic issues had been settled. This is especially true for the issue of professionalization, which translates into the question "What public are the sociologists addressing?"

Emigrants returning to Germany (René König, Max Horkheimer, Theodor W. Adorno, Siegfried Landshut, Helmut Plessner, Arnold Bergsträsser, Emmerich K. Francis, and, much later, Norbert Elias) often had been influenced by developments in America. American sociology was most influential, since books from the United States often were the only ones available. The "Young Turks" of sociology born between 1926 and 1930—Karl Martin Bolte, Rainer M. Lepsius, Burkhart Lutz, Renate Mayntz, Erwin K. Scheuch, and Friedrich Tenbruck—studied the subject in American universities.

Three of the five research centers of the period of reconstruction were financed by foreign sources: the Sozialforschungsstelle Dortmund with funds from the Rockefeller Foundation; the UNESCO Institute for Social Research in Cologne, through the initiative of Alva Myrdal; and the Institut für Sozialwissenschaftliche Forschung in Darmstadt, with American government money. The trade unions established sociology as a "democratic discipline" in Hamburg at the Akademie für Gemeinschaft. Von Wiese reopened the institute in Cologne that later was integrated into the university. With generous financing from American sources, such as the government-sponsored Voice of America, the Institut für Sozialforschung in Frankfurt resumed operations. And in Göttingen, Hans Paul Bahrdt took up the tradition of industrial sociology of the late Weimar times and founded the Soziologisches Forschungsinstitut, Göttingen—the SOFI Institut. Thus, from the resumption of sociology in Germany, there was an infrastructure for empirical social research well connected to the international community. With the exception of von Wiese's institute, however, it later proved to be impossible to integrate these institutes for empirical research into the universities, and therefore the UNESCO Institute, the Sozialforschungsstelle Dortmund, and the Darmstadt group ceased to exist.

Empirical social research at that time was largely understood to be an import from the United States. At the UNESCO Institute in Cologne and in Darmstadt, important community studies inspired by American studies of the 1930s and 1940s were carried out. The reports by Renate Mayntz and Erich Reigrotzki are still very much worth reading. Parallel to this, survey research was developed as a commercial service; here, too, the American standards of the time were immediately imported. Of great influence were the survey units that the American and British governments had begun as their troops moved into Germany. It was in these survey units that the core personnel of the later German institutes learned their techniques (Scheuch 1990b).

The 1950s were characterized by a coexistence of professors who had learned sociology largely on their own before 1945 and a larger number of sociologists born between 1926 and 1930 who were virtually identical in skill and outlook with their American contemporaries. For this generation Weimar sociology was forgotten, and the classics were read with an American selectivity and perspective.

By the end of the 1950s sociology—in terms of chairs, curricula, students, and volume of empirical research—had surpassed the level of 1933. Much against the wishes of von Wiese and

Horkheimer, the German Sociological Association had been transformed from an elitist academy into a professional association with increasingly important sections or research committees in which the Young Turks were able to attract followers. The sections for industrial sociology (for the more theoretically minded) and for methodology (for the mainly empirically oriented) offered an alternative to the plenary meetings that were still dominated by professors who were the last academic mandarins of German tradition. In research nearly everyone who later influenced the discipline worked on social stratification, which as a central topic succeeded the community studies of the first half of the 1950s. Among the Young Turks and their following a structural functional approach was the common paradigm, and Talcott Parsons was held to be the great theorist of the time.

Sociology was a deeply divided discipline. One dividing line pitted those who had emigrated against sociologists who had supported the Nazi regime. Hans Freyer, Arnold Gehlen, and Helmut Schelsky were accused of collaborating with the regime; Gunter Ipsen did more than that; and Karl-Heinz Pfeffer and Karl Valentin Müller were justly denounced as racists. In 1960 the German Sociological Association nearly split along the dividing line between collaborators with the Nazi regime and the majority led by former immigrants.

However, it was not possible simply to dismiss Gehlen and Schelsky as former Nazi sympathizers. While they had been exactly that, they now did important scholarly work. Gehlen developed an anthropology that included perhaps the best approach to the analysis of social institutions, and Schelsky had initiated many important studies on youth, the family, and social stratification. The two men published a textbook in sociology that saw four editions within three years (Gehlen and Schelsky 1955).

The second dividing line ran between the Frankfurt Institute and all others. Horkheimer, Adorno, and Pollack had been successful in the United States, the home of modern sociology. By now their Marxism had toned down to a variant of left Hegelianism that they christened "critical theory." Initially a political camouflage, it now characterized the retained commitment to cultural criticism of bourgeois society. The combination of

Marxism with cultural criticism proved to be a winning message with the cultural establishment.

The opposition to Schelsky/Gehlen and Adorno/Horkheimer crystallized around René König, whom von Wiese had invited to Cologne. Originally a pure humanist—he wrote what is considered the standard monograph on Niccolo Machiavelli (1941)—in exile he had identified with the post-Durkheim school in France. Upon returning to Germany in 1950, he recognized the need to familiarize the young generation of sociologists and sociology students with mainstream American sociology. Although himself not a quantitatively minded scholar, he encouraged quantitative social research as an antidote to the temptations of speculative grand theory. Knowing his personal preference for cultural anthropology and French culture, it is ironic that he was the key figure in thoroughly Americanizing the larger part of an academic generation in sociology.

König's *Soziologie heute* (Sociology Today, 1949), a sociological rendering of existentialist philosophy, was the first postwar best-seller in sociology. The dictionary of sociology that he edited (1958) brought together most of the Young Turks and became the largest selling sociology book ever in Germany, with more than twenty editions and almost half a million copies. Most important for the profession, however, was the two-volume handbook of empirical social research (1962) that he edited, conceived along the lines of Gardner-Lindzey's *Handbook of Social Psychology* (König 1962). The handbook is still a standard for empirical sociology and has gone through several editions. All of these works were translated into English, French, Spanish, and Italian, and some into Japanese as well.

The different positions in the first phase of sociology after 1945 were sorted into three "schools" that were to constitute sociology in Germany: the Frankfurt School, the Cologne School, and the Schelsky school. Within the discipline the Cologne school set standards for curricula and research, the *Kölner Zeitschrift* being stronger than the Dortmund-based *Soziale Welt*. The readers of these two largest social science journals do not overlap much. *Kölner Zeitschrift* is the journal for the discipline, while *Soziale Welt* is for practitioners of social science in bureaucracies and the helping professions. Thus, the publics of the three "schools"

were different and have remained so: the Frankfurt school for the cultural intelligentsia; the Cologne school for social scientists; the Schelsky school for practical applications in welfare and bureaucracy. It was largely the pressure from the respective audiences more than the preferences of the professors that for a long time caused sociology in Germany to be divided into these three camps.

THE TIME OF EXPANSION

The second most formative decade was the 1960s. It marked a return to important subjects of the classics and to some authors of that time. The Americanization of the discipline had peaked.

After the vituperous quarrels in the Deutsche Gesellschaft in the 1950s it was agreed to meet in closed session at Tübingen in 1961, to discuss basis issues in a purely scholarly atmosphere. Unexpectedly this led to a controversy between two radically different views of social science, the chief protagonists of which were Theodor W. Adorno and Karl Popper (Adorno 1962), between science as a vehicle for emancipation and a scientific view of science. Popper's work is in the philosophy of science rather conventional sociology. For Adorno empiricism means supremacy of instrumental reasoning, which subjugates reason to the rule of facts; empiricism is tantamount to "treating facts as fetishes" (Adorno 1969, p. 14). This dispute was continued by two nonsociologists—the economist Hans Albert and the philosopher Jürgen Habermas—as the "positivism controversy," Habermas representing the Frankfurt school of critical theory and Albert the Cologne school of neopositivism (Adorno 1975). This was a revival of the methodological controversies in the Verein für Socialpolitik in the decade prior to 1914.

The controversy between Habermas and Albert occurred during the 1964 sociology convention that was dedicated to the rediscovery of Max Weber. The topic that sent shock waves throughout the cultural establishment (Stammer 1965) was the revival of the debate on value judgments as part of science. The "radical" sociologists who began to appear at this time took as their central argument the charge that positivism was blind to the forces its research served.

The repercussions were much larger: the arguments of critical theory against positivism became a credo among the cultural intelligentsia. It is important for an understanding of sociology in Germany that this old controversy did not spring from developments within the discipline; rather, it became an unavoidable topic because the intellectual environment forced it onto sociology.

Meanwhile, a seeming alternative to the Cologne and Frankfurt Schools, though closely related to the latter in its concerns, became the major intellectual success: Ralf Dahrendorf with his *Gesellschaft und Demokratie in Deutschland* (1965). How was the Nazi regime possible? Could it reappear in a different guise? This topic keeps emerging in Germany as a central focus in intellectual attempts at self-analysis. In the 1980s the intellectual public expected answers from a controversy among historians; in the 1960s the expectations were focused on sociology and Dahrendorf.

Dahrendorf, trained as a philosopher, is a self-taught sociologist. By temperament he is a moralist, as is evident in his dissertation exploring the idea of justice in Marx's thought (1954). He was subsequently among the Young Turks who concentrated on industrial sociology, and published an immensely successful book on the subject (Dahrendorf 1956) that overshadowed a more original monograph by Heinrich Popitz, Hans Paul Bahrdt, Ernst-August Jüres and Hanno Kesting (1957) that is yet to be recognized internationally as a classic. Among younger sociologists Dahrendorf became a central focus of controversy as a result of his long essay on role theory, in which he characterizes modern society as a cage of obligations that prevent individuality from asserting itself (Dahrendorf 1959b). While the profession largely rejected this notion as a misperception of role theory and economics, the book *Homo Sociologicus* remained for decades the most popular sociological treatise among students (Dahrendorf, 1959b). An essay on chances for complete social equality was Dahrendorf's contribution to the topic of social stratification (Dahrendorf 1961), then dominant among the Young Turks. A much more important publication for an understanding of his concerns is his treatment of the United States as the one case where presumably there was an attempt to construct a society in the spirit of the French Enlightenment (Dahrendorf 1963). Characteristically, Dahrendorf takes as his point of departure a source of general intellectual importance, in this case Alexis de Tocqueville's report on the United States in the 1830s.

As Adorno had introduced the concerns of the cultural public into the profession, so Dahrendorf did the same for the intelligentsia concerned with public affairs. In the English-speaking world he is often included in sociological curricula as a conflict theoretician, but there is no conflict theory in his writings, except for an attempt at a taxonomy of conflicts. The label *conflict theoretician* was affixed because of his criticism of Talcott Parsons, whose structural functionalism he accused of glorifying social harmony. Dahrendorf's central theme is to explore the chances for the values of British liberalism to become the guiding principle in society. In practical life this orientation met with mixed success.

In the 1970s Dahrendorf returned to England to become the first foreign president of the London School of Economics. He later became a professor at Oxford and remains a respected commentator on public affairs with a continuing interest in sociology as an intellectual endeavor. Although frequently in error in his statements that have empirical content, he is invariably sensitive in choosing topics that relate the discipline to an intellectual public.

The mood of the times was moving away from the liberal creed of Dahrendorf. The controversies in the United States, stimulated by the Vietnam intervention, were taken up by politicized students in Germany. Marxism was believed to provide answers that the liberal promise of the postwar Western world apparently could not. The varieties of Marxism were studied with religious fervor.

At the 1968 convention of the German Sociological Association demands for an alternative to mainstream sociology, especially the "Cologne Americanism," exploded. Adorno had chosen as the congress's theme, "Late Capitalism or Industrial Society"—alternative ways of conceptualizing the same reality. The term "late capitalism" was favored by Neo-marxists as implying that the demise of bourgeois society was imminent. It also implied that the notion of a basic sameness of all industrial societies—that the United States and the Soviet Union were structurally related as industrial socieites—was wrong. The Neo-Marxist conceptualization "late capitalism" and, by contrast, critical theory implied that the social orders of the Soviet Union and the United States were dedicated to a different telos, and that this difference was what mattered most (Adorno 1969).

With the May 1968 uprising in Paris, the student movement in Germany turned into a crusade for leftism as the mandatory creed on campus, and specifically for sociologists. For a moment the adherents of the Frankfurt school could see the student movement as the realization of their hopes. Max Horkheimer had always rejected any methodological constraints on philosophizing, and on any scholarship. Methodology would restrict science to the factual, while for Horkheimer, Adorno, and Bloch the prime goal of scholarship was creative utopianism. According to Horkheimer, it was now up to science to provide the answers given earlier by religion (Horkheimer 1968). The student movement, however, accused the Frankfurt school of running away from reality, and critical theory of having only negative messages and no direction for positive action. Adorno had always maintained this view (Adorno 1969). Deposing a ruling class would not change the basic character of relations that were permeated with instrumental reasoning; there was no longer a revolutionary subject to realize the cause of emancipation. After some very ugly clashes, Adorno died in 1969. Dahrendorf turned against the student movement, as did such well-known sociologists as Helmut Schelsky and Helmut Schoeck. Erwin Scheuch's *Anabaptists of the "Affluent Society"* (1968) became a best-seller. Even Habermas, irritated by the uncompromising nature of the New Left, severed his connection by diagnosing its "left fascism" (Habermas 1969).

In the turbulent years that followed 1968, sociologists were more concerned with reacting to the New Left than with developments of their own. Sociology had been utterly surprised by a student movement that it neither predicted nor understood. Rainer Lepsius contrasts this situation with the immediate success of empirical sociology in analyzing the right-wing protest NPD party (National-Demokratische Partei Deutschlands) of the late 1960s (Lepsius 1976, p. 7).

The public, however, identified sociology with the New Left. An explosion of leftist literature, using sociological terminology, buried the output of sociologists. The public image of sociology became one of a haven for radicals opposed to bourgeois society. For about ten years after 1968,

sociology became the quarry for cultural discourse. Academic fields that were based on shared beliefs in civil society and cultural values—such as pedagogy, art appreciation, literary criticism, and political education—had their criteria damaged, even destroyed. Sociology was used to provide an alternative rationale: service to the cause of emancipation from bourgeois society. Tenbruck (1984) has charged that sociology had "colonized" the humanities, and even life in general. It actually was the other way around: as the humanities lost their belief in civil society, they raided sociology for arguments in the name of society. Professional sociology completely lost control over the use of its vocabulary—with disastrous results for the self-selection of students of sociology and the standing of the field in the world of scholarship.

The student protest movement, and various alternative cultures loosely associated with it, became a regular part of public life in Germany, as it had in the United States. It became fashionable to call a great number of protest forms *sociology* while denouncing the profession carrying out "normal science" (Kuhn 1970) as "bourgeois" sociology. Sociologists were asked to react to fashionable topics of the day, such as permissive education, Third World dependency, mind-expanding drugs, feminism, gay power, autonomous living. Many of the newly appointed professors went along, contributing to the erroneous public impression that sociology was spearheading the cultural revolution in the name of anticapitalism. The opposite was true: sociologists often caved in to demands from the protest movements.

Even in a less turbulent intellectual environment, the period between 1968 and 1973 would have been most unsettling, because it was a period of unique expansion. By the mid-1960s social democratic state governments had been convinced by proponents of the Frankfurt school that sociology should be included in the curricula of secondary education. The profession was divided on this, and as late as 1959 Dahrendorf counseled against the inclusion of sociology in degree curricula even at universities. With the youth, however, sociology was a huge success; many teachers were needed, and that meant many more professors. In 1968 there were fifty-five tenured positions as professor of sociology in the Federal Republic of Germany; in 1973 there were 190 (Lamnek 1991). From that year, the rate of expansion levelled, and by 1980 there were 252 "chairs" (Sahner 1982, p. 79).

Lepsius modified this feeling of an avalanche of sociology overwhelming academe (Lepsius 1976, p. 12). At the beginning of the 1970s, sociology had 1.3 percent of all the positions in university budgets, no larger a share than ten years earlier; 1.2 percent of the students took a major in sociology, also the percentage before the expansion; public money for sociological research had always hovered around 1 to 2 percent of all grants. The universities had expanded with explosive rapidity, and in this general explosion sociology merely kept its former share.

As a discipline, sociology, however, was among those least prepared to keep its place during an expansion that within a few years quadrupled the number of students in the Federal Republic. Consequently a great many sociologists were appointed to tenured positions who in other times would not have been. In this process the discipline lost cohesion and common scholarly standards.

THE CONSOLIDATION

After 1968 the Deutsche Gesellschaft für Soziologie was taken over by the Young Turks; from their ranks Dahrendorf, Scheuch, and Lepsius were successively president. The leadership of the association was tired of conventions serving as forums for all kinds of protests, thus further damaging the reputation of the field. Consequently, biannual sociological conventions were suspended until 1974, when a meeting was held in Kassel. While the field had a Babel of views, there was now agreement to coexist.

At the Kassel convention of 1974, a custom was started called *Theorievergleich* (comparison of theory). This is in reality a juxtaposition of sociological "denominations," not a weighing of alternative theoretical propositions (Lepsius 1976, sec. II). At that time four such denominations were defined: (a) behaviorism, the chief proponent of which in Germany was Karl-Dieter Opp; (b) action theory as represented by Hans-Joachim Hummel; (c) functionalism and systems theory, with Niklas Luhman as its prominent representative; and (d) historical materialism, which translates into Marxism. Somewhat later, parts of behaviorism and action theory amalgamated to

become rational choice; two German-speaking Dutch sociologists, Reinhard Wippler and Siegwart Lindenberg, are its best-known proponents. Phenomenological sociology has been successful especially among young sociologists, with Jürgen Helle as the chief representative.

The lines between these denominations keep shifting as new variants emerge. In general, though, this approach to theory—to choose a topic such as evolution and then listen to what each denomination has to say about it—appears to have spent itself.

Concern with theory in Germany again means reacting to theory builders, a most dissimilar pair of whom dominated the scene in the 1970s and early 1980s: Jürgen Habermas and Niklas Luhmann. Luhmann is a self-taught sociologist who studied law and became a career administrator. His first specialty was the sociology of organization, which showed a strong influence of Chester I. Barnard. Subsequently Luhmann analyzed phenomena of the *Lebenswelt* (the key term of phenomenology for the world of immediate, unreflected experience—in contrast to the world that science portrayed) at that time influenced by the phenomenologist Edmund Husserl, as in Luhmann's monograph on trust as the basis for social cohesion. Luhmann later met Talcott Parsons, whose work he understood from the perspective of a systems theorist. From then on, he focused on pure theory, going so far as to reject the application of theoretical statements to the empirical world, declaring empirical evidence to be irrelevant for his theorizing (Luhmann 1987). Since Luhmann writes prolifically in English, his views should be well known outside Germany.

It will be helpful to note his shift in emphasis over the years. The central notion was first functional differentiation as the guiding principle in evolution. This results in an increasing competence of the system if the functionally differentiated areas are allowed to develop their area-specific rationality (*Eigenlogik*). The economy is seen as a prime example of an *Eigendynamik*, provided it is not shackled by attempts at political or ethical guidance. Differentiated systems, according to Luhman, need constant feedback to permit a creative reaction. Luhman conceptualizes these feedbacks as *selbstreferenzielle Prozesse* (self-referential processes). More recently he has become interested in chaos theory and has given self-organization—which he calls *Autopoiesis*—a central place in explaining system functioning. It appears that the interest in Luhman has increased as his writings have become more abstract and his terms more outlandish—something he does self-consciously, since he can be a lucid writer.

This is less true for Jürgen Habermas, a philosopher who is self-taught in sociology. He calls his approach *critical sociology*, a choice that expresses his initial indebtedness to left Hegelianism of the Frankfurt school. While he has included Marxist terminology in his writings, he is probably best understood as a sociological disciple of the idealistic philosopher Fichte. In this perspective society is a problem for man's true calling: emancipation. He understands emancipation in the spirit of the French Enlightenment. The characteristic element of Habermas's "critical sociology" is *doppelte Reflexivität* (double feedback): the sociologist reflects on the context of discovery, and again on the context of utilization of his findings. With this attitude Habermas approaches the problematic relationship between theory and praxis (a Hegelian variant of practice) at a time when human existence is determined by a technological *Eigendynamik*. Habermas's writings, available in translation, are internationally known. Viewed over a period of around thirty years, it seems that he is sliding into a position of Great Cultural Theory, of the kind like Pitirim Sorokin's. And in becoming a synthesizer, he becomes more empirically minded, as Luhman ascends into the more abstract.

SOCIOLOGY AS "NORMAL SCIENCE"

While practically all German universities offer degrees in sociology up to the doctoral level, there are some centers in terms of number of students, research facilities, and number of teaching personnel. In terms of faculty size, these centers are Bielefeld, Berlin, and Frankfurt, Munich, Cologne, and Mannheim. If one includes among the criteria the number of degrees granted, then Bochum, Hamburg, and Göttingen must be added as centers.

There is now a very developed infrastructure for empirical research. In addition to many public service research institutes both inside and outside universities, there are some 165 commercial institutes for market and social research, the largest employing 600 academics and having a business volume of 90 million dollars. There is an academic network of three service institutions with a yearly volume of ten million dollars from the budgets of state and federal governments: the Informationszentrum, in Bonn, providing on-line information on research projects and literature abstracts; ZUMA, Zentrum für Umfragen, Methoden und Analysen, in Mannheim, doing some of the work of NORC, National Opinion Research Center, Chicago, and helping anyone in need of methodological support; and the Zentralarchiv in Cologne, which provides data for secondary analysis, as the Roper Center in the United States does. All three together form GESIS, Gesellschaft sozialwissenscaftliche Infrastruktureinrichtungen, Bonn, a package that can be used by the mostly small research institutes of German universities. There are also larger institutes, the biggest in terms of number of academics employed being the Deutsche Jugendinstitut (German Youth Institute) and the largest in terms of finance (eleven million dollars) being the Wissenschaftszentrum Berlin (Social Science Center in Berlin). All have regular budgets from tax money.

There is a yearly survey on work in progress, and between 1978 and 1988, 29,000 research projects were reported. The Zentralarchivs keeps a count on quantitative research, and limiting its attention only to such work where data are in machine readable format, the yearly academic production in quantitative research is around 900 projects. The preferred method is the personal interview, which during the years had a share of 50 percent for all projects where quantitative data were collected. The doorstep interview is being replaced by the telephone interview, although to a lesser extent than in the United States.

Among the more than 1,000 members of the German Sociological Association the attention given to applied fields is dominant. A content analysis of journal articles shows that only 15.4 percent of all published manuscripts—the rejection rate is around 80 percent of all articles submitted—deal with theory. The most important applied fields are (in order of frequency) industrial sociology, social psychology, methods of quantitative research, sociology of politics, and sociology of the family. All these have shares in publications above five percent. Twenty other fields of sociology contribute altogether 50 percent to journal publications (Sahner 1982).

Heinz Sahner's (1991) content analysis of the theoretical paradigms used in journal articles between 1970 and 1987 found the expected correlation with the intellectual climate. Marxism declined rapidly from the late 1970s, and it never dominated in German professional journals. Structural functional sociology is still the single most important theoretical paradigm, with phenomenological approaches gaining steadily. Even more so than earlier, sociology in Germany is now a multiparadigm field, including as a prominent part, "German Sociology."

REFERENCES

Abel, Theodore 1929 *Systematic Sociology in Germany.* PhD diss. Columbia University, New York.

Adair-Toteff, Christopher 1994 "Kant's Philosophical Influence on Classical German Sociology: Simmel's 'Exkurs uber das Problem: Wie ist Gesellschaft moglich?'." *Simmel Newsletter* 4:308.

Adorno, Theodor W. 1962 "Zur Logik der Sozialwissenschaften." *Kölner Zeitschrift für Soziologie und Sozialpsychologie* 14:249–263.

—— 1975 *Der Positivismusstreit in der deutschen Soziologie,* 4th ed. Neuwied: Luchterband.

——, (ed.) 1969 *Spätkapitalismus oder Industriegesellschaft. Verhandlungen des 16. Deutschen Soziologentages.* Stuttgart: Entee.

Alemann, Heine von 1978 "Geschichte und Arbeitsweise des Forschungsinstituts für Sozialwissenschaften in Köln." In Erwin K. Scheuch and Heine von Alemann, eds., *Das Forschungsinstitut.* Erlangen: Universität, Institut für Gesellschaft und Wissenschaft.

Aron, Raymond 1935 *La sociologie allemande contemporaine.* Paris: pr. univer. de France. Translated into English as *German Sociology.* New York, 1964.

Barnes, Harry E., and Howard Becker 1938 *Social Thought from Love to Science,* vol. 2. New York: D. C. Heath.

Bernhard Schafers 1995 *Soziologie in Deuthschland. Entwicklung, Instituionalisierung und Berufsfeder. Theorietische Kontroversen (Sociology in Germany. Development, Institutionalization and Professional Fields. Theoretical Controversies).* Oplanden, Germany: Leske and Budrich.

Best, Heinrich and Renate Ohly 1994 "From Paradigms to Eclecticism: Thematic Profiles of German Language Core Sociology Journals 1984–1991." *BMS, Bulletin de Methodologie Sociologique* 42:95–113.

Coser, Lewis A. 1977 *Masters of Sociological Thought,* 2nd ed. New York: Harcourt Brace Jovanovich.

Dahrendorf, Ralf 1954 *Marx in Perspektive.* Hannover: Dietz.

—— 1956 *Industrie- und Betriebssoziologie.* Berlin: De Gruyter.

—— 1959a "Betrachtungen zu einigen Aspekten der gegenwärtigen deutschen Soziologie." *Kölner Zeitschrift für Soziologie und Sozialpsychologie* 11:132–153.

—— 1959b *Homo sociologicus.* Opladen: Westdeutscher Verlag.

—— 1961 *Über den Ursprung der Ungleichheit unter den Menschen.* Tübingen: Mohr.

—— 1963 *Die angewandte Aufklärung.* Munich: Piper.

—— 1965 *Gesellschaft und Demokratie in Deutschland.* Munich: Piper.

Durkheim, Emile 1887 "La philosophie dans les universités allemandes." In *Revue internationale de l'enseignement,* Bd. 13.

Eisenstadt, Shmuel Noah, and Miriam Curelaru 1976 *The Form of Sociology.* New York: Wiley.

Fletcher, Ronald 1971 *The Making of Sociology,* 2 vols. London: Nelson.

Freund, Julien 1978 "German Sociology in the Time of Max Weber." In Tom Bottomore and Robert Nisbet, eds., *A History of Sociological Analysis.* New York: Basic Books.

Gehlen, Arnold, and Helmut Schelsky 1955 *Sociologie: Ein Lehr- und Handbuch.* Düsseldorf Köln: Diederich Verlag.

Gephardt, Werner 1982 "Soziologie im Aufbruch." *Kölner Zeitschrift für Soziologie und Sozialpsychologie* 34:1–24.

Gumplowitcz, Ludwig 1883 *Der Rassenkampf: Sociologische Untersuchungen.* Innsbruck: Wagner.

Habermas, Jürgen 1969 *Protestbewegung und Hochschulreform.* Frankfurt a.M.: Suhrkamp.

——, and William Regh 1996 *Between Facts and Norms: Contributions to a Discourse Theory of Law and Democracy.* Cambridge, Mass.: MIT Press.

Hagemann-White, Carol 1997 "Current Debates in German Social Science." *Contemporary Sociology* 26:556–559.

Hartmann, Jurgen 1992 "Portrait. In Memoriam Rene Konig (1905–1992)." *International Sociology* 7:481–483.

Holub, Robert C. 1991 *Jurgen Habermas: Critic in the Public Sphere.* New York: Routledge.

Horkheimer, Max 1968 *Kritische Theorie.* In Alfred Schmidt, ed., *Eine Dokumentation.* Frankfurt: S. Fischer. a.M.

Hradil, Stefan 1993 "New German Social Structure Analysis." *Schweizerische Zeitschrift fur Soziologie / Revue Suisse de sociologie* 19:663–688.

Jay, Martin 1973 *The Dialectical Imagination*. London: Heinemann.

Käsler, Dirk 1984 *Die frühe deutsche Soziologie 1909–1934*. Opladen: Westdeutscher Verlag.

—— 1985 *Soziologische Abenteuer*. Opladen: Westdeutscher Verlag.

Kettler, David, and Volker Meja 1994 "That Typically German Kind of Sociology which Verges towards Philosophy: The Dispute about Ideology and Utopia in the United States." *Sociological Theory* 12:279–303.

King, Michael, and Anton Schutz 1994 "The Ambitious Modesty of Niklas Luhmann." *Journal of Law and Society* 21:261–287.

König, René 1941 *Niccolo Machiavelli: Zur Krisenanalyse einer Zeitenwende*. Erlenbach-Zürich: Rentsch.

—— 1949 *Soziologie heute*. Zürich: Regio-Verlag.

—— 1958 *Soziologie*. Frankfurt: Fischer.

—— 1962 *Handbuch der empirischen Socialforschung*. Stuttgart: Enke.

—— 1987 *Soziologie in Deutschland*. Munich: Hauser-Verlag.

—— (ed.) 1978 *Soziologie*, 11th ed. Frankfurt: Fischer.

Kuhn, Thomas Samuel 1970 *The Structure of Scientific Revolutions*. Chicago: University of Chicago Press.

Lamnek, Siegfried 1991 "Gesellschaftliche Interessen und Geschichte der Ausbildung." In Harald Kerber, and Arnold Schmieder, eds., *Soziologie Theorien, Arbeitsfelder, Ausbildung: Ein Grundkurs*. Reinbek and Hamburg: Rowolt.

Lepenies, Wolfgang (ed.) 1981 *Geschichte der Soziologie*, 4 vols. Frankfurt: Suhrkamp.

Lepsius, Mario Rainer (ed.) 1976 *Zwischenbilanz der Soziologie*. Stuttgart: Enke.

—— 1987 "Sociology in the Interwar Period." In Volker Meja, Dieter Misgeld, and Nico Stehr, eds., *Modern German Sociology*. New York: Columbia University Press.

Luhmann, Niklas 1987 "Soziologische Aufklärung." In vol. 4, *Beiträge zur funktionalen Differenzierung der Gesellschaft*. Opladen: Westdeutscher Verlag.

—— 1995 *Social Systems*. Translated by John Bednarz, Jr., with Dick Baecker. Stanford, Calif.: Stanford University Press.

Meja, Volker, Dieter Misgeld, and Nico Stehl (eds.) 1987 *Modern German Sociology*. New York: Publisher.

Muller, Hans-Peter 1992 "German Sociology at the Beginning of the 90s." Schweizerische Zeitschrift fur Soziologie / Revue Suisse de sociologie 18:751–762.

—— 1995 "Fateful Encounter? German Sociology Meets Culture." Schweizerische Zeitschrift fur Soziologie / Revue Suisse de sociologie 21:189–198.

Muller, Harro 1994 "Luhmann's Systems Theory as a Theory of Modernity." *New German Critique* 61:39–54.

Nisbet, Robert A. 1966 *The Sociological Tradition*. London: Heinemann.

Oberschall, Anthony 1965 *Empirical Social Research in Germany, 1848–1914*. Paris: Mouton.

—— 1972 *The Establishment of Empirical Sociology*. New York: Harper and Row.

Paterson, John 1997 "An Introduction to Luhmann." *Theory, Culture and Society* 14:37–39.

Popitz, Heinrich, et al. 1957 *Das Gesellschaftsbild des Arbeiters*. Tübingen: Mohr.

Ratzenhofer, Gustav 1893 *Wesen und Zweck der Politik*. Leipzig: F. A. Brockhaus.

Sahner, Heinz 1982 *Theorie und Forschung*. Opladen: Westdeutscher Verlag.

—— 1991 "Paradigms Gained—Paradigms Lost: Die Entwicklung der Nachkriegssoziologie im Spiegel der Fachzeitschriften." In *Soziale Welt*, Index for vols. 1–40.

Salomon, Albert 1945 "German Sociology." In Georges Gurvitch and Wilbert E. Moore, eds., *Twentieth Century Sociology*. New York: Basic Books.

Salter, Michael 1997 "Habermas's New Contribution to Legal Scholarship." *Journal of Law and Society* 24:285–305.

Schad, Susanna Petra 1972 *Empirical Social Research in Weimar Germany*. Paris: Mouton.

Schäffle, Albert 1885 *Gesammelte Aufsätze*. Tubingen: J. C. B. Mohr.

Scheuch, Erwin K. 1968 *Anabaptists of the "Affluent Society."*

—— 1990a "Von der deutschen Soziologie zur Soziologie in Deutschland." Österreichische Zeitschrift für Soziologie 15:30–50.

—— 1990b "Von der Pioniertät zur Institution." In Dieter Franke and Joachim Scharioth, eds., *40 Jahre Markt- und Sozialforschung in der Bundesrepublik Deutschland*. Munich: Oldenbourg Verlag.

Simmel, Georg 1890 *Über Soziale Differenzierung: Soziologie und psychologie Untersuchungen*. Leipzig: Duncker and Humblod.

Stammer, Otto (ed.) 1965 *Max Weber und die Soziologie heute: Verhandlungen des 15. Deutschen Sociologentages*. Tübingen: Mohr.

Tenbruck, Friedrich H. 1984 *Die unbewältigten Sozialwissenschaften oder die Abschaffung des Menschen*. Graz: Styria.

Tönnies, Ferdinand (1887) 1912 *Gemeinschaft und Gesellschaft*. 2nd ed. Berlin: Carl Curtius.

Vanberg, Viktor 1975 *Die Zwei Soziologien: Individualismus und Kollektivismus in der Sozialtheorie*.

Vierkandt, Alfred 1931 *Handwörterbuch der Soziologie*. Stuttgart: Entze.

Wagner, Gerhard 1997 "The End of Luhmann's Social Systems Theory." *Philosophy of the Social Sciences* 27:387–409.

Wiese, Leopold von 1926 *Soziologie: Geschichte und Hauptprobleme*. Berlin: de Gruyter.

—— 1959a "Die Deutsche Gesellschaft für Soziologie." *Kölner Zeitschrift für Soziologie und Sozialpsychologie* 11:11–20.

—— 1959b "Deutsche Gesellschaft für Soziologie." In *Handwörterbuch für Sozialwissenschaften*, vol. 2. Stuttgart: Fischer.

Zeitlin, Irving M. 1981 *Ideology and the Development of Sociological Theory*, 2nd ed. Englewood Cliffs, N.J.: Prentice-Hall.

ERWIN K. SCHEUCH

GLOBAL SYSTEMS ANALYSIS

See Globalization and Global Systems Analysis.

GLOBALIZATION AND GLOBAL SYSTEMS ANALYSIS

Since the early 1960s, mounting empirical pressure has forced sociology to abandon the assumption that national societies could be understood without looking beyond their borders. The nation-state remains a crucial unit of analysis, but it must be analyzed as intertwined with the operations of a larger global social system. Global flows of culture, technology, people, goods, and capital determines to an ever larger degree how societies change at the national level. The dynamics of transnational social, economic and political structures have become a focus of study in their own right.

The value of international trade has grown more rapidly than the value of goods and services produced and sold within national boundaries. Manufacturing means assembly of components from around the globe. Electronic youth culture in the United States revolves around Japanese cartoon characters, while a generation of Third World television viewers take their cultural cues from North American TV serials. Capital markets operate around the globe and around the clock as trading moves from Tokyo to London to New York over the course of each day. Sociologists cannot yet claim to understand the working of this global system, but a number of fruitful avenues of analysis have emerged since about 1960.

The approaches favored by sociologists have differed from the study of "international relations" as it has been traditionally defined. International relations approaches have seen the global system as structured primarily by interactions in which nations are unitary actors (see Waltz 1979). The global system is presumed to be structured largely by the distribution of national power among the advanced nations. Sociologists, on the other hand, have been very interested in how the global system is structured by flows of resources, people, ideas, and attitudes across geographic boundaries, flows that often occur without, or even in spite of, national actors.

Within sociology itself, "globalization" has been transformed from a relatively narrow field of study, largely within the political economy of development, to a central theme across a wide range of subfields within the discipline. The topic of globalization has also often drawn sociologists into interdisciplinary debates with political scientists, anthropologists, geographers, and even occasionally economists, among others. As recently as the late 1980s, a number of central approaches to global systems analysis could be identified—Marxism, modernization theory, dependency theory, and world-system theory. However, although these research traditions continue to be elaborated, studies of globalization have proliferated and research perspectives have become fragmented. This article reviews the early and continuing contributions of these perspectives and outlines the main themes that current global systems analyses are exploring.

MARXISM AND MODERNIZATION THEORY

In the years after World War II, Marxism and modernization theory debated vigorously the problems and consequences of capitalist development.

However, despite their ideological opposition, they shared some basic assumptions regarding the character of this development. In particular, they shared the assumption that the global system is dominated by processes of diffusion. In the words of the *Communist Manifesto*, the expansive character of capitalist production "draws all, even the most barbarian, nations into civilization." Warren (1980) argues from a Marxist perspective that it is only by the expansion of economic ties to core countries, principally in the form of importing more foreign capital, that poor nations are likely to be able to reduce the gap that separates them from rich nations. Sklair (1991) argues that a world-system organized through nation states is being superseded by a "global system" dominated by transnational economic, political, and social structures. He points to the emergence of a transnational capitalist class that organizes the world economy to its own benefit, in contrast to the world systems view of contending national capitalist classes (for an empirical study, see Bottomore and Brym 1989). Robinson (1998) argues that sociology must move beyond nation–state based analytical approaches to make "transnational social structure" its proper object of study, since individuals are predominantly defined by their position in such transnational economic, political, and cultural structures rather than by national or local characteristics—transnational structures dominated by capital. Other Marxist-oriented theorists emphasize the irrationality of capitalist competition on a global scale, since competition between national capitalisms creates a crisis of profitability for capital due to global overcapacity, which in turn leads to declining conditions for labor (R. Brenner 1998; Walker 1999). Nonetheless, the emphasis remains the dilemmas of the diffusion of capitalism—the fact of that diffusion is presumed.

Investigating the prevalence of that complex of ideas and attitudes associated with "modernity" provided an important impetus for modernization theorists to take a global look at the diffusion of culture and social structures. In a classic study, Inkeles and Smith (1974) analyzed the attitudes of citizens in six Third World countries spread around the globe. Modern attitudes were found in social contexts more characteristic of advanced industrial countries. The more time respondents had spent living in cities or working in factories, the more their attitudes resembled those associated with the culture of advanced industrial countries. The findings suggested a global system structured largely by processes of diffusion. The implicit model was one of gradual convergence around a similar set of "modern" values and attitudes. The spread of modern social institutions helps inculcate the values and attitudes, and the values and attitudes reinforce the institutions.

The work of Meyer and associates (Meyer 1980; Meyer et al. 1997a) shows how ideas and institutions originating in the advanced industrial countries become embodied in a global culture, which in turn shapes local institutions in all countries. Beginning from the surprising homogeneity of national political and economic institutional forms around the world, Meyer and associates (1997a) argue that contemporary actors, including nation-states, organize and legitimate themselves in terms of highly rationalistic, universalistic, world-cultural models. These models largely conform to the prescriptions of modernization theory, with core values such as citizenship, rationality, socioeconomic development, and so on. These models are diffused through the world system largely through the organizations and associations of "world society"—intergovernmental and nongovernmental transnational organizations which act to promote a "shared modernity" rooted in scientific rationalism and in which scientists and professionals are particularly dominant (Boli and Thomas 1999; Meyer et al. 1997a). Nation-states are not destroyed by globalization but, in contrast, the nation-state cultural form is diffused around the world through the institutions of world society.

An extensive body of empirical work has been developed in support of these theoretical insights. Boli-Bennett (1979), for example, examines the way in which national constitutions reflect global legal norms rather than local conditions. Ramirez and Boli (1982) look at the ways in which schools take on similar shapes around the globe as conceptions of what constitutes an effective educational institution come to be shared with surprising speed across geographical boundaries. Meyer and associates (1992) argue that world-society connections diffused mass education to former colonies, rather than education systems developing simply as a function of level of economic development. Meyer and associates (1997b) examine how a world environmental regime emerged in recent decades through world-society associational processes, facilitated by the statelessness of this world society.

The interaction of these world-cultural forms with local contexts is unclear, however, as Meyer and associates (1997a) argue that there may be significant "decoupling" of these symbolic forms from the social practices in each contexts. Escobar (1995) argues that development discourses have relied exclusively on Western knowledge systems to the extent that non-Western knowledge systems are inherently marginalized by these "modernization" discourses. Ferguson (1990) shows that in Lesotho, the effect of modernization-inspired development policies was not to produce development but to depoliticize poverty and the further entrenchment of the state and Western modernizing influences. Other empirical work suggests that there are in fact a number of contesting models of the global economy, implying a more conflictual process than that depicted by Meyer and associates (Wade 1998).

Other social theorists take a more critical view of modernization while still placing the condition of modernity at the center of their analyses. Beck and associates (1994) have argued that advanced industrial societies are undergoing a new "reflexive modernization" that is closely tied to globalization. These authors see modernization bringing increased control over nature and society, as orthodox modernization theory predicts, but further rounds of modernization generating problems based precisely on its own success. The advance of rationalism and scientism remains central to their theories, but they are more skeptical about the ability of the experts to anticipate or control the side effects of their innovations. Pollution and other ecological disasters are critical political issues but also examples of how technical and social change can result in unanticipated system-level crises.

Giddens (1991) argues that modernity is inherently globalizing. Both are linked by the process of "disembedding"—the lifting out of social relations from local contexts of interaction. There are two main mechanisms of disembedding: symbolic tokens (universal media such as money) and expert systems (bodies of technical knowledge

that can be applied across a range of different contexts). Each produces a homogenization of social life across different contexts and relies on trust in absent repositories of expertise. With this trust, therefore, comes a strong element of risk, a risk that is an inherent element of the globalization process.

Beck (1992) places risk squarely at the center of his approach. For Beck, the populations of the advanced capitalist countries are living in a post-scarcity age where the major dilemmas are the side effects of success. Risks such as pollution are also inherently global in that they are not limited to the local contexts in which they are produced and also in that they have a tendency to affect all members of society relatively equally. We are also becoming increasingly conscious of these risks and therefore of our global interdependence with other societies. There is a new politics of risk—a politics that is concerned with the distribution not of "goods" but of "bads," a politics that is not limited by territory and in which multiple groups of experts struggle to legitimate their expertise as the potential solution to risk management.

The globalization of modernist worldviews and their primary agents—scientists and professionals—is once again placed at the center of the analysis. However, Giddens and Beck add an understanding of the dilemmas associated with such globalized rationalist institutions. Lash and Urry (1994) point up the postmodernist emphasis on aesthetic symbols and signs, in contrast to the modernist emphasis on rationalism and the power of scientists and professionals. They direct our attention toward cultural consumption on a global scale rather than toward the diffusion of rationalist worldviews and their effects.

Sociologists concerned with modernity and modernization emphasize the diffusion of rationalistic organizational principles (such as the nation-state form) on a global scale rather than the spread of global capitalism. Individuals are culturally constituted by the global system as rationalized, individualized actors rather than as workers or members of classes, while capitalists take second place to experts as the prime movers of the historical process of globalization. Nonetheless, theorists of modernization and modernity share with Marxists the view of an increasingly rationalized world, for better or worse.

DEPENDENCY THEORY

In contrast, sociologists who analyzed the global system from a dependency perspective emphasized the extent to which Third World political economies evolve differently from those of First World countries because they confront a world dominated by already industrialized countries. Deriving their initial inspiration from economists such as Prebisch (1950) and Baran (1957), the dependency approach saw the global system as consisting of a "core" of advanced industrial countries connected both economically and politically to a larger "periphery" of poor nations, rather than as consisting simply of a set of nations that can be ranked along various continua according to individual characteristics such as size and wealth. The structure of the global system was conceptualized primarily in terms of trade and capital flows reinforced by political domination. The principal concern was with the consequences of these ties for social, political, and economic change in the countries of the periphery.

Cardoso and Faletto's *Dependency and Development in Latin America* (1979 [1969]) is still the classic exemplar of this tradition. Their analysis shows that the way in which economic elites are connected to the global economy shapes not only their strategies of investment but also their willingness to make political alliances with other groups and classes. For example, Latin American countries whose primary ties to the core were formed by mineral exports under the control of foreign capital experienced a different political history from countries who relied on agricultural exports controlled by local elites.

The expectations of the dependency approach with regard to changes in the structure of the global system over time stand in sharp contrast to those of both traditional Marxist and modernization approaches. The dependency perspective emphasizes the ways in which economic elites and their allies in the periphery have an interest in preventing the full diffusion of economic capacities from core to periphery. For example, those who have an interest in the system of trading agrarian exports for core-country manufactures may consider nascent local industrialists to be competitors for both labor and political power.

Empirical work generated by the dependency perspective suggested that the consequences of core–periphery capital flows, rather than being the most important stimulus to the growth of the periphery as Marxists like Warren suggested, might in fact create obstacles to growth. Korzeniewicz and Moran (1997) show that overall world income inequality increased between 1965 and 1992, particularly in the 1980s—the most significant component of that inequality being between-country inequality. Initial cross-national quantitative analyses discovered that the buildup of stocks of foreign capital had negative, rather than the expected positive, consequences for growth (Bornschier et al. 1978; Chase-Dunn 1975). Firebaugh (1992, 1996), however, shows that the negative effects of foreign investment are in part a result of methodological problems with the analyses and that, while foreign investment is less beneficial than domestic investment, it has a generally positive short-term effect on growth. Dixon and Boswell (1996a, 1996b) reformulate the dependency argument to emphasize the negative externalities associated with foreign investment that dampen the productivity of domestic investment. Kentor (1998) finds that dependency on foreign capital has particularly harmful effects on growth over the long term (thirty years) through the distortion and disarticulation of the domestic political economy. Crowly and associates (1998), in a review of cross-national quantitative studies in economics and sociology, find that foreign investment has a short-term positive effect on growth but plays a more negative role over the long term. However, the dynamics through which foreign investment generates negative externalities within a political economy are not well understood (Dixon and Boswell 1996b). While the findings of these studies are still contested, they clearly demonstrate that the results of transnational capital flows are not those predicted by a simple diffusionist model.

The impact of trade liberalization has been just as controversial as that of foreign investment. O'Hearn's (1990) longitudinal analysis of the Republic of Ireland shows that while foreign investment did not have a direct negative effect, free trade (which was inextricably tied to the foreign-investment policy) had substantial negative effects on growth and inequality. Crowly and associates (1998) review studies of the impact of trade on growth and find that while export reliance is generally positively related to growth, this positive effect is reduced or reversed under conditions that approximate to those theorized as "unequal exchange" (Emmanuel 1972). Rodrik (1997), reviewing the economics literature, finds that unskilled workers are likely to experience increased labor-market insecurity in the face of free trade, that nations may have legitimate reasons to limit trade, and that national systems of social security are indeed threatened by trade liberalization.

Again, quantitative cross-national studies played a valuable role in specifying the consequences of industrializing in an already industrialized world. Chase Dunn (1975) found that a greater role for foreign capital was associated with high levels of inequality, and his findings were confirmed by a variety of subsequent studies (e.g., Evans and Timberlake 1980; Rubinson 1976). These studies also confirm the political consequences of global economic ties. Delacroix and Ragin (1981) show that peripheral status in terms of trade relations is associated with weak state apparatuses. Bornschier and Ballmer-Cao (1979) argue on the basis of cross–national data that core-peripheral capital flows strengthen the political position of traditional power holders at the expense of labor and middle-class groups.

One of the criticisms that can be leveled against the dependency approach is that it has focused too much on capital and not enough on labor. Whereas dependency theorists have been concerned with the consequences of transnational capital flows for labor in both periphery and core (e.g., Frobel et al. 1981), the tradition contains no series of cross-national quantitative analyses of either wage levels or the structure of international labor flows studies comparable to the literature on international capital flows. With some notable exceptions (e.g., Portes and Walton 1981) the global structure of labor flows and their consequences is understudied. The 1990s saw a series of valuable case studies of work under globalization, although the consequences of work organization patterns in shaping patterns of dependency has not been explored in detail (Bonacich et al. 1994; Hodson 1998; Salzinger 1997).

Even within a global economy that is becoming more polarized, there have been significant cases of upward mobility. Spain and Portugal, which once formed the core, later moved to the semiperiphery, where they are joined by Taiwan and Korea, which have moved up from the periphery (Korzeniewicz and Moran 1997). Although dependency theory has concentrated on the obstacles to mobility facing peripheral economies, it has also stimulated a wide range of research on the causes of mobility within the world-system. Analysts of "dependent development" (Cardoso 1974; Evans 1979) argue that intensification of ties with core countries is a dynamic element in reshaping the political economies of Third World countries. Dependent development shares with classic Marxist approaches the assumption that capital flows between core and periphery can play a significant role in generating industrialization in the Third World. It emphasizes, however, that both the economic character of this industrialization and its social and political concomitants are likely to be different from the experience of core countries.

The question of domestic dynamics is particularly important in relation to explanations of the mobility of individual nations from one position to another. While such mobility depends in part on changes in the system as a whole, it also depends on the outcome of domestic political struggles. In his work on Chile, for example, Zeitlin (1984) argues that the outcome of political struggles among economic elites in the nineteenth century was determinative of Chile's retaining its role as an exporter of raw materials rather than moving in the direction of trying to transform its mineral resources into more processed exports. Zeitlin's analysis of Chile shows how the outcome of domestic political contests can perpetuate peripheral status.

Brenner's (1976, 1977) interpretation of England's rise to the core provides another example of the domestic roots of systemic mobility. In Brenner's view, the differences between the agrarian strategies of England on the one hand and Spain and Portugal on the other were not simply the result of trade possibilities generated by changes at the level of the world-system. They depended crucially on interactions between peasant communities and agrarian elites at the local level, which in turn were rooted in longstanding historical characteristics of the peasant communities themselves.

Likewise, Taiwan and Korea are used as examples of the way in which internal dynamics may allow construction of more effective state apparatuses, which in turn enable a country to improve its position in the global system (Evans 1987). In the East Asian developmental states, and especially in Japan and Korea, the state sat at the center of an alliance between the large business groups, domestic banks, and certain key state agencies—prodding and poking firms and banks in more developmental directions, organizing political alliances, and mobilizing social resources (Amsden 1989; Evans 1995; Wade 1990). Research stimulated by the dependency perspective has been both a powerful corrective to views of globalization as an inevitable, relatively even process of diffusion from the core to the periphery. Recognizing the obstacles to diffusion has also problematized the cases where mobility has occurred and has focused analysts' attention on the forces shaping a nation's ability to overcome these obstacles.

WORLD-SYSTEM THEORY

The dependency approach's contribution to our understanding of the international system has, however, been limited by the fact that it does not focus directly on the structure of the global system itself. The "world-system" approach, launched by Immanuel Wallerstein (1974) and others (see Chase-Dunn 1989) at the beginning of the 1970s, took the overall structure of the system as its starting point. Wallerstein's contribution lay not only in directing attention to analysis of the global system itself, but also in setting the contemporary capitalist world-system in the context of previous systems spanning more than one society.

In Wallerstein's world-system, the hierarchical structure is postulated as essential for its survival. The geographic expansion of northwestern Europe's economic and political influence beginning at the end of the "long" fourteenth century was, in Wallerstein's view, essential to the transformation of productive organization in that region. Subsequent interchange among regions with different modes of extraction has been central to sustaining the process of accumulation in the system as a whole. Wallerstein envisions at least three structural positions within the system. Defined in terms of the nature of their exchange relations with other regions, they are (1) the "core," which exports goods produced by processes more intensive in their use of capital and new technology; (2) the

periphery, which relies on the production of labor and resource-intensive goods; and (3) the semiperiphery, which "trades both ways". Arrighi (1994) emphasizes the role of finance in the world-system as a complement to the Wallersteinian focus on trade and the division of labor. He traces the process of capital accumulation across four systemic cycles of accumulation in the world-system. Each one is associated with a different hegemonic (state) power that coordinates the securing of the conditions for capital accumulation on a world scale.

Quantitative cross-national analysis provides support for the idea that countries can be categorized according to their interactions with other nations and that countries in the same position experience shared benefits (or costs). Snyder and Kick (1979), using "block modeling" techniques, found a block of nations whose characteristics corresponded roughly to those of the core, several blocks that corresponded to the periphery, and a set of nations with the intermediary properties attributed to the semiperiphery. Smith and White (1992) used a similar methodology but improved on Snyder and Kick by examining longitudinal changes in the structure of the system. They were able to demonstrate changes in the structure of relations within and between blocks of nations and chart the mobility of individual nations within the system. Van Rossem (1996), however, using an analysis of the role structure of the world economy, argues that world-system position has little direct effect on growth but is better seen as a framework within which nations can act rather than as a determining force in national economic development.

Some of the most interesting work stimulated by world-system thinking has involved analysis of systems that antedated the emergence of the contemporary one (e.g., Abu-Lughod 1989). Wallerstein argues that systems prior to the current one were primarily of two types. "Minisystems" extended across boundaries defined by unified political control and ethnic solidarity but did not come close to being global in scope. These minisystems have been the subject of a number of recent studies, with interesting comparisons across different world-systems (Chase-Dunn and Hall 1997; Chase-Dunn and Mann 1998). "World empires" joined various ethnic and social groups in a single division of labor by extending political control over a broader geographic area. Only the contemporary capitalist world-system, however, unites such a broad geographic region (essentially the entire globe) in a single division of labor without unified political control of corresponding scope. Frank (1998) has challenged the Eurocentrism of world-systems theory, arguing that the Western European capitalist heyday is but an interlude in the dominance of Asia in the world economy. Arrighi and Silver (1999) compare the contemporary period to the two major hegemonic transitions—from Dutch to British power in the 1700s and from British to U.S. power in the early twentieth century . They argue that the financial expansion of the last two decades of the twentieth century, is not so much a sign of deepening globalization as of systemic crisis, with an uncertain outcome which depending largely on the response of the declining hegemonic power, the United States. The comparative perspective across geographic scales and historical time periods that world-systems theory can provide gives valuable insight into the novelty or otherwise of contemporary globalization processes.

Another interesting trend in current sociological work on the global system is the increasing concern of sociologists with the politics of international relations among states. The third volume of Wallerstein's (1989) epic analysis of the modern world-system makes it clear that the world-system perspective, often accused in the past of being excessively "economistic," is now focusing much more on the logic of interstate politics, an emphasis that is also central to Arrighi's work. At the same time, other major sociological figures have turned their attention to the political and military aspects of the international system (e.g., Giddens 1985; Mann 1988; Tilly 1992). There has also been some attempt within world-systems theory to incorporate the dynamics of households (Smith and Wallerstein 1992) and of social movements. The emphasis within the tradition remains firmly on structural, macro-level processes, despite an increasing attention to cultural constructions (Wallerstein 1990). World-systems theory does analyze how the core countries are affected by the development of the world-system—unlike in the previous perspectives. However, this analysis is concentrated on the struggle among core nations for hegemonic power within the world system.

There is very little analysis of the impact of peripheral development, or even of globalization processes more generally, on the core within any of the perspectives discussed so far.

A quite different systems perspective on globalization has been advanced by Robertson (1992). Building on a concern to link a Parsonian concept of social systems to an analysis of international relations, Robertson posits that globalization involves the structuration of a social system at the global level. He argues that this process of globalization has been underway since the early fifteenth century and has resulted in ever-increasing global complexity within the social system. He shares with world-systems theory a "long view" of the development of globalization tendencies. However, he rejects the "reductionism" and "economism" of world-systems theory in favor of an analysis of the cultural and social conditions of social order within a global system. Robertson argues that there is an intensification of global consciousness in the sense that individuals increasingly orient toward the world as a whole. This rise in global consciousness is sustained both by the greater material interdependence of people around the world and by the interplay of four components of the global social system: the individual self, the national society, the world-system of societies, and humankind (1992, p. 27). The self-definition of each element can no longer be sustained in isolation from the other elements—under conditions of globalization each component is constituted relative to the others, providing the defining feature of globalization.

CURRENT GLOBAL SYSTEMS ANALYSIS

Each of the "classical" perspectives on globalization has therefore generated insights into the process and continues to sustain a research tradition of its own. However, the theme of globalization has spread beyond the confines of these traditions to become a central organizing concept across a wide range of sociological perspectives and research. Since approximately the early 1980s, globalization has had an increasingly visible impact on the core countries themselves, shaping the concerns of sociologists located in those countries. Sociology itself has been at least partially globalized—both by the emergence of "indigenous" sociological communities around the world and by the growing international communication between these communities (Albrow 1996). Previous eras of sociological research into the global system had been shaped by a concern for the impact of the core on the periphery. However, these new patterns of globalization and new locations and perspectives of sociologists have generated an interest in how specific components of that system are being rearticulated and in particular how the global, the local, and the national are being reconstituted (Waters 1995). This diverse body of research typically examines globalization by generating "theories of the middle range," often as a reaction against what was seen as overly abstract or deterministic systems-level theories (Portes and Walton 1981). The diffusion of the concept of globalization through sociology and this concern for revealing the mechanisms of globalization were reflected in a fragmentation of perspectives in the 1990s. In the rest of this article, we will review some of this recent research, focusing on the issues of the globalization of production, the constitution of a "global culture" and the future of the state in a global economy.

Over the course of the 1970s and 1980s, a growing body of work emerged that took the influence of the global system seriously in its analysis of change at the domestic level while at the same time using analysis of domestic political struggles and their economic consequences to explain changing ties with the global system (see Evans and Stephens 1988). These attempts to integrate international and comparative analysis are not unique to sociology. A parallel trend can be observed in political science as well (see Gourevitch 1986; Putnam 1988).

In the 1990s, work on global and local production systems, while often informed by dependency theory, also took a somewhat different approach. Reich (1991) argues that "national champion" corporations are rapidly being transformed into "global webs," or "virtual corporations," that coordinate knowledge inputs from around the globe. Castells (1997) argues that the structural logic of society is increasingly expressed through a "space of flows" that stretches across the globe. Flows of capital, information technology, organizational interaction, images, sounds, and symbols are the expression of the dominant processes of global society. They are based on an electronic infrastructure,

supported through key nodes or locations, and directed by a dominant, managerial elite. Most people continue to live in the "space of places" where local context dominates their experience. However, the space of flows tends to dominate the space of places as function and power are increasingly organized in flows while experience remains rooted for the most part in places (Castells 1997, p. 428).

Organizational theory suggests, however, that the model of the virtual corporation is likely to be problematic as home and host country effects, corporate cultures, and sectoral characteristics still shape corporate strategies in significant ways. Gereffi advances the concept of "global commodity chains" (GCCs) as the organizational structure that ties together these various social and institutional contexts in a global production network (Gereffi 1994; Gereffi and Korzeniewicz 1994; Harrison 1994). These GCCs are dominated either by key producers or by dominant brand name marketing firms, creating "producer-driven" and "buyer-driven" GCCs. The overall organization of the GCCs and location within the GCC shape workers' wages, conditions, and power in the workplace (Bonacich et al. 1994).

This perspective therefore goes well beyond perspectives that simply warn about capital mobility and virtual corporations. It also allows us to provide more nuanced accounts of the dynamics involved in territories' dependency on foreign capital, although the analysis of the political contexts of GCCs has not yet been fully developed. This more nuanced analysis of global production structures also holds the potential for improved integration of the role of domestic dynamics in determining the position of individual nations within the system and, by extension, shaping the structure of the system itself.

Increased attention is also being paid to how, even in an era of globalization, long-established patterns of interaction and cultural forms can profoundly shape a nation's ability to compete globally. The success of Japan, Korea, and Taiwan can, for example, be argued to be due in part to the contribution of communitarian, patrimonial, and patrilineal cultural logics to creating the organizational networks that are at the heart of these countries' economic success (Orrú et al. 1997). A country's historically shaped 'logic of social organization' can make it better suited to competition in particular industries—for example, a more decentralized, less hierarchical culture such as that of the United States may be more suitable for industries, such as software, that are based on knowledge sharing (Biggart and Guillen 1999; Guillen 1994).

Theorists of "industrial districts" have made a somewhat different point regarding the importance of local social and cultural practices in shaping global competitiveness. They argue that in an era of post-Fordist production, where information processing is critical and the need for "flexible specialization" central to competitiveness, local face-to-face relationships are necessary to build up the trust that supports such competitiveness (Piore and Sabel 1984). Initial versions of this approach pointed to long-established civic traditions, craft traditions, and kin relations as underpinning such organizational forms, in Italy in particular (Piore and Sabel 1984; Putnam 1993). Later research has explored the emergence of such cooperation and trust in "new" regions, such as Silicon Valley (Saxenian 1994), Hollywood (Storper 1997), Southern California (Scott 1993), and numerous other regions identified in a huge range of studies (Castells and Hall 1994). Sabel has explored at a theoretical level how such "constitutional orders" can develop or even be promoted by policy (Sabel 1996a).

Sassen explicitly attempts to integrate these local and global perspectives through an analysis of how labor flows are shaped by capital flows (Sassen 1988, 1998), how "global cities" arise as centralized nodes of control over decentralized production systems (Sassen 1990), how domestic structures of inequality are created by the demand for high-wage professionals and low-wage service workers (Sassen 1988, 1990), and how the state comes to play a critical role in globalization, even as it is transformed by the process (Sassen 1996, 1998). She extends this analysis to begin to analyze the incorporation of women into the global economy and the opportunities and threats posed for them by this process (Sassen 1998). Sassen demonstrates the interaction between transnational corporate networks and labor flows and territorial entities such as global cities and local and national states in shaping global capitalism.

This creative tension between local and global is also visible in research on "global culture." For many authors, the global reach of markets has brought with it the cultural construction of actors around the world as individualized consumers, often in association with the more general spread of U.S. cultural norms internationally (Barber 1995; Featherstone 1990; Ritzer 1993; Sklair 1991). Others see a reaction against this process in a return to "tribalism," in the increase in ethnic and nationalist conflicts and atrocities, and in the general struggle between "locals" caught in the space of places and "cosmopolitans" operating in the space of flows (Barber 1995; Castells 1997).

Each of these implies a vision of global culture as a homogenizing force, with local identites surfacing as a reaction against this domination or, in certain cases, exclusion. However, other authors emphasise how global cultural forms become transformed in the local culture and how local cultures form part of a more varied and heterogenous global culture. Appadurai (1996) argues that global cultural flows are shaped by the multiplicity of perspectives generated by flows of people, money, technologies, ideologies, and media technologies and symbols. Working through these varied cultural landscapes, local cultures work to incorporate global symbols but in ways specific to the local context. There is no pure local culture that is untainted by global culture but rather a variety of local cultures that are increasingly interpenetrated and constantly remade out of elements of global cultural flows (Appadurai 1996; Hall 1991).

Research on migration and transnational communities provides an opportunity to examine the interaction of local and global forces in shaping "global culture." Hodagneu-Sotelo (1994) shows how migration can present opportunities for women to play a more central role in their communities and in mediating relations between the community and the state. Transnational communities of migrants emerge that may have huge economic and social impacts on the home and host countries by creating new identities and structuring flows of social and financial resources (Massey and Parrata 1998; Portes 1996). Another social group that has received much research attention, but rarely under the rubric of globalization, is professionals, who, as we have seen, are central to the process of globalization and are most likely to be integrated into global networks in the workplace (Reich 1991) or in their migration patterns (Castells 1997). Finally, research into virtual communities promises to provide insights into the nature of community and shared culture in an ostensibly placeless cyberspace (Turkle 1995; Wellman et al. 1996).

Finally, we turn to the state, which is often claimed to be a doomed social actor in the face of globalization as mobile corporations, finance, migrants, and symbols undermine its economic, political, and cultural authority (Esping-Andersen 1996). Furthermore, globalization is one factor shifting the focus of politics away from the state and established interests and toward "new social movements" organized around new identities forged from "codes" from around the world (Melucci 1996). A variety of research, mainly in political economy, has aimed to show the continuing national diversity in socioeconomic organization and the persistent power of the state to shape economic outcomes (Boyer and Drache 1996; Hirst and Thompson 1996; Wade 1996). Indeed, globalization has in many ways been produced by states. Sassen (1998) argues that the state has played a key role in creating the international and local conditions for global production and capital accumulation. States have negotiated new legal regimes that secure the rights of capital on a global scale and have supported the strategic sites through which the global economy is organized. Economic sociology's improved understanding of the social and political construction of markets can be applied very usefully to the continuing national diversity in state–market relations (Berger and Dore 1996). Fligstein (1990), for example, shows the domestic conditions for the increased U.S. corporate emphasis on finance, an emphasis that, at the end of the 1990s, threatened the East Asian economies (Wade 1998). The particular property rights and exchange rules underpinning the construction of a single market within the European Union have also been profoundly shaped by interstate negotiations (Fligstein and Mara-Drita 1996).

Neil Brenner (1998, 1999) argues that state structures and strategies are being reconstituted in order to mediate the global and local processes discussed above. The "glocal state" attempts to promote the global competitiveness of its major urban regions through increased ties to both local and international actors. Sassen (1999) points out that this remaking of certain parts of the state

apparatus to promote global competitiveness begins to shape the character of the state as a whole, as even those sections of the state still predominantly concerned with national social policy become accountable to the new priorities and as the national legal and institutional structure is changed to accommodate international capital. These processes are not inevitable, however, as the international hegemony of Anglo-American economic ideology contributes to the creation of a "leaner, meaner" state that retains the institutional capability to support capital even as its capacity to provide social services or to support civil society weakens (Evans 1997). This excessive global liberalization and integration of financial markets is likely to have a corrosive effect on domestic state capacities and social welfare (Block 1996).

The state is therefore remade by globalization, even as it plays a critical role in constituting the global economy. Sociologists are beginning to explore the implications of this reconstitution of the state for economic sovereignty and citizenship. Castells (1997) argues that a "network state" is emerging, a state in which sovereignty is pooled between increasingly intertwined local, national, and international levels of governance, such as in the European Union. Debates persist as to whether this network state means the eclipse of local or national institutions as European Union institutions increasingly come to predominate (Streeck and Schmitter 1991) or even as a "postnational society" is created in Europe (Habermas 1998). There are persistent examples within Europe, however, that local and national institutions continue to play a central role in generating economic and social progress. Recent examples include national corporatist institutions in the Netherlands (Visser and Hemerijck 1996), local "micro-corporatism" in Italy (Locke 1995; Regini 1995), and a combination of the two in the Republic of Ireland (Sabel 1996b).

States are clearly being transformed by both the localization and globalization of economic life. Boyer and Hollingsworth (1996) argue that economic action is best conceived of as "nested" within a combination of local, national, and international institutions, rather than as "embedded" within national regimes. Indeed, formal sovereignty is shifting away from the state in many cases—toward both privatized transnational legal regimes (such as international commercial arbitration) and increasingly legitimate international human rights codes and instruments. These developments are also transforming the character of citizenship—on the one hand weakening certain provisions around economic and social citizenship (Sassen 1996) while on the other universalizing certain human rights (Soysal 1994). In short, then, the state remains a vital actor within the global system but one whose role, purpose, and structure are being transformed in new and unexpected ways.

Sociology itself is being transformed and globalized, if only partially up to this point. In the process, global systems analysis has moved from the specialization of a number of key theories to perhaps becoming a defining element of sociology in the twenty-first century. New methodologies are being developed to counter the abstraction of systems analysis and to provide insights into the process of globalization as revealed in local contexts and as practiced by social actors (Burawoy et al. forthcoming). What new theoretical and methodological traditions will emerge from this period of change remains unclear. Overall, our understanding of the global system must still be considered a project "under construction" rather than a finished set of tools easily applied to specific problems.

This is all the more true given the rapid changes in the global system itself. Some things are clear nonetheless. We know that trajectories of change in national societies cannot be analyzed without reference to the global system in which they are embedded any more than the analysis of change in individual communities can be attempted without awareness of the national society in which they are embedded; but we also know that the character of relations between an individual state and the larger system is shaped not just only by the evolution of the global system but also by the outcome of political struggles at the local level. We know that the nations located at the bottom of this structure are disadvantaged economically as well as politically, but we also know that mobility is possible. We know that diffusion of ideas and norms throughout the global system has a powerful influence on how social institutions are structured in individual nations, but we also know that this diffusion takes place within a system that has a very hierarchical structure. Increasingly, we understand that local

societies incorporate global cultural forms in complex and contested ways.

We know that the contemporary global system is an invention of the last half-dozen centuries; predicting how long it will endure is another question. For some, the future seems gloomy as the market threatens to undermine both state and society and lead to barbarism, as Polanyi (1944) suggested. For others, the future holds the possibility of the re-creation of civilizing institutions on a more comprehensive global scale. Still others seek to identify spaces for action within globalization processes, hoping to shape alternatives to the pessimistic Polanyian vision of creeping barbarism.

REFERENCES

Abu-Lughod, J. 1989 *Before European Hegemony*. New York: Oxford University Press.

Albrow, M. 1996 *The Global Age*. Stanford, Calif.: Stanford University Press.

Amsden, A. H. 1989 *Asia's Next Giant: South Korea and Late Industrialization*. Oxford: Oxford University Press.

Appadurai, A. 1996 *Modernity at Large*. Minneapolis: University of Minnesota Press.

Arrighi, G. 1994 *The Long Twentieth Century*. London: Verso.

——, and B. Silver 1999 *Chaos and Governance in the Modern World System*. Minneapolis: University of Minnesota Press.

Baran, P. 1957 *The Political Economy of Growth*. New York: Monthly Review Press.

Barber, B. R. 1995 *Jihad vs. McWorld*. New York: Times Books.

Beck, U. 1992 *Risk Society: Towards a New Modernity*. London: Sage.

——, A. Giddens, and S. Lash 1994 *Reflexive Modernization*. Stanford, Calif.: Stanford University Press.

Berger, S., and R. Dore, eds. 1996 *National Diversity and Global Capitalism*. Ithaca, N.Y.: Cornell University Press.

Biggart, N., and M. Guillen 1999 "Developing Difference: Social Organization and the Rise of the Automotive Industries in South Korea, Taiwan, Spain, and Argentina." *American Sociological Review*, forthcoming.

Block, F. 1996 *The Vampire State: And Other Myths and Fallacies About the US Economy*. New York: The New Press.

Boli, J., and G. M. Thomas 1999 *Constructing World Culture : International Nongovernmental Organizations Since 1875*. Stanford, Calif.: Stanford University Press.

Boli-Bennett, J. 1979 "The Ideology of Expanding State Authority in National Constitutions, 1870–1970." In J. Meyer and M. Hannan, eds., *National Development and the World System*. Chicago: University of Chicago Press.

Bonacich, E., et al., eds. 1994 *Global Production: The Apparel Industry in the Pacific Rim*. Philadelphia: Temple University Press.

Bornschier, V., and T.-H. Ballmer-Cao 1979 "Income Inequality: A Cross-National Study of the Relationships Between MNC-Penetration, Dimensions of Power-Structure and Income Distribution." *American Sociological Review* 44:487–506.

Bornschier, V., C. Chase-Dunn, and R. Rubinson 1978 "Cross-National Evidence of the Effects of Foreign Investment and Aid on Economic Growth and Inequality: A Survey of Findings and a Re-analysis." *American Journal of Sociology* 84:651–683.

Bottomore, T., and R. J. Brym, eds. 1989 *The Capitalist Class: An International Study*. New York: New York University Press.

Boyer, R., and D. Drache 1996 *States Against Markets: The Limits of Globalization*. London: Routledge.

Boyer, R., and J. R. Hollingsworth 1996 "From National Embeddedness to Spatial and Institutional Nestedness" In R. Boyer and J. R. Hollingsworth, eds., *Contemporary Capitalism*. Cambridge, U.K.: Cambridge University Press.

Brenner, N. 1998 "Global Cities, Glocal States: Global City Formation and State Territorial Restructuring in Contemporary Europe." *Review of International Political Economy* 5(1):1–37.

—— 1999 "Beyond State-Centrism? Space, Territoriality and Geographical Scale in Globalization Studies." *Theory and Society* 28(1):39–78.

Brenner, R. 1976 "Agrarian Class Structure and Economic Development in Pre-Industrial Europe." *Past and Present* 70:30–75.

—— 1977 "The Origins of Capitalist Development: A Critique of Neo-Smithian Marxism." *New Left Review* 104:24–92.

—— 1998 "The Economics of Global Turbulence." *New Left Review* 229:1–264.

Burawoy, M., et al. forthcoming *Global Ethnography*. Berkeley: University of California Press.

Cardoso, F. H. 1974 "As tradicoes de desenvolvimento-associado." *Estudos Cebrap* 8:41–75.

——, and Enzo Faletto 1979 (1969) *Dependency and Development in Latin America*. Berkeley: University of California Press.

Castells, M. 1997 *The Information Age*, 3 vols. Oxford: Blackwell.

——, and P. Hall 1994 *Technopoles of the World*. London: Routledge.

Chase-Dunn, Christopher 1975 "The Effect of International Dependence on Development and Inequality: A Cross-National Study." *American Sociological Review* 40(6):720–738.

—— 1989 *Global Formation: Structures of the World Economy*. New York: Blackwell.

——, and T. D. Hall 1997 *Rise and Demise: Comparing World-Systems*. Boulder: Westview Press.

——, and K. M. Mann 1998 *The Wintu and their Neighbors: A Very Small World-System in Northern California*. Tucson: University of Arizona Press.

Crowly, A. M., J. Rauch, S. Seagrove, and D. A. Smith 1998 "Quantitative Cross-National Studies of Economic Development: A Comparison of the Economics and Sociology Literatures." *Studies in Comparative International Development* 33(2):30–57.

Delacroix, J., and C. Ragin 1981 "Structural Blockage: A Cross-National Study of Economic Dependence, State Efficacy and Underdevelopment." *American Journal of Sociology* 86:1311–1347.

Dixon, W. J., and T. Boswell 1996a "Dependency, Disarticulation and Denominator Effects: Another Look at Foreign Capital Penetration." *American Journal of Sociology* 102(2):543–562.

—— 1996b "Differential Productivity, Negative Externalities, and Foreign Capital Dependency: Reply to Firebaugh." *American Journal of Sociology* 102(2):576–584.

Emmanuel, A. 1972 *Unequal Exchange: A Study of the Imperialism of Trade*. New York: Monthly Review Press.

Escobar, A. 1995 *Encountering Development: The Making and Unmaking of the Third World*. Princeton, N.J.: Princeton University Press.

Esping-Andersen, G., ed. 1996 *Welfare States in Transition: National Adaptations in Global Economies*. Thousand Oaks, Calif.: Sage.

Evans, P. B. 1979 *Dependent Development: The Alliance of Multinational State and Local Capital in Brazil*. Princeton, N.J.: Princeton University Press.

—— 1987 "Class, State, and Dependence in East Asia: Some Lessons for Latin Americanists." In F. Deyo, ed., *The Political Economy of the New Asian Industrialism*. Ithaca, N.Y.: Cornell University Press.

—— 1995 *Embedded Autonomy*. Princeton, N.J.: Princeton University Press.

—— 1997 "The Eclipse of the State? Reflections on Stateness in an Era of Globalization." *World Politics* 50(1):62–87.

——, and John Stephens 1988 "Development and the World Economy." In Neil Smelser, ed., *The Handbook of Sociology*. Beverly Hills, Calif.: Sage Publications.

——, and Michael Timberlake 1980 "Dependence, Inequality and the Growth of the Tertiary: A Comparative Analysis of Less Developed Countries." *American Sociological Review* 45:531–53.

Featherstone, M., ed. 1990 *Global Culture*. London: Sage.

Ferguson, J. 1990 *The Anti-Politics Machine: 'Development', Depoliticization and Bureaucratic Power in Lesotho*. Cambridge, U.K.: Cambridge University Press.

Firebaugh, G. 1992 "Growth Effects of Foreign and Domestic Investment." *American Journal of Sociology* 98(1):105–130.

—— 1996 "Does Foreign Capital Harm Poor Nations? New Estimates Based on Dixon and Boswell's Measures of Capital Penetration." *American Journal of Sociology* 102(2):563–575.

Fligstein, N. 1990 *The Transformation of Corporate Control*. Cambridge, Mass.: Harvard University Press.

——, and I. Mara-Drita 1996 "How to Make a Market: Reflections on the Attempt to Create a Single Market in the European Union." *American Journal of Sociology* 102(1):1–33.

Frank, A. G. 1998 *Re-Orient: Global Economy in the Asian Age* Berkeley: University of California Press.

Frobel, F., J. Heinrich, and O. Kreye 1981 *The New International Division of Labor: Structural Unemployment in Industrialized Countries and Industrialization in Developing Countries*. Cambridge, U.K.: Cambridge University Press.

Gereffi, G. 1994 "The International Economy." In N. Smelser and R. Swedberg, eds., *The Handbook of Economic Sociology*. Princeton, N.J.: Princeton University Press/Russell Sage Foundation.

——, and M. Korzeniewicz 1994 *Commodity Chains and Global Capitalism* Westport, Conn.: Greenwood Press.

Giddens, A. 1985 *The Nation-State and Violence*. Berkeley: University of California Press.

—— 1991 *The Consequences of Modernity*. Cambridge, U.K.: Cambridge University Press.

Gourevitch, P. 1986 *The Politics of Hard Times*. Ithaca, N.Y.: Cornell University Press.

Guillen, M. F. 1994 *Models of Management: Work, Authority, and Organization in a Comparative Perspective*. Chicago: University of Chicago Press.

Habermas, J. 1998 *The Inclusion of the Other*. Cambridge, Mass.: MIT Press.

Hall, S. 1991 "The Local and the Global: Globalization and Ethnicity" In A. D. King, ed., *Culture, Globalization and the World-System*. Binghamton: Department of Art and Art History, State University of New York–Binghamton.

Harrison, B. 1994 *Lean and Mean*. New York: Basic Books.

Hirst, P., and G. Thompson 1996 *Globalization in Question*. Cambridge, Mass.: Blackwell.

Hodagneu-Sotelo, P. 1994 *Gendered Transitions*. Berkeley: University of California Press.

Hodson, R., ed. 1997 *The Globalization of Work*. Greenwich, Conn.: JAI Press.

Inkeles, A., and D. Smith 1974 *Becoming Modern: Individual Change in Six Developing Countries*. Cambridge, Mass.: Harvard University Press.

Kentor, J. 1998 "The Long-Term Effects of Foreign Investment Dependence on Economic Growth, 1940–1990." *American Journal of Sociology* 103(4):1024–1046.

Korzeniewicz, R. P., and T. P. Moran 1997 "World-Economic Trends in the Distribution of Income, 1965–1992." *American Journal of Sociology* 102(4):1000–1039.

Lash, S., and J. Urry 1994 *Economies of Signs and Space*. London: Sage.

Locke, R. 1995 *Remaking the Italian Economy*. Ithaca, N.Y.: Cornell University Press.

Mann, M. 1988 *States, War and Capitalism*. Oxford: Blackwell.

Massey, D. S., and E. A. Parrado 1998 "International Migration and Business Formation in Mexico." *Social Science Quarterly* 79(1):1–20.

Melucci, A. 1996 *Challenging Codes: Collective Action in the Information Age*. Cambridge, U.K.: Cambridge University Press.

Meyer, J. W. 1980 "The World Polity and the Authority of the Welfare State." In A. Bergesen, ed., *Studies of the Modern World-System*. New York: Academic Press.

—— J. Boli, G. M. Thomas, and F. O. Ramirez 1997 "World Society and the Nation-State." *American Journal of Sociology* 103(1):144–181.

——, D. Frank, A. Hironaka, E. Schofer, N. B. Tuma 1997 "The Structuring of a World Environmental Regime, 1870–1990." *International Organization* 51(4):623–651.

——, F. O. Ramirez, and Y. N. Soysal 1992 "World Expansion of Mass Education, 1870–1980." *Sociology of Education* 65(2):128–149.

O'Hearn, D. 1990 "TNCs, Intervening Mechanisms and Economic Growth in Ireland: A Longitudinal Test and Extension of the Bornschier Model." *World Development* 18(3):417–429.

Orrù, M., N. Biggart, and G. Hamilton 1997 *The Economic Organization of East Asian Capitalism.* Thousand Oaks, Calif.: Sage.

Piore, M., and C. Sabel 1984 *The Second Industrial Divide.* New York: Basic Books.

Portes, A. 1996 "Global Villagers: The Rise of Transnational Communities" *The American Prospect* (March–April):74–77.

——, and J. Walton 1981 *Labor, Class and the International System.* New York: Academic Press.

Prebisch, R. 1950 "The Economic Development of Latin America and its Principal Problems." *Economic Bulletin for Latin America* 7(February):1–22.

Putnam, R. 1988 "Diplomacy and Domestic Politics: The Logic of Two-Level Games." *International Organization* 42(Summer):427–460.

—— 1993 *Making Democracy Work: Civic Traditions in Modern Italy.* Princeton, N.J.: Princeton University Press.

Ramirez, F., and J. Boli 1982 "Global Patterns of Educational Institutionalization." In P. Albach et al., eds., *Comparative Education.* New York: MacMillan.

Regini, M. 1995 *Uncertain Boundaries: The Social and Political Construction of European Economies.* Cambridge, U.K.: Cambridge University Press.

Reich, R. 1991 *The Work of Nations.* New York: Vintage Books.

Ritzer, G. 1993 *The McDonaldization of Society.* Thousand Oaks, Calif.: Pine Forge.

Robertson, R. 1992 *Globalization.* London: Sage

Robinson, W. I. 1998 "Beyond Nation-State Paradigms: Globalization, Sociology, and the Challenge of Transnational Studies." *Sociological Forum* 13(4):561–594.

Rodrik, D. 1997 *Has Globalization Gone Too Far?* Washington, D.C.: Institute for International Economics.

Rubinson, R. 1976 "The World Economy and the Distribution of Income within States." *American Sociological Review* 41:638–659.

Sabel, C. 1996a "Constitutional Orders: Trust Building and Response to Change "In R. Boyer and J. R. Hollingsworth, eds., *Contemporary Capitalism.* Cambridge, U.K.: Cambridge University Press.

—— 1996 *Ireland: Local Partnerships and Social Innovation.* Paris: Organization for Economic Cooperation and Development, Paris.

Salzinger, L. 1997 "From High Heels to Swathed Bodies: Gendered Meanings Under Production in Mexico's Export-Processing Industry." *Feminist Studies* 23(3):549–574.

Sassen, S. 1988 *The Mobility of Labour and Capital.* Cambridge, U.K.: Cambridge University Press.

—— 1990 *The Global City.* Princeton, N.J.: Princeton University Press.

—— 1996 *Losing Control? Sovereignty in an Age of Globalization.* New York: Columbia University Press.

—— 1998 *Globalization and its Discontents.* New York: The New Press.

—— 1999 "Cracked Casings: Notes Towards an Analytics for Studying Transnational Processes." Mimeo, Department of Sociology, University of Chicago.

Saxenian, A. 1994 *Regional Advantage: Culture and Competition in Silicon Valley and Route 128.* Cambridge, Mass.: Harvard University Press.

Scott, A. J. 1993 *Technopolis.* Berkeley: University of California Press.

Sklair, L. 1991 *Sociology of the Global System.* Hemel Hempstead, U.K.: Harvester Wheatsheaf.

Smith D. A., and D. R. White 1991 "Structure and Dynamics of the Global Economy: Network Analysis of International Trade, 1965–1980." *Social Forces* 70(4):857–893.

Smith, J., and I. Wallerstein 1992 *Creating and Transforming Households: The Constraints of the World-Economy.* Cambridge, U.K., and Paris: Cambridge University Press and Maison des Sciences de l'Homme.

Snidal, D. 1985 "The Limits of Hegemonic Stability Theory." *International Organization* 39(4):580–614.

Snyder, D., and E. Kick 1979 "Structural Position in the World System and Economic Growth, 1955–1970: A Multiple Network Approach." *American Journal of Sociology* 84(5):1096–1126.

Storper, M. 1997 *The Regional World: Territorial Development in a Global Economy.* London: Guilford Press.

Streeck, W., and P. Schmitter 1991 "From National Corporatism to Transnational Pluralism: Organized Interests in the Single European Market." *Politics and Society* 19(2):133–164.

Soysal, Y. 1994 *Limits of Citizenship.* Chicago: University of Chicago Press.

Tilly, C. 1992 *Coercion, Capital and European States, AD 990–1990.* Cambridge, Mass.: Blackwell.

Turkle, S. 1995 *Life on the Screen*. New York: Touchstone/Simon and Schuster.

Van Rossem, R. 1996 "The World System Paradigm as General Theory of Development—A Cross-National Test." *American Sociological Review* 61(3):508–527.

Visser, J., and A. Hemerijck 1996 *A Dutch Miracle*. Amsterdam: Amsterdam University Press.

Wade, R. 1990 *Governing the Market*. Princeton, N.J.: Princeton University Press.

—— 1996 "The Limits of Globalization." In S. Berger and R. Dore, eds., *National Diversity and Global Capitalism*. Ithaca, N.Y.: Cornell University Press.

—— 1998 "The Coming Fight Over Capital Flows." *Foreign Policy* 113:41–54.

Walker, R. A. 1999 "Putting Capital in Its Place: Globalization and the Prospects for Labor." *Geoforum*, forthcoming.

Wallerstein, I. 1974 *The Modern World-System I: Capitalist Agriculture and the Origins of the European World Economy*. New York: Academic Press.

—— 1989 *The Modern World-System, III: The Second Era of Great Expansion of the Capitalist World Economy, 1730's–1840's*. New York: Academic Press.

—— 1990 "Culture as the Ideological Battleground of the Modern World-System" In M. Featherstone, ed., *Global Culture*. London: Sage.

Waltz, K. 1979 *Theory of International Relations*. Reading, Mass.: Addison-Wesley.

Warren, B. 1980 *Imperialism: Pioneer of Capitalism*. London: New Left Books.

Waters, M. 1995 *Globalization*. London: Routledge.

Wellman, B., et al. 1996 "Computer Networks as Social Networks." *Annual Review of Sociology* 22:213–238.

Zeitlin, M. 1984 *The Civil Wars in Chile (or the Bourgeois Revolutions That Never Were)*. Princeton, N.J.: Princeton University Press.

Seán Ó Riain

Peter B. Evans

GOVERNMENT REGULATION

Government regulation is part of two larger areas of study, one encompassing all *state* policy making and administration, whether regulatory or not, the other encompassing all *regulatory* and *deregulatory* activity, whether by the state or by some other institution. Viewed either way, the subject remains an interdisciplinary growth industry, with contributions made by political scientists, economists, legal scholars, historians, and sociologists. Scholarly emphasis in the 1990s on economic globalization and its consequences has added to an already rich literature on government regulation, deregulation, and re-regulation. Now attention is focused on the supranational as well as the national level. Cross-national, comparative studies of government regulation complement a large literature focused on the United States.

WHAT IS GOVERNMENT REGULATION?

There is no uniformly agreed-upon concept of regulation that separates it from other kinds of government activity. Mitnick (1980, pp. 3–19) offers a good overview of concepts of regulation. On the one hand, narrow definitions typically focus on government action affecting private business by policing market entry and exit, rate or price, and profit structures and competitive environment. Some narrow definitions confine regulatory activity to that undertaken by administrative agencies (see also Majone 1994). If courts are the exclusive site for state rule making and enforcement, it is not considered government regulation. On the other hand, the broadest definitions conceive of regulation as government action affecting private businesses or citizens. Government regulation then becomes virtually coterminous with all government policy making and administration, whether by legislatures, administrative agencies, courts, or some combination.

Mitnick (1980) shows that American scholarship has provided for much variation in the conceptualizing of government regulatory activity. However, Majone (1994) suggests that in the past, American concepts typically were narrower than those adopted explicitly or implicitly by European scholars. For example, self-labeled *regulation theory* is a "quasi-Marxist theory [in which] the notion of regulation . . . refers to institutions and norms that permit the reproduction of conflictual or contradictory social relations" (see Steinmetz 1996, p. 346). In this predominantly European tradition, modes of regulation are broad political-economic and cultural governance forms. They revolve around capital accumulation and involve state action, including macroeconomic, social, and labor-market policies, but also involve systems of interest intermediation in the workplace, economic rule making by banks and other nongovernmental institutions, and cultural schemata followed and taught in families and schools. Lange and Regini (1989) and Regini (1995) reject such an all-encompassing definition of regulation in favor of a somewhat narrower one. But they also call attention to how regulatory action structures and reconciles conflicts and allocates resources, as well as coordinates interaction and relationships in production and distribution.

Lange and Regini (1989) argue that regulatory principles and regulatory institutions must be separated analytically. Both economic and political institutions regulate or engage in governance. We tend to equate market exchange principles with economic institutions and legal rulings and administrative decrees with the state. However, as Lange and Regini (1989) demonstrate, economic institutions also employ command and control logic, while the state may employ the logic of exchange. Most recently, European scholars have moved away from equating regulation with the realm of *all* institutional governance or of *all* government legislation and social control. Many now distinguish "the regulation issue" both from other modes of institutional governance and from other modes of state action, including nationalization and government planning (Majone 1994, p. 77).

Sabatier (1975) has offered a useful definition of *government* regulation in between the broad and narrow extremes. His definition is based on the goals and content of government policy, not on the means of enforcement. It highlights the distinction between government policing of behavior and government allocation of goods and services. Distributive (e.g., defense contracts) and redistributive policies (e.g., the income tax, social welfare policies) allocate goods and services. Government policing is self-regulatory if it polices behavior to the benefit of the group whose behavior is policed. It is regulatory if it "seek(s) to change the behavior of some actors in order to benefit others" (Sabatier 1975, p. 307). Pollution control, antidiscrimination, consumer protection, occupational safety and health, employment relations, and antitrust are examples of regulatory policies.

Sociologists often distinguish between economic and social regulation. Where economic regulation controls market activities, such as entry and exit or price controls, social regulation controls aspects of production, such as occupational safety and health standards and pollution control (e.g., Szasz 1986). The term *social regulation* is also used to signal regulation that directly affects people rather, or more than, markets (Mitnick 1980, p. 15). In the 1990s literature on European economic integration, a distinction has been made between regulation (governance oriented to making markets) and reregulation (governance oriented to constraining markets) (e.g., Streeck 1998). But the term *reregulation* is also used more broadly, to signal regulatory reform that both liberalizes markets and institutes new rules to police them (Vogel 1996).

Regulation is dynamic. It is "an ongoing process or relation" between regulator and regulated parties (Mitnick 1980, p. 6). Because of the nature of the legal system in the United States, regulation U.S.-style tends to involve issuing and applying legal rules (Sabatier 1975, p. 307). For example, Congress has legislated federal statutes to promote competitive markets, to prevent race and gender discrimination in employment, and to increase workplace safety. These laws have been interpreted and enforced by the appropriate federal administrative agencies and by the federal courts. Federal regulatory agencies include the Interstate Commerce Commission (ICC), Federal Trade Commission (FTC), Federal Communications Commission (FCC), Securities and Exchange Commission (SEC), Equal Employment Opportunity Commission (EEOC), National Labor Relations Board (NLRB), Environmental Protection Agency (EPA), Food and Drug Administration (FDA), and Occupational Safety and Health Administration (OSHA). (For case studies of many of these agencies, see Derthick and Quirk 1985; Wilson 1980b.)

Consistent with the U.S. emphasis on legal rules as implementing mechanisms, the institutional forms used to reach regulatory goals are varied. Breyer (1982) provides an overview of the ideal-typical workings of various government regulatory forms, including cost-of-service rate making (e.g., public utility regulation), standard setting (e.g., administrative rule making and enforcement by the EPA and OSHA), and individualized screening (e.g., the FDA regulations pursuant to which food additives can be marketed). Mitnick (1980) also provides an overview of government regulatory forms and contrasts regulation by directive (e.g., administrative and adjudicative rule making) with regulation by incentive (e.g., tax incentives, effluent charges, and subsidies).

It is no accident that European scholars in the 1990s are devoting heightened attention to government regulation and are also beginning to conceive of it more similarly to their U.S. counterparts (see, e.g., Majone 1994; Scharpf 1997a; Vogel 1996). European economic integration has been accompanied by concern that national governments would compete to lessen business costs in part by lowering standards for environmental, health and safety, financial, and other regulations. European integration has also involved a cumulative process of European Court of Justice rule making geared to constructing and policing the integrated market (see e.g., Leibfried and Pierson 1995; Scharpf 1997a). Thus, European integration has created a situation in which courts and judicial review are more important than they were in the past.

According to Majone (1994, p. 77), "regulation has become the new border between the state and the economy [in Europe] and the battleground for ideas on how the economy should be run." In addition, since national courts in ordinary administrative and civil proceedings apply the market-making and market-policing rules formulated by the supranational European Court, regulatory *law* is beginning to become visible to ordinary citizens of European countries as it has been for some time to citizens of the United States. These developments do *not* mean that we can assume a future convergence of either the concept or the reality of the "regulatory state" in Europe and the United States. They *do* mean that there is increasing potential for the cross-fertilization of scholarly concepts, theories, and empirical work from both sides of the Atlantic. These developments also provide new opportunities for informative comparative studies of government regulation.

THEORIES OF REGULATION

There are various general theoretical approaches to government regulation. Most are concerned with regulatory origins or processes, but often they also address questions of impact, at least implicitly. Because regulation is not just an object of scholarly inquiry but also an ongoing political process, it is easy to confuse normative perspectives on regulation with explanations for the empirical phenomenon. Here, I focus on the latter, that is, on positive as opposed to normative theories. Mitnick (1980) and Moe (1987) provide detailed exposition and evaluation of a large range of these positive theories. All are theories of "interest." Majone (1994) reviews the predominant normative perspective. The latter holds that corrective government action to improve economic efficiency is justified by such diverse types of market failure as natural monopoly, imperfect information and negative externalities (see also Breyer 1982).

Bernstein's classic life-cycle theory argues that regulatory agencies designed in the public interest become captured by the powerful private interests they are designed to regulate (see Mitnick 1980, pp. 45–50). The diffuse majority favoring government regulation loses interest once the initial statute is legislated. This leaves the regulatory agency with few political resources to confront strong, well-organized regulatory parties with a large stake in agency outcomes.

Arguing that regulatory agencies are not simply captured by private interests but are designed from the beginning to do their bidding, Stigler (1971) and others have developed the economic theory of regulation. This theory assumes that all actors behave rationally in their own self-interest and so try to use government to achieve their own ends. But economic interest does not necessarily result in effective mobilization of resources. Because "there is a mobilization bias in favor of small groups, particularly those having one or more members with sizable individual stakes in political outcomes," concentrated business interests have great advantages over diffuse groups in mobilizing for regulatory legislation (Moe 1987, pp. 274–275). Regulatory capture results when the costs of regulation fall upon a concentrated group (e.g., a particular industry such as railroads or airlines) and the benefits of regulation fall upon a diffuse group (e.g., consumers). Similarly, when benefits fall upon a concentrated group and costs on a diffuse one, regulation will be designed to benefit regulated parties.

The economic theory of regulation does not always predict capture. Generally, regulatory policies result from a chain of control running from economic groups to politicians to bureaucrats. These policies reflect the underlying balance of power among economic groups, whatever that balance may be. Considering different distributions of regulatory costs relative to regulatory benefits, Wilson (1980a, pp. 364–374) sketches four different scenarios for the origins of regulation. Exemplified by the origin and operation of the Civil Aeronautics Board, "client politics" is consistent with Stigler's prediction that regulation reflects the regulated industry's desires. Client politics result when costs are widely distributed and benefits are concentrated. When both costs and benefits are narrowly concentrated, both sides have strong incentives to organize and exert influence, so "interest group politics" results. Wilson views passage of the Commerce Act in 1886 as a product of conflict over rate regulation, in which interest group participants included railroads, farmers, and shippers.

According to Wilson, when both costs and benefits are widely distributed, interest groups have little incentive to form around regulatory issues because none can expect to capture most of the benefits or to avoid most of the costs. "Majoritarian politics," in which the mobilization of popular opinion is likely to play an important role, governs passage of such legislation. Finally, "entrepreneurial politics" characterizes the dynamics of mobilization around policies that offer widely distributed benefits but narrowly concentrated costs. Here, although policy opponents benefit from the mobilization bias of small numbers and have strong incentives to organize, a "policy entrepreneur" can "mobilize latent public sentiment . . . [and] put opponents" on the defensive (Wilson 1980a, p. 370). For Wilson, pollution-control laws enforced by the EPA exemplify entrepreneurial politics. Although the traditional economic theory of regulation predicts ultimate capture of agencies created by entrepreneurial politics, Sabatier (1975) argues that such agencies can avoid capture by concentrated business interests if they actively develop a supportive constituency able to monitor regulatory policy effectively.

Economic theories of government regulation have much to say about the political dynamics of social groups seeking and resisting regulation, but they do not attend to political and administrative institutions. In contrast, the positive theory of institutions "traces the congressional and bureaucratic linkages by which interests are translated into public policy" (Moe 1987, p. 279). This theory is one of a large group of more specific theories falling under the burgeoning "new institutionalism" in the social sciences (Eisner 1991; Powell and DiMaggio 1991). Like all variants of institutionalism, the positive theory of institutions argues that political institutions and rules of the game matter. Although actors try to create rules that lead to outcomes they favor, institutionalized rules may well be out of sync with underlying economic interests. Whether the regulatory policies of the U.S. Congress reflect any given economic interest depends on the distribution of that interest across congressional districts, the location of members of Congress who support that interest on particular committees with particular prerogatives and jurisdictions, and the rules of the congressional game.

The positive theory of institutions ordinarily begins with and focuses on the self-interest of actors in Congress and the regulatory agencies rather than that of actors outside these legislative and administrative institutions. It argues that legislative choice of regulatory forms as well as of regulatory content can be modeled as a function of the costs and benefits to legislators of selecting particular regulatory strategies (see, e.g., Fiorina 1982). These costs and benefits are a function of the distribution of economic interests across districts and the political-institutional rules of the game. In general, electoral incentives prevent members of Congress from placing high priority on controlling administrative agencies. The principal-agent models of control employed by the positive theory of institutions "suggest . . . that even when legislators do have incentives to control agencies toward specific ends" they probably will fail "owing to . . . conflicts of interest, information asymmetries, and opportunities for bureaucratic 'shirking'" (Moe 1987, p. 281). Game-theoretic models of regulatory enforcement developed in this theory indicate ample opportunity for the capture of the regulators by regulated parties (Ayres and Braithwaite 1989). However, where some forms of capture are economically undesirable, others are economically (Pareto) efficient.

Other theoretical perspectives used by sociologists to study regulation include various forms of neo-marxist political economy or class theory (see Levine 1988; Steinmetz 1997; Yeager 1990) and the political-institutionalist view developed by Theda Skocpol and others (Skocpol 1992; Weir et al. 1988). Where the former parallels the economic theory of regulation in focusing on the organization and mobilization of nongovernmental actors—specifically classes and segments of classes—in support of their interests, the latter parallels the positive theory of institutions in stressing the import of political structures and rules of the game. But in contrast to economic and positive theories, which largely model comparative statics (Moe 1987), class and political-institutional theories ordinarily focus on historical dynamics.

Political institutionalists stress, for example, the importance of feedback from prior to current regulatory policies and of political learning by government actors (see Pedriana and Stryker 1997). Feedback and political learning can help account for deregulation as well as for regulation (see Majone 1994). Class theorists stress how regulatory enforcement and cycles of regulation and deregulation evolve over time in response both to the structural constraints of a capitalist economy and to active struggles over regulation by classes and class segments. For example, Yeager (1990) argues that because government in a capitalist society depends on tax revenues from the private accumulation of capital, it tends to resolve conflict conservatively over such negative consequences of production as air or water pollution, so as not to threaten economic growth. Many aspects of U.S. regulatory processes make it likely that laws passed against powerful economic actors will be limited in impact or will have unintended effects that exacerbate the problems that initially caused regulation.

The effectiveness of regulatory statutes may be limited by implementation decisions relying on cost-benefit considerations because ordinarily costs are more easily determined than benefits and because cost-benefit analyses assert the primacy of private production. Moreover, government relies upon signals from private business to gauge when regulation is preventing adequate economic growth. Limited effectiveness of regulation also results from enforcement procedures tilted in favor of regulated parties that have the technical and financial resources needed to negotiate with agency officials. Corporate organizational forms encourage leniency and negotiations about compliance.

Corporate officials seldom are prosecuted for criminal violations because the corporate form makes it hard to locate individual culpability. Because courts emphasize proper legal reasoning when reviewing agency decisions, regulatory agencies may focus on procedure rather than substance. Ambiguous statutes are likely to heighten a procedural approach to regulatory enforcement (see Edelman 1992). In turn, focus on procedures over substance will tilt enforcement toward the interests of regulated parties. Finally, because no unit of government has complete control over any given policy from legislation through funding and implementation, parties bearing the cost of regulation need thwart regulation at only one point in the process, while supporters of regulation must promote it effectively at all points. In implementation, advocates of tough enforcement are likely to lose to more resource-rich segments of business seeking to limit regulation (Yeager 1990).

Notwithstanding forces that load regulatory processes in favor of the regulated business community and particularly the larger, more powerful corporations at the expense of smaller firms, consumers, environmentalists, and labor, class theorists also see limits on regulatory leniency. For example, Yeager (1990) argues that pollution-control enforcement biased toward large corporations dominating the U.S. economy will reproduce both the dominance of this business segment and of large-scale pollution. Regulatory ineffectiveness may lead to a loss of legitimacy for government as the public responds to higher risk and to perceived governmental failure by pressuring for additional pollution-control efforts.

Finally, although the concept of interest is central to theories of regulation, sociologists studying regulation are sensitive to the causal role of cultural schemata, norms, ideas, values, and beliefs as well as of economic and political interests and political institutions. For example, elaborating on Swidler's (1986) notion of culture as a tool kit, Pedriana and Stryker (1997) examine the diverse cultural strategies involved in the symbolic framing of regulatory enforcement efforts in U.S. equal employment law. They show that these frames are cultural resources developed by social and institutional actors in variable ways as a function of their variable political-economic, political-cultural, and legal circumstances. They also show how actors' mobilization of cultural resources affects the subsequent path of regulatory policy making. Construction of cultural resources, then, is one key mechanism through which policy feedbacks occur and political learning is given effect. Meidinger (1987), too, highlights the role of culture, focusing on the way understandings—including understandings about costs, benefits, and appropriate trade-offs—are negotiated and enacted by actors in regulatory arenas. Because statutes are indeterminate, regulators always possess some discretion. In addition, the mutual interdependence among regulated parties and regulators calls attention to the formation of regulatory communities in which shared cognitive and normative orientations develop, forming the basis for ongoing regulatory cultures.

Ayres and Braithwaite (1989) harness the notion of regulatory culture to their search for economically efficient regulatory schemes. They approach the problem of regulatory capture through a synthesis of economic interest and socialization mechanisms. Seeking a social framework to facilitate economically efficient forms of capture while deterring inefficient capture, they point to benefits obtainable if all participants in regulatory processes that empower public interest groups adhere to a culture of regulatory reasonableness. For example, social and self-disapproval sanctions in a regulatory ethic that is firm but reasonable will inhibit regulators from capitulating to law evasion by industry and from punitive enforcement when industry is complying with regulatory law. Yeager (1990) has a somewhat different view of regulatory reasonableness. He views limits on regulatory laws controlling pollution as a function of prevailing cultural belief systems as well as of class and group relations. Notions of regulatory responsiveness and reasonableness are negotiated in enforcement interactions between regulators and regulated parties within an overall cultural framework attributing moral ambivalence rather than unqualified harm to regulated conduct. This facilitates adoption of a technical orientation to solving "noncompliance" problems rather than of a more punitive approach. Because the regulation of business has to be justified constantly within highly market-oriented cultures like the United States, administering market-constraining regulation itself becomes morally ambivalent and contributes to less aggressive enforcement.

FROM REGULATION TO DEREGULATION AND REREGULATION

Discussions of dynamism and change, whether through structural contradiction and class conflict as stressed by neo-Marxist perspectives, or through policy feedback and political learning as stressed by political-institutionalists, lead naturally toward explicit theorization and empirical research on periods or cycles of regulation and deregulation or reregulation. As Majone (1994) points out, deregulatory ideologies and politics in the United States were preceded by decades of scholarship on the economics, politics, and law of government regulatory processes. In Europe, by contrast, the term "deregulation" gained much more "sudden currency" (Majone 1994, p. 98). Unsurprisingly, on both sides of the Atlantic, the concepts and perspectives used to study deregulation parallel the alternative economic interest and political interest/political-institutional foci of theories of regulation themselves.

On the one hand, for example, Szasz (1986) analyzes deregulatory social movements in the United States through the lens of presumed accumulation and legitimation functions of the capitalist state. He suggests that changing economic circumstances provided political opportunity for the deregulatory movement in occupational safety and health. In the 1970s, a substantially worsening economy altered the balance of class forces and changed the political situation confronting the state. Deteriorating economic conditions weakened the economic and political power of organized labor, a major supporter of occupational safety and health legislation. These same conditions encouraged big business to join the already existing but to this point unsuccessful small business attacks on the Occupational Safety and Health Administration. Where small business argued for the complete elimination of OSHA, big business relied on cost-benefit analyses to argue that sound economics required reforming the implementation process. Though economic conditions made deregulation possible, the success it achieved and the form it took required business interests to mount a conscious, ideological campaign to mold favorable public opinion.

On the other hand, Derthick and Quirk (1985), examining deregulatory processes in the realm of *economic*, as opposed to *social* regulation, criticize non–state-centered analyses of deregulation. They argue that, at least in the United States, regulated industries with a putative stake in deregulation did not ask to be deregulated. Nor were consumers' movements a major force. Instead, the deregulatory push emanated predominantly from within state regulatory agencies and courts, with commissioners and judges acting as policy entrepreneurs. Deregulatory politics and deregulation itself were only later and often quite reluctantly accepted by regulated industries such as airlines, trucking, and communications.

The foci of Derthick and Quirk (1985) and Szasz (1986) converge to highlight the role played by academic and policy think-tank experts in paving the way for and promoting pro-competitive regulatory reform. Szasz shows how U.S. economists and political scientists built a rationale for deregulation in the 1970s (see Breyer 1982 for a sophisticated but very readable overview of economic justifications and analyses of regulation and of economic justifications for deregulation). Derthick and Quirk (1985) push the role played by these experts further back in time, albeit noting that the earliest promoters of regulatory reform would never have anticipated the successful political movement for which they helped paved the way. Nonetheless, U.S. administrative law and public administration experts long had found fault with government regulatory structures and procedures. By the 1960s, economists had joined the chorus, attacking economic regulation for fostering costly inefficiencies and for shielding industries from competition. Economists also attacked economic and social regulation for producing costs in excess of benefits.

As Majone (1994) points out, where the United States tended to create regulated industries, allowing critics to catalogue subsequent *regulatory* failures, Europe traditionally tended toward public ownership, with its own set of corresponding failures to interpret and experience. When deregulatory ideologies were produced in Europe or diffused from the United States, privatization became the rallying point. But neither privatization nor the search for "less restrictive" or "less rigid" government intervention necessarily means the retreat of the state (Majone 1994, p. 80).

Deregulation is most precisely conceptualized as *reduction in the level of government regulation*. It involves eliminating or reducing government rules or lessening their strictness (Vogel 1996). Strictly speaking, deregulation moves institutional governance toward *self*-governed markets. But according to Vogel (1996), much scholarship is remiss in equating deregulation with *any* kind of liberalization or pro-competitive regulatory reform (see, e.g., Derthick and Quirk 1985). Equating deregulation with market liberalization is undesirable because it forecloses by definitional fiat the question of whether and how liberalization may involve *more* government rule making rather than less. Liberalization may involve *changing* government rules rather than eliminating them (Vogel 1996).

Indeed, Vogel (1996) argues that across capitalist democracies the trends are toward what he terms reregulation rather than deregulation. Rather than reduce their levels of regulation of the private sector, governments have reorganized their control over it. When governments privatize previously nationalized industries and when they liberalize regulated markets to introduce more competition, ordinarily this involves both the reformulation of old rules and the creation of new ones. As the title of Vogel's book suggests, then, the price of "freer markets" is "more rules" (Vogel 1996; see also, e.g., Majone 1994; Streeck 1998). Increased conceptual precision helps Vogel solve what otherwise appears as a puzzle and paradox: that, as noted by Derthick and Quirk (1985), state actors themselves promote a great deal of deregulatory activity. To the question of why governments would take action apparently against their own interests, Vogel answers "they don't." Instead, as political-institutional perspectives on regulation would suggest, governments initiate regulatory *reform* and shape *reregulation* in their own interests. Pro-competitive regulatory reform represents neither "the triumph of markets over government" nor "the triumph of [economic] interests over government" (Vogel 1996, pp. 10, 13).

Vogel rejects exclusively economic theories of deregulation that argue either that increasingly integrated global markets force governments to deregulate or that interest groups, especially regulated industries, orchestrate reform. Instead, he provides a synthesis of sorts between economic and political-institutional views. He hypothesizes that, on the one hand, governments of advanced capitalist democracies *do* face a common set of economic and cultural pressures. Technologically induced global market changes in particularly dynamic sectors like telecommunications and financial services compel governments to respond in *some* way, but without setting the terms of the response. Diffusion of market and deregulatory ideologies from the United States also exerts pressures—albeit somewhat less strong—for a response. In addition, this ideological diffusion helps explain why governments across the advanced capitalist world adopt similar reform *rhetorics*. It does *not* explain when and why they undertake reform action or the form their reregulation takes. Finally, governments do face a common politics of economic slowdown, in which they find that "the growth in demand for government services outpaces the growth of government resources for meeting this demand (Vogel 1996, p. 40). This creates political opportunity. But it does not explain why conservative and even left political parties take that opportunity in some countries, while neither left nor even conservative parties do so in others.

In short, according to Vogel's theory of deregulation, there are a set of common forces for change—some stronger, some weaker, some broader, some narrower—that set the stage for specific national responses. However, "states themselves, even more than private interest groups, have driven the reform process" (Vogel 1996, p. 4). Governments in the advanced industrial world cannot ignore private groups' interests and demands, but they take the initiative in shaping reform and constructing politically acceptable compromises. In this, governments do *not* converge in a common deregulatory trend. Instead, they adopt particular types and distinctive styles of reregulation as they achieve liberalized markets to different degrees. At its core, so-called deregulation is about "finding new ways to raise government revenue and designing new mechanisms of policy implementation" (Vogel 1996, p. 19). These goals typically concern states more than private interests, so it becomes no surprise that state actors actively mobilize to shape regulatory reform.

Vogel categorizes diverse reregulatory styles and processes in terms of two dimensions: whether the emphasis is more on liberalization or more on reregulation, and whether the reregulation undermines or enhances government control over industry. In turn, the diverse reregulatory styles and processes emerge as a function of variation across countries in political-institutional regulatory regimes, developed over time as a function of each country's own unique history, especially its history of industrialization. Regulatory regimes are "comprised of specific constellations of ideas and institutions" (Vogel 1996, p. 20). The ideas, or *regime orientation*, involve "state actors' beliefs about the proper scope, goals and methods of government intervention in the economy and about how this intervention affects economic performance" (Vogel 1996, p. 20). Diverse regime orientations cause government officials to define the public interest in varied ways, to interpret common economic and ideological pressures and trends differently, and to conceive of different kinds of responses to such pressures and trends as appropriate. *Regime organization* involves how state regulators concerned with a given industry are structured internally and how they are linked to the private sector. In contemplating reform, government actors will assess how diverse alternatives are likely to affect existing institutions and arrangements. Differences in regime organization affect especially *who*—whether political parties, bureaucrats, and so forth—will control reform processes, *whether* government officials will try to refrain state capabilities, and *what* capabilities government officials will try to retain or develop for themselves in the reform process.

Vogel's (1996) framework fundamentally reorients scholars to distinguish concepts of deregulation and reregulation and to approach both in terms of an overarching perspective that considers regulation, deregulation, and reregulation as part of the broader study of regulatory change. (Parallel efforts to integrate explanations of welfare development and retrenchment into a broader theory of change in social policy are equally underway [see, e.g., discussions in Steinmetz 1997; Stryker 1998]). Vogel's framework is conducive to investigating the interaction of international pressures and domestic politics, as well as the interaction of governments and private actors. It is likewise conducive to investigating how institutional and cultural boundaries between public and private have been variably articulated across countries and over time, and to investigating how globalization shapes opportunities for and constraints on national-level government regulation and on the development of supranational regulatory institutions.

EMPIRICAL STUDIES

Empirical research on regulation includes studies of regulatory origins (e.g., Majone 1994; Sanders 1981, 1986; Steinberg 1982), processes (e.g., Edelman 1992; Eisner 1991; Moe 1987; Yeager 1990), and impact (e.g., Beller 1982; Donahue and Heckman 1991; Mendelhoff 1979). It also includes studies of deregulation and reregulation (e.g., Derthick and Quirk 1985; Streeck 1998; Szasz 1986; Vogel 1996). Studies of processes look at the evolution of regulatory forms (e.g., Majone 1994; Stryker 1989, 1990) as well as at the substance of regulatory rules (e.g., McCammon 1990; Melnick 1983; Vogel 1996). Researchers employ a variety of methodologies. These include quantitative assessment of causes and consequences of regulation (e.g., Donahue and Heckman 1991; Mendeloff 1979; Steinberg 1982) and quantitative models of regulatory processes (e.g., Edelman 1992; Edelman et al. 1999; Yeager 1990). They also include qualitative, case-oriented legal, historical, or comparative accounts of regulatory, deregulatory, and reregulatory evolution (e.g., Majone 1994; Melnick 1983; Sanders 1981; Stryker 1990; Szasz 1986; Vogel 1996). It is hard to generalize about findings from empirical studies of regulation. A few things, however, are reasonably clear.

First, no general theory or perspective on regulation enjoys unqualified support when stacked up against the variety and complexity of regulatory experiences. Second, all extant theories have something to offer the empirical analyst. Third, in response to the first and second points, the field seems to be moving away from accounts that focus on either economic interests or political-institutional rules to more integrative or synthetic accounts that encompass a role for both. Fourth, European Union integration has increased interest in empirical research on supranational regulatory bodies, as a key part of the broader study of multitiered governance structures. Fifth, empirical building blocks are being constructed for overarching concepts and theories that account for variation in regulatory regimes and for regulatory change, whether toward increased or decreased regulation or from one institutional principle (e.g., command and control) to another (e.g., market incentives). The rest of this article elaborates on these points.

Empirical studies suggest that economic interests and resources are a major factor but not the sole one, in the dynamics of political struggles over regulatory origins and administration (Moe, 1987; Sanders 1986; Stryker 1989, 1990; Szasz 1986; Yeager 1990). Political structures and rules of the game matter because they are the mechanisms through which economic and social actors must translate their interests into regulatory policy (Moe 1987). But for legislative, administrative, and judicial participants in policy processes, these institutional mechanisms also create independent interests in, and resources for, regulatory policy making. Sanders (1981) shows that the regulation of natural gas in the United States has been a function of four sets of regionally based economic interests, including gas producer regions of the United States and gas consumer regions, as well as of electoral rules and structures. Regulatory outcomes have resulted from a dynamic relationship among political actors who reflect the changing market positions of their constituents. "The potential for sectional conflict is exacerbated by the territorial basis of elections, the weakness of the party system, and a federal structure that not only encloses different political cultures and legal systems, but also supports fifty sets of elected officials sensitive to encroachments on their respective turfs" (Sanders 1981, p. 196).

Current regulatory structures and policies *do* have feedback effects constraining and providing opportunities for subsequent regulatory policies as well as for subsequent action by parties with interests at stake in regulation (Sanders 1981; Steinberg 1982; Stryker 1990). Feedbacks occur through cultural as well as political-institutional mechanisms and political learning (e.g., Pedriana and Stryker 1997; Vogel 1996). In this regard, Vogel's (1996) comparative study of deregulation and regulation of telecommunications and financial services in the United States, the United Kingdom, France, Germany, and Japan highlights the mediating role of nationally specific regime orientations. State actors interpret situations and conceive of responses through the lens of regime orientation. Their cognitive and normative interpretive work then shapes the form and content of regulatory reform. Pedriana and Stryker (1997) demonstrate that both general equal opportunity values and the specific language in which they are expressed provide raw materials for construction of symbolic resources by actors struggling over the enforcement of equal employment and affirmative action law in the United States. The work of Majone (1994) and Boyer (1996), among others, suggests that political learning occurs through the experience and interpretation of regulatory failures as well as of market failures.

In addition, the legal structures and culture through which most regulation is administered in the Untied States significantly shape regulatory processes and outcomes. For example, Melnick (1983) shows how the narrow, highly structured, reactive, and adversarial legal processes through which pollution control takes place in the United States have led to court decisions that simultaneously extend the scope of EPA programs and lessen agency resources for achieving pollution control goals. Appellate judges tend to promote stringent antipollution standards because they are removed from local concerns and are likely to be inspired by broad public goals. In a different institutional location, trial judges observe the impact on local businesses and citizens of imposing strict regulation. Their flexibility in response to the perceived harm of strict regulation generates an equity-balancing enforcement that counteracts what is accomplished in standard setting.

Likewise, because legal mandates are not self-executing and many are ambiguous, the response of regulated parties is an important mediator of regulatory impact. This response includes actions taken by organizations to demonstrate their compliance with law. For example, Edelman (1992) and Edelman and colleagues (1999) show that organizations respond to federal equal employment law in the United States by creating equal employment opportunity policies, organizational units, and grievance procedures. These both promote symbolism over substance and shape later court constructions of what constitutes compliance and what will insulate organizations from liability. More obviously, the response of regulated parties also includes whether and how public and private institutions and individuals invoke regulatory law on behalf of aggrieved parties (e.g., Burstein 1991). Additionally, it includes how public and private actors mobilize the values and language encapsulated *in* the law as political-cultural and legal resources to *change* the law (e.g., Pedriana and Stryker 1997).

Yet another insight from empirical studies is that regulatory implementation is influenced by internal agency politics as well as by the agency's external environment. Likewise, technical experts play an important role in shaping regulatory evolution. Stryker (1989, 1990) has shown how, in conjunction with class and political institutional factors, intra-NLRB conflict between agency economists and lawyers over the proper administrative use of social science caused Congress to abolish the NLRB's economic research unit. Katzmann (1980) and Eisner (1991) have shown how internal jockeying by economists within the FTC changed enforcement priorities and outcomes over time. Even more generally, empirical studies of regulation and deregulation point to the justificatory and mobilizing import of diverse kinds of scientific and technical expertise (e.g., Derthick and Quirk 1985; Eisner 1991; Szasz 1986). While heavily relied upon to promote deregulation and pro-competitive regulatory reform, economic analysis also can be mobilized to promote more stringent regulation and diverse types of reregulation (e.g., Rose-Ackerman 1992; Stryker 1989).

Empirical studies of regulation also show that regulation often has unintended effects. Yeager (1990) shows how EPA sanctioning decisions and processes, while rational in the face of economic, political, and legal constraints on the agency, reproduce private sector inequality by favoring large corporations that have financial and technical resources. Large companies have greater access to agency proceedings than do small companies. Agency proceedings often change pollution-control requirements in favor of regulated firms, so that ultimately large corporations have fewer pollution violations. In decisions to apply the harshest sanctions—criminal and civil prosecutions—the EPA may well avoid tangling with the most resource-rich firms for fear of losing in court. Melnick (1983, p. 354) indicates a similar dynamic. Ostensibly neutral procedures, then, create inequitable law enforcement and may also help reproduce the problems that led to the initial pollution-control legislation.

Yet another important message emphasized by empirical studies of regulation in the 1990s is the need to consider the growth of supranational mechanisms of governance and how these interrelate with national government regulation. Majone

(1994), for example, shows that with minimal explicit legal mandate and with very limited resources, there has nonetheless been continuous growth in the final three decades of the twentieth century in regulation by the European Community (EC, now the European Union, or EU). Economic and social regulation is "the core" of EU policy making (Majone 1994, p. 77). It is undertaken by the European Commission (Commission) in tandem with the European Court of Justice (ECJ), now supplemented with a court of first instance (see Leibfried and Pierson 1995). Between 1967–1987, for example, even *before* the Single European Act recognized EC authority to legislate to protect the environment, there were close to "200 environmental directives, regulations and decisions made by the European Commission" (Majone 1994, p. 85). Consumer product safety, banking and financial services, and medical drug testing also have been areas of high-volume Commission regulatory activity. Regulation has provided a way for the Commission to expand its role in spite of tight EC budgets and the serious political-institutional constraints embedded in the EC's legal framework, at the same time as EC member states have been willing to delegate to a supranational authority because agreements among the EC national governments had low credibility (Majone 1994).

In the regulatory arena, the ECJ has been as important as, or even more important than, the Commission (see, e.g., Leibfried and Pierson 1995). Ostner and Lewis (1995), for example, stress the *inter-relationship* of the Commission and the ECJ. Even before the Single European Act in 1987, "gender policies . . . evolved through the intricate interplay between these two supranational bodies, within the range of outcomes tolerated by member states. By the late 1980s the Court's interpretations of article 199 [of the Treaty of Rome], Commission-fostered directives that [gave] the article concrete form and extend[ed] it, and the Court's subsequent rulings about the meaning of the directives yielded a body of gender-related policies of substantial scope" (Ostner and Lewis 1995, p. 159). No wonder scholars have characterized the EU as a "state of courts and technocrats" (Leibfried 1992, p. 249) and have highlighted "the rise of the regulatory state in Europe" (Majone 1994, p. 77). In turn, European scholars' awareness of the import of Commission and ECJ regulatory activity has fueled their growing research interest in American-style regulation (Majone 1994; see also Leibfried and Pierson 1995).

Finally, although capture of government regulators by regulated parties can and does occur (see Sabatier 1975; Sanders 1981), it need not. Enactment of regulatory legislation can also lead to cycles of aggressive enforcement alternating with periods of capture or, similarly, to enforcement that oscillates between or among the interests at stake in regulation or between periods of regulation and deregulation or reregulation. For example, over time, FTC enforcement has alternated between favoring big or small business and core or peripheral economic regions of the United States (Stryker 1990). Sanders's (1981) study of natural gas regulation in the United States shows that the initial federal legislation mixed goals of consumer protection and of industry promotion. Federal Power Commission interaction with its environment did not result in stable capture by gas producers but rather in oscillation between capture by gas consumers and capture by gas producers. Clearly, consumers, labor, and other subordinate groups can be, and have been, benefited by regulation (see, e.g., Sanders 1981; Steinberg 1982; Stryker 1989). But the political economy of capitalism also sets structural and cultural limits to these benefits (McCammon 1990; Szasz 1986; Yeager 1990).

In this regard, economic globalization and European economic integration enhance the political and economic resources of business groups at the expense of labor, providing pressures and opportunities for governments to undertake market-liberalizing regulatory reforms (Streeck 1995, 1998; Stryker 1998; Vogel 1996). However, these same processes also may generate counterpressures and counteropportunities. As Streeck (1998) shows, European integration has been a process of economic liberalization by international means. In this process, national-level regulations are exposed to competitive market pressures, including the threat of "regulatory arbitrage"—business corporations moving capital or firms from countries with less favorable regulations to countries with a more favorable regulatory climate. Competitive market pressures then further advance liberalization. But liberalization likewise "calls forth demands" from individuals and communities for market-constraining reregulation, so that they can "cope with the uncertainties of free markets and stabilize their social existence in dynamically changing economic conditions" (Streeck 1998, p. 432).

A major challenge to theories and empirical research on government regulation in the future is to model and explain the historical and comparative dynamics of both economic and social regulation at intersecting subnational, national, and supranational levels. Further work should continue to address diversity and change over time and place in regulatory scope, levels, institutional forms, and cultural justifications. Ideally, further juxtaposition of abstract theory and concrete historical and comparative research, both qualitative and quantitative, can lead to integrated theories of regulatory origins, processes, and impact. Ideally, as well, these theories can explain not just regulation but also deregulation and reregulation. This is a tall order, but the seeds have been planted in scholarship like that of Vogel (1996), which is equally sensitive to economic and organizational interests and resources, to political structures and rules, and to regulatory cultures (see also the empirically informed analytic frameworks offered in, e.g., Scharpf 1997b; Stryker 1996). Seeds also have been planted in research programs, like Vogel's (1996), that are sensitive to periods or cycles in which different economic and other institutional arrangements, incentives, and constraints operate, and to feedback effects from past to future regulatory policies and processes (see also Boyer 1996).

Whether or not such an integrative and synthetic theory is achieved, a combination of unfolding social processes, including globalization, courtled European integration, and democratization and marketization in eastern Europe and elsewhere all will continue to enhance interest in the study of government regulation. All these processes simultaneously promote economic liberalization and the regulatory state. Whatever else these current political-economic changes bring, they certainly should enhance scholarly dialogue and also synergy across national borders in the study of regulation.

REFERENCES

Ayres, Ian, and John Braithwaite 1989 "Tripartism, Empowerment and Game-Theoretic Notions of Regulatory Capture" (American Bar Foundation Working Paper No. 8902). Chicago: American Bar Foundation.

Beller, Andrea 1982 "Occupational Segregation by Sex: Determinants and Changes." *Journal of Human Resources* 17:371–392.

Breyer, Stephen 1982 *Regulation and Its Reform*. Cambridge, Mass.: Harvard University Press.

Boyer, Robert 1996 "State and Market: A New Engagement for the Twenty-First Century?" In R. Boyer and D. Drache, eds., *States Against Markets: The Limits of Globalization*. London: Routledge.

Burstein, Paul 1991 "Legal Mobilization as a Social Movement Tactic: The Struggle for Equal Employment Opportunity." *American Journal of Sociology* 96:1201–1225.

Derthick, Martha, and Paul Quirk 1985 *The Politics of Deregulation*. Washington D.C.: Brookings Institution.

Donahue, John J., III, and James Heckman 1991 "Continuous versus Episodic Change: The Impact of Civil Rights Policy on the Economic Status of Blacks." *Journal of Economic Literature* 29:1603–1643.

Edelman, Lauren 1992 "Legal Ambiguity and Symbolic Structures: Organizational Mediation of Civil Rights Law." *American Journal of Sociology* 97:1531–1576.

——, Christopher Uggen, and Howard S. Erlanger 1999 "The Endogeneity of Legal Regulation: Grievance Procedures as Rational Myth." *American Journal of Sociology* 105:406–454.

Eisner, Mark Allen 1991 *Antitrust and the Triumph of Economics: Institutions, Expertise and Policy Change*. Chapel Hill: University of North Carolina Press.

Fiorina, Morris P. 1982 "Legislative Choice of Regulatory Forms: Legal Process or Administrative Process?" *Public Choice* 30:33–66.

Katzmann, Robert A. 1980 *Regulatory Bureaucracy: The Federal Trade Commission and Antitrust Policy*. Cambridge, Mass.: MIT Press.

Lange, Peter, and Marino Regini 1989 "Interests and Institutions: Forms of Social Regulation and Public Policy Making." In P. Lange and M. Regini, eds., *State, Market and Social Regulation: New Perspectives on Italy*. Cambridge, U.K.: Cambridge University Press.

Leibfried, Stephan 1992 "Towards a European Welfare State? On Integrating Poverty Regimes into the European Community." In Z. Ferge and J. E. Kolberg, eds., *Social Policy in a Changing Europe*. Boulder, Colo.: Westview Press.

——, and Paul Pierson, eds. 1995 *European Social Policy: Between Fragmentation and Integration*. Washington D.C.: Brookings.

Levine, Rhonda 1988 *Class Structure and the New Deal: Industrial Labor, Industrial Capital and the State*. Lawrence: University of Kansas Press.

Majone, Giandomenico 1994 "The Rise of the Regulatory State in Europe." *West European Politics* 17:77–101.

McCammon, Holly J. 1990 "Legal Limits on Labor Militancy: U.S. Labor Law and the Right to Strike Since the New Deal." *Social Problems* 37:206–229.

Meidinger, Errol 1987 "Regulatory Culture: A Theoretical Outline." *Law & Policy* 9:355–385.

Melnick, R. Shep 1983 *Regulation and the Courts: The Case of the Clean Air Act.* Washington, D.C.: Brookings Institution.

Mendeloff, John 1979 *Regulating Safety: An Economic and Political Analysis of Occupational Safety and Health Policy.* Cambridge, Mass.: MIT Press.

Mitnick, Barry M. 1980 *The Political Philosophy of Regulation: Creating, Designing and Removing Regulatory Forms.* New York: Columbia University Press.

Moe, Terry 1987 "Interests, Institutions and Positive Theory: The Politics of the NLRB." *Studies in American Political Development* 2:236–299.

Ostner, Ilona, and Jane Lewis 1995 "Gender and the Evolution of European Social Policies." In S. Leibfried and P. Pierson, eds., *European Social Policy: Between Fragmentation and Integration.* Washington, D.C.: Brookings Institution.

Pedriana, Nicholas, and Robin Stryker 1997 "Political Culture Wars 1960s Style: Equal Opportunity–Affirmative Action Law and the Philadelphia Plan." *American Journal of Sociology* 103:633–691.

Powell, Walter W., and Paul J. DiMaggio, eds. 1991 *The New Institutionalism in Organizational Analysis.* Chicago: University of Chicago Press.

Regini, Marino 1995 *Uncertain Boundaries: The Social and Political Construction of European Economies.* Cambridge, U.K.: Cambridge University Press.

Rose-Ackerman, Susan 1992 *Rethinking the Progressive Agenda: The Reform of the American Regulatory State.* New York and Toronto: The Free Press.

Sabatier, Paul 1975 "Social Movements and Regulatory Agencies: Toward a More Adequate—and Less Pessimistic—Theory of 'Clientele Capture'." *Policy Sciences* 6:301–342.

Sanders, M. Elizabeth 1981 *The Regulation of Natural Gas: Policy and Politics, 1938–1978.* Philadelphia: Temple University Press.

—— 1986 "Industrial Concentration, Sectional Competition, and Antitrust Politics in America, 1880–1980." *Studies in American Political Development* 1:142–214.

Scharpf, Fritz 1997a "Economic Integration, Democracy and the Welfare State." *Journal of European Public Policy* 4 (March):18–36.

—— 1997b *Games Real Actors Play: Actor-Centered Institutionalism in Policy Research.* Boulder, Colo.: Westview Press.

Skocpol, Theda 1992 *Protecting Soldiers and Mothers: The Political Origins of Social Policy in the United States.* Cambridge, Mass.: Belknap.

Steinberg, Ronnie 1982 *Wages and Hours: Labor and Reform in Twentieth Century America.* New Brunswick, N.J.: Rutgers University Press.

Steinmetz, George 1997 "Social Class and the Reemergence of the Radical Right in Contemporary Germany." In John R. Hall, ed., *Reworking Class.* Ithaca, N.Y.: Cornell University Press.

Stigler, George 1971 "The Theory of Economic Regulation." *Bell Journal of Economic and Management Science* 2:3–21.

Streeck, Wolfgang 1995 "From Market Making to State Building? Reflections on the Political Economy of European Social Policy." In S. Liebfried and P. Pierson, eds., *European Social Policy: Between Fragmentation and Integration.* Washington D.C.: Brookings Institution.

—— 1998 "The Internationalization of Industrial Relations in Europe: Prospects and Problems." *Politics & Society* 26:429–459.

Stryker, Robin 1989 "Limits on Technocratization of the Law: The Elimination of the National Labor Relations Board's Division of Economic Research." *American Sociological Review* 54:341–358.

—— 1990 "A Tale of Two Agencies: Class, Political-Institutional and Organizational Factors Affecting State Reliance on Social Science." *Politics & Society* 18:101–141.

—— 1996 "Beyond History vs. Theory: Strategic Narrative and Sociological Explanation." *Sociological Methods and Research* 24:304–352.

—— 1998 "Globalization and the Welfare State." *International Journal of Sociology and Social Policy* 18:1–49.

Swidler, Ann 1986 "Culture in Action." *American Sociological Review* 51:273–286.

Szasz, Andrew 1986 "The Reversal of Federal Policy Toward Worker Safety and Health." *Science and Society* 50:25–51.

Vogel, Steven K. 1996 *Freer Markets, More Rules: Regulatory Reform in Advanced Industrial Countries.* Ithaca, N.Y.: Cornell University Press.

Weir, Margaret, Ann Shola Orloff, and Theda Skocpol 1988 "Understanding American Social Politics." In M. Weir, A. Orloff, and T. Skocpol, eds., *The Politics of Social Policy in the United States.* Princeton, N.J.: Princeton University Press.

Wilson, James Q. 1980a "The Politics of Regulation." In J. A. Wilson, ed., *The Politics of Regulation.* New York: Basic Books.

—— ed. 1980b *The Politics of Regulation.* New York: Basic Books.

Yeager, Peter C. 1990 *The Limits of Law: The Public Regulation of Private Pollution.* Cambridge, U.K.: Cambridge University Press.

ROBIN STRYKER

GROUP COHESIVENESS

See Interpersonal Attraction; Small Groups.

GROUP CONFLICT RESOLUTION

To understand conflict resolution among groups it is helpful first to consider the role of conflict in and among groups. Conflict analysis of groups is divided between the study of *intra*group conflict, that which happens within a group among its members, and *inter*group conflict, that which happens between one or more groups where the conflict is viewed as involving the group as a whole. The study of these phenomena is closely related to the study of both group dynamics and cross-cultural relations. A further distinction is made according to the group level being studied. Here the separation is generally between group conflicts and international conflicts. Group conflicts include both communal group conflicts and workplace conflicts. Communal group conflicts can involve just about any group that provides people with social identity. Social identity is itself a group-level concept, since it is defined as the identity we gain from being part of a collectivity, a group. Since most of the hours of our days are organized around group membership, the study of groups and their interactions is central to the work of sociologists.

When groups are in conflict, the very presence of the group intensifies and changes the way conflict between individuals is perceived. Membership in the group affords the individual two perceptions that impact on the conflict: (1) that the individual is right and justified to engage in and attempt to win the conflict and (2) that the individual will be evaluated and either further embraced or rejected based on his or her performance in a conflict situation. Within groups, conflict often results in patterns of splintering or perhaps a coup d'état and expulsion. Between groups, conflict can encourage deindividuation, ethnocentrism, and diabolical imaging of the enemy. Groups often provide individuals with a way to rationalize their involvement in a conflict and perhaps to take actions they might otherwise avoid. Conflict resolution is likewise changed in a group situation.

Defining exactly what a conflict is has also been an important part of the analysis of conflict and its resolution. There are generally two accepted ways of defining "conflict": (1) realistic and (2) perceived. The former involves tangible, verifiable competing interests. The latter refers to situations where it is believed by one or both parties that the other stands in the way of achieving what is desired. Conflicts occur over resources, power distribution, and values. They are classified as latent (yet to be noticed) or manifest. A final method of defining "conflict" is as destructive or constructive. Although viewed by most people as risky and something to be avoided, conflict is often seen differently by conflict analysts. Most who study conflict and its resolution argue that conflict holds the potential to be constructive, to create positive social change. These theorists and practitioners argue that how one copes with conflict is the important distinction. If the proper structures exist (such as skilled trainers or participants), conflict can actually have creative and constructive outcomes.

CONFLICT RESOLUTION

The area of conflict resolution is itself an interdisciplinary field of research. Despite the great diversity of scholars involved in this work, they are brought together by a common interest in understanding how and when conflicts are resolved. What to call the work varies, including such terms as "conflict management," "conflict resolution," and "conflict transformation." A variable here is to what extent and in what way one might get involved to eliminate a conflict. Scholars in this area favor searching for nonviolent and noncontentious methods for ending conflicts, perhaps because these methods are felt to be more permanent than the cycle of escalation likely to emerge with aggressive measures for "ending" conflicts. Avoidance and repression are also considered to be negative responses to conflict.

Here we focus not generally on the field of conflict resolution but specifically on it in relation to groups. While there is much application of theory and research across the levels of study, there is not much agreement on the transferability of ideas from the interpersonal level to the group or international level. Conflict resolution among groups remains an important but understudied social process. Great strides have been taken in developing various models of conflict resolution at the interpersonal level, but among groups the process remains less easily identifiable. At the international level, only small inroads have been made in developing and testing possible methods. War or military threats remain the most common responses to conflict among nations.

Another variable is when and how conflict might be a positive social phenomenon. Functionalists may wonder about the purpose of the conflict in the larger social construct. Although much more writing exists on the negative impact of conflicts, there are many who argue for the creative potential of conflict. The positive view generally takes one of two tacks. Most common are those scholars who argue that conflict leads to greater understanding, relaying of information, and potentially new ideas and stronger relationships. For them, what matters is how conflict is handled. With proper training and skills, one can learn to turn conflict into a creative interaction. A second group argues that conflict in the form of competition can improve work quality, increase production, and improve unity. They are quick to point out that task conflict especially has this effect; interpersonal conflict rarely yields this positive effect.

INTERPERSONAL VERSUS GROUP CONFLICT

Conflicts happen at all levels of society. The major classifications of levels of conflict include interpersonal, intergroup, and international. The primary distinction between intergroup and international conflicts is that nationalism provides a particular framework for and gives an intensity to conflicts that distinguish them from group conflicts in general. Intergroup conflicts may be organization based

or community based, or they may stem from racial, ethnic, or class differences among groups not recognized at the nation-state level. Fisher (1990) argues that the study of group and international conflict is not nearly as well developed as the research on conflict at the interpersonal level. He cautions against assuming that analysis derived from interpersonal experiences can be generalized to other levels. He points to basic information about how groups affect conflict and suggests that these differences necessitate different strategies for addressing and reducing conflict among groups and nations.

IMPACT OF GROUPS ON CONFLICT

Group conflict is typically divided into two categories: (1) intragroup and (2) intergroup. Conflict within groups is viewed as potentially harmful since it can lead to competition for leadership, loss of focus on group purpose, and membership loss. Intragroup conflicts are typically about power and control over content, purpose, and goals. It can also emerge out of recognition of intragroup inequalities that are found unacceptable by those with less power.

The primary means of limiting intragroup conflict is maintaining a strong normative structure with effective member socialization. When conflicts arise, avoidance often leads the group to dissolve. Methods for solving conflicts within groups include facilitation or problem solving led by an external professional or perhaps a skilled insider, capitulation by one party, subdivision of the group, or re-prioritization of group goals. The latter often occurs in the presence of an outside threat. In fact, a useful response to internal conflict is the identification of a common fear or enemy. External threat increases the sense of homogeneity within the group, encourages commitment to ensuring group survival, and rationalizes stern measures to limit internal challenges to the status quo.

Intergroup conflicts are typically about control and distribution of resources (objective conflicts) or threats to identity or values (perceptual, or subjective, conflicts). Realistic group conflict theory (RCT) focuses on rational mechanisms for understanding group conflict. Social identity theory (SIT) focuses on the idea that the mere perception of belonging to a discrete group is sufficient to produce intergroup discrimination. According to SIT, groups are the major basis for the formation of an individual's sense of identity. And groups produce a positive social identity by being favorably compared to other groups (Fisher 1990). As suggested above, intergroup conflicts can also emerge when there is a desire to quell intragroup conflict through the creation of an enemy.

Usually intergroup conflict is considered more dynamic, more likely to be intractable, quicker to escalate, and more in need of external intervention than interpersonal conflict. According to White, escalation of intergroup conflict is fed by (1) a diabolical image of the enemy, (2) a virile self-image, and (3) a moral self-image (cited in Fisher 1990). Misperceptions and stereotypes of those outside the group are confirmed by group members in an effort to solidify group identity and establish the boundaries of membership. According to balance theory, groups tend to minimize intragroup differences and exaggerate intergroup differences.

Social psychologists suggest that the magnification process stems from an audience effect. In a group, one has confirmation and support for one's position as right and justified. In a group, a clear leader often emerges as external threats grow. Because groups in conflict tend to prefer more aggressive leaders, leaders of groups find themselves pushed to take stances more extreme than they would as individuals. They are expected to succeed (win) or lose power or membership in the group. Leaders often find it difficult to negotiate on behalf of a group with diverse opinions about priorities. Members of the group are more inclined to follow orders in the face of an external threat and to be convinced to commit acts (sometime heinous) to ensure group survival. This may help individuals' involvement in genocide, torture, and other crimes they would not consider participating in for individual gain.

RESPONSES TO CONFLICT

Scholars in the field point to five possible responses to conflict. The actual names of these responses vary, but they are well represented by the following terms: contending, yielding, avoiding, compromising, and problem solving (integrative solutions). These categories are appropriate for all levels of conflict—interpersonal, intergroup, and international. The first three (contending, yielding, and avoiding) tend to escalate conflict. The last two fall clearly within the purview of creative conflict resolution.

Contending behavior is when a party to a conflict seeks to solve the conflict at the other party's expense. Rubin and colleagues (1994) suggest that contentious tactics range from light to heavy, where "light" tactics result in acceptable or neutral consequences for the other party and "heavy" tactics impose or threaten severe consequences. Contending behavior is a key part of the upward spiral of escalation, since it usually evokes a defensive response from the other party. As long as a party believes it can win (benefits outweigh costs), it is likely to practice contending behavior.

Yielding responses are sometimes the partner to contending behavior. A party will yield when it is more important that the conflict be over than that the party wins. Yielding may be an initial strategy to lay the basis for getting something else that is a priority at a later time. Or perhaps the concern is just not an issue for the party that yields.

Avoiding conflict is practiced by a party that does not want to encourage the conflict to become manifest. Usually the hope is that if avoided, the conflict will become unimportant over time. While sometimes avoiding does allow space for conflict to fade, it rarely works to actually resolve those issues underlying the conflict. Therefore there is commonly a resurgence of conflict in another way or at a later time. Avoiding conflict can also be perceived by the initiating party as an act of escalation. As such, it can cause the upward spiral of conflict to begin.

Compromising about a conflict is the outcome that most people associate with conflict resolution processes. For some analysts, compromise is a sufficient method to diffuse conflict; others argue that it still falls short of the goal of a "win–win" solution. In a compromise, parties to the conflict are expected to give up some part of their needs or goals if they stand in the way of the other party's reaching important needs or goals. Each party is partially successful in achieving what it sets out to gain or protect at the beginning of the conflict. Neither one completely loses and neither one completely wins.

Problem-solving behavior entails engaging in a process with the goal of achieving a win–win solution to the conflict. A win–win solution is also called an "integrated solution" when the parties' needs and goals are different but a resolution is found that meets the concerns of both. The process of problem solving is designed to encourage conflicting parties to think creatively to establish possible joint needs and goals and to work cooperatively to solve their problems. There are various methods, such as log-rolling, expanding the pie, and bridging, that can assist in achieving a win–win solution. Log-rolling encourages parties to prioritize their needs and preferences so that lower priority requirements can be negotiated as trade offs in a win–win solution. Expanding the pie requires the infusion of additional resources—often by a party external to the conflict. This makes it possible to satisfy competing needs. In bridging, parties discover mutual definitions of their needs and a single solution leave both satisfied.

ACHIEVING CONFLICT RESOLUTION

A central question in the study of conflict and its resolution involves the conditions that support constructive outcomes to conflict. According to Deutsch (1973), a cooperative environment breeds cooperation and a competitive environment encourages groups to compete. He also suggests that there are three conditions that encourage problem-solving behavior: (1) the arousal of the desire to solve the conflict; (2) conditions that permit reformulation of the issues of the conflict; and (3) the availability of diverse and flexible ideas. Rubin and colleagues (1994) suggest (as do many other scholars) that to turn from contentious behavior to problem solving, the parties must believe that the costs outweigh the benefits if they continue to fight. This may happen because resources are scarce, because the parties fear a permanent loss of their relationship, or perhaps because another party intervenes and provides an incentive (or threat) that encourages seeking a resolution. Sometimes parties in conflict are moved to problem solving by the introduction of a superordinate goal or by the emergence of a common or shared threat.

Establishing communication between the parties is an essential part of turning competitive conflict into cooperative problem solving. The dynamics of groups can make this particularly challenging to accomplish. Leaders will not want to admit that they exaggerated stereotypes and negative associations to encourage diabolical imaging of the enemy. And leaders that emerged during the escalation of conflict will worry about damaging their credibility by agreeing to enter negotiations. For most people, negotiations mean compromise, which means appearing to have lost, at least partially. Communication and understanding can also be challenging across cultures. Lederach (1995) suggests that while the general progression of a conflict and its resolution remains fairly similar from one culture to the next, the specific processes and techniques for solving problems are dramatically different from one cultural group to the next.

Although it might prove challenging to establish, in any conflict communication is essential to building trust, eliciting interests, and defining the problems and possible solutions. Trust is also built through reciprocity of positive initiatives. As Kriesberg (1998) suggests, changes at three levels—within the group, between the groups, and in the larger social context—all contribute to the initiation of deescalation. Ongoing case studies help us understand how seemingly intractable conflicts can be softened through the transformation of interparty relationships and the intraparty absorption of those changes.

APPLICATIONS OF CONFLICT RESOLUTION FOR GROUPS

Contact Theory. Much effort has gone into identifying conditions that encourage the deescalation of conflict. Organized and well-structured contact between group members is regarded as essential for breaking down stereotypes and assumptions that prevent initiating discussion of the conflict(s). It is thought that this contact needs to be not simply positive but genuinely cooperative, so that new methods of interacting can be learned. Also, the parties need to enter into the contract as equals. Two studies of groups—by Sherif and by Blake and Mouton—suggest that building trust between competing groups requires the creation of superordinate goals if the groups are to move beyond stereotypes and negative assumptions (cited in Fisher 1990). Furthermore, many researchers (Fisher 1990; Rubin et al. 1994) point to the positive function of superordinate goals or shared tasks in reducing intergroup tensions, especially bias or ethnocentrism. The cooperative nature of this structured contact can decrease perceived threat from the other group, thus supporting the reduction of bias and ethnocentrism. Much of the work in cross-cultural conflict resolution and sensitivity or diversity training operates from this belief that structured contact can be used to challenge people's assumptions about other groups.

Third-Party Intervention (Intermediaries). Here, an intermediary intercedes with the goal of influencing or facilitating the settlement of a conflict. Historically force has been the common form of intervention. However, Princen (1992) argues that the intermediary role is becoming much more diverse in the contemporary international system. As an intermediary, a party does not impose a solution or have a direct stake in the outcome. However, it is possible that an intermediary has an indirect interest that the problem be solved. Thus Princen (1992) distinguishes those with an indirect stake (principal mediator) from those with no stake at all (neutral mediator). He suggests that the motivation to intervene shapes the form and content of the intervention made by a third party.

A typology of the forms of third-party intervention in conflict resolution would certainly include the following:

- Peacekeeping. Placement of military forces from a third party within another country on behalf of the third party or an international organization (e.g., the United Nations) to enforce or maintain a cease-fire and/or a peace agreement. While soldiers are typically armed, they limit their use of weapons to self-defense and defense of the peace agreement.

- Arbitration. An individual or a board of arbitrators is appointed (usually by a court or someone in a position of higher power) to listen to the concerns of the parties and elicit their suggested solutions. The arbitrator crafts an agreement to address these concerns. Parties who go to an arbitrator agree to abide by the decision, regardless of whether the outcome is considered favorable to one's concerns (binding arbitration).

- Mediation. Parties in conflict meet with an intermediary who facilitates a discussion about the conflict and each party's concerns. The mediator is expected to be neutral on the outcome of the issue and typically is a stranger to each party. There are exceptions in some international situations, where it is often a preference of the parties to know and trust the mediator prior to the meeting. And in some cases the international mediator may have an indirect interest in the outcome of the conflict (principal mediator). Regardless, the philosophy of mediation is that the parties solve their own conflict while the mediator encourages the process, especially the initiation of communication early in the discussions.

- Conciliation. Sometimes also known as "shuttle diplomacy" or "track-two diplomacy," this is mediation work that happens without bringing the parties face-to-face. Often this is the first step in developing enough trust for the parties to meet (especially at the international level). These intermediaries must establish high levels of trust and legitimacy with the parties in order to be succeed. Often they are known to the parties, or are powerful international players, or are generally recognized for their success in international mediation.

- Consultation. In this approach, parties are brought together by a conflict resolution specialist in a workshop format to learn problem-solving skills. Usually the entire group (or significant leadership in the group) is involved. The workshop leader works with the groups to encourage a positive motivation for solving the conflict, to improve communication between the members of the groups, to help the groups define the conflict, and to regulate interaction as the groups discuss their problems. Whereas in much arbitration and mediation the concern is for agreement, here the concern is for building new, positive relationships between the parties by changing their interactions in a controlled setting (Fisher 1990).

These workshops are commonly organized around issues such as communication skills, group decision making, and cross-cultural understanding. They are commonly used with community groups or in work settings where a long-term cooperative relationship is either necessary or desirable.

Unilateral Mechanisms. Even without the intervention by a third party, sometimes a player in a conflict will initiate the deescalation process. This most likely occurs when there is apparently little to be gained (and much to be lost) by continuing the conflict. Unilateral moves typically begin with small confidence-building measures. These actions stand on their own and are done without the requirement of reciprocation (although that may be the hope). The goal is to break the upward spiral of conflict by opening a channel of communication or establishing a foundation for trust.

- GRIT. This is the acronym for "graduated and reciprocated initiatives in tension-reduction," a strategy designed by Charles Osgood in the early 1960s that is intended to streamline unilateral measures (cited in Rubin et al. 1994). Some of his guidelines include announcing the series of unilateral initiatives ahead of time with a clear time line and continuing the announced steps even if the other party does not reciprocate. At the same time, the initiating party maintains its ability to retaliate in case the opposition responds with contentious behavior. The initiatives should reward the other party for cooperating and thus become increasingly favorable to the other party (Fisher 1990; Kreisberg 1998; Rubin et al. 1994).

- Dialogue groups. This long-term approach to building understanding between groups entails bringing members of groups together on a regular basis for general discussion. Often these meetings bring together people not directly engaged in the conflict. Hubbard (1997) reports the use of these groups in many communities in the United States to bring together Israelis and Palestinians. The groups typically also include members unrelated to either of the conflict groups. The groups discuss issues generally or specifically, depending on local, national, or international events. Dialogue groups have also been used in international conflicts to bring together the "average, everyday" people who must learn once again to live side-by-side once the hostilities have ceased.

CURRENT STATUS OF THE FIELD AND RECOMMENDATIONS FOR FURTHER RESEARCH

The field of conflict resolution is clearly interdisciplinary. With the end of the Cold War and the changing nature of conflict internationally, the field has become increasingly influential. Sociologists and social psychologists have contributed to theory building and the development of practical applications at all levels (interpersonal, group, international). The particular concern that sociologists have for group relations and for the alleviation of social inequalities (a common source of conflict) has made a natural fit between the areas of research. Conflict analysts are heirs to the work of Marx, Weber, Simmel, and many other influential sociologists.

A primary interest in both research and in the application of the field is in the area of ethnic conflict. Sociologists are working on these issues both in urban communities and at the international level. Another important area of interest is teaching conflict resolution theory and skills to young people. Mediation became well established both in the schools (elementary through university levels) and in the judicial system in the 1990s. There is also interest in an alternative to the adjudication system, an approach called "restorative justice."

A challenge to researchers and practitioners is that each conflict has its unique elements. While we have been able to isolate basic concepts and "rules" of the escalation and deescalation of conflict, the nature of human beings resists a single approach to the science of conflict resolution. Most scholars acknowledge that there is more need for study of individual cases of conflicts and for the comparison of specific conflict and conflict resolution processes. This would certainly provide more resources for the teachers and learners of conflict resolution techniques. At the same time, there is strong resistance to developing a monolithic model, since cultural, historical, and individual characteristics must be taken into account with each conflict. Much of the success of the application of the knowledge gained in the field is dependent upon the skill of the conflict resolution specialist and his or her willingness to respond to case-specific information. There is also a concern that while research is necessary to increase our understanding, the most significant work is done by those who work as practitioners of the conflict resolution process.

REFERENCES

Deutsch, Morton 1973 *The Resolution of Conflict.* New Haven, Conn.: Yale University Press.

Fisher, Ronald 1990 *The Social Psychology of Intergroup and International Conflict Resolution.* New York: Springer-Verlag.

Hubbard, Amy 1997 "Face-to-Face at Arm's Length: Conflict Norms and Extra-Group Relations in Grassroots Dialogue Groups." *Human Organization* 56(3):265–274.

Kriesberg, Louis 1998 *Constructive Conflicts.* Lanham, Md.: Rowman and Littlefield.

Lederach, John Paul 1995 *Preparing for Peace.* Syracuse, N.Y.: Syracuse University Press.

Osgood, Charles 1962 *An Alternative to War or Surrender.* Urbana, Ill.: University of Illinois Press.

Princen, Tom 1992 *Intermediaries in International Conflict.* Princeton, N.J.: Princeton University Press.

Rubin, Jeffrey, Dean Pruitt, and Sung Hee Kim 1994 *Social Conflict: Escalation, Stalemate, and Settlement.* New York: McGraw-Hill.

Simmel, Georg 1955 *Conflict and the Web of Group Affiliations.* New York: Free Press.

LYNNE WOEHRLE

GROUP PROBLEM SOLVING

See Decision Making Theory and Research; Group Conflict Resolution; Interpersonal Conflict Resolution; Small Groups; Social Psychology.

GROUP SIZE

Some of the earliest and most basic ideas about groups in sociology concern group size. Cooley (1922) described how people universally are members of primary groups, which are small in size, face-to-face, highly intimate, cooperative, and enduring. Prototypes include families and groups of friends. Although people also participate in secondary groups, which are typically larger, less personal, more formally organized, and more limited in duration and purpose, primary group participation appears necessary for teaching children the requisites for participating in society, including language, basic social skills, values, and identities. Simmel (1950) described the profound effects on interpersonal relations when the smallest group, the dyad (pair), expands to a triad. The dyad is unique because it can be destroyed by the loss of a single member, and this feature often leads to a degree of intimacy and closeness not found in larger groups. Adding another person, a third party, to form a triad dramatically transforms the character of the relations. Simmel noted three different roles served by a third party. One role is as a nonpartisan or mediator, which can serve to draw the members of the pair closer together. For example, the birth of a child may enhance the emotional bond between the parents, or a third person may try to settle a dispute between two friends. Another role is as the *tertius gaudens* ("the third party who enjoys"). The third party benefits when two members in conflict try to win the third party's support. For example, parents who are in conflict may compete to win the affection of their child by using gifts and favors. A third role is to divide and conquer. Here the third party benefits by actively encouraging conflict in the pair. For example, a parent may gain greater control over two children by having them compete for the parent's favors and affection. Simmel thus drew attention to the fact that the triad (and larger groups) brings into play processes that are impossible in the dyad. A systematic account of the effects of group size, however, awaited the emergence of an experimental research tradition.

In sociology the term *group* has been used very loosely, referring at one extreme to small aggregations of people whose members are mutually aware of each other and can potentially interact (McGrath

1984) and at the other extreme to enormous aggregations whose members simply share some characteristic, as in the case of an "ethnic group." In studies of group processes, the more restricted definition has been used. The groups studied have generally been created explicitly for the purpose of research, rather than being ones that existed naturally for other purposes.

Group size has been studied in groups facing two very different circumstances. The first concerns groups that are formed to achieve some common purpose or goal. Interest has focused on how people behave in such groups and conditions that enhance or impede their effectiveness in achieving the goal. The second concerns groups facing collective dilemmas, where each member chooses between two actions with contrasting consequences. One action maximizes each member's own interest, whereas the other action maximizes collective interests, that is, the interests of the group as a whole. The dilemma is that each member profits more from the selfish choice, but if all members make that selfish choice each is worse off than if all chose to maximize collective interests (Komorita and Parks 1994).

GOAL-ORIENTED GROUPS

As Steiner (1972) notes, purposes for which groups are formed can vary on a continuum from task performance at one extreme (e.g., solving a problem, creating some product) to sociability at the other (e.g., simply enjoying one another's company). Groups whose purpose is primarily sociability have been little studied. Assuming that sociability is defined by spontaneous, reciprocal conversation, enjoyment should be highest in groups with no more than five or six members, the largest group size in which this kind of interaction occurs easily. This rule may be qualified in larger groups, however, if the situation is arranged so that people interact in smaller subgroups.

Most experimental research has focused on groups that are more task oriented. Here the most consequential feature is the nature of the task, or *task structure*. The first major program studying task-oriented groups experimentally was conducted by Bales and associates (Bales 1950). Bales and other early researchers focused on groups attempting to solve decision or judgmental tasks, problems for which there is no correct answer and

where differences of opinion are likely regarding the resolution (e.g., a personnel issue facing an administrator in an organization). Groups were told to discuss the assigned problem for a few minutes and then arrive at a group recommendation. Bales's method of interaction process analysis (IPA) coded verbal and nonverbal communication among group members as they addressed two basic ongoing concerns: the task and the relationships among the members. Research by Bales and associates showed the feasibility of measuring ongoing behavior in discussion groups and was instrumental in the emergence of small-group research as a distinctive field in the social sciences.

Group size is a fundamental consideration in discussion groups because the number of possible symmetrical relations between pairs of members increases much more rapidly than the number of members added to the group. The formula is where x=the number of symmetrical relationships and n=number of members (Bossard 1945). In addition to the pair relations, there are also relations between each group member and the group as a whole. If group members interact for a fixed amount of time, adding group members forces changes in the nature of existing relations and limits the number and nature of new relations (e.g., time available with each member, degree to which conversation is reciprocal).

As group size increases, groups tend to adopt a more direct and organized approach in soliciting information, and a task leader is more likely to emerge or be chosen. The top communicator initiates a greater proportion of the group's communications, and the differences in amount of communication by other members diminish (Bales et al. 1951). An increasing proportion of communication is directed toward the group as a whole, and the number of members who participate minimally by simply listening and giving emotional expressions increases (Bales and Borgatta 1955). In addition, the larger the group, the greater the conflict, the less likely members are to reach agreement on controversial issues, the less the conformity to group norms is, and the less the members are satisfied with the group and its activities (Levine and Moreland 1998; Thomas and Fink 1961).

Latané and L'Herrou (1996) suggest that group size is important in determining whether or not subgroups holding a minority opinion are likely to form and persist over time. As the number of members grows larger, the larger the number of members who may hold minority views, and hence the greater the opportunity for them to interact with each other and avoid exposure to majority views. The emergence of minority subgroups in groups is also affected by whether the group has an odd or even number of members. When opinion is divided, odd-numbered groups (e.g. 3, 5, or 7 members) are more likely to break into majorities and minorities, avoiding the possible even splits of even-numbered groups. With this pattern, odd-numbered groups should have fewer deadlocks and should reach decisions more quickly than even-numbered ones (Bales and Borgatta 1955).

The ideal size of discussion groups is often considered to be four to six members, a number large enough to ensure some diversity in member resources but small enough so that everyone can participate. Groups naturally occurring in public are rarely larger that five or six people, and more often contain two or three (Moreland et al. 1996).

Juries are discussion groups entrusted by the state to make decisions of the utmost consequence for the accused. Because legislation now permits juries smaller than twelve members, jury size has emerged as a variable of interest in studies of actual and mock (experimenter-created) juries. Although twelve-person juries should be less likely to reach unanimous verdicts (or verdicts based on a two-thirds majority) than smaller juries (e.g., six or eight members), the predicted difference is small and it has not been found in the studies themselves (Davis 1989).

Group size affects performance for other types of tasks as well. Steiner (1972) describes the effects for tasks having products or solutions whose adequacy can be judged objectively. Tasks are *unitary* when they cannot be readily divided into subtasks and where mutual assistance is impractical (e.g., working one arithmetic problem, hammering a nail). Tasks are *divisible* when they can be divided into subtasks, allowing different group members to work on the parts before the final product is assembled (e.g., working ten arithmetic problems, assembly-line production). Steiner identified several types of unitary tasks. A task is *disjunctive* when any single member can supply the group's product (e.g., the answer to a question). Here potential

group productivity depends on the resources of the most competent member. The larger the group, the greater the likelihood that at least one member will have the needed resources. As the group grows larger, however, each additional person adds a smaller increment to the group's potential. Productivity gains are thus a decelerating function of group size. A task is *conjunctive* when the resources of the least competent member determine group productivity (e.g., mountain climbers trying to reach the summit while roped together). Here the larger the group, the greater the likelihood that at least one member will be low in competence. As the group grows larger, productivity decreases, with each additional person adding a smaller decrement to the group's potential. Productivity losses are thus a decelerating function of group size. A task is *additive* when individual resources are added to obtain the group product (e.g., stacking firewood, offering ideas to improve a product). Here, the larger the group, the greater the group productivity.

For divisible tasks, variation can occur both in the nature of the subtasks and in the way that subtasks are combined to form the final product. A subtask can be disjunctive, conjunctive, or additive if two or more group members are working on it, and the process of assembling the subtasks can be disjunctive, conjunctive, or additive, thus creating a large number of possibilities. Where the rule for combining subtasks is additive or disjunctive, group productivity should be a positive, decelerating function of group size. The larger the group, the more likely it is that the subgroups can be staffed optimally, but communication, coordination, and matching members to the subtasks most appropriate for their interests and skills can become increasing problems. An increase in group size has the opposite effect, however, where the rule for combining subtasks is conjunctive, For tasks where the labor is divided and it is critical that each member make the correct response (e.g., an airline crew, a team of surgeons), the larger the group, the greater the chance that one of the critical members (or subgroups) will fail to perform adequately, and hence the group will perform poorly.

Steiner notes that actual task productivity often fails to reach potential productivity because groups use faulty or limiting processes to address the task and may also fail to motivate members sufficiently. Both problems typically increase with group size. With divisible tasks, for example, assignments given to members may not provide a good match between member skills and the subtasks they are to perform. In face-to-face groups where each member contributes orally (e.g., giving novel ideas on some topic), larger groups derive decreasing benefits as group size increases simply because only one person can talk at a time. The best-studied example of motivational losses involves additive tasks where individual performances are simultaneous and anonymous. For example, where group members each make some response on cue (e.g., pulling on a rope, shouting), individual contributions are smaller the larger the group, an effect that is termed "social loafing."

In addition to a task structure, most groups also have a *reward structure*—the arrangement of payoffs or rewards that motivate members to work on the task. The type and nature of the reward structure may be imposed by a third party (e.g., a supervisor, leader), be part of the group's history, or be chosen by the group itself. In most experimental studies of task-oriented groups, the reward structure is *cooperative*: The payoff or reward is a result of the group's efforts in meeting some criterion and is shared by all members (although not necessarily equally). The payoff may be intangible (e.g., the satisfaction of solving the problem or completing the product) or tangible (e.g., money or prizes). Reward structures can also be *competitive*, where rewards are distributed unequally to members based on *relative* individual performance. Cooperative and competitive contingencies are often compared with a third alternative, *individual* contingency, where a member receives a reward when he or she meets an individual performance criterion; this is the case in most work-for-pay groups in industry.

These reward structures are not equally appropriate for all tasks. In particular, cooperative rewards are effective across a range of tasks (Johnson et al. 1981; Qin-Zhining et al. 1995) and are uniquely appropriate when the task requires collaborative activities such as response coordination, task subdivision, or information sharing. Collaboration is rewarded with cooperative rewards, increasing the likelihood that the criterion for the group reward will be met. By contrast, competitive rewards are effective only where task responses can be made independently by each person. With competitive rewards, blocking another's responses, not collaboration, is likely to lead to winning. When competition is appropriate, though, it is often more cost-effective (more responses made per unit of reward), easier to implement, and capable of producing short-term performance rates that are higher than those of the other conditions (Schmitt 1987). Competitive motivation can also arise outside of the formal reward structure. Under cooperative conditions, members may work harder simply to be the best performer in the group.

A group member's motivation to perform a task can vary greatly depending on reward structure, and group size affects important aspects of that structure. With a cooperative structure, all members are rewarded, but inequities may exist in the size of the rewards received (e.g., some people contributing to a task may get more money than others). In general, people working on tasks expect their rewards to be proportional to their contributions (Homans 1974; Walster et al. 1978). Thus, if person A and person B have similar task skills, A will be upset if A and B contributed equally to the task but A received a reward half the size of B's. Person A will not be upset, however, if A made a contribution half the size of B's to the task. People who are inequitably underpaid relative to their contributions often work less hard on future tasks and may choose to leave the group (Marwell and Schmitt 1975). In the 1990s professional sports revealed a number of cases where athletes earning millions of dollars per year refused to play for their teams (or played less energetically) because comparable performers on their own or other teams earned more. In cases where the total amount of the cooperative reward for completing a task is proportional to the number of group members (e.g., $50 for a five-member group and $100 for a ten-member group), the larger the group, the greater the potential for larger inequities, that is, several of the members receiving a large share of the reward. If large inequities are present, productivity gains are likely to be a decelerating function of group size (and member discontent may provoke a change in distribution).

In arranging for competition, the reward structure is defined by the unequal rewards distributed to winners and losers at the end of the contest. In most contests the distribution is fixed in advance and is known to the competitors. As with inequitable cooperative structures, the variety of competitive structures depends on the number of competitors in the group, assuming that the total contest amount is proportional to the number of group members (i.e., the larger the group, the larger the contest amount). Two properties of the distribution are relevant. One is the proportion of competitors receiving rewards in each contest. At one extreme, only one competitor receives a reward; at the other extreme, all competitors are rewarded, but in varying amounts. With a single winner, the larger the size of the group, the larger the competitive reward. As has been shown with large lottery prizes, the larger the competitive reward, the greater the motivation of group members to compete, at least in a single contest. However, if there is a series of contests and a difference in competitive skills causes some members to lose continually, the lack of earnings will lead to their withdraw from the group, thus lowering group productivity (Schmitt 1998). Maximizing the proportion of competitors rewarded should encourage poorer performers to remain in contests regardless of group size. When more than one competitor is rewarded, variation can occur in a second property—reward differential or spread, that is, the difference between the highest and lowest reward amounts in each contest. Again, the larger the size of the group, the larger the total competitive reward, hence the larger the possible differential. Maximizing reward differential more highly motivates those who have a chance of winning but gives those who lose frequently less incentive to continue over a series of contests. In sum, group size is a factor when competitive reward structures specify that few are rewarded or have reward differentials that are extreme. Although increasing group size (and the reward pool) is likely to increase member motivation and productivity in initial contests, over a series of contests these gains are likely to be a decelerating function of group size, as those who earn little contribute less or quit.

With individual reward structures, the potential effects of group size are similar to those for cooperative structures. Again assuming that the total reward amount for the group is proportional to the number of members, the larger the group, the greater the size of the reward inequities that are possible in arranging the individual rewards.

With large inequities, productivity gains are likely to be a decelerating function of group size.

SOCIAL DILEMMAS

Several types of social dilemmas have been investigated. The best-known type is prisoners' dilemma. Originally conceived as a two-person game, an *n*-party prisoners' dilemma in which the number playing the game can be varied has been used to study the effects of group size (Komorita and Parks 1994). Each group member has two choices: to cooperate (C), which maximizes payoffs for the group as a whole, or to defect (D), which maximizes the individual's own payoff. The actual payoffs for each member depend both on own and others' choices. Payoffs for each choice increase with the proportion of members who make the C choice, but the D always produces the higher individual payoff. Finally, the payoff if everyone chooses C is greater than the payoff if everyone chooses D, the selfish choice. Each group member chooses repeatedly over a number of trials. This basic dilemma has numerous everyday counterparts, as when commuters each prefer to use a private automobile instead of a bus, but if each does so the resulting chaos leaves everyone dissatisfied.

Other types of social dilemmas involve a pool of sources to which the group members have access (Pruitt 1998). One is the commons dilemma, based on the Tragedy of the Commons (Hardin 1968), in which a village's common land is overgrazed because of the selfish actions of the individual herdsmen. As studied experimentally, subjects take turns removing resources (e.g., money) from a pool that is replenished periodically based on the amount remaining. The pool can be productive indefinitely, provided that the subjects don't destroy it by taking all the resources. Another is the public goods dilemma, in which the resource pool is built up through individual contributions, as when people contribute money to support public television or some charity. Here the temptation is for individuals to "free ride" and let others make the contribution. As studied experimentally, subjects take turns contributing resources to a pool that is later enhanced by the experimenter and then divided equally.

Studies have found that the larger the group in social dilemmas, the less the cooperation and the greater the selfish behavior, although there is little change in groups larger than eight members (Pruitt 1998). Various explanations of this relation have been proposed (Komorita and Parks 1994; Pruitt 1998). One possibility is that any defection breaches the trust required for cooperation, and that if one person defects, others view cooperation as unlikely and follow suit. The possibility of one person defecting increases as the group grows larger. In addition, as the group grows larger, each selfish individual response becomes less identifiable and may be seen as less responsible for the lower group payoffs. By the same logic, a cooperative response may also be seen as contributing less to the group product as the group grows larger. Finally, any opportunities by the group to communicate the group's cooperative interests or to sanction defectors are more difficult to carry out in larger groups.

CONTEXT

Any social interaction among group members must take place in some context, for example, people standing, seated at a table, at stations on an assembly line, or in separate offices linked by a computer network. Physical contexts are very important because they affect both the nature of the interaction among members and the ease with which various members can interact. The nature of interaction among group members is determined in part by the number and kind of stimuli presented by those who interact. Stimuli may be verbal in the form of oral or written communication, or they may be nonverbal—information transmitted without using language (e.g., facial expressions, gestures, posture, appearance, voice quality, rate and temporal patterning of speaking).

The context in which a group functions determines whether verbal and nonverbal stimuli are transmitted among group members. If the context includes face-to-face contact, speakers can deliver messages using both verbal and nonverbal stimuli. Nonverbal stimuli add elements that can be both enriching and distracting. For example, a speaker's facial expressions and gestures can reveal the strength with which a position is held, the truthfulness of a message, or the degree of intimacy sought by the speaker. Aspects of the speaker's demeanor or appearance can also distract listeners from paying close attention to the message.

People differ, however, in how they use such stimuli and hence the meaning given to a message. This variability is greatly reduced if the messages are written. In addition, the quality of interaction may differ, depending on the presence of the verbal and nonverbal stimuli. For example, people are more likely to harm others (e.g., deliver punishment or bad news) when communication is restricted and nonverbal behavior is absent compared with face-to-face contact (where people are more fully personalized). In general, restricted communication does not lead to the full development of interpersonal relations, and it minimizes cues that reveal differences in status, power, and prestige among group members. Hence, differences in interaction and influence among group members tend to be less extreme than those in face-to-face groups (McGrath, 1984). Restricted communication is more likely as groups become large and more formally organized.

Another aspect of context concerns the timing of information transmitted among group members. When people interact, verbal and nonverbal stimuli may be presented synchronously (i.e., immediately and in real time), or asynchronously (i.e., at the member's own time, place, and pace). Face-to-face interaction, telephone conversations, and video conferences are synchronous. Letters, memos, videotapes, electronic mail, and answering machine messages are asynchronous. Synchronous interaction, whether in person or electronically mediated, constrains interaction because only one person normally talks at a time. With an increase in group size, a few members typically lead or dominate the conversation. Asynchronous interaction, by contrast, typically permits any number of messages to any or all members, and the fact that the messages are necessarily recorded means that they are normally available for comparison and review later.

Asynchronous communication has increased enormously in popularity in recent years as computer-mediated electronic mail has become available in all organizations and many households. Computer-mediated communication has unique facilitating features: the ability to link anyone who has a network connection and the opportunity to send messages instantaneously to any number of people at very low logistical and social cost. For some tasks, the use of asynchronous communication changes the effects of group size on productivity, compared with traditional face-to-face synchronous communication. For example, Valacich and associates (1995) investigated groups formed to generate new ideas, that is, to "brainstorm," where different group members have the potential for generating different ideas. In face-to-face interaction, larger groups derived decreasing benefits as group size increased from five to ten members. In computer-mediated groups, where members communicated via typed messages, larger groups derived increasing benefits as group size increased. Computer-mediated groups appear to use the advantage of reviewing the ideas of others to avoid redundant ideas and build new ones. The study of computer-mediated groups with other tasks promises to reveal further distinctions between synchronous and asynchronous interaction (see Kiesler 1997 for discussion of a number of computer- and Internet-related issues).

An intriguing and potentially distinguishing feature of computer-mediated compared with face-to-face groups is that group size itself may become difficult to define and detect (Sproull and Faraj 1997). People in face-to-face groups take up space, and their physical presence and nonverbal reactions can affect others' behavior even if a group member says nothing. By contrast, the readers of computer-mediated messages are typically invisible, and speakers may have little notion of who has seen or read a message.

In both industry and education, computers have been used to create humanlike partners who interact with people in various ways. Kiesler and associates (1996) investigated subjects' responses in a prisoners' dilemma game where the "partner" was known by the subject to be either a person or computer based. In both conditions, the subject and partner discussed options on each trial, and the partner asked the subject for commitments. For both types of partners, discussion and agreements with the subjects facilitated cooperation, although the effect was stronger with the human partner. Thus, nonhuman partners can produce "social" responses in people provided that the partners make humanlike use of social stimuli and responses.

Much of the early research on context concerned constraints on who could communicate with whom in small groups. These constraints determine the group's communication network (for a summary, see Shaw 1981). For example, two contrasting networks in groups of three or more members are the circle, where each member can communicate with two adjacent members, and the wheel, where one member occupies a central position and others can communicate only with that central person (the "hub"). Wheels and circles are examples of highly centralized and decentralized networks, respectively. Groups studied in such networks have typically been small (e.g., three to five members), and communication has usually occurred via written notes. Comparisons of group problem solving using various networks have found that when tasks are relatively simple and require that members collect their information, centralized networks are more efficient than decentralized ones (with fewer messages and errors). Where tasks are more complex and require that members perform additional operations on their information, decentralized networks are more efficient than centralized ones (Shaw 1981). With complex tasks the communication overload (termed "saturation") experienced by the member in the central position slows the attainment of a solution. Saturation is likely to be a problem in all networks as the group increases in size, and it should emerge more rapidly when interaction is synchronous.

Communication networks arrange the contacts among group members in a decisive manner, but even where members are in face-to-face contact, aspects of the setting can make interaction between some members more likely than others, thus producing networklike effects. Seating arrangement is an example. Groups discussing problems are frequently seated at tables. One of the earliest findings was that people tend to communicate with others across the table and facing them instead of with those seated alongside them (Steinzor 1950). As groups grow larger, people are frequently seated at rectangular tables. Studies have found that people at the table's end positions tend to participate more, are seen a having more influence, and are more likely to be chosen as leaders than those on the sides (for a summary, see Shaw 1981). Networklike arrangements can also be created if group members are instructed to follow a particular communication pattern in a discussion (e.g., "Talk only with the leader."). Instructions can also be used to limit style of expression (e.g.,

"Give ideas for solving the problem but don't criticize others' ideas.").

In conclusion, differences in group size pose both opportunities and problems for the members. Because the nature of the consequences depends on the type of group task, reward structure, context, and the skills of the group members, little can be said about a group if only its size is known. Under certain circumstances, however, group size is highly consequential for the group's performance and stability. It should be noted that for groups that form in everyday life, unlike those created for experimental purposes, problems posed by size do not necessarily condemn a group to subpar performance. Everyday groups usually have both pasts and futures, and are often skillful in identifying problems and in making changes that help mitigate them.

REFERENCES

Bales, R. F. 1950 *Interaction Process Analysis: A Method for the Study of Small Groups*. Cambridge, Mass.: Addison-Wesley.

Bales, R. F., and E. F. Borgatta 1955 "Size of Group as a Factor in the Interaction Profile." In A. P. Hare, E. F. Borgatta, and R. F. Bales, eds., *Small Groups: Studies in Social Interaction*. New York: Knopf.

Bales, R. F., F. L. Strodtbeck, T. M. Mills, and M. E. Rosenborough 1951 "Channels of Communication in Small Groups." *American Sociological Review* 16:461–468.

Bossard, J. J. S. 1945 "The Law of Family Interaction." *American Journal of Sociology* 50:292–294.

Cooley, C. H. 1922 *Human Nature and the Social Order*. New York: Chas. Scribner's Sons.

Davis, J. 1989 "Psychology and the Law: The Last Fifteen Years." *Journal of Applied Social Psychology* 19:199–230.

Hardin, G. 1968 "The Tragedy of the Commons." *Science* 162:1243–1248.

Homans, G. 1974 *Social Behavior: Its Elementary Forms*, 2nd ed. New York: Harcourt Brace Jovanovich.

Johnson, D. W., G. Maruyama, R. Johnson, D. Nelson, and L. Skon 1981 "Effects of Cooperative, Competitive, and Individualistic Goal Structures on Achievement: A Meta-Analysis." *Psychological Bulletin* 89:47–62.

Kiesler, S. (ed.) 1997 *Culture of the Internet*. Mahwah, N.J.: Erlbaum.

——, L. Sproull, and K. Waters 1996 "A Prisoner's Dilemma Experiment on Cooperation with People and Human-Like Computers." *Journal of Personality and Social Psychology* 70:47–65.

Komorita, S. S., and C. D. Parks 1994 *Social Dilemmas*. Dubuque, Iowa: Brown and Benchmark.

Latané, B., and T. L'Herrou 1996 "Spatial Clustering in the Conformity Game: Dynamic Social Impact in Electronic Groups." *Journal of Personality and Social Psychology* 70:1218–1230.

Levine, J. M., and R. L. Moreland 1998 "Small Groups." In D. T. Gilbert, S. T. Fiske, and G. Lindsley, eds., *The Handbook of Social Psychology*, vol. II, 4th Ed. Boston: McGraw-Hill.

Marwell, G., and D. R. Schmitt 1975 *Cooperation: An Experimental Analysis*. New York: Academic Press.

McGrath, J. E. 1984 *Groups: Interaction and Performance*. Englewood Cliff, N.J.: Prentice-Hall.

Moreland, R. L., J. M. Levine, and M. L. Wingert 1996 "Creating the Ideal Group: Composition Effects at Work." In E. H. Witte and J. H. Davis, eds., *Understanding Group Behavior*, vol. II. Mahwah, N.J.: Erlbaum.

Pruitt, D. G. 1998 "Social Conflict." In D. T. Gilbert, S. T. Fiske, and G. Lindsley, eds., *The Handbook of Social Psychology*, vol. II, 4th ed. Boston: Mcgraw-Hill.

Qin-Zhining, D. W. Johnson, and R. T. Johnson 1995 "Cooperative Versus Competitive Efforts and Problem Solving." *Review of Educational Research* 65:129–143.

Schmitt, D. R. 1987 "Interpersonal Contingencies: Performance Differences and Cost-Effectiveness." *Journal of the Experimental Analysis of Behavior* 48:221–234.

Schmitt, D. R. 1998 "Effects of Reward Distribution and Performance Feedback on Competitive Responding." *Journal of the Experimental Analysis of Behavior* 69:263–273.

Shaw, M. E. 1981 *Group Dynamics*, 3rd ed. New York: McGraw-Hill.

Simmel, G. 1950 *The Sociology of George Simmel*; Translated, edited, and with an introduction by Kurt H. Wolff. Glencoe, Ill.: Free Press.

Sproull, L., and S. Faraj 1997 "Atheism, Sex, and Databases, The Net as a Social Technology." In S. Kiesler, ed., *Culture of the Internet*. Mahwah, N.J.: Erlbaum.

Steiner, I. D. 1972 *Group Process and Productivity*. New York: Academic Press.

Steinzor, B. 1950 "The Spatial Factor in Face-to-Face Discussion Groups." *Journal of Abnormal and Applied Psychology* 45:552–555.

Thomas, E. J., and C. F. Fink 1961 "Effects of Group Size." *Psychological Bulletin* 60:371–385.

Valacich, J. S., B. C. Wheeler, B. E. Mennecke, and R. Wachter 1995 "The Effects of Numerical and Logical

Group Size on Computer-Mediated Idea Generation." *Organizational Behavior and Human Decision Processes* 62:318–329.

Walster, E., G. W. Walster, and E. Berscheid 1978
Equity: Theory and Research. Boston: Allyn and Bacon.

DAVID R. SCHMITT

H

HAWTHORNE EFFECT

See Industrial Sociology; Quasi-Experimental
Research Designs.

HEALTH AND ILLNESS BEHAVIOR

Health and illness behaviors are associated with
level of disability, quality of life, patterns of illness,
and risk of death. It is tempting to view such
health-related outcomes solely through the lenses
provided by the biomedical sciences; however, the
behaviors that importantly shape individuals' experiences of sickness or wellness, and life or death,
are more completely understood from a sociological perspective. The confluence of individuals' life
histories, their personality characteristics and social experiences, and their social positions influences health and illness behaviors and tells us
much about how to enhance health and well-
being, and mitigate disability and sickness. An
examination of health and illness behaviors, therefore, has important public health implications.

HEALTH BEHAVIORS

Health behavior usually refers to preventive orientations and the positive steps people take to enhance their physical well-being and vitality. Traditionally, work in health behavior has focused on
the use of preventive services such as immunizations,
medical checkups, hypertension screening, and
prophylactic dentistry (Becker 1974). It also includes research on such behaviors as cigarette
smoking, seat-belt use, medication adherence, substance abuse, nutritional practices, and exercise
(Janz and Becker 1994).

The conventional approach to health behavior has been limited, focusing on the origins of
particular behaviors damaging to health and strategies to modify them. The most widely used general
model—the health belief model—conceptualizes
preventive health action within a psychological
cost-benefit analysis (Rosenstock 1974). The health
belief model conceptualizes decisions to take positive health actions as motivated by perceived threat
(either susceptibility to a particularly condition or
perceptions that the condition is severe) and judgments about the barriers and benefits associated
with specific changes in behavior. Behavior change
is seen as following motives that are salient, in
situations where people have conflicting motives,
following those that are perceived as yielding valuable benefits. An important component of the
model involves cues to action, since an activating
stimulus often appears to be necessary in the
initiation of a new behavioral sequence. Both internal (e.g., feelings of symptoms) and external
(e.g., suggestions from doctors, peers, or the media) stimuli may act as cues motivating change.
Over the years, this model has been expanded
(Becker and Maiman 1983), but it serves more as
an organizing framework for the study of preventive health behavior than as a successful predictive
model. An analysis of studies that have used the
health belief model to explain a variety of health

behaviors indicates that the predictive value of the model is, at best, modest; the average variance in health behaviors explained is approximately 20 percent (Harrison, Mullen and Green 1992).

A second commonly used model to explain health decisions is the theory of planned behavior, originally developed as the theory of reasoned action (Ajzen 1991; Ajzen and Fishbein 1977). Like the health belief model, the theory of planned behavior conceptualizes changes in behavior as products of the saliency of individuals' beliefs about the potential costs and benefits associated with an outcome or action. The theory of planned behavior, however, places greater weight on persons' intentions, arguing that behavior is centrally motivated by intentions that are shaped by normative beliefs, feelings of control, and judgments about the barriers and benefits associated with potential change. Again, however, the model has had only modest success in predicting an array of health behavior; the association between intentions and behavior is typically about .40 (Conner and Norman 1994).

There are many other models and theories proposed to predict health behaviors, and much has been written comparing the relative efficacy of each for predicting health behaviors (Conner and Norman 1994; Mullen et al. 1987; Weinstein 1993). It appears that efforts to develop a general theory are limited by the fact that behavior conducive to health derives from diverse and sometimes conflicting motives. Consistently, research indicates that health behavior, or a healthy lifestyle, is not a unitary construct (Johnson et al. 1998; Sobal et al. 1992). One study of health behaviors among a nationally representative sample of adult Americans examined the clustering of four health behaviors: diet quality, alcohol use, tobacco use, and physical exercise (Patterson et al. 1994). The results (based on data from the late 1980s) suggest that approximately 10 percent of Americans live a "healthy" lifestyle, defined by a good diet, low use of tobacco and alcohol, and engaging in regular physical exercise. In comparison, about 2 percent of the population practice unhealthy behavior on all four of these dimensions. Thus, most Americans fall somewhere between the two extremes, practicing some positive health behaviors while neglecting others. Research that has attempted to establish specific clusters of related health behaviors has proved inconclusive. Some studies have identified many apparently interrelated clusters of behaviors—for example, smoking/drinking and exercise/diet—and others have identified few (cf.Johnson et al. 1998; Sobal et al. 1992). In short, the research indicates that there is no simple identifiable positive health orientation that can serve as a basis for promoting risk aversion and health maintenance.

The lack of such a general orientation results because most behaviors with important implications for health arise from motives not related to health and are significantly programmed into the daily patterns and institutional life of communities and families (Mechanic 1990). Health-protective behaviors that are consequences of accepted, everyday, conventional activities require neither conscious motivation nor special efforts to be sustained. The favorable health experience of Mormons, for example, is a product of their belief systems and patterns of activity reinforced by the way of life of this cultural community (Mechanic 1990). To the extent that health behaviors are more the result of habits than cognitive decisions, we might expect that past health behaviors are robust predictors of current health behaviors. Yet neither the theory of reasoned action nor the health belief model adequately incorporates past behavior in its model, an omission that might partially explain their lack of predictive power (Conner and Norman 1994).

Promoting health may be more a matter of changing culture and social structure than of modifying personal motives or intentions. Patterns of behavior that depend on sustained conscious motivation are less stable than those that are a natural consequence of the accepted norms and understandings within a community. Expectations not only affect the prevalence of varying behaviors but also establish constraints on the acquired behaviors of children and adolescents. Changes in the social constraints on smoking, and the growing unacceptability of smoking in varying social contexts, may have more significance than any program to change personal behavior for explaining the dramatic decline from about 42 percent of the U.S. adult population being current smokers in 1965 to 25 percent in 1995 (National Center for Health Statistics 1998).

Although there is no evidence for a unitary health orientation, some social factors, particularly socioeconomic status (SES), predict good outcomes across a wide range of health indicators (Bunker et al. 1989; Marmot 1998; Ross and Wu 1995). Occupational status, income, and education each reflect some part of SES, and all are associated with health behaviors, whether one is comparing the health behaviors of populations or of individuals. Generally, wealthy nations show the highest rates of preventative health practices, such as child immunization, routine dental care, and the use of mammography, compared with less wealthy nations. But the importance of SES may be indirect, through social conditions. Indeed, as Caldwell (1986, 1993) has argued, mothers' educational attainment appears to be particularly important, influencing health outcomes net of its relationship to per capita income. Caldwell suggests that maternal education increases women's autonomy, enhances their ability to interact efficaciously with available health services and technology (even when such technology is not advanced), and enables women to increasingly control their own health and that of family members.

Within nations, there are also important SES differences in health behaviors. Table 1 presents some examples of SES differences in the U.S. population; the behaviors presented are meant to illustrate the gap and are not an exhaustive list of possible health behaviors. As shown in Table 1, Americans with lower SES are more likely to engage in health-risk behaviors and less likely to engage in health-promoting behaviors. The precise ways in which SES affects these outcomes are not fully understood, but the consistent findings point to an explanation of health behaviors that goes beyond personal responsibility and free choice. Research that examines the impact of SES over the life course illustrates the fallacy of relying on "choice" explanations to account for SES differences in health behaviors. In a sample of Finnish men, Lynch and his colleagues (1997) examined the effects of SES during childhood (parents' occupation), adolescence (education), and adulthood (occupation) on psychosocial characteristics, such as hostility and hopelessness, that are important to health and on health behaviors, including smoking and alcohol use. They found that lower SES in childhood and adolescence is associated with greater health-risk behaviors in adulthood, in addition

to greater feelings of hopelessness and hostility. Given that childhood SES is not a matter of choice, their findings support an explanation of SES differences in health behavior rooted in persistent structural disadvantages and the accompanying differential opportunities and constraints. Others have also demonstrated that higher SES provides not only obvious economic advantages and related opportunities but also enhanced personal autonomy, increased sense of control, and greater social participation (Marmot 1998; Ross and Wu 1995, 1996), all of which also influence health outcomes.

A variety of behaviors noxious to health (smoking, drug use, and drinking) develop or increase during adolescence and young adulthood. However, young people who have a good relationship with their parents and who are attuned to parent-oriented values—as measured by school performance, attendance at religious services, and participation in meals with parents—do relatively well across a variety of health measures (Hansell and Mechanic 1990). In contrast, high engagement with peer-oriented social activities is associated with increases in behavior associated with health risk. In addition, children model their parents' health behaviors, an effect that persists at least into young adulthood (Lau et al. 1990).

Although it is apparent that adolescence is a time of life where there are likely to be changes in health behaviors, we know very little about other stages of the life course or the life transitions that may be especially important (Prohaska and Clark 1997). Prohaska and his colleagues propose a "stages of change" model that recognizes important transitions in the life course as explanations for changes in health practices (Prohaska and Clark 1997; Prohaska et al. 1994). They argue that individuals go through a number of steps, from not thinking there is a need for change to maintaining the new behavior after change. Public health efforts, therefore, could benefit from understanding what motivates or hinders a person's progression through the steps. For instance, life transitions such as motherhood may motivate progression toward positive health practices, while transitions such as death of a spouse may make it difficult to maintain health practices and, therefore, may explain deterioration of positive health behaviors among persons recently widowed. Moreover, according to this model, persons may be differently prepared to progress through the steps depending

Socioeconomic Status and Health Behaviors in the United States

Behavior	Education		Year
	Less Than 12 Years %	16 or More Years %	
Cigarette smoking (person 25 years and older)	35.7	13.6	1995
Dental visit last year (persons 25 years and older)*	38.0	73.8	1993
Prenatal care in first trimester (mothers 20 years and older)	68.0	93.9	1996
Heavy alcohol use (men 25–49 years)	16.3	6.1	1994/96
Overweight (women 25–74 years)	45.8	26.3	1988/94

	Income/Poverty		Year
	Below Poverty %	At or Above Poverty %	
Mammography use past two years (women 40 years and older)	44.4	64.8	1994
Dental visit past year (persons 25 years and older)	35.9	64.3	1993
No physician visit in last year (children under 6 years)**	11.2	5.2	1994/1995
Vaccination (children 19–35 months)	69.0	80.0	1996

Table 1

SOURCE: National Center for Health Statistics (1998).

NOTE: *Comparison is less than 12 years versus 13+ years.

**Comparison is poor versus nonpoor.

on their stage in the life course; for example, older persons may be better prepared to contemplate the health risks of smoking or heavy alcohol use, while adolescents are not. The important point for our purposes is that understanding how to modify health practices requires appreciation of how stages in the life course and transitions may influence when people are willing or able to make changes.

ILLNESS BEHAVIOR

The study of illness behavior, in contrast to health behavior, is concerned with the way people monitor their bodies, define and interpret bodily indications, make decisions about needed treatment, and use informal and formal sources of care (Mechanic 1986, 1995). Like other behavior, illness behavior is learned through socialization in families and peer groups and through exposure to the mass media and education. There is great diversity of attitudes, beliefs, knowledge, and behavior, all of which affect the definitions of problematic symptoms, the meanings and causal attributions that explain them, socially anticipated responses, and the definition of appropriate remedies and sources of care. Motivation and learning affect the initial recognition of symptoms, reactions to pain, the extent of stoicism and hypochondriasis, and the readiness to seek release from work, school, and other obligations and to seek help (Mechanic 1978).

Illness behavior begins prior to the use of services with the recognition of illness or sickness. While a complex array of variables might explain variations in interpretation of sickness, they can be summarized in ten general categories: (1) the visibility, recognizability, or perceptual salience of deviant signs and symptoms; (2) the extent to which the person perceives the symptoms as serious (that is, the person's estimate of the present and future probabilities of danger; (3) the extent to which symptoms disrupt family, work, and other social activities; (4) the frequency of the appearance of deviant signs and symptoms, or their persistence, or their frequency of recurrence; (5) the tolerance threshold of those who are exposed to and evaluate the deviance signs of symptoms; (6) the information available to, the knowledge of, and the cultural assumptions and understanding of the evaluator; (7) the degree to which autistic psychological processes (perceptual processes that distort reality) are present; (8) the presence of needs that conflict with the recognition of illness or the assumptions of the sick role; (9) the possibility that competing interpretations can be assigned to the symptoms once they are recognized; and (10) the availability of treatment resources, their physical proximity, and the psychological and monetary costs of taking action (including not only physical distance and costs of time, money, and effort, but also stigmatization, resulting social distance, and feelings of humiliation resulting from a particular illness decision) (Mechanic 1978).

In short, illness appraisal is a two-step process (Mechanic 1972). In the initial step, persons monitor their bodies to assess the location, duration, intensity, and persistence of discomfort. In the second stage, which may occur almost concurrently, they seek explanations for perceived changes. If an obvious explanation is not available, or is disconfirmed by further checking, individuals look to their environment for new cues and explanations. These interpretations, in light of knowledge and other beliefs, may then play a role in the formal initiation of care.

Individuals' appraisals of symptoms vary importantly. Processes of symptom appraisal are influenced by the manner in which symptoms occur and their characteristics, by knowledge, and by past experiences with illness (Leventhal 1986; Mechanic 1972). Some symptoms are so painful and incapacitating that they inevitably lead to intervention without significant inquiry. Others are so familiar and generally understood as self-limited that they also are dealt with routinely. Many symptoms, however, are neither familiar nor easily understood, resulting in a process of interpretation within the context of personality, situational cues and stressors, and environmental influences. Only a small proportion of symptoms lead to formal consultation or care. The vast majority are denied, normalized, or evaluated as having little significance

Much research has focused on how persons come to make judgments of their own health status. One approach is to study health appraisals among children and adolescents who have little serious illness. In a prospective study of adolescents, those who were more competent and more engaged in age-related activities, as measured by school performance and participation in sports and other exercise, rated their health more highly (Mechanic and Hansell 1987). Adolescents' health assessments are shaped by their overall sense of functioning, and they do not seem to differentiate among physical and psychological aspects of well-being in making general assessments of how they feel.

This finding is consistent with the body of research examining the impact of global judgments of health on mortality and disability. Several longitudinal studies of the elderly have found that subjective self-assessments of health predict future mortality after taking account of known risk factors and sociodemographic measures (Idler and Angel 1990; Idler and Benyamini 1997; Idler and Kasl 1995; Mossey and Shapiro 1982). Likewise, some research suggests that global assessments of health predict future level of functioning or disability (Farmer and Ferraro 1997; Idler and Kasl 1995). It is remarkable that simple self-assessments of health prospectively predict longevity and disability better than physicians' assessments or known health-risk factors. Many studies suggest that judgments of health and well-being and interpretations of sickness are shaped by factors beyond those traditionally captured by biomedical conceptions of illness. Individuals' appraisals of their health appear to depend as much on their global sense of well-being as they do on specific patterns of illness. The identification of the exact psychological and social factors responsible for self-assessed health, however, remains elusive. Some have suggested that individuals take into account important social and psychological resources, such as social support, feelings of control, and optimism, when making judgments of their own health—and that these psychosocial resources provide protection against morbidity and mortality (Idler and Benyamini 1997; Kaplan and Camacho 1983).

One of the most consistent research findings has been that perceptions of physical illness depend on the person's psychological well-being or level of psychological distress (Aneshensel et al. 1984; Farmer and Ferraro 1997; Tessler and Mechanic 1978). Individuals tend to assess their health holistically in terms of vitality and capacity to perform their social activities and roles. Psychological distress often diminishes vitality and functioning as much as serious medical conditions. The RAND Medical Outcomes Study found that depressive symptoms were more disabling than many chronic physical conditions that physicians view as extremely serious (Wells et al. 1989).

Persons seeking medical care commonly express their distress and lowered sense of well-being through many diffuse physical complaints, such as fatigue, insomnia, and aches and pains in different bodily systems, a process referred to as somatization (Kleinman 1986). Although much of the existing literature focuses on somatization as a problematic process, it is by far the predominant pattern for expressing distress. Until the last forty or fifty years, it was uncommon to conceptualize distress in psychological terms, and even now such expressions are used primarily among well-educated populations receptive to psychological interpretations. General distress has both physical and psychological concomitants; the language that people use to characterize distress depends on the cultural context, the perceived appropriateness of psychological complaints, and the stigma attached to emotional disorder.

There is controversy as to whether psychological idioms are inaccessible to many people due to cultural factors or limited schooling, or whether somatization represents a choice among alternative idioms because such presentations are seen as more consistent with the medical care context. Rates of reported depression in Chinese cultures, for example, are extremely low, although "neurasthenia" is a common diagnosis in Chinese medical care settings (Kleinman 1986). Psychiatrists in China routinely view neurasthenia as a "disorder of brain function involving asthenia of cerebral cortical activity," but the symptoms reported are strikingly similar to the physical manifestations of depressive disorders more commonly seen in Western countries. It remains unclear whether these diagnoses characterize the same underlying disorders that are expressed differently in varying cultural groups or whether they are fundamentally different. Kleinman (1986) treated Chinese patients diagnosed as neurasthenic who met the American diagnostic criteria for major depression with antidepressant drugs but found on follow-up that while a majority showed significant improvements in clinical psychiatric symptoms, they continued to be impaired, to function badly, and to seek help for their condition. They also remained skeptical of the drug treatment they received. Kleinman links these responses to the patients' needs for the medical legitimization of their "illness" to explain past failures and to justify continuing difficulties in meeting social expectations.

Similar examples are provided within the American context when "new" disorders become part of our popular understanding of what is (and is not) physical illness. For example, in recent years we have seen much debate around the legitimacy of chronic fatigue syndrome and Gulf War illness as physical disorders (Abbey and Garfinkel 1991; NIH 1994; Presidential Advisory Committee 1996). The case definitions associated with these conditions are not well specified, and the etiology of each remains undetermined. Those suffering from the symptoms of each condition have benefited greatly from the efforts of interest groups who have lobbied to have the conditions treated as unique clinical disorders. The status of disorder often brings access to insurance coverage and other entitlement programs. Equally important, recognition of a group of symptoms as a specific disorder or distinct illness acts to reduce stigma for those suffering and provides some legitimacy to persons disabled by the symptoms. Studies of patients diagnosed with chronic fatigue syndrome highlight the important role of attribution in the experience of illness. Some research indicates that patients who view their illness as essentially physical have less favorable outcomes than those who attribute the cause of their illness to social or psychological factors (Joyce et al. 1997).

In situations where there are no obvious explanations for the occurrence of symptoms, individuals seek meanings for changes in their feeling states. The commonsense theories they apply may either be idiosyncratic or drawn from socially prevalent conventional explanations such as stress, lack of sleep, overwork, and overeating. These lay explanations are influential on subsequent behavior such as care seeking and use of medication (Kleinman 1980; Leventhal et al. 1980; Leventhal et al. 1985). For example, it is commonly believed that stress increases blood pressure and that relaxation reduces it. Most individuals, however, cannot assess whether their blood pressure is high or low on the basis of available cues, yet many believe they can. Persons with hypertension, an asymptomatic condition, commonly use self-assessments of their stress levels or relaxation as an indicator of their blood pressure levels and adjust their medication accordingly, despite medical advice to the contrary (Leventhal et al. 1985). Similarly, many patients with limited understanding of the biological processes through which drugs such as antibiotics or antidepressants act increase or decrease medication in relation to changes in how they feel and environmental cues.

The decision to seek medical care in response to symptoms also depends on prevailing norms about the conditions that are within the purview of the medical field. Such norms differ across cultures and time. In recent years, the role of the popular media in influencing help-seeking appears to have increased. In the late 1980s, Prozac was widely advertised and discussed as a treatment for a wide range of symptoms ranging from clinical depression to shyness, self-criticism, low self-esteem, or just feeling blue (Barondes 1994; Kramer 1993). It became the most quickly accepted drug in U.S. history (Kramer 1993). In April 1998 Viagra was introduced to the market, and the popular press was inundated with stories of the potential of the drug to increase sexual pleasure. It replaced Prozac as the fastest-selling pharmaceutical in history, and by the end of the year approximately 7 million prescriptions had been written for some 3 million patients in the United States (Pfizer Inc. 1999). Unmet need partially explains the rapid acceptance of both drugs. However, it is also likely that variations in human feelings or behavior that would previously have been normalized were more likely to be viewed as medical conditions requiring treatment.

Sickness is an accepted role in society, bringing sympathetic attention and legitimate release from expected performance (Parsons 1951). Determinations of what is (and what is not) illness may involve intense negotiations about individuals' claims that, when legitimized, may justify failure to meet expectations or allow escape from onerous obligations (Mechanic 1978). In some situations, the sick role becomes a point of tension and conflict between the claimant, who seeks legitimation of sickness with its special privileges, and other interested parties, including families, employers, and welfare administrators, who may seek to limit release from social obligations or diminish special privileges granted to the sick and disabled (Field 1957). Most illness situations are neither problematic nor sources of conflict, but the contested cases make evident the social assumptions and expectations around which illness is organized.

Certification of illness becomes a public issue when physicians, government bureaucrats, or managed care companies have moral and legal authority to define illness and disability and to sanction the sick role. Such influence is found in certifying justified absenteeism for employers, in litigation, and in decisions on eligibility in insurance and disability entitlement programs. Efforts are often made to maintain the illusion that these are objective decisions based solely on medical expertise and clinical experience, but judgments often depend on whom the physician represents. The state or other formal organizations may thus attempt to control physicians by limiting their discretion, as happened in the Soviet Union when physicians were viewed as allowing people excuses to escape work too easily (Field 1957).

American examples of the processes involved in legitimization of illness come from observations of legislative changes affecting definitions of what is (and is not) disability. For example, in 1996 Congress passed legislation that removed substance use as a disability qualifying for Supplemental Insurance Income (SSI). Approximately 140,000 people lost their official status as "disabled" under the Social Security Act and concomitantly lost the right to income and medical benefits (Gresenz et al. 1998). Similarly, substance-use disorders associated with illegal drugs are explicitly excluded from the classes of disorders covered by the Americans with Disability Act (Mechanic 1998a). The removal or exclusion of a class of illness from the definition of disability highlights the importance of societal norms and values in sanctioning which groups of persons may legitimately occupy the sick role. Moreover, much of the debate surrounding implementation of both acts concerned judgments of personal responsibility and "badness" and "goodness," rather than the clinical significance of substance-use disorders as disabling conditions. In contrast, veterans of the Persian Gulf War have been awarded medical and disability entitlements based on Gulf War illness, despite the weight of medical evidence suggesting that there is no such unique clinical entity (NIH 1994; Presidential Advisory Committee 1996). Both examples illustrate the point that the certification of persons as legitimately sick (and thus deserving of public benefits) is not always the result of clinical judgments. Definition of illness and disability is the "rope" in a tug of war in which competing parties seek determinations in their own interest.

The study of illness behavior has many applications in research, clinical care, public health, and social policy (Mechanic 1998b). Such patterns of behavior substantially affect pathways into care and selectively shape the samples studied in clinical contexts. Failure to understand these selection effects and how they operate leads to erroneous conclusions about the nature of basic disease processes. A common error is to attribute to the etiology of the illness influences triggering use of services, a problem that plagues much research on stress and illness. At the clinical level, awareness of how people construe illness, present symptoms, and respond to care can improve understanding and communication and help health professionals to guide the treatment regimen more effectively.

Health and illness behavior studies make clear that the forces affecting health and treatment outcomes transcend medical care and the transactions that take place between doctor and patient. In recent decades there have been increasing tendencies toward the medicalization of social problems and a failure to address the complicated attitudinal needs of patients with serious chronic conditions and disabilities. Moreover, the problems in managing the frailties of old age, characterized by a combination of medical, instrumental, and social needs, increasingly challenge assumptions of treatment focused on narrow definitions of disease and care. Studies of health and illness behavior teach the importance of moving beyond initial complaints and narrow definitions of problems and toward examining the broad context of individuals' lives and the factors that affect social

functioning and quality of life. They point to the diverse adaptations among persons with comparable social and physical debility and potential. They reinforce the need to take account of the environmental and social context of people's lives, their potential assets, and their disease. A medical care system responsive to these broad concerns would be better prepared for the impending health care challenges of the new millennium.

REFERENCES

Abbey, S. E., and P. E. Garfinkel 1991 "Neurasthenia and Chronic Disease Syndrome: The Role of Culture in the Making of a Diagnosis." *American Journal of Psychiatry* 148:1638–1646.

Ajzen, I. 1991 "The Theory of Planned Behavior." *Organizational Behavior and Human Decision Processes* 50:179–211.

——, and M. Fishbein 1977 "Attitude-Behavior Relations: A Theoretical Analysis and Review of Empirical Research." *Psychological Bulletin* 84:888–918.

Aneshensel, Carol S, Ralph R. Frerichs, and George Huba 1984 "Depression and Physical Illness: A Multiwave, Nonrecursive Causal Model." *Journal of Health and Social Behavior* 25:350–371.

Barondes, Samuel H. 1994 "Thinking About Prozac." *Science* 263:1102–1103.

Becker, Marshall, (ed.) 1974 *The Health Belief Model and Personal Health Behavior*. Thorofare, N.J.: Slack.

——, and Lois Maiman 1983 "Models of Health Related Behavior." In D. Mechanic, ed., *Handbook of Health, Health Care and the Health Professions*. New York: Free Press.

Bunker, John, Deanna Gomby, and Barbara Kehrer, (eds.) 1989 *Pathways to Health: The Role of Social Factors*. Menlo Park, Calif.: Kaiser Family Foundation.

Caldwell, John 1986 "Routes to Low Mortality in Poor Countries." *Population and Development Review* 12:171–220.

—— 1993 "Health Transition: The Cultural, Social, and Behavioural Determinants of Health in The Third World." *Social Science and Medicine* 36:125–135.

Conner, Mark, and Paul Norman 1994 "Comparing the Health Belief Model and the Theory of Planned Behavior in Health Screening." In D.R. Rutter and Lyn Quine, eds., *Social Psychology and Health: European Perspectives*. Brookfield, Vt.: Avebury.

Farmer, Melissa M., and Kenneth F. Ferraro 1997 "Distress and Perceived Health: Mechanisms of Health Decline." *Journal of Health and Social Behavior* 39:298–311.

Field, Mark G. 1957 *Doctor and Patient in Soviet Russia.* Cambridge, Mass.: Harvard University Press.

Gresenz, Carole Roan, Katherine Watkins, and Deborah Podus 1998 "Supplemental Security Income (SSI), Disability Insurance (DI) and Substance Abusers." *Community Mental Health Journal* 34(4): 337–346.

Hansell, Stephen, and David Mechanic 1990 "Parent and Peer Effects on Adolescent Health Behavior." In Klaus Hurrelman and Friedrich Losel, eds., *Health Hazards in Adolescence.* New York: DeGruyter.

Harrison, J. A., P. D. Mullen, and L. W. Green 1992 "A Meta-Analysis of Studies of the Health Belief Model with Adults." *Health Education Research* 7:107–116.

Idler, Ellen L., and Ronald J. Angel 1990 "Self-Rated Health and Mortality in the NHANES-I Epidemiologic Follow-Up Study." *American Journal of Public Health* 80:446–452.

Idler, Ellen L., and Yael Benyamini 1997 "Self-Rated Health and Mortality: A Review of Twenty-Seven Community Studies." *Journal of Health and Social Behavior* 38:21–37.

Idler, Ellen L., and Stanislav V. Kasl 1995 "Self-Ratings of Health: Do They Also Predict Change in Functional Ability?" *Journal of Gerontology: Social Sciences* 50B:S344–S353.

Janz, Nancy K, and Marshall H. Becker 1984 "The Health Belief Model: A Decade Later." *Health Education Quarterly* 11:1–47.

Johnson, Marilyn F., Jeanne F. Nichols, James F. Sallis, Karen J. Calfas, and Melbourne F. Hovell 1998 "Interrelationships Between Physical Activity and Other Health Behaviors Among University Women and Men." *Preventative Medicine* 27:536–544.

Joyce, J., M. Hotopf, and S. Wessely 1997 "The Prognosis of Chronic Fatigue and Chronic Fatigue Syndrome. "*Quarterly Journal of Medicine* 90:223–233.

Kaplan, George, and Terry Camacho 1983 "Perceived Health and Mortality: A Nine-Year Follow-Up of the Human Population Laboratory Cohort." *American Journal of Epidemiology* 117:292–504.

Kleinman, Arthur 1980 *Patients and Healers in the Context of Culture.* Berkeley: University of California Press.

——, 1986 *Social Origins of Distress and Disease: Depression, Neurasthenia, and Pain in Modem China.* New Haven, Conn.: Yale University Press.

Kramer, Peter D. 1993 *Listening to Prozac.* New York: Viking.

Lau, Richard R., Marilyn Jacobs Quadrel, and Karen A. Hartman 1990 "Development and Change of Young Adults' Preventative Health Beliefs: Influences from Parents and Peer." *Journal of Health and Social Behavior* 31:240–259.

Leventhal, Howard 1986 "Symptom Reporting: A Focus on Process." In Sean McHugh and T. Michael Vallis, eds., *Illness Behavior: A Multidisciplinary Model.* New York: Plenum.

——, Daniel Meyer, and David Nerenz 1980 "The Common-Sense Representation of Illness Danger." In Stanley Rachman, ed., *Contributions to Medical Psychology.* New York: Pergamon.

——, Thomas Prohaska, and Robert Hirschman 1985 "Preventive Health Behavior Across the Life Span." In James Rosen and Laura Solomon, eds., *Prevention in Health Psychology.* Hanover, N.H.: University Press of New England.

Lynch, J. W., G. A. Kaplan, and J. T. Salonen 1997 "Why Do Poor People Behave Poorly? Variation in Adult Health Behaviours and Psychosocial Characteristics by Stages of the Socioeconomic Lifecourse." *Social Science and Medicine* 44(6):809–819.

Marmot, Michael G. 1998 "Contributions of Psychosocial Factors to Socioeconomic Differences in Health." *The Milbank Quarterly* 76:403–448.

Mechanic, David 1972 "Social Psychological Factors Affecting the Presentation of Bodily Complaints." *The New England Journal of Medicine* 286:1132–1139.

—— 1978 *Medical Sociology*, 2nd ed. New York: Free Press.

—— 1986 "Illness Behavior: An Overview." In S McHugh and T. M. Vallis, eds., *Illness Behavior: A Multidisciplinary Model.* New York: Plenum.

—— 1990 "Promoting Health." *Society* 27(2): 16–22.

—— 1995 "Sociological Dimensions of Illness Behavior." *Social Science and Medicine* 34:1345–1350.

—— 1998a *Mental Health and Social Policy: The Emergence of Managed Care*, 4th ed. Allyn and Bacon.

—— 1988b "Cultural and Organizational Aspects of Application of the Americans with Disabilities Act to Persons with Psychiatric Disabilites." *The Milbank Quarterly* 76:5–23.

——, and Stephen Hansell 1987 "Adolescent Competence, Psychological Well-Being and Self-Assessed Physical Health." *Journal of Health and Social Behavior* 28:364–374.

Mossey, Jana M, and Evelyn Shapiro 1982 "Self-Rated Health: A Predictor of Mortality Among the Elderly." *American Journal of Public Health* 72:800–808.

Mullen, Patricia D., James C. Hersey, and Donald C. Iverson 1987 "Health Behavior Models Compared." *Social Science and Medicine* 11:974–981.

National Center for Health Statistics 1998. *Health, United States, 1998, with Socioeconomic Status Health Chartbook.* Hyattsville, Md.: Author.

NIH Technology Assessment Workshop Panel 1994 "The Persian Gulf Experience and Health." *Journal of the American Medical Association* 274:391–396.

Parsons, Talcott 1951 *The Social System.* New York: Free Press.

Patterson, Ruth E., Pamela. S. Haines, and Barry M. Popkin 1994 "Health Lifestyle Patterns of U.S. Adults." *Preventative Medicine* 23:453–460.

Pfizer Inc 1999 "Pfizer Inc Fourth-Quarter Total Revenues Increased 26 Percent; Net Income from Continuing Operations, Excluding Unusual Items, Increased 42 Percent." Company Press Release, January 19.

Presidential Advisory Committee on Gulf War Veteran's Illness 1996 *Presidential Advisory Committee on Gulf War Veteran's Illness: Final Report.* Washington, D.C.: U.S. Government Printing Office.

Prohaska, Thomas R., and Melissa A. Clark 1997 "Health Behavior and the Human Life Cycle." In David S. Gochman, ed., *Handbook of Health Behavior Research. Vol. III. Demography, Development, and Diversity* New York: Plenum.

Prohaska, Thomas R., W. Velicer, J. Rossi, M. Goldstein, B. Marcus, W. Rakowski, C. Fiore, L. Harlow, C. Redding, D. Rosenbloom, and S. Rossi 1994 "Stages of Change and Decisional Balance for 12 Problem Behaviors." *Health Psychology* 13:39–46.

Rosenstock, Irvin 1974 "The Health Belief Model and Preventive Health Behavior." In Marshall Becker, ed., *The Health Belief Model and Personal Health Behavior.* Thorofare, N.J.: Slack.

Ross, Catherine E., and Chia-ling Wu 1995 "The Links Between Education and Health." *American Sociological Review* 60:719–745.

—— 1996 "Education, Age and the Cumulative Advantage in Health." *Journal of Health and Social Behavior* 37:104–120.

Sobal, Jeffery, Dennis Revicki, and Bruce R. DeForge 1992 "Patterns of Interrelationships Among Health-Promotion Behaviors." *American Journal of Preventative Medicine* 8:351–359.

Tessler, Richard, and David Mechanic 1978 "Psychological Distress and Perceived Health Status." *Journal of Health and Social Behavior* 19:254–262.

Weinstein, Neil D. 1993 "Testing Four Competing Theories of Health-Protective Behavior." *Health Psychology* 12:324–333.

Wells, Kenneth, Anita Stewart, Ron D. Hays, Audrey Burnam, William Rogers, Marcia Daniels, Sandra Berry, Sheldon Greenfield, and John Ware 1989 "The Functioning and Well-Being of Depressed Patients: Results from the Medical Outcomes Study." *Journal of the American Medical Association* 262:914–919.

DAVID MECHANIC
DONNA D. MCALPINE

HEALTH AND THE LIFE COURSE

Health and *the life course* are two broad concepts of interest to sociologists. Each of these concepts must be nominally defined.

CONCEPTIONS OF HEALTH

Health can be conceptualized in three major ways: the medical model (or physical definition); the functional model (or social definition); and the psychological model (or the subjective evaluation of health: Liang 1986). In the medical model, health is defined as the absence of disease. The presence of any disease condition is determined by reports from the patient, observations by health practitioners, or medical tests. The social definition of health is derived from Parsons's (1951) work and refers to an individual's ability to perform roles, that is, to function socially. Illness or impairment is a function of reduced capacity to perform expected roles, commonly measured in terms of activities of daily living (ADLs—eating, dressing, bathing, walking, grooming, etc). The psychological model, or the subjective evaluation of health, is often based on the response to a single question asking one to rate one's health on a scale from poor to excellent. The definition of health used by the World Health Organization since 1946 reflects this multidimensional perspective: "a state of complete physical, mental, and social well-being and not merely the absence of disease or infirmity."

It has been suggested (e.g., Schroots 1988) that a distinction be made between *disease* and *illness*. It is argued that disease refers to an objective diagnosis of a disorder, while illness refers to the presence of a disease plus the individual's perception of and response to the disease. Thus, one may have a disease, but as long as one does not acknowledge it and behave accordingly (e.g., take medicine), one will perceive oneself as healthy (Birren and Zarit 1985).

A distinction should also be made between *acute* and *chronic* conditions. These two types of health conditions are differentially related to older and younger age groups (discussed more below). That is, there is a morbidity shift from acute to chronic diseases as an individual ages. In addition, Western societies experienced a dramatic shift from infectious diseases (a form of acute condition) to chronic, degenerative diseases in the late nineteenth century and the first half of the twentieth century.

CONCEPTIONS OF THE LIFE COURSE

The life course is a progression through time (Clausen 1986), in particular, social time. Social time is a set of norms governing life transitions for particular social groups. These transitions may vary from one group to another (e.g., working class versus middle class) and from one historical period to another. The life-course approach focuses on "age related transitions that are *socially created*, *socially recognized*, and *shared*" (Hagestad and Neugarten 1985, p. 35). Historical time plays a key role in life-course analysis because of the emphasis on social time and social transitions (Elder 1977; Hareven 1978). Changes that take place in society lead to a restructuring of individual life courses. Thus, life courses will vary from one cohort (generation) to the next.

The life-course perspective should be differentiated from the life-span perspective or other developmental models of psychology. In these latter approaches the focus is on the individual, especially on personality, cognition, and other intrapsychic phenomena (George 1982). In these developmental approaches, change results from within the individual, and this change is universal—it is a function of human nature. Typically, developmental changes are linked to chronological age, with little or no reference to the social context or the sociohistorical or individual-historical context. The life-course perspective, in contrast, focuses on transitions when the "social persona" (Hagestad and Neugarten 1985, p. 35) undergoes change.

CONCEPTIONS OF AGING

In order to understand health and the life course it is also important to understand the aging process. Aging is best understood in a life-course perspective. Persons do not suddenly become old at age sixty or sixty-five or at retirement. Aging is the result of a lifetime of social, behavioral, and biological processes interacting with one another. While genetics may play a part in predisposing individuals to certain diseases or impairments, length and quality of life have been found to be highly dependent on behaviors, lifestyles, and health-related attitudes (e.g., Haug and Ory 1987).

A distinction is often made between primary and secondary aging (see Schroots 1988). Primary aging, or normal aging, refers to the steady declines in functioning in the absence of disease or despite good health. Secondary aging, or pathological aging, refers to the declines that are due to illnesses associated with age but not to aging itself. This suggests that secondary aging can be reversed, at least in principle (Kohn 1985).

VARIATIONS IN HEALTH AND LIFE EXPECTANCY

The largest cause of death in America for people under age forty-five is accidents and adverse effects (National Center for Health Statistics [NCHS] 1999). For people five to fourteen years of age and twenty-five to forty-four years of age, malignant neoplasms (tumors) rank second as a cause of death. For persons fifteen to twenty-four years of age, homicide, followed closely by suicide, are the next leading causes of death.

For adults ages sixty-five and over the causes of death are quite different. Cardiovascular disease, malignant neoplasms, cerebrovascular disease, and chronic obstructive pulmonary disease are the most common causes of death (NCHS, 1999). Older persons, too, are more likely to suffer from chronic, and often limiting, conditions. Most common among these are arthritis, hypertension, hearing impairments, heart conditions, chronic sinusitis, visual impairments, and orthopedic impairments (e.g., back). Interestingly, these same conditions are among the most commonly mentioned by persons ages forty-five to sixty-four, though their prevalence is generally considerably less than among persons sixty-five and older.

At the turn of the century, life expectancy was about 48 years. By 1950, life expectancy was 68 years (66 years for males and 71 years for females). By 1997, life expectancy had increased to 76.5 years (74 years for males and 79 for females). Many of the improvements in life expectancy came about before large-scale immunization programs. These programs largely affected the health of those born during the 1940s and 1950s. These programs have, however, reduced infant mortality and reduced the likelihood of certain debilitating diseases (e.g., polio).

The chance of surviving to old age with few functional disabilities is strongly related to socioeconomic position, educational level, and race (Berkman 1988). People in lower classes and with less education have higher mortality risk and have higher incidence and prevalence of diseases and injuries. They have more hospitalizations, disability days, and functional limitations.

Life expectancy also varies by social class. At age twenty-five life expectancy, for those with four or fewer years of education, is forty-four years for men and almost forty-seven years for women. For men and women with some college education, life expectancy is forty-seven years and fifty-six years respectively. After age sixty-five, however, this relationship becomes less clear-cut, suggesting that for older cohorts a different set of factors is involved.

Another area where health and the life course intersect is that of health inequalities in the life course. Increasing evidence indicates that many illnesses in middle and later life have their beginnings in childhood or prior to birth (Wadsworth 1997). For example, low birthweight indicates poor prenatal growth, and both are associated with higher risk of respiratory problems in adult life. Further, lower birthweight is associated with poorer health practices of expectant mothers, suggesting that these babies will be born into family/ household/social environments that do not facilitate optimal health.

Life course trajectories vary by key social characteristics such as age, gender, race, and socioeconomic status (SES) (Bartley et al. 1997). Further, these life-course trajectories are related to disease risk. For example, an individual born into a poorer or working-class family will have a different trajectory of disease over the life course than an individual born into a family with better financial and social means. The former individual accumulates risks or disadvantages over the life course that begin to show up in adulthood.

ISSUES AND IMPLICATIONS

Differences in health conditions by age raise at least two issues regarding the analysis and understanding of health. First, it has been suggested that in trying to understand the health and health behavior of the elderly, especially as our models become more complex, the *individual* is the critical unit of analysis (Wolinsky and Arnold 1988). That is, we must focus on individual differentiation over the life course. Aging is a highly individual process, resulting from large inter- and intraindividual differences in health and functioning.

The second issue concerns the extent to which many processes thought to be life-course processes may in fact be cohort differences (see Dannefer 1988). An assumption is often made that the heterogeneity within older cohorts is an intracohort, life-course process: Age peers become increasingly dissimilar as they grow older. This conclusion is, however, often based on cross-sectional data and may lead to a life-course fallacy. Age differences may reduce to cohort differences. If each succeeding cohort becomes more homogeneous, older cohorts will display greater heterogeneity compared to younger cohorts. Evidence suggests that for several cohort characteristics this may be the case. For example, there has been increasing standardization of years of education, age of labor-force entry and exit, age at first marriage, number of children, and so on. Thus, younger age groups would exhibit less diversity than older cohorts.

Not all health deterioration is a normal process of aging. Some of it appears to be the result of an accumulation of life experiences and behaviors. Many of the experiences and behaviors are different for older and younger cohorts, suggesting that an understanding of factors affecting health for older cohorts may not hold for younger cohorts as they age.

Two possible scenarios exist. One is that older people in the future will experience less morbidity than today's elderly, even though later life will be longer. That is, they will be older longer, sick for a very short period of time, and then die. An alternative situation is one in which elderly live longer and are sick or impaired for many of those years. That is, they will be sick for an extensive period of their later life. Given the fact that more people are living longer, the general expectation is that the demand for health care by the elderly will be greater in the future. The extent of the demand will depend, in part, on which of these two scenarios is closer to the truth. The conservative approach, and the one generally adopted, is that estimates of tomorrow's needs for care are based on data from today's elderly. However, a life-course perspective might yield quite a different picture because the life experiences, behaviors, and health attitudes of today's elderly may be quite different from those of younger cohorts, tomorrow's elderly.

Health is a lifelong experience of an individual, composed of accumulations of risk. Logically, reducing health problems in middle and later years will be more successful the earlier attempts are made to reduce these risks (Wadsworth 1997). Similarly, health inequalities exist, and these are associated with social and biological characteristics of individuals (e.g., gender, race, SES). Reducing health inequalities will require reducing risk factors for these different groups of individuals and doing so early in life.

(SEE ALSO: *Aging and the Life Course*; *Health and Illness Behavior*; *Life Course*; *Life Expectancy*)

REFERENCES

Bartley, Mel, David Blane, and Scott Montgomery 1997 "Health and the Life Course: Why Safety Nets Matter." *British Medical Journal* 314:1194–1196.

Berkman, Lisa F. 1988 "The Changing and Heterogeneous Nature of Aging and Longevity: A Social and Biomedical Perspective." In G. L. Maddox and M. P. Lawton, eds., *Varieties of Aging*, vol. 8 of *Annual Review of Gerontology and Geriatrics*. New York: Springer.

Birren, James E., and Judy M. Zarit 1985 "Concepts of Health, Behavior, and Aging." In J. E. Birren and J.

Livingston, eds., *Cognition, Stress and Aging*. Englewood Cliffs, N.J.: Prentice-Hall.

Clausen, John A. 1986 *The Life Course: A Sociological Perspective*. Englewood Cliffs, N.J.: Prentice-Hall.

Dannefer, Dale 1988 "Differential Gerontology and the Stratified Life Course: Conceptual and Methodological Issues." In G. L. Maddox and M. P. Lawton, eds., *Varieties of Aging*, vol. 8 of *Annual Review of Gerontology and Geriatrics*. New York: Springer.

Elder, Glen H., Jr. 1977 "Family History and the Life Course." *Journal of Family History* 2:279–304.

George, Linda K. 1982 "Models of Transitions in Middle and Later Life." *Annals of the Academy of Political and Social Science* 464:22–37.

Hagestad, Gunhild O., and Bernice L. Neugarten 1985 "Age and the Life Course." In R. H. Binstock and E. Shanas, eds., *Handbook of Aging and the Social Sciences*. New York: Van Nostrand Reinhold.

Hareven, T. K. 1978 *Transitions: The Family and the Life Course in Historical Perspective*. New York: Academic Press.

Haug, Marie R., and Marcia G. Ory 1987 "Issues in Elderly Patient-Provider Interactions." *Research on Aging* 9:3–44.

Kohn, R. R. 1985 "Aging and Age-Related Diseases: Normal Processes." In H. A. Johnson, ed., *Relations Between Normal Aging and Disease*. New York: Raven Press.

Liang, Jersey 1986 "Self-Reported Physical Health among Aged Adults." *Journal of Gerontology* 41:248–260.

National Center for Health Statistics (NCHS) 1999 "Deaths: Final Data for 1997." *National Vital Statistics Report*. Vol. 47 No. 19. Hyattsville, Md.: Public Health Service.

Parsons, Talcott 1951 *The Social System*. New York: Free Press.

Schroots, Johannes J. F. 1988 "Current Perspectives on Aging, Health, and Behavior." In J. J. F. Schroots, J. E. Birren, and A. Svanborg, eds., *Health and Aging: Perspectives and Prospects*. New York: Springer.

Wadsworth, M. E. J. 1997 "Health Inequalities in the Life Course." *Social Science and Medicine* 44:859–869.

Wolinsky, Fredric D., and Connie Lea Arnold 1988 "A Different Perspective on Health Services Utilization." In G. L. Maddox and M. P. Lawton, eds., *Varieties of Aging*, vol. 8 of *Annual Review of Gerontology and Geriatrics*. New York: Springer.

DONALD E. STULL

HEALTH CARE FINANCING

See Health Care Utilization and Expenditures; Health Policy Analysis; Medical Sociology.

HEALTH CARE UTILIZATION AND EXPENDITURES

The U.S. health care system is unique among industrialized nations because it lacks a national health insurance program. The United States relies instead on private health insurance that individuals or companies must purchase. The public insurance system is limited to those who are aged or disabled (Medicare) and to some individuals who are poor (Medicaid). The delivery system for health care in the United States is almost entirely private, with only a small sector of government providers who primarily target the poor and uninsured population. Moreover, the U.S. health care system is largely unplanned and has limited regulation, even though the government is a large payer of services. In contrast, other industrialized nations have national health systems that provide coverage for their populations that are generally independent of employment (Blendon et al. 1995). These systems are more comprehensive and less expensive than the U.S. system, which excludes 43 million people (U.S. Bureau of the Census 1998b). This article examines the factors that have contributed to a system that severely limits access to millions of individuals in the United States.

We first examine health care utilization and expenditure patterns at the macro level. This approach is used by public policy makers at the federal, state, and local levels and by private insurers in decision making about the allocation and control of public and private resources for health care services. The second approach is a micro-level focus on the patterns of use and expenditures by individuals or groups of people in society and the factors that limit (or improve) access to services.

GROWTH IN EXPENDITURES

The most significant feature of health care in the United States during the 1980s and 1990s was its overall high growth rates and its total expenditures. Total national health expenditures increased by 283 percent between 1980 and 1990 (Smith et al.

1998). Although the annual growth rate in spending slowed from 11 percent in 1990 to 4.8 percent in 1997 (Levit et al. 1998), expenditures were over $1 trillion in 1996 and are projected to exceed $2 trillion by the year 2007 (Smith et al. 1998). Health care expenditures in 1997 amounted to $4,000 per capita (Table 1).

Health expenditures increased from 12.2 percent of the gross domestic product (GDP) to 13.5 percent in 1997 (Levit et al. 1998), and they are expected to reach 16.6 percent of GDP in the year 2007 (Smith et al. 1998). The devotion of a large percentage of the total GDP to health costs is a concern because such dollars are then not available for other needs.

Factors Increasing Expenditure Growth. Levit and colleagues (1998) have examined three basic components in the growth of health spending. The first component is the economy-wide increase in prices and inflation (about half of the total increases in the 1995–1997 period). The second is the change in volume and intensity of services. Levit and colleagues (1998) found that the volume and intensity of service use were about the same in the 1990s (about one-third of the total expenditure increases in 1997). Finally, there is medical price inflation over and above these other factors. In the 1990–1995 period, excess medical prices were important factors—almost one-third of the total increases. Between 1995 and 1997, this factor was only about one-sixth of the total increase (Levit et al. 1998). Even so, excess medical prices, or the "greed factors," are an important focus for policy makers because they represent the area where savings may be targeted.

Although health economists rarely focus on administrative costs, some scholars are now paying attention to the role of high administrative costs in the United States. For example, Hellander and colleagues (1994) estimated that administrative overhead accounted for 25 percent of total U.S. health system expenditures in 1993. This included the costs of insurance overhead, hospital administration, nursing home administration, and physicians' billing and overhead. There is some evidence that such costs are increasing. The excess bureaucracy is related to the complex payment and billing systems that have been created in the United States. Consolidating the 1,500 insurers in the United States could reduce overhead costs.

National Health Expenditures by Category of Funds for 1990, 1997 and Projected for 2007

(in millions)

Source of Funds	Year		
	1990*	1997*	2007**
Total health expenditures	$699.4	$1,092.4	$2,133.3
Total health services and supplies	674.8	1,057.5	2,085.3
Hospital care	256.4	371.1	649.4
Physician services	146.3	217.6	427.3
Other professional services	40.7	160.0	229.7
Nursing home care	50.9	82.8	148.3
Home health care	13.3	32.3	66.1
Prescription drugs	37.7	78.9	171.1
Other personal care services	69.4	26.3	167.3
Other supplies and services	60.1	88.5	226.1
Other expenditures			
Research and construction	24.5	34.9	48.0
Other expenditures not included above			
Program administration and net cost of private health insurance	40.5	50.0	151.3
Government public health	19.6	38.5	74.9

Table 1

SOURCE: Adapted from *Levit et al. (1998); **Smith et al. (1998).

Kenkel (1993) found that health maintenance organizations (HMOs) reported that 18 percent of their revenues were used for overhead and profits, compared with traditional insurance plans (14 percent) and Medicare (only 3.5 percent).

Economic analysts argue that the slower spending during the latter part of the 1990s reflected several factors. First, where employers sponsored health plans, there was a shift of many workers from indemnity health plans into managed care (Levit et al. 1998), where premiums may have been lower. Second, managed care was successful in negotiating discounts with providers because there was an excess capacity of providers. Growth in managed care enrollment was found to have only a small effect on the volume and intensity of services. Finally, the general and medical-specific inflation rates declined (Levit et al. 1998).

Ginsburg and Gabel (1998) argue that spending was down in the 1990s because of a sharp decline in provider revenues and payrolls. They show that hospital and physician spending increases in 1997 were less than the growth rate in the GDP (which was 2.8 percent in 1997). Although there was a slight increase in payroll costs between 1996 and 1997 in hospitals, most of the growth was due to increases in hours worked, and not in number of employees. At the same time, drug costs had increased by 11.5 percent, primarily because of increases in the use of drugs rather than the price (Ginsburg and Gabel 1998). Premiums for health insurance increased by only 3.3 percent between 1997 and 1998 (Ginsburg and Gabel 1998). The premium increases showed substantial profit margins in 1992–1994, but lagged behind expenditures while profit margins in health plans dropped in 1996–1997 (Ginsburg and Gabel 1998).

Health care spending increases are expected to continue because of the growing demand for medical services, continued economy-wide inflation, and medical price inflation. See Table 1. Most of the expenditure growth is expected to take place in the private sector, with lower spending in the public sector (Smith et al. 1998).

The high growth rate for health expenditures has had several consequences. First, the growth rate has dominated the attention of policy makers at all levels as they have attempted to struggle with cost containment. Most policy efforts have been directed toward reducing program utilization and expenditures. This focus on cost containment has set the national political agenda, relegating issues of access to health care and the quality of care to a second level of consideration. This agenda is of great concern because the number of uninsured is increasing and the quality of health care urgently needs to be improved (Chassin et al. 1998). Moreover, the high expenditure rates continue to be used as a rationale by some policy makers for why the expansion of public programs and a national health insurance policy are not financially feasible in the United States.

Growth Through Consolidations, Mergers, and Acquisitions. Overall health expenditures are increasing in part because of the changing structure of health care financing and delivery systems. Kassirer (1996) documented the rapid trends in consolidation of the health care industry, creating larger corporations during the 1990s. Srinivasan and colleagues (1998) reported that, in 1997 alone, there were 483 mergers and acquisitions involving health services companies totaling $27 billion and 33 mergers and acquisitions involving HMOs totaling $13 billion. The big winners in mergers and acquisitions are the corporate executives of these large organizations, the stockholders, the lawyers who broker the consolidations, and the health care consultants. The losers are the physicians and nurses who may lose income and even jobs. It is not clear that these mergers and acquisitions are resulting in any overall savings to the system or in improvements in the quality of care. Rather, they appear to be increasing profits and market power (Kassirer 1996).

Srinivasan and colleagues (1998) reported that the growth rate in for-profit health service companies and HMOs has increased rapidly in recent years. Between 1981 and 1997, for-profit HMOs grew from 12 to 62 percent of total HMO enrollees and from 18 to 75 percent of all health plans. Between 1987 and 1997, there were 210 offerings for health services companies valued at $6.7 billion and 23 HMO public offerings for $1.4 billion. Health services capitalization was $113 billion and HMO capitalization was $39 billion in 1997, showing dramatic growth rates. Stock prices for health care industry firms generally outperformed the overall stock market over the decade. As these changes occurred, there were also many conversions of nonprofit health care organizations to for-profit status in order to obtain capital and survive in a highly competitive environment. In 1997, there were 81 conversion foundations with assets of $9 billion as a result of the conversions to for-profit status (Srinivasan et al. 1998).

Every year *Forbes* magazine lists the largest health care corporations in the United States and details their stock performance. Gallagher (1999) reported $10 billion in mergers and acquisitions in 1998, including many in the HMO and long term care sectors. The managed care stocks were reportedly healthy in 1998, climbing 15 percent over 1997 (Gallagher 1999). HMO mergers and acquisitions were slower in 1998 than in the previous year. By comparison, hospital stocks were off 22 percent on average and long-term care providers were off 56 percent (Gallagher 1999).

What scholars and policy makers have generally thus far ignored are both the economic and the social costs of these changes in the structure of the health care system. The costs associated with mergers, consolidations, and profits are not identified in the analyses of health care costs (Levit et al. 1997). As long as the health industry is profitable, we can expect growth in the private profit-making sector.

PRIVATE PAYERS

The payers of health services dominate the policy decision-making process in the United States. At the same time, the payers of health care have shifted over the past decade.

Private health insurance corporations dominate the health system because they have the lion's share of the resources and power in the health industry. For instance, private health insurance firms earned $348 billion in premium income in 1997 in the United States (Levit et al. 1998). See Table 2. Private health insurance companies include both the traditional indemnity insurance plans as well as managed care plans. The private health insurance industry—including managed care organizations—spent $34.5 billion (or 10 percent) of their premium income in 1997 on administration and profits.

Light (1992) has documented many of the problems with private indemnity health insurance plans. These plans have practice medical underwriting that excludes individuals with medical problems (e.g., chronic diseases) or raises the premiums for such policies to levels where individuals

National Health Expenditures by Source of Funds for 1990, 1997 and Projected for 2007

(in millions)

Source of Funds	Year		
	1990*	1997*	2007**
Total health expenditures	$699.5	$1,092.4	$2,133.3
Private funds			
Private health insurance	239.6	348.0	754.4
Out of pocket	145.0	187.6	310.7
Other private funds	31.6	49.7	80.8
Public funds			
Medicare	111.5	214.6	415.6
Medicaid	75.4	59.9	337.0
Other public	96.3	132.7	234.8

Table 2

SOURCE: Adapted from *Levit et al. (1998); **Smith et al. (1998).

cannot afford to purchase them. There are indirect approaches to reducing risk, such as waiting periods, copayments, and payment ceilings, along with the exclusion of certain procedures, tests, or drugs. Light (1992) also documented the problems with inaccurate or manipulative premiums and discrimination, which includes policy churning (switching policies before the waiting period ends) within group underwriting for those individuals at high risk, renewal underwriting (increasing the costs for those with new medical conditions), and selective marketing. There are many techniques to deny or delay payment for services. All these practices have negative consequences for individuals and groups seeking insurance. These problems are the result of a health care system geared toward profit and cost containment and of ineffective regulation of health insurance companies at the state level, although states do vary in their regulatory activities.

In 1996, Congress passed the Health Insurance Portability and Accountability Act (HIPAA). This legislation, sponsored by Senators Edward Kennedy and Nancy Kassebaum, was designed to address some of the problems with health insurance by making it easier for persons who have lost employer-provided insurance to qualify for other coverage. However, Kuttner (1999) concludes that HIPAA is of little help because there are no regulatory controls on insurance premiums and no subsidies for those persons who need the insurance because most have lost their jobs and the ability to

pay for the insurance. Similarly, the 1985 Consolidated Omnibus Budget Reconciliation Act (COBRA) allowed people leaving employment to pay insurance premiums out of pocket for up to eighteen months to retain their coverage, but again, this is of little help for those without the resources to pay for the insurance (Kuttner 1999).

Managed care organizations (MCOs) had the most dramatic growth in health care in the 1990s. As one study reported, "Managed care isn't coming; it has arrived" (Jensen et al. 1997). In 1995, 73 percent of insured U.S. workers received their coverage through an HMO, a preferred provider organization (PPO), or a point-of-service plan (POS) (Jensen et al. 1997, p. 126). See Table 3. HMOs are health plans that provide care from an established panel of providers to an enrolled population on a prepaid basis. PPOs are health plan arrangements where networks of providers agree to accept plan payment rates and utilization controls. POS plans are HMOs where members may self-refer outside the established network but are required to pay deductibles and other costs. This means that conventional, or fee-for-service (FFS), plans have experienced a precipitous decline in recent years. Between 1993 and 1995, the percentage of workers in conventional health plans dropped from 49 to 27 percent (22 percent), while significant growth occurred in HMOs (6 percent), PPOs (5 percent), and POSs (11 percent) (Jensen et al. 1997, p. 126). Eighty-five percent of the U.S. work force was covered by some type of managed care plan in 1997 (Levit et al. 1997).

**Percentage of Workers in Various
Types of Plans, 1993–1995**

Plan Type	Year	
	1993	1995
Conventional	48.9%	27.4%
Health maintenance organization (HMO)	22.4%	27.5%
Preferred provider organization (PPO)	19.6%	25.0%
Point-of-service plan (POS)	9.1%	20.1%

Table 3

SOURCE: Jenson et al. (1997).

There have been numerous studies of HMOs and their performance (Miller 1998; Miller and Luft, 1994, 1997). Davis and colleagues (1995) surveyed individuals in FFS plans in comparison to those in managed care. They found that many individuals (54 percent) had changed plans within the past three years. Of those who changed plans, 73 percent had done so involuntarily, either because of employment coverage changes or changes in jobs or moves. Of those persons in managed care who had changed plans, 41 percent also reporting having to change physicians involuntarily, compared with only 12 percent of enrollees in fee-for-service coverage.

Although most respondents were reasonably satisfied with their health insurance, those in managed care were more likely to rate their plan as "fair" or "poor" and were less like to rate their plan as "excellent." Those individuals in managed care plans reported less access to specialty care, less availability of emergency care, more waiting times for appointments, and less overall plan satisfaction (Davis et al. 1995).

Other research on the quality of managed care services points to concerns for populations with particular health needs. Miller (1998) found mixed results for access to care in HMOs among enrollees with chronic conditions and diseases. He found enough negative results to raise serious concerns about access. Nelson and colleagues (1997) found less satisfaction with the amount of services received among enrollees who used HMO services. For populations with a variety of needs, the concerns are also mounting. For example, studies of elderly ill persons revealed that HMO enrollees report poor quality of care and lower utilization

than FFS enrollees (Clement et al. 1994; Shaughnessy et al. 1994). The problems that the elderly confront reveal spaces where government programs (i.e., Medicare) and private institutional practices (HMOs) need expanded coverage and improved coordination.

Between 1989 and 1995, the enrollment of Medicare beneficiaries in HMOs grew rapidly, so that HMOs covered about 10 percent of the total beneficiaries and the remaining persons received traditional FFS care (Welch, 1996). The Balanced Budget Act of 1997 made a number of changes in the Medicare program, called Medicare+Choice, that were intended to expand Medicare beneficiaries' options (Christensen 1998). These included: (1) PPOs, where networks of providers agree to accept plan payment rates and utilization controls; (2) provider-sponsored organizations (PSOs), which are plans organized by affiliated health care providers; and (3) medical saving accounts (MSAs) established by enrollees to receive the Medicare amount that would be paid to an HMO. Enrollees must pay all costs out of the MSA that would be covered by Medicare as well as out-of-pocket expenses (Christensen 1998). Congress expected that the Balanced Budget Act would accelerate the growth in HMO enrollment to nearly 34 percent by 2005. In spite of these changes to implement this new program, growth may be slower than projected because some HMOs are unwilling to accept Medicare members because they consider Medicare rates to be too low. In 1998, HMOs announced that they were dropping approximately 400,000 of their 6 million enrollees because they consider the rates too low (Pear 1998).

There are two advantages of HMO enrollment for Medicare beneficiaries. The first is that premium costs have generally been minimal and the second is that some HMOs include prescription drug coverage and other benefits not covered by Medicare. Recently, however, drug benefits for Medicare beneficiaries have been reduced or capped by a number of HMOs (Kuttner 1999).

HMOs have also dramatically captured the Medicaid enrollment in many states. President Bill Clinton streamlined the process that allowed states to have waivers of the federal regulations that provide mandatory enrollment of Medicaid beneficiaries in HMOs (Iglehart 1995). The expectation was that HMOs would control Medicaid costs and encourage more coordinated forms of care by increasing the likelihood of having a primary care physician. The Kaiser Commission on the Future of Medicaid (1995) summarized 139 articles, books, and reports on Medicaid managed care and found mixed results. They found that the use of specialty services and emergency room care declined, but there was not a consistent increase or decrease in use of physicians' services or hospital care. The issue of cost savings was mixed, and quality and satisfaction rates were considered to be comparable. On the other hand, Iglehart (1995) documented serious problems with the implementation of Medicaid managed care in some states, including Florida and Tennessee.

Pauly (1998) argues that for-profit health plans enjoy monopsony power in the health care market. And while a monopsony can result in lower provider premiums, it may also reduce benefits as the providers reduce their spending on care. Pauly concludes that traditional antitrust policies have not addressed the problem of monopsony or monopoly power.

Woolhandler and Himmelstein (1995) view the growth in HMOs as a transformation that not only places physicians at financial risk because of cost-containment practices but also pressures physicians to withhold needed care. These financial arrangements encourage physicians to collaborate in risk selection by seeking to avoid patients who may have high care needs. Mechanic and Schlesinger (1996) have argued that the impact of managed care has had a negative impact on patients' trust of medical care and their physicians. The insurance industry and the managed care organizations hold great power and authority over the care provided to individuals and groups. They also have a great deal of influence over physicians, other health professionals, and health care workers. The current trends can have serious negative consequences for access and the health status of the population.

PUBLIC PAYERS

The two major public payers are Medicare and Medicaid, programs established in 1965. Medicare pays for those individuals who are aged or disabled under Title 18 of the Social Security Act. Medicaid is generally provided to persons age 65 and over who are entitled to Social Security and to individuals who are disabled for a period of at least 24 months. There were 38 million people eligible in 1997. Medicaid, under Title 19 of the Social Security Act, is funded jointly by federal, state, and local governments. It provides coverage to those persons who are eligible for Supplemental Security Income, for low-income individuals who are aged, blind, or disabled. It also pays for recipients and their children under the Aid to Families with Dependent Children, which is now the Temporary Assistance for Needy Families program. The program provided assistance to 36 million persons in 1996 (Waid 1998). There are other public payers, such as the Veterans' Administration and local governments, that are not discussed here in detail.

Medicare. In 1997, Medicare paid $214.6 billion for its 38.4 million aged and disabled enrollees (Levit et al. 1998). Medicare is the single largest public program, accounting for 20 percent of the nation's health expenditures. See Table 2. The growth rates in Medicare spending declined from 12.2 percent in 1994 to 7.2 percent in 1997. This decline was the result of slower price inflation and policy changes. Physician payments were limited, and fraud and abuse detection programs were increased. Limits on payments and aggressive abuse detection programs are credited with decreasing home health care spending (Levit et al. 1998). Future declines in nursing home spending are expected because of the adoption of a prospective payment system that was implemented in 1998.

In the 1980s and 1990s, Medicare spending growth had been much lower than private health insurance annual growth rates. But in 1997, Medicare spending growth rates were 5.8 percent compared with 3.8 percent for private health insurance (Levit et al. 1998). Unfortunately, this growth in spending has contributed to public policy attention on reducing spending for the Medicare program.

And although spending for Medicare has increased, the program pays for only a limited amount of health insurance for those who are aged and disabled. Data from the 1997 Current Population Survey indicate that Medicare beneficiaries paid 67 percent of their total expenditures. Private insurance paid for only 10 percent of the bills, even though a large proportion of beneficiaries have private supplemental insurance. The remainder was paid out of pocket by beneficiaries (Carrasquillo et al. 1999).

When the Medicare, Medicaid, and other public programs are combined, their expenditures represent 46 percent of total national expenditures. Because this is such a large percentage of the total, the large increases in public spending per year contribute to the public policy focus on cost containment.

Medicaid. Medicaid is a program designed for the poor as a safety net. Medicaid spending was $159.9 billion in 1997, or a 3.8 percent increase over the previous year (Levit et al. 1998). Other governmental expenditures for health care (federal, state, and local) totaled $132.7 billion. These public programs represented 27 percent of total U.S. expenditures. See Table 2. There was a rapid growth in Medicaid expenditures in the 1988–1994 period, related to the growth in (1) the number of enrollees, (2) the spending per enrollee, and (3) increases in spending for hospitals with disproportionate shares of Medicaid patients. The spending slowed in the 1994–1997 period because the number of Medicaid enrollees dropped during this period. The states also were allowed to have waivers to implement mandatory enrollment in managed care plans.

Congress passed welfare reform legislation in 1996 that replaced the Aid to Families With Dependent Children (AFDC) with Temporary Assistance for Needy Families (TANF). This legislation broke the link between welfare and Medicaid eligibility, but states must continue to provide benefits to persons who met the eligibility requirements for Medicaid prior to the legislation. The law changed the definition of childhood disability under the Supplemental Security Income (SSI) program, curtailed benefits to legal immigrants, and banned Medicaid eligibility for qualified aliens admitted to the United States after the legislation. Some benefits were restored to legal immigrants under the Balanced Budget Act of 1997 (Levit et al. 1998).

The passage of TANF means that welfare limits will gradually become effective in most states during 1999, and millions of women will lose their eligibility for welfare benefits. Although states may

continue to offer Medicaid eligibility to those individuals who go off welfare and are working in low-income jobs, many former welfare recipients are not informed of their eligibility for Medicaid services and thus have not retained their benefits. Those former welfare recipients who successfully obtain employment will generally be placed in relatively low-wage occupations that will probably not offer health insurance or job security. Overall, the legislation will result in a loss of health insurance for many women and children (Kuttner 1999).

In response to the health needs of children, Congress passed the Children's Health Insurance Program (CHIP) as a part of the 1997 Balanced Budget Act. This program provided states with $24 billion over five years to expand coverage of Medicaid for children or to establish a new children's health insurance program. The new insurance program is complex and difficult for people to understand and gain access to. In 1998, it was reported that the program was dramatically undersubscribed for a number of reasons across the country. California, for example, had enrolled only about 4 percent of the 580,000 children eligible for the program (Kuttner 1999). Some immigrants were reported to be concerned that enrollment of their children could affect their immigration status.

Several barriers restrict access to this program, particularly for immigrant populations. First, a large state bureaucracy and complicated application process have limited access to services. Second, eligibility coverage varies for children of different ages, so that one child may be covered while another is not in a single family. Many immigrant parents declined to participate in the program because they felt that providing health care for one child while not obtaining coverage for another was immoral (Altman 1998). Finally, eligibility for this program was initially tied to citizenship, which created access problems because, although their children were often documented and legal residents, undocumented immigrant parents declined to apply to the program for fear of deportation by immigration authorities (Korenbrot et al. 1999).

The Congressional Budget Office estimated that the Children's Health Insurance Program and the Medicaid expansions could extend coverage to

2 million of the 10.6 million uninsured children in l997 (Kuttner 1999). It is uncertain if more than a fraction of this total will ever receive coverage.

CONSUMER POWER

Consumers have seen a drop in their out-of-pocket spending for medical care over the past two decades. In l980, out-of-pocket spending was 24 percent of the total expenditures in contrast with 17 percent of spending in l997 (Levit et al. 1998). The total out-of-pocket spending was $187.6 billion in l997. Out-of-pocket costs include premiums for insurance, copayments, and deductibles for services use, and direct costs for services not covered by insurance, such as outpatient drugs and long-term care. The reason that out-of-pocket spending is lower is that some consumers are also paying a lower proportion of their income on premiums for health insurance. Managed care plans generally had more limited copayments and deductibles than indemnity insurance, and more individuals were enrolled in managed care (Ginsburg and Gabel 1998). Out-of-pocket costs did, however, go up in l997 because some HMOs were reportedly increasing their copayment and deductible charges (Levit et al. 1998). Consumer spending for drugs increased as well.

Some studies have reported that 61 percent of the population has employment related coverage (AHCPR 1998; Levit et al. 1998). These estimates group individuals who have public and private employment together and tend to count anyone with private insurance even if that insurance is not the primary payer of health care. New data from the 1997 Current Population Survey showed that only 43 percent of the population had their health insurance paid for by private-sector employers, 34 percent have publicly funded insurance, 7 percent purchased their own insurance, and 16 percent were uninsured (Carrasquillo et al. 1999). Employers also contribute to the Medicare Hospital Insurance Trust Fund through Social Security payroll taxes, but these account for only a small amount of the total expenditures.

Carrasquillo and colleagues (1999) point out that the role of employers in paying for insurance has been exaggerated and, as a consequence, employers have played a dominant role in public policy discussions related to health insurance. For example, President Clinton's national health insurance plan proposed to link health insurance to that paid for by private employers, even though employers are not the major payers of insurance. Employers played a role, along with many other interest groups, in defeating the Clinton plan because of fears that their costs would be increased and they would lose control over their work force (Navarro 1995). At the same time, employers are given an estimated $100 billion in tax subsidies in order to cover the costs of employer-sponsored health insurance (Reinhardt 1997). The $100 billion in subsidies could be eliminated if a national health insurance plan were paid directly by the government.

TYPES OF UTILIZATION AND EXPENDITURES

National expenditures for health care reveal how health resources are utilized and allocated to provide care in the United States. The patterns are not necessarily the way the public would allocate the resources. Instead, the expenditure patterns reflect historical decisions about how public and private dollars should be spent.

The patterns of expenditures changed rapidly in the latter half of the 1990s because of the growth in managed care. Managed care plans have instituted their own cost controls on the providers that they pay. The health industry has also been consolidating through a large number of mergers and acquisitions. These changes have resulted in fewer larger health care provider organizations.

Hospital Care. Hospital care has historically been and continues to be the largest component of health spending, accounting for 38 percent of total spending ($371 billion) in 1997. See Table 1. The spending for inpatient care dropped considerably and marked increases occurred in outpatient services. This shift represents a restructuring to outpatient care, which is less costly. In the l990–1997 period, there was a 6-percent reduction in hospital admissions per capita and a 16-percent decline in inpatient days in community hospitals (American Healthcare Infosource 1998).

As result of the restructuring and downsizing, U.S. hospitals closed 88,000 beds (10 percent) and occupancy rates fell from 64.5 percent in 1990 to 59.6 percent in 1997 (Levit et al. 1998). Although utilization fell and price increases were controlled, hospitals were able to keep profit margins high, since almost all their revenue is from third-party insurance (consumers paid directly for only 3 percent of hospital costs).

Physician Services. Costs of physicians' services were $218 billion in 1997, or 21 percent of total health services and supplies. Spending increases for physicians were associated with the increasing dominance of managed care organizations. The American Medical Association (AMA) reported that 92 percent of all physicians were in managed care, and these contracts accounted for 49 percent of their income (Levit et al. 1998). Physicians are also expected to pay for an increasing share of ancillary services under the capitated managed care contracts. Physicians have reacted to managed care cost controls by expanding the sizes of their practices to large group practices. These practices allow for greater leverage in negotiating contracts, economies of scale, and increases in capital. More research on the effects of the changing structure of medical practices on health care access, costs, and quality is needed.

Drugs and Medical Nondurables. Drugs and medical nondurables accounted for $108.9 billion in 1997, or 10 percent of total national expenditures (Levit et al. 1998). Prescription drugs as a subset grew faster than other types of health care. These costs grew at 14.1 percent in 1997 compared to 4.8 percent for health spending in 1989. Out-of-pocket drug costs were 51 percent of total payments in 1989, later dropping to only 29 percent in 1997, and the rest were paid by third parties. The switch to managed care has increased the amount of covered outpatient drugs with relatively low copayments (Levit et al. 1998). Thus, the growth in drug costs was associated with increases in the number of prescriptions—not price increases, as had been the case in the 1980s (Levit et al. 1998).

The demand for drugs continues to increase. The Food and Drug Administration (FDA) approved fifty-three new drugs in 1996 and thirty-nine in 1997—both record highs. These approvals, along with increased advertising efforts by pharmaceutical firms, may lead to increases in demand. Drug makers reported spending $21 billion on research and development in 1998, compared with $8 billion in 1990 (Herrera 1999). They also increased spending on advertising to $1.3 billion

in 1998, having great successes with Viagra (for impotence), Claritin (for allergies), and Propecia (for baldness) (Herrera 1999).

Other Services. Nursing homes represented about 8 percent of total health service and supply expenditures in 1997, and this is projected to decline to 7 percent in 2007. Other professional services were 4.6 percent of expenditures, home health care was 3 percent, dental services were 4.6 percent, and vision products and other durable medical equipment were only 1.4 percent in 1996. These expenditures were expected to remain about the same percentage of the total over the next ten-year period (Smith et al. 1998). Governmental public health activities were estimated to be about $35.5 billion in 1996, representing 3.4 percent of total U.S. health expenditures. Research expenditures were 1.6 percent of the total in 1996, and construction was 1.4 percent of the total (Smith et al. 1998); these were also projected to remain the same over the next ten-year period.

LONG-TERM CARE IN THE UNITED STATES

The only segment of the U.S. population whose cost of long-term care is fully covered is made up of those individuals below the poverty threshold who are enrolled in the state-run, federally supported Medicaid plans (Harrington et al. 1991). Many persons of moderate incomes needing long-term care are unable to afford the costs of long-term care services, which can be as much as $50,000 per year for nursing home care. If individuals "spend down" to the poverty threshold, they can become Medicaid eligible as a last resort (Wiener 1996). This not only constitutes a hardship to the patient but creates dependence on federal and state assistance, which would be unnecessary if the entire population were insured, with premiums derived from sources other than the government.

In contrast, the nonpoor elderly enrolled in Medicare are entitled only to a limited number of skilled nursing care days (up to 100 days) if medically required following hospitalization. With some exceptions, the rest of the population must either pay for care out of pocket or purchase private long-term care insurance (Levit et al. 1997).

In 1996, national estimates for long-term care spending were $125.5 billion (Levit et al. 1997). Of the total expenditures, 30 percent ($38 billion) was for home health care (including hospitals and freestanding agencies) and 70 percent was for nursing home care ($87.5 billion; including hospital and freestanding facilities) (Levit et al. 1997). Home health expenditures are expected to double between 1996 and 2007, while nursing homes are expected to grow by 50 percent during the same period (Smith et al. 1998).

Medicaid paid for 48 percent of all nursing home care and 14 percent of all home health care in 1996 (Levit et al. 1997). Medicare paid for 45 percent of home health care and 11 percent of nursing home care. Overall, the government paid 59 percent of home health costs and 61.5 percent of nursing home costs (Levit et al. 1997). Most of the burden for government spending is from general taxes used to pay for Medicaid and a combination of general taxes and payroll taxes that support the Medicare program.

Private health insurance paid only an estimated 5 percent of nursing home care and 10.6 percent of home health care expenditures in 1996 (Levit et al. 1997). The remainder of the expenditures was paid directly out of pocket by those needing long-term care (31.5 percent for nursing home care and 19.5 percent for home health care) (Levit et al. 1997).

Private, voluntary long-term care insurance is not a viable approach to financing long-term care (Wiener 1994). Although private long-term care insurance has been available since the late 1980s, only 4.5 million long-term care insurance policies had been sold by 1994 (and not all of these policies were still in effect) (Cohen and Kumar 1997). Sold on an individual basis, private long-term care insurance is primarily attractive to persons whose health condition places them at high risk and makes them likely candidates for long-term care. Only about 10 to 20 percent of the elderly can afford to purchase long-term care insurance (Wiener 1994). Premiums for two policies purchased at age 65 were estimated to cost an average of $3,500 per year, which would be about 13 percent of a median elderly couple's income (Consumer Reports 1997, p. 46). These models determined that private long-term care insurance is unlikely to have a significant impact on public spending for long-term care, even though such insurance is expected to increase (Wiener and Illston 1994; Wiener et al. 1994).

A mandatory social insurance program for long-term care would have many advantages (Harrington et al. 1991). If everyone paid into the system, then individuals would have access to coverage when they are chronically ill or disabled without the humiliation of having to become poor (i.e., to "spend down") to receive services. The program might be more appealing if enrollees could have the advantage of paying in advance (prefunding) so that services would be available when needed. No stigma would be attached to receiving services, and such a program should have wide public support. The program could also reduce the access problems that are currently experienced by those who are in the Medicaid program. The financial risk would be spread across the entire population so that individual premium costs or taxes would be relatively low, in comparison to the costs of insurance purchased when individuals are older and at risk of needing long-term care.

Although many have argued that the United States cannot afford to adopt a public social insurance program, Germany mandated a social insurance program for long-term care in 1995 (Geraedts et al. 1999). This program was funded through a combination of public taxes and payroll taxes paid by employers and employees (.08 percent of wages for each or a total of 1.6 percent) (Geraedts et al. 1999). During the first three years of this program, it maintained its financial solvency and expanded long-term care to the entire population who have disabilities. This example demonstrates that such public insurance programs, if paid for by the entire population, can ensure coverage at a reasonable cost. This approach avoids restricted access, the stigma, and the stress placed on those individuals needing long term care and their families who do not have sufficient funds to pay for them in the United States (Harrington et al. 1999).

THE UNINSURED AND THEIR HEALTH: MICRO-LEVEL ISSUES

An estimated 43 million individuals in the United States have no private health care insurance (Kuttner 1999; U.S. Bureau of the Census 1998b). These individuals have no Medicare, Medicaid, or other public insurance coverage. The percent of the population without insurance increased from 14.2 in 1995, to 15.3 percent in 1996, and to 16.1 percent in 1997 (Kuttner 1999). This represents a steady increase in the number of uninsured since the 1980s, when the Reagan administration first began cutbacks in public health expenditures. The U.S. Bureau of the Census (1998b) also estimated that about 71.5 million individuals lacked insurance for at least part of the year in 1996.

The uninsured are primarily those who are poor and members of minority groups. Of those with incomes of less than $25,000, 24 percent had no health insurance compared with only 8 percent of those with incomes over $75,000 (Kuttner 1999). For those from minority groups, 50 percent of Hispanics and 37 percent of blacks had at least one month without insurance coverage compared to only 25 percent of whites (Kuttner 1999). Moreover, approximately one in three children had no health insurance for part of the year during 1995 and 1996 (Families USA 1997). The rate of children lacking insurance rose between 1989 and 1996 (U.S. Bureau of the Census 1998a). Lack of insurance for children was closely correlated with income. The group with the highest uninsured rate was young adults (38 percent, or twice the rate for other Americans), because many of them are dependent on their parents, who are working in low-wage jobs (AHCPR, 1998).

REASONS FOR THE GROWING NUMBERS OF UNINSURED

There are many reasons why individuals do not have health insurance, but the primary one is that private health insurance rates are too high relative to the incomes of those who are poor. The costs of insurance would represent about 26 to 40 percent of incomes of those who are poor, so many of these individuals are unable to afford coverage (Kuttner 1999). Another major problem is that 44 percent of those individuals who lost their jobs in the 1993–1995 period also lost their health insurance coverage.

The Medicaid program does not provide health insurance to all those individuals living below the U.S. poverty rate. State Medicaid programs are allowed to establish their own eligibility standards for those on welfare (TANF) in order to limit the number who can be served. The Census Bureau reported that 49 percent of people who were fully

employed but living below the poverty line had no Medicaid or private insurance, and this number increased to 52 percent in 1996 (Kuttner 1999). Due to reductions in Medicaid coverage, the rate of poor children with insurance fell from 16.5 million to 15.5 million between 1995 and 1996 (U.S. Bureau of the Census 1998a). A U.S. General Accounting Office study (1996) found that nearly 3 million children who were eligible for Medicaid were not enrolled in the program because of inadequate outreach, fears by immigrants about immigration problems, and other barriers. Additionally, the combination of immigration reform and welfare reforms has produced a "chilling effect" on many immigrants and their health care providers (Korenbrot et al. 1999).

Another reason that health insurance coverage is eroding is the rising cost of health insurance premiums, especially for people who purchase individual premiums privately rather than through the job (Kuttner 1999). Kuttner (1999) also cites the trends toward temporary and part-time employment, where most workers do not have insurance. The rising costs of Medigap premiums for the elderly who are on Medicare is also a major problem. Finally, the trend away from community rating of insurance to individual and group ratings makes the costs substantially higher for individuals and some groups that have higher injury or illness rates. Employers are also reducing their supplemental health coverage for retirees (from 60 percent to only 40 percent of retirees in 1995) (Kuttner 1999).

There has been a reduction in benefit coverage, particularly for pharmaceutical benefits. Many health plans are capping their outpatient drug benefits, although prescription drugs are the largest category of out-of-pocket costs for the elderly and the costs are increasing rapidly (Kuttner 1999). As noted earlier, drugs costs have been increasing rapidly (Levit et al. 1997) and many cannot afford to pay these costs. Many HMOs and insurance companies have been reducing drug benefits because of these cost increases. One study found that 84 percent of Medigap policies for the elderly had no drug coverage (McCormack et al. 1996). The result is that many elderly individuals are unable to afford drugs that are prescribed for them.

Another problem has been limited health insurance coverage for persons with mental health problems and mental illness. Mechanic and Rochefort (1992) document the deinstitutionalization of the mentally ill from public mental hospitals and the problems associated with inadequate mental health services. Inadequate housing and community health services, as well as the limits on mental health insurance coverage have all contributed to a general decline in mental health services.

CONSEQUENCES OF LIMITED ACCESS TO HEALTH CARE

The United States and South Africa continue to hold the unenviable distinction as the only two existing industrialized countries without national health insurance. Thus, when the high U.S. expenditures per capita are compared with those of other industrialized counties, the majority of these nations have their populations covered by insurance, while the United States is excluding 43 million individuals. The lack of health insurance leads to a number of serious problems in access to health care services.

There are many other health-related problems that plague the U.S. population in comparison to those of other nations. Among the top twenty-four industrialized nations, the United States ranks sixteenth in life expectancy for women and seventeenth for men, while it ranks twenty-first in infant mortality (Andrews 1995, p. 38). Although there were substantial reductions in childhood mortality in the United States between 1950 and 1993 (Singh and Yu 1996), the United States is well behind many other industrialized countries in childhood mortality (two to four times higher than Japan and Sweden) not only because of higher mortality from medical causes (e.g., heart disease) but also because of injuries and violence. Moreover, there are large differences across groups, with male children experiencing higher mortality rates and African-American children experiencing rates of more than twice that of white children (Singh and Yu 1996).

A number of studies have been conducted on the barriers to access related to the inability to pay for services (Berk et al. 1995; Braveman et al. 1989; Berk et al. 1995; Hafner-Eaton 1994; Mueller et al. 1998; Weissman et al. 1991). Mueller and colleagues (1998) confirmed that lack of health insurance—regardless of race or ethnicity, or living in a rural environment—is the major determinant of the utilization of health care services.

Approximately 12 percent of all American families (12.8 million) experienced barriers to receiving needed health care services in 1996. Sixty percent of these families reported that the barrier to care was their inability to afford the care, and 20 percent cited insurance-related problems (AHCPR 1997). The barriers to health care included difficulties finding care, delays, or not receiving the care that was needed.

Nearly 46 million Americans were without a regular source of health care such as a doctor's office, clinic, or health center in 1996 (AHCPR 1997). Those persons without insurance were two to three times more likely to have no regular source of health care and two to three times more likely to have encountered barriers in receiving needed health care than those persons with health insurance (AHCPR 1997). Hispanics (30 percent), the uninsured under age 65 (38 percent), and young adults (34 percent) were more likely to lack a stable source of health care. Those individuals with a history of serious medical illness were twice as likely to be unable to obtain care. African Americans and Hispanics were also more likely to be unable to obtain care than whites and others (Himmelstein and Woolhandler 1995).

OTHER BARRIERS TO HEALTH CARE ACCESS

There are many other barriers to access to care. One is the lack of providers in areas close to people who need care. This is a problem for those persons living in rural areas as well as for those in central- or inner-city areas (Clarke et al. 1995). Weisgrau (1995) reviewed the myriad problems rural Americans confront in obtaining health care and mental health services due to the shortages of health care providers and the continued closures of rural hospitals. The stigma of obtaining mental health services in rural areas was also considered to be a problem.

Studies by Wennberg and colleagues (1989) have documented the wide geographic variations in health outcomes. These outcomes are considered to be, in part, related to variations in provider practices. A recent study by the Department of

Veterans' Affairs found that even though the system predominantly serves low-income men, they found substantial geographic variation in service use for different diagnoses in hospitals and clinic use across the United States which they attribute to different practice styles (Ashton et al. 1999).

Another problem is cultural barriers to care. These include language differences between patients and providers and other communication problems. Escarce and colleagues (1993), Gornick and colleagues (1996), Friedman (1994), and Korenbrot and colleagues (1999) have identified these problems. Many studies have found persistent disparities across racial and ethnic groups in access to care (Escarce et al. 1993). Racial and ethnic minorities and rural residents were less likely to use physician services. This pattern was even stronger for rural Latinos and Asians (Mueller et al. 1998), particularly refugee populations. Mortality rates for black Americans are about 50 percent higher than for white Americans, and Native Americans also show very high death rates, especially among the young (Nickens 1995). In part, the high mortality rates are related to lower socioeconomic status (SES) measured by occupation, income, and education attainment, which are generally lower for minorities. Mortality rates were more strongly related to SES in 1986 than in 1960. The substantial black and white differentials in infant mortality have been well documented (NCHS, 1994). High infant mortality rates for minorities are a function not only of poverty and low SES, but also of racial segregation in housing markets that are in close proximity to industrial pollution generators (incinerators, factories, etc.). These sources of pollution produce poor air quality in many communities of color and have a direct effect on infant mortality rates and adult morbidity (Hurley 1995).

In addition to poverty, low SES, and poor environmental quality, infant mortality rates of minorities are also influenced by continuing discrimination in society. The discrimination accumulates over time and results in perceived powerlessness, frustration, and negative self-images that in turn contribute to higher mortality rates. Discrimination against minority group members by health care providers may be a contributing factor that has not been eliminated. Using simulated video interviews of patients and physicians, a recent study documented that the race and sex of patients have an independent influence on physician decisions regarding how to manage care for chest pain. Women, blacks, and younger patients were less likely to be referred for diagnostic tests (cardiac catheterization), and the interaction effects were also significant (Schulman et al. 1999).

SOCIOLOGICAL MODELS OF ACCESS TO SERVICE USE

Much of the study of health care utilization and access has been developed using the theoretical model adopted by Andersen, Aday, and colleagues at the University of Chicago (Aday and Andersen 1974, 1991; Andersen 1995; Andersen and Aday 1978).

Andersen's (1995) original model was designed to predict or explain the use of health services. Three major components were developed for the model. First, predisposing characteristics were considered to include those that were endogenous to use including (1) demographics, such as age, gender, and race; (2) social structure, such as education, occupation, and ethnicity; and (3) health beliefs, including attitudes, values, and knowledge about health. Various critics have suggested (and Andersen 1995 agreed) that social networks, social interactions, and culture are all concepts that can be incorporated into the social structural factors. Genetic makeup might also be added to the list of predisposing factors. Second, enabling factors were considered to be those community and personal resources that may enable an individual or family to use health services. These include the supply of health personnel and organizations or facilities to provide care. Enabling factors also include income, health insurance, regular source of care, travel and waiting times, and other such factors. Social relationships, or "social support," are also important enabling factors according to Andersen (1995).

Finally, the original model included the need for health care services. "Need" included both the perceived need and the need as evaluated by health professionals. In the original model, the outcomes included the amount of physician, hospital, and other health services used. This model is one of the most widely used approaches by scholars, with hundreds of articles presenting the results of testing these factors. In Andersen's original model, access was described as potential access and realized access (actual use) of services. Access could be found to be equitable or inequitable, depending on value judgments. Inequitable access occurred when predisposing factors (such as race, ethnicity, or gender) or enabling factors (e.g., health insurance) determine who receives services rather than services determined by need. In later models, the health care system was incorporated, including national health policy, resources, and organizations. Outcomes of health services were revised to include consumer satisfaction about convenience, availability, financing, providers, and quality (Aday and Andersen 1974). The model was expanded further to include ethical criteria to measure equity, such as freedom of choice, equal treatment, and decent basic minimum care. Subsequently, the model has included understandings of effective and efficient access to services and improved health status as outcomes (Andersen 1995). Finally, Andersen sees the model as interactive and dynamic, with utilization and outcomes influencing predisposing, enabling, and need factors.

As a test of the importance of the behavioral model, a study in the late 1990s examined its use in the social science literature between 1975 and 1995. The study found 139 empirical research articles that used the model; of these articles, 45 percent included environmental variables and 51 percent included provider-related variables (Phillips et al. 1998). Extensive work has been done to examine health status as measures of health service outcomes. These include mortality, morbidity, well-being, and functioning. Outcomes can also include equity of service access. More elaborate conceptual models have been developed by the Institute of Medicine (Gold 1998; Millman 1993).

ISSUES RAISED BY TRENDS IN HEALTH CARE UTILIZATION AND EXPENDITURES

The macro-level and micro-level patterns of health care utilization and expenditure suggest that consumers, workers, the poor, people of color, the elderly, nurses, and even physicians are losing ground with respect to access to care and decision making within the health care system. Each year—indeed, every month—thousands more individuals join the ranks of the uninsured and thousands more remain *under*insured (Kuttner 1999). At the same time, expenditures for the nation's health

care system are expected to rise steeply in the first decade of the twenty-first century. While most policy makers and health policy analysts regard the American health care system as characterized by "private insurance," less than 50 percent of health insurance is in fact paid for by private employers—and these payments are subsidized by the government at a total of $100 billion (Carrasquillo et al. 1999). Thus, the role of employers in paying for insurance has been overstated and employers have played a prominent role in health policy discussions. And while the number of employers offering their employees health insurance has either remained unchanged or even decreased in recent years, the cost of these plans has been prohibitive for many workers, who then go without coverage. The result is a nationwide decline in persons with employer-sponsored health coverage (NCH Statistics 1994).

These trends raise questions about the role of the U.S. health care system in providing care to the nation's population. What becomes clear is that while the system is heavily supported by public funds, the benefits are accruing more and more to private corporations. Thus, we suggest that in order to understand changing patterns in health care utilization and expenditure, a political economy perspective is useful. A political economy perspective recognizes the enduring underlying conflicts among different interest groups (workers, purchasers, providers, doctors, insurers, nurses, the elderly) in gaining access to the myriad benefits a health care system provides. For example, many scholars argue that while the U.S. medical system is officially designed to provide the best possible care to any person who needs it and can pay for services, health care is actually only a secondary or tertiary function of this system (Navarro 1976; Relman 1980; Waitzkin 1983). Profit, above all else, is the "driving force" behind the health care system (Woolhandler and Himmelstein 1995).

The benefits and costs of health care in the United States are hotly contested, and stakeholders are engaged in a continuous struggle to gain access to the former and to externalize the latter. Doctors and nurses have organized unions; consumers have demanded a "patient's bill of rights" and a long list of other legislative reforms, producing a "managed care backlash"; health care providers and insurers have consolidated in a flurry of mergers and acquisitions in the 1990s; pharmaceutical and other health care firms have sought out markets around the globe; and managers of health care systems have slashed wages and jobs in an effort to contain costs (Andrews 1995). The results have been: (1) less regulation of the health care industry; (2) increasing profits for industry; (3) declining consumer satisfaction and less access to care and insurance under managed care; (4) loss of control and autonomy by doctors and nurses; (5) rising health care expenditures; and (6) no discernible improvement in the quality of health care. Our health care system is transforming rapidly without a coherent national approach to either the structure of the delivery of care or to the problem of rising expenditures. It is incumbent upon sociologists studying the health care system of this nation and others to provide a counterbalance to the currently dominant economic cost-benefit analytical approach to this topic. A sociological perspective offers a balanced understanding of the social basis on which the health care system operates and can, therefore, lead the way toward improvements in both theory and policy making in the areas of health and health care.

REFERENCES

Aday, L. A., and R. M. Andersen 1974 "A Framework for the Study of Access to Medical Care." *Health Services Research* 9(2):208–220.

—— 1991 "Equity to Access to Medical Care." *Medical Care* 19(12):4–27.

Agency for Health Care Policy and Research (AHCPR) 1997 *Access to Health Care in America, 1996*. Medical Expenditure Panel Survey, May (3):1–3.

—— 1998 *Health Insurance Coverage In America – 1996*. Medical Expenditure Panel Survey, May (4):1–3.

Altman, D. 1998 "The Kaiser Family Foundation: Our Mission." Paper presented to the Robert Wood Johnson Foundation Scholars in Health Policy Research Program, University of California, Berkeley.

American Healthcare InfoSource, Inc. 1998 *Hospital Statistics*. Chicago: American Hospital Association.

Andersen, R. M. 1995 "Revisiting the Behavioral Model and Access to Medical Care: Does it Matter?" *Journal of Health and Social Behavior* 36:1–10.

——, and L. A. Aday 1978 "Access to Medical Care in the U.S.: Realized and Potential." *Medical Care* 16(7):533–546.

Andrews, C. 1995 *Profit Fever: The Drive to Corporatize Health Care and How to Stop it*. Monroe, Maine: Common Courage Press.

Ashton, C. M., N. J. Petersen, J. Souchek, et al. 1999 "Geographic Variations in Utilization Rates in Veterans Affairs Hospitals and Clinics." *New England Journal of Medicine*. 340(1):32–39.

Berk, M. L., C. L. Schur, and J. C. Cantor 1995 "Ability to Obtain Health Care: Recent Estimates from the Robert Wood Johnson Foundation National Access to Care Survey." *Health Affairs* 14(3):139–146.

Blendon, R. J., J. Benson, K. Donelan, R. Leitman, H. Taylor, C. Koeck, and D. Gitterman 1995 "Who Has the Best Health Care System? A Second Look." *Health Affairs* 14(4):220–230.

Braveman, P., G. Oliva, M. A. Miller, R. Reiter, and S. Egerter 1989 "Adverse Outcomes and Lack of Health Insurance Among Newborns in an Eight-County Area of California, 1982 to 1986." *New England Journal of Medicine* 321(8):508–513.

Carrasquillo, O., D. U. Himmelstein, S. Woolhandler, and D. H. Bor 1999 "A Reappraisal of Private Employers' Role in Providing Health Insurance." *New England Journal of Medicine* 340(2):109–114.

Chassin, M. R., R. W. Galvin, and the National Roundtable on Health Care Quality 1998 "The Urgent Need to Improve Health Care Quality." *Journal of the American Medical Association* 280(11):1000–1005.

Christensen, S. 1998 "Medicare+Choice Provisions in the Balanced Budget Act of 1997." *Health Affairs* 17(4):224–231.

Clarke, L. L., C. A. Bono, M. K. Miller, and S. C. Malone 1995 "Prenatal Care Use in Nonmetropolitan and Metropolitan America: Racial/Ethnic Differences." *Journal of Health Care for the Poor and Underserved* 6(4):410–433.

Clement, D. G., S. M. Retchin, R. S. Borwn, and M. H. Stegall 1994 "Access and Outcomes of Elderly Patients Enrolled in Managed Care." *Journal of the American Medical Association* 271(19):1487–1492.

Cohen, M. A., and A. K. N. Kumar 1997 "The Changing Face of Long-Term Care Insurance in 1994: Profiles and Innovations in a Dynamic Market." *Inquiry* 34:50–61.

Consumer Reports 1997 "Long Term-Care Insurance: Special Report." *Consumer Reports* (October):36–50.

Davis, K., K. S. Collins, C. Schoen, and C. Morris 1995 "Choice Matters: Enrollees' Views of Their Health Plans." *Health Affairs* :99–112.

Escarce, J. J., K. R. Epstein, D. C. Colby, and J. S. Schwartz 1993 "Racial Differences in the Elderly's

Use of Medical Procedures and Diagnostic Tests." *American Journal of Public Health* 83 (July):948–954.

Families USA 1997 *One Out of Three: Kids Without Health Insurance, 1995–1996.* Washington, D.C.: Families USA.

Friedman, E. 1994 "Money Isn't Everything: Nonfinancial Barriers to Access." *Journal of the American Medical Association.* 271(19):1535–1538.

Gallagher, L. 1999 "Health Care Services: The Big Money is in Small Towns." *Forbes* 163(1):182–183.

Geraedts, M., G. V. Heller, and C. Harrington 1999 "Germany's Long Term Care Insurance: Putting A Social Insurance Model into Practice." Manuscript submitted for publication.

Ginsburg, P. B., and J. R. Gabel 1998 "Tracking Health Care Costs: What's New in 1998." *Health Affairs* 17(5):141–146.

Gold, M. 1998 "Beyond Coverage and Supply: Measuring Access to Healthcare in Today's Market." *Health Services Research* 33(3):625–652.

Gornick, M. E., P. W. Eggers, T. W. Reilly, R. M. Mentnech, L. K. Fitterman, L. E. Kucken, and B. C. Vladeck 1996 "Effects of Race and Income on Mortality and Use of Services Among Medicare Beneficiaries." *The New England Journal of Medicine* 335(11):791–799.

Hafner-Eaton, C. 1994 "Patterns of Hospital and Physician Utilization Among the Uninsured." *Journal of Health Care for the Poor and Underserved* 5(4):297–315.

Harrington, C., C. Cassel, C. L. Estes, et al. 1991 "A National Long-Term Care Program for the United States." *Journal of the American Medical Association* 266(21):3023.

——, G. V. Heller, and M. Geraedts 1999 "Commentary on Germany's Long Term Care Insurance Model: Lessons for the United States." Manuscript submitted for publication.

Hellander, I., D. U. Himmelstein, S. Woolhandler, and S. Wolfe 1994 "Health Care Paper Chase, 1993: The Cost to the Nation, the States, and the District of Columbia." *International Journal of Health Services* 24(1):1–9.

Herrera, S. 1999 "Health Care Products." *Forbes* 163(1):180–181.

Himmelstein, D. U., and S. Woolhandler 1995 "Care Denied: US Residents Who Are Unable to Obtain Needed Medical Services." *American Journal of Public Health* 85(3)341–344.

—— 1986 "Cost Without Benefit: Administrative Waste in the U.S." *New England Journal of Medicine* 314:440–441.

Hurley, A. 1995 *Environmental Inequalities: Race, Class, and Industrial Decline in Gary, Indiana 1945–1980.* Chapel Hill: University of North Carolina Press.

Iglehart, J. K. 1995 "Medicaid and Managed Care." *The New England Journal of Medicine* 332(25):1727–1731.

Jensen, G. A., M. A. Morrisey, S. Gaffney, and D. Liston 1997 "The New Dominance of Managed Care: Insurance Trends in the 1990s." *Health Affairs* 16:125–136.

Kaiser Commission on the Future of Medicaid 1995 *Medicaid and Managed Care: Lessons from the Literature.* Menlo Park, Calif.: Henry J. Kaiser Family Foundation.

Kassirer, J. P. 1996 "Mergers and Acquisitions—Who Benefits? Who Loses?" *The New England Journal of Medicine* 334(11):722–723.

Kenkel, P. J. 1993 "Provider Based Managed-Care Plans Continue Growth Trend." *Modern Healthcare* (May 19):26–34.

Korenbrot, C., L. S. Park, R. Sarnoff, J. Greene, and C. Bender 1999 *Impact of Recent Welfare and Immigration Reforms on Low-Income Pregnant Women and Their Health Care Providers.* Unpublished report to the California Endowment. Institute for Health Policy Studies, University of California at San Francisco.

Kuttner, R. 1999 "The American Health Care System: Health Insurance Coverage." *The New England Journal of Medicine* 340(2):163–168.

Levit, K. R., C. Cowan, B. R. Braden, B.R., et al. 1998 "National Health Expenditures, 1997: More Slow Growth." *Health Affairs* 17(5):99–110.

——, H. C. Lazenby, B. R. Braden, et al. 1997 "National Health Expenditures, 1996." *Health Care Financing Review* 19(1):161–200.

Light, D. W. 1992 "The Practice and Ethics of Risk-Rated Health Insurance." *Journal of the American Medical Association* 267(18):2503–2508.

McCormack, L. A., P. D. Fox, T. Rice, and M. L. Graham 1996 "Medigap Reform Legislation of 1990: Have the Objectives Been Met?" *Health Care Financing Review* 18(1):157–174.

Mechanic, D., and D. A. Rochefort 1992 "A Policy of Inclusion for the Mentally Ill." *Health Affairs* 11(1):128–150.

——, and M. Schlesinger 1996 "The Impact of Managed Care on Patients' Trust in Medical Care and Their Physicians." *Journal of the American Medical Association* 275(21):1693–1697.

Miller, R. H. 1998 "Healthcare Organizational Change: Implications for Access to Care and Its Measurement." *Health Services Research* 33(3):653–680.

——, and H. S. Luft 1994 "Managed Care Plan Performance Since l980: A Literature Analysis." *Journal of the American Medical Association* 271(19):1512–1519.

——, and H. S. Luft 1997 "Does Managed Care Lead to Better or Worse Quality of Care?" *New England Journal of Medicine* 16(5):1–18.

Millman, M. (ed.) 1993 *Access to Health Care in America. Institute of Medicine Committee on Monitoring Access to Personal Health Services*. Washington, D.C.: National Academy Press.

Mueller, K. J., K. Patil, and E. Boilesen 1998 "The Role of Uninsurance and Race in Healthcare Utilization by Rural Minorities." *Health Services Research* 33(3):597–610.

National Center for Health Statistics (NCHS) 1994 *Health, United States, 1993*. Hyattsville, Md.: U.S. Public Health Service.

Navarro, V. 1995 "Why Congress Did Not Enact Health Care Reform." *Journal of Health Politics, Policy and Law* 20:455–461.

—— 1976 *Medicine Under Capitalism*. New York: Prodist.

Nelson, L., R. Brown, M. Gold, A. B. Ciemnecki, and E. Docteur 1997 "Access to Care in Medicare HMOs, 1996." *Health Affairs* 16(2):148–156.

Nickens, H. W. 1995 "The Role of Race/Ethnicity and Social Class in Minority Health Status." *Health Services Research*. 30(31):151–162.

Pauly, M. V. 1998 "Managed Care, Market Power, and Monopsony." *Health Services Research* 33(5):1439–1460.

Pear, R. 1998 "HMOs are Retreating from Medicare, Citing High Costs." *New York Times* (October 2):A20.

Phillips, K. A., K. R. Morrison, R. Andersen, and L. A. Aday 1998 "Understanding the Context of Healthcare Utilization: Assessing Environmental and Provider-Related Variables in the Behavioral Model of Utilization." *Health Services Research* 33(3):571–596.

Reinhardt, U. E. 1997 "Wanted: A Clearly Articulated Social Ethic for American Health Care." *Journal of the American Medical Association* 278:1446–1447.

Relman, A. S. 1980 "The New Medical-Industrial Complex." *New England Journal of Medicine* 303:963–970.

Schulman, K. A., J. A. Berlin, W. Harless, J. F. Kerner, et al. 1999 "The Effect of Race and Sex on Physicians' Recommendations for Cardiac Catheterization." *The New England Journal of Medicine* 340(8):618–626.

Shaughnessy, P. W., R. E. Schlenker, and D. F. Hittle 1994 "Home Health Care Outcomes Under Capitated and Fee-For-Service Payment." *Health Care Financing Review* 16(1):187–221.

Singh, G. K., and S. M. Yu 1996 "US Childhood Mortality, 1950 Through 1993: Trends and Socioeconomic Differentials." *American Journal of Public Health* 86(4):505–512.

Smith, S., M. Freeland, S. Heffler, D. McKusick, and the Health Expenditures Projection Team 1998 "The Next Ten Years of Health Spending: What Does the Future Hold?" *Health Affairs* 17(5):128–140.

Srinivasan, S., L. Levitt, and J. Lundy 1998 "Wall Street's Love Affair with Health Care." *Health Affairs* 17(4):158–164.

U.S Bureau of the Census 1998a *Census Brief: Children Without Health Insurance*. Washington, D.C.: U.S. Government Printing Office.

—— 1998b *Health Insurance Coverage, 1997*. Washington, D.C.: U.S. Government Printing Office.

U.S. General Accounting Office 1996 *Health Insurance for Children: Private Insurance Coverage Continues to Deteriorate*. GAO/HEHS 96-129. Washington, D.C.: U.S. General Accounting.

Waid, M. O., U.S. Health Care Financing Administration (USHCFA) 1998 Overview of the Medicare and Medicaid Programs. *Health Care Financing Review* 1998 Statistical Supplement.

Waitzkin, H. 1983 *The Second Sickness: Contradictions of Capitalist Health Care*. New York: Free Press.

Weisgrau, S. 1995 "Issues in Rural Health: Access, Hospitals, and Reform." *Health Care Financing Review* 17(1):1–14.

Weissman, J. S., R. Stern, S. L. Fielding, and A. M. Epstein 1991 "Delayed Access to Health Care: Risk Factors, Reasons, and Consequences." *Annals of Internal Medicine* 114(4):325–331.

Welch, W. P. 1996 "Growth in HMO Share of the Medicare Market, 1989–1995." *Health Affairs* 15(3):201–214.

Wennberg, J. E., J. L. Freeman, R. M. Shelton, and T. A. Bubolz 1989 "Hospital Use and Mortality Among Medicare Beneficiaries in Boston and New Haven." *New England Journal of Medicine* 321:1168–1173.

Wiener, J. M. 1996 "Can Medicaid Long-Term Care Expenditures for the Elderly Be Reduced?" *The Gerontologist* 36(6):800–811.

——, and L. H. Illston 1994 "How to Share the Burden: Long-Term Care Reform in the l990s." *The Brookings Review* 12(2):17–21.

——, and R. J. Hanley 1994 *Sharing the Burden: Strategies for Public and Private Long-Term Care Insurance*. Washington, D.C.: Brookings Institution.

Woolhandler, S., and D. U. Himmelstein 1995 "Extreme Risk—The New Corporate Proposition for

Physicians." *New England Journal of Medicine* 333(25):1706–1708.

CHARLENE HARRINGTON
DAVID N. PELLOW

HEALTH POLICY ANALYSIS

Health policy analysis is of increasing interest to sociologists in the areas of medical sociology and health services research. Health policy analysis draws on perspectives from across the social science disciplines: from anthropology and economics to political science and sociology, as well as law, medical ethics, and the applied fields of public health, public administration, and public policy. Leading sources of policy analysis are scholars in twenty to thirty university-based health policy and health services research centers and institutes and the myriad and growing number of private sector "think tanks" such as the Brookings Institution, the Urban Institute, RAND, the National Bureau of Economic Research, Project Hope, and the American Enterprise Institute. An early indicator of advances in the field of policy studies was the publication of the *Policy Studies Review Annual*, which commenced in 1977 (Nagel 1977) and continues to cover the field with an editorial advisory board made up of distinguished social scientists.

Major federal agencies that both sponsor and conduct health policy analysis include the National Center for Health Statistics (NCHS); the Health Care Financing Administration (HCFA); the Agency for Health Care Policy and Research (AHCPR); the Alcohol, Drug Abuse, and Mental Health Administration (ADMHA); the Social Security Administration; the National Institute on Aging (NIA); and the Office of the Assistant Secretary for Planning and Evaluation. Federal research funding is the mother's milk of health policy analysis; although limited, it has assured the slow but gradual accumulation of health services research knowledge.

Several journals are sources for the latest developments in health policy analysis: *Health Affairs, Health Care Financing Review, Health Services Research, Journal of Health and Social Behavior, Journal of the American Medical Association, Milbank Quarterly, International Journal of Health Services, New England Journal of Medicine,* and *Journal of Health Politics, Policy and Law.* A recent, comprehensive text, *Understanding Health Policy* (Bodenheimer and Grumbach 1998), though written by physicians and with a clinical orientation, is nonetheless critical of chronic systemic tensions and inequalities in U.S. health care delivery. The authors integrate social science literature throughout, one indication of a growing consensus regarding salient problems among scholars, practitioners, and "patients" alike, in a nation shaken by unprecedented corporate intrusions into health and medical encounters.

There are multiple paradigms in and approaches to health policy analysis in schools of public policy, public health, public administration, and social work. The same diversity is present in sociology and other social science disciplines. However, we detect and discuss important areas of convergence between current controversies in U.S. health policy and perspectives and methods that are well established in sociology. We believe these areas of convergence are likely to enhance the stature and usefulness of the discipline in the analysis of health policy, in public as well as in academic life.

The various disciplines, substantive specializations, and methodologies represented in such work have contributed an array of perspectives to the definition of health policy analysis, how it is conducted, and how professional training is oriented and organized. As the number of programs offering health and related policy training has increased, the academic respectability of such work has grown apace. In sociology, vestiges of an invidious distinction between "basic" and "applied" research are still with us, and policy research is both less visible and less valued than is warranted, given its potential public impact. Nonetheless, an expanded topical definition of health policy analysis, following from the recent political and cultural tumult over changes in health care, is conducive to research in several vibrant research genres in sociology, including political economy (see, e.g., *International Journal of Health Services*), constructionist approaches to medical encounters and social problems (Brown 1995; Spector and Kitsuse 1987), phenomenology of illness and medical practice (Benner 1994), community-based studies (Israel et al. 1998), and comparative sociocultural studies of health systems (Mechanic 1996; Kleinman 1980). The latter, bordering medical anthropology, encompasses conventional treatment regimen, as well as "self-help" and various nonbiomedical, "alternative" health practices, be they traditional or sacred (Baer 1995). Such topical breadth is also evident in "mainstream," medically oriented outlets. In recent years, the *Journal of the American Medical Association (JAMA)* has devoted sustained attention to public health issues such as gun violence (Sinauer et al. 1996), domestic violence, motor vehicle accidents, and terrorism.

For sociologists, the primary point of entry into health policy analysis has been medical sociology, which has long been sustained by its applied relevance to and sponsorship by agencies in government and medicine (Cockerham 1988). Other contributing subfields include aging/social gerontology, political sociology, gender studies, and social stratification. Despite productive cross-pollination between these related fields of scholarship, the number of sociologists working in health policy analysis is small relative to those involved overall in studies of health care and of social policy, broadly conceived. Though medical sociologists continue to comprise one of the largest sections of the American Sociological Association (ASA)—with more than 1,000 members—their presence in the smaller Association for Health Services Research (AHSR), a major professional association, is modest: only 5 percent of its 1,400 members report primary disciplinary training in sociology, compared to 20 percent from medicine and 14 percent from economics (other members were trained in other social sciences, the allied health fields, and business). Health policy analysis is not, however, confined to conventional research roles and careers; many working in health policy analysis hold master's degrees, are employed on the staffs of governmental and private agencies, and are not oriented toward academic theory or publication (Luft 1999).

Sociologists' limited involvement in health policy analysis reflects the sources of, and agendas driving, health services research funding. Many problems in the planning and administration of large, complex programs favor orientations and methodological skills others can best provide, primarily those in economics and business. It reflects as well an unfortunate trend in which "the division of intellectual labor in our discipline tends to replicate program divisions. Experts on aging study

Social Security; experts on health care study Medicare; experts on poverty study Aid to Families with Dependent Children" (Quadagno 1999, p. 8). More generally, the American health care system is itself increasingly governed by business principles of cost control and administrative efficiency, under corporate managed care. The dramatic growth of for-profit health maintenance organizations (HMOs), "now accounting for 75 percent of all HMOs and enrolling over 50 percent of all subscribers" (Fein 1998, p. 10), has intensified public debate over quality, access, and humanity in health care.

The products of health policy analysis range from journalistic and descriptive accounts to sophisticated quantitative analyses and projections. But over the last decade or more, health policy analysis has reflected a societal struggle to come to terms with a secular change in the organization and financing of medical care, away from solo, fee-for-service practice toward corporate managed care. Given the current emphasis on cost savings and efficiencies, and on mechanisms for achieving them such as capitation, risk adjustment, and "utilization management" or "practice guides" for physicians' clinical discretion, economic models and analyses have been paramount in health policy analyses funded by government agencies and large corporate entities. The justification advanced for these competitive efforts has typically been a need to check inflationary costs and "excessive" demands for medical services by consumers, ostensibly free to operate in a "market" for such services.

Consequently, traditional foci of sociological interest—including professional status and autonomy, access to and stratification of health care services, and continuity Federal safety-net policies rooted in the postwar *social contract* (Quadagno 1999; Rubin 1996)—have been pushed to the margins of public and policy debates. However, sociological perspectives are both rejuvenated and needed at this time. One important line of critique has been to challenge attributions of market choice and consumer autonomy in the face of corporate managed care (Freidson 1994; Freund and McGuire 1999). Another is to reject the very notion of "system" in relation to health care and medical coverage in the United States and instead to document, as does Diamond (1995), the collective vulnerability and implications arising from the arbitrary and confusing patchwork quilt that is American health policy—a paradox of "excess and deprivation" (Bodenheimer and Grumbach 1998). Yet another is to demonstrate how health care professions may act to mediate between users of health services and their often remote provider organizations. In an important analysis of how doctors are implicated in this process, Freidson (1994) argues for a rebirth of *professionalism*, based on client service and trust, as bases for health care reform. Although one may question the likelihood of this scenario, given the mistrust of doctors at the heart of the consumer backlash of recent decades, the answers are sure to be significant both for social theory and policy. These are but a few examples of the distinctive contributions sociologists are making to health policy analysis, broadly defined.

Consistent with this public spotlight, sociological research on health policy and other segments of the welfare state is gaining momentum. The 1998 president of the American Sociological Association devoted her address to a historical analysis of changes in welfare policy provision, including social security and medicare, as central to understanding the erosion of the postwar social contract in the United States (Quadagno 1999). Furthermore, the demographic aging of America, along with a dramatic increase since mid-century in women's labor-force participation (with resultant strains in traditional sources of familial care), are propelling the neglected problems of chronic illness, community-based care, and allocation of resources—that is, between capital-intensive hospital treatments and more equitable provision of basic health care—to the forefront of the national and research agendas.

In recent years, then, the inventory and scope of topics subsumed under the heading *health policy analysis* have expanded in ways that energize and demand the attention of sociologists. The legislative failure of the Clinton administration's national health plan demonstrated the necessity for a coherent set of principles—moral and political, as well as technocratic—in order to implement large-scale policy reform; resistance to "environmental racism" by those unduly exposed to hazardous jobs and industrial toxins has assumed global dimensions; and such widely publicized conflicts as those over public versus corporate liability for the expense of tobacco-related illness (Glantz et al.

1996) and firearms and other forms of violence (Prothrow-Stith 1998; Sinauer et al. 1996)—all these have underscored the political, economic, and cultural forces that shape the health problems, as well as the spectrum of policy options, that analysts address. Indeed, health policy analysts have periodically been buffeted directly by political currents. During the Reagan administration, conservative forces in Congress sought to curtail sharply the collection of health-related data at the federal level; and spokespersons for the failed Clinton plan were attacked as proponents of a federal "takeover" of health care. This attack reflected and accelerated the devolution of federal discretion and responsibility for health care and other policies to state and local governments. Thus, health policy analysis, like health policy itself, has become increasingly politicized.

Research in health policy analysis necessarily concerns itself most directly with timeliness, pragmatism, and specificity in an effort to improve health and health care delivery. Research and analysis are conceived to inform social policy by (1) illuminating features of social organization and social action that are relevant to health policy planning, (2) identifying the social and health problems that require formulation in attempts to develop health policy, and (3) organizing and interpreting data that monitor the effects and outcomes of health policy decisions and the relative impact of programmatic alternatives.

In response to this mission, health services research contributes two major types of knowledge: *engineering* and *enlightenment* knowledge (Weiss 1978). In turn, these models imply distinctly different roles for analysts in the policy process (Marris 1990). In the *engineering* model, researchers seek to provide instrumental knowledge for practical assessment of alternatives and problem solving, accepting the values and goals inherent in existing policies largely as givens. Many influential health policy analyses first appear as fugitive documents directed to internal governmental audiences, addressing particularistic needs and interests of government agencies and actors, and are based on reports designed with an evaluative purpose. Policy analysis of this kind is, again, primarily funded and supported by government, with a lesser role played by such private foundations as the Robert Wood Johnson Foundation.

In the *enlightenment* model, researchers critically—even irreverently—scrutinize the implicit empirical, moral, and political assumptions embedded either in discrete policies or in broader debates (e.g., about the "right to die" or national health insurance). Rather than dealing with how policies work in a technical or engineering sense, enlightenment research contributes to the root understanding of how, by whom, and with what unintended consequences problems in health policy are socially constructed. Often, enlightenment research promotes shifts in what Thomas Kuhn (1970) calls "paradigms," that is, fundamental ways of looking at problems. The enlightenment model is rooted as well in a critical, Weberian tradition in which the *formal rationality* of internal program functioning is juxtaposed with the *substantive rationality* of such programs, as they affect individual freedom and social equity.

As Marris (1990) shows, the engineering model is most effective and appropriate when policies have clear goals, enjoy broad consensual support, and can be linked directly to social outcomes. At the macro level especially, such conditions have rarely obtained regarding health policy in the United States. Moreover, experienced observers have concluded that however well conceived and conducted, research has had a limited direct role on the adoption and implementation of health policy (e.g., Lee 1998; Mechanic 1974). Important, though less often discussed, is that analysts in the engineering model are dependent on access to reliable, comprehensive, and timely data sets. Such a research infrastructure is difficult to develop and maintain, even where data collection is mandated at state or federal levels of government (Mechanic 1974). Given the present trend of privatization in the management and delivery of health services, sources, collection, and linkage of data are correspondingly more varied and less subject to public oversight. For example, while public health departments have a responsibility to serve the population at large, HMOs, however carefully they document utilization of services among their thousands of subscribers, have no such obligation to the public. This poses serious questions regarding the coordination of public and private health entities (Goldberg 1998).

Among other fertile research questions being posed in the expanding, multidisciplinary field of health policy analysis are the following: How is the global resurgence in infectious disease—termed the *third epidemiologic transition* (Barret et al. 1998)—linked to our more global economy and consumer culture, and what strains is it likely to impose on outdated public health networks? To what extent is globalization leading to convergence in the organization of health care systems internationally (Mechanic 1996)? How are the successes of the American health care system in increasing human longevity creating new conceptions of and practices in medical ethics? Inasmuch as chronic illnesses are often peripheral to direct treatment by doctors, what roles are nurses and other medical practitioners playing in the revision of medical ethics and practice (Thomasma 1994)? What is the place and role of communities in our increasingly corporate health care system? And how might we rethink research practices to better conceptualize and tap community-level perspectives and dynamics (Israel et al. 1998)? Many contemporary problems in health care—from mechanisms by which AIDS and other diseases are transmitted, to discrimination against minority groups seeking care—would seem to rest on understanding community-level dynamics.

Sociology has a long tradition of reformism and interest in finding solutions to applied problems. Robert Lynd's *Knowledge for What?* (1986) called sociologists to the task, and a long line of American sociologists have worked within the applied tradition. Particular examples are from the Chicago School (Bulmer 1984; Deegan 1988; Deegan and Burger 1981; Park 1952) and Columbia University, where Lazarsfeld and his colleagues advanced the field of applied research after World War II. These efforts were followed by work on the uses of sociology (Lazarsfeld et al. 1967) and a burgeoning of critical scholarship in the wake of the "counterculture" of the 1960s. These forerunners laid the foundation for what has become an increasingly exciting enterprise: the study of health policy. Freeman's (1978) observation on the nature of health policy analysis as a scientific enterprise remains applicable: that policy studies are rather specialized and "content limited," demonstrating few attempts to develop overriding conclusions about the policy process; hence, "there is practically no effort at 'grand theory' and little at 'middle-range theory' either" (Freeman 1978, p.

11). Nevertheless, narrow, highly specialized studies are not policy studies if they have no use beyond the most limited and specialized areas of concern. "Policy studies . . . need to be broad in implications, insightful to those beyond the narrow band of experts in a particular field, and intermeshed with work in related areas" (Freeman 1978, p. 12). The stimulation of and funding for policy analyses has been driven largely by the immediacy of existing (rather than emerging) problems that catch the attention of policy makers. Therefore, there is tension between the need to conduct carefully controlled definitive studies and the need to enlarge the focus of such research to contribute broader application and significance.

The growth of health policy analysis was shaped by the social problem definitions of health care from the 1960s to the 1980s (Rist 1985), and these, in turn, have been shaped by the political and economic exigencies of these periods. Health care was defined in the 1960s by the crisis of access, in the 1970s by the crisis of fragmentation and lack of comprehensive planning, and in the 1980s by the crisis of cost and the resurgence of market forces in health care. The widening reverberations of these forces throughout the 1990s presents sociology with an urgent and relevant research agenda. The cost of medical care continues to rise at two or three times the rate of inflation; the costs to business, government, and individuals skyrocket; more and more Americans are uninsured each year; the annual expenditure on the medical-industrial complex climbs above $600 billion; and the population is aging. In the wake of these dramatic developments, the health care system and the policies creating it have been increasingly exposed to criticism and investigation. The key health policy issues for the new century are the cost, quality, and outcomes of care; the organization, financing, and delivery of acute and long-term care services; and expanding access to care.

(SEE ALSO: *Health-Care Utilization and Expenditures*; *Health Promotion and Health Status*; *Medical-Industrial Complex*; *Medical Sociology*)

REFERENCES

Baer, Hans A. 1995 "Medical Pluralism in the United States: A Review." *Medical Anthropology Quarterly* 9(4):493–502.

Barrett, Ronald, et al. 1998 "Emerging and Re-Emerging Infectious Diseases: The Third Epidemiologic Transition." *Annual Review of Anthropology* 27:247–271.

Benner, Patricia, ed. 1994 *Interpretive Phenomenology: Embodiment, Caring, and Ethics in Health and Illness.* Thousand Oaks, Calif.: Sage.

Bodenheimer, Thomas, and Kevin Grumbach 1998 *Understanding Health Policy: A Clinical Approach*, 2nd ed. Stamford, Conn.: Appleton and Lange.

Brown, Phil 1995 "Naming and Framing: The Social Construction of Diagnosis and Illness." *Journal of Health and Social Behavior* 33:267–281.

Bulmer, Martin 1984 *The Chicago School of Sociology: Institutionalization, Diversity and the Rise of Sociological Research.* Chicago: University of Chicago Press.

Cockerham, William C. 1988 "Medical Sociology." In Neil J. Smelser, ed., *Handbook of Sociology.* Newbury Park, Calif.: Sage.

Deegan, Mary Jo 1988 *Jane Addams and the Men of the Chicago School, 1892–1918.* New Brunswick, N.J.: Transaction Books.

——, and John S. Burger 1981 "W. I. Thomas and Social Reform: His Work and Writings." *Journal of the History of Behavioral Sciences* 17:114–125.

Diamond, Timothy 1995 "Breaking the Dichotomy Between Theory and Research: The Method of Institutional Ethnography." Paper presented at the annual meeting of the American Sociological Association, Washington, D.C.

Fein, Rashi 1998 "The HMO Revolution" (Part 1). *Dissent*, 45 (2):29–36.

Freeman, Howard E., ed. 1978 *Policy Studies Review Annual*, vol. 2. Beverly Hills, Calif.: Sage.

Freidson, Eliot 1994 *Professionalism Reborn.* Chicago: University of Chicago Press.

Freund, Peter E. S., and Meredith B. McGuire 1999 *Health, Illness, and the Social Body: A Critical Sociology*, 3rd ed. Upper Saddle River, N.J.: Prentice-Hall.

Glantz, Stanton A., et al. 1996 *The Cigarette Papers.* Berkeley: University of California Press.

Goldberg, Bruce W. 1998 "Managed Care and Public Health Departments: Who Is Responsible for the Health of the Population?" *Annual Review of Public Health* 19:527–537.

Israel, Barbara A., et al. 1998 "Review of Community-Based Research: Assessing Partnership Approaches to Improve Public Health." *Annual Review of Public Health* 19:173–202.

Kleinman, Arthur 1980 *Patients and Healers in the Context of Culture*. Berkeley: University of California Press.

Kuhn, Thomas 1970 *Structure of Scientific Revolutions*, 2nd ed. Chicago: University of Chicago Press.

Lazarsfeld, Paul F., William H. Sewell, and Howard L. Wilensky 1967 *The Uses of Sociology*. New York: Basic Books.

Lee, Philip R. 1998 "Health Policy: A Fifty-Year Perspective." Unpublished manuscript, Institute for Health Policy Studies, University of California San Francisco.

Luft, Harold S. 1999 (Director, Institute for Health Policy Studies, University of California San Francisco) Personal communication.

Lynd, Robert S. 1986 *Knowledge for What The Place of Social Science in American Culture*. Middletown, Conn.: Wesleyan University Press.

Marris, Peter 1990 "Witnesses, Engineers, or Storytellers? Roles for Sociologists in Social Policy." In Herbert J. Gans, ed., *Sociology in America*. Newbury Park, Calif.: Sage.

Mechanic, David 1974 *Politics, Medicine, and Social Science*. New York: John Wiley & Sons.

—— 1996 "Comparative Medical Systems." *Annual Review of Sociology* 22:239–270.

Nagel, Stuart S., ed. 1977 *Policy Studies Review Annual*, vol. 1. Beverly Hills, Calif.: Sage.

Park, Robert Ezra 1952 *Human Communities*. Glencoe, Ill.: Free Press.

Prothrow-Stith, Deborah 1998 *Peace by Piece: A Violence Prevention Guide for Communities*. Boston: Harvard School of Public Health.

Quadagno, Jill 1999 "Creating a Capital Investment Welfare State." *American Sociological Review* 64(1):1–11.

Rist, Ray C. 1985 "Introduction." In Ray C. Rist, ed., *Policy Studies Review Annual*, vol. 7. New Brunswick, N.J.: Transaction Books.

Rubin, Beth A. 1996 *Shifts in the Social Contract*. Thousand Oaks, Calif.: Pine Forge.

Sinauer, N., J. L. Annest, and J. A. Mercy 1996 "Unintentional, Nonfatal Firearm-Related Injuries: A Preventable Public Health Burden." *Journal of the American Medical Association* 275(22)1740–1743.

Spector, Malcolm, and John I. Kitsuse 1987 *Constructing Social Problems*. New York: Aldine de Gruyter.

Thomasma, David C. 1994 "Toward a New Medical Ethics: Implications for Ethics in Nursing." In Patricia Benner, ed., *Interpretive Phenomenology*. Thousand Oaks, Calif.: Sage.

Weiss, Carol H. 1978 "Research for Policy's Sake: The Enlightenment Function of Social Research." In Howard Freeman, ed., *Policy Studies Review Annual*, vol. 2. Beverly Hills, Calif.: Sage.

CARROLL L. ESTES
CHRISTOPHER WELLIN

HEALTH PROMOTION AND HEALTH STATUS

Health promotion, a general term, refers to a wide range of health-enhancing activities that seek to maintain health and functional ability, increase longevity, and reduce the prevalence and consequences of disease. These diverse activities include distributing free needles to substance abusers, identifying and modifying genes such as those linked to the development of Alzheimer's disease, proposing laws that seek to deter cigarette smoking, and offering blood pressure and cholesterol screening. They also include personal health practices whereby individuals engage in healthy lifestyles, consume vitamins, and the like. Therefore, these wide-ranging activities are conducted by persons trained in the field of public health, traditional health care workers, practitioners of complementary medicine, basic science researchers, politicians, health policy experts, and the individuals who practice health-enhancing behavior, to name but a few.

Long ignored in favor of medical, surgical, and pharmaceutical treatments that seek to cure or arrest health problems, health promotion information is now a prominent feature of popular magazines and nightly newscasts. Indicative of its rising importance, the United States Public Health Service has expanded the official title of the Centers for Disease Control to the Centers for Disease Control and Prevention.

The significance of health promotion activity is well known to the medical community. It offers the best, if not cheapest, method of reducing the burden of life-threatening conditions and maintaining a healthy, well-functioning, long-lived population (Pope and Tarlov 1991). As has been stated, "many of the most serious disorders. . . can be prevented or postponed by immunizations, chemoprophylaxis, and health life-styles. To an unprecedented extent, clinicians now have the opportunities, skills, and resources to prevent disease and promote health, as well as cure disease" (Office of Disease Prevention and Health Promotion 1994). Thus, health promotion is the ounce of prevention to avoid the pound of disease/disability/decline.

THE RANGE OF HEALTH PROMOTION ACTIVITIES

Activities that constitute health promotion are conducted on macro and micro levels. They address many spheres of society including: (1) the physical environment, (2) political/economic institutions, (3) health and medical care systems, (4) the social environment, (5) the fields of human biology, molecular medicine, and genetics, and (6) human behavior.

Macro-level efforts range from the international arena (e.g., drafting treaties about water safety), to the national level (e.g., policies about smoking and air pollution standards), and further to the local level (e.g., offering services of the city or county public health agency). They also include the private sector. Some of these activities address the training of medical personnel, the financing and delivery of medical care at private and public sites, the provision of health screening services, the development of active surveillance systems about disease threats, the provision of immunization programs, the offering of health education programs, and the scientific discovery of pathways to disease.

Micro-level health promotion involves individuals and small units. A single person's actions to maintain a healthy body, forestall the development of disease, achieve a longer life, or reduce emotional stress are micro-level health-promoting activities. Also included in this category are behaviors of the patient–health provider dyad. Such behavior often pertains to establishing a set of health-promoting practices and complying with this plan.

In a narrower approach to health promotion, disease control is the focus. This has resulted in distinguishing health promotion activities according to their potential for primary, secondary, and tertiary prevention of disease. The terms are used in relationship to the stage of a disease or condition; thus primary prevention includes the pre-disease phase and applies to the period prior to onset or diagnosis of a disease. In contrast, secondary and tertiary prevention occur after a disease has manifested itself. Efforts to detect the disease and keep it controlled, contained, and manageable are included (secondary prevention) as well as medical treatment activity addressed to preventing disability, improving life quality, and delaying death during the course of well-established disease.

Primary prevention can begin at any time during the life course. Directed toward individuals without disease manifestations, it seeks to help them maintain well-functioning, disease-free bodies. One of the oldest primary prevention practices is handwashing to prevent spread of communicable disease. One of the newest is testing women for the BRCA1 gene for breast cancer. If it is detected in an individual, she may be prescribed a drug that has been observed to have cancer-prevention potential. This type of primary prevention activity reflects cutting-edge medical technology from the fields of molecular medicine and genetic therapy. It is growing exponentially as a health promotion strategy. Indeed, $25 million of macro-level prevention efforts were recently announced to prevent or curb the spread of infectious diseases by using state-of-the-art technology (*New York Times*, December 27, 1998).

Avoiding exposure to agents that cause disease, injury, or defects is clearly the focus of much of the primary prevention activity. Public health agencies achieve this by offering immunization programs to children and adults alike. Health policy and health law personnel propose laws to prohibit cigarette advertisements. Physicians offer general and condition-specific health education, such as teaching patients about the value of weight control. Laboratory personnel seek to develop new vaccines or analyze the genetic characteristics of bacteria linked to certain infectious diseases.

Personal behavior is often the target of primary prevention efforts. Individuals with a family history of heart disease may be advised about dietary change from fatty foods or the need to engage in exercise, stress reduction, smoking cessation, and/or weight reduction programs. Given recent data, these activities appear to be quite important in preventing the development of a heart attack (myocardial infarction) and blockage of the coronary arteries. Even reducing one of the modifiable risk factors for heart disease (smoking, high blood pressure, obesity, physical deconditioning, high lipid count, impaired glucose tolerance) significantly reduces the risk of developing this disease (Herd et al. 1987; Kannel et al. 1987). Since more than half of the men and women over age 65 currently die of heart disease, such activity could have profound effects. Indeed, the development of a major heart condition may take fifty years, beginning in childhood with unhealthy food and exercise habits (Fries and Crapo 1986). Therefore, the individual is responsible for this type of primary prevention, which can actually begin with parental efforts to offer low-fat diets to their children. The idea is that the person would then carry on healthy living behavior throughout the life cycle.

The importance of personal behavior in health promotion and disease prevention was established in a recent effort to reconceptualize the causative factors for death (mortality). Previously, mortality data listed specific diseases as primary or secondary causes of death. The new approach designates specific health-risk behaviors (e.g., smoking and exercise behavior, food habits, alcohol use) as actual causes of death (McGinnis and Foege 1993). These behaviors accounted for half of all U.S. deaths in 1990. The three leading risk behaviors were tobacco use (400,000 deaths) and diet and activity patterns (300,000 deaths). By now considering this health-risk behavior to be the cause of death, the prevailing disease-centered approach is diminishing in importance. Reducing the prevalence of these behaviors is becoming a goal of interventive efforts and can facilitate the shift to primary prevention efforts.

Secondary prevention is undertaken after a disease has been detected. This may occur a half century after the causal agent or offending behavior initiated the disease process (Fries and Crapo 1986). For example, a heart attack at age 70 may have as its etiology poor dietary habits beginning at age 15, smoking behavior that started at 20, and at ages 30, 40, and 45, respectively, physical deconditioning, job stress, and the development of hypertension.

In contrast to primary prevention, secondary prevention involves control of a disease or condition. Aims are to ensure early detection, follow this with prompt and effective treatment, and educate the individual about risk-reduction behavior. Such efforts seek to halt, slow, or possibly reverse the progression of a condition and to prevent secondary effects or complications. Therefore, the heart patient would not only receive medication that might improve functional capacity of the heart but also receive referral to a smoking-cessation program.

Secondary prevention efforts are addressed to all acute and chronic conditions, but five chronic diseases account for most of the deaths, hospital care, and disability of the U.S. population. In order of prevalence they are arthritis, high blood pressure (hypertension), heart disease, chronic bronchitis, and diabetes. These chronic diseases are readily amenable to preventive action (Pope and Tarlov 1991). Physicians can treat these conditions medically, pharmaceutically, and surgically to prevent complications or arrest disease progression. The individuals suffering from these conditions can engage in a series of health behaviors and modify their lifestyles. For example, persons with diabetes can be asked to visit their doctor regularly, have frequent tests of blood and urine to detect disease progression, and visit specialists for control of diabetes complications involving eyes, kidneys, nervous system, skin, and so forth. Simultaneously, they can be taught to monitor and control their conditions, engage in dietary change, and actively pursue weight-control and exercise programs.

One of the most important tools for secondary prevention is health screening. This procedure seeks to detect disease, abnormal body states, and sensory loss. It comprises activities as diverse as mammography; Pap smears; and blood pressure, glaucoma, blood sugar, prostate specific antigen (PSA), and hearing tests. These secondary prevention services may be offered in physician's offices, at community sites (such as health fairs or churches on Sunday), or at work sites.

Secondary prevention procedures are immensely valuable, especially if they allow a disease to be detected in its early stages. Through early detection, medical and personal care can begin before the disease has progressed. Complications may be avoided, dangerous clinical thresholds may be averted, and the downward trajectory to disability and death may be prevented. For example, mammography that detects a small breast tumor may be responsible for saving a woman's life, preventing disfigurement from mastectomy (seldom performed in the early stages of cancer), averting the need for chemotherapy and its severe side effects, and enabling the patient to have hope for complete remission. In contrast, if a tumor is detected by clinical breast examination by a physician or breast self-examination, it will be larger than one identified through mammography. A tiny tumor or precancerous breast tissue change will not be apparent, through clinical breast examination and the cancer detected may be larger or have metastasized.

Physicians and nurses are the predominant practitioners of secondary prevention. Physician assistants, pharmacists, nutritionists, health educators, and physical therapists are among others who form the secondary prevention medical team. Unfortunately, there is much less use of this health promotion strategy than is optimal, or even desirable. Studies have shown that fewer than half of all physicians indicated they schedule proctoscopic examinations and chest x-rays for asymptomatic patients with no personal history of cancer (American Cancer Society 1990). This study also showed that specialists in internal medicine offer their patients the most cancer screening relative to other medical specialties (Pap tests; mammograms; stool blood determinations; chest x-rays; and breast, digital rectal, and proctoscopic examination).

Tertiary prevention is the last type of disease-focused prevention. It seeks to provide good health care to persons with diseases that have progressed beyond their initial stages. Therefore, since it is too late to prevent illness or arrest its progression to a more serious phase, tertiary prevention includes medical and surgical interventions that can prevent functional decline, improve life quality, or delay death.

The U.S. medical care system has focused on tertiary prevention and uses an increasingly large medical and surgical armamentarium. Breakthrough technology is at the basis of these efforts. It features replacement of organs with mechanical, animal, or other human parts; using genetically engineered products to alter disease agents; and cloning or otherwise duplicating disease-free cells to replace unhealthy tissue. These efforts are unprecedented and unique to the U.S. health care system. No other nation offers a comparable level of advanced medical care. Unfortunately, these tertiary prevention services have made our health care system the most costly in the world on a per capita basis but have not improved our life expectancy to the level of most of the industrialized world. In 1994 life expectancy at birth in the United States was 75.9 years, compared with 80.1 years in Hong Kong, 79.3 in Japan, 78.2 in France, and 78.1 in our neighbor, Canada (U.S. Bureau of Census 1994). Men, in particular, have failed to experience major gains in life expectancy. Women of all racial groups have outlived men since 1900, and white females currently have a seven-year advantage in length of life (U.S. Bureaus of Census 1994).

The fact that the gender gap in survival is occurring simultaneously with a major decline in mortality from conditions such as heart disease may speak to the limitations of tertiary prevention. Some attribute lower mortality from heart disease to procedures such as replacing valves and arteries, heart transplantation, removing blockages in coronary arteries and introducing stents, or offering pharmacological treatment in the form of clot-reducing drugs. Yet others suggest that medical measures have been less effective than those that involve change in health-risk behavior. It is proposed that the reduction in heart disease mortality has been achieved mainly through primary and secondary prevention practices. Since males are less likely to have good dietary practices, and more likely to ingest foods that contribute to artery blockages, use tobacco and have poor exercise habits, this may be affecting their mortality rates. Men may not be living as long as women because they fail to engage in health-promoting behavior, relying instead on medical treatment for an existing condition.

Tertiary prevention is clearly important. The vast majority of individuals suffering from cancer, severely debilitating disease, or life-threatening heart problems seek, or await the development of, advanced medical care. Medical journal articles about life-saving, and sometimes life-enhancing, treatments, are reported regularly on evening news programs. Only a small number of people refuse to have organ transplants or kidney dialysis, and many wait for new AIDS or cancer drugs to be offered for clinical trials. Canadian citizens routinely cross the U.S. border to avail themselves of medical, surgical, and technological procedures that are unavailable in their country or subject to waiting lists.

As stated in a classic medical sociology article, medical care in this country has not been responsible for a decline in mortality rates; rather, the primary causes of the reduction are public health measures that lessen the risk of acquiring disease (McKinlay and McKinlay 1977). We need to refocus our efforts toward heavier emphasis on primary and secondary prevention, and reduce our reliance on costly and technology-heavy tertiary interventions.

THE ROLE OF THE INDIVIDUAL IN HEALTH PROMOTION

As presented above, the responsibility for health promotion rests with several agents; the national and international health care systems, health law and health policy experts, public and private health facilities, health professionals, and individuals. However, the individual is often the center of attention as the burden of health promotion is shifted to the person.

This approach rests on the premise that a person's actions account for whether he or she remains healthy and does not experience progression of or complications from disease. The corollary to this is that persons who fail to exert control over health behaviors are contributing to disease, disability, and death. Movements to empower people and help them take charge of their medical conditions reflect this emphasis on the person's responsibility for health.

Indicative of this trend is that patient noncompliance with the medical regimen is considered to be a cause of medical treatment failure. Clearly, many people fail to adhere to the treatment plan prescribed by their physician. They may fail to have their prescriptions filled, take the amount of medication prescribed, keep medical follow-up appointments, or adhere to a dietary program necessary for a controlling a condition. Only 57

percent of persons with elevated cholesterol levels actually visited a physician after being notified of their state. Gender is an important part of compliance. Women visit physicians more than men, especially for preventive care (Verbrugge 1990). They also act as gatekeepers to the medical system for children and husbands, offering suggestions and advice, and sometimes making medical appointments without the consent of the latter.

This line of reasoning—patients are largely responsible for poor health outcomes because they do not follow the doctor's advice—ignores the fact that health professionals may create situations that foster noncompliance. Presenting an ultimatum about smoking cessation to heart patients, informing people with diabetes they must avoid sugar for the rest of their lives, or telling people diagnosed with hypertension they must fill a costly prescription for a condition that does not cause them physical distress seldom results in compliance. People do not like to be given lists of do's and don'ts. If reasons for the recommended procedures, medications, or behavioral changes are not given, compliance may fail to materialize. Asymmetric models of the patient–physician encounter (Bloom 1974) pose physician authority on the one hand and childlike response on the other. These models have lost their impact, especially among educated middle-class patients, and compliant behavior as an automatic response by the patient is becoming much less widespread.

Another reason that health promotion should not be considered the sole responsibility of the individual is that knowledge is the foundation for action. However, individuals may have little knowledge of appropriate health-promoting behavior. They are consumers of health information. As such, they must either depend on others for information or take the initiative for self study. While knowledgeable, enlightened patients can certainly help to control and/or contain their medical problems, only medically trained persons familiar with that patient's health problems can offer appropriate recommendations! To illustrate, the heart patient's physician is responsible for educating the patient about specific exercises to reduce the risk of a second heart attack because it is the physician who is intricately familiar with the functional and/or anatomical state of that person's heart. Physicians must educate their patients and, in doing so, carefully explain the regimen. It is only when patients receive adequate information and careful explanation about a particular regimen that they can be held accountable.

BARRIERS TO HEALTH PROMOTION

Reducing barriers to health service use helps considerably to promote health and reduce disease prevalence (Orlandi 1987). Analysis of the major barriers to health service utilization shows that they are both societal and individual. Societal impediments are known as structural barriers and refer to variables that originate in the economic, political, and medical organizational spheres of society. Individual, or personal, barriers refer to behavioral variables that seek to avoid, delay, or underutilize health care.

Structural barriers limit access to health promotion programs, as they do to medical service utilization. They can act at several levels. At the economic and health insurance level, absence of such resources make it unlikely that patients will receive some recommended screening or early detection tests. Even for those persons with health insurance coverage, policies may not cover the recommended tests. Constraints on health promotion services are also due to policies or factors that reflect how health care services are organized. To illustrate, political decisions that reduce the availability of public transportation in turn reduce access to sites offering health promotion services. Another example would be health policies that encourage medical sites with state-of-the-art equipment to proliferate in suburban areas. If the newest mammography equipment is available only to women in affluent areas, while inner-city sites have machines that may be old and of poor quality, clearly mammography screening will be less likely in these latter areas.

Personal barriers to health promotion activity include several factors that relate to an individual's perceptions, beliefs about cause and cure, and/or attitudes toward use of formal health care services. These barriers influence whether people will seek health care, follow the advice of medical professionals, and comply with a health promotion regimen and are reflected in the health belief model (Rosenstock 1974). This model of health services utilization proposes that people seek medical services according to: (1) perception of the threat posed by a health problem, and beliefs about their susceptibility to it (e.g., "heart attacks are serious but no one in my family died of heart disease"); (2) the possible inconvenience of the health-related activity versus potential rewards ("I can't manage without a morning cigarette, and besides my heart can't be in such bad shape since I only smoke half a pack a day"); and (3) response cues ("Did you have your annual prostate cancer checkup?").

Cultural factors affect the likelihood that persons will engage in recommended health promotion activity. Beliefs and practices handed down through the generations prescribe alternative health behaviors and nutrition habits. Some are harmless, others may be beneficial (chicken soup for colds, for example), and still others may exacerbate illness or even cause death (refusing blood transfusions on religious grounds). Beliefs also affect primary prevention; for example, some cultural traditions associate obesity with beauty or strength, not risk for chronic disease.

Denial is a particularly important personal barrier that can be added to this model, since denial of illness is directly related to avoidance of medical care. Many women fail to have a mammogram or delay the procedure because they seek to deny the possible threat of cancer. Some of these women have intense fear of the disease, others believe it is incurable, still others fear the surgical or chemotherapeutic treatment involved (Young 1998). In either case, they avoid thinking about it and feel they are better off not knowing whether they have a breast tumor. Delay in scheduling mammograms is a current interest of people seeking to improve rates of mammography compliance (Rimer et al. 1996).

Belief in one's own ability to control one's life also relates to health promotion. Health locus of control measures indicate whether individuals are internally controlled or whether they believe control is due to chance or the actions of powerful others (Wallston et al. 1978). Thus, individuals with internal health locus of control are the best candidates for health promotion programs because they believe in exerting control over their health status. They represent, on a conceptual level, the action stage of Prochaska and DiClemente's

(1984) transtheoretical model of health behavior. Using this same framework, persons who are not engaging in risk-reduction behavior might be considered to be in precontemplation or contemplation stages and may never move to action.

HEALTH PROMOTION FOR OLDER PEOPLE

Health promotion and disease prevention programs generally target working-age people rather than older adults (Young 1994). This is quite unfortunate, since approximately 85 percent of people aged 65 and over suffer from chronic disease and the three most prevalent conditions are arthritis, high blood pressure, and heart disease (National Center for Health Statistics 1996). When considered simultaneously with the three leading causes of death in this population (heart disease, cancer, and stroke), the need for preventive care is quite apparent. These five conditions are largely amenable to risk-factor reduction practices. Indeed, readily available and well-known health promotion and disease prevention practices can alter the course of most, if not all, chronic and killer diseases of older people. There is great potential for improving the health of older adults by including them in health promotion programs (Pope and Tarlov 1991).

Health promotion efforts for older people should certainly involve risk-reduction behavior. As they are taught about behavioral and lifestyle changes, these efforts can result in a sharp drop in the medical consequences of chronic disease. Heart disease provides an important example. Rates of coronary heart disease are at least ten times as high in persons aged 65 and over as among their counterparts under age 45. Women as well as men show a dramatic rise in heart disease rates after they reach age 65. It has clearly been shown that much heart disease can be prevented by diet, exercise, smoking cessation, and similar healthy living practices. Furthermore, some of these same practices can reduce the likelihood of death, development of secondary complications of heart disease, and occurrence of a second heart attack (Kannel et al. 1987). Such behavioral change also brings psychological and social benefits to heart patients and results in gains in several areas of their lives. Yet older people recovering from heart attacks have been found to be significantly less likely to receive preventive behavior advice than their younger counterparts (Young et al. 1987). Particularly absent for persons aged 60 and over is advice to cease smoking and enroll in a cardiac rehabilitation exercise program. The question then emerges, "How can older people engage in health-promoting behavior that may prevent another heart attack, if not given the proper information from their physicians?"

Another way health promotion can be achieved is through following recommendations of major authorities for periodic administration of specific tests, examinations, and immunizations. The guidelines for adult preventive care offered by the U.S. Preventive Service Task Force (1989) include specific age-related tests. The set of recommendations for people aged 65 and over includes annual influenza shots; breast, thyroid, mouth, skin, ovarian, testicular, lymph node, rectal, and prostate cancer examinations; and dental examinations. Tests to determine blood pressure and visual ability should be conducted every two years. There are also recommendations for periodic tests of urine, hearing, estrogen levels in women, and cholesterol. Of course all of these recommendations apply to persons without specific health problems (those who are asymptomatic and of normal risk). Cholesterol and blood pressure tests for older people with heart disease would need to be performed frequently.

Thus, health promotion for older people can be achieved if (1) physicians conduct specific examinations and tests at defined periods of time and (2) if older people engage in risk-reduction behavior. For either to be successful, the older person must follow a recommended plan for medical visits and for individual behavior. This plan must be carefully explained to the older patient. However, studies show that patient-physician interaction in later life is poor (Coe 1987), and physicians may communicate poorly with their older patients and fail to offer a recommended illness-management plan (Young et al. 1987). Clearly, if older people are to change poor dietary habits, they must first be informed about good food choices. Since this information is condition-specific, it needs to be provided by the physicians who treat the individuals or their medical agents, such as nurses or physician assistants.

Older individuals also bear responsibility for behavioral change. They must be willing to engage in health behaviors that prevent illness or modify high-risk profiles. Even when these behaviors represent change in lifelong habits, they must be willing to pursue them. However, for effective risk-reduction practices to be targeted to older people, patient–physician partnerships must be formed (Hess 1991). Including the older patient in the health promotion program is essential.

HEALTH PROMOTION FOR MINORITIES

Significant advances in understanding, managing, and treating chronic disease have failed to eliminate the excess death and disability found in older minorities. African Americans, for example, have a five-year deficit in life expectancy (U.S. Bureau of the Census 1994). They have higher mortality rates for cancer and heart disease (Polednak 1989) and twice the risk of severe complications from diabetes, such as blindness, neurological decline, and illnesses that require dialysis or amputation (Lieberman 1988). Other ethnic minorities such as Hispanic Americans, Native Americans, and some Asian Americans also have a major gap in mortality and morbidity, compared with whites; death rates for heart disease and stroke, two leading causes of death, are twice as high for older minorities as for whites (Polednak 1989). Indeed, the health gap of minorities in the United States is wide and shows no signs of being bridged.

This bleak prognosis is certainly a call for massive efforts at treatment, on the one hand, and extensive health promotion efforts, on the other. Yet despite the fact that health needs vary across populations, health promotion efforts have usually been generic (Young and Olson 1993). Often they focus on the needs of white, middle-class adults (Gottlieb and Green 1987).

Programs to target ethnic minorities must be culturally sensitive; they must also be specific to a particular population (Tseng and Ellyne 1990). One-size-fits-all programs will not fit ethnic minorities as a whole, or individual ethnic groups. The cultural background of the particular target population must be taken into account, along with educational level, health beliefs, and attitudes toward health providers (Young and Olson 1993).

The need to modify generic health promotion program for minority groups is increasingly recognized. Without targeted programs, it is doubtful that health promotion efforts can achieve high success. Knowledge about and appreciation of specific cultural norms, values, and beliefs should be a major component of health promotion programs for minorities (Leavitt 1990).

An example of a health promotion program that targeted a particular ethnic minority was conducted among African Americans with coexistent diabetes and hypertension (Waller et al. 1994). Sixty subjects were randomly assigned to an educational/self-care intervention group or an observation group. The former were instructed by a health educator, using culturally relevant materials. Diet and food preparation information were specific to the food habits of lower-income African Americans and focused on culturally acceptable food and cooking changes. Materials prepared reflected the average educational level of the target population. After one year, high-risk behavior among the intervention group was significantly less than among the observational group. Risk for complications of diabetes, heart disease, and stroke all declined. Furthermore, the diseases were considered to be controlled.

The determinants of success of health promotion programs are clearly their effect on (1) health-risk behavior and (2) medical outcome (control over the condition, laboratory test values within acceptable ranges, etc.). Programs that can change behavior and also effect better outcome for ethnic minorities cannot be generic. They must be culturally sensitive and appropriate to the population they seek to serve. Otherwise, there will be little effect on the mortality and morbidity status of the minority group.

HEALTH STATUS ASSESSMENT

Health promotion goals are often measured in terms of reduction in the prevalence of specific diseases or decline in death rates for a particular condition. The sciences of epidemiology and biostatistics and the field of medical sociology propose several ways to determine health status. They use measurements and statistics for populations, subgroups, and individual cases.

Health status data are collected by epidemiologists, agencies, and medical professionals. Among multiple strategies used are disease surveillance, population surveys, and conducting probability and nonprobability studies of the health of subpopulations (Friedman 1988). Surveys that assess health-risk behavior (e.g., Behavioral Risk Factor Surveys from the Centers for Disease Control and Prevention) are well accepted means of collecting health status data.

Measurements often used to assess health status include rates, ratios, counts, proportions, distributions, ranges, and quantiles. These measurements may indicate prevalence of a particular disease (number of persons with the disease in proportion to the total number in the group); incidence (number of new cases in a given period); or number of persons of a particular age, gender, or ethnic group with the disease. They can also indicate ranking systems and represent change over time in disease or death rates.

Rates are often calculated as the number of cases per 1,000, 10,000, or 100,000 persons. They are also standardized to take factors such as age into consideration. Therefore, since age increases risk of lung cancer, epidemiologists can eliminate this potential bias by using appropriate statistical techniques. They may use age adjustment or age standardization procedures to calculate the expected rate of lung cancer (Friedman 1988). This enables them to assume nonsmokers are the same age composition as smokers.

After rate comparisons are made, the relative and attributable risks of a disease can be determined. In these calculations, biostatisticians evaluate prevalence or incidence of a disease in a particular population and may then compare risks of two different populations. Other analyses may be of change in risk over time, or the lifetime risk of acquiring a disease such as cancer.

A frequently encountered health indicator is the proportion of cases that fall into a particular quantile. This generic term refers to several tiers,

each representing a proportion of the population. To illustrate, people may be categorized into four quartiles, representing cholesterol levels. Each 25 percent segment of the population may then be compared. In these analyses, the association of an outcome variable, such as a second heart attack, with membership in a high-cholesterol-level group (quartile 1, for example) is clearly shown.

From a public health perspective, important indicators of health status are infant mortality and life expectancy rates. Low infant mortality and high life expectancy are considered to represent good health in a society. The premise is that societies that can reduce unnecessary maternal and child deaths and increase the average life expectancy at birth have established good medical care procedures and may have health practices that reduce the burden of illness and premature death.

In the United States, infant mortality rates have declined over the past century. In 1991 the overall infant death rate in the United States was 8.9/1,000 births (National Center for Health Statistics 1996). This represented a decline from 20/1,000 in 1970. Among certain subpopulations infant mortality was much higher than for the population at large. Blacks, for example, had infant death rates of 17.6, versus 7.3 for whites.

Life expectancy at birth is approximately 76 years in the United States. However, it is close to 80 years for white women and 73 years for white men. These figures represent a rise in life expectancy for men and women alike, and although there is a major racial gap, nonwhites have also shown an increase over the past 90 years.

In comparison with industrialized countries that offer all or most of their citizens publicly funded health care, U.S. men and women show up to a four-year gap in life expectancy (U.S. Bureau of Census 1994). U.S. infants are also more likely to die than those in several industrialized nations.

Sociologists use a different approach to assess health status than epidemiologists or biostatisticians They measure functional ability, perceived health status, emotional and psychological health, and quality of life, to name a few. Medical measures are used infrequently, and statistics are seldom expressed in rates. Rather, sociologists assess health status by tabulating scale scores of health-specific indices and/or calculating frequency distributions of individual health status questions. In the case of the latter, the investigator might determine presence/absence of a specific health problem (e.g., Do you have arthritis?) and measure central tendencies and variance in the data.

Functional ability is considered to an important indicator of health status in a sociological context. While the level of functioning can be measured as physical, mental, or social impairment, most of the interest is in physical functioning. This approach conceptualizes functional ability as ability to conduct activities of daily living (ADLs) or instrumental activities of daily living (IADLs) without assistance from others. Instruments used include measures suitable for older people (e.g., the OARS instrument of Duke University 1978), disease-specific measures (e.g., the arthritis functioning measure of Patrick and Deyo 1989), and instruments that assess cognitive functioning as a component of physical functioning (e.g., Keller et al. 1993).

The individual's perception of his or her health is often measured. In these investigations, the concern is with how the person assesses general health status at the present time or in reference to other people and other times. Thus, they may be asked "Is your health generally excellent, good, fair, poor, bad?" or "How does your health compare with that of people your own age?" or "Is your health better or worse than one year ago?" They may also be asked about perceived functional ability (Duke University 1978; Lawton et al. 1982).

Emotional and psychological health are also measured. Well-validated instruments such as the CES-D of the Center for Epidemiological Studies or the Zung Depression Measure are used for depression (DeForge and Sobal 1988). Investigators also seek to determine mood (Profile of Mood States of McNair et al. 1971), positive and negative effect (Bradburn 1969), morale (Lawton et al. 1982), and subjective well-being (Dupuy 1984).

Quality of life indicators are among the least well validated instruments used to assess health status. There are many different approaches to quality of life that represent medical, psychological, and social models of illness. Since sociologists prefer a multidimensional view, Levine and Croog (1984) presented five components of quality of life: social-role performance, physiologic state, emotional state, intellectual function, and general satisfaction or feeling of well-being. Also considered to measure quality of life are some subscales of the Sickness Impact Profile (Bergner 1984). The full 134-item instrument assesses physical, social, psychological, and interactional aspects of illness, but some scales are specific to pain or impairment level and tend to reflect a medical, rather than psychosocial, view of quality of life. Indeed, the medical approach may concentrate exclusively on disease-specific or treatment-specific variables. It may measure, for example inability to eat or excessive fatigue among cancer patients undergoing chemotherapy, or frequency of urination among individuals with hypertension who are prescribed medications to expel fluids from the body. Still other medically focused approaches to quality of life may focus on the experience of pain, as in the previously mentioned Sickness Impact Profile.

Health status assessment is clearly a broad field. It includes measurement of disease patterns in a population, self-reports by individuals of generalized health status, and middle-level health measurements. These latter measurements are neither macro level, like population-based mortality and morbidity statistics, nor micro level, like individual reports. Rather, they include validated scales, indices, or series of questions that may be widely used among general or specific populations. Many, if not most, measures have been found to be reliable and valid indicators of health status. The medical sociologist or related researcher thus has a wide range of instruments to assess health status.

CONCLUSION

Health promotion includes a wide-ranging set of activities that (1) enhance health status, (2) prevent disease, (3) seek to control the spread of chronic or infectious disease, and (4) attempt to arrest or delay deterioration that occurs as the result of these conditions. Health-promoting activities occur at the societal and individual levels and include a long list of agents. Essentially, health promotion represents the principle that maintaining health, preventing disease, and avoiding decline or complications of progressive illness are all achievable goals. For any society to have a healthy, vital citizenry, it must reduce the financial, social, and medical burdens of illness. All these are accomplished with health-promoting practices.

REFERENCES

American Cancer Society 1990 "1989 Survey of Physicians' Attitudes and Practices in Early Cancer Detection." *Ca-A Cancer Journal for Clinicians* 40:77–101.

Bergner, M. 1984 "The Sickness Impact Profile (SIP)." In N.K. Wenger, M. Mattson, C. Furberg, and J. Elinson, eds., *Assessment of Quality of Life in Clinical Trials of Cardiovascular Therapies*. New York: Le-Jacq.

Bloom, S. W. 1974 *The Doctor and His Patient*. New York: Free Press.

Bradburn, N. 1969 *The Structure of Psychological Well-Being*. Chicago: Aldine.

Coe, R. M. 1987 "Communication and Medical Care Outcomes: Analysis of Conversations Between Doctors and Elderly Patients." In R. Ward, and S. Tobin, eds., *Health and Aging: Socioissues and Policy Directions*. New York: Springer.

DeForge, B.R., and J. Sobal, 1988 "Self-Report Depression Scales in the Elderly: The Relationship Between the CES-D and Zung." *International Journal of Psychiatry in Medicine* 18:325–338.

Duke University Center for the Study of Aging and Human Development 1978 *Multidimensional Functional Assessment: The OARS Methodology*. Durham, N.C.: Duke University Medical Center.

Dupuy, H. J. 1984 "The Psychological General Well-Being (PGWB) Index." *In N. Wenger, M. Mattson, C. Furberg, and J. Elinson, eds., Assessment of Quality of Life in Clinical Trials of Cardiovascular Therapies*. New York: Le-Jacq.

Friedman, G.D. 1988 *Primer of Epidemiology*, 3rd ed. New York: McGraw-Hill.

Fries, J. F., and L. M. Crapo, 1986 "The Elimination of Premature Disease." In Ken Dychtwald, ed., *Wellness and Health Promotion for the Elderly*. Rockville, Md.: Aspen.

Gottlieb, N. H., and L.W. Green, 1987 "Ethnicity and Lifestyle Health Risk: Some Possible Mechanisms." *American Journal of Health Promotion* 2(1):37–51.

Herd, J. A., J. J. W. Alastair, J. Blumenthal, J. E. Daugherty, and R. Harris, 1987 "Medical Therapy in the Elderly." *Journal of the American College of Cardiology* 10:29–34.

Hess, J. W. 1991 "Health Promotion and Risk Reduction for Later Life." In R. Young and E. Olson, eds.,

Health, Illness, and Disability in Later Life: Practice Issues and Interventions. Newbury Park: Sage.

Kannel, W. B., J. T. Doyle, R. J. Shepard, et al. 1987 "Prevention of Cardiovascular Disease in the Elderly." *Journal of the American College of Cardiology* 10A:25–28.

Keller, D. M., M. G. Kovar, J. B. Jobe, and L. G. Branch, 1993 "Problems Eliciting Elder's Reports of Functional Status." *Journal of Aging and Health* 5:306–318.

Lawton, M. P., M. Moss, M. Fulcomer, and M.H. Kleban, 1982 "A Research and Service-Oriented Multilevel Assessment Instrument." *Journal of Gerontology* 37:91–99.

Leavitt, R. 1990 "The Appreciation of Cultural Diversity. How to Integrate Content into Curriculum." In G. Price and P. Fitz, eds., *Issues in Aging: Cultural Diversity and the Allied Health Curriculum*. Hartford, Conn.: University of Connecticut.

Levine, S., and S. H. Croog 1984 "What Constitutes Quality of Life? A Conceptualization of the Dimensions of Life Quality in Healthy Populations and Patients With Cardiovascular Disease." In N. Wenger, M. Mattson, C. Furgerg, and J. Elinson, eds., *Assessment of Quality of Life in Clinical Trials of Cardiovascular Therapies*. New York: Le-Jacq.

Lieberman, L. S. 1988 "Diabetes and Obesity in Elderly Black Americans." In J. S. Jackson, ed., *The Black Elderly: Research on Physical and Psychosocial Health*. New York: Springer.

McGinnis J. M., and W. H. Foege, 1993 "Actual Causes of Death in the United States." *Journal of the American Medical Association* 270(18): 2207–2212.

McKinlay, J.B., and S.M. McKinlay, 1977 "The Questionable Contribution of Medical Measures to the Decline of Mortality in the United States in the Twentieth Century." *Health and Society* 55(3):405–426.

McNair, D., M. Lorr, and L. Doppleman, 1971 *Manual for the Profile of Mood States*. San Diego: Educational and Industrial Testing Service.

National Center for Health Statistics 1996 *Vital Statistics of the United States 1991*, vol. 2. Hyattsville, Md.: U.S. Government Printing Office.

New York Times. "Clinton Plans 125 Million Initiative on Infectious Disease." December 27, 1998.

Office of Disease Prevention and Health Promotion, U.S. Department of Health and Human Services Public Health Service 1994 *Clinician's Handbook of Preventive Services*. Washington D.C.: U. S. Government Printing Office.

Orlandi, M. A. 1987 "Clinical Perspectives. Promoting Health and Preventing Disease in Health Care Settings: An Analysis of Barriers." *Preventive Medicine* 16:119–130.

Patrick, D. L., and R. A. Deyo 1989 "Generic and Disease-Specific Measures in Assessing Health Status and Quality of Life." *Medical Care.* 27 (Suppl. 3):S217–S232.

Polednak, A.P. 1989 *Racial and Ethnic Differences in Disease*. New York: Oxford University Press.

Pope, A. M., and A. Tarlov 1991 *Institute of Medicine Disability in America*. Washington, D.C.: National Academy Press.

Prochaska, J. O., and C. C. DiClemente 1984 *The Transtheoretical Approach: Crossing the Traditional Boundaries of Therapy*. Chicago: Dow Jones/Irwin.

Rimer, B. K., J. M. Schildkraut, C. Lerman, T. H. Lin, and J. Audrain, 1996 "Participation in a Women's Breast Cancer Risk Counseling Trial: Who Participates? Who Declines? *Journal of American Cancer Society* 77(11):2348–2355.

Rosenstock, I. M. 1974 "Historical Origins of the Health Belief Model." *Health Education Monographs* 2:344.

Tseng, R. and D. Ellyne, 1990 "Perspectives on Developing a Course in Multicultural Health Promotion." *Issues in Aging*, 44–48.

U.S. Bureau of Census 1994 *Current Population Reports*. Washington, D.C.: U.S. Government Printing Office.

U.S. Preventive Services Task Force 1989: *Guide to Clinical Preventive Services*. Baltimore: Williams and Wilkins.

Verbrugge, L. M. 1990 "The Twain Meet: Empirical Explanations of Sex Differences in Health and Mortality." In M. G. Ory and H. R. Warner, eds., *Gender, Health, and Longevity*. New York: Springer Publishing Company.

Waller, J. B., R. Young, and J. R. Sowers, 1994 *Frail Elderly* (Report to National Institutes of Health, NIA No. 10428). Washington, D.C.: U.S. Government Printing Office.

Wallston, K. A., B. S. Wallston, and R. DeVellis, 1978 "Development of the Multi-Dimensional Health Locus of Control MHLC Scales." *Journal of Health Education Monographs*. 6(2):160–170.

Young, R. F. 1994 "Older People as Consumers of Health Promotion Recommendations." *Generations* 18(1):69–73.

—— 1998 "Delay in Breast Cancer Screening." Report to Karmonos Cancer Institute.

——, E. Kahana, and M. Rubenfire, 1987 "Preventive Health Behavior Advice: A Study with Older Myocardial Infarction Patients." *Evaluation and the Health Professions*. 10:4394–4407.

Young R. F., and E. A. Olson, 1993 "Health Promotion Among Minority Aged: Challenges for the Health Professions." *Journal of Continuing Education in the Health Professions* 13:235–242.

ROSALIE F. YOUNG

HEALTH STATUS MEASUREMENT

See Health and Illness Behavior; Health Promotion and Health Status; Quality of Life; Medical Sociology.

HETEROSEXUAL BEHAVIOR PATTERNS

See Courtship; Sexual Behavior in Marriage and Close Relationships; Sexual Behavior Patterns; Sexual Orientation; Sexual Violence and Exploitation.

HIERARCHICAL LINEAR MODELS

Hierarchical linear models are applicable in situations where data have been collected from two (or more) different levels. Sociology's initial interest in such multilevel relationships can be traced back to Durkheim's research into the impact of community on suicide (Durkheim [1898] 1951). More recently, these models have been related to the topic of contextual analysis (Boyd and Iversen 1979), where researchers are interested in investigating linkages between micro-level and macro-level variables. Sociological theories have been classified into three groups according to the degree to which they incorporate multilevel variables (Coleman 1986). In one group, variation in a dependent variable is explained through independent variables obtained from the same social level (e.g., country, community, individual). In a second group, attempts are made to account for differences in a dependent variable at one level by examining variation in an independent variable at a higher level; and in a third group, variations in a dependent variable are explained by variations in an independent variable at a lower level. Theories that fall into either the second or third group are multilevel theories and can be explored using hierarchical linear models.

SPECIFICATION OF THE HIERARCHICAL LINEAR MODEL

A wide variety of hierarchical models can be specified. However, in order to outline the basic features of such models, a simple example will be developed. Assume that a researcher is interested in modeling the length of hospital stay (LOS) for a specific individual (Y_i) as a function of the severity of that individual's illness (X_i) and the bed occupancy rate for the institution in which that individual is hospitalized (G_j). In this hypothetical model we have one criterion (or dependent) variable, Y_i, at the micro level, one micro-level predictor (or independent) variable, X_i, and one macro predictor (or independent) variable, G_j. This produces a two-level hierarchical model. The technique is quite flexible and can be expanded to include multiple predictor variables at either (or both) the micro- and macro-levels and additional levels. In the given example, an index of individual comorbidity could be included as an additional micro-level predictor, type of hospital (e.g., public vs. private) could be included as an additional macro-level predictor, and an additional level of the gross national product (GNP) of the country in which the hospital is located could be added to create a three-level model.

The first step in developing hierarchical models is to specify a model for the micro-level variables that is identical for all contexts. In the present example a linear model relating LOS as a function of severity of illness is specified for each of the hospitals.

$$Y_{ij} = \beta_{0j} + \beta_{1j} X_{1ij} + \varepsilon_{ij} \qquad (1)$$

Where $j=1, 2, \ldots, j$ denotes the macro-level contexts (e.g., the hospitals) and $i=1, 2, \ldots, n_j$ denotes micro-level observations within contexts (e.g., individuals within hospitals). The intercepts from Equation 1 (β_{0j}) provide estimates of the expected LOS for individual i in hospital j whose severity of illness is zero, whereas the slopes (β_{1j}) provide estimates for the effect of a unit change in the severity of the illness for individual i in hospital

j. Finally, the β_{ij}'s represent random errors or residuals. It is assumed that these errors are normally distributed within each context with a mean of zero and a constant variance σ^2. This is a standard linear model with the exception that the coefficients (i.e., the β_j's) are allowed to vary across contexts (hospitals).

In situations where separate regression equations are estimated for various contexts, four different patterns can emerge. These patterns are depicted in Figures 1a, 1b, 1c, and 1d. In Figure 1a, the functional relationship between the micro-level variables is identical for all the contexts, and thus the intercepts and slopes are the same for all contexts. In Figure 1b, the degree of linear relationship between the micro-level variables is equivalent across contexts; however, the initial "location" (i.e., the intercept) of this relationship varies across contexts. In Figure 1c, the degree of linear relationship between the micro-level variables varies as a function of context, although the initial "location" is consistent across contexts. Finally, in Figure 1d, both the initial location and the relationship between the micro-level variables vary significantly across contexts.

Systematic differences across contexts are reflected in three of the figures (viz., Figures 1b, 1c, and 1d). The presence of these differences leads to questions of whether there are contextual or macro-level variables that could be associated with the varying micro-level coefficients (i.e., the slopes and/or intercepts). Questions of this type are addressed by specifying a second-level model. For example, if there is significant variation among the micro-level coefficients, then this variation could be modeled as a function of contextual or macro-level variables as follows:

$$\beta_{0j} = \gamma_{00} + \gamma_{01} G_j + U_{0j} \qquad (2)$$

$$\beta_{1j} = \gamma_{10} + \gamma_{11} G_j + U_{1j} \qquad (3)$$

where G_j is a contextual (or macro-level) variable, γ_{00} and γ_{10} are the intercepts from the second-level models, γ_{01} and γ_{11} are the slopes from the second-level model, and U_{0j} and U_{1j} are the second-level residuals. It is assumed that the residuals are distributed multivariate normal with mean vector **0** and variance-covariance matrix **T**. In the present example, Equation 2 would be used to model differences across hospitals among the intercepts

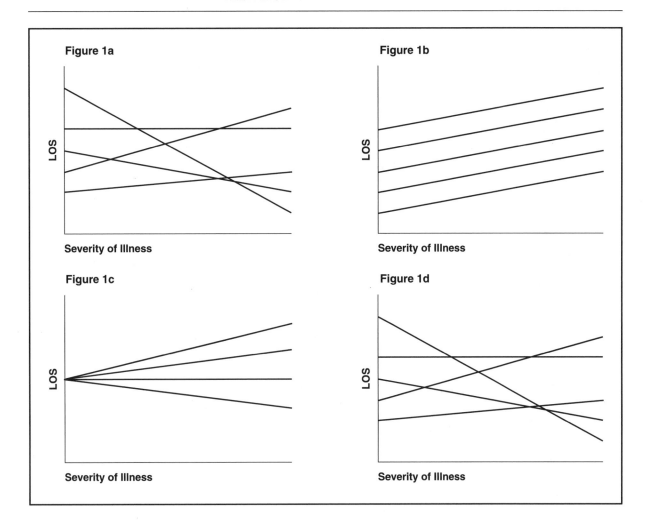

of the micro-level equations (cf. Figures 1b and 1d), whereas Equation 3 would be used to model differences across hospitals in the slopes of the micro-level equations (cf. Figures 1c and 1d).

Depending on the actual variability of the micro-level coefficients (i.e., the β_j's), different second-level models would be justified. For example, in situations where there is no variation in the slopes across contexts (see Figure 1b), the inclusion of G_j in Equation 3 would not be meaningful given that β_{1j} is the same across all contexts. Similarly, in situations where there is no variation in the intercepts across contexts (see Figure 1c), the inclusion of G_j in Equation 2 would not be meaningful given that β_{0j} is the same across all contexts.

By substituting Equations 2 and 3 into Equation 1, we can obtain a single equation form of the hierarchical model as follows:

$$Y_{ij} = \gamma_{00} + \gamma_{01} G_j + \gamma_{10} X_{1ij} + \gamma_{11} G_j X_{1ij} + (U_{0j} + U_{1j} X_{1ij} + \varepsilon_{ij}) \tag{4}$$

The model represented by Equation 4 is a mixed model with both fixed coefficients (viz., the γ's) and random coefficients (viz., the U's and the ε's). Further, since the random coefficients are allowed to covary across contexts, it can be called a variance component model.

The approach to investigating relationships occurring across hierarchical levels represented by the equations above is not new. Burstein and colleagues (1978) discussed a similar approach under the conceptualization of "slopes as outcomes." Conceptually, this is an accurate description, given that the regression coefficients estimated within each context at the micro level are used as criterion (or dependent) measures in the macro-level (or second-level) model (cf. Equations 2 and 3). However, while this conceptualization of the relationship between micro- and macro-level variables has been understood for a number of years, concerns about the adequacy of estimating such models using traditional statistical techniques (viz., ordinary least squares, OLS) have been expressed. However, separate statistical advances throughout the 1980s improved the estimation procedures for these models (for reviews see Burstein and colleagues 1989; Raudenbush 1988), with the advances resulting in several different software packages being developed specifically for the estimation of hierarchical linear models (e.g., GENMOD, HLM, ML3, and VARCL).

ESTIMATION OF HIERARCHICAL LINEAR MODELS

In estimating the various components of the hierarchical linear model, a distinction is made among fixed effects, random effects, and variance components. Specifically, fixed effects are those parameter estimates that are assumed to be constant across contexts (e.g., the γ's from Equations 2 and 3), whereas random effects are parameter estimates that are free to vary across contexts (e.g., β_{0j} and β_{1j} from Equation 1). Hierarchical linear models also allow for the estimation of the variance components of the model. These include (1) the variance of the residuals from the micro-level model (i.e., the variance of the ε_{ij}'s identified as σ^2 above); (2) the variance of the second-level residuals (i.e., U_{0j} and U_{1j}); and (3) the covariance of the second-level residuals (i.e., the covariance of U_{0j} and U_{1j}). The variance–covariance matrix of the second-level residuals was previously defined as **T**.

Estimation of Fixed Effects. One approach that could be used to estimate the γ's from Equations 2 and 3 is traditional OLS regression. However, because the precision of estimation of these parameters will vary as a function of contexts, the usual OLS assumption of equal error variances (i.e., homoscedasticity) will be violated. In order to deal with this violation the second-level regression coefficients (the γ's) are estimated using a more sophisticated procedure, generalized least squares (GLS). GLS techniques provide weighted estimates

of the second-level regression coefficients such that the contexts that have more precise estimation of the micro-level parameters receive more weight in the estimation. That is, those contexts in which there is greater precision in estimating the parameters (the slopes and the intercepts) receive more weight in estimating the second-level regressions.

Estimation of Variance–Covariance Components. The components of the variance–covariance matrix **T** include the variance of the micro-level residuals, and the variance and covariance of the second-level residuals. These components are used in the GLS estimation of the fixed effects of the second-level model. However, the values of the components of this matrix are typically not known and must be estimated. The best methods for doing this are iterative methods that alternatively estimate the parameters of the models and then estimate the variance–covariance matrix **T** until a convergence is reached. Hierarchical linear models adopt the EM algorithm (Dempster et al. 1977) that produces maximum likelihood estimates for the variance–covariance components of **T**.

Estimation of Random Effects. The simplest way of estimating the coefficients for the micro-level model (i.e., Equation 1) is to compute an OLS regression for a specific context. In the present example, this would involve obtaining a regression equation relating expected LOS to severity of illness for all individuals within a specific hospital. If there are reasonably large sample sizes within each context, this analysis would provide relatively precise estimates of the coefficients of interest. These estimates will not be stable, however, if sample sizes are smaller. Further, inspection of the second-level models reveals that there is a second estimate of the coefficients from the micro-level models. Thus, for any particular observational unit there are two separate estimates of the micro-level regression coefficients: one from the micro-level regressions themselves and the other from the second-level regression model. The question that this leaves is which of these provides a more accurate estimate of the population parameters for the particular observational unit.

Rather than forcing a choice between one of these two estimates, hierarchical linear models use empirical Bayes estimation procedures (Morris

1983) to compute an optimally weighted combination of the two estimates. The empirical Bayes estimates are a weighted composite of the two estimates discussed above. The micro-level regression coefficients (the ß$_j$'s) estimated by OLS are weighted according to the precision with which they are estimated (i.e., their reliability). In cases where the OLS estimates are not very reliable (e.g., due to small sample size), the empirical Bayes procedure allots greater weight to the second-level estimates. Essentially, then, the weighted composite "shrinks" the micro-level estimate toward the second-level estimate, with the level of shrinkage being determined by the reliability of the micro-level estimate. It has been demonstrated that, in general, the empirical Bayes estimates have smaller mean squared errors than OLS estimates.

Statistical Tests. A variety of statistical tests for hypothesis testing are provided by the various computer programs used to estimate hierarchical linear model. For example, HLM (Bryk et al. 1994) computes a *t*-test to evaluate the hypothesis that the second-level regression parameters depart significantly from zero. In addition, chi-square tests are provided for tests of whether or not there is significant variation in the second-level residuals. These latter tests allow the researcher to determine the model that best fits the observed data. For example, it might be that there is no significant variation in the slopes across contexts; however, there might be significant variation in the intercepts (as in Figure 1b).

FURTHER ISSUES WITH HIERARCHICAL LINEAR MODELS

Centering. Often, as in the present example, interpretation of the intercepts is not straightforward, since a value of zero for the independent variable (in the present case, severity of illness) is not meaningful. In situations like this, it is possible to "center" the independent variable as a deviation from the mean level of that variable in the sample as follows.

$$Y_{ij} = \beta_{0j} + \beta_{1j}(X_{1ij} - \overline{X}_{1j}) + \varepsilon_{ij} \qquad (5)$$

With this specification, the intercepts now represent estimates of the expected length of stay for individuals in a specific hospital whose severity of

illness is at the mean. The interpretation of the other parameters remain unaltered.

Longitudinal Data. Hierarchical linear models can also be used to analyze longitudinal data collected in order to examine questions regarding the assessment of change (Bryk and Raudenbush 1987). Under this approach, there are repeated observations within an observational unit and there is a sample of different units. This allows for a two-level conceptualization of development such that change in the individual units is modeled as a function of time and differences in the patterns of change across individual units can be modeled as a function of measurable characteristics of the individual units. Under this conceptualization, interest is in between-individual (unit) differences in within-individual (unit) change.

Statistical Software. As previously noted, a number of different software programs have been specifically developed in order to estimate hierarchical linear models. Kreft and colleagues (1994) reviewed five of the then-available packages. While they recommended ML3 (Prosser et al. 1991) for the "serious" user, they concluded that HLM's main advantage is its ease of use. Since that time, both programs have been updated and now versions for Windows '95 are available (viz., HLM 4 and MlwiN. Information on the latest version of these programs is available from the following Web sites: go to http://www.ssicentral.com/hlm/mainhlm.htm for information on HLM 4; go to http://www.ioe.ac.uk/mlwin for information on MlwiN.).

CONCLUSION

Hierarchical linear models provide statistically sophisticated ways for dealing with analyses in which data are obtained from multiple levels. Such data are common in sociological research, especially if the investigation deals with contextual effects or longitudinal designs. For more detailed discussions of hierarchical linear models, the interested reader is directed to the following sources that provide more in-depth coverage: Bryk and Raudenbush (1992); Goldstein (1995); or Hox (1995). (At the time of publication, a complete, on-line version of this text was available from: http://ioe.ac.uk/multilevel.what-new.html.

REFERENCES

Boyd, L. H., and G. R. Iversen 1979 *Contextual Analysis: Concepts and Statistical Techniques.* Belmont, Calif.: Wadsworth.

Bryk, A. S., and S. W. Raudenbush 1987 "Application of Hierarchical Linear Models to Assessing Change." *Psychological Bulletin* 101:147–158.

—— 1992 *Hierarchical Linear Models: Applications and Data Analysis Methods.* Newbury Park, Calif.: Sage.

——, and R. J. Congdon 1994 *Hierarchical Linear Modeling with the HLM/2L and HLM/3L Programs.* Chicago: Scientific Software International.

Burstein, L., K. S. Kim, and G. Delandshere 1989 "Multilevel Investigations of Systematically Varying Slopes: Issues, Alternatives, and Consequences." In R. D. Bock, ed., *Multilevel Analysis of Educational Data.* New York: Academic Press.

Burstein, L., R. L. Linn, and F. J. Capell 1978 "Analyzing Multilevel Data in the Presence of Heterogeneous Within-Class Regressions." *Journal of Educational Statistics* 3:347–383.

Coleman, J. S. 1986 "Social Theory, Social Research, and a Theory of Action." *American Journal of Sociology* 91:1309–1336.

Dempster, A. P., N. M. Laird, and D. B. Rubin 1977 "Maximum Likelihood from Incomplete Data Via the EM Algorithm." *Journal of the Royal Statistical Society*, Series B 39:1–8.

Durkheim, E. (1898) 1951 *Suicide.* Glencoe Ill.: Free Press.

Goldstein, H. 1995 *Multilevel Statistical Models.* New York: Halstead.

Hox, J. J. 1995 *Applied Multilevel Analysis.* Amsterdam: TT-Publikaties.

Kreft, I., J. de Leeuw, and R. van der Leeden 1994 "Review of Five Multilevel Analysis Programs: BMDP-5V, GENMOD, HLM, ML3, VARCL." *The American Statistician* 48:324–335.

Morris, C. 1983 "Parametric Empirical Bayes Inference: Theory and Applications." *Journal of the American Statistical Association* 78:47–65.

Prosser, R., J. Rasbash, and H. Goldstein 1991 *ML3: Software for Three-Level Analysis.* London: Institute of Education, University of London.

Raudenbush, S. W. 1988 "Educational Applications of Hierarchical Linear Models: A Review." *Journal of Educational Statistics* 13:85–116.

GEORGE ALDER

HIGHER EDUCATION

Colleges and universities seem to defy the maxim that only highly rationalized institutions can succeed in the modern world. Only the Catholic Church has a longer continuous existence among Western institutions. Higher education has done more than survive; it is in many ways a pivot of key developments in the social structure and culture. It is central for the generation of research and technological innovations. It is also central in the selection, training, and credentialing of young men and women for higher-level positions in the occupational structure.

Among the most important sociological questions surrounding higher education are the following: (1) To what extent have advanced industrial societies become based on a "knowledge economy" closely related to university research and training? Related to this question is another: To what extent do we see the rise of a "new class" of "knowledge workers" with advanced training—differing in interest and outlook from both business elites and earlier aristocracies of labor? (2) To what extent do institutions of higher education reproduce social inequalities by certifying the cultural advantages of children from the upper classes, or reshuffle the social hierarchy by rewarding intellect and ability independent of students' social-class background? (3) Do institutions of higher education, with their traditions of collegial control and tenure, represent an alternative model to corporate forms of organization? These issues can be addressed only after examining the historical development, the existing organizational structures, and the contemporary pressures on higher education.

First, it is necessary to define the dimensions of higher education. Formal educational systems are conventionally divided between primary (the first six years), secondary (the next four to six years), and postsecondary education. Some postsecondary schools offer courses of study that are narrowly vocational and very short in duration. These institutions (including secretarial, business, and vocational–technical colleges) are not usually considered to be part of higher education. Institutions must award degrees that are recognized by baccalaureate-granting colleges and universities to be considered part of higher education. By this criterion, community colleges in the United States,

Fachhochschulen in Germany, and the "further education" colleges in the United Kingdom represent bottom tiers of their respective national higher education systems. These are all short-cycle, vocationally oriented institutions, but some of their degrees are transferable to higher-level colleges and universities. Above these lower-tier institutions are a vast array of colleges, universities, and specialized institutions (for example, seminaries and art schools) that constitute the core of the higher education sector in all contemporary societies. Levels in this institutional hierarchy are structured, most fundamentally, by the type of credentials offered. In the United States, for example, levels are marked by movement from the associate to the baccalaureate to the master's to the doctoral degree.

HISTORICAL DEVELOPMENT

The distant relatives of today's institutions of higher education go back in the West to the Greek academies of the fourth and fifth centuries B.C.E. In these academies, young men from the governing classes studied rhetoric and philosophy (and lesser subjects) as training for public life (Marrou [1948] 1982). In the East, the roots of higher education go back to the training of future government bureaucrats at the feet of masters of Confucian philosophy, poetry, and calligraphy. In both East and West, a close relationship existed among social class, high culture, and preparation for public life.

However, modern institutions of higher education trace a more direct lineage from the medieval *studium generale*. In the first European universities of the twelfth and early thirteenth centuries (notably Salerno, Bologna, and Paris), students and masters came together to pore over the new knowledge discovered in ancient texts and developed by the Arab scholars of Spain. These gatherings of students and teachers were a product of the revival of scholarly inquiry in what has been called the "twelfth-century Renaissance." The medieval universities were similar to modern higher education in that they were permanent institutions of learning with at least a rudimentary formal organization. Courses of study were formally organized, lectures and examinations were given at scheduled times, administrative officials presided, graduation ceremonies were held, and students lived in lodgings near the university buildings. The *studium generale*, or leading universities, were recognized as such because they housed at least one of the "higher faculties" in law, medicine, or theology in addition to faculties of the arts. Courses in the arts, typically with an emphasis on logic and philosophy, were common preparation for study in the three learned professions. Thus, from the beginning, a certain vocational emphasis is evident in the university. Degrees awarded on the completion of professional studies certified accomplishments that made their recipients worthy of entry into professional life. Nevertheless, the spirit of inquiry was equally important in the medieval universities; these were places renowned for famous teachers, such as Abelard in Paris and Irnerius in Bologna. Civic competition led to a proliferation of universities. By the end of the Middle Ages, eighty had been founded in different parts of Europe (Rashdall [1985] 1936).

In the seventeenth and eighteenth centuries, the fortunes of colleges and universities waned. The causes for decline are numerous, including the attractiveness of commercial over scholarly careers, the interference (in some places) of religious and political authorities, and the insularity of faculty who jealously guarded their guild privileges but resisted new currents of thought. During this period, colleges and universities became places concerned with the transmission of ancient texts rather than the further advance of knowledge. Professional training moved out of the universities: into Inns of Court, medical colleges, and seminaries. New elites interested in technical and scientific progress established entirely new institutions rather than allying with the colleges and universities. Napoleon, for example, founded elite professional training institutions, the *grandes ecoles*, and the early investigators in the natural sciences created separate elite societies to encourage research and discussion.

The revived university is the product of nineteenth-century European reform movements, led in the beginning by intellectually oriented aristocrats and eminent philosophers and theologians. The University of Berlin, founded in 1810, was the first reformed university, and others shortly followed in its wake. The new university was founded on the "Humboldtian principles" of the unity of teaching and research (meaning that both functions were performed by the professoriate) and the freedom to teach and learn without fear of outside interference. The development of new academic components, such as the research seminar and the specialized lecture, created an environment in which path-breaking researchers, such as Leopold Ranke in history and Justus von Liebig in chemistry, emerged (McClelland 1980). By mid-century, the German research universities had become a model for reformers throughout Europe and from as far away as the United States and Japan. The first research university in the United States, Johns Hopkins University, founded in 1876, was explicitly modeled on the German research university.

Higher education's current emphasis on training for a wide range of applied fields has an equally important history. Here the United States, rather than Germany, was the decisive innovator. The Morrill Acts (passed in 1862 and 1890) provided funds for states to establish "land grant" universities to provide both general education and practical training in agricultural and mechanical arts for all qualified applicants. Such institutions encouraged both the democratization of American higher education and a closer connection between universities and emerging markets for educated labor. The American university's role in society was further enhanced by its willingness to work collaboratively with government, professional associations, and (somewhat later) business and community organizations. The "Wisconsin Idea" encouraged close connection between university experts and government officials during the period before World War I. Universities also cooperated closely with professional associations to raise educational training standards. Connections between university and state were extended, particularly in the sciences, during World War II and the Cold War, when government grants for university-based scientific research became a very large source of support. These developments encouraged a new view of higher education. In the 1960s, Clark Kerr (1963) coined the term "multiversity" to describe institutions, like his own University of California, as service-based enterprises specializing in training, research, and advice for all major sectors of society. Junior colleges, first established just after the turn of the twentieth century, were by the 1960s even more systematically tied than universities to local and regional markets for semiprofessional and technical labor (Brint and Karabel 1989). In terms of growth, these two-year colleges are the great success story of twentieth-century higher education, and their influence is now evident even in four-year institutions. The utilitarian approach of American educators was resisted for some time in Europe and Asia, where access to higher education was strictly limited to those students who passed rigorous examinations and where higher degrees had long served as important badges of social status linked to cultural refinement. However, by the last quarter of the twentieth century, the entrepreneurial multiversity had become an important model throughout the developed world (Clark 1998).

Institutions of higher education rarely shed their earlier identities completely; instead, they incorporate new emphases through reorganizing and adding new components and new role expectations. Today, all major historical stages of university development remain very much in evidence. Much of the nomenclature, hierarchy, and ritual of the medieval university remains and is in full display at graduation ceremonies. Although the major fields of study have changed dramatically, the underlying liberal arts emphasis of the ancient academies has remained central in the first two years of undergraduate study (the lower division). The nineteenth-century emphasis on specialization is evident in the second two years of undergraduate study (the upper division) and in graduate and professional programs. The nineteenth-century emphasis on research remains an absorbing occupation of faculty and graduate students. The twentieth-century emphases on ancillary training, service, and advisory activities are organized in separate components (as in the case of university extension programs, agricultural experiment stations, university-based hospitals, and collegiate sports teams) or performed by research faculty in their capacity as consultants and lecturers in the community.

ACADEMIC ORGANIZATION

Contemporary institutions of higher education are organized horizontally by divisions among fields of knowledge and vertically by ranks of authority. The dual hierarchy of professors and administrators is a structural feature of academic organization with particularly important consequences.

Knowledge is divided among discipline-based departments and interdisciplinary programs and research centers. Interdisciplinary programs have become increasingly important in the organization of research activity. However, academic appointments remain based in departments. For this reason, departments must be considered fundamental to academic organization. In chair systems, characteristic of continental European universities, one or two senior professors hold chairs and organize research programs, while the other professors serve in subsidiary roles under the direction of the chair. In American universities, departmental faculty operate independently, pursuing their own research programs, only occasionally in collaboration.

The larger structures of knowledge-based organization are the colleges and professional schools. A college of humanities will, for example, typically include all departments in the fine arts (such as music and theatre) and the humanities disciplines (such as philosophy and English). Colleges and professional schools are administrative units. The number of colleges and professional schools varies by the size of the campus. A very large campus will have separate divisions for the arts, humanities, social sciences, biological sciences, and physical sciences. It may also have half a dozen or more professional schools. A small campus may have only a single college of arts and sciences.

Colleges and universities are under no obligation to represent all fields of basic and applied knowledge, and most do not. (The term "university" does not, as many believe, refer to the universe of all fields of knowledge. Originally, it meant simply "an aggregate of persons.") New disciplines must fight for a place in the university, and old disciplines sometimes fragment or disappear altogether. Sociology and psychology, for example, both broke away from philosophy, while the nineteenth-century discipline of political economy eventually divided into political science and economics. Today the fate of disciplines in particular colleges and universities depends on a number of factors, including, most notably, student demand for courses in the department, the strength of the departmental faculty in national ratings, the ability of faculty to bring in grants and contracts, the exodus or retirement of "star" faculty, and the effectiveness of the department in making its case for new hiring. These factors have little to do with

any purely objective intellectual principles of value. Over the long run, disciplines with a strong profile in the labor market and those with access to large research grants have been least vulnerable to retrenchments. One might even argue that the modern university is moving away from a liberal arts core in the direction of a "practical arts core" composed of departments closely tied to technological and economic advance or to national security (such as economics, molecular biology, physics, and international affairs) and professional schools providing training for the highest-income occupations (such as medicine, law, and finance). Strength in this practical arts core does not necessarily come at the expense of strength in traditional liberal arts disciplines, however. In the larger universities, powerful disciplines help to subsidize less powerful ones, which, in turn, may teach a disproportionate share of students.

Modern institutions of higher education are far from *collegiua* in their authority structure, but they also do not fit an ideal-type corporate model of top-down control. Instead, decision-making practices are based, at least in principle, on divided spheres of power and ongoing consultation among the major "branches" of institutional governance. In this dual structure, both administrative and knowledge-based authority are represented. The authority structure of knowledge is constituted by the departments and, within the departments, by the professorial ranks. Advancement in the professorial hierarchy is based in principle on the quality of a faculty member's professional accomplishments (typically involving assessments of research, teaching, and service). Differences in rank are associated with both deference and income. This hierarchy moves from the temporary ranks of lecturer and instructor to the regular ranks of assistant, associate, and full professor. Highly visible full professors may be appointed to named chairs that provide both additional symbolic recognition and a separate budget for research and travel.

The top level of the administrative hierarchy is composed of a president or chancellor, who is responsible for fund-raising and interaction with important resource providers as well as overall supervision; a provost or executive vice chancellor, who is responsible for internal academic matters; and the deans of the colleges and schools. Top administrators are usually drawn from members of the faculty, although an increasing number of lower-tier institutions now hire professional managers at the presidential level. Top administrators make the ultimate decisions about budget allocations, hiring and promotion, and planning for the future. However, the faculty, at the leading authorities in their specialized domains of knowledge, retain a decisive say at least in the better institutions, over all decisions involving curricular organization and instruction. They also retain the predominant say in hiring and promotion decisions within the academic departments, expecting only very rare overrules by administrators. The faculty typically play a significant advisory role in the development of new programs and centers and in discussions of institutional priorities. Top universities depend for prestige and resources on the accomplishments of their faculty; as a general rule, the less distinguished the faculty, the more powerful the administration (Blan 1973). Faculty in nonelite institutions have, consequently, sometimes chosen to organize in collective bargaining units to control administrative discretion through contractural means (Rhoades 1998).

The unique institution of tenure greatly enhances the influence of faculty. After a six-year probationary period, assistant professors come up for a decision on promotion to tenure and accompanying advancement in rank. Tenure, a conventional rather than a legal status, guarantees lifetime employment for those who continue to hold classes and act within broad bounds of moral acceptability. Together, dual authority and tenure guarantee opposition to any administrative efforts to abandon existing programs or to downgrade the work conditions and privileges of faculty.

The primary funding for colleges and universities varies by national circumstances. Most institutions of higher education in Europe and in the developing world are state-supported. Modest fees are sometimes charged students enrolling in expensive or high-demand fields. However, the idea of tuition is only now developing. In the United States, public colleges and universities are primarily supported by state appropriations, but they also charge tuition and fees. Private colleges and universities, lacking state appropriations, charge substantially higher tuitions and, therefore, attract a larger proportion of students from the higher social classes. They also use interest from their investments to support the operating budget. In both public and private universities, research contracts and grants are another important source of funds.

COMPARISON OF NATIONAL SYSTEMS

Sociologists frequently use the term "system" to describe national patterns of higher education. This term should be used advisedly, since many national "systems" are not in fact highly coordinated. Societies with strong traditions of state planning have relatively centralized systems. The Russian, French, and Swedish systems remain among the most centralized today. But even in these countries, some private institutions operate independently of the centrally organized public system. Societies with weak traditions of state planning and strong traditions of voluntarism have decentralized and highly diverse systems. American higher education is a clear example of this pattern. Colleges and universities have been organized by religious bodies, secular elites, state legislators, and individual entrepreneurs. The result is a system of some 4,000 largely independent institutions. Institutions emulate and compete with one another in a complex ecological setting whose major dimensions are defined by level of selectivity, by institutional identity (for example, denominational or nondenominational, residential or commuter), and, perhaps most of all, by geography. One of the few forms of regulation is the requirement that curricular programs meet accreditation standards.

It is possible to classify national systems in many ways. Clark (1965) proposed dividing them by the primary influence on the coordination of the system. He placed the former Soviet Union near the pole of state-based coordination and the United States near the pole of market-based coordination. He classified Italy as the clearest example of coordination by an "academic oligarchy." Here powerful academics were the decisive influence in the development of rules and policies for the system as a whole. Clark argued further that the dominant mode of coordination has important consequences for the ethos and structure of the system. State-based systems place a strong and focused emphasis on manpower planning objectives and scientific and technical development. Market-coordinated systems place consumer interests first and compete to satisfy simultaneously the social, vocational, and educational interests of students. In "oligarchical" systems, faculty traditions and privileges are jealously preserved and institutions do not change easily.

Clark's framework remains useful. Depending on the question of interest, however, other dimensions of comparison may be equally important. National systems, for example, can also be characterized in relation to their (1) size and openness, (2) institutional diversity, and (3) interinstitutional stratification structure. Countries vary significantly across these three dimensions. The United States represents an unusually large, diverse, and stratified system. Two-thirds of secondary school students enter higher education, but they enter a very heterogeneous set of institutions that are highly stratified by acceptance rates. Germany, by contrast, represents a still relatively small, homogeneous, and unstratified structure. About one-third of German high school students enter higher education. Four-year institutions are designed to be quite similar to one another, and there is no clear ranking system among them. In the United States, therefore, life fates are determined within the system; in Germany, they are determined to a greater degree by inclusion in or exclusion from the system. Some systems in the industrialized world remain relatively small but nonetheless include also a highly differentiated elite track. This is true, for example, in France, where the *grandes ecoles* represent a clearly defined upper tier reserved for the very best students. It is also true in Japan, where an institution such as the University of Tokyo retains very close linkages to elite positions in the Japanese state and private economy. Differences across these dimensions have important implications for student consciousness. The highly educated are, for example, more likely to be seen as a separate status group in societies in which access to higher education is relatively restricted. By contrast, opportunity consciousness tends to replace class consciousness in more open systems.

SOURCES AND CONSEQUENCES OF GROWTH

Since the 1960s, the trend in the industrialized world has been in the direction of the American model, with an increasing proportion of students entering higher education but with stratification among institutions and major subjects also increasing. In most countries of Europe, for example, access to higher education is now possible from all secondary school tracks (including vocational tracks) and once-rigorous secondary school–leaving examinations have been relaxed to allow a larger flow of students into higher education. Nevertheless, both attendance and graduation rates in most of the industrialized world remain at about half that in the United States. Thus, higher education in Europe and East Asia is no longer class education, but it has not reached the level of mass education found in the United States.

Theorists of postindustrial society have suggested that the growth of the knowledge sector in the economy is behind this expansion of higher education. Estimates vary on the rate of growth of the "knowledge sector," depending on the definition used. Industries employing high proportions of professionals are growing faster, by and large, than other industries, but some estimates show them slowing down over time (Rubin and Huber 1986). Every estimate shows that they do not as yet contribute a dominant share of the gross national product or even a dominant share of the most dynamic export industries.

The growth of the knowledge sector is undoubtedly an important factor in the expansion of graduate and professional education. Its importance at the undergraduate level is more debatable. In relation to undergraduate enrollments, at least three other sources of growth must be given proper emphasis. One is the interest of states in expanding educational opportunities for their citizens. Another is the interest of students, given these opportunities, to differentiate themselves in the labor market. As secondary school completion approaches universality and higher education attendance becomes more feasible, more students have a motive to differentiate themselves by pursuing higher degrees (Meyer et al. 1979). Finally, and perhaps most important, is the increasing role played by educational credentials as a means of access to desirable jobs in the economy. Credentials are not simply (or in many cases primarily) a guarantee of technical skills. They also signal that their holders are likely to have cultural and personality characteristics sought by employers. These characteristics include middle-class manners, a competitive outlook, literacy and communication skills, and persistence. Colleges both reward and inculcate these qualities (Collins 1979).

Sociologists agree that restrictive systems of higher education tend to reproduce the social inequalities of the larger society, because the cultural information, motivation, and academic skills needed to pass rigorous examinations are highly correlated with social class. Social-class advantages do not disappear in more open systems, but these systems do generally allow a higher proportion of academically able students from the lower classes to advance. The sheer size of a system does not, however, guarantee decreasing inequality (Blossfeld and Shavit 1993). Much depends on the circumstances of students in the system and the levels of stratification within in the system. Since 1980, the number of college graduates in the United States has continued to grow, but this growth has occurred almost exclusively from among students whose families are in the top quartile of household income. Students from families in the bottom quartiles are entering at higher rates, but they have not graduated at higher rates. The reasons are clear: These students are often less prepared and less motivated to succeed, more likely to feel the press of work and family responsibilities, and more likely to struggle financially with the high cost of four years of college. They are also more likely to enter two-year institutions emphasizing job-related training.

CONTEMPORARY PRESSURES

Colleges and universities are increasingly costly operations. In state-organized systems, growth is subject to fiscal circumstances and state priorities. In market-organized systems, developments are pushed to a considerable degree by the value of college degrees in the labor market and by competition among colleges and universities. To finance the growth that allows for development of new fields without sharp cutbacks in older fields, colleges and universities compete vigorously for research funds, private gifts, and preeminence in markets for educational services. They also compete vigorously for top faculty and students, the foundations for an institution's reputation.

The high costs of operation and the increasingly competitive environment have led to several important developments. In the broad field of institutions of higher education, two quite separate market segments tend to develop: one for largely well-to-do students who can afford an expensive four-year residential experience and another for largely moderate- to lower-income students who desire convenience and flexibility as they juggle school, family, and work. In the former, the liberal arts tradition remains strong at the undergraduate level. In the latter, the emphasis is on practical, "consumer-friendly" job-relevant training. As a result of this bifurcation of market segments, the lower tier of liberal arts colleges has begun to disappear in the United States. In most cases, these institutions have transformed themselves into comprehensive colleges with large undergraduate professional programs in areas such as business, engineering, technology, and education (Breneman 1994). The same general trend toward practical, job-relevant training is evident at all but the most selective public four-year colleges and universities.

The size of operations and the increasing competition among institutions have strengthened the influence of top administrators. Managers have started to think strategically about areas of comparative advantage, a striking departure from the model of the past, which emphasized representation of all major fields of study. As a result of this strategic thinking, most departments can no longer depend on automatic replacements for departing faculty, even at the senior level. Administrators have also added resources to student services and development offices to strengthen their relations with key resource providers. For the first time in the postwar period, close partnerships have been developed at some institutions with private firms, which can provide new sources of research funding (Cohen et al. 1998). The ability to attract top students and sizable research grants has improved the position of some departments and schools while weakening the relative position of others. Within institutions, power and influence has continued to shift in the direction of the major professional school faculties and faculties in scientific disciplines with access to large federal research grants. Although still far from completely rationalized along market and bureaucratic-hierarchical lines, institutions of higher education moved significantly in this direction in the last decades of the twentieth century. Far from reinforcing the position of universities as an alternative to corporate organizations, this movement suggests a tendency for academic institutions to become more like corporations, with power concentrated in the hands of managers, who are conscious, above all, of the markets for their organization's services. Nevertheless, as long as subject-area experts remain central to research and instruction, dual authority will be necessary for academic organization—and academic and corporate forms of organization will never completely converge.

These organizational developments help to explain weaknesses of "new-class" theories. "Knowledge workers" (including professors) do not represent a stratum with social and political interests distinct from those of business elites and nonprofessional workers. Instead, the interests of the knowledge workers are decisively influenced by their particular occupational, organizational, and market circumstances (Brint 1994). This is also true within universities. Those faculty located in professional programs are usually closely allied with top administrators, as are "star" faculty, while those in traditional liberal arts are more likely to express an independent, and somewhat critical, outlook.

All segments of the faculty do, however, share certain guild-like interests in maintaining control over recruitment, employment, and working conditions. The development of new electronic technologies of learning (such as distance learning, "virtual universities," and Web-based courses) may pose a more significant long-run threat to these guild interests than any of the recent managerial efforts to rationalize campus operations. Studies thus far have not shown consistently significant differences in learning between students taking courses off-site in technologically mediated settings and those taking conventional, on-site courses. This tends to raise questions about the most powerful faculty rationale for the current campus-based organization of academic work. In the future, campuses will undoubtedly continue to exist for elite students, because of the importance of face-to-face contact for building networks that carry over into adult life. They will also be necessary for coursework and research requiring laboratory equipment. It is possible, however, that the number of campuses serving nonelite students will shrink over the long run, with campus-based instruction shifting toward still more convenient and flexible computer-mediated technologies.

REFERENCES

Blan, Peter M. 1973 *The Organization of Academic Work.* New York: John Wiley and Sons.

Blossfeld, Hans-Peter, and Yossi Shavit 1993 "Persisting Barriers: Changes in Educational Opportunities in 13 Countries." In Yossi Shavit and Hans-Peter Blossfeld, eds., *Persistent Inequalities.* Boulder, Colo.: Westview Press.

Breneman, David W. 1994 *Liberal Arts Colleges–Thriving, Surviving or Endangered?* Washington, D.C.: Brookings Institution Press.

Brint, Steven 1994 *In an Age of Experts: The Changing Role of Professionals in Politics and Public Life.* Princeton, N.J.: Princeton University Press.

——, and Jerome Karabel 1989 *The Diverted Dream: Community Colleges and the Promise of Educational Opportunity, 1900–1985.* New York: Oxford University Press.

Clark, Burton R. 1965 *The Higher Education System.* Berkeley: University of California Press.

—— 1998 *Creating Entrepreneurial Universities: Organizational Pathways of Transformation.* New York: Pergamon.

Cohen, Wesley M., et al. 1998 "Industry and the Academy: Uneasy Partners in the Cause of Technological Advance." In Roger G. Noll, ed., *Challenges to Research Universities.* Washington, D.C.: Brookings Institution Press.

Collins, Randall 1979 *The Credential Society.* New York: Academic Press.

Kerr, Clark 1963 *The Uses of the University.* New York: Harper and Row.

Marrou, Henri [1948] 1982 *A History of Education in Antiquity.* Madison: University of Wisconsin Press.

McClelland, Charles E. 1980 *State, Society, and Univeristy in Germany, 1700–1914.* Cambridge, U.K.: Cambridge University Press.

Meyer, John W., Francisco O. Ramirez, Richard Rubinson, and John Boli-Bennett 1979 "The World Education Revolution, 1950–1970." In John W. Meyer and Michael T. Hannan, eds., *National Development and the World System.* Chicago: University of Chicago Press.

Rashdall, Hastings [1895] 1936 *The Universities of Europe in the Middle Ages*, ed. F. M. Powicke and A. B. Emden, vol. 1. Oxford: Oxford University Press.

Rhoades, Gary 1998 *Managed Professionals: Unionized Faculty and Restructuring of Academic Labor.* Albany, N.Y.: SUNY Press.

Rubin, Michael R., and Mary Taylor Huber 1986 *The Knowledge Industry in the United States, 1960–1980.* Princeton, N.J.: Princeton University Press.

Steven Brint

HISPANIC AMERICANS

Despite their common linguistic heritage, Hispanic Americans are a heterogeneous and rapidly growing population that includes no less than twenty-three distinct national identities and combines recent legal and undocumented immigrants with groups whose ancestors predate the formation of the United States as we know it today. The label *Hispanic* is derived from *Hispania*, the Latin word for Iberia. In 1973 the U.S. Department of Health, Education and Welfare adopted the term "Hispanic" at the recommendation of the Task Force on Racial/Ethnic Categories to designate U.S. residents who trace their origins to a Spanish-speaking country. Following suit, the U.S. Census Bureau adopted this label as a statistical shorthand for the Hispanic national-origin groups (del Pinal and Singer 1997; Haverluk 1997). Originating in the western United States, the term "Latino" has been adopted as an alternative by groups that view "Hispanic" as a conservative pan-ethnic label imposed by the government that ignores their political and economic struggles for equality and representation. These distinctions notwithstanding, both labels serve as umbrellas for a highly diverse segment of the U.S. population.

Hispanics are one of the fastest growing segments of the U.S. population. High levels of immigration combined with high fertility rates yield a growth rate for Hispanics that is seven times that of the non-Hispanic population (U.S. Department of Commerce 1993). In 1990 the U.S. Census Bureau enumerated 22.4 million Hispanics, representing 9 percent of the aggregate population, but the 1997 population estimate reached 29.7 million, accounting for 11 percent of the national total (U.S. Department of Commerce 1998). Hispanics accounted for about one-third of national population growth during the 1980s, and their contribution to aggregate demographic growth is expected to increase in the future. Census Bureau projections made in 1995 predicted that by the year 2000 the Hispanic population would reach 31.4 million, but this estimate is conservative because annual estimates since that time have consistently been exceeded (U.S. Department of Commerce 1996). Hispanics are projected to surpass blacks as the largest minority by 2003—perhaps sooner, depending on the volume of legal and undocumented immigration from Central and South America and the Spanish-speaking Caribbean. Already in 1998, Hispanic children outnumbered black children.

Although immigration has figured prominently in the growth of the Hispanic population since 1941, its influence on demographic growth, ethnic diversification and renewal, and population replenishment has been especially pronounced during the 1980s and 1990s. Immigration was responsible for approximately one-third of the phenomenal growth of the Hispanic population in the 1980s and 1990s. At the end of the 1990s, two-thirds of the population were immigrants or children of immigrants (del Pinal and Singer 1997), and trends in fertility and immigration suggested higher growth of the Hispanic population well into the twenty-first century. By the year 2020, the U.S. Hispanic population is projected to reach 52.6 million, representing approximately 16 percent of the national total (U.S. Department of Commerce 1996).

Nearly two-thirds of all U.S. Hispanics (64 percent) are of Mexican origin, while 11 percent trace their origins to Puerto Rico, 4 percent to Cuba, and 14 percent to other Central and South American nations. An additional 7 percent of Hispanics are of unspecified national origin, which includes mixed Spanish-speaking nationalities, Spaniards, and "Hispanos," the descendants of the original Spanish settlers in what came to be known as Colorado and New Mexico. This national-origin profile of the Hispanic population has evolved since 1970 because of the differential growth of selected groups. In particular, since 1970 the Mexican, Central American, and South American population shares have increased, while the Cuban, Puerto Rican, and other Hispanic shares have declined (Bean and Tienda 1987; del Pinal and Singer 1997). Differential growth rates derive from rising immigration flows combined with high fertility among the foreign-born.

Defining features of the U.S. Hispanic population, in addition to vigorous growth, include increasing diversity, segmented integration, and rising political influence. Among the more salient aspects of diversity are immigrant and generational status, national origin, residential distribution, socioeconomic status, political participation, and reproductive behavior. Segmented integration is evident in the emergence of a solid middle class coupled with rising poverty, especially among children and immigrants, and greater geographic dispersion coupled with persisting residential concentration—nationally in a few large metropolitan areas and locally in ethnic neighborhoods within major cities (Haverluk 1997). As the number of Hispanics increases, politics also becomes increasingly important in determining their social and economic destiny. Greater political influence is already evident in the growing presence of Hispanics among elected officials. However, Hispanic voter turnout remains exceedingly low, suggesting that the potential political impacts of population growth have not fully unfolded.

The continued rapid growth of U.S. Hispanic population coupled with increased diversification raises concerns about long-term prospects for their social integration, particularly recent arrivals from Mexico, Central and South America, and the Spanish-speaking Caribbean. Among casual observers who note the emergence of ethnic neighborhoods where Spanish is spoken publicly as well as privately, the growing Hispanic presence has raised fears about the potential "Latinization" or "Hispanicization" of the United States. However, larger numbers are not likely to be the most decisive force shaping the Hispanic imprint on the U.S. social and economic landscape, for size automatically confers neither power nor status. Therefore, to evaluate the recent past and future imprint of Hispanics in the United States, what follows summarizes several themes that have developed in the sociological literature on Hispanic Americans. These include: (1) the origin of current ethnic labels, (2) the roots of diversification, (3) the changing social, demographic, and economic composition of the population, and (4) the implications for societal integration of recent social and economic trends. A concluding section summarizes key lessons from existing studies and identifies areas for future investigation.

EVOLVING LABELS

Ethnic labels are partly imposed by the host society and partly chosen by immigrant groups who wish to preserve their national identity. The labels "Spanish origin" and "Hispanic" originally were coined as terms of convenience for official reporting purposes. Before the mid-1960s, Hispanics were unfamiliar to most observers outside the Southwest, where persons of Mexican ancestry were well represented, and the Northeast, where Puerto Rican communities began to flourish after World War II. Therefore, until 1960 the "Spanish surname" concept was adequate for identifying persons of Mexican origin residing in the Southwest, and "Puerto Rican stock" was used to identify persons who resided in the Northeast (predominantly New York) and who were born in or whose parents were born in Puerto Rico. However, with increasing intermarriage, residential dispersion, and generational succession, these concepts became progressively less viable to identify persons from Mexico and Puerto Rico. Furthermore, the influx of immigrants from Central and South America and the Spanish-speaking Caribbean into areas traditionally inhabited by Mexicans and Puerto Ricans necessitated labels that could more adequately represent the growing diversity along national-origin lines.

In recognition of the growing residential, marital, and generational heterogeneity of the Spanish-speaking population, in 1970 the U.S. Census Bureau adopted the "Spanish origin" concept, which was based on self-identification and could be administered to the U.S. population on a national level (Bean and Tienda 1987). Symbolically, this decision, which was also an important political gesture, recognized Hispanics as a national minority group rather than as regionally distributed subgroups. And in 1980 the term "Hispanic" accompanied the "Spanish origin" item on the census schedule to identify persons from Latin America, Spain, and the Spanish-speaking Caribbean. However, through the 1980s the term "Latino" came into popular use as an alternative to "Hispanic." As a symbol of self-determination and self-definition, "Latino" is the label preferred by many ethnic scholars.

Despite their popular use and administrative legitimacy, pan-ethnic terms such as "Latino" or "Hispanic" are less desirable than specific national-origin designations, such as Puerto Rican,

Venezuelan, Cuban, or Mexican, which better reveal the appreciable socioeconomic and generational diversity of Hispanic Americans. Not surprisingly, diversity along national-origin lines became a major intellectual theme in the scholarly writings about Hispanics during the mid- to late 1980s and remained so at the turn of the century as the powerful forces of international and internal migration continued to diversify the composition of this rapidly growing population.

ROOTS OF DIVERSIFICATION

Social science interest in Hispanic Americans has increased greatly since 1960, and the scope of topics investigated has expanded accordingly. Whereas studies conducted during the 1960s and through the mid-1970s tended to focus on regionally localized populations, the 1980s witnessed a proliferation of designs that compare group experiences. This shift in the research agenda, which coincided with the designation of Hispanics as a national population, also brought into focus the theme of diversity and inequality among national-origin groups. More recent studies have focused on economic opportunities afforded by geographic dispersal and the changing fortunes of the burgeoning second generation—especially the children of recent immigrants.

The Hispanic presence in the United States predates the formation of the nation as we currently know it. Over a decade before the Pilgrims landed at Plymouth Rock, Spaniards had already settled in present-day New Mexico. Several subsequent events shaped the Hispanic imprint on the United States. These include (1) the Louisiana Purchase, which provided a powerful impetus for westward expansion during the 1800s; (2) the Treaty of Guadalupe Hidalgo, which ended the Mexican-American War and ceded all Mexican territories north of the Rio Grande to the United States; (3) the Mexican Revolution, which propelled thousands of Mexicans north to seek refuge from the bloody conflict; (4) the Cuban Revolution, which provided the impetus for several unprecedented refugee flows; (5) the political instability in Central America during the 1980s, which has augmented legal and undocumented migrant streams from El Salvador, Guatemala, and Nicaragua; and (6) the economic crisis of the 1980s, which encouraged higher levels of documented and undocumented migration from South America, especially Colombia, Peru, and Ecuador (U.S. Department of Commerce 1993). International events in Latin America continue to influence the U.S. Hispanic population by altering immigration streams and their reception as refugees or labor migrants.

The uneven integration experiences of the various national-origin groups are as powerful in diversifying the U.S. Hispanic population as are migration streams of largely unskilled workers from Latin America. The cultural and socioeconomic diversity of Hispanic Americans can be traced partly to the diverse modes of their incorporation into the United States and partly to the changing opportunities to become Americanized. Nelson and Tienda (1985) proposed a framework for conceptualizing the emergence, consolidation, and persistence of distinct Hispanic ethnic groups. They identified three domains of immigrant incorporation that are pertinent for understanding the socioeconomic stratification of Hispanics: (1) the mode of entry, namely, the conditions of migration as voluntary labor or as political migrants; (2) the mode of integration, that is, the climate of reception at the time of mass entrance to the host society; and (3) the circumstances that precipitate reaffirmation of national origin. The latter emphasizes the distinction between the cultural or symbolic content of Hispanic origin and the economic consequences of ethnicity that result in the formation of minority groups. This distinction between the economic and the cultural underpinnings of Hispanic ethnicity is pertinent for theorizing about the long-term integration prospects of specific nationality groups.

Along these three domains of ethnic incorporation, the major national-origin groups exhibit considerable diversity. For example, the origin of the Mexican and Puerto Rican communities can be traced to annexation, although the timing and particulars of the two cases were quite distinct. The annexation of Mexican territory resulted from a political settlement subsequent to military struggle and was followed by massive and voluntary wage-labor migration throughout the twentieth century, but particularly after 1960. The Puerto Rican annexation, which was formalized at the culmination of the Spanish-American War, will remain an incomplete process until statehood or independence is achieved. However, like the Mexican experience, the Puerto Rican presence on the U.S. mainland was characterized by a massive wage-labor flow after World War II that has ebbed and flowed according to economic conditions on both the island and the mainland.

Mexico has been the leading source country for Latin American immigrants since 1820, but the Mexican flow began in earnest during the time of the Mexican Revolution. The Bracero Program, which was a binational agreement that allowed entry of temporary agricultural workers, institutionalized migrant streams that persisted long after the formal agreement was terminated in 1964. Also, Mexico is the leading source of undocumented migrants to the United States. Although 2.3 million Mexicans obtained legal status under the provisions of the Immigration Reform and Control Act (IRCA) of 1986, undocumented migrant workers continue to enter the United States and are currently settling in such nontraditional areas as North Carolina, Atlanta, New Jersey, and New York.

These distinct modes of incorporation are sharpened by the experience of Cubans, whose socioeconomic success is as striking as the limited socioeconomic achievements of Puerto Ricans and Mexicans. Although the U.S. Cuban community was established before Fidel Castro's rise to power, Cuba's internal politics are largely responsible for the dramatic growth of the Cuban population in the United States since 1960. The Cuban Revolution created a wave of U.S.-bound political refugees who were themselves differentiated by social classes. The so-called golden exile cohort, which virtually gutted the Cuban middle class, was followed by the exodus of skilled and semiskilled workers who made up the vast majority of Cuban emigrés. Although the distinction between political and economic migrants is murky, political refugees, unlike wage-labor migrants, usually command immediate acceptance from the host society. The Cuban experience, however, stands in sharp contrast to that of later political refugees from Central America (primarily El Salvador, Nicaragua, and Guatemala), whose refugee story is one of clandestine entry and extended legal and political struggles for recognition. Probably this difference reflects the fact that Cubans were fleeing a communist regime while this was not the case for Central American refugees.

Immigration from Central and South America and the Spanish-speaking Caribbean has continued to diversify not only the national-origin composition of the Hispanic population but also the socioeconomic position of the various groups. The Dominican Republic, a country of only 8 million inhabitants, was the fourth-largest source of U.S. immigrants in 1995, including many who entered without documentation (del Pinal and Singer 1997). Although internal political problems precipitated Dominican emigration after 1960, declining economic conditions fueled the migrant stream during the 1970s. Likewise, the Central American wage labor-flow has been propelled by poor economic conditions coupled with political upheavals, especially during the 1980s and 1990s. That more than two-thirds of Central Americans residing in the United States in 1995 entered after 1980 testifies to the recency and intensity of this wage-labor flow. South American immigration to the United States derives mainly from Colombia, but there is a growing presence of Ecuadorians and Argentineans among this stream. Compared to Mexican, Central American, and Dominican flows, undocumented migrants are less common among South American immigrants.

The future role of immigration in stratifying the Hispanic population is highly uncertain, as it depends both on changes in U.S. foreign policy toward Central and South America and on revisions in immigration policy concerning the disposition of undocumented aliens and quotas on admissions of close family members of legal residents. Equally important is the role of expanded social networks in drawing new migrants to U.S. shores. Trends in the 1990s indicate that these flows are likely to continue into the foreseeable future. A comparison of wage-labor migration histories of Hispanics clearly illustrates how diverse modes of entry and integration have fueled the diversification of Hispanic Americans.

Ethnic reaffirmation and consolidation can best be understood as immigrant minority communities define themselves vis-à-vis the host society. For groups that were relatively successful in adapting to the host society, such as Cubans, national heritage acquired a highly symbolic character that is used for economic relationships when expedient and downplayed otherwise. Alternatively, class position and national origin become inextricably linked when immigrants are destined for the lower ranks of the social hierarchy, as seems to have occurred for Mexicans, Puerto Ricans, and Central Americans, or when illegal status forces many underground. Thus, the distinction between symbolic ethnicity and minority status revolves around the degree of choice groups have in controlling their socioeconomic destiny (Vincent 1974).

SOCIAL, DEMOGRAPHIC, AND ECONOMIC TRENDS

Until the 1960s, the U.S. Hispanic population was overwhelmingly Mexican and almost exclusively located in the Southwest (Haverluk 1997). But migration from Puerto Rico to the Northeast during the 1950s and the arrival of thousands of Cubans in south Florida and the Northeast following the 1959 Cuban Revolution led to the establishment of distinct Hispanic communities in Miami and New York City. Heavy migration from Mexico and other Latin American countries since the 1970s has altered the regional landscape and created a more geographically and socially heterogeneous Hispanic population whose imprint reaches well beyond the traditional states of residence.

Although Hispanics reside in all states, historically the population has been concentrated in nine states, where 85 percent of Latinos reside. These include the five southwestern states of California, Texas, Arizona, New Mexico, and Colorado, as well as New York, Florida, Illinois, and New Jersey. Two states—California and Texas—were home to more than half of all Hispanics in 1995, with Mexicans and Central Americans disproportionately concentrated in these states. Despite residential dispersion of Hispanics during the 1980s and 1990s, the visibility of distinct Hispanic communities is reinforced by persisting regional concentration along national origin lines. Puerto Ricans remain concentrated in the Northeast—predominantly in major cities of New York and New Jersey—while Cubans have become bimodally distributed in south Florida and large northeastern cities (Bean and Tienda 1987). Mexicans remain disproportionately concentrated in the major cities of the Southwest and Chicago.

Cities with large Hispanic populations witnessed the greatest growth during the 1990s (Frey 1998). The ten metro areas with the largest Hispanic populations experienced the largest population gains. These include Miami, New York City, and Chicago as well as others close to the Mexican border. In San Antonio, Miami, and El Paso, Hispanics are the majority population. In 1996, more than 6 million Hispanics resided in Los Angeles, making it the second largest Latino city in the world (behind Mexico City). Residential segregation further compounds geographic concentration by spatially isolating Hispanics of low socioeconomic status and recent immigrants from non-Hispanic whites. This segregation reinforces the cultural distinctiveness of Hispanics in regions where visible communities have been established even as increased residential dispersion concurrently fosters national integration. It is in this sense—increasing geographic dispersion combined with persisting concentration—that Hispanics experience segmented residential integration.

The demography of the Hispanic population helps in understanding other characteristics, such as educational standing and economic well-being. For instance, the high immigrant composition of the population means that many have not had the opportunity to acquire a U.S. education, or much education at all. The youthful age structure also means that Hispanic school enrollment rates are higher and retirement rates lower compared to other population groups.

A social and economic profile of the Hispanic population since 1960 provides signals of both optimism and pessimism for the long-term economic prospects of distinct nationality groups. Because education is key for economic and social mobility, as well as for integration of new arrivals, trends in educational attainment are quite revealing about the diverse futures facing Hispanics. On the one hand, from 1960 to 1996 Hispanics witnessed an unmistakable improvement in their educational attainment. Whereas only 30 percent of Hispanics aged 25 and over had completed a high school education or more in 1970, by 1996 more than 53 percent had done so (del Pinal and Singer 1997; U.S. Department of Commerce 1993). However, there have been very modest gains in educational progress since 1980. More disturbing is evidence that educational gaps between Hispanics and non-Hispanics have widened because gains of the latter have been faster. These widened gaps are evident at all levels of educational attainment, beginning in preschool. Because Hispanics average less pre-school experience, they begin elementary school with fewer social skills. Furthermore, high school noncompletion rates remain distressingly high for Mexicans and Puerto Ricans—the two groups with the longest history in the United States.

That Cubans outperform Mexicans and Puerto Ricans in educational attainment undermines simplistic explanations that immigration and language are the reasons for the continued educational underachievement of the latter. The continued arrival of new immigrants with very low levels of education also contributes to the slow educational progress of Hispanics. However, this is only a partial explanation because even among the native-born, Hispanics lag behind African Americans and non-Hispanic whites in educational attainment. Low socioeconomic status and especially the preponderance of parents with low educational attainment are major forces driving the persisting educational underachievement of Mexicans and Puerto Ricans (Bean and Tienda 1987). Most research shows that Hispanics with family backgrounds comparable to those of non-Hispanic whites are less likely to withdraw from high school and as likely to continue on to college. Unfortunately, the current educational distribution implies intergenerational perpetuation of educational disadvantages well into the future.

These educational disadvantages carry over into the labor market, yet Hispanics have higher age-specific labor-force participation rates than most groups. This labor-market advantage exists largely because immigrants have very high rates of labor-force participation and they comprise a large and growing share of the working-age Hispanic population (Bean and Tienda 1987). However, relatively low skills and limited proficiency in English channel Hispanic immigrants to low-wage jobs with few benefits. Yet because Hispanic immigrants themselves are highly diverse along national origin lines, group experiences in the U.S. labor market are equally varied.

The 1960s and 1970s witnessed a deterioration of the labor-market standing of Puerto Rican men and women, while Cubans became virtually indistinguishable from non-Hispanic whites in terms of participation rates, unemployment rates, and occupational profiles. Mexicans stand somewhere between these extremes, with greater success than Puerto Ricans in securing employment, but usually at low wages owing to their low levels of human capital. Therefore, Mexicans are more highly represented among the working poor than are non-Hispanic whites, but Puerto Ricans are more likely than other Hispanic groups to join the ranks of the nonworking poor. Puerto Rican men witnessed unusually high rates of labor-force withdrawal during the 1970s, and their labor-force behavior converged with that of economically disadvantaged blacks (Tienda, 1989).

Numerous explanations have been provided for the deteriorating labor-market position of Puerto Ricans. These include the unusually sharp decline of manufacturing jobs in the Northeast; the decline of union jobs in which Puerto Ricans traditionally concentrated; increased labor-market competition with Colombian and Dominican immigrants; and the placement of Puerto Rican workers at the bottom of a labor queue. Direct empirical tests of these working hypotheses—all with merit—have not been forthcoming. However, the dramatic improvement in the labor-market standing of Puerto Ricans during the 1990s as a result of tight labor markets and vigorous economic growth suggest that Puerto Ricans are, like blacks, located at the bottom of a hiring queue and hence more vulnerable to dislocation in accordance with the business cycle.

Less debatable than the causes of Hispanics' labor-market status are the associated economic consequences. The median family incomes of Hispanic families place them below white and above African-American families (Bean and Tienda 1987). Although this socioeconomic ranking by groups has been in place since the 1970s, in 1995 Hispanic median family income actually fell below that of African Americans (del Pinal and Singer 1997). However, the emergence of a solid middle class supports the view of segmented economic integration wherein some groups experience upward mobility while others do not.

Trends in poverty rates also indicate that Hispanics are losing ground relative to African Americans. Not only have Hispanic poverty rates risen over time, but they appear resistant to improvement when the economy rebounds. Although black poverty rates have historically exceeded Hispanic poverty rates, this situation changed during the 1990s, when black poverty dropped faster than Hispanic poverty. Thus, by 1995 black and Hispanic family poverty rates had converged, and for some population subgroups (e.g., single-mother families and children), Hispanic poverty rates exceeded those of blacks for the first time.

Poverty rates are higher among immigrants compared to native-born Hispanics; and, among specific national origin groups, Mexicans and Puerto Ricans experience the highest risk of poverty. In 1995 more than one in three Puerto Rican families had incomes below the poverty level, compared to 22 to 28 percent for the other Hispanic groups. Even Cubans, the most highly educated of the Hispanic groups, experienced poverty rates double those of non-Hispanic whites in 1995—16 versus 6 percent, respectively (del Pinal and Singer 1997). Puerto Rican families headed by single women have the highest poverty rates, as nearly two of every three such families were poor in 1995 compared to only 30 percent of Cuban and 50 percent of Mexican mother-only families. In part, these differences among national origin groups reflect the groups' nativity composition. That is, because recent arrivals have relatively low skills, even their high rates of labor-force participation cannot shield them from poverty wages. A working poverty explanation also is consistent with the failure of Hispanic poverty to rebound during periods of economic recovery. Puerto Ricans are a possible exception, inasmuch as their poverty derives more from nonwork than that of Mexicans or Central/South Americans.

INTEGRATION PROSPECTS

The changing demography of Hispanics has direct implications for the integration of Hispanic immigrant minority groups and raises questions about assimilation prospects. The rapid growth and residential concentration of the groups, coupled with the rising salience of immigration as a component of demographic growth, revitalizes Hispanic cultures and fosters maintenance of Spanish. That Hispanics have some of the lowest naturalization rates of all immigrant groups hinders their political participation and, for some observers, raises questions about their commitment to becoming American.

Puerto Ricans are U.S. citizens by birth and enjoy most of the privileges that citizenship confers, while Mexican and other Latin American immigrants who enter legally must wait at least five years to apply for citizenship. Those who enter illegally have an uncertain status in the United States as long as they remain undocumented. That Puerto Ricans have been less successful economically than Mexicans raises questions about the significance of citizenship as a requisite for socioeconomic integration. The newest wage-labor migrants—Colombians, Dominicans, and Central Americans—appear to fare better than Puerto Ricans, posing yet another challenge to conventional understandings about immigrant assimilation processes. However, it is too early to determine their long-term prospects, which likely will depend more on changes in labor market opportunities and the educational achievement of the second generation than on processes of discrimination and social exclusion. Furthermore, the growing number of undocumented migrants among these groups could undermine their social and political leverage over the short to medium term.

Although it is difficult to predict the long-term integration prospects of any group, the diversity of the Hispanic experience complicates this task further because of the uncertain future of immigration and the economy, and because the political participation of Hispanics has traditionally been low. While the spatial concentration of Hispanics allows native languages to flourish and under some circumstances promotes ethnic cohesion, some observers interpret the rise and proliferation of ethnic neighborhoods as evidence of limited integration prospects, irrespective of whether the segregation is voluntary or involuntary. An alternative interpretation of high levels of residential segregation among Hispanics, particularly recent arrivals, is that of ethnic resilience. This perspective maintains that in the face of inter-ethnic tensions and economic adversity, individuals rely on their ethnic compatriots for social supports and hence promote solidarity along ethnic lines. One implication of this view is that ethnic resilience is the *consequence* rather than the *cause* of unequal integration prospects—that Hispanics' tendency toward elaborate ethnic ties reflects their tentative acceptance by the dominant society. As such, ethnic traits become enduring rather than transitional features of Hispanic neighborhoods.

A similar debate over the integration prospects of Hispanics clouds the issue of Spanish-language retention, which is politically significant because it provides a ready target for policies designed to assimilate linguistically diverse populations and because Spanish-language retention is a ready scapegoat for the poor educational achievement of Hispanics. Spanish is the second most common language spoken at home in the United States, but it is also a limiting attribute because two of five Hispanics reported that they did not speak English well or at all in 1990 (del Pinal and Singer 1997). Although this circumstance could prohibit labor-market integration, this is not necessarily the case in ethnic neighborhoods where virtually all business transactions can be conducted in Spanish. According to Lopez (1996), in Los Angeles, Spanish has become the *lingua franca* of the city's working class. As such, the public use of Spanish symbolizes and reinforces the ethnic stratification of the Hispanic population, particularly in areas of high residential concentration. Public use of Spanish by the poorer segments of the Hispanic population not only reinforces stereotypes about poverty and immigration but also reinforces beliefs about the limited integration prospects of Hispanics.

Furthermore, considerable controversy about the socioeconomic consequences of bilingualism exists, yet the preponderance of research shows that Spanish retention and bilingualism per se are not the sources of Hispanic underachievement. Rather, the failure to acquire proficiency in English is the principal culprit (Bean and Tienda 1987). In support of the distinction between bilingualism and lack of proficiency in English, there is some evidence that bilingualism may be an asset, albeit only among the middle classes who are able to convert this skill into social and financial resources (Tienda 1982). The failure of many Hispanics to achieve proficiency in English certainly limits their economic opportunities, but it is facile to equate lack of proficiency in English with bilingualism, which does not preclude proficiency in English. Although Spanish maintenance among Hispanics is more pervasive than is the maintenance of Asian languages among respective national origin groups, language shifts clearly indicate linguistic assimilation toward English dominance (Lopez 1996). Bilingualism is pervasive among second-generation Hispanics, but by the third generation bilingualism is less common than English monolingualism (Lopez 1997b). In short, language trends indicate that Hispanics are becoming assimilated to U.S. society and culture.

Finally, the long-term integration prospects of Hispanics depend on whether and how groups from specific localities or national-origin groups mobilize themselves to serve ethnic interests. Despite the convenience of the pan-ethnic label for statistical reporting purposes, Hispanics do not represent a unified political force nationally, and the fragility of their coalitions is easily undermined by demographic, economic, and social diversification. Hispanic populations of all ages and citizenship statuses affect routine electoral politics and contribute to the electoral power of registered Hispanic voters by the weight of numbers, which is the basis of redistricting. However, greater numbers are insufficient to guarantee increased representation, particularly for a population with a large number of persons under voting age, low rates of naturalization and voter registration, and, among registered voters, a dismal record of turning out at the polls. Most important is the low adult citizenship rate of 54 percent, compared to 95 percent for non-Hispanic whites and 92 percent for blacks (Rosenfeld 1998). That voter turnout also varies by national origin further divides the fragile Hispanic political alliances, such as the Hispanic congressional caucus, by splitting the Hispanic vote along class and party lines.

In the 1992 U.S. elections, Mexican Americans cast only about 16 votes per 100 persons compared to 50 for every 100 non-Hispanic whites. Cubans cast 29 votes for every 100 persons in the 1992 election; and despite their high citizenship rate (93 percent), Puerto Ricans cast only 24 votes for every 100 residents on the U.S. mainland. Other Hispanics, with an adult citizenship rate of 43 percent, cast 17 votes for every 100 residents in 1992. Despite low rates of voting relative to population shares, Hispanics have increased their representation at all levels of political office. Rosenfeld (1998) analyzed changes in Hispanic elected officials in the five southwest states from 1960 to 1995, a period that captures the entire trajectory of Hispanic electoralism in all states except New Mexico. The analysis considered the universe of elected officials in each state, including statewide and legislative offices as well as U.S. House and Senate seats relative to the voting-age population. Empirical trends indicate the emergence of Hispanic electoralism, which he characterizes as the achievement of a steady and significant level of

Hispanic representation throughout the political system.

Thus, political behavior also points to greater political integration, albeit slow and with some uncertainty for the future. This is because most of the gains in political representation and Hispanic electoralism occurred prior to 1980, and the rapidly changing demographic and socioeconomic profile is less predictable. The political status of Hispanics underwent rapid changes during the 1990s, and the eventual outcomes are far from certain. Low rates of naturalization are beginning to reverse. For Mexicans, this has been facilitated by changes in Mexican law that permit dual citizenship in Mexico and the United States. Furthermore, legislative changes that tie access to welfare benefits to citizenship status have also encouraged many immigrants to naturalize. Finally, the higher priority given to citizens in sponsoring relatives for admission to the United States also intensified demand for naturalization. However, there persist large differentials by national origin (del Pinal and Singer 1997), with Mexicans lagging far behind Cubans and Central/South Americans.

CONCLUSIONS

Several lessons can be culled from the scholarly literature and public discourse about the social and economic future of Hispanic Americans. One is that generic labels, such as "Hispanic" and "Latino," are not useful for portraying the heterogeneous socioeconomic integration experiences of specific national-origin groups. A second major lesson is that the evolving differentials in economic standing of Hispanic national origin groups are rooted in the distinct *modes of incorporation* of each group, which in turn have profound implications for short- and long-term integration prospects. A third major lesson, which is related to the second, is that the socioeconomic imprint of Hispanic Americans will be as varied as the population itself. Changes in immigrant composition and residential segregation will play decisive parts in determining how Hispanics shape the ethnic landscape of the United States into the twenty-first century.

The nagging question is: Why does there persist a close association between Hispanic national origin and low social standing? On this matter there is much debate, but both sides accord great emphasis to the role of immigration in deciding the socioeconomic destiny of Hispanic Americans. One interpretation—the replenishment argument—emphasizes how immigration continues to diversify the composition of the population by introducing new arrivals on the lower steps of the social escalator, even as earlier arrivals experience gradual improvements in their economic and social statuses. The recency of immigration of a large share of the Hispanic population has direct implications for other demographic, social, and economic characteristics. They are younger, and less proficient in English, and many cannot vote because they are not citizens. Immigrants are also more likely than native-born Hispanics to be working class and to have lower education levels. Consistent with the predictions of classical assimilation theory, the replenishment hypothesis implies that observed differences in socioeconomic standing among Hispanics will disappear with time, irrespective of country of origin or period of arrival. Lending support to this prediction is a growing body of evidence showing that later arrivals fare better in the U.S. labor market and social institutions than do earlier arrivals.

Despite some compelling aspects of the replenishment argument, it falls short of accounting for the limited social mobility of Mexicans and Puerto Ricans, the two groups with the longest exposure to U.S. institutions and traditions. These experiences challenge the immigrant-replenishment hypothesis and place greater emphasis on the complex set of circumstances that define distinct modes of incorporation for the major national-origin groups and subsequent entry cohorts. The structural interpretation emphasizes the role of unique historical circumstances in which each national origin group established its presence in the United States and acknowledges that social opportunities depend greatly on the state of the economy and public receptiveness toward new arrivals.

Unfortunately, it is too early to evaluate the relative merits of the two hypotheses, especially in the absence of the longitudinal data required to trace socioeconomic trajectories of successive generations. That the future of immigration (its volume, source countries, and composition) is highly indeterminate further aggravates the difficulties of assessing these hypotheses. Of course, the greatest uncertainty about immigration concerns the volume and sources of illegal migrants. Finally, the socioeconomic fate of Hispanic Americans as a whole and as separate national origin groups will also depend on the extent to which Hispanic elected and appointed officials use ethnicity as a criterion for defining their political agendas. The early decades of the twenty-first century will be pivotal in resolving these uncertainties.

(SEE ALSO: *Discrimination; Ethnicity*)

REFERENCES

Bean, Frank D., and Marta Tienda 1987 *The Hispanic Population of the United States*. New York: Russell Sage Foundation.

del Pinal, Jorge, and Audrey Singer 1997 "Generations of Diversity: Latinos in the United States." *Population Bulletin* 52(3):2–48.

Frey, William H. 1998 "The Diversity Myth." *American Demographics* (June):39–43.

Haverluk, Terrence 1997 "The Changing Geography of U.S. Hispanics, 1850–1990." *Journal of Geography* 96(3):134–145.

Lopez, David E. 1996 "Language: Diversity and Assimilation." In Roger Waldinger and Mehdi Bozorgmehr, eds., *Ethnic Los Angeles*. New York: Russell Sage Foundation.

Nelson, Candace, and Marta Tienda 1985 "The Structuring of Hispanic Ethnicity: Historical and Contemporary Perspectives." *Ethnic and Racial Studies* 8:49–74.

Rosenfeld, Michael 1998 "Mexican Immigrants and Mexican American Political Assimilation." In *Migration Between Mexico and the United States: Binational Study*, vol. 3. Washington, D.C.: U.S. Commission on Immigration Reform.

Tienda, Marta 1982 "Sex, Ethnicity, and Chicano Status Attainment." *International Migration Review* 16:435–472.

—— 1989 "Puerto Ricans and the Underclass Debate." *Annals of the American Academy of Political and Social Sciences* 501:105–119.

U.S. Department of Commerce 1993 *We the American Hispanics*. Washington, D.C.: Bureau of the Census, Economics and Statistics Administration.

—— 1996 "Population Projections of the United States by Age, Sex, Race and Hispanic Origin: 1995–2050." *Current Population Reports*, P25-1130. Washington, D.C.: Bureau of the Census, Economics and Statistics Administration.

—— 1998 *The Hispanic Population in the United States: March, 1997. Detailed Tables for Current Population Reports P20-511*. Washington D.C.: Bureau of the Census, Ethnic and Hispanic Statistics Branch.

Vincent, Joan 1974 "The Structuring of Ethnicity." *Human Organization* 33:375–379.

MARTA TIENDA

HISTOGRAMS

See Statistical Graphics.

HISTORICAL ANALYSIS

See Comparative-Historical Analysis; Event-History Analysis; Historical Sociology.

HISTORICAL SOCIOLOGY

Used as a category to identify social scientific research that constructs or illustrates theory by careful attention to culturally, geographically, and temporally located facts, historical sociology (or, from the historian's vantage point, sociological history) exists as a self-conscious research orientation within both of its parent disciplines. Popular assertions in the 1950s and 1960s that history involved the study of particular facts while sociology involved the formulation of general hypotheses (see Franzosi and Mohr 1997, pp. 133–139 [for the historians' view]; Lipset 1968, pp. 22–23; McDonald 1996; cf. Mills 1959, pp. 143–164) had turned around by the early 1980s, at which time Abrams claimed that "sociological explanation is necessarily historical" (Abrams 1982, p. 2; see Burke l980, p. 28). While this integrative interpretation of the two disciplines reflects the attitudes of many researchers in the respective disciplines, a few persons remain extremely cautious about the merits of integrating them (see Ferrarotti 1997, pp. 12–13).

Abrams's claim is true for much of sociological theorizing, and sociologists realize that seminal research in their discipline has been informed by careful attention to historical information. Nonetheless, fundamental differences exist between history and sociology regarding the choice of research strategies and methodologies. Historical research emphasizes the sociocultural context of events and actors within the broad range of human culture, and when examining events that occurred in early periods of the human record it borrows from archaeology and cultural anthropology, two companion disciplines. Historians, therefore, who examine premodern material often borrow anthropological rather than sociological insights to elucidate areas where the historical record is weak, under the assumption that preindustrialized societies share basic similarities that sociological theory rarely addresses (Thomas 1963, 1971; cf. Thompson 1972). Historians are likely to choose research topics that are culturally and temporally delimited and that emerge "from the logic of events of a given place and period" (Smelser 1968, p. 35; see Bonnell 1980, p. 159). They tend to supplement secondary sources with primary texts or archival data (see Tilly 1981, p. 12).

In contrast, sociological research stresses theory construction and development, and its heavy emphasis on quantification limits most of its research to issues that affect societies after they begin to modernize or industrialize (and hence develop accurate record keeping that researchers can translate into data [see Burke 1980, p. 22]). Many of their methodological techniques—including surveys, interviews, qualitative fieldwork, questionnaires, various statistical procedures, and social-psychological experimentation—have little if any applicability to historians (Wilson 1971, p. 106). (Interestingly, however, a number of historical sociologists are utilizing narratives to elucidate sociologically traditional issues like capital–state relations and urban development [Gotham and Staples 1996; see Isaac 1997; Kiser 1996.]) Given their orientation toward theory, sociologists are likely to choose research topics that are "rooted in and generated by some conceptual apparatus" (Smelser 1968, p. 35; see Bonnell 1980, p. 159). Their data sources infrequently involve archival searches (see Schwartz 1987, p. 12) or heavy dependence on primary texts. Sociologists seem more willing than historians both to "undertake comparative analysis across national and temporal boundaries" and to present generalizations that relate to either a number of cases or universal phenomena (as opposed to a single case [Bonnell 1980, p. 159]). Reflecting these basic differences, social history, which developed out of the historical discipline, concentrates on speaking about lived experiences, while traditional historical sociologists concentrate on analysing structural transformations (Skocpol 1987, p. 28).

Although some historical sociological studies attempt either to refine concepts or rigorously to test existing theoretical explanations, more often they attempt "to develop new theories capable of providing more convincing and comprehensive explanations for historical patterns and structures" (Bonnell 1980, p. 161). When testing existing theories, historical sociologists argue deductively (by attempting to locate evidence that supports or refutes theoretical propositions), case-comparatively (by juxtaposing examples from equivalent units), or case-illustratively (by comparing cases to a single theory or concept [Bonnell 1980, pp. 162–167]). Both case comparisons and case illustrations can show either that cases share a common set of "hypothesized causal factors" that adequately explain similar historical outcomes or that they contain crucial differences that lead to divergent historical results (Skocpol 1984, pp. 378–379). In any case, historical sociologists occasionally need reminding that, in both their quantitative and qualitative research, they must avoid the "common tendency . . . to play fast and loose with time" (Jensen 1997, p. 50), since the temporal dimensions of events have profound implications for the validity of comparisons.

Sociology's founding figures—Marx and Engels, Weber, Tocqueville, and, to a limited degree, Durkheim—utilized history in the formulation of concepts and research agendas that still influence the discipline. In various works Marx and Engels demonstrated adroit sociohistorical skills, particularly in *The Eighteenth Brumaire of Louis Bonaparte* (Marx [1885] 1963) and *The Peasant War in Germany* (Engels [1870] 1926). In these studies they moved deftly among analyses of "short-term, day-to-day phenomena" of sociopolitical life, the underlying structure of that life, and "the level of the social structure as a whole" (Abrams 1982, p. 59) to provide powerful examples of historically grounded materialist analysis (see Abrams 1982, p. 63; Sztompka 1986, p. 325).

Weber, who was steeped in the ancient and medieval history of both the East and West, believed that, through the use of heuristically useful ideal types, researchers could "understand on the one hand the relationships and cultural significance of individual events in their contemporary manifestations and on the other the causes of their being historically *so* and not *otherwise*" (Weber 1949, p. 72). However much contemporary researchers have faulted his *Protestant Ethic and the Spirit Of Capitalism* (1930) for misunderstanding

Puritan religious traditions (Kent 1990; MacKinnon 1988a, 1988b) and interpreting them through preexisting philosophical categories (Kent 1983, 1985), it remains the quintessential example of his historically informed sociological studies (see Marshall 1982). Weber's extensive contribution to many aspects of historical sociology (including the linkage between "agency and structure," multicausality, ideal types, and various methodology and substantive issues) receives extensive attention in Kalberg (1994).

Variously assessed as a historian and a political scientist, Tocqueville also contributed to historical sociology with books that examined two processes—democratization (in the United States) and political centralization (in France)—that remain standard topics of historical sociological research (Tocqueville [1835] 1969, [1858] 1955; see Poggi 1972; Sztompka 1986, p. 325). Similar praise for historical sensitivity, however, has not always gone to a fellow Frenchman of a later era, Emile Durkheim, whose concepts were scornfully called by one historical sociologist an "early form of ahistoricism" (Sztompka 1986, p. 324). Bellah, nevertheless, asserted that "history was always of central importance in Durkheim's sociological work" (Bellah 1959, p. 153) and even argued that, "at several points Durkheim went so far as to question whether or not sociology and history could in fact be considered two separate disciplines" (Bellah 1959, p. 154). Indeed, recent research has identified Durkheim's cross-disciplinary sensitivity in his analysis of the history of French education (Emirbayer 1996a) and "the structures and processes of civil society" (Emirbayer 1996b, p. 112). Nevertheless, Abrams's compromise interpretation may be most accurate concerning most of Durkheim's work. He acknowledges that Durkheim identified the broad process of the Western transition to industrialization, even though his "extremely general framework" demands specific historical elaboration (Abrams 1982, p. 32).

Despite the prominence of history within major studies by sociology's founding figures, subsequent sociologists produced few historically informed works until the late 1950s (cf. Merton 1938). Also during this period (in 1958) the historian Sylvia Thrupp founded the *Journal of Comparative Studies in Society and History*, and since then other journals have followed that are sympathetic to historical sociology (including *Journal of Family History*, *Journal of Interdisciplinary History*, *Journal of Social History*, *Labor History*, *Past and Present*, *Social History*, and *Social Science History* [Bart and Frankel 1986, pp. 114–116]). The output of interdisciplinary books continued growing throughout the 1960s, and by the 1970s "the sociological study of history achieved full status within the discipline" (Bonnell 1980, p. 157, see p. 156; see Smith, 1991 [for a clear historical overview]).

Studies of capitalist expansion examine such topics as the emergence and consequences of the Industrial Revolution, the rise of the working class, population growth, and the developmental operations of the modern world system. Exemplary studies include Smelser's *Social Change in the Industrial Revolution* (1959) and Wallerstein's *The Modern World System* (1974). Basing his middle-range model on Parsons's general theory of action, Smelser deduced a supposedly universal sequence through which all changes move that involve structural differentiation in industrializing societies (see Bonnell 1980, p. 162; Skocpol 1984, p. 363). He illustrated the applicability of his framework by drawing examples from the economic changes within the British cotton industry during the nineteenth century, followed by additional examples of changes to the lives and activities of workers in that industry. These historical facts, however, were secondary to the model itself.

Wallerstein borrowed from Marxism and functionalism to devise a "world system" theory of the global economy that purports to be universal in its interpretive and explanatory power. He argued that after the late fifteenth and early sixteenth centuries, a "world economy" developed in which economically advantaged and politically strong areas, called "core states," dominated other economically nondiversified and politically weak "peripheral areas." Through "semi-peripheral areas" that serve as "middle trading groups in an empire," resources flow out of the peripheral areas and into the core states for capitalist development, consumption, and often export back to their areas of origin (Wallerstein 1974, pp. 348–350). Within this model Wallerstein mustered a phalanx of historical facts in order to demonstrate the emergence of the world economy above the limited events in various nation-states, and in doing so he "has promoted serious historical work within sociology" (Tilly 1981, p. 42).

E.P. Thompson's exemplary study (1963) took the sociological concept of "class" and presented its historical unfolding in England between 1780 and passage of the parliamentary Reform Bill in 1832 (Thompson 1963, p. 11). He argued that "the finest-meshed sociological net cannot give us a pure specimen of class . . . . The relationship [of class] must always be embodied in real people and in a real context" (p. 9). By the end of the era that he examined, "a more clearly-defined class consciousness, in the customary Marxist sense, was maturing, in which working people were aware of continuing both old and new battles on their own" (p. 712). His study stands among the finest examples of historically careful development of a sociological concept.

In contrast to the economic focus on issues involving capitalist expansion, studies of the growth of national states and systems of states examine political topics such as state bureaucratization, the democratization of politics, revolutions, and the interaction of nations in the international arena. Three heralded historical sociology studies in this genre are Eisenstadt (1963), Moore (1966), and Skocpol (1979). Eisenstadt studied twenty-two preindustrial states that had centralized, impersonal, bureaucratic empires through which political power operated. After a tightly woven and systematic analysis of comparative social, political, and bureaucratic patterns, he concluded that "in any of the historical bureaucratic societies, their continued prominence was dependent upon the nature of the political process that developed in the society: first, on the policies of the rulers; second, on the orientations, goals, and political activities of the principal strata; and third, on the interrelations between these two" (Eisenstadt 1963, p. 362).

Moore's case studies of revolutions in England, France, the United States, China, Japan, and India sought "to understand the role of the landed upper classes and peasants in the bourgeois revolutions leading to capitalist democracy, the abortive bourgeois revolutions leading to fascism, and the peasant revolutions leading to communism" (Moore 1966, p. xvii). His own sympathies, however, lay in the development of political and social systems that fostered freedom, and he realized the importance of "a violent past" in the development of English, French, and American democracies (pp. 39, 108, 153). He concluded "that an independent nobility is an essential ingredient in the growth of democracy" (p. 417) yet realized that a nobility's efforts to free itself from royal controls "is highly unfavorable to the Western version of democracy," unless these efforts occur in the context of a bourgeois revolution (p. 418).

Skocpol scrutinized the "causes and processes" of social revolutions in France, Russia, and China "from a nonvoluntarist, structural perspective, attending to international and world-historical, as well as intranational, structures and processes." While doing so she moved "states—understood as potentially autonomous organizations located at the interface of class structures and international situations—to the very center of attention" (Skocpol 1979, p. 33). She concluded that "revolutionary political crises, culminating in administrative and military breakdowns, emerged because the imperial states became caught in cross-pressures between intensified military competition or intrusions from abroad and constraints imposed on monarchical responses by the existing agrarian class structures and political institutions" (p. 285).

Underappreciated by theorists of historical sociology is the growing number of studies that apply sociological categories and concepts to the emergence and development of historically significant religious traditions (see Swatos 1977). By doing so, these scholars have surpassed the traditional sociological and historical colleagues who limit their efforts primarily to political and structural issues, especially ones arising during the late eighteenth to twentieth centuries. Swanson (1960), for example, coded material on fifty hunting-and-gathering societies in an effort to connect religion and magic to social structure, and subsequently analyzed relationships between constitutional structures and religious beliefs around the period of the Protestant Reformation (Swanson 1967). The emergence and early development of major religious traditions has received considerable sociological attention. They include, for example, analyses of early Christianity as a social movement (Blasi 1988), as a millenarian movement (Gager 1975; see Lang 1989, p. 339; Meeks 1983, pp. 173–180), and as a dramatically expansive young religion during the first centuries of the Common Era (Stark 1996). Concepts from sociological studies of modern sectarianism have informed historical studies of Mahayana Buddhism (Kent 1982) and

Valentinian Gnosticism (Green 1982). Weberian examinations continue to influence historically grounded studies of numerous world religions, including ancient Judaism (Zeitlin 1984), Islam (Turner 1974), and other religious traditions from around the world (see Swatos 1990). On a grand scale, religion figures prominently in the work of globalization theorist Roland Robertson (e.g., Robertson 1985; see Robertson 1992).

The historically grounded research in the sociology of religion, along with the works of Eisenstadt and others, suggests that future historical sociological studies will continue pushing beyond the confines of modern, macrosociological topics and into a wide range of premodern historical areas. Likewise, historical issues likely will become more consciously developed in microsociological studies (see Abrams 1982, pp. 227–266), and there will appear more sociologically informed historical examinations of cultural development (still exemplified by Elias 1978). Nonetheless, considerable macrosociological research still needs to be performed on historical issues affecting preindustrializing and Third World countries as well as on recent international realignments between forms of capitalism and communism.

Sometimes coupled with communism's collapse is the reappearance of nationalism and ethnic violence in various parts of the world. The deterioration of the Balkans in what (under Soviet influence) was Yugoslavia, for example, prompted Veljko Vujacic (1996) to develop "a comparative examination of contemporary Russian and Serbian nationalism" by attempting "to demonstrate the usefulness of some of Weber's key theoretical ideas on nations, nationalism, and imperialism"(p. 789). Specifically, he tried "to show how long-term historical and institutional legacies, shared memories, and defining political experiences, played themselves out in the contemporary period, influencing the different availability of mass constituencies in Russia and Serbia for nationalist mobilization under the auspices of new 'empire-saving coalitions'" (p. 789). Despite being faced with the difficult task of utilizing Weberian theory in this comparative context, Vujacic warned, "there is no need to gloss over the frequently bloody and unpredictable consequences of [people's] struggles with unduly abstract sociological generalizations. Instead, we should theorize our narrative, while giving contingency its place" (p. 790). In essence,

narrative accuracy must not be compromised by the demands of theory building.

Innovative methodological techniques continue to enter the historical sociology realm. As outlined by Roberto Franzosi and John Mohr, two such methodologies are network analysis (mapping "the connectivities among people, groups, and organizations" [Franzosi and Mohr 1997, pp. 145–154]) and content analysis ("the use of formal methods for extracting meanings from textual materials" [Franzosi and Mohr 1997, p. 149; see Tilly 1997, pp. 219ff.]). These and other methodologies contribute to the production of respected historical sociology studies on such topics as capitalist expansion, "the growth of national states and systems of states," collective action (Tilly 1981, p. 44; and see Tarrow 1996 for a review of Tilly's work), and the sociology of religious development. (Not to be overlooked, however, are studies of both capital–state relations and urban development and poverty [Gotham and Staples 1996].) Discussion will continue over the relative merits of globalization theory, world systems theory, and modernization theories (see Mandalios 1996), and globalization theory likely will expand and modify to include greater emphasis on regional world systems, particularly in East–Southeast Asia (Ikeda 1996). The extent to which Michel Foucault's historically grounded, poststructuralist work on the relationships among cultural meanings, self-identities, and social control extend into the historical sociology corpus (for example, Foucault 1979, 1980; Dean 1994; see Seidman 1994, pp. 212–233) remains to be seen.

As older sociological methodologies disseminate within history and newer ones enter the discipline, we will continue to appreciate "the importance of historical sociology in enlarging our understanding of the historical variations in class, gender, revolutions, state formation, religion, and cultural identity" (Somers 1996, p. 53). On a practical level, the profile of historical sociology in its respective disciplines will be enhanced as universities extend cross-appointments of faculty, cross-list courses in methodologies and other topics, share theses and dissertation supervisory responsibilities among history and sociology faculties; encourage interdepartmental co-sponsorship of visiting speakers, and generally enhance the learning and training environments for graduate students and staff. On a professional level, the American Sociological Association continues to sponsor a section in its annual conference entitled "Comparative and Historical Society."

(SEE ALSO: *Comparative-Historical Sociology*; *Event History Analysis*)

REFERENCES

Abrams, Philip 1982 *Historical Sociology*. Shepton Mallet, U.K.: Open House.

Bart, Pauline, and Linda Frankel 1986 *The Student Sociologist's Handbook*, 4th ed. New York: Random House.

Bellah, Robert N. 1959 "Durkheim and History." *American Sociological Review* 24:447–461. Reprinted in Robert A. Nisbet, ed., *Emile Durkheim*, Englewood Cliffs, N.J.: Prentice-Hall, 1965.

Blasi, Anthony J. 1988 *Early Christianity as a Social Movement*. New York: Peter Lang.

Bonnell, Victoria E. 1980 "The Uses of Theory, Concepts, and Comparison in Historical Sociology." *Comparative Studies in Society and History* 22:156–173.

Burke, Peter 1980 *Sociology and History*. London: George Allen and Unwin.

Dean, Mitchell 1994 *Critical and Effective Histories: Foucault's Methods and Historical Sociology*. London: Routledge.

Eisenstadt, S. N. 1963 *The Political System of Empires*. New York: Free Press.

Elias, Norbert 1978 *The Civilizing Process: vol. 1. The History of Manners*, trans. Edmund Jephcott. New York: Urizen Books.

Emirbayer, Mustafa 1996a "Durkheim's Contribution to the Sociological Analysis of History." *Sociological Forum* 11:263–284.

—— 1996b "Useful Durkhiem." *Sociological Theory* 14:109–130.

Engels, Frederick (1870) 1926 *The Peasant War in Germany*, 2nd ed., trans. Moissaye J. Olgin. New York: International Publishers.

Ferrarotti, Franco 1997 "The Relation Between History and Sociology: Synthesis or Conflict?" *International Journal of Contemporary Sociology* 34:1–16.

Foucault, Michele 1979 *Discipline and Punish: The Birth of the Prison*. New York: Vintage.

—— 1980 *The History of Sexuality: vol. 1. An Introduction*. New York: Vintage.

Franzosi, Roberto, and John W. Mohr 1997 "New Directions in Formalization and Historical Analysis." *Theory and Society* 26:133–160.

Gager, John G. 1975 *Kingdom and Community: The Social World of Early Christianity*. Englewood Cliffs, N.J.: Prentice-Hall.

Gotham, Kevin Fox, and William G. Staples 1996 "Narrative Analysis and the New Historical Sociology." *The Sociological Quarterly* 37:481–501.

Green, Henry A. 1982 "Ritual in Valentinian Gnosticism: A Sociological Interpretation." *Journal of Religious History* 12:109–124.

Ikeda, Satoshi 1996 "The History of the Capitalist World-System vs. the History of East-Southeast Asia." *Review* (Fernand Braudel Center) 19:49–77.

Isaac, Larry W. 1997 "Transforming Localities: Reflections on Time, Causality, and Narrative in Contemporary Historical Sociology." *Historical Methods* 30:4–12.

Jensen, Gary F. 1997 "Time and Social History." *Historical Methods* 30:46–57.

Kalberg, Stephen 1994 *Max Weber's Comparative-Historical Sociology*. Oxford: Polity Press.

Kent, Stephen A. 1982 "A Sectarian Interpretation of the Rise of Mahayana." *Religion* 12:311–332.

—— 1983 "Weber, Goethe, and the Nietzschean Allusion: Capturing the Source of the 'Iron Cage' Metaphor." *Sociological Analysis* 44:297–319.

—— 1985 "Weber, Goethe, and William Penn: Themes of Marital Love." *Sociological Analysis* 46:315–320.

—— 1990 "The Quaker Ethic and the Fixed Price Policy: Max Weber and Beyond." In William H. Swatos, ed., *Time, Place, and Circumstance: Neo-Weberian Studies in Comparative Religious History*. Westport, Conn.: Greenwood Press.

Kiser, Edgar 1996 "The Revival of Narrative in Historical Sociology: What Rational Choice Theory Can Contribute." *Politics and Society* 24:249–271.

Lang, Graeme 1989 "Oppression and Revolt in Ancient Palestine: The Evidence in Jewish Literature from the Prophets to Josephus." *Sociological Analysis* 49:325–342.

Lipset, Seymour Martin 1968 "History and Sociology: Some Methodological Considerations." In Seymour Martin Lipset and Richard Hofstadter, eds., *Sociology and History: Methods*. New York: Basic Books.

MacKinnon, Malcolm H. 1988a "Calvinism and the Infallible Assurance of Grace: The Weber Thesis Reconsidered." *British Journal of Sociology* 39:143–177.

—— 1988b "Weber's Exploration of Calvinism." *British Journal of Sociology* 39:178–210.

Mandalios, John 1996 "Historical Sociology." In Bryan S. Turner, ed., *The Blackwell Companion to Social Theory*. Oxford: Blackwell.

Marshall, Gordon 1982 *In Search of the Spirit of Capitalism: An Essay on Max Weber's Protestant Ethic Thesis*. New York: Columbia University Press.

Marx, Karl (1885) 1963 *The Eighteenth Brumaire of Louis Bonaparte*, 3rd ed. New York: International Publishers.

McDonald, Terrence J. 1996 "What We Talk About When We Talk about History: The Conversation of History and Sociology." In Terrence J. McDonald, ed., *The Historic Turn in the Human Sciences*. Ann Arbor: University of Michigan Press.

Meeks, Wayne A. 1983 *The First Urban Christians: The Social World of the Apostle Paul*. New Haven, Conn.: Yale University Press.

Merton, Robert 1938 "Science, Technology, and Society in Seventeenth-Century England." *Osiris* 4:360–632. Reprinted with a new preface, New York: Harper Torchbooks, 1970.

Mills, C. Wright 1959 *The Sociological Imagination*. New York: Oxford University Press.

Moore, Barrington, Jr. 1966 *Social Origins of Dictatorship and Democracy*. Boston: Beacon Press.

Poggi, Gianfranco 1972 *Images of Society: Essays on the Sociological Theories of Tocqueville, Marx, and Durkheim*. Stanford, Calif.: Stanford University Press.

Robertson, Roland 1985 "The Sacred and the World System." In Phillip E. Hammond, ed., *The Sacred in a Secular Age*. Berkeley: University of California Press.

—— 1992 *Globalization: Social Theory and Global Culture*. London: Sage.

Schwartz, Mildred A. 1987 "Historical Sociology in the History of American Sociology." *Social Science History* 11:1–16.

Seidman, Steven 1994 *Contested Knowledge: Social Theory in the Postmodern Era*. Oxford: Routledge.

Skocpol, Theda 1979 *States and Social Revolutions*. London: Cambridge University Press.

—— 1984 "Emerging Agendas and Recurrent Strategies in Historical Sociology." In Theda Skocpol, ed., *Vision and Method in Historical Sociology*. Cambridge, U.K.: Cambridge University Press.

—— 1987 "Social History and Historical Sociology: Contrasts and Complementarities." *Social Science History* 11:17–30.

Smelser, Neil, J. 1959 *Social Change in the Industrial Revolution: An Application to of Theory to the British Cotton Industry*. Chicago: University of Chicago Press.

—— 1968 *Essays in Sociological Explanation*. Englewood Cliffs, N.J.: Prentice-Hall.

Smith, Dennis 1991 *The Rise of Historical Sociology*. Oxford: Polity Press.

Somers, Margaret R. 1996 "Where Is Sociology After the Historic Turn? Knowledge Cultures, Narrativity, and Historical Epistemologies." In Terrence J. McDonald, ed., *The Historic Turn in the Human Sciences*. Ann Arbor: University of Michigan Press.

Stark, Rodney 1996 *The Rise of Christianity: A Sociologist Reconsiders History*. Princeton, N.J.: Princeton University Press.

Swanson, Guy 1960 *The Birth of the Gods: The Origin of Primitive Beliefs*. Ann Arbor: University of Michigan Press.

—— 1967 *Religion and Regime: A Sociological Account of the Reformation*. Ann Arbor: University of Michigan Press.

Swatos, William H., Jr. 1977 "The Comparative Method and the Special Vocation of the Sociology of Religion." *Sociological Analysis* 38:106–114.

—— ed. 1990 *Time, Place and Circumstance: Neo-Weberian Studies in Comparative Religious History*. Westport, Conn.: Greenwood Press.

Sztompka, Piotr 1986 "The Renaissance of Historical Orientation in Sociology." *International Sociology* 1:321–337.

Tarrow, Sidney 1996 "The People's Two Rhythms: Charles Tilly and the Study of Contentious Politics. A Review Article." *Comparative Studies in Society and History* Vol. 38, 3:586–600.

Thomas, Keith 1963 "History and Anthropology." *Past and Present* 24:3–24.

—— 1971 *Religion and the Decline of Magic*. New York: Scribner's.

Thompson, E. P. 1972 "Anthropology and the Discipline of Historical Context." *Midland History* 1:41–55.

—— 1963 *The Making of the English Working Class*, 1966 ed., New York: Vintage Books.

Tilly, Charles 1981 *As Sociology Meets History*. New York: Academic Press.

—— 1997 *Roads from Past to Future*. Oxford: Rowman and Littlefield.

Tocqueville, Alexis de (1835) 1969 *Democracy in America*, 2 vols., trans. George Lawrence. London: Collins.

—— (1858) 1955 *The Old Regime and the French Revolution*, 4th ed., trans. Stuart Gilbert. Garden City, N. Y.: Doubleday.

Turner, Bryan S. 1974 *Weber and Islam: A Critical Study*. London: Routledge and Kegan Paul.

Vujacic, Veljko 1996 "Historical Legacies, Nationalist Mobilization, and Political Outcomes in Russia and Serbia: A Weberian View." *Theory and Society* 25:763–891.

Wallerstein, Immanuel 1974 *The Modern World System*. New York: Academic Press.

Weber, Max 1930 *The Protestant Ethic and the Spirit of Capitalism*, trans. and ed. Talcott Parsons. New York: Scribners. 1976 Reprint. (originally published in German in 1920).

—— 1949 *The Methodology of the Social Sciences*, trans. and eds. E. Shils and F. Finch. New York: Free Press.

Wilson, B. R. 1971 "Sociological Methods in the Study of History." *Transactions of the Royal Historical Society* (5th ser.) 21:101–118.

Zeitlin, Irving 1984 *Ancient Judaism: Biblical Criticism from Max Weber to the Present*. New York: Polity Press.

STEPHEN A. KENT

HOMELESSNESS

Literal homelessness—lacking permanent housing of one's own—is a condition that has been present throughout human history. It has always been dangerous as well, given the necessity of shelter for survival. Nevertheless, the routine occurrence of homelessness in the past probably prevented the problem from generating any extraordinary degree of collective concern. Members of premodern societies often experienced losses or disruptions of residence as a result of food scarcity, natural disaster, epidemic disease, warfare, and other environmental and self-inflicted circumstances. Such forces contributed to the likelihood, if not the expectation, that most people would be homeless at some point in the life cycle.

Ironically, now that homelessness is relatively rare in Western societies, it has achieved a special notoriety. When shelter security becomes the norm, the significance of housing evolves beyond the purely functional. Homes, like jobs, constitute master statuses, anchoring their occupants in the stratification system. Hence, being without a home portends a more general and threatening *disaffiliation*, defined as "a detachment from society characterized by the absence or attenuation of the affiliative bonds that link settled persons to a network of interconnected social structures" (Caplow et al. 1968, p. 494). This is the broadest meaning associated with the concept of homelessness, at the opposite end of the continuum from its literal definition.

Homelessness, broadly construed, first appeared on the American scene during the early stages of colonial settlement, with paupers, indentured servants, petty criminals, unemployed seamen, and the mentally impaired forming a pool of individuals at risk of vagrancy. It began to assume major proportions as a social problem in the United States near the end of the nineteenth century. Over the several preceding decades, urban homeless populations had emerged in response to a series of events at the national level, including Civil War displacement; the arrival of impoverished European immigrants; seasonal employment patterns in agriculture, construction, and the extractive industries; and severe economic setbacks in the early 1870s and 1890s (Rooney 1970).

As a makeshift remedy, downtown warehouses and old hotels were converted into inexpensive, dormitory-style lodging facilities. The proximity of the lodging facilities to one another, along with the distinctive mix of commercial and recreational establishments growing up around them, helped to concentrate the homeless physically in areas that came to be known as *skid rows* (supposedly named for a "skid road" in Seattle used to slide logs downhill). At the turn of the century, these areas were less burdened by the seedy images later evoked by the term "skid row." Instead, they were vibrant neighborhoods offering a temporary resting place and a range of services to thousands of tramps, the mobile workers who laid the foundation for the U.S. industrial economy.

The manpower needs created by World War I subsequently drained skid row districts, but a pool of footloose veterans replenished them at war's end. An even greater surge in homelessness—one extending well beyond the boundaries of skid row—was soon sparked by the Great Depression. The widespread hardship of the period forced previously domiciled individuals into a migrant lifestyle, and shantytowns (dubbed "Hoovervilles") sprang up in urban and rural settings alike. These new manifestations of homelessness in turn stimulated the first generation of sustained research on the subject among sociologists. Anderson (1940), Sutherland and Locke (1936), and other scholars conducted studies of different segments of the homeless population as part of the Depression-era relief effort.

A second generation of research started in the 1950s. Large-scale single-city surveys—many of which were funded by urban renewal agencies—informed the debate over what to do about deteriorating skid row areas (Bahr and Caplow 1974; Bogue 1963). Demographic data obtained during the surveys showed homeless respondents to be predominantly male, white, single, older, and of local origins. The surveys also lent credibility to the popular view of the homeless as deviant "outsiders." Depending on the city under examination, between one-fourth and one-half reportedly were problem drinkers, a higher percentage had spent time in jail or prison, most were unable or unwilling to hold down steady employment, many suffered from poor health, and few were enmeshed in supportive social networks. This negative profile based on the survey findings was countered by a parallel body of ethnographic evidence. Field observers like Wallace (1965) portrayed the homeless of skid row in subcultural terms, as a cohesive group with their own language, norms, and status hierarchy. Participation in the subculture was believed to help members cope with a problem more serious than their presumed deviance: extreme poverty.

In the 1970s, almost a century after skid row became a recognizable entity in the American city, its demise seemed imminent. Urban renewal and redevelopment projects had eliminated much of the infrastructure of skid row, while slackening demand for short-term unskilled labor was eroding one of the few legitimate economic roles the area could claim to play. Consequently, several investigators predicted skid row's disappearance and, by implication, the decline of the U.S. homeless population (Lee 1980). Yet within a decade of such forecasts, homelessness had resurfaced as an important national issue. During the 1980s media coverage of the so-called *new homeless* increased dramatically, and federal legislation (most notably the McKinney Act) was formulated to address their plight. The amount of social scientific inquiry rose as well. Indeed, the recent outpouring of scholarly monographs on the topic has surpassed that of any prior generation of research.

Despite this renewed interest, what is known about contemporary homelessness remains limited, for several reasons. Unlike most groups surveyed by sociologists, the homeless are not easily reached at residential addresses or telephone numbers. The demolition of skid row districts in general and of single-room-occupancy (SRO) hotels in particular, accompanied by social control measures designed to reduce the public visibility of drunks, panhandlers, and other "undesirables," has intensified the difficulties involved in finding homeless people, pushing a higher percentage of them into more dispersed, obscure locations. Those referred to as the *doubled up*, who stay with settled relatives or friends, are virtually inaccessible to investigators. Also poorly captured by surveys are the many individuals for whom homelessness is of brief duration or episodic in character. Even among the homeless who can be found, participation rates fall far short of perfect. The prospect of further stigma and humiliation keeps some from admitting their condition, thus excluding them from sample membership, while others are too suspicious or incoherent to take part in an interview.

Finally, the political context surrounding the latest wave of research magnifies the significance of each methodological obstacle just identified. Because the homelessness issue has been transformed into a referendum on the ability of the state to meet its citizens' needs, liberals and conservatives both use the slightest technical shortcoming as ammunition with which to attack any study unfavorable to their own position. Similarly, members of both camps—not to mention the media, advocacy groups, government agencies, and other actors—selectively draw on research results to frame the homelessness problem in a way that attracts (or diverts) public attention. Thus, apparently straightforward "facts" about homelessness—and there are few of these to begin with—become matters open to debate.

"Snapshot," or single-point-in-time, data on the size of the national homeless population illustrate the uncertain nature of the existing knowledge base. According to an early assertion by advocates, the number of homeless in the United States as of 1982 stood at 2.2 million, or approximately 1 percent of the total population of the country (Hombs and Snyder 1982). However, only two years later the U.S. Department of Housing and Urban Development (HUD) (1984) compiled a series of estimates, extrapolated from street counts and surveys of informants and shelter operators, that yielded a "most reliable" range of 250,000 to 350,000. A 1987 Urban Institute study arrived at a figure—500,000 to 600,000 homeless nationwide on a single day—that fell between the advocate and HUD extremes (Burt and Cohen 1989). More recently, the Census Bureau enumerated 240,000 homeless people in the course of its massive yet heavily criticized 1990 S-night (street and shelter) operation (U.S. Bureau of the Census 1992).

Although most experts now dismiss the advocate-generated 2 million figure as groundless, the remaining estimates vary considerably. One explanation for this variation is that all are *point estimates*, depicting the size of the homeless population at a specific moment (e.g., a particular day or week). To the extent that the number of homeless changed during the 1980s, studies conducted on different dates should produce different results. Indeed, the trend retrospectively uncovered by several investigators (Jencks 1994)—slow growth early in the decade, rapid increase in the middle, and decline after 1987–1988—seems consistent with the magnitudes of the HUD, Urban Institute, and Census estimates. Others believe that the homeless population grew rapidly throughout the decade, by as much as 25 percent annually in some places. That growth rate could be inflated, though, given the relative stability documented in one of the few large cities (Nashville, Tennessee) for which longitudinal observations are available (Lee 1989).

It is hard to know whether the most credible point estimates accurately reflect the true scope of homelessness. If the homeless population is marked by high turnover, with many people entering and exiting quickly, the total number who experience homelessness over a longer period will be grossly underestimated by a point estimate. Two recent *period-prevalence* studies illustrate this dynamic. In the first study, counts of unduplicated shelter users in New York and Philadelphia suggest that roughly 1 percent of the residents of both cities are homeless each year, and the figure rises to 3 percent for a three-to-five-year interval (Culhane et al. 1994). In the second, 15 percent of the respondents to a nationally representative telephone survey reported that they had been literally homeless or had doubled up with someone else during their lifetimes (Link et al. 1995).

While definitional and methodological differences underlie much of the disagreement over the magnitude of the homeless population, generalizations about its composition have been complicated by (1) the selective emphasis of many inquiries on atypical "slices" of the whole (homeless veterans, the mentally ill, etc.) and (2) real variation in the characteristics of the homeless across communities. Contrary to media reports and popular perceptions, the modal homeless individual is still an unattached male with local roots, similar in fundamental ways to his skid row counterpart of the 1950s or 1960s. Yet there clearly have been significant compositional shifts during the intervening period. Blacks and other minorities, rarely found on skid row, are now overrepresented among the homeless, and women, children, young adults, and high school graduates constitute larger segments of the population both absolutely and proportionally than they once did (Burt 1992; Rossi 1989). Family groupings, usually headed by the mother alone, have become more common as well. Taking these elements of demographic continuity and change together, perhaps the safest conclusion to be drawn is that a trend toward greater diversity distinguishes the new homelessness from the old.

The same conclusion applies with respect to deviant characteristics. Alcoholism, which previously constituted the most noticeable form of deviance among the homeless, is now rivaled by other kinds of substance abuse, and mental illness has surpassed physical illness as an object of public concern. Beyond a rough consensus regarding the greater variety of such problems in the current homeless population, little of a definitive nature is known about them. For example, a review of nine studies cited mental illness prevalence rates that run from a low of one-tenth to a high of one-half of all homeless (U.S. General Accounting Office 1988), and occasional reports suggest that as many as 90 percent are at least mildly clinically impaired. This wide range leaves room for opposing arguments: on the one hand, that pervasive mental illness is the principal cause of contemporary homelessness; on the other, that its presumed causal role represents a stereotypic myth created by the visibility of a small minority of disturbed folk.

Even if the extent of mental illness has been exaggerated, there can be no doubt that the general well-being of the homeless remains low. This is hardly surprising in light of the stresses that accompany life on the street. The absence of shelter exposes homeless persons to the weather, violence, and other threatening conditions. They have trouble fulfilling basic needs that most Americans take for granted, such as finding a job, obtaining nutritionally adequate meals, getting around town, washing clothes, storing belongings, and locating toilet and bathing facilities. To cope with these difficulties, homeless people draw on a repertoire of subsistence strategies (Snow and Anderson 1993). One of the most common is temporary low-wage employment, often as a day laborer. For some, *shadow work*—engaging in unconventional activities outside the formal economy (scavenging, panhandling, selling blood, trading junk)—offers a means of survival. Others resort to crime, especially petty theft, prostitution, and drug dealing, or become dependent on service providers.

While frequently creative, such strategies heighten the physical health risks to which the homeless are subjected. Compared to the settled population, a larger percentage of homeless individuals suffer from chronic disorders, and rates for most infectious diseases are at least five to six times greater (Wright et al. 1998). The collective consequence of these conditions is a drastically shortened life expectancy. However, to identify homelessness as the direct cause of higher morbidity and mortality would be an oversimplification. Preexisting health problems can reduce a person's employability, prompting a downward "drift" toward homelessness and lessening the chances of returning to a normal life. Homelessness can also be a complicating factor in the provision of health care. In part because of their circumstances (e.g., lacking transportation, distrusting authorities, being unable to store medicine), many homeless miss appointments and do not follow through with their prescribed treatment. They are, in short, less than ideal patients from the perspective of health professionals, whose goal is to insure continuity of care.

Poor health and other disadvantages associated with homelessness tend to worsen as the length of time on the streets increases. Some people still experience the longer-duration bouts common in the skid row era; close to 10 percent may be homeless for five continuous years or more. These "chronics," by virtue of their visibility, disproportionately influence public perceptions of who the homeless are, but they now constitute the exception rather than the rule. Results from most surveys indicate that the median episode of homelessness lasts between two months and one year (Burt 1992; Link et al. 1995). Of the persons who fall into this "temporary" category, some are homeless only once in their lives. Many, though, exhibit a more complex pattern marked by frequent exits from and returns to homelessness (Piliavin et al. 1996). For such individuals, being without shelter is just one manifestation of prolonged residential instability.

Whether temporarily or chronically homeless, few prefer to be in that state. But if preference can be ruled out, what forces account for the new homelessness? Among the numerous answers elicited by this question so far, two general classes are discernible. *Structural* explanations treat homelessness as a function of large-scale trends that constrain people's chances for success and that are beyond their immediate control. Scholars point in particular to (1) the decreasing availability of affordable housing; (2) the growth of the poverty population; (3) changes in the economy (e.g., deindustrialization and the expansion of the service sector) resulting in fewer decent-paying, limited-skill jobs; (4) intensifying competition among members of the baby boom cohort during their adult years; (5) the declining appeal of marriage (and the heightened vulnerability of unmarried women and men); (6) the deinstitutionalization movement in mental health care policy; and (7) wider access to controlled substances, dramatically illustrated by the crack cocaine "epidemic" (Burt 1992; Jencks 1994; Wright et al. 1998). The rise of the new homeless is typically attributed to the convergence of two or more of these trends in the 1980s.

The availability of affordable housing has probably received the most attention of any structural factor, in part because all the other trends are thought to operate in conjunction with this one to produce homelessness. The thrust of the housing thesis is that government action, a supply–demand imbalance, inner-city revitalization, and related events have not only priced many low-income households out of rental status but have also eliminated a key fallback option historically open to them: SRO units in downtown residential hotels (Hoch and Slayton 1989; Ringheim 1990). With the depletion of the SRO stock, displacement from other sectors of the housing market may lead directly to a homeless outcome.

In contrast to the structural approach, *individualistic* explanations posit traits, orientations, or experiences specific to the person as the main causes of homelessness. Few researchers have found much evidence that lacking permanent residence is a freely chosen lifestyle. Nevertheless, the enlargement of the emergency shelter system in recent years has made it easier for poor people who are exposed to domestic conflict or doubled up in a crowded unit to voluntarily head for a shelter as a way of coping with their untenable housing situations. In similar fashion, older thinking about the inherent immorality and wanderlust of skid row denizens has given way to revisionist claims that the primary antecedents of homelessness are deficits in talent or motivation or the debilitating effects of mental illness or substance abuse. Traumatic life events, either in childhood (e.g., sexual violence, placement in foster care or an orphanage) or adulthood (divorce, job loss, a serious health problem), can increase the likelihood of homelessness as well.

Interestingly, many experts who subscribe to some version of the individualistic view have had to invoke associated structural trends—deinstitutionalization in the case of mental illness, for example—in order to explain the size and compositional changes that have occurred in the homeless population in recent years. The tendency to draw on both individualistic and structural perspectives has grown more pronounced with the realization that a theory of homelessness, like that of any social phenomenon, can never be fully satisfying when cast in exclusively micro- or macrolevel terms. To date, the work of Rossi (1989) offers the most compelling cross-level synthesis. He contends that structural changes have put everyone in extreme poverty at higher risk of becoming homeless, especially those poor people who exhibit an "accumulation of disabilities," such as drug abuse, bad health, unemployment, and a criminal record. Being "disabled" forces one to rely on a network of friends and family for support, often over prolonged periods. If the strain placed on this support network is too great and it collapses, homelessness is the likely result.

Though Rossi's central idea—that structural factors and individual problems combine to make certain segments of the poor more vulnerable to homelessness than others—seems reasonable to social scientists, it could prove less acceptable to members of the general public. Based on previous research into public beliefs about the causes of poverty, most Americans might be expected to hold the homeless responsible for their lot. However, the small amount of evidence that bears directly on this expectation contradicts rather than confirms it. Findings from a local survey, supplemented with data from a national opinion poll, indicate that (1) more people blame homelessness on structural variables and bad luck than on individualistic causes and (2) many hold a mixture of structural and individualistic beliefs, consistent with the complex roots of the condition (Lee et al. 1990).

The relative frequency of the two types of beliefs is a matter of substantial political significance, since the study just cited shows that each type implies a distinctive set of policy attitudes. As a rule, members of the public who believe in structural causes consider homelessness a very important problem, feel that the response to it has been inadequate, and endorse a variety of corrective proposals, including a tax increase and government-subsidized housing. This policy orientation stands at odds with that for individualistic believers, who tend to devalue homelessness as an issue and favor restrictive measures (vagrancy enforcement, access limitation, etc.) over service provision. Regardless of which orientation ultimately registers the greatest impact on policy making, the sharp contrast between them says much about how homelessness has managed to stay near the top of the U.S. domestic social agenda for the past two decades.

Homelessness also persists as an issue because it is so hard to solve. Out of frustration, many communities have resorted to controlling the homeless. Historically, mechanisms to achieve this goal have included expulsion, spatial containment, and institutionalization (the latter for the sake of monitoring, rehabilitation, or punishment). Other efforts have been aimed at amelioration. For example, the Stewart B. McKinney Homeless Assistance Act recognizes the responsibility of the federal government to meet the basic needs of the "down and out." Since the McKinney Act was signed into law in 1987, it has authorized billions of dollars for food, shelter, health care, and other forms of aid (Foscarinis 1996). However, most of the funding is used to support emergency relief programs. The act designates only modest amounts for reintegration initiatives (for example, moving people into transitional or permanent housing) and virtually nothing for prevention. In short, it treats symptoms but not causes.

The effectiveness of legislation like the McKinney Act is further hindered by our federal system of government, which requires an unrealistically high degree of coordination among units at different levels to insure successful and equitable implementation. The current political climate does not bode well for such legislation, either. Repeated challenges have been made to the McKinney Act; critics want to reduce the size of the federal commitment, redirect the homeless toward existing social services (although many do not appear eligible to receive benefits), and give local government more flexibility. In practice, this is likely to mean a continuation of the piecemeal approach already taken in many places, with an assortment of non-profit organizations, religious groups, advocates, volunteers, and state and municipal agencies attempting to do their part. As long as communities lack specific intervention strategies for keeping at-risk residents from losing their housing and for equipping them with essential skills, there will be little change in the status quo.

The United Nations' designation of 1987 as the "Year of Shelter for the Homeless" attests that homelessness has been an international as well as an American concern. The situation in Europe resembles that in the United States in several respects. Although rates of homelessness appear to be slightly lower across the dozen or so European countries for which data are available, the number of people affected annually (at least 2.5 million) is large (Wright et al. 1998). The compositional profile of the European homeless population looks familiar: Its members are disproportionately single, male, from disadvantaged socioeconomic backgrounds, and in poor physical and mental health. Like their American counterparts, they have become homeless as a result of both structural pressures (e.g., a poverty and affordable housing "squeeze") and individual experiences (family breakup, substance abuse, etc.). Remedies for these causes are no easier to come by in Europe than

they are in the United States. The primary response thus far has been to offer emergency relief, with the burden of service provision falling on the private sector.

Homelessness takes a different, more acute form in the developing countries of the Third World, where rapid population growth outstrips the expansion of the housing stock and the economy by a wide margin. Compounding the growth-housing mismatch are prevailing patterns of spatial redistribution: Rural-to-urban migration streams have created huge pools of homeless people in tenements, in squatter communities, and on the streets of many large cities. Besides such demographic trends, periodic events of the kind that once created literal homelessness in premodern societies—drought, earthquakes, food shortages, and the like—still contribute to the problem today outside the West. War (including "ethnic cleansing") and political instability add to the toll.

What is perhaps most striking about homelessness in the Third World context is its youthful face. Visitors to developing nations cannot help but notice the ubiquitous street children; UNICEF estimates that there may be as many as 100 million globally (Glasser 1994). A majority are "on the street" during the daytime, typically performing some sort of economic activity (begging, vending, etc.), but they have a family and dwelling to return to at night. Perhaps 10 percent qualify as literally homeless or "of the street." The children belonging to this group may have run away from difficult family circumstances, been discarded as "surplus kids" by parents unable or unwilling to care for them, or been discharged from an orphanage or other institutional setting. Because children of the street must hustle to survive, they are occasionally romanticized as savvy and resilient. But they also lack adequate diets, are susceptible to criminal victimization, and engage in behaviors such as drug use and prostitution that jeopardize their health.

Sadly, the prospects for weaving a safety net to catch homeless children and adults—let alone for targeting the sources of the problem—must be judged slim in the face of the financial debts, service demands, and other burdens under which Third World governments operate. Possibly because these burdens are so overwhelming, homelessness—while important—has yet to achieve dominant-issue standing. As one informed observer put the matter, "neither the resources to address the plight of the homeless nor the degree of aroused public sympathy present in the United States are in evidence in the developing world" (Knight 1987, p. 268). However, that is the sector of the world in which a vast majority of all homeless persons will continue to live for the foreseeable future.

REFERENCES

Anderson, Nels 1940 *Men on the Move*. Chicago: University of Chicago Press.

Bahr, Howard M., and Theodore Caplow 1974 *Old Men Drunk and Sober*. New York: New York University Press.

Bogue, Donald J. 1963 *Skid Row in American Cities*. Chicago: Community and Family Study Center, University of Chicago.

Burt, Martha R. 1992 *Over the Edge: The Growth of Homelessness in the 1980s*. New York: Russell Sage Foundation.

——, and Barbara E. Cohen 1989 *America's Homeless: Numbers, Characteristics, and the Programs That Serve Them*. Washington, D.C.: Urban Institute.

Caplow, Theodore, Howard M. Bahr, and David Sternberg 1968 "Homelessness." In David L. Sills, ed., *International Encyclopedia of the Social Sciences*, vol. 6. New York: Macmillan.

Culhane, Dennis P., Edmund F. Dejowski, Julie Ibanez, Elizabeth Needham, and Irene Macchia 1994 "Public Shelter Admission Rates in Philadelphia and New York City: The Implications of Turnover for Sheltered Population Counts." *Housing Policy Debate* 5:107–140.

Foscarinis, Maria 1996 "The Federal Response: The Stewart B. McKinney Homeless Assistance Act." In Jim Baumohl, ed., *Homelessness in America*. Phoenix, Ariz.: Oryx.

Glasser, Irene 1994 *Homelessness in Global Perspective*. New York: G.K. Hall.

Hoch, Charles, and Robert A. Slayton 1989 *New Homeless and Old: Community and the Skid Row Hotel*. Philadelphia: Temple University Press.

Hombs, Mary E., and Mitch Snyder 1982 *Homelessness in America: A Forced March to Nowhere*. Washington, D.C.: Community for Creative Non-Violence.

Jencks, Christopher 1994 *The Homeless*. Cambridge, Mass.: Harvard University Press.

Knight, Rudolph H. 1987 "Homelessness: An American Problem?" In Richard D. Bingham, Roy E. Green, and Sammis B. White, eds., *The Homeless in Contemporary Society*. Newbury Park, Calif.: Sage.

Lee, Barrett A. 1980 "The Disappearance of Skid Row: Some Ecological Evidence." *Urban Affairs Quarterly* 16:81–107.

—— 1989 "Stability and Change in an Urban Homeless Population." *Demography* 26:323–334.

——, Sue Hinze Jones, and David W. Lewis 1990 "Public Beliefs About the Causes of Homelessness." *Social Forces* 69:253–265.

Link, Bruce, Jo Phelan, Michaeline Bresnahan, Ann Stueve, Robert Moore, and Ezra Susser 1995 "Lifetime and Five-Year Prevalence of Homelessness in the United States: New Evidence on an Old Debate." *American Journal of Orthopsychiatry* 65:347–354.

Piliavin, Irving, Bradley R. Entner Wright, Robert D. Mare, and Alex H. Westerfelt 1996 "Exits from and Returns to Homelessness." *Social Service Review* 70:33–57.

Ringheim, Karin 1990 *At Risk of Homelessness: The Roles of Income and Rent*. New York: Praeger.

Rooney, James F. 1970 "Societal Forces and the Unattached Male: An Historical Review." In Howard M. Bahr, ed., *Disaffiliated Man: Essays and Bibliography on Skid Row, Vagrancy, and Outsiders*. Toronto: University of Toronto Press.

Rossi, Peter H. 1989 *Down and Out in America: The Origins of Homelessness*. Chicago: University of Chicago Press.

Snow, David A., and Leon Anderson 1993 *Down on Their Luck: A Study of Homeless Street People*. Berkeley: University of California Press.

Sutherland, Edwin H., and Harvey J. Locke 1936 *Twenty Thousand Homeless Men*. Chicago: J.B. Lippincott.

U.S. Bureau of the Census 1992 *Statistical Abstract of the United States: 1992* (112th ed.). Washington, D.C.: U.S. Government Printing Office.

U.S. Department of Housing and Urban Development 1984 *A Report to the Secretary on the Homeless and Emergency Shelters*. Washington, D.C.: Office of Policy Development and Research, U.S. Department of Housing and Urban Development.

U.S. General Accounting Office 1988 *Homeless Mentally Ill: Problems and Options in Estimating Numbers and Trends*. Washington, D.C.: Program Evaluation and Methodology Division, U.S. General Accounting Office.

Wallace, Samuel E. 1965 *Skid Row as a Way of Life*. Totowa, N.J.: Bedminster.

Wright, James D., Beth A. Rubin, and Joel A. Devine 1998 *Beside the Golden Door: Policy, Politics, and the Homeless.* New York: Aldine de Gruyter.

BARRETT A. LEE

HOMICIDE

See Crime Rates; Criminology.

HOMOSEXUALITY

See Alternative Life Styles; Sexual Orientation; Sexually Transmitted Diseases.

HUMAN ECOLOGY AND ENVIRONMENTAL ANALYSIS

With the growing awareness of the critical environmental problems facing the world today, ecology, the scientific study of the complex web of interdependent relationships in ecosystems, has moved to the center stage of academic and public discourse. The term *ecology* comes from the Greek word *oikos* ("house") and, significantly, has the same Greek root as the word *economics*, from *oikonomos* ("household manager"). Ernst Haeckel, the German biologist who coined the word *ecology* in 1868, viewed ecology as a body of knowledge concerning the economy of nature, highlighting its roots in economics and evolutionary theory. He defined *ecology* as the study of all those complex interrelations referred to by Darwin as the conditions of the struggle for existence.

Ecologists like to look at the environment as an ecosystem of interlocking relationships and exchanges that constitute the web of life. Populations of organisms occupying the same environment (habitat) are said to constitute a *community*. Together, the communities and their abiotic environments constitute an *ecosystem*. The various ecosystems taken together constitute the *ecosphere*, the largest ecological unit. Living organisms exist in the much narrower range of the *biosphere*, which extends a few hundred feet above the land or under the sea. On its fragile film of air, water, and soil, all life depends. For the sociologist, the most important ecological concepts are diversity and dominance, competition and cooperation, succession and adaptation, evolution and expansion, and carrying capacity and the balance of nature. Over the years, the human ecological, the neo-Malthusian, and the political economy approaches and their variants have come to characterize the field of human ecology.

CLASSICAL HUMAN ECOLOGY

The Chicago sociologists Louis Wirth, Robert Ezra Park, Ernest W. Burgess, and Roderick McKenzie are recognized as the founders of the human ecological approach in sociology. In the early decades of the twentieth century, American cities were passing through a period of great turbulence due to the effects of rapid industrialization and urbanization. The urban commercial world, with its fierce competition for territory and survival, appeared to mirror the very life-world studied by plant ecologists. In their search for the principles of order, human ecologists turned to the fundamental process of *cooperative competition* and its two dependent ecological principles of *dominance* and *succession*. For classical human ecologists, such as Park (1936), these processes determine the distribution of population and the location and limits of residential areas. City development is then understood in terms of succession—an orderly series of invasion–resistance–succession cycles in the course of which a biotic community moves from a relatively unstable (primary) to a more or less permanent (climax) stage. If resistance fails and the local population withdraws, the neighborhood eventually turns over and the local group is succeeded by the invading social, economic, or racial population. Each individual and every community thus finds its appropriate *niche* in the physical and living environment. In the hands of the classical human ecologists, human ecology became synonymous with the ecology of space. Park and Burgess identified the natural areas of land use, which come into existence without a preconceived design. Quite influential and popular for a while was the "Burgess hypothesis" regarding the spatial order of the city as a series of concentric zones emanating from the central business district. However, Hawley (1984) has pointed out that with urban characteristics now diffused throughout society, one in effect deals with a system of cities in which the urban hierarchy is cast in terms of functional rather than spatial relations.

Since competition among humans is regulated by culture, Park (1936) made a distinction between the biotic and cultural levels of society: above the symbiotic society based upon competition stands the cultural society based upon communication and consensus. Park identified the problematic of human ecology as the investigation of the processes by which biotic balance and social equilibrium are maintained by the interaction of the three factors constituting what he termed the *social complex* (population, technological culture [artifacts], and nonmaterial culture [customs and beliefs]), to which he also added a fourth, the natural resources of the habitat. However, while human ecology is here defined as the study of how the interaction of these elements helps maintain or disrupts the biotic balance and the social equilibrium, human agency and the cultural level are left out of consideration by Park and other human ecologists.

NEOCLASSICAL HUMAN ECOLOGY

Essentially the same factors reappear as the four POET variables (population, organization, environment, and technology) in Otis Dudley Duncan's (1964) *ecological complex*, indicating its point of contact with the early human ecological approach. In any case, it was McKenzie who, by shifting attention from spatial relations to the analysis of sustenance relations, provided the thread of continuity between the classical and the neoclassical approaches. His student Amos Hawley, who has been the "exemplar" of neoclassical human ecology since the 1940s, defines human ecology as the attempt to deal holistically with the phenomenon of organization.

Hawley (1986) views the *ecosystem* as the adaptive mechanism that emerges out of the interaction of population, organization, and the environment. *Organization* is the adaptive form that enables a population to act as a unit. The process of system *adaptation* involves members in relations of interdependence in order to secure sustenance from the environment. *Growth* is the development of the system's inner potential to the maximum size and complexity afforded by the existing technology for transportation and communication. *Evolution* is the creation of greater potential for resumption of system development through the incorporation of new information that enhances the capacity for

the movement of people, materials, and messages. In this manner, the system moves from simple to more complex forms.

Hawley (1984) has identified the following propositions, which affirm the interdependence of the demographic and structural factors, as constituting the core of the human ecological paradigm:

1. Adaptation to environment proceeds through the formation of a system of interdependences among the members of a population,

2. system development continues, *ceteris paribus*, to the maximum size and complexity afforded by the existing facilities for transportation and communication,

3. system development is resumed with the introduction of new information that increases the capacity for movement of materials, people, and messages and continues until that capacity is fully utilized. (p. 905)

The four ecological principles of *interdependence, key function, differentiation*, and *dominance* define the processes of system functioning and change. A system is viewed as made up of functioning parts that are related to one another. Adaptation to the environment involves the development of interdependence among members, which increases their collective capacity for action. Differentiation then allows human populations to restore the balance between population and environment that has been upset by competition or improvements in communication and transportation technologies. As adaptation proceeds through a differentiation of environmental relationships, one or a few functions come to mediate environmental inputs to all other functions. Since power follows function in Hawley's view, dominance attaches to those units that control the flow of sustenance into the ecosystem. The productivity of the key function, which controls the flow of sustenance, determines the extent of functional differentiation. As a result, the dominant units in the system are likely to be economic rather than political.

Since the environment is always in a state of flux, every social system is continuously subject to change. Change alters the life condition of all participants, an alteration to which they must adapt in order to remain in the system. One of the most significant nonrecurrent alterations is *cumulative change*, involving both endogenous and exogenous changes as complementary phases of a single process. While evolution implies a movement from simple to complex, proceeding through variation and natural selection, cumulative change refers to an increase in scale and complexity as a result of increases in population and territory. Whether the process leads to growth or evolution depends on the concurrent nature of the advances in scale and complexity.

Generalizing the process of cumulative change as a principle of *expansion*, Hawley (1979, 1986) applies this framework to account for growth phases that intervene between stages of development. When scale and complexity advance together, the normal conditions for growth or expansion arise from the colonization process itself. Expansion, driven by increases in population and in knowledge, involves the growth of a center of activity from which dominance is exercised. The evolution of the system takes place when its scale and complexity do not go hand in hand. Change is resumed as the system acquires new items of information, especially those that reduce the costs of movement away from its environment. Thus an imbalance between population and the carrying capacity of the environment may create external pressures for branching off into colonies and establishing niches in a new environment. Since efficiencies in transportation and communication determine the size of a population, the scope of territorial access, and the opportunity for participation in information flows, Hawley (1979) identifies the technology of movement as the most critical variable. In addition to governing accessibility and, therefore, the spread of settlements and the creation of interaction networks among them, it determines the changes in hierarchy and division of labor. In general, the above process can work on any scale and is limited only by the level of development of the technologies of communication and transportation.

Hawley (1986, pp. 104–106) points out how with the growth of a new regional and international division of labor, states now draw sustenance from a single biophysical environment and are converted to subsystems in a more inclusive world system by the expansive process. In this way, free trade and resocialization of cultures create a far more efficient and cost-effective global reach. The result is a global system thoroughly interlinked by transportation and communication networks. The key positions in this international network are occupied by the technologically advanced nations with their monopoly of information and rich resource bases. However, as larger portions of system territories are brought under their jurisdiction, the management of scale becomes highly problematic. In the absence of a supranational polity, a multipolar international pecking order is then subject to increasing instability, challenge, and change. With mounting costs of administration, the system again tends to return to scale, resulting in some degree of decentralization and local autonomy, but new information and improvements in the technologies of movement put the system back into gear and start the growth process all over again. In the modern period of "ecological transition," a large portion of the biophysical environment has progressively come under the control of the social system. Hawley, therefore, believes that the growth of social systems has now reached a point at which the evolutionary model has lost its usefulness in explaining cumulative change.

Hawley points out that while expansionism in the past relied on political domination, its modern variant aims at structural convergence along economic and cultural axes to obviate the need for direct rule by the center. The process of modernization and the activities of multinational corporations are a prime example of this type of system expansion, which undermines traditional modes of life and results in the loss of autonomy and sovereignty by individual states. Convergence of divergent patterns of urbanization is brought about by increased economic interdependence among nations and the development of compatible organizational forms and institutional arrangements. This approach, as Wilson (1984, p. 300) points out, is based on the assumption that convergence is mainly a result of market forces that allow countries to compete in the world on an equal basis. He cites evidence that shows how the subordinate status of non-Western nations has hindered their socioeconomic development, sharpened inequalities, increased rural-to-urban migration and rural–urban disparities, and led to the expansion of squatter settlements.

Human ecological theory accounts for the existence of an international hierarchy in terms of functional differences and the operation of its universal principles of ecosystem domination and expansion. Quite understandably, underdevelopment is defined by Hawley simply in terms of inferiority in this network. Since not all can enjoy equal position on scales of size, resources, and centrality with respect to information flows, Hawley believes that the resulting "inequality among polities might well be an unavoidable condition of an international division of labor, whether built on private or state capitalist principles" (1986, pp. 106, 119).

As the process moves toward a world system, all the limiting conditions of cumulative change are reasserted at a higher level. On the one hand, a single world order with only a small tolerance for errors harbors the seeds of totalitarianism (Giddens 1990). On the other, there is also the grave danger that a fatal error may destroy the whole system. Human ecologists, however, rely on further expansion as the sure remedy for the problems created by expansion. To restore ecological balance, they put their faith in the creation of value consensus, rational planning, trickle-downs, market mechanisms, technological fixes and breakthroughs, native "know-how," and sheer luck.

The real irony of this relentless global expansion elaborated by Hawley lies, however, in the coexistence of the extreme opulence and affluence of the few with the stark poverty and misery of the majority at home and abroad. The large metropolitan centers provide a very poor quality of life. The very scale of urban decay underscores the huge problems facing the city—congestion, polluted air, untreated sewage, high crime rates, dilapidated housing, domestic violence, and broken lives. One therefore needs to ask: What prospect does this scale and level of complexity hold for the future?

HUMAN ECOLOGY AND THE PROBLEMATICS OF "CHAOS"

Chaos theory is the latest attempt to unravel the hidden structure in apparently random systems and to handle chaos within and between systems. In this view, order and disorder (chaos) are seen as two dimensions of the same process: Order generates chaos and chaos generates order (Baker 1993, p. 123). At the heart of both lies a dynamic element, an "attractor," that creates the turbulence

as well as re-creates the order. In the human–social realm, Baker has identified center–periphery, or *centriphery*, as the attractor. Baker, however, uses the concepts of center and periphery more broadly to cover not only their application in the dependency approach (which views the exploitation and impoverishment of the non-Western peripheral societies as basic to the rise of the dominant Western capitalist center), but also to carry the connotation of humans as "world-constructors." Centriphery is, then, the universal dynamic process that creates both order and disorder, as well as accounts for the pattern of human social evolution. The center has an entropic effect on the periphery, causing increasing randomness and denuding it of its resources. But as the entropic effects mount, they are fed back to the center. Beyond a certain point, the costs of controlling the periphery become prohibitive. Should the center fail to come up with new centering strategies, it may split off into subcenters or be absorbed by another more powerful center. Baker is thus led to conclude that "although the effect of feedback is unpredictable, the iteration of a pattern leads to turbulence. The mechanism for change and evolution are endemic to the centriphery process" (Baker 1993, p. 141).

Several things need to be noted about this approach. For one, since these eruptive episodes are random, "the emergence of repeated patterns . . . must be seen as random . . . not as mechanically predictable occurrences. Among other things, the precise character of the emergent pattern cannot be predicted, even though we would no longer be surprised to find a new thing emerging" (Francis 1993, p. 239). For another, Baker's centriphery theory is essentially Hawley's human ecological theory recast in the language of chaos theory, with the important difference that a specific reference is now made both to the role of *agency* as "world-constructors" involved in "categorizing, controlling, dominating, manipulating, absorbing, transforming, and so on," and to their devastating impact on the peripheralized "others," the victims of progress, who suffer maximum entropy, exploitation, impoverishment, death, and devastation. Even so, Baker's is the latest, though undoubtedly unintended, attempt to generalize and rationalize Western expansionism and its "chaotic (unpredictable) . . . devastating, and now increasingly well known, impact on native peoples" (Baker

1993, p. 137). As such, the centriphery process, said to explain both order (stability) and disorder (change), is presented not only as evolutionary and irreversible, but also as natural and universal: "Thus, the Western world became a center through the peripheralization of the non-Western world. And within the Western world, particularly in North America, the city, which peripheralized the rural hinterland, became the megapolis whose peripheralizing effects were simultaneously wider and greater." (p. 136)]

Not only the recurrent iteration of this pattern but even its "unpredictable" outcomes (new strategies of control, splitting off into new subcenters, absorption into a larger center, etc.), are also prefigured in Hawley (1986). Its process is expansion, and its "attractor" is none other than the old master principle of sociology: domination or control (Gibbs 1989). While Friedmann and Wolff (1982) characterize world cities as the material manifestation of the control functions of transnational capital in its attempt to organize the world for the efficient extraction of surplus, Lechner (1985) leaves little doubt that Western "[materialism] and the emphasis on man's relation to nature are not simply analytical or philosophical devices, but are logically part of an effort to restore world-mastery" (p. 182).

"ECOLOGICAL DEMOGRAPHY"?

Since the study of organizational dynamics as well as the structure and dynamics of population are at the core of sociology, Namboodiri (1988) claims that rather than being peripheral to sociology, human ecology and demography constitute its core. As a result, he contends that the hybrid "ecological demography" promises a more systematic and comprehensive handling of a common core of sociological problems—such as the analysis of power relations, conflict processes, social stratification, societal evolution, and the like—than any other competing sociological paradigm. However, although human ecologists recognize the possibility of other pairwise interactions in addition to competition, and even highlight the points of convergence between the human ecological and the Marxist point of view (Hawley 1984), human ecology as such does not directly focus on conflict in a central way. In this connection, Namboodiri (1988) points out how the very

expansionist imperative of human and social systems, identified as a central postulate by human ecologists, generates the possibility of conflict between the haves and the have-nots far more in a milieu of frustrated expectations, felt injustice, and a growing awareness of entitlements, which includes claims to their own resources by nations and to a higher standard of living by deprived populations. How these factors affect the development of and distribution of resources and the relationships among populations by sex, race, ethnicity, and other stratifiers should obviously be of concern to a socially responsible human ecology, one that moreover should be responsive to Borgatta's call for a "proactive sociology" (1989, 1996).

The general neglect of cultural factors and the role of norms and agency in human and organizational interaction has also been a cause for concern to many sociologists. While some latitude is provided for incorporating social norms in specific analyses (e.g., in the relationship between group membership and fertility behavior), their macro-orientation and focus on whole populations compels human ecologists and demographers to ignore the role of the subjective values and purposes of individual actors in ecological and demographic processes (Namboodiri 1988, pp. 625–627).

THE HUMAN ECOLOGICAL APPROACH: AN EVALUATION

While the human ecological approach has strong theoretical underpinnings and proven heuristic value in describing Western expansionism and the colonizing process in supposedly objective terms, its central problem is one of ideology. Like structural functionalism, it is a theory of the status quo that supports existing institutions and arrangements by explaining them as the outcome of invariant principles: "Its concerns are the concerns of the dominant groups in society—it talks about maximizing efficiency but has nothing to say about increasing accountability, it talks of maintaining equilibrium through gradual change and readjustment and rules out even the possibility of fundamental restructuring" (Saunders 1986, pp. 80–81). Not surprisingly, human ecologists downplay the role of social class by subsuming it under the abstract concept of a "categoric unit." They also fail to analyze the role of the state and of the interlocking power of the political, military, and economic establishment, which are centrally involved in the process of expansion and colonization of peoples and cultures. These omissions account for their total lack of concern for the fate of the "excluded others" and the "dark side of expansionism": colonial exploitation, war, genocide, poverty, pollution, environmental degradation, and ecological destruction. Hutchinson (1993) blames the human ecologists for neglecting or downplaying the role of socioeconomic practices and government policies in creating rental, economic resource, and other differentials. He claims that their analyses tend to be descriptive because they take for granted the existence of phenomena such as socioeconomic or racial and ethnic segregation rather than looking at them in terms of spatial processes that result from the competition between capital and labor.

ENVIRONMENTAL SOCIOLOGY AND THE NEW HUMAN ECOLOGY

The mounting public concern since the 1970s about fuel shortages, oil spills, nuclear power plant accidents, acid rain, dying lakes, urban smog, famine and death in the Sahel, rainforest destruction, and the like has made social scientists realize that overexploitation of the ecosystem may destroy the very basis of our planetary survival. Many environmentalists have blamed the voracious appetite of industrial societies and their obsession with growth for the destruction of the fragile balance among the components of the ecological complex.

Having encountered a seemingly unlimited frontier and an expanding economy, the West has come to believe that expansion is in the nature of things. A major reason for the neglect of the physical environment by American sociologists has, therefore, been the anti-ecological worldview of the dominant social paradigm that has been shaped by this belief. At the same time, the exaggerated emphasis by human ecologists on culture, science, and technology as "exceptional" human achievements has led to the illusion that humans are "exempt" from bioecological constraints to which all species are subject. This awareness has led Catton and Dunlap (1978) to develop the fields of new human ecology (Buttel 1987) and environmental sociology to deal with the reciprocal interaction between human activities and the physical environment. They believe that the POET model, broadened to include the role of human agency and culture, provides a useful analytical framework for grounding environmental sociology in the ecological perspective.

In a comprehensive review of the new field, Buttel (1987) has pressed for shifting the focus of environmental sociology from the imbalance of population and resources, emphasized by Catton, to the reality of the unequal distribution of these resources. Allan Schnaiberg's idea of the "treadmill of production" (1980), which emerges from a dialectical relationship between economic growth and ecological structures, points to the need to focus on production institutions as the primary determinants of economic expansion and to incorporate a conflict dimension in environmental analysis. Buttel's own work in environmental sociology draws on the "political economy tradition" of the neo-Marxists and the neo-Weberians. Catton's major contributions, on the other hand, are in the neo-Malthusian tradition. While the problem of order created by the harsh realities of industrial life and expansionism had earlier defined the central problematic of sociology and human ecology, the problem of survival now defines the central problematic of environmental sociology and the neo-Malthusian new human ecology: to the earlier question of how social order is possible is now added the more urgent concern with survival itself.

THE POLITICAL ECONOMY APPROACH AND THE NEW URBAN SOCIOLOGY

The conservative nature of the classical and neoclassical human ecology paradigms has also come under attack from theorists who focus on the internal contradictions and the global reach of capitalism to understand urban phenomena.

Smith (1995) has argued that a new urban sociology paradigm, which draws on neo-Marxist sociological theory, urban political economy, dependency theory, world-system analysis, and critical theory, has now become dominant and largely supplanted human ecology and the old urban sociology approach to the study of urban phenomena. The conflict between the two approaches is an aspect of the old conflict between the structural-functional and the neo-Marxist (conflict) perspectives in the field of sociology generally. Whereas human ecology's main concern is with how technological change enables population aggregates to adapt to their environment through changes in social and spatial organization, the new perspective underplays the role of technological determinants or functional imperatives in shaping the urban landscape. It focuses instead on social inequality and conflict, and highlights the role of economic and political elites, states and other institutional actors, and powerful global forces in order to analyze the problematic "underside" of modern city life: urban poverty, housing segregation by race and social class, urban fiscal crises, deindustrialization, structured inequality in the built environment, and the massive level of human misery associated with the rapid growth of megacities in the Third World (Smith 1995, p. 432.) The new approach looks at urban growth within the context of the international division of labor engendered by the global reach of the expansionary logic of competitive capitalism. This process, which translates aspects of competitive capitalism into geographic space, involves "the creation and destruction of land and built environments we term 'cities.' [Moreover,] this leads to concentrations and locational shifts of human populations, infrastructure, and buildings within the urban landscape (resulting in suburbs, neighborhoods, slums, etc.)" (Feagin 1988, p. 23, quoted in Smith 1995, p. 438).

A "new urban paradigm" in the political economy tradition has been put forward by Gottdiener and Feagin (1988) as an alternative to the human ecological and the expansionist paradigms discussed earlier. Rather than treating societies as mere population aggregates or as unified biotic communities, the new urban paradigm treats them as specified by their mode of production. In this view, crisis tendencies and profit generation constitute the core of societal development, which is seen as dominated by the process of capital accumulation. Thus, to take one example, conventional human ecologists like to regard central-city restructuring as a consequence of adaptation to increasing population size and the growing complexity of social organization. They then relate these changes to the size of the metropolitan hinterland. The new urban paradigm, on the other hand, emphasizes the impact of the global economy, multinational corporations, the shift to functional specialization in world-system financial and administrative activities, the constant subsidization by the state, the efforts of pro-growth coalitions, and changes in labor-force requirements leading to some renovation and central-city gentrification. It tends to focus on power and inequality, the production and reproduction of capital accumulation, crisis adjustment in sociospatial organizations, and such other processes. The following are some of the basic questions that the new urban sociology paradigm seeks to answer: What is the character of power and inequality? How do they relate to "ecological" patterns? How do production and reproduction processes of capital accumulation, as well as the processes of crisis adjustment, manifest themselves in sociospatial organization?

THE CRISIS OF THE NEW URBAN SOCIOLOGY

However, having apparently supplanted human ecology, the new urban sociology itself appears to be in a state of deep crisis (Hutchinson 1993). Among other things, many of its practitioners are now claiming that the new urban sociology lacks a paradigm equivalent to that of human ecology; that its contribution is critical rather than substantive; that its viewpoint is far more ideological than empirical; and that it lacks a unifying focus, there being as many new urban sociologies as there are its practitioners (La Gory 1993, p. 113). At the same time, while asserting that "what is most salient about the new approach is . . . its direct challenge to the theory and method of ecology," Gottdiener and Feagin (1988) deride the attempt "to pick and choose from some of the new literature . . . areas of compatibility, thereby turning the new approach into a mere footnote of the old" (p. 167). However, in view of the inadequacy of both approaches, La Gory (1993) suggests the use of network analysis as the preferred strategy for devising a revised urban paradigm that is informed by both the strengths and shortcomings of these two perspectives. And noting the considerable conceptual convergence between the two approaches, Smith (1995) argues for a *synthesized* urban theory that will require the fleshing out of Hawley's theory of social organization, technology, and population distributions by incorporating the contributions of the new urban theory regarding the nature and content of the global competitive capitalist system. Thus, Smith claims that while the new urban sociology can provide human ecology with a better understanding of power and dominance and how class interests play a central role in shaping urbanization, human ecology can help the new urban theory pay more attention to the demographic processes and variables in order to develop a theory of demographic change under global capitalism.

ECO-CATASTROPHE AND ENVIRONMENTAL COLLAPSE

Industrial and industrializing nations are now beset with more or less the same devastating problems of air, land, and water pollution and environmental destruction. Large numbers of lakes and rivers that were not naturally eutrophic have now become so as a result of pollution and chemical runoffs. In the United States, Love Canal and Times Beach, Missouri, made headlines in the 1980s as much as Chernobyl did in 1986 in the Soviet Union. Sulfur dioxide emissions from industrial and power plants cause acid rain that inflicts irreparable damage on buildings, monuments, marine life, trees, and plants. More than 60,000 synthetic chemicals are now on the market, of which a sizable number contaminate the environment and pose health hazards. Over half a million tons of toxic wastes are produced each year in the United States, while the five-year cost of cleaning nuclear waste, which remains dangerously radioactive for thousands of years, may well exceed $30 billion. The soil, lake water, and groundwater near nuclear power and weapons plants are heavily contaminated with such toxins as mercury, arsenic, and many types of solvents, as well as with deadly radioactive materials such as plutonium, tritium, and strontium-90. The contamination is so bad in eight states that huge tracts of land are said to be totally unfit for human habitation and pose serious health hazards for the surrounding communities. The siting of dump sites in minority communities and the international shipment of hazardous waste to non-Western nations raise serious issues of environmental justice. With an annual production of solid waste that doubled between 1960 and the late 1990s to nearly 225 million tons, the United States is producing more garbage than any other nation in the world and will soon be facing a huge problem of disposal as its 2,300 landfills run out of room and their leachates pose serious threats of toxicity.

The environmental destruction is far more serious and widespread in eastern Europe and the republics of the former Soviet Union. These countries are the sites of some of the world's worst pollution. Lakes and rivers are dead or dying. Water is so contaminated in some areas that it is undrinkable. Chemical runoff and sewage and wastewater dumping have created serious groundwater contamination. Lignite (brown coal), the major source of energy for industry and homes in some of these nations, is responsible for the heavy concentration of sulfur dioxide and dust in the air that has caused serious respiratory problems and additional health damage. The haze-covered cities are an environmental disaster. According to Worldwatch estimates, the former Soviet Union alone accounted for a fifth each of global carbon dioxide and sulfur dioxide emissions—the former are implicated in global warming; the latter are the principal ingredient of acid rain. These environmental problems thus not only span transboundaries, they also cut across ideological labels.

In non-Western nations, a million people suffer acute poisoning and 20,000 persons die every year from pesticides. Pesticides are a major source of environmental and health problems in the United States as well. But the United States alone exports more than half a billion pounds of pesticides that are restricted in or banned from domestic use. The ecology, natural environment, and resources of these non-Western nations are being destroyed and contaminated at a frightening rate. Irreversible damage is being done by large-scale destruction of rainforests and the intensive use of marginal lands, as well as by the imbalances that result from population pressures and the practices of multinational firms and national elites. Desertification now threatens a third of the earth's land surface. Poverty, hunger, starvation, famine, and death are endemic throughout much of the world.

RELATION BETWEEN POPULATION AND THE ENVIRONMENT

What lends urgency to the current population–resource crisis for the West is the fact that while human numbers are declining or standing still at most in industrial societies, they are increasing disproportionately in the rest of the world, a world divided today not only economically and sociopolitically, but also demographically. The technological mastery of the world has resulted in a higher material standard of living in the West, but it has also spelled economic polarization, ecological ruin, and environmental disasters worldwide. At the same time, hunger, famine, poverty, and overpopulation in the rest of the world have raised critical issues of equity, justice, security, and human survival. While the close link among poverty, population growth, and environmental degradation is invariably highlighted by the neo-Malthusians and the media, the impact of unsustainable patterns of consumption and production on the environment does not receive equal emphasis. Much more disconcerting is the fact that the use of the population argument tends to divert attention away from the role of exploitative and oppressive social institutions and arrangements. Schnaiberg and Gould (1994) find the lack of control over industrial production systems rather than population growth to be the main factor contributing to the underdevelopment of Southern societies. Without minimizing the danger of overpopulation, they find clear historical evidence that the worldwide environmental disruption has been caused not by population growth but by the enormous expansion of production, profits, and surplus in the past century. And based on available evidence, Humphrey and Buttel (1982) have been led to conclude that "[one] of the most important findings to come from the study of the relationship between population size and the environment is the misplaced importance given to world population size as cause of natural resource scarcities and pollution.... [We do not] imply that world population growth should be... neglected as a cause of environmental problems, [but] a fixation on it as the major reason for pollution and energy crises would be sociologically misguided" (p. 60).

Depending on their consensus or conflict orientation, we find that the dominant perspectives on the population–resource dynamic place differential emphasis on the alternative modes of resolving competition over scarce resources. In this respect, the modern division of labor, highlighted by Durkheim, is but one of several modes of resolving competition over scarce resources. Schnore (1965, pp. 12–13) offers a number of alternative survival strategies, which may involve one or a combination of the following: (1) demographic changes resulting in the elimination of excess numbers (increase in the death rate, decrease in the birthrate, and migration); (2) technological changes that allow for the expansion of the resource base (the exploitation of unused or existing resources, availability of new areas and new resources, resource substitutions, etc.); and (3) organizational changes that allow for the support of larger numbers (occupational and territorial differentiation, revolutionary changes that redistribute the surplus among the many, and reduction in the general level of living to support increased numbers).

For human ecology, the most salient aspect of the population–environment relationship is the way it affects human survival and the quality of human life. Under the impact of the interlocking crises of overpopulation, resource depletion, and environmental degradation, issues of sustainability and survival have come to occupy center stage. Corresponding to the main approaches in human ecology, three broad positions may be identified for discussion: the pro-growth (expansionist), the neo-Malthusian, and the political economy perspectives. Our discussion of these positions is followed by a consideration of the Brundtland Report, issued by the World Commission on Environment and Development, and of the traditional-Gandhian view of the ecological crisis. Extended treatment of the issues involved may be found in Catton (1980), de la Court (1990), Humphrey and Buttel (1982), Mellos (1988), and Schnaiberg and Gould (1994).

The Pro-Growth (Expansionist) Perspective. To explain the growth patterns of modern society, this approach builds on the foundations of "the new synthetic theory developed in the biological sciences in the last forty years, ... mixing in elements of neo-Malthusian theory, Marx's historical materialism, and modern systems theory" (Lenski 1979, p. 14). It seems quite likely, however, that the basic elements of expansionism, now presented as a natural universal process, were derived from the fundamental American experience of abundance and an open frontier conceived as a process. As Avery O. Craven (1937) put it more than sixty years ago, the basic idea was "that American history ... presents a series of recurring social evolutions in diverse geographical areas as a people advance to colonize a continent. The chief characteristic is expansion; the chief peculiarity of institutions, constant readjustment.... Into... raw and differing areas men and institutions and ideas poured from older basins, there to return to a more or less primitive state and then to climb slowly back toward complexity .... The process was similar in each case, with some common results but always with 'essential differences' due to time and place" (quoted in Potter 1954, p. 145–146.)

In expansionist thinking, scale, complexity, and acceleration—that is, the constant broadening of the limits of the maximum permitted by prevailing circumstances—mark the human–environment encounter. Hawley's version of human ecology, with its focus on population growth and differentiation as significant processes of continuous change, provides a concise exposition of the pro-growth or expansionist view on the population–resource problematic. Hawley believes that industrial systems have no known upper limits on either the number of specializations or the size of the populations that can be supported. Similar pro-growth sentiments are expressed by other expansionist thinkers. Asserting that resource supplies are finite but unbounded, Hawley (1986, pp. 110–111) questions the neo-Malthusian assumption that overpopulation and overuse will soon exhaust a declining supply of fixed resources. While acknowledging the threat of overpopulation and pollution to the quality of the environment, he points to the inherently expansive nature of populations, technology, and organization that has resulted in a long history of resource expansion through more efficient extraction and use of new and existing resources, new resource development, and resource substitutions. With regard to global food-producing resources, he presents evidence to show that the size of arable land, its productivity, and its agricultural output can be increased beyond the rate of population growth. He blames poverty and the structural conditions that generate it for the chronic food shortages in parts of the world and points to the indispensability of further increments of growth and the creation of central organizations capable of tackling these and other environmental problems. Contrary to the view of the Malthusians, he holds that the expansive power of populations by itself does not cause war, resource depletion, or environmental degradation; it does so only under specific organizational circumstances. Hawley (1986, p. 26) views

these outcomes as the result of the maladaptation or malfunctioning of organization, with disequilibrium opening the possibility for evolutionary change through a movement to a higher level of complexity.

While Colin Clark directly links population numbers to power, Herman Kahn (1974) views population increase as a necessary stimulus to economic growth and believes the earth can easily support 15 billion people at $20,000 per capita for a millennium. In fact, he believes that the wider the gap between the rich and the poor, the more the riches will percolate downward. In any case, he is unconvinced that the rich would agree to part with their income to ensure a more equitable distribution of wealth. Roger Revelle (1974) believes the earth can actually support nearly thirty times the present population in terms of food supplies and that it would take almost 150 years to hit that mark. While economic development is necessary to provide people with the basis to control their fertility, Revelle is certain the world would drown in its own filth if most of the people in the world were to live at Western standards. Finally, the postindustrial sociologist Daniel Bell (1977) is convinced that economic growth is necessary to reduce the gap between the rich and poor nations. He has little doubt that the "super-productivity society," with less than 4 percent of its labor force devoted to agriculture, could feed the whole population of the United States, and most of the world as well. In his opinion, pollution exists because the market principle has never been applied to the use of collective goods. Actually, Bell suggests that the government itself could utilize the market to demand a public accounting from all parties on issues of public interest, levy effluent charges for pollutants, and bring effective compliance through the price mechanism.

However, while corporations have shown greater sensitivity and self-regulation, there is evidence that attempts to enforce the "polluter-pays" principle are likely to be resisted or the costs passed on to the public. The negative impact of governmental policies that alleviate energy and resource scarcities is more likely to be felt at the lower socioeconomic levels (Morrison 1976). Dunlap (1979) presents evidence to show that the effects of pollution and the costs of cleaning the environment are borne disproportionately by the poor and may actually serve to reinforce class inequalities.

The Neo-Malthusian Perspective. Within the context of actual and perceived resource scarcities worldwide, neo-Malthusianism has gained ascendance since the 1970s over the earlier theories of demographic transition and neoclassical human ecology (expansionism), which were dominant through the 1960s. Based on the Malthusian notion that population invariably outruns food supply because of a lag between the simple arithmetical increases in resources and the exponential rates of population growth, the neo-Malthusians bring in the notion of *carrying capacity* to identify overpopulation as the main threat to human planetary survival. However, in spite of the fact that there is no exact or objective formula for determining the *optimum population*, the neo-Malthusians tie in the notion of carrying capacity—the optimum population that a given environmental resource base can support at a given time—with the idea of an acceptable quality of life that one *insists* on living. Sometimes the theory of demographic transition, discussed below, is also invoked to explain why Western societies have been able to avoid the Malthusian apocalypse by joining declining death rates and birthrates with increasing standards of living, while non-Western societies cannot, given the least likelihood of their ever achieving Western levels of industrial and economic development, and the sheer impossibility of the whole world living at U.S. standards within the constraints imposed by the finite nature of the earth's resources (Daly 1979).

Compounding the environmental effects of the poverty-stricken and "food-hungry" populations of the world are the impacts of massive consumption and pollution by the "energy hungry" nations (Miller 1972, p. 117). The latter rise sharply with even a slight growth in the population of Western nations, where one-quarter of the world's population is responsible for more than 85 percent of worldwide consumption of natural resources and the environmental sinks. Within the United States, a bare 6 percent of the world's population consumes more than half of the world's nonrenewable resources and more than a third of all the raw materials produced. G. Tyler Miller, Jr. (1972, p. 122) believes that the real threat to our life-support system, therefore, comes not from the poor but from the affluent megaconsumers and megapolluters who occupy more space, consume more natural resources, disturb the ecology more,

and directly and indirectly pollute the land, air, and water with ever-increasing amounts of thermal, chemical, and radioactive wastes. While the Club of Rome (Meadows et al. 1972) and the other neo-Malthusians gave a grace period of thirty or so years, Catton (1980) believes we have already overshot the maximum carrying capacity and are now on a catastrophic downward crash course. In any case, he is convinced that our best bet would be to act as if a crash were imminent and to take advance measures to minimize its impact.

However, the basic premises of Malthusian theory have not stood the test of time. With each technological breakthrough, the Western nations have so far been able to raise their carrying capacity through extending their territorial and environmental reach, which now reaches to the ends of the globe. The social and economic forces unleashed by the Industrial Revolution not only telescoped the doubling of human population within a shorter time span, they also brought about ever-rising material standards of living due to astronomical increases in the scale and speed of agricultural and industrial production in the advanced nations. While the Malthusian theory predicts the fall in growth rates of population as a result of rising death rates, this prediction failed to apply during the period of industrial growth. The theory of *demographic transition* was proposed to cover the anomalous results. The theory specifies declining fertility as a consequence of modernization and economic development. However, in the West itself, smaller families became a clear option only after the newly affluent had suffered a major setback in higher living standards during the Great Depression. On the other hand, the downward transition of fertility worldwide appears to be the result of a complex of factors, including the declining role of tradition and religion, rising levels of income, the increasing role of women's education and outside employment, urban residence and industrialization, and the awareness and availability of fertility-control measures (Weinstein 1976, p. 85). Many of the generalizations based on the demographic-transition theory have thus proved to be culturally and historically specific.

At the same time, the "development" of poor nations has created a new set of claimants for the resources needed to maintain the high material standard of living of affluent nations. As the poor nations begin to assert control over their own resources, try to set terms of their exchange, or resist outside pressures to transform them into "environmental preserves" or the "global commons," the prospects of conflict, particularly over critical water, mineral, forest, and energy resources, are greatly magnified. Amartya Sen (1981) has looked at the famine situation as essentially a "crisis of entitlement," not so much because there is lack of food but because many are denied any claims to it because of the very nature of the market economy. In the West, the entitlement revolution has entailed huge welfare expenditures, which could be financed either by economic growth or by direct redistribution of income (Bell 1976, p. 20). For Bell and the neo-Malthusians, the latter is out of the question.

To restore the population–resource balance—with global economic development, equitable distribution of resources, and the perfectibility of man and society now largely ruled out—the neo-Malthusians rely on sophisticated computer models to predict the end to development and limits to economic and demographic growth for the non-Western nations; others favor "sustained environment development". Still others despair of the effort to avert disaster through population control or the *preventive checks* of moral restraint proposed by Malthus. Instead, they invoke the operation of the Malthusian *positive checks* (wars, famines, pestilence, and natural disasters) and raise the specter of massive famines and die-offs to justify triage, war, secessionist movements, adding sterilants to drinking water, forced sterilization, violent and coercive contraceptive technologies for women, even genocide. In a piece published in 1969 in the Stanford Alumni Almanac, and appropriately titled "The Immorality of Being Softhearted," Garrett Hardin is quite clear that food would be the worst thing to send to the poor. Nothing short of the final solution will do. "Atomic bombs would be kinder. For a few moments the misery would be acute, but it would soon come to an end for most of the people, leaving a very few survivors to suffer thereafter." These solutions, which would bring about the decimation of entire populations, have been called ecofascist. Such sentiments are by no means uncommon among the neo-Malthusians.

To revert to the neo-Malthusian argument: The tragedy of numbers is compounded by the "free rider," who derives personal benefits from the collective efforts of others, and the more serious "tragedy of the commons" (Hardin 1966), where each herdsman will add cattle without limit, ignoring the costs imposed on the others and degrading the land held in common. The "tragedy of the commons" is really the tragedy of individualism run amuck, an individualism from which all constraints of private and common morality have been removed. However, others have been quick to point to the equal or far greater extent of environment pollution and ecological destruction in socialist countries as one more evidence of the inevitable convergence of capitalism and socialism!

Many environmental problems are clearly transideological and transnational. Acid rain, oil spills, the destruction of the ozone layer, the threat of global warming—all call for common responsibility and joint regulation. Ironically, it appears that the expressed concern about the destruction of the global commons through overpopulation or industrial pollution is seldom matched by a parallel commitment by powerful nations to preserve or clean up the environment or provide support for international population-control efforts. Instead, one witnesses a mad scramble to divide up the remaining oceanic and other planetary resources without regard to equity, ecology, or environment. As a result, the air and the oceans, as well as the forests and lands of other nations, are being overexploited or used as garbage and toxic dumps with impunity.

Of no small consequence globally is the environmental impact of waste, widespread corruption at all levels, hoarding and price-fixing, and poor storage, distribution, and transportation networks. Not surprisingly, "formidable mafias based on a triangular alliance between the corrupt bureaucrat, the corrupt politician and the corrupt businessman emerged in all [Indian] States and became a most powerful threat to the conservation of the country's tree cover" (Vohra 1985, p. 50). When one adds to this list the role of political and economic elites and multinational corporations, and of huge debts, huge dams, and huge arms stockpiles, it becomes clear that poverty, hunger, malnutrition, and starvation may have far more to do with political, cultural, and socioeconomic components of food shortages than with sheer numbers alone. This is not to underestimate the immensity of the population problem or to minimize the difficulty of its solution.

The Political Economy Perspective. With the rise of the "consumer society" and the "welfare state" in the West, and the coupling of the "revolution of rising expectations" and the "entitlement revolution" with the impossibility of generalizing Western levels of consumption worldwide, the problematic nature of the relationship between consumption and production has again come to the fore. On the one hand, food aid and food supply have become powerful political weapons globally; on the other, welfare programs constitute a potentially deprivational means of control (Gibbs 1989, p. 453). Saunders points out that today the basic class divisions centered in the relations of production are increasingly being overlaid by "a division, which cuts right across the class structure, between those with access to individual forms of consumption and those who are reliant on collective provision" (1986, p. 232).

Arguing that the issues of collective consumption must be separated from issues of production and class struggle and that urban struggles develop around the question of social consumption, Saunders contends that by recognizing that consumption may generate its own effects, Castells (1985) opens up the possibility of identifying nonclass bases of power and popular mobilization, as well as nonclass forms of popular aspiration and identity (Saunders 1986, p. 226). It is precisely for this reason that the anticonsumerism of the counterculture during the 1960s was both hailed as a true "revolution without Marx or Jesus" and also seen as a threat to the very existence of a mass-production society. On the other hand, the current neo-Malthusian demands centered on the impossibility of generalizing Western standards of living (level of consumption) to the rest of the world, or on stabilizing consumption at some "optimum" level for achieving a steady state within western societies, also rest on the possibility of regulating production by manipulating mass-consumption patterns.

Barry Commoner (1974) faults socialist as much as capitalist economic theories for neglecting the biosphere as a major factor of production but regards both poverty and population growth as outcomes of colonial exploitation. The world, he believes, has enough food and resources to support nearly twice its present population. The problem, in his view, is a result of gross distributive imbalances between the rich and the poor, and

requires a massive redistribution of wealth and resources to abolish poverty and raise standards of living in order to wipe out the root cause of overpopulation. The alternative to this humane solution is the unsavory one of genocide or natural destruction. A study of environmental destruction in southern Honduras by Susan Stonich (1989) illustrates the power of a perspective that combines the concerns of political economy, ecology, and demography. Her conclusion is that environmental degradation arises from fundamental social structures and is intricately connected to problems of land tenure, unemployment, poverty, and demography.

Stonich identifies political and economic factors and export-promotion policies of international lending institutions and aid agencies as the key elements of a development policy for the whole of Central America that is likely to lead to destruction of the remaining tropical forests, worsen poverty and malnutrition, and increase inequality and conflicts within and between nations. Government policies encourage commercial agriculture in order to earn foreign exchange in the face of mounting external debt, which rose by 170 percent in just seven years to equal three-fourths of the 1986 gross national product. The expansion of export-oriented agriculture and the integration of resource-poor rural households into the capitalist sector, often by ruthless and violent means, concentrates the highest population densities in the most marginal highland areas and encourages intensive land-use and adaptive strategies that accelerate ecological decline. Between 1952 and 1974, as a result of changes in land-use patterns, forest land declined by more than two-fifths and the area lying fallow by three-fifths. In the same period, food-crop production was reduced drastically while pasture area rose by more than half regionally and by more than 150 percent in the highlands, where the number of cattle rose by about 70 percent. By 1974, a third of all rural families were landless; two-fifths were below the subsistence level in 1979.

The result has been the evolution of a class of rich peasants raising export-oriented cattle and cash crops, a class of land-poor and landless peasants and wage laborers, and a class of middlemen operatives who serve as transportation links in an expanding regional and national network. The whole socioeconomic structure has an extremely deleterious effect on the regional ecology and environment. These patterns are being repeated all over Africa and Asia. Even the "green revolution," which uses the model of American agribusiness to commercialize agriculture in non-Western countries, provides only a temporary respite. Its recurrent and increasingly high capital requirements for seed, fertilizer, insecticide, water, land, and machinery wipe out the small farmers and landless laborers. It destroys peasant agriculture, exposes the monocultures to destruction by disease and pests, magnifies inequality, and sows the seeds of social instability and rural strife. To those who subscribe to the political economy perspective, the bioecological explanation thus appears to be too simplistic. It overlooks the social context of development and land distribution within which worldwide destruction of traditional agriculture and the rainforests is now occurring.

In sum, these considerations bring out the fact that debates surrounding resource distribution and the control of population and consumption patterns are neither entirely scientific nor purely ecologically inspired. As Barry Commoner (1974) points out, they are political value positions. Will the changes come voluntarily, or will they involve totalitarian nightmares? "Sustainable development" and "traditional ecology" hold out two contrasting possibilities for the future.

THE BRUNDTLAND REPORT AND THE PROMISE OF SUSTAINABLE DEVELOPMENT

At the heart of the Brundtland Report of the World Commission on Environment and Development (1987) is the idea of *sustainable development* that has become the rallying point for diverse agendas linking poverty, underdevelopment, and overpopulation to environmental degradation and "environmental security." The report defines sustainable development as "development which meets the needs of the present without compromising the ability of future generations to meet their own needs." Its popularity lies in its ability to accommodate the opposing idea of limits to growth within the context of economic expansion, but with a new twist. As pointed out by Gro Brundtland (1989), the "central pivot" of the notion of sustainable development remains "progress, growth, the generation of wealth, and the use of resources." The imposition of limits on consumption is then

justified in order to protect the resource base of the environment both locally and globally. At the same time, continuous economic growth is considered essential to meeting the needs of the world's neediest. In fact, the Brundtland Report indicates that "a five-to-tenfold increase in world industrial output can be anticipated by the time world population stabilizes sometime in the next century" (World Commission on Environment and Development 1997).

Sustainable development is also seen as a strategy to enhance global security by reducing the threat posed by conflict and violence in an inequitable and resource-hungry world. To this end, it promotes a commitment to multilateralism, with a call for strong international institutions to ward off the new threats to security and for the collective management of global interdependence (Brundtland 1989, p. 14). As a result, the interests of economic growth and the environment are seen as mutually reinforcing rather than contradictory. The World Commission Report (1987) duly notes that ecology and economy "are becoming ever more interwoven—locally, regionally, nationally, and globally—into a seamless net of causes and effects." And the 1990 Worldwatch Institute Report predicts that the world will have a sustainable society by the year 2030 (Brown et al. 1990, p. 175). Meanwhile, the challenge, as Arnold (1989, p. 22) states, is to ensure that the sustainability vision "is not trivialized or, worse, used as one more way to legitimize the exploitation of the weak and vulnerable in the name of global interest and solidarity."

To its credit, the Brundtland Report singled out some forms of economic growth that destroy resources and the environment. The present $1 trillion expenditure on armaments, for example, constitutes "more than the total income of the poorest half of humanity." According to 1990 United Nations estimates, military expenditures in developing countries, which account for 75 percent of the arms trade, had multiplied by seven times since 1965 to almost $200 billion, compared with a doubling by the industrialized countries. In addition, burgeoning debt, adverse trade policies, and internal instability constitute the overwhelming obstacles to sustained development. The fifty-two poorest nations of the world are now burdened with nearly a $400 billion debt. With Africa's total debt approaching $200 billion (half of its overall gross national product and three to four times its annual income from exports), its average debt repayments amount to more than half the export income. The debt burden forces the African nations to concentrate on monocrop export agriculture to the detriment of food-crop production and pushes hungry and landless farmers and nomads to marginal lands that they overgraze and overexploit in order to survive. However, with respect to fixing the responsibility for deforestation, the Brundtland Report appears to be of two minds (de la Court 1990). In asserting that to most farmers, especially the poor ones, "wood is a 'free good' until the last available tree is cut down," the report partly sides with the "tragedy of the commons" argument, accusing the poor farmers of being "both victims and agents of destruction." On the other hand, it also points to a different cause: "The fuelwood crisis and deforestation—although related—are not the same problems. Wood fuels destined for urban and industrial consumers do tend to come from the forests. But only a small proportion of that used by the rural poor comes from forests. Even in these cases, villagers rarely chop down trees; most collect dead branches or cut them from trees" (quoted in de la Court 1990, p. 68). In any case, the Brundtland Report became the focal point for global environmental efforts in the 1990s, even though in the United States it remained "America's best-kept secret." It undoubtedly played a crucial role in the United Nations conference on the global environment held in Brazil in 1992.

SOCIAL CHAOS AND THE PROBLEMATICS OF SOCIAL AND ECOLOGICAL INTEGRATION

Dennis Wrong (1994, pp. 295–296) has pointed out how the globalization of the world economy and the accompanying spread of communication and transportation systems to embrace more of the world represent an unprecedented increase in the dissociation of system from social integration, and how the fear of disorder has become more acute in a greatly interdependent world suffering from persistent economic scarcity and a limited capacity for human sympathy with others.

To Scott Greer (1979), the rapid growth of American society, made possible by the increase in societal scale, has led to the following Durkheimian dilemma: "Increasing interdependence requires more cultural integration than we can manage; growth itself has undermined the cultural support system. While bureaucratization may increase order within a segment of the society, what is to guarantee order among segments?" In the absence of the spirit of consensus generated by war, economic disaster, or a universalized humanity, Greer feels that symbiosis rather than cultural integration may best remedy the fragmentation accompanying the discontinuities of societal growth. Such an approach would not only emphasize trading partners, controlled markets, and formal and informal co-optation, but "given the increasing number of role players who do not 'know their place,' from white working-class men to black college-educated women, such a system will take an awful lot of work by leaders, middlemen, and fixers, as well as some luck" (Greer 1979, pp. 315–316).

Daniel Bell (1976) has made the critical point that while the dominant nineteenth-century view of society as an interrelated web, a structured whole unified by some inner principle, still rules Marxist and functionalist thought, it is no longer applicable. On the contrary, society today is composed of three distinct realms—the technoeconomic structure, the polity, and the culture—each obedient to a different axial (value) principle, each having different rhythms of change, and each following different norms that legitimate different and even contradictory types of behavior. The discordances between these realms are responsible for various contradictions within society. Bell has proposed the creation of a "public household" to overcome the disjunctions among the family, the economy, and the state through the use of modified market mechanisms to further social goals. And given his conviction that the crisis is really a spiritual one of belief and meaning, he recommends the return in Western society of some conception of religion to restore the continuity of generations and provide a ground for humility and care for others. This presents a formidable challenge, however, for Bell is painfully aware that one can neither manufacture such a continuity nor engineer a cultural revolution.

It is doubtful that the problems of order created by the "normal" but dangerous nonrelation between the life-sustaining (ecology–economy) and order-maintaining (sociopolitical) systems of contemporary society can be corrected, as Bell believes, by the creation of a miraculous hybrid—a "public household"—protected and nurtured by both the polity and the household to serve the interests of the technoeconomic structure and by the side-door entry of the "religious" to provide for the integrative and "higher"-order needs of a socially disjointed and spiritually vacuous society. Even the frantic use of a "holistic" ecological approach is bound to fail if its actual goal is somehow to dominate or desperately hold on to a sundered reality in which everything is so hopelessly *unrelated* to everything else. Since a dependent part cannot grow infinitely at the expense of the others, or usurp the whole for its own purposes without undermining the very conditions of its own existence, the high-powered technoeconomic structure, driven by the insatiable demand for energy, resources, and markets, is inherently disorder-producing and anti-ecological. Its immensity of scale and utilitarian thrust not only destroy traditional structures and sociocultural diversity but also set in motion irreversible and ecologically damaging global processes whose attempted solutions greatly magnify the problems.

That the philosophy and ideology of progress may promote activities inconsistent with sound ecological management and the prospects of human survival is also increasingly being recognized (Peck 1987). But the fact that "'history' is not on our side, has no teleology, and supplies us with no guarantees" does not mean to Giddens (1990) "that we should, or that we can, give up in our attempts to steer the juggernaut . . . . For we can envisage alternative futures whose very propogation might help them be realised. What is needed is the creation of models of utopian realism" (p. 154). Unwilling and unable to abandon the world-constructionist project, he offers a "post-scarcity" system as perhaps the only possibility but is also bothered by the "dark side of modernity," the creation of totalitarian power, based on his original insight that totalitarianism and modernity are not just contingently but inherently connected (Giddens 1990, p. 172).

In the stark asymmetry between the disorder-producing and the order-creating powers of the centriphery lies the real "nightmare of reason" and the roots of the current crisis and worldwide chaos. The process is not only incomprehensible

("complex"), but totally out of control. In this state of affairs, "what is there to love or preserve in a universe of chaos? How are people supposed to behave in such a universe? If that is the kind of place we inhabit, why not go ahead with all our private ambitions, free of any fear that we may be doing special damage" (Worster 1994, p. A3).

TRADITIONAL ECOLOGY AND THE ENVIRONMENT

Patterns of human social organization and technology use reflect the vision a people have of themselves and of their place in the universe. According to Karl Polanyi ([1947] 1974), the question of how to organize human life in a machine society confronts us with a new urgency:

> *Behind the fading fabric of competitive capitalism there looms the portent of an industrial civilization with its paralyzing division of labor, standardization of life, supremacy of mechanism over organism, and organization over spontaneity. Science itself is haunted by insanity. This is the abiding concern."* (pp. 213–214)

A. K. Saran (1978) does not doubt in the least that the ecological crisis is a self-inflicted one, because an entropic environmental system and an infinitely expanding economy and technology are mutually incompatible. His main argument is that the modern system does not provide a coherent worldview or the proper regulative principle to satisfy the needs of the different orders in a unitive way. In such a system, only a technological solution to the problem of order in the sociopolitical realm can be contemplated, and a piecemeal approach will be relied on to deal with the consequences of a discordant and disharmonious order. In addition to generating tremendous violence, universal disorder, and planetary destruction in the desperate attempt to hold the parts together under its hegemony, such an approach is bound to fail. Since the symbolic is not an integral part of the modern literal consciousness, the attempt to appropriate Mother Earth or other symbols, such as that by the proponents of Gaia, may be ideologically seductive but is both scientifically irrelevant and spiritually vacuous. Neo-Malthusian disclaimers notwithstanding, since evolution has been the master concept to organize and rearrange the world in human terms, the ontology of modern science is necessarily anthropocentric. Saran's conclusion, therefore, is that there can be no ecological science unless it is grounded in traditional cosmology.

In a study of the Tukano Indians of the northwest Amazon, G. Reichel-Dolmatoff (1977) shows how aboriginal cosmologies, myths, and rituals

> represent in all respects a set of ecological principles . . . that formulate a system of social and economic rules that have a highly adaptive value in the continuous endeavor to maintain a viable equilibrium between the resources of the environment and the demands of society. The cosmological myths which express the Tukano world-view do not describe Man's Place in Nature in terms of dominion, or mastery over a subordinate environment, nor do they in any way express the notion of what some of us might call a sense of "harmony with nature". Nature, in their view, is not a physical entity apart from man and, therefore, he cannot confront it or oppose it or harmonize with it as a separate entity. Occasionally man can unbalance it by his personal malfunctioning as a component, but he never stands apart from it. Man is taken to be a part of a set of supraindividual systems which—be they biological or cultural—transcend our individual lives and within which survival and maintenance of a certain quality of life are possible only if all other life forms too are allowed to evolve according to their specific needs, as stated in cosmological myths and traditions. . . . This cosmological model . . . constitutes a religious proposition which is ultimately connected with the social and economic organization of the group. In this way, the general balance of energy flow becomes a religious objective in which native ecological concepts play a dominant organizational role. To understand the structure and functioning of the ecosystem becomes therefore a vital task to the Tukano. (pp. 9–11)

However, modernity in its essence has been totally destructive of the traditional vision of human nature, our proper place in the "web of life," and our conception of the ultimate good. Polanyi ([1947] 1974) points out how with the modern separation of "economy" as the realm of hunger and gain,

> [our] animal dependence upon food has been bared and the naked fear of starvation permitted to run loose. Our humiliating enslavement to the "material", which all human culture is designed to mitigate, was deliberately made more rigorous. This is the root of the "sickness" of an acquisitive society that Tawney warned of . . . . [The task of] adapting life in such surroundings to the requirements of human existence must be resolved if man is to continue on earth. (p. 219)

The post–World War II creation of the global economy through the idea of "development" is the other half of the story. As pointed out by Wolfgang Sachs (1990), and in line with Hawley's observation, the concept of development provided the United States with the vision of a new global order in which the former colonies were held together not through political domination but through economic interdependence. But to "define the economic exploitation of the land and its treasures as 'development' was a heritage of the productivist arrogance of the 19th century. Through the trick of a biological metaphor, a simple economic activity turns into a natural and evolutionary process. [Soon] traditions, hierarchies, mental habits—the whole texture Of societies—were all dissolved in the planner's mechanistic models . . . patterned on the American way of life" (p. 42).

However, even after nearly two decades of development work, the results were far from heartening. Instead of declining, inequality, poverty, unemployment, hunger, and squalor actually increased manyfold in all "developing" countries. To summarize: While the expansionist vision tries to tie ecology, economy, and polity together, and the neo-Malthusians add biology to the list, it is in *sustainable development* that all these orders are firmly knit together—but at a price. The paradoxical nature of the term *sustainable development* arises from the fact that it attempts to combine the contradictory notions of limits to growth and active growth promotion. However, if the key to maintaining ecological integrity is economic self-sufficiency and production for use, then the problem today is surely one of the inhuman scale of enterprise based on the "techniques of degradation" (Marcel 1952), which serve nothing higher than human self-interest, and of the concept of man as having an economically rather than a spiritually determined nature (Coomaraswamy 1946, p. 2).

Roy Rappaport (1976) has documented how the Maring of New Guinea support as many as 200 people per square mile by cultivating nearly forty-five acres of cleared forest at a time without damaging the environment. But then they look at the world and its "resources" through very different eyes!

A PROACTIVE ENVIRONMENTAL SOCIOLOGY

Heightened concern with ecology and the environment has now moved into the mainstream of public life as a major priority at the national and international levels. This provides important opportunities for environmental sociologists to contribute to the understanding and solution of these problems. Constance Holden (1989) has highlighted the report of the National Academy of Sciences that outlines an agenda for both micro and macro social scientific studies of "anthropogenic" stresses on the resources and the environment in the north circumpolar region and that has general application. The fragile Arctic region has a great wealth of natural resources. It comprises one-tenth of the earth's area and has a population of 8 million people, of whom a quarter are natives. The report placed major emphasis on interdisciplinary studies, particularly those linking the social and physical sciences and basic and applied research. It emphasized the need for drawing on native knowledge and put urgent priority on issues such as cultural survival and the allocation of scarce resources. It also asked the social scientists to come up with models generalizable to other areas.

An interesting insight concerns how each of the several identities of the Arctic (e.g., as homeland for the natives, as a "colony" exploited for its natural resources, and as the last wilderness) results in a distinctive approach to human–environment relationships. "These approaches have come increasingly into conflict as subsistence hunters and commercial interests vie for limited stocks of fish and game; communities are shaken by boom and bust cycles in scrambles for mineral resources; and rapid modernization has inflicted trauma on native cultures" (Holden 1989, p. 883). The committee identified three areas of interest to the social scientist. In the area of human–environment

relationships, there is a need for studies on conflict resolution to strike a balance between commercial needs and the interests of subsistence hunters, sportsmen, and conservation. The second area pertains to community viability, for which a systematic approach is needed to help develop a physical and social services infrastructure to meet the special climatic needs of the region. A final area pertains to the study of the impact of rapid social change (single-industry cash economy, the snowmobile revolution), which is exacting a heavy price from the local inhabitants in terms of higher rates of alcoholism, suicide, stress, loneliness, accidents, and violence.

The shift from expansionist to neo-Malthusian thinking seemingly implies an attempt to come to terms with the finitude of the total ecosphere and changed global realities, but the underlying assumptions and contradictions are again not made explicit. The overriding concern has been with the protection of industrial and commercial interests, even where these interests clearly come in conflict with the interests of individuals, communities, and their environment. The commitment to protect growth or a certain way of life at any cost has led human ecologists and neo-Malthusians to disregard the minimum well-being or sheer survival of the rest of humankind. In fact, Hawley (1986) admits that while "competition," resulting from demand exceeding the carrying capacity, may account for the exclusion of some contestants from access to their share of a limited resource, it does not shed "any light on what happens to the excluded members of a population after their exclusion" (p. 127). This serious neglect of the concern for the underdog and the undermined is matched by the self admitted tendency of the human ecologists "not [to] confront policy matters directly" (Hawley 1986, p. 127). Given its reliance on large-scale macro forces to explain other macro-level phenomena, the human ecological approach does not readily lend itself to policy considerations. Even otherwise, since it views spatial patterns as the natural outcome of ecological processes rather than as the result of power relations, it becomes a conservative force in policy applications (La Gory 1993, p. 112).

Edgar Borgatta (1989, 1996) has sought to develop an important field called "proactive sociology," with a view to closing the wide gap between sociological theory and practice and to save sociology from sheer irrelevance. Sociological approaches, even when application-oriented, have been largely timid, inactive, or merely reactive. They have restricted their focus to studying how changes in social policy may alter behavior and social situations, but they have refrained from making policy recommendations for designing social structures to serve accepted values. Proactive sociologists, on the other hand, would have the task not only of clarifying values and specifying their meaning but also of assuming the responsibility for making policy recommendations based on an understanding of appropriate models of change. In stark contrast to the pretended value-neutral and value-free stance of mainstream sociology, Borgatta (1996) would, therefore, push to include the consideration of values, as well as the examination of possible structures to implement preferred values, among the central tasks for proactive sociologists.

In human ecology, for instance, it is with reference to the population–consumption problematic that questions of value and their interpretation become evident. Rather than waiting to study only the aftereffects of "all in the path"—the Three Mile Island radiation leak or the Exxon Valdez oil spill—or stepping in at the end of the "issue-attention" cycle, when the problem is historically interesting but socially irrelevant, a proactive sociology would concern itself with the dynamics out of which problems arise, anticipating potential problem areas and their alternative solutions as the means to translate desired values into effective policy. This would involve identifying possible futures and the consequences of action or inaction for their attainment—a policy dimension ignored by sociologists, despite their belief that this may make all the difference in a fast-changing and turbulent world in which the ability to handle and manage change requires the ability to anticipate change and to adapt social structures to changing requirements. To this end, the sociologist would need to ask whether what he or she was doing would make an impact and be useful to society. The fundamental assumption here is that if we know something about the impact of social structure on behavior, we should be able to propose models for changes in social structures that will effectively implement values that have priority status in society (Borgatta 1989, p. 15). Sociologists would then be obligated to "address societal

values more directly by providing alternate models of potential changes and exploring the consequences these changes may produce if identified values are implemented" (Borgatta and Hatch 1988, p. 354).

Following this lead, a "proactive environmental sociology" would have particular application to the "sociology of environmental issues," which is concerned with the study of environmental movements, resource management problems, and the like. It would broaden the scope of the sociology of environmental issues by focusing specifically on the changes that are required to effectively implement stated values such as equity, environmental justice, rights of the deprived and of "future generations," resource conservation, equitable sharing of the global commons, the right to clean and healthy environment, sustainable lifestyles and consumption patterns, and the like, and by exploring the possible consequences of these changes. Thus David Mahar, an adviser to the World Bank, has argued that blaming peasant colonists for deforestation is "tantamount to blaming the victim" for "misguided public policies" that promote road building, official colonization of the forest, and extensive live-stock development, and that "purposely or inadvertently encourage rapid depletion of the forest." This *definition of the situation* led Mahar to propose an "alternative development model" that would put government action on hold so that, based on land-use surveys, lands "found to have limited agricultural potential— virtually whole of terra firme [*sic*] of Amazonia— would be held in perpetuity as forest reserves." These and other unconventional conclusions are stated by Mahar as his own and carry the disclaimer that they do not necessarily represent the views and policies of the World Bank itself (cited in Hildyard 1989).

This example also brings out Borgatta's point that a proactive stance may involve the espousing of unpopular positions. It may lead a proactive environmental sociologist to examine the role of established institutions and values (crass individualism and the impact of "anthropocentric," "cowboy," "superpower," and "commercialized conservation" approaches to the use of finite resources and a fragile environment; wasteful consumption patterns; draconian measures of population control; corporate nonaccountability and the global impact of multinationals, the state, and the like) in order to facilitate the creation of ecologically sustainable social structures that implement positive environmental values. On this basis, a systematic concern with morality and the application of knowledge would lead to a "proactive environmental sociology" that would prompt the sociologist to formulate alternative policies with respect to the set of environmental values or goals that are to be implemented (Borgatta and Cook 1988, p. 17). This approach would also ensure that the applied aspects of "environmental sociology" would flourish within the discipline and not become detached from sociology, as has been the fate of industrial sociology and many other areas in the past (Borgatta 1989).

OVERVIEW

Environmental sociologists have complained of the lack of a unifying focus within the field and have noted its specialized, fragmented, and dualistic tendencies, which hinder concept and theory development (Buttel 1987, p. 466). This should be a cause for serious concern insofar as the new human ecology is supposed to provide a holistic, integrated understanding of human–environment interactions. In addition to the problems surrounding functionalist as well as Marxist categories and assumptions is the difficulty of adapting bioecological concepts to the human context. Notions such as ecosystem, niche, succession, climax communities, balance of nature, even evolution—none have clear social referents and all pose formidable problems of inappropriate or illegitimate transferal of concepts. Thus, while one finds constant reference to urban or social "ecosystems" in the literature, the wide-ranging, even global, energy-exchange patterns make the boundaries so diffuse that it becomes impossible to locate an urban ecosystem in time and space, at least in biological terms (Young 1983, p. 195). Or, if humans are defined as niche dwellers, the term *niche*, "if adopted directly from biology would produce only one worldwide niche for the entire global species, a result that would render the concept useless. How can the species problem be overcome in adapting such a concept to human ecology?" (Young 1983, p. 795).

Terms such as *the environment* are not easy to define or conceptualize; nor are ecological chain reactions, multiple causal paths, and feedback mechanisms in complex ecosystems easy to delineate. In recognition of the substantial difference between human and bioecological orders, some human ecologists, such as Hawley, have moved away from bioecological models. Thus, Hawley (1986) is highly critical of the neo-Malthusian application of the "carrying-capacity" notion, on the ground that "while the argument may be suitable for plants and animals, its transfer to the human species is highly questionable" (p. 53). While still shying away from assigning a critical role to human agency, or even a policy-making role to the human ecologist, Hawley has nonetheless broadened the scope of his theory by incorporating culture and norms as ecosystem variables. However, as a commentary on Western-style development and its total disregard for limits, Rappaport has raised more basic objections: To treat the components of the environment as if they were mere resources is to view them exclusively in economic terms and invite "the use and abuse of biological systems of all classes and the neglect of moral and aesthetic considerations in general. Whatever may be meant by the phrase 'quality of life,' exploitation does not enhance it" (1978, pp. 266–267).

Human ecologists, in general, have not dealt adequately with such concerns, nor with the problems of power, domination, and the role of the state and of "values" in human–environmental relationships. At a minimum, one needs to know the role of the state in the regulation, maintenance, expansion, suppression, and "resocialization" of peoples and societies. If ecosystems are constituted of interdependent parts, one needs to know the nature of the reciprocal relationships among the parts and among the parts and the ecosystem. Rappaport (1978) has drawn attention to the maladaptive tendency of subsystems to become increasingly powerful and to dominate and use the larger system for their own benefit, to the detriment of the general interest and the adaptive flexibility of the system. He mentions the dominating positions occupied by huge corporations and the "military industrial complex" as examples. More broadly, Rappaport ties pollution, "resource" depletion, and the diminution of the quality of life and the destruction of its meanings to the scale of modern societies and the voracious appetites of their industrial metabolisms. Thus, while he does not deny that population increase may have a negative impact on the quality of life, he has little doubt that the real cause of ecosystem destruction and the deterioration of the quality of life is to be found in the way societies are organized, not in their population trends. If that is so, what alternative do humans have?

Within the human ecological perspectives, environmental problems are seen as arising either from the unplanned nature of growth and expansionism, from its attendant externalities and "commons" tragedies, from growth and market restrictions (the pro-growth, expansionist perspective), or from the excess of population over the carrying capacity of the environment (the neo-Malthusian perspective). To restore ecological balance and environmental health, human ecologists place their faith in value consensus, rational planning, systems theory, computer models, economic growth, trickle-downs, market mechanisms, and technological fixes (the pro-growth perspective) or in limits to growth, sustainable development, sticks and carrots, benign neglect, triage, die-offs, outright compulsion, and even genocide (the neo-Malthusian perspective). Within the political economy perspective, on the other hand, the emphasis is on internal contradictions, uneven development, center–periphery relations, capitalist exploitation, the role of multinationals and the state, trade imbalances, and the treadmill of production. To ensure environmental and ecological protection, equitable distribution, and social justice, the proposals from a political economy standpoint range from social revolution to conflict and confrontation, from redistribution to social welfarism and mixed economies.

The political economy perspective is critical of the basic assumption of the Chicago ecologists that changes in population, organization, and the technologies of movement explain expansionary movements and territorial arrangements. By allowing planners to alter spatial forms to dissipate class conflict and social unrest, Smith (1979, p. 255) believes, the perspective becomes a powerful depoliticizing weapon in their hands. He favors "client-centered" planning, which does not assume that "physical structure determines social structure," but holds that both are shaped by the economic and political structures of society, which

provide selective access to opportunities and further discriminatory patterns of land use and investment. Smith therefore offers "conflictual planning" on behalf of the poor and the powerless in order to call attention to the hidden social costs of development and to increase the political costs of pursuing repressive policies disguised as rationally planned allocational, locational, and investment choices. This approach poses three basic questions: "Whose values, interests, and social actions will determine the purpose, pace, and direction of historical change? Can the costs and benefits of historical change be distributed fairly? Can the changes that do occur further the cause of social justice?" (Smith 1979, p. 288).

Schnaiberg (1980) has identified three responses to the contradiction between production expansion and ecological limits: (1) the expansionist, which will be temporary, increasingly unequal, environmentally stressful, and authoritarian; (2) the business-as-usual, which will be unstable, socially regressive, unequal, and of limited environmental value; and (3) the ecological, involving appropriate technology, reduced consumption, and reduced inequality, which will be the most durable but also the most socially disruptive and the least desirable. Schnaiberg's own preference, short of a social revolution, is for a mixed social democratic system like Sweden's, with some production expansion and improved welfare distribution under close state supervision.

However, this solution does not quite address the critical concerns of the environment or the needs of three-fourths of humanity. It presents to the world the anti-ecological model of the "treadmill of production" under a more benign form. It ignores the reality of global inequity, environmental injustice, and global-resource wars—the fact that behind every environmental struggle of today lies a struggle over the expansion of the treadmill of production. It is worth noting that at least in the case of sustainable-yield forestry, Schnaiberg and Gould (1994) no longer look to Sweden as the model. With more than 90 percent of Sweden's native forest now extinct, and its native species replaced by North American tree species, the authors decry that "native plants and animals have been exterminated, sacrificed for an economically-sustainable industry. The Swedish treadmill is sustained at the expense of the Swedish environment" (1994, p. 210). The real thrust, therefore, is not sustainable development at all but what Vandana Shiva (1990) has called *commercialized conservation*, which puts a dollar value on biodiversity and "justifies conservation in terms of present or future commercial returns" (p. 14). Smith (1979) believes that the environmental problem, like the problem of poverty, has arisen and remains insoluble because of our commitment to existing economic arrangements and institutions and because wealth and power are valued over persons and human need. In fact, the global treadmill operates in such a way that the poor countries often end up financing the development of the rich ones. Thus, during the period from 1982 to 1990, Foster (1995) reports how Third World nations became a net exporter of hard currency to developed countries to the tune of about $30 billion per year, while also remitting almost $12.5 billion in monthly payments on debt alone to their creditors in wealthy nations.

While the West is busy presiding over a general reorganization of the global economy and the ways of living throughout the world, the common problem, as Hilary French (1990) points out, is that of finding the proper balance between sufficiency and excess, which she says will be as difficult for the former socialist nations as it has been for the West. In this context, she points out how Czechoslovakia's president, Vaclav Havel, has identified the omnipresent dictatorship of consumption, production, advertising, commerce, and consumer culture as the common enemy.

The uncontrolled greed of the global treadmill has been blamed for the frightening global environmental degradation and for overpowering our sense of responsibility to future generations. "How much is enough" for living a good life (Durning 1992) has become the critical issue today. This concern with sufficiency should lead us to question the equation of consumption with meaningful existence and of the good life with the material standard of living. But such an equation cannot be avoided in a society of abundance, which has to follow the imperative of consumption if its expanding productive capacities are to be put to use. However, since redistribution or any real systemic changes are ruled out, Daly (1979) recommends a control from within based on obedience

to objective value, warning that "if interior restraints on will and appetite diminish, then exterior restraints, coercive police powers, and Malthusian positive checks must increase." (p. 53)

Gandhi, aware both of the fatal attraction and the destructive potential of wanton materialism, saw it as constituting the gravest threat to human freedom, survival, and environmental security. He therefore opted for a simple, nonexploitative, and ecologically sustainable social order. Such a decentralized social order, based on truth and nonviolence, was to be governed by the metaphysically determined optimum levels of wants, technology, and resource use fitted to the requirements of the human scale. In the interim, he demanded that the rich become trustees of the poor in order to serve justice, to mitigate the negative impacts of the differentials of wealth and power, and to avoid class conflicts. His radical vision of a normal social order, nowhere realized as yet, provides a useful yardstick for measuring how ecologically sound and environmentally sustainable a society is in its actual operation. Noting that the world has enough for everyone's needs but not for everyone's greed, Gandhi was convinced that such a social order would come about

> *only if the means of production of the elementary necessaries of life remain in the control of the masses. These should be freely available to all as God's air and water are or ought to be; they should not be made a vehicle of traffic for the exploitation of others. Their monopolization by any country, nation or group of persons would be unjust. The neglect of this simple principle is the cause of the destitution that we witness today not only in this unhappy land but in other parts of the world too.* (quoted in Sinha 1976, p. 81.)

From this point of view, while there is little disagreement that overpopulation aggravates environmental and other problems, the attempts to eradicate the root causes of social instability, inequality, and poverty are bound to be far more effective in the long run than the impressive but partially effective approaches to population control. Brian Tokar (1988) has pointed out that, historically, rapid increases in population occur when people become dislocated from their traditional land base and become less secure about their personal and family survival. On the other hand, populations become stable when the future is secure, the infant mortality rate is low, social choices for women are expanding, and parents are not worried about who will support them in their old age.

How to effect the radical changes required to restore the proper ecological balance and preserve the biocultural integrity and diversity of the global "household," but "without the most fantastic 'bust' of all time" (Ehrlich 1968, p. 169), is the formidable challenge and the urgent task facing humankind. This will involve a redirection of the vast, creative human energies away from a self-defeating and ecodestructive expansionist and wasteful orientation, and their rechanneling into life-giving and life-promoting forms of human action and human social organization.

REFERENCES

Arnold, Steven H. 1989 "Sustainable Development: A Solution to the Development Puzzle." *Development, Journal of SID* 2/3:21–24.

Baker, Patrick L. 1993 "Chaos, Order, and Sociological Theory." *Sociological Inquiry* 63:123–149.

Bell, Daniel 1976 *The Cultural Contradictions of Capitalism.* New York: Basic Books.

—— 1977 "Are There 'Social Limits' to Growth?" In Kenneth D. Wilson, ed., *Prospects for Growth: Changing Expectations for the Future.* New York: Praeger.

Borgatta, Edgar F. 1989 "Towards a Proactive Sociology." Paper presented at the 29th International Congress of the International Institute of Sociology, Rome.

—— 1996 "Proactive Sociology: The Need for Relevance in Sociology." *The Annals of the International Institute of Sociology* (New Series, vol. 5). Trieste, Italy: University of Trieste.

——, and Karen S. Cook 1988 "Sociology and Its Future." In Edgar F. Borgatta and Karen S. Cook, eds., *The Future of Sociology.* Newbury Park, Calif.: Sage.

——, and Laurie R. Hatch 1988 "Social Stratification." In Edgar F. Borgatta and Karen S. Cook, eds., *The Future of Sociology.* Newbury Park, Calif.: Sage.

Brown, Lester R., Christopher Flavin, and Sandra Postel 1990 "Picturing a Sustainable Society." In Lester R. Brown and associates, *State of the World 1990: A Worldwatch Institute Report on Progress Toward a Sustainable Society.* New York: W. W. Norton.

Brundtland, Gro Harlem 1989 "Sustainable Development: An Overview." *Development, Journal of SID* 2/3:13–14.

Buttel, Frederick H. 1987 "New Directions in Environmental Sociology." *Annual Review of Sociology* 13:465–488.

Castells, Manuel 1985 "From the Urban Question to the City and the Grassroots." *Urban and Regional Studies* (Working Paper No. 47). University of Sussex, U.K.

Catton, William R., Jr. 1980 *Overshoot.* Urbana: University of Illinois Press.

——, and Riley E. Dunlap 1978 "Environmental Sociology: A New Paradigm." *American Sociologist* 13:41–49.

Commoner, Barry 1974 "Interview on Growth." In Willem L. Oltmans, ed., *On Growth: The Crisis of Exploding Population and Resource Depletion.* New York: Capricorn Books.

Coomaraswamy, A. K. 1946 *The Religious Basis of the Forms of Indian Society.* New York: Orientalia.

Craven, Avery O. 1937 "Frederick Jackson Turner." In William T. Hutchinson, ed., *Marcus W. Jernegan Essays in American Historiography.* Chicago: University of Chicago Press.

Daly, Herman E. 1979 "Ethical Implications of Limits to Global Development." In William M. Finnin, Jr. and Gerald A. Smith, eds., *The Morality of Scarcity: Limited Resources and Social Policy.* Baton Rouge: Louisiana State University Press.

de la Court, Thijs 1990 *Beyond Brundtland: Green Developments in the 1990s.* New York: New Horizon Press.

Duncan, Otis Dudley 1964 "Social Organization and the Ecosystem." In Robert E. L. Faris, ed., *Handbook of Modern Sociology.* Chicago: Rand McNally.

Dunlap, Riley E. 1979 "Environmental Sociology." *Annual Review of Sociology* 5:243–273.

Durning, Alan 1992 *How Much Is Enough.* New York: W.W. Norton.

Ehrlich, Paul R. 1968 *The Population Bomb.* New York: Ballantine Books.

Feagin, Joe R. 1988 *The Free Enterprise City: Houston in Political-Economic Perspective.* New Brunswick, N.J.: Rutgers University Press.

Foster, John Bellamy 1995 "Global Ecology and the Common Good." *Monthly Review* 46(9):1–10.

Francis, Roy 1993 "Chaos, Order, and Sociological Theory: A Comment." *Sociological Inquiry* 63:239–241.

French, Hilary F. 1990 *Green Revolution: Environmental Reconstruction in Eastern Europe and the Soviet Union* (Worldwatch Paper No. 99). Washington, D.C.: Worldwatch Institute.

Friedmann, J., and G. Wolff 1982 "World City Formation: An Agenda for Research and Action." *International Journal of Urban and Regional Research* 6:309–344.

Gibbs, Jack P. 1989 *Control: Sociology's Central Notion.* Urbana: University of Illinois Press.

Giddens, Anthony 1990 *The Consequences of Modernity.* Stanford, Calif.: Stanford University Press.

Gottdiener, M., and Joe Feagin 1988 "The Paradigm Shift in Urban Sociology." *Urban Affairs Quarterly* 24:163–187.

Greer, Scott 1979 "Discontinuities and Fragmentation in Societal Growth." In Amos H. Hawley, ed., *Societal Growth: Processes and Implications.* New York: Free Press.

Hardin, Garrett 1968 "The Tragedy of the Commons." *Science* 162:1243–1248.

Hawley, Amos H. 1979 "Cumulative Change in Theory and in History." In Amos H. Hawley, ed., *Societal Growth: Processes and Implications.* New York: Free Press.

—— 1984 "Sociological Human Ecology: Past, Present, and Future." In Michael Micklin and Harvey M. Choldin, eds., *Sociological Human Ecology: Contemporary Issues and Applications.* Boulder, Colo.: Westview.

—— 1986 *Human Ecology: A Theoretical Essay.* Chicago: University of Chicago Press.

Hildyard, Nicholas B. 1989 "Adios Amazonia? A Report from Altimira Gathering." *The Ecologist* 19:53–67.

Holden, Constance 1989 "Environment, Culture, and Change in the Arctic." *Science* 243:883.

Humphrey, Craig R., and Frederick H. Buttel 1982 *Environment, Energy, and Society.* Belmont, Calif.: Wadsworth.

Hutchinson, Ray 1993 "The Crisis of Urban Sociology." In Ray Hutchinson, ed., *Urban Sociology in Transition: Research in Urban Sociology* 3. Greenwich, Conn.: JAI Press.

Kahn, Herman 1974 "Interview on Growth." In Willem L. Oltmans, ed., *On Growth: The Crisis of Exploding Population and Resource Depletion.* New York: Capricorn Books.

La Gory, Mark 1993 "Spatial Structure and the Urban Experience: Ecology and the New Urban Sociology." In Ray Hutchinson, ed., *Urban Sociology in Transition: Research in Urban Sociology* 3. Greenwich, Conn.: JAI Press.

Lechner, Frank, J. 1985 "Modernity and its Discontents." In Jeffrey C. Alexander, ed., *Neofunctionalism.* Beverly Hills, Calif.: Sage.

Lenski, Gerhard 1979 "Directions and Continuities in Social Growth." In Amos H. Hawley, ed., *Societal Growth: Process and Implications.* New York: Free Press.

Marcel, Gabriel 1952 *Men Against Humanity.* London: Harvill Press.

Meadows, Donella, Dennis Meadows, Jorgen Randers, and William Behrens 1972 *The Limits to Growth: A Report for the Club of Rome's Project on the Predicament of Mankind.* New York: Universe Books.

Mellos, Koula 1988 *Perspectives on Ecology: A Critical Essay.* New York: St. Martin's Press.

Miller, G. Tyler, Jr. 1972 *Replenish the Earth: A Primer in Human Ecology.* Belmont, Calif.: Wadsworth.

Morrison, Denton E. 1976 "Growth, Environment, Equity and Scarcity." *Social Science Quarterly* 57:292–306.

Namboodiri, Krishnan 1988 "Ecological Demography: Its Place in Sociology." *American Sociological Review* 53:619–633.

Park, Robert E. 1936 "Human Ecology." *American Journal of Sociology* 42:1–15.

Peck, Dennis L. 1987 "Introduction to Science and Technology: Critical Assessments of Progress." *Quarterly Journal of Ideology* 11(2):i–iii.

Polanyi, Karl (1947) 1974 "Our Obsolete Market Mentality." *The Ecologist* 4:213–220.

Potter, David M. 1954 *People of Abundance: Economic Abundance and the American Character.* Chicago: Phoenix Books.

Rappaport, Roy A. 1976 "Forests and Man." *The Ecologist* 6:240–246.

—— 1978 "Biology, Meaning, and the Quality of Life." In J. Milton Yinger and Stephen J. Cutler, eds., *Major Social Issues: A Multidisciplinary View.* New York: Free Press.

Reichel-Dolmatoff, G. 1977 "Cosmology as Ecological Analysis: A View from the Rain Forest." *The Ecologist* 7:4–11.

Revelle, Roger 1974 "Interview on Growth." In Willem L. Oltmans, ed., *On Growth: The Crisis of Exploding Population and Resource Depletion.* New York: Capricorn Books.

Sachs, Wolfgang 1990 "On the Archeology of the Development Idea." *The Ecologist* 20:42–43.

Saran, A. K. 1978 "The Traditional Vision of Man." Paper presented at UNESCO Seminar, Hyderabad, India. Mimeo.

Saunders, P. 1986 *Social Theory and the Urban Question.* New York: Holmes and Meier.

Schnaiberg, Allan 1980 *The Environment: From Surplus to Scarcity.* New York: Oxford University Press.

——, and Kenneth A. Gould 1994 *Environment and Society: The Enduring Conflict.* New York: St. Martin's Press.

Schnore, Leo F. 1965 *The Urban Scene: Human Ecology and Demography.* New York: The Free Press.

Sen, Amartya K. 1981 *Poverty and Famines: An Essay on Entitlement and Deprivation.* Oxford: Clarendon Press.

Shiva, Vandana 1990 "Biodiversity, Biotechnology and Profit: The Need for a Peoples' Plan to Protect Biological Diversity." *The Ecologist* 20/2 (March/April).

Sinha, Radha 1976 *Food and Poverty: The Political Economy of Confrontation.* London: Croom Helm.

Smith, David A. 1995 "The New Urban Sociology Meets the Old: Rereading Some Classical Human Ecology." *Urban Affairs Review* 30(3):432–458.

Smith, Michael P. 1979 *The City and Social Theory.* New York: St. Martin's Press.

Stonich, Susan C. 1989 "The Dynamics of Social Processes and Environmental Destruction: A Central American Case Study." *Population and Development Review* 15:269–296.

Tokar, Brian 1988 "Social Ecology, Deep Ecology and the Future of Green Political Thought." *The Ecologist* 18:132–141.

Vohra, B. B. 1985 "Why India's Forests Have Been Cut Down." *The Ecologist* 15:50–51.

Weinstein, Jay A. 1976 *Demographic Transition and Social Change.* Morristown, N.J.: General Learning Press.

World Commission on Environment and Development 1987 *Our Common Future* (The Bruntland Report). New York: Oxford University Press.

Worster, Dennis 1994 "Chaos Theory Seeps Into Ecology Debate, Stirring Up a Tempest." In Dennis Farney, Great Divides: Scenes From the Politics of American Culture. *The Wall Street Journal* July 11.

Young, Gerald, ed. 1983 *Origins of Human Ecology.* Stroudsburg, Pa.: Hutchinson Ross.

LAKSHMI K. BHARADWAJ

HUMAN NATURE

Debates over the nature of human nature have characterized social theory since it emerged in the Renaissance. As Thomas Sowell has argued, these debates generally take two forms: the optimistic and the pessimistic (Sowell 1987). The former position, associated with Rousseau and anarchists such as William Goodwin, holds that humans are essentially good but are turned bad by the institutions of their society. The latter position is rooted in the assumption that humans are fundamentally egoistic and selfish, thereby requiring either a strong state to regulate them or, in a less pessimistic account, an institution like the market to guide their affairs toward an optimal result.

For sociologists, neither position became the dominant way of thinking about human nature; instead, the plasticity of human experience was emphasized. Durkheim (1973) wrote the most important defense of a pluralistic approach to the subject, one that remains unsurpassed to this day in its clarity of presentation. Human nature is dualistic, he argued, speaking to the needs of both body and soul, the sacred and the profane, the emotional and the cognitive, and other such dualities. We are, in short, what we make ourselves. This version of a flexible approach to human nature would come to characterize contemporary theorists such as Parsons, who spoke of "much discussed 'plasticity' of the human organism, its capacity to learn any one of a large number of alternative patterns of behavior instead of being bound by its generic constitution to a very limited range of alternatives" (1951, p. 32).

In current sociological debates, the plasticity of human nature is emphasized by the general term *social construction*. If one argues that we ought to speak of gender roles rather than sex roles—the former is recognized to be the product of how people arrange their cultural rules, whereas the latter is understood to be fixed biologically—one is making a case for plasticity (Epstein 1988). Indeed, given the importance of feminism in contemporary theory, which tends to argue that "nothing about the body, including women's reproductive organs, determines univocally how social divisions will be shaped" (Scott 1988, p. 2), the strength of a plasticity approach to human nature is probably stronger than ever before.

Current research in many areas of sociology is premised on a social construction approach. Work stimulated by ethnomethodology is one clear case. In contrast to a Chomskian understanding of language as originating in rules hard-wired in the brain, the tradition of conversation analysis examines how human beings in real conversation twist and shape their utterances to account for context and nuance (Schegloff and Sacks 1979; Scheff 1986). Moreover, since the language we use is a reflection of the way we think, it is possible to argue that the mind itself is socially constructed, that the a priori nature of the way we think is relatively minimal (Coulter 1979). Accounts of sociological practice based on the assumption of plasticity do not end there. It has been argued that homosexuality is not driven by biological destiny but is a socially constructed phenomenon (Greenberg 1988). Morality, as well, can be understood as socially constructed (Wolfe 1989). Underlying a wide variety of approaches to sociology—from symbolic interactionism to social problems—is an underlying premise that human nature is not driven by any one thing.

The only dissent from a general consensus about human nature's plasticity is rational choice theory. At least among economists who believe that economic methodologies can be used to study social institutions such as the family, there is a belief that "human behavior is not compartmentalized, sometimes based on maximizing, sometimes not, sometimes motivated by stable preferences, sometimes by volatile ones, sometimes resulting in an optimal accumulation, sometimes not" (Becker 1976, p. 14). Yet there are many versions of rational choice theory; at least one of them, that associated with Jon Elster, is committed to methodological individualism but is also willing to concede the existence of a "multiple self" (Elster 1986). It is far more common in contemporary sociology to speak of egoism and altruism as existing in some kind of unstable combination rather than giving the priority totally to one or the other (Etzioni 1988).

Arguments about human nature, in turn, are related to the philosophical anthropology that shaped so much social theory. It has been a consistent theme of the sociological enterprise to argue that humans are different from other species. From the emphasis on *homo faber* in Marx and Engels, through Weber's notions about the advantages of culture, to Mead's account of why dogs and other animals are incapable of exchanging significant symbols, humans have been understood to possess unique characteristics that determine the organization of their society. Twentieth-century theorists such as Arnold Gehlen or Helmuth Plessner carried forward this tradition and are increasingly translated and read (for an overview, see Honneth and Joas 1988). Even Niklas Luhmann,

whose work is heavily influenced by biology and cybernetics, can still claim that "the decisive advantage of human interaction over animal interaction stems from this elemental achievement of language" (1982, p. 72).

The most important shift in philosophical anthropology in recent years is a shift from an essentially materialist understanding of human capacities to an essentially mental one. Powers of interpretation and narrative, it has been argued, constitute the essential features of the human self (Taylor 1989). Just as an argument about the plasticity of human nature enables sociology to avoid reduction into psychological categories, an emphasis on the interpretive powers of humans prevents a reduction of sociology to sociobiology and other basically algorithmic ways of thinking about evolution.

As with the issue of plasticity, not all sociologists agree either that there are specific human characteristics or that, if there are, they ought to be understood as primarily mental and interpretive. Sociobiologists argue not only that humans are driven by their genetic structure more than they would like to believe but also that other animals also possess cultural skills. There is therefore no fundamental difference between human and nonhuman species, they are merely points along a continuum (Lumsden and Wilson 1981). Both sociologists and anthropologists, consequently, have argued for the use of sociobiological approaches in the social sciences (Lopreato 1984; Rindos 1986; Wozniak 1984), although there are also critics who question such an enterprise (Blute 1987).

In the 1990s, sociobiology, now often called evolutionary psychology, was something of a growth industry. Edward O. Wilson, who did so much to originate the field, sees the possibility of a unified approach to knowledge, one in which the laws of human interaction could eventually be deduced from the physical and the biological sciences (Wilson 1998). In the meantime, others influenced by evolutionary psychology have argued that cultural products such as language and mind can be understood through the laws of evolution (Blackmore 1999; Lynch 1996). Even such specific cultural products as novels and works of art are formed by processes of cultural selection, it has been argued (Taylor 1996). While still something of a minority point of view, trends such as these are premised on the idea that the natural sciences, especially biology, offer a better model for understanding human societies than the sociological tradition as dervived from Durkheim, Weber, and Mead.

Another challenge to the anthropocentric view that social scientists have taken toward humans has arisen with cognitive science and artificial intelligence. Whereas classical sociological theory compared humans to other animal species, we can now compare them to machines. Computers, after all, process information just as human brains do, use language to communicate, and reason, and can, especially in new approaches to artificial intelligence called connectionist, learn from their mistakes. There are, consequently, some efforts to apply artificial intelligence to sociology just as there are efforts to use the insights of sociobiology (Gilbert and Heath 1986), although here, again, there are strong critical voices (Wolfe 1991; Woolger 1985). In the more recent work of Niklas Luhmann, as well as in the writings of some other theorists, emphasis is placed on information science, systems theory, even thermodynamics—all of which are approaches based on a denial that human systems require special ways of understanding that are different from other systems (Bailey 1990; Beniger 1986; Luhmann 1989).

In spite of efforts to develop sociological theory on the basis of algorithmic self-reproducing systems, it is unlikely that assumptions about the unique, interpretative, meaning-producing capacities of humans will be seriously challenged. It is the capacity to recognize the contexts in which messages are transmitted and thereby to interpret those messages that make human mental capacities distinct from any organism, whether natural or artificial, that is preprogrammed to follow explicit instructions. One reason humans are able to recognize contexts is precisely the plasticity of their mental capacities. The plastic theory of human nature, in short, overlaps with an emphasis on philosophical anthropology to produce an understanding of human behavior that does not so much follow already-existing rules so much as it alters and bends rules as it goes along.

Both understandings of human nature and accounts of specifically human capacities will be relevant to future efforts in sociological theory to reconcile micro and macro approaches. Although there has been a good deal of effort to establish a micro–macro link (Alexander et al. 1987), the more interesting question may turn out not to be not whether it can be done but whether (and how) it ought to be done. Systems theory and the information sciences provide a relatively easy way to make a link between parts and wholes: Each part is understood to have as little autonomy as possible, so that the system as a whole can function autonomously with respect to other systems. The micro, like a bit of information in a computer program, would be structured to be as dumb as possible so that the macro system itself can be intelligent. Nonhuman enterprises—computers on the one hand and the structure of DNA in other animal species on the other—show that there is a major bridge between the macro and the micro. But the cost of constructing that bridge is the denial of the autonomy of the parts, a high cost for humans to pay.

But the conception of human beings as preprogrammed rule followers is not the only way to conceptualize micro sociological processes. The traditions of ethnomethodology and symbolic interactionism, which are more compatible with notions emphasizing the plasticity of human nature, imagine the human parts of any social system as engaged in a constant process of renegotiating the rules that govern the system. When the micro is understood as plastic, the macro can be understood as capable of existing even in imperfect, entropy-producing states of disorder. Indeed, for human systems, as opposed to those of machines and other species, disorder is the norm, integration the exception. If there is going to be a micro–macro link in sociology, it may well come about not by denying human plasticity and uniqueness, but rather by accounting for the particular and special property humans possess of having no fixed nature but rather a repertoire of social practices that in turn make human society different form any other kind of system.

(SEE ALSO: *Evolution: Biological, Social, Cultural; Intelligence; Sex Differences*)

REFERENCES

Alexander, Jeffrey C., Bernhard Giesen, Richard Munch, and Neil J. Smelser 1987 *The Macro–Micro Link.* Berkeley: University of California Press.

Bailey, Kenneth D. 1990 *Social Entropy Theory*. Albany: State University of New York Press.

Becker, Gary 1976 *The Economic Approach to Human Behavior*. Chicago: University of Chicago Press.

Beniger, James R. 1986 *The Control Revolution: Technological and Economic Origins of the Information Society*. Cambridge, Mass.: Harvard University Press.

Blackmore, Susan 1999 *The Meme Machine*. Oxford: Oxford University Press.

Blute, Marion 1987 "Biologists on Sociocultural Evolution: A Critical Analysis." *Sociological Theory* 5:185–193.

Coulter, Jeff 1979 *The Social Construction of Mind*. London: Macmillan.

Durkheim, Emile 1973 "The Dualism of Human Nature and Its Social Conditions." In Robert N. Bellah, ed., *Emile Durkheim on Morality and Society: Selected Writings*. Chicago: University of Chicago Press.

Elster, Jon, ed. 1986 *The Multiple Self*. Cambridge, U.K.: Cambridge University Press.

Epstein, Cynthia 1988 *Deceptive Distinctions: Sex, Gender, and the Social Order*. New Haven, Conn.: Yale University Press.

Etzioni, Amitai 1988 *The Moral Dimension*. New York: Free Press.

Gilbert, C. Nigel, and Christian Heath, eds. 1986 *Social Action and Artificial Intelligence: Surrey Conferences on Sociological Theory and Method 3*. Aldershot, U.K.: Gower.

Greenberg, David 1988 *The Construction of Homosexuality*. Chicago: University of Chicago Press.

Honneth, Axel, and Hans Joas 1988 *Social Action and Human Nature*. Cambridge, U.K.: Cambridge University Press.

Lopreato, Joseph 1984 *Human Nature and Biocultural Evolution*. Boston: Allen and Unwin.

Luhmann, Niklas 1982 *The Differentiation of Society*, trans. Stephen Holmes and Charles Larmore. New York: Columbia University Press.

—— 1989 *Ecological Communication*, trans. John Bednarz. Chicago: University of Chicago Press.

Lumsden, Charles J., and Edward O. Wilson 1981 *Genes, Mind, and Culture: The Coevolutionary Process*. Cambridge, Mass.: Harvard University Press.

Lynch, Aaron 1996 *Thought Contagion: How Beliefs Spread Throughout Society*. New York: Basic Books.

Parsons, Talcott 1951 *The Social System*. New York: Free Press.

Rindos, David 1986 "The Evolution of the Capacity for Culture: Sociobiology, Structuralism, and Cultural Selectiveness." *Current Anthropology* 27:315–332.

Scheff, Thomas J. 1986 "Micro-Linguistics and Social Structure: A Theory of Social Action." *Sociological Theory* 4:71–83.

Schegloff, Emmanuel, and Harvey Sacks 1979 "Opening Up Closings." In Ray Turner, ed., *Ethnomethodology: Selected Readings*. Baltimore: Penguin.

Scott, Joan Wallach 1988 *Gender and the Politics of History*. New York: Columbia University Press.

Sowell, Thomas 1987 *A Conflict of Visions*. New York: William Morrow.

Taylor, Charles 1989 *Sources of the Self: The Making of the Modern Identity*. Cambridge, Mass.: Harvard University Press.

Taylor, Gary 1996 *Cultural Selection: Why Some Achievements Survive the Test of Time–and Others Don't*. New York: Basic Books.

Wilson, Edward O. 1998 *Consilience: The Unity of Knowledge*. New York: Knopf.

Wolfe, Alan 1989 *Whose Keeper?: Social Science and Moral Obligation*. Berkeley: University of California Press.

—— 1991 "Mind, Self, Society, and Computer: Artificial Intelligence and the Sociology of Mind." *American Journal of Sociology* 96:1073–1096.

Woolger, Steve 1985 "Why Not a Sociology of Machines?: The Case of Sociology and Artificial Intelligence." *Sociology* 19:557–572.

Wozniak, Paul R. 1984 "Making Sociobiological Sense out of Sociology." *Sociological Quarterly* 25:191–204.

ALAN WOLFE

HUMAN RIGHTS, CHILDREN'S RIGHTS, AND DEMOCRACY

Sociology has existed in universities and as a research and scholarly profession for more than a century, but it has serious problems in justifying its existence in terms of demonstrating that the knowledge it produces is useful. In its early stages of development, sociology was often coupled with social work or with other fields such as anthropology, political science, and economics. However, as universities grew, the social and behavioral science fields became differentiated, and in the post–World War II period sociology not only grew but flourished and developed a major identity in the universities. However, more important, within the field applied interests were often disparaged. In large part, fields such as social work, family studies, industrial relations, systems analysis, administration, criminology, penology, and others became independent major entities as sociologists denigrated the notion of being involved in applied research and practice. In fact, in the last decades of the twentieth century sociologists appear more often to be seen as possible peripheral members in social research rather than the organizers of major social research, which is frequently motivated by practical, applied considerations.

Still, it is occasionally noted that sociology has been useful, but it is frequently and necessarily a quite modest statement. For example, it is often pointed out that sociology led much of the development and diffusion of statistical and other analytic procedures in the social sciences. Sociology also led the way in developing procedures for systematic data collection, which it has not only shared with other academic disciplines but which has become a part of common daily life, such as polling, investigative reporting, and so on. And the interest in social problems, consistent but peripheral for sociology over the years, has led to some involvement in race and ethnic relations, women's rights, and human rights more generally. Incidentally, while sociology has failed to move in the direction of applied science, psychology has virtually exploded in that direction, leading to concern over the years that that discipline might detach its academic and research interests from the applied professional and clinical aspects. Indeed, the field of psychology has moved into areas of application neglected by sociology, such as family relations, group counseling and therapy, and environmental and ecological studies; other sister disciplines, such as anthropology, economics, and political science have made a similar move in order to increase the scope of development of applied interests.

THE RELEVANCE OF SOCIOLOGY

It is not unreasonable to raise the question: If sociology is presumed to be adding to the knowledge of the world, how can it be useful? This question has been raised throughout the history of the discipline, but that does not mean it has gotten serious attention. As a recent positive example, note the work of Turner (1998) and the subsequent comments on the topic. Another recent consideration of "The Value of Sociology" that provides perspective is the article by Snow (1999), but to some extent much of the discussion about the value of sociology is abstract, albeit broader than some earlier particularistic orientations, which took the view that if sociology was not valuable, it would not be in the college or university curriculum. Two sentences from the abstract of Turner's article (p.243) provide an orientation to answering the question: "It is argued that sociological theory and its applications to real world problems should constitute the core of the discipline . . . . Sociology should redefine and reorient its practice to create an engineering discipline where abstract theoretical principles are boiled down to rules of thumb and used to build or tear down social structures" (p. 243). This is a more direct statement of the idea that sociology should be useful.

Part of the reason for the hesitancy of sociologists to become interested in applied research is the way the field was defined—as "the science of society." Scientists study and analyze their subject matter, but they do not determine what is right and proper for society. The task of determining laws, custom, and mores is not seen by them as being their task, and indeed there is commonly great concern that the values of social scientists should not influence their research and scholarly work. Thus, applied research in sociology has often been defined as examining what is going on in a social situation, in order to determine the underlying social forces at work. If a social policy is involved, the aim of the research may be to see if it is working; with the introduction of a new social policy, research is most typically aimed at seeing whether stated objectives can be confirmed. Much of the interest in applied research in the social sciences became associated with the concept of "evaluation research," particularly in the post–World War II period, with stimulus from sociologists such as Donald Young and Leonard S. Cottrell, Jr., at Russell Sage Foundation. However, stimulus for evaluation research occurred in other ways as well, such as through laboratories and research centers in educational psychology, social psychology, and other behavioral and social sciences, with research often being supported by such government agencies as the National Institute of Mental Health. These thrusts led to two important developments for the social and behavioral sciences.

The first was the growth of methodological sophistication, often identified with the classic codifying work on quasi-experimental research design by Campbell and Stanley (1963) and Cook and Campbell (1979). The second was the notion that evaluation research could be of two types: conventional research, in which the disinterested researcher merely seeks to describe what happens when policy changes are introduced, and "formative" research, wherein the social scientist is not only involved in the evaluation of the consequences of policy changes but is a consultant in the process of identifying the changes needed to accomplish the goals of proposed policy, often with sequential evaluations and changes when the desired results do not materialize with the initial changes.

Throughout this history of social science involvement in applied research, evaluations have often produced negative (i.e., no change) findings, and in some cases even retrogression or reversal on the intended change direction and/or unintended consequences. But, independently of all these results, it can be asked whether the presumed knowledge of sociology and the social sciences is being used effectively, and the answer has been that this does not appear to be the case, at least in the context of one type of criticism. This critique has been advanced many times in different ways, and in the context of this article it will be phrased as not satisfying options of "proactive sociology" (see Borgatta 1991, 1994, 1996). In particular, do sociologists evaluate the social and behavioral structures that exist in society and put them in a comparative perspective? Do sociologists examine the values that exist and describe them objectively, presumably correctly interpreting what they are? Do sociologists examine stated values and see how well social structures that exist implement the identified values? Before proceeding to further consideration of these questions, consider one relevant case.

DEMOCRACY AND INDIVIDUAL RIGHTS

While no form of government can effectively be defined as maximizing the provision of human rights and children's rights, there is a strong basis for arguing that democratic forms are more likely to do so in the long run than other governmental forms. There are a fair number of nations that at this juncture appear to be reasonably well oriented to protecting human and children's rights, but attention to a little bit of history should keep one from becoming complaisant about the prospect. For example, in the United States slavery existed until the end of the Civil War, less than a century and a half ago. Until the amendments that followed the Civil War, if one read the Constitution of the United States one might have thought women were entitled to the same rights as men, but they were not. The assumption that women were not entitled to the same rights as men was so ingrained in the culture that it was not even necessary that it be made explicit. It was a world in which men governed; women did not even get the right to vote until half a century after the end of the Civil War. And the history of the expansion of the United States and its relationship with Mexico and with the American Indians may give pause to those who think that simply having a government that is labeled a democracy is one in which "social justice" writ small and large is to be expected.

In a democracy the de facto rules do not necessarily provide equal protection under the law for all persons, and the majority or even a smaller segment of society may define the rules. In more recent times, there have been examples of restrictive abuse in the United States, as in the passing of the constitutional amendment that established "prohibition" of alcohol. Aside from attempting to restrict the choice behavior of citizens, the amendment created the era of gangsters and racketeers. Although that constitutional amendment was repealed, there remain numerous laws prohibiting access to certain substances among the most obvious of which are the laws restricting "drugs." More than the outlawing of alcohol during prohibition, the drug laws have created the circumstances leading to the incarceration of the overwhelming majority of the roughly 1.5 million people in the U.S. prison system today. But more generally, in a democracy, all kinds of laws may be passed that restrict individual rights. Germany's progression from a democratic government to Hitler's dictatorship, although an extreme case, should never be forgotten. Similarly, the cases in which liberal or "socialist" regimes have been overthrown with the help of the great American Democracy, only to be followed by totalitarian regimes, may be seen as disturbing.

To continue with the example of the United States, the McCarthy period in the 1950s is an example of rampant political witch hunts. But consider even the more recent partisan political situation, also termed a witch hunt by some, involving a person as powerful as the president of the United States. A Republican majority in the House of Representatives voted to impeach the president, sending two articles of impeachment to the Senate, which was to "try" the president to determine his guilt or innocence, with a guilty finding by two-thirds of the Senate requiring removal from office. Here we will not discuss the constitutional issues involved, or the moral and legal failings of the president in the matter, but only pay analytical attention to the strange articles of impeachment to show how subtly the power of a majority can create a situation that counters "fairness" and fails to protect even the rights of a president (see *Congressional Record*, December 19, 1998).

Two articles of impeachment were passed in the House of Representatives by an essentially partisan vote of the Republican majority; here *attention will be given only to the question of what is minimally necessary to arrive at a guilty verdict by two-thirds, or 67, of the 100 senators*. Article I states in part: "Contrary to that oath, William Jefferson Clinton willfully provided perjurious, false and misleading testimony to the grand jury concerning one or more of the following . . . ." Then four alleged "testimonies" were noted. Now, any sociologist or statistician should be able to analyze the charge and ask the question, "What would the minimum guilt attribution be to create a majority of 67 senators voting guilty?" Simple, since only one alleged testimony is required to judge the president guilty, if 16 senators voted guilty on the first testimony and 17 different (nonoverlapping) senators voted guilty on each of the three other testimonies, the majority of 67 would be created to judge the president guilty of Article I. Thus, the extraordinary situation exists that *theoretically the president could be judged guilty by no more than 17 senators on any of the four testimonies, but he could be judged guilty by 67 senators because of the way the question was formulated!* What a strange way for a democracy to operate. Of course, the situation is even more ridiculous with regard to Article II, which is also defined in the "one or more" fashion, but involves seven "acts," leading to the situation that theoretically the minimum number of senators needed (nonoverlapping) is 9 for three "acts"

and 10 for each of the other four to get a cumulative majority of 67 senators voting guilty. Thus, it can be seen how the Republican congressmen were able to structure a vote in any way they wished, since they constituted the majority in the House of Representatives. It has been said many times that an effective democracy requires constant attention to how power is used and how the rights of all individuals, even of the president, are protected.

Democracy is a common topic of study, and topics relevant to issues of human rights are implicit in many presentations, as, for example, those in a special issue of *International Sociology* ("Democratic Culture," 1999).

HUMAN RIGHTS AND CHILDREN'S RIGHTS

With regard to human rights and children's rights, attention must be given to providing, as much as possible, for the protection for all persons, and presumably this can happen most dependably in a democracy. However, some things need to be emphasized. Special rights can be legislated for particular individuals or groups, and because they are often accepted as reasonable, this may lead to some abuses and strange situations. For example, *it has been repeatedly stated that with regard to human rights, the attribution of status on an inherited basis does not correspond to a concept of equal opportunity and equal treatment*. If this is the case, then how do equal opportunity and equal treatment operate with regard to other aspects of inheritance? If a parent is rich, owning $70 billion of assets, the child could inherit roughly $30 billion in the United States under current law. If the parent is poor, the child may not inherit anything. Further, in being raised in the rich family, the child may have extraordinary forms of support and access to resources that the poor child does not have. The capitalist system may provide the possibility of upward mobility in a democracy, but considering the advantages of the wealthy, the playing fields for the rich and the poor are not equal. Thus, even if the state mandates a strong support system for all children, human rights and children's rights are still subject to a relative notion of the importance of inherited status. *Question: How much attention do sociologists give to this kind of analysis and identification of the values involved?* The sociologist, of course, should be able to note that the general system even in a democracy can provide a very strong support of inherited status. The acceptance of inherited status is still rampant in much of the world, beginning with any nation in which there is a notion of royalty, which of course includes Great Britain and some other developed nations that are classed as democracies.

This article began by noting that sociologists and other social scientists should become more concerned with the possibility of proactive involvement in social change. As regards the above example, a major concern of the sociologist would be not only to consider and analyze the consequences of existing social policy, but also to *realistically represent* the value system that presumably underlies the social policy. As has been implicit thus far, social policy often does not correspond to the values that are espoused. There is reason for concern in being involved in this proactive orientation, since often values are not consistently aligned and may conflict. *Most dramatically, a traditional view of the family may conflict with the notion that children are due equal opportunity and access to resources in society, the provision of which necessarily becomes a community or state function. The tradition of parental "ownership" of children simply may conflict with providing children with equal access to the resources that exist in the society.* Thus, the analysis of values becomes a critical area for sociological research. Beyond this, if there is a thrust for moving toward "universal" values regarding human and children's rights, then in the proactive orientation sociologists and other social scientists who are ostensibly knowledgeable about how social structures operate should be able to model and propose social structures in order to implement these values.

HUMAN RIGHTS

Human rights, or the rights and privileges that every person should expect and receive in a just or "good" society, have been a concern of philosophers through the ages, and commonly this interest has been reassociated with such concepts as "social justice." Although this philosophical topic has also been addressed in religious and political codes and documents, the first really broad and broadly supported international statement on the topic is to be found in the United Nations Universal Declaration of Human Rights (1949), which was approved by the U.N. General Assembly on 10 December 1948. Sociologists might give this document critical attention. Are the rights that are noted consistent with each other; if not, what are the inconsistencies and how might they be resolved? Thus, the study of implicit values becomes a vital area for sociologists. Questions that become obvious include questions about the priorities of the values. The Universal Declaration begins with a preamble that states: "Whereas recognition of the inherent dignity and of the equal and inalienable rights of all members of the human family is the foundation of freedom, justice and peace in the world . . ." It goes on to elaborate on these rights and then states: "The General Assembly proclaims this Universal Declaration of Human Rights as a common standard of achievement for all peoples and all nations, to the end that every individual and every organ of society, keeping this Declaration constantly in mind, shall strive by teaching and education to promote respect for these rights and freedoms and by progressive measures, national and international, to secure their universal and effective recognition and observance, both among the peoples of Member States themselves and among the peoples of territories under their jurisdiction." There followed thirty articles that can be summarized as follows:

1. "All human beings are born free and equal in dignity and rights . . ."

2. All are entitled ". . . without distinction of any kind, such as race, colour, sex, language, religion, political or other opinion, national or social origin, property, birth or other status . . ."

3. "Everyone has the right to life, liberty and the security of person."

4. "No one shall be held in slavery or servitude; slavery and the slave trade shall be prohibited in all their forms."

5. "No one shall be subjected to torture or to cruel, inhuman or degrading treatment or punishment."

6. "Everyone has the right to recognition everywhere as a person before the law."

7. "All are equal before the law and . . . equal protection before the law . . . ."

8. "Everyone has the right to . . . national tribunals . . . ."

9. "No one shall be subjected to arbitrary arrest, detention or exile."

10. Elaboration is provided for entitlement to ". . . fair and public hearing . . . ."

11. "Everyone charged with a penal offence has the right to be presumed innocent until proved guilty . . . . No one shall be held guilty of any penal offence on account of any act or omission which did not constitute a penal offence . . . ."

12. "No one shall be subjected to arbitrary interference with his privacy, family, home or correspondence, nor to attacks upon his honour and reputation . . . ."

13. "Everyone has the right to freedom of movement and residence within the borders of each state. Everyone has the right to leave any country, including his own, and to return to his country."

14. "Everyone has the right to seek and to enjoy in other countries asylum from persecution."

15. "Everyone has the right to a nationality . . . ."

16. "Men and women of full age, without any limitation due to race, nationality, or religion, have the right to marry and to found a family. They are entitled to equal rights . . . entered into only with the free and full consent of the intending spouses. The family is the natural and fundamental group unit of society and is entitled to protection by society and the State."

17. "Everyone has the right to own property alone as well as in association with others . . . ."

18. "Everyone has the right to freedom of thought, conscience and religion . . ."

19. "Everyone has the right to freedom of opinion and expression . . . ."

20. "Everyone has the right to freedom of peaceful assembly and association . . . ."

21. "Everyone has the right to take part in the government . . . ."

22. "Everyone . . . has the right to social security . . . ."

23. "Everyone has the right to work, to free choice of employment, to just and favourable conditions of work and to protection against unemployment . . . ."

24. "Everyone has the right to rest and leisure . . . ."

25. "Everyone has the right to a standard of living adequate for health and well-being . . . ."

26. "Everyone has the right to education. Education shall be free, at least in the elementary and fundamental stages. Elementary education shall be compulsory. Technical and professional education shall be made generally available and higher education shall be equally accessible to all on the basis of merit. Education shall be directed to the full development of the human personality and to the strengthening of respect for human right and fundamental freedoms . . . . Parents have a prior right to choose the kind of education that shall be given to their children."

27. "Everyone has the right freely to participate in the cultural life . . . . Everyone has the right to the protection of the moral and material interests resulting from any scientific, literary or artistic production of which he is the author."

Articles 28 to 30 deal with (1) the rights to an international community in which these rights are realized; (2) respect for the rights and freedoms of others; and (3) maintenance of morality, public order, and the general welfare of a democratic society, in a manner that is not contrary to the purposes and principles of the United Nations.

It is not until Article 29 that one realizes that the Universal Declaration of Human Rights implicitly assumes a democratic form of government in all nations. Therefore, the approval of the Universal Declaration in 1948 by a vote of 48 to 0 with 8 abstentions—from the U.S.S.R., Ukraine, Byelorussia, Poland, Czechoslovakia, Yugoslavia, Saudi Arabia, and the Union of South Africa—is not ununderstandable. However, what is important for sociologists is that this is an attempt at identifying of universals, which presumably can be the basis for examining existing social structures and dealing with explorations of how social structures can be made to support the values involved. But before getting into such an enterprise, it is necessary to reiterate the idea that the values incorporated into the Universal Declaration themselves need to made explicit.

Before going on to subsequent developments in the area of human rights, a few remarks about the Universal Declaration are appropriate. First, human rights in this document are allocated specifically to individuals. This is in keeping with the notion that only individuals have status before the law. Of course, throughout history, particularly with the beginning of industrialization, the law has given status to entities other than individuals, most obviously corporate structures, including religious organizations, schools and foundations, and unions. Provision of rights before the law to such entities has consequences for individual human rights. Second—and this is a consideration that will become more prominent in subsequent comments—the rights provided are ambiguously allocated to adults, but the Universal Declaration provides no definition of adult status. Thus the definition of a vital concept is omitted—but quite a few other important concepts are also named but not defined. Implicitly, the concepts are subject to definition in the state where the individual resides. To give an example of the ambiguity, let us look at Article 16: "Men and women of full age, without limitation due to race, nationality or religion, have the right to marry and to found a family." It is not clear what full age means. Is it twelve years of age, fifteen, sixteen, eighteen, or twenty-one? Men and women have a right to marry, but does that mean one of each, or any combination of men and women? In terms of history and ethnic/religious variations, this is not a trivial question. "The family is the natural and fundamental group unit of society and is entitled to protection by society and the State." What is a family? There is so much variation in any anthropological view of the family as to make this a very vague concept, and the definition is continuing to change in modern industrial societies, what with the arrival of birth control and divorce and sequential multiple marriage. Sociologists and other social scientists obviously can provide some bases for clarification of these statements of rights and values. Other issues that arise with United Nations documents are emphasized in subsequent sections.

At this point it is appropriate to note that when the Universal Declaration of Human Rights was voted on, it was emphasized that it did not have the status of a treaty. A treaty was in preparation, however, and the International Covenant on Civil and Political Rights (1966), which incorporated much of the Universal Declaration, was adopted by the U.N. General Assembly, in 1966.. By 1985, 80 of the 159 members had ratified the treaty. The treaty changed some of the orientation, however, as can be seen by Article 1, which states: "All people have the right to self-determination. By virtue of that right they freely determine their political status and freely pursue their economic, social and cultural development. The States . . . shall promote the realization of the right of self-determination . . . ." The treaty begins with an ambiguous statement on how states are to operate, not on individual human rights. Unfortunately, it also contains language that responds to political entities, and one radical interpretation of the language suggests that any political entity effectively has the right to become independent. It needs to be emphasized that human rights—and closely topics related such as genocide, women's rights, and children's rights (to be considered below)—have been the subject of many actions in the U.N. General Assembly.

The literature in the field of human rights does not appear to have a major sociological component, but some sociological studies do exist (Buergenthal 1997; Gros Espeill 1998; Magnarella 1995; Pace 1998).

CHILDREN'S RIGHTS

The issues associated with children's rights are anticipated in part in the movement from the Universal Declaration to the International Covenant. Article 26 of the Universal Declaration states that everyone has the right to education but that parents have a prior right to choose the kind of education to be given to their children. In the International Covenant, more is said about the parental role. Article 18, for example, states: "The States . . . undertake to have respect for the liberty of parents . . . to ensure the religious and moral education of their children in conformity with their own convictions." Further, Article 23 states:

"Every child shall have . . . the right to such measures of protection required by his status as a minor, on the part of his family, the society and the State." This elaboration on the involvement of the society and the State raises many questions about the rights of children. Let us look at this in terms of education issues.

First, some attention must be given to the question of what constitutes education. A primary concept obviously is that there should be access to literacy—the ability to read and write. But other skills can also be important, as is exposure to what is classed as knowledge. Using a simplistic index, such as the one used in "Why Family Planning Matters" (1999), it is estimated that, of 4.8 billion people in developing countries, 45 percent of females and 54 percent of males of the relevant age group are in secondary school, suggesting that education is still relatively primitive in most of the world. Possibly more striking is that in twenty-six of the thirty-nine sub-Saharan African nations for which data are reported, less than 20 percent of females of the relevant age group are in secondary school. So, somehow much of the world is not yet in tune with the values in the U.N. treaties with regard to education. For sociologists, even these facts can be a challenge. Assuming that the value of education is seen as an important "universal" value, what is necessary to implement it in developing countries?

The question of the education of children goes beyond such components as literacy, and basic knowledge bases to other values that need attention to be clarified. For example, consider the allocation of rights ". . . of parents . . . to ensure the religious and moral education of the their children in conformity with their own convictions." This is indoctrination, and it is directly inconsistent with the notion that the children should be educated. To state the matter crassly, children are subject to indoctrination into specific belief systems, with no opportunity for choice. Children are not exposed to competing belief systems. Beyond indoctrination into belief systems, children are subject to behavior restrictions and physical practices. For example, circumcision of male children is a common form of irreversible mutilation that is imposed by parents and often by the dominant culture. Health-based rationale are sometimes advanced for the practice, without apparent support, and in addition it is suggested that the

practice does little harm. The same cannot be said about the "circumcision" of female children, in which the mutilation involves the removal of sensitive sexual tissue. While there has been substantial negative reaction to female circumcision, it is prevalent in a number of less developed countries. It has to be noted that the "community" and the governing bodies in these countries often support the indoctrination of children. This is not surprising, since many of these countries tend to be either formally or informally theocratic and children are indoctrinated not only through their parents but also through other community support systems. By contrast, in developed countries, where education is more widespread and substantial, belief systems may persist through parents and some community support systems, but modifications are obvious. For example, in Italy, where most of the population are Roman Catholic, the birthrate is the lowest among all developed countries, in spite of the papal condemnation of birth control methods other than abstention or rhythm. It would be naive to believe that Italians are not using modern techniques of birth control.

The treaty basis for children's rights, the Convention on the Rights of the Child (1989), was adopted by the U.N. General Assembly on 20 November 1989. The document contains fifty-four articles, but the greater detail does not alter the problem of value clarification, and in some ways some of the statements of rights create greater ambiguity. For example, Article 14 states: "States . . . shall respect the right of the child to freedom of thought, conscience and religion." From where will the child have acquired thought, conscience and religion?" Note also the role of the parents in Article 18: "Parents . . . have the primary responsibilities for upbringing and development of the child." Much of the document seems to consist of platitudinous statements that the parents will be good and the state will help them. However, sociologists and other social scientists may find it challenging to try to assess structures that might facilitate this. Situations in different nations may be quite different because of underlying differences in the social and economic circumstances. For example, much current political rhetoric in the United States focuses on strengthening the family so that it can better serve children. How is this to be done? Presumably, sociologists would examine the current dichotomy between reality and rhetoric, noting the shift over the course of the twentieth century from large families with a single working head to small families, sometimes with two working parents, sometimes with single parent. How could the family be strengthened? The conventional/conservative notion of the mother staying home might not be the right answer. One possible answer that needs to be looked at is discarding school patterns that have their roots in the rural past and replacing them with patterns that meet current needs, such as full-day, year-long schooling, which recognizes that parents are not available until the end of the workday and do not have three-month summer vacations. Another possible answer would be to provide supervision and instruction at a level that corresponds to what research says is needed: rather than acquiescing to the economics of minimum support and unrealistic expectations about what schools as now constituted can produce. When something like the latter is suggested, too often the response is that it is not realistic because of cost and convention. On the contrary, and this is an important point: *If that is what the analysis of social scientists finds, there should be insistence that it is realistic.*

While there has been a substantial amount written about the rights of the child, one particularly accessible source is especially recommended—the 1996 issue of the *American Psychologist* that is devoted in large part to the topic (Limber and Wilcox 1996; Melton 1996; Murphy-Berman and Weisz 1996; Saks 1996) With regard to the Convention on the Rights of the Child, it should be noted that at this writing the treaty has been ratified by all member nations of the United Nations except two: Somalia and the United States.

CONCLUSION

Human rights and children's rights are topics that provide rich potential for research and applied involvement for sociologists and other social scientists. The United Nations has given considerable attention to issues of human rights, and this brief consideration has barely scratched the surface. Sociologists have given attention to some aspects of human rights in detail, including issues of women's rights and racial and other discrimination, but even in these topics the focus has often been narrow considering the varieties of problems and issues in the world.

Special circumstances bring issues of human rights to prominence, and at the end of the twentieth century the issue of genocide has been given substantial attention. Even this issue should be carefully examined by sociologists and social scientists. For example, in a syndicated column Alexander Cockburn wrote: "In 1996, [Madeleine] Albright was asked the following question on CBS-TV's '60 Minutes' by Lesley Stahl: 'We have heard that half a million children have died [in Iraq]. I mean, that's more children than died in Hiroshima. And you know, is the price worth it?' Albright infamously replied, 'I think this is a very hard choice, but the price—we think the price is worth it.' So, back in Nuremburg time, Albright would certainly have been condemned and maybe hanged, if the standards applied to Seyss-Inquart had been leveled against her and if she had been on the losing side. So would her commanding officer, Bill Clinton" (*Seattle Times,* June 3, 1999). The winning side has always defined what is acceptable, but its actions should be subject to objective analysis. Cockburn went on to note: "The protocols of the Geneva Convention of 1949 prohibit bombing not justified by clear military necessity. If there is any likelihood the target has a civilian function, then bombing is forbidden. NATO's bombers have damaged and often destroyed hospitals and healthcare centers, public housing, infrastructure vital to the well-being of civilians, refineries, warehouses, agricultural facilities, schools, road and railways. If Slobodan Milosevic goes on trial before before the International Criminal Court, Clinton, Albright and Defense Secretary William Cohen should have their place on the court's calendar, too." It has also been pointed out that the NATO bombings in Serbia were carried out with the defined expectation that there would be no NATO military casualties, and there were none. The Serb military was to be reduced in effectiveness, meaning the destruction not only of military physical resources but also of personnel in barracks and persons in government centers and other related circumstances; there was also the expectation that there would be "collateral damage," that is, civilian casualties. Of course, the Serbs killed Kosovo Albanians during the forced expulsion, but the irony was that after the collapse of the Serbs, the process was reversed. The agenda for social scientists in such matters is one of requiring objectivity in the analysis of the values and the documents and in the reporting of the events. While Cockburn's critique may be rejected, it should be done so on the basis of the objective facts and the relevance of defined values, not on the basis of the interpretation of the winning side. History is full of uncomfortable facts, and in retrospectively looking at questions of human rights, we have to remember such things as that victory over Japan in World War II came by means of nuclear destruction of two Japanese cities, not two Japanese armies.

Sociologists have not focused sufficiently on human and children's rights with regard to clarifying the "universal" values that the United Nations has promulgated and in which the international community has concurred. Some issues are very complex, loaded with traditional and religious values that directly conflict with those in the Universal Declaration, which tend to be stated in broad and/or general humanistic terms. For example, in a nation that is dominated by a single religion—one that is virtually actually a theocracy—dogmas and traditions supported by the community and in families, may dictate highly restricted status for behavior by women. In a modern industrial nation, this may be viewed as depriving women of their human rights.

The conflict between values that emphasize the good of the broader community and those presumed to be individual human rights is also a critical area for attention by sociologists. One such conflict exists in the values involved in family planning and fertility control. From the community point of view, which may be phrased as "for the good of the society at large," there may be a need for fertility control. For example, although the world (or a nation) may be able to support a tremendous increase in population, such population growth also carries the potential for catastrophic famines and epidemics. The potential problems may result in a general value being placed on the importance of family planning and fertility control by both developed and less developed nations. How is population growth to be attenuated? "Educational" programs have had some success in less developed nations, especially those with a potential for modernization and industrialization. In China, with a tradition of valuing large families, especially male children, the government decided that a strict policy of one child only was necessary to stay population growth. When this policy was implemented, the population was about 90 percent rural, and it currently is still predominantly so. Is such a policy reasonable, and how can it be implemented? The implementation was possible through the form of government that existed, but not without some abuses and also some relaxations of the policy. Here the sociologist can be asked the practical question. How could the policy be implemented without some problems, that is, what would the sociologist instruct the policy makers to do to get the same effect as was accomplished? How are people to be made to adhere to a "one-child-family" policy? Many different types of suggestions can be advanced, including questioning the premise that such a policy is necessary or even appropriate. The argument may shift to empirical questions and estimates, and the like, while the world population continues to increase from 6 billion at the beginning of the twenty-first century to estimates as high as 15 billion by the year 2050. Then the question of quality of life comes into play. At this point, roughly 1.5 billion people live in more or less developed nations and 4.5 billion in less developed nations. What would happen if those in less developed nations used resources at the same rate as those in developed nations? What would happen if, in fifty years, 15 billion people used resources at the level they are currently used in the United States today? The critical analyst might point out that population control is more essential in developed nations, since one additional person there might use twenty (or as much as one hundred) times the resources as one person in a less developed nation. Sociologists obviously have fertile ground for research in examining how social structures might support values that are advanced as "universals" for human and children's rights.

REFERENCES

Borgatta, Edgar F. 1991 "Towards a Proactive Sociology." In *Annals of the International Institute of Sociology*. New Series, Vol. 1. Rome, Italy: University of Rome.

Borgatta, Edgar F. 1994 "Sociology and the Reality of the Press on Environmental Resources." In William V. D'Antonio, Sasaki Masamichi, and Yoshio Yonebayashi, eds., *Ecology, Society, and the Quality of Social Life*. New Brunswick, N.J.: Transaction Publishers.

Borgatta, Edgar F. 1996 "The Relevance of Sociology in Coping with Societal Problems." In *Annals de L'Institute Internationale de Sociologie*. Vol. 5, pp. 125 – 136. Trieste, Italy: University of Trieste.

Buergenthal, Thomas 1997 "The Normative and Institutional Evolution of International Human Rights." *Human Rights Quarterly* 19:703–723.

Campbell, Donald T., and Julian C. Stanley 1963 "Experimental and Quasi-Experimental Designs for Research on Teaching." In N. L. Gage, ed., *Handbook of Research on Teaching*. Chicago: Rand McNally.

Congressional Record. December 19, 1998, 105th Congress, 2nd Session, H.Res. 611 in the Senate of the United States. Washington, D.C.: U.S. Government Printing Office. (http://thomas.loc.gov/cgi-bin/query/D?c105:3:./temp/~c105uc7qTc::).

"Convention on the Rights of the Child" 1989 *United Nations Document A/Res/44/25*. New York: United Nations.

Cook, Thomas D., and Donald T. Campbell 1979 *Quasi-Experimentation: Design and Analysis Issues for Field Settings*. Chicago: Rand McNally.

"Democratic Culture: Ethnos and Demos in Global Perspective" 1999 *International Sociology* 14(3).

Gros Espiell, Hector 1998 "Universality of Human Rights and Cultural Diversity." *International Social Science Journal* 50:523–534.

"International Covenant on Civil and Political Rights" 1966 *Department of State, Selected Documents, No. 5. (revised)* (1978). Washington, D.C.: U.S. Government Printing Office.

Limber, S. P., and B. L. Wilcox 1996 "Application of the U.N. Convention on the Rights of the Child to the United States." *American Psychologist* 51:1246–1250.

Magnarella, Paul J. 1995 "Universal Jurisdiction and Universal Human Rights: A Global Progression." *Journal of Third World Studies* 12:159–171.

Melton, G. B. 1996 "The Child's Right to a Family Environment." *American Psychologist* 51:1234–1238.

Murphy-Berman, V., and V. Weisz 1996 "Convention on the Rights of the Child." *American Psychologist* 51:1231–1233.

Pace, John P. 1998 "The Development of Human Rights Law in the United Nations, Its Control and Monitoring Machinery." *International Social Science Journal* 50:499–511.

Saks, M. J. 1996 "The Role of Research in Implementing the U. N. Convention on the Rights of the Child." *American Psychologist* 51:1262–1266.

Snow, David A. 1999 "The Value of Sociology." *Sociological Perspectives* 42(1):1–22.

Turner, Jonathan H. 1998 "Must Sociological Theory and Sociological Practice Be So Far Apart?: A Polemical Answer." *Sociological Perspectives* 41(2):243–277.

"Universal Declaration of Human Rights" 1949 *Department of State Publication 3381*. Washington, D.C.: U.S. Government Printing Office. (Note: Copies of U.N. publications and documents can be located on the Internet, both at U.N. sites and university sites, e.g., http://www.un.org/overview/rights.html.)

"Why Family Planning Matters" 1999 *Population Reports*, Series J, Number 49, Vol. 27.

EDGAR F. BORGATTA

HUMANISM

Humanism in its broadest sense can be traced to the philosophical movement that originated in Italy in the second half of the fourteenth century and that affirmed the dignity of the human being. Although over the centuries there have been numerous varieties of humanism, both religious and nonreligious, all have been in agreement on the basic tenet that every human being has dignity and worth and therefore should be the measure of all things.

Humanism, as practiced in sociology, starts from two fundamental assumptions. The first of these is that sociology should be a moral enterprise, one whose fundamental purpose is to challenge the views and conditions that restrain human potential in a given society. The second is that sociology should not be defined as a scientific discipline that embraces "positivism"—the position that facts exist independently of the observer and that the observer should be a value-neutral compiler of facts.

Sociologists operating in the humanist tradition hold that the study of society begins with the premise that human beings are free to create their social world and that whatever impinges on that freedom is ultimately negative and destructive. They argue that the use of one of the traditional methodological tools of science—dispassionate observation—has not only taken sociology away from its Enlightenment origins in moral philosophy but is based on a faulty epistemology.

Although diverse theoretical frameworks, such as Marxism, conflict theory, phenomenology, symbolic interaction, and feminist sociology, can all be said to have some form of a humanistic orientation as a part of their overall framework's, humanism in sociology is most readily identified with those sociologists who in their teaching, research, and activism gravitate around the Association for Humanist Sociology (AHS), which was founded in 1976 by Alfred McClung Lee, Elizabeth McClung Lee, and Charles Flynn.

The fundamental underpinnings of sociological humanism can be traced back to two traditions that came out of the Enlightenment: moral philosophy and empiricism. Although Modern sociologists see these traditions as separate, to the Enlightenment French and Scottish philosophers (collectively known as the *philosophes*) they were intertwined and interdependent. The *philosophes* called for a fusion of morals and science, for a social science that sought to liberate the human spirit and ensure the fullest development of the person. It is this emphasis on moral philosophy and empiricism, as modified by German idealism and more recently by the American philosophical tradition of pragmatism, that constitutes the foundations of humanism in sociology, today.

THE ENLIGHTENMENT AND THE LEGACY OF SOCIOLOGICAL HUMANISM

Although the Enlightenment *philosophes* initiated the enterprise of modern sociology through their call for the application of scientific principles to the study of human behavior (Rossides 1998), humanist sociologists stress that the *philosophes* were first and foremost moral philosophers. Science and morality were to be fused, not separated; the "is" and the "ought" were to be merged into a moral science, a science for the betterment of humankind. It was Jean Jacques Rousseau, with his arguments against inequality and for the dignity of the person, who best represents this tradition of moral science tradition Rousseau (1755–1985) started with the fundamental assumption that all people are created equal and from this formulated a radical system of politics. Rousseau and the *philosophes* were wedded to the idea that individual liberty and freedom prospered only under conditions of minimal external constraint that had to be consensually based. In the eighteenth century, the *philosophes* articulated their doctrine of individual liberty and freedom chiefly in the idiom of natural rights (Seidman 1983).

The *philosophes* held that the most important value was the freedom of the individual in a humane society that ensured this freedom. Not having any developed psychology of the individual, of the subjective side of human behavior, or of how institutions are formed, they could not go beyond this modest beginning. They could not fashion a full-blown vision of the free individual within a society based on the principle of human freedom.

This tradition of a moral science is overlooked by contemporary sociologists, who instead focus on the empiricism of the *philosophes*; but although empiricism without doubt played the greatest role in the rise of social science, it is only one part of what the *philosophes* advocated. In their dismissal of the moral science tradition and in their virtually unquestioning embrace of the positivism of Comte, Spenser, Durkheim, and the other early founders of sociology as a discipline, contemporary sociologists overlook the *philosophes'* concern that there was an epistemological dilemma inherent in the new empirical science they envisioned. If a social science was to arise out of the Enlightenment, it had to have a new conception of knowledge, one that rejected Greek and medieval Christian epistemology. The Aristotelian view held that a definite entity resided within the human body, an entity that passively observed what was going on in the world, just as a spectator does. The observer sees a picture of the world, and it is this passive observation that constitutes *experience*. Science, in the Aristotelian model, was the process of observing objects as they were thought to be conceived in the human mind. Following Newton, the world was to be understood in terms of mathematical equations by means of axioms that were put in the minds of humans by God and that enabled the mind to picture reality. John Locke's *Essay Concerning Human Understanding* ([1690] 1894) represented an early attempt to show that the extreme rationalist notion that the world precisely followed mathematical axioms was in error. Locke argued that first principles did not exist a priori but came from the facts of experience. Locke, however, became caught up in the epistemological dilemma that experience was mental, and not physical, and therefore still had to be located in the "unscientific" concept of mind. This led Locke, like David Hume (1711–1776), to conclude that an exact science of human behavior was unattainable (Randall 1976). Only probabilistic knowledge could be arrived at, and this could only modestly be used to guide humankind.

Although the epistemological dilemma posed by Locke and other Enlightenment thinkers was real to them, the development of sociology in France, England, and later in the United States discarded these concerns and embraced positivism as the cornerstones of the discipline. Sociology, however, developed differently in Germany, and it is through German social science that the tradition of humanism in sociology was kept alive.

GERMAN IDEALISM

German social science, unlike its English, French, and later American counterparts, was much more influenced by idealism than by empiricism. This influence is due to two giants of philosophy: Immanuel Kant and Georg William Freidrich Hegel.

Immanuel Kant (1724–1804). Kant ([1781] 1965) was interested in answering the basic question of how autonomy and free will were possible in a deterministic Newtonian universe. His answer led him back to Locke's epistemological dilemma. According to Kant, there is a *phenomenal* and a *neumenological* self. Kant called the world as experienced by the individual *phenomena* and the thing in itself *neumena*. Since science is concerned with experience, Kant relegated it to the study of phenomena. The neumenon is beyond the scientist's realm of inquiry, because Kant wanted to claim the neumenon for the moral philosopher. For Kant, the basis of moral philosophy was to be found in the human mind; moral law located a priori in the mind and can be deduced rationally. Kant, like Locke before him, was faced with the dilemma of how the mind works.

Kant's explanation was that objects of scientific investigation are not simply discovered in the world but are constituted and synthesized a priori in the human mind. The external world that human beings experience is not a copy of reality, but something that can only be experienced and understood in light of a priori forms and categories. According to Kant, these forms and categories determine the form but not the content of external reality. Causation is a product of the mind and is a necessary precondition for the conception of an orderly universe.

Kant believed that he had solved the problem of knowledge through the forms and that he could do the same for ethics. Morally right action, too, is located in the mind. Going back to Rousseau and before him to the fourteenth-century humanists, Kant ([1788] 1949) focused on the dignity of the human being. His notion of the *categorical imperative*, that each person be treated as an end and never as a means, solidifies the importance of the person as the cornerstone of philosophical inquiry and of humanism. Natural rights are part of the neumenal world, part of the moral self. Kant thus began to look to the mind, to the self, as the primary origin of society. Moral values come from human consciousness: but, lacking a viable theory of consciousness, Kant could go only so far. It was Hegel who took up the challenge and subsequently made further progress toward the development of a humanistic orientation in sociology.

Georg Wilhelm Freidrich Hegel (1770–1831). Hegel was well versed in the social and moral philosophy of his day, and was particularly steeped in the work of Kant, who was the dominant figure in Germany philosophy at the time. Although Hegel ([1821] 1967) held that Kant's epistemology was successful in explaining how scientific knowledge was possible, he differed with Kant by rejecting Kant's belief that the categories were innate and therefor ahistorical. For Hegel, the human mind has to be understood in the context of human history. Human reasons is the product of collective action and as such is constantly evolving toward an ultimate understanding of its own consciousness. There are adumbrations of the sociology of knowledge in Hegel's view, specifically in his arguments that the Kantian categories, which are used to make sense of the world, change as the political and social climate changes. Hegel is very close to modern sociology in other aspects of his thought, and it is extremely unfortunate that he is so often dismissed because of his ultimate reliance on the metaphysical assumption that total understanding would only come with the realization of the absolute spirit in human history. When Hegel's contributions are mentioned, it is usually only as having had an influence on Marx, and even then it is inevitably pointed out that Marx turned Hegel "upside down." These interpretations overlook the fact that Hegel was the first modern theorist to develop an antipositivistic critical approach to society. Hegel rejected positivism because of its overreliance on empiricism, which forces the individual to find sense impressions meaningful. As was Kant's philosophy, Hegel's philosophy was humanist at its core.

Also overlooked is the fact that Hegel not only offered an active epistemology but a social one as well. This socially based epistemology (the categories are conditioned by social and political factors) also led him to conceive of a socially based moral philosophy. Whereas Kant held that the concept of freedom was based in the mind of the individual, Hegel, like Rousseau, believed that freedom could only be expressed in terms of a supportive community.

Perhaps Hegel's most important contribution to modern social science is that he was among the first theorists to look at the social development of self, something that makes him a forerunner of humanist sociology. For Hegel ([1807] 1967), the self must be understood as a process, not as a static reality. The self develops as the mind negotiates intersubjectivity. We experience ourselves as both an intending subject and as an object of experience. The mind develops and strives for ultimate truth in this context, which, to Hegel, is freedom. The essence of being is, therefore, a self-reflexive struggle for freedom. Hegel's idealism led him to conclude that objective analysis is always mediated by subjective factors and points toward freedom. In Hegel, there is the outline of a critical, humanistic sociology. He offered an active, antipositivistic, socially conditioned epistemology, with an emphasis upon freedom through the seeking of self knowledge, along with a critique of any non-morally based society.

PRAGMATISM AND HUMANISM

The importance of pragmatism for a humanistic orientation in sociology lies in its assumption of an active epistemology that undergirds an active theory of the mind, thereby challenging the positivistic behaviorism of the time made popular by the likes of John B. Watson. For the pragmatists, how the mind comes to know cannot be separated from how the mind actually develops.

George Herbert Mead ([1934] 1974) exemplifies the pragmatists' view concerning the development of mind. Consciousness and will arise from problems. Individuals ascertain the intentions of others and then respond on the basis of their interpretations. If there were no interactions with others, there would be no development of the mind. Individuals possess the ability to modify their own behavior; they are subjects who construct their acts rather than simply responding in predetermined ways. Human beings are capable of reflexive behavior: that is, they can turn back and think about their experiences. The individual is not a passive agent who merely reacts to external constraints, but someone who actively chooses among alternative courses of action. Individuals interpret data furnished to them in social situation. Choices of potential solutions are only limited by the given facts of the individual's presence in the larger network of society. This ability to choose among alternatives makes individuals both determined and determiners (Meltzer et al. 1977).

What Mead and the pragmatists stressed was the important notion that the determination of ideas—in particular, the impact of social structure on the mind of an individual—is a social-psychological process. Thinking follows the pattern of language. Language is the mechanism through which humans develop a self and mind, and language is social because words assume meaning only when they are interpreted by social behavior. Social patterns establish meanings. Language sets the basis for reason, logic, and by extension all scientific and moral endeavors. One is logical when one is in agreement with one's universe of discourse; one is moral when one is in agreement with one's community. Language is a mediator of social behavior in that with a language come values and norms. Value judgments and collective patterns exist behind words; meaning is socially bestowed.

Although Mead was the most important pragmatist for understanding the development of self, the epistemology of pragmatism was most precisely formulated by John Dewey (1929, 1931). Dewey's epistemology represented a final break with the notion that the mind knows because it is a spectator to reality. For Dewey, thought is spatiotemporal. Eternal truths, universals, *a priori* systems are all suspect. Experience is the experience of the environment—an environment that is physical, biological, and cultural. Ideas are not Platonic essences but rather are functional to the experience of the individual (Dewey 1931). This position is antipositivistic in that the mind deals only with ideas and, therefore, does not ponder reality, but only ideas about reality. Truth is not absolute but is simply what is consistent with experience.

The individual is engaged in an active confrontation with the world; mind and self develop in a social process. The pragmatists provided an epistemological justification for freedom (the basic tenet of humanism). The mind develops in a social context and comes to know as it comes into being. Any restriction on the freedom of the mind to inquire and know implies a restriction on the mind to fully develop. The pragmatists rounded out Hegel's ([1807] 1967) view that ultimate truth is freedom by showing that the mind needs freedom to develop in a social context. Epistemology and freedom are inseparable.

Pragmatism, by joining epistemology and freedom via the social development of mind, also provides a solution for the seeming incompatibility between an instrumental and an intrinsic approach to values. The value of freedom is instrumental in that it is created in action (the action of the developing mind); but it is also intrinsic in that the mind cannot fully develop without the creation of an environment that ensures freedom. This integrated epistemological framework provides the basis for a humanistic methodology for sociology.

PRAGMATISM, METHODOLOGY, AND HUMANISM

Dewey and Mead developed a methodology that gave social scientists a different frame of reference from that of the "traditional scientific methodology." Flexibility was the main characteristic of their pragmatic methodology—it did not offer specific forms or languages to which social problems had to be adapted. Instead, the form and language of the method grew out of the problem itself. The social scientist, thus, fashions his or her own methodology depending upon the problem studied. New concepts and methodologies arise from efforts to overcome obstacles to successful research. Techniques are developed that enable the researcher to be both a participant in and observer of social structures. There is an instrumentalist linkage between theory and practice as it is incorporated into the humanist sociologist's life. This is what Alfred McClung Lee (1978), a leading humanist sociologist, meant when he wrote: "Sociologists cannot be persons apart from the human condition they presumably seek to understand" (p. 35). This is what C. Wright Mills (1959) meant when he wrote: "The most admirable thinkers within the scholarly community . . . do not split their work from their lives." (p. 195).

For the humanist sociologist, the main purpose in amassing a body of knowledge is to serve human needs; knowledge must be useful. By accepting this dictum, humanist sociologists extend the analysis of what *is* to the analysis of what *ought* to be. Knowledge should provide answers for bringing about a desired future state of affairs, a plan that can be achieved through the methodological insights of pragmatism whereby the researcher is both participant and observer.

The dilemma of which values to choose is answered by opting for the pragmatist's emphasis upon responsibility as a moral standard which assumes that a fundamental quality of human beings is their potentiality for ethical autonomy. People not only *are* but *ought* to be in charge of their own destiny within the limits permitted by their environment. Individual character development takes place to the extent that persons can and do decide on alternative courses of action (Dewey 1939).

Pragmatism is grounded upon an assumption of freedom of choice. However, choice among alternatives is always limited. It is in pointing out these limitations in the form of power relations and vested interests behind social structures that humanist sociology builds upon pragmatism and thereby confronts the basic sociological criticism of pragmatism—that it lacks a viable notion of social structure. Humanist sociology seeks to fashion a full-blown vision of the free individual within a society based on the principle of human freedom.

HUMANIST SOCIOLOGY TODAY

Humanist sociology has moved beyond pragmatism via its attempt to spell out the social structural conditions for the maximization of freedom. Humanist sociology is based on moral precepts, the foremost of which is that of *freedom*—"the maximization of alternatives" (Scimecca 1995, p.1). This is assumed to be *the* most desirable state for human beings—and the goal of sociology is to work toward the realization of conditions that insure this freedom. Given its Meadian theory of self (an active theory of self that chooses between alternatives), humanist sociology is concerned with how this is best realized within a community. Humanist sociology begins with the fundamental assumption that all varieties of humanism hold—that individuals are the measure of all things. Using a nonpositivistic epistemological foundation, humanist sociologist's employ their methods of research to answer the most important question that can be asked by a humanist sociologist about human behavior, the one originally raised by the Enlightenment *philosophes*: How can social science help to fashion a humane society in which freedom can best be realized?

REFERENCES

Dewey, John 1929 *The Quest for Certainty*. New York: Minton, Balch and Company.

——1931 Context and Thought. Berkeley: University of California Press.

——1939 *Freedom and Culture*. New York: G.P. Putnam's Sons.

Flynn, Charles 1976 *Association for Humanist Sociology Newsletter* 1(1) pp 1–2.

Hegel, Georg Wilhelm Freidrich (1807) 1967 The *Phenomenology of Mind*. New York: Harper Colophon Books.

——(1821) 1967. *The Philosophy of Right*. Oxford: Clarendon Press.

Kant, Immanuel (1788) 1949 *The Critique of Practical Reason*. Chicago: University of Chicago Press.

——(1781) 1965 *The Critique of Pure Reason*. New York: St. Martin's Press.

Lee, Alfred McClung 1978 *Sociology for Whom?* New York: Oxford University Press.

Locke, John (1690) 1894 *Essay Concerning Human Understanding*. Oxford: Oxford University Press.

Mead, George Herbert (1934) 1974 *Mind, Self and Society*. Chicago: University of Chicago Press.

Meltzer, Bernard N., John W. Petras, and Larry T. Reynolds 1977 *Symbolic Interactionism: Genesis, Varieties, and Criticisms*. Boston: Routledge and Kegan Paul.

Mills, C. Wright 1959 *The Sociological Imagination*. New York: Oxford University Press.

Randall, John Herman, Jr. 1976 *The Making of the Modern Mind*. New York: Columbia University Press.

Rossides, Daniel W. 1998 *Social Theory: Its Origins, History, and Contemporary Relevance*. Dix Hills, N.J.: General Hall.

Rousseau, Jean Jacques (1755) 1985 *Discourse on Human Inequality*. New York: Penguin Books.

Scimecca, Joseph A. 1995 *Society and Freedom*, 2nd ed. Chicago: Nelson-Hall.

Seidman, Steven 1983 *Liberalism and the Origins of European Social Thought*. Berkeley: University of California Press.

JOSEPH A. SCIMECCA

HYPOTHESIS TESTING

See Scientific Explanation; Statistical Inference.

I

IDEAL TYPES

See Typologies.

IDENTITY THEORY

Identity theory, in the present context, has its referent in a specific and delimited literature that seeks to develop and empirically examine a theoretical explanation, derived from what has been called a structural symbolic interactionist perspective (Stryker 1980), of role choice behavior. It is only one of a large number of formulations—social scientific, therapeutic, humanistic—in which the concept of identity plays a central role, formulations having their roots in a variety of disciplines ranging from theology through philosophy to political science, psychology, social psychology, and sociology. Further mention of these diverse formulations will be forgone in order to focus on identity theory as specified above; those who desire leads into the literature of sociology and social psychology to which identity theory most closely relates will find them in McCall and Simmons (1978); Stryker (1980); Weigert (1983); Stryker and Statham (1985); Hewitt (1997a, 1997b); MacKinnon (1994); and Burke and Gecas (1995).

The prototypical question addressed by identity theory, phrased illustratively, is: Why is it that one person, given a free weekend afternoon, chooses to take his or her children to the zoo while another person opts to spend that time on the golf course with friends? The language of this prototypical question implies a scope limitation of the theory that is important to recognize at the outset of the discussion. The theory is intended to apply to situations where alternative courses of action are reasonably, and reasonably equivalently, open to the actor. A defining assumption of the symbolic interactionist theoretical framework is that human beings are actors, not merely reactors. Identity theory shares this assumption, which recognizes the possibility of choice as a ubiquitous feature of human existence. At the same time, however, identity theory recognizes the sociological truth that social structure and social interaction are equally ubiquitous in constraining—not in a strict sense "determining"—human action. That constraint is variable. It may be true in an abstract and philosophical sense that people are "free" to act in any way they choose in any situation in which they may find themselves, including choosing to endure great punishment or even death rather than to behave in ways demanded by others; but surely it is entirely reasonable to presume that jailed prisoners have no viable options with respect to many—likely most—facets of life and in any event have fewer viable options than persons who are not jailed. Identity theory has more to say on those the latter persons than on the former, and more to say on those—perhaps few—aspects of life about which the former do have reasonable choice than on those many aspects of prisoner life where options, as a practical matter, do not exist.

As a derivative of a symbolic interactionist theoretical framework, identity theory shares a number of the assumptions or premises of interactionist thought in general. One, that human beings are actors as well as reactors, has already been suggested. A second is that human action and interaction are critically shaped by definitions or interpretations of the situations of action and interaction, which definitions and interpretations are based on shared meanings developed in the course of interaction with others. A third premise is that the meanings which persons attribute to themselves, their self-conceptions, are especially critical to the process producing their action and interaction. And a fourth premise is that self-conceptions, like other meanings, are shaped in the course of interaction with others and are, at least in the initial instance and at least largely, the outcomes of others' responses to the person.

The fourth premise has sometimes been phrased as "self reflects society." Taken in conjunction with the third premise, it gives rise to the basic theoretical proposition or formula of symbolic interactionism: Society shapes self, which shapes social behavior. That formula, it must be noted, admits of and, indeed, insists upon the possibility of reciprocity among its components—social behavior impacts self and society, and self can impact society. Identity theory builds upon refinements of the traditional symbolic interactionist framework and specifications of its basic formula.

The refinements essentially have to do with three facets of the traditional symbolic interactionist framework as it evolved from Mead ([1934] 1962), Cooley ([1902] 1983), Blumer (1969), and others: the conceptualization of society, the conceptualization of self, and the relative weight to be accorded social structure versus interpretive processes in accounts of human behavior. The traditional framework tends to view "society" as unitary, as a relatively undifferentiated and unorganized phenomenon with few, if any, internal barriers to the evolution of universally shared meanings. It also tends to a view "society" as an unstable and ephemeral reflection, even reification, of relatively transient, ever-shifting patterns of interaction. In this view of society, social structures, as these are typically conceived of by sociologists, have little place in accounts of persons' behaviors. These accounts tend to be innocent of a coherent sense of extant social constraints on those behaviors, and there are few means of linking the dynamics of social interaction in reasonably precise ways to the broader social settings that serve as context for persons' action and interaction.

Further, and enlarging this theme of an inadequate conceptualization and consequent neglect of social structure, this view of society tends to dissolve social structure in the universal solvent of subjective definitions and interpretations, thus missing the obdurate reality of social forms whose impact on behavior is undeniable. To say this does not deny the import for social life of the definitional and interpretative processes central to interactionist thinking and explanation. It is, however, to say that seeing these processes as in large degree unanchored and without bounds, as open to any possibility whatsoever without recognizing that some are much more probable than others, results in visualizing social life as less a product of external constraints and more a product of persons' phenomenology than is likely warranted. Finally, on the premise that self reflects society, this view of society leads directly to a view of self as unitary, as equivalently internally undifferentiated, unorganized, unstable, and ephemeral.

Contemporary sociology's image of society is considerably different from that contained in traditional symbolic interactionism, and it is the contemporary sociological conceptualization of society that is incorporated into the structural symbolic interactionist frame from which identity theory derives. This contemporary conceptualization emphasizes the durability of the patterned interactions and relationships that are at the heart of sociology's sense of social structure. It emphasizes social structure's resistance to change and its tendency to reproduce itself. The contemporary image differs as well by visualizing societies as highly differentiated yet organized systems of interactions and relationships; as complex mosaics of groups, communities, organizations, institutions; and as encompassing a wide variety of crosscutting lines of social demarcation based upon social class, age, gender, ethnicity, religion, and more. This vast diversity of parts is seen as organized in multiple and overlapping ways—interactionally, functionally, and hierarchically. At the same time, the diverse parts of society are taken to be sometimes highly interdependent and sometimes relatively independent of one another, sometimes implicated in close and cooperative interaction and sometimes conflicting.

The symbolic interactionist premise that self reflects society now requires a very different conceptualization of self, one that mirrors the altered conception of society. Self must be seen as multifaceted, as comprised of a variety of parts that are sometimes interdependent and sometimes independent of other parts, sometimes mutually reinforcing and sometimes conflicting, and that are organized in multiple ways. It requires a sense of self in keeping with James's ([1890] 1990) view that persons have as many selves as there are other persons who react to them, or at least as many as there are groups of others who do so.

Equally important, viewing both society and self as complex and multifaceted as well as organized opens the way to escaping the overly general, almost banal, and essentially untestable qualities of the basic symbolic interactionist formula by permitting theorization of the relations between particular parts of society and particular parts of self, and by permitting reasonable operationalizations of those parts.

In identity theory, this theorization proceeds by specifying the terms of the basic symbolic interactionist formula, doing so by focusing on particulars hypothesized as especially likely to be important in impacting role choice. That is, first of all, the general category of social behavior is specified by taking role choice—opting to pursue action meeting the expectations contained in one role rather than another—as the object of explanation. Role choice is hypothesized to be a consequence of identity salience, a specification of the general category of self, and identity salience is hypothesized to be a consequence of commitment, a specification of society. Identity theory's fundamental proposition, then, is: Commitment impacts identity salience impacts role choice.

The concept of identity salience develops from the multifaceted view of self articulated above. Self is conceptualized as comprised of a set of discrete identities, or internalized role designations, with persons potentially having as many identities as there are organized systems of role relationships in which they participate. Identities require both that persons be placed as social objects by having others assign a positional designation to them and that the persons accept that designation (Stone 1962; Stryker 1968). By this usage, identities are self-cognitions tied to roles and, through roles, to positions in organized social relationships; one may speak of the identities of mother, husband, child, doctor, salesman, employee, senator, candidate, priest, tennis player, churchgoer, and so on. By this usage, too, identities are cognitive schemas (Markus 1977), structures of cognitive associations, with the capacity of such schemas to impact ongoing cognitive and perceptual processes (Stryker and Serpe 1994).

Self is not only multifaceted; it is also postulated to be organized. Identity theory takes hierarchy as a principal mode of organization of identities; in particular, it assumes that identities, given their properties as cognitive schemas, will vary in their salience, and that self is a structure of identities organized in a salience hierarchy. Identity salience is defined as the probability that a given identity will be invoked, or called into play, in a variety of situations; alternatively, it can be defined as the differential probability, across persons, that a given identity will be invoked in a given situation. Identity theory's fundamental proposition hypothesizes that choice between or among behaviors expressive of particular roles will reflect the relative location in the identity salience hierarchy of the identities associated with those roles.

The concept of commitment has its basic referent in the networks of social relationships in which persons participate; as such, commitment is a social structural term. Associated with the "complex mosaic of differentiated parts" image of society is the recognition that persons conduct their lives not in the context of society as a whole but, rather, in the many contexts of relatively small and specialized social networks, networks made up of persons to whom they relate by virtue of occupancy of particular social positions and the playing of the associated roles. To say that persons are committed to some social network is to say that their relationships to the other members of that network depend on their playing particular roles and having particular identities: To the degree that one's relationships to specific others depend on being a particular kind of person, one is committed to being that kind of person. Thus, commitment is measured by the costs of giving up meaningful relations to others should an alternative course of action be pursued. Commitment, so defined and measured, is hypothesized by identity theory to be the source of the salience attached to given identities (Stryker 1968, 1980, 1987a).

Two analytically distinct and possibly independent dimensions or forms of commitment have been discerned: interactional and affective (Serpe 1987; Stryker 1968). The former has its referent in the number of relationships entered by virtue of having a given identity and by the ties across various networks of relationships (for instance, one may relate as husband not only to one's spouse, her friends, and her relatives but also to members of a couples' bridge club and other such groups). The latter has its referent in the depth of emotional attachment to particular sets of others.

Reciprocity among the three terms of the identity theory formula is again recognized; but the dominant thrust of the process is hypothesized to be as stated by the proposition, on the grounds that identity, as a strictly cognitive phenomenon, can change more readily than can commitment, whose conceptual core is interaction rather than cognition.

The empirical evidence brought to bear on the hypotheses contained in the fundamental identity theory formula has been supportive. Stryker and Serpe (1982) demonstrate that both time spent acting out a religious role and preferred distribution of time to that role are tied to the salience of the identity associated with the role; they demonstrate as well that the salience of the religious identity is tied to commitment (in this case, the measure of commitment combines interactional and affective commitment) to others known through religious activities. Burke and various associates (Burke and Hoelter 1988; Burke and Reitzes 1981; Burke and Tully 1977) show the link between identity and gender, academic attainment and aspirations, and occupational aspirations, finding evidence that the linkage reflects the commonality of meaning of identity and behavior. Lee (1998) finds that the correspondence of meanings of students' personal identities and meanings they attach to those occupying positions in scientific disciplines predicts interest in science as well as appreciably accounting for gender differences in intention to become scientists. Serpe and Stryker (1987), using data on student-related identities obtained at three points in time from students

entering a residential college, provide evidence that the salience of these identities is reasonably stable over time; that in a situation in which earlier commitments have been attenuated by a move to a residential university, high identity salience leads to efforts to reconstruct social relationships that permit playing the role associated with the salient identity, efforts taking the form of joining appropriate organizations; and that when such efforts are not successful, the level of salience of the identity subsequently drops and self-structure is altered. Callero (1985), Callero and associates (1987), and Charng and associates (1988) show that commitment and identity salience add appreciably to the ability to account for the behavior of repeated blood donors. Sparks and Shepherd (1992) find, to their considerable surprise, that identity theory–based predictions stand up well in accounting for behavioral intentions with regard to green consumerism, the predicted relationships holding when examined in the context of the variables of a theory of planned behavior. Serpe (1987) shows that over time there is indeed a reciprocal relationship between commitment to various student role relationships and the salience of identities associated with those roles, and that the identity theory hypothesis arguing the greater impact over time of commitment on salience than vice versa is correct.

The success of identity theory attested to in this brief and incomplete review of empirical evidence notwithstanding, however, there is reason to believe that the theory requires development and extension beyond the basic proposition that has been the major focus of attention to this point. Indeed, such work has begun; and it has a variety of thrusts. How to incorporate varying degrees of situational constraint into the theory—the impact that variations in "choice" have on the ways in which the relationships among commitment, identity salience, and role performances play themselves out—is one such thrust (Serpe 1987). Another seeks to explore mechanisms underlying the linkages among commitment and identity salience, and identity salience and behavior; to this end, work (especially by Burke and Reitzes 1981, 1991) exploits the basic symbolic interactionist idea that it is commonality of meaning which makes social life possible. Some attention has been given to extending the applicability and predictive power of identity theory by incorporating into it other than strictly role-based identities; in particular, the concern has been with what have been termed "master statuses" (such as age, gender, and class) and personal traits (such as aggressiveness and honesty), and the suggestion is that master statuses and traits may affect identity processes by modifying the meaning of the roles from which identities derive (Stryker 1987a). Stryker and Serpe (1994) treat the conceptual and measurement confusion of the importance ranking of identities and identity salience, in the process showing that both importance and salience respond to commitment, that importance and salience are related, and that both contribute to the prediction of role-related behavior.

An effort is being made to correct the almost totally cognitive focus of identity theory (as well as its parent and grandparent interactionist frameworks) by recognizing the importance of affect and emotion to the processes with which the theory is concerned. The earliest statement of the theory (Stryker 1968) posited a cathectic modality of self that parallels the cognitive modality from which the emphasis on identity flows; however, subsequent work on the theory has not pursued that idea. Stryker (1987b) has attempted to integrate emotion into the theory by arguing, with Hochschild (1979), that emotional expressions carry important messages from self and, beyond Hochschild, that the experiences of emotions are messages to self informing those who experience those emotions of the strength of commitments and the salience of identities.

Finally—and here work has barely begun—it is time to make good on the promise to provide more adequate conceptualization of the linkages between identity theory processes and the wider social structures within which these processes are embedded. From the point of view of structural symbolic interactionism, structures of class, ethnicity, age, gender, and so on operate as social boundaries making it more or less probable that particular persons will form interactional networks; in this way, such social structures enter identity theory directly through their impact on commitments. However, the relation of such structures to identity processes clearly goes beyond this direct impact; they affect not only the probabilities of interaction but also the content (meanings) of the roles entailed in interaction and, thus, the meanings of identities, the symbolic and material resources available to those who enter interaction with others, and the objectives or ends to which interactions are oriented. Explication of these impacts, both direct and indirect, of social structure on the processes that relate commitment, identity salience, and role performance remains to be accomplished.

REFERENCES

Blumer, Herbert 1969 *Symbolic Interactionism: Perspective and Method*. Englewood Cliffs, N.J.: Prentice-Hall.

Burke, Peter J., and Viktor Gecas 1995 "Self and Identity." In Karen Cook, Gary A. Fine, and James House, eds., *Sociological Perspectives on Social Psychology*. Needham Heights, Mass.: Allyn and Bacon.

Burke, Peter J., and Jon W. Hoelter 1988 "Identity and Sex–Race Differences in Educational and Occupational Aspirations Formation." *Social Science Research* 17:29–47.

Burke, Peter J., and Donald C. Reitzes 1981 "The Link Between Identity and Role Performance." *Social Psychology Quarterly* 44:83–92.

—— 1991 "An Identity Theory Approach to Commitment." *Social Psychology Quarterly* 54:239–251.

Burke, Peter J., and Judy Tully 1977 "The Measurement of Role/Identity." *Social Forces* 55:880–897.

Callero, Peter L. 1985 "Role-Identity Salience." *Social Psychology Quarterly* 48:203–215.

——, Judith A. Howard, and Jane A. Piliavin 1987 "Helping Behavior as Role Behavior: Disclosing Social Structure and History in the Analysis of Pro-Social Action." *Social Psychology Quarterly* 50:247–256.

Charng, Hong-Wen, June Allyn Piliavin, and Peter L. Callero 1988 "Role-Identity and Reasoned Action in the Prediction of Repeated Behavior." *Social Psychology Quarterly* 51:303–317.

Cooley, Charles H. (1902) 1983 *Human Nature and Social Order*. New Brunswick, N.J.: Transaction Books.

Hewitt, John P. 1997a *Dilemmas of the American Self*. Philadelphia: Temple University Press.

—— 1997b *Self and Society*, 7th ed. Needham Heights, Mass.: Allyn and Bacon.

Hochschild, Arlie R. 1979 "Emotion Work, Feeling Rules, and Social Structure." *American Journal of Sociology* 85:551–575.

James, William (1890) 1990 *Principles of Psychology*. Chicago: Encyclopedia Britannica, Inc.

Lee, James D. 1998 "What Kids Can 'Become' Scientists? The Effects of Gender, Self-Concepts, and Perceptions of Scientists." *Social Psychology Quarterly* 61:199–219.

MacKinnon, Neil J. 1994 *Symbolic Interaction as Affect Control*. Albany: State University of New York Press.

Markus, Hazel 1977 "Self-Schemas and Processing Information About the Self." *Journal of Personality and Social Psychology* 35:63–78.

McCall, George, and J. S. Simmons 1978 *Identities and Interaction*, rev. ed. New York: Free Press.

Mead, George H. (1934) 1963 *Mind, Self and Society*. Chicago: University of Chicago Press.

Serpe, Richard T. 1987 "Stability and Change in Self: A Structural Symbolic Interactionist Explanation." *Social Psychology Quarterly* 50:44–55.

——, and Sheldon Stryker 1987 "The Construction of Self and the Reconstruction of Social Relationships." In Edward J. Lawler and Barry Markovsky, eds., *Advances in Group Processes*, vol. 4. Greenwich, Conn.: JAI Press.

Sparks, Paul, and Richard Shepherd 1992 "Self-Identity and the Theory of Planned Behavior: Assessing the Role of Identification with 'Green Consumerism.'" *Social Psychology Quarterly* 55:388–399.

Stone, Gregory P. 1962 "Appearance and the Self." In Arnold M. Rose, ed., *Human Behavior and the Social Process*. Boston: Houghton Mifflin.

Stryker, Sheldon 1968 "Identity Salience and Role Performance." *Journal of Marriage and the Family* 30:558–564.

—— 1980 *Symbolic Interactionism: A Social Structural Version*. Menlo Park, Calif.: Benjamin/Cummings.

—— 1987a "Identity Theory: Developments and Extensions." In Krysia Yardley and Terry Honess, eds., *Self and Society: Psychosocial Perspectives*. New York: Wiley.

—— 1987b "The Interplay of Affect and Identity: Exploring the Relationships of Social Structure, Social Interaction, Self and Emotion." Paper presented at annual meeting of the American Sociological Association, Chicago.

——, and Richard T. Serpe 1982 "Commitment, Identity Salience, and Role Behavior: Theory and Research Example." In William Ickes and Eric S. Knowles, eds., *Personality, Roles, and Social Behavior*. New York: Springer-Verlag.

——, and Richard T. Serpe 1994 "Identity Salience and Psychological Centrality: Equivalent, Overlapping, or Complementary Concepts?" *Social Psychology Quarterly* 57:16–35.

——, and Ann Statham 1985 "Symbolic Interactionism and Role Theory." In Gardner Lindzey and Eliot Aronson, eds., *The Handbook of Social Psychology*, 3rd ed. New York: Random House.

Weigert, Andrew J. 1983 "Identity: Its Emergence Within Sociological Psychology." *Symbolic Interaction* 6:183–206.

SHELDON STRYKER

ILLEGAL ALIENS/ UNDOCUMENTED IMMIGRANTS

See International Migration.

ILLEGITIMACY

Until the 1960s, it was widely assumed that marriage was a universal or nearly universal institution for licensing parenthood. Marriage assigned paternity rights to fathers (and their families) and guaranteed social recognition and economic support to mothers and their offspring. According to Malinowski (1930), who first articulated "the principle of legitimacy," and to Davis (1939, 1949), who extended Malinowski's theory into sociology, marriage provides the added benefit to children of connecting them to a wider network of adults who have a stake in their long-term development.

This functional explanation for the universality of marriage as a mechanism for legitimating parenthood became a source of intense debate in anthropology and sociology in the 1960s. Evidence accumulated from cross-cultural investigations showed considerable variation in marriage forms and differing levels of commitment to the norm of legitimacy (Bell and Vogel 1968; Blake 1961; Coser 1964; Goode 1961). More recently, historical evidence indicates that the institution of marriage was not firmly in place in parts of Western Europe until the end of the Middle Ages (Glendon 1989; Goody 1983).

The accumulation of contradictory data led Goode (1960, 1971) to modify Malinowski's theory to take account of high rates of informal unions and nonmarital childbearing in many New World nations and among dispossessed cultural minorities. Goode (1971) argued that the norm of legitimacy was likely to be enforced only when fathers possessed wealth and property or when their potential economic investment in child rearing was high. Therefore, he predicted that when Agiving a name" to children offers few material, social, or cultural benefits, the norms upholding marriage will become attenuated.

So vast have been the changes in the perceived benefits of marriage since the 1960s in the United States and most Western nations that even Goode's modification of Malinowski's theory of legitimacy now seems to be in doubt (Cherlin 1992; Davis 1985). Indeed, the term "illegitimacy" has fallen into disfavor precisely because it implies inferior status to children born out of wedlock. Both legal and feminist scholars have been critical of the notion that the presence of a father confers status on the child (Burns and Scott 1994; Mason et al. 1998). The nuclear unit (biological parents and their offspring)—once regarded as the cornerstone of our kinship system—remains the model family form, but it no longer represents the exclusive cultural ideal, as was the case in the mid-1960s. The incentives for marriage in the event of premarital pregnancy have declined, and the sanctions against remaining single have diminished (Cherlin 1999; McLanahan and Casper 1995). In the 1990s, considerable scholarly attention and public policy debate has been devoted to ways of restoring and reinvesting in the institution of marriage (Furstenberg 1996; McLanahan and Sandefur 1994; Popenoe et al. 1996).

TRENDS IN NONMARITAL CHILDBEARING

Premarital pregnancy has never been rare in the United States or in most Western European nations (Burns and Scott 1994; Goode 1961; Smith 1978; Vinovskis 1988). Apparently, the tolerance for pregnancy before marriage has varied over time and varies geographically at any given time. Throughout the first half of the twentieth century, premarital pregnancy almost always led to hasty marriages rather than out-of-wedlock births—even for very young women (O'Connell and Moore 1981; Vincent 1961). In 1940, illegitimacy was

uncommon in the United States, at least among whites. Nonmarital births were estimated at about 3.6 per 1,000 unmarried white women, while the comparable rate for nonwhites was 35.6. For all age groups, among whites and nonwhites alike, a spectacular rise occurred over the next five decades (Clague and Ventura 1968; Cutright 1972; McLanahan and Casper 1995).

In the 1960s and the 1970s, nonmarital childbearing rates continued to increase for younger women, albeit at a slower pace, while for women in their late twenties and thirties rates temporarily declined. Then, in the late 1970, nonmarital childbearing rates rose again for all age groups and among both whites and African Americans. This rise continued until the mid-1990s, when levels of nonmarital childbearing stabilized or even declined (Ventura et al. 1996). Since the early 1970s, rates of marriage and marital childbearing have fallen precipitously. Thus, the ratio of total births to single women has climbed continuously (Smith et al. 1996). Nearly a third of all births (32.4 percent) in 1996 occurred out of wedlock, more than seven times the proportion in 1955 (4.5 percent) and more than twice that in 1975 (14.3 percent). The declining connection between marriage and parenthood is evident among all age groups but is especially pronounced among women in their teens and early twenties. Three out of four births to teens and nearly half of all births to women ages twenty to twenty-four occurred out of wedlock. Virtually all younger blacks who had children in 1995 (more than 95 percent) were unmarried, while two-thirds of white teens and more than a third of white women twenty to twenty-four were single when they gave birth.

Nonmarital childbearing was initially defined as a problem among teenagers and black women (Furstenberg 1991). But these recent trends strongly suggest that disintegration of the norm of legitimacy has spread to all segments of the population. First the link between marriage and sexual initiation dissolved, and now the link between marriage and parenthood has become weak. Whether this trend is temporary or a more permanent feature of the Western family system is not known. But public opinion data suggest that a high proportion of the population finds single parenthood acceptable. A Roper study ("Virginia Slims American

Women"s Opinion Poll" 1985) revealed that 49 percent of women agreed that "There is no reason why single women should not have children and raise them if they want to."

Citing similar attitudinal evidence from the National Survey of Families and Households in 1987–1988, Bumpass (1990) concludes that there has been an "erosion of norms" proscribing nonmarital childbearing. He concludes that this behavior is not so much motivated by the desire to have children out of wedlock as it is by the reduced commitment to marriage and the limited sanctions forbidding nonmarital childbearing. Bumpass argues that much of the nonmarital childbearing is unplanned and ill timed.

THE CONSEQUENCES OF NONMARITAL CHILDBEARING

Although extensive research exists on the economic, social, and psychological sequelae of single parenthood for adults and children, relatively little of this research has distinguished between the consequences of marital disruption and nonmarriage (Furstenberg 1989; Furstenberg and Cherlin 1991; Garfinkel and McLanahan 1986; Maynard 1997). A substantial literature exists on the consequences of nonmarital childbearing, but it is almost entirely restricted to teenage childbearers (Chilman 1983; Hofferth and Hayes 1987; Institute of Medicine 1995; Miller and Moore 1990; Moore et al. 1986). It is difficult, then, to sort out the separate effects of premature parenthood, marital disruption, and out-of-wedlock childbearing on parents and their offspring.

Nonmarital childbearing most certainly places mothers and their children at risk of long-term economic disadvantage (Institute of Medicine 1995; Maynard 1997; McLanahan and Booth 1989). Out-of-wedlock childbearing increases the odds of going on welfare and of long-term welfare dependency (Duncan and Hoffman 1990). The link between nonmarital childbearing and poverty can probably be traced to two separate sources. The first is "selective recruitment," that is, women who bear children out of wedlock have poor economic prospects before they become pregnant, and their willingness to bear a child out of wedlock may reflect the bleak future prospects of many unmarried pregnant women, especially younger women

(Furstenberg 1990; Geronimus 1987; Hayes 1987; Hogan and Kitagawa 1985; Maynard 1997). But is also likely that out-of-wedlock childbearing—particularly when it occurs early in life—directly contributes to economic vulnerability because it reduces educational attainment and may limit a young woman's prospects of entering a stable union (Furstenberg 1991; Hofferth and Hayes 1987; Hoffman et al. 1993; Trussell 1988).

If nonmarital childbearing increases the risk of lengthy periods of poverty for women and their children, it is also likely that it restricts the opportunities for intra- and intergenerational mobility of families formed as single-parent units. Growing up in poverty restricts access to health, high-quality schools, and community resources that may promote success in later life (Ellwood 1988; Wilson 1987). Apart from the risks associated with poverty, some studies have shown that growing up in a single-parent family may put children at greater risk because they receive less parental supervision and support (Amato and Booth 1997; Dornbush 1989; McLanahan and Booth 1989; McLanahan and Sandefur 1994). As yet, however, researchers have not carefully distinguished between the separate sources of disadvantage that may be tied to nonmarital childbearing: economic disadvantage (which could restrict social opportunities or increase social isolation) and psychological disadvantage (which could foster poor parenting practices or limit family support).

Even though nonmarital childbearing may put children at risk of long-term disadvantage, it is also possible that over time the advantages conferred by marriage may be decreasing in those segments of the population that experience high rates of marital disruption (Bumpass 1990; Edin 1998; Furstenberg 1995). Moreover, the social and legal stigmata once associated with nonmarital childbearing have all but disappeared in the United States and many other Western nations (Glendon 1989). Over time, then, the hazards associated with nonmarital childbearing (compared with ill-timed marital childbearing) for women and their children may have declined. Whatever the reasons for these trends, it appears that nonmarital childbearing may have peaked by the mid-1990s. Whether the leveling off in rates of nonmarital childbearing signals a shift in family formation patterns or is merely a response to the robust economy of the 1990s remains to be seen.

NONMARITAL CHILDBEARING AND PUBLIC POLICY

Growing rates of nonmarital childbearing in the United States and many other Western nations suggest the possibility that the pattern of childbearing before marriage or between marriages may be spreading upward into the middle class. In Scandinavia, where marriage has declined most dramatically, it is difficult to discern whether formal matrimony is being replaced by a de facto system of informal marriage (Hoem and Hoem 1988). If this were to happen, the impact on the kinship system or the circumstances of children might not be as dramatic as some have speculated. But if the institution of marriage is in serious decline, then we may be in the midst of a major transformation in the Western family.

The weakening of marriage has created confusion and dispute over parenting rights and responsibilities. A growing body of evidence indicates that most nonresidential biological fathers, especially those who never marry, typically become disengaged from their children (Arendell 1995; King and Heard 1999; Seltzer 1991; Teachman 1990). Most are unwilling or unable to pay regular child support, and relatively few have constant relationships with their children. Instead, the costs of child rearing have been largely assumed by mothers and their families, aided by public assistance. A minority of fathers do manage to fulfill economic and social obligations, and some argue that many others would do so if they had the means and social support for continuing a relationship with their children (Marsiglio 1998; Smollar and Ooms 1987).

The uncertain relationship between biological fathers and their children has created a demand for public policies to shore up the family system (Garfinkel et al. 1996; Popenoe 1996). Widespread disagreement exists over specific policies for addressing current problems. Advocates who accept the current reality of high levels of nonmarriage and marital instability propose more generous economic allowances and extensive social support to women and their children to offset the limited economic role of men in disadvantaged families (Ellwood 1988). Critics of this approach contend that such policies may further erode the marriage system (Vinovskis and Chase-Lansdale 1987). Yet few realistic measures have been advanced for strengthening the institution of marriage (Furstenberg and Cherline 1991).

Enforcement of child support has attracted broad public support. A series of legislative initiatives culminating in the Family Support Act of 1988 have increased the role of federal and state governments in collecting child support from absent parents (typically fathers) and standardizing levels of child support. There has been a steady but modest improvement in the collection of child support in the 1990s. It is much less clear whether the strengthening of child support has worked to the benefit of children (Furstenberg et al. 1992; Garfinkel et al. 1996). It is too early to tell whether these sweeping measures will succeed in strengthening the economic contributions of fathers who live apart from their children. And, if it does, will greater economic support by absent parents reinforce social and psychological bonds to their children (Furstenberg 1989; Garfinkel and McLanahan 1990)? The other great experiment of the 1990s was the Welfare Reform Act in 1996, which replaced the longstanding entitlements to public assistance with temporary provisional support. It is much too early to tell what, if any, the effects of this policy will be on marriage and fertility practices. Advocates of welfare reform claimed that it would reduce out-of-wedlock childbearing and help restore marriage (Murray 1984). But the link between welfare payments and marriage patterns has never been strong (Moffitt 1998). Still, it may be possible to devise a test of the consequences of the different policies given the large state variations in program implementation.

As for the future of marriage, few, if any, sociologists and demographers are predicting a return to the status quo or a restoration of the norm of legitimacy. Short of a strong ideological swing favoring marriage and condemning nonmarital sexual activity and childbearing, it is difficult to foresee a sharp reversal in present trends (Blankenhorn et al. 1990). Predicting the future, however, has never been a strong point of demographic and sociological research.

(SEE ALSO: *Deviance Theories; Law and Society*)

REFERENCES

Amato, P.R., and A. Booth 1997 *A Generation at Risk: Growing Up in an Era of Family Upheaval.* Cambridge, Mass.: Harvard University Press.

Arendell, T. 1995 *Fathers and Divorce.* Thousand Oaks, Calif.: Sage Publications.

Bell, N. W., and E. F. Vogel (eds.) 1968 *A Modern Introduction to the Family.* New York: Free Press.

Blake, J. 1961 *Family Structure in Jamaica.* New York: Free Press.

Blakenhorn, D., S. Bayne, and J. B. Elshtain 1990 *Rebuilding the Nest.* Milwaukee, Wis.: Family Service America.

Bumpass, L. 1990 "What's Happening to the Family? Interactions Between Demographic and Institutional Change." *Demography* 27:483–498.

Burns, A., and C. Scott 1994 *Mother-Headed Families and Why They Have Increased.* Hillsdale, N.J.: Lawrence Erlbaum.

Cherlin, A. J. 1992 *Marriage, Divorce, Remarriage,* rev. and enl. ed. Cambridge, Mass.: Harvard University Press.

—— 1999 *Public and Private Families,* 2nd ed. Boston: McGraw-Hill.

Chilman, C. S. 1983 *Adolescent Sexuality in a Changing American Society: Social and Psychological Perspectives for the Human Services Professions.* New York: Wiley.

Clague, A. J., and S. J. Ventura 1968 *Trends in Illegitimacy: United States 1940–1965.* (Vital and Health Statistics, Public Health Service Publication no. 1000, ser. 21, no. 15.) Washington, D.C.: U.S. Government Printing Office.

Coser, R. L., (ed.) 1964 *The Family: Its Structures and Functions.* New York: St. Martin's Press.

Cutright, P. 1972 "Illegitimacy in the United States, 1920–1968." In C. Westoff and R. Parks, eds., *Demographic and Social Aspects of Population Growth.* Washington D.C.: U.S. Government Printing Office.

Davis, K. 1939 "Illegitimacy and the Social Structure." American Journal of Sociology 45:215–233.

—— 1949 *Human Society.* New York: Macmillan.

—— 1985 *Contemporary Marriage: Comparative Perspectives on a Changing Institution.* New York: Russell Sage Foundation.

Dornbush, S. M. 1989 "The Sociology of Adolescence." The Annual Review of Sociology 15: 233–259.

Duncan, G. J., and S. D. Hoffman 1990 "Teenage Welfare Receipt and Subsequent Dependance Among Black Adolescent Mothers." Family Planning Perspectives. 22:219–223.

Edin, K. 1998 "Why Don't Poor Single Mothers Get Married (or Remarried)?" Paper presented at the Russell Sage Foundation, New York, May.

Ellwood, D. T. 1988 *Poor Support.* New York: Basic Books.

Furstenberg, F. F., Jr. 1989 "Supporting Fathers: Implications of the Family Support Act for Men." Paper presented at the forum on the Family Support Act sponsored by the Foundation for Child Development, Washington, D.C., November.

—— 1990 "Coming of Age in a Changing Family System." In F. Feldman and G. Elliott, eds., *At the Threshold: The Developing Adolescent.* Cambridge, Mass.: Harvard University Press.

—— 1991 "As the Pendulum Swings: Teenage Childbearing and Social Concern." *Family Relations* 40:127–138.

—— 1995 "Fathering in the Inner-City: Paternal Participation and Public Policy." In W. Marsiglio, ed., *Fatherhood: Contemporary Theory, Research, and Social Policy.* Thousand Oaks, Calif.: Sage Publications.

—— 1996 "The Future of Marriage." *American Demographics* (June): 34–40.

——, and A. Cherlin 1991 *Divided Families: What Happens to Children When Their Parents Part.* Cambridge, Mass.: Harvard University Press.

K. E. Sherwood, and M. L. Sullivan 1992 *Caring and Paying: What Fathers and Mothers Say About Child Support.* New York: Manpower Demonstration Research Corporation.

Garfinkel, I., J. L. Hochschild, and S. McLanahan (eds.) 1996 *Social Policies for Children.* Washington, D.C.: Brookings Institution.

Garfinkel, I., and S. McLanahan 1986 *Single Mothers and Their Children.* Washington, D.C.: Urban Institute Press.

—— 1990 "The Effects of the Child Support Provisions of the Family Support Act of 1988 on Child Well-Being." *Population Research and Policy Review* 9:205–234.

Geronimus, A. T. 1987 "On Teenage Childbearing in the United States." *Population and Developmental Review* 13:245–279.

Glendon, M. A. 1989 *The Transformation of Family Law.* Chicago: University of Chicago Press.

Goode, W. J. 1960 "A Deviant Case: Illegitimacy in the Carribean." American Sociological Review 25:21–30.

—— 1961 "Illegitimacy, Anomie, and Cultural Penetration." *American Sociological Review* 26:319–325.

—— 1971 "Family Disorganization." In R. K. Merton and R. Nisbet, eds., *Contemporary Social Problems*, 3rd ed. New York: Harcourt Brace Jovanovitch.

Goody, J. 1983 *The Development of the Family and Marriage in Europe.* Cambridge, U.K.: Cambridge University Press.

Hayes, C. D. 1987 *Risking the Future,* vol. 1. Washington, D.C.: National Academy Press.

Hoem, B., and J. M. Hoem 1988 "The Swedish Family: Aspects of Contemporary Development." *Journal of Family Issues* 9:397–424.

Hofferth, S. L., and C. D. Hayes 1987 *Risking the Future,* vol. 2. Washington, D.C.: National Academy Press.

Hoffman, S. D., E. M. Foster, and F. F. Furstenberg, Jr. 1993 "Re-Evaluating the Costs of Teenage Childbearing." *Demography* 30:1–13.

Hogan, D. P., and E. Kitagawa 1985 "The Impact of Social Status, Family Structure, and Neighborhood on the Family Structure of Black Adolescents." *American Journal of Sociology* 90:825–855.

Institute of Medicine 1995 *The Best Intentions: Unintended Pregnancy and the Well-Being of Children and Families.* Washington, D.C.: National Academy Press.

King, V., and Heard, H. E. 1999 "Nonresident Father Visitation, Parental Conflict, and Mother's Satisfaction: What's Best for Child Well-Being?" *Journal of Marriage and the Family* 61:385–396.

Malinowski, B. 1930 "Parenthood, the Basis of Social Structure." In R. L. Coser, ed., *The Family: Its Structure and Functions.* New York: St. Martin's Press.

Marsiglio, W. 1998 *Procreative Man.* New York: New York University Press.

Mason, M. A., A. Skolnick, and S. D. Sugarman (eds.) 1998 *All Our Families: New Policies for a New Century.* New York: Oxford University Press.

Maynard, R. A. (ed.) 1997 *Kids Having Kids: Economic Costs and Social Consequences of Teen Pregnancy.* Washington, D.C.: Urban Institute Press.

McLanahan, S., and K. Booth 1989 "Mother-Only Families: Problems, Prospects, and Politics." *Journal of Marriage and the Family* 51:577–580.

McLanahan, S., and L. Casper 1995 "Growing Diversity and Inequality in the American Family." In R. Farley, ed., *State of the Union: America in the 1990s,* vol. 2. New York: Russell Sage Foundation.

McLanahan, S., and G. Sandefur 1994 *Growing up with a Single Parent: What Hurts, What Helps.* Cambridge, Mass.: Harvard University Press.

Miller, B. C., and K. A. Moore 1990 "Adolescent Sexual Behavior, Pregnancy, and Parenting." *Journal of Marriage and the Family* 524:1025–1044.

Moffitt, R. A. (ed.) 1998 *Welfare, the Family and Reproductive Behavior.* Washington, D.C.: National Academy Press.

Moore, K. A., M. C. Simms, and C. L. Betsey 1986 *Choice and Circumstance: Racial Differences in Adolescent Sexuality and Fertility.* New Brunswick, N.J.: Transaction Books.

Murray, C. 1984 *Losing Ground.* New York: Basic Books.

O'Connell, M., and M. J. Moore 1981 "The Legitimacy Status of First Births to U.S. Women Aged 15–24, 1939–1978." In F. F. Furstenberg, Jr., R. Lincoln, and J. Menken, eds., *Teenage Sexuality, Pregnancy, and Childbearing.* Philadelphia: University of Pennsylvania Press.

Popenoe, D. 1996 *Life Without Father.* New York: Free Press.

——, J. B. Elshtain, and D. Blankenhorn (eds.) 1996 *Promises to Keep: Decline and Renewal of Marriage in America.* Lanham, Md.: Rowman & Littlefield.

Seltzer, J. A. 1991 "Relationships Between Fathers and Children Who Live Apart: The Father's Role after Separation." Journal of Marriage and the Family 53:79–101.

Smith, H. L., S. P. Morgan, and T. Koropeckyz-Cox 1996 "A Decomposition of Trends in the Nonmarital Fertility Ratios of Blacks and Whites in the United States, 1960–1992." *Demography* 33:141–151.

Smollar, J., and T. Ooms 1987 *Young Unwed Fathers: Research Review, Policy Dilemmas, and Options.* Washington, D.C.: Maximus.

Teachman, J. D. 1990 "Still Fathers? The Reorganization of Parental Obligations Following Divorce." Paper presented at the Albany Conference of Demographic Perspectives on the American Family: Patterns and Prospects, April.

Trussel, J. 1988 "Teenage Pregnancy in the United States." *Family Planning Perspectives* 20:262–272.

Ventura, S. J., J. A. Martin, S. C. Curtin, and T. J. Matthews 1996 "Report of Final Natality: Statistics." *Monthly Vital Statistics Report* 45 (11) (supp. 2) Hyattsville, Md.: National Center for Health Statistics.

Vincent, C. E. 1961 *Unmarried Mothers.* New York: Free Press.

Vinovskis, M. 1988 *An "Epidemic" of Adolescent Pregnancy? Some Historical and Policy Considerations.* New York: Oxford University Press.

——, and P. L. Chase-Lansdale 1987 "Should We Discourage Teenage Marriage?" *Public Interest* 98:23–37.

"Virginia Slims American Women's Public Opinion Poll" 1985 A study conducted by the Roper Center for Public Opinion.

Wilson, W. J. 1987 *The Truly Disadvantaged*. Chicago: University of Chicago Press.

FRANK F. FURSTENBERG JR.

IMPERIALISM, COLONIALISM, AND DECOLONIZATION

The colonial expansion of European states into the Americas, Asia, Africa, and the Pacific, followed by the collapse of these empires and their replacement by sovereign nation-states, is a double movement of great historical importance. The following briefly reviews the larger contours of this history and outlines some central arguments about its causes and consequences.

IMPERIALISM AND COLONIALISM

The term "imperialism" was first used in the 1830s to recall Napoleonic ambitions. It gained its core contemporary meaning around the turn of the century as a description of the feverish colonial expansion of Britain, France, Germany, Russia, the United States, and Italy. But the term is not confined to formal colonial expansion; in particular, the continuing dependence of much of the Third World on Western states and multinational corporations is often understood as neocolonialism or neoimperialism (Magdoff 1969; Nkrumah 1966).

Contemporary efforts to distill these diverse usages generally define imperialism as the construction and maintenance of relationships of domination between political communities. Such relations are often seen as explicitly political, either in the narrow sense of direct administrative control or more broadly as formal or informal control over state policy. Economic conceptions of imperialism sometimes develop an analogue to these notions, where relations of economic control or exploitation replace political domination.

"Imperialism" has also been appropriated in a much narrower sense to support particular lines of argument. Lenin's statement that "imperialism is the monopoly stage of capitalism" ([1917] 1939, p. 88) may be understood as a move of this sort. Arrighi, among others, argues that Lenin is better understood as formulating a substantive proposition; he suggests the interpretation "imperialism, or the tendency to war between capitalist countries, is a necessary consequence of the transformation of capitalism into monopoly or finance capital" (1978, p. 14).

Even when imperialism is equated with the establishment and maintenance of political domination, an awkward relationship between *imperialism* and *empire* persists. Classically, "empire" refers to the great agrarian bureaucracies that dominated antiquity, from the Aztec to the Chinese, from ancient Sumer to Imperial Rome. It is not clear how much these structures have in common with the overseas colonial empires of Western states, much less with contemporary structures of dependence on foreign investment. Agrarian bureaucracies involved ethnic divisions that separated classes (most importantly separating warriors and peasant producers) rather than entire communities or nations (Gellner 1983).

A second historical use of "empire" is the medieval image of a temporal parallel to the Roman Church (Folz 1969; Guenee 1985). Rather than an alien and illegitimate structure, empire was seen as a political order unifying the Christian world. Revived by Charlemagne, the notion of a universal polity lived on, in an increasingly ghostly fashion, through the Holy Roman Empire. It receded into the background as a real political force with the construction of absolutist states and was lost as a compelling image with the rise of the nation-state.

In contrast to these historical understandings of empire, modern conceptions of imperialism rest on the notion that popular sovereignty forms the basis of political community. Only with the notion of popular sovereignty does domination refer to relationships between rather than within communities. If the criteria that the United Nations uses today to identify colonialism were to be applied before 1700, all territories would be parts of empires and all peoples would be dependent subjects. It is thus no accident that the notion of imperialism arose with the nation-state; it connotes the expansionary drive of a community that is internally organized around (the myth of) popular sovereignty.

European Political Expansion. European overseas expansion can be described crudely as occurring in two stages, the colonial and the imperial. In the fifteenth and sixteenth centuries, seagoing powers constructed networks of colonial enclaves along the route to the East Indies. Less than half a century after the voyages of Columbus, the conquistadores had laid waste to the Incan and Aztec empires and were sending gold and silver back to Spain. In the following two centuries, Spain, Portugal, Great Britain, France, and the Netherlands colonized virtually the whole of the Caribbean, Central and South America, and the North Atlantic seaboard. The colonial period per se came to a close with the wars of national independence in the Americas between 1776 and 1830, leaving European states in control of little more than trading posts and exhausted sugar plantations.

The second period of expansion, one of imperial rather than colonial expansion, began after an interregnum marked by British naval hegemony. In the three decades after 1880, a scramble for territory partitioned Africa, Southeast Asia, and the Pacific among Great Britain, France, Germany, Belgium, and Portugal, while the United States annexed the remains of the Spanish Empire. None of this expansion involved much metropolitan emigration; colonial officials, traders, planters, and missionaries formed a thin veneer on indigenous societies.

The sources of the political structures of imperial rule lie in both metropolitan and indigenous traditions. Colonies tended to be formally organized along metropolitan lines (Fieldhouse 1966). Settler colonies mirrored domestic political structures quite directly (Lang 1975), while nonsettler colonies recall metropolitan structures in a more abstract fashion. For example, the British tried to fashion systems of local rule (Lugard [1922] 1965), while the French strove to create a unified, centralized administration. But the superficiality of most imperial rule led to great variation in actual administrative arrangements. Even empires whose guiding rationale was assimilation (the French and the Portuguese, especially) depended heavily on indigenous authorities and traditions.

Overseas colonies also varied in the strength and character of their economic relationship to the metropolis. Only a few colonies were the source of great riches for the metropolitan economy: most prominently, the American settler and plantation colonies, British India, and the Dutch East Indies. Others had a largely strategic value; much

of the British Empire, for instance, was acquired in the effort to maintain lines of communication to India. The great majority of colonies acquired after 1880 had rather little importance for the metropolis, either as markets for imperial products or as sources of raw materials (Fieldhouse 1973).

Theories of Imperialism. The starting point for modern theories of imperialism is John Hobson's *Imperialism: A Study* ([1902] 1965). A liberal critic of the Boer War, Hobson saw imperial expansion as a search for new outlets for investment. He found the source of this search in the surplus capital amassed by increasingly monopolistic corporate trusts. Hobson viewed imperial expansion as costly for the nation as a whole and sought to expose the special interests promoting imperialism. He also contended that capital surpluses could be consumed domestically by equalizing the distribution of income.

Lenin's *Imperialism: The Highest Stage of Capitalism* ([1917] 1939) provides the most influential statement of an economic analysis of imperialism. Lenin agreed with Hobson that imperialism flowed from the need to invest outside the domestic economy, drawing explicitly on Hilferding's ([1910] 1981) analysis of finance capital as a stage of capitalism. He was concerned to show that imperialism was a necessary consequence of the dynamics of capitalism (in contrast to Hobson's anticipation of Keynes) and that the expansionary impulse could not be globally coordinated (versus Kautsky's notion of an ultra-imperialism). Lenin argued that the unevenness of development makes imperialist war inevitable, as "late starters" demand their own place in the sun.

More contemporary writers like Baran and Sweezy (1966), Frank (1967), and Wallerstein (1974) drew upon both the Marxist tradition and Latin American theories of *dependencia* to suggest an alternative economic analysis of imperialism. They argued that international economic relations involve a net transfer of capital from the "periphery" to the "core" of the economic system and point to the continuities in this process from early colonial expansion to contemporary neoimperialism. This is in sharp contrast with the Leninist tradition, which argues that colonial forays bring noncapitalist societies into the world economy.

Other writers consider political ambitions or relationships to be the taproot of imperialism. In perhaps the most interesting account of this sort, Schumpeter (1951) turned the Marxist perspective on its head. He noted that the characteristic motif of the ancient empires is military expansion for its own sake. Schumpeter argued that imperialism appears as an atavistic trait in the landed aristocracy of modern societies, stressing the mismatch between the social psychology of the warrior and the industrious, calculating spirit of the entrepreneur. A more political perspective treats imperial activity as flowing from the anarchical structure of the Western state system (Cohen 1973; Waltz 1979). In the absence of an enforceable legal order, states are motivated to expand when possible or endure decline relative to more aggressive states. This perspective explains European imperialism in the nineteenth century as the product of increasing levels of international competition and conflict.

Whether economic or political, most analyses of imperialism find its sources in the logic of the West, ignoring indigenous peoples in the process. John Gallagher and Ronald Robinson led a historiographic revision aiming to redress this imbalance. Their seminal essay "The Imperialism of Free Trade" (1953) emphasized the continuity in British policy between the informal imperialism of the mid-eighteenth century and the rush for colonies after 1880. In *Africa and the Victorians*, Robinson and colleagues (1961) argued that it was increasing indigenous resistance to European influence that led Britain to replace informal domination with formal empire. In later work, Robinson (1972) emphasized the other side of the coin—the extent to which Western empires as political systems were dependent on local collaboration.

DECOLONIZATION

"Decolonization" refers to a polity's movement from a status of political dependence or subordination to a status of formal autonomy or sovereignty. In modern usage, it is generally assumed that the imperial or metropolitan center is physically separated from the dependency and that the two societies are ethnically distinct. The term refers specifically to the disintegration of Western overseas empires and their replacement by sovereign states in the Americas, Asia, and Africa.

There are several routes by which decolonization can take place. Most frequently, the dependency becomes a new sovereign state, a political entity recognized in the international arena as independent of other states and as possessing final jurisdiction over a defined territory and population. Less often, decolonization may occur through the dependency's full incorporation into an existing polity, such that it is no longer separate and subordinate.

It is often unclear when (or whether) decolonization has occurred. Puerto Rico's relation to the United States can be described as one of colonial dependency or as free association. In the 1960s, Portugal claimed to have no colonies, only overseas territories formally incorporated into a unitary Portuguese state (Nogueira 1963). And where political relations are not contested, the absence of overt conflict makes it difficult to know when sovereignty has been achieved. For example, arguments can be made for dating Canadian independence at 1867, 1919, 1926, or 1931.

European Political Contraction. Virtually all of the decolonization of Western overseas empires occurred in two historical eras (Bergesen and Schoenberg 1980). The major American colonies became independent during the late eighteenth and early nineteenth centuries. The mid-twentieth century witnessed a more rapid and complete wave of decolonization worldwide. The types of colonies in existence in each period and the nature of the decolonization process varied greatly across the two periods (Fieldhouse 1966; Strang 1991a).

The first wave of decolonization began with the independence of Britain's thirteen continental colonies as the United States of America. The French Revolution touched off a slave uprising that led ultimately to the independence of the French colony of Saint Domingue as Haiti. Portuguese Brazil and Spanish Central and South America became independent after the Napoleonic Wars, which had cut Latin America off from the Iberian peninsula.

While the first period of decolonization was limited to the Americas, twentieth-century decolonization was global in scope. It included the independence of most of the Indian subcontinent, Southeast Asia and Australasia, the Middle East, Africa, and the Caribbean. Between the world wars, some of Britain's settler colonies and a number of loosely held protectorates became fully sovereign. Soon after World War II, the major

Asian colonies—India, Indonesia, Indochina, and the Philippines—achieved independence. The pace of change rapidly accelerated during the 1960s, which saw the decolonization of nearly all of Africa. By the 1980s, nearly all Western colonies had become independent or had been fully incorporated into sovereign states.

One fundamental difference between the two eras of decolonization has to do with who sought independence. Early American decolonizations were creole revolutions, as the descendants of European settlers sought political autonomy from the "mother country." The American Revolution and the Spanish Wars for Independence were political rather than social revolutions. Slave revolt in Haiti provided the sole exception, to the horror of creole nationalists as well as loyalists elsewhere.

By contrast, twentieth-century decolonization was rooted in indigenous rather than creole movements for independence, as decolonization came to mean freedom from racially alien rule. After World War II, settler minorities opposed decolonization, since national independence spelled an end to their privileged political, economic, and social position. Only in South Africa did a racialist minority regime survive decolonization.

The first and second waves of decolonization also differed importantly in the amount of violence involved. Early decolonization in the Americas was won through military combat between settler and imperial forces. Wars for independence raged in Britain's thirteen continental colonies, in Spanish Central and South America, and in Haiti. Only in Portuguese Brazil was independence achieved without a fight, largely because Brazil was several times richer and more populous than Portugal.

During the twentieth century, protracted wars for independence were fought in Indochina, Indonesia, Algeria, and Angola. But these were the exceptions to the rule. Most colonies became independent with little or no organized violence between the imperial state and colonial nationalists. In much of Africa, imperial powers virtually abandoned colonies at the first sign of popular opposition to the colonial regime. By the mid-1960s, decolonization had become a rather routine activity for many imperial powers, often achieved through institutionalized expressions of popular will such as plebiscites.

Causes of Decolonization. A variety of arguments have been developed about factors contributing to decolonization. While most treatments have dealt with a single dependency or empire, there have been a number of efforts to develop explicitly comparative analyses (see Albertini 1982; Anderson 1983; Bergesen and Schoenberg 1980; Boswell 1989; Emerson 1960; Grimal 1978; Lang 1975; Smith 1978; Strang 1990).

Decolonization is often seen as the result of structural change in the dependency itself. Settler colonies are thought to undergo a natural process of maturation, well expressed in the physiocratic maxim that colonies are like fruit that fall from the tree when they are ripe. Indigenous populations are also importantly affected by contact with Western economic and political structures.

In both kinds of colonies, the specific condition that seems to precipitate decolonization is the emergence of peripheral nationalism. Settler colonies generally began as economic corporations chartered by European states. Non-Western peoples were generally tribal or segmental societies prior to colonization, and imperial structures were fundamentally dependent on the collaboration of indigenous elites (Robinson 1972). Decolonization required a new vision of the colonial dependency as a national society (Anderson 1983; Diamond 1958).

Colonial powers contributed unintentionally to the formulation of a national vision. They did so partly by spurring the rise of new social groups—indigenous bourgeois, landless workers, civil servants, teachers—who proved to be the carriers of colonial nationalism and independence. Contact with the colonial power exposed these groups to the notions and institutions of the Western nation-state while simultaneously denying them participation rights. Settlers, of course, carried notions of these rights with them (see Bailyn 1967 and Greene 1986 on the ideological origins of the American Revolution). Under these conditions, nationalism was a weapon easily turned on its creators (Emerson 1960; Strang 1992).

While pressures for decolonization invariably stemmed from the dependency itself, the response of the metropolitan power played a crucial role in the outcome. The classic contrast in imperial policy is between British "association" and French "assimilation" (though parallel contrasts between the imperial policies of the United States and Portugal are even more striking). The British empire was administratively structured around indirect rule and local autonomy, which permitted considerable flexibility in the imperial reaction to pressures for decolonization. By contrast, the French aimed at the assimilation of their colonies into a unitary republic, which led to firmer resistance to decolonization.

Some decolonization occurred because the balance of military capacity shifted against metropolitan states. This was crucial to the decolonization of the Americas, as increasingly vigorous creole societies could not be controlled from across the Atlantic. After World War II, metropolitan weakness was a contributing factor as European colonial states found themselves reduced to the position of second-rate powers. At critical junctures after 1945, metropolitan governments were unable to project sufficient military power abroad to control events: the British in Suez, the French in Indochina and Algeria, the Dutch in Indonesia.

Finally, several systemic factors or processes may be linked to decolonization. One is the presence of a state that is economically and politically dominant on the world stage. It has been argued that "hegemonic" states seek to construct a global free-market system that provides them access to markets more cheaply than does formal control (Bergesen and Schoenberg 1980; Boswell 1989; Krasner 1976). This argument has much in common with Gallagher and Robinson's (1953) notion of an "imperialism of free trade" that metropolitan states preferred to the overhead costs of empire. Both Britain and the United States supported the collapse of rival empires and avoided empire building themselves during the periods of their global hegemony.

A second systemic factor is the contagiousness of decolonization. The American Revolution served as a model for insurrection in both Haiti and Latin America. After World War II, the independence of India, Indochina, and Indonesia had a substantial impact on colonized peoples everywhere. The contagiousness of independence is most apparent in the rapidity with which decolonization swept across Africa, where thirty-three colonies became independent between 1957 and 1966.

Finally, global political understandings and discourse play a critical role in decolonization (Strang 1990). After 1945, the two superpowers were ideologically opposed to colonialism, though each accused the other of imperialism. Even the major imperial powers (Great Britain, France, the Netherlands) found it difficult to reconcile colonial possessions with the political ideas and institutions of the evolving national polity. As a result, the rationale for colonialism crumbled under pressure, with imperialism being formally denounced by the United Nations in 1960.

The social construction of a society or administrative unit as a "colonial dependency" is thus crucially important to mobilization around national independence, particularly given contemporary political understandings. A sharp distinction is generally drawn between the overseas empires of European states and "internal colonies" such as Wales, Armenia, or Eritrea. While the empirical basis for such a distinction is sometimes shaky, it is real in its consequences. Identification as a colonial dependency greatly increases the chances of mobilizing internal and external support for indigenous nationalism; it also vastly reduces the compulsion that the metropolitan state can legitimately bring to bear.

Consequences of Decolonization. The implications of decolonization for more general notions of international domination or exploitation are strongly contested. Dependency and world systems theorists view decolonization as producing change in the mere form, but not the content, of core–periphery relations (Chase-Dunn and Rubinson 1979). The argument is that contact between more and less developed economies tends generally to reinforce the differential between them, even in the absence of explicit political controls. Dependence on foreign capital has been argued to slow long-term economic growth (Bornschier et al. 1978) and more generally to shape the political and economic structure of the dependent society (Amin 1973; Cardoso and Faletto 1979).

Despite these concerns, it is clear that decolonization involves a fundamental shift in the structures regulating international exchange, especially in the post–World War II era. Contemporary states are armed with widely accepted rights to control economic activity within their boundaries, including rights to nationalize foreign-owned industries and renegotiate contracts with multinational corporations (Krasner 1978; Lipson 1985). Third World nations mobilize around these rights (Krasner 1985), and the negative impact of economic dependency seems to decrease when the peripheral state is strong (Delacroix and Ragin 1981).

While notions of dependency and neocolonialism are the subject of vigorous debate, a straightforward consequence of decolonization is the worldwide expansion of an originally European state society. Most of the present members of the United Nations became sovereign through decolonization (McNeely 1995). And historically, the political units emerging from decolonization have been strikingly stable. Few ex-dependencies have been recolonized or annexed or have merged or dissolved (Jackson and Rosberg 1982; Strang 1991b). Against much expectation, decolonization has produced states that figure as core players in the contemporary international economic and political order.

REFERENCES

Albertini, Rudolf von 1982 *Decolonization: The Administration and Future of the Colonies 1919–1960.* New York: Holmes and Meier.

Amin, Samir 1973 *Neo-Colonialism in West Africa.* London: Monthly Review Press.

Anderson, Benedict 1983 *Imagined Communities: Reflections on the Origins and Spread of Nationalism.* London: Verso.

Arrighi, Giovanni 1978 *The Geometry of Imperialism.* London: New Left Books.

Bailyn, Bernard 1967 *The Ideological Origins of the American Revolution.* Cambridge, Mass.: Harvard University Press.

Baran, Paul, and Paul Sweezy 1966 *Monopoly Capital.* New York: Monthly Review Press.

Bergesen, Albert, and Ronald Schoenberg 1980 "The Long Waves of Colonial Expansion and Contraction 1415–1970." In A. Bergesen, ed., *Studies of the Modern World System.* New York: Academic Press.

Bornschier, Volker, Christopher Chase-Dunn, and Richard Rubinson 1978 "Cross-National Evidence of the Effects of Foreign Investment and Aid on Economic Growth and Inequality: A Survey of Findings and a Reanalysis." *American Journal of Sociology* 84:651–683.

Boswell, Terry 1989 "Colonial Empires and the Capitalist World-Economy: A Time Series Analysis of Colonization, 1640–1960." *American Sociological Review* 54:180–196.

Cardoso, Fernando H., and Enzo Faletto 1979 *Dependency and Development in Latin America.* Berkeley: University of California Press.

Chase-Dunn, Christopher, and Richard Rubinson 1979 "Toward a Structural Perspective on the World-System." *Politics and Society* 7:453–476.

Cohen, Benjamin J. 1973 *The Question of Imperialism.* New York: Basic Books.

Delacroix, Jacques, and Charles C. Ragin 1981 "Structural Blockage: A Cross-National Study of Economic Dependency, State Efficacy, and Underdevelopment." *American Journal of Sociology* 86:1311–1347.

Diamond, Sigmund 1958 "From Organization to Society." *American Journal of Sociology* 63:457–475.

Emerson, Rupert 1960 *From Empire to Nation.* Cambridge, Mass.: Harvard University Press.

Fieldhouse, David K. 1966 *The Colonial Empires.* New York: Dell.

—— 1973 *Economics and Empire, 1830–1914.* Ithaca, N.Y.: Cornell University Press.

Folz, Robert 1969 *The Concept of Empire in Western Europe from the Fifth to the Fourteenth Century.* London: Arnold.

Frank, Andre Gunder 1967 *Capitalism and Underdevelopment in Latin America.* New York: Monthly Review Press.

Gallagher, John, and Ronald Robinson 1953 "The Imperialism of Free Trade." *Economic History Review* S5:1–15.

Gellner, Ernest 1983 *Nations and Nationalism.* Oxford: Basil Blackwell.

Greene, Jack P. 1986 *Peripheries and Center: Constitutional Development in the Extended Polities of the British Empire and the United States 1607–1788.* Athens: University of Georgia Press.

Grimal, Henri 1978 *Decolonization.* London: Routledge and Kegan Paul.

Guenee, Bernard 1985 *States and Rulers in Later Medieval Europe.* Oxford: Basil Blackwell.

Hancock, William K. 1950. *The Wealth of Colonies.* Cambridge: Cambridge University Press.

Hilferding, Rudolf (1910) 1981 *Finance Capital.* London: Routledge and Kegan Paul.

Hobson, John A. (1902) 1965 *Imperialism: A Study.* New York: Allen and Unwin.

Holland, R. F. 1985 *European Decolonization 1918–1981.* New York: St. Martin's Press.

Jackson, Robert, and Carl Rosberg 1982 "Why Africa's Weak States Persist: The Empirical and the Juridical in Statehood." *World Politics* 35:124.

Krasner, Stephen D. 1976 "State Power and the Structure of International Trade." *World Politics* 28:317–343.

—— 1978 *Defending the National Interest*. Princeton, N.J.: Princeton University Press.

—— 1985 *Structural Conflict*. Berkeley: University of California Press.

Lang, James 1975 *Conquest and Commerce: Spain and England in the Americas*. New York: Academic Press.

Lenin, Vladimir Ilich (1917) 1939 *Imperialism: The Highest Stage of Capitalism*. London: International Publishers.

Lipson, Charles 1985 *Standing Guard: Protecting Foreign Capital in the Nineteenth and Twentieth Centuries*. Berkeley: University of California Press.

Lugard, Frederick J. D. (1922) 1965 *The Dual Mandate in British Tropical Africa*, 5th ed. London: Cass.

Magdoff, Harry 1969 *Age of Imperialism*. New York: Monthly Review Press.

McNeely, Connie L. 1995 *Constructing the Nation-State: International Organizations and Prescriptive Action*. Westport, Conn.: Greenwood.

Nkrumah, Kwame 1966 *Neo-Colonialism: The Last Stage of Imperialism*. London: International Publishers.

Nogueira, Franco 1963 *The United Nations and Portugal: A Study of Anti-Colonialism*. London: Sidgwick and Jackson.

Robinson, Ronald 1972 "Non-European Foundations of European Imperialism: Sketch for a Theory of Collaboration." In Roger Owen and Bob Sutcliffe, eds., *Studies in the Theory of Imperialism*. Bristol, U.K.: G. B. Longman.

——, John Gallagher, and Alice Denny 1961 *Africa and the Victorians: The Official Mind of Imperialism*. London: St. Martin's Press.

Schumpeter, Joseph 1951 "The Sociology of Imperialism." In *Imperialism and Social Classes*. New York: Kelley.

Smith, Tony 1978 "A Comparative Study of French and British Decolonization." *Comparative Studies in Society and History* 20:70–102.

Strang, David 1990 "From Dependency to Sovereignty: An Event History Analysis of Decolonization." *American Sociological Review* 55:846–860.

—— 1991a "Global Patterns of Decolonization 1500–1987." *International Studies Quarterly* 35:429–454.

—— 1991b "Anomaly and Commonplace in European Political Expansion: Realist and Institutional Accounts." *International Organization* 45:142–161.

—— 1992 "The Inner Incompatibility of Empire and Nation: Popular Sovereignty and Decolonization." *Sociological Perspectives* 35:367–384.

Wallerstein, Immanuel 1974, 1980, 1989 *The Modern World-System*, 3 vols. Cambridge: Cambridge University Press.

Waltz, Kenneth 1979 *Theory of International Politics*. Reading, Mass.: Addison-Wesley.

Weber, Max 1958 *The Protestant Ethic and the Spirit of Capitalism*. New York: Scribners.

DAVID STRANG

IMPRESSION FORMATION

See Affect Control Theory and Impression Formation; Social Psychology.

INCEST

Incest is illicit sex or marriage between persons socially or legally defined as related too closely to one another. All societies have rules regarding incest. Incest is conceptualized in four ways: as a proscribed or prescribed marriage form, as a taboo, as prohibited coitus, and as child abuse. The first three conceptualizations are most closely related to early scholars (mid-1800s to mid-1900s), who tended to overlap them. The last conceptualization has become prominent more recently.

Incest-as-marriage rules are usually proscriptive ("Thou shalt not"). Prescriptive ("Thou shalt") incestuous marriage rules have been documented for royalty in Old Iran and ancient Egypt and for Mormons in the United States (Lester 1972). Some groups historically encouraged brother–sister incest. Cases in point were the ruling families of Egypt and Polynesia, where preservation of family resources and ethnic identity took precedence over political alliances with other groups (Firth 1936, 1994).

That some groups proscribe while others prescribe incestuous marriages has caused some to be skeptical of many theories about incest, especially theories that assume that incest avoidance is natural, that close inbreeding is genetically disadvantageous, or that there is an incest taboo. John F. McLennan ([1865] 1876), a lawyer, coined the terms *endogamy* (within-the-group marriage) and *exogamy* (outside-the-group marriage). He defined incest as endogamy. Based on his analyses of marriage in Ireland, Australia, ancient Greece, and other societies, he concluded that rules proscribing endogamy evolved as a group survival mechanism. He reasoned that as members of one tribe or group married into others, "blood ties" emerged. These blood ties encouraged reciprocity between groups and cooperation and harmony within groups.

Anthropologist Lewis Henry Morgan ([1877] 1964) generally agreed with McLennan's definition of incest as endogamy and with McLennan's assumption that proscribing incest promoted both exogamy and group survival. Morgan assumed, however, that incest originally became prohibited due to the presumed deleterious effects of inbreeding. That is, Morgan assumed that at some point, humans developed the capacity to see that exogamy increased the "vigor of the stock" (p. 65). Moreover, in agreement with sociologist Herbert Spencer's ([1876] 1898, pp. 623–642) earlier critique of McLennan's application of the terms "endogamy" and "exogamy," Morgan ([1877] 1964) contended that given the very contradictory nature by which kinship is recognized and organized among humans, McLennan's "terms and his conclusions are of little value" (p. 432). Finally, Morgan contended that practices such as brother–sister and father–daughter marriage among Hawaiians, for instance, spoke to earlier, savage stages of human existence. To Morgan, human groups evolve through three basic epochs: savagery, barbarism, and civilization. The first two epochs each have two stages, the last one only one stage. In Morgan's schema of the evolution of humankind, at the very first stage there is promiscuous intercourse and the marriage of brothers and sisters. In the second stage, brother–sister marriage is prohibited. The third stage of evolution sees prominence given to the Gentile pattern of social organization, which includes monogamy. The patriarchal family characterizes the fourth stage. The fifth, and final, stage in the schema, arising with the concept of property, is hallmarked by the monogamian family and the superiority of the "Aryan, Semitic, and Uralian system of consanguinity and affinity" (Morgan [1877] 1964, pp. 421–422). To Morgan, the Aryan family represented the highest level of human evolution, and thus the epitome of civilized humans. This high civilization was attributed to the "providence of God" (p.

468). To Morgan, in this civilized arrangement, cousin marriage is prohibited. In reading Morgan's work, one gets the impression that he saw this last stage as the best and the highest, and seemed to personally identify with it. Thus, it is somewhat curious that he married his cousin, Mary Elizabeth Steele.

Tylor (1889) elaborated on McLennan's notion of exchange and reciprocity among exogamous groups. He noted that men made political alliances with men in other groups by exchanging women in marriage. Spencer ([1876] 1898) argued that endogamy was probably the original practice among early peoples, especially among peaceful tribes. Exogamy probably began through wife stealing. He assumed that some early groups probably stole wives from other groups because they faced a scarcity of women. Other groups forcefully captured wives in the process of war. Thus, Spencer positioned exogamy as originally speaking to extremely brutal treatment of women. He assumed that as time passed and circumstances changed, exogamy would be seen as advantageous to groups who could make the linkages between sexual intercourse and procreation. That is, these groups might come to see exogamy as leading to a healthier stock of people. In addition, he assumed that, over time, such exchanges also would be seen as creating bonds among groups who otherwise might compete for scarce resources or else annihilate each other through warfare.

The common thread among these theories is the focus on incest rules as social organizational principles. A shared weakness is the reliance on analyses of primitive or premodern groups. These inclinations are also found in varying degrees in writings by Sir James Frazer (1927), Brenda Seligman (1929, 1932), Robert Briffault (1930), Bronislaw Malinowksi (1922, 1927, 1929), George Murdock (1949), and Claude Levi-Strauss ([1949] 1969). Many of these and other writers also fail to differentiate between incest rules and exogamy rules. What one group calls incestuous marriage may not biologically be such. Likewise, some groups' exogamy rules permit biologically incestuous marriage. Recognizing that incest rules are socially defined, Sumner (1906) presaged today's sociobiologists. Sumner argued that incest rules should be modified as researchers gathered genetic evidence that dispelled fallacious beliefs that all incestuous matings are deleterious.

Sociologist Emile Durkheim's *Incest: The Nature and Origin of the Taboo* ([1898] 1963) is an infrequently cited magnum opus. Based on ethnographic research in Australia, this book emphasized and illustrated the social and moral origins of incest taboos. Durkheim noted the ways in which prohibitions against incest and penalties for rule violations organize social groups internally. Cooperation and alliances with other groups via exogamy are consequently prompted. Durkheim contended that the incest taboo has a religious origin. It is derived from the clan's sentiments surrounding blood, specifically menstrual blood. While blood is taboo in a general way, contact with the blood of the clan is taboo in specific ways. Durkheim reasoned that menstrual blood represents a flowing away of the clan's lifeblood. This renders women taboo for and inferior to men of the same clan. The taboo relates to intercourse in general and to marriage in particular. Blood and incest are presumed to be related such that a man violating the taboo is seen as a murderer. Thus, in a real sense, Durkheim posited women as having a dual nature, being at once both sacred and profane. That women bear children, thus rendering a clan immortal, made them sacred. However, since they spilt blood, which itself is sacred, they had a profane nature to them. To marry a clan's women to another group kept the clan sacred, while at the same making it possible for other clans to perpetuate themselves.

Durkheim contended that the origin of the taboo is lost to the consciousness of clans over time but that the taboo itself is replaced by a generalized repugnance of incest. This repugnance prompts men to exchange women with other groups, thus facilitating political alliances between men of different groups. In addition, in his *The Division of Labor in Society* ([1893] 1963), Durkheim posited that when incest loses its religiously based criminal status, prohibitions against it are or will be codified into law.

While brother–sister marriages are negatively sanctioned in many parts of the world, the United States contrasts sharply with European and other nations in having civil laws that prohibit cousin marriage as well (Ottenheimer 1990). Roughly 60 percent of U.S. states prohibit cousin marriage. Many of the states have prohibitions placed on marriages other than brother–sister or cousin–cousin. For instance, Alaska prohibits marriage to persons more closely related than the fourth degree of consanguinity, regardless of whether this relationship is whole- or half-blood. Both Rhode Island and South Carolina forbid men to marry their stepmother, grandfather's wife, wife's daughter, and various other affinal or blood kin. Both states forbid women to marry their husband's grandfather, son's daughter's husband, daughter's husband, stepfather, or grandmother's husband (Kessinger 1990). Many of these laws no doubt were influenced by persons such as Morgan, with his emphasis on social evolution and his contention that civilized people simply don't engage in incestuous pairings. It is probably also the case that the eugenics movement, of the late 1800s through roughly the early 1900s, had some effect on maintaining such laws. The word "eugenics" was coined by biologist Francis Galton and meant improvement in the human race through selective breeding (Parrinder 1997). Galton and his followers were concerned with an array of social issues that they thought could be minimized if not eradicated through eugenics. These included overpopulation caused by high fertility rates of immigrants, poor people, and other classes of people deemed to be of inferior stock. Given a belief that criminals biologically inherited their antisocial tendencies, proponents of eugenics also believed that sterilization and birth control were necessary among some people so that they did not bring forth more generations of criminals (Rafter 1997). Fears of the negative effects of human inbreeding were also high at this time, resulting in several U.S. states passing laws that made cousin–cousin marriage a criminal offense (Gibbons 1993). The eugenics movement is also associated with social Darwinism and the Nazi regime. However, both of these topics are beyond the purview of this article.

Marriage laws and moral crusades aside, endogamous unions have continued to occur in the United States. An analysis of marriage patterns in Madison County, Virginia, 1850–1939, revealed a rather high rate of marriage between first cousins and first cousins once-removed (Frankenberg 1990). Possible reasons for these patterns may include restricted physical mobility and preference for socially similar others. Relying on U.S. Census data, another study revealed a fairly high rate of endogamy among Louisiana Cajuns (Bankston and Henry 1999). Partial explanations for this endogamy include restricted residential mobility, ethnic identity emphases of the subculture, and a preference for social-class homogamy. The rate of biologically incestuous unions among this group, however, was not made clear in the report.

The concern over genetic transmission of physical and mental defects through marriage to close relatives continues today. In an analysis of consanguineous marriage and health profiles of offspring from these unions, researchers in Dammam City, Eastern Province, Kingdom of Saudi Arabia, found that of the 1,307 unions studied, 52 percent were consanguineous. The most common consanguineous union was among first cousins. These consanguineous unions are associated with culture values and efforts to keep property and resources in the family. The study revealed that babies born of a consanguineous union tended to be smaller than those born of a nonconsanguineous union (Al-Abdulkareem and Ballal 1998). A recent American study focused on the relationship between consanguinity and childhood mortality in an Old Order Amish settlement. It was found that the Amish in the Lancaster, Pennsylvania, area are at risk for genetically transmitted defects that result in increased mortality rates. In addition, consanguineous unions resulted in higher neonatal and postnatal death rates than did nonconsanguineous unions (Dorsten et al. 1999).

Sigmund Freud focused on the incest taboo ([1913] 1950) and infantile sexuality ([1905] 1962). Through his tale of the primal horde, Freud posited that in the original family there was a jealous and violent father who engaged his daughters in incest. The jealous brothers banded together, killed, and ate the father. Horrified by their deeds, the brothers made incest taboo. For Freud, this (the moment when humans created incest rules) was when humans became social. He assumed that very young (Oedipal) children sexually desire their opposite-sex parent. Little boys then suffer from castration anxiety, fearing that the father will become aware of their desires and punish them. While little girls see their mothers as inferior to men, they also know them to be more powerful than they are.

Thus, little girls resignedly align themselves with their mothers, repress their incestuous impulses, and experience penis envy. Even though Freud's theories were based on conjecture and focused on the bourgeois nuclear family of his day, they have nonetheless influenced many social scientists, including French anthropologist Jean Claude Levi-Strauss ([1949] 1969) and American sociologist Talcott Parsons (1954).

Levi-Strauss agreed with Freud that humans became social with the creation of incest rules. Borrowing from the emphasis on the exchange of women, found in the works of Durkheim and Marcel Mauss, and Durkheim's assumption that women of a clan become the symbol (totem) for the clan, Levi-Strauss posited that exogamy represents a special form of alliance-creating reciprocity. Since incest involves sexuality, incest rules and the exchange of women represent a unique social connection between the biological and the cultural. Although frequently lauded by social scientists, the work of Levi-Strauss adds little to previous theories about incest.

Parsons incorporated Freud's theory of infantile sexuality into his structural-functionalist view of the American nuclear family. Like functionalists before him, he assumed that incest rules exist to prevent role confusion within the nuclear family and to encourage alliances with other families (see also Malinowski 1927, 1929). He contended that the mother was to exploit her son's Oedipal desires as if she had him on a rope. At earlier ages she was to pull him toward her, encouraging heterosexuality. At later ages she was to push him away, encouraging him to establish relationships with nonrelated females. Tugging and pulling on the rope were also designed to assist the son in internalizing society's incest rules and guide him in creating his own nuclear family. Parsons assumed that little girls also experience an erotic attachment to their mothers. He argued that as the mother severed this attachment, it was her responsibility to instill in the daughter an aversion to both father–daughter and brother–sister incest. Failure to do this would result in family disorganization and in the daughter's inability to become a normatively functioning adult. Parsons contended that incest aversion would be realized if the mother kept the erotic bond with her husband intact.

Parsons's analysis has thus assisted in perpetuating what child abuse researchers have sought to eradicate: placing blame on mothers when fathers incestuously abuse their daughters (see Finkelhor 1984; Russell 1986; Vander Mey and Neff 1986).

Psychologist Edward Westermarck ([1891] 1922) contended that family and clan members develop a sexual aversion to one another due to the dulling effects of daily interaction and the sharing of mundane tasks. This aversion prompts the development of laws and customs proscribing incest among persons with a shared ancestor and set of obligations based on clan membership. Westermarck noted that failure to develop this aversion and the propensity to violate incest laws were due to alcoholism, membership in the lower social classes, inability to control the sex drive, lack of alternative sexual outlets, social and geographic isolation, and failure to have developed normative, family-like feelings of duty. Variations on Westermarck's thesis appear in writings today. Some focus on a learned aversion that Oedipal children develop because their fantasies cannot be realized, due to their lack of full sexual maturation. Westermarck's thesis is weak because if there were a natural aversion to incest, then laws prohibiting it would be unnecessary. Furthermore, a growing body of literature suggests that persons who share mundane tasks and interact daily do not necessarily develop a sexual aversion to one another (see Vander Mey and Neff 1986).

Sociobiologists (e.g., Parker 1976; van den Berghe 1980) variously incorporate Freudian theses, Westermarck's thesis, and the assumption that human social behavior follows a fitness maxim to argue that groups establish prescriptive or proscriptive incest rules to enhance a group's survival by facilitating genetic advantages. Sociobiologists typically use the functionalist assumption that incest rules regulate the internal dynamics of the procreating group and encourage affiliation with other nuclear groups. Violations of incest rules are assumed to be caused by the factors identified by Westermarck. Many sociobiologists link intercourse directly to procreation. The assumption has no merit when one tries to explain why adult–child and child–child intercourse occurs. Equally problematic is the frequent reliance on the rules prescribing incest among royals. Dismissed is the role that

ethnocentrism plays in such rules. Finally, serious questions arise when research on primates, birds, or other nonhumans is extrapolated to human social behavior and organization. In sum, it is questionable whether the sociobiological arguments for, and data supporting the existence of, incest-avoidance mechanisms in humans can be confidentially accepted (Leavitt 1990).

A new twist on sociobiological discourse on the incest taboo comes from the field of genetic psychology. It is proposed that the taboo exists to protect children's "mating-strategy template." It is assumed that humans have a mating-strategy template that effectively gears females toward attracting men who can provide for them and their children. The human biogram also orients males toward being able to garner valuable resources for themselves, which they can then share with mates and children. It is assumed that should adult–child incest occur, male and female children who experience it will have disruptions in their mating-strategy template. In effect, if incest occurs, then the developing girl child will suffer various psychopathologies and will be unable to adequately compete for suitable mates. This will make her less attractive as a potential mate. Boys who experience father–son incest will lose the ability to be instigators of mating since it already has been imposed on them. Boys then become targets. It is assumed that by lowering children's attractiveness as mates, their reproductive success is also lowered. With this lowered reproductive success, future generations are negatively affected as well. Therefore, it is argued that incest taboos have been instituted as a way to avoid these long-term consequences for greater intergenerational success in mating outside one's own group (Immerman and Mackey 1997).

Prefiguring more recent research on incest as child abuse, Durkheim wrote that incest violations are most likely to occur in families in which members do not feel morally obligated to be dutiful to one another and to practice moral restraint ([1898] 1963). In many parts of the world today, incest is seen as a serious and severe type of child abuse. As child abuse, incest is any form of sexual touching, talking, or attempted or actual intercourse between an adult and a child or between two children when the perpetrator is significantly older than the victim or forces the victim to engage in actions against his or her will. The perpetrator and victim are related either by consanguinity or affinity. Incest is abuse because it harms the victim and violates the child's basic human rights. Its negative effects linger throughout victims' lives (Russell 1986). That the sexual victimization of children is nothing new, but rather ancient, is well documented (deMause 1982; Rush 1980). Public recognition of incest as child abuse, however, has its roots in research and public discourse dating from roughly the early 1970s.

Had Freud not abandoned his first psychoanalytical paper, "The Aetiology of Hysteria" ([1896] 1946), he could have been heralded as the savior of children. In this paper he described incest and other sexual abuse experienced by eighteen patients when they were children. He linked his adult patients' problems to their experiences of childhood sexual trauma. However, when his paper was coldly received and then ignored by senior psychologists, and Freud faced professional ostracism, he dismissed these findings (see Jurjevich 1974; Masson 1984). He reasoned that his patients were incorrectly recalling masturbatory childhood fantasies of sexual encounters with adults (Freud [1905] 1962). Freud then associated adult neurosis and hysteria with unfulfilled childhood incest fantasies.

Freud's revamped theories quickly became popular. Several writers then recounted case studies of children who had experienced sex with an adult. The children were described as seductive and provocative. They were not seen as victims; rather, they were seen as sexual initiators (see Vander Mey and Neff 1986). Although Swedish sociologist Svend Riemer (1940) and American sociologist S. Kirson Weinberg (1955) tried to bring attention to incest as a form of family deviance that sometimes resulted in harm to victims, Freudian theory held fast until the late 1960s. The "discovery" of child abuse, in conjunction with the civil rights movement, the anti–Vietnam War movement, and the resurgence of the women's rights movement, refocused attention such that the physical abuse of children and rape of women became seen as serious wrongs inflicted on other humans and as special types of social problems (Vander Mey and Neff 1986). Since that time, theories and research have explored in great detail why and how incestuous abuse occurs and its lasting negative effects. Laws protecting children against such abuse have been enacted. These laws mandate that treatment services be available for victims, perpetrators, and families (Fraser 1987). They also stipulate penalties (fines, imprisonment) for convicted abusers. These operate on a sliding scale, with harsher penalties applied to cases in which the victim is very young or has suffered serious physical or psychological trauma because of the abuse. Some cases are handled in family courts. Others, especially those involving serious harm to the child, are heard in criminal courts. Although variable in scope, laws in European nations prohibit and punish incestuous child abuse (Doek 1987). As with statutes in the United States, applicable penalties often depend on the victim–perpetrator relationship, the age of the victim, and the seriousness of harm to the victim. Efforts to refine legal statutes and penalties continue. Laws are also needed that more specifically define and punish child–child incestuous abuse. While the bulk of research on incestuous abuse has focused on adult–child incest, there is accumulating evidence to the effect that sibling incest is more common than previously thought and also can be traumatizing (Adler and Schutz 1995; Vander Mey 1988).

Feminists usually focus on father–daughter incest. They refer to it as rape to emphasize the specific type of abuse that it is. The term "rape" also illustrates the point that if an adult male forced another person to engage in intercourse with him, he could be arrested. However, if he rapes his own child, it is called incest, which is often seen as a disgusting, private, family problem (Brownmiller 1975). Feminists see incest as commonplace, originating in and perpetuated by patriarchy (Rush 1980). A general feminist approach to father–daughter incest incorporates a discussion of the sex-role socialization of males and the male-as-superior patriarchal ideology as causal factors in incest. The contention is that females ultimately are rendered second-class citizens, the property of men, and sexual outlets for men (see Rush 1980). Problems with a general feminist perspective on incest include a focus limited to father–daughter incest, the monocausal linkage of patriarchy to incest, the portrayal of all incest perpetrators as male and all incest victims as female, and the oversimplified view of male sex-role socialization (Vander Mey 1992; see also Nelson and Oliver 1998). American feminist sociologist Diana Russell (1986) extends and refines the general feminist approach to incest. She argues that males are socialized to sexualize the power given them by virtue of the fact that they are male. This includes sexualizing the power they have over their own children. Moreover, Russell recognizes that mothers and children can be incest perpetrators. She advocates androgynous socialization of children, more equality between men and women, and more public awareness of the harsh realities of incestuous abuse.

Welsh psychologist Neil Frude (1982) relied on existing empirical and clinical research to articulate a five-factor explanatory model of father–daughter incest. These five factors are sexual need (of the perpetrator), attractive partner, opportunity, disinhibition, and sexual behavior. A strength of Frude's model is the attention paid to the interweaving of sex and power. Weaknesses include the fact that incest perpetrators are not usually sexually deprived, victim attractiveness is often irrelevant, and families are not usually closed systems today. American sociologist David Finkelhor (1984) offers a somewhat similar model, although it differs from Frude's model in that Finkelhor pays keen attention to the myriad ways in which larger social forces and cultural ideology are related to child sexual abuse. Finkelhor's model has the added strength of being applicable to several types of incest and other sexual abuse.

American sociologists Brenda Vander Mey and Ronald Neff (1986) constructed a research-based ecological model of father–daughter incest. They begin with the assumption that there is no incest taboo. Rather, there are rules proscribing adult–child incest. They contend that characteristics of the society, the neighborhood, the family and the marital dyad, and the father–daughter dyad differentially affect the probability that a daughter will be sexually abused by her father. These levels of influence interact in complicated ways. Father–daughter incest is associated with dominance in society and in the family, residence in a violent neighborhood, social isolation of the family, family disorganization, and the father's lack of empathy for his wife and children. Mitigating factors decreasing the likelihood of incest include a father's conformity to rules against incest, sex education of the daughter, and media attention to adult–child incest as wrong and illegal. This model is strong in its reliance on research and theoretical principles. Although this model is limited to father–daughter incest, it does provide

information that can assist in identifying children at risk for incestuous abuse.

Incestuous abuse of children, male and female alike, is associated with an array of problems for victims. These problems include bulimia, self-mutilation, alcohol abuse, criminal behavior such as assault and shoplifting, psychological impairment, sexually aggressive behavior, and sexual hyperarousal (Araji 1997; Green 1993; Kinzl and Biebl 1992; Ryan et al. 1996; Wonderlich et al. 1996).

Incestuous abuse is seen as an international social problem today. At least four journals frequently carry the latest research on this topic: *Child Abuse and Neglect, Journal of Family Violence, The Journal of Interpersonal Violence,* and *The Journal of Child Sexual Abuse.*

However, not everyone sees adult–child sexual contact as abusive. It has been argued that American and European cultures have long tended to deny that children have a sexuality. That is, experts on child development have for many decades focused on every other aspect of human development but have ignored child sexuality. In addition, audiences have been less than receptive to the idea that children might enjoy sexual contact with other children—or with adults—and that this contact might be conducive to their development in a constructive way. It has been argued that taking the cultural constraints away from children's need to develop their sexuality is part of a child's right (Martinson 1973, 1994; Yates 1978). Due to the very sensitive nature of the topic, few empirical studies on child sexuality have been conducted. Of the few available studies, one was a longitudinal study of sexual experiences in early childhood. It revealed that most of the children focused on in the study had engaged in some form of sex play by age six (Okami et al. 1997). However, another extensive study of college students revealed that among those who had experienced sexual contact while children, sexual contact with an adult was more often seen as unwanted, unwelcome, and/or abusive (Nelson and Oliver 1998).

Organizations such as the North American Man Boy Love Association contend that the child abuse laws constrain children's liberty. Some parents, particularly in the United States and Europe, have resisted the child sexual abuse laws as infringing on their right to rear their children in ways they see as most appropriate (for elaboration, see Beckett

1996; Hechler 1988). Thus, just as marriage laws and cultural groups vary in their definitions of what constitutes incestuous marriage, we now are seeing public discourse on how best to define sexual contact with children.

REFERENCES

Adler, Naomi A., and Joseph Schutz 1995 "Sibling Incest Offenders." *Child Abuse and Neglect* 19:811–819.

Al-Abdulkareem, Abdulkareem A., and Seifeddin G. Ballal 1998 "Consanguineous Marriage in an Urban Area of Saudi Arabia: Rates and Adverse Health Effects on the Offspring." *Journal of Community Health* 23:75–83.

Araji, Sharon Kay 1997 *Sexually Aggressive Children: Coming to Understand Them.* Thousand Oaks, Calif.: Sage.

Bankston, Carl, III, and Jacques Henry 1999 "Endogamy Among Louisiana Cajuns: A Social Class Explanation." *Social Forces* 77:1317–1338.

Beckett, Katherine 1996 "Culture and the Politics of Signification: The Case of Child Sexual Abuse." *Social Problems* 43:57–76.

Briffault, Robert 1930 *Rational Evolution: The Making of Humanity.* New York: Macmillan.

Brownmiller, Susan 1975 *Against Our Will: Men, Women and Rape.* New York: Simon and Schuster.

deMause, Lloyd 1982 *Foundations of Psychohistory.* New York: Creative Roots.

Doek, Japp E. 1987 "Sexual Abuse of Children: An Examination of European Criminal Law." In P. B. Mrazek, and C. H. Kempe, eds., *Sexually Abused Children and Their Families.* New York: Pergamon.

Dorstein, Linda Eberst, Lawrence Hotchkiss, and Terry M. Kind 1999 "The Effect of Inbreeding on Early Childhood Mortality: Twelve Generations of an Amish Settlement." *Demography* 36:263–272.

Durkheim, Emile (1893) 1963 *The Division of Labor in Society*, trans. G. Simpson. New York: Free Press.

—— (1898) 1963 *Incest: The Nature and Origin of the Taboo*, trans. A. Ellis. New York: Lyle Stuart.

Finkelhor, David 1984 *Child Sexual Abuse: New Research and Theory.* New York: Free Press.

Firth, Raymond 1936 *We, the Tikopia: A Sociological Study of Kinship in Primitive Polynesia.* London: Allen Unwin.

—— 1994 "Contingency of the Incest Taboo." *MAN* 29:712–713.

Frankenberg, Susan R. 1990 "Kinship and Mate Choice in a Historic Eastern Blue Ridge Community, Madison County, Virginia." *Human Biology* 62:17–35.

Fraser, Brian G. 1987 "Sexual Child Abuse: The Legislation and the Law in the United States." In P. B. Mrazek and C. H. Kempe, eds., *Sexually Abused Children and Their Families.* New York: Pergamon.

Frazer, Sir James George 1927 *Man, God and Immortality.* New York: Macmillan.

Freud, Sigmund (1896) 1946 "The Aetiology of Hysteria." In E. Jones, ed., and J. Riviere, trans., *Collected Papers.* New York: International Psycho-Analytic Press.

—— (1905) 1962 "My Views on the Part Played by Sexuality in the Aetiology of the Neurosis." In P. Reiff, ed., *Sexuality and the Psychology of Love.* New York: Collier Books.

—— (1913) 1950 *Totem and Taboo*, trans. J. Strachey. New York: Norton.

Frude, Neil 1982 "The Sexual Nature of Sexual Abuse: A Review of the Literature." *Child Abuse and Neglect* 6:211–223.

Gibbons, Ann 1993 "The Risks of Inbreeding." *Science* 259(5099): 1252.

Green, Arthur H. 1993 "Child Sexual Abuse: Immediate and Long-Term Effects and Intervention." *Journal of the American Academy of Child and Adolescent Psychiatry* 32:890–992.

Hechler, David 1988 *The Battle and the Backlash: The Child Sexual Abuse War.* Lexington, Mass.: Lexington Books.

Immerman, Ronald S., and Wade C. Mackey 1997 "An Additional Facet of the Incest Taboo: A Protection of the Mating-Strategy Template." *Journal of Genetic Psychology* 158:151–164.

Jurjevich, Ratibor-Ray M. 1974 *The Hoax of Freudism: A Study of Brainwashing the American Professionals and Laymen.* Philadelphia: Dorance.

Kessinger, Roger A. 1990 *Marriage Licensing Laws: A State by State Guide.* Boise, Idaho: Kessinger Publishing Company.

Kinzl, Johannes, and Wilfried Biebl 1992 "Long-Term Effects of Incest: Life Events Triggering Mental Disorders in Female Patients with Sexual Abuse in Childhood." *Child Abuse and Neglect* 16:576–573.

Leavitt, Gregory C. 1990 "Sociobiological Explanations of Incest Avoidance: A Critical Review of Evidential Claims." *American Anthropologist* 92:971–993.

Lester, David 1972 "Incest." *The Journal of Sex Research* 8:268–285.

Levi-Strauss, Claude (1949) 1969 *The Elementary Structure of Kinship*, trans. J. H. Bell, J. R. von Sturmer, and R. Needham. Boston: Beacon Press.

Malinowksi, Bronislaw 1922 *Argonauts of the Western Pacific.* New York: E. P. Dutton.

—— 1927 *Sex and Repression in Savage Society*. London: Routledge and Kegan Paul.

—— 1929 *The Sexual Life of Savages in North-Western Melanesia*. London: Routledge and Kegan Paul.

Martinson, Floyd M. 1973 *Infant and Child Sexuality: A Sociological Perspective*. St. Peter, Minn.: The Book Mark.

—— 1994 *The Sexual Life of Children*. Westport, Conn.: Greenwood Press.

Masson, Jeffrey M. 1984 *The Assault on Truth: Freud's Suppression of the Seduction Theory*. New York: Farrar, Straus, and Giroux.

McLennan, John F. (1865) 1876 *Primitive Marriage: An Inquiry into the Origin of the Form of Capture in Marriage Ceremonies*. London: Bernard Quaritch.

Morgan, Lewis Henry (1877) 1964 *Ancient Society*, ed. Leslie A. White. Cambridge, Mass.: The Belknap Press of Harvard University Press.

Murdock, George Peter 1949 *Social Structure*. New York: Macmillan.

Nelson, Andrea, and Pamela Oliver 1998 "Gender and the Construction of Consent in Child–Adult Sexual Contact: Beyond Gender Neutrality and Male Monopoly." *Gender and Society* 12:554–577.

Okami, Paul, Richard Olmstead, and Paul R. Ambramson 1997 "Sexual Experiences in Early Childhood: 18-Year Longitudinal Data from the UCLA Family Lifestyles Project." *The Journal of Sex Research* 34:339–347.

Ottenheimer, Martin 1990 "Lewis Henry Morgan and the Prohibition of Cousin Marriage." *Journal of Family History* 15:325–334.

Parker, Seymour 1976 "The Precultural Basis of the Incest Taboo: Toward a Biosocial Perspective." *American Anthropologist* 78:285–305.

Parrinder, Patrick 1997 "Eugenics and Utopia: Sexual Selection from Galton to Morris." *Utopian Studies* 8:1–11.

Parsons, Talcott 1954 "The Incest Taboo in Relation to Social Structure and the Socialization of the Child." *British Journal of Sociology* 5:101–117.

Rafter, Nichole Hahn 1997 *Creating Born Criminals*. Champaign: University of Illinois Press.

Riemer, Svend 1940 "A Research Note on Incest." *American Journal of Sociology* 45:566–575.

Rush, Florence 1980 *The Best Kept Secret: Sexual Abuse of Children*. New York: McGraw-Hill.

Russell, Diana E. H. 1986 *The Secret Trauma: Incest in the Lives of Girls and Women*. New York: Basic Books.

Ryan, Gail, Thomas J. Miyoshi, Jeffrey L. Metzner, Richard D. Krugman, and George E. Fryor 1996 "Trends in a National Sample of Sexually Abusive Youths."

Journal of the American Academy of Child and Adolescent Psychiatry 35:17–25.

Seligman, Brenda Z. 1929 "Incest and Descent: Their Influence on Social Organization." *Royal Anthropological Institute of Great Britain* 59:231–272.

—— 1932 "The Incest Barrier: Its Role in Social Organization." *British Journal of Psychology* 22:250–276.

Spencer, Herbert (1876) 1898 *The Principles of Sociology*, vol. 1. New York: D. Appleton and Company.

Sumner, William Graham 1906 *Folkways: A Study of the Sociological Importance of Usages, Manners, Customs, Mores, and Morals*. Boston: Ginn.

Tylor, Edward B. 1889 "On the Method of Investigating the Development of Institutions; Applied to Laws of Marriage and Descent." *Journal of the Royal Anthropological Institute* 18:245–269.

van den Berghe, Pierre 1980 "Incest and Exogamy: A Sociobiological Reconsideration." *Ethology and Sociobiology* 1:51–162.

Vander Mey, Brenda J. 1988 "The Sexual Victimization of Male Children: A Review of Previous Research." *Child Abuse and Neglect* 12:61–72.

—— 1992 "Theories of Incest." In W. O'Donohue, and J. Geer, eds., *The Sexual Abuse of Children: Research, Theory, and Therapy*. Hillsdale, N.J.: Erlbaum.

——, and Ronald L. Neff 1986 *Incest as Child Abuse: Research and Applications*. New York: Praeger.

Weinberg, S. Kirson 1955 *Incest Behavior*. New York: Citadel Press.

Westermarck, Edward (1891) 1922 *The History of Human Marriage*. New York: Allerton.

Wonderlich, Stephen, Mary Ann Donaldson, David K. Carson, Dennis Staton, Linda Gertz, Laurie R. Leach, and Maureen Johnson 1996 "Eating Disturbances and Incest." *Journal of Interpersonal Violence* 11:195–207.

Yates, Alayne 1978 *Sex Without Shame: Encouraging the Child's Healthy Sexual Development*. New York: William Morrow.

BRENDA J. VANDER MEY

INCOME DISTRIBUTION IN THE UNITED STATES

As the twentieth century drew to a close, the gap between rich and poor in the United States, and between the wealthy and impoverished nations of the world, continued to widen. This entry extends the analysis presented in the 1992 edition of the

Encyclopedia (largely based on 1988 data) to include information on income, wealth, and poverty gathered from studies conducted in the mid- and late 1990s by various government departments, academic economists, and private research institutions.

INCOME DISTRIBUTION

Data on money income for households, families, and persons in the United States are collected yearly by the Bureau of the Census, based on a national probability sample of approximately 50,000 households. The official definition of "income" is money income before taxes, including some government transfers (Social Security benefits, welfare payments, worker's compensation), returns on investments, and pensions, but excluding capital gains or health insurance supplements paid by employers. In recent years, the Census Bureau has also published computations based on fourteen alternative definitions of income; for example, after deducting a range of taxes or after adding the earned income credit, the value of noncash government benefits such as food stamps, school lunches, and Medicare or Medicaid reimbursements to providers. Some of these alternative measures reduced the level of income inequality, while others increased it, but the general finding is that government transfers have a significantly stronger effect on reducing inequality than does the current tax system. For the sake of simplicity and consistency, this entry will primarily use data based on the official definition.

Household Income. In 1997, the median income for all 102 million U.S. households was $37,005, an increase of almost 2 percent over 1996, continuing an upward trend from a low of $34,700 in 1993. Adjusted for inflation, however, the 1997 median was slightly lower than the previous high of $37,303 in 1989. As Table 1 indicates, there are significant differences among subgroups in median income, and while all but male nonfamily householders and Asian/Pacific Islanders experienced an increase in real income over the previous year, data covering the entire period 1989–1997 present a mixed picture. Gains between 1989 and 1997 were highest for black households, for both married-couple family households and those headed by a female householder, and for persons aged

55–64. Losing ground over the eight years were male family householders without a wife, male nonfamily householders, Hispanic households, and households headed by young adults age 15–24 as well as by those 35–54 years old.

With respect to region and place of residence, households outside metropolitan areas and in the South and Midwest experienced income gains; metropolitan households and those in the Northeast and West suffered declines. In absolute numbers, however, the South continues to lag well behind the Northeast, while at the extremes of the distribution, median household income in Alaska is almost twice that in West Virginia.

Because a "household" can consist of one person, often a young adult at the onset of the work life or an elderly retiree, household medians are typically lower than those for families, officially defined as two or more persons related by blood, marriage, or adoption. The advantages of family households, especially those comprising a married couple, over nonfamily households is shown in Table 1. Clearly, some of the other differences seen in Table 1—by race, ethnicity, region, and residence—can be accounted for by variations in the proportion of married-couple family households.

Per Capita Income. Table 1 also reports on per person income, which has risen by close to 7 percent since 1989 in constant dollars, with black gains outstripping those for whites, although white per capita income remains roughly 40 percent higher that that of blacks. In addition, that part of per capita income which is accounted for by earnings continues to show a gender gap in wages, but one that has narrowed from a 31 percent advantage for male workers in 1989 to 25.8 percent in 1997. In part, this narrowing is due to a 3 percent increase in real earnings for women over the eight years, but also an even more significant decline of more than 4 percent for men during the same period. The loss in real earnings for men reflects the general decline in employment in high-paying unionized jobs in the blue-collar sector as well as corporate downsizing at the managerial level.

Although not shown in Table 1, per capita income also varies directly with years of schooling. Since 1980, the adjusted median wage for workers with only a high school education fell by 6 percent, while the median for college graduates rose by 12

Summary Measure of Income by Selected Characteristics: 1989, 1996, and 1997

CHARACTERISTICS	1997 Median income (dollars)	Median income (in 1997 dollars) 1996	Median income (in 1997 dollars) 1989	Percent change in real income 1996 to 1997	Percent change in real income 1989 to 1997
HOUSEHOLDS					
All households	37,005	36,306	37,303	*1.9	−0.8
Type of Household					
Family households	45,347	44,071	44,647	*2.9	*1.6
Married-couple families	51,681	51,002	49,925	*1.3	*3.5
Female householder, no husband present	23,040	22,059	22,315	*4.4	3.3
Male householder, no wife present	36,634	36,476	39,108	0.4	*−6.3
Nonfamily households	21,705	21,454	22,221	1.2	*−2.3
Female householder	17,613	16,774	17,865	*5.0	−1.4
Male householder	27,592	27,892	29,036	−1.1	*−5.0
Race and Hispanic origin of householder					
White	38,972	38,014	39,241	*2.5	−0.7
White, not Hispanic	40,577	39,677	40,166	*2.3	1.0
Black	25,050	24,021	23,583	*4.3	*6.2
Asian and Pacific Islander	45,249	44,269	46,611	2.2	−2.9
Hispanic origin[1]	26,628	25,477	28,192	*4.5	*−5.5
Age of Householder					
15 to 24 years	22,583	21,930	24,027	3.0	*−6.0
25 to 34 years	38,174	36,711	38,442	*4.0	−0.7
35 to 44 years	46,359	45,439	48,554	*2.0	*−4.5
45 to 54 years	51,875	51,630	53,738	0.5	*−3.5
55 to 64 years	41,356	40,729	39,946	1.5	*3.5
65 years and over	20,761	19,894	20,402	*4.4	1.8
EARNINGS OF FULL-TIME, YEAR-ROUND WORKERS					
Male	33,674	32,882	35,179	*2.4	*−4.3
Female	24,973	24,254	24,237	*3.0	*3.0
PER CAPITA INCOME					
All races	19,241	18,552	17,999	*3.7	*6.9
White	20,425	19,621	19,088	*4.1	*7.0
White, not Hispanic	21,905	20,991	(NA)	*4.4	(X)
Black	12,351	12,172	11,231	1.5	*10.0
Asian and Pacific Islander	18,226	18,332	(NA)	−0.6	(X)
Hispanic origin[1]	10,773	10,279	10,605	*4.8	1.6

Table 1

SOURCE: U.S. Bureau of the Census (1998d): vii.

percent. This differential signifies the growing wage gap between unskilled and skilled workers in an economy increasingly geared to processing information rather than to manual labor. For example, according to the Bureau of Labor Statistics, in 1982 workers in the top decile earned roughly four times the wages of workers in the lowest decile; by 1996, this difference had spread to almost five times (Pierce 1998).

Income Dispersion by Households. In 1997, 11 percent of households had income below $9,000, while 9.4 percent reported income of $100,000 or more. Adjusted for inflation, these numbers indicate a decline of 9 percent in households at the lowest level and an increase of 21 percent in the proportion at the top over the decade since 1987. Also showing a slight increase were households with incomes in both the $75,000–$99,999 and $10,000–$14,999 brackets. In contrast, the proportion of households with incomes between $15,000 and $50,000 declined from 45.2 percent of the total to 44.5 percent. It would appear, then, that the "middle" continues to "disappear," but that the overall distribution of household income moved upward, with the greatest gains among those in the highest income categories (U.S. Bureau of the Census 1998d, Table B-2).

Income Dispersion by Families. A similar pattern characterizes the distribution of income by families rather than households: a modest decline in the proportion with incomes below $10,000, from 7.3 percent in 1987 to 6.8 percent in 1997, a 20 percent increase, from 9.3 to 11.8 percent, at the $100,000+ level, and declines in the proportion in the $25,000–74,999 range (U.S. Bureau of the Census 1998d, Table B-4). For both families and households at the lower end of the distribution, much of the gain in income over the decade can be attributed to the longer hours worked by both wives and husbands, as well as the tight labor market that allowed workers to bargain for higher wages (Mishel et al. 1998). Nonetheless, the major gains in family income accrued to the top 10 percent, who realized 85 percent of the increase in the value of stocks.

Income Inequality. Although the Census Bureau's press releases in the late 1990s focused almost entirely on the overall gain in median household income since 1994, especially for black and female-headed households, the data also showed a marked increase in inequality on the two measures tabulated by the Bureau.

1. *Shares of aggregate income received by households.* When income groups are divided into quintiles, the share of aggregate income received by the lowest one-fifth of households fell from a high of 4.4 percent in 1977 to a low of 3.6 percent in 1997, while the share going to the highest fifth rose from 43.6 to 49.4 percent. Declines over the past two decades also characterized the three middle quintiles. In other words, the top 20 percent of households accounted for an ever-higher share of the nation's aggregate income, with that of the top 5 percent increasing from 16.1 to 21.7 percent.

2. *Index of income concentration.* Another way of measuring inequality is through an index of income concentration called the Gini coefficient or ratio. A Gini score of 0 would indicate complete equality, where there are no differences among units; a score of 1 indicates complete inequality, whereby one unit has all of whatever is being measured and the other units have none. Figure 1 tracks the percentage change in Gini ratios for household income since 1967. As you can see, the period from 1967 to 1980 was one in which income differences among households rose slowly, held in check largely by increases in government transfers to the poor and a relatively progressive tax structure. Inequality rose more sharply between 1978 and 1989, stabilized briefly during the recession of 1990–1992, and then shot upward in the mid- and late 1990s. Some of this increase can be accounted for by a change in Census methodology, but most is very real, and there was no indication that the trend had abated in 1998.

As striking as are the data on household income inequality shown in Figure 1, the story for *family* income is even more dramatic. After declining during the 1960s, the percent change in Gini coefficients for family income has risen sharply higher than for households, reaching the 20–25

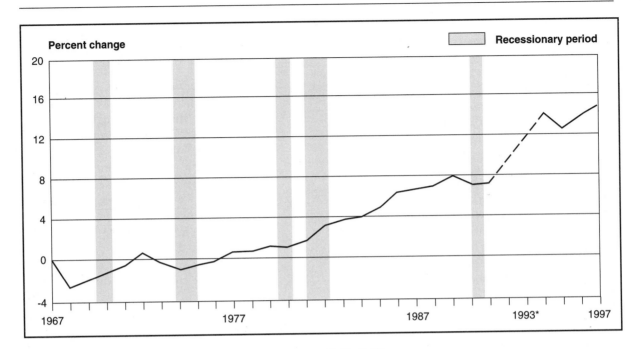

Figure 1. Percent change in Household Gini Coefficients: 1967–1997

SOURCE: U.S. Bureau of the Census (1998d): xiii.

NOTE: *Computer-assisted personal interviewing (CAPI) was introduced in January 1994. As part of the conversion, increases were made in the limits for some income sources. This change in methodology increased measured income in 1993 for the highest income households by considerably more that their actual incomes rose. See Current Population Reports, Series P60–191, "A Brief Look at Postwar U.S. Income Inequality."

percent range by the mid-1990s (U.S. Bureau of the Census 1996, 1998a).

Other Benefits. In addition to money income and government transfers, the well-being of households and families is also affected by employee benefits such as health insurance coverage, vacation pay, sick leave, and pensions. Although it was once thought that fringe benefits would tend to reduce inequality within the labor force, since such compensation represents a larger proportion of lower-wage workers' income than of high-income earners, quite the opposite appears to be the case.

While government-sponsored programs such as Social Security and workers' compensation insurance do indeed have an equalizing effect throughout the labor force, employer-sponsored benefits, in contrast, have "substantially increased compensation dispersion," especially at the lower end of the wage scale, according to data from the Bureau of Labor Statistics (Pierce 1998). This is so because less skilled workers are most likely to be employed

in jobs that do not provide benefits, particularly in the small businesses providing most of the new jobs and in workplaces where employers can find a number of ways to limit coverage and/or exclude dependents. Benefits can be denied to entry-level employees and to those classified as "contingent." This latter category—covering all types of part-time employment—also accounts for growing numbers of white-collar workers without employer-sponsored health insurance and pension plans.

As Table 2 indicates, even the proportion of workers at the top of the wage scale with health insurance coverage has declined since 1982, while that of low-wage employees has shrunk from half to one-fourth.

Taxes and Transfers. Thus, although government transfers, most notably Social Security and the earned income credit, have had a moderating effect on income dispersion, the impact of the tax system has been less so, as rates have become less progressive than in the 1960s. At the federal level, the Taxpayer Relief Act of 1997 might benefit

Percentage of Employees with Employer-Provided Health Insurance

	1982	1996
Bottom 10% of wage earners	49	26
Middle 50% of wage earners	90	84
Top 10% of wage earners	98	90

Table 2

SOURCE: Pierce (1998); see also U.S. Bureau of the Census (1998b).

lower-income taxpayers through a $500 per child tax credit, but the major new programs—education and retirement savings accounts—will lighten the tax burden only of those who can afford to put money aside for the future. The big winners are the top 1 percent of wealthholders, who will receive, on average, more than $7,300 in tax relief from a cut in the capital gains rate, compared with savings of about $7 for the lower 60 percent of taxpayers (Congressional Budget Office 1998).

In addition, the FICA payroll tax, which takes a bigger bite out of the incomes of a majority of American families than does the federal income tax, is regressive in that most workers will pay the tax on 100 percent of income, while higher-income earners will be taxed on only the first $72,600 of wages. Also regressive in their impact are the types of levies currently favored by state governments—sales and sin taxes. As a consequence, the current tax structure has done more to reinforce than to moderate the trend toward income inequality in the United States.

Explanatory Variables. A number of other secular trends have been advanced to explain the long-term increase in income inequality in family and household income.

1. *Labor-market factors.* One set of explanatory variables focuses on changes in the economy: (a) the shift in employment from manufacturing to service-related jobs, and the further division among service jobs between high- and low-skilled; (b) a concomitant decline in organized labor and the power of unions to negotiate favorable wage and benefit packages; (c) global competition and immigration patterns that depress wages of low-skill workers; and (d)

growth of the contingent labor force, such as temporary, part-time, and contract workers, who are typically ineligible for fringe benefits.

All these trends have contributed to an extremely skewed wage structure in which a few at the top crowd out the rest of the field, a "winner take all" situation that characterizes all occupations but is most notable in professional sports and in the compensation package of chief executive officers (Frank and Cook 1995). With the exception of a handful of millionaire athletes, almost all the benefits of economic growth and changes in tax system since the mid-1970s have been reaped by a small stratum of Americans already enriched by education, opportunity, and social capital.

2. *Lifestyle factors.* A second set of variables concerns long-term changes in patterns of marriage and living arrangements: (a) an increase in nonfamily and single-parent households due to later age at first marriage, high rates of divorce and separation, nonmarital births, and increased life expectancy, especially for widows in single-person households; and (b) the tendency toward endogamy among high-earning men and women, thus concentrating incomes and widening the split between the few at the top and the rest of the population.

Interestingly, the widening gap between top and bottom in income shares is not fully reflected in data on the distribution of wealth.

WEALTH

The methodological difficulties in measuring income are minor compared to those encountered in the study of *net worth*: the total value of all assets owned by a household, family, or person, less the debt owed by that unit. Such assets include investment portfolios, bank accounts, trusts, businesses, real estate, homes and their furnishings, insurance policies, annuities, pension equity, vehicles, works of art, jewelry, and other contents of safe deposit boxes. Because public records of such assets are minimal and/or difficult to trace, researchers are largely dependent on self-reports. In addition, because very few extremely wealthy units would appear in a national random sample, special frames must be constructed. As a result, data reported by the Bureau of the Census, the Federal Reserve Board, and the Internal Revenue Service are not always comparable because of differences in sampling, the type of assets being counted, and the way in which they are measured and weighted. In this section, we will briefly review the history of studying wealth in America, current data, and the generalizations that can be most confidently drawn.

The first systematic study of wealthholding was conducted in 1963 by the Federal Reserve Board (FRB), which found that the wealthiest one-half of 1 percent of households ("superrich") owned 25 percent of the aggregate net assets of the nation. The next one-half of 1 percent ("very rich") accounted for an additional 7 percent of net worth, and the next 9 percent (plain "rich"), accounted for one-third of the total, leaving 35 percent of the total net worth in the hands of the remaining 90 percent of households.

Although comparable data were not collected until 1983, evidence from the Internal Revenue Service (IRS) estate tax records suggests that the share of assets owned by the superrich declined between 1965 and 1976 to a low of 14.4 percent. This drop was due in part to an extended stock market slump and in part to changes in tax policy, as well as the growth of social welfare programs such as Aid to Families with Dependent Children, Medicare and Medicaid, and the liberalization of Social Security benefits, all of which shifted resources from the affluent to the more needy.

Interest in research on wealth picked up again in the mid-1980s, when both the Bureau of the Census and the FRB conducted studies designed to yield data comparable to the 1963 survey, although with different sampling frames and asset measures. The common finding, however, was that between 1976 and 1983 the downward trend of asset ownership by the superrich was dramatically reversed: from owning less than 15 percent of aggregate wealth to accounting for more than 30 percent just six years later. This doubling of asset ownership reflected an upward swing in the value of stocks, reinforced by Reagan administration policies on taxes and welfare favoring the more affluent. It must be noted, however, that these

numbers are subject to considerable error due to sampling, nonresponse, and missing data.

Recent Studies of Household Wealth. In a major effort to standardize research findings, the FRB adopted a consistent weighting formula for adjusting data on household wealth from the Board's Survey of Consumer Finances for 1989, 1992, and 1995 (Kennickell and Woodburn 1997). According to these calculations, shown in Table 3, the share of net worth held by the superrich remained constant between 1989 and 1992 at about 23 percent, then rose to 27.5 percent between 1992 and 1995. At the other end of the distribution, the share owned by the 90 percent less well-off households also remained stable—at about 32 percent—over the entire 1989–1995 period. The 1992–1995 increase in the share of net worth of the top one-half of one percent, then, has come largely from the share of the 90–99 percentile "plain rich," which declined from 37 to 33 percent. In other words, there is little evidence that the rich have become richer at the expense of nonaffluent households.

There are marked contrasts between the few at the top and the rest of American households in the types of assets held. Wealth for the bottom 90 percent consists primarily of a principal residence, vehicles, and cash-value life insurance, and has been considerably diluted by rising debt (mortgage and credit card) in the 1990s. In contrast, stocks and bonds, trusts, and equity in businesses account for the bulk of the accumulated wealth of the top decile. By 1997, when stock ownership replaced the value of real estate as the leading component of aggregate wealth, the top 1 percent held more than half of all such investment instruments, with the bottom 80 percent holding 3 percent of the total value (Wyatt 1998). Yet even at this relatively low level of stock ownership, primarily through pension plans, low-wealth households will be especially vulnerable to sudden downturns in the market value of their investments.

Another set of numbers comes from the Bureau of the Census, which has, since 1990, conducted a panel study of households—the Survey of Income and Program Participation (SIPP)—that permits following the economic status of units over time. These data differ from those collected by the FRB in three crucial respects: the sample

Percentage of Total Net Worth Held by Different Percentiles: 1989, 1992, and 1995

| YEAR | Percentile of Net Worth | | | |
	0–89.9	90–99	99–99.5	99.5–100
1989	32.5	37.1	7.3	23.0
1992	31.9	36.9	7.5	22.7
1995	31.5	33.2	7.6	27.5

Table 3

SOURCE: Kennickell and Woodburn (1997): 22.

frame does not yield many very high income households; a different set of assets are counted; and the distribution of wealth is measured differently. In the SIPP study, the distribution of "asset ownership" is computed on the basis of the median net worth of households at each quintile of monthly income. For both 1991 and 1993, the one-fifth of households with the lowest monthly income owned about 7 percent of the total net worth of all households, while those in the top fifth owned 44 percent (U.S. Bureau of the Census 1995). Unfortunately, comparable data for the next wave (1995–1996) have not yet been published, nor can the SIPP numbers be used for historical comparisons.

Personal Wealth. In addition to studies of household wealth by the Census and Federal Reserve Board, the Internal Revenue Service periodically publishes reports on individual wealth-holding, based on estate tax returns. These data are also subject to error—from sampling, from calculating mortality rates, and from underreporting, since not all assets can be tracked and since high-income earners have ways of dispersing and hiding assets prior to death. The most recent data come from surveys of estate tax returns of the very wealthy carried out by the IRS's Statistics of Income Division (SID) in 1992 and 1995 (Johnson 1997).

In 1992, it was estimated that 3.7 million adults, or 2 percent of Americans aged 21 or older, had gross assets of at least $600,000, which accounted for 28 percent of the aggregate personal wealth of the nation. In 1995, the number of wealthy persons had increased (to 4.1 million), as had their total net worth, but once adjusted for inflation, these differences were minimal. Indeed, looking at the very wealthiest—persons with a net

worth of at least $1 million—in terms of numbers, total assets, and net worth, there was a sharp decline between 1989 and 1992, due primarily to the recession of 1990–1992. Between 1992 and 1995, however, the number of millionaires increased slightly (to 1.32 million), as did their total assets and net worth, but both still remained below the levels of 1989.

The SID also computed the percent of total U.S. net worth held by the top 1 percent and one-half of 1 percent of individual wealthholders. As shown in Figure 2, the share of total wealth owned by the wealthiest individuals rose from 1989 to 1992 before declining to 1989 levels. Clearly, according to these data, there was no dramatic shift in net worth from the less affluent to the top, although the dollar amount of their assets did appreciate. Between 1989 and 1995, then, the pattern for individual wealthholders was similar to that for household net worth in showing minimal increases in the concentration of wealth.

At the time of publication, detailed reports from the IRS and FRB on trends between 1995 and the end of the decade were unavailable, but material from *Forbes* magazine's yearly compilation of the 400 wealthiest individuals suggests that the fortunes of the very affluent have increased significantly (*Forbes*, October 12, 1998). In 1998, the minimum needed to appear on the list of the 400 wealthiest individuals in the United States was $500 million, up 5 percent from 1997 and more than double that of a decade earlier. Most dramatic was the increase in the proportion with a net worth of more than $1 billion, up from 170 persons in 1997 to 186 in 1998, almost half the total, compared to only 23 in 1986. Ten of the billionaires had fortunes in excess of $10 billion, including the five children of the founder of Walmart Stores, and Bill Gates, the founder of Microsoft, whose net worth almost equals the gross domestic product of New Zealand. Thus, while the very rich may not be getting richer at the expense of the less affluent, they received the lion's share of wealth created in the economic boom years of the mid-1990s.

POVERTY

Interesting changes are also taking place at the lower end of the income distribution, among the persons, families, and households officially designated as living below the poverty threshold. In the

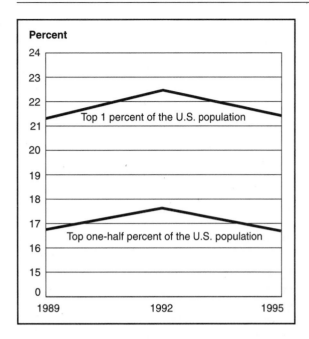

Figure 2. Percent of Total U.S Net Worth Held by the Top 1 Percent and Top ½ Percent of the U.S. Population

SOURCE: Johnson (1997: 79.

early 1930s, Franklin Delano Roosevelt could speak movingly of one-third of the nation being ill-housed, ill-clad, and ill-nourished in a society without an extensive social welfare system. Yet three decades later, in the early 1960s, despite the introduction of Social Security and other programs designed to minimize the effects of unemployment, more than 20 percent of Americans could still be defined as lacking a minimally adequate standard of living.

Defining Poverty. By 1964, as the nation geared up for Lyndon Johnson's War on Poverty, the Social Security Administration (SSA) was pressed to construct clear parameters for measuring impoverishment. The SSA turned to research conducted by the by the Department of Agriculture (DoA) in 1955, which found that families typically spent one-third of their income on food and which also computed the cost of a least expensive nutritionally adequate food plan. The SSA simply multiplied the cost of the DoA's food basket by three and, with some corrections for family size, age and sex of householder, and rural/urban residence, arrived at a dollar figure for yearly income—the poverty level—that neatly demarcated the poor from the nonpoor.

The value of the minimal food plan is adjusted each year to the cost-of-living index, but it no longer distinguishes rural from urban residence (the rural threshold had been higher, since it was thought that country folk could grow some of their own food) or female from male heads of household (on the grounds that women ate less than men). Only number of children and age of householder have been retained in the calculations. Nor has there been an adjustment for the fact that the cost of housing today typically exceeds that for food.

By the official yardstick, the poverty threshold for a single person in 1997 was $8,183, slightly higher for those under age 64 and slightly lower for someone aged 65 or older on the assumption that an older person eats precisely $276 worth less food per year than does a younger person. The poverty line was $12,802 for a family of three and $16,400 for a family of four. These are the dollar amounts considered adequate to house, feed, and clothe household members. Income in excess of the threshold officially lifts the unit out of poverty and therefore makes the unit ineligible for additional benefits, including both income supports (the former Aid to Families with Dependent Children and its successors, and Supplemental Security Income) and in-kind programs (food stamps, Medicaid, school lunch assistance, and housing subsidies). At the urging of conservative critics, the Bureau of the Census also publishes computations that include the cash value of these in-kind benefits in the definition of income, thus automatically reducing the poverty rate by about 25 percent. Nonetheless, at this writing, the official poverty level is still calculated on the basis of money income earned or received.

As Figure 3 indicates, the number of people below the poverty level was cut in half between 1959 and 1973—from 22.4 to 11.1 percent of the population—as a result of federal programs designed to assist the elderly, low-income families, and single-parent households. As the domestic War on Poverty fell hostage to the war in Vietnam, poverty rates began to rise, reaching a high of 15.2 percent during the recession of the early 1980s, and again in 1993, before declining to the current 13.3 percent, or 35.5 million persons.

In its 1998 report, the Census Bureau drew special attention to the fact that poverty declines in 1995–1997 have been much steeper for black

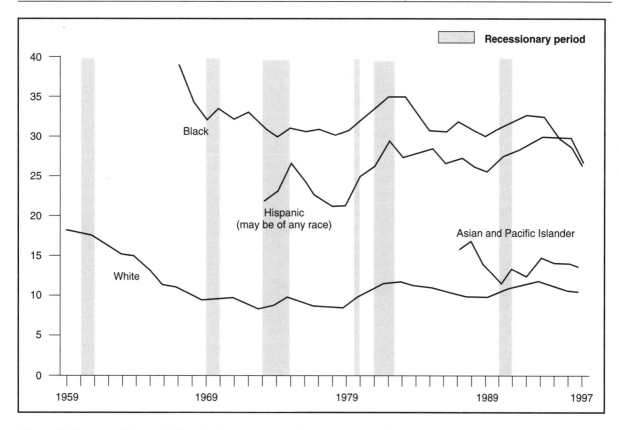

Figure 3. Percent of Persons Below the Poverty Level, by Race and Ethnicity

SOURCE: U.S. Bureau of the Census (1998):45.

and Hispanic persons than for Asian/Pacific Islanders and whites, but this effect is partly due to the fact that blacks and Hispanics were much further behind to begin with, so that any income increase will translate into a higher percentage compared to those initially less disadvantaged. Nonetheless, poverty among African Americans is at an all-time low, though the rate remains more than twice that for whites. The three factors most responsible for declining poverty rates today are: (1) The rise in the minimum wage that took effect in 1996, which accounts for the increased incomes of black and Hispanic single mothers, most of whom are hourly workers; (2) the earned income tax credit (EITC) now available to low-income workers, which has been particularly helpful to low-wage married-couple families; and (3) the economic boom that has generated a large number of jobs at the lower-skill level of the service sector, thus reducing unemployment and allowing low-wage workers to bargain for higher wages and benefits. In 1998, however, Congress voted down

further raises in the minimum wage and failed to expand the EITC, thus leaving low-skill workers increasingly dependent on market forces.

The Census also computes the "ratio of income to poverty level"; that is, the number of Americans in families whose income is under half the poverty level, the "severely poor," as well as those with incomes 25 percent above the threshold, the "near poor." In 1997, 14.6 million persons, or 41 percent of the poor, were "severely poor." Another 12.3 million were "near poor," including many full-time workers, since the earnings of a year-round, full-time minimum-wage-worker would still fall below the poverty threshold for a couple with one child.

Who are America's poor? Forty percent are children under age 18, whose poverty rate of about 20 percent is unchanged since 1989. Especially disadvantaged are the 59 percent of children under age six living with a female householder, no husband present. And while the poverty rate for all such households has hovered at slightly under one-third since 1987, there was a significant decline in poverty from 1996 to 1997 for black female householders. Even so, four in ten black female householders and almost half of Hispanic female householders were officially poor in 1997.

The most powerful variable affecting poverty status, however, is not race or ethnicity, but sex. It is women of all ages, especially those without husbands, from teenage mothers to elderly widows, who are most at risk of being poor. If economic well-being depends on working full time, remaining married, and being free of child-care responsibilities, then single mothers with limited education and job skills will be especially disadvantaged (U.S. Bureau of the Census 1998e). Yet it is precisely these women, many of whom were dependent for survival upon the income provided by Aid to Families with Dependent Children (AFDC), who came to be blamed for their own misfortune and to symbolize the failure of public welfare programs.

The Poverty Debate of the Mid-1990s. Although poverty programs absorbed less than 5 percent of the national and state budgets, they became a focal point for political debate in the mid-1990s. The public had come to believe, contrary to empirical studies, that AFDC families remained on the welfare rolls for generations, that poor women had additional children in order to increase their monthly benefit, and that it was characteristics of the poor themselves (laziness, substance abuse, sexual immorality) that accounted for poverty. In fact, fewer than 10 percent of the poor can be considered long-term welfare recipients, primarily women who entered the system as very young unwed mothers and who have been unable to develop the job skills or to find employment near their home that pays enough to lift the family above the poverty level. Nor is there any consistent relationship between benefit levels and the fertility of poor women.

As the SIPP data clearly show, poverty is a transitory state for the great majority who fall below the threshold. For example, although 21.4 percent of Americans were poor at some point in 1994, the proportion who were poor for all of 1993 and 1994 was only 5.3 percent. Almost half of all spells in poverty (47.3 percent) lasted 2–4 months, and 75 percent lasted less than one year (U.S.

Bureau of the Census 1988f). People fall into poverty when a marriage ends, when employment stops, or when children become ill; they are lifted out of poverty when they remarry, when they are employed, and when family members are restored to health.

As part of their attack on all government programs to which entire classes of citizens are entitled, conservative critics of the American social welfare system have long maintained that there is a "culture of poverty," whereby maladaptive attitudes toward work and family are transmitted across generations (e.g. Murray 1984). In this view, welfare dependency itself is the problem, and the solution is to remove income supports, so that employment becomes the more attractive alternative. In contrast, most sociologists would focus on the structural conditions that produce unemployment, family dissolution, educational failure, and homelessness, with people's behavior perceived more as a response to than as a cause of their situation.

The debate was won by those seeking radical change in the welfare system, and in 1996 the Personal Responsibility and Work Opportunity Act replaced AFDC and several other federal assistance programs with block grants to the states for Temporary Assistance for Needy Families (TANF). The states were given relative freedom to construct their own programs for moving former welfare recipients into the paid labor force.

It is too early to tell what effect the new systems will have on poor women and their children. Some states will be more effective than others in providing the job training and child care required for full-time labor-force participation; others will be more or less punitive. It will also be very difficult to disentangle the effects of the business cycle from those of public policy, or to determine whether people leaving welfare would have done so anyway given the transitory nature of most poverty spells. At the moment, welfare rolls have dropped dramatically, as a function of both economic growth and tighter eligibility requirements. And although the poverty rate also fell in 1997, the decline was minimal. Much will depend on whether the private sector can continue to generate jobs that former recipients can find and hold—and that will pay a family wage.

COMPARATIVE PERSPECTIVES

Any discussion of wealth, poverty, and income inequality within a society must take into account the vast differences between modern industrial and the less developed nations. Poor people in high-income societies are rarely as deprived of the basic necessities of survival as are most people in the Third World, where income inequality is typically much greater than in the industrialized countries. But Americans do not compare themselves to Sudanese; rather, they compare themselves to other Americans to whom they feel similar. It is a sense of relative rather than absolute deprivation that tends to fuel resentment. At this writing, despite the extent of income inequality in the United States, there are few appreciable signs of anger directed toward the top wealthholders. Rather, whatever ill will has been generated by blocked opportunity appears to be directed toward racial and ethnic minorities at the same or lower social-class level.

Yet, when compared with other Western democracies, the United States has the most unequal distribution of income and highest poverty rate. For example, while the percentage of American children in poverty was among the highest in the developed world, proportionately fewer were lifted out of poverty by government aid (Atkinson et al. 1995; United Nations 1998). This is so because the United States has the least extensive social welfare system of any modern state, and since 1996 even this limited "safety net" has been reduced. Alone among its industrialized peers, the United States is without a comprehensive family policy, lacks a national health insurance system, and provides minimal assistance to the most needy. As a consequence, there are few institutionalized mechanisms other than Social Security—which has also come under attack from those who would turn it into a private rather than public responsibility—for the redistribution of income that might narrow the gap between the very rich and very poor or that might substantially reduce both the likelihood and impact of poverty. In the absence of a revitalization of a sense of collective responsibility, income inequality will continue to characterize the United States. Indeed, all signs point to a continuation of economic, social, and political trends that elevate individual over collective interests and that reinforce the power of the market and weaken that of government.

REFERENCES

Atkinson, Anthony B., Lee Rainwater, and Timothy M. Smeeding 1995 *Income Distribution in OECD Countries: Evidence from the Luxembourg Income Study*. Washington, D.C.: OECD (Organization for Economic Cooperation and Development) Publications and Information Center.

Congressional Budget Office 1988 Data provided to Citizens for Tax Justice, Washington, D.C.

Frank, Robert H., and Philip J. Cook 1995 *The Winner Take All Society: How More and More Americans Compete for Ever Fewer and Bigger Prizes, Encouraging Economic Waste, Income Inequality, and an Impovershed Cultural Life*. New York: Free Press.

Johnson, Barry W. 1997 "Personal Wealth, 1992–1995." *Internal Revenue Service Statistics of Income Bulletin* 16(3):70–95.

Kennickell, Arthur B., and R. Louise Woodburn 1997 *Consistent Weight Design for the 1989, 1992, and 1995 SCFs, and the Distribution of Wealth*, Revision II. Washington, D.C.: Federal Reserve Board.

Mishel, Lawrence, Jared Berbstein, and John Schmitt 1998 *The State of Working America*. Washington, D.C.: Economic Policy Instutute.

Murray, Charles 1984 *Losing Ground*. New York: Basic.

Pierce, Brooks 1998 *Compensation Inequality*. Washington, D.C.: Bureau of Labor Statistics.

United Nations 1998 *Human Development Report 1998*. New York: United Nations.

U.S. Bureau of the Census 1995 *Asset Ownership of Households: 1993*. Current Population Reports, Series P70, No. 47. Washington, D.C.: U.S. Government Printing Office.

—— 1996 *A Brief Look at Postwar U.S. Income Inequality*. Current Population Reports, Series P60, No. 191. Washington, D.C.: U.S. Government Printing Office.

—— 1998a *Changes in Median Household Income: 1969 to 1996*. Current Population Reports, Special Studies, Series P23, No. 196. Washington, D.C.: U.S. Government Printing Office.

—— 1998b *Health Insurance Coverage: 1997*. Current Population Reports, Series P60, No. 202. Washington, D.C.: U.S. Government Printing Office.

—— 1998c *Measuring 50 Years of Economic Change Using the March Current Population Survey*. Current Population Reports, Series P60, No. 203. Washington, D.C.: U.S. Government Printing Office.

—— 1998d *Money Income in the United States: 1997*. Current Population Reports, Series P60, No. 200. Washington, D.C.: U.S. Government Printing Office.

—— 1998e *Moving Up and Down the Income Ladder.* Current Population Reports, Series P70, No. 65. Washington, D.C.: U.S. Government Printing Office.

—— 1998f *Trap Door? Revolving Door? Or Both?* Current Population Reports, Series P70, No. 63. Washington, D.C.: U.S. Government Printing Office.

Wyatt, Edward 1988 "Share of Wealth in Stock Holdings Hits 50-year High." *New York Times* January 11, p. 1ff.

BETH B. HESS

INDEX

See Measurement.

INDIAN SOCIOLOGY

The reviewers of Indian sociology generally trace its origin to the works of several British civil servants, missionaries, and Western scholars during the eighteenth and nineteenth centuries (Dhanagere 1985; Mukherjee 1979; Rao 1978; Singh 1986; Srinivas and Panini 1973). British administrators wanted to understand the customs, manners and institutions of the people of India to ensure the smooth running of their administration. Christian missionaries were interested in learning local languages, folklore, and culture to carry out their activities. The origin, development, and functioning of the various customs and traditions, the Hindu systems of caste and joint family, and the economy and polity of the village/tribal community were some of the prominent themes of study by the British administrators and missionaries as well as other British, European, and Indian intellectuals. The first all-India census was conducted in 1871. Several ethnographic surveys, monographs, census documents, and gazetteers produced during this period constitute a wealth of information that is of interest to sociologists even today. Mukherjee (1979) observes that the works of the civil servants, missionaries, and others during the colonial rule in India "provided the elements from which the British policy for ruling the subcontinent crystallized and also in turn helped to produce the pioneers in Indian sociology" (p. 24). Further, the available studies of Indian society and culture became an important source for testing various theories by scholars such as Marx and Engles, Maine, and Weber.

Although the first universities in India were established in 1857 in Bombay, Calcutta and Madras, formal teaching of sociology began only in the second decade of the twentieth century—at the University of Bombay in 1914, at Calcutta University in 1917 and at Lucknow University in 1921. By this time the observations and impressions of the census commissioners and civil service officials about the caste system, family structure and functions, age at marriage and widowhood, and so forth. had already begun to be published, along with statistical tables based on the population counts. Prior to India's independence in 1947, only three other universities (Mysore, Osmania, and Poona) were teaching sociology. There was no separate department of sociology; it was joined with the department of economics (Bombay and Lucknow), economics and political science (Calcutta), anthropology (Poona), or philosophy (Mysore). Almost all the pioneers in sociology in the first half of the twentieth century were trained in disciplines other than sociology. Only a limited number of courses in sociology, as fashioned by teachers according to their interest, were taught. Sociology courses included such topics as social biology, social problems (such as crime, prostitution, and beggary), social psychology, civilization, and prehistory. "In the case of teaching of Indian social institutions the orientation showed more Indological and philosophical emphasis on the one hand and a concern for the social pathological problems and ethnological description on the other. Strong scientific empirical traditions had not emerged before Independence" (Rao 1978, pp. 2–3).

Although many of the pioneers in sociology were educated at Calcutta, substantial impact on Indian sociology during the first half of the twentieth century was made at Bombay University and Lucknow University. Patrick Geddes, the first chairperson of the department of sociology and civics at Bombay University, was a city planner and human geographer. His reports on the city planning of Calcutta, Indore, and the temple cities of south India contain much useful information and demonstrate his keen awareness of the problems of urban disorganization and renewal (Srinivas and Panini 1973, p. 187). G. S. Ghurye succeeded

Geddes in 1924. During his thirty-five year teaching career at Bombay University, he guided about eighty research students. Several of his students (e.g., M. N. Srinivas, K. M. Kapadia, I. P. Desai, Y. B. Damle, A. R. Desai, and M. S. A. Rao) later on had a great impact on the development of sociology in India. Trained as a social anthropologist at Cambridge University, he addressed a wide range of themes in his research work and writings: from castes, races, and tribes in India to cities and civilization, from Shakespeare on conscience and justice to Rajput architecture, and from Indian Sadhus to sex habits of a sample of middle-class people of Bombay. He drew attention to several unexplored dimensions of Indian society, culture, and social institutions.

R. K. Mukherjee and D. P. Mukherji, both trained in economics at Calcutta University, taught sociology at Lucknow University. R. K. Mukherjee made a series of micro-level analyses of problems concerning rural economy, land, population, and the working class in India as well as the deteriorating agrarian relations and conditions of the peasantry, intercaste tensions, and urbanization. D.P.Mukherji's interest was diverse; they ranged from music and fine arts as peculiar creations of the Indian culture to the Indian tradition in relation to modernity. A professed Marxist, he attempted a dialectical interpretation of the encounter between the Indian tradition and modernity, which unleashed many forces of cultural contradiction during the colonial era (Dhanagare 1985).

B. N. Seal and B.K. Sarkar were two of the leading sociologists of that time at Calcutta University. Seal was a philosopher, interested in comparative sociology. He wrote on the origin of race, positive sciences, and the physicochemical theories of the ancient Hindus, as well as made a comparative analysis of Vishnavism and Christianity. He stressed the need for a statistical approach, inductive logic, and methodology to appraise the contextual reality comprehensively. Sarkar, a historian and economist by training, opposed the persistent general belief that Hinduism is "other worldly." He was also one of the few who discussed Marx, Weber, and Pareto at a time when they were not fashionable with sociologists either in India or abroad (Mukherjee 1979). S. V. Ketkar and B. N. Dutt, both of whom specialized in Indological studies in United States, and K.P.

Chattopadhyay, a social anthropologist trained in the United Kingdom, are some of the other noteworthy pioneers of Indian sociology.

Mukherjee (1979) points out that the goals set by the pioneers ranged from an idealized version of Oriental culture to the materialist view of social development. They were involved in bibliographical research to establish the historical database and strongly advocated empirical research. But in the days of the pioneers, the interaction between theoretical formulations and the database remained at a preliminary stage.

Some of the outstanding trends in the development of Indian sociology since India's independence have been the organization of professional bodies of sociologists, a lack of rigid distinction between sociology and social anthropology, debates regarding the need for indigenization of sociology and the relevance of Indian sociology, diversification and specialization into various subfields, and participation of sociologists in interdisciplinary research.

There has been a tremendous increase in the number of universities, colleges, and institutes teaching sociology. In most universities, the teaching of sociology started first at the graduate level and then at the undergraduate level. Universities and institutions offering degrees in interdisciplinary areas—such as management, rural development, planning, communication, and nursing—include some sociology courses in their training program. In the 1990s, some states have also introduced sociology courses at the higher secondary level. There was no professional body of sociologists during the colonial period. Ghurye was instrumental in establishing the Indian Sociological Society in 1951, and R. N. Saksena was instrumental in organizing the first All-India Sociological Conference in 1956. These organizations merged in 1967 as a single all-India professional body of sociologists. The Indian Sociological Society has more than a thousand life members. Several regional associations of sociologists was also formed during the 1980s and 1990s.

The development of sociology in India, from the viewpoint of theory, methodology, and research interests, has been significantly influenced by sociology in Western countries. Several Western scholars, a majority of them initially from the

United Kingdom and Europe, and later on also from the United States, have carried out studies in India. Similarly, many of the leading sociologists in India have been trained in the United Kingdom and the United States. However, with a rise in the cost of higher education and a fall in the availability of financial assistance in the Western universities, there has been of late a decline in the number of Indian students going to the United Kingdom and the United States for advanced study in sociology. There has, however, been a steady increase in the participation of Indian sociologists in various international seminars, workshops, and conferences. The holding of the eleventh World Congress of Sociology in New Delhi in 1986 is indicative of the recognition of the development of Indian sociology and its contribution.

Two journals of sociology—*The Indian Journal of Sociology*, started in 1921 by Alban G. Widgery (a British professor at Baroda College), and *The Indian Sociological Review*, started in 1934 with R. K. Mukherjee as its editor—were short-lived. There are now only a few all-India journals of sociology: *Sociological Bulletin* (a biannual journal of the Indian Sociological Society since 1952), *Contributions to Indian Sociology* (edited by two French scholars, Louis Dumont and D. F. Pocock, from its inception in 1957 to 1963, when its editorship was passed on to Indian sociologists), and *Social Change* (published by the Council for Social Development since 1971). Occasionally, articles with sociological content and relevance are published in other journals, such as *Economic and Political Weekly* and the journals published by some universities and regional associations. Several sociological articles are published in the journals of some institutions and university departments with a focus on interdisciplinary training and research. For example, since the beginning of the 1980s, the National Institute of Rural Development in Hyderabad has published a quarterly (*Journal of Rural Development*), and the National Institute of Urban Affairs in New Delhi has published a biannual journal (*Urban India*). Also, the Center for Women's Development Studies in New Delhi publishes a biannual journal called *Indian Journal of Gender Studies*.

Initially, no rigid distinction was made between social anthropology and sociology, but they separated as teaching disciplines in the 1950s. In the field of research, however, the distinction between social anthropology and sociology continues to be blurred. Ghurye, Srinivas, S. C. Dube, and Andre Beteille, among others, have argued that sociologists in the Indian context cannot afford to make any artificial distinction between the study of tribal and folk society on the one hand and advanced sections of the population on the other; nor can they confine themselves to any single set of techniques. Yogesh Atal (1985) points out that this is true of several countries in Asia and the Pacific; social anthropologists have extended the scope of their investigation to micro communities in rural as well as urban settings in their own country, and sociologists have found the anthropological method of fieldwork and participant observation useful in their research. Even the Indian Council of Social Science Research (ICSSR) treats both these disciplines together in its two surveys of research, the first covering the period upto 1969 (ICSSR 1972–1974) and the other from 1969 to 1979 (ICSSR 1985–1986); the same approach continues for the third survey, now under way, for the period 1979 to 1987.

There have been continuous debates regarding the need for indigenization of sociology, or "sociology for India" and the relevance of Indian sociology (Sharma 1985; Unnithan et al. 1967). One side of the debate started with the suggestion of Dumont and Pocock (1957) that "in principle, . . . a sociology of India lies at the point of confluence of Sociology and Indology" (p. 7). The proponents of an Indological approach in sociology emphasize that the contextual specificity of Indian social realities could be grasped better from the scriptural writings. Gupta (1974) points out the need for separating normative and actual behavior. Oommen (1983) pleads that "if sociology is to be relevant for India as a discipline it should endorse and its practitioners should internalize the value-package contained in the Indian Constitution" (p. 130), that is, socialism, secularism, and democracy rather than hierarchy, holism, pluralism, and so forth as pointed out by the Indologists. Another side of the debate is identified with a paradigm of Indian sociology free from academic colonialism—that is, borrowed packages of concepts and methods from other cultures, particularly the West, that supposedly do not have relevance for the Indian social, historical, and cultural situation (Singh 1986). However, although most sociologists are not hostile to using Western concepts, models, and analytical categories, they want their adaptations to suit the Indian sociocultural setting. Singh (1986) analyzes the contents and salient orientations of the presidential addresses delivered by M. N. Srinivas, R. N. Saksena, Ramkrishna Mukherjee, S. C. Dube, A. R. Desai, and M. S. Gore at the conferences of the Indian Sociological Society. He observes that there is a deep concern with the issue of relevance in the contexts of social policies, normative analysis of these policies, and the role of sociologists in understanding, critical appraisal, and/or promotion of these normative objectives of development and change in India.

In the 1950s and 1960s, several micro-level studies of caste, joint families, and village communities, mostly from the viewpoint of structural-functional aspects and change, were carried out. Srinivas introduced the concepts of dominant caste, Sanskritization, Westernization, and secularization to understand the realities of intercaste relations and their dynamics (Dhanagare 1985). Change in the structural and functional aspects of family in different parts of India was the focal point of most studies in the area of marriage, family, and kinship. The village studies focused on stratification and mobility, factionalism and leadership, the jajmani (patron–client) relationship, contrasting characteristics of rural and urban communities, and linkages with the outside world.

Indian sociology in the last quarter of the twentieth century shows both continuity and change in research. Caste and stratification, village communities, and social change have continued to be themes of research, but the approach has shifted from the functional to the conflict viewpoint. Descriptive studies of a single village community or other unit in a single social setting have been replaced by analytical comparative studies of social structure across time and space. Interest in the area of marriage, family, and kinship has declined. Women's studies have increased greatly. Several studies have been conducted in the fields of education, urban sociology, social movements, voting behavior, communication, and industrial relations. Sociologies of medicine, law, science, and other professions have also begun to develop. Now the thrust is on studying various processes. For example, with a concern for equality and distributive justice, there is an increasing emphasis on examining the process of education as a vehicle of social change as it affects the existing system of stratification, women, and less favored segments of the population.

A steady trend of out-migration of entrepreneurial and educated Indians, particularly to Western countries, has led to a modest beginning of sociological studies of the Indian diaspora (Motwani et al. 1993). Such studies attempt to understand the sociocultural dynamics of the Indian diaspora. Some of these studies are influenced primarily by the phenomenological and the symbolic interactionist perspectives (Jayaram, 1998). Interest in the study of changing patterns of marriage and family relations due to international migration, both among the out-migrants and among the aged and others who continue to reside in India, is slowly increasing. A genealogical study of an Asian Indian, covering nineteen generations, is a notable illustration of efforts to trace roots and study intergenerational socioeconomic changes (Desai 1997).

India started its first Five-Year Plan in 1952. Since then social scientists, particularly economists, sociologists, and demographers, have been involved in conducting diagnostic, monitoring, and evaluative studies concerning a variety of developmental programs at micro as well as macro levels. For example, the interest and financial support of the Indian government and international agencies have been instrumental, since the early 1950s, in encouraging and sponsoring research in the field of population and family planning (Visaria and Visaria 1995, 1996). Policies and programs concerning urban and rural community development, Panchayati Raj, education, abolition of untouchability, uplift of weaker sections (scheduled castes, scheduled tribes, and other backward castes), and rehabilitation of people affected by large-scale projects (constructions of large dams, industrial estates, capital cities, etc.) have been some of the other important areas of research by sociologists. At times, the various ministries of the central and the state governments, the ICSSR, and other funding agencies have sponsored all-India studies that have tended, albeit in a small way, to strengthen interdisciplinary approaches in social research. For example, in 1975–1976 the Indian Space Research Organization conducted a one-year satellite instructional television experiment in 2,330 villages spread over twenty districts of six states (Agrawal et al. 1977); the ICSSR sponsored a nationwide study of the educational problems of students from scheduled castes and tribes (Shah 1982).

During the 1970s and 1980s, several social research institutes were established in different parts of India. Also, many universities established interdisciplinary women's studies. Most prominent sociology departments and/or social research institutes are located in Delhi, Bombay, Ahmedabad, Jaipur, Chandigarh, Poona, Banglore, Hyderabad, and Trivandrum.

Several universities have gradually switched over to the use of the regional language as a medium of instruction at the undergraduate level, and some at the graduate level also; however, inadequate availability of textbooks in regional languages has been a major handicap in the teaching–learning process. Statistics has as yet not become an integral component of sociology curricula in a large number of colleges and universities. Although the survey approach is widely used in sociological research, most research publications hardly go beyond the use of descriptive statistics. There has been a strong plea for developing concepts and measurements that fit the Indian situation, but concerted efforts in this matter are still lacking. At the end of the twentieth-century, there is a frequently mentioned concern about an emergent paradoxical trend in sociological teaching and research in India. On the one hand, sociology has been accepted as one of the core subjects in almost all colleges and universities and several interdisciplinary institutions; on the other hand, a severe problem obstructing the growth and development of sociology in India due to a dearth of qualified teachers and falling standards, which may be due to a lack of teaching material in the regional languages and the inability of a large number of students to read textbooks and reference material in English. With a democratic polity, a developing economy, and a socioculturally diversified population, questions of applying even fairly good social science research findings get shrouded in the complex processes of the state policy and administration.

REFERENCES

Agrawal, Binod C., J.K.Doshi, Victor Jesudason, and K.K.Verma 1977 *Satellite Instructional Television Experiment: Social Evaluation–Impact on Adults, Parts I–II*. Bangalore: Indian Space Research Organization.

Atal, Yogesh 1985 "Growth Points in Asian and Pacific Sociology and Social Anthropology." In *Sociology and Social Anthropology in Asia and the Pacific*. Paris: UNESCO. New Delhi: Wiley Eastern.

Desai, D. K. 1997 *A Genealogical Study of an Asian Indian* Delhi: Himalaya Publishing House.

Dhanagare, D. N. 1985 "India." In *Sociology and Social Anthropology in Asia and the Pacific*. Paris: UNESCO. New Delhi: Wiley Eastern.

Dumont, Louis, and D. F. Pocock 1957 "For a Sociology of India." *Contributions to Indian Sociology* 1:7–22.

Gupta, Krishna Prakash 1974 "Sociology of Indian Tradition and Tradition of Indian Sociology." *Sociological Bulletin* 23:14–43.

Indian Council of Social Science Research (ICSSR) 1972–1974 *A Survey of Research in Sociology and Social Anthropology*, 3 vols. Bombay: Popular Prakashan.

—— 1985–1986 *Survey of Research in Sociology and Social Anthropology 1969–1979*. 3 vols. New Delhi: Satvahan Publications.

Jayaram, N. 1998 "Social Construction of the Other Indian: Encounters Between Indian Nationals and Diasporic Indians." *Journal of Social and Economic Development* 1:46–63.

Motwani, Jagat K., Mahin Gosine, and Jyoti Barot-Motwani, eds. 1993 *Global Indian Diaspora: Yesterday, Today and Tomorrow*. New York: Global Organization of Poeple of Indian Origin.

Mukherjee, Ramkrishna 1979 *Sociology of Indian Sociology*. New Delhi: Allied Publishers.

Oommen, T. K. 1983 "Sociology in India: A Plea for Contextualisation." *Sociological Bulletin* 32:111–36.

Rao, M. S. A. 1978 "Introduction." In *Report on the Status of Teaching of Sociology and Social Anthropology, Part I: Recommendations*. New Delhi: University Grants Commission.

Shah, Vimal P. 1982 *The Educational Problems of Scheduled Caste and Scheduled Tribe School and College Students in India*. New Delhi: Allied Publishers.

Sharma, Surendra 1985 *Sociology in India: A Perspective from Sociology of Knowledge*. Jaipur: Rawat Publications.

Singh, Yogendra 1986 *Indian Sociology: Social Conditioning and Emerging Concerns*. New Delhi: Vistar Publications.

Srinivas, M. N., and M. N. Panini 1973 "The Development of Sociology and Social Anthropology in India." *Sociological Bulletin* 22:179–215.

Unnithan, T. K. N., Yogendra Singh, Narendra Singhi, and Indra Deva, eds. 1967 *Sociology for India*. New Delhi: Prentice Hall.

Visaria, Leela, and Pravin Visaria 1995 *India's Population in Transition.* (Population Bulletin 50: 3). Washington, D.C.: Population Reference Bureau.

—— 1996 *Prospective Population Growth and Policy Options for India, 1991–2101.* New York: Population Council.

VIMAL P. SHAH

INDIGENOUS PEOPLES

For well over a century claims have been advanced that Native Americans, and indigenous peoples in general, are about to vanish (Bodley 1990, 1994; Dippie 1982). Apparently, however, indigenous peoples have neither read nor followed these scripts. In fact, quite the opposite has occurred. In the United States and around the world there has been a resurgence of indigenous consciousness, political mobilization, and cultural renewal (Cornell 1988; Nagel 1996; Snipp 1988a, 1989, 1992; Thornton 1987; Wilmer 1993). Groups in Canada, the United States, Australia, Brazil, Southeast Asia, and elsewhere are making land claims, petitioning for political rights, and demanding control of resources with remarkable success given their nearly universal paucity of votes, money, or military means. Interestingly, these indigenous movements are occurring while the number of people who live "traditional" or "tribal" lifestyles has diminished under the onslaught of expanding national and global industrialism and capitalism. A full description and explanation of these contradictory trends would require several volumes. Here we offer a summary of current understanding of the state of indigenous peoples in North America and around the world, and we suggest why such issues are of vital concern to sociology.

TERMINOLOGY

Ethnic terminology is notoriously politically controversial and loaded. Terms such as "tribe," "clan," "ethnic entity," and "nation" have been used over the last few centuries as weapons of both the strong and the weak in wars of words, laws, and often guns, to attack or defend the rights and survival of indigenous peoples. Even the term "indigenous peoples" is problematic—after all, everyone is indigenous to some place, and indigenousness sometimes can be a matter of

when the clock starts. We use the term "indigenous" to refer to those peoples who either live, or have lived within the past several centuries, in nonstate societies, although these indigenous societies may well have existed within the boundaries of state societies. We eschew the term "pre-state" because it implies, even sometimes unintentionally, that there is a necessary, progressive evolution from nonstate to state societies. We hasten to add that although some states have existed for several millennia (Sanderson 1999) in a variety of forms, the diversity of types among nonstate societies is far greater. This why there is a plethora of terms to refer to them: clans, bands, macrobands, tribelets, tribes, chiefdoms, segmentary lineages, and so forth. Virtually all these terms entail an attempt to organize this diversity (for discussion of the terms and concordance of the various meanings, see Chase-Dunn and Hall 1997, chs. 4, 7).

The most problematic in this litany of terms is "tribe." As much as anthropologists and others have argued that "tribe" has become so general as to be useless (Fried 1975), it often is used in efforts to communicate with the general public or beginning students. The problem is especially salient for those peoples who inhabited North America before Europeans arrived, since the tribe–nation distinction has often been used politically to support or to deny autonomy or sovereignty for indigenous groups. To further confuse matters some, indigenous communities officially and legally call themselves "tribes," though many have replaced "tribe" with "nation." Even the designation "Native American" is not without problems, since legally, anyone born in the United States is a "native"[-born] American. For all these reasons we use "nonstate society" as a generic term, and for those peoples indigenous to the Americas, we alternate among Native Americans, American Indians, native peoples, and indigenous peoples.

When referring to a specific indigenous community, we use the name of the group—but even that is often problematic. There are four broad problems in regard to group names that we discuss here because of the light these difficulties shed on the issues facing indigenous peoples generally. Our discussion deals specifically with North America, although the issues we raise often are faced by native peoples elsewhere. First, membership in indigenous groups may change over time as various forms of identity and political organization change in response to internal processes or encounters with outsiders. In early periods of contact with Europeans, North American native peoples often shared a broad sense of identity but were not ruled by any single social or political organization (Cornell 1988). Through years of contact, this situation frequently reversed itself. The need for unified resistance to European, then American, encroachments often necessitated the formation of sociopolitical structures that encompassed individuals and communities that had not necessarily shared historical cultures or identities (for examples, see Champagne 1989, 1992; Dunaway 1996; Faiman-Silva 1997; Fenelon 1998; Hall 1989; Himmel 1999; Meyer 1994).

Second, many historical indigenous cultures and communities have been destroyed, either by outright genocide, the devastations of disease, assimilation into European societies, or merger or amalgamation with other indigenous groups. As a survival strategy, many native groups found themselves greatly transformed, in particular through the consolidation of diverse individuals and communities. At times these amalgamated communities represented a form of "ethnogenesis," that is, the creation of new native groups.

Third, a great deal of ethnographic and ethnohistorical investigation shows that the symbolic, demographic, and social boundaries of nonstate groups are extremely permeable (as, indeed, are those of many states and empires). Thus, the expectation of fixed, clear, rigid boundaries or borders is an artifact of the creation of the modern European nation-state, and of the needs of European and American negotiators to identify "leaders" of native societies for purposes of treaty-making and land acquisition. Hence naming a group often gave a false sense of unity, solidity, and organization.

Finally, there are the historical accidents of naming and the vagaries of spelling that stemmed from a lack of clear understanding of indigenous languages. One of the most notorious is the naming of the Lakota peoples as "Sioux," which is a French corruption of an Anishinaabe [Chippewa or Ojibwa] word, "nadowasieux," which translates into something like "slimy snake people" (Tanner 1987, p. 4)—certainly, not a name many Lakotas would wish to be known by. Many Native American groups are shifting back to their own names

for themselves, rather than continuing to use those assigned them by outsiders. For instance, Diné is increasingly used to refer to Navajo institutions and people, and the former "Winnebagos" of Wisconsin are now officially the "Ho Chunks."

SOCIOLOGICAL SIGNIFICANCE OF INDIGENOUS PEOPLES

There are several reasons that the study and understanding of indigenous peoples and the challenges they face are of special interests to sociology and to sociologists. First, in the United States (and every country in the Americas and in many others elsewhere) indigenous peoples are part of an ethnically diverse social, political, cultural, and economic landscape. Despite their often relatively small numbers, placing indigenous peoples into the ethnic mosaic of contemporary nations and states puts later settler and immigrant groups into a more accurate and larger historical context. This is a point that goes beyond "political correctness" or broad "multiculturalism." The history and current conditions of native peoples often highlight questions of group rights, nation formation, justice, and social change that are relevant to all ethnic communities, not just indigenous groups. To ignore any group in academic discussion of majority–minority relations is itself a form of racism that denies the existence or legitimacy of that group.

Second, of considerable importance in developing general theoretical accounts of intergroup relations is the fact that indigenous peoples present a wide variety of social structures that are not found among state groups, such as Americans, or immigrant groups within states, such as Cuban Americans. Thus, all theories of intergroup relations that study only state peoples will lack dimensions unique to indigenous peoples, such as particular spiritual traditions or patterns of social relations. For instance, most sociologists are familiar with the U.S. racial classification norm called the "one-drop rule": If an individual has any African ancestry, then that person is considered African American no matter what the person's appearance or skintone. But for Native Americans—another colonized, conquered, and oppressed group—the same rule does not apply. Often standards require much more than "one drop" for an individual to be officially considered an "Indian."

A common standard requires one-quarter Indian ancestry (or "blood quantum"), that is, that an individual must have one grandparent or two great-grandparents who are American Indian to qualify as a "real" Indian. Sometimes such ancestry rules are official U.S. government regulations, and more than occasionally they are tribal government rules (see Meyer 1994 for a detailed discussion). No such "one drop" or "blood quantum" rules apply to other U.S. immigrant or ethnic groups.

Third, since the formation of the United States, Native Americans have had a very special political and social relationship with the U.S. government. They are the only ethnic community that has legal right to direct federal action and accountability that bypass city, county, and state governmental authority. This "government-to-government" tribal–federal relationship generates many politically and sociologically interesting interactions and exceptions. One example can be found in the controversies about gaming on Indian reservations that emerged in the last quarter of the twentieth century; another involves treaty-based Indian hunting and fishing rights.

Fourth, theories of long-term social change and social evolution that do not include analysis of indigenous peoples will be inherently defective due to a biased sample of societies examined. There is another danger—that of assuming that surviving indigenous people, even those who live "traditionally," are models or "living artifacts" of earlier societies. Contemporary indigenous peoples have survived centuries—and in parts of Asia, millennia—of contact and interaction with state societies. Their contemporary social structures have been shaped by their responses to those interactions. Indeed, Ferguson and Whitehead (1992) argue persuasively that these state/nonstate contacts so profoundly change both types of societies that scholars must view even the earliest first-hand accounts of indigenous societies with considerable skepticism. This is because typically by the time a representative of state society who produces written records observes an indigenous group, there has already been considerable interaction, and what that observer sees already has been shaped by that interaction. This is not denying that there are occasional observations that reflect very little interaction and change, but they are very rare. This raises questions, for example, about the accuracy

of depictions of western U.S. tribes by such early travelers (1804) as Meriwether Lewis and William Clark.

In summary, to ignore indigenous peoples leads to bad sociology in the form of theories and explanations that are based on biased samples, that cover only a truncated range of processes and relations found in societies, and that lead to a distorted picture of ethnic, cultural, social, political, and economic diversity in any society with indigenous communities. This is why it is important to overcome the nineteenth century legacy of the division of labor between anthropology and sociology in their objects of study. This is no easy task given the great diversity of indigenous groups in the world, or even in the continental United States.

DEMOGRAPHIC ISSUES

One of the more formidable problems in studying indigenous peoples is describing their demography. Here, too, there are several interesting challenges, even if discussion is restricted to the United States. First, there is the politics of numbers. This derives from changes, and in some cases, improvements in historical demography in the twentieth century and the uses to which numbers are put. Stiffarm and Lane (1992) argue persuasively that there is an inherent tendency to minimize the historical population of Native Americans prior to European contact in order to support the argument that destruction of the indigenous American population was not extreme and mostly accidental. While estimates for the indigenous population of North American (United States and Canada) range from 1 million to 30 million, Thornton (1987) argues for a figure in the neighborhood of 7 million, based on careful reconstruction of population densities, early population counts, and the effects of known epidemics. From 1492 on, Native populations declined drastically, primarily, but not exclusively, because of exposure to "Old World" diseases. For the continental United States, the absolute population nadir of about a quarter million was reached around the turn of the twentieth century. Thereafter, population has grown steadily, so that at the end of the twentieth century the Native American population is approximately 2 million, or between one-third and one-half of what it likely was in 1492. An important point here is that various studies show that more than disease was involved in the initial depopulation. That outright genocide contributed to the nearly total destruction of the Native American population is now well-documented (see Thornton 1987; Stannard 1992).

The impressive population recovery of the post–Second World War period is worth some mention. From 1960 to 1970, the number of Americans who reported their race to be "American Indian" in the U.S. census grew by 51 percent (from 523,591 to 792,730); from 1970 to 1980, the American Indian population grew faster, by 72 percent (to 1,364,033); and from 1980 to 1990, the American Indian population increased by 37 percent (to 1,878,285). Several reasons are given for this growth, including improved enumeration techniques, a decreasing death rate, and an increasing willingness of individuals to identify themselves as Native American. An important feature of the contemporary Native American population is the extensive intermarriage of indigenous peoples with non-Indians. Intermarriage has given rise to three distinct types of U.S. Indian population (Snipp 1986). First, there are "American Indians," persons who claim to be Indian racially and ethnically (having a specific tribal identification). Second, there are "American Indians of multiple ancestry," persons who claim to be Indian racially but have significant non-Indian ancestry. Third, there are "Americans of Indian descent," who do *not* claim to be Indian racially but report an Indian component in their background. The second two categories contain a number of individuals whose ethnic and racial identities readily shift with political, economic, and social contexts. By 1990 many, if not most, Indians were marrying outside their tribal group, and many were marrying non-Indians. As the number of individuals of ambiguous, and often ambivalent, Indian identity has increased, questions about membership in Indian tribes and definitions of who is and is not really an Indian have been raised by tribal governments, federal officials, and Indian communities and individuals. "Indianness" has become an empirical measurement issue, a political issue, and a theoretical issue. With the financial successes of some native community enterprises (in gaming, natural resources, and tourism), questions of tribal membership have become an economic issue as well.

ECONOMIC DEVELOPMENT

In the twentieth century, political incorporation, assimilation, and economic interaction have tended to attenuate cultural processes and heighten political processes of tribal governments (Cornell 1988; Cornell and Kalt 1999). Access to wealth from mineral resources, gaming, and tourism has helped economic development. Snipp (1988b) shows, however, that many differences between Indian nations with energy resources and those without such resources tend to be minimal. A key problem in economic development—and one that is especially salient among indigenous communities—is how to participate in and benefit from economic development without simultaneously undermining or destroying traditional Indian values (Cornell and Kalt 1992; Ward and Snipp 1996, especially Ward's chapter). Not surprisingly, these issues are enmeshed in indigenous political action globally (Wilmer 1993).

AMERICAN INDIAN POLITICAL ACTIVISM

The urbanization, intermarriage, education, increased participation in the paid labor force, and bicultural character of the American Indian population during the post–Second World War period gave rise to the most politically active period in American Indian history. The 1960s, 1970s, 1980s, and 1990s saw Native Americans organize themselves into political activist organizations (the American Indian Movement, Women of All Red Nations), protest movements ("Red Power," Camp Yellow Thunder in the Black Hills), legal defense organizations (Native American Rights Fund, Native Action), and lobbying groups (National Congress of American Indians, National Tribal Chairmen's Association). These organizations and movements were established and grew in the fertile political soil of the civil rights era ethnic politics in the United States. The following decades were marked by a range of Native American protest events, from the "fish-ins" in the Pacific northwest in the mid-1960s, to the nineteen-month occupation of Alcatraz Island beginning in 1969, to the seventy-one-day siege at Wounded Knee on the Pine Ridge Reservation in South Dakota in 1973, to the occupation of Camp Yellow Thunder in the Black Hills in the 1980s, to the protests against Indian athletic mascots of the 1980s and 1990s (see Johnson 1996; Nagel 1996). Against this backdrop of marches, occupations, protests, and sometimes open conflict, many legal battles were waged in U.S. and tribal courtrooms across the country. Out of both the protest and the legal battles came a new "self-determination" era in federal Indian policy. Self-determination opened the way to increased tribal control of budgets and decision making, to the development of tribally owned natural resources, to the establishment of casinos and gaming on tribal land, and to opportunities for self-rule and economic development by Indian communities. These political and economic opportunities have raised social questions about the rules for tribal membership, which will remain a subject for debate well into the twenty-first century because of the projected continued growth of the Indian population.

OTHER CONTEMPORARY NATIVE ISSUES

Two of the major contemporary issues facing Native Americans are debates over gaming and renewed interest in indigenous religion. Because of their special relationship with the U.S. federal government, reservation governments are able to sponsor gaming over the opposition of state authorities; to sell gasoline and cigarettes without paying local and state taxes; and to sell other products, such as fireworks, that are typically regulated or made illegal by state or local governments. Of all these, the most controversial has been the establishment of gaming facilities. Indeed, these bingo parlors and casinos have spawned social movements that are nominally antigaming but are often very thinly disguised anti-Indian movements, and in some cases reflecting a conflict of interest, as when state authorities see Indian gaming as unfair competition to state-run lotteries and other gaming enterprises. Similar non-Indian opposition has resulted from renewed Indian land claims (such as by the Oneidas in upstate New York in 1998–1999). These controversies have heightened the stakes of identity politics both within native groups and between native groups and the general population.

Initially, one might expect that renewed interest in and presumably respect for native religions by non-Indians might have been received positively by Native Americans. However, this is generally *not* the case. Often non-Indian appropriation of Indian spiritual traditions is perceived by native

people as a final theft. After stealing Indian land, mineral rights, water rights, and fishing rights, the final non-Indian assault on native peoples is to usurp and subvert Indian culture. This has not been helped by the number of charlatans and hucksters (a few of whom are of native ancestry) involved in assorted "New Age" appropriations of Indian cultural elements, typically lifted entirely out of their indigenous context (see Churchill 1994, 1996; Rose 1992). The spread of New Age and "world" music, which uses elements and occasionally performers from various indigenous populations, has spawned analogous controversies at a global level (Feld 1991). Not the least of the subcontroversies is that it is non-Indian performers and producers who are making the large profits from the use of indigenous instruments, themes, music, and performances. Such controversies will not disappear quickly. They have, however, generated a new interest in relations with indigenous peoples and new attempts to reexamine the long and often tawdry history of Indian/non-Indian relations.

CONCLUSION

The sociology of indigenous peoples, including their relations to state peoples, is multifaceted, and fascinating. It is also a vital and necessary component to the study of the sociology of intergroup relations. Many complex and important sociological processes occur primarily, and sometimes only, in relations between state and nonstate peoples. In order to develop robust theories of intergroup relations, of social movements, and of globalization and resistance to its negative consequences, the study of indigenous peoples in indispensable. Theories built solely on the study of immigrant populations are necessarily flawed; those that include indigenous peoples are much richer.

A NOTE ON REFERENCES

The literature on indigenous peoples is immense, even in sociology. We have cited works which contain extensive bibliographies. We also suggest that those interested in this area use the World Wide Web to search for information on Native American studies, American Indian studies, and individual tribes—many of which have their own Web pages. The History Net list, H-AMINDIAN, is also an excellent resource. Some useful scholarly journals are: *American Indian Culture and Research Journal, American Indian Quarterly, Native America, Wicazo Sa Review,* and *Cultural Survival Quarterly.*

REFERENCES

Bodley, John H. 1990 *Victims of Progress,* 3rd ed. Mountain View, Calif.: Mayfield Publishing.

——— 1994 *Cultural Anthropology: Tribes, States, and the Global System.* Mountain View, Calif.: Mayfield Publishing.

Champagne, Duane 1989 *American Indian Societies: Strategies and Conditions of Political and Cultural Survival.* Cambridge, Mass.: Cultural Survival.

——— 1992 *Social Order and Political Change: Constitutional Governments Among the Cherokee, the Choctaw, the Chickasaw, and the Creek.* Stanford, Calif.: Stanford University Press.

Chase-Dunn, Christopher, and Thomas D. Hall 1997 *Rise and Demise: Comparing World-Systems.* Boulder: Westview Press.

Churchill, Ward 1994 *Indians Are Us: Culture and Genocide in Native North America.* Monroe, Maine: Common Courage Press.

——— 1996 "Spiritual Hucksterism: The Rise of the Plastic Medicine Men." In Ward Churchill, ed., *From a Native Son: Selected Essays on Indigenism, 1985–1995.* Boston: South End Press.

Cornell, Stephen 1988 *The Return of the Native: American Indian Political Resurgence.* New York: Oxford University Press.

Cornell, Stephen, and Joseph Kalt 1992 *What Can Tribes Do?: Strategies and Institutions in American Indian Economic Development.* Los Angeles: American Indian Studies Center, University of California.

——— 1999 "Sovereignty and Nation-Building: The Development Challenge in Indian Country Today." *American Indian Culture and Research Journal* 22(3):87–214.

Dippie, Brian W. 1982 *The Vanishing American: White Attitudes and U.S. Indian Policy.* Lawrence: University Press of Kansas.

Dunaway, Wilma A. 1996 *The First American Frontier: Transition to Capitalism in Southern Appalachia, 1700–1860.* Chapel Hill: University of North Carolina Press.

Faiman-Silva, Sandra L. 1997 *Choctaws at the Crossroads: The Political Economy of Class and Culture in the Oklahoma Timber Region.* Lincoln: University of Nebraska Press.

Feld, Steven 1991 "Voices of the Rainforest." *Public Culture* 4(1):131–140.

Fenelon, James 1998 *Culturicide, Resistance, and Survival of the Lakota (Sioux Nation).* New York: Garland Publishing.

Ferguson, R. Brian, and Neil L. Whitehead, eds. 1992 *War in the Tribal Zone: Expanding States and Indigenous Warfare.* Santa Fe, N.Mex.: School of American Research Press.

Fried, Morton 1975 *The Notion of Tribe.* Menlo Park, Calif.: Cummings.

Hall, Thomas D. 1989 *Social Change in the Southwest, 1350–1880.* Lawrence: University Press of Kansas.

Himmel, Kelly D. 1999 *The Conquest of the Karankawas and the Tonkawas: A Study in Social Change, 1821–1859.* College Station: Texas A & M University Press.

Johnson, Troy 1996 *The Indian Occupation of Alcatraz Island: Self-Determination and the Rise of Indian Activism.* Urbana: University of Illinois Press.

Meyer, Melissa L. 1994 *The White Earth Tragedy: Ethnicity and Dispossession at a Minnesota Anishinaabe Reservation, 1889–1920.* Lincoln: University of Nebraska.

Nagel, Joane 1996 *American Indian Ethnic Renewal: Red Power and the Resurgence of Identity and Culture.* New York: Oxford University Press.

Rose, Wendy 1992 "The Great Pretenders: Further Reflections on Whiteshamism." In M. Annette Jaimes, ed., *The State of Native America: Genocide, Colonization, and Resistance.* Boston: South End Press.

Sanderson, Stephen K. 1999 *Social Transformations: A General Theory of Historical Development,* 2nd ed. Boulder: Rowman and Littlefield.

Snipp, C. Matthew 1986 "Who Are American Indians? Some Observations About the Perils and Pitfalls of Data for Race and Ethnicity." *Population Research and Policy Review* 5:237–252.

——— (ed.) 1988a *Public Policy Impacts on American Indian Economic Development.* Albuquerque: Native American Studies (Development Series No 4).

——— 1988b. "Public Policy Impacts and American Indian Economic Development." In C. Matthew Snipp, ed., *Public Policy Impacts on American Indian Economic Development.* Albuquerque: Native American Studies (Development Series No 4).

——— 1989 *American Indians: The First of This Land.* New York: Russell Sage Foundation.

——— 1992. "Sociological Perspectives on American Indians." *Annual Review of Sociology* 18:351–370.

Stannard, David E. 1992 *American Holocaust: Columbus and the Conquest of the New World.* New York: Oxford University Press.

Stiffarm, Lenore A., with Lane, Phil, Jr. 1992 "The Demography of Native North America: A Question of American Indian Survival." In M. Annette Jaimes, ed., *The State of Native America: Genocide, Colonization, and Resistance.* Boston: South End Press.

Tanner, Helen H., ed. 1987 *Atlas of Great Lakes Indian History.* Norman: University of Oklahoma Press.

Thornton, Russell 1987 *American Indian Holocaust and Survival.* Norman: University of Oklahoma Press.

Ward, Carol, and C. Matthew Snipp, eds. 1996 *Research in Human Capital and Development: Vol. 10, American Indian Economic Development.* Greenwich, Conn.: JAI Press.

Wilmer, Franke 1993 *The Indigenous Voice in World Politics: Since Time Immemorial.* Newbury Park, Calif.: Sage.

THOMAS D. HALL
JOANE NAGEL

INDIVIDUALISM

Individualism is a doctrine concerning both the composition of human society and the constitution of sociocultural actors. The term was invented in the 1820s, apparently, in France (Swart 1962). Its first appearance in English dates from the 1835 translation of Alexis de Tocqueville's study of the United States (Tocqueville [1850] 1969, p. 506). The basic notion conveyed by the newly coined word, that the individual is sovereign vis-à-vis society, was intensely controversial, for it stood on the grave of one established order, proclaiming the rise of another. As an early French critic saw it, individualism "destroys the very idea of obedience and of duty, thereby destroying both power and law," leaving nothing "but a terrifying confusion of interests, passions and diverse opinions" (cited in Lukes 1973, p. 6).

Individualism should be distinguished from historically specific constitutions of the individuality of human beings. The word "individual," used to discriminate a particular human being from collectivities ("family," "state"), had been in circulation for centuries prior to Tocqueville (albeit mainly as an adjective), and individualizations had been practiced under one description or another long before that, at least as evidenced in the oldest surviving texts of human history. However, premodern constitutions of individuality did not become the foci of a distinctive doctrine of individualism. That development came in response to the profound changes of social structure and consciousness that had been slowly accumulating during the seventeenth and eighteenth centuries. In the transformation from a medieval to a modern world, new transparencies of meaning evolved— among the most important, a particular conception of "the individual." The enormous power of that conception is reflected in the fact that people of modern society have generally had no doubt as to what an "individual" *is*. The reference has been self-evident because the object referred to, an *individual*, has been self-evident, pregiven, natural.

But one must remember that "the individual" is a construct. Like all constructs, it is historically variable. The meaning of individualism's "individual" was formed under specific historical circumstances that, in practice as well as in ideology, increasingly prized values of rational calculation, mastery, and experimentation; deliberate efforts toward betterment of the human condition; and a universalism anchored in the conviction that "human nature" is basically the same everywhere at all times and that rationality is singular in number. These commitments were manifested in the doctrine of individualism (as, indeed, in the formation of the modern social sciences). By the time of Tocqueville and the newly coined word, individualism's individual had become integral to much of the practical consciousness of modern society. Human beings were being objectified as instances of "the individual"—that is, as instances of a *particular kind* of individuality.

The forces created during that formative period wrought great changes in the fabric of society, many of which continue to reverberate. Of course, as historical circumstances have changed, both "the individual" of individualism and the constitution of individuality have changed. Nonetheless, a certain transparency of meaning remains still today in our practical consciousness of "the individual," and it is still informed by a doctrine of individualism. Thus, when a sociologist says that "a natural unit of observation is the individual" (Coleman 1990, p. 1), he can assume without fear of failure that most of his readers will know exactly what he means.

The remainder of this article offers brief accounts of (1) the development of individualism during the seventeenth, eighteenth, and nineteenth centuries, (2) recent shifts of emphases in individualism's conception of "the individual," and (3) some current issues and concerns. More extended treatments can be found in Macpherson (1962), Lukes (1973), Abercrombie and colleagues (1986), Heller and colleagues (1986), and Hazelrigg (1991), among others.

THE SELF-REPRESENTING INDIVIDUAL

While elements of individualism can be seen in expressions of practical affairs as early as the twelfth-century renaissance (Macfarlane 1978; Ullmann 1966), the first more or less systematic statement of the doctrine came during the 1600s. Scholars such as René Descartes, Thomas Hobbes, and John Locke believed that in order to understand a whole (e.g., society) one had first to understand the parts of which it is composed. In the case of society, those parts, the building blocks of a society, were instances of "the individual." Although disagreeing on various specific issues—for example, whether human agency is distinct from a natural world of causal necessity (Descartes) or a product of that causal necessity (Hobbes)—these seventeenth-century scholars displayed a remarkable confidence in their understandings of "the individual" as a presocial atom. Their individual was a highly abstract being, squatting outside the world.

In the premodern order of European society, social relations had been organic, corporate, and mainly ascriptive. Sovereignty was a complex relation of duty, responsibility, and charity, focused on a specific location in the hierarchical order of organic community. Certainly members of the community were individualized, but the distinction was constituted primarily by ascriptive position in the hierarchical order. It is clear from surviving documents of the twelfth century, for example, that one individual knight was discriminable from any other in ways that we would describe as "personality." With rare exceptions, however, the discrimination was local. Otherwise, knights were discriminable mainly by pedigree, lines of fealty, and quality of chivalry. Individuals could rise (and fall) through gradations of rank, but vertical movement was first within the family or household group. A knight who aspired to still higher standing had first to be retained in another, more powerful family. Similarly, while there is no reason

to doubt that residents of a twelfth-century village or town could reliably discriminate one another by physiognomic features, the portrayal of human beings in paintings concentrated on matters of costume, placement, and posture to signal social distinctions among virtually lifeless mannequins. Even in the revolutionary works attributed to Giotto (1267–1337), whose use of subtle gestures and glances began to individualize portrayals sufficiently to be called portraits in the modern sense, such facial features as warts, wens, moles, wrinkles, lines, scars, and sagging skin were still quite irrelevant to, and therefore absent in, the visualized identity or character of a person. But by the end of the 1400s we see, most notably in Domenico Ghirlandaio's *Portrait of Old Man and Boy* (c. 1490), depictions that to the modern sensibility count as realistically individualized faces. The art of portraiture gradually developed into advertisements of a new actor, front and center—modernity's sovereign individual (Haskell 1993).

In this new order, by contrast to its predecessor, social relations were conceived as contractual rather than organic, based on achieved rather than ascribed traits of individuals liberated from constraints of community. City life was once again the center of gravity in territorial organization, having displaced the manorial system. What would become the modern nation-state was beginning to take shape during the period of relative peace inaugurated by the several Treaties of Westphalia in 1648. Within this context of invention and experimentation with new (or renewed) organizational forms, the new individual was conceived as a wholly separate entity of self-identical integrity, a "bare individual" who could freely consent to enter into concert with other, equivalently constituted individuals, each propelled by self-interest. This was, as Macpherson (1962) described it, the advent of "possessive individualism," and it correlated well with the developing motivations of capitalism.

By the end of the eighteenth century, individualism had attained mature statement in treatises by David Hume, Adam Smith, and Immanuel Kant, among others. This mature statement, worked out in the context of rapidly changing political-economic institutions, emphasized the centrality of a "self-representing individual." The chief claim—that "every individual appears as the autonomous subject of his [or her, but primarily his] decisions and actions" (Goldmann [1968] 1973, p. 20)—served as the linchpin to formalized explanations of the political and economic rights of members of society, especially the propertied members. Expressions of the chief claim in moral and legal rights of the individual became enshrined in newly invented traditions, in legitimizing principles such as "popular sovereignty" and "inalienable rights," and in documents of public culture such as the Declaration of the Rights of Man and the Constitution of the United States of America (Hobsbawm and Ranger 1983; Morgan 1988). The prayerful injunction "God bless the squire and his relations and keep us in our proper stations" had been replaced by the almost wholly secular "*I* pledge allegiance to the flag" (i.e., to an abstract sign). While the claim of autonomy emphasized the universality of rights and the particularity of the "I," the practical emphasis on a self-representing individual was formulated in political-economic terms that "necessitated" elaborate definitions and procedures for the defense of "property rights" long before equivalent attention would be given to, say, "rights of the handicapped."

Much like the individual of organic community, the self-representing individual is a substantial presence, manifest as the embodiment of a uniform human nature, and as such is the bearer of various traits, dispositions, and predications. However, the site of the self-representing individual's capacity of agency and potential for autonomy is neither the community nor the accumulated traits, dispositions, and predications. Rather, it is deeply interior to what became a new "inner nature" of the human being. Beneath the faculty of reason, beneath all feeling and emotion and belief, there is "the will." Emile Durkheim ([1914] 1973) described it as the egoistic will of the individual pole of *homo duplex*, for George Herbert Mead (1934) it was "the principle of action." But before either of those sociologists, the master theorizer of the self-representing individual, Immanuel Kant, had formulated the basic principle as the pure functioning of the "I" through time. Only because I can unite a variety of given representations of objects in *one* consciousness, Kant ([1787] 1929, B133) argued, is it possible that I can "represent to myself the *identity of consciousness*," throughout those representations. In other words, the very possibility of a knowledge of the external world is dependent on the temporal continuity of the "I."

The individual is absolute proprietor of this pure functionality, this willing of the "I" as basic principle of action; the individual owes absolutely nothing to society for it.

By conceiving the essential core of human individuality to be a deeply interiorized, radically isolated pure functionality, connections between the individual and the substantive traits that he or she bears become arbitrary. The individual is formally free to exercise choice in which traits to bear, free to be mobile geographically, socially, culturally, personally. Ascriptive traits are devalued in favor of achieved traits, and one set of achieved traits can always be exchanged for yet another set. This principle of freely exchangeable traits, an aspiration directing progress toward "the good society," depended on new means of socialization (or "internalization of norms"), so as to insure sufficient regularity in processes of exchange. Indeed, the self-representing individual was central to a distinctive regimen of behavior, a new practical meaning of "discipline" (Foucault [1975] 1977). As the doctrine of individualism saw it, the contractual, associative forms of social relation, though looser fitting in their normative constraints than the old organic community, were complemented by the figure of "the self-made man" who had internalized all the norms of rectitude and propriety so nicely as to merit life in an unprecedentedly free society. When reality failed the image, there were courts and legal actions for deciding conflicts of interest and the clash of individuals' rights. Notably, not a single book on the law of torts had been published in English by the mid-1800s; the explosive growth of tort law and third-party rules was only beginning (Friedman 1985, pp. 53–54).

Because the doctrine of individualism provided a set of answers to questions that were foundational to sociology (as to the social sciences in general)—What is the individual? How is society possible? and so forth—virtually every topic subsequently addressed by sociology has in one way or another involved aspects of individualism. Given the composition of individualism's self-representing individual, the most prominent issues have often centered on questions of relationship between the rise of individualism and the development of new forms of political-economic organization as manifested in capitalism, bureaucracy, and the modern state. Indeed, that relationship was focus of one of the great controversies occupying many early sociologists (Abercrombie et al. 1986). Hardly anyone doubted the existence or importance of a relationship. Rather, the debates were about such issues as causal direction (which caused which?), periodizations (e.g., when did capitalism begin?), and whether ideas or material conditions (each category conceived as devoid of the other) were the primary motive force. In many respects the debates were a continuation of the struggles they were about.

Other, more specific topics addressed by sociologists have also involved aspects of the rise of individualism. Several have already been mentioned (e.g., a new regimen of discipline). Additional examples are the development of sectarian (as opposed to churchly) religions, followed by an even more highly privatized mystical-religious consciousness of the isolated individual; changes in domestic architecture, such as greater emphasis on individualized spaces of privacy and functionally specialized rooms; changes in table manners, rules of courtesy, and other "refinements of taste"; the emergence of a "confessional self" and practices of diarykeeping; increased emphasis on romantic love ("affective individualism") in mate selection; new forms of literary discourse, such as the novel and autobiography; the rise of professionalism; and the rise of the modern corporation as an organizational form that, having gained standing as a legal actor comparable to a flesh-and-blood person, cast into doubt reliance on understandings of "the will" as foundation and motive force of contractual relations (see Abercrombie et al. 1986; Horwitz 1992; Perrot [1987] 1990).

THE SELF-EXPRESSING INDIVIDUAL

The figure of the self-representing individual proved to be unstable, even as the meaning of representation gradually changed. This was mainly because the same factors that had produced this version of individualism's individual also led to dissolution of the transparent sign. For example, whereas clothing, manners, bodily comportment, and similar traits had been, in the old order, reliable signs (representations) of a person's rank or station in life, the sign became increasingly arbitrary in its relationship to ground. This loosening of the sign, together with a proliferation of signs in exchange,

led to a new universalism of "the empty sign." The prototype was money and the commodity form: Devoid of intrinsic value and capable of representing everything, it represents nothing in particular. As one recent scholar has described the process, borrowing a clause from Karl Marx, "all that is solid melts into air" (Berman 1983).

At the same time, the rhetoric of transhistorical forms of value (e.g., the commodity, inalienable rights) allows for an enormous amount of individual variation in the sociocultural conditions under which it can succeed. Individualism's emphasis on the bare individual was being increasingly generalized, further reducing the import of group-based relations and traits. In the mid-1800s, for instance, the distinction between public affairs and private matters was drawn at the door of home and family. Family life provided the chief "haven" of organic relations, nurturant domesticity, and refuge from the trials of work and politics. But soon the haven itself became a site of struggle toward still greater individuation. Of the many factors contributing to this rebellion against the traditional restraints of family, one of the most important was a new culture of sexuality, which manifested a more general and growing concern for the interior interests and needs of the individual.

Precedent for this concern can be seen in Kant's conception of the self-representing individual (because of the transcendental "I," every individual has in common a potential for *self-actualization*) as well as in romanticist movements of the early 1800s. However, the development of a new "inner discourse of the individual" has been mostly a twentieth-century phenomenon. The psychology of Sigmund Freud and his disciples formed part of that development, certainly; but another part was formed by the conception of a new "social citizenship" (Marshall 1964), which emphasized an individual's rights of social welfare in addition to the earlier mandates of political and economic rights. A new figure of individualism's individual gradually emerged, the "self-expressing individual."

The individualism of the self-representing individual promoted the idea that all interests are ultimately interests of the bare individual. The new version of individualism both extends and modifies that idea. Whereas the self-representing individual puts a premium on self-control and hard work, the self-expressing individual generalizes the value of "freedom of choice" from political-economic exchange relations to matters of personal lifestyle and consumption preferences (Inglehart 1990). The central claim holds that "each person has a unique core of feeling and intuition that should unfold or be expressed if individuality is to be realized" (Bellah et al. 1985, p. 336), and each person has the right to develop his or her unique capacities of self-expression. A recent change in divorce law partly illustrates the import of that claim. Prior to the 1960s one of the few organic relations still surviving in modern society was the marital bond; few conditions were deemed grave enough to have legal standing as grounds for breaking it. With the invention of "no fault" divorce (relatively noncontroversial legislation that spread rapidly from state to state; Jacob 1988), the marital relation became a civil contract much like any other, and a spouse's freedom to choose divorce in the interest of satisfying unfulfilled needs of self-expression gained recognition.

Another manifestation of this self-expressing individual is the recent development of a specialized field, the sociology of emotions (e.g., Barbalet 1998; Thoits 1989). Certainly earlier scholars (e.g., Georg Simmel) had recognized emotive dimensions of sentiment, tradition, trust, and the like, and had assumed motivations such as fear of power, anxiety about salvation, envy of success, frustrated ambition, and eponymous glory. No one imagined that persons of premodern societies did not experience emotions—though usually this would have been in an idiom of "the passions," and scholars disagreed whether these were in fact ahistorical, noncultural formations. But emotions had rarely been treated as important topics of inquiry by sociologists until the latter decades of the twentieth century. The emotive dimensions of life had typically been regarded as subordinate to other dimensions, just as the passions had been treated as dangerous when unbridled—energies which belonged properly in the harness of reason or "the rational faculty." (Most of the seven deadly sins, remember, were emotional states or effects of emotional states.) When rightly yoked by reason, emotive energies of the self-representing individual could achieve highly valued public outcomes even if the particular emotion itself was classified as a vice. Thus, avowed Adam Smith among others, private greed or avarice could become, through the device of market transaction, a public benefit. For the self-expressing individual, on the other hand, emotive aspects of life are, or should be, valued in themselves, not only for what might result from them. Whereas the eighteenth-century "pursuit of happiness" (one of the self-representing individual's inalienable rights) was idiomatic for the unfettered formal liberty of the individual to pursue self-interest in commerce (an inherently outward-looking, social activity), for the self-expressing individual the pursuit of happiness refers to a much more introspective, privately evaluated emotional state, "being happy with who one is."

Individualism's self-expressing individual remains a trait-bearing substantial entity, to be sure. The variety of bearable traits is greatly expanded by the shift in emphasis from self-control to self-expression through lifestyle experimentation ("the person as work-in-progress-from-within," as it were). Moreover, this shift in emphasis is accompanied by the stipulation that only those traits that an individual can freely choose to assume, and then jettison, should be relevant criteria by which to discriminate and evaluate individuals. Criteria falling outside the bounds of individual choice ("immutable" traits, whether biological or sociocultural) are deemed to be both irrelevant and, increasingly, a violation of an individual's rights. In conjunction with the "entitlements" logic of social citizenship, this stipulation of a radically individualistic freedom of reversible choice has been linked to the emergence of a generalized expectation of "total justice" (Friedman 1985).

By the same token, the doctrine of individualism has always contained a large fictive component. Long after the doctrine proclaimed the sovereignty of the bare individual, for example, the actual individuality of human beings continued to be heavily marked by ascriptive traits (e.g., gender, race) and by sociocultural inheritances from one's parents. The shift to an expressive individualism reflects efforts to situate the agency of a "free individual" outside the separately conceived domain of relations of domination. Rather than attempt to change those relations, the self-expressing individual would "transcend" them by concentrating on a logic of rights pertaining to the free expression of individual will in a domain of "personal culture" (Marcuse [1937] 1968).

Fictions can be productive in various ways, however. The fictions of individualism have often been made taskmasters, as women, African Americans, persons with disabilities, and other human beings discriminated primarily by ascriptive or group-based criteria have struggled to make reality conform to doctrinal image.

SOME CURRENT ISSUES

Because individualism has been one of the professional ideologies of the social sciences ("methodological individualism"), a perennial issue concerns the proper structure of explanation—specifically, whether explanation of any sociocultural phenomenon must ultimately refer to facts about individuals, and if so, what precisely that means (Coleman 1990; Hazelrigg 1991; Lukes 1973). No one denies that collectivities are composed of individuals. But that truism settles neither the question of how "composition" is to be understood nor the question of what constitutes "the individual." In short, the methodological issue involves a number of theoretical-conceptual issues, including several that are located at the intersection between individualism's "individual" and historical variations in the actual constitution of individuality (Heller et al. 1986). The doctrine of individualism has consistently conceptualized "the individual" as a distinct and self-contained agent who acts within, yet separate from, a constraining social structure. Rather than being an ensemble of social relations, individualism's individual is the substantial atom out of which any possible social relations are composed. This has certain implications for the empirical field.

How, for instance, does one understand the category "rational action"? What minimal criteria must be satisfied in order that a particular action can count as "rational"? The individual who stands forth in individualism tends to the heroic—self-made, self-reliant, and self-governing, rising above circumstances, taking charge of one's own destiny, and, in the aggregate of similar atoms, building a better world. This individual was soon accorded central place as the chief fount of rational action. Whereas late eighteenth-century scholars such as Adam Smith continued to remind readers that rational action could and did stem from nonrational motivations (e.g., moral sentiment, the ethos of tradition, even the simple inertia of habit), pride of place in the list of motivational sources increasingly shifted to that part of the "faculties of mind" called "the rational faculty," conceived as an instrument of the will. The emphasis on rationality as faculty, an "instrumental rationality," was no doubt encouraged by, and at the same time promoted, a growing list of successes in the inventiveness of carefully deliberated, calculated designs, plans, and projects of human engineering. (Recall the success of Dutch efforts, beginning on an ever larger scale in the 1600s and 1700s, to push back the sea and create thousands of square miles of new land—for most of us a barely remembered fact of history, but in those earlier times a truly audacious undertaking.) Are the limits of rational action therefore as closely circumscribed as the limits of an individual actor's rational deliberations, calculations, and intentions? Most sociologists today are agreed in answering "no" to that question, although they diverge, sometimes sharply, in particulars of the answer (Coleman 1990; Kuran 1995; Sica 1988).

Social action can be highly rational in the aggregate, both in outcome and in process, even when individual actors, attending more to nonrational or irrational than to rational motivations and intentions, behave in ways that hardly fit the doctrinal image of "heroic actor." People do learn from experience (if fitfully and slowly), and part of the accumulated fund from that learning consists in organizational forms that have rationalities built into them. This "rationality as form"—a materialized intelligence in the same way that a hand-held calculator, an airplane, or a magnetic resonance imager is a materialized solution to a set of problems—enables many more people to use, benefit from, and even operate the rationalities built into such devices than have the understanding ("rationality as faculty") required to design their architectures or to convert design into working product. Moreover, whereas the examples just cited can be readily interpreted as immediate and punctual products of some specific individual's rational faculty (thus fitting the heroic-actor model of the inventor or discoverer as genius), many other examples of rationality-invested organizational forms—family structures, markets, bureaucracy, and so forth—are as much or more the gradual accretions of indirection, sentiment, habituation, and happenstance than the intended consequences of rationally deliberated, calculated, instrumental actions of particular individuals. The doctrine of individualism has often slighted the importance of these latter wellsprings of rational action, as if the actions they motivate do not quite count, or do not count in quite the same way, as action that directly manifests the willful force of an individual's reasoned intentions.

In a related vein, if the individual owes nothing to society for the "I" as principle of action, where should the distinction be drawn between determinants of action that are social and those that are psychological? Consider, for instance, a person suffering the characteristics clinically (and thus socially) categorized as "depression." Are these characteristics proper to the individual only, or are they also in some way descriptive of a social condition that is integral to the individual so characterized? If Willy Loman, of Arthur Miller's *Death of a Salesman*, is depressed, does that description say anything about the circumstances of a life Loman shared with countless others, or is it the description only of a misery interior to an isolated individual? Each of these accounts of what is under description has had its proponents. The popularity of a medicative regimen that emphasizes direct palliation or amelioration of psychic state (as in chemical applications, whether Prozac or psilocybin) suggests a growing preference for the second account.

Some sociologists contend that individualism's self-expressing individual is an accurate depiction of contemporary reconstitutions of individuality, and that in this new form of "the individual" the substance of selfhood, an individual's self-identical integrity, is being evacuated. Bellah and colleagues (1985) indict the emergence of "a language of radical individual autonomy" in which people "cannot think about themselves or others except as arbitrary centers of volition (p. 81)." Others argue that the emphasis on individual autonomy and separation is an expression of masculine, patriarchal values, as contrasted to feminine values of social attachment (Gilligan 1982). Still others see the development of an entirely new "order of simulacra" (Baudrillard [1976] 1983), in which simulation or the simulacrum substitutes for and then vanquishes the real (e.g., television images establish the parameters of reality). The alleged result is a collapse of "the social" into the indifference of "the masses," who no longer care to discriminate among "messages" (beyond their entertainment effects) since one simulation is as good as another.

Equally contentious issues surround the evident growth in people's sense of entitlement and in the array of legal rights claimed and often won on behalf of "individual choice." Individualism's figure of the self-expressing individual is held by some to be the harbinger of a new age of democracy, by others to be the confirmation of a continuing trend toward greater atomization (Friedman 1985). Both assessments point to the emergence of a "rights industry" that promotes the invention of new categories of legal right pertaining to everything from a guaranteed freedom to experiment with unconventional lifestyles without risk of discrimination or retribution, to the rights of animals both individually and at the species level, to the possibility of endowing genes with "subject-like powers" and thus legal standing (Glendon 1991; Norton 1987; Oyama 1985). Some critics contend that the expansion of concern for increasingly particularized and "arbitrary" individual choices comes at the expense of a diminished concern for social outcomes. "Unless people regain the sense that the practices of society represent some sort of natural order instead of a set of arbitrary choices, they cannot hope to escape from the dilemma of unjustified power" (Unger 1976, p. 240). The conviction recalls that of the early French critic quoted in the opening paragraph.

REFERENCES

Abercrombie, Nicholas, Stephen Hill, and Bryan S. Turner 1986 *Sovereign Individuals of Capitalism*. London: Allen and Unwin.

Barbalet, J. M. 1998 *Emotion, Theory, and Social Structure*. Cambridge, U.K.: Cambridge University Press.

Baudrillard, Jean (1976) 1983 *In the Shadow of the Silent Majorities*. New York: Semiotext (e).

Bellah, Robert N., Richard Madsen, William M. Sullivan, Ann Swidler, and Steven M. Tipton 1985 *Habits of the Heart*. Berkeley: University of California Press.

Berman, Marshall 1983 *All That Is Solid Melts into Air*. London: Verso.

Coleman, James S. 1990 *Foundations of Social Theory*. Cambridge, Mass.: Harvard University Press.

Durkheim, Emile (1914) 1973 "The Dualism of Human Nature and Its Social Conditions." In Robert Bellah, ed., *Emile Durkheim on Morality and Society*. Chicago: University of Chicago Press.

Foucault, Michel (1975) 1977 *Discipline and Punish*, trans. Alan Sheridan. New York: Pantheon.

Friedman, Lawrence 1985 *Total Justice*. New York: Russell Sage Foundation.

Gilligan, Carol 1982 *In a Different Voice*. Cambridge, Mass.: Harvard University Press.

Glendon, Mary Ann 1991 *Rights Talk*. New York: Free Press.

Goldmann, Lucien (1968) 1973 *Philosophy of the Enlightenment*, trans. Henry Maas. Cambridge, Mass.: MIT Press.

Haskell, Francis 1993 *History and Its Images*. New Haven, Conn.: Yale University Press.

Hazelrigg, Lawrence 1991 "The Problem of Micro-Macro Linkages: Rethinking Questions of the Individual, Social Structure, and Autonomy of Action." *Current Perspectives in Social Theory* 11:229–254.

Heller, Thomas C., Morton Sosna, and David E. Wellbery 1986 *Reconstructing Individualism*. Stanford, Calif.: Stanford University Press.

Hobsbawm, Eric, and Terence Ranger, eds. 1983 *The Invention of Tradition*. Cambridge, U.K.: Cambridge University Press.

Horwitz, Morton J. 1992 *The Transformation of American Law, 1870–1960*. New York: Oxford University Press.

Inglehart, Ronald 1990 *Cultural Shift in Advanced Industrial Society*. Princeton, N.J.: Princeton University Press.

Jacob, Herbert 1988 *Silent Revolution*. Chicago: University of Chicago Press.

Kant, Immanuel (1787) 1929 *The Critique of Pure Reason*, 2nd ed., trans. Norman Kemp Smith. London: Macmillan.

Kuran, Timur 1995 *Private Truths, Public Lies*. Cambridge, Mass.: Harvard University Press.

Lukes, Steven 1973 *Individualism*. Oxford: Basil Blackwell.

Macfarlane, Alan 1978 *The Origins of English Individualism*. Oxford: Basil Blackwell.

Macpherson, C. B. 1962 *The Political Theory of Possessive Individualism*. Oxford: Oxford University Press.

Marcuse, Herbert (1937) 1968 "The Affirmative Character of Culture." In *Negations*, trans. Jeremy J. Shapiro. Boston: Beacon.

Marshall, T. H. 1964 *Class, Citizenship, and Social Development*. New York: Doubleday.

Mead, George Herbert 1934 *Mind, Self, and Society*, ed. Charles W. Morris. Chicago: University of Chicago Press.

Morgan, Edmund S. 1988 *Inventing the People*. New York: Norton.

Norton, Bryan G. 1987 *Why Preserve Natural Variety?* Princeton, N.J.: Princeton University Press.

Oyama, Susan 1985 *The Ontogeny of Information*. Cambridge, U.K.: Cambridge University Press.

Perrot, Michelle, ed. (1987) 1990 *A History of Private Life*, vol.4, trans. Arthur Goldhammer. Cambridge, Mass.: Harvard University Press.

Sica, Alan 1988 *Weber, Irrationality, and Social Order*. Berkeley: University of California Press.

Swart, Koenraad W. 1962 "'Individualism' in the Mid-Nineteenth Century (1826–1860)." *Journal of the History of Ideas* 23:77–90.

Thoits, Peggy A. 1989 "The Sociology of Emotions." *Annual Review of Sociology* 15:317–342.

Tocqueville, Alexis de (1850) 1969 *Democracy in America*, 13th ed., J. P. Mayer, ed., George Lawrence, trans. New York: Doubleday.

Ullmann, Walter 1966 *The Individual and Society in the Middle Ages*. Baltimore: Johns Hopkins University Press.

Unger, Roberto Mangabeira 1976 *Law in Modern Society*. New York: Free Press.

LAWRENCE HAZELRIGG

INDUSTRIAL SOCIOLOGY

The term *industrialization* connotes the development of social organizations, generally in nation-states in which large manufacturing enterprises loom large and in which adjunctive legal institutions supporting laissez-faire philosophies of market relationships and providential public and private services grow with them in tandem. Adam Smith's *Wealth of Nations* became early on, after its appearance in 1776, a kind of founding blueprint for the exploitation of private interests and initiatives in the service of the "general good." Industrial sociological studies accordingly focus on the "causes" or prerequisites for, the correlates of (in family, community, and other social settings), and the consequences of the industrialization process, largely in social systems governed in accord with eighteenth-century liberalism, with its emphases on the economic rights of property owners and their agents.

The key consequences under examination have been the "rights, privileges, and immunities" of parties to labor contracts; the characteristic social and economic relationships among investors, producers, workers, and consumers in Western societies and, in turn, the circumstances of dependents, communities, and regions; and, finally, the resulting stabilities and changes in the social, economic, and political structures of the nations in which all these persons live.

Those whose research and teaching agendas include several of these broad domains draw very heavily on specialists in "world systems," economic development, economic determinism, legal institutions, social stratification, public policy, organizations, urban sociology and community studies, labor markets, and economic sociology. A number of issues treated elliptically in these lines of research, especially those addressed by French, German, British, Italian and Japanese scholars, are discussed in relevant articles in this Encyclopedia.

Industrial sociology as a distinguishable if very broad field of study may truly be said to have been born in the late 1770s, so continuous with their forebearers' interests have been many of the specific subjects of concern of modern investigators. Systematic studies of social organizations in industrial societies date from the long-celebrated if not always carefully read analyses by Adam Smith, who addressed philosophical issues having to do with economic activities and related "moral sentiments" early in his writings and then turned to his widely known and enduring work on the social (macroscopic) and organizational (microscopic) roles in society of capitalists and, more famously, of labor. Smith regarded labor and its effective mobilization and utilization, not the fruits of mercantilism (i.e., the quantity of gold and silver imported from colonies and the exportation of finished goods), as the real sources of what he termed the wealth of nations. Smith's studies of the superiority of specialized divisions of labor in a pin factory became a template for studies of the personal and social costs and benefits of manufacturing enterprises by scholars of all political colors.

Furthermore, Smith's analyses and urgings about the benefits of free trade, of constraining the role of government in economic affairs, of the critical roles of increasingly differentiated divisions of labor, and of the emergence of the "factory system" in late-seventeenth and early-eighteenth-century England staked out most of the basic subjects of modern industrial sociologists' research

studies: economic organizations; managers' and workers' ways; the correlates of technology and divisions of labor; economic exchange and trade; questions about the roles of central governments in economies, and about innumerable regulatory measures affecting workplaces; and, finally, the distributive effects of industrialization on national stratification systems.

Industrial sociologists can also trace their roots to Charles Dickens's very popular literary treatments of life in early-nineteenth-century England and to other early and more pointedly social, economic, and political reformers in Europe. Thus, investigators now undertake studies with debts to English and French critics, commentators, and philosophers whose works are captured in the term "the Enlightenment"; to Henri St. Simon's urgings about the application of scientific rationality to social organization; to Karl Marx's historicist treatments of capitalism's problematical "maturer" states; to the pros and cons in arguments about nascent trade union movements; to debaters arguing over alternative welfare, trade, and other initiatives by governments; and to assessments of the philosophical legitimacy of the emerging stratification of societies, as variant forms of aristocracy gave way to variant forms of more representative governments. Dickens's characterization of an employers' association that resisted safety guards on moving machine parts as "The Association for the Mangling of Operatives" and his and his audiences' concerns about the improvement of working conditions presaged a great deal of the work of industrial sociologists in the twentieth century, most of whom have been critical of unfettered markets. Continuities since the nineteenth century, meantime, in all but methods of research, have been notable. The subjects pursued include the forces that virtually compel ever more differentiated divisions of labor; the effects of different patterns of national income distribution; and the contributions of these forces to the rise, expansion, and characters of both "blue-collar" labor forces and, overlapping with them, the expansion of middle classes in urban centers; the forces that contribute to the rise of trade unions and the resulting growth of new systems of law that have changed the nature of property and property claims to include more than physical capital and realty; the forces that have contributed to the decline in small agricultural holdings, small towns, and rural areas; and, withal, the forces that generally make social life more secular, political life more democratic or undemocratic, and working life more bureaucratic.

During the period from 1900 to 1950, much of the macro-level research that continued to add to present-day conceptions of the body of industrial sociological literature was actually performed by institutional economists—in the United States principally students of labor, management, and the "legal foundations of capitalism", in the tradition of the "Wisconsin" or (J.R.) "Commons School" (Commons and associates 1926, 1935, 1936). These investigators also founded the field of industrial relations, whose practitioners' work has perennially overlapped with that of industrial sociologists. In more recent times, sociologists have essentially inherited what has come to be seen as the "institutional tradition" in economics, a longtime tradition in that discipline that has given way, in the post–World War II world, to mathematical modeling and econometrics. Parallel works in western Europe have similarly been informed by Sydney and Beatrice Webb and by pre–World War I Christian democratic and secular left-liberal traditions in France and Germany.

In the period after World War I, industrial sociologists gave increasing attention to the positive and negative social effects of business cycles: "Busts" undoubtedly helped to purge national economies of many types of waste and inefficiencies and thus contributed to subsequent "booms." At the same time, however, busts sparked unwelcome recessions and depressions, with their subversive effects on growth, employment levels, and thus on the living standards, attitudes, and behavior of most citizens. Researchers' attentions, in the 1930s especially, focused correlatively on the growth of large corporations in the Western democracies; the pros and cons of aggressive price competition; and the possibly leavening effects of unions and of interventions by the "positive state" against the centralization of economic and thus, potentially, of political power in private hands, such that some of the less admirable correlates of capitalist systems could be controlled. Generally the researchers sought not so much to traduce "big business" as to identify constraints on private economic power that would not reduce the benefits to societies of large corporations' productive capacities. The emergence of fascism in Germany in the 1930s embodied widespread apprehensions about both big government and the reach of the communist revolution in what became the USSR.

Systematic attention toward the middle of this period was also given to what is now termed the global economy, often in the form of studies of the effects of the international trade barriers that contributed so significantly to the collapse of the Western industrial economies—the so-called Crash of 1929 and the Great Depression. The political and economic interdependencies among nations—and those among classes of economic actors within them—became increasingly palpable to researchers, who began to see economies more clearly in terms of the structures of individual industries and industry groupings—new chapters in the all-important story of the causes and correlates of the division of labor (Brady 1943). Additionally, unions were gaining in their appeal, beyond skilled tradesmen, to industrial, "mass-production" assembly workers. Among the questions pursued by sociologists were those having to do with the prospects that a coherent working class would emerge in the United States out of the ferment of the pre–World War II era. Incipient "class warfare" could be tamed, if not quashed, by reforms that are collectively referred to nowadays as revisions in the (Jean-Jacques Rousseau's) "social contract" and by the construction of social "safety nets" of types that are currently being critically assessed in both the United States and in western Europe; renewed and very vigorous industrial price competition has contributed significantly to concerns about expansion of central government "welfare" budgets in competition with funds for private investment.

Finally, by the 1920s and into the 1940s, there were growing concerns about whether Benito Mussolini's "corporate state" and Adolf Hitler's Third Reich represented a kind of conspiracy of fascists with Italy's and Germany's financial and manufacturing leaders (Neumann 1942) against those, especially in the three Communists Internationals, who were perceived by conservatives to be urging workers to turn to the revolutionary political left. This subject earned much increased attention after World War II; joined by historians' work in the 1950s, the social scientific literature on the social sources of totalitarian systems has become extensive, one of the recurring questions in this literature being whether the seeds of "totalitarianism of the right" germinate especially well in "capitalist" soil (Moore 1973). The answers from sociologists' studies, however, have tended to focus on the fragility of support for democratic institutions in most societies. These studies have analyzed the vulnerabilities of democracies to losses of the confidence of large numbers of citizens victimized by major and long-enduring economic collapses, rather than on markets' preoccupation with putative contradictions in capitalism per se, as a key reason for the appeal of social movements on the political right. Suffering from traumatic social, political, and economic discontinuities, sociologists reported, could all too easily contribute to the delivery of the loyalties of many—from Rome and Naples in Italy, to Marienthal in Austria, to Berlin in Germany, and to Buenos Aires in Argentina—to demagogues and "scapegoaters". Indeed, these studies led social psychologists among sociologists to important and widely influential discoveries about scapegoating phenomena that could generate poisonous race and ethnic relations (Adorno et al. 1950).

At what we may call the "mesoscopic"—middle—levels of analyses, industrial sociologists, in loose confederation with the more institutionally oriented scholars among labor economists, turned their attention in the pre–World War II period to the implications of the levels of aggregate demand (and deficiencies thereof) for the structures and experiences of communities before and during the Great Depression [as in Muncie, ("Middletown"), Indiana, in the United States]; to the disinclinations of unemployed Americans to "blame the system" (rather than themselves) for their sad circumstances during the Great Depression; and to the pros and cons of government intervention in national economies and of the construction of the aforementioned "safety nets" for victims of economic downturns.

Not least among sociologists' interests were those in the stratification of societies, especially respecting the distribution of wealth and income among individuals and families; the behavior of economic elites in local communities; and the causes and correlates of social mobility. In the latter matter, evidence mounted that the economic successes and failures of individuals could not be attributed simply to their ambition, "drive," and hard work—or their lack of these oft-praised qualities. Indeed, many successes and failures are

grounded in opportunity structures, not the least important of which are individuals' access to third-party "bonding" agents and access to formal education and training. While most economists have equated their educational achievement, or lack thereof, to earners' incomes without further ado, sociologists have urged that imperfections in markets enabled American employers to assume that better-educated workers were more productive and to pass on the costs of such an assumption to consumers (Berg 1970). For economists, better-educated workers are paid more because they are more productive, but their measure of productivity is income, not actual output, as a supposedly valid measure of output.

The advent of World War II brought many industrial sociologists to focus, not without a degree of patriotic fervor, on organizational arrangements in relation to the need to heighten productivity gains in what President Franklin D. Roosevelt called the world's arsenal of democracy. Studies of workers' groups in industry in the late 1920s, many conducted by applied sociologists linked to academic business schools (at Harvard University especially), had already indicated that most workers were as responsive to work-group "peer pressures" to fix production quotas at rates below those contemplated by managers and by their time-and-motion experts as they were to economic incentives. These findings were replicated many times between 1929 and 1985. This view of workers' motives continues to inform the urging by many sociologists that we go beyond conventional economic studies of wage administration in seeking to understand the ways of citizens in their workplaces. At issue are the respective roles of communitarian and of individualistic predispositions among workers.

With a few very noble exceptions, and for the majority's own good reasons, economists conceive of production organizations as essentially unproblematic "givens" into which resources are pumped and from which outputs flow. Sociologists' lessons about organizations as social systems, which balanced the valuable lessons taught by economists, were widely applied in the electrical appliances industry, the airframes industry, and in automobile, steel, and other industrial settings. The lesson: Identify work groups and win over workers' groups and their leaders to corporate aims; then reap the benefits of the support of not-so-rugged individualists in workplaces, who often respond more favorably to group norms than to group-disrupting industrial incentive-type pay plans. As it turned out, these lessons were perhaps applied somewhat more assiduously from 1960 to 1990 in Japan than in the United States, where worker participation in organizational decision making and work reforms have appealed to comparatively fewer employers despite the possible benefits of "humanized" personnel policies. Researchers have discovered that U. S. managers' interest in worker participation tends to wax when there labor market conditions are "tight"—that is, high demand for workers—and wane when they are "loose." In Western managers' theory at least, human resources are factors of production—commodities—and the treatments of these factors are functions more of short-run market conditions than of long-term concern about the qualities of work life (O'Toole 1974). The latter concerns find more expression in collective bargaining relationships and in remedial legislation, with the endorsement and help of many sociologists who are skeptical of managers as patrons, than in initiatives by employers who are skeptical of the benefits of "codeterminative" relations with workers, such as those requiring worker representations on boards of directors under laws in Germany and the Scandinavian countries.

THE CONTEMPORARY SCENE

In present-day industrial sociology, the main subjects of study have been (1) the increasingly important roles of education and training in shaping Americans' opportunities (Jencks et al. 1979); (2) the relationships between the significant differences in circumstances between managers and workers in "core" industries and managers and workers in "internal labor markets" on the one hand, and the lower-paid, appreciably less capitalized, smaller, more vulnerable establishments in the "peripheries" of economies on the other (Kalleberg 1983); (3) in the correlates—income and otherwise—of discrimination against women and minorities; and (4) the problems of those who simply are not well integrated into the labor force, the so-called underclass (Wilson 1987). These newer topics have taken their places with continuing studies of work groups; industrial conflict; mobility patterns; the evolving roles of public policies and the state; the politics of income distribution;

and intramural studies of organizations, their decision-making arrangements, and, more recently, their "cultures."

Studies by industrial sociologists are increasingly comparative in character, as these researchers seek to identify cultural and political factors—such as belief systems and constitutional arrangements, respectively—that influence the effectiveness of different nations' populations in efforts to mobilize human and other resources, motivate leaders and their human charges, design productive organizations, and make and provide goods and services (Cole 1989; Lincoln and Kalleberg 1990).

Overall, industrial sociologists have contributed to the delineation of options facing leaders in government but less so to enterprises, unions, and urban communities. During the period until 1970, industrial sociologists' investigations moved in increasingly specialized directions.

One thrust brought a large group of the field's leaders to concentrate on organizations (Coleman 1982; Stinchcombe 1990; Thompson 1967). In rich elaborations and embellishments on Max Weber's pioneering work on bureaucracies, sociologists in the United States and western Europe have ventured into "the Japanese factory"; the Tennessee Valley Authority; banks; mental hospitals; British coal mines; a gypsum mine; a state employment agency; schools, prisons and equivalent "total institutions"; a foundry; the U.S. Military Academy; steel mills (in the United States and Europe); German, Soviet, and Czech manufactories; the military establishment; French family firms; social movements; labor unions; merchant ships; American soldiers' organized experiences in and out of World War II combat; and the YMCA—to mention just a few contexts and populations about which studies were completed (Hall 1987; Perrow 1986).

While the vast body of literature produced by the observers in this disparate array of organizations has received little acclaim in the media, it is a sign of the importance of these investigators' findings, assessments, and consequent theories that their work is basic to the curricula of the very influential graduate schools of business and management, from Harvard to Berkeley, from Seattle to Miami, and from Maine to Los Angeles—and in Scandinavia; Germany; France; the United Kingdom; Japan; and, by the 1990s, Moscow. The lessons learned: It is possible to design a great many optional variations on the specific structures of hierarchical organizations, their intramural arrangements, and the "production relations" therein, to meet the exigencies confronting managers and their charges in dealings with each other; with competitors, clients, customers, suppliers, subcontractors, regulators, third-party insurers, and community forces; and with labor market developments.

Industrial sociologists—whether "majors" from colleges or holders of masters and doctoral degrees, some of whom work as consultants or as technicians or managers in corporate settings—offer prescriptions for improving employee morale and marketing programs (from demographic assessments to surveys of customer attitudes); for designing optimal "mixes" of wage and salary schedules with supplementary benefits; for reducing supplementary benefits; for reducing absenteeism and turnover; for productivity "enhancement"; for designing therapeutic (rather than custodial) environments in mental health care agencies; and for constructing occupational safety programs, grievance machinery, and quality control programs.

A second group moved away from these more microscopic studies of organizations to study the social, economic, and political development of whole societies, some in historical terms during the post–World War II era, including India's, China's, Italy's, Japan's, and Germany's (actually "redevelopment" in the latter two cases), and the USSR's systems. Among the lessons were important guidelines to understanding the stabilities of some and the flexibilities of other social-cultural values that gave distinctive national shape to individual countries' brands of industrialization. It is clear that while the "common denominators" in the paths to both growth and development—the latter a matter of the degree of distributive justice in a society and the former a matter of increases in gross national product—are numerous, there are instructive differences as well (Inkeles and Smith 1974).

Indeed, a consortium of scholars, many of them sociologists studying "industrialization and industrial man" in comparative-international terms, produced well over forty volumes and a great many shorter pieces on the convergences and divergences among industrial and industrializing nations over the period 1955–1975 (Dunlop et al. 1975; Kerr and Dunlop 1973). These works of scholarship have helped thousands of leaders in governments, large corporations, labor unions, and international agencies to make judgments about investments (both public and private); social, political, and economic policies; and the aptness of designs of organizations in what is now truly a global economy in which nations' planning efforts are turning, more and more, toward market and away from command economies (Yergin and Stanislaw, 1998). The conclusions at the end of 1990, in a continuing body of research following the preceding twenty-four months of changes in eastern Europe and the USSR, were that the "marketizing" and democratization movements in previously planned economies would assuredly reduce divergences among industrial systems but would by no means eliminate entirely the influence of discrete national cultures in shaping the practices and institutions, from child rearing to legal structures, that help, in turn, to shape social relations in a given nation's enterprises, as some sociologists have long argued.

A third constituency moved "below" organizational levels to study the dynamics of work groups within organizations, picking up on the work of the previously mentioned human relations school before, during, and after World War II. This group of scholars drew heavily on earlier sociologists' insights and theories—from Georg Simmel, Charles Cooley, and George Herbert Mead, and especially from the massive number of post–World War II publications of data and analyses from one of the first very-large-sample and sophisticated social scientific surveys of wartime American soldiers (Inkeles 1964). These reports gave abundant corroboration to the findings in industry, by earlier human relations investigators, concerning the critical importance of small groups and their norms in efforts to understand individual attitudes and behavior (Homans 1950). The applications of these findings—in studies of satisfaction, leadership, morale, productivity, grievances, absenteeism, turnover, and incentive systems—have become staples in training programs for supervisors and foremen in the United States and in delineating jobs and designing work flows across American industries (Perrow 1986; Porter et al. 1975). A new group of business school educators in western Europe has generated very similar programs tailored to take account of the historical and cultural imperatives of managers and workers in different countries. The growing integration of Europe's economies and the mobility of their citizen promises to add to the convergence in the ways and means of financing and directing economic organizations.

A fourth group has focused on industries and occupations as special and highly significant aspects of organizations' "external environments" and as subsets of America's systems of social stratification. Sociological studies of whole industries—their personnel and collective bargaining policies especially—have often informed public agencies' regulations, legislators' bills, and judges' decisions. Analyses of differences among industries and occupations have helped leaders in government, business, and labor unions to understand better the dynamics of industrial conflict; the character and effectiveness of organizations; and the complexities in identifying the effects of physical technology—capital—in the spinning of "webs of rules" (Kerr et al. 1973) that, for all of their de facto and even informal character, function very much like governance systems in the workaday world (Kalleberg and Berg 1987). In their most formal states, these systems—arbitration procedures, for example—sometime mature into what the U. S. Supreme Court in 1960, in a "trilogy" of cases that defined the role of arbitration in industrial relations, called "systems of industrial common law" (i.e., as legal systems virtually unto themselves). Otherwise, more implicitly, as with work rules that establish "how fast is fast, how fair is fair, and how reasonable is reasonable", the webs of rules define relationships and codes applicable to both employers and employees that afford a kind of lubrication to the mechanics of human interactions in bureaucratic machines, with their close tolerances, involving millions of persons in hundreds of thousands of workplaces. Sociological studies of the costs and benefits to employees and employers (and ultimately to the public) of work rules, for example, have helped transform emotionally charged arguments about "featherbedding", "soldiering," and "goldbricking" (all efforts to escape irksome chores) into coherent and constructive debates about nonmonetary dimensions of working conditions. Studies of work rules suggest that "informal organizations" within parent organizations are really not so much informal as they are what Durkheim long ago called "the noncontractual element of contracts"; sociologists have demonstrated that though these patterned, enduring, and bilaterally honored arrangements do not appear on an organization's wall charts, they are significant components of organizational life unto themselves, not mere shadows of more familiar and more palpable structures.

Meanwhile, the discoveries in international comparisons of data on grievances and strikes—that there are numerous short strikes and many grievances in the United States and few but long strikes and virtually no grievance procedures in western Europe for example—have led researchers, employers, and union leaders to appreciate the value of expeditious "on-site" bargaining relationships, on a day-to-day basis, such that emotional affect in disagreements may be drawn off and tensions relaxed before out-and-out conflicts disrupt production and social relations. It seems clear that these day-to-day adjustments and accommodations occur even as the efficacy of unions has declined in the United States and will likely wane in the "Euro" countries.

At the same time, the costs as well as the benefits of federal laws requiring that unions be democratic have helped us to make more realistic estimates about democratic arrangements' capacities to function as panaceas; democracy, for example, offers no guarantees against corruption, nor does it assure harmonious relations between parties to collective bargaining agreements. Sociologists have also documented a kind of (perhaps understandable) hypocrisy regarding democracy: Many lay observers and most labor columnists are delighted by unionists who vote to ratify contracts or to "decertify" their bargaining agents but are appalled by "strike votes."

Still another group of specialists have concentrated their attentions on worker satisfactions, dissatisfactions, and work experiences, by use of survey research designs that involve both periodic "snapshots" of different working Americans (and Japanese and west Europeans) and repeated observations of these same respondents, in "panel studies," over long time periods. These designs also make it possible to study "cohort effects," that is, the effects of reaching a given age in different time periods, each with their different qualities regarding a variety of social realities (Quinn et al.

1974). Thus there are significant differences, for example, in the experiences (and their attitudes about them) of workers, depending on whether they entered the labor force in 1960, 1970, 1980, or 1990. Sociologists can accordingly raise thoughtful questions about the implications, for public and private policies, of changing *social* definitions of aging, for example, in juxtaposition and contrast with essentially arbitrary public *policies* that fix eligibilities for a number of services and benefits on the basis of the chronological ages of individuals; not all those now 65 years old think, act, or want to be treated as a homogeneous class of senior citizens, nor have they had the same life histories, on average, as those who reached that age in 1940, 1960, or 1980.

Finally, the advent and continuing engagements of the civil rights movements have sparked the expenditure of a great deal of research effort on the comparative socioeconomic opportunities of men and women, and of minority group members in these groups (Jacobs 1989; Jaynes and Williams 1989). The findings by sociologists in these investigations have figured prominently in the drafting of legislation, legal suits, and employment policies, as well as in landmark civil rights decisions in courts at all levels.

In their work, as noted at the outset, a shrinking population of traditional industrial sociologists have drawn on work by sociologists in virtually every one of the profession's own major areas of interest with alacrity and have, in turn, seen much of their work inform the work of these other specialists. There has been similar intellectual commerce with social psychologists, industrial relations practitioners, and with full-time nonacademic social scientist practitioners in private enterprises, public agencies, universities, and research and other organizations in foreign lands, especially in the United Kingdom; Yugoslavia; Germany; Japan; France; Scandinavia; Canada; Italy; and what has, for so long, been called eastern Europe (Adams 1991; Barr, 1994; Freeman, 1994).

Industrial sociologists will likely grow in numbers in the years ahead, despite the growth of service sectors and information technology across the globe, as the global economy's structures will tend to be more related to multilateral regional pacts among nations with shared currencies, laws, and macroeconomic policies that will reshape the political, economic, and social characters of member nations.

REFERENCES

Adams, Roy J., ed. 1991 *Comparative Industrial Relations: Contemporary Research and Theory*. London: HarperCollins Academic.

Adorno, T. W., et al. 1950 *The Authoritarian Personality*. New York: Harper.

Barr, Nicholas, ed. 1994 *Labor Markets and Social Policy in Central and Eastern Europe*. New York: Oxford University Press.

Berg, Ivar 1970 *Education and Jobs: The Great Training Robbery*. New York: Praeger.

Brady, Robert A. 1943 *Business as a System of Power*. New York: Columbia University Press.

Cole, Robert E. 1989 *Strategies for Learning: Small Group Activities in American, Japanese, and Swedish Industry*. Berkeley: University of California Press.

Coleman, James 1982 *The Asymmetric Society*. Syracuse, N.Y.: Syracuse University Press.

Commons, John R., et al. 1926, 1935, 1936 *History of Labor in the United States*. New York: Macmillan.

Dunlop, John, et al. 1975 *Industrialism and Industrial Man Reconsidered*. Princeton, N.J.: Inter-University Study of Human Resources in National Development.

Freeman, Richard B., ed. 1994 *Working Under Different Rules*. New York: Russell Sage Foundation.

Hall, Richard 1987 *Organizations: Structures, Process and Outcomes*. Englewood Cliffs, N.J.: Prentice-Hall.

Homans, George 1950 *The Human Group*. New York: Harcourt, Brace.

Inkeles, Alex 1964 *What is Sociology?* Englewood Cliffs, N.J.: Prentice-Hall.

——, and David H. Smith 1974 *Becoming Modern: Industrial Change in Six Developing Countries*. Cambridge, Mass.: Harvard University Press.

Jacobs, Jerry 1989 *Revolving Doors: Sex Segregation and Women's Careers*. Stanford, Calif.: Stanford University Press.

Jaynes, Gerald David, and Robin M. Williams, Jr., eds. 1989 *A Common Destiny: Blacks and American Society*. Washington, D.C.: National Academy Press.

Jencks, Christopher, et al. 1979 *Who Gets Ahead? Determinants of Economic Success in America*. New York: Basic Books.

Kalleberg, Arne, ed. 1983 "Capital Labor and Work: Determinants of Work-Related Inequalities." (special issue). *International Sociology Journal*. August.

——, and Ivar Berg 1987 *Work and Industry Structures, Markets, and Processes*. New York: Plenum.

Kerr, Clark, John T. Dunlop, Fredrick Harbison, and Charles A. Meyers 1973 *Industrialization and Industrial Man*. London: Penguin.

Lincoln, James R., and Arne L. Kalleberg 1990 *Culture, Control and Commitment: A Study of Work Organization and Work Attitude in the U. S. and Japan*. Cambridge, U.K.: Cambridge University Press.

Moore, Barrington 1973 *Social Origins of Dictatorship and Democracy: Lord and Peasant in the Making of the Modern World*. Boston: Beacon Press.

Neumann, Franz 1942 *Behemoth: The Structure and Practice of National Socialism*. New York: Oxford University Press.

O'Toole, James, ed. 1974 *Work and the Quality of Life: Resource Papers for Work in America*. Cambridge, Mass.: MIT Press.

Perrow, Charles 1986 *Complex Organizations: A Critical Essay*. New York: McGraw-Hill.

Porter, Lyman W., et al. 1975 *Behavior in Organizations*. New York: McGraw-Hill.

Quinn, Robert P., et al. 1974 *Job Satisfaction: Is There a Trend?* Monograph 30. U.S. Department of Labor, Washington D.C.: U.S. Government Printing Office.

Stinchcombe, Arthur L. 1990 *Information and Organization*. Berkeley: University of California Press.

Thompson, James D. 1967 *Organizations in Action*. New York: McGraw-Hill.

Wilson, William J. 1987 *The Truly Disadvantaged: The Inner City, the Underclass and Public Policy*. Chicago: University of Chicago Press.

Yergin, Daniel, Joseph Stanislaw 1998 *The Commanding Heights*. New York: Simon and Schuster.

IVAR BERG

INDUSTRIALIZATION IN LESS DEVELOPED COUNTRIES

In the two and a half centuries since the Industrial Revolution in England, the process of industrialization has perhaps had more impact on all the nations of the world than any other complex set of forces. This process has not been uniformly introduced in all countries, nor has it occurred at the same time or at the same rate. Despite the common features of industrialization, these differences in its introduction and adoption have produced inequities among nations and among people on a scale never before experienced.

In describing various countries and regions of the world, certain terms have been adopted, first by official agencies such as the United Nations and national governments, and then more generally by scholars, journalists, and those interested in making sense of international relations. According to a now commonly used United Nations classification, *more developed countries* (MDCs, or developed countries) comprise all of Europe, North America (excluding Mexico), Japan, Australia, and New Zealand. Other countries (e.g., Singapore, Taiwan, and Israel) constitute recent additions, while many of the former Soviet-bloc countries (including the Russian Federation) are now in a developing, or "transition," phase. *Less developed countries* (LDCs, or developing countries) make up the remainder. The distinction between MDCs and LDCs mirrors the famous "North–South divide," a phrase coined by former West German chancellor Willy Brandt (1980) in his Commission's report to the World Bank. LDCs have also been referred to as the Third World, a term devised in post–World War II Europe to distinguish the politically nonaligned, underdeveloped nations of the world from the industrialized capitalist nations (First World) and the industrialized communist countries (Second World) (Worsley 1984, pp. 306–315).

In some cases, the underlying variable upon which these distinctions are based is economic, in other cases it is political, and in still others it is unspecified. However, generally speaking, MDCs are "rich" and LDCs are "poor." In 1996, the per capita gross national product (GNP) among all MDCs was US$25,870, while in the LDCs it was only US$1,183 (World Bank 1998, p. 38). The major explanation for this vast discrepancy is that MDCs are fully industrialized whereas LDCs are not. In 1994, the industrial market economies produced 81.4 percent of total world manufactures (World Bank 1997, p. 152). Considering that LDCs comprise 84 percent of the world's population (World Bank 1997, p. 36), their industrial output and, consequently, their standard of living are dramatically lower than in MDCs.

INDUSTRIALIZATION DEFINED

Industrialization is a complex process comprised of a number of interrelated dimensions (Hedley

1992, pp. 128–132). Historically, it represents a transition from an economy based on agriculture to one in which manufacturing represents the principal means of subsistence. Consequently, two dimensions of industrialization are the work that people do for a living (economic activity) and the actual goods they produce (economic output). Other dimensions include the manner in which economic activity is organized (organization), the energy or power source used (mechanization), and the systematic methods and innovative practices employed to accomplish work (technology). Table 1 specifies these dimensions and also lists indicators commonly used to measure them.

According to these indicators, MDCs are fully industrialized. On average, close to one-third of the labor forces in these countries are employed in industry (three-fifths work in the service sector); manufacturing makes up approximately one-quarter of the gross domestic product; the overwhelming majority of workers are employees of organizations; commercial energy consumption is high (5,100 kilograms of oil equivalent per capita); and professional and technical workers comprise on average 15 percent of the work force. Furthermore, more than 95 percent of all receipts for royalty and license fees are collected in the MDCs (Hedley 1992, pp. 128–133; United Nations Development Programme [UNDP] 1998; World Bank 1997). Industrial activity and the services associated with it constitute the major driving force and source of income in these more developed economies.

In contrast, none of the LDCs is fully industrialized as measured by these five dimensions of industrialization. Although manufacturing accounts for a significant proportion of many of these countries' total output, most do not achieve industrial status on any of the other dimensions. Manufacture in these countries is accomplished largely by traditional methods that have varied little over successive generations. Consequently, although manufacturing (transforming raw materials into finished goods) is an essential component of industrialization, there is considerably more to the process. Because industrialization is multidimensional, it cannot be measured by only one indicator.

In general, LDCs may be classified into three major groups according to how industrialized they are. The first and smallest group, referred to as *newly industrializing countries* (NICs), contains the most industrialized countries in that they achieve industrial status on at least two dimensions listed in Table 1. Located mainly in East Asia (e.g., South Korea, Malaysia, Thailand, Indonesia) and Latin America (e.g., Mexico, Brazil, Argentina, Venezuela), these eight NICs accounted for more than 40 percent of all merchandise exports from developing countries in 1995 (World Bank 1997, pp. 158–160). Although China and, to a lesser degree, India (because of their huge population bases) contribute significantly to the merchandise exports of LDCs, they have not developed their industrial infrastructures to the same extent as these NICs and therefore do not belong in the most industrialized group of LDCs.

A subgroup of NICs are high-income, oil-exporting nations (e.g., the United Arab Emirates, Qatar, Bahrain, Kuwait, and Saudi Arabia). Although they do not have large manufacturing bases, they do have significant proportions of their labor forces involved in industry (oil exploration and refining), a substantial component of professional and technical workers (many of them imported), and high per capita commercial energy consumption (World Bank 1998, pp. 34–35, 42–43). Although concentrated in just one industry, they are more industrialized than most other LDCs according to the criteria specified in Table 1. As a result of their petrodollars, they have acquired an industrial infrastructure that in other countries has taken many decades to establish.

The second, very large group of LDCs in terms of industrialization are those with a traditionally strong manufacturing base that also have a substantial agricultural component. Their economies straddle the agricultural and industrial modes of production. China and India are in this group, as are most of the non-European nations that form the Mediterranean basin. The goods that these LDCs predominantly manufacture (e.g., apparel, footwear, textiles, and consumer electronics) are essential to their own domestic markets and, because they are labor-intensive, also compete very well in the international market. In addition, they export natural resources and agricultural products. Other countries included in this semi-industrial group are most of the nations in Central and South America as well as many in South and East Asia.

Dimensions and Measures of Industrialization

1. Economic Activity
    a. Percentage of labor force in manufacturing
    b. Percentage of labor force in industry

2. Economic Output
    a. Manufacturing as a percentage of gross domestic product (GPD)
    b. Industry as a percentage of gross domestic product
    c. Gross output per employee in manufacturing
    d. Earnings per employee in manufacturing

3. Organization
    a. Wage and salary earners as a percentage of the labor force
    b. Number of manufacturing establishments employing fifty or more workers per capita

4. Mechanization
    a. Commercial energy consumption per capita
    b. Total cost of fuels and electrical energy per employee in manufacturing

5. Technology
    a. Percentage of professional and technical workers in labor force
    b. Registered patents in force per capita
    c. Registered industrial designs in force per capita

Table 1

The third and final group of LDCs are not industrialized on any of the five dimensions listed in Table 1. On average, less than 10 percent of their labor forces are employed in industry; most (76 percent) work in agriculture. Manufacturing contributes only 20 percent to their national economies; the bulk of income derives from natural resources and cash crops grown exclusively for export. Per capita gross national product is very low (US$215). Most of these nonindustrial LDCs are located in sub-Saharan Africa and Asia (UNDP 1998).

Of these groups of LDCs, the semi-industrial cluster of nations is by far the largest, constituting just over half the world's population. China and India alone make up two-thirds of this group. The second-largest group, comprising between 10 and 15 percent of the world population, is the nonindustrial countries; NICs (including high-income oil exporters) comprise less than 10 percent. Thus, approximately one-quarter of the world is fully industrialized, another 10 percent are industrializing, half are semi-industrial, and the remaining 15 percent are nonindustrial.

CORRELATES OF INDUSTRIALIZATION

Research has demonstrated that industrialization is directly related to national and individual income, urbanization, the development of an infrastructure (e.g., communication and transportation networks, education, and health and welfare programs), and the overall quality of life (Hedley 1992, pp. 133–146). These relationships occur because industrialization results in huge productivity gains, which in turn raise individual and national income. For example, when Britain was industrializing, total national income increased by more than 600 percent between 1801 and 1901 (Mitchell 1962, p. 366). In 1850, workers in industrial nations earned eleven times more than their counterparts in nonindustrial countries. Moreover, the advantages of industrialization have been cumulative: today per capita income is more than fifty-two times greater in developed than less developed countries (World Bank 1995, p. 53), thus magnifying what one author has termed a *Global Rift* (Stavrianos 1981). For a variety of reasons, the direct relationship between industrialization and income is continuing to increase.

In an annual survey of all countries in the world, the United Nations Development Programme (UNDP) measures "human development" based on the combination of three, admittedly crude, criteria: longevity, knowledge, and a decent standard of living. Table 2 provides a summary of its most recent results grouped by level of industrialization. Of the 174 countries examined, MDCs consistently scored at the top of all three dimensions that comprise human development, while LDCs, particularly the *least* developed (nonindustrial) countries, scored at the bottom of the scales. The composite Human Development Index ranged from a high of 0.960 for Canada to a low of 0.185 for Sierra Leone.

According to the UNDP (1998, p. 2):

Well over a billion people are deprived of basic consumption needs. Of the 4.4 billion people in developing countries, nearly three-fifths lack basic sanitation. Almost a third have no access to clean water. A quarter do not have adequate housing. A fifth of children do not attend school to grade 5. About a fifth do not have enough dietary energy and protein. Micronutrient deficiencies are even more widespread. Worldwide, 2 billion people are anaemic, including 55 million in industrial countries. In developing countries only a privileged minority has motorized transport, telecommunications and modern energy. Inequalities in consumption are stark. Globally, the 20% of the world's people in the highest-income countries account for 86% of total private consumption expenditures–the poorest 20% a minuscule 1.3%. More specifically, the richest fifth:

- *Consume 45% of all meat and fish, the poorest fifth 5%.*

- *Consume 58% of total energy, the poorest fifth less than 4%.*

- *Have 74% of all telephone lines, the poorest fifth 1.5%.*

- *Consume 84% of all paper, the poorest fifth 1.1%.*

- *Own 87% of the world's vehicle fleet, the poorest fifth less than 1%.*

Although annual GNP growth rates were higher overall in LDCs (4.1 percent) than MDCs (2.2 percent) between 1980 and 1995 (UNDP 1998, p. 210), the *least* developed of these LDCs did not fare so well. Not only were their GNP growth rates (2.1 percent) lower than those of MDCs, they were also significantly below their 1970–1995 average annual population growth rate (2.6 percent) (UNDP 1998, p. 209), which means that these countries are actually falling behind in what little progress they have made (Estes 1988). For example, of the 50 countries that comprise sub-Saharan Africa

(Cunningham 1998), two-thirds have been evaluated as "least developed," that is, targeted for priority international development assistance by the Nations Nations (UNDP 1998, p. 226). Consequently, some experts have openly questioned whether these countries will ever reach the level of industrialization and quality of life now enjoyed in the capitalist countries of the North (South Commission 1990, p. 19).

DEVELOPMENT GOALS: A VIEW FROM THE SOUTH

World War II marked the end of one era and the beginning of another. Among the more notable turning points following the war were the establishment of the United Nations (and its subsequent Universal Declaration of Human Rights), the onset of the Cold War between East and West, the emergence of many new independent states following the end of colonial rule, and the sudden realization that the income and development gaps between MDCs and LDCs were growing at a precipitous rate. In turn, these events sparked the generation of theories on international development (see, for example, *Modernization Theory, Convergence Theories, Dependency Theory, Global Systems Analysis*), the creation of organizations such as the International Monetary Fund (IMF) and the World Bank to design an open and stable global monetary system and to establish development and investment programs (IMF 1985), and the formation of various world commissions to address issues of global development (e.g., Brandt Report 1980; Pearson Report 1969; World Commission on Environment and Development 1987).

These activities were initiated largely in MDCs by Northern-based scholars and practitioners. Although there have been several prominent writers from the South who have viewed relations between MDCs and LDCs from a Southern perspective, (Cardoso and Faletto [1969] 1979; Said 1993; Sen 1990, 1992); it was not until 1990 that delegates from the South expressed their concerns in a representative and comprehensive manner. The South Commission (1990), initially formed in 1987, was comprised of twenty-eight members from twenty-six LDCs located on all continents of the South. Chaired by Julius K. Nyerere, former president of Tanzania, the South Commission "has its origins in a recognition within the South that developing

Human Development Index (HDI) by Level of Industrialization (1995)

HDI Measures	Industrial Countries[1] (N = 50)	Developing Countries (N = 124)	Least Developed Countries[2] (N = 43)	World (N = 174)
Life expectancy at birth (years)	74.2	62.2	51.2	63.6
Adult literacy rate (%)	98.6	70.4	49.2	77.6
Combined 1st; 2nd; and 3rd-level gross enrolment ratio (%)	82.8	57.5	36.4	61.6
Real GDP per capita (purchasing power parity US$)	16,337	3,068	1,008	5,990
Human Development Index	0.91	0.54	0.34	0.77

Table 2

SOURCE: Adapted from United Nations Development Programme (1998): p. 130.

NOTE: [1]Including the former Soviet-bloc nations.

NOTE: [2]Designated by the United Nations as LDCs targeted for priority international development assistance.

countries have many problems and much experience in common, but that no one in the South was responsible for looking at these things in a comprehensive manner, or at the lessons about appropriate development strategies which could be drawn from them" (Nyerere 1990, p. v). Consequently, *The Challenge to the South* (South Commission 1990) is an attempt to articulate from a Southern perspective what needs to be done "to help the peoples and governments of the South to be more effective in overcoming their numerous problems, in achieving their ambition of developing their countries in freedom, and in improving the lives and living conditions of their peoples" (Nyerere 1990, p. vi).

As part of its initial mandate, the South Commission (1990) first defined its development goals:

Development is a process of self-reliant growth, achieved through the participation of the people acting in their own interests as they see them, and under their own control. Its first objective must be to end poverty, provide productive employment, and satisfy the basic needs of all the people, any surplus being fairly shared. This implies that basic goods and services such as food and shelter, basic education and health facilities, and clean water must be available to all. In addition, development presupposes a democratic structure of government, together with its supporting individual freedoms of speech, organization,

and publication, as well as a system of justice which protects all the people from actions inconsistent with just laws that are known and publicly accepted. (p. 13–14)

To achieve these development goals, the South Commission (1990) identified three interrelated task areas:

1. *National self-reliance.* Individual countries of the South must realize their own unique potential through united and sustained efforts on the part of *all* people working toward clearly defined interim and long-term objectives. However, because there are external factors (e.g., the current structure of the global economy) that impede progress, solidarity among nations of the South is crucial.

2. *South–South cooperation.* "By joint endeavours to use to the maximum their different resources of expertise, capital, or markets, all would be able to address their separate and differing needs more effectively, thereby widening their development options . . . By exploiting these openings for co-operation, the South as a group can also become stronger in its negotiations with the North" (p. 16).

3. *An organized South for meaningful North–South negotiations.* In their relations with the North, the South must "establish common priorities in keeping with the

development interests of all," "share technical and negotiating expertise," and "hold constructive South–South discussions in advance of negotiations" (p. 21). Also, the South should actively support the growing initiative to establish international regulatory frameworks for the enforcement of global economic relations (including finance and trade) that are in the best interests of *all* nations and *all* peoples.

From this brief review of the report of the South Commission, it is possible to identify several key features of sustained development, *as perceived by those affected*:

- The South must play an active role in its own self-reliant development,

- Democratic grassroots participation is essential,

- Cooperation must occur at several levels (e.g., community, nation, and region),

- International regulatory codes must be renegotiated between North and South.

Although it is too soon to assess what results the recommendations of the South Commission will achieve, there are indications that some progress is being made. For example, President James Wolfensohn of the World Bank proposed a *Challenge of Inclusion* (1997) during a recent annual meeting of the Bank. Wolfensohn's "challenge" is similar to the objectives of the South Commission: "Our goal must be to reduce . . . disparities across and within countries, to bring more and more people into the economic mainstream, to promote equitable access to the benefits of development regardless of nationality, race, or gender" (p. 6). Moreover, the key elements of his challenge also resemble those offered by the South Commission:

- First and foremost, the governments and the people of developing countries must be in the driver's seat—exercising choice and setting their own objectives for themselves . . .

- Second, our partnership must be inclusive—involving bilaterals and multilaterals, the United Nations, the European Union, regional organizations, the World Trade Organization, labor organizations, NGOs [nongovernmental organizations], foundations, and the private sector . . .

- Third, we should offer our assistance to all countries in need. But we must be selective in how we use our resources. There is no escaping the hard fact: More people will be lifted out of poverty if we concentrate our assistance on countries with good policies than if we allocate it irrespective of the policies pursued . . .

- Finally, all of us in the development community must look at our strategies anew (Wolfensohn 1997, pp. 9–11).

Whether *The Challenge to the South* and *The Challenge of Inclusion* represent realistic steps toward meaningful North–South dialogue, cooperation, and beneficial action remains to be seen. However, if we do not tear down the many institutionalized structures of exclusion that are currently in place, all of us may eventually lose.

A NEW TECHNOLOGICAL REVOLUTION

Another set of challenges confronting LDCs is the new information and communications technology (ICT) revolution. Beginning in the late 1960s with breakthroughs in microelectronics and fiber-optic transmission (Diebold 1990; Gilder 1989), the ICT revolution is still very much in its genesis and is limited primarily to the developed countries (Hedley 1998). In 1994, just five G-7 nations (the United States, Japan, Germany, France, and United Kingdom) accounted for 80 percent of the information technology market, and American and Japanese corporations dominate the industry (Organization for Economic Co-Operation and Development [OECD] 1996, pp. 7, 37). Table 3 presents the stark facts of information communication by both traditional and modern means. Particularly with regard to telephones and personal computers, essential ingredients for electronic communication, the less developed, low- and middle-income countries are barely represented. In sub-Saharan African countries, for example, 51 percent of all telephones are located in the largest cities (7 percent in MDCs), and the average waiting time for a telephone connection is 15.2 years (Aggor 1998, p. 9). Inadequate infrastructure, low purchasing power, lack

Information Communication by National Level of Income

Means of Information Communication	High-Income Countries	Middle-Income Countries	Low= Income Countries	World
Daily newspapers per 1,000 people (1994)	303	62	12	98
Television sets/1,000 (1996)	611	252	47	211
Telephone main lines/1,000 (1996)	540	78	11	133
Mobile telephones/1,000 (1996)	131	8	0	28
Fax machines/1,000 (1995)	33.7	1.5	0.2	6.3
Personal computers/1,000 (1996)	224	2	..	50
Internet hosts/10,000 (July 1997)	203.5	2.4	0.1	34.8

Table 3

SOURCE: World Bank (1997): p. 286; World Bank (1999): p. 227.

of technological skills, and poor competition and regulation mean that particularly in the least developed countries, it will take years to realize much benefit from the ICT revolution (World Bank 1999, pp. 62–64). By some measures, the knowledge and information gap between MDCs and LDCs is larger than the income gap.

Various development scenarios have been proposed in anticipation of the impact of a full-scale ICT revolution (Hedley 1999; Howkins and Valantin 1997). The basic question addressed is whether this revolution will "help level the international playing field in terms of opportunities for social and economic development" or whether it will "lead to increasing disparities in incomes and information access" (Baranshamaje et al. 1995). In order to address this question, a high-powered workshop comprised of twenty-seven experts in technology and development from five MDCs and eight LDCs was convened in 1996 (Howkins and Valantin 1997). Sponsored by the U.N. Commission on Science and Technology for Development and the Canadian-based International Development Research Centre, the delegates attempted to establish the parameters of worldwide ICT development. Four possibilities emerged, based on the inclusivity and openness of the global community and the proactive or reactive responses of individual countries (Howkins and Valentin):

1. *The march of follies.* "The global community is exclusive and fragmented," and "most developing countries respond only partially and reactively to acquisition and use of ICTs." In this scenario, the global rift between MDCs and LDCs widens.

2. *Cargo cult.* "The global community is inclusive and supportive," but "most developing countries respond only partially and reactively to the acquisition and use of ICTs." This scenario results in cultural imperialism in which a few transnational corporations dominate the ICT industry. Developing countries have little input.

3. *Netblocs.* "The global system is exclusive and fragmented"; however "developing countries take an active approach to the acquisition and use of ICTs and develop a complete set of policies." This scenario produces regional groups or blocs based on shared cultures, religions, and languages. "At the end of the scenario period, the blocs have achieved much. They have created information societies and economies that reflect their own histories, traditions, cultures, and ways of doing business. But their insistence on their own regional laws, regulations, and trading principles creates centripetal forces that lead to a highly unstable situation."

4. *Networld.* "The global community is inclusive and supportive," and "developing countries have a complete and proactive set of policies toward the acquisition and use of ICTs." This is a global village scenario in which corporations from developed countries operate out of "enlightened self-interest as they seek ways of working with companies and institutions in the developing world . . . Their awareness is matched by a realization in

developing countries that they should work with global corporations to create their own national information society and economy."

The workshop delegates did not attempt to predict which of these four development scenarios was most probable. Rather, based on their two sets of parameters, they indicated the various possibilities, what would be required to reach each, and some of the development consequences that would likely flow from them. In other words, if the global community is not inclusive and supportive, and if developing countries do not develop a complete and proactive set of policies toward the acquisition and use of ICTs, then we may expect various consequences that are inimical to comprehensive and sustained development worldwide. As Herbert Simon (1987, p. 11) has observed:

Technological revolutions are not something that "happen" to us. We make them, and we make them for better or for worse. Our task is not to peer into the future to see what computers will bring us, but to shape the future we want to have–a future that will create new possibilities for human learning, including, perhaps most important of all, new possibilities for learning to understand ourselves.

Thus, if we wish to take up *The Challenge of Inclusion*, there are certain courses of action to follow. If we do not take up this challenge, then, according to the founding editor of *Scientific American*, the very survival of our species is at stake (Piel 1992).

REFERENCES

Aggor, Adolphine Y. 1998 *African Development via the Internet: A New Wave or More of Same?* Master's thesis, University of Victoria, Canada.

Baranshamaje, Etienne, et al. 1995 *Increasing Internet Connectivity in Sub-Saharan Africa: Issues, Options, and World Bank Group Role.* Available on the Internet at http://www.worldbank.org/aftdr/connect/incrint.htm.

Brandt Report 1980 *North-South: A Program for Survival.* Report of the Independent Commission on International Development Issues. Cambridge, Mass.: MIT Press.

Cardoso, F. H., and E. Faletto (1969) 1979 *Dependency and Development in Latin America.* Berkeley: University of California Press.

Cunningham, R. 1998 *Sub-Sahara Africa: Links to Sites by Country.* Available on the Internet at http://www.staff.uiuc.edu/~rcunning/ssa.htm.

Diebold, John 1990 "The Fiber-Optics Breakthrough: The Communications Society." In John Diebold, ed., *The Innovators: The Discoveries, Inventions, and Breakthroughs of Our Time.* New York: Truman Talley Books/Plume.

Estes, Richard J. 1988 *Trends in World Social Development: The Social Progress of Nations, 1970–1987.* New York: Praeger.

Gilder, George 1989 *Microcosm: The Quantum Revolution in Economics and Technology.* New York: Simon and Schuster.

Hedley, R. Alan 1992 *Making a Living: Technology and Change.* New York: HarperCollins.

—— 1998 "Technological Diffusion or Cultural Imperialism? Measuring the Information Revolution." *International Journal of Comparative Sociology* 39(2):198–212.

—— 1999 "The Information Age: Apatheid, Cultural Imperialism, or Global Village?" *Social Science Computer Review* 17(1):78–87.

Howkins, John, and Robert Valantin (eds.) 1997 *Development and the Information Age: Four Global Scenarios for the Future of Information and Communication Technology.* Ottawa: International Development Research Centre and the United Nations Commission on Science and Technology for Development. Available on the Internet at http://www.idrc.ca/books/835/index.html.

International Monetary Fund (IMF) 1985 *The Role and Function of the International Monetary Fund.* Washington, D.C.: International Monetary Fund.

Mitchell, B. R. 1962 *Abstract of British Historical Statistics.* Cambridge, U.K.: Cambridge University Press.

Nyerere, Julius K. 1990 "Chairman's Preface." In South Commission, *The Challenge to the South: The Report of the South Commission.* Oxford, U.K.: Oxford University Press.

Organization for Economic Co-operation and Development (OECD) 1996 *Information Technology Outlook 1995.* Paris: Organisation for Economic Co-operation and Development.

Pearson Report 1969 *Partners in Development: Report of the Commission on International Development.* New York: Praeger.

Piel, Gerard 1992 *Only One World: Our Own to Make and Keep.* New York: Freeman.

Said, Edward W. 1993 *Culture and Imperialism.* New York: Knopf.

Sen, Amartya K. 1990 *The Political Economy of Hunger.* Oxford, U.K.: Clarendon Press.

—— 1992 *Inequality Reexamined.* New York: Russell Sage Foundation.

Simon, Herbert A. 1987 "The Steam Engine and the Computer: What Makes Technology Revolutionary?" *Computers and People* 36(11–12):7–11.

South Commission 1990 *The Challenge to the South: The Report of the South Commission.* Oxford, U.K.: Oxford University Press.

Stavrianos, L. S. 1981 *Global Rift: The Third World Comes of Age.* New York: William Morrow.

United Nations Development Programme (UNDP) 1998 *Human Development Report 1998.* New York: Oxford University Press.

Wolfensohn, James D. 1997 "The Challenge of Inclusion." Address to the Board of Governors, Hong Kong, China, September 23, 1997.

World Bank 1995 *World Development Report 1995.* Oxford, U.K.: Oxford University Press.

—— 1997 *1997 World Development Indicators.* Washington, D.C.: International Bank for Reconstruction and Development, World Bank.

—— 1998 *1998 World Bank Atlas.* Washington, D.C.: International Bank for Reconstruction and Development, World Bank.

—— 1999 *World Development Report: Knowledge for Development.* Oxford, U.K.: Oxford University Press.

World Commission on Environment and Development 1987 *Our Common Future.* Oxford, U.K.: Oxford University Press.

Worsley, Peter 1984 *The Three Worlds: Culture and World Development.* London: Weidenfeld and Nicolson.

R. Alan Hedley

INFANT AND CHILD MORTALITY

Mortality affects the volume of a population. Deaths are not equally distributed among all groups; rather many unique patterns have been identified. For example, the probability of dying is high among both extremes of a population's age structure—the very young and the very old. As a general pattern, the death rate is relatively high at age zero, reaches a minimum in the range from ages ten to fifteen, and then begins to increase gradually with increasing age. This increase becomes marked after age forty-five or fifty (Coale 1965).

Infant and child mortality are important because the largest mortality risk differentials between a society with high mortality and one with low mortality are always found within infancy and childhood. Because infant and child mortality are often related to general levels of health and living conditions, they are often thought of as measures by which nations can gauge their current level of socioeconomic development and societal cohesiveness. Comparisons can then be made with past mortality estimates, along with those of neighboring nations, allowing a country to make projections concerning its future development and public policy programs. Assuming this general precept, researchers investigate historical mortality trends in an attempt to isolate general patterns of infant and child mortality. The goal is to provide information for policy makers, raise standards of living for residents of a nation, thereby reducing early childhood mortality.

MEASURES AND DATA SOURCES

The *infant mortality rate* (IMR) is defined by demographers as the probability that a newborn infant will die before it reaches its first birthday. This probability is generally computed by calculating the ratio of the number of infant deaths under one year of age in a given year per number of births in that given base year. This approach is termed a *period* IMR because it only utilizes data from one year to arrive at its estimate. This method is not entirely accurate in that it 1) utilizes infant deaths *of* those born in the preceding year and 2) misses those infant deaths that occur in the following year. If the number of births and deaths does not change drastically from year to year, then this method results in a close approximation of an infant's probability of survival to age one (Shryock and Siegel 1976).

A more accurate measure of infant mortality is a ratio that involves the use of infant birth and death data for two years. In this instance, a researcher is able to calculate more precisely the true probability of infant death by identifying all infant births in the base year of interest and linking them to their respective infants' deaths at less than one year of age in *both* the base year and the following year. This method is referred to as the *cohort* IMR for a given year and population. Infant mortality rates are expressed in terms of infant deaths per 1,000 live births (Shryock and Siegel 1976).

In order to capture different causes that are known to affect the timing of infant deaths within the first year of life, researchers often decompose infant mortality into various components. *Neonatal mortality* usually refers to deaths of infants under 28 days of age, whereas *postneonatal mortality* involves the deaths of infants aged 28 to 364 days. Due to the large proportion of pregnancies that result in fetal deaths, and the existing similarity between the causes of death for fetuses and for neonates, other complementary measures have been constructed. *Fetal mortality* refers to fetal deaths at a gestational age greater than 28 weeks, and *perinatal mortality* is defined as fetal mortality plus infant deaths at less than 7 days of age. All corresponding rates are constructed in much the same manner as the IMR, including the use of either the period or cohort method of estimation. For both the fetal and perinatal mortality rates, researchers usually include the number of fetal or perinatal deaths (whichever may be the rate of interest) within the denominator of the rate along with the number of births for the population of interest (Shryock and Siegel 1976).

Conventionally, the number of deaths that occur among children aged one to four is a general measure of *child mortality*. In some cases, though, the child mortality rate may include the IMR (in which case it takes into account all deaths under five years of age). As a rule, most researchers interested in child mortality separate out infant mortality in order to arrive at a clearer picture of the specific causes of death that affect children who survive infancy. Child mortality rates are generally calculated by dividing the number of deaths of children aged one to four by the total number of children aged one to four in the population and multiplying by a 1,000 (Shryock and Siegel 1976).

The most common source of data on infant and child mortality in more developed countries (MDCs) is national vital statistics registries, which were established in some countries as early as the beginning of the eighteenth century (e.g., Sweden). Researchers are able to access detailed birth and death records for both infants and children and analyze their trends and patterns. Throughout the world, the most stable data on infant and child mortality have come from those countries with established vital registration programs. For those MDCs that do not have adequate systems of vital registration and for the majority of less developed countries (LDCs) that do not have a vital statistics system in place, other techniques exist for estimating infant and child mortality (Palloni 1981). In most of these countries, population censuses and surveys of a sample of the total population are utilized to indirectly estimate mortality rates and trends (Hill 1991). Techniques developed in the late 1960s and early 1970s have been refined and improved upon in a variety of ways (United Nations 1990). Most techniques involve the use of birth histories collected from women in the population.

EPIDEMIOLOGIC TRANSITION AND INFANT AND CHILD MORTALITY

Early research on infant mortality revealed an array of factors that presumably led to infant mortality declines in certain countries, specifically certain Western European MDCs. The experiences of these nations are the basis for a set of general hypotheses regarding the decline of infant mortality. These nations serve as test cases because of the nature of the available data and the familiarity of researchers with them. Ideas have been developed concerning the relationship among certain economic, social, and technological developments and the reduction of adult, childhood, and infant mortality. Epidemiologic transition theory, as elucidated by Omran (1971, 1977), gives researchers a theoretical framework for understanding these processes as they have occurred throughout different time periods and within different nations. This theory outlines several stages that specific nations have moved through on their way to their current mortality patterns. Many have used this theory to investigate current infant mortality levels among various countries and within specific ones (Frenk et al. 1989; Pampel and Pillai 1986).

In applying the precepts of epidemiologic transition theory to the case of infant mortality, researchers have used diverse historical sources. Epidemiologic transition theory outlines three stages through which various Western European nations moved through as they advanced toward a higher state of economic and technological development. The first two stages, termed the Era of Pestilence and Famine and the Era of Receding

Pandemics, characterize most of human existence. Within these eras, infant and child mortality were relatively high and primarily due to the prevalence of infectious disease. In the third stage, the Age of Degenerative and Man-Made Diseases, infectious diseases receded and came under medical control. Infant and child mortality fell accordingly. Other causes of death now became important, and interest in them rose. In this sense, infectious infant mortality is currently associated with countries that are less developed and populations within countries that live at disadvantaged socioeconomic levels (Omran 1971, 1977).

To better understand changes in infant mortality according to epidemiologic transition theory, researchers must be able to access data that detail the cause of infant mortality death. But as has been noted, very few countries possess the data repositories, either current and past, to adequately examine infant mortality declines and their component causes. The use of neonatal and postneonatal IMRs were one way of moving forward with these types of studies without having the necessary data for detailed analyses. Neonatal and postneonatal mortality became associated with cause-of-death groupings according to general preconceived notions of etiologic mechanisms.

Bourgeois-Pichat (1951) presumed that infectious infant mortality was primarily due to environmental factors that were wholly amenable without medical intervention. This category was termed "exogenous" infant mortality (e.g., infectious, parasitic, and respiratory diseases), while "endogenous" infant mortality was defined as those causes of infant death that were primarily due to natal and antenatal factors (e.g., congenital malformations, prematurity). Neonatal mortality became a proxy for endogenous causes of death while postneonatal mortality was associated with exogenous mortality. All that was now minimally required to continue analyses of infant mortality transitions was information on the timing of infant death (Bogue 1969; Bouvier and Van der Tak 1976). Although these conceptual distinctions probably held true throughout most of human history, debates exist as to the current validity of these conceptualizations and the continued value of their use. The introduction of neonatal technologies and other factors in MDCs have led to further discussion and reconceptualization (Sowards 1997).

INFANT AND CHILD MORTALITY THROUGH HISTORY

Among historians such different academic spheres as demography, sociology of the family, and public health, there is an interesting debate concerning the timing and factors that have led to a decline in infant and childhood mortality. There are some interpretative similarities that may offer us a foundation with which to begin this discussion.

Historically, the size of the human population remained fairly constant until the first half of the eighteenth century. One hypothesis states that until then, although periods of low mortality were common, a population was still vulnerable to famines and epidemics, thus rendering population size stable. Before the Neolithic period (c. 9500 b.c.), it is estimated that infants had a 50 percent chance of surviving to adulthood (Stockwell and Groat 1984). It is thought that the first real decline in infant and child mortality came after the Neolithic revolution, when agriculture and animal domestication became more common, despite the increased spread of infectious diseases among now clustered and sedentary populations (Creighton-Zollar 1993). Within the framework of demographic transition theory, the staggering growth of the human population registered during the last 250 years is mainly explained by a combination of significant decrements in mortality and constant fertility rates (Kitagawa 1977; Stolnitz 1955).

Interestingly, some historians have found a link between the decline in infant mortality and the greater significance of children within the family organization. In the second half of the twentieth century, a discussion about the history of the family properly began with Philippe Ariès's *L'Enfant en la Vie Familiale sous L'Ancient Régime* (Van de Walle and Van de Walle 1990). Ariès suggests that the recognition of childhood as an independent stage of the life cycle occurred first during the sixteenth and seventeenth centuries. Other family historians have argued that infant mortality was so high that parents preferred not to "invest too much emotional capital in such ephemeral beings" (quoted by Van de Walle and Van de Walle 1990, p. 151).

For these authors, the British aristocracy's movement toward the increased domesticity of women redefined the role of the mother within the domestic economy. British aristocratic mothers now spent an increasing significant proportion of their time with their infants and children, forming strong parent–child bonds, which had previously been weak. These mothers were the first social group to conceive of a child as a treasure above and beyond the small utilitarian value children may have previously possessed (Van de Walle and Van de Walle 1990).

These authors suggest that from the seventeenth through the nineteenth centuries, the interest in children became increasingly mother-centered. Feelings of empowerment over the health and well-being of infants and children rose to such a level that women began demanding that the medical community and government pay more attention to children. Children thus passed from a "private" realm of familial responsibility to a "public" one, withe the community now expressing a vested interest in improving the health and well-being of children. These historical changes in the power structure of the family may have operated in conjunction with various other social and economic factors that led to the decreasing rate of infant and child mortality among Western developed countries (Van de Walle and Van de Walle 1990).

TWENTIETH-CENTURY MORTALITY TRENDS IN DEVELOPED COUNTRIES

Developed and developing countries are comprised of different population histories worthy of individual historical analysis, even though the only available and reliable documents that allow the reconstruction of demographic transitions are found in Europe. For some local Western European populations, studies have revealed that mortality levels decreased slightly between 1840 and 1860, but several scholars agree that the radical decline of mortality among the MDCs took place during the period 1880–1910 or even up to 1930 (Kitigawa 1977; Preston 1992; Stolnitz 1956). Although it is generally believed that this decrease in mortality levels was primarily due to a reduction of deaths during childhood, the causes of that change are still nonetheless a matter of controversy.

Epidemiologic transition theory's main argument is that the socioeconomic development achieved by those countries was fundamental in the reduction of mortality (Omran 1971). From this perspective, socioeconomic factors such as improved health and hygienic habits, diet and standards of living, were the main determinants of the transition from high to low mortality in Western nations. The sanitary revolution played an auxiliary role within this process of transition. Some other scholars suggest that although the improvement of economic conditions in Western nations was important, but this was more a permissive element than a precipitating factor. For them, the introduction of hygienic measures that helped to control communicable diseases was the leading cause of the decreased mortality rate (Preston 1992; Preston and Haines 1991; Spiegelman 1956; Stolnitz 1956).

According to Stolnitz (1956), in the mid-1800s reliable estimates for France and England show that real per capita income was rising rapidly but declines in mortality were still rather negligible. On the contrary, when mortality declined clearly after 1870, the West had already experienced a diverse set of economic circumstances. For instance, in France and Sweden the decrease in mortality appears to have occurred at a time when economic growth was slower than in earlier decades, while in Great Britain standards of living may have been slightly declining. Simultaneously, great changes occurred in the field of bacteriology, including the discoveries of Pasteur, and the large-scale public health programs were implemented. At the end of the nineteenth century in England, the main reason for the reduction in mortality levels was due to the lower prevalence of diseases resulting from these health innovations.

A study of the importance of different causes of death during the transition to a lower mortality rate shows interesting findings (Preston and Nelson 1974). Among 165 local populations (from 43 countries around the world) from the period 1861–1964, approximately 60 percent of the total decline in death rates was attributed to declining mortality from infectious diseases—25 percent due to influenza, pneumonia, and bronchitis; 10 percent due to respiratory tuberculosis; 10 percent due to diarrheal diseases; 15 percent due to other infectious and parasitic diseases; another 20 percent was attributed to a decrease in vascular diseases.

Many Western countries experienced a steady decline in mortality rates after 1930. Spiegelman (1956) suggests that during the period 1930–1950, these nations were experiencing a reduction in mortality at all stages of life. According to the author, from 1946 to 1954 most countries of Western Europe achieved a reduction of up to 33 percent in their IMRs. In Table 1 we reconstruct infant mortality trends for some selected countries during a period of forty-five years. In 1948, Sweden already had a relatively low IMR (23.2 per 1,000); by 1993 it had decreased to 4.8

Japan is a striking case. Japan, Australia, and New Zealand are included in Table 1 among the developed countries following the suggestion of the World Bank (1983), although they do not share the historical experience and culture of the Western countries included in the same group. The reduction of infant mortality has been explained by specific health measures first taken during the U.S. occupation after World War II and continued later by the Japanese government. During the 1930s, life expectancy at birth (life expectancy at birth represents the average number of years to be lived for a newborn, given a specific pattern of mortality in a country in a given moment) in Japan was similar to that in Western countries at the end of the nineteenth century. However, between 1948–1950 and 1951–1953, the increase in life expectation was about 5.5 years at age 0, 4 to 5 years at age 15, and 2 years at age 45. This was far and away the greatest average annual increase in demographic history (Stolnitz 1956). Table 1 shows a Japanese decrease in infant mortality from 61.7 per 1,000 in 1948 to 30.4 in 1960. This accelerated decrease continued to 13.1, 7.4, and 4.3 in 1970, 1980 and 1993, respectively, giving Japan the lowest IMR in the world.

In the United States, child mortality had been declining in the two decades before 1900 for the total population, although the decline was greater among whites than among blacks. It is difficult to estimate the magnitude of this differential because of data problems (Preston and Haines 1991). Preston and Haines find that between 1899 and 1900, 88 percent of deaths among those under age 15 were children aged 0 to 4 and 59 percent of these were infant deaths. Regarding the three main causes of infant mortality, 25 percent of deaths were due to gastrointestinal diseases, 20 percent to respiratory diseases (e.g., influenza, pneumonia, and bronchitis), and 27 percent to malformations and a wide array of causes, such as premature birth, debility and atrophy, inanition, and

hydrocephalus. The main causes of child mortality (deaths below age five) were basically the same, but with a slightly different distribution: 21 percent were due to gastrointestinal diseases, 23 percent respiratory diseases, and 20 percent to malformations.

In comparing eighteen developed countries, Pampel and Pillai (1986) found the United States to have a relatively high IMR despite its leading economic position. Indeed, the United States has the highest IMR among developed countries. Table 1 shows that in 1948 the American IMR was half that of Japan. By 1993, however, that ratio had reversed; for every Japanese infant death there were 2 in the United States. Although this 2:1 does not exist between the United States and other developed countries, most of the countries shown in the table had higher IMR rates than the United States before World War II and have achieved significant declines since that time.

To briefly highlight some other developed countries, we take Spain as an example. According to Spiegelman (1956), acute infectious diseases were not totally under control there before World War II. This country began the forty-five-year period covered in Table 1 with an IMR of 70 in 1948. Infant mortality has continually decreased, reaching 6.7 in 1993.

Another case that may be worthy of highlighting is that of Germany, which is included in the group of Western countries because of its reunification and the general adoption of a market economy. Interestingly, in 1948 the Democratic Republic (East Germany) had a considerably higher IMR than the Federal Republic (West Germany), 94.0 versus 70.1. East Germany's rate was slightly higher in 1960, but in 1970 the trend reversed. In later years, both countries experienced equal rates. In 1993, unified Germany's IMR was 5.8, the third lowest of this selected group of developed countries.

TWENTIETH-CENTURY MORTALITY TRENDS IN EASTERN EUROPE

It is difficult to obtain comparable data for Eastern Europe; Table 1 shows only a few examples. In Romania in 1948 the IMR was particularly high. From 1948 to 1960 the IMR was almost halved, decreasing from 142.7 to 75.7. That pace of decrease could not be sustained, and in 1993 it

Infant Mortality Rates for some Selected Countries and Years

	Infant Mortality Rate				
	1948	1960	1970	1980	1993
Developed Countries					
Canada	44.4	27.3	18.8	10.4	6.3
United States	32.0	26.0	20.0	12.5	8.4
Japan	61.7	30.4	13.1	7.4	4.3
Austria	76.2	37.5	25.9	14.1	6.5
France	55.9	27.4	18.2	9.9	6.5
Germany					5.8
Democratic Republic	94.0	38.8	18.5	12.1	
Federal Republic	70.1	33.8	23.6	12.6	
Italy	72.1	43.9	29.6	14.3	7.1
Spain	70.0	43.7	26.5	11.1	6.7
Sweden	23.2	16.6	11.0	6.7	4.8
United Kingdom	36.0	22.5	18.4	12.2	6.3
Australia	27.8	20.2	17.9	11.0	6.1
New Zealand	27.5	22.6	16.7	30.2	7.2
Eastern Europe					
Czechoslovakia	83.5	23.5	22.1	16.6	8.5
Poland	110.7	56.1	33.2	21.2	16.2
Romania	142.7	75.7	49.4	29.3	23.3
Yugoslavia	102.1	87.7	55.5	32.8	21.9
Latin America					
Argentina	69.5	62.4	58.9	33.2	22.9
Bolivia	131.3	74.3	—	124.4*	75.0
Brazil	—	—	—	70.6*	47.0
Costa Rica	90.4	74.3	61.5	20.2	13.7
Cuba	40.1	35.4	38.7	19.6	9.4
El Salvador	100.4	76.3	66.6	42.0	44.0
Mexico	101.7	74.2	68.5	53.0*	34.0
Peru	109.0	92.1	64.6	98.6*	74.9
Venezuela	97.8	53.9	49.3	27.7*	22.0
Africa					
Egypt	138.6	109.3	116.3	76.0	117.0
Kenya	—	—	81.2	80.2*	71.0
Liberia	—	—	159.2	132.5*	200.0
Mauritius	186.2	70.9	58.5	28.4*	19.9
Mozambique	48.8	34.2	41.6	153.5*	118.0
South Africa				83.3	53.0
Asian	77.1	59.6	36.4		
Black	133.2	128.6	132.6		
White	36.0	29.6	21.6		
Asia					
Afghanistan	—	—	—	193.8*	163.0
Bangladesh	—	—	—	128.2*	91.0
China	—	—	—	39.3*	44.0
India	130.1	86.5	122.0	113.9	74.0
Iraq	97.6	17.7	19.7	77.1*	127.0
North Korea	—	—	—	54.1*	28.8
South Korea	—	—	—	29.7*	12.3
Philippines	114.4	73.1	60.0	50.6	40.0
Saudi Arabia	—	—	—	66.1*	29.0
Singapore	80.8	34.8	19.7	11.7	4.7
Sri Lanka	92.1	56.8	45.1	34.4	16.5

Table 1

SOURCE: United Nations (1979, 1982, 1987, and 1996).

NOTE: *Data from 1983.

reached 23.3, the highest IMR among the Eastern European countries shown.

In the cases of Poland and Yugoslavia, both countries had a high IMR in the immediate postwar period (110.7 and 102.1, respectively). Despite its lower starting level, Yugoslavia consistently experienced higher rates thereafter: 87.7 in 1960, 55.5 in 1970, 32.8 in 1980, and 21.9 in 1993, whereas in Poland such rates have been 56.1, 33.2, 21.2, and 16.2 for the same years.

In 1948, Czechoslovakia had the lowest IMR among the Eastern bloc countries shown in Table 1, but it was still higher than that of Western countries. The decrease observed from 1948 to 1960 is very significant: from 83.5 to 23.5 in twelve years. This pace decelerated but continued to decline. By 1993, it had achieved an IMR similar to that of the United States: 8.5 deaths 1,000/ live births.

TWENTIETH-CENTURY MORTALITY TRENDS IN DEVELOPING COUNTRIES

In the developing countries of Latin America, Asia, and Africa, reduction in mortality levels began around the beginning of the twentieth century. Scholars have found only fragmented information to reconstruct the demographic history of such countries. They can affirm, however, that the pace of declining mortality was slow until 1940 and accelerated after World War II (Kitagawa 1977; Meslé and Vallin 1996; Preston and Nelson 1974). According to Stolnitz (1956), the decline in mortality in developing countries during the postwar period, which was highly accelerated, has no parallels in the Western experience. The common explanation, found in numerous studies (Arriaga 1970; Kitigawa 1977; Preston 1976; Stolnitz 1956), is that access to medical innovations coming from developed countries and the implementation of specific programs of disease control were the main cause of the mortality reduction, especially in infant mortality.

Since the changes in those regions have not been uniform, currently there is a convergence of the mortality patterns in developing countries, whereas in the developed areas there is a marked divergence (Meslé and Vallin 1996). Indeed, trends of mortality just described for developed countries show variations, but among developing countries such heterogeneity is even greater. It would be impossible in this space to describe the mosaic of infant mortality experiences in developing countries; however, we can point out some major tendencies and outstanding cases during the forty-five years period covered by Table 1.

In order to understand the scope of differences among developing countries, it is important to consider a general characteristic of populations with high mortality: The younger the age, the larger the absolute change in mortality rates (Arriaga 1970). At the beginning of this transition toward a low mortality pattern, drastic changes are observed in infant and child mortality among different populations. For many developing countries, infant and child mortality trends throughout history cannot be known because there are no available data. Although this issue will be discussed below, usually the more socioeconomically disadvantaged countries are the ones for whom the data are lacking.

Latin America. During the 1930s Latin America had a high mortality pattern. For instance, a newborn baby had less than a 50 percent chance of living to the age of thirty; consequently, no country had a life expectancy more than forty years at birth (Arriaga 1970). The main decline was registered between 1940 and 1960. The largest decline could be found during the 1940s; there was a slower pace of decrease in the 1950s (Arriaga 1989; Camposortega Cruz 1989a).

Brazil and Mexico are the two most highly populated countries in Latin America, and they experienced similar processes of industrialization up until the 1970s. Brazil had a military government and Mexico did not; however, both have high economic inequality, possibly Brazil the more so. Unfortunately there are no data available for Brazil prior to the 1980s, but Table 1 shows that its IMR was higher than that of Mexico in both 1983 and 1993. Mexico's IMR decreased by 25 percent between 1948 and 1960; it continued to decline even in the midst of a drastic economic recession that began in the 1980s. By 1993, the persistently high rate had been reduced to 34.0 infant deaths per 1,000 live-births; the Brazilian IMR was 47.0 in that year.

Argentina provides an example of early industrialization as well as early demographic transition in the region. During the immediate postwar period, this country had an IMR similar to those of several Western countries (69.5 in 1948); considering this fact, the rate in 1993 (22.9) was relatively high, even higher than the IMR (22.0) of Venezuela, a country that had a rate 30 percent higher than Argentina in 1948.

El Salvador, Bolivia, and Peru, some of the poorest countries in the region, had high IMRs in 1948. For example, in El Salvador a tenth of all infants died in 1948, but this rate had decreased 25 percent by 1960 to 76.3 infant deaths per 1,000 live births. This pace of decline slowed in subsequent years, reaching 42.0 in 1980. However, by 1993 this indicator of general well-being had reversed, and the IMR had increased slightly to 44.0, perhaps because of severe economic conditions during the 1980s.

In Bolivia, if the data in Table 1 are correct, the decrease in infant mortality between 1948 and 1960 was spectacular: from 131.3 deaths to 74.3 deaths per 1,000 within twelve years. Information for the 1970s is unavailable. In 1983 the rate was again high (124.4), but ten years later it had dropped to 75.0. These significant shifts give rise to concerns about the quality of the data. In any case, the IMR in 1993 was higher than the Salvadorian rate and similar only to the Peruvian one.

Bolivia and Peru have the highest IMRs among the selected countries (75.0 and 74.9, respectively). In this region, such a rate might be surpassed only by Haiti, for which information is not available. Interestingly, Peru had a decrease in its IMR from 1948 (109.0) to 1970 (64.6). But in 1983 the IMR was even higher that it had been twenty years earlier: In 1983 it was 98.6, up from 92.1 in 1960. Although the IMR had decreased to 74.9 in 1993, Peru still has one of the highest rates of infant mortality in all of Latin America.

In contrast, Cuba and Costa Rica have the lowest and the second lowest IMRs, respectively. The public health systems in both countries have good reputations throughout the region. Costa Rica shows a steady decrease from 1948, when its IMR was 90.4. By 1970, it had declined 30 percent, reaching 61.5. Contradicting Arriaga (1989) and Camposortega Cruz (1989a), this country achieved a steeper decrease in infant mortality during the 1970s: In 1970 the rate was 61.5 and in 1980, 20.2, showing a decrease of 33 percent. In 1993, the Costa Rican IMR was 13.7.

The Cuban IMR was already the lowest in the region in 1948 (40.1) among those countries shown in Table 1. Up until 1970 there was only a small and unsteady decrease to (38.7). During the 1970s and afterward, the country achieved significant decreases: The rate reached 19.6 in 1980 and 9.4 in 1993. The decrease in infant mortality has been one of the main goals and achievements of the Cuban health system, despite the country's unfavorable economic situation. Cuba now has the lowest IMR in Latin America, being only slightly higher than that of Czechoslovakia and the United States.

Asia. Infant mortality rates in Asia are quite diverse. As regards of India, Jain and Visaira (1988) argue that even though several studies suggest that the infant mortality rate in 1920 was 240 per 1,000 live births, this might have been understated, and the IMR could have been between 200 and 225 during the 1940s. This finding is in contrast to the estimations of Arriaga (1989) and other researchers. Using different sources of information and techniques, Jain and Visaira construct a trend of infant mortality with higher rates than those shown in Table 1, with the rates coinciding only since the 1970s. Jain and Visaira (1988) and Arriaga (1989) found that as a result of implementing a specific program of hygiene among mothers, infant mortality did decline after 1970. Between that year and 1993, the IMR decreased from 122.0 to 74.0.

Although there is no complete direct information for China that allows us to construct a complete infant mortality trend since the postwar period, some estimations are provided in a study by Banister (1986). From the mid-1960s to 1977–1978, the author and her colleagues found a constant decrease in infant mortality (from 70 to 40 deaths), although the trend was later reversed. Their calculation for 1981–1982 was 61 deaths per 1,000 live births, which does not match the information from the United Nations: 39.3 in 1983 and 44.0 a decade later (Table 1). Banister and her team examined the possibility of measurement errors in order to discern whether the estimation was fatally biased and changed the direction of the trend. They confirmed that such was not the case

(Banister 1986). There may have been an over- or underestimation between both calculations, but either way, the direction of the tendency toward an increasing IMR seem to be correct.

According to Banister (1986), there are three reasons that may explain this inversion. First, in 1978 a general economic reform began and the availability of preventive and curative health services was somehow affected, which may have been detrimental to the survival of some infants. Second, at the same time China's severe family-planning reached rural couples. In 1981, 53 percent of all births corresponded to second and higher-order births; therefore, if mothers of these unauthorized babies lacked prenatal care, not surprisingly their infants would experience higher risk of early death. Additionally, the provision of medical care had been tilted intentionally toward the only child, which may have implied the deterioration of the health care available for children in multichild families. Third, a decrease in the proportion of breast-feeding combined with the use of contaminated water used to mix formula might have adversely affected infant survival. Although these researchers did not have precise information on the proportion of breast-feeding, based on fragmentary data that proportion seems to have decreased (in 1982 22 percent of the babies in urban areas and 60 percent in rural settlements were breast-fed). A possible fourth factor is infanticide, but the distribution of infant deaths by sex did not show a bias toward more female deaths (it is said that there exists in China a preference for male babies). Hence, if infanticide played an important role in increasing the IMR, Banister's evidence suggest either that the incidence of female infanticide is not statistically significant or that respondents reported neither the birth nor the death of female victims of infanticide.

Sri Lanka is a rare case of a developing country's retaining records from nearly the beginning of the twentieth century. Stolnitz (1956) refers to Sri Lanka (formerly Ceylon) as one example of rapidly declining infant mortality; more recently, Meegama (1986) offers an overview of mortality trends since the beginning of the twentieth century. According to this latter author, during the second half of the nineteenth century, the IMR started to decrease because of a reduction in the number of famines and the control of cholera epidemics.

During 1911–1915, the IMR was 201 deaths per 1,000 live births, fifteen years later it had decreased to 175 deaths. In 1945, at the end of the World War II, the IMR was recorded at 140 infant deaths per 1,000 live births. Prior to the war, there was a decrease in the mortality rate for both sexes and all age groups in both endemic and nonendemic malarial zones. One of the main reasons for this decline was the expansion of maternity and child welfare services, which decreased both infant and maternal mortality (Meegama 1986). It might have been the combination of that preexisting decline and the introduction of a wider range of medical measures that caused a steady decrease in mortality after the war. As shown in Table 1, in 1948 Sri Lanka had an IMR of 92.1. This was halved by the beginning of the 1970s (45.1) and was again reduced to a third of the 1970 rat by 1993 (16.5).

South Korea and Singapore are two cases of recent industrialization and fast decline in mortality patterns. Information is not available to reconstruct the South Korean mortality history; however, what can be seen in Table 1 is a decrease of more than 50 percent from 1983 to 1993. In 1983 the country had an IMR of 29.7, which had declined to 12.3 ten years later.

Singapore is another impressive case of accelerated reduction in infant mortality. In 1948, it had a relatively low IMR among Asian countries (80.8), but its rate was greater than that of Japan. By 1960, the rate had been reduced by more than 50 percent, reaching 34.8. The trend continued, and by 1993 Singapore's IMR was 4.7, similar to the Swedish and very close to the Japanese rate.

Africa. Mortality in Africa is the highest of any major region in the world and historically has had the least reliable information, with certain exceptions. Through the application of special techniques, mortality trends have been reconstructed. The pattern of mortality in Africa is characteristic of populations with a high mortality schedule: It is dominated by mortality among children under five years of age, and infectious, parasitic, and respiratory diseases are the major causes of death. Concerning infant mortality in Africa, we examine some cases from this region displayed in Table 1.

Kenya lacks a usable vital registration system, but the application of indirect techniques has helped in reconstructing mortality trends there. In 1948, when the country began its transition toward lower mortality, it might have had an IMR of 184 per 1,000 live births, according to some estimates (Ewbank et al. 1986). In 1970 that rate had dropped to 81.2, but in the following decades the pace of change was considerably slower; in 1993 the rate was 71.0. For an African country, this is a low mortality pattern, but it is comparable to some Asian countries and to the poorest in Latin America.

Mauritius has a mortality pattern that is gradually approaching that of Western Europe (United Nations 1984). It has the lowest IMR of African countries shown in Table 1. In the period immediately after the World War II, Mauritius had an IMR of 186.2 deaths per 1,000 live births; this decreased 62 percent in twelve years to 70.9 in 1960. That steady rate of decrease was maintained, with the IMR falling to 19.9 by 1993.

The South African case presented some different data analysis challenges because prior to the 1980s information on mortality was not available for the country as a whole but rather by ethnic group, showing the effect of apartheid on vital statistics but also allowing us to see ethnic differentials in the levels of infant mortality. As shown in Table 1, the white population had always been better off than their fellow South Africans; the IMR of the black population held relatively constant until 1970 and the IMR of the Asian population was located between that of the white and black populaces. The ratio of deaths between ethnic groups illustrates social differences: In 1948 there were approximately 4 black infant deaths for each white one and 1.7 black infant deaths for each Asian one. The ratio for Asian to white deaths was approximately 2-to-1 for babies under the age of one year. In 1970 the gap between blacks and the other races widened: There were 6.1 black infant deaths for each white death, 3.6 black infant deaths for each Asian death, and 1.7 Asian infant deaths for each white infant death. By the 1980s the information from the *Demographic Yearbook* was no longer classified by ethnic group; it shows that the general IMR decreased between 1983 and 1993, from 83.3 to 53.0, but it does not show the ethnic differential during those years.

DIFFERENTIALS IN INFANT AND CHILD MORTALITY

Numerous studies have documented and examined various differences in infant and child mortality among different groups along various socioeconomic and ecological spectrums. For most of the earliest periods under investigation, ecological and geographic factors seemed to account for most of the observed differences in infant and child mortality rates (Preston and Haines 1991). Current research on this topic is guided by a theoretical framework put forth by Mosley and Chen (1984). Their original intent was to outline an analytical framework for studying child survival in developing countries, but many researchers have found this framework to be extremely suitable for studying infant and mortality differentials within various contexts.

Mosley and Chen (1984) propose that all socioeconomic determinants, or exogenous factors, of child mortality operate through a set of biological mechanisms that they call "proximate determinants" or "intermediate variables." That is, social and economic factors influence infant and child mortality through a set of biological factors that an infant is born with. Many studies have identified numerous variables and factors that influence both the biological viability of an infant at birth and the health and well-being of the infant *ex utero*, thereby increasing or decreasing the probability that an infant will die before its first birthday or that a child will die before its fifth. These social and economic factors range from individual-level characteristics to household- and community-level factors.

Research has identified three main infant birth outcomes that exert major influences on infant survival chances and through which many exogenous factors operate: infant birthweight, gestational age, and the interaction of the two, sometimes referred to as intrauterine growth retardation (IUGR). Infants weighing less than 2,500 grams at birth (low birthweight, LBW) and infants of short gestation (less than thirty-seven weeks' gestation=premature) have been consistently found to be at dramatically higher risk of infant mortality (Hummer et al. 1999). Interactions between these two outcomes have also been found to affect infant mortality rates significantly (Frisbie et al. 1996). These relationships hold for both MDCs and LDCs (UN 1984).

Of the set of proximate and exogenous determinants originally outlined by Mosley and Chen (1984), most have been identified as having significant effects on infant mortality. Smoking, alcohol, and illicit drug use have all been shown to adversely affect infant and child mortality (Chomitz et al. 1995; Petitti and Coleman 1990). Maternal weight gain has been found to be negatively correlated with infant mortality risk; that is, the more weight a woman gains during her pregnancy, the lower the infant mortality risk (Hummer et al. 1999). The birth order of the infant is associated with differential infant mortality risks, while shorter interpregnancy intervals are linked to higher mortality risks (Kallan 1993; Miller 1991). Male infants have always had higher mortality risks (Rumbaut and Weeks 1996). The role of prenatal care has been debated in recent times, but most researchers agree that adequate prenatal care produces beneficial effects for the health and well-being of mothers, infants, and ultimately young children (Fiscella 1995). The effect on infant mortality risk of maternal age had previously been thought to be constantly negative in direction, but more recent analyses indicate that many interaction effects may work specifically through maternal age, making the conceptual picture much more complex (Geronimus 1987).

Exogenous factors have also been investigated and analyzed. One factor that has captured the continued interest of researchers is the role that race and ethnicity play in explaining infant and child mortality differentials. In both MDCs and LDCs consisting of multiracial and/or multiethnic populations, racial and ethnic infant and child mortality differentials often exist. For example, in 1996 the black population in the United States experienced an IMR of 14.1 while the white population experienced an IMR of 6.1 (MacDorman and Atkinson 1998). In 1990, the indigenous population of Mexico experienced a higher risk of infant mortality 1.5 times higher than the nonindigenous population (Fernández-Ham 1993). Although the role that race and ethnicity may play in IMR differentials is complex, there is agreement that such differences are based on social, economic and historical inequalities (Cooper and David 1986; David 1990). In LDCs those historical inequalities are also related to place of residence, which in most of these countries imply a more disadvantaged position for rural populations (Camposortega Cruz 1989b).

More direct socioeconomic indicators are currently being tested to identify their effects on mortality risks. Increases in maternal education have consistently been shown to decrease both infant and child mortality risk at both the individual and national levels (Hummer et al. 1992; Pampel and Pillai 1986). Marital status has also been linked to differential infant mortality risks; unmarried mothers have a higher risk for infant mortality. This may reflect the fact that single mothers often must bear the costs of both child-rearing and day-to-day living expenses with limited assistance (Frisbie et al. 1997). Studies have also identified the important role that income plays in influencing infant and child mortality risk (Geronimus and Korenman 1988). Cramer (1995) finds evidence of this association even when controlling for a wide array of other sociodemographic risk factors. Many others have explored the effects of various public health assistance and intervention programs, either by governmental or nonprofit agencies. In both MDCs and LDCs, some evidence exists to support the creation and implementation of such intervention programs, such as the Women, Infants and Children (WIC) program in the United States and governmental health programs in Guatemala (Moss and Carver 1998; United Nations 1984). According to Frenk and associates (1989), in certain developed countries there may exist two populations divided by their differential infant and child mortality risk. These researchers point to existing differences between insured and uninsured populations in Mexico as an example of the divergent character of national infant mortality profiles in both high- and middle-income countries (Frenk et al. 1989).

With the development of new theoretical frameworks and statistical methodologies, infant and child mortality research has traveled down new paths. One interesting development has been analyses based upon characteristics of both the individual and the neighborhood or community in which individuals live. Determinants of infant and child mortality are hypothesized to emerge from conflation of personal, household, and neighborhood factors. Collins and David (1997) find that violent neighborhoods may adversely effect an expectant mother's pregnancy outcome, in spite of the measured personal characteristics of the mother. Guest (1998) finds that the neighborhood unemployment level has an important effect on infant mortality beyond effects due to other socioeconomic indicators and race.

PROSPECTS

The search for solutions to reduce levels of infant and child mortality will require the joint participation of multiple actors: governments, international agencies, nongovernmental organizations, and individuals within the scientific and policy communities. Predicting future trends in infant and child mortality remains a rather difficult task given the complexity of this phenomenon. However, scientific knowledge gathered at both the aggregate and individual levels should make reduction of the significant gap between the developed and developing world possible. The multiple differences that exist in mortality patterns within groups in both developed and developing countries are illustrated by the current age structure of mortality. In 1990-1995, life expectancy at birth was 74.4 years in developed countries and 62.3 years in the less developed world. This indicator is consistent with the corresponding IMRs: 10 versus 70 infant deaths per 1,000 live births for MDCs and LDCs, respectively.

It is noteworthy that infant and child mortality rates fell so drastically in the twentieth century. But even so, there remains the need to determine the next course of action in order to combat the mortality differentials between less and more developed nations and among various socioeconomic groups within nations. Continued successes will depend on identifying problem areas and creating innovative solutions to these health, and ultimately, social problems.

REFERENCES

Arriaga, E. E. 1970 *Mortality Decline and its Demographic Effects in Latin America* (Population Monograph Series No. 6). Berkeley: University of California Press.

—— 1989 "Changing Trends in Mortality Decline during the Last Decades." In L. Ruzicka, G. Wunsch, and P. Kane, eds., *Differential Mortality: Methodological Issues and Biosocial Factors*. Oxford: Clarendon Press.

Banister, J. 1986 *China: Recent Trends in Health and Mortality*. Washington, D.C.: Center for International Research, U.S. Bureau of the Census.

Bogue, D. J. 1969 *Principles of Demography*. New York: John Wiley and Sons.

Bourgeois-Pichat, J. 1951 "La Mesure de la Mortalité Infantile. I. Princepes et Methodes." *Population* 2:1–17.

Bouvier, L. F., and J. Van der Tak 1976 "Infant Mortality: Progress and Problems." *Population Bulletin* 31:3–33.

Camposortega Cruz, S. 1989a "La evolución de la mortalidad en México, 1940–1980." *Estudios Demográficos y Urbanos* 4(2):229–264.

—— 1989b "Mortalidad en México. Algunas Consideraciones Sobre Los Diferenciales Urbano-Rurales." *Estudios Demográficos y Urbanos* 4(3):573–593.

Chomitz, V. R., L. W. Cheung, and E. Lieberman 1995 "The Role of Lifestyle in Preventing Low Birth Weight." *Future of Children* 5(1):121–138.

Coale, A. J. 1965 "Birth Rates, Death Rates, and Rates of Growth in Human Population." In Mindel C. Sheps and Jeanne C. Ridley, eds., *Public Health and Population Change*. Pittsburgh, Pa.: University of Pittsburgh Press.

Collins, J. W., and R. J. David 1997 "Urban Violence and African-American Pregnancy Outcomes." *Ethnicity and Disease* 7:184–190.

Cooper, R., and R. David 1986 "The Biological Concept of Race and its Application to Public Health and Epidemiology." *Journal of Health Politics, Policy and Law* 11:97–116.

Cramer, J. C. 1995 "Racial and Ethnic Differences in Birthweight: The Role of Income and Family Assistance." *Demography* 27:413–430.

Creighton-Zollar, A. 1993 "Infant Mortality by Socioeconomic Status and Race: Richmond, VA 1979–1981." *Sociological Spectrum* 10:133–142.

David, R. 1990 "Race, Birthweight, and Mortality Rates [editorial]." *Journal of Pediatrics* 116:101–102.

Ewbank, D., R. Henin, and J. Kekovole 1986 "An Integration of Demographic and Epidemiologic Research on Mortality in Kenya." In United Nations, *Determinants of Mortality Change and Differentials in Developing Countries* (Population Studies No. 94). New York: United Nations.

Fernández-Ham, P. 1993 "La Mortalidad Infantil en la Población Indígena: Atrasos y Contrastes." *Demos* 6:12–13.

Fiscella, K. 1995 "Does Prenatal Care Improve Birth Outcomes? A Critical Review." *Obstetrics & Gynecology* 85(3):468–479.

Frenk, J., J. Bobadilla, J. Sepulveda, and M. Lopez 1989 "Health Transition in Middle-Income Countries: New Challenges for Health Care." *Health Policy and Planning* 4(1):29–39.

Frisbie, W. P., M. Biegler, P. deTurk, D. Forbes, and S. G. Pullum 1997 "Determinants of Intrauterine Growth

Retardation and Other Compromised Birth Outcomes: A Comparison of Mexican Americans, African Americans, and Non-Hispanic Whites." *American Journal of Public Health* 87(12):1977–1983.

Frisbie, W. P., D. Forbes, and S. G. Pullum 1996 "Compromised Birth Outcomes and Infant Mortality Among Racial and Ethnic Groups." *Demography* 33(4):469–481.

Geronimus, A. T. 1987 "On Teenage Childbearing and Neonatal Mortality in the United States." *Population and Development Review* 13(2):245–279.

——, and S. D. Korenman 1988 "Comment on Pampel and Pillai's 'Patterns and Determinants of Infant Mortality in Developed Nations, 1950–1975.'" *Demography* 25(1):155–158.

Guest, A. M. 1998 "The Ecology of Race and Socioeconomic Distress: Infant and Working-Age Mortality in Chicago." *Demography* 35(1):23–34.

Hill, K. H. 1991 "Approaches to the Measurement of Childhood Mortality: A Comparative Approach." *Population Index* 57(3):368–382.

Hummer, R. A., M. Biegler, P. deTurk, D. Forbes, W. P. Frisbie, Y. Hong, and S. G. Pullum 1999 "Race/Ethnicity, Nativity and Infant Mortality." *Social Forces* 77(3):1083–1118.

Hummer, R. A., I. A. Eberstein, and C. B. Nam 1992 "Infant Mortality Differentials Among Hispanic Groups in Florida." *Social Forces* 70(4):1055–1075.

Jain, A. K., and P. Visaira (eds.) 1988 *Infant Mortality in India. Differentials and Determinants.* New Delhi: Sage Publications.

Kallan, J. E. 1993 "Race, Intervening Variables, and Two Forms of Low Birthweight." *Demography* 30:489–506.

Kitagawa, E. M. 1977 "On Mortality." *Demography* 14(4):381–389.

MacDorman, M. F., and J. O. Atkinson 1998 "Infant Mortality Statistics from the 1995 Period Linked Birth/Infant Death Data Set." *Monthly Vital Statistics Report* 46(12s):1–24.

Meegama, S. A. 1986 "The Mortality Transition in Sri Lanka." In United Nations, *Determinants of Mortality Change and Differentials in Developing Countries* (Population Studies No. 94). New York: United Nations.

Meslé, F., and J. Vallin 1996 *Mortality in the World: Trends and Prospects.* Paris: Centré Francais sur la Population et le Développement.

Miller, J. E. 1991 "Birth Intervals and Perinatal Health: An Investigation of Three Hypothesis." *Family Planning Perspectives* 23:62–70.

Mosley, W. H., and L. C. Chen 1984 "An Analytic Framework for the Study of Child Survival in Developing Countries." *Population Development and Review* 10(supplement):25–48.

Moss, N. E., and K. Carver 1998 "The Effect of WIC and Medicaid on Infant Mortality in the United States." *American Journal of Public Health* 88(9):1354–1361.

Omran, A. R. 1971 "The Epidemiologic Transition. A Theory of Population Change. Part 1." *The Milbank Fund Quarterly* 49(4):509–538.

Omran, A. R. 1971 "Epidemiologic Transition: A Theory of the Epidemiology of Population Change." *Milbank Memorial Fund Quarterly* 49(4):509–538.

Omran, A. R. 1977 "Epidemiologic Transition in the U.S.: The Health Factor in Population Change." *Population Bulletin* 32(2):3–42.

Palloni, A. 1998 "A Review of Infant Mortality Trends in Selected Underdeveloped Countries: Some New Estimates." *Population Studies* 35(1):100–119.

Pampel, F. C., and V. K. Pillai 1986, "Patterns and Determinants of Infant Mortality in Developed Nations, 1950–1975." *Demography* 23(4):525–542.

Petitti, D. B., and C. Coleman 1990 "Cocaine Use and the Risk of Low Birthweight." *American Journal of Public Health* 80:25–27.

Preston, S. H. 1976 *Mortality Patterns in National Populations.* New York: Academic Press.

—— 1992 "Infant and Child Mortality." In E. F. Borgatta and M. L. Borgatta, eds., *Encyclopedia of Sociology*, vol. 2. New York: Macmillan.

——, and M. R. Haines 1991 *Fatal Years: Child Mortality in Late Nineteenth-Century America.* Princeton, N.J.: Princeton University Press.

——, and V. E. Nelson 1974 "Structure and Change in Causes of Death: An International Summary." *Population Studies* 28(1):19–51.

Rumbaut, R. G., and J. R. Weeks 1996 "Unraveling a Public Health Enigma: Why Do Immigrants Experience Superior Perinatal Health Outcomes." *Research in the Sociology of Health Care* 13B:337–391.

Shryock, Henry S., and J. Siegel 1976 *The Methods and Materials of Demography.* Washington, D.C.: U.S. Government Printing Office.

Sowards, K. A. 1997 "Premature Birth and the Changing Composition of Newborn Infectious Disease Mortality: Reconsidering 'Exogenous' Mortality." *Demography* 34(3):399–409.

Spiegelman, M. 1956 "Recent Trends and Determinants of Mortality in Highly Developed Countries." In F. G. Boudreau and C. V. Kiser, eds., *Trends and*

Differentials in Mortality. New York: Milbank Memorial Fund, pp. 26–34.

Stockwell, E. G., and H. T. Groat 1984 *World Population: An Introduction to Demography*. New York: Franklin Watts.

Stolnitz, G. J. 1955 "A Century of International Mortality Trends: I." *Population Studies* 9(1):24–55.

—— 1956 "Comparison Between Some Recent Mortality Trends in Underdeveloped Areas and Historical Trends in the West." In F. G. Boudreau and C. V. Kiser, eds., *Trends and Differentials in Mortality*. New York: Milbank Memorial Fund, pp. 51–60.

United Nations 1979 *Demographic Yearbook. Historical Supplement*. New York: United Nations.

—— 1982 *Demographic Yearbook*. New York: United Nations.

—— 1984 "The Influence of Developmental-Related Change on Infant and Child Mortality in Africa." In United Nations, *Mortality and Health Policy: Proceedings of the Expert Group on Mortality and Health Policy, Rome, 30 May to June 1983*. New York: United Nations.

—— 1987 *Demographic Yearbook*. New York: United Nations.

—— 1990 *Step-by-Step Guide to the Estimation of Child Mortality*. New York: United Nations.

—— 1996 *Demographic Yearbook*. New York: United Nations.

Van de Walle, E., and F. Van de Walle 1990 "The Private and the Public Child." In J. Caldwell, S. Findley, P. Caldwell, G Santow, W. Cosford, J. Braid, and D. Broers-Freeman, eds., *What We Know About Health Transition: The Cultural, Social and Behavioural Determinants of Health*, Vol. 1. Australia: The Australian National University, pp. 150–164.

World Bank 1983 *World Development Report*. New York: Oxford University Press.

Georgina Rojas-García
Samuel Echevarría

INFORMAL ECONOMY, THE

Informal economic activity can only be understood in relationship to its counterparts in the institutions of the formal economy, most notably in markets for labor, goods, and services. In most modern, industrial, capitalist societies, economic activity occurs in the form of exchanges of cash for labor, consumer goods, and services within well-regulated economic institutions located within the formal economy. The labor market, in particular, provides the framework for regulating the exchange of work and wages between sellers and buyers of labor (workers and employers) under the auspices of a legal and regulatory environment enforced by the state. At the same time, it is also widely recognized that livelihood strategies may entail all manner of exchange outside these formal institutions and regulations. That is, exchanges may occur in the informal economy. Goods and services may be bartered, traded for nonmonetary compensation, or produced under conditions that flaunt health and safety regulations. Earned income may go unreported and untaxed. Individuals may self-provision, using their own resources to produce and consume household necessities even when they are readily available for purchase. Credit may be extended on the basis of kinship and trust. Numerous other types of unrecognized exchanges create value "under the table," that is, in the informal economy.

In some societies the informal economy is the dominant mode of economic activity. It is especially prominent in developing countries where the majority of the population may engage in various types of economic exchanges outside any formal regulation, cash economy, or state supervision. Yet informal activity is not limited to developing nations. Increasingly, economists, sociologists, and others who study work and labor markets recognize that the informal economy is very much present in first world industrial and postindustrial economies. The *shadow, black, gray, underground, subterranean,* or *parallel economy* are among the common euphemisms for an informal economy that exists side by side with its more studied and theorized counterparts in developed as well as developing nations, first and third worlds, urban and rural communities, and everything in between.

DEVELOPMENT OF THE CONCEPT

History. The term *informal economy* has numerous uses and meanings and few precise definitions. Its original formulation is attributed to an anthropologist, Keith Hart, studying emerging urban labor markets in Africa for the International Labour Office (ILO) (Hart 1973). Hart distinguished between waged employment in large firms or government agencies and self-employment in his studies of the urban labor force, noting the wide variety of small-scale entrepreneurial activities that were central to the livelihood strategies and economic life of residents of urban centers in Africa. Small traders, food vendors, and sellers of goods or services from shoe shines to haircuts are the familiar mainstays of urban economies. Subsequent use of the term by the ILO came to mean self-employment and small-scale family enterprise correlated with poverty, underemployment, and low productivity, particularly in poor, developing nations. This view was widely adopted by analysts and policy makers for whom the informal economy was a phenomenon of poverty and underdevelopment, with the implication that development of a modern economy decreases the need for and significance of informal activity. Ultimately, informal work should be absorbed into the regulated economy.

More recently, assumptions about the scope, location, and importance of informal work have come under scrutiny, since it has been recognized that informal work is neither unique to impoverished Third World countries nor necessarily diminishing in size or importance. Several developments in diverse areas of economic sociology, but all of them linked to global economic restructuring, have led to renewed interest in informal work and a growing understanding that it is both more widespread and less understood than previous accounts suggested. Studies of urban ethnic enclaves, patterns of employment for new immigrants, and the explosion of the global division of labor in "world cities" have generated interest in informal work. Similarly, there has been a corresponding interest in livelihood and income-generating strategies of both the urban and rural poor, and in wide-scale economic restructuring that sought increased flexibility in production processes and labor practices, as well as recognition of the persistence of noncash exchanges in communities of all sizes and locations. Additionally, periodic headline-grabbing media accounts of sweatshops, child and immigrant labor abuses, and other gross violations of labor law and workplace protections have fueled broad awareness of the persistence and pervasiveness of informal activity.

Definitions. Despite growing awareness of the ubiquity of the informal sector, a precise definition remains elusive, and numerous issues remain unresolved. Typically, informal activity is defined by what it is not; that is, it is not formal, it is not regulated, and it is not counted in official statistics and national accounting schemes. Castells and Portes (1989) provide an influential definition using this approach: "The informal economy is . . . a process of income-generation characterized by one central feature: it is unregulated by the institutions of society, in a legal and social environment in which similar activities are regulated" (p. 12).

While broadly inclusive, this definition provides little guidance for distinguishing between different types of activities conducted under different circumstances. For example, should overtly criminal activities, such as drug dealing, be classified in the same way as work that is otherwise legal, such as flea market sales, except that is unreported and untaxed? Should both production and consumption processes be classified as part of the informal sector? In other words, are the goods that are produced in sweatshops comparable to those produced at home for private consumption? When do self-employment and the use of family labor become informal work? These questions illustrate both the diverse approaches found in the literature and the confusion that exists there.

Other analysts emphasize specific defining characteristics of the informal economy rather than focusing on what it is not. For example, Roberts (1994), while accepting the basic outline of the standard definition, argues that the key feature of informality is not the absence of regulation but instead the existence of a specific type of regulation that dominates the activity. Thus, the informal sector is marked by the dominance of regulation based on personal relations and networks embedded in family, community, friendship, or ethnicity rather than on regulation organized on formal, legal, or contractual bases. Similarly, Mingione (1991) suggests that income strategies organized around reciprocal networks, such as those found in family and household labor and relations, characterize the informal sector. These analysts emphasize the interpersonal networks that create obligations and responsibilities that permit exchanges that bypass formal institutions. This approach has found expression in the many studies of immigrant labor and ethnic enclave enterprise where kinship and co-ethnic personal ties are the means for conducting business.

A number of taxonomies and typologies have been proposed in an effort to codify characteristics of informal activity. Feige (1990) distinguishes between illegal, unreported, unrecorded, and informal categories of a more encompassing *underground economy*. While there is much overlap, these categories appear to represent a continuum ranging from those most thoroughly in violation of the law to those that merely forgo its protections. Castells and Portes (1989) clearly differentiate informal from illegal by separating processes of production and distribution from the product itself. Thus, a perfectly legitimate product or service may be produced informally in violation of the law. Cappechi (1989) cross-classifies three types of labor markets (nonmonetary, informal monetary, official) with the equivalent three markets for goods and services to derive a nine-cell typology. Informality in either labor or product markets creates five types of informality.

Still other analysts argue that, fundamentally, informality can only be understood on a case-specific basis. For example, Gaughan and Ferman (1987) contend "that the term *informal economy* will mean different things in advanced industrial nations from what it does in developing countries. . . . poor communities as opposed to middle-class communities, or in an urban as opposed to a rural setting" (p. 18). In keeping with this notion of the variability of forms of informal activity, Miller (1987) discusses informal economies in the plural rather than the singular.

Regardless of specific emphasis, virtually all analysts agree that informal economies, sectors, activities, and labor can only be understood vis-à-vis their relationship to their formal counterparts and in the context of their relationship to the state (Roberts 1994). There is no such thing as an informal economy in the absence of a formal economy. Portes (1994) even suggests that the extent of informal activity depends on the degree of state regulation, with greater informal development representing a response to an overly restrictive formal sector. Furthermore, while many analysts discuss informal activity as outcomes or in terms of structural elements that comprise a form of economic institution, there appears to be greater utility in conceptualizing it as a process that varies in time and space. Thus, the concepts of informality and informalization, in which economic activity is evaluated in terms of its degree of adherence to state regulation and particular labor practices, permit an assessment of variation in levels and development of informal sectors and their shares of the larger economy.

Forms of Informal Activity. Empirical studies of informal activity identify a wide range of actual practices. Ultimately, what is included and what is excluded depends on the specific definition and the specific context for the activities, as discussed above. Nevertheless, certain broad categories are regularly found in the literature. They can be categorized in terms of what type of exchange relationship is involved and the specific kinds of goods and services transacted. Thus, goods and services can be exchanged for income that goes unreported in any official venue, as exemplified by the babysitter or maid who gets paid in cash that is not taxed or reported by either employer or employee. They may be bartered and exchanged directly for the same or other goods or services, as in the trade of child-care services or child care for firewood. They may be supplied and consumed to save money or to self-provision, as when members of a household raise a garden and preserve food for home consumption.

Specific goods, services, and activities vary from place to place. Urban dwellers are unlikely to raise livestock or cut wood for home consumption, but they are no less likely than their rural counterparts to engage in child care or household and auto repair (Tickamyer and Wood 1998). Sweatshops and street vendors are most likely to be found in large urban labor markets (Gaber 1994; Sassen-Koob 1989), but industrial subcontracting and home assembly operations are well documented in rural communities as well (Gringeri 1994).

One of the problems in specifying types of informal activity is distinguishing informal from related forms of work and exchange. At the margins it may be extremely difficult to draw this line. For example, where does engaging in an activity for recreation or personal satisfaction end and self-provisioning begin? Should the avid gardener whose vegetable consumption is a by-product of the hobby be classified as engaged in informal work? Where should volunteer work done for charitable purposes be classified? Informal labor overlaps with many other forms of waged and unwaged labor, including social and generational reproduction, self-provisioning and subsistence activities, consumption work, and community service as well as simple commodity production, self-employment, and subcontracting.

SOCIAL, SPATIAL, AND TEMPORAL DIMENSIONS

The expanding literature demonstrates that informality is not limited to a particular time, place, type of economy, or population group. Nevertheless, clear themes that focus on specific groups and places emerge in the research literature. Some of it is empirically based; some is speculative and yet to be tested or verified regarding who participates, where, and under what circumstances; and some is contradictory or unfounded. The most common assumption is that informal labor involves categories of workers who are disadvantaged in some manner and, therefore, are shut out from the opportunities available in the formal sector. For example, informal workers have been identified as particularly prevalent among racial and ethnic minorities, immigrants, women, and children (Hoyman 1987; Portes et al. 1989; Sassen-Koob 1984). Other studies would add rural residents (Fitchen 1981; Jensen et al. 1995) and the urban poor (Edin and Lein 1998).

While there are many specific accounts and case studies to illustrate the importance and workings of informal labor and sectors among these specific populations and locations, there is little evidence at this time to suggest that informal work is any more prevalent in one group compared to another. Furthermore, it is not always clear from these accounts whether informality adheres to the group or to the type of jobs certain groups are more likely to hold. For example, women are sometimes identified as more likely to operate in the informal sector, as is work that is typically female, such as child care and domestic service. If it is the case that women are more likely to work informally, is it because of gender or because they hold gendered jobs?

Informalization is often assumed to be increasing in both developing and developed countries as a response to the social and economic restructuring that has transformed and linked core and peripheral economies in the last several decades. Globalization, the growth of transnational capitalism, and increased international competition have led capital to seek more flexible production processes, to escape from state regulation and taxation, and to reduce labor costs. This puts pressure on labor–capital agreements, benefits available from the welfare state, and the general availability of employment that pays a living wage, has social benefits, and observes rules and regulations. The result is increased self-employment, subcontracting, and, presumably, informal employment as employers seek to cut the costs of doing business and employees are forced to find any means of subsistence. Yet here, too, there is little empirical confirmation of what are largely untested hypotheses. For example, it is not yet established whether informal activity is more prevalent among different class and income groups, whether it is in fact a substitute for formal work, or whether it serves as a supplement to increase or stretch income. Instead, there is a rich tradition of case studies of different regions, communities, and industries that are informative but case-specific, lacking both comparability or comprehensiveness. Thus, it is premature to conclude that informality is increasing or that it is especially prevalent in some groups or places compared to others.

RELATIONSHIP TO THE ETHNIC ECONOMY

While informal economic activity is not limited to a particular market segment or group, researchers have shown particular interest in those forms of informal activity that occur in ethnic economies. Part of the reason for this is that the extensive literature on the ethnic economy offers a unique view of informal work given by researchers whose main purpose is not to examine the informal economy per se but to study ethnic exchange relationships (rather than class relationships) in the secondary labor market. This research shows that ethnic economies provide opportunities for unique forms of informal activity not commonly found in other sectors. However, the importance that is placed on informalization in the ethnic economy literature should in no way imply that the two economies are always congruent, although some enclave economies are almost entirely informal (Stepick 1989).

Ethnic economies are labor markets characterized by sectoral specialization of industries owned and operated by entrepreneurs from the same ethnic or immigrant group and their co-ethnic workers. While ethnic and informal economies are not synonymous, the prevalence of work outside the formal sector within ethnic economies suggests that conditions in these labor-market areas necessitate, or at least are particularly well suited for, informal economic activity.

The reasons for this vary. Since most workers in the ethnic economy are immigrants from developing countries or ethnic minorities that face discrimination in the formal labor market, they often provide a pool of available cheap labor for the informal market. That is, the labor supply is cheap as long as the work remains part of the informal economy, since the cost of labor rises when wages are regulated. Enterprising businessmen and women can make use of this inexpensive labor, keeping their costs low by hiring "off the books" or paying piece rates for contracted work that may or may not be reported by the worker as income.

Since ethnic economies are also marked by subcultural norms and preferences, informal activity may also allow for cultural variation in working conditions. In the case of Latin American immigrant women, for example, the myriad home working opportunities within the ethnic economy allow mothers to earn needed income while still tending to their children and other domestic tasks. In fact, there is evidence that some home-based industries emerged in response to the demands of experienced female laborers who wanted to earn extra income but expressed a cultural preference to stay at home (Fernandez-Kelly and Garcia 1989).

While the magnitude of informal economic activities within ethnic economies is not known, studies of the garment industry in New York and Los Angeles, a sector that is almost exclusively part of the informal economy, suggest that many of the workers in the industry are unregistered and working out of their homes (Fernandez-Kelly and Garcia 1989; Sassen-Koob 1989; Stepick 1989). This is also true of the home-based electronics production industry (Lozano 1989). Latin American immigrant women comprise the largest portion of this work force that engages in the unreported assembling of electronic components at home on a piece-rate basis. The informal economy may also be responsible for the viability of these industries.

While the garment industry faltered in the 1980s, textile businesses owned by immigrants who subcontracted homeworkers thrived.

Ethnic enclaves are a special condition of the ethnic economy that arises when an ethnic economy is located in a geographically concentrated area. This geographic concentration can also give rise to unique opportunities within the informal sector. In enclaves such as Washington Heights in New York City, Chinatown in Los Angeles, and Little Havana in Miami, the demand for capital for entrepreneurial ventures has created possibilities for informal money-lending operations. These tend to take the form of either rotating credit associations, whereby residents contribute small sums of money that are pooled and then loaned at low interest rates to other residents, or personal loans from one wealthy entrepreneur to a potential small-business owner. These lending transactions occur outside of state and federal lending laws and are often made without any written agreement by the participants. Social pressure alone seems sufficient to guarantee repayment. This is consistent with Roberts's (1994) contention that interpersonal networks regulate the informal economy.

Ethnic enclaves also generate a heightened demand for goods typical of those widely available in an immigrant's home country. This demand for ethnically defined goods creates unique opportunities for informal work. Enterprising men and women often produce foodstuffs and other products for sale out of their homes. Some also find customers among other immigrants who agree to resell their products in their retail shops and *bodegas*. The informal production of goods insures that costs to both the retailer and the customer remain low, insuring future demand.

WAYS OF MEASURING AND STUDYING

This brief discussion of informal activity in ethnic economies illustrates only one variation in the form and scope of this phenomenon and underscores the importance of further research to gain a greater understanding of how informal economic processes impact individuals, households, and labor markets. As previously noted, recognition that informal economic activity is widespread in developed as well as developing, urban as well as rural, contexts is just beginning to emerge. Consequently, what is known about the size of the informal economy, its participants, its determinants, and its relationship to the formal sector remains limited.

Most of what we currently know about informal work comes from ethnographic and field studies using in-depth interviews and other qualitative data-collection techniques. These provide a rich and varied collection of information about the nature and meaning of informal work in different regions. These regions include remote rural areas such as the Ozarks (Campbell et al. 1993), rural Pennsylvania (Jensen et al. 1995), and the Southwest (Roberts 1994). Other researchers have also looked at urban subpopulations, including Latin American immigrants in New York City (Sassen-Koob 1989) and in Miami (Stepick 1989). These studies offer a intensive look at the kinds of informal activities that occur, who does them and why, and when people engage in informal economic activities.

Case studies and other qualitative methodologies have provided a rich source of data on specific groups and locales, but their limited geographic scope means that there is little information on informal economic activity in larger populations and subpopulations, thus limiting our understanding of the prevalence of such activities across rural and urban places. Furthermore, there appear to be inconsistencies about the nature of informal work across areas, and case studies can only begin to explore these seeming differences. For example, studies of informalization in rural areas suggest that bartering and self-provisioning are both a means of supplementing a meager income and a normative way of life. On the other hand, urban studies depict informal work as an activity engaged in when the avenues to work in the formal labor market are blocked.

Attempts to quantify informal activity for use in policy making have been made by several national and international agencies, although the methods employed are often crude. Portes (1994) separates these strategies into categories based on the following approaches: (1) the labor market, (2) the very small enterprise, (3) macroeconomic discrepancies, and (4) household consumption.

The first three approaches rely on data taken from industry reports and measures of national economic activity such as the gross domestic product. The labor-market approach entails assigning all labor as informal if it is reported as self-employment in areas not typically assumed to be high status or high paying. The very small enterprise (VSE) approach, like the labor-market approach, is also based on industry data. Instead of focusing on self-employment, however, VSE-based estimates are predicated on the notion that all businesses employing fewer than ten workers are engaging in informal activity. In the third approach, discrepancies in different measures of similar economic activity are attributed to the informal economy.

The household consumption approach was developed in 1987 in an effort to surpass the limitations involved in estimating informal activity based on reported, presumably formal, production activities. Estimates of informal economic activity, using this approach, are based on consumer reports of "the amounts spent . . . on goods and services acquired off the books or on the side" (Smith 1987). This method is unique in that it focuses on consumption; however, it is also limited in that it assumes that all products are consumed by individuals rather than firms.

In recognition of the inability to generalize to larger geographic areas based on ethnographic data, in acknowledgment of the limitation of the assumptions entailed in current estimation strategies, and in order to limit the costs entailed in labor-intensive qualitative methodologies, some researchers are turning to more direct survey methodology to examine informal economic processes. Recent studies using survey methodology include work by Jensen and colleagues (1995), Tickamyer and Wood (1998), and Tolbert and colleagues (1996). They note that in order to provide systematic, representative, and comparable data across different locales on who participates and how extensively, where and when participation occurs, and under what circumstances, different data are needed. The goal of these researchers is to provide the baseline data that will enable future researchers to determine if informal activity is increasing or decreasing over time and with changing economic conditions. They are also interested in exploring the relationship between informal work and other social processes, including the relationship to formal labor-market participation, to household, family, and community structures and processes, and to human and social capital formation.

These newer studies are significant because they demonstrate that collecting direct information on informal work using structured survey techniques is possible despite the elusive nature of such activities, their often semilegal status, and respondents' seeming lack of awareness of the extent of their participation in informal work. These studies also underscore the need for better, more extensive tests of survey methods both to determine optimal strategies for using survey methodology on this topic and to provide definitive answers to the many questions posed about informal labor.

CONCLUSIONS

While sociologists, economists, and other researchers continue to provide information on informal work, there are many issues that remain unaddressed. These issues include questions regarding the prevalence, importance, and nature of informal activities. Why do people participate in the informal economy? How important is it to their economic survival? Is it vital or is it more socially driven, carrying little expectation for immediate economic reward? What percent of households engage in informal work, and which members of the household are most likely to be the workers? What are the economic returns to participation? Do formal and informal work complement or substitute for each other? Do people turn to the informal economy as a last resort in times when formal work is curtailed, or are certain types of people likely to engage in both formal and informal labor? And, finally, how is the probability of informal work shaped by individual, household, and labor-market characteristics?

Future research will need to address these issues. Furthermore, more studies will be needed at the national and international level (including comparative research) in order fully to understand the importance of the informal economy in shaping the larger economy as a whole. In order to understand this, it is essential to understand where the informal economy fits vis-à-vis the formal economy and how it has evolved. Is the informal economy merely a pure market response to unwanted government interference in commerce, or is it merely a reflection of expected social relationships in a given place and time? Most likely, the informal economy arises from a combination of factors including poverty and normative pressures to help neighbors and for self-provision. A purely formal economic focus, however, limits our understanding of the range of possibilities entailed in informal work and the impact that such work has on shaping interpersonal processes. Furthermore, by limiting our measures of economic growth, household and individual well-being, inequality, and production to official statistics of formal economic activity, we see only a fraction of the entire picture. This is particularly problematic when policies that attempt to address these issues are shaped from these fragmented images.

Since modern economic policy has been shaped almost exclusively by focusing on the formal economy, conventional definitions of employment, unemployment, poverty, and economic growth may be insufficient to explain the myriad of issues that emerge when informal work is added to the picture. As it has become increasingly recognized that informal economic activity is vital to many individuals and households in both developed and developing countries, the need for more research has become more pressing. By addressing many of the unanswered questions that remain about the informal economy, policy makers can begin to address the labor-market problems that may force workers into informal economic activity, to regulate those activities that exploit certain segments of the work force, and to understand the importance of both formal and informal work as a means of improving living standards.

REFERENCES

Campbell, R. R., J. C. Spencer, and R. G. Amonker 1993 "The Reported and Unreported Missouri Ozarks: Adaptive Strategies of the People Left Behind." In T. Lyson and W. Falk, eds., *Forgotten Places: Uneven Development in Rural America*. Lawrence: University Press of Kansas.

Cappechi, Vittorio 1989 "The Informal Economy and the Development of Flexible Specialization in Emilia-Romagna." In A. Portes, M. Castells, and L. A. Benton, eds., *The Informal Economy: Studies in Advanced and Less Developed Countries*. Baltimore: Johns Hopkins University Press.

Castells, Manuel, and Alejandro Portes 1989 "World Underneath: The Origins, Dynamics, and Effects of the Informal Economy." In A. Portes, M. Castells, and L. A. Benton, eds., *The Informal Economy: Studies in Advanced and Less Developed Countries*. Baltimore: Johns Hopkins University Press.

Edin, Kathryn, and Laura Lein 1998 *Making Ends Meet*. New York: Russell Sage Foundation.

Feige, Edgar 1990 "Defining and Estimating Underground and Informal Economics: The New Institutional Economics Approach" *World Development* 18(7):989–1002.

Fernandez-Kelly, M. P., and A. M. Garcia 1989. "Informalization at the Core: Hispanic Women, Homework, and the Advanced Capitalist State." In A. Portes, M. Castells, and L. A. Benton, eds., *The Informal Economy: Studies in Advanced and Less Developed Countries*. Baltimore: Johns Hopkins University Press.

Fitchen, Janet M. 1981 *Poverty in Rural America: A Case Study*. Boulder, Colo.: Westview.

Gaber, John 1994 "Manhattan's fourteenth Street Vendors' Market: Informal Street Peddlers' Complementary Relationship with New York City's Economy." *Urban Anthropology*. 23(4):373–407.

Graughan, Joseph, and Louis Ferman 1987 "Toward an Understanding of the Informal Economy." *Annals of the American Academy of Political and Social Science* 493 (September): 15–25.

Gringeri, Christina 1994 *Getting By: Women Homeworkers and Rural Economic Development*. Lawrence: Kansas University Press.

Hart, Keith 1973 "Informal Income Opportunities and Urban Employment in Ghana." *Journal of Modern African Studies* 11:61–89.

Hoyman, Michele 1987 "Female Participation in the Informal Economy: A Neglected Issue." *Annals of the American Academy of Political and Social Science* 493 (September):64–82.

Jensen, Leif, Gretchen T. Cornwell, and Jill L. Findeis 1995 "Informal Work in Nonmetropolitan Pennsylvania." *Rural Sociology* 60(1):67–107.

Lozano, B. 1989 *The Invisible Work Force: Transforming American Business with Outside and Home-Based Workers*. New York: Free Press.

Miller, S. M. 1987 "The Pursuit of Informal Economies." *Annals of the American Academy of Political and Social Science* 493 (September):26–35.

Mingione, Enzo 1991 *Fragmented Societies: A Sociology of Economic Life Beyond the Market Paradigm*. Cambridge, Mass.: Basil Blackwell.

Portes, Alejandro 1994 "The Informal Economy and Its Paradoxes." In N. J. Smelser and R. Swedberg, eds., *The Handbook of Economic Sociology*. Princeton, N.J.: Princeton University Press.

——, Manuel Castells, and Lauren A. Benton, eds. 1989 *The Informal Economy: Studies in Advanced and Less Developed Countries*. Baltimore: Johns Hopkins University Press.

Roberts, Brian 1994 "Informal Economy and Family Strategies." *International Journal of Urban and Regional Research* 18(1):6–23.

Sassen-Koob, Saskia 1989 "New York City's Informal Economy." In A. Portes, M. Castells, and L. A. Benton, eds., *The Informal Economy: Studies in Advanced and Less Developed Countries*. Baltimore: Johns Hopkins University Press.

Smith, James D. 1987 "Measuring the Informal Economy." *Annals of the American Academy of Political and Social Science* 493 (September):83–99.

Stepick, Alex 1989 "Miami's Two Informal Sectors." In A. Portes, M. Castells, and L. A. Benton, eds., *The Informal Economy: Studies in Advanced and Less Developed Countries*. Baltimore: Johns Hopkins University Press.

Tickamyer, Ann R., and Teresa A. Wood 1998 "Identifying Participation in the Informal Economy Using Survey Research Methods." *Rural Sociology* 63(2):323–339.

Tolbert, Charles, L. Tobin, and D. Haynie 1996. "Informal Economic Activity in Louisiana Farm and Rural Households." Paper presented at the annual meetings of the Rural Sociological Society, Des Moines, Iowa.

ANN TICKAMYER
STEPHANIE BOHON

INFORMATION SOCIETY

Increased reliance on activities directly associated with the production, distribution, and utilization of information has led to characterizing many advanced countries of the world as information societies. The term *information society* and related concepts, such as information age and knowledge economy, describe a social system greatly dependent on information technologies to produce and distribute all manner of goods and services. In contrast to the industrial society, which relied on internal combustion engines to augment the physical labor of humans, the information society relies on computer technologies to augment mental labor.

Trends in labor-force composition both define and measure the extent to which a nation can be described as an information society. Machlup

(1962) was perhaps the first to describe U.S. society in these terms. He estimated that nearly one-third of the labor force in 1958 worked in information industries such as communications, computers, education, and information services, which accounted for 29 percent of the gross national product (GNP). Using a slightly different methodology, Porat (1977) estimated that information activities had risen to just under half of the U.S. GNP by 1967.

A defining attribute of the information society is the search for improvements in productivity through substituting information for time, energy, labor, and physical materials. In practical terms, this means supplying workers with computerized workstations that are networked to other workstations through intranets as well as the Internet. It allows the use of software to reprogram equipment in distant locations, and it often eliminates the physical delivery of messages and even products. These changes are aimed at making organizational production, distribution, and management decisions more efficient. An early indicator of the extent to which industries sought productivity improvements through the use of information equipment is that whereas only 10 percent of all U.S. investments in durable equipment was spent on the purchase of computers and communications equipment in 1960, that investment increased to 40 percent in 1984 (U.S. Congress 1988) and is now much higher.

The concept of postindustrial society, developed most notably by Daniel Bell (1973), anticipated development of the information society. The term *post-industrial* described the decline of employment in manufacturing and an increase in service and professional employment noted by Machlup (1962) and Porat (1977). Knowledge and information were viewed by Bell as the strategic and transforming resources of postindustrial society, just as capital and labor were the strategic and transforming resources of industrial society.

Advances in the capabilities of information technologies to process large quantities of information quickly have been a crucial factor in the development of the information society. These technologies are of two types, computer power and transmission capability. Development of inexpensive silicon integrated circuits containing as many as a million transistors on a single chip had

already been achieved by the mid-1980s, making it possible to pack enormous information processing power into very little space. As a result, desktop microcomputers gained the processing power comparable to the largest mainframe computers of the previous decade. Computational power continued to increase by a factor of ten every five to seven years in the 1990s (Martin 1995). Improvements in microprocessor technology, coupled with developments in parallel processing, storage methods, input–output devices, and speech recognition and synthesis, have continued to increase dramatically the nature, scale, and speed of tasks that can be accomplished on computers. All this has happened while prices for computers declined in an equally dramatic way.

Corresponding advancements have occurred in photonics as a result of the development of laser technology and ultra-pure glass fiber. These developments resulted in the ability to transmit enormous quantities of information long distances on tiny optic fibers without amplification. By the mid-1980s, AT&T Laboratories had transmitted 420 million bits per second of information over 125 miles without amplification. Advancements of this nature, as well as the use of satellites, made it possible for computers located thousands or tens of thousands miles apart to share large amounts of information nearly as quickly and effectively as would happen if they were located in the same building. Like the price for computing power, the price for transmitting large amounts of information from one place to another also has declined.

These changes in computational and transmission power have made possible new ways of interacting and doing business. Automatic teller machines located on one continent can dispense cash from a bank located on another continent. Cash registers and gasoline pumps are connected to a telecommunications system so that credit card balances can be checked before making a sale. By pressing numbers on a touch tone telephone and without talking to another human being, products can be purchased, library books can be renewed, newspaper delivery can be started or stopped, survey questionnaires can be answered, and money can be transferred from one account to another. These examples illustrate not only the substitution of information technology applications for human labor, but also the creation of services that could not previously be provided.

However, these developments pale beside the huge capability being unleashed by development of the World Wide Web. Once a system for the exchange of simple text messages among scientists, it has now expanded to a required form of communication for many, if not most, businesses and professionals. It is estimated that as many as 160 million users are now connected to the Internet, of which nearly half are in the United States and Canada. The rapid growth in Internet use in the mid-1990s has led to increases in connections among geographically dispersed work groups and to new methods for the selling of goods and services.

Development of the information society happened neither suddenly nor without warning. According to Beniger (1986), its roots go back to a crisis of control evoked by the Industrial Revolution in the late 1800s. Industrialization speeded up material-processing systems. However, innovations in information processing and communications lagged behind innovations in the use of energy to increase productivity of manufacturing and transportation systems. Development of the telegraph, telephone, radio, television, modern printing presses, and postal delivery systems all represented innovations important to the resolution of the control crisis, which required replacement of the traditional bureaucratic means of control that had been depended on for centuries before.

However, an entirely new stage in the development of the information society has been realized through advances in microprocessing technology and the convergence of mass-media telecommunications and computers into a single infrastructure of social control (Beniger 1986). An important factor in this convergence was digitalization of all information, so that distinctions between types of information such as words, numbers, and pictures become blurred, as does communication between persons and machines on the one hand, and between machines on the other. Digitalization, therefore, allowed the transformation of information into a generalized medium for processing and exchange by the social system, much as common currency and exchange rates centuries ago did for the economic systems of the world. Combining

telephone, television, and computer into a single device represents an important likely and practical consequence of this convergence.

Quite different views exist about the possible effects of the development of a full-fledged information society (Lyon 1988). One view is that it will empower workers, providing direct access to opportunities unavailable to them in an industrial society except by high organizational position and proximity to centralized positions of power. In 1985, Harlan Cleveland described information as being fundamentally different from the resources for which it is being substituted; for example, it is not used up by the one who consumes it, hence making its use possible by others. It is also easily transportable from one point to another, a characteristic made strikingly clear by the rapid rise of the World Wide Web. Cleveland argued that the information society would force dramatic changes in longstanding hierarchical forms of social organization, terminating taken-for-granted hierarchies based on control, secrecy, ownership, early access, and geography. A similar view was provided by Masuda (1981), writing in a Japanese context, who envisioned the development of participatory democracies, the eradication of educational gaps between urban and rural areas, and the elimination of a centralized class-based society.

A more pessimistic view of the consequences of knowledge as the key source of productivity was offered by Castells (1989). Fundamentally, the new information infrastructure that connects virtually all points of the globe to all others allows for great flexibility in all aspects of production, consumption, distribution, and management. To take advantage of the efficiencies offered by full utilization of information technologies, organizations plan their operations around the dynamics of their information-generating units, not around a limited geographic space. Individual nations lose the ability to control corporations. Information technologies, therefore, become instrumental in the implementation of fundamental processes of capitalist restructuring. In contrast to the view offered by Cleveland, the stateless nature of the corporation is seen as contributing to an international hierarchical functional structure in which the historic division between intellectual and manual labor is taken to an extreme. The consequences for social organization are to dissolve localities as functioning social systems and to supersede societies.

There can be no doubt that the use of information technologies is significantly changing the structures of advanced societies. Yet it would be a mistake to think of the use of information technologies as a cause only, and not a consequence, of changes in societal structures. Laws have evolved in the United States in an attempt to regulate rates that can be charged for cable television, how much can be charged by providers for telecommunications services to schools and libraries, and what levels of telephone transmission services must be provided to individual households as a part of universal service. The influence of people's values is also being exerted on the extent and means by which confidentiality of data records must be protected; it also is being exerted through state and local laws mandating the accessibility of computers to schoolchildren.

Our rapid evolution to an information society poses many important sociological questions about how our increased dependence upon information technologies influences social interaction and other aspects of human behavior. The ability to transmit work across national boundaries, even the high likelihood that information essential to the operation of a nation will be stored outside rather than within a country, raises important questions about what is essential for preserving national sovereignty. The ability to control operations at long distance encourages an even greater division of labor among nations. As a result, labor unions may become powerless in the face of the ability of corporations to move production activities across national boundaries (Lyon 1988). And, just as elements of national society have weakened in the face of globalization, a set of counterforces have been unleashed whereby identity-based social movements compete to fill the void of power and control (Castells 1997). It is important for sociologists to seek an answer to the question of how the increased reliance on information technologies affects the sovereignty of individual nations and related social movements.

The information age provides new challenges for nearly all areas of sociology. It influences how and from whom we learn, with lifelong distance education changing the once essential learning triangle of professor, student, and classroom. New types of crime, such as creating and spreading computer viruses, have been elevated from curiosities to major threats to the functioning of organizations, society, and the world order. The impact on people's self-concepts may also be substantial. From preschool on, computers have become part of the sociological and psychological development of children, the potential effects of which have yet to be fully understood (Turkle 1984). This interaction with computers now extends via the Internet to others with computers, so that the core sociological concept of social interaction must make room for electronic, long distance interaction and its consequences. Many adults now spend far more of their lives in interchange with computers than with another technological development, the automobile, which also dramatically changed people's lives in the industrial society.

Information technologies also have the potential for breaking down boundaries of individual communities, making it possible for people to bypass forming traditional community ties, unless extraordinary efforts are made to maintain them (Allen and Dillman 1994). Thousands of new job titles are added to the occupational structure of countries, while other job titles disappear. Robert Reich, for example, describes the evolution of jobs into three broad types—routine work, in-person service workers, and symbolic analysts (1991). The latter are theorized to be the creators of "value" in the information age, replacing land, plants, and equipment as the most valued production resource. These anticipated changes, to the extent they occur, provide the basis for evolution of a new class structure in society, based more upon educational accomplishment than upon the ownership of material resources.

Some have argued that we are evolving into a world of the information-rich and information-poor, with computer access and skills forming the great divide (Castells 1997; Lyon 1988). Even though computers seem omnipresent in society, they are present in only a minority (about 40 percent) of U.S. households and only half of those households have e-mail or Web access (National Telecommunications Information Administration [NTIA] 1998). To the extent that computers with Web connections shift from an optional way of accessing important information and purchasing good and services to a mandatory means of obtaining competitive prices, a case can be made that class differences will expand.

It's appropriate that Daniel Bell, besides being one of the earliest prognosticators of the information age, also has more recently described quite different ways in which it could evolve (1989). He points out that the telecommunications revolution makes possible an intense degree of centralization of power if the society decides to use it in that way. However, because of the multiplicity, diversity, and cheapness of the modes of communication, decentralization is also possible. One of the important challenges for sociology is to understand which of these visions will prevail and why.

REFERENCES

Allen, John C. and Don A. Dillman 1994 *Against All Odds: Rural Community in the Information Age.* Boulder, Colo.: Westview Press.

Bell, Daniel 1973 *The Coming of Postindustrial Society: A Venture in Social Forecasting.* New York: Basic Books.

—— 1989 "Communication Technology: For Better or for Worse." In Jerry L. Salvaggio, ed., *The Information Society: Economic Social and Structural Issues.* Hillsdale, N.J.: Lawrence Erlbaum Associations.

Beniger, James R. 1986 *The Control Revolution: Technological and Economic Origins of the Information Society.* Cambridge, Mass.: Harvard University Press.

Castells, Manuel 1989 *The Information City.* Cambridge, U.K.: Basil Blackwell.

Castells, Manuel 1997 *The Information Age Economy, Society and Culture: Volume II. The Power and Identity.* Malden, Mass.: Blackwell Publishers.

Cleveland, Harlan 1985 "The Twilight of Hierarchy: Speculation on the Global Information Society." *Public Administration Review* 45:185–196.

Lyon, David 1988 *The Information Society: Issues and Illusions.* London, U.K.: Polity Press.

Machlup, Fritz 1962 *The Production and Distribution of Knowledge in the United States.* Princeton, N.J.: Princeton University Press.

Martin, William J. 1995 *The Global Information Society.* London: Aslib Gower.

Masuda, Yoneji 1981 *The Information Society as Postindustrial Society.* Tokyo: Institute for the Information Society; Bethesda, Md.: World Future Society.

National Telecommunications Information Administration 1999 "Falling Through the Net: Defining the Digital Divide." Available at: http://www.ntia.doc.gov/ntiahome/net2/falling.html

Porat, M.U., et al. 1977 *The Information Economy. OT Special Publication 77-12.* Washington, D.C.: U.S. Department of Commerce.

Reich, Robert 1991 *The Work of Nations.* New York: Alfred A. Knopf.

Turkle, Sherry 1984 *"The Second Self": Computers and the Human Spirit.* New York: Simon and Schuster.

U.S. Congress, Office of Technology Assessment 1988 *Technology and the American Transition: Choices for the Future.* OTA-TET-ZA3. Washington, D.C.: U.S. Government Printing Office.

DON A. DILLMAN

INHERITANCE

NOTE: *Although the following article has not been revised for this edition of the Encyclopedia, the substantive coverage is currently appropriate. The editors have provided a list of recent works at the end of the article to facilitate research and exploration of the topic.*

Statutory and common laws governing inheritance have a profound effect on the formation or dissolution of household structures and the patterns of inheritance transfers over generations. A society, for any political or social reason, can initiate and promulgate a law or civil code controlling inheritance; inevitably, new laws or codes cause drastic change in the structure and functions of family systems.

In order to understand the subject of inheritance, it will be necessary to define many terms. To *inherit* is by law to receive property, resources, or, often, status from an ancestor at her or his decease or to take by intestate succession or by will. *Intestate succession* is a transfer of resources according to legal procedures that control distribution of the resources when there is no will. A person is *intestate* when he or she has not made a will. In a *will*, usually a written document, a person (or *testator*) makes a deposition of his or her property, and the deposition takes effect, at least in modern societies, upon the testator's death. A will is changeable and revocable during the lifetime of a testator.

Takers are successors or beneficiaries. *Impartible inheritance* is a situation, established by statute, in which the property and resources are indivisible and are given to one person *(devisee)*; this type of inheritance is likely to occur within family households primarily in rural areas of most historic societies, especially in Eastern and Western Europe. *Partible inheritance*, dividing assets for conveyance to one's heirs, is linked to nuclear family households found in those locations where there is accelerated industrialization and urbanization.

Any system of inheritance promotes the continuity of family and societal structures over generations. The transfer of resources from the older to the younger generation helps maintain a family's position and power in the social order. Such transfers also provide stability to existing societal caste and class arrangements and ordinarily are ensconced deeply in tradition and myth. It is more likely that inheritance systems function to perpetuate existing social structures than to change society's organizations and institutions.

INHERITANCE, LAWS, AND CHANGE

Those most affected by changes in laws are persons with little power in society. This is evident in eighteenth- and nineteenth-century European societies, in which the promulgation of laws and decrees drastically affected the structure and practices of rural families. For example, Gaunt (1983) indicates that in nineteenth-century central Europe, in a section that is now part of Czechoslovakia, the decree to conscript unmarried men for military duty caused parents of serf families to encourage early marriage of their children. As a consequence, the incidence of complex family households increased, and there were changes in the patterns of inheritance succession. During a labor shortage in eighteenth-century Poland, fiefdom rulers encouraged endogamous marriage and attempted to restrict their chattels from leaving their villages. The economy was based on household unit sharecropping. The peasants encouraged complex family households consisting of two or more conjugal units, while the Polish lords favored neolocal household residence (Kochanowicz 1983). The inheritance outcomes of these efforts to circumvent political, economic, and social measures, often repressive in intent, affected existent family structures, their forms, and inheritance patterns.

The possession of equities, property, possessions, resources, and land (especially in the case of European peasants) determined whether these would compose an impartible or partible inheritance. For example, an impartible inheritance pattern is most likely when land is the primary family asset. In addition, the transfer of authority over these rights depended upon the timing of "stepping down," a process deeply embedded in the cultural traditions of the society (Gaunt 1983; Plakans 1989). Stepping down usually occurred through a retirement contract, which was essentially a will that indicated the conditions of the transfer from parents to children. This *inter vivos* phenomenon, a conveyance of property and other equities while the individual was alive and engaged in stepping down, was "one made of preserving intergenerationally the match between family and the property that provides its livelihood" (Sorensen 1989, p. 199). Stepping down, or disengaging, usually occurred when the oldest son married or when the parents were near or at retirement age. Stepping down was invoked by law or tradition, and it resulted in variations in inheritance patterns and in the organization of the life course of various family members.

Sorensen (1989) provides a detailed retirement contract of his great-grandfather on his mother's side, a prosperous farm family in the western part of Jutland, Denmark. The transfer of this medium-sized farm, substantially undervalued, when Laurids Poulsen was fifty-six, was apparently to make certain that the property remained in the family to buttress its position in the society.

It is not explicitly stated in the Poulsen retirement agreement that the heir, Alfred, would care for his parents in their declining years. The contract's provisions enabled Laurids and his wife, Maren, to be independent. Yet in this situation and, as Sorensen (1989) indicates, in Scandinavia since before the Middle Ages, transferring property to a son implied the promise of care in old age. Thus, there existed two motivations for conveying property to a son, but the stronger proved to be the hope of maintaining the property in the family over generations.

In former ages, conveying property and its accompanying position, status, and power was the intent of inheritance patterns. The preservation and maintenance of the family unit was the goal.

Impartible inheritance expressed this intent of maintaining the family property and social position, but it created obvious winners and losers. The transfer of a family's property to a single heir meant that other family members could leave to seek opportunities elsewhere or remain with the family enterprise in a subservient position.

The possibilities for fuller expression of family members' abilities, where talent and skills and not family membership determined the individual's life course trajectory, would come at a later period. Partible inheritance reduced the requirement that family members subordinate their desires, interests, and expectations to those of the family unit. Changes in a society's demographics, such as fertility and mortality, and changes in the means of producing goods and services resulted in lessened need for impartible inheritance. Partible inheritance became identified with the modern period of Western civilization.

MODERN PERIOD

Rules for succession and rules for inheritance of property are related but distinct from one another. Inheritance of property usually follows lines of succession to social position. Codified systems of secular law governing inheritance and status succession emerge in complex societies and are sufficiently precise and uniform to meet the majority needs of the population (Radcliffe-Brown 1935).

For urbanites in complex societies such as those in Europe and the United States, the transfer of land, dwelling unit, tools, and equipment is less critical to the survival and maintenance of the family over generations than it is for the rural resident. Economic assets other than land and buildings—that is, personal mementos and possessions—become the content of such transfers.

Rural landholders of modest means were unable to effect a pattern of impartible inheritance. Increasing societal complexity nurtured corporate agriculture in preference to the family farm. The reduction in the number of family-owned farms, the increasing dependence of farm family members upon the larger, mostly urban society for jobs that are not located close to the farm dwelling, price supports, and payment for nonproduction have diminished the possibilities for maintaining the family farm over generations. Partible inheritance has become the norm.

This shift to partible inheritance under new rules of succession meant that for the first time the claims of the surviving spouse outweighed those of the surviving kin of one's lineage, a reversal of the pattern found in eighteenth- and nineteenth-century Europe and in primitive societies (Benedict 1936; Hoebel 1966). Under U.S. state statutes governing intestacy the surviving spouse and children share in the estate. The spouse receives at least one-third, depending on the number of surviving children and the specifics of the state law governing inheritance. If there is no surviving spouse the children share and share alike. Where there is no surviving spouse or children the estate passes to grandchildren. In the absence of grandchildren the next to receive are grandparents, then siblings, then more distant relatives.

Where testacy exists the estate usually passes to the surviving spouse. This horizontal transfer in the generational line of succession is uniquely modern and represents an evolution from the Roman definition of inheritance as "succession to the entire legal position of a deceased man" (Maine 1963, p. 208). In Rome the heir functioned as a guardian or executor of the estate to perpetuate the honor and status of the deceased and family survivors and to keep intact and extend the estate's holdings. The stepwise shift from decedent to surviving spouse and subsequent vertical transfer of equities to children after the death of the surviving spouse resulted in a family system based more on individual relationships, feelings, perceptions, and interactions and less on tradition, primogeniture, and maintaining properties and estates.

The pattern of conveying all property to the spouse, to be discussed further in this article, is a practice seemingly not in consonance with the concept and exercise of testamentary freedom.

TESTAMENTARY FREEDOM

Testamentary freedom, the individual's right to will away property to persons outside the family or to distribute to a number of heirs and legatees related by blood, consanguinity, or adoption, is a fundamental Anglo-American concept of the U.S. inheritance system. The primogeniture system, which passed all property to a single heir and was most suited for the wealthy, was replaced in eighteenth-century England by a new law of the land—testamentary freedom. This occurred at the time England disposed its feudal land tenure system. The 1789 French Revolution, in keeping with its ideology of justice, freedom, equality, and fraternity, and for more concrete social and political reasons, enacted laws requiring equal distribution of a deceased person's assets among surviving children. Colonial settlers in the United States undoubtedly inspired by and enamored of the changes in English and French societies, brought with them this notion of testamentary freedom as part of their intellectual and cultural heritage.

At first blush the practice of testamentary freedom would seem at least to contradict if not destroy the major intent of an inheritance system. According to Edmund Burke, "the power of perpetuating our property in families is one of the most valuable and interesting circumstances belonging to it, and that which tends the most to the perpetuation of society itself" (1910, p. 121). The major question is whether testamentary freedom as it is practiced negates what Burke suggests is a most critical process for generational and societal continuity.

Testamentary freedom, like justice or liberty, is a relative and not an absolute condition. In practice it accommodates to family continuity over generations; a multilineal descent system; a highly differentiated society where the majority of assets owned by individuals are moveable; and values that espouse rationality, choice, freedom, and democracy. The right of an individual to dispose of property according to her or his wishes is recognized if the individual disposes property in a responsible fashion—when one takes care of one's kin, thus maximizing the possibilities of family continuity and orderly social relationships among family members. Testamentary freedom is not exercised absolutely. It accommodates to the norms of responsibility. Empirical data support the idea that compromise occurs among the interests of the individual's family and state in the exercise of testamentary freedom (Sussman, Cates, and Smith 1970).

Courts, social norms, and societal economic patterns limit the expression of testamentary freedom. Courts use the soundness of mind principle in determining if an individual acts in a responsible fashion. Knowing what one possesses, the nature of the business in which one is engaged, and the natural objects of one's bounty are the essential components of the legal definition of a sound mind. In practice, courts almost universally consider the well-being of the family in addition to considering whether an individual has knowledge of his or her assets and successors (Cates and Sussman 1982). Neglecting or abandoning the family is viewed as unnatural, and being unnatural is equated with being of unsound mind. The media abound with cases regarding will contests involving decedents' bequests to loved pets, charities, strangers, or acquaintances. Preventing a distant relative from taking from or receiving an adequate share of an estate may result in legal action. Sussman, Cates, and Smith (1970) report a case in which charities were the major beneficiaries. The sole surviving relative, a niece, contested the will and lost, but she received a large out-of-court settlement of $150,000. Courts, plaintiffs, and defendants normally favor out-of-court settlements because of lower economic and psychic costs. In 1965, when this case occurred, a settlement of $150,000 was judged to be ample compensation. The settlement was also an indication that the well-being of a distant family member had been considered.

Prevalent social norms foster concern for the well-being of surviving family members. Believing that families should take care of their own and that family members should not be pauperized, the state has more than a legal interest in seeing that testamentary freedom be exercised with regard for the well-being of the family.

PATTERNS OF GENERATIONAL DISTRIBUTIONS

Complex societies have developed systems of statewide resource transfers that have replaced in part some of the functions of the family inheritance system. These large-scale transfer systems, based on the principle of serial service, are society's way of taking care of those deemed dependent, those unable to contribute to the gross national product through gainful employment. Preponderant numbers of the very young and the elderly receive support from such transfers. The preeminent philosophical notion is that the young adult and middle age generations, individuals ages sixteen to sixty five, pay through their earnings for government-initiated entitlement and needs programs such as Social Security, Medicare, Medicaid, educational grants, welfare payments, and so forth, programs to maintain and enhance the lives of the less fortunate. These generations may participate in these programs somewhat grudgingly, but they do so with the knowledge that they were supported during their childhood and with the expectation of being supported by these same programs in their old age. This pattern of society-wide transfers is characteristic of serial service.

Such massive transfers have reduced the economic burden of families in caring for dependent members. In some instances these programs have diminished the need for family members to provide extensive and intensive social and emotional support (Kreps 1965). Social Security pensions and other vested retirement programs, in both the private and public sectors, provide sufficient income for an increasing number of retirees. Most of them will be able to live independently or with minimal support from their relatives during their later adult years. Being economically independent or quasi-independent in old age with little need to rely upon the family's financial resources is a radical shift from earlier periods, when older relatives depended on the determinations of the inheritance system.

The society-wide transfer system based on universal taxation has not completely replaced the family inheritance system. One can view the former as an impersonal, bureaucratized, and universal system enacted primarily by statute or charter and monitored by official regulations. Participants become part of a large formal system and once they qualify are treated in a uniform manner. The use of computers and identification numbers increases the impersonality of support systems.

The family inheritance system, on the other hand, is influenced but not controlled by large-scale economic transfers. It exists and functions within a set of norms that extoll interpersonal relationships, continuity of marriage and blood lines, symbolic meanings, feelings of filial piety, nurturance, support, care, distributive justice, and reciprocity.

These institutional systems and programs that mutually support families probably condition the bases upon which individual inheritance dispositions are made. Sussman, Cares, and Smith (1970) indicate that as a consequence of the growth of society-wide transfer programs,

> Inheritance transfers may be less a consequence of acts of sexual reciprocity, based upon what specific individuals of one generation in a family do for others of another generation, but more a function of serial service. Serial service (a concept elaborated by William Moore, 1967) involves an expected generational transfer that occurs in the normal course of events. It is expected that parents have to help their young children, and middle aged children may be called upon to give care or arrange for care of an aged and often ailing parent. This is within the cycle of life, and services of this kind are expected and are not based upon reciprocal acts. Whatever parents have in the way of worldly possessions will in due course be passed on to lineal descendants. (p. 10)

Since the 1970s there has been a strong movement to reduce, or at best not increase, taxation to support benefit systems that assure society-wide economic transfers across generational lines. Those who support a reduction in such transfers strongly believe that the society has reached its absorptive capacity to pay increasingly higher costs for retirement and a variety of services to dependent family members. The cutback in government programs coupled with the exhortation that the government "should get off the back of family members" and the reglorification of the myth that families in ancient times cared for their own have resulted in increasing burdens for families in the care of their elderly and dependent members. This shift away from society to family responsibility for family members suggests a new look at family economic transfers and the role such inheritance plays in intergenerational relationships and in the solution of long-term care of aged and other dependent members.

INHERITANCE ISSUES FOR THE 1990S

Believing they do not want to be a burden to their children, older adults with economic resources and few relatives for whom to function as primary caregivers when needed are spending their inheritance on travel and other leisure activities and for total medical and physical care as they move from independent to dependent living. A likely result is the diminishing of available funds to heirs and legatees and increased importance of family heirlooms. These gifts express the meaning and significance of the relationships between family members prior to the death of the testator.

The increasing unavailability of relatives, especially children, to care for aged family members will result in the assignment of heirs and legatees who are not related by blood or marriage. These are friends and service providers who supply social support, care, and nurturance and are "like family." Elders in the latter part of this century and well into the twenty-first, that is, members of the World War II baby boom generation, will be searching for a relative or someone to care for them in their declining years. Their drastically low reproduction rates and the consequences of the gender revolution begun in the 1960s will result in the availability of a severely limited number of immediate family members or distant relatives able or willing to provide care. Elderly people will turn to persons not related by blood or marriage—members of the individual's wider family (Marciano 1988). Wider family members are not a certain age, nor must they conform to traditional social norms; they are not related by blood or marriage. Bondings express deep friendship and voluntary informal contracted obligations and expectations. Wider family members today are on call and respond to requests for assistance immediately. They act and feel that they are at home in each other's household.

The consequence is an increasing incidence in the naming of such persons in wills and the probability that courts in the future will uphold their right to share the estate even in the case of intestacy. The courts may rule that traditional patterns of distribution to surviving family beneficiaries be modified to include those who provided care and nurturance to the deceased. The basis for such action is the notion of distributive justice, which invokes fairness. Those who have voluntarily provided services, intimacy, friendship, and care should be recognized and even rewarded. They have fulfilled the role of filial responsibility.

The dark side of this pattern is the exploitative friend, surrogate, or service provider who manipulates the care receiver and takes over the estate through an *inter vivos* transfer or by a rewriting of the will. This sorcerism, coupled with an increasing number of will contests, will keep attorneys in good financial stead and courts very busy for a long time.

Distributive justice, a just and fair distribution of resources as perceived by a testator or promulgated by the laws of intestacy, will be characteristic of transfers to family and kin as well as wider family members in the coming decades. A component of distributive justice is equality (Piaget 1932), a standard that is invoked by statutes governing intestacy. Equality is determined by the degree of relationship of the deceased to the survivor. Thus, upon the death of a parent intestate, equal shares are given to surviving children. If a spouse survives, she or he usually receives one-third of the estate, and the remaining two-thirds are distributed to surviving children.

Equity is another component of distributive justice. It implies a just and fair condition. It is not the same as equality. It is the "distribution of rewards and costs between persons" (Homans 1961, p. 74). Equity is the component most suited to arrangements for payment of rewards for incurred costs. Hence, both family and nonfamily members can expect rewards in property inheritance in relation to the costs incurred in caregiving and related activities. Such exchanges will become normative and generally accepted. Reciprocity is to be recognized and rewarded.

Portending the future, testators will increasingly enter into contracts with either family or nonfamily (wider) members, setting forth conditions and expectations of needed supports and caregiving (Hanks and Sussman 1990). Such contracts, seemingly as legal as any other contract, are likely to be challenged in the courts by those who stand to inherit under the laws of descent and succession. The rootedness of these contracts in distributive justice, with its fairness and equity principles, suggests that their validity will be sustained.

Contracts can involve *inter vivos* transfers or declarations in a will. For example, a middle-aged testator can give resources to a young relative or member of a wider family with a pay-back arrangement of care and service when needed by the benefactor. A will provision can readily be made.

The exact instrument that will enhance its legality needs to be developed in consultation with attorneys. Such contracts, similar to prenuptial agreements, drawn with both parties of sound mind, should be legal. These contracts will have provisions for modification and cancelation, like any other contract. The major point is that such contracts can reduce the concerns of an aging population regarding their life-style in very old age and diminish their total dependence upon institutional forms of care. The "inheritance contract" fosters independence and utilization of one's resources in meeting health and social needs. Caretaking as a family enterprise can reduce potentially the outlay of public monies currently expended for health and social service programs. This reduction in the economic burden of government is not tantamount to the elimination of current universal support programs. At best the inheritance contract helps provide meaningful relationships, establishes a procedure for planning and expending one's resources, and encourages individuals to rely less upon governmental institutions.

Openness in discussing wills is a new departure from the past and leads to forthrightness in discussing other family matters. Hanks (1989) reports in her sample of 111 corporate family members that 88 percent discussed their wills and 60 percent their funeral arrangements. Such openness with relatives can reduce future will contests and result in conversations and negotiations regarding foreseeable generational transfers and caregiving arrangements. The symbolic meaning attached to the passing on of jewelry, paintings, furniture, books, and other household items has been given very little attention (Sussman, Cates, and Smith 1970). Allocations of these items demonstrated to the recipients the kind of emotional and affective relationship they had with the deceased. More individuals experienced pain and depression from not receiving a promised or expected heirloom than from receiving a lesser share of property or equities. Strong feelings are aroused because of the memories connected with these heirlooms, and the deceased cannot be asked regarding her or his feelings and emotions toward the heir. Openness in discussing wills and related matters can reduce misunderstandings and misinterpretations regarding the meaning attached to the transfer of heirlooms and the trauma of not knowing.

In the 1990s and future decades inheritance will continue its patterns of transfer and distribution of properties and equities over generations. It will be a different system from that found in rural areas in historic or current time. It will continue to be insignificant in the generational transfer of status and power except for the wealthy classes. Things that will distinguish inheritance in the future from that of the past is the emergence of the inheritance contract; openness in discussing will contents with potential beneficiaries; greater inclusion of distant family relatives in wills; increased number of will contests; and increased incidence in the number of older adults who spend money on leisure activities or on their own health care rather than contribute it to their children's inheritance.

(SEE ALSO: *Intergenerational Resource Transfers*)

REFERENCES

Benedict, Ruth 1936 "Marital Property Rights in Bilateral Society." *American Anthropologist* 38:368–373.

Burke, Edmund 1910 *Reflections on the French Revolution and Other Essays*. New York: DuHon.

Cates, Judith, and Marvin B. Sussman 1982 *Family Systems and Inheritance Patterns*. New York: Haworth Press.

Gaunt, David 1983 "The Property and Kin Relationships of Retired Farmers in Northern and Central Europe." In Richard Wall, Jean Robin, and Peter Laslett, eds., *Family Forms in Historic Europe*. Cambridge: Cambridge University Press.

Garrett, Mario D. 1995 "Filial Piety or a Filial Pie: Capital Transfer from the Elderly to Their Offspring within Southeast and Eastern Asia." In Stanley R. Ingman, Pei Xiaomei, Carl D. Ekstrom, Hiram J. Friedsam, and Kristy R. Bartlett, eds., *An Aging Population in an Aging Planet, and a Sustainable Future*. Denton, Tex.: Center Texas Studies.

Gross, Stephen J. 1996 "Handing Down the Farm: Values, Strategies, and Outcomes in Inheritance Practices among Rural German Americans." *Journal of Family History* 21:192–217.

Hanks, Roma 1990 "Inheritance and Caregiving: Perceptions in Veteran and Corporate Families." Unpublished paper, College of Human Resources, University of Delaware.

——, and Marvin B. Sussman 1990 "Inheritance Contracting: Policy Implications of Inheritance and Caregiving Patterns." Unpublished paper, College of Human Resources, University of Delaware.

Hill, Gretchen J. 1995 "Inheritance Law in an Aging Society." *Journal of Aging and Social Policy* 7:57–83.

Hoebel, Edgar A. 1966 *Anthropology*. New York: Mc-Graw-Hill.

Homans, George C. 1961 *Social Behavior: Its Elementary Forms*. New York: Harcourt, Brace and World.

Hooyman, Nancy R. 1989 "Women as Caregivers of the Elderly: Implications for Social Welfare Policy and Practice." In David E. Bregel and Arthur Bloom, eds., *Aging and Caregiving*. Newbury Park, Calif.: Sage.

Kochanowicz, Jasalav 1983 "The Peasant Family as an Economic Unit in the Polish Feudal Economy of the Eighteenth Century." In Richard Wall, Jean Robin, and Peter Laslett, eds., *Family Forms in Historic Europe*. Cambridge: Cambridge University Press.

Kreps, Juanita 1965 "The Economics of Intergenerational Relationships." In Gordon F. Streib and Ethel Shanas, eds., *Social Structure and the Family*. Englewood Cliffs, N.J.: Prentice-Hall.

Maine, Henry S. 1963 *Ancient Law*. Boston: Beacon Press.

Marciano, Teresa D. 1988 "Families Wider Than Kin." *Family Science Review* 1:115–124.

Niraula, Bhanu B. 1995 "Old Age Security and Inheritance in Nepal: Motives versus Means." *Journal of Biosocial Science* 27:71–78.

Peart, Nicola 1996 "Towards a Concept of Family Property in New Zealand." *International Journal of Law, Policy and the Family* 10:105–133.

Piaget, Jean 1932 "Retributive and Distributive Justice." In *Moral Judgement of the Child*. New York, Harcourt, Brace and World. Reprinted in Edgar Borgatta and Henry J. Meyer, eds., *Sociological Theory*. New York: Alfred A. Knopf, 1956.

Plakans, Andrejs 1989 "Stepping Down in Former Times: A Comparative Assessment of Retirement in Traditional Europe." In David I. Kertzer and K. Warner Schaie, eds., *Age Structuring in Comparative Perspective*. Hillsdale, N.J.: L. Erlbaum.

Radcliffe-Brown, Alfred R. 1935 "Patrilineal and Matrilineal Succession." *Iowa Law Review* 20:286–303.

Rosenfeld, Jeffrey P. 1991 "The Heir and the Spare: Evasiveness, Role-complexity, and Patterns of Inheritance." In Judith R. Blau and Norman Goodman, eds., *Social Roles and Social Institutions: Essays in Honor of Rose Laub Coser*. Boulder, Colo.: Westview Press.

Schwartz, T. P. 1996 "Durkheim's Prediction about the Declining Importance of the Family and Inheritance: Evidence from the Wills of Providence, 1775–1985." *Sociological Quarterly* 37:503–519.

Sorensen, Aage B. 1989 "Old Age, Retirement, and Inheritance." In David I. Kertzer and K. Warner Schaie, eds., *Age Structuring in Comparative Perspective*. Hillsdale, N.J.: L. Erlbaum.

Sussman, Marvin B., Judith N. Cates, and David T. Smith 1970 *The Family and Inheritance*. New York: Russell Sage Foundation.

Tsikata, Dzodzi 1996 "Gender, Kinship and the Control of Resources in Colonial Southern Ghana." In Rajni Palriwala and Carla Risseeuw, eds., *Shifting Circles of Support: Contextualizing Kinship and Gender in South Asia and Sub Saharan Africa*. Walnut Creek, Calif.: AltaMira.

Van-Houtte, Jean, Marc Keuleneer, and Kathelijne Vanden-Brande 1995 "Inheritance Law and Practice in the USA and Belgium." *Sociologia-del-Dritto* 22(3):75–106.

MARVIN B. SUSSMAN

IN-LAW RELATIONSHIPS

See American Families; Intergenerational Relationships; Kinship Systems and Family Types.

INSTITUTIONS

See American Society.

INTEGRATION

See African-American Studies; Segregation and Desegregation.

INTELLECTUALS

NOTE: *Although the following article has not been revised for this edition of the Encyclopedia, the substantive coverage is currently appropriate. The editors have provided a list of recent works at the end of the article to facilitate research and exploration of the topic.*

Modern societies face a growing dilemma posed by the fact that key institutions and their elites are increasingly dependent upon intellectuals, particularly those in universities, research institutes, and the cultural apparatus generally. Yet, the leaders in these same social units are among the major critics of the way in which the society operates, sometimes calling into question the legitimacy of the social order and its political structure. A ruling elite, even one that is conservative and anti-intellectual, cannot respond to such challenges by crushing the intellectuals, unless it is willing to incur the punitive costs which such suppression entails. As the Polish "revisionist" philosopher Leszek Kolakowski (1968, p. 179) wrote while still a member of the Communist party, "the spiritual domination of any ruling class over the people ... depends on its bonds with the intelligentsia ... ; for the less one is capable of ruling by intellectual means, the more one must resort to the instruments of force." Decades earlier, the classically liberal (laissez-faire) economist and sociologist Joseph Schumpeter (1962, p. 150) argued that under capitalism the dominant economic class must protect the intellectuals, "however strongly disapproving" they are of them, because they cannot suppress intellectual criticism without initiating a process of repression which will undermine their own freedom.

The word *intellectual* is fraught with ambiguities. The meanings attached to it are diverse (Lipset and Dobson 1972, pp. 137–140). In the loosest sense in which the word is used in common parlance today, intellectuals may be said to be all those who are considered proficient in and are actively engaged in the creation, distribution, and application of culture. Edward Shils (1968, p. 179) has suggested a comprehensive definition: "Intellectuals are the aggregate of persons in any society who employ in their communication and expression, with relative higher frequency than most other members of their society, symbols of general scope and abstract reference, concerning man, society, nature and the cosmos." For analytic purposes, however, it is desirable to distinguish between several types. It is particularly useful to emphasize the much smaller category of "creative intellectuals," whose principal focus is on innovation, the elaboration of knowledge, art, and symbolic formulations generally. Included in this group are scholars, scientists, philosophers, artists, authors, some editors, and some journalists, as distinguished from the more marginally intellectual groups who distribute culture, such as most teachers, clerics, journalists, engineers, free professionals, and performers in the arts, as well as those who apply knowledge in the course of their work, such as practicing physicians, lawyers, and engineers. To differentiate them from the intellectuals, they may be categorized as the *intelligentsia*.

The creative intellectuals are the most dynamic group within the broad stratum: Because they are innovative, they are at the forefront in the development of culture. The intelligentsia are dependent upon them for the ideational resources they use in their work. Much of the analytic literature dealing with intellectuals has emphasized their seemingly inherent tendency to criticize existing institutions from the vantage point of general conceptions of the desirable, ideal conceptions which are thought to be universally applicable. Thus, Joseph Schumpeter (1950, p. 147) stressed that "one of the touches that distinguish [intellectuals] ... from other people ... is the critical attitude." Raymond Aron (1962, p. 210) argued that "the tendency to criticize the established order is, so to speak, the occupational disease of the intellectuals." Richard Hofstadter (1963, p. 38) noted: "The modern idea of the intellectual as constituting a class, as a separate social force, even the term *intellectual* itself, is identified with the idea of political and moral protest." Lewis Coser (1970, p. viii) in defining the term stated: "Intellectuals are men who never seem satisfied with things as they are. . . . They question the truth of the moment in higher and wider truth."

These concerns are iterated by the fact that "intelligentsia" and "intellectuals," the two words most commonly used to describe those in occupations requiring trained or imaginative intelligence, were used first in the context of describing those engaged in oppositional activities. "Intelligentsia," first began to be used widely in Russia in the 1860s, referring to the opposition to the system by the educated strata. It was generally defined as "a 'class' held together by the bond of 'consciousness,' 'critical thought,' or 'moral passion'." (Malia 1961 p. 5) "Intellectual" as a noun first secured wide usage in France during the infamous Dreyfus case in 1898. A protest against Dreyfus's unjust imprisonment (after a biased court-martial), signed by a variety of writers and professors, was published as the "Manifesto of the Intellectuals." The anti-Dreyfusards then tried to satirize their opponents as the self-proclaimed "intellectuals" (Bodin 1962, pp. 6–9; Hofstadter 1963, pp. 38–39). The term was picked up in the United States in the context of characterizing opponents to World War I.

The American intellectual also has been seen as a source of unrest. Many have called attention to this phenomenon, seeing it as a continuing one in

American history (May 1963; Hayek 1949, pp. 417–433). Richard Hofstadter (1965, pp. 111–112) described their stance of alienation as "historical and traditional," and pointed out that "even the genteel, established intellectuals of the mid-nineteenth century were in effect patrician rebels against the increasing industrialization and the philistinism of the country. So that it has been the tradition of American intellectuals of all kinds and stamps to find themselves at odds with American society: this, I think, to a degree that is unusual elsewhere." A century ago, Whitelaw Reid (1873, pp. 613–614), the editor of the *New York Tribune*, pointed to the role of the American "Scholar in Politics" as a foe of the "established," and a leader of the "radicals."

The reader should not get the impression that intellectual and student involvement in protest is confined to left-wing or progressive movements. This is not true, as witnessed, for example, by the intellectuals and students who constituted a core segment of activist support for the Fascist party of Mussolini, and of the National Socialist party of Hitler, before they took power, as well as among fascist and assorted anti-Semitic right-wing extreme groups in France and various countries in Eastern Europe up to World War II (Hamilton 1971; Röpke 1960, pp. 346–347). In Eastern Europe and the Soviet Union, intellectuals have been in the forefront of the struggles against Communist regimes, behavior that is perceived as left, i.e. opposition to statism, authoritarianism, and severe stratification.

In the United States, although scattered groups of right-wing intellectuals have emerged at times, the record seems to validate Richard Hofstadter's (1963, p. 39) generalization that for almost all of this century the political weight of American intellectuals has been on the progressive, liberal, and leftist side. Quantitative data derived from attitude surveys, the earliest dating back to before World War I, plus assorted other reports of the political orientations of the American professoriate, down to the present, strongly indicate that American intellectuals have consistently leaned in this direction (Lipset and Dobson 1972, pp. 211–289; Lipset 1991). This bias, to a considerable extent, reflects the absence or weakness of a legitimate national conservative tradition in America. National identity and national ideology are linked to a value system that emphasizes egalitarianism and populism, stemming from an elaboration of

principles enunciated in the Declaration of Independence. Thus, when American intellectuals point up the gap between the real and the ideal, whether the latter is represented by what was in a bygone Jeffersonian laissez-faire era (a utopia of equal yeoman farmers) or what it should be (a classless participatory future), they challenge the system for not fulfilling the ideals implicit in the American Creed.

Still, the argument is frequently made that inherent in the structural changes since World War II, which have been described as leading to a "postindustrial society," has been a growing interdependence between political authority and intellectualdom, which should have reduced the critical stance. Modern developed socioeconomic systems are highly dependent on superior research and development resources, which mean better support for universities, and research centers, and the much larger component of persons who have passed through the higher education system—thus creating a mass, high-culture market that pays for the institutions and products of the artistic community (Bell 1973). Governments are increasingly a major source of financing for intellectualdom, ranging from artists to scientists. Recognition and financial rewards from the polity conceivably should help to reduce the historic tensions and the intellectual's sense of being an outsider. A further trend pressing in this direction is the fact that the complexities involved in "running" an advanced industrial or postindustrial society forces laymen, both political and economic leaders, to seek advice in depth from, to defer to, the scholarly-scientific community (Dahl 1989, pp. 334–335; Gagnon 1987). Many, therefore, have seen these trends as fostering the role of the intellectual as participant, as leading to the "interpenetration" of scholarship and policy (Shils 1968; Brint 1991).

These developments, however, have not led to the decline in the critical role of the intellectual in the United States, although patterns elsewhere appear somewhat different (Lerner, Nagai, and Rothman 1990, p. 26). A number of analyses of different American scholarly disciplines have emphasized the significant presence of political radicals among them and their greater alienation from the powers than in Western European societies (Lipset 1991). In seeking to explain this trans-Atlantic difference, a Swedish scholar, Ron Eyerman (1990) notes that unlike the situation in America,

Swedish (and I would add European) intellectuals are not an "alienated stratum" opposed to the state "because the avant-garde tradition was absorbed through a reformism [that] put intellectual labor to use in service of society," that is, largely through the labor and socialist movements. While the overwhelming majority of American intellectuals view themselves as outsiders, and have had little experience in directly influencing power that could moderate their sense of alienation, many European intellectuals have worked in a somewhat more integrated context. And most are, it should be noted, still on the left politically, though less radical relative to their national spectrums than their American counterparts.

The dilemma remains for intellectuals everywhere of how to obtain the resources necessary to pursue creative activity without "selling out," without tailoring creative and intellectual work to the demands of employer, patron, or consumer. In modern times in the West, the emphasis on originality, on innovation, and on following the logic of development in various creative fields— be they painting, music, literature, physics, or sociology— has been responsible for a recurrent conflict between intellectuals and those who pay for their works or exert control through the state, churches, businesses, the market, or other institutions. Intellectuals have often felt themselves to be dependent on philistines while wanting to do whatever they liked according to the norms of their field.

Much of the discussion has focused on the tensions created for unattached intellectuals. It has been asserted "that free-lance intellectuals are more receptive to political extremism than are other types of intellectuals . . . [since] the freelance intellectual . . . has been dependent on an anonymous and unpredictable market. . . . Rewards are much less certain to be forthcoming for the freelance intellectual, the form of reward less predictable, and the permanence of the recognition more tenuous. . . . [They] tend to be more dependent on their audience, over which they have relatively little control, and to feel greater social distance from it (Kornhauser 1959, pp. 186–187)."

To understand the continued anti-establishment emphasis of intellectuals, even when well rewarded, it is important to recognize the relationship of this emphasis to their concern for creativity or innovation. The capacity for criticism, for rejection of the status quo, is not simply a matter of preference by some intellectuals. Rather, it is built into the very nature of their occupational role. The distinction between integrative and innovative roles implies that those intelligentsia involved in the former, like teachers, engineers, and exponents of mass culture, use ideas— scholarly findings—to carry out their jobs; those in the latter activities, like scholars, poets, and scientists, are concerned with the creation of *new* knowledge, *new* ideas, *new* art. To a considerable extent, in such endeavors, one is much more rewarded for being original than for being correct —an important fact, a crucial aspect of the role insofar as we consider that such intellectuals tend to be socially critical.

(SEE ALSO: *Postindustrial Society*)

REFERENCES

Allen, Norm R., Jr. 1996 "Religion and the New African American Intellectuals." *Nature, Society, and Thought* 9:159–187.

Aron, Raymond 1962 *The Opium of the Intellectuals*. New York: Norton.

Beaud, Paul, and Francesco Panese 1995 "From One Galaxy to Another: The Trajectories of French Intellectuals." *Media Culture and Society* 17:385–412.

Bell, Daniel 1973 *The Coming of Post-Industrial Society*. New York: Basic Books.

Bodin, Louis 1962 *Les Intellectuels*. Paris: Presses Universitaires de France.

Brint, Stephen 1991 "The Powers of the Intellectuals." In William Julius Wilson, ed., *Sociology and the Public Agenda*. Newbury Park, Calif.: Sage.

Coser, Lewis 1970 *Men of Ideas*. New York: The Free Press.

Dahl, Robert A. 1989 *Democracy and Its Critics*. New Haven: Yale University Press.

Drake, W. Avon 1997 "Black Intellectuals and the Politics of Race: The Affirmative Action Debate." *Research in Race and Ethnic Relations* 10:147–168.

Eyerman, Ron 1990 "Intellectuals and the State: A Framework for Analysis; with special reference for the United States and Sweden." Unpublished paper, Department of Sociology, University of Lund, Sweden.

Gagnon, Alain (ed.) 1987 *Intellectuals in Liberal Democracies*: Political Influence and Social Involvement. Westport, Conn.: Greenwood Press.

Hamilton, Alastair 1971 *The Appeal of Fascism: A Study of Intellectuals and Fascism, 1919–1945*. London: Anthony Blond.

Hofstadter, Richard 1963 *Anti-Intellectualism in American Life*. New York: Alfred A. Knopf.

——1965 "Discussion." In A. Alvarez, ed., *Under Pressure*. Baltimore: Penguin Books.

Hollander, Paul 1998 *Political Pilgrims: Western Intellectuals in Search of the Good Society*. New Brunswick, NJ: Transaction.

"Intellectuals and Social Change in Central and Eastern Europe." 1992 *Partisan Review* 59:525–751.

Karabel, Jerome 1996 "Towards a Theory of Intellectuals and Politics." *Theory and Society* 25:205–233.

Kellner, Douglas 1997 "Intellectuals, the New Public Spheres, and Techno-Politics." *New Political Science* 169–188.

Kempny, Marian 1996 "Between Politics and Culture. Is a Convergence between the East-European Intelligentsia and Western Intellectuals Possible?" *Polish Sociological Review* 4:297–305.

Kolakowski, Leszek 1968 *Marxism and Beyond*. London: Pall Mall Press.

Kornhauser, William 1959 *The Politics of Mass Society*. New York: Free Press.

Lepenies, Wolf 1994 "The Future of Intellectuals." *Partisan Review* 61:111–119.

Lerner, Robert, Althea K. Nagai, and Stanley Rothman 1990 "Elite Dissensus and Its Origins," *Journal of Political and Military Sociology* 18 (Summer): 25–39.

Lipset, Seymour Martin 1991 "No Third Way: A Comparative Perspective on the Left." In Daniel Chirot, ed., *The End of Leninism and the Decline of the Left*. Seattle: University of Washington Press.

——, and Richard Dobson 1972 "The Intellectual as Critic and Rebel: With Special Reference to the United States and the Soviet Union." *Daedalus* 101 (Summer 1971):137–198.

Malia, Martin 1961 "What is the Intelligentsia?" In Richard Pipes, ed., *The Russian Intelligentsia*. New York: Columbia University Press.

May, Henry 1963 *The Discontent of the Intellectuals*. Chicago: Rand McNally.

Misra, Kalpana 1997 "From 'Capitalist Roaders' to 'Socialist Democrats': Intellectuals in Post-Mao China." *China Report* 33:267–295.

Petras, James 1991 "The Metamorphosis of Latin America's Intellectuals." *International Journal of Contemporary Sociology* 28:3–4.

Reid, Whitelaw 1873 "The Scholar in Politics." *Scribner's Monthly*, vol. 6.

Röpke, Wilhelm 1960, "National Socialism and the Intellectuals." In George B. de Huszar, ed., *The Intellectuals*. New York: Free Press.

Royce, Edward 1996 "The Public Intellectual Reconsidered." *Humanity and Society* 20:3–17.

Schumpeter, Joseph 1950 *Capitalism, Socialism and Democracy*. New York: Harper Torchbooks.

Shils, Edward 1968 "Intellectuals." In David L. Sills, ed. *International Encyclopedia of the Social Sciences*, vol. 7. New York: Macmillan and Free Press.

Smith, James-Allen 1991 *The Idea Brokers: Think Tanks and the Rise of the New Policy Elite*. New York: The Free Press.

Torpey, John C. 1995 *Intellectuals, Socialism, and Dissent: The East German Opposition and Its Legacy*. Minneapolis: University of Minnesota Press.

Weijers, Ido 1997 "Educating the Modern Intellectuals." *International Journal of Contemporary Sociology* 34:81–91.

Seymour Martin Lipset

INTELLIGENCE

In everyday life people commonly refer to each other as being smart or slow. The perception that individuals differ widely in mental adeptness—in intelligence—long preceded development of the IQ test, and there is indeed a large vernacular for brilliance, stupidity, and the many points in between. There has been much sparring over the scientific meaning and measurement of intelligence, both in the rowdy corridors of public debate and in the sanctums of academe. But what do we actually know about intelligence? A lot more in the last decade, and some of it surprising even to experts. Moreover, the data form a very consistent pattern showing that differences in intelligence are a biologically grounded phenomenon with immense sociological import.

MEASUREMENT OF INTELLIGENCE

The effort to measure intelligence variation among individuals is a century old. Two strategies for measuring such differences have emerged, the *psychometric* and the *experimental*. Both spring from the universal perception that, although all people can think and learn, some are notably better at both than others. Accordingly, intelligence research focuses on how people *differ* in cognitive competence, not on what is common to all of us. (Other disciplines such as neuroscience and cognitive psychology specialize in the commonalities.) The aim of intelligence research is thus much narrower than explaining the intricacies of how brains and minds function. These intricacies are relevant to intelligence experts, but generally only to the extent that they illuminate why people in all cultures differ so much in their ability to think, know, and learn.

Psychometric (Mental Testing) Strategy. The IQ test represents the psychometric approach to measuring intelligence. Alfred Binet devised the first such test in France to identify children who would have difficulty profiting from regular school instruction. Binet's idea was to sample everyday mental competencies and knowledge that were *not* tied to specific school curricula, that increased systematically throughout childhood, and that could reliably forecast important differences in later academic performance. The result was a series of standardized, age-graded test items arranged in increasing order of difficulty. A child's score on the test compared the child's level of mental development to that of average children of the same age. Binet's aim was pragmatic and his effort successful.

Innumerable similar tests have been developed and refined in the intervening century (Anastasi 1996; Kaufman 1990). Some are paper-and-pencil tests, called *group tests*, that can be administered cheaply to many individuals at once and with only a small sacrifice in accuracy. Others, such as the various Wechsler tests, are *individually administered tests* that require no reading and are given one-on-one. Today, individually administered intelligence tests are typically composed of ten to fifteen subtests that vary widely in content. The two major categories are the *verbal* subtests, such as vocabulary, information, verbal analogies, and arithmetic, which require specific knowledge, and the *performance* subtests, such as block design, matrices, and figure analogies, which require much reasoning but little or no knowledge. The highly technical field that develops and evaluates mental tests, called *psychometrics*, is one of the oldest and most rigorous in psychology. Its products have

been found useful in schools, industry, the military, and clinical practice, where they are widely used.

Professionally developed mental tests are highly *reliable*, that is, they rank people very consistently when they are retested. A great concern in earlier decades was whether mental tests might be culturally biased. *Bias* refers to the systematic over- or underestimation of the true abilities of people from certain groups—a "thumb on the scale"— favoring or disfavoring them. There are many specific techniques for uncovering test bias, and all mental tests are screened for bias today before being published. IQ tests generally yield different average scores for various demographic groups, but the consensus of expert opinion is that those average differences are not due to bias in the tests. The consensus among bias experts, after decades of research often trying to prove otherwise, is that the major mental tests used in the United States today do not systematically understate the developed abilities of native-born, English-speaking minorities, including American blacks. The American Psychological Association affirmed this consensus in its 1996 task force report, "Intelligence: Knowns and Unknowns" (Neisser et al. 1996).

The biggest remaining question about IQ tests today is whether they are *valid*, that is, whether they really measure "intelligence" and whether they really predict important social outcomes. As will be shown later, IQ tests do, in fact, measure what most people mean by the term "intelligence," and they predict a wide range of social outcomes, although some better than others and for reasons not always well understood.

Experimental (Laboratory) Strategy. The experimental approach to measuring differences in general intelligence is older than the psychometric but little known outside the study of intelligence. It has produced no tests of practical value outside research settings, although its likely products could someday replace IQ tests for many purposes. The approach began in the late 1800s when the great polymath Francis Galton proposed that *mental speed* might be the essence of intelligence. He therefore set out to measure it by testing how quickly people respond to simple sensory stimuli such as lights or tones. Galton's measures did not clearly correlate with "real-life" indicators of mental ability, such as educational success, so his *chronometric* approach was quickly dismissed as wrong-headed and far too simplistic to capture anything important about the beautiful complexity of human thought.

Advances in statistics after the mid-twentieth century, however, showed that Galton's data actually had shown considerable promise. New medical and computer technology have since allowed researchers to measure elements of mental processing with the necessary precision that Galton could not. The revival of his approach in the 1970s has revolutionized the study of intelligence. It is the new frontier in intelligence research today. No longer producing "fool's gold" but the real thing, the study of elementary cognitive processes has attracted researchers from around the world. It now appears that some differences in complex mental abilities may, in fact, grow from simple differences in how people's brains process information, including their sheer speed in processing.

There is no single experimental approach, but perhaps the dominant one today is the chronometric, which includes studies of inspection time (IT) and reaction time (RT). Chronometric tasks differ dramatically from IQ test items. The aim is to measure the *speed* of various elementary perceptual and comprehension processes. So, instead of scoring how well a person performs a complex mental task (such as solving a mathematics problem or defining a word), chronometric studies measure how quickly people perform tasks that are so simple that virtually no one gets them wrong. These *elementary cognitive tasks* (ECTs) include, for example, reporting which of two briefly presented lines is the longer or which of several lights has been illuminated. In the former, an IT task, the score is the number of milliseconds of exposure required to perceive the difference. In the latter, an RT task, the score is the number of milliseconds the subject takes to *release* a "home button" (called "decision time") in order to press the lighted response button (called "movement time").

Both average speed and variability in speed of reaction are measured over many trials. It turns out that brighter people are not only faster but more consistent in their speed of stimulus apprehension, discrimination, choice, visual search, scanning of short-term memory, and retrieval of information from long-term memory. In fact, variability in speed is more highly correlated with IQ (negatively) than is average speed. ECT performance correlates more highly with IQ as the tasks become more complex, for example, when the number of lights to distinguish among increases from two to four to eight (respectively, one, two, and three "bits" of information). Composites of various speed and consistency scores from different ECTs typically correlate −.5 to −.7 with IQ (on a scale of −1.0 to 1.0, with zero meaning no relation), indicating that both chronometric and psychometric measures tap much the same phenomena. Psychometric and chronometric measures of mental capacity also trace much the same developmental curve over the life cycle, increasing during childhood and declining in later adulthood. Debates among the experimentalists concern how many and which particular elementary cognitive processes are required to account for differences in psychometric intelligence.

MEANING OF INTELLIGENCE.

The meaning of intelligence can be described at two levels. Nonexperts are usually interested in the *practical meaning* of intelligence as manifested in daily life. What skills does it reflect? How useful are they in school, work, and home life? In contrast, intelligence researchers tend to be interested in the more *fundamental nature* of intelligence. Is it a property of the brain and, if so, which property exactly? Or is it mostly a learned set of skills whose value varies by culture? Personnel and school psychologists, like other researchers concerned with the practical implications of mental capability, are often interested in both levels.

Practical Definitions of Intelligence. The practical meaning of intelligence is captured well by the following description, which was published by fifty-two leading experts on intelligence (Gottfredson 1997a). It is based on a century of research on the mental behavior of higher- versus lower-IQ people in many different settings.

Intelligence is a very general mental capability that, among other things, involves the ability to reason, plan, solve problems, think abstractly, comprehend complex ideas, learn quickly and learn from experience. It is not merely book learning, a narrow academic skill, or test-taking smarts. Rather, it reflects a broader and deeper capability for comprehending our surroundings–"catching on," "making sense" of things, or "figuring out" what to do. (p. 13)

The concept of intelligence refers specifically to an *ability* that is *mental*. It does not encompass many of the other personal traits and circumstances that are important in people's lives. It does not include, for instance, strictly physical skills, creativity, or traits of personality and character such as conscientiousness and drive. IQ tests are not intended to measure these other traits. Three practical definitions that are more specific may illuminate better what intelligence means in daily affairs. Each can be translated into the others, but each highlights a different practical aspect of intelligence: the ability to deal with complexity (Gottfredson 1997b), learn (Carroll 1997), and avoid making cognitive errors (Gordon 1997).

Intelligence as the ability to deal with complexity. IQ test items vary widely in content and format, but they often seem esoteric or narrowly academic. Many people in the past took these superficialities as guides to the nature of what IQ tests measure and therefore mistakenly concluded that they cannot be measuring anything of real consequence, at least outside schools. IQ tests' superficial characteristics, however, are irrelevant to their ability to measure intelligence. What matters is the *complexity*, the amount of mental manipulation, their tasks require: contrasting, abstracting, inferring, finding salient similarities and differences, and otherwise turning things over in one's mind to accomplish the mental task. Complexity is the active ingredient in tests that call forth intelligence. People who score higher on IQ tests are people who deal better with complexity, that is, are more adept at understanding and effectively solving more complex mental challenges.

Any kind of test *vehicle* or content (words, numbers, figures, pictures, symbols, blocks, mazes, and so on) can be used to create different levels of complexity. IQ tests typically do, in fact, contain subtests with different kinds of content. Forward and backward digit span (two memory subtests) illustrate clearly the notion of mental manipulation and task complexity. In digits forward, individuals are asked to repeat a string of from two to nine digits (say, 3-2-5-9-6) that is presented orally at one digit per second. In digits backward, the individual simply repeats the numbers in reverse order (in this case, 6-9-5-2-3). The one extra element in the second task (mentally reversing the list) greatly increases its complexity, nearly doubling its correlation with IQ.

Number series completion subtests can also seem trivial, but they illustrate how the same simple content can be varied to build increasingly complex mental demands. Consider the following three series: 4, 6, 8, 10, 12,— (easy item); 2, 4, 5, 7, 8, 10,— (moderate); and 9, 8, 7, 8, 7, 6,— (difficult). One must discern the relations between succeeding numbers in order to complete the series, and those relations become increasingly complex across the three series (respectively, add 2 to each successive digit; add 3 to each successive set of two digits; subtract 1 from each successive set of three digits). These are similar to the items found in one of the fifteen subtests of the Stanford–Binet Intelligence Scale (SBIS–IV) for school-aged youth. They require very little knowledge. Instead, their challenge is to use that simple information effectively—to contrast and compare, find relations, and infer rules—in order to solve logical problems in the test setting. IQ tests that require this on-the-spot problem solving are referred to as tests of *fluid intelligence*—of mental horsepower, if you will.

Some IQ subtests require test takers to bring considerable knowledge into the test setting in order to perform well, but they, too, illustrate the principle that the active ingredient in IQ tests is the complexity of their mental demands. Vocabulary, for example, is one of the very best subtests for measuring intelligence. The reason is that people do not learn most words (*love, hate*) by memorization or direct instruction, but rather by *inferring* their meanings and their fine nuances in meaning (*love, affection, infatuation, devotion,* and *ardor; hatred, loathing, abhorrence, antipathy,* and *contempt*) from the way other people use them in everyday life. Learning vocabulary is largely a process of distinguishing and generalizing concepts in natural settings.

Table 1 illustrates how vocabulary level reflects differences in the ability to deal with complexity. These results are from an earlier version of the Wechsler Adult Intelligence Scale (WAIS). All the adults tested were able to provide at least a tolerable definition of concrete items such as *bed, ship,* and *penny,* but passing rates dropped quickly for more abstract and nuanced concepts such as *slice* (94 percent), *sentence* (83 percent), *domestic* (65 percent), and *obstruct* (58 percent). Only half could define the words *remorse, reluctant,* and *calamity.* Fewer than one in five knew the words *ominous* and *tirade*, and only 5 percent could provide even a partial definition of *travesty*. Anyone who has attended high school, read newspapers and magazines, or watched television will have encountered these words. Vocabulary tests thus gauge the ease with which individuals have routinely "picked up" or "caught onto" concepts they encounter in the general culture. So, too, do the general information subtests that are included in many IQ test batteries ("Why do homeowners buy home insurance?").

Vocabulary, information, and other tests that require considerable prior knowledge are referred to as tests of *crystallized intelligence* because they measure the knowledge that has formed or crystallized from past problem solving. The greater the mental horsepower, the greater the accumulation. Only knowledge that is highly general and widely available is assessed, however, because otherwise IQ tests would also be measuring the opportunity to learn, not success when given the opportunity to do so. Tests of fluid and crystallized intelligence correlate very highly, despite their very different content, because the key active ingredient in both is the complexity of the problems people must solve.

Intelligence as the ability to learn. One of life's unremitting demands is to learn—that is, to process new information sufficiently well to understand it, remember it, and use it effectively. This is especially so in education and training, but it is also the case in meeting the challenges of everyday life, from learning to use a new appliance to learning the subtle moods of a friend or lover.

IQ level is correlated with speed, breadth, and depth of learning when learning requires thinking, specifically, when it is intentional (calls forth conscious mental effort), insightful (requires "catching on"), and age-related, that is, when older children learn the material more easily than do younger children (because they are mentally more mature) and when the material to be learned is meaningful and hierarchical (mastering earlier elements is essential for learning later ones, as in mathematics). Learning is also correlated with intelligence level when the learning task permits using past knowledge to solve new problems, the amount of time for learning is fixed, and the material to be learned is not unreasonably difficult or complex (which would cause everyone to fall back on trial-and-error learning). In short, intelligence is the

Percentage of Adults Age 16–65 Passing[a] WAIS Vocabulary Items

ITEM	% PASSING	ITEM	% PASSING
1. Bed	100	21. Terminate	55
2. Ship	100	22. Obstruct	58
3. Penny	100	23. Remorse	51
4. Winter	99	24. Sanctuary	49
5. Repair	98	25. Matchless	47
6. Breakfast	99	26. Reluctant	50
7. Fabric	92	27. Calamity	50
8. Slice	94	28. Fortitude	36
9. Assemble	90	29. Tranquil	36
10. Conceal	87	30. Edifice	22
11. Enormous	89	31. Compassion	29
12. Hasten	87	32. Tangible	30
13. Sentence	83	33. Perimeter	26
14. Regulate	80	34. Audacious	20
15. Commemce	79	35. Ominous	20
16. Ponder	64	36. Tirade	17
17. Cavern	68	37. Encumber	19
18. Designate	63	38. Plagiarize	13
19. Domestic	65	39. Impale	14
20. Consume	61	40. Travesty	5

Table 1

SOURCE: Matarazzo (1972), Table 5, p. 514.

NOTE: [a]Passing includes getting at least partial credit.

ability to learn when the material to be learned is moderately complex (abstract, multifaceted, and so on), as distinct from learning by rote or mere memorization.

People learn at very different rates. In school, the ratios of learning rates are often four or five to one, and they can go much higher depending on the material. The military has likewise found that recruits differ greatly in how well they learn, which it calls *trainability*. One 1969 (Fox, Taylor, and Caylor 1969) study done for the U.S. Army found, for example, that enlistees in the bottom fifth of ability needed two to six times as many teaching trials and prompts as did their higher-ability peers to reach minimal proficiency in rifle assembly, monitoring signals, combat plotting, and other basic soldiering tasks. Figure 1 illustrates the major differences in trainability at different levels of IQ. People with IQs of about 115 and above can not only be trained in a college format but can even gather and infer information largely on their own. Training for people with successively lower IQs, however, must be made successively less abstract, more closely supervised, and limited to simpler tasks. Low levels of trainability limit not only how much can be learned in a set amount of time but also the complexity of the material that can be mastered with unlimited time.

Intelligence as the ability to avoid *common cognitive errors.* Intelligence can also be conceived, for practical purposes, as the probability of *not* making cognitive errors. The notion is that all people make cognitive errors but that brighter people make fewer of them in comparable situations. They make fewer errors in learning, for example, because they learn more quickly and thoroughly. And they make fewer errors of judgment in new and unexpected situations because they are better able to look ahead, assess the likely consequences of different actions and events, spot incongruities and problems, factor more information into their decision making, and perceive alternative courses of action.

Just as items on intelligence tests are scored right versus wrong or better versus worse, so, too, can many decisions in everyday life be classified in this manner. And just as intelligence tests must use many items to assess intelligence level accurately, so, too, does the meaning of intelligence in daily life manifest itself in the accumulation of good and bad decisions, large and small, throughout one's life. The lifetime advantages of higher intelligence are explored later. The point here is simply that intelligence can also be described as the ability to avoid making common errors in judgment and accumulating a harmful record of them.

These three workaday definitions give an intuitive sense of what it means at the level of personal experience to be more versus less intelligent. Intelligence researchers seek to understand intelligence differences in their more fundamental sense, below the surface of everyday observation. As described next, most have adopted a new working definition of intelligence for this purpose.

Psychometric *g* (Not IQ) as the Research Definition of "Intelligence." The psychometric approach to measuring intelligence cannot by itself tell us what intelligence is fundamentally, say, neurologically. However, it has greatly narrowed the possibilities. Most importantly, it has shown that intelligence is a highly general ability and that it is the backbone or supporting platform for the more specific mental abilities. This finding rests in turn on the discovery of a single, common, and replicable means for isolating for study what most people mean by intelligence. As explained, it is not the IQ but *g*, which is short for the *general mental ability factor* (Jensen 1998). The latter has replaced the former as the gold standard for measuring intelligence. Researchers do not yet know exactly what aspect of mind or brain *g* represents, but *g* has become the de facto definition of intelligence for most intelligence researchers, some of whom would drop the term "intelligence" altogether.

From the earliest days of mental testing, researchers observed that people who do well on one test tend to do well on all others. That is, all mental tests intercorrelate to some degree. This prompted Charles Spearman, Galton's student and one of the earliest theorists of intelligence, to invent the statistical technique of factor analysis to isolate that common component from any set of mental tests. Once the common factor, *g*, is statistically extracted from a large, diverse set of tests, each individual's standing on it (the person's *g* level) can then be calculated. So, too, conversely, can the ability of different tests to measure *g* (their *g-loadings*). Among mental tests, IQ tests provide the most accurate measures of *g*. Scores on the great variety of IQ tests are all highly *g*-loaded, that is, they all correlate highly with *g* (with .9 being a typical value for tests of the Wechsler variety). This high correlation means that IQ scores are quite adequate for most practical purposes; therefore, *g* scores are generally actually calculated only for research purposes.

The replicability of g. Research reveals that the same *g* dimension characterizes all demographic groups yet studied. Virtually identical *g* factors have been extracted from all large, diverse sets of mental tests, regardless of which method of factor analysis was used and regardless of the age, sex, or race of the test takers. The same *g* is called forth by tests that require much cultural knowledge as by ones requiring virtually none. It can be called up

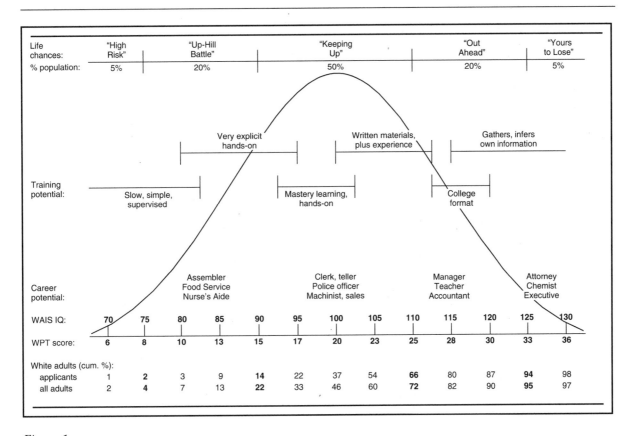

Life chances:	"High Risk"		"Up-Hill Battle"			"Keeping Up"			"Out Ahead"		"Yours to Lose"
% population:	5%		20%			50%			20%		5%

| | Very explicit hands-on | | Written materials, plus experience | | Gathers, infers own information | |

| Training potential: | Slow, simple, supervised | | Mastery learning, hands-on | | College format | |

Career potential:		Assembler Food Service Nurse's Aide		Clerk, teller Police officer Machinist, sales		Manager Teacher Accountant		Attorney Chemist Executive
WAIS IQ:	70	75	80	85	90	95	100	105	110	115	120	125	130
WPT score:	6	8	10	13	15	17	20	23	25	28	30	33	36
White adults (cum. %):													
applicants	1	2	3	9	14	22	37	54	66	80	87	94	98
all adults	2	4	7	13	22	33	46	60	72	82	90	95	97

Figure 1

by any kind of item content (numbers, letters, shapes, pictures, blocks, and the like), a phenomenon that Spearman called *indifference of the indicator*.

Mental tests often measure more specific aptitudes in addition to g (say, verbal or spatial ability), but g is the crucial backbone of all mental tests. Efforts to create useful mental tests that do not measure g (for example, verbal aptitude tests that do not tap g) have all failed. Although mental tests are suffused by a common factor, no analogous common factor can be found among different personality tests (which test for extroversion, conscientiousness, sociability, and so on). The absence of a general personality factor illustrates that the general mental ability factor g is not an artifact of factor analysis but a real phenomenon.

To be sure, the existence of the g factor can be obscured by inappropriate testing (for example, when some test takers do not know the language well) and by narrow sampling (when all test takers are similar in intelligence). When allowed to manifest itself, however, the g factor clearly shows itself

to transcend the particulars of content and culture. This is not to say that culture cannot affect the development of g or its social significance, but only that culture does not determine its fundamental nature. The nature of g seems to be surprisingly independent of culture, as other sorts of research have confirmed.

The generality of g. The great generality of g is perhaps psychometrics' most crucial discovery about the nature of intelligence. As noted, the identical g factor is the major distinction in mental abilities in all groups of people and tests, regardless of cultural context or content. As also noted, all mental ability tests measure mostly g, no matter what specific abilities they were intended to measure (verbal aptitude, mathematical reasoning, memory, intelligence, and so on). The manifest skills most associated with intelligence in both fact and public perception—reasoning, problem solving, abstract thinking, and learning—are themselves highly general, context-independent thinking skills. The psychometric vehicles (tests and test items) for measuring *g* are necessarily culture-bound to some degree, but the *g* abstracted from them appears not to be.

There are, of course, other mental aptitudes, but, unlike *g*, they seem specific to particular domains of knowledge or activity (language, music, mathematics, manipulating objects in three-dimensional space). Moreover, none of these narrower abilities seem so integral as *g* to the expression of all the others. Many decades of factor-analytic research on human abilities have confirmed what is called the hierarchical structure of mental abilities (Carroll 1993). As shown in the simplified version in Figure 2, abilities are arrayed from the top down, with the most general placed at the top. Research always finds *g* at the top of this generality hierarchy for mental abilities.

The generality of intelligence was less clear when researchers relied on IQ as their working definition of intelligence. The reason is that all IQ tests are imperfect measures of *g* and each often captures the flavor of some specialized ability or knowledge in addition to *g*. That is, all IQ tests share a large *g* component, but their small non-*g* components often differ in size and content. Attempting to understand intelligence by studying IQ scores has been akin to chemists trying to understand the properties of a particular chemical element by each studying samples that were impure to different degrees and with different additives. This ensured a muddied and fractious debate about the essence of intelligence. In contrast, the *g* factor is a stable, replicable phenomenon. When researchers study *g*, they can be confident they are studying the same thing, even when the *g*'s they use were extracted from different sets of tests. Moreover, *g* has the advantage over IQ that it cannot be confused with the attributes or contents of any particular test, because *g* is always extracted from some large, mixed set of them. One must look below the surface characteristics of IQ tests, to *g*, to explain the core phenomenon they measure.

The g-loadings of tests and tasks. The ability to classify tests according to their correlation with *g* is also a major advance in the study of intelligence. It allows research on why tasks vary in their ability to call forth *g* and thus helps predict where in life higher levels of intelligence are most useful. Stated another way, mental tests can now be used to

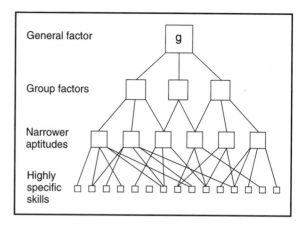

Figure 2

compare environments, not just people, and figure out why some environments are more cognitively demanding than others.

Evidence suggests that tasks are more *g*-loaded when they require more complex information processing, for example, when there are more pieces of information, when there are more operations to perform, and when the information is abstract, nested or incomplete. For instance, spelling and arithmetic tests pose much less complex and *g*-loaded tasks for adolescents and adults than do vocabulary and mathematical reasoning tests. Spelling and computing well in adolescence and beyond depends less on *g* level than does comprehending higher-level verbal and mathematical concepts, despite their superficially similar content.

As will be seen, many work tasks and occupations have been ranked in their demands for *g*. In theory, a *g* loading can be calculated for virtually everything we do in daily life. Life is like a series of mental tests in the sense that its demands vary considerably in complexity and consequent *g*-loading. This means that the advantages of being brighter will vary systematically across different life settings according to their cognitive complexity.

The finding that the subtests in an IQ test battery differ systematically in their ability to measure *g* has been cleverly used to explore the biological as well as the sociological meaning of *g*. By the method of *correlated vectors*, the *g*-loadings of IQ subtests are themselves correlated with other attributes of the subtests. For example, tests' *g*-loadings have been found to predict the genetic heritability of their scores, degree of inbreeding depression, and the subtests' correlations with brain size, faster glucose metabolism in the brain, and greater complexity and speed of onset of various electroencephalogram (EEG) brain waves. This pattern of correlations reinforces other findings which suggest that *g* is a biologically grounded capability to process complex information regardless of its explicit content.

Mental test scores—including the IQ—are composed of both *g* and non-*g* components, however. The non-*g* component might reflect more specific abilities, specific bits of cultural knowledge, aspects of personality or the testing situation, or other unspecified impurities that are independent of *g*. The decomposition of test scores into their *g* versus non-*g* components is also an enormously important development for understanding the meaning of intelligence. For example, it has been shown that it is almost exclusively the *g* component, not the non-*g* components, of tests that accounts for their ability to predict later school achievement and job performance. This considerably narrows the range of possible explanations for why IQ tests predict differences in individuals' later achievement. The explanation cannot reside mostly in the context-specific bits of knowledge that an IQ might reflect, but in the highly general mental capability that *g* represents in all contexts and cultures.

Experimental Study of the Components of *g*. If psychometrics has discovered that *g* is a very general information-processing capability, laboratory studies of intelligence are aimed at teasing out its components or building blocks. The debate among experimentalists has been about whether individual differences in general intelligence are more like differences in computer hardware or computer software. Both views, however, perceive differences in *g* or IQ as differences among individuals in the speed and quality of their information processing.

The "software" view argues that differences in intellectual performance originate in the better or worse use of the same hardware, for example, in the use of better strategies or algorithms for using information and solving problems. These *metacognitive* skills might include better allocation of time to the different components of a problem, monitoring of progress or responding to feedback, and otherwise better controlling how the different components of a task are executed. Such studies might look, for example, at the kinds of planning subjects use in solving verbal analogies or the ways they use their time in comprehending a passage of text. In this view, the general factor *g* reflects not a general underlying ability but the greater conscious use of separate planning and control strategies of general value, in all of which individuals could presumably be trained.

The "hardware" view postulates that differences in the speed and quality of information processing originate in differences in basic brain physiology, such as nerve conduction velocity. The great enthusiasm over the "top-down" software view during the 1970s and 1980s waned as research began more and more to support the claims of the "bottom-up" hardware view of intelligence. People can indeed be observed to use different strategies in solving problems, but differential motivation, effort, or strategy use do not seem to account for IQ differences, and the successful strategies are fairly task-specific.

Although research has not yet proven that differences in lower-level information processing abilities actually *cause* differences in higher-level ones, measures closer to the physiological level offer more promising explanations of *g* (Vernon 1993). For example, simultaneous recordings of subjects' RTs and brain-wave activity (specifically, average evoked potentials [AEP] measured by the EEG) have shown that speeds of ECT responses are moderately to highly correlated with complexity and speed of onset of certain brain waves, both of which occur in less time than required for *conscious* awareness of a stimulus. Much other research shows that both ECT and AEP responses are, in turn, moderately to highly correlated with IQ scores and, most importantly, with *g* itself. The *g* factor is the only mental ability with which ECT scores correlate.

Accordingly, some intelligence researchers now argue that intelligence may not be an ability per se, but rather a chemical, electrical, or metabolic property of the brain. Specific aptitudes, such as verbal and spatial ones, appear to reside in particular regions of the brain, but *g* may represent a global property permeating all regions. Nerve conduction velocity is currently being investigated as one such possible global property. Differences in velocity may in turn result from differences in nerve myelination (myelin is the fatty sheath around nerve axons). While still speculative, the velocity and myelination hypotheses are consistent with a well-established pattern of differences that any putative cause of intelligence will have to explain, namely, both the steady rise and then fall of fluid intelligence over the life cycle as well as the enduring differences in *g* among people at any single age.

Popular Contending Theories. Any theory of intelligence must take into account the basic facts about intelligence, whether it is measured as IQ or *g*. These include its high generality, heritability (discussed shortly), and correlations with elementary perceptual and physiological processes of the brain. Some of the theories that are most popular outside expert circles contradict or ignore these facts and thus are not viable contenders to the emerging *g* theory of intelligence. Others remain untested hypotheses. The major contenders to *g* theory can be characterized as either *specificity* or *multiplicity* theories of intelligence.

Specificity theories. Some scholars have argued that intelligence is not an underlying ability but merely the accumulation of specific *bits of knowledge*. For them, being "smart" is nothing more than knowing a lot, no matter how much time and effort went into that learning or what was learned. It is akin to the accumulation of marbles in a jar, signifying nothing other than that many marbles have been collected by whatever means. The apparent assumption is that people do not differ in their ability and efficiency in gathering marbles. However, intelligence has to be more than knowledge per se because, among other reasons, differences in intelligence show up on tests that require no knowledge whatsoever. Moreover, as noted, people differ greatly in their ability to acquire knowledge even when given the same opportunity to learn. There are "fast" students and "slow" students, irrespective of motivation and quality of instruction. For many experts, differences in the ability to *acquire* knowledge are at the heart of intelligence.

Another variant is the *cultural specificity* theory, which is that intelligence is merely the display of traits, whatever they may be, that are highly regarded in a particular culture. For example, one

claim is that because IQ tests are typically developed by white European males, they inevitably measure beliefs, behavior, and knowledge that white European males value but that may have no intrinsic value. Intelligence, they say, might be defined completely differently in another culture, such as skill at hunting, navigating, or cooperating for the general good. The first claim is false and the second is irrelevant, even if true. As noted, the same *g* is extracted from all diverse sets of mental tests and for all cultural groups. (Besides, Asians tend to do better than whites on tests developed by the latter.) Whether different cultural groups recognize, value, and reward the phenomenon represented by *g* is interesting and important, but it does not erase the phenomenon itself as a scientific fact any more than rejecting the concept of evolution brings evolution to a halt.

Perhaps the best-known variant is the *academic specificity* theory, which says that IQ and intelligence are simply "book smarts," a narrow "academic" skill that is useful inside but not outside schools and bookish jobs. According to this theory, intelligence may be an enduring personal trait, but only a narrow one. As will be shown, *g* is indeed highly useful in education and training. However, the very generality of *g*—the ability to deal with complexity, to learn, and to avoid mistakes—argues against the narrow "book smarts" conception of intelligence. So, too, does much research, discussed later, on the many practical advantages conferred by higher levels of *g*. Carpenters as well as bank tellers, sales agents as well as social scientists, routinely deal with complexity on the job and are aided by higher levels of *g*.

Multiplicity theories. Robert Sternberg (1985) argues that there are several intelligences, including "analytical," "practical," and "creative." Howard Gardner (1983) is famous for postulating eight and possibly nine intelligences: linguistic, logical-mathematical, musical, spatial, bodily-kinesthetic, intrapersonal, interpersonal, naturalist, and (possibly) existential. Daniel Goleman's 1995 book on "emotional intelligence" has taken the country by storm. All three theories are engaging, are popular in lay circles, and describe undeniably important skills, knowledges, and achievements. All three theories suggest that *g*, if it exists, is only one of various coequal abilities. This is, indeed, why multiple intelligence theories are so popular. They are often interpreted—wrongly—as suggesting that everyone can be smart in some useful way.

The question, however, is whether the "intelligences" these theories describe are actually comparable to g in any fundamental way. Specifically, are they even abilities, or might they be the *products* (literary, scientific, or artistic) of exercising g together with specific abilities in specific settings with specific kinds of training and experience? Are the purported intelligences even *mental* rather than, say, physical abilities or aspects of personality? And for those that are mental abilities, are they comparable to g in their *general applicability*? Unfortunately, the research necessary for answering these questions credibly has not been conducted. Almost none of the "multiple intelligences" has actually been measured, and none have been shown independent of g in representative samples of the population. Verbal descriptions of them leave many experts doubtful that they are comparable to g in any important way.

Some of them, like emotional intelligence, seem to be a combination of many different traits, some being abilities and others not, some being mental and others not. Verbal definitions suggest that practical intelligence (like "street smarts") may be the accumulation of highly context-specific knowledge gathered through strictly informal experience (for example, knowing the special argot and norms of a particular neighborhood, occupation, or other subculture). Gardner's intelligences are different forms of highly valued cultural accomplishment. As such, they require not only the ability to succeed but also the personality traits, such as drive and persistence, needed to transform that potential into a valued product. This is not to deny that personality is important for great accomplishment, but only that it is useful to distinguish between the separate ability, personality, and other factors contributing to it.

In addition, some of Gardner's intelligences seem to mirror more specific and psychometrically well-studied traits, such as verbal, mathematical, and spatial aptitude. Much research has shown that these so-called group factors are highly correlated with g but appear below it in the hierarchical structure of human mental abilities (see Figure 2). Gardner himself has stated that exemplary levels of all his intelligences require IQ levels over 120,

meaning that the eight intelligences are not alternatives to g but narrower abilities pervaded by it. In short, they appear to be different cultural playgrounds for the cognitively rich. All the purported "multiple intelligences" are important topics for study, but they cannot be assumed to be comparable to g in either generality or practical importance by virtue of being labeled "intelligences."

HERITABILITY AND ENVIRONMENTALITY OF INTELLIGENCE

Behavioral genetics is a method for studying the influence of *both* genes and environments on human behavior. In recent decades the field has shown that mental abilities, personality, vocational interests, psychopathology, and even social attitudes and life events are shaped by both genes and environments (Loehlin 1992; Plomin et al. 1997). More research has been conducted on the heritability of intelligence than on any other psychological trait, and much of it has been longitudinal.

Behavioral genetics focuses on explaining *variation* in a particular population. Its basic method is to look at similarities between relatives of different degrees of genetic and environmental relatedness: identical twins reared apart, adopted siblings reared together, identical versus fraternal twins, and so on. Such research can also test, among other things, whether *specific* environmental factors create IQ similarities and differences and, if the research is longitudinal, whether change (and stability) in IQ ranking is due to the operation of genes, environments, or both. It can also test whether two heritable traits or behaviors, such as IQ and academic achievement, share the same genetic and environmental roots.

Such research does not reveal *how* genes affect intelligence, only that they do. Explanations of how genes influence intelligence will come from molecular genetics, which has only recently isolated the first gene for intelligence. Molecular genetic research also holds promise for detailing exactly how environments might influence the actions of genes.

Individual Differences. Behavioral genetics has focused historically on explaining differences among individuals *within* a population. The following such findings should be generalized only to the sorts of populations studied so far, most of them Western and none extreme in terms of either deprivation or privilege.

IQ is substantially heritable. Heritability (h²) refers to the percentage of observed differences in a trait (in *phenotypes*) that is due to differences in genes (*genotypes*). Estimates of the heritability for IQ typically range between .4 and .8 (on a scale from 0 to 1.0). This means that from 40 percent to 80 percent of the observed differences in individuals' IQs are due to the genetic differences among them. This means, conversely, up to 20 percent to 60 percent of IQ differences are environmental in origin. Aptitudes measured by the most *g*-loaded tests are the most heritable. Aptitudes measured by tests of more specific abilities, such as verbal and spatial visualization, are moderately heritable, but less so than *g*.

IQ heritability rises with age. This discovery was a surprise even to behavioral geneticists because, like virtually all social scientists, they had assumed that environmental effects cumulate over a lifetime to reduce the influence of genes. Not so, apparently. The heritability of IQ is about .4 in the preschool years, rises to .6 by adolescence, and increases to about .8 in late adulthood. The reason for this increase is unclear. The major hypothesis, however, is that "genes drive experience" and lead people to seek different social niches. That is, different genotypes tend to choose, create, and elicit different environments in childhood and beyond, which in turn shape intellectual development. For example, bright and dull youth receive different encouragement and opportunities. They also tend to choose different experiences for themselves, especially as they become more independent of parents, teachers, and other authorities. As individuals take a greater hand in shaping their environments, for better or worse, their IQ phenotypes begin to mirror their IQ genotypes more closely. The correlation between IQ phenotypes and genotypes (which is the square root of heritability) rises to .9 by later adulthood.

The surprising rise in heritabilities is consistent with the disappointing results of socioeducational interventions (similar to Head Start) that were designed to raise low childhood IQs. To date, all have exhibited *fade-out*, meaning that the initial improvements in IQ dissipated within a few years. Improvements in more malleable outcomes (such as fewer children being held back a grade) may be observed, but permanent rises in *g* are not. The same IQ fade-out occurs with genetically at risk children adopted into more advantaged families: By adolescence, their early favorable IQs fall back to the average for their nonadopted biological relatives.

IQ-relevant environments are partly genetic in origin. Social scientists have tended to think of environments as conditions strictly "out there" to which people are passively "exposed." Children's environments correlate with their genes, however, partly because they passively receive both from their parents. People's environments are also heritable to some degree because people choose, make, remake, elicit, and interpret them. Because people's genetic proclivities help shape their environments, real and perceived, behavioral geneticists often refer to people's proximal environments as, in effect, their *extended phenotypes*. That is, people's near environments are to some degree an extension of themselves because they are partly *products* of the person's genotype for intelligence, personality, and the like.

When people's environments are studied with the same behavioral genetic techniques as are their psychological traits and behaviors, research consistently shows that rearing environments, peer groups, social support, and life events are, in fact, moderately heritable. For example, one measure of individual infant and toddler rearing environments found that those environments were 40 percent heritable. Moreover, half of the environmental measure's ability to predict cognitive development could be accounted for by that measure's genetic component. In other words, IQ-relevant environments are partly genetic in origin. This is an example of what behavioral geneticists refer to as the operation of nature *via* nurture.

Shared family effects on IQ dissipate by adolescence. Behavioral genetic research confirms that environments have substantial influence in creating IQ differences. However, providing yet another surprise, the research showed that environmental influences had been completely misunderstood. Psychologists–behavioral geneticists David Rowe (1994) and Sandra Scarr (1997) call this mistaken view, respectively, "family effects theory" and "socialization theory." This is the still widespread but false assumption that differences between families in their socioeconomic circumstances (income, parental education, occupation, income, and so on) and child-rearing styles (cold, authoritative, and so on) create differences between their children in ability and personality. These presumed effects are called *shared* or *between-family* influences because they affect all children in the family in the same way and thus make children in the same families more alike and children in different families less alike.

As it turns out, such shared effects influence IQ (but not personality) in early childhood, but they are disappear by adolescence. Nor is it known what these temporary influences are. The only environmental effects that continue to influence IQ beyond adolescence are *nonshared* or *within-family* effects on IQ. Nonshared effects are factors that influence one sibling but not others in a family. What they consist of regarding IQ is not yet known, but they could include random biological events, illness, and differential experiences in parent–child or sibling relationships. Nonshared effects help to explain why biological siblings who grow up together are so different in IQ. They differ by about 12 IQ points, on the average, compared to the average 17-point IQ difference between any two random strangers. Much of that difference is due to their genetic differences, however, because biological siblings share, on the average, only 50 percent of their segregating genes.

The dissipation of "family effects" and the rising influence of genes with age can be seen clearly in adoption research. The IQs of adopted siblings are similar in childhood but not in adolescence. By adolescence, their IQs also cease to resemble the IQs of their adoptive parents but become more like the IQs of the biological parents they have never known.

Special abilities, ECTs, and school achievement have common genetic roots with g. As noted, there are many mental abilities, whether at the level of ECTs, such as choice reaction time, or at the level of group factors, such as verbal ability. However, they all correlate with g. To the extent that they overlap each other and g phenotypically, that overlap is due almost entirely to a common genetic source. Conversely, only a small portion of the genetic component of specific aptitudes—such as verbal skills, memory skills, and speed of processing—is not g-related. The same general pattern is found for the sizable correlation between academic achievement and IQ. To the degree that they correlate, that similarity is almost entirely genetic; to the degree that they diverge, the cause is mostly environmental.

IQ stability is mostly genetic in origin whereas age-to-age change in IQ rank originates mostly in nonshared environments. Rank in IQ relative to agemates is highly stable. Genes and shared environments both contribute mostly to IQ stability rather than to age-to-age change. It is the nonshared environment that causes age-to-age change. Marked change is rare and tends to be idiosyncratic, transient, and difficult to attribute to any particular event.

Cautions in interpreting heritabilities. High heritabilities do *not* mean that a trait is not malleable. Heritability and malleability are separate phenomena. Certain heritable conditions (such as diabetes) are treatable and certain nongenetic effects (such as those of lead poisoning) are not. All that a high heritability means is that current differences in environmental conditions do not create much intelligence variation beyond that owing to genetic differences. If environments were equalized for everyone, phenotypic variation might be reduced somewhat, but heritability would rise to 100 percent. In contrast, if environments could be individually tailored to compensate for genetic differences (by providing insulin for diabetics, changing the diets of those with phenylketonuria, providing the best education to the least intelligent, and the like), both heritability and variability would fall.

Moreover, heritability is the degree to which genes explain phenotypic *variance* in a trait, so a high heritability does not rule out shifts in population *averages* over time. Something that affects everyone can change a group's average without changing its variability. Recent generations have been getting taller, but height is still highly heritable within generations. The same is true for IQ levels, which have been increasing several points a decade this century in developed countries. Both increases are still scientific puzzles, but some scholars have suggested a common explanation—societywide improvements in nutrition, reduction in disease, and the like. Researchers have yet to establish, however, to what extent the rises in IQ reflect increases in the g versus non-g components of mental tests and thus an increase in g itself.

What is clear, however, is that *shared* family environments that vary within the *normal* range of family environments in the developed world do *not* have create lasting differences in IQ. Within the normal range of variation, different families have basically the same effects in promoting mental growth. The key to understanding how environments create IQ differences among age peers lies in understanding *nonshared* effects. These are the environments, whether biological or social, and both within and outside family settings, that affect siblings differently and make them less alike. The shattering of shared effects theory as an explanation for adult differences in IQ is a revolutionary development, albeit one yet to be accepted by many social scientists. The discovery of lasting nonshared influences opens exciting new ways of thinking about IQ-relevant environments. We may have been looking in all the wrong places. Behavioral genetics provides the best tools at present for ferreting out what those nongenetic factors are.

To reiterate a cautionary note, we do *not* know the effects of environments that are extreme or that do not allow individuals the personal freedoms that most Westerners enjoy. We do not know, either, what the effects of entirely novel environments or interventions would be, whether social or biological. We can predict, however, that any social or educational intervention would have to fall outside the normal range of variation already studied in order to change the distribution of IQs very much. For instance, supplying a typical middle-class family environment to all lower-class children cannot be expected to narrow the average IQ gap between middle- and lower-class adolescents. Middle-class children themselves range across the entire IQ spectrum (as do lower-class children) despite the advantages (or absence thereof) of middle-class life.

Group Differences. There is little scientific debate anymore about whether valid *phenotypic* differences exist among races, ethnicities, and social classes. Average group differences in IQ are the rule, not the exception, both worldwide and in the United States. To the extent that the matter has been investigated, group IQ differences appear to reflect differences in *g* itself and are mirrored by group differences in performance on the simple laboratory tasks described earlier.

Group IQ differences can be pictured as the displacement of the IQ bell curves of some social groups somewhat upward or downward on the IQ continuum compared to others. All groups' bell curves overlap greatly; the differences consist in where along the IQ continuum each group is centered. Ashkenazic Jews tend to score as far above average (about IQ 112) as American blacks score below average (about IQ 85), with most other groups spread in between. It should be noted, however, that black cultural subgroups differ among themselves in average IQ, as do the constituent subgroups of Jews, gentile whites, Asians, Hispanics, and Native Americans.

The most contentious debate regarding intelligence is whether average group IQ differences are partly genetic in origin. The favored assumption in the social sciences for the last half-century has been that race differences are entirely environmental. However, research designed to prove this has not done so. It has succeeded in finding environmental factors that might possibly explain at most a third of the American black–white average difference. This failure does not rule out an entirely environmental explanation based on factors yet to be assessed. It does rule out several factors, however, that were once assumed to account for the bulk of the average difference, namely, family income and social class. Large average IQ differences between black and white children are found at all levels of family income and social class.

Behavioral geneticists have recently developed statistical methods for estimating the extent to which average differences among social groups (races, sexes, and so on) might be due to genetic differences among them. Perhaps not surprisingly, few behavioral geneticists have actually applied those methods to available data, and those who have been willing to do so have experienced unusual barriers to publishing their results. As a result, there is little direct published evidence one way or the other. When surveyed in 1988, about half of IQ experts reported a belief that race and class differences result from *both* genetic and environmental influences. This should be considered a reasonable but unproven hypothesis.

The earlier caution should be repeated here. Research has so far studied only the normal range of environmental variation within any race or ethnic group. American minority children may more often grow up in extremely deprived environments. Studies of very low-IQ Appalachian communities suggest that biologically unhealthy and cognitively retarded family environments can permanently stunt cognitive development.

Some people fear that any evidence of genetic differences between groups would have dire social consequences. This fear is unwarranted. A demonstration of genetic differences would not dictate any particular political reaction. Both liberal and conservative social policy can humanely accommodate such an eventuality, as some policy analysts and behavioral geneticists have illustrated (Kaus 1992; Rowe 1997). Depending on one's politics, for example, genetic differences by race could be used to argue either for forbidding or for requiring racial preferences in education and employment. Moreover, environmentalism and hereditarianism have both on occasion helped undergird tyrannical regimes that practiced mass murder, for example, respectively, the Stalinist Soviet Union and Nazi Germany. Political extremism (or moderation) is neither guaranteed nor precluded by scientific conclusions one way or the other. Scientific facts and political reactions to them are independent issues. Developing *effective* social policy does depend, however, on working in concert with the facts, not against them, whatever they may be.

SOCIAL CORRELATES AND CONSEQUENCES OF DIFFERENCES IN INTELLIGENCE

Much research has focused on how *individuals'* own behavior and life outcomes are affected by their intelligence level. There has been little research yet on what may ultimately interest sociologists more, namely, the ways in which *interpersonal contexts* and *social institutions* are shaped by the cognitive levels of the individuals populating them.

Individual Level. American adults clearly value intelligence highly because they rate it second only to good health in importance. Differences in intelligence do, in fact, correlate to some extent with just about everything we value, including mental and physical health, success in school and work, law-abidingness, emotional sensitivity, creativity, altruism, even sense of humor and physical

coordination. The scientific question, however, is whether differences in intelligence actually *cause* any of these differences in people's behaviors and outcomes. Or might intelligence as often be their consequence as their cause?

Questions of causality. Most IQ variability is genetic from adolescence on, meaning that it cannot be mostly "socially constructed." Moreover, to the extent that it has nongenetic sources, evidence leans against their being the usual suspects in social research (parents' income, education, child-rearing practices, and the like). If intelligence is not caused (much) by its major social correlates, does it cause them?

Pieces of an answer are available from experimental and quasi-experimental research conducted by educational, employment, and training psychologists in public, private, and military settings for more than a half-century. Differences in *prior* mental ability are strong—in fact, the strongest—predictors of *later* performance in school, training, and on the job when tasks are at least moderately complex. Moreover, the correlations are stronger with objective than subjectively measured performance outcomes (for example, standardized performance rather than teacher grades or supervisor ratings). The military services also have extensive experience attempting to nullify the effects of ability differences on recruits' later performance in training and on the job. Their failed attempts testify to the stubborn functional import of such differences—as does the failure of lengthy job experience to neutralize differences in worker intelligence.

IQ is moderately highly correlated with a nexus of good outcomes—higher education, high-status jobs, and income growth over a career. In view of the *g*-loadedness of the educational and occupational worlds, it would be surprising were IQ not found to be an important precursor to these outcomes. IQ is, in fact, the best predictor of later educational level attained, and it helps predict occupational status and income growth even after controlling for education and family background.

IQ is also correlated to varying degrees (negatively) with a nexus of bad outcomes—dropping out of school, unemployment, incarceration, bearing illegitimate children, dependence on welfare, and living in poverty as an adult. This nexus of social pathology has been the focus of recent lively debates about the role of intelligence, where protagonists typically pit intelligence against an array of external factors, including various aspects of family background, to see which is the stronger predictor. Intelligence generally equals or exceeds the predictive ability of any small set of such variables, although the relations tend to be modest in both cases. One possible explanation for the relation of IQ to social pathology is that lack of socioeconomic competitiveness may precipitate a downward social spiral.

However, IQ may play a direct role, too. Committing crimes, bearing illegitimate children, and other such personal behavior may result in part from errors of judgment in conducting one's life, perhaps due in part to lack of foresight and ability to learn from experience. Conversely, higher g may help insulate people from harmful environments. Research has shown, for instance, that higher intelligence is a major attribute of "resilient" children, who prosper despite terrible rearing conditions, and of those who avoid delinquency despite living in delinquent environments. The hypothesis is that their greater ability to perceive options and solve problems constitutes a buffer.

Either the genetic or nongenetic components of phenotypic intelligence might be responsible for its causal impact. Because intelligence is highly genetic, it is reasonable to assume that its causal impact is mostly due to its genetic component. This has, in fact, been found to be the case with its effect on standardized academic achievement. The latter shares all its genetic roots with IQ. Similar *multivariate genetic analyses* are now accumulating for various socioeconomic outcomes that depend on mental competence. Educational and occupational level are both moderately genetic in origin, with estimates (for males) ranging from .4 to .7 for education and .3 to .6 for occupation. Part of that genetic portion overlaps the genetic roots of IQ. In the best study so far (Lichtenstein and Pedersen 1997), occupational status was more than half genetic in origin. Half that *genetic* portion was shared jointly with the genetic roots of *both* IQ and years education, and half was independent of both. The remaining variability in phenotypic occupational status was split between *nonshared* environmental effects that (1) were shared with education (but not IQ) and (2) were unique to occupation.

One of the biggest confusions in the debate over the causal role of intelligence results from the mistaken equating of intelligence with genetic factors and of social class with nongenetic factors by some of the most visible protagonists in the debate. While the former assumption has some justification owing to the high heritability of g, it nonetheless muddies the conceptual waters. The latter assumption is even less warranted, however, because many social "environments" turn out to be moderately genetic. All social "environments" must now be presumed partly genetic until proven otherwise. Not being genetically sensitive, virtually all current research on the effects of social and family environments is actually uninterpretable. Progress in the causal analysis of environments and their relation to g will come only when more social scientists begin using genetically sensitive research designs.

Principles of importance. Although the causal role of intelligence has yet to be clarified, research leaves no doubt that people's life chances shift markedly across the IQ continuum. Those shifts in specific life arenas will be discussed later, but it would help first to state four principles that summarize what it means for intelligence to have *practical importance* in individuals' lives.

First, importance is a matter of better *odds*. Being bright is certainly no guarantee of happiness and success, nor does being dull guarantee misery and failure. Most low-IQ people marry, work, have children, and are law-abiding citizens. Being brighter than average does, however, systematically tilt the odds toward favorable outcomes. Higher levels of intelligence always improve the odds, sometimes only slightly but often substantially, depending on the outcome in question.

Second, importance *varies systematically* across different settings and life arenas. Intelligence level tilts the odds of success and failure more in some arenas of life (such as academic achievement) than others (such as good citizenship). For instance, the correlations of IQ with years of schooling completed (.6) and composites of standardized academic achievement (.8) are over twice that for IQ correlations with delinquency (−.2 to −.3). Correlations in the same life arena can also vary depending on complexity of the tasks involved. For instance, correlations of job performance with test scores range from .2 in unskilled work to .8 in the most cognitively demanding jobs.

Third, importance is *relative* to other known influences and one's particular aims. Many personal traits and circumstances can affect the odds of success and failure in different arenas of life. Intelligence is never "everything" in the practical affairs of life. Depending on the outcome in question, personality, experience, peers, family background, and the like can tilt the odds of success, sometimes more than intelligence does and sometimes less. As noted earlier, IQ predicts standardized achievement better than it does persistence in education, probably because personality and circumstances affect the latter much more than the former. Weak prediction at the individual level does not mean the predictor is unimportant in a pragmatic sense, as illustrated by the relation between delinquency and social class. The correlation is generally below −.2 but usually thought quite important for policy purposes, as is the similarly low correlation at the individual level between smoking and various health risks.

Fourth, importance is *cumulative*. Small individual effects can be quite important when they cumulate across the many arenas and phases of one's life. Many of g's daily effects are small, but they are consistent and ubiquitous. Like the small odds favoring the house in gambling, people with better odds win more often than they lose and can thus gradually amass large gains. Likewise, although smart people make "stupid" mistakes, they tend to accumulate fewer of them over a lifetime. Although the odds of any particular unfavorable outcome may not always be markedly higher in the lower IQ ranges, lower-IQ people face worse odds at every turn in life, meaning that their odds for experiencing *at least one* destructive outcome may be markedly higher.

Education and training. Schooling is the most *g*-loaded setting through which citizens pass en masse. Its unremitting demand is to learn and, moreover, to learn increasingly complex material as young people progress through it. It therefore highlights the intellectual distinctions among citizens better than does any other life setting and in ways plainly visible to the layperson. To be sure, schools enhance everyone's cognitive development, but they currently seem to have little impact on making

people either more alike or less alike in intelligence. Sociologist Christopher Jencks estimated in 1972 that if quantity and quality of schooling were made identical for everyone, such equalization would reduce the variance in test scores by only 20 percent. When Poland's Communist government rebuilt Warsaw after World War II, it allocated housing, schools, and health services without regard to residents' social class. This far-reaching equalization of environments did little or nothing either to equalize the IQs of the next generation of children or to reduce the correlation of their IQs with parental education and occupation (Stein, Susser, and Wald 1978).

As already noted, brighter students and military recruits learn much more from the same learning opportunities and often require less than one-fourth the exposure than do their less able peers for the same degree of learning. This difference in ability to capitalize on learning opportunities also greatly influences the maximum level of attainment youngsters are likely to reach. People with an IQ of 75 (the threshold for mental retardation) have roughly only a 50–50 chance of being able to master the elementary school curriculum; an IQ of about 105 is required for the same odds of getting grades good enough in high school to enter a four-year college; and an IQ of 115 is required for 50–50 odds of doing well enough in college to enter graduate or professional school.

Figure 3, similarly to Figure 1, summarizes accumulated employer experience about the most effective sorts of training for people at different ranges of IQ. Figure 3 is based on research with the Wonderlic Personnel Test (WPT), a short group intelligence test. Above the WPT equivalent of IQ 115–120 (which includes about 10 to 15 percent of the general white population), people can basically train themselves; the middle half of the IQ distribution (IQ 91–110) can learn routines quickly with some combination of written materials, experience, and mastery learning; but people below IQ 80 (10 percent of the general white population) require slow, concrete, highly supervised, and often individualized training. The military is prohibited by law from inducting anyone below this level because of inadequate trainability, and current minimum standards exclude anyone below the equivalent of IQ 85.

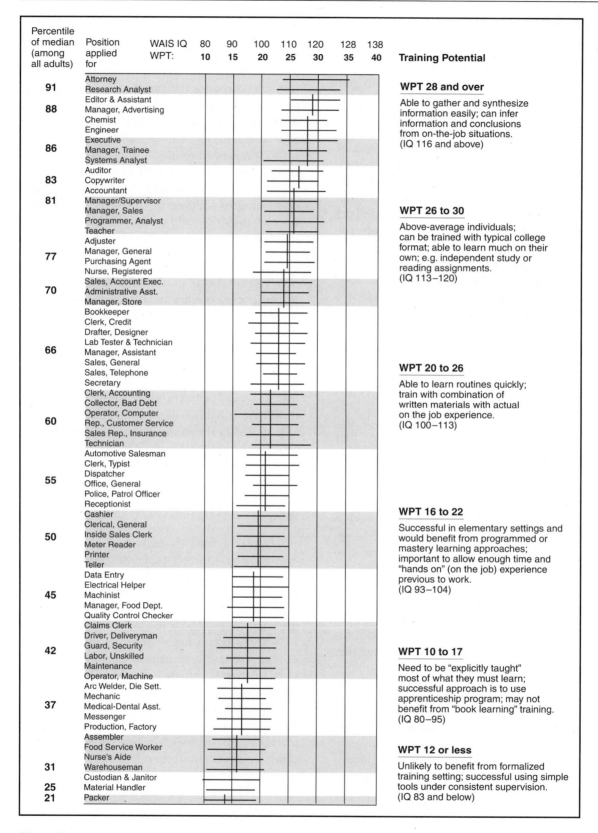

| Percentile of median (among all adults) | Position applied for | WAIS IQ | 80 | 90 | 100 | 110 | 120 | 128 | 138 | Training Potential |
		WPT:	10	15	20	25	30	35	40	
91	Attorney Research Analyst									**WPT 28 and over**
88	Editor & Assistant Manager, Advertising Chemist Engineer									Able to gather and synthesize information easily; can infer information and conclusions from on-the-job situations. (IQ 116 and above)
86	Executive Manager, Trainee Systems Analyst									
83	Auditor Copywriter Accountant									
81	Manager/Supervisor Manager, Sales Programmer, Analyst Teacher									**WPT 26 to 30**
77	Adjuster Manager, General Purchasing Agent Nurse, Registered									Above-average individuals; can be trained with typical college format; able to learn much on their own; e.g. independent study or reading assignments. (IQ 113–120)
70	Sales, Account Exec. Administrative Asst. Manager, Store									
66	Bookkeeper Clerk, Credit Drafter, Designer Lab Tester & Technician Manager, Assistant Sales, General Sales, Telephone Secretary									**WPT 20 to 26**
60	Clerk, Accounting Collector, Bad Debt Operator, Computer Rep., Customer Service Sales Rep., Insurance Technician									Able to learn routines quickly; train with combination of written materials with actual on the job experience. (IQ 100–113)
55	Automotive Salesman Clerk, Typist Dispatcher Office, General Police, Patrol Officer Receptionist									
50	Cashier Clerical, General Inside Sales Clerk Meter Reader Printer Teller									**WPT 16 to 22**
45	Data Entry Electrical Helper Machinist Manager, Food Dept. Quality Control Checker									Successful in elementary settings and would benefit from programmed or mastery learning approaches; important to allow enough time and "hands on" (on the job) experience previous to work. (IQ 93–104)
42	Claims Clerk Driver, Deliveryman Guard, Security Labor, Unskilled Maintenance Operator, Machine									**WPT 10 to 17**
37	Arc Welder, Die Sett. Mechanic Medical-Dental Asst. Messenger Production, Factory									Need to be "explicitly taught" most of what they must learn; successful approach is to use apprenticeship program; may not benefit from "book learning" training. (IQ 80–95)
31	Assembler Food Service Worker Nurse's Aide Warehouseman									**WPT 12 or less**
25	Custodian & Janitor Material Handler									Unlikely to benefit from formalized training setting; successful using simple tools under consistent supervision. (IQ 83 and below)
21	Packer									

Figure 3

Employment. Many studies have found that the major distinction among occupations in the U.S. economy is the cognitive complexity of their constituent tasks. The most complex jobs are distinguished by their greater requirements for dealing with unexpected situations, learning new procedures and identifying problems quickly, recalling task-relevant information, reasoning and making judgments, and similar higher-order thinking skills that are prototypical of intelligence. Other job attributes that correlate highly with the *occupational complexity factor* include writing, planning, scheduling, analyzing, decision making, supervising, negotiating, persuading, instructing, and self-direction. So, too, do responsibility, criticality, and prestige. As already noted, mental ability test scores correlate most highly with performance in the most complex jobs. That is, differences in intelligence have a bigger impact on performance—"more bang for the buck"—when work is more *g*-loaded.

Not surprisingly, then, an occupation's overall complexity level correlates extremely highly with the average IQ of its incumbents. As Figure 3 illustrates, all occupations draw applicants from a wide range of IQ, but the minimum and average IQ levels rise with job level. Although wide, the typical IQ recruitment ranges for different occupations do not overlap at the extremes of job level (professional versus unskilled). The average IQ of applicants to middle-level jobs (about IQ 105), such as police work, is 15 IQ points (one standard deviation) lower than for applicants to professional jobs but 15 IQ points higher than for applicants to semiskilled work, such as food service worker. No occupation seems to recruit its workers routinely from below IQ 80.

The foregoing results for jobs suggest a high practical utility for higher intelligence in other aspects of life. Many jobs (child care, sales, accounting, teaching, managing) pose the same mental challenges (persuading, instructing, organizing, and ministering to people) that pervade nonpaid activities (parenting, home and financial management, civic responsibilities, friendships, and so on).

Daily life. Daily life has become considerably more complex during the twentieth century. Increased size, bureaucratization, and regulation of social institutions and services, together with greater reliance on continually changing information technologies, have greatly increased the cognitive complexity of daily life. Life may be physically easier, healthier, and more pleasant today, but it has become mentally more challenging in developed societies. Some of this complexity is captured well by the U.S. Department of Education's 1992 National Adult Literacy Survey (NALS; Kirsch et al. 1993). Although the NALS was not designed as an intelligence test, it closely mimics the key attributes of an IQ test battery: Its intent was to measure complex information-processing skills by sampling a broad range of tasks from universally relevant contexts and contents; the relative difficulty of its items stems from their complexity, not their manifest content; and its three scales reflect one general factor.

Figure 4 illustrates items at different levels of the three NALS subscales; Figure 1 translates the NALS scores into IQ equivalents. These items do not involve esoteric "book smarts" but represent practical, everyday skills in dealing with banks, restaurants, transportation systems, and social agencies; understanding the news and one's options; and providing basic information about oneself. Nonetheless, about 15 percent of white adults and 40 percent of black adults routinely function no higher than Level 1 (225 or less), which corresponds to 80 percent proficiency in skills such as locating an expiration date on a driver's license and totaling a bank deposit. Another 25 percent of whites and 36 percent of blacks routinely function no higher than Level 2 (226–275), which includes proficiency in such skills as locating an intersection on a street map, entering background information on an application for a Social Security card, and determining the price difference between two show tickets.

These are examples of the myriad daily tasks that require some independent learning and reasoning as one navigates life. None may be critical by itself, but the more often one fails such tasks, the more one is hampered in grasping opportunities, satisfying one's needs and desires, and assisting family and friends. A national education panel concluded, in fact, that Level 1 and 2 skills are not sufficient for competing successfully in a global economy or exercising fully the rights and responsibilities of citizenship. Consistent with this, the

PROSE	DOCUMENT	QUANTITATIVE
149 Identify country in short articles	69 Sign your name	191 Total a bank deposit entry
210 Locate one piece of information in sports article	151 Locate expiration date on driver's license	
224 Underline sentence explaining action stated in short article	180 Locate time of meeting on a form	
	214 Using pie graph, locate type of vehicle having specific sales	
226 Underline meaning of term given in government brochure on supplemental security income	232 Locate intersection on a street map	238 Calculate postage and fees for certified mail
250 Locate two features of information in sports article	245 Locate eligibility from table of employee benefits	246 Determine difference in price between tickets for two shows
	259 Identify and enter background information on application for social security card	270 Calculate total costs of purchase from an order form
275 Interpret instructions from an appliance warranty		
280 Write a brief letter explaining error made on a credit card bill	277 Identify information from bar graph depicting source of energy and year	278 Using calculator, calculate difference between regular and sale price from an advertisement
304 Read a news article and identify a sentence that provides interpretation of a situation	296 Use sign out sheet to respond to call about resident	308 Using calculator, determine the discount from an oil bill if paid within 10 days
316 Read lengthy article to identify two behaviors that meet a stated condition	314 Use bus schedule to determine appropriate bus for given set of conditions	
	323 Enter information given into an automobile maintenance record form	325 Plan travel arrangments for meeting using flight schedule
328 State in writing an argument made in lengthy newspaper article		331 Determine correct change using information in a menu
347 Explain difference between two types of employee benefits	342 Identify the correct percentage meeting specified conditions from a table of such information	

(continued)

(continued)

PROSE	DOCUMENT	QUANTITATIVE
	348 Use bus schedule to determine appropriate bus for given set of conditions (a harder question than the similar one above)	350 Using information stated in news article, calculate amount of money that should go to raising a child
359 Contrast views expressed in two editorials on technologies available to make fuel-efficient cars		
362 Generate unfamiliar theme from short poems		368 Using eligibility pamphlet, calculate the yearly amount a couple would receive for basic supplemental security income
374 Compare two metaphors used in poem		
		375 Calculate miles per gallon using information given on mileage record chart
	379 Use table of information to determine pattern in oil exports across years	
382 Compare approaches stated in narrative on growing up		382 Determine individual and total costs on an order form for items in a catalog
	387 Use table comparing credit cards. Identify the two categorices used and write two differences between them	
410 Summarize two ways lawyers may challenge prospective jurors		405 Using information in news article, calculate difference in times for completing a race
		421 Using calculator, determine the total cost of carpet to cover a room
423 Interpret a brief phrase from a lengthy news article	396 Using a table depicting information about parental involvement in school survey to write a paragraph summarizing extent to which parents and teachers agree	

Figure 4

NALS study found that, compared to adults with Level 5 skills (376–500, reached by about 4 percent of whites and less than 0.5 percent of blacks), adults with Level 1 skills were five times more likely to be out of the labor force, ten times more likely to live in poverty, only 40 percent as likely to be employed full time, and 7 percent as likely to be employed in a managerial or professional job—if employed at all.

Two daily activities where mental competence may have life-and-death implications are driving and health behavior. A large longitudinal study of Australian servicemen found that the death rate from motor vehicle accidents for men with IQs above 100 (52 per 10,000) was doubled at IQ 85–100 (92 per 10,000) and tripled at IQ 80–85 (147 per 10,000). The study authors suggested that the higher death rates might be due to poorer ability to assess risks. Medical research has likewise documented that many nonretarded patients have difficulty reading labels on prescription medicine and following simple physician instructions about self-care and future appointments.

Nexus of social pathology. Table 2 shows how the odds of social pathology fall (or rise) the further one's IQ exceeds (or falls below) the average IQ. It shows the percentages of young white adults in five successive IQ ranges who experience certain bad outcomes. As shown, the odds of incarceration, illegitimate births, poverty as an adult, and the like all double at each successively lower IQ range. The ratios in the last column show how the odds of bad outcomes thus differ greatly even for people who are only somewhat below average (IQ 76–90) versus somewhat above average (IQ 111–125) in IQ. Among these young white adults, for instance, 17 percent of the former IQ group versus only 3 percent of the latter live in poverty as adults, for a ratio of about 5:1. The odds are less discrepant for some bad outcomes (3:2 for divorce and unemployment) but more discrepant for others (7:1 for incarceration and 88:1 for dropping out of high school). The disparities in odds across IQ groups are even more extreme at the extremes of IQ. Good and bad outcomes can be found at all IQ levels, but what is *typical* differs enormously, as was also illustrated with the NALS data.

Moreover, the odds of dropping out of school, illegitimate births, poverty, and welfare dependence all increase with lower IQ among siblings within the very same family and even when the families are intact and not poor. There is something about below-average IQ itself that puts individuals at serious social risk, whatever their family circumstances.

Overall life chances. Figure 1 and Table 2 together paint a vivid picture of how greatly overall life chances differ by IQ level. People with IQs below 75 are clearly in the "high-risk" zone, where trainability and employability are very low and the odds of various social pathologies are much elevated. Although risks fall substantially for individuals with IQs only somewhat below average (IQ 76–90), these people still face an "uphill battle" because they are not very competitive for many training programs and jobs. The middle 50 percent of the population (IQ 91–110) is competitive for many of a modern economy's jobs but likely only to be just "keeping up" relative to others. Their brethren of somewhat above-average IQ (IQ 111–125) are more likely "out ahead" socioeconomically because they are highly trainable and competitive for better jobs. Their rates of pathology are also very low. People with IQs above 125 are so competitive cognitively and so seldom hobbled by *g*-related social pathology that socioeconomic success is truly "theirs to lose."

Interpersonal Context. One of the most fascinating questions in the study of intelligence has received virtually no attention: How does the *mix* (average and variability) of intelligence levels in a

setting—its *IQ context*—affect behavior in that setting? How might one's fate be affected by the intelligence level of the *other* people in one's interpersonal settings—of one's parents, siblings, neighbors, friends, and other close compatriots?

The basic issue is this: A difference in IQ of one standard deviation (about 15 points) is socially perceptible and meaningful. Interpersonal communication becomes fraught with increasing difficulty beyond this distance because of larger gaps in vocabulary, knowledge, and ability to draw inferences or "catch on," as well as the emotional discomfort such gaps create. Figure 1 reveals how IQ ranges of about one standard deviation also mark off substantial differences in options for education, training, and career, and thus the likelihood of entering different social niches. As shown in the figure, the normal range of intelligence (IQ 70–130, which includes roughly 95 percent of the general white population) spans four standard deviations of IQ. Socially and cognitively, that is an enormous difference. How, then, do people communicate and congregate across the IQ continuum in their daily lives? The average difference between siblings and spouses is about 12 IQ points, which means that most people in a biological family fall within the range of ready cognitive communicability. Any two random people in the population, however, differ by 17 IQ points, which represents the borderline for communicating effectively and as social equals.

Communication, cooperation, and reciprocity. The ability to communicate as equals constitutes a social tie, as does the ability to trade information and assistance. Such reciprocity is the basis of longer-term cooperation. Lack of reciprocity creates not only social distance but also animosity where reciprocity had been expected. There are many bases for cooperation and reciprocity, but sharing information and helping to solve problems is crucial in many settings. Ethnographic studies of middle school children, for instance, show how patterns of mutual assistance and friendship, rather than resentment and unwillingness either to provide help to classmates or to seek it from them, evolve from similarities and differences in students' competence in answering homework and test items. Similar *g*-driven interpersonal relations can be expected in many workgroups

Percentage of Young White Adults with Particular Life Outcomes, by IQ Level

LIFE OUTCOME	IQ: 75 and Below "Very dull"	76–90 "Dull"	91–110 "Normal"	111–125 "Bright"	Over 125 "Very Bright"	Ratio of Dull to Bright
Out of labor force 1+ mo/yr (men)	22	19	15	14	10	4:3
Unemployed 1+ mo/yr (men)	12	10	7	7	2	3:2
Divorced in 5 yrs	21	22	23	15	9	3:2
% of children below IQ 75 (mothers)	39	17	6	7	–	2:1
Had illegitimate child (women)	32	17	8	4	2	4:1
Lives in poverty	30	16	6	3	2	5:1
Went on welfare after first child (women)	55	21	12	4	1	5:1
Ever incarcerated/ doing time (men)	7	7	3	1	0	7:1
Chronic welfare recipient (mothers)	31	17	8	2	0	8:1
High school dropout	55	35	6	0.4	0	88:1

Table 2

SOURCE: Herrnstein and Murray (1994): (respectively) 158, 163, 174, 230, 180, 132, 194, 247/248, 194, 146.

and other settings in which teammates depend on one another for technical competence.

People of markedly different ability levels also tend to have different interests, which further impedes their ability to develop rapport. Assortative mating studies show that individuals explicitly seek mates of similar IQ levels and that spouses' IQs are, in fact, moderately correlated (about .4), perhaps more so than any other personal characteristic (except gender). Cognitive incompatibility is certainly responsible for the extreme social isolation often experienced by both the mentally retarded and the highly gifted. Extremely gifted children, who may be four standard deviations or more above average (IQ 160 and above), often feel, and are treated as, alien. These children are as different from the borderline gifted (IQ 130) as the latter are from the average child (IQ 100). With extraordinary vocabularies for their age, the highly gifted speak virtually a different language from their agemates. Although less extreme, the same type of alienation develops across much smaller gaps in IQ. In short, cognitive similarity seems to affect the formation of social bonds, which themselves are the building blocks of "social structure."

Social separation and segregation. Because rough similarity in *g* promotes interpersonal reciprocity and rapport, it should not be surprising that people segregate themselves somewhat by cognitive ability when free to do so, marriage being the most intimate example. Segregation occurs along IQ lines for other reasons as well, many related to the functional value of intelligence in obtaining higher education and better work.

In the typical school, students enter grade 1 spanning at least mental ages four to nine, which translates quickly into markedly different grade-equivalent achievement levels. By reducing *g* variability within learning groups, ability grouping and tracking represent schools' attempt, albeit a perennially controversial one, to accommodate students of different cognitive levels. Its pedagogical merits aside, grouping reinforces friendships within IQ ranges and is but the first of many ways by which schools and employers direct individuals toward different occupational and income groups, and thence into residential neighborhoods, partly along IQ lines.

A 1933 epidemiological survey in New York City documented that the *average* IQ levels of white school children across a large sample of the city's 273 Health Areas ranged from 74 to 118, a range of three standard deviations. The parents of these children would differ even more in average IQ. Consistent with genetic expectations, parents of any ability level produce children at virtually all ability levels, but their children's average IQ is closer to the population average than is their own.

Social clustering along IQ lines can be expected to increase familiarity, communication, and mutual assistance by enhancing within-group similarity, at least when the groups are minimally competent. Enhanced similarity can elevate the risks of low IQ, however, when IQ clustering results in a *critical mass* of individuals below some *critical threshold* in IQ. That threshold may be IQ 75, which is the level below which individuals need considerable assistance from family, friends, or social agencies to live independently in modern societies. When critical mass is reached in a family or community, networks of competent help become overwhelmed by sticky webs of bad judgment, which in turn produce a physically unhealthy and socially dysfunctional environment for all members, as sympathetic social anthropologists have documented.

In any case, greater *within-group* similarity produces greater *between-group* dissimilarity and distance. A contested but reasonable hypothesis of Richard Herrnstein and Charles Murray's 1994 book, *The Bell Curve*, is that society is becoming *increasingly* stratified along cognitive lines, jeopardizing national unity. That specter raises much anxiety in democratic societies, perhaps accounting for the quick distaste the thesis roused in many quarters. Any societal divisions that g creates would, however, be softened somewhat by g's genetic basis. The laws of genetics guarantee that many children will differ substantially from their parents, producing intergenerational mobility across IQ and social-class lines and thereby assuring some cross-group ties. Whether or not it is increasing over time or permeable in nature, social clustering by g is nonetheless considerable. It is therefore a

perennial matter of public debate, whether the question be where to locate Section 8 or other public housing or how to integrate social classes and races in educational settings.

Social networks and subcultures of attitudes, behavior, and knowledge. The Bell Curve's thesis about the dangers of cognitive stratification rests in its assumption that different cognitive strata create distinct and somewhat discordant cultures. Sociologist Robert A. Gordon (1997) has outlined at the level of small groups how different IQ contexts do actually represent different subcultures. These different subcultures in turn expose their members to different experiences, risks, knowledge, opinions, assistance, and expectations, as suggested earlier. IQ-discrepant subgroups, for example, differ not so much in the social ideals they espouse as in tolerance for their violation. They also differ in the degree to which they diffuse news and information from the broader culture rather than propagate rumor, misinformation, and even the AIDS virus.

The New York City neighborhoods mentioned earlier differed not only in IQ but also in rates of birth, death, infant mortality, and juvenile delinquency, illustrating that different IQ contexts probably constitute notably different social milieus for developing children. Children of, say, IQ 100 surely live different lives with different opportunities when raised in IQ contexts of 85 versus 115, both of which are common in the United States. Not only is such a child substantially above average in the first context while below average in the second, which creates its own opportunities and obstacles for the child, but there are also significant differences across the two contexts in the quality of ambient advice, information, and personal examples. Children's IQ levels seem not to be permanently affected by their IQ contexts, but their more malleable behaviors and outcomes may be, as studies of youthful career aspirations and delinquency suggest. Epidemiological analyses of the g-related contagion of certain risky health and social behaviors would further illuminate how risks rise or fall according to the level of "local intelligence" in which one is embedded.

Societal Level. The interpersonal contexts that influence an individual's behavior are themselves shaped partly by the g levels of the people inhabiting them, as just described. IQ contexts thus represent an impact of g on an individual level that is above and beyond the effects of that individual's own IQ. IQ contexts have "macro" as well as "micro" effects in a society, however, because they create gradients of information flow, status and stigma, power and influence across a nation. These societal-level effects of g, via IQ contexts, may be the most important of all for a society, and they cry out for sociological analysis. Only a few such analyses have been done, but they illustrate the promise of a *sociology of intelligence*.

Evolution of social structures. If knowledge is power, then brighter people can be expected to advance further in any society freely allowing its accumulation. What is less obvious, except in hindsight, is that the routes to success may themselves be shaped by enduring variation in g within a population. Wide dispersion in g is a biological fact that all societies must accommodate. What norms and institutions evolve to promote such accommodation, especially where g has high functional value?

Consider the occupational hierarchy, that gradient of occupations from high to low in status, income, and educational requirements, which sociologists have shown to be replicated around the world. The consequences for individuals of their placement in it is clear, but its evolution is not. As described earlier, the major dimension underlying the hierarchy seems to be the complexity, not the content, of the tasks comprising the occupations arrayed along it. The occupational hierarchy is, then, a set of stable task configurations ranked in desirability according to their g-loadedness.

The structural question is how tasks gradually become sorted over time by their g-loadings into more g-homogeneous sets *within* occupations, thereby creating sharper distinctions in g-loading *between* occupations. This segregation of tasks by g-loading into a g-based occupational hierarchy most likely gradually arises from the natural sorting and reassignment of people *and* tasks to each other in the effort to improve aggregate performance of an organization's or society's essential functions. When workers are sorted more consistently by g level into occupations, occupational content can evolve to better fit the typical incumbent. For example, employers can gradually remove easy tasks from, and add complex tasks to, jobs whose usual incumbents are bright, and do the opposite for jobs typically peopled by less bright workers (Gottfredson 1985).

Of course, g is hardly the only contributor to job performance, and job performance is not the only basis for how work and workers are organized in firms and societies. But to the extent that g is the most functionally important worker attribute overall *and* that people become sorted to work by g level, there will arise a g-based occupational hierarchy whose distinctions gradually expand or contract when the g-related efficiency of sorting workers rises or falls. This theory illustrates how the biological fact of differences in g can constrain the evolution of social institutions. That biological fact clearly rules out common utopian fantasies in which all citizens are assigned, rotated through, or ascend to jobs of equal difficulty and status.

Racial politics. When two social groups differ substantially in average g and g has functional value, they can also be expected to differ in g-related outcomes. The average difference in outcomes will depend on, among other factors, the size of the average group difference in g and the g-loading of the outcome in question. The g-generated differences in outcome have many sociopolitical reverberations, because they are pervasive, frequently large, and sometimes involve races once subjugated. The societal-level reverberations have the power to alter many aspects of a nation's culture. This can be illustrated by the national effort in recent decades to eliminate racial disparities in education and employment despite continuing racial disparities in g.

A key practical dilemma for educators and employers is that unbiased, valid measures of mental ability are generally the best predictors of school and job performance but, owing to phenotypic differences in g across racial groups, they have considerable *disparate impact*. That is, they screen out disproportionate numbers of candidates from some races. Unless group disparities in g are eliminated, there will continue to be a trade-off between selecting the most able applicants and selecting a racially balanced student body or work force, especially in highly g-loaded settings such as graduate school and the professions. In both employment law and public perceptions, unequal selection rates by race constitute prima facie evidence of illegal discrimination, often making it risky to use g-loaded predictors.

This combination of scientific facts and legal constraints has precipitated in personnel selection psychology a desperate but unsuccessful search for non-*g* substitutes for mental tests. There turns out to be no substitute for higher-order thinking skills. This failure created additional pressure on the field to reduce employers' legal vulnerability while retaining mental tests by instituting racial preferences. Eventually the U.S. Congress banned the most efficient such "solution" as an undisguised quota (the race-norming of employment tests, which means ranking applicants on separate racial curves). That ban in turn increased the pressure to covertly reduce or eliminate the *g* component of tests (to remove crucial mental demands), the results of which led to enormous controversy—and litigation—in personnel selection psychology. The same controversial effort to reduce the *g*-loading of employee selection criteria is now occurring for college admissions in states where racial preferences have been banned or might be. Being the most *g*-loaded predictor of student performance, the SAT has been the first target. In short, *g*-related group differences in outcomes have long been driving widespread changes in standards for admission, hiring, promotion, and more, sometimes improving selection and sometimes not, but always causing controversy.

Selection psychology is only one microcosm for observing the sorts of societal waves created by *g*-related group disparities. Virtually every school practice, from instructional and grouping practices to discipline to teacher assignment and funding, has been modified in recent decades to neutralize either the reality or the appearance of racial differences in phenotypic intelligence and their real-world effects. Keen disappointment at the failure of these modifications to accomplish that neutralization has itself has sparked mutual recriminations between blacks and whites, led to more expansive definitions of discrimination and racism, and in many other ways shifted national politics. As is apparent, the societal-level ramifications of group differences in *g* hinge critically not only on how large they are and whom they affect but also on how a society explains and reacts to the differences.

Inequality and the democratic paradox. A population's IQ bell curve may bunch up or spread out somewhat with environmental change, and it may shift a bit up or down the IQ continuum over time. Nonetheless, it will remain as much a biological fact as are differences in height. The bell curves for different demographic groups may also shift somewhat relative to each other along the IQ continuum, but gaps will likely persist.

As indicated in Figure 1, the IQ continuum represents a gradient of functional advantage for the individuals and groups arrayed along it. Happiness and regard may be available to all, but money, power, and prestige all tend to flow up the continuum, especially in a free society. Accordingly, envy flows up and stigma down. The IQ continuum is thus a strong current deep within the body politic that influences its surface dynamics in myriad ways and can frustrate efforts to steer a society in certain directions. Perhaps for this reason, political efforts to regulate or defy those dynamics have sometimes been violent in spirit if not in act. A 1980 analysis of genocides earlier in the century found that all but one of the targeted groups (Gypsies) were of apparently *higher* average intelligence than those seeking to exterminate them, for instance, the Jews in Germany, Armenians in Turkey, Ibos in Nigeria, and the educated classes in Cambodia.

Any humane society will moderate the effects of unequal biological and social advantage, preventing unbridled competition and the degradation of its weaker members. If resources naturally flow up the IQ continuum, societies can consciously redistribute some of them back down it—in a word, by helping. Such is the realm of charity and, increasingly, social policy, although such measures are seldom conceived in terms of helping the less "able" because that in itself would be stigmatizing. More often today, help is couched in terms of assisting the "deprived," as though all social inequality were the result of some social groups illegitimately expropriating from others what would have otherwise naturally accrued to them. Some inequality may be, but much is not.

Extreme egalitarianism is as problematic, however, as unbridled individualism, for it hobbles talent and deadens ambition. John Gardner outlined the trade-offs between promoting individual merit and equalizing social outcomes in his 1984 book, *Excellence: Can We Be Equal and Excellent Too?*

In that eloquent little book, he asked the question that writers from both the political left and right have since tried to answer in more detail: How can we create a valued place for people of all ability levels and bring out the best in all? The proffered answers differ primarily in the difficult trade-offs the authors settle for among personal liberty, equality of socioeconomic outcomes, and an emphasis on human excellence and productivity, three principles that are somewhat inconsistent owing to meaningful differences among people.

If such are the political dilemmas that the deep current of *g* inevitably creates, the debates over their resolution seldom seem cognizant of the dilemma's roots in human variation. Democracy is itself a social leveler because its grants *political* equality to people who are in numerous ways *biologically* unequal. But this strength is also its torment, because democracy excites the desire for yet more leveling, to which biological inequalities—especially intelligence differences—pose an obstacle. Mother Nature is no egalitarian. As Alexis de Tocqueville observed almost 200 years ago ([1835, 1840] 1969), "When there is no more hereditary wealth, class privilege, or prerogatives of birth, and when every man derives his strength from himself alone, it becomes clear that the chief source of disparity between the fortunes of men lies in the mind . . . [T]here would still be inequalities of intelligence which, coming directly from God, will ever escape the laws of man" (pp. 457–458, 538).

Biological diversity in *g* is a core challenge to democratic societies and to the scholars who are responsible for helping citizens understand how their society works. The challenge is exacerbated as technology advances, because such advance favors higher-*g* over lower-*g* people owing to their better ability to capitalize on it. Western democracies view democracy and technology as their twin engines of progress, however, and so haplessly seek solutions to inequality by pursuing yet more of both. That is the *democratic paradox*. The answer to the dilemma lies not in pursuing the opposite strategy—that is, curtailing both democracy and technology, as is sometimes hinted—but most likely in better understanding how differences in *g* orchestrate and constrain social life, to the extent that they do. For sociologists of intelligence, there is much to do.

REFERENCES

Anastasi, A. 1996 *Psychological Testing*. New York: Plenum.

Brown, H., R. Prisuta, B. Jacobs, and A. Campbell 1996 *Literacy of Older Adults in America: Results from the National Adult Literacy Survey*. NCES 97-576. Washington, D.C.: U.S. Department of Education, National Center for Education Statistics.

Carroll, J. B. 1993 *Human Cognitive Abilities: A Survey of Factor-Analytic Studies*. New York: Cambridge University Press.

—— 1997 "Psychometrics, Intelligence, and Public Perception." *Intelligence* 24(1):25–52.

de Tocqueville, A. (1835, 1840) 1969 *Democracy in America*. New York: Harper Perennial.

Fox, W. L., J. E. Taylor, and J. S. Caylor 1969 *Aptitude Level and the Acquisition of Skills and Knowledges in a Variety of Military Training Tasks*. (Technical Report 69-6). Prepared for the Department of the Army by the Human Resources Research Office. Washington, D.C.: The George Washington University.

Gardner, H. 1983 *Frames of Mind*. New York: Basic Books.

Gardner, J. 1984 *Excellence: Can We Be Equal and Excellent Too?* New York: Harper.

Goleman, D. 1995 *Emotional Intelligence*. New York: Bantam.

Gordon, R. A. 1997 "Everyday Life as an Intelligence Test: Effects of Intelligence and Intelligence Context." *Intelligence* 24(1):203–320.

Gottfredson, L. S. 1985 "Education as a Valid but Fallible Signal of Worker Quality: Reorienting an Old Debate About the Functional Basis of the Occupational Hierarchy." In A. C. Kerckhoff, ed., *Research in Sociology of Education and Socialization*, vol. 5. Greenwich, Conn.: JAI Press.

Gottfredson, L. S. 1997a "Mainstream Science on Intelligence: An Editorial with 52 Signatories, History, and Bibliography." *Intelligence* 24(1):13–23.

Gottfredson, L. S. 1997b "Why Intelligence Matters: The Complexity of Everyday Life." *Intelligence* 24(1):79–132.

Herrnstein, R. J., and C. Murray 1994 *The Bell Curve: Intelligence and Class Structure in American Life*. New York: Free Press.

Jencks, C., M. Smith, H. Acland, M. J. Bane, D. Cohen, H. Gintis, B. Heyns, and S. Michelson 1972 *Inequality: A Reassessment of the Effect of Family and Schooling in America*. New York: Harper and Row.

Jensen, A. R. 1998 *The g factor: The Science of Mental Abilities*. Wesport, Conn.: Praeger.

Kaufman, A. S. 1990 *Assessing Adolescent and Adult Intelligence*. Boston: Allyn and Bacon.

Kaus, M. 1992 *The End of Inequality*. New York: Basic Books.

Kirsch, I. S., A. Jungeblut, L. Jenkins, and A. Kolstad 1993 *Adult Literacy in America: A First Look at the Results of the National Adult Literacy Survey*. Princeton, N.J.: Educational Testing Service.

Lichtenstein, P., and N. L. Pedersen 1997 "Does Genetic Variance for Cognitive Abilities Account for Genetic Variance in Educational Achievement and Occupational Status? A Study of Twins Reared Apart and Twins Reared Together." *Social Biology* 44:77–90.

Loehlin, J. C. 1992 *Genes and Environment in Personality Development*. Newbury Park, Calif.: Sage.

Matarazzo, J. D. 1972 *Wechsler's Measurement and Appraisal of Adult Intelligence*, 5th ed. Baltimore: Williams and Wilkins.

Neisser, U., G. Boodoo, T. J. Bouchard, A. W. Boykin, N. Brody, S. J. Ceci, D. F. Halpern, J. C. Loehlin, R. Perloff, R. J. Sternberg, and S. Urbana 1996 "Intelligence: Knowns and Unknowns." *American Psychologist* 51:77–101.

Plomin, R., J. C. DeFries, G. E. McClearn, and M. Rutter 1997 *Behavioral Genetics*, 3rd ed. New York: W. H. Freeman.

Rowe, D. C. 1994 *The Limits of Family Influence: Genes, Experience, and Behavior*. New York: Guilford.

—— 1997 "A Place at the Policy Table? Behavioral Genetics and Estimates of Family Environmental Effects on IQ." *Intelligence* 24(1):133–158.

Scarr, S. 1997 "Behavior-Genetic and Socialization Theories of Intelligence: Truce and Reconcilliation." In R. J. Sternberg and E. Grigorenko, eds., *Intelligence, Heredity, and Environment*. New York: Cambridge University Press.

Stein, Z., M. Susser, and I. Wald 1978 "Cognitive Development and Social Policy." *Science, 200* 23:1357–1362.

Sternberg, R. J. 1985 *Beyond IQ: A Triarchic Theory of Human Intelligence*. New York: Cambridge University Press.

Vernon, P. A. 1993 *Biological Approaches to the Study of Human Intelligence*. Norwood, N.J.: Ablex.

Wonderlic Personnel Test, Inc. 1992 *Wonderlic Personnel Test and Scholastic Level Exam: User's Manual*. Libertyville, IL: Author.

LINDA S. GOTTFREDSON

INTERGENERATIONAL RELATIONS

Throughout recorded history, concern has been expressed about relations among the generations. Historians have identified changing patterns of relationships between the old and the young, pointing out that in some epochs veneration of the aged was common, while in other eras, the aged were more likely to be held up to scorn and ridicule. In contemporary American society, these contrasts are muted, and themes of both consensus and conflict are present.

Sociologists have explored intergenerational relations extensively, using both macrosociological and microsociological approaches. Scholars who have taken a macrosociological approach have examined the discontinuity caused by the succession of different groups of individuals who were born during the same time period and therefore age together (Foner 1986). Sociologists refer to such groups as "cohorts." Many important questions have been raised regarding relations among cohorts, including: How do people differ as a result of membership in a specific cohort? How and why do cohorts come into conflict with one another? Does a "generation gap" exist?

In contrast, sociologists who have taken a microsociological approach have focused on intergenerational relations within families. These scholars have examined the content and quality of relationships among family members in different generations, posing such questions as: How much contact do adult children have with their parents? What kinds of exchanges occur between older and younger generations? What is the role of grandparents in families? Under what circumstances does conflict among the generations in families occur? To fully understand intergenerational relations, it is essential to study both levels and to draw connections between them.

MACROSOCIOLOGICAL PERSPECTIVES

Mannheim's View of Generations. Karl Mannheim provided one of the most enduring analyses of relations between cohorts (he used the term "generation," however, instead of the contemporary sociological term "cohort"). Mannheim argued that the individuals born into a given cohort experience the same set of sociopolitical events while they are growing up; this distinguishes them as a special social group. Merely by their location in a given cohort, members are likely to have certain similarities, since they are endowed with "a common location in the historical process" (1952, p. 290).

Thus, position within a cohort—like position within the socioeconomic structure—limits members to a narrow range of possible experiences and predisposes them to characteristic modes of thought. These differences can lead to conflict between the cohorts, as younger cohorts try to impose their views on society. The older cohort, on the other hand, has a major stake in preserving the existing social order. The interaction between these divergent cohort groups, according to Mannheim, is a critically important aspect of human social life.

To be sure, Mannheim did not compare belonging to a cohort with belonging to a more concrete group—such as a family—in that a cohort lacks a clear organizational framework. Further, he noted that differences may exist within cohorts. That is, within the same cohort, subgroups (in Mannheim's terms, "generational units") can form that are different from, and may even be antagonistic toward, one another. Nevertheless, Mannheim viewed location in a cohort as a powerful influence on people's lives in much the same way that class position is an influence on their lives. This concern with the continual succession of cohorts, and its effects on social life, has found its clearest contemporary expression in age-stratification theory.

Age-Stratification Theory. Age-stratification theory begins with the fundamental assumption that to understand intercohort relations, we need to see society as *stratified* by age. Consistent with Mannheim, this view holds that society is divided into a hierarchy of socially recognized age strata. Each stratum consists of members who are similar in age and whose behavior is governed by the same set of norms for behavior appropriate for their age group. Further, members of various age strata differ in their abilities to obtain and control social resources. For example, young people in most societies have less power and fewer resources than middle-aged adults.

The duties, obligations, and privileges associated with age strata vary according to individual attributes, but they are always influenced by the structural aspect of age. Thus, various cohorts in a society may have greatly divergent views on filial responsibility, expectations for independence of children, and values on other issues.

Sociologists see such differences among cohorts as the basis for possible conflicts of interest in society. In fact, conflict regarding continuity and discontinuity has been a major theme in macrosociological approaches to intergenerational relations. As Vern Bengtson (1989, p. 26) notes, members of the older cohort desire continuity: They want to transmit to younger cohorts "what is best in their own lives." Correspondingly, they fear discontinuity: that young people will choose to live by very different sets of values. What has come to be known as the "problem of generations" reflects "the tension between continuity and change, affirmation and innovation, in the human social order over time" (Bengtson 1989, p. 26).

As an example, an age-stratification perspective on intergenerational relations can be applied to the political realm. When the age-stratification system is viewed as analogous to other stratification systems (e.g., class or gender), it follows that group solidarity may develop within each age cohort and that conflict—both overt conflict and conflict of interests—may occur between two different cohorts.

On a basic level, members of older and younger cohorts find different political issues more salient; for example, the elderly are more likely to focus on old-age pensions and health benefits, while the young are concerned with issues such as educational loans or the military draft (Riley et al. 1988). Such differences in salience may result in differences in voting behavior; for example, older individuals may be less likely to support tax increases for educational spending (Button 1992).

Political ideology among older and younger cohorts has been examined, with the fairly consistent finding that the current aged cohort is generally more conservative than younger cohorts. (However, these cross-sectional differences do not highlight the fact that people change their political attitudes over time, in line with changes in the society as a whole; for a discussion of political shifts during the life course, see Alwin 1998.)

Do divergent interests and attitudes result in age-related collective political action? Sociologists have examined whether the aged constitute a self-defined political group that sets its agenda against those of other age strata. This question may be particularly important because studies have shown that older people are more likely to register and vote than younger individuals (Binstock 1997). Certainly Washington politicians and the media view the elderly as a political powerhouse; however, it is not clear that a voting block can be organized around old-age interests, as political attitudes vary greatly within the cohort. In addition, the elderly are a heterogeneous group; there are differences in socioeconomic status and racial and ethnic background within the aged cohort. Finally, the interests of the "young-old" (65–75) may differ from those of the "old-old" (over 75), with the former more concerned with retirement issues, income maintenance, and leisure opportunities, and the latter more interested in funding for medical services and long-term care. The overall evidence shows that the aged are willing to act together on some issues (like Social Security) but not on others.

A political development of the 1990s, however, may create more polarization among cohorts and thus lead to an upswing in age-based politics. This is the rising concern over "generational equity." Gordon Streib and Robert Binstock (1988) have summarized the issue in the following way. The elderly in developed nations were seen as a disadvantaged group from the 1950s to the early 1970s. They were portrayed as having low economic and social status, compared with younger persons. However, by the late 1970s, some scholarly and popular literature began to assert that old people had in fact *over*benefited, and the elderly came to be seen as potentially burdensome economically to younger generations.

The older generation has at times been viewed as a scapegoat for a number of problems (Binstock 1983). In particular, the elderly have come to be seen as demanding resources for themselves, thus depriving children of quality schooling, health care, and other services. Organizations have arisen whose goal is to advocate the interests of the young at the expense of the older cohort. These groups have the expressed goal of establishing "generational equity," by transferring resources back to the young.

In the face of such attacks, it is conceivable that the elderly will begin to coalesce into a more unified generational unit. However, in response to these claims, a countermovement has developed that encourages cooperation among advocates for youth *and* the elderly. On the level of practice, this interest has led to the development of intergenerational programs that bring old and young together.

While the macrosociological approach just discussed provides important insights into intergenerational relations and has obvious relevance for public policy on aging issues, it is also important to examine intergenerational relations on the microsocial level.

MICROSOCIOLOGICAL APPROACHES: A FOCUS ON THE FAMILY

Many sociologists have also focused on the smaller world of the family in an attempt to further our understanding of intergenerational relations. The family resembles the larger society, in that it is the locus of both intergenerational consensus and conflict. There is considerable family solidarity, indicated by feelings of affection and attachment that result from a shared history and close contact (Bengtson et al. 1990; Silverstein and Bengtson 1997), as well as inequalities of power and social resources. These twin themes of solidarity and conflict are evident throughout sociological research on the topic.

The way in which these themes are worked out in families has been affected by the dramatic changes in the age structure of American society. In particular, average life span has increased, which means that family members will spend more time than ever before occupying intergenerational family roles. Further, increased life expectancy leads to a greater likelihood that families will spend longer periods of time caring for disabled elderly relatives.

Societal changes have also increased the complexity of intergenerational relations. For example, the high divorce rate found in contemporary American society raises the likelihood that adult children will return to their parents' homes, often bringing their own young children with them. Women's unprecedented participation in the labor force and their return to college in great numbers may also affect intergenerational relations. To be sure, the acquisition of these nonfamilial roles provides new and enriching opportunities for women; however, it may alter the time that has traditionally been devoted to "kinkeeping" between the generations.

It is only possible to comment on a few major themes in this review. The most widely studied area is that of parent–child relations in later life, including patterns of intergenerational contact and factors that affect the quality of adult child–elderly parent relationships.

Contact Between Parents and Children. A major concern of researchers has been to understand patterns of contact between adult children and older parents. Research on this issue has gone through two major phases. First, there was a period in which the nuclear family was held to be isolated. This view was based in part on Talcott Parsons's analyses of family relations, which held that modernization had brought about the decline of the extended family (DeWit and Frankel 1988). During this period, it was widely believed that because of the geographic mobility of children, families abandoned their elderly relatives. This view also held that most elderly persons rarely saw their children and that family members no longer provided care for older relatives (Shanas 1979).

In the second phase, many prominent researchers devoted considerable effort to demonstrating that this view is inaccurate. Investigators such as Ethel Shanas, Marvin Sussman, and Eugene Litwak, as well as later researchers, clearly established that older persons have frequent contact with family members and that few are totally isolated from kin. Further, most aged family members are involved in a network of emotionally and instrumentally supportive relationships.

Studies have shown that in most cases parents and adult children have relatively frequent and regular contact (Umberson 1992); in fact, 40 to 50 percent of adult children see their parents at least once a week (Rossi and Rossi 1990). A major factor in determining the frequency of contact is physical proximity. Numerous studies have found that the frequency of intergenerational contact is greatly affected by geographical distance between households, with more distant children interacting less often with parents (cf. Eggebeen 1992). However, it is clear that many geographically distant children continue to interact to a significant degree with parents and that parents and children are able to maintain close ties despite being separated by great distances.

Determinants of Quality of Parent–Child Relationships. Researchers have moved beyond simply establishing patterns of contact to examining factors that affect the quality of parent–child relations in later life. For a review of this literature, see Suitor and colleagues (1995). A number of factors appear to have an impact on relationship quality.

Increased parental dependency is frequently cited as a factor that negatively affects the quality of aged parent–adult child relations. Studies have highlighted imbalanced exchanges and perceptions of inequity between the generations as major causes of family disharmony. For example, several investigations have suggested that an increase in parents' dependence upon their adult children may reduce positive feelings between the generations. Other studies have found that adult children's feelings of closeness and attachment are reduced when parents' health declines. As parents' health deteriorates, adult children are likely to need to increase their levels of support to previously independent parents, as well as to accept a lessening or termination of the parents' provision of support—thus disrupting the previously established flow of support between the generations.

A second factor affecting parent–child relations is *gender*. Research has shown that women tend to have stronger and more supportive ties with parents than do men (Silverstein et al. 1995; Spitze et al. 1994). Further, studies of the effects of gender consistently demonstrate stronger affectional ties between mothers and daughters than any other combination (Rossi and Rossi 1990). Mothers report more positive affect with adult daughters than sons and are more likely to rely on daughters than sons as confidantes and comforters. Daughters in turn report greater feelings of closeness to mothers and are more likely to turn to them as confidantes than to fathers.

Third, the *age of the child* affects relationships with parents. Theories of adult development and intergenerational relations lead to the expectation that a child's age will be negatively related to parent–child conflict and positively related to closeness. This literature suggests that maturational changes are likely to reduce differences between parents and adult children, thus minimizing the bases for conflict between them. For example, Bengtson (1979) suggests that as children mature, their orientations become more similar to those of their parents. Similarly, Gunhild Hagestad (1987) posits both that differences between parents and children become muted across time and that there is greater tolerance for differences that remain. Empirical findings have consistently supported these assertions.

Fourth, changes in the degree of *status similarity* between adult children and their parents may affect their relationship. In particular, some studies have found a pattern of increased closeness in intergenerational relations when children begin to share a larger number of adult statuses with their parents. For example, the mother–daughter relationship appears to assume greater importance from the daughters' perspective when they themselves become mothers (Spitze et al. 1994; Umberson 1992). Conversely, decreases in status similarity may negatively affect adult child–parent relations. For example, the status dissimilarity that develops when daughters surpass their mothers educationally may have particular potential for creating difficulties between the generations (Suitor 1987). For a review of research regarding parent–child relationships across the life course, see Pillemer and Suitor (1998) and Suitor and colleagues (1995).

Two other areas that have received considerable attention are relations with grandparents in the family and the importance of changing dependencies among the generations over the life course.

Grandparenthood. In recent years, sociologists have shown increasing interest in studying the role of grandparents in families (see Robertson 1995 for a review of contemporary grandparenting). The demographic shifts noted above have brought about changes in the nature of grandparenthood in several ways. First, more people now survive to become grandparents than ever before. Second, the entry into grandparenthood is likely to occur in midlife, rather than in old age; thus, the duration of grandparenthood may extend to four decades or more. Third, the role of grandparent is not clearly defined in American society, and the normative expectations, privileges, and obligations are ambiguous (Hagestad 1985).

Studies have revealed several consistent findings about grandparenthood. Contrary to popular stereotypes, most grandparents do not wish to take on a parental role toward their grandchildren. Rather, they generally prefer a more distant role in the grandchildren's lives. Nevertheless, grandparents are often a critical resource for families in times of trouble (Hogan et al. 1993).

Perhaps the most consistent finding in more than a quarter-century of research is diversity in grandparenting styles. A number of typologies have been identified, which usually array grandparents along a continuum from intense involvement and assumption of parental responsibilities, on the one hand, to relative alienation from grandchildren, on the other (Neugarten and Weinstein 1964).

The most ambitious study to date used a representative survey to examine styles of grandparenting and to uncover factors that determine the adoption of a particular style (Cherlin and Furstenberg 1986). Andrew Cherlin and Frank Furstenberg were able to identify five basic grandparenting styles. *Detached* grandparents have little contact with their grandchildren. *Passive* grandparents visit somewhat more frequently but carefully maintain a distance from their grandchildren's lives. *Supportive* grandparents have more contact and focus on providing services to the grandchildren. *Authoritative* grandparents exert parent-like influence to a relatively great degree. Finally, *influential* grandparents combine involvement both by providing services and by adopting a parental role.

Cherlin and Furstenberg found that geographical distance was the most critical factor in determining which style of grandparenting developed. Detached grandparents were much more likely to live far away, while the most involved grandparents lived in close proximity to the grandchildren. Further, grandparents practiced "selective investment" in their grandchildren. They had more intense relationships with some grandchildren and more distant relationships with others. Other studies have affirmed this finding and have also pointed to the importance of gender: Grandmothers tend to have closer relationships with grandchildren than grandfathers.

Research interest has also highlighted the effects of children's marital disruption on the relationship between grandparents and grandchildren. Despite suggestions in the popular media that relations between grandchildren and grandparents are damaged when adult children divorce, studies have shown that this is not necessarily the case. Cherlin and Furstenberg (1986) found that "custodial grandparents" (that is, those whose adult children were awarded custody of the grand- children) tended to maintain very close ties with their grandchildren, while "noncustodial grand- parents" were less likely to maintain such ties. Since custody of minor children continues to be awarded more frequently to mothers than fathers, this means that ties with maternal grandparents are more likely to be maintained or strengthened following a divorce, while ties with paternal grand- parents are more vulnerable—particularly in terms of frequency of interaction.

Jeanne Hilton and Daniel Macari (1997) also found that geographic proximity and whether the grandparents were related to the custodial parent were important factors in structuring the grand- parent–grandchild relationship. In a study of New York families, Hilton and Macari (1997) found that grandparents were more involved with their grandchildren when they lived nearby and were related to the custodial parent; they also found that grandmothers were more involved with grand- children than were grandfathers. Further informa- tion on the effect of divorce on parent, adult– child, and grandchild relationships can be found in Johnson (1993).

Changing Dependencies. Social scientists have convincingly demonstrated that children and par- ents continue to depend on one another for both emotional and instrumental support throughout the life course (Spitze and Logan 1992). The litera- ture on intergenerational relations, however, has focused more heavily on children's support to elderly parents than the reverse. Thus, before turning to a brief discussion of the issue of caregiving to the elderly, it is important to empha- size the *reciprocal* nature of intergenerational assistance.

Marvin Sussman (1985) has provided a model of parent–child relations across the life span that emphasizes the cyclical shift in relations with par- ents. In the beginning, parents provide a substan- tial amount of assistance to their offspring, even into the children's early married life. Then, as children become more independent—and possi- bly move away—there is a decrease in intergenera- tional helping. Finally, as elderly parents begin to decline in health, they come to depend more

heavily on their children. This cyclical view of support is important, in that it stresses patterns of *mutual* aid between the generations (see also Rossi and Rossi 1990). Further, it should be noted that it is usually only very late in the life course that children's provision of support exceeds that of parents, and even then only when parents become frail and disabled (Spitze and Logan 1992).

Throughout the 1990s, several hundred arti- cles were published examining the experiences of families at this stage of the life course. Research has documented the strains experienced by mid- dle-aged children when parents become depend- ent, including practical problems of managing competing demands on their time and energy as well as emotional stress, increased social isolation, guilt, and feelings of inadequacy.

Besides establishing both the prevalence of support for aged parents and problems in provid- ing care, researchers have attempted to determine who is most likely both to become a caregiver and to experience the greatest stress from caregiving. Two of the most consistent findings involve the issues of gender and the relationship to the elderly person. First, women are substantially more likely to become caregivers than are men, and the role of caretaking appears to result in more intensive "hands-on" activities for women than men (cf. Allen 1994; Arber and Ginn 1995; Coward and Dwyer 1990; Finley 1989; Lee et al. 1993). Second, when the elderly person is married, it is the spouse who almost always becomes the primary caregiver (Stoller 1992). Thus, adult children generally become caregivers only when the care recipient's spouse is not available to occupy this status. In addition, the nature of caregiving is different for spouses than for other caregivers. Spouses are more likely to have sole responsibility for caregiving and to have responsibility for providing assistance with routine activities of daily living (Stoller 1992). Further, spouses appear to experience greater physical and financial strain than do adult child caregivers and the are more likely to continue caregiving at the expense of their own well-being (Horowitz 1985). For a further discussion of caregiving, see Dwyer (1995).

Although research has focused on the detri- mental consequences of caregiving, some more recent evidence suggests that most caregivers can also identify positive consequences of caregiving.

These positive aspects usually involve feelings of gratification derived from helping someone they love and fulfilling expectations of filial responsibility. Thus, the issue of changing dependencies in later life reflects the twin themes of consensus and conflict evident throughout theory and research on intergenerational relations.

REFERENCES

Allen, Susan M. 1994 "Gender Differences in Spousal Caregiving and Unmet Need for Care." *Journal of Gerontology: Social Sciences* 49:S187–S195.

Alwin, Duane F. 1998 "The Political Impact of the Baby Boom: Are There Persistent Generational Differences in Political Beliefs and Behavior." *Generations* 12:46–54.

Arber, Sara, and Jay Ginn 1995 "Gender Differences in Informal Caring." *Health and Social Care in the Community* 3:19–31.

Bengtson, Vern L. 1979 "Research Perspectives on Intergenerational Interaction." In Pauline K. Ragan, ed., *Aging Parents*. Los Angeles: University of Southern California Press.

—— 1989 "The Problem of Generations: Age Group Contrasts, Continuities, and Social Change." In V. L. Bengtson and K. W. Schaie, eds., *The Course of Later Life: Research and Reflections*. New York: Springer.

——, Carolyn Rosenthal, and Linda Burton 1988 "Families and Aging: Diversity and Heterogeneity." In R. H. Binstock and L. K. George, eds., *Handbook of Aging and the Social Sciences*, 3rd ed. San Diego, Calif,: Academic Press.

Binstock, Robert H. 1983 "The Aged as Scapegoat." *The Gerontologist* 23:136–143.

—— 1997 "The 1996 Election: Older Voters and Implications for Policies on Aging." *The Gerontologist* 37:15–19.

Button, J. W. 1992 "A Sign of Generational Conflict: The Impact of Florida's Aging Voters on Local School and Tax Referenda." *Social Science Quarterly* 73:786–797.

Cherlin, Andrew J., and Frank F. Furstenberg, Jr. 1986 *The New American Grandparent: A Place in the Family, A Life Apart*. New York: Basic Books.

Coward, R. T., and J. W. Dwyer 1990 "The Association of Gender, Sibling Network Composition, and Patterns of Parent Care By Adult Children." *Research on Aging* 12:158–181.

DeWit, David J., and B. Gail Frankel 1988 "Geographic Distance and Intergenerational Contact: A Critical Assessment and Review of the Literature." *Journal of Aging Studies* 2:25–43.

Dwyer, Jeffery W. 1995 "The Effects of Illness on the Family." In Victoria Bedford and Rosemary Bliezner, eds., *Handbook of Aging and the Family*. Westport, Conn.: Greenwood Press.

Eggebeen, David J. 1992 "Family Structure and Intergenerational Exchanges." *Research on Aging* 14:427–447.

Finley, Nancy J. 1989 "Theories of Family Labor as Applied to Gender Differences in Caregiving to Elderly Parents." *Journal of Marriage and the Family* 51:79–86.

Foner, Anne 1986 *Aging and Old Age: New Perspectives*. Englewood Cliffs, N.J.: Prentice-Hall.

Hagestad, Gunhild O. 1985 "Continuity and Connectedness." In V. L. Bengtson and J. F. Robertson, eds., *Grandparenthood*. Newbury Park, Calif.: Sage.

—— 1987 "Dimensions of Time and the Family." *American Behavioral Scientist* 29:679–694.

Hilton, Jeanne M., and Daniel P. Macari 1997 "Grandparent Involvement Following Divorce: A Comparison in Single-Mother and Single-Father Families." *Journal of Divorce and Remarriage* 28:203–224.

Hogan, Dennis P., David J. Eggebeen, and Clifford C. Clogg 1993 "The Structure of Intergenerational Exchanges in American Families." *American Journal of Sociology* 98:1428–1458.

Horowitz, Amy 1985 "Family Caregiving to the Frail Elderly." In C. Eisdorfer et al., eds., *Annual Review of Gerontology and Geriatrics*. New York: Springer.

Johnson, Colleen L. 1993 "Divorced and Reconstituted Families: Effects on the Older Generation." In L. Burton, ed., *Families and Aging*. San Francisco: Baywood Press.

Lee, Gary R., Jeffrey W. Dwyer, and Raymond T. Coward 1993 "Gender Differences in Parent Care: Demographic Factors and Same-Gender Preferences." *Journal of Gerontology: Social Sciences* 48:59–516.

Mannheim, Karl 1952 *Essays on the Sociology of Knowledge*, trans. Paul Kecskemeti. London: Routledge and Kegan Paul.

Neugarten, Bernice L., and K. K. Weinstein 1964 "The Changing American Grandparent." *Journal of Marriage and the Family* 26:199–204.

Pillemer, Karl, and J. Jill Suitor 1998 "Baby Boom Families: Relations with Aging Parents." *Generations* 12:65–69.

Riley, Matilda White, Anne Foner, and Joan Waring 1988 "Sociology of Age." In *Handbook of Sociology*. Newbury Park, Calif: Sage.

Robertson, Joan F. 1995 "Grandparenting in an Era of Rapid Change." In Victoria Bedford and Rosemary Bliezner, eds., *Handbook of Aging and the Family*. Westport, Conn.: Greenwood Press.

Rossi, Alice S., and Peter H. Rossi 1990 *Of Human Bonding: Parent–Child Relations Across the Life Course*. New York: Aldine de Gruyter.

Shanas, Ethel 1979 "Social Myth as Hypothesis: The Case of the Family Relations of Old People." *The Gerontologist* 19:3–9.

Silverstein, Merril, and Vern L. Bengtson 1997 "Intergenerational Solidarity and the Structure of Adult Child–Parent Relationships in American Families." *American Journal of Sociology* 103:429–460.

Silverstein, Merril, T. M. Parrott, and Vern L. Bengtson 1995 "Factors That Predispose Middle-Aged Sons and Daughters to Provide Social Support to Older Parents." *Journal of Marriage and the Family* 57:465–475.

Spitze, Glenna, and J. R. Logan 1992 "Helping as a Component of Parent–Adult Child Relations." *Research on Aging* 14:291–312.

——, D. Glenn, and S. Zerger 1994 "Adult Children's Divorce and Intergenerational Relationships." *Journal of Marriage and the Family* 56:279–293.

Streib, Gordon, and Robert H. Binstock 1988 "Aging and the Social Sciences: Changes in the Field." In R. H. Binstock and L. K. George, eds., *Handbook of Aging and the Social Sciences, Third Edition*. San Diego, Calif.: Academic Press.

Suitor, J. Jill 1987 "Mother–Daughter Relations When Married Daughters Return to School: Effects of Status Similarity." *Journal of Marriage and the Family* 49:435–444.

——, Karl Pillemer, Shirley Keeton, and Julie Robison 1995 "Aging Parents and Aging Children: Determinants of Relationship Quality." In Victoria Bedford and Rosemary Bliezner, eds., *Handbook of Aging and the Family*. Westport, Conn.: Greenwood Press.

Sussman, Marvin 1985 "The Family Life of Older People." In R. Binstock and E. Shanas, eds., *Handbook of Aging and the Social Sciences*. New York: Van Nostrand Reinhold.

Umberson, Debra 1992 "Relationships Between Adult Children and Their Parents: Psychological Consequences for Both Generations." *Journal of Marriage and the Family* 54:664–674.

KARL PILLEMER
SHIRLEY A. KEETON
J. JILL SUITOR

INTERGENERATIONAL RESOURCE TRANSFERS

The transfer of resources between individuals of different generations occurs on both the societal level, as the outcome of public policy or within the context of the private sector, and the family level, as in the exchange of emotional support and material goods. This discussion of the intergenerational exchange of resources will consider, first, the flow of resources within the context of the family; second, intergenerational transfers on the societal level; and last, the issue of equity in the transfer of resources intergenerationally. In addition, brief mention will be made of special circumstances, such as cross-cultural differences or the special case of divorce and stepfamilies.

The meaning of the word *generation* varies from setting to setting. In the family environment, the reference is primarily to lines of descent (grandparents, parents, children, etc.). However, each family member is also a member of a particular birth cohort, or group of individuals born during the same period of historical time, such as 1920–1924, and, at any given time, a member of a particular age group, such as sixty-five- to sixty-nine-year-olds. Each of these is also reflected in the intergenerational exchange within the context of the family and in the intergenerational exchange of a society's resources. Finally, the exchange process may also include the concept of generation that connotes a group of individuals, usually part of the same birth cohort, who share a common set of political or social beliefs (e.g., the "Woodstock Generation").

RESOURCE TRANSFERS WITHIN THE CONTEXT OF THE FAMILY

Resources exchanged among family members vary greatly in size and type. Examples range from the ordinary, everyday exchange of care involved in child rearing or household chores to the bequest of substantial financial or material resources to descendants in a will. The latter behavior has been explored as part of a broader practice referred to as a "legacy" (Kane 1996), which includes last wills and testaments, the transfer of property, and, even more broadly, how people want to be remembered.

Over the last several decades a number of perspectives have developed regarding such familial exchanges. One such perspective views the resource-transfer process in terms of *reciprocity of exchanges among family members*. Analysts have examined reciprocity as a motivator of interdependence over time, at different points in the family structure (e.g., parent–child, sister–brother), and within the context of individual family members' perceptions of how much each member has given or received in the past. *Exchange theory* specifically views all kinds of social interactions as the exchange of rewards between individuals where the group or individual with the greater amount of *social power* regulates the exchange process (Dowd 1975). Regarding resources to older family members, Horowitz and Shindelman (1983) view reciprocity in terms of the "credits earned" by the older individual for providing resources in the past to the family member currently on the giving end.

In contrast, the *life-cycle model* of family intergenerational transfers maintains that the distribution of resources among the generations in the family takes on a curvilinear shape: Individuals in the middle generations, and most likely middle-aged, transfer the bulk of family resources to those who are either younger or older. (For an illustration, see the works of Reuben Hill [1965, 1970] regarding his study of three-generational families in the Minneapolis–St. Paul area). In contrast, the *role continuity model of family intergenerational transfers* asserts that, except in families where the older generations are financially strained, older family members redistribute their wealth to successive generations in the family (for further discussion, see Covey 1981; Kalish 1975; Riley and Foner 1971). Still another perspective used to explore the giving and receiving of resources in the family is that of *hierarchical/sequential* activities. From this perspective, individuals first seek aid from members of their nuclear family; failing that, from members of their extended family; and, only as a last resort, from institutional sources such as government programs, banks, and the educational system (viz., Morgan 1983). A final perspective is that of altruism. *Altruism* is a helping behavior that benefits the recipient but provides no benefits, and may incur costs, to the provider. In this context, then, resources are transferred from one generation to another with regard only to the benefit they provide to the recipient, without regard to the costs incurred by the provider. Research has investigated the relative importance of exchange versus altruism as motivators for intergenerational transfers (Cox and Jakubson 1995; Cox and Rank 1992; Schoeni 1997). This research finds that intergenerational transfers are more likely to be part of an exchange process rather than behaviors conducted out of altruism.

A great variety of resources, both material and psychosocial in nature, are exchanged among members of nuclear and extended families. These include the giving and receiving of material gifts of all manner and size; the provision of help during emergencies, as when a family member is ill or in need of sudden and immediate shelter; providing physical or financial resources in time of need, such as babysitting or nursing, offering advice, taking care of household maintenance, and providing financial support; the passing on of family legacies, including pictures, artifacts, recipes, and family lore; and inheriting assets of all kinds upon the death of family members.

In Western societies prior to industrialization, inheritance was a mechanism for passing on from father to son the means of family economic support, the farm or business (milling, smithing, etc.) that traditionally remained within the family for generations. With the arrival of industrialization and the movement of economic support to the factory or the office, the content and impact of inheritance grew more varied. While monetary and property assets are still very common, items with more symbolic significance, such as mementos or heirlooms, are often the most cherished (Rosenfeld 1979; Schorr 1980; Sussman et al. 1970).

The provision of care to family members is a resource transfer that occurs in every emotionally healthy family the world over. Most caregiving involves the many ordinary, everyday activities that are necessary to the survival and well-being of family members, for example, the typical care and feeding of infants and children, the performance of daily chores and house repairs, the giving of advice and emotional support, and the nursing of relatives during episodes of acute illness. In some instances family members give or receive care for conditions that are quite taxing and of an indefinite duration, such as Down's syndrome in a child or Alzheimer's disease or physical impairment or frailty in a spouse or older parent.

The intergenerational nature of this transfer is underscored in data from numerous studies, including nationally representative surveys, such as the one conducted by Louis Harris and Associates (1975) in conjunction with the National Council on the Aging, as well as many studies of family caregiving, including the National Long-Term Care Survey and the Longitudinal Survey of Aging. The general findings of this research indicate that the vast majority (perhaps as many as 80 percent) of older adults who need help with activities of daily living receive such help from relatives, particularly children or grandchildren (Stone et al. 1987; Stull 1995). A variety of motives for such care provision have been explored. Biegel and associates (1991) suggest that there are two types of explanations for the motives to provide care. Egoistic explanations argue that helping others is done with the anticipation that rewards will be forthcoming for such care provision. This includes payment for care, avoiding censure, gaining social approval, or complying with social norms. Some evidence for payments for care yields inconclusive results. For example, McGarry and Schoeni (1997) report that they found no evidence that parents provide financial assistance to their children in exchange for caregiving. On the other hand, Lillard and Willis (1997) report that in Malaysia, a country with neither Social Security nor Medicare, children are an important source of financial security in old age and that this is, in part, a repayment for parents' investments in children's education. They find further that parents and children engage in the exchange of time help for money.

A second set of explanations for providing care encompasses empathy and altruism. In these motivations, the interest is in benefiting the other, not oneself. As noted earlier, altruistic explanations of intergenerational transfers have not found much empirical support.

Noninheritance economic transfers within the family take a variety of forms: gifts, loans, payment of bills or down payments, and emergency financial help, for example. The directionality of this assistance, in both nuclear and extended families, is from parents of all ages to children of all ages and from adult children to older parents. Evidence (Schoeni 1997) indicates that people in their twenties and thirties receive more time and money assistance than do people of other ages, including the very old.

The transfer of goods and services among family members includes sharing the same household; making major purchases such as furniture, a car, or a large appliance; making smaller purchases such as clothing; and doing major repairs. Data show that substantial intergenerational transfers occur. For example, 90 percent of those Americans 65 years of age and older who had children or grandchildren gave those offspring gifts, while between 92 percent and 96 percent of adults 18 to 64 years old gave gifts to parents or grandparents (Harris and Associates 1975).

INTERGENERATIONAL RESOURCE TRANSFERS ON THE SOCIETAL LEVEL: FROM ONE BIRTH COHORT/AGE GROUP TO ANOTHER

On the societal level, the concept of intergenerational transfers shifts from resource exchanges among specific individuals of the same lineage to transfers to and from large groups of people of one birth cohort or age group to large groups of people in the same or other birth cohort or age group. These exchanges take place in several arenas: (1) the public policy arena, where the transfer is usually in the form of resources defined in statutes and laws (examples in the United States include the Social Security system, Head Start, Temporary Assistance to Needy Families, school bonds); (2) the private sector, where transfers are in the form of wages or goods (examples include jobs that support workers and nonworkers, corporate profits that supply tax revenue); and (3) the creative arena (examples of these transfers include art, music, literature, and the fruits of social and physical science research).

Products of Public Policy. The outcomes of public policy are transfers that affect everyone in a society. Frequently, these resources are multifaceted, affecting a broad range of individuals. For instance, in the United States the term *Social Security* is commonly used to refer to Old-Age and Survivors Insurance retirement income and the death survivors' component of a larger piece of legislation that also includes a disability insurance program, an unemployment insurance component, and the public assistance Supplemental Security Income program. As a totality, then, these components of the Social Security legislation go to a wide range of individuals in a number of different circumstances. Moreover, it is important to note that, while resources stemming from public policy may be received by specific individuals at a particular point in time or over a particular span of time, in another sense each has a larger impact that far exceeds that exchange. For example, the issuance of a school bond in a community directly and immediately provides educational resources to a particular cohort of school-age residents. However, indirectly, those resources affect the lives of other members of the family, resulting in improved quality of life for them as well. Additionally, from a longitudinal perspective, the resources invested in educational infrastructure and materials benefit future generations of the community's students.

Discussion about the relative contribution of public and private transfers has led to conflicting expectations. For example, if one expects altruistic motivations, then private transfers would neutralize the impact of public transfers. On the other hand, if exchange motivates transfers, then private transfers would reinforce the effects of public transfers on economic well-being. Cox and Jakubson (1995) find that private transfers can enhance public transfers, the reverse of previous expectations that public transfers merely supplant private ones.

Outcomes of the Private Sector. Intergenerational resource transfers resulting from private sector activity affect both the *active working population*, composed of individuals who are primarily in their young adult and middle years, and the so-called *dependent population*, composed of children and older people supported by the active working population. This transfer occurs through both the wages that workers earn and the tax revenues, funneling through the public sector, those workers provide. The precise age boundaries for these classifications vary from society to society according to culture and the primary means of economic support (agricultural or industrial). However, even within the age span of the active working population, one finds individuals who are part of the dependent population, such as those who are disabled or unemployed in their age groups. Moreover, within the age span of the dependent population, one finds working school-age children and retirees working part-time or part-year.

In the United States, the *total dependency ratio* is generally considered to be the number of persons under eighteen and those age sixty-five and over (together, the two dependent populations) for every 100 working-age individuals eighteen to sixty-four years of age. The *youth dependence ratio* is generally the number of persons under eighteen for every 100 individuals eighteen to sixty-four, while the *old-age dependency ratio* is the number of persons sixty-five and older for every 100 persons eighteen to sixty-four years of age. In the United States, while the youth dependency ratio has declined from 51 in 1950 to 34 in 1994, the old-age dependency ratio climbed from 13.3 in 1950 to 20 in 1994. Additionally, the old-age dependency ratio is expected to increase to 37 by 2030, at the height of the so-called baby boom retirement years (U.S. Bureau of the Census 1996).

However, none of these ratios take into consideration the possible impact of the following on intergenerational resource transfers: (1) the current and future contributions of elderly persons and youth who are employed; (2) the potential for increased labor-force participation among those sixty-five and older; (3) the changes in the Social Security Act to gradually increase the age of eligibility for full Social Security retirement benefits to sixty-seven over a twenty-seven-year period, beginning in the year 2000; (4) the growing number of working women, who have different and, as yet, somewhat uncharted labor-force participation patterns; and (5) the growing economy (Crown 1985; Kingson et al. 1986).

Current Cohorts of Children and the Heterogeneity of the Elderly: Two Special Considerations of Intergenerational Transfers. In the United States, intergenerational resource transfers that are the products of public policy and private sector activity support individuals of all ages. Of growing importance, however, is a consideration of the effect of the nature of such transfers on two groups, current cohorts of children and the elderly, at any time when they are viewed as a heterogeneous group. Regarding the former, it is clear that, at present, many children live in poverty or near poverty and, thus, are not receiving from older generations (either older family members or older generations on the societal level) the resources they need to live satisfactory lives as children. Moreover, limited access during childhood to such resources as health care and education, in particular, leads to reduced economic opportunities and productivity in adulthood. Thus, without the infusion of such resources, children are unable to prepare themselves for a productive adulthood in which they are capable of successfully joining the active working population to sustain themselves. Moreover, they will also be unable to provide support for those individuals, young and old, who will then compose a large part of the dependent population of the future. For instance, persons age seventeen and under in 1990 will be twenty to thirty-seven years of age in 2010, when the first wave of the baby boom cohort will begin to retire, and forty to fifty-seven years of age in the year 2030, when the full weight of the baby boom retirement will be felt.

Regarding the heterogeneity of the elderly, it is important to keep in mind that older people in Western societies vary greatly not only in chronological age (forty marks the onset of protection under the U.S. Age Discrimination in Employment Act; eighty-five is generally considered the beginning age of the "oldest-old") but also in income, health, and activity status. In addition, the elderly vary, on these and other factors, according to race and gender. As a result, in old age *chronological age alone is not an adequate indicator of the need for a substantial infusion of public or private sector resources.* Indeed, some older people are still greater producers than consumers of society's resources. Likewise, for any particular individual, certain times *during* old age require a greater amount of societal resources than other times.

Outcomes of Creativity. The fruits of research, music, literature, systems of jurisprudence, and other cultural and scientific products represent very important types of societal-level intergenerational transfers. As long-term transfers that cross the generations of a society and frequently move from one society to another, these are resources that traverse both time and geography. (For instance, disease-resistant hybrid strains of rice developed in the United States and used in agricultural settings around the world benefited not only Americans alive during and after the mid-1950s but also people in other societies over succeeding

decades.) Frequently, especially regarding the products of scientific research, those in the same birth cohort as the originator(s) or creator(s) do not feel the full impact, positive or negative, of the outcome themselves; this becomes part of the birthright, for better or worse, of the generations that follow. For example, those in the generation of the developers of the diphtheria/pertussis/tetanus vaccine, given routinely to infants, faced the risk of these diseases themselves during childhood. On the other hand, individuals in the same birth cohort as the developers of the atomic bomb have not lived the entire span of their lives, including childhood, coping with the implications of this scientific outcome.

THE ISSUE OF EQUITY IN THE INTERGENERATIONAL TRANSFER OF RESOURCES

In the mid-1980s, the equity of intergenerational transfers was a prominent topic of discussion in both the press and various academic settings. This topic is receiving renewed interest. Consideration usually centers on the allocation process for resources resulting from public policy. However, it is important to keep in mind that much of the time these resources affect individuals within the context of the family. While there are many perspectives regarding the justification and procedure for transferring resources across generations, four particular factors appear to underlie each of these perspectives, each one subject itself to multiple meanings. When there is disagreement about the procedure for and direction of resource distribution across generations, it is frequently due to disagreement regarding the meaning of one or more of these factors (Hirshorn 1991). These are (1) the concept of the generation, discussed previously; (2) the issue of whether the resource transfer results in one party's experiencing an absolute or relative gain or loss in comparison with others; (3) the perception of the resource "pie" to be allocated (e.g., Is it constant in size? expandable?); and (4) the idea of *distributive justice*, or fairness in the rationale for deciding how to allocate resources (e.g., transfers can be based on level of need, on merit, or on equal shares for all, among other criteria).

Intergenerational Inequity Perspective. One of the most discussed perspectives in recent years argues that there is *intergenerational inequity* in the transfer of resources in the United States, particularly resources resulting from public policy. It focuses on the relative welfare of current cohorts of youth and current cohorts of the elderly. This perspective maintains, moreover, that, in the United States in recent decades, the welfare of the young, especially those under the age of eighteen, has diminished as a result of the enhanced status of the elderly, who have been accumulating sizable proportions of the nation's personal wealth and, at the same time, been on the receiving end of the bulk of the resources stemming from social policy (Medicare and Social Security retirement funds are singled out especially). Moreover, those adhering to this view maintain, the absolute size of public expenditures directed at the elderly is a major cause of the current budget deficits and other economic problems facing the United States. The assumption is that sufficient funds will not exist in the future to ensure that those who are currently children and young adults will receive their fair share of these very resources—Social Security retirement and public sector health care support—in their own old age (Cornman and Kingson 1996). Among the problems with this perspective is that it assumes that the elderly, as a group, are all doing well in absolute terms; thus it does not take into consideration the variation within the older population that makes this group, which is quite heterogeneous regarding health status, economic status, living arrangements, and other factors. Moreover, this perspective relies on the idea that the correct concept for use in assessing the equity of public resources transferred across generations—one that would result in social justice—is *numerical equality*. Yet equal expenditures do *not* result in equal levels of return, no matter who receives the transfer. Finally, given the wide range of types of resources transferred within the context of the family and in the public and private sectors, it is meaningless even to try to arrive at an accurate measure of which generation/birth cohort/age group is faring better as a whole (Kingston et al. 1986).

Common Stake Perspective. An alternative view of intergenerational resource transfers notes the *common stake* that all generations/birth cohorts/age groups have in the wide variety of intergenerational exchanges. This perspective emphasizes the importance of using the concept of the *life course* in assessing the giving and receiving of resources at all levels and in all contexts, societal and familial. Thus, it emphasizes that, at some points along the life course, one generally takes more of certain kinds of resources than one gives, while at other points along the life course the opposite is true (e.g., hands-on care is very strong in infancy and sometimes in old age; use of tax revenues for education is very prominent during childhood). Moreover, generally we do not give the same resources from the very same people, not within the context of the family or on the societal level. For instance, usually we do not provide the unstinting, continuous, and comprehensive care we received in infancy to our *parents*, but we do to our own children.

This perspective also stresses the fact that the same intergenerational resource transfer affects some individuals directly and others indirectly. For example, the public sector program Temporary Assistance to Needy Families, provides *direct* support to children in families headed by parents who are unable to provide sufficient work-related income; thus, family funds are freed to purchase such items as needed medical supplies for, say, an ailing grandparent. *Indirectly* affected by another public transfer that flows intergenerationally is the schoolchild, living with a grandparent, whose lunch money comes from the latter's monthly Social Security check. Finally, the common stake viewpoint underscores the need for current and future generations of the elderly to concern themselves with the welfare of children and young people and vice versa—for the sake of all concerned (Kingson et al. 1986).

(SEE ALSO: *Altruism; Filial Responsibility; Inheritance; Intergenerational Relations; Social Mobility*)

REFERENCES

Biegel, David, E., E. Sales, and R. Schultz 1991 *Family Caregiving in Chronic Illness*. Newbury Park, Calif.: Sage.

Cornman, James M., and E.R. Kingson 1996 "Trends, Issues, Perspectives, and Values for the Aging of the Baby Boom Cohort." *The Gerontologist* 36:15–26.

Covey, H. 1981 "A Reconceptualization of Continuity Theory." *Gerontologist* 21:628–633.

Cox, D., and G. Jakubson 1995 "The Connection Between Public Transfers and Private Interfamily Transfers." *Journal of Public Economics* 57:129–167.

INTERGROUP AND INTERORGANIZATIONAL RELATIONS

Cox, D., and M.R. Rank 1992 "Inter-Vivos Transfers and Intergenerational Exchange." *Review of Economics and Statistics* 74:305–314.

Crown, William H. 1985 "Some Thoughts on Reformulating the Dependency Ratio." *Gerontologist* 25:166–171.

Dowd, James J. 1975 "Aging as Exchange: A Preface to Theory." *Journal of Gerontology* 30:584–594.

Harris, Louis, and Associates, Inc. 1975 "The Myth and Reality of Aging in America." Washington, D.C.: National Council on the Aging, Inc.

Hill, Reuben 1965 "Decision Making and the Family Life Cycle." In E. Shanas and G. Streib, eds., *Social Sructure and the Family*, Englewood Cliffs, N.J.: Prentice Hall.

—— 1970 *Family Development in Three Generations.* Cambridge, Mass.: Schenkman.

Hirshorn, Barbara 1991 "Multiple Views of the Intergenerational Flow of Society's Resources." *Marriage and Family Review*, special edition on intergenerational relations.

Horowitz, Amy, and L. Shindelman 1983 "Reciprocity and Affection: Past Influences on Current Caregiving." *Journal of Gerontological Social Work* 5(3):5–20.

Kalish, Richard 1975 *Late Adulthood.* Monterey, Calif.: Brooks/Cole.

Kane, Rosalie A. 1996 "From Generation to Generation: Thoughts on Legacy." *Generations*, 20:5–9.

Kingson, Eric R., B.A. Hirshorn, and J.M. Cornman 1986 *Ties That Bind: The Interdependence of Generations* (report from the Gerontological Society of America). Washington, D.C.: Seven Locks Press.

Lillard, L.A., and R.J. Willis 1997 "Motives for Intergenerational Transfers: Evidence from Malaysia." *Demography* 34:115–134.

McGarry, K., and R.F. Schoem 1997 "Transfer Behavior Within the Family: Results from the Asset and Health Dynamics Study." *Journals of Gerontology Series B–Psychological Sciences and Social Sciences* 52:82–92, Special Issue.

Morgan, James N. 1983 "The Redistribution of Income by Families and Institutions and Emergency Help Patterns." In G.J. Duncan and J.N. Morgan, eds., *Five Thousand American Families: Patterns of Economic Progress.* (Institute of Social Research 16). Ann Arbor: University of Michigan Press.

Riley, Matilda W., and A. Foner 1971 "Social Gerontology and the Age Stratification of Society, Part 1." *Gerontologist* 11:79–87.

Rosenfeld, J.P. 1979 *The Legacy of Aging: Inheritance and Disinheritance in Social Perspective.* Norwood, N.J.: Ablex.

Schoeni, R.F. 1997 "Private Interhoushold Transfers of Money and Time: New Empirical Evidence:" *Review of Income and Wealth* 4:423–448.

Schorr, Alvin 1980 ". . . Thy Father and Thy Mother . . . A Second Look at Filial Responsibility and Family Policy." Washington, D.C.: Social Security Administration.

Stone, Robyn, Gail L. Cafferata, and Judith Sangl 1987 "Caregivers of the Frail Elderly: A National Profile." *The Gerontologist* 27:616–626.

Stull, Donald E. 1995 "Caregivers (Family)." In A.R. Davis, J. Boondas, and A. Lenihan, eds., *Encyclopedia of Home Care for the Elderly.*

Sussman, Marvin, J. Cates, and D. Smith 1970 *The Family and Inheritance.* New York: Russell Sage Foundation.

U.S. Bureau of the Census 1996 "Population Projections of the United States by Age, Sex, Race, and Hispanic Origin: 1995 to 2050." *Current Population Reports*, Series P-25, No. 1130. Washington, D.C.: U.S. Government Printing Office.

DONALD E. STULL
BARBRIK HIRSHORN

INTERGROUP AND INTERORGANIZATIONAL RELATIONS

The focus here is first on the meaning of intergroup relations and next on interorganizational relations. Although the emphasis in both cases is mainly on research and conceptualizations based in the United States, we consider to some extent research based in other nations and cultures. We also occasionally consider the uses of sociological research.

INTERGROUP RELATIONS

A *group* is a collection of persons who have shared problems and act together in response to those problems, have shared expectations, and have a sense of common destiny. There are many kinds of groups, ranging from informal friendships to ethnic groups, to societies, and even to intersocietal groups. *Intergroup relations* refers to patterns of relationships that develop between groups. Extensive reviews of the literature in intergroup relations may be found in Seeman (1981) and Stephan (1985).

Although intergroup relations refers to all types of groups, it is not possible to avoid focusing on ethnic-racial group relations, because this has been the central concern in the United States since the social sciences and sociology, in particular, became established academic disciplines. Intergroup relations has been approached from the level of analysis of the group on the one hand, and from a social psychological perspective on the other.

This latter approach examines intergroup relations from the point of view of the individual and his or her relations with a group. In the latter part on the nineteenth century, the United States experienced huge immigration from southern, central, and eastern Europe. Since the new immigrants arrived from cultures that were markedly different from those of Americans who were already established here, conflicts developed, a pattern in some ways not materially different from conflicts that now exist between U.S. citizens and recent immigrants from Central and Latin American and Asia. The history of research on intergroup relations in sociology shows a profound emphasis on problems created by these massive immigrations.

Lieberson (1980) has thoroughly studied the question of why those who migrated to the United States from south, central and eastern Europe after 1880 in large numbers (such as Italians, Russians, Lithuanians, Poles) have been so much more successful than blacks. He found that blacks, in part because of their visibility, confronted much more serious social and competitive disadvantages than did these groups, even though the European groups did have many obstacles to overcome. Because of the slave period and the initial contacts with Africans, white society had and still has very unfavorable dispositions toward blacks, much more unfavorable than their dispositions toward white Europeans and even more unfavorable than their dispositions toward Asian immigrant groups. The competitive threat of Asian groups at the same time period was not nearly as great, since the Asian immigration was much smaller. Blacks also faced greater barriers than did Europeans from labor unions. Thus, Lieberson asserts that blacks and Europeans confronted intrinsically different situations that produced very different sets of opportunities for socioeconomic advancement.

Conflict and competition between groups is only one—albeit important—pattern that may develop, although it is the adaptation that is most likely to make headlines and be reported on the television news. William Graham Sumner (1906) applied the concept of ethnocentrism to explain intergroup conflict. Ethnocentrism is a "view of things in which one's own group is the center of everything, and all others are scaled and rated with reference to it" (p. 13). Sumner believed that ethnocentrism served to highlight and then exaggerate differences between groups and hence contributed to in-group cohesion and strong hostility to the out-group.

One of the oldest social-psychological theories of intergroup relations stresses personality determinants. The leading exponent of this view is Gordon Allport (1954). Allport's definition of prejudice has two components: attitude and belief. Allport defines ethnic prejudice as "an antipathy based upon a faulty and inflexible generalization" (p. 9). In his book, Allport refers to the generality of prejudice. A number of studies in this tradition report large intercorrelations of prejudices—that is, persons who are anti-Semitic are also anti-Catholic and antiblack (Epstein and Komorita 1965). The claim is that these views stem from a deep-seated personality syndrome, called by Allport "the prejudiced personality." The prejudiced person is highly moralistic and has a need for definiteness, among other features. As Seeman (1981) has noted, the evidence on cross-group generality and its personality basis is easily challenged on both methodological and theoretical grounds. In general, the trait approach has slowly given way to a more situationalist view.

A note on discrimination and prejudice is in order, since much of the intergroup relations literature concerns these concepts. *Discrimination* is typically defined as treating people unequally due to their group membership, while *prejudice* is often seen as "a rigid emotional attitude toward a human group" (Simpson and Yinger 1972, p. 24). As Seeman (1981) points out, in prejudice persons are categorized wrongly or prejudged, and this process is a complex rather than a simple one:

The error comes in misconceiving and misjudging such a group, and the individual members thereof, as a consequence of misreading the nature of the category involved. Often enough the misreading occurs because the cultural and historical sources of supposed category qualities are not taken into account or are attributed to irrelevant features of the category, that is, to blackness, Jewishness, and so on. What makes all this extremely tricky is that (a) it is difficult to demonstrate what, in fact, the appropriate characterizations are for the social categories we find it necessary to employ; and (b) given the powerful control that majorities exercise, pressures are generated that tend to socialize the members of a given category into the very features we discern: to make Jews "intellectual," blacks "hostile," Chicanos "indolent," and women "dependent." Thus, though demonstrable relevance (correctness) of the attributed qualities to the category is critical, there is typically a seeming relevance (a misread relevance) that beclouds the issue both for the participant and the analyst (p. 380).

Robert E. Park was one of the first leading sociologists of race relations and is identified with ecological theory (Park and Burgess 1921). Park viewed human beings as competing for territory much like plants and other animals. Ecological processes foster competition for limited resources. The distribution of the population is itself shaped by competition over scarce resources, and this competitive process structures the economic interdependence of groups and individuals. Competition also makes people aware of their status and induces them to view themselves as of superior or of inferior status depending on their social situation. Those who see themselves as superior express their consciousness of felt superiority and seek to maintain their privileged position through prejudice. Hence, the intergroup competitive process expresses itself through the development of moral and political order. This order is a product of such processes, in addition to competition, as conflict, accommodation, and assimilation. Racial consciousness is therefore seen as developing out of the competitive process, which is born in the competitive struggle for status. An "inferior" status group might not wish to compete and instead establish a niche within the division of labor, and this might lead to a stable equilibrium.

A dominant intergroup relations paradigm is derived from Marxist thought and is called conflict theory. In this view, race relations and their consequences emerge from the system of social stratification in the society. Societies are seen as constantly changing. Societies distinguish between and among their members and award some greater rewards, such as power, prestige, and money, than others. The result is social inequality, which becomes an essential part of the stratification system. Hence, the stratification system is simply the structured inequalities of groups or categories or individuals. The different groups in the society, such as classes or ethnic-racial groups, compete for the limited resources available. Three conditions are necessary for intergroup conflict and inequalities to result (Cox 1948; Vander Zanden 1983).

First, there must be at least two identifiable groups. People must be aware of their group and another group on the basis of some characteristic or set of characteristics. These may be physical or not—that is, beliefs or values are sufficient.

Second, the two groups must compete with one another or feel they are competing for a limited pool of resources for themselves, if necessary at the expense of members of the other group.

Third, the two groups cannot have exactly the same amount of power, so that one group can claim an advantage in obtaining resources that another group also seeks. Under these conditions, one group becomes more dominant as the competition develops. The more powerful group defines the other group as inferior. As the group with less power seeks to protect and assert its interests, the dominant group may feel threatened and aggrandize to an even greater degree, and tension may mount. Most members of the dominant group soon find it easy and appropriate to view the other group in very negative terms.

Assimilation involves adapting another culture in place of one's native culture and usually is applied to the process that occurs when person adjust to a new society and culture by adopting it. For example, many Asian groups have recently immigrated to the United States. Typically their children learn English, dress in American style, eat American food, and are seen as and regard themselves as Americans. However, many adult Asians, although completely or partially bilingual, will retain an affinity for their native culture and understandably are more comfortable conversing in their original tongue.

Accommodation refers to a decision by two or more groups to put aside a significant difference that exists between them in order to stress common interests. This leads to cultural pluralism—that is, a number of different cultural patterns coexisting in the same society. The United States is a pluralist society in that it permits many distinctive religious, ethnic, and racial groups to exist side by side. The need of new Asian groups to retain their cultural identities is reflected in the existence in many large cities of Chinatowns, Koreatowns, and Japantowns. Some areas in large cities have signs only in Chinese or in both Chinese and English. This has produced some conflict with non-Chinese residents in these communities and has sparked "English-only" movements and resistance to bilingual instruction in public schools.

A great deal of research has been undertaken examining the impact of intergroup contact on intergroup hostility and prejudice (see reviews by Stephan 1985; Williams 1977). Many of the early studies looked at naturally occurring intergroup contacts. A substantial number of laboratory and field investigations have been undertaken focusing on those characteristics of intergroup contacts that foster positive intergroup outcomes. Stephan (1985) summarizes the findings with regard to this problem in a list of thirteen propositions, such as: "Cooperation within groups should be maximized and competition between groups should be minimized" and "Members of the in-group and the out-group should be of equal status both within and outside the contact situation" (p. 643).

There is a wealth of information and research on intergroup relations. However there is a definite lack of application of this information when dealing with intergroup conflicts, especially in the area of public policy. Brewer (1997) identifies several reasons for this gap between research and practice in reducing intergroup conflicts.

There have traditionally been different approaches to researching the processes involved in intergroup conflict. Research traditions focus on different levels of aggregation, with some focusing on interpersonal processes and others focusing on the group level of analysis. Additionally there are theoretical perspectives that study intergroup conflict with a primary focus on concepts in the cognitive, affective, or behavioral realm. These different approaches tend to generate literatures that remain isolated, rarely citing research outside their own perspective.

While these separate research traditions might use different conceptual frameworks, they do have one thing in common that contributes to a lack of direct participation in the policy arena. Science has a norm of objectivity, and this leads many researchers to avoid advocating for specific action by governments or groups. Scientific research is seen as producing facts, and the role of the scientist is to produce those facts, not to decide what to do about them. The expert is hesitant to become the advocate.

History may contribute to this feeling, both for the researchers and the policy makers. In the 1950s and 1960s, much social science research (specifically the "contact hypothesis") was used as the basis for public policy designed to reduce racial tension and conflict through the integration of schools. The research outcomes on desegregation were mixed, due in part to an oversimplified application of theoretical ideas that were very specific and conditional in nature. Additionally, the social science research on which desegregation was in part based was developed in carefully controlled laboratory experimentation. In real-life situations, which are far more chaotic and complex, the mechanisms of the theories might be overwhelmed by other factors, factors the theories were never intended to deal with. While the research community might be happy to learn from the failure of experiments and to argue about the failure of the assumptions of models to be met, the policy maker sees failure of a program and an increase in conflict among constituents. So the scientists see the politicians as understanding neither the restricted nature of most theories nor the process of the growth of knowledge as including failures. The policy makers see only that the experts were wrong and that their advice created conflict (or a perception of increased conflict) when a reduction was expected.

While research on desegregation was based on the contact hypothesis and ideas of assimilation, current research is based more on ideas of pluralism and multiculturalism. This perspective focuses on promoting positive in-group attitudes by emphasizing group identities and characteristics, and trying to make these identities respected and recognized by other groups; to be proud of one's own ways while recognizing the pride of other's for their own ways. This creates some tensions and potential pitfalls when using this branch of theory and research as a basis for public policy.

Much of intergroup theory has focused on and developed from the situation in the United States; however, recently more attention and research have been applied to the problem in other areas of the world. With increasing migration and diversity in western Europe has come a concurrent increase in tension and conflict, and this has generated a surge of research. Pettigrew (1998) shows that "despite sharp differences in national histories, political systems, and minorities, this new work reveals considerable consistency across the nations of western Europe. It also largely replicates and extends, rather than rebuts, the North American literature" (p. 98). He shows similarities such as the higher level of "subtle" prejudice compared with "blatant" prejudice. Blatant prejudice is tied to perceived biological differences between groups and is "hot, close and direct" (p. 83). Subtle prejudice is tied to the "perceived threat of minority groups to traditional values" (p. 83) and the "lack of positive feeling towards minorities" (p. 83). In addition, the mechanisms of intergroup contact and relative deprivation seem to function in similiar ways in many North American and European populations.

Given the tension between Arabs and Jews in the Middle East, it should not be surprising that theories of intergroup relations should be tested there in attempts to reduce conflicts. One such study attempted to use the contact between Jewish and Arab citizens of Israel that occurred in joint medical teams to mitigate intergroup stereotypes and prejudice (Desivilya, 1998). The study found that while the contact reduced prejudice in the local work situation, that reduction was not carried into the larger societal context and overall national image and ethnic stereotypes were not changed.

INTERORGANIZATIONAL RELATIONS

An *organization* is a group with three main features: a goal or set of goals, a boundary, and a technology (Aldrich 1979). Although we say organizations have goals, what is meant is that much of what organizations actually do seems as if it is directed to a shared objective or set of objectives. This may be for the sake of appearance, and/or the organization may really be goal-oriented. The boundary feature simply refers to the distinction that an organization makes between members and nonmembers. Finally, technology refers to the organization's division of labor or to the set of activities that the organization performs as part of its daily routines in processing new materials or people.

Each of these characteristics can be illustrated by the university. Its goals are often set forth, albeit in glowing and idealized terms, in its general catalogue. These typically include teaching, research, and public service. One must apply to become a member of the university—student, faculty or staff. And such statuses are frequently difficult to come by. The university's technology includes its classrooms and laboratories as well as the lecture and discussion methods of instruction.

Interorganizational relations refers to the relations between or among two or more organizations. There have been several overviews of the field of interorganizational relations (Aldrich 1979; Aldrich and Whitten 1981; Galaskiewicz 1985; Mulford 1984; Van de Ven and Ferry 1980).

Every organization has relationships with other organizations. In the case of the university, if it is to function it must have students, and to recruit them it must have relationships with high schools, junior colleges, and other universities. These students (and faculty and staff) must eat, work, and play, so the university has relationships with food, housing, energy, and other suppliers of various kinds in the community. And, of course, the university needs other resources, especially funds, and therefore must relate to government agencies and alumni to obtain them (Clark 1983).

Organizations are ambivalent about establishing an interorganizational relationship to obtain resources (Yuchtman and Seashore 1967). On the one hand, they want and need resources if they are to survive; but on the other hand, organizations wish to maintain their autonomy, and insofar as they establish an interorganizational tie, they will be expected to reciprocate, and hence their freedom will be constrained. It is assumed that organizations want their autonomy from other organizations, but their survival needs induce them to relinquish some autonomy.

Galaskiewicz (1985) claims that interorganizational relations take place for three major reasons: to obtain and to allocate resources, to form coalitions to enhance power, and to achieve community acceptance or legitimacy.

Interorganizational relations research has been undertaken at three levels: the dyad (Hall et al. 1977), the action set (Hirsch 1972), and the network (Burt 1983; Galaskiewicz 1985). The simplest form of interorganizational relation is the dyad, which simply refers to the relationships of two organizations to each other. The action set concept developed form Merton's (1957) notion of role sets. Caplow (1964) and Evan (1966) took Merton's idea and applied it to the relationships between a focal organization, such as a university, and its pairwise relationship with other organizations with whom it interacts. One might examine the relationship between a university and the office of the mayor of the city within which it is located, and then study the effects of changes in this relationship as they influence other relationships in the set of organizations (Van de Ven and Ferry 1980). Aldrich (1979) has termed the group of organizations that constitute a temporary alliance for a particular or limited goal the "action set." Networks of organizations contain the complete set of ties that connect all the organizations in a population of organizations (Aldrich 1979; Hall 1987; Van de Ven and Ferry 1980). Although the approaches of Aldrich and Van de Ven and Ferry are not identical conceptually, both orientations toward networks focus on identifying all connections of specified kinds that take place within a particular organizational population. Hence, the analysis of networks is far more complex than that of action sets or dyads.

The body of knowledge in the area of interorganizational relationships is not extensive, and what there is has focused on social services. There exists quite a bit of theoretical information but very few large databases. With the exception of research on corporate board of directors' interlocks (Burt 1983; Burt et al. 1980), there is little work on the private sector.

An early area of interest to theorists was the general state of the organizational and interorganizational environment. Aldrich (1979) identified six dimensions of environments: capacity, homogeneity/heterogeneity, stability/instability, concentration/dispersion, domain consensus/dissensus, and turbulence. Capacity refers to the relative level of resources available in the organization's environment. A rich environment refers to one where resources are plentiful, while a lean environment is the opposite.

Homogeneity/heterogeneity refers to the extent to which organizations, individuals, or even social forces that influence resources are relatively similar or different. For example, does a focal organization deal with a relatively uniform and a highly heterogeneous population? If one contrasted the labor forces that a Japanese and an American firm draw from to recruit, one would find that the Japanese firm confronts a more homogeneous environment than does its American counterpart. This is, of course, because American workers are much more heterogeneous than are Japanese workers in education, ethnic-racial background, and many other features (Cole 1979).

Stability/instability concerns the degree of turnover in various elements of the environment. Again, if Japanese and American firms are compared, we would anticipate greater turnover in the latter than in the former. The advantage of low turnover or a stable environment is that it permits the organization to develop fixed routines and structures.

Aldrich (1979) refers to the extent to which resources are distributed evenly in the environment or concentrated in a particular area as concentration/dispersion. For example, the RTD is the major bus company in Los Angeles, and its potential ridership is dispersed over an area of more than 400 square miles. Such long transportation lanes present major problems, in contrast, for example, with the Santa Monica Bus Company, whose ridership is concentrated in a much smaller and geographically homogeneous area.

Organizations differ in the extent to which their claim to a specific domain is contested or acknowledged by other organizations. Domain consensus refers to a situation wherein an organization's claim to a domain is recognized, while domain dissensus refers to a situation where disagreement exists over the legitimacy of an organization's domain.

The final organizational dimension is turbulence. This term refers to the extent to which there are increasing environmental interconnections; the more interconnections, the greater the turbulence. Areas where many new organizations are emerging are generally areas of greater turbulence.

Some factors have been shown to be involved in the dissolution of interorganizational relations. Institutional forces, power, and competition are factors involved in the stability of these relations (Baker et al. 1998). Institutional forces reduce the likelihood of ties being broken. Personal relationships and structural attachments (such as coordination of accounting methods) represent "sunk costs" for the organization. To break ties with one organization and forge them with another takes significant effort and time. Power may increase or decrease the tendency for relations to dissolve. Given a client–provider relation, if the client has high power it increases the likelihood of the relation being broken, while high power for the provider decreases the tendency for the relation to break. Competition tends to destabilize ties between organizations, although the effect of competition is weak relative to power and structural attachments. In situations where there is much competition, there are more opportunities for defection from a relation and more incentive to do so.

A great deal of the work on interorganizational relations has concerned delivery systems and stressed coordination (Mulford 1984; Rogers and Whetten 1982). This is because a central problem in service delivery involves overcoming the segmentation and fragmentation of services created by the large number of organizations with overlapping responsibilities and jurisdictions. Bachrach (1981) has identified a number of factors that discourage coordination among organizations serving the chronically mentally ill, including budget constraints, lack of a mandate to engage in interorganizational planning, and confusion due to separate funding streams for care. Other factors also discourage coordination, such as differences in organizational activities and resources; multiple network memberships and consequent conflicting obligations felt by constituent organizations; and a lack of complementary goals and role exceptions (Baker and O'Brien 1971).

Each organization in a delivery system relies on the other organizations in the system, since no single unit can generate all the resources necessary for survival. Hence, the organization in a system enters into exchanges with other organizations and consumers. It is assumed that each organization or system seeks to better its bargaining position. This perspective on delivery systems as interorganizational networks is generally labeled the resource dependence perspective (Pfeffer and Salanick 1978).

Contingency theory (Lawrence and Lorsch 1967) assumes that organizational functioning depends on the intertwining of technological and environmental constraints and the structures that emerge to deal with these constraints. The theory assumes, as does system theory more generally, that there is no single most effective way to organize (Katz and Kahn 1966), that the environment within which an organization functions influences the effectiveness of an organization, and that different organizational structures can produce different performance outcomes.

Scott (1998) uses systems theory to describe how organizations manage their task environments and their institutional environments, and adapt to their changing organization–environment interdependencies. Scott stresses the differences between technical and institutional environmental controls.

Although there is not a great deal of comparative research on interorganizational relations, some comparisons have been done, for example, on the differences in the patterns of relations in Japan and the United States. American companies tend to be connected to more organizations, have a more formalized and more extensive body of rules for the relationship, and exchange more information across the relations than their Japanese counterparts (Aldrich et al. 1998; Jang 1997). Claims such as these must be taken with a degree of caution, as there is a great deal of influence between Japanese and American firms. For example, Japanese auto assembly plants, which started in the United States, brought both intraorganizational and interorganizational patterns of organization, for example, team-based work groups and "just-in-time" delivery of parts needed in product assembly (Florida and Kenney 1991). Since that time, these organizational characteristics have become more common in the United States, and this increasing interdependence and connection between organizations can be seen in the impact of labor disputes extending through the economy at an increasingly rapid rate. A strike at a parts production facility that makes transmissions can shut down numerous auto production plants in a few days. A strike at Federal Express or United Parcel Service leads to economic impacts nation- and world wide literally overnight.

This globalization of economic relations mirrors a globalization of international relations. Both on an ongoing basis (e.g., the G-7, or Group of Seven Economic Conferences; the European Union; the United Nations) and on a temporary basis (e.g., the Gulf War, U.N. peacekeeping missions), interorganizational relations are becoming more and more common and vital to the peace and prosperity of the world (Alter and Hage 1993).

REFERENCES

Aldrich, Howard 1979 *Organizations and Environments*. Englewood Cliffs, N.J.: Prentice-Hall.

——, Michele Kremen Bolton, Ted Baker, and Toshihiro Sasaki 1998 "Information Exchange and Governance Structures in U.S. and Japanese R&D Consortia: Institutional and Organizational Influences." *IEEE Transactions on Engineering Management*. 45(3):263–276.

——, and D.A. Whetten 1981 "Organizational Sets, Action Sets, and Networks: Making the Most of Simplicity." In P.C. Nystrom and W.H. Starbuck, eds., *Handbook of Organization Design*, vol. I. New York: Oxford University Press.

Allport, Gordon W. 1954 *The Nature of Prejudice*. Reading, Mass.: Addison-Wesley.

Alter, Catherine, and Jerald Hage 1993 *Organizations Working Together*. California: Sage Publications.

Bachrach, Leona L. 1981 "Continuity of Care for Chronic Mental Patients: A Conceptual Analysis." *American Journal of Psychiatry* 138(11):1449–1456.

Baker, Frank, and Gregory O'Brien 1971 "Intersystem Relations and Coordination of Human Service Organizations." *American Journal of Public Health* 61(1):130–137.

Baker, Wayne E., Robert R. Faulkner, and Gene A. Fisher 1998 "Hazards of the Market: The Continuity and Dissolution of Interorganizational Market Relationships." *American Sociological Review* 63(2):147–178.

Brewer, Marilyn B. 1997 "The Social Psychology of Intergroup Relations: Can Research Inform Practice?" *Journal of Social Issues* 53(1):197–212.

Burt, Ronald S. 1983 *Corporate Profits and Cooptation: Networks of Market Constraints and Directorate Ties in the American Economy*. New York: Academic Press.

——, K.P. Christman, and H.C. Kilburn, Jr. 1980 "Testing a Structural Theory of Corporate Cooptation: Interorganizational Directorate Ties as a Strategy for Avoiding Market Constraints on Profits." *American Sociological Review* 45:821–841.

Caplow, Theodore 1964 *Principles of Organzation*. New York: Harcourt, Brace, Jovanovich.

Clark, Burton 1983 *The Higher Education System*. Berkeley: University of California Press.

Cole, Robert E. 1979 *Work, Mobility, and Participation*. Berkeley: University of California Press.

Cox, Oliver C. 1948 *Caste, Class and Race: A Study in Social Dynamics*. New York: Monthly Review Press.

Desivilya, Helena S. 1998 "Jewish–Arab Coexistence in Israel: The Role of Joint Professional Teams." *Journal of Peach Research* 35(4):429–453.

Epstein, R., and S. S. Komorita 1965 "Parental Discipline, Stimulus Characteristics of Outgroups, and Social Distance in Children." *Journal of Personality and Social Psychology* 2:416–420.

Evan, William 1966 "The Organization Set: Toward a Theory of Interorganizational Relations." In J. Thompson, ed., *Approaches to Organizational Design*. Pittsburgh, Pa.: University of Pittsburgh Press.

Florida, Richard, and Martin Kenney 1991 "Transplanted Organizations: The Transfer of Japanese Industrial Organization to the U.S." *American Sociological Review* 56(3):381–399.

Galaskiewicz, Joseph 1985 "Interorganizational Relations." *Annual Review of Sociology* 11:281–304.

Hall, Richard H. 1987 *Organizations: Structures, Processes and Outcomes*, 4th ed. Englewood Cliffs, N.J.: Prentice-Hall.

——, J. Clark, P. Giordano, P. Johnston, and M. Van Roekel 1977 "Patterns of Interorganizational Relationships." *Administrative Science Quarterly* 22:457–474.

Hirsch, Paul M. 1972 "Processing Fads and Fashions: An Organization-Set Analysis of Cultural Industry Systems." *American Journal of Sociology* 77:639–659.

Jang, Ha-Yong 1997 "Cultural Differences in an Interorganizational Network: Shared Public Relations Firms Among Japanese and American Companies." *Public Relations Review* 23(1):327–342.

Katz, Daniel, and Robert L. Kahn 1966 *The Social Psychology of Organizations*. New York: Wiley.

Lawrence, Paul R., and J. W. Lorsch 1967 *Organization and Environment: Managing Differentiation and Integration*. Cambridge, Mass.: Graduate School of Business Administration, Harvard University.

Lieberson, Stanley 1980 *A Piece of the Pie: Black and White Immigrants Since 1880*. Berkeley: University of California Press.

Merton, Robert K. 1957 *Social Theory and Social Structure*. New York: Free Press.

Mulford, C. L. 1984 *Interorganizational Relations: Implications for Community Development*. New York: Human Sciences Press.

Park, Robert E., and E. W. Burgess 1921 *Introduction to the Science of Sociology*. Chicago: University of Chicago Press.

Pettigrew, Thomas F. 1998 "Reactions Toward the New Minorities of Western Europe." *Annual Review of Sociology* 24(1):77–103.

Pfeffer, Jeffery, and G. R. Salaneik 1978 *The External Control of Organizations: A Resource Dependence Perspective*. New York: Harper and Row.

Rogers, David L., and D. A. Whetten 1982 *Interorganizational Coordination: Theory, Research, Implementation*. Ames: Iowa State University Press.

Scott, W. R. 1998 *Organizations: Rational, Natural, and Open Systems*, 4th ed. Upper Saddle River, N.J.: Prentice-Hall.

Seeman, Melvin 1981 "Intergroup Relations." In M. Rosenberg and R.H. Turner, eds., *Social Psychology: Sociological Perspectives*. New York: Basic Books.

Simpson, George E., and J. M. Yinger 1972 *Racial and Cultural Minorities*, 4th ed. New York: Harper and Row.

Stephan, Walter G. 1985 "Intergroup Relations." In Gardner Lindzey and Eliot Aronson, eds., *Handbook of Social Psychology*, vol. II. New York: Random House.

Sumner, William Graham 1906 *Folkways*. Boston: Ginn.

Van de Ven, Andrew H., and D. L. Ferry 1980 *Measuring and Assessing Organizations*. New York: Wiley.

Vander Zanden, J.W. 1983 *American Minority Relations*, 4th ed. New York: Alfred A. Knopf.

Williams, Robin M. 1977 *Mutual Accomodation: Ethnic Conflict and Cooperation*. Minneapolis: University of Minnesota Press.

Yuchtman, Ephraim, and S. Seashore 1967 "A Systems Resource Approach to Organizational Effectiveness." *American Sociological Review* 32:891–903.

OSCAR GRUSKY
JEFF ERGER

INTERMARRIAGE

Intermarriage among people of different races, religions, nationalities, and ethnicities would be a subject of little concern in many societies (Degler 1971). It should be expected of a culturally diverse society such as the United States. Indeed, the United States is the most racially and culturally diverse nation in the Western, industrialized world. The heterogeneous composition of the United States should lend itself to a high degree of tolerance and acceptance of diversity in marriage patterns among its constituent groups (Spickard 1989). Since the 1960s, we have seen a rise in the number of intermarriages between different racial groups (U.S. Bureau of the Census 1998) and also an increasing number of interfaith marriages (Kalmijn 1993; Lehrer 1998). In order to discuss past, current, and future intermarriage trends, this article examines historical and contemporary trends in black/white intermarriages, past and future directions in Asian American intermarriages, the state of interfaith marriages, and reasons for the increasing number of intermarriages.

HISTORY OF BLACK/WHITE INTERMARRIAGES

Slavery had its greatest impact on the interracial relations of the Africans brought to the United States. Most of the slaves who came in the beginning were males, with the number of black females not equal to the number of males until 1840. As a result, the number of sexual relations between black slaves and indentured white women was fairly high. Some of these interracial relationships were more than casual contacts and ended in marriage. The intermarriage rate between male slaves and free white women increased to the extent that laws against them were passed as a prohibitive measure. Before the alarm over the rate of intermarriages, male slaves were encouraged to marry white women, thereby increasing the property of the slavemaster, since the children from such unions were also slaves (Jordan 1968).

The end of slavery did not give the black woman any right to sexual integrity. What slavery began, racism and economic exploitation continued to impose on the sexual lives of black women. In the postbellum South, black women were still at the mercy of the carnal desires of white men. According to historians, black women were forced to give up their bodies like animals to white men at random. Many have noted that many southern white men had their first sexual experience with black women. In some cases, the use of black women as sexual objects served to maintain the double standard of sexual conduct in the white South. Many white men did not have sexual relations with white women until they married. Some southern white men were known to joke that until they married, they did not know that white women were capable of sexual intercourse (Cash 1960; Dollard 1957).

It was the protection of the sexual purity of white women that partially justified the establishment of racially segregated institutions in the South. The southern white man assumed that black men had a strong desire for intermarriage and that white women would be open to proposals from black men if they were not guarded from even meeting with them on an equal level. As Bernard (1966) writes, "The white world's insistence on keeping Negro men walled up in the concentration camp was motivated in large part by its fear of black male sexuality" (p. 75).

The taboo on intermarriage was mostly centered on black men and white women. One reason for this is that white men and black women had engaged in coitus since the first black female slaves entered this country. Some black slave women were forced to engage in sexual relations with their white masters; others did so out of desire. Children resulting from these interracial sexual unions were always considered black, and the prevalent miscegenation of black women and white men has produced much lighter skinned American blacks than their African ancestors.

Traditionally, white fear of interracial relations has focused on the desire to avoid mongrelization of the races. Such a fear lacks any scientific basis, since many authorities on the subject of racial types seriously question that a pure race ever existed on this planet. Most authorities note it as an actual fact that the whole population of the world is hybrid and becoming increasingly so. At any rate, the rate of miscegenation in the past almost certainly casts doubt on any pure race theory for the United States (Day 1972).

Intermarriage is certainly nothing new in the United States. Its meaning and dynamics have, however, changed over the 400 years since blacks entered this country. In the era before slavery, black male and white female indentured servants often mated with each other. During the period of black bondage, most mixed sexual unions took place between white men and female slaves, often involving coercion by the white partner. A similar pattern of miscegenation occurred after slavery, with a white man and a black woman as the typical duo. When blacks moved to larger cities outside the South, the black male–white female pairing became more common. As is commonly known, legal unions between the races were prohibited by law in many states until 1967. But legal prohibitions were not the only deterrent to such biracial unions. This country's history is replete with acts of terror and intimidation of interracial couples who violated the society's taboos on miscegenation. While blacks and whites came together in love and marriage over the years, it was generally at a high cost, ranging from death to social ostracism (Stember 1976).

CONTEMPORARY BLACK/WHITE MARRIAGE

Between 1960 and 1990, black/white intermarriages increased fourfold (U.S. Census Bureau 1998). Among the reasons for this increase has been the desegregation of the public school system, the work force, and other social settings. Around 1968, American society witnessed the first significant increase in interracial dating. This was the year that blacks entered predominantly white college campuses in comparatively large numbers. Contemporaneous with this event was the sexual and psychological liberation of white women. While white society disapproved of all biracial dating, the strongest taboo was on the black male–white female bond. These bonds became the dominant figures in the increments of biracial dating. The college campus became an ideal laboratory for experiments in interracial affairs. In the university setting, the blacks and whites who dated were peers, with similar educational backgrounds, interests, and values. Young white women, who were not as racist as their parents, were liberated from parental and community control. Their student cohorts were more accepting of or indifferent to their dating across racial lines. Those changes in interracial dating practices coincided with the civil rights movement and a greater white acceptance of blacks as racial equals.

In the 1970s through 1990s, integration of work settings, neighborhoods, schools, and other public settings has meant that blacks and whites interact much more as equals than in the past. According to a Gallup poll (1997), a majority of blacks go to school, live, and work in places where the population is at least half white or even predominantly white. Only 15 percent of blacks work with mostly or all blacks and 41 percent of blacks live in a mostly or all-black neighborhood. Therefore, it is not surprising that with increasing social interaction there would also be an increasing number of interracial unions.

In addition to these systemic changes, there has been a major change in public attitudes toward biracial couples. According to a Gallup poll (1997), a majority of blacks and whites under the age of 50 say they accept and approve of interracial unions between blacks and whites. Of all the different race-related trends, this change in attitude is the most significant. In 1958, only 4 percent of white Americans approved of marriages between blacks and whites; in 1997, 61 percent approved. However, negative attitudes toward black/white intermarriages still persist. About a quarter of blacks and about 40 percent of whites say they disapprove of interracial marriage. Much of this can be attributed to how different generations view interracial marriages, as well as regional differences. Younger people approve of such marriages, while older black and white Americans are less likely to approve. According to Wilson and Jacobson (1995), age and education are strong predictors of those who are accepting of black/white intermarriages. In their study, they found younger, educated cohorts to be more accepting of such unions, compared to older, less educated cohorts. Moreover, acceptance of such marriages is much lower in certain regions of the United States, such as the South (Gallup Organization 1997). Although these changes in attitudes toward intermarriage seem positive, this poll result could be misleading. Many people tend to give the liberal answer they think is proper or expected when asked about controversial issues such as interracial marriage. However, when confronted with the issue on a very personal level, their response may be much different.

In the past, white families in particular frequently refused to have anything to do with children who entered into interracial marriages (Golden 1954; Porterfield 1982; Spickard 1989). According to Rosenblatt and colleagues (1995), white families compared to black families were most often in opposition. Opposition by white family members was most often based in racist assumptions and stereotypes, but also based in concern about the racism that the couple would face from society at large. Moreover, white families were concerned that marrying interracially meant a poor economic future. Other concerns raised by white families included issues of safety and well-being, as well as the issue of raising a biracial child. The authors found that there was less opposition in black families. Close family members might have been militantly against the marriage, but mothers in black families played a key role in providing acceptance of the interracial marriage. On the other hand, in white families, fathers were the key person in providing acceptance. In both black and white families, families were particularly concerned about their daughters' marrying interracially. Rosenblatt and colleagues (1995) explain that "for white families, the roots may include the racism of a dominant group and fear of loss in status. For black families, the roots may include the fear and pain of being connected with the oppressor" (p. 69). St. Jean (1998) discusses how black males in families may be more ambivalent about such unions. In previous studies, black women more than black men had tended to disapprove of such intermarriages (Paset and Taylor 1991); however, St. Jean (1998) found quite the opposite. She found that black men had a more difficult time accepting such marriages.

Although many black/white couples are drawn together because of nonracial factors, such as common interests and personal attraction (Lewis et al. 1997), race remains a major factor in their interactions with family, friends, and society at large. Given the persistence of racism, many interracial marriages face rough going. Based on her qualitative research findings, St. Jean (1998) found that although for the "couples the salience of color seems to diminish after marriage, race consciousness does not diminish. In their everyday lives, they are reminded by Blacks, Whites, relatives and nonrelatives of the inappropriate nature of their association" (St. Jean, p. 12). It is a fact that the scars of nearly 400 years of the worst human bondage known are not healed, and disapproval by many black and white people of interracial love affairs is one of the wounds.

PAST AND FUTURE DIRECTIONS IN ASIAN AMERICAN INTERMARRIAGES

Since 1990, fueled by immigration from Asia, the Asian and Pacific Islander population has grown at a rate of 4.5 percent per year (U.S. Bureau of the Census 1995). By the year 2000, this population had reached 12.1 million. As this group increases in size, intermarriage will probably occur more frequently (Lee and Fernandez 1998). According to Gordon (1964), the acculturation to American beliefs and values by new immigrants has meant that intermarriage would follow and is an important sign of the assimilation process. Hwang and colleagues (1997) report that Asian Americans with high levels of acculturation and structural assimilation have a high incidence of intermarriage: "Asian Americans who speak fluent English and who have lived longer in the US were found to have a higher tendency to marry persons from different racial and ethnic groups" (p. 770).

Despite the increase in population growth, the intermarriage rate for Asian Americans has declined overall. However, there are several explanations that account for these changes. According to Lee and Fernandez (1998), Asian-American outmarriage from 1980 to 1990 declined significantly from 25 percent to 15 percent based on their analysis of the 5 percent Public Use Microdata Sample (PUMS) of the 1990 U.S. census. They note that intermarriage levels dropped for Koreans, Filipinos, and Vietnamese. While outmarriage rates among American-born Asians increased, they declined for those foreign-born. They also note that Asian-American women were more likely to outmarry than men and that outmarriage was more common among Japanese Americans, Filipinos, Chinese, and Asian Indians. Lee and Fernandez (1998) further suggest that even though the Asian-American outmarriage rate overall has fallen, Asian interethnic marriages, made up of partners from two Asian ethnicities, has increased from 11 to 21 percent.

According to Shinagawa and Pang (1996), these marriage patterns can be explained through a sociohistorical framework. They define five different historical cohorts: Pre–World War II and World War II (prior to 1946), post–World War II (1946–1962), the civil rights era (1963–1974), the post-1960s (1975–1981) and the Vincent Chin cohorts (1982–1990). Because the pre–World War II and World War II cohort experienced antimiscegenation laws, they intermarried with other nonwhites. Those in the post–World War II cohort lived in an era when antimiscegenation laws were struck down and Asian immigrants could now become citizens. At the same time, American soldiers fighting wars in Asia brought back Asian wives. The civil rights era cohort experienced radical changes in terms of race. Racial groups, no longer segregated from each other, were interacting more, and laws were enacted to bar racist discrimination. Asians could now intermarry with whites, and this era saw an increasing number of Asian women marrying white men. The post-1960s cohort experienced the beginning politicization of the Asian-American community. However, intermarriages were still mostly between whites and Asians. Major changes started to happen in the Vincent Chin cohort. In 1982, Vincent Chin, a Chinese American autoworker in Detroit, was beaten to death by two whites who mistakenly identified him as a Japanese American, angering the Asian-American community and fueling community mobilization and politicization. The murder, which became symbolic of anti-Asian hate crimes and discrimination, brought diverse Asian communities together to eradicate discrimination against Asians and bring justice to Vincent Chin's family (Espiritu 1992). This era was defined by an emerging increasingly coalesced Asian-American community as well as by a growth of the Asian Pacific American population. According to Shinagawa and Pang (1996), these dramatic developments contributed to the growth of interethnic Asian marriages.

Shinagawa and Pang (1996) hypothesize six major reasons why pan-ethnic intermarriages and pan-ethnicity among Asian Americans are on the ascent: (1) the growth of the Asian-American population; (2) the growth of personal and social networks due to these population increases; (3) the growth in the number of educated, middle-class Asian Americans; (4) the acculturation of Asian Americans; (5) shared racial identity; and (6) most importantly, the growing racial consciousness among Asian Americans. According to Espiritu (1992), the construction of pan-Asian ethnicity arose out of a need for political strength and power. Shinagawa and Pang (1996) stress the importance of a pan-Asian ethnic consciousness that has shaped not only political but also marital patterns: "Deindustrialization, white flight, increased economic competition, anti-immigrant sentiments, hate violence against Asians, the growing sense of despair and hopelessness in the inner cities, and interracial conflicts not only between Whites and Asian Americans but also between racial minority groups all signify racial consciousness by Asian Americans" (p. 144).

TRENDS IN INTERFAITH INTERMARRIAGE

Although interracial marriages have increased, interfaith marriages are much more commonplace. Intermarriage between white ethnics is quite the norm (Lieberson and Waters 1988). Marriages between members of different faiths also happens much more frequently and seems to carry less stigma than interracial coupling. In fact during 1990, 52 percent of Jews were married to non-Jews, while Protestant/Catholic intermarriages have increased significantly (Kalmijn 1991). According to Kalmijn (1991), the increasing importance of similar educational levels in spouse selection and the declining importance of religious differences explains the increase in Protestant/Catholic intermarriages. Using data from the 1987–1988 National Survey of Families and Households, Lehrer (1998) also suggests that intermarriages between Protestants and Catholics have increased steadily. She identifies key variables that play a role in the decision to intermarry. She reports that those with higher levels of education are more likely to intermarry than those with lower levels of education. She also discusses how a premarital pregnancy will increase the likelihood of an intermarriage. Those who are strongly committed to their faith are least likely to intermarry. Despite these increases, Lehrer and Chiswick (1993) report that interfaith marriages are more likely to end in divorce, attributing these high divorce rates to the different religions of the couple. However, they also suggest that conversion by one spouse to the faith of the other produces less conflict and a more harmonious relationship.

FACTORS IN INTERMARRIAGES

Although the increasing trend toward intermarriage across ethnicity, religion, and race can be attributed to the increasing interaction between diverse individuals and to the elimination of institutional barriers, there are also other sociological, demographic, and psychological factors at work. According to psychotherapist Joel Crohn (1995), the decision to intermarry is not based on one single element—there may be many psychological influences operating. From his work as a therapist, he identifies four reasons that individuals from different religious, cultural, or ethnic backgrounds may be attracted to each other. First, stereotypes about a particular group may attract persons to each other; for example, black men are masculine, Jewish men are good providers, and Asian women are sexy.

Second, Crohn (1995) suggests that outmarriage can also be due to a partner's struggle with his or her identity. Those who outmarry may find members of the opposite sex from their ethnic, racial, or religious group unappealing and unattractive. Marriage can then be the arena in which individuals deal with their ambivalent attitudes toward their racial, ethnic, or religious identity: "Marriage to an outsider represents the ultimate strategy in trying to erase the stigma of a minority identity" (Crohn 1995, p. 52). At the same time, minority groups may outmarry into the dominant group to gain acceptance by that group. According to Pang (1997), Asian-American women who choose relationships with white men "participate in a language of assimilation that minimizes essential core parts of their self" (Pang 1997, p. 295). She found that Asian-American women who outmarry do not place importance on their race or culture and rather take on the identity of their white husband. According to Pang (1997), assimilation and incorporation into white society for these Asian-American women was of importance.

Third, Crohn (1995) suggests that whites may feel like they lack a particular cultural tradition and thus be attracted to a partner with a certain cultural and ethnic distinctiveness. Crohn further suggests that intermarriage is also a way for adult children to separate themselves from their family emotionally and/or physically. In fact, other studies have documented that those who chose to intermarry were more rebellious and had huge conflicts with family due to objections to their marital choice (Sung 1990).

Fourth, Crohn discusses how attraction across religious, ethnic, or racial barriers may be grounded in cultural values and traditions, such as collectivism or individualism, that the individual is attracted to.

According to social exchange theory, relationships are exchanges of valued resources and involve an analysis of costs and benefits. Pierre Van den Berghe (1960) theorizes that racial or ethnic intermarriage is an instance of such an exchange, in this case that of hypergamy. *Hypergamous* means that women marry up in status; while *hypogamous* means that the racial and ethnic status of the husband is lower than that of his wife. In the past, most black men who married white women were of a higher social status than their wives. In fact, this marrying down was so common that sociologists formulated a theory about it, hypothesizing that the black groom was trading his class advantage for the racial caste advantage of the white bride (Davis 1941; Merton 1941). Kalmijn's (1993) study of marriage license data from 33 states between 1968 and 1996 indicates that black/white intermarriages have been on the rise, most prominently between black males and white women. Kalmijn notes that these marriages involved white women and high-status black men, meaning that white women moved up in socioeconomic status.

Other factors may propel people into an interracial marriage. Some students of the subject assert that uneven sex ratios are a basic cause. Wherever a group near another group has an imbalance in sex ratio, there is a greater likelihood of intermarriage. If the groups have a relatively well-balanced distribution of the sexes, members will marry more within their own group (Guttentag and Secord 1983; Parkman and Sawyer 1967).

As for the sociocultural factors that promote or deter interracial marriages, several explanations have been put forth to explain the variation in intermarriage patterns in the United States. Tucker and Mitchell-Kernan (1990) hypothesized that certain environments are more racially tolerant of intermarriage than are others. Their hypothesis is based on findings from U.S. census data showing that interracial marriage rates are highest in the West and lowest in the South (U.S. Bureau of the Census 1985). Similar to their explanation is the argument by Blau and Schwartz (1984) that the larger the group size as a proportion of the population, the less likely it is that members will marry outside their group. Second, they suggested that the more heterogeneous an area's population, the more likely it is that people will marry outside their group. Both the aforementioned propositions imply that intermarriage is a function of environmental forces, not individual motivations.

In addition to the normal problems of working out a satisfactory marital relationship, interracial couples must cope with social ostracism and isolation. While the motivation for an interracial marriage may or may not differ from that of intraracial marriages, there are problems that are unique to interracial marriages. When researchers studied interracially married couples they discovered that courtship in most cases had been carried on clandestinely and, further, that many of them were isolated from their families following the marriage. Other outstanding social problems encountered by the couples centered on such factors as housing, occupation, and relationships with family and peers. Several of the spouses lost their jobs because of intermarriage, while others felt it necessary to conceal their marriages from their employers.

In addition to these strains, intermarried couples also face stressors within the family. Conflicts with in-laws contributed to marital instability (Chan and Smith 1995). Moreover, intermarried couples experienced not only the greatest conflict with in-laws but also differences that arose in terms of child rearing. According to Chan and Smith (1995), intermarried couples may face more problems because of their concerns with raising biracial children. They may worry about the children's psychosocial development because of their mixed heritage. The children may look more black than white and "this may create more stress for the mother who is most likely to be the primary caretaker and have to deal with the prejudice others might have about her children" (Chan and Smith 1995, p. 383).

Further research needs to be done to investigate the factors involved in intermarriages, as well to assess marital stability and instability among intermarried couples. However, there are several data problems in conducting research on intermarriages. First, marriage data collected by the National Center for Health Statistics (NCHs) is incomplete, since not all states are required to submit data and only about forty states submit such information (Besharov and Sullivan 1996). Moreover, many states do not ask questions about race on marriage licenses. Currently, only thirty-two states report race information to the NCHS (Besharov and Sullivan 1996). Even if data on race and ethnicity are available, the analysis is quite limited when conducting research on the second-generation intermarriage experience (Roy and Hamilton 1997). Moreover, data on interfaith marriage are also sparse, since the census and other government surveys rarely ask a respondent's religion (Salins 1997). In addition, the General Social Survey, which collects information on attitudes toward intermarriages, is quite limited because only two questions are presented in this survey: "How do you feel about having a close relative or family member marry a Black person?" And "Do you think there should be laws against marriages between Blacks and Whites?" According to St. Jean (1998), these questions do not adequately address current attitudes on intermarriages. Rather, St. Jean (1998) suggests that qualitative research, such as focus groups, provide more insight and information than the existing quantitative research on the topic.

SUMMARY

As barriers between different groups of people come down, intermarriage will continue to take place. This article has discussed the history and trends of black/white intermarriages, past and future directions of Asian-American intermarriages, trends in interfaith marriages, and factors involved in intermarriages. High intermarriage rates have been mostly among white ethnics (Salins 1997). Despite the increases in interracial marriage, black/white intermarriages are still quite low compared to other interracial and interfaith marriages. Racist attitudes still persist. Of these various types of intermarriage, black/white intermarriage is still one that is fraught with controversy. Those who oppose it often combine a hostility toward racial equality with invidious assessments of the private

thoughts and lives of interracial couples. Many men and women mate for no more complex reasons than meeting, liking each other as individuals, and choosing to transcend the societal barriers to their relationship. Only in societies similar to that of the United States does a biracial union take on any greater significance. For centuries, Latin American nations have undergone such a fusion of the races that only nationality, language, and religion remain as sources of identity. But the painful history of race relations in North America militates against the natural mixing of individuals from different races. Instead of regarding interracial dating and marriage as a matter of personal choice, many minorities have taken up the call for racial purity so common to their white supremacist adversaries of the past.

Despite the opposition to biracial unions, they will continue to increase as long as the social forces that set intermarriage in motion exist. There is, for example, the class factor. As long as middle-class blacks occupy token positions in the upper reaches of the job hierarchy, most of the people they meet in their occupational world will be white. Considering the fact that the job setting is the paramount place for meeting mates, it is only natural that many blacks will date and marry whites. Those whites will be the people they most often encounter and with whom they share common values, interests, and lifestyles. In the 1950s, E. Franklin Frazier (1957) predicted:

The increasing mobility of both white and colored people will not only provide a first-hand knowledge of each for the other but will encourage a certain cosmopolitanism. That means there will be a growing number of marginal people who will break away from their cultural roots. These marginal people will help create not only an international community but an international society. In becoming free from their local attachments and provincial outlook, they will lose at the same time their racial prejudices, which were a product of their isolation. Many of these marginal people will form interracial marriages because they are more likely to find suitable marriage partners in the cosmopolitan circles than within their native countries.

A careful reading of history indicates that the intermarriage rate often rises or fall for reasons related more to political and economic factors than individual desire. Within the developed world, the United States has the lowest rate of interracial marriage because it is the most racially diverse of all those nations. Due to a combination of economic factors, many white Americans feel less secure about the racial privileges they have long enjoyed and the impact intermarriage would have on their life chances and that of their children. The increasing presence of people of color and their competition for the best jobs, houses, incomes, and lifestyles heighten these insecurities. Increasingly, they are willing to turn back those challenges by racial scapegoating in the political arena, resulting in a number of reactionary voting patterns by the Anglo majority on affirmative action and immigrant issues, which largely affect African Americans, Asian Americans, and Latino citizens. In defense of their right to participate equally in the political and economic life of the United States, people of color have forged movements of racial and ethnic solidarity to counter the white backlash.

However, racial divisions are doomed to eventual failure in large part because race itself is a social construct used more as an opiate or divisive strategy than for any other purpose. Just as religion is the divisive force in much of the world, racial differences serve to mask the underlying causes of class inequality in the United States. The political and economic elite have found it expedient to exploit minor differences in physical traits among groups to detract from public consciousness of the most pronounced case of economic inequality in the developed world. Only when economic justice becomes a social reality can we expect to see dating and marriage choices based on merit and not a group's standing in the racial and class hierarchy.

REFERENCES

Bernard, Jessie 1966 *Marriage and Family Among Negroes.* Englewood Cliffs, N.J.: Prentice-Hall.

Besharov, Douglas, and Timothy Sullivan 1996 "One Flesh: America Is Experiencing an Unprecedented Increase in Black-White Intermarriage." *The New Democrat,* July/August, 8(4):20–22.

Blau, Peter, and Joseph E. Schwartz 1984 *Crosscutting Social Circles: Testing a Macrostructural Theory of Intergroup Relations.* Orlando, Fla.: Academic Press.

Cash, Wilbur Joseph 1960 *The Mind of the South.* New York: Vintage.

Chan, Anna Y., and Ken R. Smith 1995 "Perceptions of Marital Stability of Black–White Intermarriage." In Cardell K. Johnson, ed., *American Families: Issues in Race and Ethnicity.* New York: Garland Publishing.

Crohn, Joel 1995 *Mixed Matches: How to Create Successful Interracial, Interethnic, and Interfaith Relationships.* New York: Ballantine Books.

Davis, Kingsley 1941 "Intermarriage in Caste Societies." *American Anthropologist* 43:376–395.

Day, Beth 1972 *Sexual Life Between Blacks and Whites: The Roots of Racism.* New York: World Publishing.

Degler, Carl N. 1971 *Neither Black nor White.* New York: Macmillan.

Dollard, John 1957 *Caste and Class in a Southern Town.* Garden City, N.Y.: Doubleday.

Espiritu, Yen Le 1992 *Asian American Panethnicity: Bridging Institutions and Identities.* Philadelphia: Temple University Press.

Frazier, E. Franklin 1957 *Race and Cultural Contacts in the Modern World.* New York: Alfred A. Knopf.

Gallup Organization 1997 *Special Report: Black–White Relations in the US.* Princeton, N.J.: Gallup Organization.

Golden, Joseph 1954 "Patterns of Negro–White Intermarriage." *American Sociological Review* 19:144–147.

Gordon, Milton 1964 *Assimilation in American Life: The Role of Race, Religion, and National Origins.* New York, Oxford University Press.

Guttentag, Marcia, and Paul F. Secord 1983 *Too Many Women? The Sex Ratio Question.* Beverly Hills, Calif.: Sage.

Hare, Nathan, and Julia Hare 1984 *The Endangered Black Family.* San Francisco: Black Think Tank.

Hwang, Sean-Shong, Rogelio Saenz, and Benigno E. Aguirre 1997 "Structural and Assimilationist Explanations of Asian American Intermarriage." *Journal of Marriage and the Family* 59(August):758–772.

Jordan, Winthrop D. 1968 *White Over Black: American Attitudes Toward the Negro 1550–1812.* Chapel Hill: University of North Carolina Press.

Kalmijn, Matthijs 1993 "Trends in Black/White Intermarriage." *Social Forces* 72(1):119–146.

Kalmijn, Matthijs 1991 "Shifting Boundaries: Trends in Religious and Educational Homogany." 56(6):786–800.

Kosmin, Barry A., Sidney Goldstein, Joseph Waksberg, Nava Lere, Ariella Keysay, and Jeffrey Scheckner 1991 *Highlights of the CJF 1990 National Jewish Population Survey.* Washington D.C.: Council of Jewish Federations.

Lee, Sharon, and Marilyn Fernandez 1998 "Trends in Asian American Racial/Ethnic Intermarriage: A Comparison of 1980 and 1990 Census." *Sociological Perspectives* 41(2):323–343.

Lehrer, Evelyn L. 1998 "Religious Intermarriage in the United States: Determinants and Trends." *Social Science Research* 27(3):245–263.

Lehrer, Evelyn L., and Carmel U. Chiswick 1993 "Religion as a Determinant of Martial Stability." *Demography* 30(3):385–404.

Lewis, Richard, Jr., George Yancey, and Siri S. Bletzer 1997 "Racial and Nonracial Factors that Influence Spouse Choice in Black/White Marriages." *Journal of Black Studies* 28(1):60–78.

Lieberson, Stanley, and Mary Waters 1988 *From Many Strands: Ethnic and Racial Groups in Contemporary America*. New York: Russell Sage.

Merton, Robert 1941 "Intermarriage and Social Structure: Fact and Theory." *Psychiatry* 4:361–374.

Pang, Gin Yong 1997 *Asian American Intermarriage and the Language of Assimilation*. Unpublished doctoral dissertation, University of California, Berkeley.

Parkman, Margaret A., and Jack Sawyer 1967 "Dimensions of Ethnic Intermarriage in Hawaii." *American Sociological Review* 32:593–608.

Paset, Pamela, and Ronald D. Taylor 1991 "Black and White Women's Attitudes Toward Interracial Marriage." *Psychological Reports* 69(3):753–754.

Porterfield, Ernest 1982 "Black-American Intermarriage in the United States." In Garv A. Cretser and Joseph J. Leon, eds., *Intermarriage in the United States*. New York: Haworth Press.

Rosenblatt, Paul C., Terri A. Karis, and Richard D. Powell 1995 *Multiracial Couples: Black and White Voices*. Thousand Oaks, Calif.: Sage Publications.

Roy, Parimal, and Ian Hamilton 1997 "Interethnic Marriage: Identifying the Second Generation in Australia." *International Migration Review* 31(1):128–143.

Salins, Peter D. 1997 *Assimilation, American Style*. New York: Basic Books.

Shinagawa, Larry Hajime, and Gin Yong Pang 1996 "Asian American Panethnicity and Intermarriage." *Amerasia Journal* 22(2):127–152.

Spickard, Paul R. 1989 *Mixed Blood: Intermarriage and Ethnic Identity in Twentieth-Century America*. Madison: University of Wisconsin Press.

St. Jean, Yanick 1998 "Let People Speak for Themselves: Interracial Unions and the General Social Survey." *Journal of Black Studies* 28(3):398–415.

Stember, Charles Herbert 1976 *Sexual Racism*. New York: Elsevier.

Sung, Betty L. 1990 "Chinese American Intermarriage." *Journal of Comparative Family Studies* 21(3):337–352.

Tucker, M. Belinda, and Claudia Mitchell-Kernan 1990 "New Trends in Black American Interracial Marriage: The Social Structural Context." *Journal of Marriage and the Family* 52:209–218.

U.S. Bureau of the Census 1985 *Census of the Population, 1980: Vol. 2. Marital Characteristics*. Washington, D.C.: U.S. Government Printing Office.

—— 1998 *Intermarried Married Couples: 1960–present*. Washington, D.C.: U.S. Government Printing Office.

Van den Berghe, Pierre 1960 "Hypegamy, Hypergenation and Miscegenation." *Human Resources* 13:83–89.

Wilson, Deborah, and Cardell K. Johnson 1995 "White Attitudes Toward Black and White Interracial Marriage." In Cardell K. Johnson, ed., *American Families: Issues in Race and Ethnicity*. New York: Garland Publishing.

GRACE J. YOO
ROBERT E. STAPLES

INTERNAL MIGRATION

Migration is the relatively permanent movement of individuals or groups over varying distances to change places of residence; permanence and distance are its major defining dimensions. Internal migration occurs within the boundaries of a given country. (International migrants, not considered here, are called immigrants.) Internal migration, therefore, is a type of geographic mobility status.

DEFINITIONS

The following definitions are standard in the field of social demography (Bogue 1985):

Mobility status. A classification of the population based on a comparison between the place of residence (destination) of each individual in a census enumeration or survey and the place of residence (origin) at some specified earlier date. Mobility status in terms of the distance of the move falls into four main categories: nonmovers, local movers, intrastate migrants, and interstate migrants.

They may be examined more specifically in the list below:

I. *Nonmovers*, or nonmobile persons, live in the same house at the time of the census as at the date of origin.

II. *Movers*, or mobile persons, live in a different house and are further classified as to where they were living at the earlier date.

   a. *Local movers* are mobile persons who live in the same county at census time as at the date of origin.

   b. *Internal migrants* are mobile persons who live in a different county at census time than at the date of origin. Internal migrants may be further subclassified:

      1. *Intrastate migrants* live in a different county but within the same state.

      2. *Interstate migrants* live in a different state.

      3. *Interregional migrants* live in a different geographic division or census geographic region; they are also interstate migrants.

Mobility interval. The lapsed time between the date specified for previous residence and the date of enumeration is usually either one year or five years. Recent census enumerations specify five years, and the Current Population Surveys have specified intervals of one, two, three, four, and five years.

Metropolitan mobility. A system of subdividing mobile persons into categories by place of residence at the beginning and the end of the mobility interval and, according to metropolitan statistical areas (MSAs), is as follows:

1. Within the same MSA

2. Between MSAs

3. From outside MSAs to MSAs

4. From MSAs to outside MSAs

5. Outside MSAs at both dates

Mobility rates. The number of persons in a specified mobility status per 100 or 1,000 in the population of the area in which they resided at the end of the mobility interval is a mobility rate. Such rates may refer to any of the categories of nonmobile or mobile persons specified above. Mobility rates may be specific for age, race, sex, or other traits. The denominator may also be the origin date or the midpoint of the migration interval.

Migration flows. The key distinction of flows is that either the origin or the destination is unknown. There are two types of flows:

1. *In-migration* is comprised of migrants arriving at a particular place of destination, with no reference to the place of origin. In-flows could also arrive at specified types of places, such as central cities or metropolitan areas.

2. *Out-migration* is comprised of migrants departing from a particular area, with no reference to the place of destination. Outflows may also depart from specified types of places, such as places outside MSAs or suburban metropolitan rings of MSAs.

Migrations streams. These connect an origin to a destination. There are three types of migration streams:

1. *Specific streams.* Streams that connect particular places within a category, such as streams between specific cities, counties, states, or regions. This is the major use of the term.

2. *Typological streams.* Streams that connect types of places, such as streams between all central cities and suburbs in a state or the nation.

3. *Counterstreams.* When a stream between two places endures, it usually generates a counterstream, a smaller stream in the opposite direction. The stream and counterstream are referred to as an *exchange.*

Net migration. This is the difference obtained when the number of out-migrants is subtracted from the number of in-migrants in a particular place or type of place. A location that experiences a loss of population through migration is said to have a negative net migration; one that gains population through migration has a positive net migration. Because of its birth and death rates, an area may have a negative net migration and continue to have a growing population. There is no such thing as a net migrant, however.

Return migration. The census contains an item that identifies the state of birth. Return migrants are those persons who return to their state of birth during the mobility interval. There is no way of knowing how long they have been away from their state of birth when they return.

WHY STUDY MIGRATION?

Migration is important to social scientists because an increase or decrease in the size of a population, due to excess in- or out-migration, causes many social conditions to change. Community infrastructure, such as highways and schools, may become overburdened due to population growth, while public services may become difficult to maintain when population declines. Furthermore, social scientists study the equilibrating effects of population movement on national and regional economic systems. Growth or decline in the local economy is an incentive for people to move, which redistributes the population to balance the system.

The ability to predict the impacts of population growth or decline on the institutional sectors of a community and the ability to understand regional population dynamics, of course, provide many practical benefits to government and business planners.

MIGRATION RESEARCH

Net migration rates before 1940 were estimated using a survival-rate method. This method takes the population in one census as its base. It adjusts the number by adding births and subtracting deaths during the next decade. The amount of population change not accounted for is attributed to migration (Bogue and Beale 1961). The 1940 census was the first to include a mobility item. It asked where persons lived five years earlier. In 1950, after World War II, there was so much population movement that a one-year interval was substituted in the census. In 1960 the five-year mobility interval was restored and has been retained in subsequent decades. Because of these measurement

changes, the 1960 and 1970 censuses were the first from which decade changes could be derived. Thus several landmark studies appeared in the 1960s, breaking new ground and setting patterns for future migration research (Long 1988). Shryock's (1964) work showed the importance of studying gross migration flows in addition to the prevailing dependence on net migration. Lowry (1966) introduced econometric modeling to migration research. Finally, Lansing and Mueller (1967) helped introduce survey approaches to analyzing internal migration.

U.S. MOBILITY

Americans are unusually mobile (Bogue 1985). Only Canada and Australia have populations as mobile as that of the United States. In a single year, from March 1995 to March 1996, 17 percent of U.S. inhabitants moved from one domicile to another and about 6 percent changed their county of residence. At current mobility rates, average Americans live at fourteen different addresses during their lifetimes. Of these thirteen moves, three are as a dependent moving with parents and ten are of their own volition. People who have lived their entire lives at the same address account for no more than 2 or 3 percent of the adult population. Perhaps no more than 10 to 15 percent of people spend their entire lives in their county of birth.

When using the five-year mobility interval, mobility rates are not five times as large as those for a single year because persons who move several times within the interval are counted only once. Nearly one-half of the population is mobile over a five-year period, and more than one-fifth are migrants. Since 1980 there appears to have been no diminution in the tendency to migrate, but there has been an apparent reduction in local mobility.

One can discover contradictory findings in mobility literature. These contradictions are often due to the specific databases under analysis. Some databases use mortgage data and leave out renters; others, such as the Annual Housing Survey, use households; and some, such as most census publications, use individuals as units of analysis, each database giving somewhat different results. In addition, some data sources offer little information on the characteristics of migrants. The individual master file of the Internal Revenue Service includes state and county migration data but no personal characteristics, and several large moving companies provide data on their customers also without personal characteristics (Kahley 1990).

Reasons for Migration. Migration may occur in response to changing economic, social, or political conditions. Push factors are conditions in the sending population that impel or stimulate migration. Conditions that attract in-migrants are classified as pull factors (Ravenstein 1889).

Declining economic opportunities, political instability, or the weakening of place ties may stimulate out-migration. Expanding economic opportunities, potential for advancement, the presence of family members and friends, or previous vacationing or residential experience tend to attract migrants. Not surprisingly, rural communities with high birthrates and regions with limited opportunities are areas of high out-migration, whereas urban, industrial regions and communities with expanding opportunities tend to have high in-migration (Prehn 1986). Marriage, divorce, increasing or decreasing family size, and housing adequacy top the list in surveys. A sizable majority of respondents to the Annual Housing Survey reported housing or family dynamics as reasons for their move (Gober 1993).

The average age at which young adults leave home declined from the low twenties to the upper teens between 1920 and 1980, and then the median age began to rise again. These trends mirror another one; for the Vietnam cohort of young adults forward, those who return to live at home at some time holds at about 40 percent. About 25 percent had moved back in earlier cohorts. The expectation of a permanently empty nest for parents of young adults now seems a less certain one (Goldscheider and Goldscheider 1994).

Zelinski (1971) proposed a macro-level three-stage model of national internal migration. First, with the onset of modernization, the overall level of migration increases, primarily in the form of rural-to-urban moves. Second, as industrialization and modernization spread to more regions, migration may continue to increase; improved transportation and communication increase the availability of information and decrease the uncertainty of moving. Interurban moves become the majority of all moves. Finally, at advanced stages, when level-of-living differences among areas have diminished, there may be more urban-to-rural movement and more "consumer-oriented" migration toward warm climates or locations with other amenities (Long 1988).

Differential Migration. What population characteristics predict migration? Characteristics that indicate less entanglement with social obligations, greater need for employment, and higher job skills are good predictors. Men are more mobile with respect to residence than women, although the difference is small. The single migrate at higher rates than the married. For several decades, blacks have been more mobile than whites. However, in 1980 whites migrated at higher rates than blacks, although blacks continued to be more mobile locally. Hispanics migrated internally at a rate between those of the black and white populations. Persons with higher levels of education are more likely to migrate than those who are less well educated.

Age and Mobility. The shape of the age profile of migrants in the United States has been consistent for decades, changing only gradually over time. The younger children are, the more likely they are to migrate. The migration rate of children bottoms out in the early teens and does not increase rapidly until the late teens. More than one-third of Americans in their young adult years, ages twenty to twenty-four, the peak migration years during the life course, moved at least once between 1982 and 1983, and nearly one-half of this mobility was migratory. Not surprisingly, this age corresponds with college graduation and marriage for many. The increasing age of children in the home, particularly once they begin their formal schooling, dampens the attractiveness of migration for parents. The age-specific migration rate declines slowly at first, then more steeply until age thirty-five, after which it slowly declines throughout the middle years to a life-course low point just before the retirement years. The retirement migration hump between ages sixty and seventy is small by comparison to the early adulthood migration bulge. The final increase in age-specific migration rises at the end of life and relates largely to health issues. The elderly as a broad category are only about one-half as mobile as the general population.

MIGRATION AND REGIONAL DISTRIBUTION OF POPULATION

Three large interregional flows of internal migration have been occurring in the United States for many decades.

Westward Movement. For a long time, there was a high-volume flow of persons into the Pacific region, principally California, as well as a high-volume flow into the mountainous southwestern states. The 1970–1980 decade had a higher volume of westward movement than any previous one. Mountain states that previously suffered losses all made positive gains, and Colorado, Nevada, and Arizona continued the large gains of the previous decade. In the 1990s, there was a net flow out of California, largely to other western states, reversing a long-term trend for that state.

Northward Movement from the South. The southern region lost population heavily between the close of the Civil War and 1950. Industrial centers in the northeast and east-north-central regions absorbed a very large share of the migrating population. Both white and black migrants flowed along these channels in great numbers. Some southern states, however, particularly Florida and Texas, were exceptions. Between 1970 and 1980 the net outflow from the South completely disappeared. Those who left the South preferred the West to the North as a destination, and in-migrants to the South balanced the out-migrants. Every state in the northeast and north-central regions suffered a net migration loss during the decade, resulting in a major regional migration turnaround (Bogue 1985). By 1990 there were no net flows out of the South to other regions, but the Northeast, Midwest, and West all contributed to the southern region (Gober 1993).

The Southward Movement to the Gulf Coast and the Southern Atlantic Seaboard. The entire Gulf Coast, from the mouth of the Rio Grande in Texas across the coastal portions of lower Louisiana, Mississippi, and Alabama and on to include all of Florida, experienced much more rapid and intensive economic development than the southern and southeastern parts of the United States

lying away from the coast. Although this trend is a very old one, it accelerated rapidly in the 1970s.

As of 1980 there were only two regional migration streams instead of three: movement toward the South and Southwest and movement toward the West. The northeast and the north-central regions are the sources from which these migrants came (Bogue 1985). But in the 1980s, the South gained more through net migration than did the western states (Weeks 1996), a trend that accelerated by 1990. The geographic redistribution of knowledge-based industries of the information age carries in its wake a college-educated work force to the Sunbelt, including the South (Frey 1995).

Metropolitan Deconcentration. One of the macro-level processes that affects geographic mobility in our time is metropolitan deconcentration. Many nonmetropolitan counties in the United States experienced a slowing of population decline in the 1960s, and in the 1970s their net migration rates climbed above the break-even point, which signaled a genuine and widespread "rural–urban turnaround." Older people seem to have been in the vanguard of migration to nonmetropolitan counties; the turnaround for them happened in the 1960s rather than the 1970s. This reversal of a long-term trend of rural-to-urban migration is of great interest to demographers. Mounting evidence now indicates that although deconcentration continues in nonmetropolitan America as a whole, by the late 1980s metropolitan counties were outgrowing nonmetropolitan ones (Long and DeAre 1988). In the 1990s there is an uneven urban revival, with a few metropolitan areas with more flexible and diverse economies, mostly outside the Northeast and Midwest, gaining migrants. The new dominance of the suburbs over the central city is key to metropolitan deconcentration in the 1980s and 1990s. During this period, the suburbs are capturing the bulk of employment and occupational growth (Frey 1995).

RETIREMENT MIGRATION

Demography traditionally tends to focus on youthful migration, and labor-force migration in particular. Increasing attention, however, is being given to non–labor-force-motivated migration, particularly to the migration of persons of retirement age (Longino 1996). For the elderly, interstate flows are highly channelized—that is, half of the interstate migrants, regardless of their origin, flow into only eight of the fifty states. Florida dominates the scene, having received about one-quarter of all interstate migrants aged sixty or over in the five years preceding the 1960, 1970, 1980, and 1990 censuses. Although Florida, California, Arizona, and North Carolina have different major recruitment areas, they are the only states that attract several unusually large streams from outside their regions. Florida and North Carolina draw primarily from east of the Mississippi River, and Arizona and California draw from west of it. Among the elderly, the special characteristics of the destination tend to be more important than the distance. Warm climate, economic growth, and lower cost of living are still important pull factors.

Distance selectivity of elderly migration has been studied. Local movers are generally not as economically and socially well-off as nonmovers, and migrants are more well-off. Interstate migrants tend to have the most positive characteristics.

Permanence is an important but difficult dimension of migration to study. The census assumes that one's "usual place of residence" is not temporary. In reality, however, much of the migration among older people may be temporary. So far, studies of elderly seasonal migrants show them to be relatively advantaged, attracted by non–labor-force issues such as climate, cost of living, and the locations of family members and friends.

Metropolitan-to-metropolitan migration predominates among the elderly. Of the one-third who changed environmental types, no increase occurred between the 1960 and 1980 censuses in the proportion moving out of metropolitan areas in each decade. However, the movement in the opposite direction, up the metropolitan hierarchy, declined, both among older intrastate and interstate migrants. The net difference made it appear as though the flow from cities increased. Metropolitan-to-metropolitan migrants, especially those moving longer distances, tend to have more income, to be married, and to live in their own homes. A higher proportion of nonmetro-to-metro migrants is older, widowed, and living dependently, especially with their children. Coding revisions in

the 1990 census made updates of these comparisons impossible to calculate.

The cycle of migration for a job when one is young and returning to one's roots after retirement is an appealing notion to theorists. In contrast, Rogers (1990) demonstrated that elderly persons are not any more likely to return home than are the nonelderly; in fact, the probabilities of return migration by the elderly are lower than those of the general population, even after controlling for the different mobility levels of the two populations. There is wide state variability, however. The southeastern region is unusually attractive to older return migrants, and return migration is uncommonly high among the older black population moving into that region. Some evidence from the 1990 census shows that regional return migration patterns are shifting away from the Sunbelt states. Some migrants, apparently, return to their home states after an earlier retirement move (Longino 1995).

Some dubbed retirement migration as the growth industry of the 1990s. The amount of income transferred between states through retirement migration is quite substantial. Not surprisingly, economic development agencies are mounting efforts to attract mature migrants. This is leading to sharp competition among destinations for these migrants as new residents. The impact of elderly migration as a social phenomenon has yet to generate enough research to provide definite statements.

INTERNATIONAL COMPARISONS OF INTERNAL MIGRATION

Little research exists to compare countries on internal migration because measures, data sources, and units of analysis differ widely among nations. Consequently, international organizations have not published compendia of national comparative data on migration as they have on fertility and mortality. In addition, certain types of cultures conceive internal migration differently. In some small countries, such as England, lack of new housing stock limits residential movement. Migration is also limited in countries such as France, where transportation routes primarily connect the peripheral towns to a central national capital for historical reasons. Conversely, internal migration is amplified and culturally expected in nations of immigrants with widely dispersed regional centers and major cities, such as the United States, Canada, and Australia.

Nonetheless, existing studies provide some tentative generalizations that compare internal migration in the United States with that in other countries (Long 1988). The U.S. national average for moves is higher than that of most other countries because (1) cities in the South and West are growing; (2) a relatively large minority of people who repeatedly move elevates the U.S. average for lifetime moves above that for most other countries; and (3) during the 1980s and 1990s the baby boom generation in the United States has moved through the life-cycle stages that have the highest rates of geographic mobility.

Comparative studies also give attention to older migrants, although their mobility rates are lower than for the young. Rogers (1989) argues that as the populations of industrialized nations age, the internal migration patterns of elderly persons will change. Elderly migration levels are low in countries in the first stage of this population transition. In the second stage of the transition, large, long-distance flows to particular principal destination regions appear. The third stage continues to exhibit large numbers of elderly migrants, but their moves now include a significant number of short-distance moves to more dispersed inland regions. Rogers and colleagues (1990) argue from comparative data that England is in the third stage, the United States is transitioning between the second and the third stages, Italy is well into the second stage, and Japan is in the first stage.

Since 1970, for most developed countries, population aging has brought declining national rates of internal migration (Long 1988). For the United States, the decline appears to be greater for local moves than for long-distance movement. Urbanization was the dominant redistribution trend in the 1950s in fourteen European countries studied by Fielding (1989). The relationship between net migration and settlement size began to break down, however, in the 1960s—first in the countries of northwestern Europe in the mid-1960s, then in the countries and regions of the southern and western European periphery through the 1960s, and in the case of Spain, into the 1970s. By the 1970s, most of the countries of western Europe were recording counterurbanization, where the net flow was away from cities and toward small settlements. That counterurbanization became less dominant in the early 1980s but was not replaced by urbanization. Only in West Germany and Italy did the counterurbanization relationship persist. The United States experienced a similar pattern of long-term urbanization, reversed in the 1970s and then nearly reversed again in the 1980s (Frey 1990).

PREDICTING FUTURE MIGRATION

Migration rooted in labor movement will change in the future as the geographical basis of the economy changes. Robust new industry will attract migrants. Such developments in the southern region may extend several more decades into the future. On the other hand, migration not related to the labor force, such as retirement migration, is more sensitive to lifestyle issues. Eventual overcrowding, which results in a decline in the quality of life of local residents, will tend to discourage retirement migration. Florida's dominance of retirement destinations in 1990 lost 2 percent of the migrant retiree market.

Migration for better jobs increases in times of economic expansion. Thus, studies of the late 1990s may find migration to have increased in response to an improved economy. Other trends could also increase migration rates. First, the age composition is always shifting. In the 1980s, there were more persons in the twenty-to-thirty age range, their prime mobility years. The baby boom generation has a lower migration rate for long moves than others. However, because of its large size, a large number of baby boomers migrated. In the 1990s, the incidence of moving will likely dampen as baby boomers age and leave their prime mobility years. Second, the rising level of education may increase migration. Each new cohort of adults has a higher level of education than its predecessor. The third factor, household change, contains counterindicators. Married couples are increasingly likely to divorce, a situation favoring migration, but at the same time there are more dual-career couples in the population, a situation favoring nonmobility (Long 1988).

As we have seen, many factors motivate migration. These factors need further study, which will certainly generate new research hypotheses to be tested by migration researchers in the twenty-first century.

(SEE ALSO: *Population; Retirement*)

REFERENCES

Bogue, Donald J. 1985 *The Population of the United States: Historical Trends and Future Projections.* New York: Free Press.

——, and Calvin L. Beale 1961 *Economic Areas of the United States.* New York: Free Press.

Fielding, A.J. 1989 "Migration and Urbanization in Western Europe Since 1950." *The Geographical Journal* 155:60–69.

Frey, William H. 1990 "Metropolitan America: Beyond the Transition." *Population Bulletin* 45:1–51.

—— 1995 "The New Geography of Population Shifts." In R. Farley, ed., *State of the Union: America in the 1990s: Vol. 2. Social Trends.* New York: Russell Sage Foundation.

Gober, Patricia 1993 "Americans on the Move." *Population Bulletin* 48:2–39.

Goldscheider, Frances, and Calvin Goldscheider 1994 "Leaving and Returning Home in Twentieth Century America." *Population Bulletin* 48:2–35.

Kahley, William J. 1990 "Measuring Interstate Migration." *Economic Review* 75(2):26–40.

Lansing, John B., and Eva Mueller 1967 *The Geographic Mobility of Labor.* Ann Arbor: Institute for Social Research, University of Michigan.

Long, Larry H. 1988 *Migration and Residential Mobility in the United States.* New York: Russell Sage Foundation.

——, and D. DeAre 1988 "U.S. Population Redistribution: A Perspective on the Nonmetropolitan Turnaround." *Population and Development Review* 14:433–450.

Longino, Charles F., Jr. 1995 *Retirement Migration in America.* Houston: Vacation Publications.

—— 1996 "Migration." In James E. Birren, ed., *Encyclopedia of Gerontology: Age, Aging, and the Aged,* vol. 2. San Diego, Calif.: Academic Press.

Lowry, Ira S. 1966 *Migration and Metropolitan Growth: Two Analytic Models.* San Francisco: Chandler.

Prehn, John W. 1986 "Migration." In *The Encyclopedia Dictionary of Sociology,* 3rd ed. Guilford, Conn.: Dushkin.

Ravenstein, E.G. 1889 "The Laws of Migration." *Journal of the Royal Statistical Society* 52:245–301.

Rogers, Andrei 1989 "The Elderly Mobility Transition: Growth Concentration and Tempo." *Research on Aging* 11:3–32.

—— 1990 "Return Migration to Region of Birth Among Retirement-Age Persons in the United States." *Journal of Gerontology: Social Sciences* 45:S128–S134.

——, John F. Watkins, and Jennifer A. Woodward 1990 "Interregional Elderly Migration and Population Redistribution in Four Industrialized Countries: A Comparative Analysis." *Research on Aging* 12:251–293.

Shryock, Henry S. 1964 *Population Mobility Within the United States.* Chicago: Community and Family Study Center, University of Chicago.

Weeks, John R. 1996 *Population: An Introduction to Concepts and Issues,* 6th ed. Belmont, Calif.: Wadsworth.

Zelinski, Wilbur 1971 "The Hypothesis of the Mobility Transition." *Geographical Review* 61:219–249.

CHARLES F. LONGINO, JR.

INTERNATIONAL ASSOCIATIONS IN SOCIOLOGY

Founded by Rene Worms in Paris in 1893, the International Institute of Sociology (IIS) is the oldest continuous sociological association of any kind in the world. The IIS also happens to be the oldest continuous international association in the social sciences. Indeed, Worms's models for the IIS were the recently formed international institutes in law and in statistics. In the same year that he founded the IIS, Worms (1869–1926) also started ed the *Revue internationale de sociologies* (two years before Durkheimians would found the *Annee sociologigue*) and a book series, the Bibliotheque Sociologique Internationale, which would in time publish more than fifty volumes.

In 1893 Worms was twenty-four years old. His organizational skills are even more impressive when we consider where the IIS's founding falls in relation to that of other major associations in the discipline of sociology, including the discipline's only other major international association. In 1895, Worms himself founded the Societe de Sociologie de Paris, an association that held monthly meetings. A full ten years later, in 1905, C. W. A. Veditz of George Washington University founded the American Sociological Society (now the American Sociological Association) at a constituent meeting held at Johns Hopkins University. Another five years later, in 1910, the German Sociological Society held its first meeting—in Frankfurt, with Simmel presenting the opening paper. Three years after that, in 1913, Tongo Takebe founded the Japan Institute of Sociology (now the Japan Sociological Society).

Then some time passed before other major associations were formed. The Italian Society of Sociology was not founded until 1937, by Corrado Gini (who in 1926 established Italy's equivalent of the Census Bureau and who developed the Gini Scale). The International Sociological Association, which is discussed below began after World War II, in 1948—under broad sponsorship from UNESCO and informed by Cold War rivalries. Finally, the British Sociological Society was founded even later, in 1951; indeed, Britain had only one chair in sociology from 1907 through World War II, housed at the London School of Economics.

Like so many of sociology's founding figures, from Auguste Comte to George Herbert Mead, Worms was trained in philosophy and began his academic career in that discipline. The son of political economist Emile Worms, he earned his philosophy degree at the Ecole Normale Superieure and then also degrees in law and economics. His first teaching assignment was at the secondary school level while he also substituted for Henri Bergson at the College de France. And like other philosophically trained sociologists of the mid- and late nineteenth century, including Auguste Comte and Herbert Spencer, Worms's early way of thinking about society was by analogy to biological organisms. Within a decade, however, Worms moved, under increasing criticism from Gabriel Tarde (and also Dukheim), to a far more eclectic theoretical position, one that treated sociology essentially as the philosophy of the social sciences. After 1907 he taught an annual course in the history of sociology at the Ecole des Hautes Etudes Sociales. During this period he also taught on the law faculty at the University of Paris and served on important advisory bodies of the French government. By 1924 he had risen to Conseiller d'Etat.

The first World Congress of Worms's IIS was held a year after its founding, in September 1894, and the first volume of the Institute's Annales appeared a year after that. Not only scholars but also politicians and other influentials throughout the West found both the Revue and the IIS to be tolerant and supportive of heterogeneous ideas. This hospitable environment reflected Worms's own broad work experience and interdisciplinary training—along with his own general openness to differing theoretical approaches. Worms respected the work being done, for instance, by the circle around Durkheim, but he also kept a healthy independence from its influence. Thus, we find among the IIS's earliest members major figures not only in sociology but also in economics, the other social sciences, and the natural sciences: Franz Brentano, Enrico Ferri, Ludwig Gumplowicz, Achille Loria, Alfred Marshall, Carl Menger, Edward Ross, Gustav Schmoller, Georg Simmel, Albion Small, Gabriel Tarde, Edward Taylor, Ferdinand Tonnies, Alexandre Tchouprov, Thorsten Veblen, Lester Ward, Sydney and Beatrice Webbs, and Wilhelm Wundt. Indeed, in the early years sociologists were a minority among IIS members. Yet, with the exception of Durkheim, all major sociologists, Weber included, participated in the Institute at one time or another in its first three decades.

In casting his net well beyond the academy, Worms was known to play on the vanity of the famous from many walks of life in order to bring them into his international organization (D'Antonio 1994, citing Gephart). Often he granted influentials an honorary membership or officership in order to exempt them from paying dues. The first president of the IIS was Sir John Lubbock, vice president of the Royal Society of London, president of the London Chamber of Commerce, and a member of the House of Commons. A year later, Albert Schaeffle became the second IIS president, reflecting the fact that until 1914 IIS Congresses tended to be held annually. Aside from exchanging ideas frequently with Tonnies, Durkheim, and Simmel, Schaeffle served as director of the Zeitschrift fur gesammte Staatswissenschaft of Tubingen. The IIS's third president was a senator from Russia, Paul de Lilienfeld. One founding member, T.G. Masaryk of Prague, became both president of Czechoslovakia and president of the IIS. IIS vice presidents were no less successful in other pursuits: Bernardino Machada, Raymond Poincare, and Woodrow Wilson were past presidents, respectively, of Portugal, France, and the United States.

The first sociologist to serve as IIS president was Lester Ward, in 1903; two years later, Ward became the first president of the American Sociological Society. Indeed, Ward, Franklin Giddings, and Albion Small were all active in the IIS and would be prime movers in the formation of the American Sociological Society. All would serve as IIS presidents and, together, they comprised three of the American organization's ten original officers.

Worms himself was always more a technical director than a research sociologist, serving as IIS secretary general and treasurer for thirty-three years. During his tenure, eleven different countries were represented in the presidency of the IIS (and in 1924 Worms was made an honorary member of the American Sociological Society). The first French sociologist to serve as IIS president was Charles Letourneau.

In the interwar years, IIS Congresses were held biannually and IIS leadership was strongly influenced by Célestin, Bougle, Secondo Bouthoul, Corrado Gini, Maurice Halbwachs, Robert MacIver, William Ogburn, Joseph Schumpeter, Pitrim Sorokin, and Luigi Sturzo. Each World War disrupted the frequency of Congresses and, as it turned out, each of these periods also marked general passages for the institute as an organization. For instance, a Congress scheduled for Vienna in 1915 was canceled because of war, and then planning did not resume until 1925. In that year Worms became ill, and he died the following year: the Congress ended up being held in 1927. A decade passed. Then the 14th Congress, scheduled for Bucharest in 1939, had to be canceled—again due to war. It would not be held until 1950, now relocated to Rome and placed under the leadership of Corrado Gini. Earlier, in 1932, Gini had founded the Italian section of the IIS.

At the turn of the century, international associations in all scholarly disciplines typically called themselves "institutes"; they were more "traveling academies, as Scheuch (1997) put it, than bureaucratically established organizations. All drew membership by invitation, all placed numerical limits on total membership, and all organized plenary sessions around particular themes. The IIS continues this tradition to this day. Thus, the format for its biannual Congresses is quite distinct from that of today's meetings of the International Sociologi-

cal Association (ISA) held every four years. In the first place, the IIS tries to keep attendance to around 500 total participants (whereas ISA meetings draw anywhere from 3,000 to 5,000 participants). In the second place, all participants are encouraged to attend morning plenary sessions organized around a particular conceptual theme selected by each Congress's program committee. The afternoons are then devoted to working groups in which members present papers spanning a far broader range of topics.

This "traditional" format is designed to serve both interpersonal and intellectual ends: Interpersonally, IIS Congresses stage events that are designed to create a sense of community among scholars from different national traditions of training and thereby to encourage collaboration and other scholarly exchanges. This is the case not only with the collective morning plenary sessions in which presentations are simultaneously translated in three languages—the language of the host country, French, and English. It is also the case with collective lunches, dinners, receptions, and local sightseeing trips. Intellectually, themes of IIS Congresses are intended to have a cumulative impact on social science disciplines.

The *Annales* served as the IIS's official publication through 1931 (and the 10th Congress held in Switzerland in 1930), at which time it was discontinued. From this period until 1989, IIS activities were reported in the *Revue*, which also informally took over publication of IIS Congress papers. In 1989 the *Annales* were revived and the *Revue* became independent of the IIS. Recent World Congresses were held in Morelia, Mexico (1982), Albufeira, Portugal (1986), Rome (1989), Kobe (1991), Paris (1993), Trieste (1995), Cologne (1997), and Tel Aviv (1999).

The International Sociological Association was founded in 1948 under an initiative of the Social Science Department of UNESCO—as part of a broad effort that spanned comparable associations in economics, law, and political science. All of these new international bodies very much reflected the geopolitical situation of the day, and all were both considerably larger in membership and looser in thematic focus than the IIS. Today, the major scholarly contribution of the ISA revolves not around its plenary sessions but rather around nearly fifty specialized Research Committees, some of which rival in size an entire IIS Congress.

After WWII, the Allies were interested in undercutting the conditions that could foster any return to fascism, and they saw the dissemination of the social sciences as one important factor in fostering democracy. Indeed, UNESCO had already opened an Institute for Social Research in Cologne, the Rockefeller Foundation had financed another in Dortmund, and the American government still another in Darmstadt. Given that UNESCO was based in Paris, the first discussions leading to the ISA were held in that city beginning in October 1948 under the leadership of Arvid Brodersen. Also attending this first meeting were Georges Davy, Gurvitch, Gabriel Le Bras, Arie den Hollander, Rene Konig, Louis Wirth, Paul Lazarsfeld, Erik Rinde, and Otto Klineberg.

At the time, national sociological associations existed in eight countries (Belgium, Brazil, China, Germany, Italy, Japan, Netherlands, and the United States). In four other countries sociology was included in other social science associations, and in another ten the discipline was organized as institutes on the IIS model—with membership limited to selected individuals (Platt 1998). In September 1949, ISA organizers invited leading sociologists in twenty-one countries to a Constituent Congress in Oslo. Louis Wirth, the noted American sociologist of urban life, was named the first president, and Erik Rinde in Oslo was appointed Executive Secretary and Treasurer (Platt 1998). Unlike the IIS, membership in the ISA was by national association (including general social science association), not by individuals directly. As such, the rise of the ISA itself contributed to the founding of eleven national affiliates, including the British Sociological Association and its counterpart in Mexico (Platt 1998).

The ISA's first World Congress was held in Zurich in 1950, organized by Rene Konig with Wirth serving as president. One hundred fifty-four individuals participated, and eleven national associations and eighteen other bodies were admitted as members. In part, this Congress was held jointly with the newly formed International Political Science Association (and the Research Committee on Political Sociology remains a joint committee of both associations). Shortly thereafter, the ISA's

first Research Committee was formed, focusing on social stratification and mobility. This Committee's issues dominated the 2nd World Congress in 1953 in Liege, Belgium. By 1959 other Research Committees were being formed, at first referred to as subcommittees. Throughout the 1950s, another seventeen national associations were founded and joined the ISA, and then in the 1960s twelve more were added (Platt 1998). By 1952 the first issue of *Current Sociology*, the journal of the ISA, had appeared, and papers of early World Congresses were published separately as *Transactions*—a practice that ended in 1970 due to the cost and effort involved (Platt 1998). Originally, ISA World Congresses were held every three years, but beginning in 1962 they were moved to today's four-year schedule. Tracing the locations of World Congresses to this point, the 1956 Congress was in Amsterdam, the 1959 Congress in Stresa on Lake Maggiore in Italy, and the 1962 Congress in Washington, D.C.

Because the ISA relied on UNESCO for funding, its activities were heavily influenced by the agenda of UNESCO's Social Science Department (SSD). Early ISA presidents often had served earlier on SSD staff (Platt 1998). One early item on the SSD agenda was using the teaching of sociology to promote international understanding (Platt 1998). Only in the 1960s did teaching steadily lose priority to research, and this same period of transition, not coincidentally, marked the rise to preeminence of the Research Committees—at the expense of the Congress's general program topic and plenary sessions (Platt 1998). By 1970 and the World Congress in Varna, Bulgaria, there were seventeen different Research Committees (Platt 1998).

One issue facing the ISA leadership in its early years was how to deal with the earlier, well-established international association, the IIS. IIS activities had lapsed during WWII, and after the war some of its leaders were tainted with affiliations with defeated Axis regimes (Platt 1998). The same controversy split the national sociological association in Germany by 1960 but not the national associations in Italy or Japan. Regardless, as early as 1953 the leaders of sociology's two international organizations agreed to "friendly collaboration," including a willingness to schedule meetings at different times and to exchange proceedings. Relations between the two organizations have been relatively amicable ever since. Both international bodies have had to deal with the state of sociology in communist countries during the Cold War, the rising prominence of sociology in Third World countries, and addressing cases of political and scholarly repression in selected countries (Platt 1998).

In 1970 the ISA made two major changes in its founding statutes, one that introduced general individual membership and another that opened up the governance of the Research Committees. ISA leadership saw the Research Committees as a force moving the organization beyond national associations toward a grander internationalism. One result, however, is that the Research Committees became the equivalent of the internally pluralistic "sections" of the American Sociological Association (ASA), as opposed to remaining more coherent research groups. Thus, like ASA sections, the number of Research Committees has increased and many "working groups" and "thematic groups" within each Committee operate relatively independently of each other. In 1994, more than 3,000 sociologists attended the ISA World Congress in Bielefeld, Germany (76 percent from North America and Western Europe), and forty-five national associations were admitted. By 1997 there were fifty-nine identifiable research groups of one kind or another. Concerns abound, therefore, that the organization's centrifugal tendencies are overwhelming whatever centripetal forces remain (Platt 1998).

One consequence of the increasing internal pluralism of the ISA is that its funding base became and remains "increasingly problematic" (Platt 1998). ISA dues have been raised considerably for individual members, particularly for those living in economically advanced societies (Platt 1998). Throughout the 1970s and 1980s, communist bloc countries continued to support the voting rights of collective members, along with subsidies by affiliated governments. Still, the only ISA World Congress held in a socialist country was the 1970 meeting in Bulgaria. Looking back in 1994, the chair of a Constitutional Revision Committee held that the ISA's founding statutes had been premised on Cold War politics. His proposal then was that the organization needed to stress even more the importance of membership by dues-paying individuals, as opposed to relying on government

subsidies. Two years earlier, in 1992, the Research Council had voted to give the Research Committees power equal to that of member national associations. For the first time, the Research Committees voted for ISA officers (Platt 1998).

Increasingly in the 1980s, the ISA was concerned about the dominance of First World sociology to the detriment of contributions from sociologists in the Third World. With this in mind, the journal *International Sociology* was founded in 1986 with the mandate to favor scholarly submissions from "disadvantaged areas" (Platt 1998). The first ISA World Congress held in a Third World country was in 1982 in Mexico City (followed by the 1986 Congress in New Delhi).

REFERENCES

Clark, Terry N. 1967 "Marginality, Eclecticism, and Innovation: Rene Worms and the Revue Internationale de Sociologie from 1893 to 1914." *Revue Internationale de Sociologie* 3:3–18.

——1968 "Rene Worms." In *International Encyclopedia of the Social Sciences*. New York: Macmillan and Free Press.

D'Antonio, William V. 1994 "Sociology and the IIS." *Annals of the International Institute of Sociology*, Paris, France, pp. 1–19.

Platt, Jennifer 1998 *History of the ISA, 1948–1997*. International Institute of Sociology.

Rhoades, Lawrence J. 1981 *A History of the American Sociological Association 1905–1980*. Washington D.C.: American Sociological Association.

Scheuch, Erwin 1997 "Closing Report." Address delivered to the 33rd IIS World Congress, Cologne.

DAVID SCIULLI

INTERNATIONAL LAW

NOTE: *Although the following article has not been revised for this edition of the Encyclopedia, the substantive coverage is currently appropriate. The editors have provided a list of recent works at the end of the article to facilitate research and exploration of the topic.*

International law is the system of rules and principles governing relations at the interstate level. It originally developed in response to the needs of states but in recent times has grown to include international organizations and, to some extent, individuals.

International law as a systematic body of rules began in Europe in the seventeenth century. Before then, and from earliest history, rules existed governing the interrelations of various groups of people (Nussbaum 1958). But the rules were systematized in Europe only when the contacts among peoples became regular and frequent and the idea of a single ruler for all known society foundered. That occurred with the collapse of the Holy Roman Empire during the Thirty Years War (1618–1648). The state system developed in its place, characterized by a number of kingdoms and principalities, each equal to the others, sovereign within its own borders, and subject to no outside sovereign. Hugo Grotius, a Dutchman who lived during this time, wrote a seminal book, *De Jure Belli ac Pacis* (1620–1625), describing legal rules, derived from natural law, by which these states could achieve peaceful coexistence and, when they failed, how they could conduct their wars with some semblance of humanity. His book popularized international law, and he is generally considered the founder of international law.

The rules and principles Grotius described reflected the characteristics of states. The fundamental notion that states were sovereign and equal became a principle of international law. And because the rulers of states respected that principle as law, they were less likely to wage war or to annex their neighbors. International law helped create the success of the state system and in turn reflected the features of the system.

Grotius derived his rules from natural law, thus suggesting that nature was superior to states. By the nineteenth century, however, theorists abandoned natural law as a source of international law. Instead, they looked at the behavior of the states themselves as the source of international law. International lawyers became positivists, and the state became for international law the ultimate political entity. The rules of international law could guide and could set out regular procedures to ensure the smooth and peaceful conduct of international relations, but they permitted states wide prerogatives. Governments acquiesced in international legal rules because their states benefited

from an orderly system of international relations in which they gave up few of the attributes of absolute sovereignty. For example, the rules did not speak to what states did internally, no matter how egregious. Individuals were not considered subjects of international law. Nor did the rules restrain states from the use of force. International law described permissible uses of force, but states could in effect use force whenever they chose.

By the twentieth century pressures for change began to develop. Technological advances in war and communications accounted for movements aimed at restraining states in their use of force and abuse of human beings. People such as Elihu Root, U.S. Secretary of State in Theodore Roosevelt's administration, wanted international law to provide the vehicle for restraint. Governments started experimenting with dispute settlement through arbitration and courts. They formed the League of Nations to help them control states' uses of force. International law and international institutions were being substituted for unbridled state sovereignty. The concept was a radical departure from the past and came about only over the course of half a century and two world wars.

After World War II, governments were willing in theory to contemplate real restraints on their ultimate sovereign prerogatives. The United Nations was created as an entity under international law. Its charter committed states to uphold human rights, to cooperate in solving world problems, to abandon the use of force, and to follow the commands of the organization itself. The idea was to lessen state sovereignty for the good of the whole world community. Thus, the state began to lose its place as the ultimate political entity almost exactly 300 years after its rise.

Certain international legal norms are now theoretically superior to the wills of the states. In other words, a certain amount of natural law now characterizes the system again. In addition, the state is making way for other types of political institutions such as regional arrangements, although if the state should ever become finally obsolete so will international law. The current form of international law and many of its rules and principles presuppose a system of coequal entities without a single sovereign.

While the state system remains intact, however, international law has taken on an increasingly important role in governing the relations of states in an interdependent, technologically linked world. It does this even though international law has never had the institutions typical of domestic law: a legislature for making law, an executive to enforce it, and a judiciary to adjudicate and interpret it. In some respects international law still functions as it did in the nineteenth century because the system benefits the state. Nevertheless, law does get made, enforced, and adjudicated, and social movements are at work putting demands on states to form and live by new norms of international law.

Because of the informal condition in which international law exists, however, some legal thinkers argue it is not law at all but rather moral precepts or mere guidelines. Most prominent of these thinkers was John Austin, who described law as a series of commands backed by sanctions. International law has no overarching authority to issue commands, and the sanctions are irregular. But Austin's criticism depends on his definition of law. If law is defined as behavior or behavioral restraint induced by a sense of obligation, international law, in its sphere, is law. Positivist international lawyers also point out that in the end the states acknowledge that international law is law, and that is the relevant indicator.

International legal rules have two basic sources: custom and treaty. Rules of customary international law are created through practices that states engage in because they believe they have a legal obligation to do so. Treaties are the explicit agreements states make with each other to be bound. As the need for international law has grown, states have relied on treaties as a law-making vehicle more and more. The general multilateral treaty has become a common form of law making for important international concerns. For almost ten years nearly every state of the world attended a conference to negotiate a comprehensive treaty on the law of the sea. Because so many states attended and the treaty was so long in the making, the treaty began to take on the characteristics of customary international law, irrespective of its status as a treaty. A similar conference will convene in 1992 to discuss climate, and suggestions have been made to convene such a conference for trade.

When no rule of custom can be found and no treaty exists, international courts have in some disputes turned to a third source of law—general principles of law. These are principles commonly found in domestic legal systems and can serve to fill any gaps in international law, which suffers from its ad hoc law-making process. Theorists consider general principles a subsidiary source of international law because general principles are not made in a positive sense by all the states of the system, and they may be applied to a state that did not wish to be bound by them. Custom and treaty, however, generally allow states to opt out of a rule, thus reflecting the traditional view that the states are superior to the system of law. In the last thirty years, however, states have accepted that certain principles cannot be derogated from because they are considered peremptory norms or *jus cogens*. Examples of such norms are the prohibitions on genocide, the slave trade, and the use of force to advance a state's political agenda. With the concept of *jus cogens*, international law has again taken on some elements of natural law.

Jus cogens also exemplifies the extent to which international law has overcome cultural relativity. As new states emerged in the 1960s, scholars from these states questioned whether international law should be binding on them since it was a European product that had aided in perpetuating colonialism. These criticisms have faded, however, because it became clear that international law also created the thing desired most by newly independent countries—statehood. Moreover, because international law is made by states, the new majority could begin to re-create international law. The process of international law has succeeded to the point of bringing states together in accepting that certain principles are overriding, despite the particular value systems of individual states.

Like the law-making system, the law-adjudicating system in international law depends on states volunteering to use it. The system does have courts, in particular, the International Court of Justice. But no state needs to subject itself to the court unless it wishes to do so. The court does have limited compulsory jurisdiction in the case of states that agree to submit cases to it in advance of disputes arising. Nicaragua brought a case against the United States under such an agreement in

1986. States can also agree on an ad hoc basis to submit disputes to arbitral tribunals. The vast majority of international law is adjudicated informally, however. If a state violates international law, such as when Iraq invaded Kuwait in 1990, most states in the system will pronounce their views regarding the legality of the action. Assessing these evaluations leads to conclusions regarding lawfulness. Thus, states make and adjudicate the law themselves.

States also enforce international law themselves. International law is notorious for being poorly enforced. In fact, however, most international law is in fact observed most of the time. Because the states must agree to the law, they tend to make only the laws they want and are willing to live by. Otherwise they opt out of the rules, as the United States has done for some of the new law of the sea. Law is not so well observed, however, in those areas that make headlines—war, human rights, terrorism—which perhaps accounts for international law's poor reputation for enforcement.

When a rule of international law is violated, the state that is harmed is allowed to take action against the perpetrator. For example, if a fishing treaty between state A and state B is violated because state A's fishermen overfish in state B's waters, state B might be entitled to terminate the treaty and prevent future fishing by state A. This system works to some extent, but states have tried to improve on it in recent decades by, first, giving the United Nations and, in particular, the Security Council authority to police some violations of international law and to expand the ability of domestic institutions in enforcing international law by expanding the concept of universal jurisdiction.

The Security Council has authority to maintain peace. In article 42 of the U.N. Charter, it is given the power to call on member states to contribute troops to fight at the direction of the council. The idea comes very close to having an international police force. It has only been used once, however —in Korea in the 1950s. Other attempts have been stymied by the cold war antagonism of the United States and the Soviet Union, each of which has a veto over invocation of article 42. As a sort of substitute, the Secretary General has regularly sent troops, contributed voluntarily by U.N. members, to serve a peacekeeping role. Peacekeeping troops are not supposed to take enforcement action. But enforcement action may be a possibility again with the end of the cold war. Following Iraq's invasion of Kuwait in 1990, the council ordered worldwide economic sanctions and permitted the use of force, both to enforce the sanctions and to push Iraqi troops out of Kuwait.

Another solution to enforcement has been the widening of universal jurisdiction. To prevent states from interfering in each other's affairs, international law contains principles of jurisdiction defining when and where a state may enforce rules of domestic or international law. In some instances any state may take action. This concept of universal jurisdiction is as old as international law. It was originally developed to handle the problem of piracy. Pirates are defined as persons who commit crimes for profit on the high seas. Generally they do not fly any state's flag, and they act outside the territorial jurisdiction of any state. Typically, the state where the act took place or the state of the pirate's nationality would have jurisdiction, but those categories often do not exist for pirates. The state of the victim might have jurisdiction, but the international system developed the rule that any state may board a vessel that fails to fly a flag and that any state may arrest, try, and punish pirates.

After World War II, universal jurisdiction was expanded to include the concept of crimes against humanity. The victorious allied powers tried German and Japanese individuals, holding them personally responsible for human rights abuses, characterized as crimes against humanity and thus crimes for which any state in the world could take jurisdiction. The Nuremburg and Japanese War Crimes Trials broke new ground in international law by holding that individuals had rights and responsibilities not only under their nation's law but under international law and by expanding the scope of a state's jurisdiction.

Individual responsibility and expanded state jurisdiction are being included today in a variety of treaties, especially related to human rights, narcotics, and terrorism. Customary international law now permits universal jurisdiction over persons who have committed genocide or war crimes. The International Court of Justice has also suggested that important human rights may be enforced by any state regardless of its connection with the violation because the obligation to respect human rights is an obligation owed to all people; it is a right *erga omnes*.

International law will need these improvements in enforcement. The scope of questions now covered by international law grows annually with the increasing interdependence of the world and the technological advances that bring peoples into conflicting contact. The need to protect the global environment is the newest challenge for international law. States may soon decide they need an international organization to regulate the world trading system. The problems of development, health, communications, education, population, and use of space on earth and in outer space are all new problems in need of attention. Add to them the old problems of war, territorial disputes, governing international organizations, treaties, dispute resolution, refugees, human rights, diplomatic immunity, law of the sea, air space, recognition of new states, and so on, and the growing importance of international law becomes apparent. International law will continue to serve as a means of conducting smooth international relations, its traditional role, but it will also continue to assume new importance as a means of solving problems. In order to achieve this, however, international law must improve its institutions and be accepted by more states, whose own sovereignty will diminish as international law advances.

(SEE ALSO: *Genocide; Law and Legal Systems; Sociology of Law; War*)

REFERENCES

Abeyratne, Ruwantissa I. R. 1996 "International Politics and International Justice: Unity in Diversity?" *International Journal of Politics, Culture and Society* 10:291–316.

Bassiouni, M. Cherif 1993 "The History of the Draft Code of Crimes against the Peace and Security of Mankind." *Israel Law Review* 27:247–267.

Berry, David S. 1998 "Conflicts between Minority Women and Traditional Structures: International Law, Rights and Culture." *Social and Legal Studies* 7:55–75.

Binder, Leonard 1996 "The Moral Foundation of International Intervention and the Limits of National Self-Determination." *Nationalism and Ethnic Politics* 2:325–359.

Brownlie, Ian 1990 *Principles of Public International Law.* Oxford: Clarendon Press.

Buergenthal, Thomas 1997 "The Normative and Institutional Evolution of International Human Rights." *Human Rights Quarterly* 19:703–723.

Chinkin, Christine 1995 "Violence against Women: The International Legal Response." *Gender and Development* 3:23–28.

Corntassel, Jeff J. and Tomas Hopkins Primeau 1995 "Indigenous 'Sovereignty' and International Law: Revised Strategies for Pursuing Self-Determination." *Human Rights Quarterly* 17:343–365.

Dezalay, Yves and Bryant Garth 1995 "Merchants of Law as Moral Entrepreneurs: Constructing International Justice from the Competition for Transnational Business Disputes." *Law and Society Review* 29:27–64.

Dezalay, Yves, G. Garth Bryant, Pierre Bourdieu, R. C. Austin, David Bonner, Noel Whitty, Sandra Coliver, and Heinz Klug 1996 *Dealing in Virtue: International Commercial Arbitration and the Construction of a Transnational Legal Order.* Chicago: University of Chicago Press.

Gros Espiell, Hector 1998 "Universality of Human Rights and Cultural Diversity." *International Social Science Journal* 50: 525–534.

Janis, Mark 1988 *An Introduction to International Law.* Boston: Little, Brown.

Kash, Douglas A. 1998 "An International Legislative Approach to 21st-Century Terrorism." In Kushner, Harvey W., ed., *The Future of Terrorism: Violence in the New Millennium.*, Thousand Oaks, CA: Sage

Knoppers, Bartha M. and Sonia LeBris 1991 "Recent Advances in Medically Assisted Conception: Legal, Ethical and Social Issues." *American Journal of Law and Medicine* 17:329–361.

Lansky, Mark 1997 "Child Labour: How the Challenge Is Being Met." *International Labour Review* 136:233–257.

Lecuona, Rafael A. 1997 "International Law, Cuba, and the United States of America." *International Journal on World Peace* 14:37–49.

Lowe Joseph, D 1994 *Dictionary of Diplomatic, International Law, International Relations Terms,* Berkeley: Joseph D Lowe Publisher.

Max Planck Institute for Comparative Public Law and International Law 1981 *Encyclopedia of Public International Law.* New York: North-Holland.

Mendlovitz, Saul and John Fousek 1996 "Enforcing the Law on Genocide." *Alternatives* 21:237–258.

Nippold, Otfried and S. Hershey Amos 1998 *The Development of International Law after the World War.* Holmes Beach: Gaunt-Incorporated.

Nussbaum, Arthur 1958 *A Concise History of the Law of Nations.* New York: Macmillan.

Otto, Dianne 1996 "Subalternity and International Law: The Problems of Global Community and the Incommensurability of Difference." *Social and Legal Studies* 5:337–364.

Parry, Clive, and John Grant 1988 *Encyclopedic Dictionary of International Law.* New York: Ocean Publications.

Stone, Julius 1983 "A Sociolgial Perspective on International Law." In R. St. J. McDonald and D. M. Johnston, eds., *The Structure and Process of International Law: Essays in Legal Philosophy Doctrine and Theory.* The Hague: Martinus Nijhoff.

MARY ELLEN O'CONNELL

INTERNATIONAL MIGRATION

International migration is a term used to refer to change of usual residence between nations. The number of international migrants is always much smaller than the total number of persons traveling across international frontiers, because the overwhelming majority of such travelers do not intend to change their usual residence. International migration is contrasted with *internal migration*, which refers to a change of usual residence within a nation. The term *immigration* is used to denote the flow of persons establishing a usual residence in a given nation whose last residence was in some other nation. The term *emigration* is used to denote the flow of persons relinquishing a usual residence in a given nation to establish residence in some other nation. *Net international migration* denotes the difference between the number of persons immigrating to a given nation in a given period and the number emigrating from that nation in the same period.

Immigratory and emigratory events constitute two of the four components of national population change; the other two components are births and deaths. For most nations, population change is determined predominantly by the balance of births and deaths (natural increase). However, for a few nations in certain periods, the net international immigration has also been an important component of the total population change.

In determining the number of persons who have changed residence among nations, national statistical agencies must specify the meaning of a change in usual residence. The United Nations (1978) suggests that international movements with an intended stay of more than one year be classified as international migration. Unfortunately, there is considerable lack of uniformity among nations with respect to how international migration is defined. For example, according to data of the Mexican government, some 46,000 Mexicans emigrated to the United States in 1973; according to data of the U.S. government, the number of permanent legal immigrants from Mexico was about 72,000 (United Nations 1978). Also, many governments, including that of the United States, collect data on immigration but not on emigration. Finally, all data on immigration published by governments refer to legal immigration only. Data on illegal or undocumented immigration cannot be tabulated.

Certain terms useful for the study of either international or internal migration will now be explained. A *migration stream* is defined as the total number of migratory events from place A to place B during a given time. The *counterstream* is defined as the total number of migratory events from place B to place A. The sum of events in the stream and counterstream is termed the *gross interchange* between A and B. The *effectiveness of migration* is defined as the ratio of the net migration between A and B and the gross interchange between the two places. The effectiveness of migration can therefore vary from a low of 0 to a high of 1. For most pairs of geographic units, the effectiveness of migration tends to be much closer to 0 than to 1.

Petersen (1975) makes very useful distinctions among the concepts of free, impelled, and forced migrations. In free migration, the will of the migrant is the main factor. In impelled migration, the will of the migrant is subordinated to the will of other persons. In forced migration, the will of other persons is paramount, and the will of the migrant is of no weight at all. Another useful term is *return migration*, defined as migration back to a place in which one had formerly resided. *Chain migration* (MacDonald and MacDonald 1964) is also a frequently used concept. It refers to the common pattern whereby a given individual migrates to a particular destination in which he or she already has kin or friends who have previously migrated from his or her own area of origin.

MIGRATION DIFFERENTIALS

It is universally observed that the propensity for international migration is strongest among young adults. Other differentials in migration tend to be limited to particular cultures or locales. Because the highest propensity for international migration is among young adults, the contribution of international migration to population change is often considerably greater than the net international migration by itself. This is because the birthrate for migrants is higher than for the total population, and the death rate is lower.

DETERMINANTS OF THE VOLUME OF INTERNATIONAL MIGRATION

Demographers analyze the determinants of the volume of a migratory stream into two components. The first concerns the specific propensity to migrate for individuals of each given type. The second concerns the number of individuals of each given type. The volume of a migratory stream can be calculated as the sum of the products obtained by multiplying the specific propensity to migrate for individuals of each given type by the number of individuals of that type.

The determinants of the propensity to migrate may conveniently be analyzed in terms of a preference system, a price system, and the total amount of resources available for all goals (Heer 1975, 1996). The preference system describes the relative attractiveness of various places as goals for potential migrants, compared to other goals that their resources would allow them to pursue. An area's attractiveness is the balance between the positive and negative values it offers.

Among the most important of the positive values is the prospect of a better-paying job. Other positive values achieved by migration include the chance to live in a more favorable climate, freedom from persecution, opportunity for marriage, and continuation of marital ties. In the case of forced migration, the positive value achieved is simply to save one's own life.

However, international migration also creates negative values. A major disincentive to migration is that it involves a disruption of interpersonal relationships with kin and old friends. Chain migration is so attractive precisely because it mitigates the disruption of such relationships (Massey et al. 1987). Other negative values created by international migration are the necessity of learning new customs and, often, a new language. Laws restraining legal entry or departure are also, of course, very important deterrents to international migration and will be discussed later in more detail.

The price system describes the costs in money, energy, and time, which cannot be used in the pursuit of other goals, imposed by a given migration decision. Since the cost of international migration generally varies in direct proportion to the distance traveled, the number of immigrants to a given place tends to vary inversely with the distance.

The total resources available for all goals also affects the decision to migrate. If the only draw back to migration is the expense of the move, an increase in monetary income should increase the probability of migration.

MAJOR STREAMS OF INTERNATIONAL MIGRATION

Certain major streams of international migration deserve mention, either because they have had important historical consequences or because they otherwise exemplify unusual patterns. One of the earliest streams of international migration with historical significance was the westward movement of nomadic tribes in Europe and Central Asia at the time of the fall of the Roman Empire. The many tribes that moved westward during this period included those speaking Celtic, Germanic, and Ural-Altaic languages. As the easternmost tribes moved westward, they pushed forward the tribes in front of them. One suggested explanation for this extensive migration is that the grasslands of Central Asia had become desiccated. A second possibility is that an expanding Chinese Empire disrupted the life of the nomadic tribes near its borders and, thus, provoked the movement of all the other tribes (Bury 1928; Huntington 1924; Teggart 1939).

The European and African migrations to North America, South America, and Oceania have probably had more important historical consequences than any other migratory stream. This flow began slowly after Columbus's voyage to America in 1492. It has been estimated that more than 60 million Europeans have left for overseas points in the centuries since then. However, net migration was lower, since many of those leaving Europe later returned (United Nations 1953, pp. 98–102). The migration from Africa to the New World was almost wholly a forced migration of slaves. The first slaves were brought to the colony of Virginia in 1619, and the slave trade in the United States was not legally ended until 1808. During the period of slave trade, about 400,000 Africans were brought to the United States (U.S. Bureau of the Census 1909). The impact of the migration of slaves is revealed by the fact that, in 1790, 20 percent of the 4 million persons in the United States were black.

During the twentieth century, the origin of immigrants to the United States shifted drastically away from Europe and toward Asia and the Americas. This change is illustrated in Figure 1, which shows the number and percentage distribution by region of last residence of immigrants to the United States by decade from 1891–1900 to 1991–96.

The emigration from Puerto Rico to the mainland United States, of major magnitude in the years following World War II, is of interest because it exemplifies an extremely high rate. According to the 1970 census, the combined total of the population of Puerto Rico and of persons in the United States of Puerto Rican birth or parentage was about 4.1 million, of which around 1.4 million were in the United States. Thus 33.9 percent of all Puerto Ricans were on the mainland (U.S. Bureau of the Census 1971, 1973).

Immigration into Israel following World War II is likewise noteworthy because it exemplifies an extremely high rate. In 1948, when independence was established, the total population of Israel was 650,000; by 1961, after the influx of more than 1 million immigrants, it had risen to 2.2 million (Bouscaren 1963; United Nations 1966).

Perhaps the world's largest gross interchange in a short time took place in India and Pakistan following the 1947 partition of British India and the establishment of these two areas as independent states. This migration is also of interest because it was impelled rather than free. In the face

of violence, Hindus and Sikhs in Pakistan moved to India and Muslims in India moved to Pakistan. From 1947 through 1950, 10 million persons migrated from Pakistan to India and 7.5 million from India to Pakistan (Spate 1957).

The two most recent major streams of international migration exemplify what has been termed *labor migration*. Labor migration is said to occur when immigrants are legally admitted to a nation for defined time periods in order to alleviate a shortage of labor. Labor migrants are not given the right of permanent residence. The first stream was the large-scale migration of workers into the prosperous nations of northern and western Europe from poorer nations in the Mediterranean region such as Italy, Spain, Portugal, Yugoslavia, Greece, Turkey, Algeria, and Morocco (Massey et al. 1998). This stream began around 1960 and ended in 1973, following the sudden elevation of petroleum prices by the Organization of Petroleum Exporting Countries (OPEC). The proportion of the total population that was foreign increased substantially in all of the northwest European nations. For example, from 1960 to 1970, the foreign population of the German Federal Republic increased from 1 percent to 5 percent and that of Switzerland from 9 percent to 16 percent (Van de Kaa 1987). The second major stream was the large-scale migration of workers into the major oil-producing nations in the Persian Gulf region out of such nations as Jordan, Egypt, Yemen, Pakistan, and India (Massey et al. 1998). For example, from 1957 through 1975, 70 percent to 75 percent of the total labor force in Kuwait consisted of foreigners (Birks and Sinclair 1981).

CONSEQUENCES OF INTERNATIONAL MIGRATION

One may examine the possible consequences of international migration for the individual, the area of net emigration, the area of net immigration, and the larger social system, which includes areas of net emigration and net immigration. The discussion must be in part speculative, since knowledge about these topics is incomplete.

Before a move, an immigrant will have anticipated a net balance of favorable consequences. Sometimes, however, reality will fall short of expectations, and dissatisfaction will provoke the

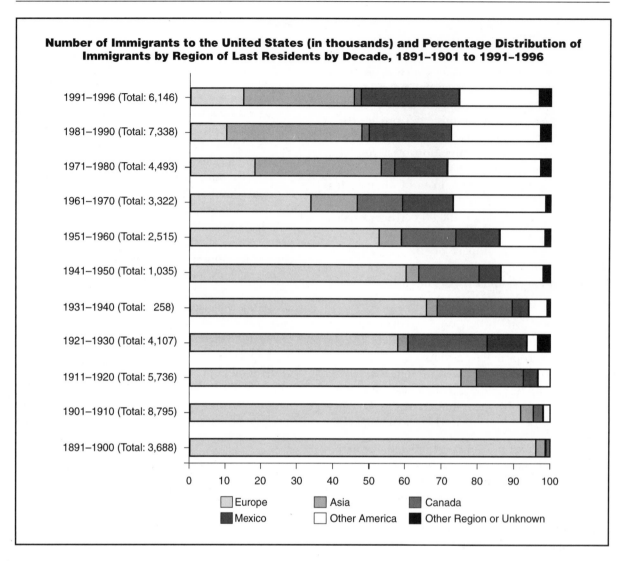

Number of Immigrants to the United States (in thousands) and Percentage Distribution of Immigrants by Region of Last Residents by Decade, 1891–1901 to 1991–1996

1991–1996 (Total: 6,146)

1981–1990 (Total: 7,338)

1971–1980 (Total: 4,493)

1961–1970 (Total: 3,322)

1951–1960 (Total: 2,515)

1941–1950 (Total: 1,035)

1931–1940 (Total: 258)

1921–1930 (Total: 4,107)

1911–1920 (Total: 5,736)

1901–1910 (Total: 8,795)

1891–1900 (Total: 3,688)

0 10 20 30 40 50 60 70 80 90 100

Europe   Asia   Canada
Mexico   Other America   Other Region or Unknown

Figure 1

immigrant to either return to the nation of origin or, on occasion, to move on to some other nation.

Net emigration may have several important consequences for an area. By relieving population pressure, it may cause the average level of wage and salary income to rise. Remittances from emigrants may also be helpful. On the other hand, net emigration may cause the value of land and real estate to decline. Moreover, areas of net emigration suffer the loss of investments made to raise and educate children who spend their productive years elsewhere. This loss is particularly large when the individual receives a higher education prior to emigration. Such a loss is termed *brain drain*.

Finally, since emigration rates are selective by age, nations with substantial net emigration may have relatively few young adults relative to the number of children and the aged.

Net immigration may also have important consequences. If the area is definitely underpopulated, the resultant population increase may help the nation to achieve economies of scale (reduction in the cost of goods obtainable by increasing the scale of production and marketing) and, thus, raise the general standard of living. Under other circumstances, net immigration may result in some decline in average wage and salary income. In either case, a net flow of immigrants tends to raise the price of land and real estate. Furthermore, in general, net immigration increases the proportion of young adults in the total population. Dependent on their composition, immigrants may receive either more or less in government benefits than the amount of their tax payments. Finally, net immigration may make the population more heterogeneous with respect to race, religion, or language.

For the system compromising the nations of both net inflow and net outflow, the direct effect of international migration is of course to promote a redistribution of population. If migrants have been responsive to differences in job opportunities, this redistribution may further the economic development of the total system. Moreover, a substantial amount of international migration responsive to job opportunities might also induce a decline in the degree to which there is economic inequality among nations. Unrestricted international migration might make the poor nations richer and the rich nations less prosperous. However, there is substantial disagreement among scholars as to what the effect of unrestricted immigration from the poor nations might be on the prosperity of the rich nations such as the United States. Simon (1984) believes that net immigration to the United States will serve to increase its average income. Davis (1981), on the other hand, takes a much more pessimistic view. Additional analysis of the consequences of immigration from poor nations to the United States is found in a study sponsored by the National Research Council (Smith and Edmonston 1997, 1998).

LEGISLATION AFFECTING IMMIGRATION AND EMIGRATION

National laws concerning immigration have varied from almost complete prohibition to positive encouragement. Laws restricting emigration are now relatively rare but have been of important consequence in modern times for at least one nation, the USSR.

In the seventeenth and eighteenth centuries, a mercantilist ideology, which saw a large population as the key to national wealth and power, encouraged many of the governments of Europe to attempt to prohibit emigration and to encourage immigration. In the late seventeenth century, the French minister Colbert enacted legislation prescribing the death penalty for persons attempting to emigrate or helping others to emigrate, except to a French colony. In 1721, Prussia passed a similar law. Moreover, the Prussian emperor Frederick the Great invested state funds in subsidizing the settlement of immigrants. In eighteenth-century Russia, both Peter the Great and Catherine the Great subsidized colonists from abroad, mostly from Germany (Glass 1940).

The nineteenth century, influenced by the economic doctrine of laissez faire, was the great period of unrestricted international migration. During this century the European governments freely permitted emigration, and the newly independent United States of America welcomed millions of immigrants.

After World War I, the United States took a more active role in restricting international immigration. The major events in this connection were changes in immigration law in 1921 and 1924 that greatly restricted the number of immigrants to the United States, establishing a quota for each of the countries outside the Western Hemisphere. Furthermore, the nations of northwestern Europe was given much larger quotas relative to their populations than those of southern and eastern Europe. This was done even though, in the immediately preceding years, rates of immigration from southern and eastern Europe had been much higher than those from northwestern Europe. The justification made at the time for the quota differentials was the presumed greater ease with which immigrants from northwestern Europe could assimilate (Eckerson 1966).

By the 1960s, a changing climate of opinion with respect to the inferiority or superiority of different ethnic groups made it possible for President Kennedy to advocate the abolition of the discriminatory national-origins quota system, and a law accomplishing this was enacted in 1965 under the Johnson administration. The 1965 law called for the abolition of the national-origins quota system as of July 1, 1968, but, nevertheless, imposed an overall annual quota of 170,000 immigrants from outside the Western Hemisphere and 120,000 from within it (exclusive of immediate relatives of U.S. citizens). This legislation granted preference to persons with relatives already in the United States, to persons with needed occupational skills, and to refugees. Additional legislation passed in 1976 abandoned the separate quotas for the two hemispheres and imposed a 20,000 limit on immigrants from any nation in the Western Hemisphere (the 20,000 limit had previously been in existence only for Eastern Hemisphere nations). The major effect of the 1976 legislation was to make it more difficult for Mexicans to enter the United States legally.

Some nations, while placing severe restrictions on immigrants in general, have made use of positive inducements to encourage immigration from selected nations or groups. Currently the best example of such legislation is that of Israel, which has committed itself to encouraging the immigration of Jews from anywhere in the world. Formerly, Canada and Australia also exemplified such policies of selective encouragement. Each of these nations subsidized immigrants from European nations while placing severe restrictions on the immigration of nonwhites (Bouscaren 1963; Petersen 1964).

The United States, Australia, Canada, and Israel have laws that allow immigrants permanent residence leading to citizenship. Since 1950, other nations, particulary in northwestern Europe and in the Persian Gulf, have had policies that encourage only labor migration, that is, migration of workers, mostly male, who were supposed to return to their native countries following a fixed term. In the case of the European nations at least, these policies had unintended results. The contract workers were allowed to bring their dependents to live with them. Hence, they became permanent immigrants even though this was not the result intended by original policy (United Nations 1982).

In many nations of the world, particularly in the United Stated, a major phenomenon is the existence of illegal, or undocumented, immigrants. A necessary condition for the existence of illegal immigration is a lack of congruence between the laws regulating the supply of legal immigrant opportunities and the demand for them. For example, the demand to immigrate to the United States from a particular nation should be a reflection of that nation's population size and the average propensity to immigrate to the United States if there were no legal restrictions. Accordingly, nations with large population size are likely to have more

immigrant demand than nations with small populations; yet all nations, without regard to population size, have the same annual quota. Furthermore, national differences in individual propensity to immigrate to the United States should be a function of such variables as the difference in standard of living compared with that of the United States, difference in degree of public safety compared to the United States, proximity to the United States, degree of similarity with the language and culture of the United Stated, and prior existence of immigrants that allows for chain migration. According to the official estimate of the U.S. Immigration and Naturalization Service, there were 5 million undocumented immigrants in the United States in October 1996. Of these, 2.7 million, more than half the total, were from Mexico. An additional 335,000 were from El Salvador and 165,000 from Guatemala (U.S. Immigration and Naturalization Service 1997, p. 198). Given Mexico's population size and presumed high average propensity for immigration to the United States, one can easily explain why such a very large proportion of all undocumented persons in the United States have been from that nation (Heer, 1990). An additional fact of interest is the high proportion of undocumented immigrants residing in California. According to the official Immigration and Naturalization Service estimate for October 1996, 40 percent of all undocumented immigrants were living in that state (U.S. Immigration and Naturalization Service 1997).

Rising concern over the extent of undocumented immigration into the United States led the U.S. Congress to enact the Immigration Reform and Control Act of 1986. The intent of the legislation was to eliminate the presence of undocumented aliens in the United States either by legalizing their status or by forcing them to leave the country. This act had two key provisions. The first was the imposition of sanctions upon employers who knowingly employed illegal aliens. The second was the provision of a process whereby undocumented persons who had lived in the United States continuously since January 1, 1982, or had worked in U.S. agriculture for ninety days in the period from May 1985 to May 1986 were allowed to become temporary legal residents. After a short time, they would be allowed to become permanent legal residents. The success of employer sanctions is problematic because sanctions can be applied only if the employer knowingly hires illegal aliens and because it is relatively easy for an undocumented person to present to the potential employer either fake documents or the documents of some other legally resident person. On the other hand, more than 3 million persons applied for legalization of status after the act was passed, among whom about 2.3 million were from Mexico (U.S. Immigration and Naturalization Service 1990).

In 1998 more than 80 percent of the world's 5.9 billion persons lived in one of the less developed nations. The annual rate of natural increase in these nations was around 1.7 percent; in the developed nations it was only 0.1 percent. In the developed nations per capita gross national product was $20,240; in the less developed nations, only $1,230 (Population Reference Bureau 1998). These facts imply a strongly increasing demand for immigration to the developed nations from the less developed. Given the current barriers to legal immigration imposed by the developed nations, undocumented immigration will be of increasing prevalence unless the governments of the developed nations take extraordinary measures to curb it.

REFERENCES

Birks, John, and Clive A. Sinclair 1981 "Demographic Settling Amongst Migrant Workers." In *International Population Conference, Manila 1981*, vol. 2. Leige, Belgium: International Union for the Scientific Study of Population.

Bouscaren, Anthony T. 1963 *International Migration Since 1945*. New York: Praeger.

Bury, B. 1928 *The Invasion of Europe by the Barbarians*. London: Macmillan.

Davis, Kingsley 1981 "Emerging Issues in International Migration." In *International Population Conference, Manila 1981*, vol. 2. Leige, Belgium: International Union for the Scientific Study of Population.

Eckerson, Helen F. 1966 "Immigration and National Origins." *Annals of the American Academy of Political and Social Science* 367:4–14.

Glass, David V. 1940 *Population Policies and Movements in Europe*. Oxford: Clarendon Press.

Heer, David M. 1975 *Society and Population*, 2nd ed. Englewood Cliffs, N.J.: Prentice-Hall.

——1990 *Undocumented Mexicans in the United States*. New York: Cambridge University Press.

——1996 *Immigration in America's Future: Social Science Findings and the Policy Debate*. Boulder, Colo.: Westview Press.

Huntington, Ellsworth 1924 *Civilization and Climate*. New Haven, Conn.: Yale University Press.

MacDonald, John S., and Leatrice D. MacDonald 1964 "Chain Migration, Ethnic Neighborhood Formation, and Social Networks." *Milbank Memorial Fund Quarterly* 52: 82–97.

Massey, Douglas, Rafael Alarcon, Jorge Durand, and Humberto Gonzalez 1987 *Return to Aztlan: The Social Process of International Migration from Western Mexico*. Berkeley: University of California Press.

Massey, Douglas S., Joaquin Arango, Graeme Hugo, Ali Kouaouci, Adela Pellegrino, and J. Edward Taylor. 1998. *Worlds in Motion: Understanding International Migration at the End of the Millennium*. Oxford: Clarendon Press.

Petersen, William 1964 *The Politics of Population*. Garden City, N.Y.: Doubleday.

——1975 *Population*, 3rd ed. New York: Macmillan.

Population Reference Bureau 1998 *World Population Data Sheet*. Washington, D.C.: Population Reference Bureau.

Simon, Julian 1984 "Immigrants, Taxes, and Welfare in the United States." *Population and Development Review* 10:55–69.

Smith, James P., and Barry Edmonston, eds. 1997 *The New Americans: Economics, Demographic, and Fiscal Effects of Immigration*. Washington, D.C.: National Academy Press.

—— eds. 1998 *The Immigration Debate: Studies on the Econommic, Demographic, and Fiscal Effects of Immigration*. Washington, D.C.: National Academy Press.

Spate, O.H.K. 1957 *India and Pakistan: A General and Regional Geography*. New York: Dutton.

Teggart, Frederick J. 1939 *Rome and China: A Study of Correlations in Historical Events*. Berkeley: University of California Press.

United Nations 1953 *The Determinants and Consequences of Population Trends*. New York: United Nations.

——1966 *United Nations Demographics Yearbook, 1965*. New York: United Nations.

——1978 *United Nations Demographic Yearbook, 1977*. New York: United Nations.

——1982 *International Migration Policies and Programmes: A World Survey*. New York: United Nations.

U.S. Bureau of the Census 1909 *A Century of Population Growth in the United States: 1790–1900*. Washington, D.C.: U.S. Government Printing Office.

——1971 *U.S. Census of Population: 1970*. Final Report PC(1)-A1. Washington, D.C.:U.S. Government Printing Office.

——1973 *U.S. Census of Population: 1970*. Final Report PC(2)1E. Washington, D.C.: U.S. Government Printing Office.

U.S. Immigration and Naturalization Service 1990 *Provisional Legalization Application Statistics, January 9, 1990*. Washington, D.C.: U.S. Immigration and Naturalization Service.

——1997 *1996 Statistical Yearbook of the Immigration and Naturalization Service*. Washington, D.C.: U.S. Government Printing Office.

Van de Kaa, Dirk J. 1987 "Europe's Second Demographic Transition." *Population Bulletin* 42:1–59.

DAVID M. HEER

INTERNET

The Internet is a curious phenomenon. It's a vast international institution of critical and growing importance, yet in another sense its properties are so evanescent that it's tempting to say that Internet does not exist; there's no *there* there except the process itself. The reason is that at heart Internet is nothing more than a highly specific collection of rules or standards for computers called communication protocols. Even the name comes from the U.S. Department of Defense standard TCP/IP (terminal control protocol/internet protocol). What we now see as institutional Internet—the fiber optics and copper cabling, the billions of dollars of computer hardware and software, the business and governmental organizations, and body of human skill and knowledge that's both on the Net and in the user community—emerged and grew with volcanic force inside the purely formal boundaries of the protocol system. What the protocols allowed, the world's social and economic system instantiated.

A critical part of this development was that the protocols in question were public and open, that they were standards and not products per se. This is in contrast to the course of other communications systems, such as the telephone, radio, and television, for which key components were held proprietary or otherwise regulated by patents,

secrecy, and both governmental and private monopolies. No one would claim that what has become the Internet was created for the common welfare of all humankind, or that it is guaranteed to work for that welfare in the future. In fact, some of the key components of the Internet came from the bowels of the Pentagon at the height of the Cold War, and the overall moral valence of the Internet is as unsettled a question as one could imagine. But it is useful to note that in many ways the Internet is government work that made good and that its ongoing success appears to depend on public and open standards. Attempts to commercially supplant the Internet or take it proprietary have so far been unsuccessful, despite the huge upsurge of Net-based commerce.

HISTORY

The history of the Internet is partly the history of technology, the hardware of the system. But more important are the social aspects of computer-mediated communication, the human networks created by the hardware system. There are two polar points of view on the social impact of the Internet on communities and society. On the one hand, enthusiasts have argued that the Internet removes barriers that have historically divided people and opens the way to unprecedented equality in social interactions and for social opportunities (Rheingold 1993). On the other hand, critics contend that the Internet removes humanity from social interaction and strands people in an impersonal virtual world without touch, dignity, or personhood (Stoll 1995). The earliest empirical research to address the actual uses and impact of the Internet in social life seems to suggest that people experience Internet interactions in ways similar to their face-to-face social experience. But the technology is young and the scope of its use has broadened only in the 1990s. A decade into the twenty-first century, the prognosis may become clear.

Hardware. If the Internet is anything physical it is a network of computers—actually, a network between networks, an internetwork. Computer networking is not new. Many of the house-sized 1960s-style computers, called mainframes, were often linked into larger networks, although this typically required that computers be in the same building if not the same room. This constraint was partly overcome by using radio-frequency messaging over coaxial cables similar to those now used for cable TV.

Computer networking using coaxial cable became common and useful in the 1960s. But a problem arose when the University of Hawaii decided to adopt a multicampus computer network. Cable connections in Hawaii would not only have to span long distances, they would have to span those distances deep under the Pacific Ocean. The cost was too high even to contemplate. Computer scientists began a search for alternatives and settled on radio-based computer communications—network messages would be broadcast on special channels. The result was called AlohaNet.

A problem immediately arose. The distance between islands in Hawaii is typically only a few hundred miles. It took only a few thousandths of a second (or less) for radio messages to span that distance, but that's a fairly long time for a computer. This meant that two computers at remote locations could start talking at once, each not hearing the other immediately, which garbled their messages. Garbling of this sort was called a message collision. To solve this problem, the AlohaNet designers had to build collision-detection circuitry into their network controllers. A computer would not only have to send messages and listen for other's messages, it would have to check for message collisions, and re-send if a collision occurred.

Such a scheme sounded awkward, but in practice it was elegant. Collision detection and retransmission overhead turned out to be a tiny part of the overall cost in time and speed of the network. Broadcast-style, collision-detecting networks have a number of advantages. First, the number of computers in network (usually called nodes) is not necessarily fixed. If rules are set up to allow it, any computer in a broadcast system can chime in and negotiate to be part of the network. Once that computer is known to the network, messages can be routed to it as if it had been there all along. Second, as long as there are two or more computers up and running in a given network segment, they can talk; their peers could go on- or off-line as it suited them without bringing down the net. The flexibility of broadcast-style networks led to a revolution in computer communication.

ETHERNET AND LOCAL AREA NETWORKS

Of course, networks actually broadcasting would soon fill up the available radio-frequency spectrum. Consequently, most systems that actually were put in use contained their transmissions inside dedicated runs of coaxial cable, or, later, telephone-like twisted-pair conductors. The most popular of these was the Ethernet system developed by a consortium of computer makers. The Ethernet system allowed a fairly high-speed (1 million bytes per second) network based on coaxial cable to span a physical space one kilometer end-to-end, longer with repeaters to boost the signal. This meant that all but the largest of buildings and many whole complexes and campuses could be served by a single, fast local area network (LAN). Originally, in the early 1980s, Ethernet was used mostly to tie together collections of mainframes and smaller minicomputers, but within a few years it was possible inexpensively to integrate most organizations' growing collections of personal computers (PCs—IBMs and clones, Macintoshes, and others) into an Ethernet system. The easy availability of fairly fast, fairly cheap Ethernet LAN systems, and the rising tide of PCs that could use them, was half the nascent Internet equation. You could call it the demand side. Computers increasingly were used not so much as solo workstations but as components in LANs; their interoperability became one of their principal virtues.

ARPAnet and DOD Connectivity. The supply side of the Internet equation actually preceded the growth of LANs by a few years. In the late 1960s, the Department of Defense (DOD) began pumping increasing amounts of money into the softer side of computer science: artificial intelligence, computer graphics, computer voice and hearing, visual processing, natural-language processing, computer-based language translation, and computer networking. The source of the funding was the Defense Advanced Research Projects Administration (DARPA, or more commonly, ARPA). The mode of funding was unusual for DOD, in that the research was mostly unclassified and public, in the form of grants to universities and think-tanks.

Public (or partly public) projects seemed to call for a method of openness and interchange different from the Pentagon's historic need-to-know procedures. The method that was suggested was the development and use of a computer network to accomplish document and data interchange and what would now be called electronic mail (e-mail). ARPAnet was built by the Massachusetts Institute of Technology (MIT) and a think-tank—Bolt, Baranek and Newman (BBN)—to link together ARPA grant sites and allow ARPA investigators and their staffs to communicate electronically. Physically, ARPAnet used high-speed and expensive leased AT&T telephone long lines to connect to fairly large computers, like the DECsystem 10s and 20s and PDP 11/70s from BBN's neighbor Digital Equipment Corporation (DEC). Human users typically used simple display terminals to interact with to their local host computers, which sent the messages out over the network. Specialized and proprietary interface gear made the whole thing work. Only members of the ARPA grant club were allowed to participate, which led to hard feelings among those excluded—although cost would have excluded many others anyway. Even in the early 1980s, after ARPAnet had been taken over by the National Science Foundation and become NSFnet (the Internet's immediate ancestor), the cost of participation included about $10,000 up front for network gear, substantial use of a $150,000 minicomputer, and quite a few hundred dollars each month for leased lines.

At least two university-based networking systems sprang up in the late 1970s and early 1980s in an attempt to provide ARPAnet-like connectivity to non-ARPA institutions. Both used a mail-drop scheme to avoid the high costs of leased phone lines. In other words, the participating computers used modest-speed, dial-up modems (like those of most contemporary home PCs in the 1990s, only slower) to phone a predetermined list of their peers at fixed intervals, usually once or twice a day after long-distance rates went down. It worked like an activist organization's telephone tree: each computer called N neighbors, who called N neighbors, and so on, until all the messages were delivered. The process was slow—e-mail sent this way might take overnight or longer to arrive—but it was much less expensive than the full-time alternatives. Mail-drop networks tended to be organized by host-machine type. Universities with big IBM mainframes tended to support Bitnet operation, while sites using the AT&T Unix operating system or clones typically adopted a scheme called Usenet.

The obvious advantages of intersite networking to university researchers and others created a strong demand for this kind of service. Full-time live service such as that provided by ARPAnet was particularly advantageous, since it allowed sharing of computer facilities and easy access to scarce computing resources, such as supercomputers. When the U.S. National Science Foundation (NSF) began supporting such supercomputer facilities at about the same time DOD was losing interest in its specialized networking, NSF essentially took over the ARPAnet infrastructure and renamed it NSFnet. (ARPAnet lived on for a while inside NSFnet.) NSFnet was initially set up along the same lines as ARPAnet—only institutions that were NSF grant recipients were welcome as members. But interest from other academic and research entities (as well as the broader scope of NSF) caused the system to grow into what is now the Internet.

The Internet in the 1980s and early 1990s was still for the most part a network between networks, the lower-level networks being the university and commercial LANs. Real participation on the Internet by a PC required a dedicated LAN connection, usually a coaxial or twisted-pair link using Ethernet technology, and a high-speed leased link to the Internet backbone. These were available in most university environments but were prohibitively costly to arrange at home. Software developers soon came up with a solution: an Ethernet emulator that ran over ordinary telephone lines using relatively low-cost commercial modems. Serial Line Interface Protocol (SLIP) and its successors allowed ordinary PCs in ordinary homes to dial into Internet Service Providers (ISPs) and function as full-fledged peers on the Internet system. Now, commercial ISPs brought the Internet into homes and small businesses at prices comparable to ordinary voice telephone service.

NSF decommissioned NSFnet in 1995 amidst political fanfare, creating a generic Internet and opening the door to a growing swell of private and commercial development. The electronic marketplace surged, with on-line shopping in the 1998 holiday season topping $1.2 billion over Amercia On-Line (AOL) alone. Private citizens routinely communicated electronically with families and strangers, and located services and information readily from PCs in libraries, schools, businesses, and homes.

Meanwhile, NSF turned its attention to development of the next wave of innovation. In partnership with MCI WorldCom, NSF created and supports the Very High Performance Backbone Network Service (vBNS), also known as Internet 2 and Next Generation Internet. This network links the two leading-edge supercomputing sites and at the end of the 1990s, connected 150 research institutions nationwide. Internet 2 seeks to accelerate Internet development and enable a new generation of applications to improve media integration, real-time collaboration, and interactivity. Although not yet generally accessible by ordinary users, Internet 2 clearly suggests that real time multimedia virtual interaction will soon be possible around the globe. (See King, Frinter, and Pickering 1997, for more detailed history of the Internet.)

INTERNET MODALITIES

E-mail. Probably the most common form of Internet communication is electronic mail, which is text-based messaging from a single computer user to one or more recipients. Internet routing services are used to send the message from a sender's address (e.g. gwjones@msn.com) to a recipient's (e.g., tbsmith@udom.edu). Individual addresses represent dedicated mailboxes—actually, special computer files—maintained by the users' ISPs. The mailbox address precedes the @ symbol, and the ISP's address follows it. E-mail has traditionally been plain, unformatted text, but newer e-mail software has the capacity to handle styled text, display graphics, even sound and video. Although these facilities are not yet universal, they suggest that e-mail will become more fluid, stylized, and expressive. In text-based e-mail, emotions are commonly expressed with "emoticons," symbol combinations with a cartoonish character such as :-) for humor or :-(for sadness.

E-mail can take a mass or bulk form. For example, persons with a common interest can sign up to be members of a mailing list under the control of a computer program called a list server, usually called a listserv or mail list. Mail sent to the listserv is relayed to all list members, so that the resulting interchanges have the form of a public broadcast to other listserv members. Some listservs automatically broadcast all messages received, while others are moderated by a member who screens messages for conformity to the group's purpose.

Sometimes mass mailings take a hostile or abusive turn, as in the case of unsolicited commercial e-mail (UCE), usually labeled spam. ("Spam" is not an acronym but an unflattering reference to the lunchmeat; apparently, the usage is an allusion to a Monty Python skit in which a restaurant patron can't get any meal that doesn't contain Spam. Most precisely, spam is abusive mass broadcasting to a Usenet newsgroup, as described below, but the term has been borrowed by the e-mail world.) UCE, or spam, is bulk mail sent inappropriately to computer users who have not requested it. UCE is abusive because it is analogous to junk surface mail sent with postage due—the UCE victim, after all, has to pay for the connection over which the message is delivered, and all Internet users pay indirectly for the infrastructure that carries spam.

Spamming is one example of cultural conflicts that emerge from the migration of commercial practice to the Internet. The Internet grew up in military and academic subcultures where norms and expectations for behavior are explicitly not-for-profit. With the commercialization of the Internet in the late 1990s, many business practices were translated to the new medium without adaptation to existing prescriptions and proscriptions. "Netiquette"—etiquette for the Internet—continues to evolve and issues of social control over the Internet are largely unsettled at the turn of this century.

People tend to assume that e-mail is a relatively private medium. Historically, no one knew an e-mail address unless the user disclosed it. Today, institutions and ISPs publish e-mail addresses, and search engines on the World Wide Web (WWW) can locate many user addresses. In some ways, the e-mail address is coming to replace the telephone number as a direct personal identifier. People seem increasingly to use e-mail instead of the telephone to reach friends, family, and business contacts. With the rise of telephone answering machines and whole-family participation in the work force in the 1990s, delayed responding to any kind of messaging has become normative. E-mail allows people to receive and respond to messages at their convenience, 24 hours per day. Because it is written, messages can be clearly stated and thoughtfully framed. For communication across long distances, e-mail is less expensive than the telephone and can communicate documents much more rapidly than any postal or delivery service. These uses plainly are not revolutionary, just partial replacements of existing communication methods (c.f. Kraut, Patterson, Lundmark, Kiesler, Mukophadhyay, and Scherlis 1998).

Unlike telephone calls, e-mail is usually archived by the servers that send and receive messages, the nodes between corresponding users. In the United States, the legal precedent is that information on the server, or on machines owned by business or government, is owned by the owner of the machine and is not private information. E-mail correspondence may be subject to review by superiors, may be subpoenaed by courts, and may even be considered public records in some states. The privacy protection of telephone wiretapping laws was not extended to e-mail.

E-mail and listservs have become important tools for passing announcements and other information among members of existing face-to-face groups. Listservs are common forums for professional communications and announcements and are often used in classroom study groups to encourage open questioning and discussion. Researchers use listservs to disseminate new findings, share resources, locate grant programs, and even to recruit study participants.

For professional and other formal communications, e-mail has successfully facilitated social contact, social networking, and information distribution (Wellman and Gulia 1999). However, in private communications with family and close friends, e-mail has increased the amount of contact people have, but has not replaced the telephone or face-to-face meetings. People sometimes e-mail even to those they see daily. But they do not replace their visits with e-mail. This suggests that people are missing something when e-mailing to their close others. Perhaps it is the experience of seeing another's face, or hearing another's voice. It remains to be seen whether voice- or video-enhanced e-mail will become accepted as a face-to-face surrogate.

Usenet. Usenet, often called the Internet news facility, is a giant messaging system through which loosely organized thematic discussion takes place on-line. Worldwide, millions of users linked to hundreds of thousands of computer sites write messages that they post to one of more than 30,000 topical newsgroups. These posts are then distributed by Usenet-serving computers to Usenet users. Usenet began in 1979 as a mail-drop messaging alternative to the then-exclusive ARPAnet (see earlier) but evolved into a broadcast-based medium on the Internet.

Usenet topical areas or newsgroups vary by seriousness, from the highly focused to the totally whimsical. Newsgroups with names like "sci.archaeology" or "comp.lang.c++" tend to be largely topic-oriented, while many others have no real purpose other than to offer forums for freewheeling electronic banter and disreputable, nuisance advertising. Newsgroups are loosely organized and vary considerably in their scope and traffic. There are newsgroups offering social support to the ill and grieving and newsgroups offering sexual information to the naive and inexperienced. Information on starting newsgroups is available in the newsgroup news.groups.

Users are not required to wade through thousands of newsgroups to find messages of interest. Most Web browsers now have news-reading functions, or specialized programs are available for this purpose. People typically subscribe to selected newsgroups that they want to examine regularly, so that when they go on-line they will see these 10 or 30 or 200 newsgroups, not 30,000. Messages posted to Usenet are organized in discussion threads, that is, messages related by reference to the same initial post or topic. Users may skip some threads on their subscribed newsgroups, reading only those threads of personal interest.

Usenet has a character similar to that of e-mail–based listservs, although its explicitly public nature gives it a somewhat different feel. Usenet newsgroups historically predate listservs, so that much of netiquette evolved from these public discussion forums. Admonitions against spam originated on Usenet, as did the tendency for people to flame norm violators and discussion rivals. Flaming involves posting a hostile and insulting message to the group, intended to shame the author of a prior post. Flaming may have had its origin in a puerile effort to enforce group norms, but it is just as often a deliberate attempt to violate them for shock value or amusement. A deliberate attempt to provoke a hostile response on Usenet is called trolling; trolling/flaming battles dominate some newsgroups.

Usenet norms are discussed and described in newsgroups devoted to this topic, and summaries are posted in news.announce.newsusers. Additionally, most newsgroups have a document called the Frequently Asked Questions list (the FAQ) that deals with local norms and standards. Beyond these formal statements, something not unlike a community character emerges and is maintained by regular participants in some newsgroups over time. New users, seeking to fit in there, need to go through a process of socialization first, usually by lurking and observing. Other newsgroups, however, are anarchic, and still others are abandoned and ignored.

Research has suggested that newsgroups provide a setting intermediate between the public and the private where stigmatized social identities can be established and supported. For example, McKenna and Bargh (1998) found that homosexuals who had never made their sexual orientation public found the courage to do so through social support on Usenet. In another domain, however, Mickelson (1997) found that mediated social support on Usenet was less helpful to parents of attention-deficit/hyperactive children than face-to-face support in therapy groups. Researchers may investigate other socially unacceptable phenomena by identifying populations and soliciting volunteers on Usenet. Moreover, the messages posted to newsgroups are considered public behavior. As such, they offer a rich resource for social researchers. There is at least one important possible problem: Usenet users may be deceiving others in their self-presentations and in their messages. However, this problem permeates all self-report research and is not specific to Internet phenomena.

Chat. Computer chat evolved from grassroots networking attempts somewhat oblique to the development of the Internet. Chat was initially a feature of old-fashioned local bulletin-board systems (BBS), in which a system operator, or sysop, with (usually) a DOS PC allowed a dozen or so outside parties to dial in with modems and read Usenet-like delayed messages, or to communicate with each other in real time, by typing messages that appeared on the screen with labels indicating from whom they came. Some of the early national time-sharing services such as Compuserve offered this feature, too, often with a name like "CB simulator," indicating the metaphor of the period,

citizen-band radio (CB). The idea was that people who were basically strangers would adopt "handles" (later called screen names) that concealed actual identity while advertising proclivities, and that these strangers would engage in streams of banter like CB radio operators out on the highway.

With the advent of mass-marketed national services such as AOL, Microsoft Network, and the like, chat facilities—now organized into topical areas or chat rooms—became one of the principal attractions. Chat and chat metaphors soon became second only to the World Wide Web as the public image of the Internet. Most users access chat facilities through commercial providers where it is implemented on private servers. There are also pure peer-to-peer Internet chat programs, such as Internet Relay Chat (IRC), that don't require a host chat provider. Participation in IRC and related free-floating chat is probably dwarfed by use of AOL and similar commercial services.

Like Usenet, topical options in chat are numerous and variously populated. Users interact in real-time with minimal constraints. As with Usenet, the degree of group norm enforcement in chat rooms varies from high to nonexistent. On commercial providers' chat facilities, broad norms of conduct often are officially enforced by staff members and user volunteers. Other hand-me-downs from Usenet were adapted to the constraints of chat. For example, the chat equivalents of Usenet's emoticons are one-letter abbreviations in angle brackets, like <g> for grin. Apparently, these are both easier to type and to parse than graphic emoticons when one is engaged in chat activity.

With the emergence of chat came a wave of real-life chatter about the development of close relationships between people who met on the Internet. People arranged marriages to others they had never met face-to-face but with whom they had chatted endlessly. The self-disclosure and narrow scope of interactions, as well as the sheer number of encounters, provided a fertile breeding ground for social relationships. Many marriages and friendships founded there have endured, while others have dissolved. While the surge of new relationships and the awe of onlookers have stabilized, chat shows no signs of losing popularity.

Another chat phenomenon, cybersex, involves graphic verbal descriptions of sex acts, exchanged in real time by couples and groups. It is the Internet equivalent of a graphic romance novel, except it is interactive and participatory. Participants may self-stimulate while generating messages to other users. Touted as an opportunity to free the libido from social restriction and personal inhibition, users may engage in unusual acts with minimal personal risk. Cybersex has been controversial. Like arguments over pornography in print, issues of access and censorship remain unsettled as we enter the twenty-first century.

Research on chat has focused primarily on two aspects of chat: the effect of anonymity in chat rooms on the negotiation of social identity (Turkle 1995); and the development of community among interacting users (Wellman and Gulia 1999). Most of this research has involved qualitative analysis or sometimes merely impressionistic characterization of chat activity. Many case studies have been conducted that describe activity in novel chat rooms or the chat experiences of particular individuals. Like Usenet, some chat is public behavior that is ripe for empirical study.

Chat is engaging, just as conversation with similar others is engaging in face-to-face interactions. But with chat, users hear all the conversations in the room, not only their own. Moreover, self-presentations can be well controlled to avoid sharing unflattering information. For these reasons, some people become obsessed with chat activity and seem to develop a dependency on this type of social contact. Others, particularly those who are homebound, have found fulfillment of their social needs through chat. Chat seems to attract a different type of user, relative to Usenet. The chat user seeks the interaction, perhaps more than the information available from topical discussion. Usenet users may seek the information and prefer not to be distracted by the interaction.

Multi-User Domains (MUDs). In the late 1970s and early 1980s, as the Net was still in its infancy, the fantasy role-playing game of Dungeons and Dragons swept through high schools and colleges. MUDs (Multi-User Domains or Multi-User Dungeons) originated as electronic platforms for similar fantasy games. They have become more elaborate and more free of goal-based game character as they have grown in popularity. They are based on different kinds of software (specified by names

such as MUSE, MOO, or MUSH) that can be accessed through the Internet.

Users, known as players, join MUDs through a command that connects their computer to the computer running the game program. Connection gives players access to a shared database of rooms, exits, and other virtual objects, which are created and manipulated through simple commands. Players create a character to play (called an avatar) by giving the character a name and a description, and enter rooms. Players interact with each other using simple commands such as "say" to talk to others in the room, "whisper" to talk to specific others, or "emote" for nonverbal expressions. Avatars grow and develop through interaction and game experience.

While some MUDs have graphical interfaces that allow characters and objects to be represented by icons, most interfaces so far have been textual. MUDs require the player's imagination to create the objects, the actions, and the outcomes of the process. There is no necessary goal, and rules can be fluid. The interactions are the thing of interest. The Usenet news group rec.games.mud periodically lists Internet-accessible MUDs with their complete network addresses.

There has been tremendous interest in MUDs because they are the most unusual modality on the Internet, most different from RL, that is, real life. Avid players remain connected for days, cycling between RL and several different MUDs. Players may be especially susceptible to Internet dependency as some are drawn deeper into the fantasy world of the MUDs. There, identity is self-described and under the complete control of the player. One may be whoever one wishes to be. And actions are free of RL consequences, so freedom is perfected in the MUDs. Finally, anonymity is complete, with no means available to identify players in RL. These features allow MUDs to offer a utopian existence in a virtual world that is forever changing and changeable.

Researchers interested in the effects of simulation and role play on the development of identity are flocking to MUDs to investigate. Researchers interested in the effect of special types of relationships, or exposure to violence, on the family are also observing MUDs. And researchers interested in Internet dependence are focused on MUDs as well (e.g. Turkle 1995).

While interesting and entertaining environments, it may be premature to generalize findings based on observations of MUDs to other types of Internet experience. Although MUDs are anonymous, as are some chats, most Internet activity is identifiable and public. Although MUDs, and some chats, are user-created and malleable fantasy forums, most Internet activity is quite constrained both by norms and technical requirements, as well as considerations of cost and practicality. MUDs will likely continue to appeal to certain subpopulations, but they are not expected to become primary activities of Internet users. In fact, the trend at the turn of the century suggests that traditional games are becoming available as network software that can be shared and played interactively with others (Monopoly, bridge, Risk, etc.). They are appealing to a broad audience, both young and old. These games involve no avatars and no explicit fantasies about social identity. It is too early to tell whether they will compete effectively with MUDs for player time in RL.

World Wide Web (WWW). E-mail, Usenet, and chat facilities are to some extent immediate and ephemeral. They depend on user activity to generate their subject matter, and they require a constant stream—in the case of chat, a stream in real time. Other Internet-based facilities arose in an attempt to provide access to more fixed corpora of text: public-domain literature, programs, documents, and so forth.

Information protocols were an attempt to link data-storage facilities and user software to make Internet-based information search and retrieval convenient. A rudimentary form was File Transfer Protocol or FTP. FTP allowed external users to go to a foreign computer—if they knew where it was, what they were looking for, and how to sign on—and retrieve some of the files to which they were given access. Gopher, another information protocol, was similar in that it put selected parts of a computer file directory on the Net in a form suitable for browsing. A network of cooperating Gopher servers built a large-scale index of their total contents that was available as an entry point. Wide-Area Information Service (WAIS) was a more industrial-strength and business-oriented approach to the problem.

Gopher, WAIS, and to a significant extent most of the rest of the Internet have been superceded by World Wide Web, a generalized hypertext facility that has submodalities corresponding to most other computer communication tasks. The idea of hypertext had been around since the 1960s—a computer-driven book with interconnected parts. Users could browse the hyperbook by following the linkages. Hypertext had been implemented on single computers or networks in various ways in the 1970s and 1980s. In 1990, at the European high-energy physics lab CERN (Conseil Européen pour la Recherche Nucléaire, Council for European Nuclear Research), Tim Berners-Lee developed a method of doing this over the Internet, which he called World Wide Web. WWW, or the Web as it is more often called, uses coded tags and descriptors (e.g. URLs, HTTP, HTML) to specify dynamic behaviors on a user's computer screen when links are invoked. This selection opens a file or otherwise triggers an event, spilling information to the user's screen.

WWW caught on explosively when inexpensive ISP access and Web service became widely available. Many individuals established WWW sites to describe their personal lives, their work, families, friends, and even their pets. For academics, Web sites typically described professional interests. Many course materials were posted to Web sites where students could retrieve them at any time. Businesses posted their personnel directories, and cities posted their public officials. Cinemas posted their playing times. It became a kind of instant, paperless desktop publishing mixed with features of a home broadcasting studio.

WWW is not socially interactive in the sense that e-mail or Usenet are interactive. Instead, interaction is scripted and restricted to some fixed set of user actions, somewhat like a video game. But the coupling of WWW with database applications and complicated scripting languages gave it a dynamic feel. Animations, sounds, and other types of sensory stimulus contribute to this feeling, and these frills will become the norm with Internet 2.

While mainstream business, institutions, and interest groups have WWW sites describing themselves, so do deviant interests. Because interaction is controlled by the Webmasters, criticism for deviance can be avoided. Militant and extremists groups, pornographers, and political interests abound and freely argue their unpopular opinions on WWW. Issues of censorship and access restrictions, particularly for children, are largely unsettled.

Information is located on the Web by search engines that use logical operations to specify criteria for matching against hypertext found on registered servers. Different search engines, such as Yahoo or AltaVista, work with different subsets of WWW sites, so search results vary. Webmasters link together related sites and improve their odds of appearing in the search results of interested users. And respectable information is very prevalent, although sometimes difficult to distinguish from the propaganda. WWW does not provide a reference librarian or tour guide, and the only requirement to post information is access to a Web-serving computer. For this reason, educators were encouraged to emphasize strategies for evaluating source credibility and information integrity in their curricula, and researchers are scrambling to understand how people may effectively discern valid information.

Professionals already disseminate their research results and theories on WWW. Many electronic journals are available only on-line; some print journals are also publish electronically. Many researchers post their own work to a personal Web page for others to easily access and reference. However, publishing a work on the Web may interfere with journals' claims to copyright on the same material, so many professional organizations are discouraging the posting of research papers prior to mainstream publication. Still, post-print abstracts and full-text articles are available in on-line databases and libraries. This wealth of information has made literature searching simpler and more useful than ever before.

Researchers have also established Web sites for data collections for studies of almost everything imaginable. Research materials (e.g., questionnaires, stimuli) are posted to a site accessed by a code provided by researchers to participants. Some studies simply recruit all comers to participation. Some research sites are scripted, so that the user follows a specified sequence of activities. Others require relatively few and simple actions. Participants prefer the convenience of WWW administrations to face-to-face meetings with researchers. But researchers cannot verify that participants are who they say they are, and some control over the situation is lost. Early comparisons of pencil-and-paper questionnaires to WWW questionnaires found no differences in responding due to administrative mediums for short, self-report data where sampling was controlled (Kardas and Milford 1996).

WWW as a platform for propaganda, commerce, and entertainment has not been lost on the public. In fact, many people are betting large sums of money in development and investment that WWW is revolutionary. Already, users can read about a new vocalist, find her latest recording, listen to it, buy it, and order tickets to her upcoming concert—all accomplished in a few minutes without leaving home or waiting in lines! For many users, WWW has replaced their telephone books, mail-order catalogues, newspapers, and libraries, as all of this information is easily accessed on the Web.

Since live audio, live video, live telephone transmissions, and similarly active content can be transmitted and manipulated inside WWW, on the Internet, we would seem to have arrived at a stage at which function does not necessarily follow the network form. The old Internet, with text-based messaging and 48-hour relay turnarounds, seems hopelessly outdated, even quaint. What we've reached seems to be a stage of pure mediation: The Internet, through the mechanism of WWW, has the capacity to be a conduit for nearly any form of information, limited only by the available network bandwidth, transmission speed, and user patience. The extent to which the social conduct of life on the Net carries traces of its ancestry remains to be seen.

REFERENCES

Kardas, E. P., and T. M. Milford 1996 *Using the Internet for Social Science Research and Practice.* New York: Wadsworth.

King, J., R. E. Grinter, and J. M. Pickering 1997 "The Rise and Fall of Netville: The Saga of a Cyberspace Construction Boomtown in the Great Divide." In S. Kiesler, ed., *Culture of the Internet.* Mahwah, N.J.: Erlbaum.

Kraut, R., M. Patterson, V. Lundmark, S. Kiesler, T. Mukophadhyay, and W. Scherlis 1998 "Internet Paradox: A Social Technology that Reduces Social Involvement and Psychological Well-Being?" *American Psychologist* 53:1017–1031.

McKenna, K. Y. A., and J. A. Bargh 1998 "Coming Out in the Age of the Internet: Identity 'Demarginalization'

Through Virtual Group Participation." *Journal of Personality and Social Psychology* 75:681–694.

Mickelson, K. D. 1997 "Seeking Social Support: Parents in Electronic Support Groups." In S. Kiesler, ed., *Culture of the Internet*. Mahwah, N.J.: Erlbaum.

Rheingold, H. 1993 *The Virtual Community*. New York: HarperCollins.

Stoll, C. 1995 *Silicon Snake Oil: Second Thoughts on the Information Highway*. New York: Doubleday.

Turkle, S. 1995 *Life on the Screen*. New York: Simon-Schuster.

Wellman, B., and M. Gulia 1999 "Net-Surfers Don't Ride Alone: Virtual Communities as Communities." In B. Wellman, ed., *Networks in the Global Village*. Oxford, England: Westview.

Diana Odom Gunn
Christopher W. Gunn

INTERPERSONAL ATTRACTION

Everyone meets many people. With some, there is a natural fit; with other, there isn't. Liking a person is quite different from liking chocolate or liking to ski. Liking someone implies feelings of warmth, intimacy, and consideration and a desire to spend time together. Interpersonal attraction plays a large part in the formation of all relationships except those into which a person is born, that is, all nonascriptive relationships. Everyone uses tactics that are expected to recruit potential partners; the specific tactics used in presenting oneself, as well as the characteristics an individual looks for in others, will vary depending on whether what is sought is friendship or love or a good working partner (McCall 1974). In earlier studies, questions of affiliation were confused with questions of attraction. You may be attracted to many people, but only those who are available in terms of physical proximity and who are defined as appropriate by social norms will actually become interaction partners (Berscheid and Reis 1998, p.204).

Even though liking someone is based on many factors that can't always be defined, a person does know, upon meeting someone, whether he or she is in fact liked. This perceived liking in turn draws us toward the other (Sprecher and Hatfield 1992).

Men and women operate differently in the area of choosing people as being attractive. For example, men are more inclined to reject a person who disagrees with them than are women and more likely to choose the same type of person as a friend and as a marriage partner (Lindzay and Aronson 1969).

First impressions don't necessarily last. Nisbett, reanalyzing Newcomb's data in 1989, found that people's liking of other people after sixteen weeks' acquaintance was not predicted very well by their initial liking of these others after one week's acquaintance (Nisbett and Smith 1989,p.72)

THEORETICAL EXPLANATIONS OF INTERPERSONAL ATTRACTION

Homans, working from the perspective of exchange theory, states that people consider the rewards versus the costs of any potential relationship (Lindzay and Aronson 1969) and are attracted to those people who provide the most reward at the least cost. From this perspective, the ideal relationship is one in which both participants have equal costs and rewards, so that neither feels cheated or exploited. Newcomb asserts that frequency of interaction is an important determinant of attraction, a view known as the *propinquity perspective*. The basic assumption is that the more frequently one interacts with others, the more attractive they become. It is expected that frequency of interaction will lead to increasing similarity of beliefs and values and that this *assumed similarity* will in turn lead to increased attraction. This perspective ignores the possibility that getting to know a person better may actually reveal many differences (Lindzay and Aronson 1969). Despite the idea's appeal to common sense, there is little evidence of increasing reciprocity of interpersonal attraction over time (Kenny and LaVoie 1982).

People do prefer those who are similar in background, interests, and values. They want to talk about things that interest them and do things familiar to them. A person who can provide social support by having similar beliefs and values is a likely potential friend. Despite the folk wisdom that opposites attract, similarity is more powerful than complementarity. The exceptions are those with strong needs on either end of the dominance–submission continuum or the nurturance-succorance continuum (Argyle 1969, p. 213); when strong needs exist in these areas, complementarity is more powerful.

TRYING TO ATTRACT OTHERS

Though different factors come into play when one is evaluating someone as a potential friend or a potential work partner or a potential romantic partner, there seem to be inferred qualities that make a stranger appear to be likable or not likable. One study found that when videotapes of women were shown to males and females to judge, those most often chosen were apt to be described as sociable, cheerful, and positive emotionally; the underchosen were more apt to be described as negative and moody (Hewitt and Goldman 1982).

In a culture, like the United States, that values openness, psychological awareness, and emotional vulnerability, self-disclosure increases likability. Those who disclose little are less apt to be found attractive by others (Montgomery 1986).

Revealing yourself to another person is a sign that you like and trust them. It also signals that you trust them to respond appropriately. There seem to be three specific links between self-disclosure and attraction and likeability: (1) the more you disclose about yourself, the more you are liked; (2) people disclose more to those they initially like; and (3) the very act of disclosing makes you like the person to whom you disclosed (Collins and Miller 1994). A modern form of self-presentation that tells quite a bit about what people think makes them appear attractive is the personal ad. No longer are these dismissed as being for the desperate; rather, they are seen as just another way to introduce oneself. A study of the responses to different sets of physical characteristics referred to in ads showed that tall men and thin women received the greatest number of responses (Lynn and Shurgot 1984). In these ads it can also be seen that people present themselves as happy, able, capable, and very successful. It is interesting to note that the richer a man claims to be, the younger, taller, and prettier a woman he wants. The younger and prettier a woman presents herself as being, the more successful a man she wishes to meet.

FORMING RELATIONSHIPS

First meetings proceed cautiously. In every cultural group there are conventions about how long the preliminaries must last. These conventions vary depending upon the age and gender of the participants, as well as where the meeting takes place. The goals of the encounter determine the interpersonal attraction tactics used. For example, when characteristics of potential dating partners were varied along two dimensions, physical attractiveness and personality desirability, undergraduate males chose physical attractiveness as the deciding variable (Glick 1985). Therefore, a female hoping for a date would find that increasing physical attractiveness would be more effective than showing what a nice personality she had. Not all inititial encounters develop into relationships. In general, whether the individual develops an expectation that future encounters will be rewarding is critical to the continuation of relationship. Several studies have shown that perceiving the relationship as being better than others' relationships facilitates commitment to and satisfaction with the relationship (Rusbult et al. 1996).

Relationship satisfaction also positively correlates with evaluating your partner more positively than he or she evaluates self. Such evaluations are also positively related to more effectively resolving any conflicts that occur and thus to continuation of the relationship (Murray and Holmes 1996).

The goals of the encounter determine the interpersonal attraction tactics used. For example, when characteristics of potential dating partners were varied along two dimensions, physical attractiveness and personality desirability, undergraduate males chose physical attractiveness as the deciding variable (Glick 1985). Therefore, a female hoping for a date would find that increasing physical attractiveness would be more effective than showing what a nice personality she had.

PLAYING AND WORKING TOGETHER

Competition has an interesting relationship with interpersonal attraction. Rees found that during intragroup competition, football players reported the most liking and respect for those who played their own position yet outperformed them (Rees and Segal 1984). Riskin also found that males, when given background data indicating both the degree of competitiveness and the degree of work mastery in target males, rated the most competitive as most attractive, as long as they were also seen as having ability. In addition, these competitive males were assumed by the male subjects to be more attractive to women (Riskin and Wilson 1982). Numerous studies have shown that emergent leaders are given high interpersonal-attraction ratings by both sexes.

The workplace provides a setting where qualities of competitiveness, ability, and leadership are displayed. It might be assumed that this leads to the formation of romantic attachments. Though this does in fact occur, the work setting also provides for additional complexity in the handling of personal attraction. Attraction and intimacy must be seen in the context of outsiders' view of the relationship. Attempts must be made to balance the demands of the job and those of the relationship. Role relationships within the workplace are expected to contain a degree of distance that is at odds with the demands of "getting closer." Despite these problems, people do get romantically involved with co-workers. One study of 295 adults (average age: thirty-two) revealed that 84 had been involved in a romantic relationship with someone at work and 123 had been aware of a romance in their workplace. Such relationships are more likely to occur in less formal organizations, especially those that are very small or very large. The person most likely to enter into such a relationship is a female who is young, new, and of low rank (Dillard and Witteman 1985, p. 113).

FRIENDSHIP

Being perceived as friendly, pleasant, polite, and easy to talk to increases a person's ability to attract potential friends. If in addition similar values, interests, and backgrounds are present, the likelihood of friendship is even greater (Johnson 1989). In ongoing relationships, friendship has nothing to do with the participants' rating of each other's physical appearance. Nevertheless, at the initial meeting stage a person judged as being too physically attractive will be avoided. In one study, sixty undergraduate males were shown a male target population (previously rated from 1 to 5 by a male and female sample) and were asked who among this group they would like to meet. The most attractive were chosen less frequently; they were judged to be more egocentric and less kind. It was the moderately attractive who were seen as being the type of person most of the subjects would like

to meet. Explaining these findings in terms of exchange theory, one would say that most people rate themselves as bringing moderate attractiveness to a relationship and feel that extreme attractiveness throws off the equality (Gailucci 1984).

Though it is often assumed that young people do not see older people as potential friends, a review of forty research reports reveals that perceived agreement in attitudes tends to neutralize young adults' general perception of older adults as unattractive. Elders may perceive young people as attractive or unattractive, but they still prefer to associate with individuals who are middle-aged or older (Webb et al. 1989).

SEXUAL ATTRACTION AND ROMANTIC RELATIONSHIPS

While males and females alike differ in their ability to distinguish between friendly and sexually interested behavior, males are more likely to see sexual intent where females see only friendly behavior. When shown videotapes of five couples, each showing a male and a female behaving in either a friendly or a sexually interested way, males consistently saw more sexual intent (Shotland and Craig 1988).

Men and women also differ as to the relative importance of physical features and personal qualities in determining the choice of romantic partners. Even though both sexes rated personal qualities as being more important than physical features, males placed greater emphasis on the physical than did women (Nevid 1984). Despite this, there seems to be a point at which attempting to increase physical appeal by dressing to reveal the body has a negative effect on one's appeal as a marital partner. Hill reports that when male and female models wore very tight clothes that displayed a great deal of skin, they were rated as being very attractive as potential sex partners but their marital potential was lowered. High-status dressing had the opposite effect for both males and females: Ratings of physical, dating, sexual, and marital attractiveness all increased as the status of clothing increased (Hill et al. 1987).

A shared sense of humor is another important component of loving and liking. When a humor test comprising cartoons, comic strips, and jokes was given to thirty college couples, along with a test that measured how much the partners loved and liked each other, a strong correlation between shared humor and a predisposition to marry was found (Murstein and Brust 1985). It can probably be assumed that the shared humor comes before the relationship, as well as serving as a factor that enhances it. How people feel about their romance at any given time tends to cause them to rewrite history. For example: When people involved in romantic relationships were asked, once a year for four years, to describe how the relationship had changed during the past year, it was found that current feelings had more to do with the ratings that actual changes (Berscheid and Reis 1998, p. 211).

(SEE ALSO: *Courtship: Exchange Theory; Love; Mate Selection Theories; Personal Relationships; Social Psychology*)

REFERENCES

Argyle, Michael 1969 *Social Interaction*. Chicago: Aldine.

Berscheid, Ellen, and Harry T. Reis 1998 "Attraction and Close Relationships." In D.T. Gilbert et. al., eds., *The Handbook of Social Psychology*, 4th ed. New York:McGraw-Hill.

Collins. N. L., and L. C. Miller 1994 "Self-Disclose and Liking: A Meta-Analytic Review." *Psychological Bulletin* 116, 457–475.

Dillard, James P., and Hal Witteman 1985 "Romantic Relationships at Work: Organizational and Personal Influences." *Human Communication Research* 12:99–116.

Gailucci, N. 1984 "Effects of Men's Physical Attractiveness on Interpersonal Attraction." *Psychological Reports* 55:935–938.

Glick, Peter 1985 "Orientations Toward Relationships: Choosing a Situation in Which to Begin a Relationship." *Journal of Experimental Social Psychology* 21:544–562.

Hewitt, J., and Morton Goldman 1982 "Traits Attributed to Over- and Under-Chosen Women." *Psychological Reports* 5:431–439.

Hill, Elizabeth, Elaine Nocks, and Lucinda Gardner 1987 "Physical Attractiveness: Manipulation by Physique and Status Displays." *Ethnology and Sociobiology* 8:143–154.

Johnson, Martin R. 1989 "Variables Associated with Friendship in an Adult Population." *Journal of Social Psychology* 129:379–390.

Kenny, David A., and Lawrence LaVoie 1982 "Reciprocity of Interpersonal Attraction: A Confirmed Hypothesis." *Social Psychology Quarterly* 45:54–58.

Lindzay, Gardner, and Elliot Aronson 1969 *The Handbook of Social Psychology*, Vol. 3. Reading, Mass.: Addison-Wesley.

Lynn, Michael, and Barbara A. Shurgot 1984 "Responses to Lonely Hearts Advertisements: Effects of Reported Physical Attractiveness, Physique, and Coloration." *Personality and Social Psychology Bulletin* 10:349–357.

McCall, George J. 1974 "A Symbolic Interactionist Approach to Attraction." In T. L. Huston, ed., *Foundation of Interpersonal Attraction*. New York: Academic Press.

Montgomery, Barbara 1986 "Interpersonal Attraction as a Function of Open Communication and Gender." *Communication Research Reports* 3:140–145.

Murstein, Bernard I., and Robert G. Brust 1985 "Humor and Interpersonal Attraction. *Journal of Personality Assessment* 49:637–640.

Murray, S. L., and J. G. Holmes 1996 "The Construction of Relationship Realities." In G. Fletcher and J. Fittness, eds., *Knowledge Structures in Close Relationships: A Social Psychological Approach*. Mahwah, N.J.: Erlbaum.

Nevid, Jeffrey F. 1984 "Sex Differences in Factors of Romantic Attraction." *Sex-Roles* 11:401–411.

Nisbett, Richard E., and Michael Smith 1989 "Predicting Interpersonal Attraction from Small Samples: A Re-Analysis of Newcomb's Acquaintance Study." *Social Cognition* 7:67–73.

Rees, C. Roger, and Mady-Wechsler Segal 1984 "Intragroup Competition, Equity and Interpersonal Attraction." *Social Psychology Quarterly* 47:328–336.

Riskin, John, and David Wilson 1982 "Interpersonal Attraction for the Competitive Person: Unscrambling the Competition Paradox." *Journal of Applied Social Psychology* 12:444–452.

Rusbult, C.E. et. al. 1996 "An Interdependence Analysis of Accommodation Processes." In G. Fletcher and J. Fittness, eds., *Knowledge Structures in Close Relationships: A Social Psychological Approach*. Mahwah, N.J.: Erlbaum.

Shotland, R., and Jane Craig 1988 "Can Men and Women Differentiate Between Friendly and Sexually Interested Behavior?" *Social Psychology Quarterly* 51:66–73.

Sprecher, Susan, and Elaine Hatfield 1992 "Self-Esteem and Romantic Attraction: Four Experiments." *Recherches de Psychologie Sociale* 4:61–81.

Webb, Lynn, Judith Delaney, and Lorraine Young 1989 "Age, Interpersonal Attraction and Social Interaction: A Review and Assessment." *Research on Aging* 11:107–123.

ARDYTH STIMSON

INTERPERSONAL CONFLICT RESOLUTION

Most of us understand conflict as a negative aspect of social interactions and therefore are inclined to avoid it if possible. Yet theorists contend that conflict is an inevitable part of human association and, to some extent, a necessary one (Straus 1979). In fact, conflict, either intrapsychic or interpersonal, is a pivotal concept in theories of human development (Shantz 1987). Even with its acknowledged importance in human development, however, research on conflict has been relatively recent. This may perhaps have been due to the perception of conflict as largely a negative occurrence and the equating of conflict with aggression (Shantz 1996). If interpersonal conflict is not aggression, what is it? How do individuals respond to interpersonal conflict? What is our theoretical understanding of individual behavior in interpersonal conflict, and what are the factors that are related to how individuals resolve conflicts with others? This entry addresses the above questions with a focus on childhood and adolescence. The term *conflict* will refer to interpersonal conflict unless otherwise stated.

WHAT IS CONFLICT?

Interpersonal conflict is an event that occurs between two individuals in the course of interactions. Thus, it requires at least two individuals for conflict to occur; conflict is not an attribute of a single individual (Shantz 1987). According to conflict theory, which draws from symbolic interactionism, exchange theory, and systems theory, conflict is defined as "a confrontation between individuals, or groups, over scarce resources, controversial means, incompatible goals, or combinations of these" (Sprey 1979, p. 134). From the sociolinguistic perspective, conflict is a "social activity, created and conducted primarily by means of talking" (Garvey and Shantz 1992, p. 93). Thus, the main elements of conflict are an interactional context, which is at least dyadic, and the presence of behavioral opposition (Joshi 1997).

An important condition for sustained interactions is the maintenance of interpersonal equilibrium. Conflict causes disequilibrium, and the individuals involved in the conflict can use different ways to move the interactions to an equilibrium. These different ways are conflict resolution strategies and can be defined as "sets of behaviors that seem to subserve a social goal. They may be either conscious, planned means to forseeable ends (as these terms usually connote), or unconscious, automatic or habitual behaviors that have the effect of subserving goals" (Shantz 1987, p. 289).

THEORETICAL MODELS RELATED TO INTERPERSONAL CONFLICT RESOLUTION

There are two theoretical models that attempt to explain how individuals respond in conflict situations—the social information processing model and the interpersonal negotiation skills model. The social information processing model focuses on the intraindividual cognitive processes that take place in social situations. The INS model, on the other hand, describes the developmental changes in conflict resolution strategies that co-occur with cognitive changes.

Social Information Processing. According to the social information processing model (Dodge et al. 1986), individuals go through a set of steps in which they process social information contained in social situations. However, the person is generally not aware of these information-processing steps. The individual must respond skillfully at every step to successfully negotiate the situation. The first step is to encode the social cues in the situation, which means that the person assesses the situation in terms of what exactly is happening. The next step is to interpret the cues in the light of previous knowledge, thus forming mental representations of the cues. Thus, the understanding of the situation—why is this conflict happening? why is the other person behaving in this way?—is constructed. Once the cues are interpreted, the individual must generate possible ways of responding to the situation, which in conflict situations would be conflict resolution strategies. This is followed by the choice of an appropriate response, and finally the individual must enact the chosen response behaviorally.

A revision of the model (Crick and Dodge 1994) highlighted the role of arousal regulation, especially between the steps of cue interpretation and generation of strategies. This means that the emotions experienced by the individual may influence the goals and responses generated, and eventually chosen. Thus, the social information processing model focuses on the intrapersonal processes that underlie interpersonal conflict resolution.

Interpersonal Negotiation Strategies Model. The interpersonal negotiation strategies (INS) model (Selman and Demorest 1984; Yeats et al. 1990) draws from both the cognitive-developmental and the information-processing perspectives. It predicts that cognitive development is accompanied by an increased sophistication in the ability to coordinate the social perspective of the self and the other. Three factors implicated in the choice of an interpersonal negotiation strategy determine the developmental level of the strategy—the understanding of the self's and the other's perspective, the purpose of the strategy, and the affective control, or the way in which individuals understand and balance the affective disequilibrium. A fourth factor, the orientation, determines the type of strategy that the individual uses, namely, self-transforming or other-transforming. Children move through four developmental levels of social perspective taking—undifferentiated/egocentric, differentiated/subjective, self-reflective/reciprocal, and third-person/mutual. At the undifferentiated/egocentric level, children are not able to differentiate between the thoughts and feelings of self and the other. Their strategies, therefore, tend to be unreflective and impulsive, using either force or obedience. The differentiated/subjective level is characterized by the recognition that different persons have different perspectives on the situation. However, children understand the perspectives only from one person's point of view. The next level, called the self-reflective/reciprocal level, is the level at which a child is able to mentally step outside the self and take the other person's perspective. Children also understand that people's actions do not have to reflect their thoughts and feelings. Finally, at the third-person/mutual level, the individual is truly able to take a third-person perspective and understand the situation in terms of mutual goals.

One of the strengths of this model is that it views interpersonal negotiation strategies in an interpersonal context, juxtaposing the understanding of the self in relation to the other. However, the focus remains on the individual, not on the interpersonal process of conflict resolution.

FACTORS RELATED TO CONFLICT RESOLUTION STRATEGIES

Age. There appear to be developmental trends in the use of certain conflict resolution strategies. In the case of aggression as a strategy, the evidence is somewhat contradictory, especially during preschool years. Some findings indicate the use of aggression (Dawe 1934), while others indicate a predominant use of insistence and rare use of aggression (Laursen and Hartup 1989). Overall, the use of power assertion decreases with age and the use of compromise increases with age. The use of compromise, however, may be restricted to hypothetical situations (Laursen and Collins 1994). Thus, adolescents may offer compromise as a solution to hypothetical situations but may report using disengagement as often as compromise (Collins and Laursen 1992). For example, a study of conflict occurring in family talk (Vuchinich 1990) revealed that adolescents are more likely to use standoff (disengagement from the conflict) or withdrawal (physical disengagement from the situation). The use of disengagement may be evident as early as middle childhood (Joshi 1997). Also, the use of compromise may emerge during middle childhood (Joshi 1998). Longitudinal studies are needed to confirm developmental patterns evinced by cross-sectional studies.

Gender. The clearest gender differences are in the use of aggression, with girls being less likely to use physical aggression than boys. During middle childhood, girls may be more likely to end conflicts with friends with disengagement (Joshi 1997). Using the INS framework, an investigation of adolescents reporting hard-drug use suggested that boys are more likely to use other-transforming strategies, whereas girls use both self-transforming as well as other-transforming strategies (Leadbeater et al. 1989). Overall there appear to be no clear gender differences other than in the use of aggression.

The Relationship. The relationship as the context of the conflict is another factor that influences how the conflict is resolved. Relationships that are defined by kinship norms may be considered by individuals as a "safer" context in which to disagree and argue, since there is no immediate threat of dissolution of the relationships (Berscheid 1985; Laursen 1993). Thus, adolescents may be more likely to use compromise with friends than with adult family members (Laursen and Collins 1994). Another dimension along which relationships vary is the distribution of power. Peer relationships are more egalitarian, while a hierarchy typifies parent–child relationships (Maccoby and Martin 1983). We could, therefore, hypothesize that children are more likely to use negotiation and compromise with peers than with parents. How does the resolution of conflict differ between peers and between parents and children?

CONFLICT RESOLUTION WITH PEERS

Research on conflict resolution with peers reveals some general patterns. In one of the earliest observational studies on conflict resolution, Dawe (1934) found that in naturally occurring conflicts in 2- to 5-year-olds, the use of aggression increased with age. Aggression was expressed in behaviors such as pushing, pulling, and striking. Talking during conflict also increased with age. Children resolved most conflicts themselves. When preschoolers' conversations were examined, Eisenberg and Garvey (1981) found that children used verbal strategies such as insistence and repetition, reasoning, and asking for explanations. Subsequent observations of preschoolers (Killen and Turiel 1991) indicated that in a natural setting as well as a lab setting, children ended more conflicts without active resolutions. Laursen and Hartup (1989) found somewhat similar results from their observations of preschoolers. Insistence was the most frequently used strategy, negotiation and aggression were rarely used, and most conflicts were resolved without adult intervention.

At an older age (7 years), children report using predominantly direct strategies (50 percent), such as leaving the scene of interaction, using physical force, or getting help from a third person (Shantz 1993). About 28 percent of the strategies reported were conventional, such as saying "please" or apologizing, and about 20 percent of the strategies used involved reasoning and/or compromise. As mentioned earlier, the use of compromise increases during adolescence but may be restricted to hypothetical situations.

CONFLICT BETWEEN FRIENDS AND NONFRIENDS

Children, at least until middle childhood, may not be able to understand that friendships can be both supportive and conflictual (Berndt and Perry 1986). Conflict between friends and nonfriends does appear to proceed differently, especially the strategies used to resolve the conflict. An observational study (Hartup et al. 1988) of young children (approximately 3.5 years to 5.5 years of age) revealed that the frequency with which children used disengagement strategies, such as mutual turning away, was greater with friends than with nonfriends. This resulted in different outcomes, with equality occurring with greater frequency with friends than with nonfriends. Also, conflict with friends was more intense than conflict with nonfriends.

In another study, Hartup and colleagues (1993) found that 9- and 10-year-olds showed differences in management of conflict with friends and nonfriends in a closed-field situation, that is, "a situation in which the children cannot choose with whom, what and where their interaction will occur and how long their interaction will last" (p. 446). Children in a dyad were taught conflicting versions of a board game. In this situation, friends disagreed more frequently than nonfriends, and their disagreements lasted longer. Conflict resolution per se was not a focus of the study.

Regarding conflict resolution strategies specifically, young adolescents aged 11 to 14 years showed a greater skill at generating alternatives for resolving conflicts by reacting to hypothetical situations with friends than with nonfriends (Caplan et al. 1991). Similarly, in another study investigating differences in conflict resolution strategies used with friends and acquaintances, Vespo and Caplan (1993) found that children were more likely to use conciliatory gestures with friends than with acquaintances.

At least three reasons can contribute to differences in young adolescents' conflict resolution skills with friends and nonfriends (Caplan et al.

1991). First, friendship is characterized by intimacy and tolerance. Second, children learn and practice conflict resolution in the context of friendship. Third, friendships shape young adolescents' understanding of conflict and expectations regarding outcome (p. 105).

Thus, no clear patterns emerge regarding developmental changes in conflict resolution strategies, except for a decline in the use of aggression. Perhaps individuals use a range of strategies depending on contextual factors, such as the issue of the conflict. Whether this is true is an important question that needs to be answered. Research has indicated that children who are able to resolve conflicts skillfully are more likely to be socially better adjusted (Asher et al. 1982). Theoretically, the use of compromise is considered both desirable and developmentally more sophisticated. How is it, then, that compromise is not one of the strategies frequently used until adolescence? Skillful conflict resolution may be more a matter of the using a strategy more appropriate for a particular conflict than of using a particular conflict resolution strategy.

CONFLICT RESOLUTION WITHIN THE FAMILY

The context of family relationships is a powerful influence in the development of social skills. Interactions with different family members foster the development of the ability to understand others' feelings (Dunn 1988). During the second year of life, children begin to get into conflict with their parents and siblings with increased intensity and frequency (Dunn and Slomkowski 1992). During the elementary school years, children are most likely to use assertion or insistence at the beginning of a conflict and end the conflict with submission (Joshi 1997). As noted earlier, adolescents may use standoff or withdrawal in their conflicts with parents and siblings (Vuchinich 1990). There is a need for replication of these findings to trace developmental trends, if any, in the use of conflict resolution strategies with family members.

While individuals might use different strategies to resolve conflicts in different relationships, it could be argued that conflict resolution skills learned in the family may transfer to other contexts. Every relationship is embedded in a network of relationships, and thus it must affect and be affected by other relationships (Hartup and Laursen 1991; Hinde 1981; Lewis et al. 1984). How does conflict resolution in one context relate to conflict resolution in another?

LINKAGES IN CONFLICT RESOLUTION BETWEEN CONTEXTS

Studies indicate that patterns of interactions with parents serve as models for children that they can use with peers (Parke et al. 1992). The level of conflict in the family was found to be predictive of adjustment in school (Tesser et al. 1989). Most of the research related to conflict resolution between parents and children uses parental disciplinary style as the indicator of parents' conflict resolution strategies with children. Also, these studies are conducted within the social information processing framework. Overall, the findings indicate that children who experience power-assertive styles of discipline are likely to misinterpret social cues and use ineffective conflict resolution strategies (Dodge et al. 1990; Hart et al. 1990; Weiss et al. 1992). However, these studies examine conflict resolution at a more general level, with some emphasis on aggression. When the correspondence between the conflict resolution strategies parents use with children and strategies that children use with peers is examined, some interesting findings are revealed (Joshi 1997). First, parents use different strategies depending on the issue of the conflict. Second, both children and parents use more than one strategy to resolve conflict. For example, a child may use assertion to begin with and then resort to reasoning, and if the conflict does not get resolved, eventually withdraw from the conflict. The use of multiple strategies makes the one-on-one mapping of conflict resolution strategies used in two contexts a difficult task. The one correspondence that was found was between the last strategy that mothers used with children and the last strategy that children used with peers. Specifically, children who used reasoning as the last strategy with a friend had mothers who used reasoning as a last strategy with them (Joshi 1997).

FUTURE DIRECTIONS IN RESEARCH AND THEORY

One of the features of the research and theory in the area of interpersonal conflict resolution, at least during childhood and adolescence, is that it focuses more on intraindividual processes than it does on interindividual processes. We still need more research on how individuals involved in a conflict situation influence each other's behavior. The risk of focusing on the individual lies in its inevitable outcome—that the strategy that the person uses comes to be denoted as the person's attribute, which is a stable characteristic. If we know that individuals may use different strategies in different conflict situations, and that they use a combination of strategies, then it would be erroneous to describe conflict resolution styles in terms of single strategies. Thus, the important variables that need to be examined along with conflict resolution strategies are the issue of the conflict, the relationship between the individuals, and the strategies of the other individual.

The conceptualization of interpersonal conflict resolution as a process will be better accomplished by measurement that reflects process. Therefore, interpersonal interactions must be characterized by the assessment of the behavior of one person as contingent on the behavior of the other person. This would require the development of newer models that would predict individual behavior in conflict based on the aforementioned contextual variables.

Besides achieving the goal of depicting conflict resolution with greater accuracy, the study of contextual variables will help us better understand what exactly constitutes general conflict resolution skills. This knowledge will be particularly useful in planning interventions for individuals who find interpersonal conflict situations challenging.

REFERENCES

Asher, S. R., P. D. Renshaw, and S. Heymel 1982 "Peer Relations and the Development of Social Skills." In S. G. Moore, ed., *The Young Child: Reviews of Research*, vol. 3. Washington, D.C.: National Association for the Education of Young Children.

Berndt, T. J., and T. B. Perry 1986 "Children's Perceptions of Friendships as Supportive Relationships." *Developmental Psychology* 22(5):640–648.

Berscheid, E. 1985 "Interpersonal Attraction." In G. Lindzey and E. Aronson, eds., *Handbook of Social Psychology*. New York: Random House.

Caplan, M., L. Bennetto, and R. P. Weissberg (1991). "The Role of Interpersonal Context in the Assessment of Social Problem-Solving Skills." *Journal of Applied Developmental Psychology* 12:103–114.

Collins, W. A., and B. Laursen 1992 "Conflict and Relationships During Adolescence." In C. U. Shantz and W. W. Hartup, eds., *Conflict in Child and Adolescent Development*. New York: Cambridge University Press.

Crick, N. R., and K. A. Dodge 1994 "A Review and Reformulation of Social Information-Processing Mechanisms in Children's Social Adjustment." *Psychological Bulletin* 115(1):74–101.

Dawe, H. C. 1934 "An Analysis of Two Hundred Quarrels of Preschool Children." *Child Development* 5:139–157.

Dodge, K. A., J. E. Bates, and G. Pettit 1990 "Mechanisms in the Cycle of Violence." *Science* 250(4988):1678–1683.

Dodge, K. A., G. S. Pettit, C. I. McClaskey, and M. Brown 1986 "Social Competence in Children." *Monographs of the Society for Research in Child Development*, 51 (2, serial no. 213).

Dunn, J. 1988 *The Beginnings of Social Understanding*. Cambridge, Mass.: Harvard University Press.

——, and C. Slomkowski 1992 "Conflict and the Development of Social Understanding." In C. U. Shantz and W. W. Hartup, eds., *Conflict in Child and Adolescent Development*. New York: Cambridge University Press.

Eisenberg, A. R., and C. Garvey 1981 "Children's Use of Verbal Strategies in Resolving Conflicts." *Discourse Processes* 4:149–170.

Garvey, C., and Shantz, C. U. 1992 "Conflict Talk: Approaches to Adversarial Discourse." In C. U. Shantz and W. W. Hartup, eds., *Conflict in Child and Adolescent Development*. Cambridge, U.K.: Cambridge University Press.

Hart, C. H., G. W. Ladd, and B. R. Burleson 1990 "Children's Expectations of the Outcomes of Social Strategies: Relations with Sociometric Status and Maternal Disciplinary Styles." *Child Development* 61:127–137.

Hartup, W. W., D. C. French, B. Laursen, M. K. Johnston, and J. R. Ogawa 1993 "Conflict and Friendship Relations in Middle Childhood: Behavior in a Closed-Field Situation." *Child Development* 64:445–454.

Hartup, W. W., and B. Laursen 1991. "Relationships as Developmental Contexts." In R. Cohen and A. W. Siegel, eds., *Context and Development*. Hillsdale, N.J.: Lawrence Erlbaum.

Hartup, W. W., B. Laursen, M. I. Stewart, and A. Eastenson 1988 "Conflict and the Friendship Relations of Young Children." *Child Development* 59:1590–1600.

Hinde, R. 1981 "The Bases of a Science of Interpersonal Relationships." In S. Duck and R. Gilmour, eds., *Personal Relationships: Studying Interpersonal Relationships*. London: Academic Press.

Joshi, A. 1997 *Children's Conflict Resolution Strategies with Friends: Relations to Parent–Child and Interparental Conflict Resolution Strategies*. Unpublished doctoral dissertation, Purdue University, West Lafayette, Ind.

—— 1998 "On the Brink? Some Initial Findings on the Beginnings of the Use of Compromise in Interpersonal Conflict." Poster presented at the meeting of the Society for Research on Adolescence, San Diego.

Killen, M., and E. Turiel 1991 "Conflict Resolution in Preschool Social Interactions." *Early Education and Development* 2(3):240–255.

Laursen, B. 1993 "The Perceived Impact of Conflict on Adolescent Relationships." *Merrill-Palmer Quarterly* 39(4):535–550.

——, and W. A. Collins 1994 "Interpersonal Conflict During Adolescence." *Psychological Bulletin* 155(2):197–209.

——, and W. W. Hartup 1989 "The Dynamics of Preschool Children's Conflicts." *Merrill-Palmer Quarterly* 35(3):281–297.

Leadbeater, B. J., I. Hellner, J. P. Allen, and J. L. Aber 1989 "Assessment of Interpersonal Negotiation Strategies in Youth Engaged in Problem Behaviors." *Developmental Psychology* 25(3):465–472.

Lewis, M., C. Feiring, and M. Kotsonis 1984 "The Social Network of the Young Child: A Developmental Perspective." In M. Lewis, ed., *Beyond the Dyad*. New York: Plenum Press.

Maccoby, E. E., and J. A. Martin 1983 "Socialization in the Context of the Family: Parent–Child Interaction. In P. H. Mussen (series ed.) and E. M. Hetherington (vol. ed.), *Handbook of Child Psychology: Vol. 4. Socialization, Personality, and Social Development*. New York: Wiley.

Parke, R. D., J. Cassidy, V. M. Burks, J. L. Carson, and L. Boyum, 1992 "Familial Contribution to Peer Competence Among Young Children: The Role of Interactive and Affective Processes." In R. D. Parke and G. W. Ladd, eds., *Family–Peer Relationships: Modes of Linkages*. Hillsdale, N.J.: Lawrence Erlbaum.

Selman, R. L., and A. P. Demorest 1984 "Observing Troubled Children's Interpersonal Negotiation Strategies: Implications of and for a Developmental Model." *Child Development* 55:288–304.

Shantz, C. U. 1987 "Conflicts Between children." *Child Development* 58:283–305.

—— 1993 "Children's Conflicts: Representations and Lessons Learned." In R. R. Cocking and K. A. Renninger, eds., *The Development and Meaning of Psychological Distance*. Hillsdale, N.J.: Lawrence Erlbaum.

—— (1996). "Introduction." *Merrill-Palmer Quarterly* 42(1):iii–vii.

Sprey, J. 1979 "Conflict Theory and the Study of Marriage and the Family." In W. R. Burr, R. Hill, F. I. Nye, and I. L. Reiss, eds., *Contemporary Theories About the Family*, vol. 2. New York: Free Press.

Straus, M. A. 1979 "Measuring Intrafamily Conflict and Violence: The Conflict Tactics (CT) Scales. *Journal of Marriage and the Family* 41:75–88.

Tesser, A., R. Forehand, G. Brody, and N. Long 1989 "Conflict: The Role of Calm and Angry Parent–Child Discussion in Adolescent Adjustment." *Journal of Social and Clinical Psychology* 8(3):317–330.

Vespo, J. E., and M. Caplan 1993 "Preschoolers' differential Conflict Behavior with Friends and Acquaintances." *Early Education and Development* 4(1):45–53.

Vuchinich, S. 1990 "The Sequential Organization of Closing in verbal Family Conflict." In A.D. Grimshaw, ed., *Conflict Talk: Sociolinguistic Investigations of Arguments in Conversations*. Cambridge, U.K.: Cambridge University Press.

Weiss, B., K. A. Dodge, J. E. Bates, and G. S. Pettit 1992 "Some Consequences of Early Harsh Discipline: Child Aggression and a Maladaptive Social Information Processing Style." *Child Development* 63:1321–1335.

Yeats, K. W., L. H. Schultz, and R. L. Selman 1990 "Bridging the Gaps in Child-Clinical Assessment: Toward the Application of Social-Cognitive Developmental Theory. *Clinical Psychology Review* 10:567–588.

ANUPAMA JOSHI

INTERPERSONAL POWER

In its broadest sense, interpersonal power refers to any cause of any change in the behavior of one actor, B, which can be attributed to the effect of another actor, A. It sometimes refers to the capacity to cause such change (Weber [1918] 1968), sometimes to actual use of that capacity (Dahl 1957; Simon 1953) but always to overcoming the "resistance" of B (Weber [1918] 1968), hence causing B to do something B would not otherwise do (Dahl 1957). Interpersonal power is therefore the power of one individual "over" another as opposed to an individual's power to do something, the capacity of an actor to attain some goal (as in Russell 1938). "Power over" always implies a relation between two actors rather than referring to an attribute of an actor. It is sometimes thought of as "micro" power and contrasts with "power to," which is attributed to collectives (Hawley 1963; Parsons 1963) and is thought of as "systemic" or "macro" power.

Adequate description of a power relation will typically refer to: (1) the *bases* of power (the bases of A's power over B are the resources that are possessed by A that are instrumental to the goals of B); (2) the *means* of power (the ways in which A uses these resources to change the behavior of B); (3) the *strength* of power (the costs to B if B does not comply with demands by A); (4) the *costs* of power (the costs of A of having to exercise power over B); (5) the *amount* of power (the extent to which A is able to get B to do something that B would not otherwise have done); (6) the *scope* of power (the acts with respect to which the amount of A's power over B is greater than zero); and (7) the *domain* of power (the persons over whom the amount of A's power is greater than zero). However, there is a great deal of disagreement over which of these constitute power and what kinds of bases, means, costs, and particularly compliance the word covers.

CONCEPTS OF POWER

In his work on power, Simon (1953) treats the effects rather than the causes of power and covers by the one word a whole family of concepts describing the effects of all the human causes of human conduct. Force, power, influence, authority, and manipulation all have a strong family resemblance to each other, and Dahl (1957), March (1955), and Simon (1953) have all treated them as one process. But French and Raven (1959) have pointed out important ways in which the dynamics of different kinds of power differ, and March (1966) has shown compellingly that treating them all as one unitary process leads only to a dead end.

The laws of *force*, for example, differ in a fundamental way from the laws governing power. In using force, A does not require B to choose between compliance or noncompliance. A kills B, imprisons B, drags B, wrestles B to the ground, but does not require choice by B. Threat of force requires a choice, but threat of force is a different process (Goode 1972). A threat may be futile if B has decided to die for a cause; the threat may not accomplish its purpose. Actual force will accomplish its purpose whether B chooses to comply or not. It simply removes B as a factor opposed to A's wishes.

Like force, *manipulation* does not require that B choose between complying or not complying with the wishes of A. A may control B by controlling the information at B's disposal, by preventing certain choices being open to B, or by activating motives of B known to lead B to do what A wants. In some sense, B may be said to make choices (hence the difference from force), but A does not require B to choose between compliance and noncompliance. A controls the conditions that govern how B analyzes the choice to be made.

Although there are more than one narrow senses of the term *power*, all are distinguished from force and manipulation by the fact that power involves a choice by B between compliance and noncompliance. But this is true also of influence and authority. What distinguishes power is that it involves external sanctions. In Blau (1964) B is coerced to do something, X, by threat of a penalty for noncompliance. In Festinger (1953), B is induced to do X by a promise of reward for compliance or coerced to do X by threat of a penalty for noncompliance. Both rewards and penalties are external to the actor. They make no internal change, no change in the actor's state of mind. B does not change views privately, even if B conforms publicly. *Influence*, on the other hand, persuades B that X is right according to B's own interests; hence B complies privately as well as publicly. Compliance is willing in the case of influence, "forced" (Festinger 1953) in the case of power. If compliance were not observable to A, B would still comply in the case of influence but would not in the case of power. Hence, power is highly dependent on observability, but influence is not (French and Raven 1959).

Authority differs from both: It refers to a claim by A, accepted by B, that A has a legitimate right to expect compliance by B, even if compliance runs counter to B's own preferences (Barnard 1938). It differs from influence because whether B likes or does not like X is irrelevant. It differs from power in that B is expected to comply (and, if B accepts A's authority, does comply) because it is right, not because it is expedient. If B accepts A's legitimate authority, then B complies with A's commands whether compliance is observable to A or not. Furthermore, the power that legitimate authority makes possible has different effects because it is legitimate. Power exercised outside the scope of legitimate authority creates "reactance" (Brehm 1966), but power exercised inside the scope of legitimate authority does not (French and Raven 1959).

French and Raven (1959) also distinguish reward from punishment power and hence inducement from coercion. Coercion causes reactance; inducement does not. But they are so indissolubly connected that it becomes difficult to treat them as distinct processes. A reward forgone is a cost, and a penalty forgone is a reward. Hence, withholding a reward is equivalent to imposing a penalty, and withholding a penalty is equivalent to giving a reward. In order to distinguish the two, one would have to be able to separate giving something from withholding something. This might be possible in principle, but not in the case of power. Power depends on the contingency of sanctions; that is, A must be able to give *or* withhold something, depending on whether B does not comply. It is difficult to have one without the other. Thus, probably the most satisfactory concept of interpersonal power is Festinger's forced compliance (1953), compliance that is public but not private, caused either by threat of penalty or promise of reward.

This still leaves the question of whether power is potential or actual. Weber ([1918] 1968) emphasized the capacity of one actor to overcome the resistance of another whether or not the capacity is actually used. Simon (1953) and Dahl (1957) have objected to making inferences from a potential that might or might not actually be used. Research in fact consistently shows that not all potential power is used (see below), and Dahl in particular has argued that power has an effect only if used. On the other hand, Friedrich (1937) has argued that B might comply with the preferences of A because of anticipated reward or punishment, even if A says or does nothing that overtly demands compliance by B. Bachrach and Baratz (1963) go further and argue that certain kinds of acts that involve B doing nothing (nondecisions) occur without B even needing to know what A will

do, simply because B knows what A *could* do (a hypothesis confirmed by Zelditch and Ford, 1994). Both arguments imply that sheer existence of potential power has an effect whether used or not. The effect does not even have to be intended.

The issue of intentionality is another of the disputed questions in conceptualizing power, but not only can potential power have an effect without being used, there are even theories, such as those of Cartwright (1959) and Emerson (1962, 1972), in which "use" of power occurs without necessarily being intended by anyone.

The dispute over potential versus actual power refers more to causes, the dispute over broad versus narrow concepts of power more to effects. Thus, another ambiguity of power is whether one is referring to causes, effects, or the process relating the two.

THE CAUSAL APPROACH TO POWER

As process, power most typically refers to an exchange of "resources" (characteristics or objects instrumental to the attainment of goals). The only exception is the "causal" approach to power. Simon (1953) pointed out the similarity between the concept of "power over" and causality, leading to a longstanding tradition in which the former is defined in terms of the latter (as in Dahl 1957; Nagel 1975). But this led to so many difficulties that March (1966) concluded that the concept of power was superfluous. Although Nagel (1975) attempted to give the concept more explanatory power by narrowing it (to the effects of A's preferences on B), this led to little further advance, possibly because causal modeling gives one little insight into the process relating causes to effects.

But "process" theories themselves divide into four types: field theory; rational choice, or decision, theories of exchange; behavioral exchange theory; and a neo-Weberian "resistance" theory of exchange.

THE FIELD THEORY OF POWER

In field theory, power is the ability to activate forces in the life space of another in the direction of X (Cartwright 1959). The capacity to activate such forces depends on the motive base of B, thought of as a tension system, which, when activated by A, produces a vectored force that reduces the tension. Thus, power depends on the needs of B as much as on the wishes of A. It was this approach that gave rise to the concept of a "resource": Transferable resources give rise to power. But use of power by A faces not only opposing forces leading B away from X but also resistance due to the exercise of power itself. (This resistance was later termed *reactance* by Brehm 1966 to distinguish it from resistance due to B's dislike of doing X itself.) A's "control" over B is the outcome of the opposing forces acting on B. Thus, the outcome of the reduction of tension in the force field is distinguished from A's power in a manner corresponding to the distinction between actual versus potential power. In field theory, therefore, success—that is, actual compliance by B—is not the measure of A's power since there are many forces other than A affecting B's behavior.

Field theory, like the causal approach to power, treats the whole family of power concepts as power, excluding only physical force. But research in this tradition was much concerned with differences between different types of power, including reward power, punishment power, expert power, legitimate power, and referent power (power arising from B's attraction to A, which causes a desire to be similar to A). It was found that both reward and punishment power depend on A's ability to observe B's behavior, while the other forms of power do not. Coercion increased but reward decreased reactance. Legitimacy normatively constrained power so that using it outside its legitimate scope reduced its effect. Use of coercion when it is legitimate decreased reactance, while use of rewards when they are not legitimate increased reactance (French and Raven 1959). Because of reactance, use of coercion depends on restraints that prevent B from leaving the field.

EXCHANGE THEORIES OF POWER

The most important difference between field theory and exchange theories is that in the latter alternatives become the most important factor in the analysis of power. The reason is that, assuming voluntary relations, an actor may do things that she or he would prefer not to do because they are nevertheless preferable to any available alternative. Thus, an abused wife may not leave her husband because separation or divorce are either even less desirable or even more costly. But exchange theories themselves come in three somewhat distinct forms: rational choice, or decision, theory; behavioral exchange theory; and resistance theory.

Rational Choice Theories of Exchange and Power. Thibaut and Kelley (1959) offer perhaps the earliest rational choice model of the exchange process applied to power. They treat all interaction by analogy to the exchange of goods and services, each actor's participation in exchange being determined by choice among alternatives, the outcomes of which are characterized by their rewards and costs. Rewards are simply the positive values, costs the negative values, associated with the consequences of choosing an alternative. The value that results from the algebraic sum of rewards and costs is the payoff for a given act. Given interaction between two actors, A and B, payoffs are a joint function of the choices made by each. A matrix of joint payoffs for alternative actions by A and B formulates the conditions determining interaction between the two, in particular whether a relation forms and persists. Thibaut and Kelley treat payoffs in terms of their subjective value for the actors, hence in terms of their "utility" (although they do not use the term). In general, actors are assumed to maximize utility and continue in a relation only if for each actor a course of action is better than the best available alternative.

Thibaut and Kelley deal largely with stable relations rather than with particular acts. Power in a relation arises out of the "dependence" of the actors on each other. It can take either (or both) of two forms: A may be able to control the outcomes of B independently of any act by B, hence controlling B's fate, or A may be able to make rewards and costs contingent on B's behavior, hence controlling B's behavior. But an important principle of the theory is that control of an individual's fate can be converted into behavioral control.

There are many variants of the decision-theoretic approach to exchange, each differing with respect to how they treat the choice that underlies it. Value can be treated as objective (e.g., in monetary terms) or subjective (e.g., in terms of the meaning of money to the actor). The latter gives rise to a utility theory, such as in Thibaut and Kelley (1959), Blau (1964), and Bacharach and

Lawler (1981). The relation between choice of an alternative and its outcome can be treated deterministically (as is true of all three of the utility theories just cited) or probabilistically. If value is treated objectively and outcomes probabilistically, one has an *expected utility* theory as in Harsanyi (1962). Among probabilistic theories, probability itself can be treated objectively or subjectively: In March (1955) the probabilities are objective, in Nagel (1968) and Tedeschi and colleagues (1973) they are subjective. In the latter case one has a *subjective expected utility* theory. In all these variants of decision theory, the central axiom is that the actor maximizes whatever the theory's criterion of choice.

Despite the variations among these theories, in general they predict that, given a conflict of interest, A is more likely to use power when more is at stake, when the cost of exercising power is less, when the likelihood of compliance is greater, and when there are fewer alternative means of obtaining compliance. The costs of exercising power include the relative depletion of A's stock of resources, the likelihood of retaliation, and the effect of reactance on subsequent relations with B. In general, the evidence supports these predictions, although "use" sometimes refers to whether or not A prefers to impose his or her will on B; sometimes to whether or not, if A does have such a preference, it is accomplished by manipulating rewards and punishments rather than by other means; and sometimes to whether or not A's behavior is overt and explicit, communicating threats or promises, or is covert. Rational choice theories will also in general predict that B is more likely to comply with A's preferences the larger the reward attached to compliance, the larger the penalty attached to noncompliance, the greater the credibility of A's promises of reward or threat of penalty, and the fewer the alternatives available to B. Again, the evidence largely supports these predictions. But it is well to keep in mind that with respect to both use and compliance, the evidence deals largely with voluntary relations.

Unlike other decision theories, subjective expected utility theory (especially Nagel 1968) makes use of Friedrich's (1937) "law of anticipated reactions," in which compliance occurs without directives, threats, or promises by A. In the case of punishment, not only is there no visible exercise of power by A, but compliance by B may appear to be willing because there is no visible resistance. In addition, if one takes into account that the law of anticipated reactions can be applied to A as well as to B, A may know in advance that B will comply and therefore know that it is unnecessary visibly to exercise power in order to achieve A's objective (Samuel and Zelditch 1989).

Bacharach and Lawler (1981) have pointed out that even though relative power in a relation is necessarily zero-sum, meaning that a gain by one actor implies loss by the other, relative power can be distinguished from absolute power, the sheer quantity of resources controlled by an actor. Hence, relative power can be distinguished from total power, the sum of the resources possessed by A and B. Total power, unlike relative power, is a variable that can increase for both actors at the same time. Bacharach and Lawler argue that total power has an effect independent of relative power, especially on the use of punitive power capabilities. Given a conflict of interest, if punitive power is an available tactic, the likelihood of its use by the more powerful actor increases as his or her relative power increases but decreases as total power increases.

Thibaut and Kelley note that all these ideas are more useful as the pattern of exchange becomes more stable; hence, the focus of exchange theory is often not only on the fact that power is relational, which is true even at the level of a unit act, but on the structure of relations arising from enduring patterns of repeated exchanges. The most influential theory of this kind has been Emerson's theory of power–dependence relations (1962, 1972). Though it originally grew out of Thibaut and Kelley's work, this theory has come to be associated more recently with behavioral exchange theory, a theory originating in the work of Homans.

Behavioral Exchange Theory. Homans (1961) behaviorized exchange theory by transforming rewards and costs into reinforcement contingencies and the process of exchange into mutual operant conditioning. Many fundamental concepts of decision theory, however, survive in behavioral exchange theory. Choices are determined by maximizing profit, which is the difference between rewards and costs. Costs in Homans take a form more like costs in economics than in Thibaut and Kelley, becoming opportunity costs, that is, profit forgone by choosing X over not-X. But, as in

Thibaut and Kelley, exchange occurs at a point at which for both actors exchange is more profitable than each actor's best available alternative. Thus, A uses power in Homans—where "use" means attempts to direct the behavior of another—when it is more profitable than any alternative available to A, and B complies when compliance is more profitable than noncompliance. Homans, however, gives more emphasis than do Thibaut and Kelley to the effect of satiation on the value of a reward: Accumulation of rewards brings diminishing returns. Hence, poor actors are more responsive than are rich ones to offers of any given level of reward for doing an otherwise undesired act.

Emerson's power–dependence theory, perhaps the most influential theory of interpersonal power, was originally a utility theory of relations like Thibaut and Kelley's (Emerson 1962). But Emerson (1972) followed Homans in behaviorizing exchange theory, except that, unlike Homans, Emerson again dealt with relations rather than acts. Power–dependence theory is formulated in terms of two actors whose social relations entail ties of mutual dependence. "Power" is the amount of B's resistance that can be overcome by A: It is potential rather than actual power that is used to describe the relation. Power is a function of dependence, which arises from the control by one actor of resources on which another depends for achieving his or her goals. Dependence varies directly with an actor's motivational investment in goals but inversely with the availability of alternative sources of resources outside the relation. The "power advantage" of one actor over another is a function of the net balance of each one's dependence on the other. If the net balance is zero, power is equal, or "balanced." A relatively unique feature of Emerson's theory is that balanced power is assumed to be stable, while imbalance creates pressures to change the power relation in the direction of balance. There are four kinds of balancing operations. B may (1) reduce motivational investment in the goals mediated by A, withdrawing from the relation; (2) increase the number of alternative sources of the resource (extend networks); (3) increase A's motivational investment in goals mediated by B (e.g., by offering status to A); or (4) deny to A alternative sources of resources mediated by B (coalitionformation). Attention to these operations leads one to distinguish use of power from change of power—increasing or decreasing

dependence in the relation. These assumptions about balance have had a major impact on the study of organizations (beginning with Thompson 1967), but other exchange theories have tended to reject the balance assumption, especially Blau (1964), who instead treats the balance mechanisms as means by which A maintains or increases power over B.

"Use" in power–dependence theory comes to mean something quite different from what it means in decision or field-theoretic formulations: It refers now to asymmetries in the outcomes of reciprocal exchange. It is assumed that use of power, in the more usual sense, increases until an equilibrium is reached, at which point the less powerful actor is receiving no more benefits than the best alternative source could provide. While power imbalance does in fact increase asymmetry of exchange, it has been consistently found that its use is suboptimal. It is constrained in part by search costs (Molm 1987s) and in part by commitment to the other and concern for equity (Cook and Emerson 1978). Furthermore, use of punishment power depends not only on punishment capability but also on reward capability: Those weaker in reward power are, other things being equal, more likely to use punishment power (Molm 1997). Molm argues they have more to gain and less to lose by the use of coercion than those with more reward power: It is muggers, who gain nothing at all without coercion, who have nothing to lose by using it.

Molm also finds that, given mutual dependence, the effectiveness of coercion is directly proportional to its use, providing that its use is: (1) instrumental rather than symbolic, that is, a specific consequence of a specific behavior rather than a personal challenge; (2) highly contingent on the undesired behavior; and (3) consistent, that is, the punishment of equivalent behavior is equivalent. Coercion is perceived as more symbolic if it is noncontingent, inconsistent, or threatened but not actually used, increasing the side effects of coercion (resistance, negative affect, retaliation, loss of the relation). If it is perceived as instrumental, on the other hand, a high probability of punishment for a specific behavior, because it is effective in the short run, actually increases the net frequency of rewards in the long run, while "weak"—that is, sporadic—coercion decreases the long-run net frequency of rewards and increases the side effects of coercion.

The most significant development in the behavioral exchange theory of power has been its extension to networks of dyadic relations. Interpersonal power is not necessarily confined to a dyadic relation, as Coleman (1973) has shown. But except for Coleman, interpersonal power has usually been treated as dyadic. More complex structures are possible, however, by connecting dyads into networks (Emerson 1972). Study of such networks has rapidly developed as a central preoccupation of research on interpersonal power, especially preoccupation with the question of determinants of power at a position within a network. Most of this research has been concerned with negatively connected networks. A negative connection is one such that exchange in one relation decreases the value of exchange in another, while a positive connection increases its value. Thus, if A must choose which of two offers of exchange to accept from two others, B and C, AB is negatively connected to AC because choice of AB excludes exchange between A and C. Subsequent research has concentrated on the effects of varying structures of negatively connected networks. Centrality of a position turns out not to predict asymmetry of exchange very well; hence, much theory and research has been directed at discovering what alternative concept of power of a position does predict asymmetry of exchange. Cook and Emerson (1978) proposed "vulnerability" as an alternative and defined it as the effect that removing a position would have on the total quantity of resources available for exchange in a network. An intuitively appealing concept, this idea works well for many networks, though Markovsky and colleagues (1988) have objected that there are certain structures for which it does not accurately predict asymmetries. Their alternative conception derives from resistance theory.

Resistance Theory. Willer's (1981) resistance theory objects to the importance of satiation in behavioral exchange theory and as an alternative goes back to Weber's concept of power as overcoming resistance. Willer conceives of interaction as exchange of sanctions. The value of a sanction is a function of its objective value multiplied by its quantity, but value is not itself a function of quantity; hence, there is no satiation effect. Willer focuses instead on the "preference alteration state" of the actor (P_A), consequent on sanctions, and defines resistance as the ratio of two differences: the best possible outcome minus the value of P_A is divided by P_A minus the worst possible outcome B will accept, called P_A at confrontation. Exchange occurs at equiresistance.

The emphasis on resistance leads the theory to incorporate coercion and conflict more easily within the same framework as voluntary exchange. But in addition it leads to a different understanding of power at a position in a network. As in Cook and Emerson (1978), power at a position depends on alternatives, but Markovsky and colleagues (1988) propose a graph-theoretic index of power based on exclusion—B, bidding for exchange with A, is "excluded" if, having no alternatives, B does not exchange at all if outbid by another. The difference between the two is that in Markovsky and colleagues, exclusion is relative to the number of exchanges sought, while in Cook and Emerson actors seek to make a single exchange at a given point in time. It is "advantageous" in resistance theory to be connected to positions that have few alternatives relative to the number of exchanges sought and disadvantageous to be connected to positions that have many alternatives relative to the number sought. In exclusive networks, an odd number of positions is advantageous because in them a position has alternatives or a partner's alternatives have alternatives. An even number is disadvantageous because a position has one or more rivals for exchange with a partner. The ratio of advantageous to disadvantageous paths leading out from a point in a network (counting overlapping paths only once) gives the graph-theoretic index of power at that point in the network. The logic of the argument can be extended to inclusion as well as to exclusion. An inclusive connection is one such that exchange in one cannot occur until exchange in another also occurs. Inclusive relations, for example, increase the power of peripheral positions in a network. However, in mixes of the two, exclusion overwhelms inclusion and power is as centralized as in exclusive networks (Szmatka and Willer 1995).

Exclusion is more certain in some networks than others, and the magnitude of outcome differentials is sensitive to the certainty of exclusion. Outcome differentials are greater in "strong power" networks, in which the less powerful have no alternatives if they reject the terms of exchange of the more powerful, than in "weak power" networks, in which no position is assured of excluding another without cost to itself (Markovsky et al. 1993). Markovsky and colleagues argue that, in general, the strength of power is inversely proportional to the density of a network because the greater the density of a network, the more alternative opportunities for exchange. Hence, outcome differentials should be inversely proportional to the density of a network. They also show that weak power networks are more sensitive to strategy. Strong power maximizes outcome differentials even if the powerful are passive. In weak power networks, structural forces keep the division of profits more nearly equal, but strategy makes a difference: The more experienced demand more if they are in powerful positions and yield more if they are in less powerful positions, thus magnifying outcome differentials. Weak power networks are also more sensitive to the actual experience of exclusion (Skvoretz and Willer 1993): Potential exclusion, determined by structure, determines outcomes in strong power networks, but (given full information) outcomes are sensitive to both the potential and actual experience of exclusion in weak power networks.

(SEE ALSO: *Decision-Making Theory and Research; Exchange Theory*)

REFERENCES

Bacharach, Samuel B., and Edward J. Lawler 1981 *Bargaining: Power, Tactics, and Outcomes*. San Francisco: Jossey-Bass.

Bachrach, Peter, and Morton S. Baratz 1963 "Decisions and Nondecisions: An Analytical Framework." *American Political Science Review* 57:632–642.

Barnard, Chester I. 1938 *The Functions of the Executive*. Cambridge, Mass.: Harvard University Press.

Blau, Peter M. 1964 *Exchange and Power in Social Life*. New York: Wiley.

Brehm, Jack W. 1966 *A Theory of Psychological Reactance*. New York: Academic Press.

Cartwright, Dorwin 1959 "A Field Theoretical Conception of Power." In Dorwin Cartwright, ed., *Studies in Social Power*. Ann Arbor: University of Michigan Press.

Coleman, James S. 1973 *The Mathematics of Collective Action*. Chicago: Aldine.

Cook, Karen S., and Richard M. Emerson 1978 "Power, Equity, and Commitment in Exchange Networks." *American Sociological Review* 43:721–739.

Dahl, Robert A. 1957 "The Concept of Power." *Behavioral Science* 2:201–215.

Emerson, Richard M. 1962 "Power–Dependence Relations. *American Sociological Review* 27:31–41.

——1972 "Exchange Theory." In Joseph Berger, Morris Zelditch, and Bo Anderson, eds., *Sociological Theories in Progress*, vol. 2. Boston: Houghton Mifflin.

Festinger, Leon 1953 "An Analysis of Compliant Behavior." In Musafir Sherif and Milbourne O. Wilson, eds., *Group Relations at the Crossroads*. New York: Harper.

French, John R. P., and Bertram Raven 1959 "The Bases of Social Power." In Dorwin Cartwright, ed., *Studies in Social Power*. Ann Arbor: University of Michigan Press.

Friedrich, Carl J. 1937 *Constitutional Government and Politics: Nature and Development*. New York: Harper and Bros.

Goode, William J. 1972 "The Place of Force in Human Society." *American Sociological Review* 37:507–519.

Harsanyi, John C. 1962 "Measurement of Social Power, Opportunity Costs, and the Theory of Two-Person Bargaining Games." *Behavioral Science* 7:67–80.

Hawley, Amos 1963 Community Power and Urban Renewal Success." *American Journal of Sociology* 68:422–431.

Homans, George C. 1961 *Social Behavior: Its Elementary Forms*. New York: Harcourt Brace Jovanovich.

March, James G. 1955 "An Introduction to the Theory and Measurement of Influence." *American Political Science Review* 49:431–451.

——1966 "The Power of Power." In David Easton, ed., *Varieties of Political Theory*. Englewood Cliffs, N. J.: Prentice-Hall.

Markovsky, B., J. Skvoretz, D. Willer, M. Lovaglia, and J. Erger 1993 "The Seeds of Weak Power: An Extension of Network Exchange Theory." *American Sociological Review* 58:197–209

Markovsky, Barry, David Willer, and Travis Patton 1988 "Power Relations in Exchange Networks." *American Sociological Review* 53:220–236.

Molm, Linda 1987 "Linking Power Structure and Power Use." In Karen S. Cook, ed., *Social Exchange Theory* Newbury Park, Calif.: Sage.

——1997. *Coercive Power in Social Exchange*. New York: Cambridge University Press.

Nagel, Jack H. 1968 "Some Questions About the Concept of Power." *Behavioral Science* 13:129–137.

——1975 *The Descriptive Analysis of Power*. New Haven, Conn.: Yale University Press.

Parsons, Talcott 1963 "On the Concept of Political Power." *Proceedings of the American Philosophical Society* 107 (3):232–262.

Russell, Bertrand R. 1938 *Power: A New Social Analysis*. London: Allen and Unwin.

Samuel, Yitzhak, and Morris Zelditch, Jr. 1989 "Expectations, Shared Awareness, and Power." In Joseph Berger, Morris Zelditch, Jr., and Bo Anderson, eds., *Sociological Theories in Progress: New Formulations*. Newbury Park, Calif.: Sage.

Simon, Herbert 1953 "Notes on the Observation and Measurement of Political Power." *Journal of Politics* 15:500–516.

Skvoretz, J., and D. Willer 1993 "Exclusion and Power: A Test of Four Theories of Power in Exchange Networks." *American Sociological Review* 58:801–818.

Szmatka, J., and D. Willer 1995 "Exclusion, Inclusion, and Compound Connection in Exchange Networks." *Social Psychology Quarterly* 58:123–131

Tedeschi, James T., Barry R. Schlenker, and Thomas V. Bonoma 1973 *Conflict, Power, and Games*. Chicago: Aldine.

Thibaut, John W., and Harold H. Kelley 1959 *The Social Psychology of Groups*. New York: Wiley.

Thompson, James D. 1967 *Organizations in Action*. New York: McGraw-Hill.

Weber, Max (1918) 1968 *Economy and Society*. Guenther Roth and Claus Wittich, eds.; trans. Ephraim Fischoff et al. New York: Bedminster Press.

Willer, David 1981 "Quantity and Network Structure." In David Willer and Bo Anderson, eds., *Networks, Exchange, and Coercion*. New York: Elsevier/Greenwood.

Zelditch, M., and Ford, J. 1994 "Uncertainty, Potential Power, and Nondecisions." *Social Psychology Quarterly* 57:64–73.

MORRIS ZELDITCH, JR.

ITALIAN SOCIOLOGY

The birth of sociology in Italy is variously dated, depending on the causes that are adduced for it or on the perspective from which it is viewed. Indeed, even the conceptualization of sociology differs; hence, in a certain sense it is more important to determine when *each* "sociology" was born. We can distinguish two types of sociology and two corresponding ways of providing cultural and professional training. The first type is positivist (or neopositivist) sociology, tied to quantitative empirical research, which aims to discover the laws and the causal relationships that can be drawn from the data and from experience; the second type is humanistic sociology, which interprets its role as a critical science, raises questions, is more an approach to science than a science proper, and places social phenomena in their historical context. The two places for training professional sociologists are the research center and the university, respectively; each type of institution has an ambivalent and fluctuating relationship with the two sociologies.

Both types of sociology and both kinds of training, together with their origins, take on specific meanings according to the historical period; and hence they depend on the process of complexification of Italian society and the parallel development of different Italies (at least the three indicated by Bagnasco 1977).

THE ORIGINS OF ITALIAN SOCIOLOGY

Many historians of sociology see Italian sociology as deriving from the political thought of Niccolò Macchiavelli (1469–1527), because of his interest in leadership and its connection with the structures within which the prince must exercise his will. The political sociology of Vilfredo Pareto, Gaetano Mosca, Scipio Sighele, Roberto Michels, and Camillo Pellizzi can also be seen as belonging to this current of thought. This school, largely academic in origin, is based in political science, the philosophy of politics, and the philosophy of law. Associated with and grafted onto it is a sociology of law, also rooted in the universities, reflected by the great number of articles published in the first issues of *Quaderni di sociologia (Notebooks of Sociology)*, a review founded in 1951. Philosophy (Roberto Ardigò), political science (Gaetano Mosca), and law (Carlo Francesco Gabba, Rodolfo Laschi, Enrico Ferri, Icilio Vanni) became "godfathers" to Italian sociology. This may be explained by its dominant themes: the legitimation, explanation, and order that accrue to leadership and political structures as they develop. There were also economists, often (though not always) with a socialist background and orientation—Ginseppe Toniolo, Achille Loria, and Pareto—always attempting to study society in macroscopic terms in a way closely linked to political science.

Besides these currents concerned with the sphere of public action, there was the study of the private sphere as it deviated from the established order, as examined from the perspectives of political science, philosophy, and economics. Cesare Lombroso, Enrico Morselli, Scipio Sighele, and Alfredo Niceforo—some of them with medical training—studied the criminal personality, constructed typologies of the "delinquent man," elaborated pseudobiological explanations of deviant behavior, and thus attempted to interpret the relationship between society and the deviant (the duty of society being to lock up and prevent the deviant from causing further harm).

The sociological bent of these Italian protosociologists, who were generally university professors, was rooted in the work of Auguste Comte and Herbert Spencer. Hence, in their work we find a search for the laws underlying the social phenomena studied, the confidence that one can understand these phenomena by means of an inductive method borrowed from the natural sciences, and the belief that it is possible to describe and explain social reality with the positivist method. Italian sociological positivism (from 1865 to the rise of Fascism) worked out a paradigm of social analysis that was fairly homogeneous and characterized by naturalistic determinism in the form of evolutionary organicism. It was carried out by means of a positivist inductive method, although the basis of determinism varied during the history of positivism. For Lombroso, Niceforo, and others, the bases of such determinism were in biology and evolution (the theories of instinct and atavism), while for Pareto the structure of social activity took its model from economics. Another distinctive characteristic of this positivism was to consider society, social phenomena, and subjects in normative but exclusively objective terms. Roberto Ardigò worked along these lines as a theorist of human action, but after a certain point he became increasingly aware of the importance of "nonlogical" actions, of interiorization, and of socialization—the possibility of a voluntaristic theory. It is thus possible, in his case, to speak of a positivism of the subject, which foreshadows the work of Pareto.

The positivist approach was used by Socialist and Catholic scholars, as well as by liberals. This perspective was shared by the founders of *Rivista italiana di sociologia (Italian Review of Sociology)*, which was published from 1897 to 1922.

Positivism, mainly a French and English current of thought, began to decline when its naturalistic–determinist presuppositions were left behind and other variables had been introduced, thus leading to interpretations of society in more complex terms (Mosca, Pareto, Michels, Gaetano Salvemini); also, it was questioned when a progressive and optimistic determinism was replaced by a pessimistic determinism (as in Michels, with his iron law of oligarchy). Positivism was reborn with the formation of the Chicago School of urban and ecological studies at the end of the 1930s.

In Italy, positivism was replaced by the idealism of Benedetto Croce and Giovanni Gentile, who were strongly critical of positivism's main ideas and naturalistic research methods. The polemical debate in 1900–1901 between Pareto and Croce in the pages of *Il giornale degli economisti (The Journal of Economists)* is emblematic.

The technologically hard core of positivism is the research method, particularly "the experimental method that has given such brilliant results in the natural sciences," as Pareto wrote in his "Discorso per il Giubileo" (Borgatta 1917; "Discourse for the Jubilee").

This explains why, among the positivist sociologists, there were many demographers and statisticians (including Angelo Messedaglia, Loria, Niceforo, and Livio Livi) during the years of Fascism (1920–1940) and why the preeminence of idealism—the point of reference for sociology—lay primarily in statisticians such as Corrado Gini, Vittorio Castellano, Marcello Boldrini, and Nora Federici.

Gini, in particular, was active in founding the Istituto Centrale di Statistica (Central Institute of Statistics) in 1926; this agency was set up to organize census taking in Italy. In 1928 he founded the Comitato Italiano per lo Studio dei Problemi della Popolazione (Italian Committee for the Study of Population Problems), the school of statistics at the University of Rome (1929), the Italian section of the Institut International de Sociologie (1932), the Società Italiana di Sociologia (Italian Society of

Sociology) in 1937, and the Facoltà di Scienze Statistiche, Demografiche e Attuariali (Faculty of Statistical, Demographic, and Actuarial Sciences) at the University of Rome (1936). In this period Gini also founded, or was a founding member of, many journals, such as the *Bollettino bibliografico di scienze sociali e politiche* (1924; *Bibliographical Bulletin of Social and Political Sciences*), *La vita economica italiana* (1926; *Italian Economic Life*), and *Gems* (1934).

To sum up, Italian sociology was born through the importation of positivist ideas, paradigms, and methodological creeds, and it tried to solve the problems that society or the classes in power considered important in the second half of the nineteenth century and the first half of the twentieth—the existing forms of power and their legitimation, as well as the control of deviance. Its content therefore concerned the philosophy of law, political doctrines, socialism, the social thought of the Catholic Church, criminality and alienation, and related matters. In the first half of the twentieth century, in particular during the Fascist period, the study of demographics and statistics remained alive, as did the study of the charismatic components and fatal distortions of power (Michels) and investigation of the irrational and subjective element in society, in the form of residues and derivations (Pareto).

The themes and problems of concern were closely linked to the period in which Italian sociology developed. Socially, Italy was still traditional, and sociology was developed within the universities, in the context of more or less formally recognized courses.

1945 TO THE 1960S

The postwar period witnessed a profound rupture in Italian society, in its culture, and hence in its sociology. That society became much more complex, and its emerging culture became part of sociological study. Thus problems such as those in the South of Italy—urbanization, migration, the large concentrations of workers—were brought to the forefront. In addition, Italian sociologists were very receptive to foreign ideas and schools of thought. Thus, alongside the survival in academic circles of the influence of Comte, Spencer, and Darwin and the work of Gini, Livi, and Castellano, the American influence became dominant and the

German tradition regained importance, primarily in research institutes.

In other words, there was first an accumulation of theory and research that was incorporated into university sociology courses; later came the first chair of sociology, which was awarded to Franco Ferrarotti, at Rome in 1962. Scholars did not yet have sociological training, since no academic structures for that purpose existed; therefore they came from fields such as classical studies, political science (still very much oriented toward law), economics and commerce, medicine, law, and so forth.

One effect of this complexity was the subdivision of sociology into many branches: development and modernization; urban and rural sociology; the sociology of labor, of the economy, of migrations.

This period lasted from the end of World War II to the founding of the first faculty of sociology at Trento and the reform of the faculties of political sciences; it saw the incubation of a new direction in Italian sociology. Since that time there has been the development of the faculty of sociology at the University of Rome, and many other universities have acquired significant faculty strength in sociology. Let us now examine these currents.

The Sociology of Development and the Mezzogiorno. One of the problems the new Italy had to face was how to the reduce the developmental gap between North and South, in particular how to enable the society of the South and of Sicily and Sardinia to overcome their state of underdevelopment. Even before World War II the "Southern question" had been posed and announced by the actions and writings of Guido Dorso and Salvemini, among others. But it was only after 1946 that the problem became a subject of study and institutional intervention. Some of the institutions that deal with intervention and training, as well as with sociological research on the problems of the Mezzogiorno, are the Associazione per lo Sviluppo dell'Industria nel Mezzogiorno (SVIMEZ; Association for the Development of Industry in the Mezzogiorno), the CENTRO per la Formazione e studi per il Mezzogiorno (Center for Professional Training and Studies of the Mezzogiorno), the Associazione Nazionale per gli Interessi del Mezzogiorno (ANANI; National Association for the Interests of the

Mezzogiorno), the Movimento di Collaborazione Civica (Movement of Civic Collaboration), the Unione Nazionale per la Lotta contro l'analfabetismo (National Union for the Fight Against Illiteracy), and UNRRA-Casas (Instituto per lo Sviluppo dell'ediliza Sociale; the Institute for the Development of Public Housing).

Projects and plans were drawn up within and in cooperation with these agencies. They include the pilot project for the Abruzzi, the Sardinia project, the Center for Studies and Initiatives in western Sicily, the Center for Community Development at Palma di Montechiaro, and the Molise and Avigliano projects. It was in these institutions that sociological and anthropological studies on development, modernization, and the community were carried out. Tullio Tentori (1956), Guido Vincelli (1958), Danilo Dolci (1955, 1957, 1960), Gilberto Antonio Marselli (1963), Lidia de Rita (1964), Maria Ricciardi Ruocco (1967), Luca Pinna (1971), Gualtiero Harrison and Maria Callari Galli (1971), and Giovanni Mottura and Enrico Pugliese (1975) are among those whose works reveal a social commitment together with testing of the theories of modernization. They show an awareness of their limits as well, as elaborated by the English-language sociological tradition; moreover, there was a strong element of utopianism in this mixture of social commitment and scientific rigor.

It was not just the ideas of American and northern European scholars that were studied and applied to the modernization of the South of Italy; scholars themselves were committed to the task. At the same time, some classic research was carried out, important both because it was cited by Italian scholars and because it was rejected by them (in particular by Alessandro Pizzorno and Marselli). One of the books that became an object of controversy was Edward C. Banfield's *The Moral Basis of a Backward Society* (1958). Other frequently cited foreign research works included Joseph Lopreato's "Social Stratification and Mobility in a South Italian Town" (1961), Feliks Gross's "Value Structure and Social Change" (1970), and Johann Galtung's *Members of Two Worlds: A Development Study of Three Villages in Western Sicily* (1971).

Sociological study of modernization also entered the universities through sociology courses that took their place alongside courses in rural economics. The most important center for these courses was the Faculty of Agriculture at Portici, and the most significant sociologists were Marselli, Pugliese, Mottura, and Emanuele Sgroi.

The Sociology of Work and Economics. The sociology of work and economics arose in the research agencies, in research centers of large industries, and in labor unions.

One very important research center for the training of Italian sociologists was Olive Hi's Ufficio Studi e Relazioni Sociali (Research and Social Relations Office) at Ivrea. Adriano Olivetti, building a company and a community, surrounded himself with sociologists, economists, communications experts, and planners. Ferrarotti, Pizzorno, Luciano Gallino, Paolo Ceri, and Antonio Carbonaro worked and studied at the facility. They, and many more, devoted themselves to industrial relations and the rationalization of staff selection in large industries operated by enlightened and paternalistic entrepreneurs like Olivetti. Very often, however, the left-wing slant of their training and their impression of being manipulated led these sociologists to leave the research center after a short stay and to continue their sociological training at universities in the United States. In this cultural climate, which also was indebted to nineteenth-century models of integration of the company, the community, and territorial planning, the review *Comunità* (Community) published essays with a strong cultural and social commitment. The publishing house of the same name made available to the Italian public the classics of German and, especially, American sociology.

Another forum for the training of sociologists (especially in the sociology of labor) was the research offices of the labor unions (and, to a lesser extent, of the political parties). In particular, future sociologists such as Aris Accornero, Guido Baglioni, Gian Primo Cella, and Guido Romagnoli were directed toward studies of factory work. The factory and labor union conflicts were the main subjects of their volume, with a consequent tendency to identify the "organization" with the factory (a pamphlet on the sociology of organizations by G. Bonazzi is, significantly, entitled *Dentro e fuori la fabbrica* (1982); *Inside and Outside the Factory*) and the labor union. These sociologists had few contacts with foreign scholars; when they did, such contacts were oriented toward France and particularly toward the Institut des Sciences Sociales du

Travail (Institute of the Social Science of Labor) in Paris.

Urban Sociology and the Sociology of Planning. Other institutions in which sociologists (this time urban sociologists) were trained in the 1950s and 1960s were the planning offices set up by the territorial governments (large municipalities and provinces in northern Italy), particularly the Istituto Lombardo di Studi Economici e Sociali (ILSES; Lombard Institute of Economic and Social Studies) in Milan and the Centro Studi Sociali e Amministrativi (CSSA; Center for Social and Administrative Studies) in Bologna. The former trained the sociologists Pizzorno, Gianni Pellicciari, Massimo Paci, Alberto Martinelli, Guido Martinotti, Paolo Guidicini; the latter, Achille Ardigò, Paolo Guidicini, Giuliano Piazzi, and Pietro Bellasi. There was also the Ufficio Studi Sociali e del Lavoro (Office for Social and Labor Studies) in Genoa, where Luciano Cavalli carried out his *Inchiesta sugli abituri* (1957; *Survey on Slums*).

ILSES dealt with research on neighborhoods, on participation in neighborhoods, and, in general, on the structure of the city. The approaches were borrowed from the concepts and research of the Chicago School and the group that had formed around Paul Henry Chombart de Lauwe. Thus, among other things, Ernest W. Burgess's model of concentric areas was verified for Italian cities (in Rome and Milan), as was Hoyt's model of sectors. The results of these researches found expression in anthologies on the Chicago School: such as Guido Martinotti's *Città e analisi sociologica* (1968; *The City and Sociological Analysis*); manuals of urban sociology, such as Franco Demarchi's *Società e spazio* (1969; *Society and Space*); and a manual of urban research based largely on that carried out by ILSES and CSSA, Paolo Guidicini's *Manuale della ricerca sociologica* (1968, 1987; *Manual of Sociological Research*).

The sociologists who worked at ILSES developed close contacts with the United States (particularly Martinotti, Paci, and Martinelli) and with the United Kingdom (Guidicini).

International Sociology. Sociology entered the universities where both theoretical and empirical sociologists were trained but no attention was given to international sociology. International sociology in Italy was developed by the Istituto di Sociologia Internazionale di Gorizia (ISIG; Institute of International Sociology of Gorizia), founded by Demarchi in 1969. This branch of sociology seeks its identity in the synthesis of ideas from political sociology; the sociology of international relations; and the sociology of ethnic relations, of borders, of towns, and of territories. Relations were developed with scholars from the United States, from Eastern Europe, and from the countries of the European Economic Community. From the United States, the institute took the research methodology of multivariate analysis, under the direction of Edgar F. Borgatta; it was one of the first institutions in Italy to adopt these techniques. Its researchers later held important positions in various universities: Renzo Gubert, Alberto Gasparini, Raimondo Strassoldo, Bruno Tellia, Bernardo Cattarinussi, and Giovanni Delli Zotti.

Among the cited research organizations, ISIG is one of the few that carries out an active program that is not encompassed by university activities. There are at least two reasons for this. First, Italian sociology has tended not to be interested in international relations. Second, there has been an acceleration of international interdependence; in recent years there has been great change in the relations between Western and Eastern Europe, and between Europe and the rest of the world. Under the direction of Alberto Gasparini, ISIG has responded to the need for such study, with an emphasis on Eastern Europe and the countries of the former USSR.

Academic Institutionalization of Italian Sociology. The most intense activity of the research agencies occurred in the 1950s and 1960s; it was scientific in the full sense of the word, since concrete problems were tackled empirically, starting from a theory (generally developed abroad) and ultimately returning to the theory. This way of doing research, and of training for research, is quite different from the method adopted in the universities, because it is tied to concrete problems and specific deadlines.

Moreover, in this period, together with the ideas and plans designed to establish sociology in the universities (the first chair in sociology was awarded to Ferrarotti in 1962), sociology was taking on an identity as an academic discipline. The first issue of *Quaderni di sociologia* (*Notebooks of Sociology*) was published in 1951, edited by Nicola

Abbagnano and Ferrarotti, and in 1957 the Associazione Italiana di Scienze Sociali (AISS; Italian Association of Social Sciences) was founded. In 1959 the Centro Nazionale di Prevenzione e Difesa Sociale (National Center for Prevention and Social Defense) in Milan, together with AISS, organized the Fourth World Congress of Sociology at Stresa; and from then until 1974 Italian sociologists (Angelo Pagani and Guido Martinotti) held the post of secretary of the International Sociological Association. Italian sociology was now mature and ready to enter the universities with its own sociologists, their empirical experience, and their theoretical preparation; hence it was able to extend the discipline.

SOCIOLOGY IN THE UNIVERSITIES (SINCE 1960)

Italian sociology, as a discipline and as scientific research, has developed strongly. The heart of this development lies more in the universities and university teachers than in the nonacademic institutes that played such a large role until the 1960s. All this happened with the consolidation of sociology in the university system (which had the function of training young researchers and became the channel for legitimizing the scientific character of sociological research). Subsequent developments included the publication of dictionaries and encyclopedias of sociology, the foundation of the Associazione Italiana di Sociologia (Italian Association of Sociology), and the formation and coordination of sociological interests in specific areas.

Sociology in the Italian Universities. The complexity of Italian society requires a strong sociological reading of reality, and the nonacademic agencies discussed above could not long meet this need. Moreover, a strong impulse to legitimize sociological analysis came from the student protest movement, which in the mid-1960s reached Europe from the United States.

Thus sociology entered the universities mainly with the establishment in Trento of the Istituto Universitario di Scienze Sociali (University Institute of Social Sciences, later the Faculty of Sociology) in 1962 and with the reform of political science faculties in 1968.

The Faculty of Sociology at Trento. The Istituto Universitario di Scienze Sociali was officially founded on September 12, 1962, on the initiative of the Provincia Autonoma di Trento (the Autonomous Province of Trento), the Istituto Trentino di Cultura (the Trento Institute of Culture), and of Professor Giorgio Braga, lecturer at the Università Cattolica in Milan. The governing body is composed of ten professors: three jurists, two economists, one statistician, one mathematician (the director, Mario Volpato), one ethicist, and the sociologists Braga (vice director) and Franco Ferrarotti. The first sociologists to teach there were not from the Milan area. Later Milanese came to Trento: Francesco Alberoni and Guido Baglioni. The first teachers at Trento were from several regions: Giorgio Braga (from the Università Cattolica in Milan), Franco Ferrarotti (Rome), Filippo Barbano (Turin), Sabino Acquaviva (Padua), Franco Demarchi (Trento), and Achille Ardigò (Bologna). The students who enrolled in the first year (226), and even more in the immediately following years, were strongly motivated to study social problems and came increasingly from regions far from Trento.

The Faculty of Sociology, with its four-year program, grants two types of degrees in sociology: general and special. The general course in the sociological disciplines trains teachers and researchers who will work in universities, international institutions, and centers of research on economic and social problems. The special sociology course prepares students for management careers in public administration and in private firms (in particular, for research, public relations, and personnel), social insurance offices, agencies for agricultural development, welfare agencies, labor unions and political parties, business consultancy agencies, marketing research offices, and town planning bodies.

As can be seen, this university planning aimed at the extension of the university; moreover, it set out to deal with a society that was both complex and predictable in its organization of problems and phenomena to be studied and, if possible, solved.

Things changed with the arrival of the student protest movement. At the University of Trento, different models of teaching and organization were experimented with, leading it to occupy a unique position in the Italian university system. A "critical university," managed by a joint committee of teachers and students, was formed. The director of the institute and experimenter with this model was Francesco Alberoni, who attracted other teachers interested in this project, in particular from Milan. This situation lasted until 1970; meanwhile, it triggered experimentation at other Italian universities and to some extent contributed to the reform of the faculties of political science. In subsequent years, when the institute was transformed into the first Faculty of Sociology in the Italian university system, corsi di laurea (degree courses) in sociology emerged, often within existing facoltà di magistero (education faculties) at Rome, Naples, Salerno, and Urbino.

The Reform of the Faculties of Political Science. Sociology was offered in twenty-three Italian universities in 1964–1965, a total of thirty-eight courses taught by twenty-seven professors. It was episodically and marginally introduced into the faculties of law, letters, arts, economics, and political science, and often the same person was asked to teach several courses; for example, Alberoni taught four different courses in sociology at the same time at the Università Cattolica of Milan. The courses were scattered throughout Italy: four courses each in Rome and Milan (Università Cattolica); three courses each in Bari and Florence; two courses each in Bologna, Cagliari, Milan (Università Statale), Naples, and Palermo; and one course each at the universities of Catania, Ferrara, Genoa, Messina, Milan (Polytechnic), Padua, Pavia, Pisa, Salerno, Siena, Turin, Trieste, Urbino, and Venice. For the most part the teachers were "masters": Achille Ardigò, Gianfranco Morra, Anna Anfossi, Franco Leonardi, Camillo Pellizzi, Giovanni Sartori, Luciano Cavalli, Renato Treves, Francesco Alberoni, Sabino Acquaviva, Eugenio Pennati, Agostino Palazzo, Franco Ferrarotti, Vittorio Castellano, Antonio Carbonaro, Filippo Barbano, Angelo Pagani, and Alessandro Pizzorno.

At the end of the 1990s, the situation has completely changed, both in terms of the number of universities in which sociology is taught (now forty-two), obviously expanded by the establishment of new universities—and in terms of the number of courses and teachers (now 827). Moreover, some very substantial centers of sociology have been established, and sociology is taught in all the Italian universities. The universities with the greatest numbers of sociology courses are (in descending order): Rome (eighty-four), Bologna (thirty-nine), Turin (sixty-three), Milan (forty-three),

and Trento (fifty-two). Those with fewer than twenty but at least ten courses are Padua (seventeen), Naples (sxteen), Calabria (fourteen), Florence (thirteen), Salerno (twelve), Catania (eleven), and Palermo (ten).

One very important technical reason for these profound changes in the teaching of sociology was the reform of the faculties of political science. The first faculty of political science in Italy was established in 1875 at Florence (and called Cesare Alfieri). It was designed to train public officials and, in general, it prepared men for an active life and public debate. As time passed, while it kept these functions, this faculty tended to become transformed into a faculty of social science. After World War II the need was increasingly felt to reform the faculties of political science, detaching them from other faculties (particularly from the law faculties) and giving them an updated cultural core. Subsequently such faculties were divided into two two-year courses of study: The first is based on fundamental courses (including sociology), and the second is organized into five indirizzi (courses of study)—international, historical, economic, administrative, and social. In this last course (political-social) some true sociological curricula are offered; they are obviously more concentrated in the faculties of political science at Rome, Bologna, Turin, Padua, and Milan. At present, the political-social course of studies is available in the following universities: Turin, Milan (Università Statale and Università Cattolica), Pavia, Trieste, Padua, Bologna, Florence, Pisa, Cambrino, Rome (LUISS), Naples, Bari, Messina, Catania, and Palermo.

The Future of Sociology in the Universities. At present, the teaching of sociology is concentrated in the Faculties of Sociology at Trento, Rome, Naples, Milan, Urbino, Salerno; in the degree courses in sociology at others universities; and in the several faculties of political science. Sociology courses are also offered by other faculties (such as economics and commerce, architecture, medicine, letters and philosophy, and arts), but the current tendency is to reduce this spread. There are at least two reasons for this: the "zero growth" of sociology (i.e., sociology departments have the right only to replace sociologists who leave the university or switch to other disciplines) and other disciplines' expansion of their number of chairs.

In the future, there will therefore be a tendency to strengthen sociology where it is already strong (in the faculties of political science) or through the creation of new degree courses in sociology; however, it is likely to disappear or to be excluded from the mainstream where it is peripheral (in the faculties of economics and commerce, architecture, and others). There are other ways in which the universities can train sociologists, such as Ph.D. programs (they are at the moment thirty-one: thirteen in the North; twelve in the center of the country; five in the South, one in Sicily and Sardinia) courses or schools of specialization for those who already have a degree and special-purpose schools or diploma courses for those who plan to attend the university for only two years after their secondary schooling.

THE 1990S: IN THE SHADOW OF INTERNATIONAL CHANGE AND SOCIAL CHANGE IN ITALY

The themes explored by Italian sociology, like those of any national sociology, are closely tied up with the contemporary state of society.

Italian society in the 1990s is undergoing profound changes. Of these, the most evident has resulted from the fall of communism in the Soviet Union and its satellites. The Christian Democratic party, whose raison d'être was as a bastion against communism, lost this purpose and no longer found itself "condemned to govern." Because of the increasing secularization of Italian Catholicism, the Christian Democrats also lost their function as the party of the Church, and it became widely acknowledged that the party was corrupt, as were the other parties. "Tangentopoli" ("Bribe City"—the name given to the massive system of the political fixing of public contracts in return for cash from industry) was uncovered, and "Mani pulite" ("Operation Clean Hands"—the attempt to eradicate it) was launched by the magistrature. The alliances between large organizations and their joint vested interests (large-scale capitalists, big trade unions, protected labor), the "Soviet" component of the state economy (state-owned industries), and the big political parties lost legitimacy with the birth of new political players (the Northern League), new economic players (Small and Medium-Sizes Enterprises), and new trade unions (smaller, autonomous, and more trade-specific) that claimed resources and reduced the size and authority of the large organizations.

The fall of the Iron Curtain has de-ideologized international relations between Eastern and Western Europe, establishing national or ethnic identity as the criterion of statehood. But in Italy, the fall of the great central organizations has made obvious the importance of the role of highly fragmented local political, social, cultural, and economic forces. The burgeoning importance of ethnicity and local parties (more in the North than the South) and demands for federalism (especially in taxation) and even independence point to a new society, with the marks of the postmodern.

Growing of affluence has put an end to internal emigration and emigration abroad and directed interest toward women's rights, communications, and information technology, and new religious solutions within and outside the traditional Western religions. By contrast, however, the welfare state, designed and constructed by the society of large organizations and by "big" government, has entered a massive solvency crisis, burdened as it is with a level of debt that is unsustainable in comparison with other developed countries and that it cannot pay. Solutions have been sought in cuts in public spending and pensions, the growth of the service sector, the involvement of individual citizens, and the campaign for convergence to the Maastricht criteria.

Sociology has responded to these changes with the expansion of some areas of study and the contraction of others. The former have shifted to incorporate related disciplines such as political science, theology, computer science, constitutional law, and migration; the latter have been subsumed into disciplines such as economics. Research institutes have regained an important position, both inside and outside universities, and the spread of sociology courses in universities has stopped.

One relatively new theme for sociological research and reflection is national identity, both in terms of establishing whether an Italian national identity actually exists in the minds of Italians and in terms of exploring the local identities that may drive toward claims for independence or forms of federalism. A classical study in this regard is Gian

Enrico Rusconi's "*Se Cessiamo di Essere uma Hazioue*" ("*If We Cease to be a Nation*"), which carries the emblematic subtitle *Regional Ethno-Democracies and European Citizenship*. Here the theme of national identity is combined with ethnic and European identity, and accentuated localism with accentuated cosmopolitanism. Work has also been produced in this field by Carlos Barbe, Loredana Sciolla, Carlo Tullio-Altan, and Riccardo Scartezzini. The futures studies journal *Futuribili* has devoted an edition to the future of Italy and the Italians entitled "The Italians Are Here, When Will Italy Be?"

Another theme of political sociology centres on changes in the structure of parties and consensus in the wake of the "discovery" that the existing political system is illegal. Much research has been conducted into the mechanisms of political corruption (Donatella Della Porta, Mauro Magatti, Vaclav Belohradsky), the renewal of the political class, and the formation of new ruling classes as a result of the transformation of the original illegalities into new legalities (Belohradsky 1994). These political transformations have changed the way voters feel about politics. Increases in the numbers of floating voters and nonvoters have given new life and direction to electoral sociology. Opinion polls have become a tool of fundamental importance, and sociologists are studying voting behavior in specialized institutes set up outside universities. Another dimension in the relaunching of political sociology is international relations, especially the study of post-communist Eastern Europe, including scenario building and forecasts of the workings, duration, and results of the transition there. In this field, too, research and studies have been carried out and conferences organized by institutes, both independent of universities or based in them. The funds used for these initiatives are provided by European programmes—such as Phare, Tacis, Intas, and Democracy—with the aim of creating international scientific and fact-finding networks.

Such scientific institutions have been set up in a large number of Italian towns, first and foremost ISIG in Gorizia, which has specialized for the last thirty years in the ethnic, border, and international questions in the Balkan–Danube area and the former Soviet area. ISIG has established a Forum for European Border Towns, an Ethnic Minorities Observatory, an Italian Futures Studies Academy, and a Permanent Forum for peace initiatives specializing in pilot studies, databases, and the organization of parallel diplomatic meetings for the solution of conflicts. These initiatives frequently result in the publication of journals and books. Heading the journals are *Futuribili*, (along the lines of *Futuribles* and *Futures*,) devoting each issue to special themes. *ISIG Magazine* is a journal, published in English and Italian, that also deals with particular themes on a monographic basis. Books frequently tackle international subjects: *International Solidarity and National Sovereignty* (Picco and Delli Zotti 1995) discusses the increasing intrusion upon national sovereignty by international organisations (the UN, NATO, and the EU); "The Future of the Moment Before" (Gasparini 1993) deals with Russia and its future. Other studies analyze: the factors driving toward the formation of a new Russian empire and the persistent character of Russian religiosity and mysticism; the Balkans and the solution of conflicts through international solidarity to bring in a new order based on protectorates (Mroljub Radojkovic, Kosta Barjaba, Alberto Gasparini); ethnic groups and borders in Europe (Luca Bregantini, Alessandro Pannuti, Moreno Zago, Alberto Gasparini); Arab and Israeli nationalism in the Middle East (Elie Kallas); the transition of the former socialist countries in Eastern Europe.

Other themes undergoing strong development are connected with the modern affluent society: They include women and their position with regard to work, equality, self-fulfilment outside the family, and the family as an institution (Chiara Saraceno, Laura Balbo, Pierpaolo Donati); poverty, and extreme poverty in cities rather than widespread poverty (Paolo Guidicini, Giovanni Pieretti); and the role played by poverty in immigration from the Balkans, Eastern Europe, and the Mediterranean Arab countries (Umberto Melotti, Maurizio Ambrosini, ISMU). Connected to these developments and to the relationship between politics and civil society as seen in an increasingly crisis-bound welfare state are studies (Pierpaolo Donati, Ivo Colozzi, Guido Lazzarini, Giuliano Giorio) that seek solutions to the crisis through the service sector and that explore Europe and its new forms of citizenship. Other emerging themes indicating change in Italian society and the need for certainties in an uncertain situation are to be found in the relaunching of studies on Italian religion and religiosity (Roberto Cipriani, Franco Garelli, Stefano Martelli, Salvatore Abruzzese) and the solutions offered by traditional religions and new movements (also dealt with in an edition of *Futuribili*).

Another important theme is the relationship between communications and a changing society, with specific reference to the role of communications in mass emergency risk management (Bruna De Marchi, Luigi Pellizzoni, Daniele Ungaro, Alberto Abruzzese, Laura Bovone, Mario Morcellini). Community studies show a prevalence of territorial belonging and a decline in metropolitan expansion in favor of restricted urban areas forming a city system in which individuals retain their own identity while relating to other people (Alberto Gasparini, Reuzo Gubert, Gabriele Pollini).

Finally, a theme reemerging after the explosion and subsequent decline of the studies launched in the early 1970s by the Club of Rome is prediction. Here again, ISIG and *Futuribili* are at the fulcrum heart of an interest that is particularly strongly felt at a time of uncertainty and transition toward a society that is as yet unclear (Eleonora Masini, Giorgio Nebbia, Alberto Gasparini, Luca Bregantini, Moreno Zago).

In contrast to these themes, produced by contingent and transient situations, others have been declining in the 1990s. Less attention has been devoted to large companies, and the factory and the trade union movement have lost some of their importance as an area of study. The same applies to the study of social classes. These fields have felt the effects of a crisis in the culture of the defense of workers' rights and in the paradigm—very often a Marxist one—use to explain social classes and the relations between them.

In short, the profound external and internal changes overtaking Italian society have worked to the advantage of some themes of study and undermined the previous importance of others. As was the case with postwar sociology, the driving force in this development has been institutes outside universities (especially in international studies) or at least consortia and niches inside universities but only loosely tied to their teaching function. This has produced a strong movement to strengthen existing journals and create new ones; these include *Futuribili, Ikon, Polis, Quaderni di sociologia* (*Notebooks of Sociology*), *Rassegna italiana di sociologia* (*Italian Review of Sociology*), *RES* (*Ricerca e sviluppo per le politiche sociali: Research and Development for Social Policies*), *Religioni e società* (*Religions and Society*), *La Società* (*The Society*), *Sociologia del lavoro* (*The Sociology of Work*), *Sociologia della comunicazione* (*The Sociology of Communication*), *Sociologia e politiche sociali* (*Sociology and Social Policies*), *Sociologia e professione* (*Sociology and Profession*), *Sociologia e ricerca sociale* (*Sociology and Social Research*), *Sociologia urbana e rurale* (*Urban and Rural Sociology*), *Studi di sociologia* (*Sociology Studies*), and *Teoria sociologica* (*Sociological Theory*).

REFERENCES

Accornero, Aris, and Francesco Carmignani 1986 *I paradossi della disoccupazione*. Bologna: Il Mulino.

Acquaviva, Sabino, and Enzo Pace, eds. 1984 *Dizionario di sociologia e antropologia culturale*. Assisi: Cittadella.

Alberoni, Francesco ed., 1966 *Questioni di sociologia*. Brescia: La Scuola.

—— 1968 *Statu nascenti*. Bologna: Il Mulino

Amendola, Giandomenico, and Antonio Tosi, eds. 1987 "La sociologia dell'abitazione." *Sociologia e ricerca sociale* 22:1–173.

Ammassari, Paolo 1970 *Worker Satisfaction and Occupational Life*. Rome: University of Rome.

Ardigò, Achille 1980 *Crisi di governabilità e mondi vitali*. Bologna: Cappelli.

—— 1988 *Per una sociologia oltre il post-moderno*. Bari: Laterza.

Ardigò, Roberto 1918 *Opere filosofiche*. Paduva: Draghi.

Associazione Italiana di Sociologia 1989 *L'Italia dei sociologi: Problemi, prospettive, indirizzi di ricerca*. Bologna: AIS.

Bagnasco, Arnaldo 1977 *Tre Italie*. Bologna: Il Mulino.

Banfield, Edward C. 1958 *The Moral Basis of a Backward Society*. Glencoe, Ill.: Free Press.

Barbano, Filippo, and Giorgio Sola 1985 *Sociologia e scienze sociali in Italia, 1861–1890*. Milan: Angeli.

Barberis, Corrado 1988 *La classe politica municipale*. Milan: Angeli.

Barjaba, Kosta, ed. 1996 "Albania. Tutta d'un pezzo, in mille pezzi . . . e dopo?". *Futuribili* 2–3:453.

Belohradsky, Vaclav, ed. 1994 "Illegalità-legalità e nuovi patti sociali. Dalla Russia all'Italia per l'Europa." *Futuribili*, 3:239.

Bestuzhev-Lada, Igor, and Luca Bregantini, eds. 1995 "Balcanizzazione euro-asiatica vs. nuovo impero russo." *Futuribili* 1–2:336.

Bettin Lattes, Gianfranco, ed. 1995 *La società degli europei*. Bologna: Monduzzi.

Boileau, Anna Maria, and Emidio Sussi 1981 *Dominanza e minoranze*. Udine: Grillo.

Borgotta, G. 1917 *L'opera sociologica e le fests guibilari di V. Pareto*, Torino: SE.

Bonazzi, Giuseppe 1982 *Dentro e fuori della fabbrica*. Milan: Angeli.

Bregantini, Luca and Alessandro Pannuti, eds. 1997 "Etnia? Sia se volete che sia." *Futuribili*, 1-2:351.

Burgalassi, Silvano, and Gustavo Guizzardi, eds., 1983 *Il fattore religione nella società contemporanea*. Milan: Angeli.

Caizzi, Bruno, ed. 1962 *Nuova antologia della questione meridionale*. Milan: Comunità.

Castellano, Vittorio 1968 *Introduzione alla sociologia e primi elementi de morfologia sociale*. Rome: Ilardi.

Cattarinussi, Bernardo, and Carlo Pelanda, eds. 1981 *Disastro e azione umana*. Milan: Angeli.

Cavalli, Luciano 1957 *Inchiesta sugli abituri*. Genoa: Office of Social and Labor Studies.

Cella, Gian Primo, ed. 1979 *Il movimento degli scioperi nel XX secolo*. Bologna: Il Mulino.

Cipolla, Costantino 1997 *Epistemologia della tolleranza*. Milan: Angeli.

Crespi, Franco, ed. 1987 *Sociologia e cultura*. Milan: Angeli.

De Finis, Giorgio and Riccardo Scartezzini, eds., 1996 *Universalità e differenza*. Milan: Angeli.

De Marchi, Bruna, ed. 1994 "Rischio, gestione del rischio, comunicazione del rischio" (Risk, risk management, risk communication). *Isig-Magazine*, III:4–16.

De Rita, Lidia 1964 *I contadini e la televisione*. Bologna: Il Mulino.

Delli Zotti, Giovanni 1983 *Relazioni transnazionali e cooperazione transfrontaliera*. Milan: Angeli.

Demarchi, Franco 1969 *Società e spazio*. Trento: Istituto Superiore di Scienze Sociali.

——, Aldo Ellena, and Bernardo Cattarinussi, eds., 1987 *Nuovo dizionario di sociologia*. Rome: Paoline.

Dolci, Danilo 1955 *Banditi a Partinico*. Bari: Laterza.

—— 1957 *Inchiesta a Palermo*. Turin: Einaudi.

—— 1960 *Spreco*. Turin: Einaudi.

Donati, Pierpaolo 1983 *Introduzione alla sociologia relazionale*. Milan: Angeli.

—— 1993 *La cittadinanza societaria*. Bari: Laterza.

Ferrarotti, Franco 1972 *Trattato di sociologia*. Turin: Utet.

Gallino, Luciano 1978 *Dizionario di sociologia*. Turin: Utet.

—— 1980 *La società. Perché cambia, come funziona*. Turin: Paravia.

——, ed. 1992 *Percorsi della sociologia italiana*. Milan: Angeli.

——, ed. 1992 *Teoria dell'attore e processi decisionali*. Milan: Angeli.

Galtung, Johan 1971 *Members of Two Worlds: A Development Study of Three Villages in Western Sicily*. Oslo: Universitetforlaget.

Garelli, Franco, and Marcello Offi 1996 *Fedi di fine secolo*. Milan: Angeli.

Gasparini, Alberto 1975 *La casa ideale*. Venice: Marsilio.

—— 1982 *Crisi della città e sua reimmaginazione*. Milan: Angeli.

——, and Paolo Guidicini, eds., 1990 *Innovazione tecnologica e nuovo ordine urban*. Milan: Angeli.

—— 1993 *The Future of the Moment Before*. Gorizia: ISIG.

——, and Miroljub Radojkovic, eds. 1994 "Oltre le guerre balcaniche. Cosa può succedere quando i piccoli dei hanno grandi sogni". *Futuribili* 2:22.

——, and Moreno Zago, eds. 1995 "Al di là dei nuovi muri. L'Europa collaborativa che viene dalle città di confine." *Futuribili* 1-2:352.

——, and Vladimir Yadov, eds. 1995 *Social Actors and Designing the Civil Society of Eastern Europe*. Greenwich, Conn.: JAI Press.

Gini, Corrado 1960 *Organismo e società*. Rome: Ilardi.

Giorio, Giuliano 1985 *Società e sistemi sociali*. Milan: Angeli.

Gross, Feliks 1970 "Value Structure and Social Change." *Revue Internationale de Sociologie* 1(3):85–120.

Gubert, Renzo 1972 *La situazione confinaria*. Trieste: Lint.

—— 1976 *L'identificazione etnica*. Udine: Del Bianco.

——, ed. 1999 *Territorial Belonging Between Ecology and Culture*. Trento: Università degli Studi di Trento.

Guidicini, Paolo 1987 *Manuale per le ricerche sociali sul territorio*. Milan: Angeli (Revised Edition).

——, and Giovanni Pieretti, eds. 1998 *Città globale e città degli esclusi*. Milan: Angeli.

Harrison, Gualtiero, and Maria Callari Galli 1971 *Né leggere, né scrivere*. Milan: Feltrinelli.

Izzo, Alberto 1977 *Storia del pensiero sociologico*. Bologna: Il Mulino.

La Rosa, Michele 1986 "La sociologia del lavoro in Italia." *Sociologia del lavoro* 26-27:1–137.

Lentini, Orlando 1981 *La sociologia italiana nell'età del positivismo*. Bologna: Il Mulino.

Lopreato, Joseph 1961 "Social Stratification and Mobility in a South Italian Town." *American Sociological Review* 4.

Lotti, Luigi, and Gianfranco Pasquino 1980 *Guida alla facoltà di scienze politiche.* Bologna: Il Mulino.

Magatti, Mauro, ed. 1997 *Per la società civile.* Milan: Angeli.

Marselli, Gilberto Antonio 1963 "American Sociologists and Italian Peasant Society: With Reference to the Book of Banfield." *Sociologia Rurale* 3:15–32.

Martinotti, Guido, ed. 1968 *Città e analisi sociologica.* Padua: Marsilio.

Melotti, Umberto, ed. 1988 "Dal terzo mondo in Italia. Studi e ricerche sulle imigrazioni straniere." *Quaderni del Terzo Mondo* 31–32: 1–18.

Mosca, Gaetano 1962 *Storia delle dottrine politiche.* Bari: Laterza.

Mottura, Giovanni, and Enrico Pugliese 1975 *Agricoltura, Mezzogiorno e mercato del lavoro.* Bologna: Il Mulino.

Negrotti, Massimo 1979 *Uomini e calcolatori.* Milan: Angeli.

Niceforo, Alfredo 1953 *Avventure e disavventure della personalità e della umana società.* Milan: Bocca.

Pagani, Angelo, ed. 1960 *Antologia di scienze sociali.* Milan: Angeli.

Pareto, Vilfredo 1964 *Trattato di sociologia generale.* Milan: Comunità.

Pellizzi, Camillo 1964 *Rito e linguaggio.* Rome: Armando.

Picco, Giandomenico, and Giovanni Delli Zotti, eds., 1995 *International Solidarity and National Sovereignity.* Gorizia: ISIG.

Pinna, Luca 1971 *La famiglia esclusiva: parentela e clientelismo in Sardegna.* Bari: Laterza.

Pinto, Diana, ed. 1981 *Contemporary Italian Sociology.* Cambridge, U.K.: Cambridge University Press.

Pirzio Ammassari, Gloria 1997 *L'Europa degli interessi.* Roma: Euroma.

Pizzorno, Alessandro 1960 *Comunità e razionalizzazione.* Turin: Einaudi.

Pollini, Gabriele 1987 *Appartenenza e identità.* Milan: Angeli.

Regini, Marino, ed. 1988 *La sfida della flessibilità.* Milan: Angeli.

Ricciardi Ruocco, Maria 1967 *Inchiesta a Marsala.* Manduria: Lacaita.

Rusconi, Gian Enrico 1993 *Se cessiamo di essere una nazione.* Bologna: Il Mulino.

Savelli, Asterio 1989 *Sociologia del turismo.* Milan: Angeli.

Scaglia, Antonio 1988 *Sociologia: Dalle scienze della natura alla scienza dell'agire umano.* Milan: Angeli.

—— 1992 *La sociologia europea del primo Novecento.* Milan: Angeli.

Scivoletto, Angelo, ed. 1983 *Sociologia del territorio.* Milan: Angeli.

Sgroi, Emanuele 1991 *La questione ambientale da allarme a progetto: Le nuove professionalità.* Naples: CUEN.

Strassoldo, Raimondo 1976 *Ambiente e società.* Milan: Angeli.

—— 1979 *Temi di sociologia delle relazioni internazionali.* Gorizia: ISIG.

—— 1993 *Le radici dell'erba.* Napoli: Liguori.

Sturzo, Luigi 1960 *La società, sua natura e leggi.* Bologna: Zanichelli.

Sussi, Emidio, and Danilo Sedmak 1984 *L'assimilazione silenziosa.* Trieste: Editoriale Stampa Triestina.

Tentori, Tullio 1956 *Il sistema di vita nella comunità materana.* Rome: UNRA-Casas.

Tullio-Altan, Carlo 1995 *Ethnos e civiltà.* Milan: Feltrinelli.

Ungaro, Daniele 1997 *La transizione italiana.* Roma: Armando.

Urpis, Ornella 1998 *Nuove identità e secolarizzazione.* Gorizia: ISIG.

Vincelli, Guido 1958 *Una comunità meridionale. Montorio dei Frentani.* Turin: Taylor.

Visentini, Luciano 1984 *Tra mestiere e vocazione: La sociologia del lavoro in Italia.* Milan: Angeli.

ALBERTO GASPARINI

ISBN 0-02-864850-1

90000